Cases and Materials on Civil Procedure

Cases and Materials on Civil Procedure

SEVENTH EDITION

David Crump
John B. Neibel Professor of Law, University of Houston

Kevin O. Leske
Associate Professor of Law, Barry University

Keith W. Rizzardi
Professor of Law, St. Thomas University, Florida

William V. Dorsaneo, III
Chief Justice John and Lena Hickman Distinguished Faculty
Fellow and Professor of Law
Southern Methodist University Dedman School of Law

Rex R. Perschbacher
Professor and Daniel J. Dykstra Chair in Law
University of California at Davis

Debra Lyn Bassett
Justice Marshall F. McComb Professor of Law
Southwestern Law School

Carolina Academic Press
Durham, North Carolina

ISBN 978-1-5310-1398-1
eISBN 978-1-5310-1399-8
LCCN 2018959316

Carolina Academic Press, LLC
700 Kent Street
Durham, North Carolina 27701
Telephone (919) 489-7486
Fax (919) 493-5668
www.cap-press.com

Printed in the United States of America
2020 Printing

Contents

Preface to the Seventh Edition

What This Casebook Is About. This is the casebook for professors who want their students to explore the purposes and policies of our procedural system. But it's also the casebook for those who want their students to become capable trial lawyers and litigators. It features innovative ways to get students to think deeply about the issues, and it contains special materials for teaching litigation strategies. It's designed to help you prepare your students to enter the profession.

Organization and Methodology. As with earlier editions, the Seventh Edition is organized in a traditional manner. It begins with an introductory chapter that gives an overview of the litigation process. Later chapters cover the stages of a civil suit, in order. Although each chapter contains one or more problems or exercises, the Seventh Edition primarily uses the court opinion method, supplemented with copious notes and questions. Law professors will recognize all of the "old favorite" cases, but there are plenty of newer ones from the twenty-teens too, so that students using this book will not have to deal only with cases decided before they were born. Careful editing of the cases makes coverage of a wide variety of issues possible.

Revisions and Additions. The Seventh Edition contains particularly strong coverage of subjects that create major issues today, such as discovery, pleadings, and jurisdiction. Every chapter emphasizes up-to-date cases and materials.

Special Features. The Seventh Edition also includes the following special features:

- *An Introduction to the Practice through Actual Litigation Documents.* Unlike most Civil Procedure books, the Seventh Edition includes documents adapted from actual cases. Complaints and answers, motions, briefs, orders, and in the discovery chapter, a deposition, are all excerpted for the student to review and study. A set of self-initiated disclosures adapted from a real case is also included. In some instances, a series of related papers paints a complete picture. For example, Chapter 2 ends with an appendix containing all of the major pleadings, motions, and briefs generated in a typical forum contest, with explanatory notes and questions. Likewise, Chapter 9 contains the documents presented by both sides in an actual summary judgment proceeding, as well as President Clinton's successful motion for summary judgment in *Jones v. Clinton.* Chapter 10 contains fascinating excerpts from the jury selection, court's charge, and final arguments in *Pennzoil Co. v. Texaco Inc.*—the case that produced the largest jury verdict in history. These unique "real world" materials help students to understand both the theory and practice of civil litigation.
- *"Chapter Summary Problems."* Most of the chapters contain "Chapter Summary Problems." These comprehensive problems call for application of the students'

composite knowledge of the difficult parts of each chapter, requiring students to "put the chapter together" and to apply what they have learned. These problems are placed early in the chapter, encouraging the student to think about the issues beforehand, but they are to be answered only after the student has studied the materials in the chapter. These Chapter Summary Problems will increase your students' comprehension, retention, and use of the doctrines in each chapter, and you'll get better ultimate performance, because these problems encourage the kinds of analysis that a law school final examination requires.

- *"Improving the System."* We have included sections at the ends of most chapters entitled "Improving the System." These sections are designed to help students think critically about current discussions of proposals for change. Our experience has been that this method encourages better critical thought about the purposes of procedural rules and statutes. It not only facilitates mastery of the materials, but also tends to engage students more effectively in discussions of policy issues than episodic questions raised for the first time in class.
- *Supplementation of Traditional Federal Materials Though Comparison with State Practices; Use of Florida, California, and Texas as "Benchmark" States.* It is traditional to emphasize the federal system in first-year Procedure courses. Accordingly, this casebook provides thorough coverage of federal practice, but it also supplements federal materials with a comparative explanation of laws in three benchmark states: Florida, California, and Texas. We selected these states because of their size and because their procedural systems are well developed. In every chapter, the treatment of state practice is brief and is designed to enhance comprehension without detracting from the book's major federal theme.
- *A "User Friendly" Book.* The Seventh Edition is also designed to be user friendly. Although Civil Procedure may be the most difficult course in the first-year curriculum, we have done our best to make fundamental concepts easier for students to comprehend. For example, we have selected cases with interesting fact patterns, and particularly difficult cases are preceded by notes pointing the students in the right direction. The cases are also edited with student comprehension in mind, but without oversimplification. Our philosophy is that it is best for the student to come to class with a basic comprehension of the material in the book, so that the professor can cover more sophisticated issues during class.
- *An Appendix Concerning the Quality of Life for a Litigation Lawyer.* In recent years, litigators have encountered increasing difficulty in combining quality of life with professional practice in the adversary system. For this reason, the Seventh Edition contains a unique Appendix that deals with whether and how an ethical and competent litigator can live a full life. The Appendix is designed to help students avoid, or at least minimize, some of the more negative aspects of real-world litigation. Also, sections within the chapters titled "Real Life as a Lawyer" are designed to help students confront some of these difficulties: financial issues that limit options, obstreperous opponents, clients, and

co-counsel, and dangerous problems of time management that arise in an era of adjudication by deadline.

We hope and expect that you and your students will enjoy using the Seventh Edition. We know that they will find it interesting, challenging, and entertaining.

DAVID CRUMP
KEVIN O. LESKE
KEITH W. RIZZARDI
WILLIAM V. DORSANEO III
REX R. PERSCHBACHER
DEBRA LYN BASSETT

Cases and Materials on Civil Procedure

Chapter 1

An Overview of the Procedural System

I. What a Civil Procedure Course Is About

A course in civil procedure concerns itself principally with the way in which people litigate in the civil courts. In the federal courts, this process is governed mainly by a set of rules called the "Federal Rules of Civil Procedure." These rules traditionally are a major component of the civil procedure course. In a larger sense, the course may be about various processes through which civil disputes are resolved, including such mechanisms as negotiation and arbitration.

There are several objectives to such a course. First, and most obviously, the course can help you to begin learning how to handle litigation. Secondly, you need a knowledge of civil procedure to understand the subjects taught in your other courses. If a case in your contracts or torts casebook has been decided as it has because the complaint was inadequate or because the evidence does not support the verdict, you can understand the case better by understanding the underlying procedure.

Finally, a procedure course should make you aware of ways in which our system of justice can be improved. How strict, or how flexible, should be our standards for the sufficiency of papers filed with a court? Questions like these involve deeper issues, and the people best equipped to answer them are those who are thoroughly familiar with our procedural system.

II. The Stages in a Civil Suit: An Introduction

Let us use a simple hypothetical dispute to illustrate a civil suit. Imagine that Priscilla Nongrata is alleged to have punched Hart Hertz in the nose in Las Vegas, Nevada. Hart Hertz suffered a (fortunately) non-fatal heart malfunction, and he is considering suit against Priscilla.

Priscilla lives in San Francisco, California (in precise legal terms, let us say that she is a "citizen" of California, "residing" in San Francisco). At the time of the incident, she owned a chain of restaurants, and she wanted to expand her operations. One of the restaurants she owned was in Dallas, and she wanted to open another in Houston. She telephoned Hart, a citizen of Texas residing in Houston, in an effort to undertake the venture cooperatively with him. Priscilla suggested to Hart that they both fly to Las Vegas and meet at the Starlight Hotel. While the two tycoons were meeting, they had a disagreement, and that is when Priscilla allegedly assaulted Hart.

The following discussion is sprinkled with problems, each of which gives you a simple example. At the end of this section, you will find a brief answer for each problem.

[A] The Pre-Litigation Phase of a Civil Dispute

A great deal can happen *before* Hart files his lawsuit. In a procedure course, which is likely to focus on court decisions, there may be little that directly concerns this first stage of dispute resolution, simply because it is rarely memorialized in a reproducible form. You should be aware, however, that actions taken at this stage can affect outcomes.

Before suit, Hart Hertz must have recognized that a potential dispute has arisen. Ordinarily, he will have consulted an attorney, a process that creates an attorney-client relationship. The characterization of the dispute—is it a contract claim, or a tort, or some kind of statutory violation?—is a sophisticated undertaking in some cases. At least some investigation must precede the filing of a suit. Finally, many disputes are settled without suit, because of the expense, delay and uncertainty of litigation. In fact, it might be said that settlement is the norm and that the small percentage of cases that are judicially resolved are the exception.

[B] What Court Can Hear the Suit, and Where?: "Jurisdiction" and "Venue"

Subject-Matter Jurisdiction. One of the first questions that will face Hart Hertz's lawyer is, "What kind of court (if any) can hear this type of case?" We say that a court having power to decide a particular type of dispute has "subject-matter jurisdiction" over it.

Subject-Matter Jurisdiction in State and Federal Courts. There are state court systems, and there is a system of federal courts. Much of what each court system does is similar to what the other does. In fact, it is not unusual for *both* the federal and the state courts to have potential jurisdiction over the subject-matter of a particular dispute. In that event, the claimant has a choice. One kind of case that is within the jurisdiction of both federal courts and state courts is "diversity" cases, as they are called: cases in which the parties are citizens of different states, and in which more than $75,000 is in controversy. If Hart's suit is for more than $75,000, his lawyer will have this option, since the parties are citizens of different states. Thus, Hart's suit may be filed in either a state or a federal court.

Trial Courts and Appellate Courts. Within a given court system, there are different kinds of courts. For example, there are "trial" courts and "appellate" courts. The trial courts are the "intake" point. There, complaints and answers are filed, witnesses are heard, and juries render verdicts. A record is made of the proceedings, and the function of the appellate court is to review that record. In addition to this trial-appellate distinction, there are specialized courts, such as probate courts, domestic relations courts, or other particularized courts in given states.

A Diagram of the Court System. Figure 1A shows a bird's-eye view of our court system. At the top is the United States Supreme Court, which can review federal issues decided by state courts as well as judgments of lower federal courts. On the right side is the federal court system. On the left side is a prototypical state court system, with trial courts at the bottom, intermediate appellate courts, and a state supreme court.

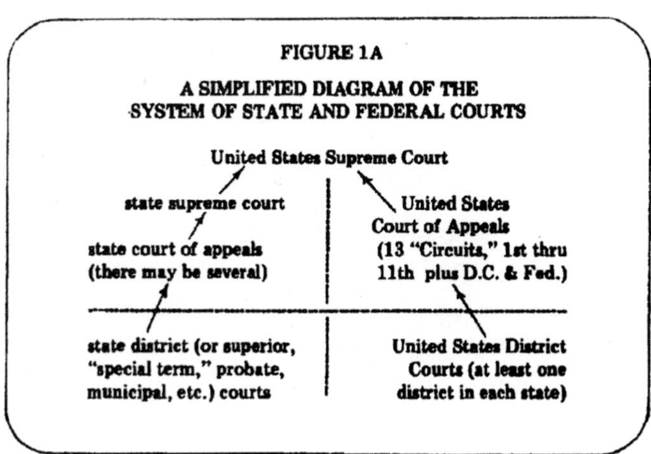

Different State Court Systems: Three States as Examples. There are many variations upon this model. In New York, for example, the "Supreme Court" (which is not supreme at all) is the general trial court; the "Appellate Division" is an intermediate court; and the "New York Court of Appeals" is the court of last resort, analogous to a state supreme court. In California, the "superior court" is the general trial court, several "district courts of appeal" comprise the intermediate level, and the California Supreme Court is at the top. In Texas, state "district" courts render judgments that are appealed to courts of appeals, and from there, a civil case can sometimes go to the Texas Supreme Court. The three systems are structurally similar, with different terminology.

A Second Jurisdictional Requirement: Jurisdiction Over the Person of the Defendant. In addition to jurisdiction over the subject-matter, the court must have jurisdiction over the person of the defendant. While subject-matter jurisdiction means power to decide this type of dispute, jurisdiction over the person means power to render a decree enforceable against this individual defendant. One of the concerns inherent in personal jurisdiction is distant forum abuse. A person who has had no contact with another state cannot properly be sued in the state courts there. If, for example, Priscilla has never had any dealings with anyone in Massachusetts, and has never been there, Hart could not file his suit there and force Priscilla to answer. In that event, the Massachusetts court might have jurisdiction over the subject-matter, but it would not have "jurisdiction over the person" of defendant Priscilla. However, there are several proper choices open to Hart. He can file suit in California (where Priscilla is a citizen) or in Nevada (where the claim is related to the state). In either state, he can choose either a state or a federal court (because of diversity of citizenship). He might want to file suit in Texas because he would have the "home court advantage" there, but as we will see later, he probably could not succeed in obtaining jurisdiction over Priscilla in Texas, because she is not "at home" there.

Serving the Papers on the Defendant. Hart must "serve" the defendant, Priscilla, with "process" (*i.e.*, with the suit papers) in a manner that conforms to law. The method varies with the situation; the traditional method is for a sheriff, marshal or other appropriate person to hand-deliver a copy of the suit papers to the defendant. This step, which gives the defendant notice of the litigation, is also necessary to the court's jurisdiction over the person of the defendant.

Venue. There may be many courts in different places with potential jurisdiction over a given dispute. Within the states of California, Texas, and Nevada, for example, there would be many courts that could acquire both subject-matter and personal jurisdiction over Hart's and Priscilla's dispute. Venue statutes provide a series of rules for determining which, among these courts, would be the most appropriate.

Forum Contests: The Motion to Dismiss. It sometimes happens that a plaintiff files suit in a given court, but the defendant does not agree that this court is a proper forum. In that situation, the defendant may wish to file what is called a "motion to dismiss" or, in appropriate circumstances, a "motion to transfer." The plaintiff, of course, can dispute these initiatives by the defendant. A "forum contest" results. The choice of forum is important because some courts may have more advantageous rules for one side or the other, may be inconveniently distant, or may have a jury pool that is likely to result in higher damages. It occasionally happens that after a forum contest is resolved, the parties know what their lawsuit is "worth," and they settle.

Problem A

Amanda sues Barney for $1,000,000 in a small claims court. It should be obvious to you that there is something inappropriate about this choice of forum. What is the technical name of the concept that tells you so (*i.e.*, what is it that the court lacks)? What can Barney do about the plaintiff's choice of forum, and what will be the court's probable response?

Problem B

In Rochester, New York, Chauncey was driving a car manufactured by United Motors when he was seriously injured because of its allegedly defective design. United Motors is one of the nation's largest manufacturers of automobiles, selling many thousands of vehicles annually in every state. United is a citizen of Michigan with its principal place of business in Detroit, and Chauncey is a citizen of New York, residing in Rochester. In what court(s) could Chauncey properly sue United Motors?

A federal district court in Detroit?

A state trial court in Rochester?

A state trial court in Buffalo?

[*A possible outcome:* Chauncey will file suit in a state trial court in Rochester (not Detroit, because he wants it in his home court). United may prefer federal procedures and, if so, will "remove" the case to federal court. United may also move for a transfer of venue to Detroit, but the Rochester federal judge will probably not grant it.]

Problem C

A state court of appeals "reverses" a decision by a trial court and "remands" the case to that court for a new trial. The state supreme court refuses to grant a writ of error, thereby declining to review the case. What does all of this jargon mean?

[C] The "Size" of the Lawsuit: Multiple Parties and Claims

The Simplest Situation: One "Plaintiff" Sues One "Defendant." On appeal, the appealing party (that is, the loser at trial) becomes the "Appellant." The other party is the "Appellee."

Multiple Parties in One Case. It is also possible for there to be more than one plaintiff in a case, or for the plaintiff(s) to sue more than one defendant. If, for example, Hart thinks that the Starlight Hotel was at fault in furnishing inadequate security (so that his injuries at Priscilla's hands were more serious than they otherwise might have been), he can claim against both Priscilla and the Hotel Corporation. If Hart's wife, Sarah, has a valid claim for the loss of his companionship, she may join as a plaintiff.

Multiple Claims in One Case. Sometimes a lawsuit may contain different kinds of claims. For example, if Priscilla contends that Hart assaulted her (rather than the other way around), she may file a "counterclaim." If Priscilla believes that a co-defendant is really at fault, she may file a "cross claim" (against the Starlight Hotel, for example). If she believes that a third person who is not a party to the suit should be liable, she can bring that person into the dispute by filing a "third party claim." If there is someone left out of the suit who wants to join it (example: Hart's wife, Sarah), that person may be able to "intervene." In summary, the plaintiff is not always the only party who wants to make a claim, and the rules accommodate others' doing so.

"Compulsory" Joinder. It sometimes happens that a person left out of a suit has such an important interest in it that it would be unfair for the suit to proceed without him or her. The omitted person would be a "person[] required to be joined if feasible," in the terminology of the Federal Rules. The court then has the authority to force the parties to include the absent person or, in an unusual case, to abort the proceedings.

Complex Devices. There are other procedures designed to handle cases with very large numbers of parties or cases in which multiple inconsistent claims are asserted. A "class action" is perhaps the best known of these devices.

Problem D

Harriet and Ida were injured in a three-car collision when Harriet's car came into contact with cars driven by Jim and Ken, respectively. Harriet and Ida think that Jim, Ken, or both, were negligent; Jim, who was also injured, thinks that the other two drivers were negligent. What is likely to happen (that is, what claims will be brought)?

[D] The "Suit Papers": Pleadings and Motions

The Complaint. Hart Hertz would commence his action against Priscilla by filing what is called a "complaint." In some states, this document is called a "petition." It sets forth in general terms the contentions upon which the plaintiff bases his legal theory, and it also states what the plaintiff wants ("a demand for the relief sought").

The Answer: The Defendant's Response to the Plaintiff's Suit. The defendant responds with an "answer" (or, in some circumstances, a motion or other procedural device), which may raise several different kinds of issues. For example, it may allege that there were procedural deficiencies in the way the action was brought, such as a lack of jurisdiction. Alternatively, it may attack the sufficiency of the complaint.

Answers "On the Merits": Admissions, Denials, and Affirmative Defenses. Finally, the defendant may attack the validity of the plaintiff's claim itself. This last kind of answer is described as an answer "on the merits." There are two basic kinds of answers on the merits: first, admissions and denials, which agree with or rebut facts claimed by the plaintiff; and secondly, affirmative defenses, which say that even if the plaintiff can prove the elements of the claim, there is an external reason why the plaintiff should not recover. Contributory negligence and the statute of limitations are examples of affirmative defenses. In Hart and Priscilla's case, for instance, Priscilla might file an answer admitting her presence with Hart at the Starlight Hotel, but denying the alleged assault (if those were the facts as she claimed them). She might also plead the affirmative defense of self-defense, if she contended that Hart had started the fight.

Motions. A "motion" is an application to the court for an order of a particular kind. We say that a lawyer "files a motion" for, or "moves" for, action by the court. The motions to dismiss discussed above are examples, and there are also other common motions. For example, if Priscilla fails to file an answer, Hart can file a "motion for default judgment," which is the kind of judgment that is available in that situation. If Priscilla answers by admitting all of Hart's allegations, Hart might file what is called a "motion for judgment on the pleadings." There are infinitely many kinds of orders that a court could be asked, by motion, to grant.

Motion for Summary Judgment. If the undisputed facts developed before trial show that one side or the other is clearly entitled to judgment, a "motion for summary judgment" may be granted. "Summary judgment" disposes of the case without a trial. It is available, however, *only* when there is no reasonable way in which the opposing party could prevail. For example, if Priscilla were to stipulate to the amount of Hart's damages and also were to testify in a pretrial deposition to facts admitting that she did assault Hart and cause his injuries, Hart might be able to obtain a summary judgment.

Problem E

[Taken from a tragic case, reported in the newspapers:] Larry has a terminal disease, and the only apparent way to preserve his life is a transplant of bone marrow from his relative, Marty. But Marty refuses to consent to the operation that would take the bone marrow from him. Larry therefore sues Marty. He sets out these facts in his complaint and requests that the court issue an order requiring Marty to submit to the operation. Assume that there is no legal principle enabling a person to invade the body of another for these purposes. The complaint thus cannot be the basis of any relief, even if entirely true. What procedural step is defendant Marty likely to take?

Problem F

Natalie files suit against Philip, alleging that Philip's negligence in stopping his car on a public road caused Natalie certain injuries. The court has jurisdiction and the complaint is pleaded sufficiently, but Philip's position is that the facts are not as Natalie alleges them. Specifically, although Philip agrees that he did stop on a public road, he contends that he was not negligent in stopping. Further, Philip believes that Natalie herself was negligent and caused her own injuries. What pleading(s) does Philip file to get these positions considered by the court?

Problem G

After the pleadings are all complete in the case of *Natalie v. Philip*, Natalie testifies in a pretrial deposition that she was traveling in her automobile at 100 miles per hour on the occasion in question and that she ran into Philip from behind while he was stopped at a stop sign. What should Philip do and what is the likely result?

[E] Discovery, Disclosures, Investigation, and Pretrial Conferences

Discovery. The term "discovery" refers to pretrial procedures by which a litigant may obtain information from opponents and witnesses. Some basic information, called "initial disclosures," must be provided by one litigant to the other without awaiting a discovery request. Other discovery methods are also available. In the case of *Hertz v. Nongrata*, for example, it is likely that each party would want to take the "oral deposition" of the other. This procedure allows an attorney to question a party or witness in the presence of a court reporter, who records the questions and answers. Another discovery device, called written interrogatories, consists of written questions. Priscilla might want to direct written interrogatories to Hart, asking for such information as the identities of physicians he has consulted. Still another device, called a request for production or inspection, allows a party to obtain documents or tangible items. Priscilla might use this device to obtain Hart's medical records. A request for admissions requires the opponent to admit or deny facts and is useful for establishing undisputed matters; for example, Hart might ask Priscilla to admit that she was present at the Starlight Hotel.

The Scope of Discovery. The rules of discovery allow for broader inquiry than the evidence that will be admissible at trial. After all, discovery is part of the investigative stage of the proceeding. Even if a particular piece of information is not admissible, it may help to find other admissible information. In general, discovery extends to information that is relevant and "proportional to the needs of the case." For instance, Hart can inquire in a deposition whether Priscilla was arrested or interrogated by the police concerning this incident, even though the arrest may not be admissible at trial. But Hart probably would exceed the proper scope of discovery if he demanded production of every medical record of Priscilla's throughout her life, because the discovery would not be proportional to the needs of the case.

Investigation. A lawyer usually does a large part of the investigation in a lawsuit on his or her own, rather than through discovery. For example, one does not usually depose a friendly witness, because that procedure would be tantamount to cross-examining him in front of the adversary. Instead, it may be better simply to interview the witness. (There is risk in this method, however, because the written interview notes will probably be inadmissible at trial. If there is danger that the witness may be unavailable, taking a deposition would be better.)

Pretrial Conference. In many jurisdictions, the judge meets with the lawyers informally to discuss the way the trial is to be conducted, to explore and encourage settlement, or to rule on pretrial matters such as discovery disputes. In *Hertz v. Nongrata*, the court might hold a pretrial conference to discuss who the witnesses would be, what documents might be offered, how the jury might be instructed, and like matters.

Problem H

While taking Priscilla's deposition, Hart's lawyer asks her what, if anything, she has heard other people say about the alleged assault that is the focus of the suit. Priscilla's lawyer correctly interjects that the question calls for hearsay. Hart's lawyer, in response, points out that although the answer might not be admissible at trial, it might allow him to interview useful witnesses. Is the question properly within the scope of discovery?

Problem I

What would be the best method(s) to obtain information from the following persons?

a. Information about how an automobile accident happened from the opposing party in the suit, who is expected to be evasive in answering questions.

b. Information as to what doctors the opposing party consulted, and what charges he paid for what services.

c. Information from the physician your own client consulted (the physician is forthcoming with answers and will be available for trial).

d. The exact appearance and condition of the vehicle that was involved in the accident, which is in the control of the opposing party.

e. Verification that the defendant was indeed the person driving the accident vehicle.

[F] The Trial Itself

Functions of the Judge and of the Jury. The judge presides over the trial and decides questions of law. The proper definition of an assault and the admissibility or exclusion of evidence are examples of questions of law that might come up in *Hertz v. Nongrata*. The jury, on the other hand, decides disputed questions of fact. Whether Priscilla's conduct amounted to an assault as defined, and whether her representations of self-defense are credible, are examples of factual issues that the jury might resolve. Sometimes, a trial may be held before the judge sitting without a jury (a "non-jury trial").

Jury Selection. Potential jurors are summoned at random to create an array or panel. These potential jurors, or "venire members," are subject to examination by the judge (or by the lawyers, or by both) to determine their fitness to serve. The attorneys can "challenge" any juror they believe is disqualified (for example, one who has an unacceptable bias against a party). The number of challenges for this reason, called "challenges for cause," is unlimited. In addition, the attorneys have a specified number of "peremptory" challenges, by which they may remove a certain number of venire members without stating any reason. In the trial of *Hertz v. Nongrata*, for instance, if a potential juror said she disliked Priscilla so much that she could not judge the case fairly, Priscilla's lawyer would exercise a challenge for cause to remove her. If Hart's lawyer senses that a particular venire member is unlikely to award damages in a significant amount, he can use a peremptory challenge to remove this individual.

Opening Statements and Presentation of the Case. After the jury is empanelled and sworn, the lawyers make opening statements, explaining to the jurors the testimony they expect to offer. The plaintiff, Hart, would then present his witnesses and evidence, followed by Priscilla. Both sides may offer rebuttal or surrebuttal evidence.

Rules of Evidence. Not every sort of information may be heard by the jury. For example, with certain exceptions, hearsay is excluded. Thus, if Hart were to offer to testify that other individuals had made informal statements to him about the alleged assault, Priscilla's lawyer could object to, and probably have the judge exclude, this testimony.

Burden of Proof. Hart Hertz would have the "burden of proving" the elements of his assault and battery claim. This burden of proof, in turn, implies two different kinds of obligations. First, Hart must introduce evidence that is at least minimally sufficient to support a finding by the jury. If he produces no evidence, he loses. Thus, we say that Hart has the "burden of producing evidence" or the "burden of production." Furthermore, Hart has the burden of persuading the jury that his claim is probably correct. This "burden of persuasion" is by the "preponderance of the evidence"; in other words, the jury must be satisfied by the preponderance, or the greater weight, of the credible evidence that Hart's claim is correct.

Motion for Judgment as a Matter of Law (or, in Some States, for a "Directed Verdict"). If Hart Hertz were to testify that he could not remember the incident because it all happened quickly, and if he were to rest his case without producing any other evidence, he would not have carried his burden of production. The jury could not reasonably make a finding by the preponderance of the evidence in his favor. In this situation, defendant Priscilla could move for, and the court could grant, a "judgment as a matter of law" (sometimes called a "directed verdict" or "instructed verdict"). This procedure aborts the trial. The standard, understandably, is stringent: the judge must be satisfied that there is no reasonable way for the jury to decide in Hart's favor. In that circumstance, we say that the movant is entitled to judgment "as a matter of law," and the judge decides the issues by the law.

Jury Arguments, the Court's Charge, and the Verdict. After all of the evidence has been presented, the parties' attorneys may make arguments to the jury. They tell the jury what they think the evidence shows and explain how they think their factual inferences fit with the law. The judge then "charges" the jury, giving it definitions of necessary terms. The jury returns an answer (or answers) called its "verdict."

Problem J

In a case tried before a jury, the plaintiff has introduced some evidence that a person could within reason believe, covering each issue required to be proved by the plaintiff. However, the judge believes that the preponderance of the evidence favors the defendant—that is, the defendant would win if the judge were hearing the case in a non-jury trial. If the defendant files a motion for judgment as a matter of law, how should the court rule on it, and why?

[G] The Post-Trial Stage

Post-Trial Motions: Renewing the Motion for Judgment as a Matter of Law. If the verdict loser believes that the verdict is unsupported by the evidence, she may renew her "motion for judgment as a matter of law" (sometimes called a "motion for judgment notwithstanding the verdict" when requested post-verdict). This procedural device is the same as the motion for judgment as a matter of law requested before the jury leaves the courtroom: it can be granted only if there is no reasonable way to infer support in the evidence for the jury's decision.

Motion for New Trial. In the alternative, the verdict loser may make a "motion for new trial." The function of this procedure is different from that of the post-trial motion for judgment as a matter of law; it seeks relief from trial errors or other procedural miscarriages. For example, if the jury has found in Hart's favor, but Priscilla persuades the judge that he gave the jury an erroneous charge, the court may grant her a new trial.

Judgments and Remedies. The court will, in the final analysis, issue a "judgment" (either based on the verdict or contrary to it) stating what relief is granted or refused. The relief may be money damages ordered to be paid, or an injunction—or it may be a judgment for defendant, stating that plaintiff shall "take nothing."

Enforcement of Judgment. The issuance of a judgment does not always result in its satisfaction. If the defendant fails to pay, the court may issue a "writ of execution," ordering an officer to seize and sell his non-exempt assets, if any. There are enforcement procedures in addition to execution.

The Binding Effect of Judgments: Res Judicata. A judgment, once entered and final, can be asserted as a bar to a later suit raising the same claim. This doctrine is called "res judicata," which is Latin for "the thing has been adjudicated."

Problem K

The jury has found defendant Tom negligent and has also found that his negligence proximately caused $50,000 in damages to Ursula. Tom finds an opinion of the state supreme court disapproving the definition of negligence that the judge used in his instructions to the jury. Does this mean that Tom is entitled to a judgment as a matter of law? Why or why not? If not, what should Tom do to assert his rights? Assuming Ursula gets a judgment, what if Tom has no unusual assets, but has a house and a car (both of which are exempt from execution under controlling law) and a bank account containing $2,000? If, after the judgment becomes final, Ursula brings another suit on the same claim because she thinks she should have recovered a larger amount, what can Tom do?

[H] A Side Issue: One Jurisdiction Applies Another's Law

The Law Binding a Court. A state trial court is bound by statutes passed by the state legislature, by the ruling of appellate courts over it, and by the state constitution. All courts are bound by federal law, including the United States Constitution. (In fact, there is nothing anomalous about a state court's deciding a claim that is based upon federal law; that happens frequently.) But by the same token, courts in one state are not generally bound by the rulings of courts in another state. If, in one of your casebooks, there appears an opinion of the California Supreme Court alongside an opinion of the New York Court of Appeals that reaches the opposite conclusion, this does not mean something is wrong.

Conflict of Laws (or "Choice" of Law). Sometimes courts apply the law of another state in deciding a case. For example, if Hart's suit against Priscilla is heard in a California state court, it might be appropriate for that court to apply the law of Nevada in defining assault and battery or self-defense. The parties were in Nevada when the conduct at issue took place.

State Law in the Federal Courts (and Vice Versa). As we have seen, Hart's suit could have been brought in either a state or a federal court. But there is no federal law prohibiting this alleged assault and battery; the law governing a garden-variety brawl in Nevada (or any other state) is state law. Accordingly, a federal court would use state law in these matters. If, for example, Hart's suit were brought in a federal court located in Nevada, that court would try to apply the law the way a Nevada state court would.

Problem L

Arnold, a citizen of Massachusetts, and Billy, a citizen of New York, drove to Florida. While in Florida, they had an accident in which Billy was injured and which he attributes to Arnold's negligence. Billy later files suit for $500,000 against Arnold in a Massachusetts state court. Incidental question: Does the Massachusetts state court have jurisdiction? Principal question: What state's legal principles should the Massachusetts state court use to decide whether Arnold should pay Billy?

[I] Appeals

The Functions of an Appellate Court. An appellate court does not normally hear evidence or decide disputed questions of fact. It has two functions: to decide whether the case was tried in accordance with the law and to determine whether the evidence in the record supports the verdict according to legal standards.

An Appellate Court's Review of the Evidence. In reviewing the evidence, moreover, the appellate court cannot reverse merely because it disagrees with the jury. It must determine that the evidence is not reasonably capable of interpretation so as to support the verdict under the applicable law. Thus, when an appellate court speaks of "the facts" in the case, it may be speaking only about the set of inferences that best support the verdict.

Problem M

George has lost a jury trial in which all of the issues were hotly disputed in the evidence. George believes that the opponent's witnesses did not tell the truth, that the jury was hoodwinked, and that the opposing lawyer thus obtained a verdict that does not conform to the true facts. Can he use these arguments to obtain a reversal on appeal?

Brief Answers to Problems in This Section

A. The small claims court lacks subject-matter jurisdiction. Barney can make a motion to dismiss, which the court should grant. Amanda can then file suit in the proper court.

B. A federal court in Detroit has both personal jurisdiction (United has its "home" there) and subject-matter jurisdiction (there is diversity of citizenship, and the "serious injury" will exceed $75,000). The state court in Rochester also has both kinds of jurisdiction (United sells automobiles there). So, probably, does the state court in Buffalo; venue rules may, however, enable United to challenge this forum.

C. This jargon means that the court of appeals has nullified the trial court's judgment, it is sending the case back for retrial, and the state supreme court has refused to consider reversing the reversal.

D. Harriet and Ida can join their claims against Jim and Ken. Jim can counterclaim against Harriet and cross-claim against Ken. (In fact, given human nature, everybody may wind up claiming against everybody else.)

E. Marty can file a motion to dismiss for failure to state a claim upon which relief can be granted.

F. Philip would file an answer denying negligence and causation (and, if required in this jurisdiction, admitting other facts claimed by Natalie that he believes are true). He should also include the affirmative defense of contributory negligence in his answer.

G. Philip should move for summary judgment, because the only reasonable interpretation of the undisputed evidence is that he was not causally negligent as Natalie alleged.

H. Priscilla's answer to this question is discoverable because the information, although it is hearsay, is reasonably calculated to lead to the discovery of admissible evidence.

I. (a) Oral depositions are the superior means of obtaining controversial information from an opponent. (b) Interrogatories are useful for obtaining this sort of specific information. (c) It may be best first to interview this cooperative witness rather than depose him. (d) A request for production and inspection obtains access to the vehicle in the opponent's possession. (e) A request for admissions efficiently establishes non-controversial facts.

J. The court cannot grant judgment as a matter of law because the standard for this procedure is that there must be no way a reasonable juror could find for the opponent. (The judge's inferences about the preponderance of the evidence are irrelevant here; that's the jury's job.)

K. Tom is not entitled to judgment as a matter of law. He would have to show that he is entitled to judgment as a matter of law (meaning that no reasonable person could find for Ursula on the evidence). Tom may succeed, however, in a motion for new trial. If there was no error, the judge would grant judgment in accordance with the jury's verdict. Tom's exempt assets cannot be executed upon, but a writ of garnishment may be used with respect to the bank account. Tom should plead res judicata to bar Ursula's assertion of the same claim after final judgment.

L. The Massachusetts state court would have jurisdiction. It *might* very well apply Florida law in deciding the merits; it is impossible, however, to provide a definitive answer. A *federal* court located in Massachusetts would apply whatever state's law a Massachusetts *state* court would apply—including Florida law, if that were the case.

M. In most jurisdictions, an appellate court has no authority to consider the factual disputes George seeks to raise.

III. Jurisdiction: The Court's Power to Act

How to Read the Case of Strawbridge v. Curtiss

As you read the case that follows, you should take care to understand its procedural history. In what court was the suit filed? Where did it go from that court? What is the procedural issue that controls the disposition of the case? What are the sources of the law that the court uses to decide it, and how is its reasoning explained? (Specifically, is it an interpretation of the Constitution, of a rule of court, of a statute, or of that court-generated law called "common law"?)

The case concerns the scope of diversity jurisdiction. If a plaintiff who is a citizen of one state sues a defendant who is a citizen of another state, the problem is straightforward. But what is to be done if a plaintiff sues one defendant of diverse citizenship and, in the same suit, also sues another who is of the same citizenship as the plaintiff? The Constitution is the ultimate source of diversity jurisdiction, but it does not provide much guidance in this case. It simply says that the "judicial power shall extend . . . to Controversies . . . between citizens of Different States." U.S. Const. art. III, § 2. This constitutional provision is implemented by a statute passed by Congress, which (in its present form) says that the federal district courts have jurisdiction over "all civil actions where the matter in controversy exceeds the sum or value of $75,000, . . . and is between . . . Citizens of different States." 28 U.S.C. § 1332. The dispute in *Strawbridge v. Curtiss* is controlled by an earlier version of this statute, but the outcome does not depend on that difference. (Incidentally, the "circuit" court at that time was the federal trial court.)

Strawbridge v. Curtiss is a venerable case, decided by one of this nation's most famous chief justices, and the principle that it enunciates is still good law today.

> Read 28 U.S.C. § 1332 (the diversity statute) and U.S. Const. art. III, § 2 (the constitutional diversity provision).

Strawbridge v. Curtiss

7 U.S. (3 Cranch) 267 (1806)

THIS was an appeal from a decree of the circuit court, for the district of Massachusetts, which dismissed the complainants' bill in chancery, for want of jurisdiction.

Some of the complainants were alleged to be citizens of the state of Massachusetts. The defendants were also stated to be citizens of the same state, excepting Curtiss, who was averred to be a citizen of the state of Vermont, and upon whom the *subpoena* was served in that state. . . .

MARSHALL, CH. J. delivered the opinion of the court.

The court has considered this case, and is of opinion that the jurisdiction cannot be supported.

The words of the act of congress are, "where an alien is a party; or the suit is between a citizen of a state where the suit is brought, and a citizen of another state."

The court understands these expressions to mean, that each distinct interest should be represented by persons, all of whom are entitled to sue, or may be sued, in the federal courts. . . . That is, each of the persons . . . must be competent to sue, or liable to be sued, in those courts. . . .

Decree affirmed.

Notes and Questions

(1) *What Kind of Jurisdiction?* This case concerns a jurisdictional issue. But what kind of jurisdiction is at issue—subject-matter jurisdiction or jurisdiction over the person of the defendant? [Note: Don't be confused by the fact that diversity jurisdiction has something to do with the state affiliations of the parties. Subject-matter jurisdiction is power to decide the generic type of dispute, while personal jurisdiction concerns the court's power to bind a particular defendant.]

(2) *Constitutional Versus Statutory Interpretation.* Is this decision an interpretation of the Constitution or of the diversity statute passed by the Congress? What difference would it make? [Note: If it is a Constitutional decision, could Congress *ever* provide for jurisdiction in this situation? If it is not based on the Constitution, couldn't Congress do so simply by rewriting the statute?]

(3) *Who "Won"?* What does this decision mean to the parties? Who has "won," and what does it mean to say that the party has "won"? What can the plaintiff do now?

How to Brief the Case of Strawbridge v. Curtiss

Within your first week in law school, you will probably be introduced to the concept of "briefing" a case. A case brief is just a set of notes about the case, abstracting its important elements, which usually include such aspects as the parties, the issues, the court's holding and the reason for the court's decision. There are an infinite variety of ways to go about briefing, and you should use the method that your instructor prefers. In the alternative, you should use the method that you find most useful. Briefing is a means of undertaking systematic analysis.

With these qualifications in mind, you should consider Figure 1B. It contains a brief of *Strawbridge v. Curtiss*, done in one of the many possible ways that it could be done. Having seen this sample, you should brief the next case yourself.

How to Read the Case of Wyman v. Newhouse

Remember that the plaintiff must have the suit papers "served" upon the defendant. Remember, too, that the defendant must have some kind of relationship to the court, such as contacts with the state in which it is located. Another way for jurisdiction to attach is for the plaintiff to have the defendant served *while he is within* the state.

In essence, that is what *Wyman v. Newhouse* is about. But it is about a great deal more. The foulest of treachery, the scandal of a "meretricious relationship," and the triumph of justice through good legal advice, all combine to make this a wonderful case. As you read it, ask yourself: Why did Ms. Wyman engage in the treachery that so unfortunately characterized her actions? What advantage did she hope to gain?

FIGURE 1B

Strawbridge v. Curtiss (S. Ct. 1806)

I. ~~Facts~~ Procedure: citizens of Massachusetts sued citizens of Vermont and Massachusetts in a "circuit" court (then the federal trial court). That court dismissed for lack of jurisdiction; appeal to S. Ct.

II. Issue: Must all parties be of diverse citizenship from all adverse parties for diversity jurisdiction to exist in the federal courts?

III. Narrow holding: Dismissal affirmed. No jurisdiction.

IV. Broad holding: The diversity statute as passed by Congress required complete diversity among all adverse parties.

V. Reasoning: The Act of Congress conferring jurisdiction said that a diversity suit could be brought "between a citizen of a state . . . and a citizen of another state." The Court interpreted this language to mean that all claimants must be qualified to sue all defendants.

Wyman v. Newhouse

93 F.2d 313 (2d Cir. 1937)

[Sarah Wyman sued Edgar Newhouse in a Florida state court. Her complaint included claims for "money loaned, money advanced . . . , and for seduction under promise of marriage." Following his lawyer's advice, Newhouse did not answer the suit, and a default judgment was entered against him.

[Because Newhouse had no assets in Florida, the Florida judgment was itself of no value to Wyman. However, she filed an "action on the judgment" in a federal District Court in New York. An action on the judgment is a suit of a peculiar kind: it pleads that the plaintiff has a judgment from another state, and it asks the court to enter a judgment enforceable within its jurisdiction.

[The Full Faith and Credit Clause of the Constitution requires courts to honor "the public Acts, Records, and Judicial Proceedings of every other State." U.S. Const. art. IV, § 1. This clause is implemented by a Congressional Act requiring that duly authenticated judicial proceedings "shall have the same full faith and credit in every court within the United States . . . as they have by law or usage in the courts of such State, Territory or Possession from which they are taken." 28 U.S.C. § 1738. Thus, if the Florida judgment would be enforceable in Florida, the New York federal court was required to enforce it in New York. However, the court dismissed Wyman's action, agreeing with Newhouse that the Florida judgment was unenforceable. Wyman appealed.

[The Court of Appeals therefore considers the validity of the Florida judgment. Its validity depends upon the effectiveness of the service of process on Newhouse in Florida. He claims it was ineffective because Wyman had fraudulently enticed him into Florida for the sole purpose of serving him with process.]

Appellant and appellee were both married, but before this suit appellant's husband died. They had known each other for some years and had engaged in meretricious relations.

The affidavits submitted by the appellee . . . established that he was a resident of New York and never lived in Florida. On October 25, 1935, while appellee was in Salt Lake City, Utah, he received a telegram from the appellant, which read: "Account illness home planning leaving. Please come on way back. Must see you." Upon appellee's return to New York he received a letter from appellant stating that her mother was dying in Ireland; that she was leaving the United States for good to go to her mother; that she could not go without seeing the appellee once more; and that she wanted to discuss her affairs with him before she left. Shortly after the receipt of this letter, they spoke to each other on the telephone, whereupon the appellant repeated, in a hysterical and distressed voice, the substance of her letter. Appellee promised to go to Florida in a week or ten days and agreed to notify her when he would arrive. This he did, but before leaving New York by plane he received a letter couched in endearing terms and expressing love and affection for him, as well as her delight at his coming. Before leaving New York, appellee telegraphed appellant, suggesting arrangements for their accommodations together while in Miami, Fla. She telegraphed him at a hotel in Washington, D.C., where he was to stop en route, advising him that the arrangements requested had been made. Appellee arrived at 6 o'clock in the morning at the Miami Airport and saw the appellant standing with her sister some 75 feet distant. He was met by a deputy sheriff who, upon identifying appellee, served him with process in a suit for $500,000. A photographer was present who attempted to take his picture. Thereupon a stranger introduced himself and offered to take appellee to his home, stating that he knew a lawyer who was acquainted with the appellant's attorney. The attorney whom appellee was advised to consult came to the stranger's home and seemed to know about the case. The attorney invited appellee to his office, and upon his arrival he found one of the lawyers for the appellant there. Appellee did not retain the Florida attorney to represent him. He returned to New York by plane that evening and consulted his New York counsel, who advised him to ignore the summons served in Florida. He did so, and judgment was entered by default....

These facts and reasonable deductions therefrom convincingly establish that the appellee was induced to enter the jurisdiction of the state of Florida by a fraud perpetrated upon him by the appellant..., when her sole purpose and apparent thought was to induce him to come within the Florida jurisdiction so as to serve him in an action for damages....

...A judgment procured fraudulently [in Florida], as here, lacks jurisdiction and is null and void [citing Florida decisions]. A fraud affecting the jurisdiction is equivalent to a lack of jurisdiction [citing Florida decisions].... The appellee was not required to proceed against the judgment in Florida....

Judgment [dismissing Wyman's action] affirmed.

Notes and Questions

(1) *Non-Fraudulent Contact or Injury.* How would the result differ if Wyman's entreaties and professions of affection for Newhouse had been genuine? Imagine that he came to Florida and stayed for several pleasant days until a disagreement erupted, and Wyman filed suit and had him served before he left Florida. What result? Alternatively, imagine that during this pleasant visit, a disagreement occurred and resulted in Newhouse's injuring Wyman—he struck her and broke her nose, for example—and he left Florida before she could sue. Is Wyman required to go to New York to file suit for this injury inflicted by Newhouse in Florida?

(2) *The Claimed Basis for Jurisdiction.* Why, then, did Wyman lure Newhouse to Florida? If she were to attempt to explain why she thought the Florida court had power to act, what would she give as the general principle on which that power could be based?

(3) *Where Can Wyman Properly Bring Suit?* Is there anywhere that Wyman can properly sue Newhouse now, if she believes her claim is valid? What were the reasons she didn't sue there in the first place?

IV. Pleadings: The Complaint and Answer

Read Rule 8(a), (e) of the Federal Rules of Civil Procedure.

Note: The Federal Rules of Civil Procedure and Their Effects on Pleadings

The Federal Rules of Civil Procedure govern many procedural matters in federal court (although, as you have seen, there are also matters that are governed directly by the Constitution or by statutes). Typically, rule changes originate in an Advisory Committee to the Supreme Court and are promulgated by that Court and by Congress to govern the district courts.

Rules of Pleading. The cases in this section deal with the question: just what does a plaintiff have to say in a complaint in order to have it survive the first wave of attack by the defendant? The most relevant provisions are contained in Rule 8: The complaint "must contain . . . a short and plain statement of the claim showing that the pleader is entitled to relief," "[n]o technical form is required," and pleadings "must be construed so as to do justice." But these general provisions don't tell pleaders and those responding to pleadings just how much factual detail is required in the "statements of the claim" or how informative the statement must be. These issues have been hotly contested for years.

Two Standards for Pleading a Complaint. The Supreme Court has found that this general language contains two more specific standards. First, the plaintiff, in the complaint, must set out sufficient factual allegations. Second, these sufficient factual allegations must amount to a substantively sufficient legal claim. The two requirements are closely related, and the courts often put them together.

First, Facts That Show Plausibility. The standard for factual sufficiency, as you will see from the case below, requires the plaintiff to provide "sufficient factual matter. . . . to state a claim for relief that is *plausible on its face.*" To take an extreme example, a complaint that says only, "Defendant owes plaintiff money" would not meet this "sufficient facts" standard.

Second, if the Facts Are Assumed True, a Claim That Is Valid. The second standard, the standard for substantive sufficiency, requires the reviewing court to accept the allegations in the complaint as true and to read them in the light most favorable to the plaintiff. Then, even if the complaint is highly specific, the court can dismiss if the law does not provide any claim under the facts pleaded. To take another extreme example, if the complaint contains a long list of facts but includes information that shows that the law does not allow the plaintiff to recover, this standard is not met. Often, the two standards are stated together in a single sentence, as a requirement that plaintiff must plead sufficient facts to make the claim plausible if the allegations are assumed true. Consider the following case.

Bell v. HCR Manor Care Facility

432 Fed. Appx. 908 (11th Cir. 2011)

PER CURIAM:

. . . [Renee] Bell, as personal representative of Sylvia C. Fann's ("Fann") estate, sued Defendants for medical malpractice and wrongful death, under 42 U.S.C. § 1983 [the federal civil rights relief statute] and the Federal Tort Claims Act ("FTCA"), 28 U.S.C. § 1346. [These statutes provide claims for harm done through governmental action. The defendants, however, did not include any governmental entities; the plaintiffs only sued two private nursing homes and a private doctor.] The district court granted Defendants' motions to dismiss. . . . [W]e affirm . . . .

. . . When reviewing a motion to dismiss under 12(b)(6) for failure to state a claim, we must accept the allegations in the complaint as true and construe them in the light most favorable to the plaintiff. *See Ironworkers Local Union 68 v. AstraZeneca Pharms., LP*, 634 F.3d 1352, 1359 (11th Cir. 2011). We need not, however, accept the legal conclusions in the complaint as true. *See Sinaltrainal* [*v. Coca-Cola Co*,], 578 F.3d [1252] at 1260 [11th Cir. 2009)]. "[T]he complaint must . . . contain sufficient factual matter, accepted as true, to state a claim to relief that is *plausible on its face.*" *AstraZeneca Pharms.*, 634 F.3d at 1359 (quotation marks omitted); *see also Ashcroft v. Iqbal*, ___ U.S. ___, 129 S.Ct. 1937, 1949 (2009); *Bell Atlantic Corp. v. Twombly*, 550 U.S. 544, 570, 127 S. Ct. 1955, 1974 (2007).

"To state a claim for relief in an action brought under § 1983, [a plaintiff] must establish that [she was] deprived of a right secured by the Constitution or laws of the United States, and that the alleged deprivation was committed under color of state law." *American Mfrs. Mut. Ins. Co. v. Sullivan*, 526 U.S. 40, 49–50, 119 S.Ct. 977, 985 (1999); *see also Griffin v. City of Opa–Locka*, 261 F.3d 1295, 1303 (11th Cir. 2001). "A person acts under color of state law when he acts with authority possessed by virtue of his employment with the state." *Griffin*, 261 F.3d at 1303. "The dispositive issue is whether the official was acting pursuant to the power he/she possessed by state authority or acting only as a private individual." *Id.* (quotation marks omitted). ". . . § 1983 excludes from its reach merely private conduct, no matter how discriminatory or wrong." *Sullivan*, 526 U.S. at 49–50, 119 S.Ct. at 985 (quotation marks omitted). "[T]he inquiry must be whether there is a sufficiently close nexus between the State and the challenged action of the regulated entity so that the action of the latter may be fairly treated as that of the State itself." *Sims v. Jefferson Downs, Inc.*, 611 F.2d 609, 611 (5th Cir. 1980).

In Bell's complaint, she alleges that Defendants acted under color of state law while caring for her mother because they were "licens[ed] by the state of Florida to run [a] nursing care facility." The fact that a nursing home is licensed or regulated by a state, however, does not alone establish state action. *See Blum v. Yaretsky*, 457 U.S. 991, 1011–12, 102 S.Ct. 2777, 2789–90 (1982) (concluding that privately owned and operated nursing homes' state licensure, regulation and partial funding did not render decisions to discharge or transfer patients state action under the Fourteenth Amendment) . . . .

Bell challenges the medical treatment that two private nursing homes and a physician in a private hospital provided to Fann. Specifically, Bell argues that Defendants improperly cleaned and cared for an open wound on Fann's back such that the wound became infected. Bell also argues that Defendants' negligence caused Fann's death. . . .

Bell's complaint targets merely private conduct, which § 1983 does not reach.... Bell's § 1983 claim fails to establish a claim for relief that is plausible on its face. *See AstraZeneca Pharms.*, 634 F.3d at 1359; *see also Iqbal*,129 S. Ct. at 1949; *Twombly*, 550 U.S. at 570, 127 S.Ct. at 1974.

Although Bell also sued Defendants under the FTCA, that claim fails because defendants are neither federal agencies nor federal officials and were not acting on the federal government's behalf.... Dismissal of that claim, therefore, is appropriate under Rule 12(b)(6). *See Iqbal*, 129 S.Ct. at 1949; *Twombly*, 550 U.S. at 570, 127 S.Ct. at 1974. [The court therefore AFFIRMS the dismissal of these two federal claims.]

Notes and Questions

(1) *What if Plaintiff Had Pleaded Medical Malpractice Claims?* If the court in *Bell* had been considering a complaint containing medical malpractice claims against these defendants, maybe the result would have been different. Can you explain why? You should frame your answer to this question in terms of the standards governing the complaint, and you should be sure that you can explain those standards. [In fact, the plaintiff did plead other claims in addition to the two federal claims considered in this case, and the court of appeals remanded those claims for the district court to consider.]

(2) *What if the Court Simply Does Not Believe the Plaintiff's Factual Allegations?* Imagine that a judge reads a complaint containing medical malpractice claims—and the judge says, "I simply don't believe a word of these factual allegations." Can the district court dismiss, then? You should recognize that the answer is no, after considering the question in light of the standards for pleadings.

Then, another question arises. Why are the rules set up so that a district court can't dismiss, if it disbelieves what the plaintiff says in the complaint? Consider this: the suit is at its earliest stage. No evidence has been produced. There are no witnesses, and there is no jury. All that the court has, and all that it can consider, is the complaint. And if it is going to dismiss without evidence, shouldn't it accept the facts in the complaint as true?

(3) *Prisoner Litigation Inarticulately Alleging Civil Rights Violations: An "Acid Test" for Pleading Rules.* Dismissal of invalid claims is of considerable importance to state officials, who may reasonably see themselves as hampered in essential duties by a blizzard of complaints drafted by inmates *pro se* in their spare time. Many of these complaints display no awareness of either substantive law or procedure, and many are inarticulate or even unintelligible. But the discovery and other procedures necessary for dealing with even an unfounded complaint entail significant additional expense and time away from other duties. On the other hand, a *pro se* inmate sometimes has a real gripe (or even a valid claim) that is masked by his draftsmanship, and presumably it is preferable for him to air even an invalid dispute in the courts than to seek redress by extrajudicial means. Consider the following excerpts

from Stancill, *Inmate Lawsuits Mushroom: Court Costs Whopping $630,000 in 12-Month Period*, Houston Chronicle (1985):(*)

> The winter doldrums must have hit TDC prisoner Joseph Anthony Parker particularly hard.
>
> From December through February, Parker, an inmate at the Darrington unit of the Texas Department of Corrections, stayed busy by filing 21 federal lawsuits alleging that prison officials and others violated his civil rights.
>
> Parker, in handwritten complaints from his Rosharon cell, contended that TDC officials were responsible for defective snacks and provisions he bought from a prison store, such as stale corn chips and bitter coffee that gave him "sinus headaches, stomach and chest pains."
>
> W.C. Davis, an inmate at the Harris County rehabilitation center, filed only one federal lawsuit in February but it was a memorable one.
>
> Davis claims he is wrongfully imprisoned because a key witness in his trial "had sex with me while I was asleep and she lied to cover up her transgressions." . . .
>
> Taxpayers spent a whopping $630,000 to cover court costs of handling inmate lawsuits filed in federal district court in Houston and Galveston over the past 12 months ending in February, says Max Brown, a management analyst in U.S. District Court Clerk Jesse Clark's office. . . .
>
> [One magistrate's] example of a case without merit is a case filed by a prisoner who alleged civil rights violations because he was served three meatballs in the lunch line while other inmates got four.
>
> But he also points out he has seen cases that should be aired, such as prisoner beatings and other mistreatment. One such case that recently ended in a settlement, he says, was one by two men who were bitten severely when they served as "dog boys" to help train prison dogs.

The judges in this district have considered involuntary appointment of attorneys without fee to such cases, using the court's authority over admission of attorneys to practice before it as a means of enforcement. Is this solution appropriate (if appointed, how would you counsel your client in the "meatballs" case)? Should taxpayer dollars be used for the payment of attorneys who take such cases voluntarily? Or should such suits be more readily subject to dismissal?

After enduring this phenomenon for many years, Congress passed the Prisoner Litigation Reform Act in 1996. The Act requires that prisoners exhaust all administrative remedies available to them before suing, authorizes judges to screen all suits before ordering a hearing, allows revocation of good time credits for frivolous suits, and provides that inmates must pay substantial filing fees (in the past, filing for

---

indigents was free). *See Prison Suits Drop Under New Federal Restrictions*, S.F. Daily Journal, June 19, 1997, at 1 (reporting 25% decrease in some locations).

Litigation Document Example 1.1: Pleadings and Decision in *Wytinger v. Two Unknown Police Officers*

How to Read the Pleadings in Wytinger v. Two Unknown Police Officers

On February 20, 1980, William David Wytinger committed suicide by hanging himself in the London City jail in the State of West York (a hypothetical city in a typical state of the United States). Shortly thereafter, Wytinger's surviving parents brought a civil rights suit, naming as defendants two police officers and the City of London. The underlying claim is based on 42 U.S.C. § 1983, often referred to by lawyers as "1983" or "the civil rights statute."

Section 1983 gives redress for deprivation of constitutional rights under color of state law, such as the right to due process under the Fourteenth Amendment and the right to not be subjected to cruel and unusual punishment under the Eighth Amendment. Very often, as shown here, plaintiffs bring Section 1983 actions when seeking compensation for the alleged wrongful conduct of police, prison guards, or other government agents.

Section 1983 liability may be imposed in cases involving prisoners or pretrial detainees if the individual officers acted with deliberate indifference to the person's serious medical needs. *Estelle v. Gamble*, 429 U.S. 97, 104–05 (1976). Proof of an official city policy or a persistent widespread municipal custom is required to hold a municipality accountable for the decedent's injuries and death. *Monell v. Department of Social Services*, 436 U.S. 658, 690–91 (1978). Hence, the plaintiff must allege acts or omissions sufficiently harmful to evidence a deliberate indifference to serious medical needs, and in order to state a claim against the City of London, the plaintiff must allege that the City caused the decedent's injury through an official policy or pursuant to a widespread custom that is so well-settled that, though not officially adopted, it can be said to fairly represent municipal policy. As you read the following materials, you should keep these legal standards in mind, together with the standard for dismissal of a complaint.

These documents are taken from a real case. The "business" parts of the documents are closely similar to the original ones in the real case, but they have been edited and the names are changed.

The Complaint

IN THE UNITED STATES DISTRICT COURT FOR
THE MIDDLE DISTRICT OF WEST YORK
LONDON DIVISION

BARRY WYTINGER and PAULA WYTINGER, Plaintiffs v. TWO UNKNOWN POLICE OFFICERS and the CITY OF LONDON, WEST YORK, Defendants.	CIVIL ACTION NO. ________ COMPLAINT FOR DAMAGES JURY DEMAND

PLAINTIFFS' ORIGINAL COMPLAINT

Come now BARRY WYTINGER and PAULA WYTINGER, Plaintiffs, complaining of TWO UNKNOWN POLICE OFFICERS and THE CITY OF LONDON, WEST YORK, and would show as follows:

PARTIES, JURISDICTION, AND VENUE

1. Plaintiffs are the surviving parents of WILLIAM DAVID WYTINGER, deceased. Decedent died intestate in, and while a resident of, the County of Manero, State of West York. During all times mentioned in this complaint, Plaintiffs were, and still are, citizens of the United States, and they resided, and still reside, in London, Manero County, West York. Plaintiffs are the sole heirs at law of decedent WILLIAM DAVID WYTINGER.

2. Defendant UNKNOWN POLICE OFFICERS were, at all times material to this complaint, duly appointed, employed, and acting police officers of the Defendant CITY OF LONDON, and were acting under color of the statutes and ordinances of the City of London and the State of West York. Though the identity of Defendant UNKNOWN OFFICERS is unavailable to Plaintiffs at this time, Plaintiffs will request discovery of their names from Defendant CITY OF LONDON. Plaintiff alleges that the deprivation of Decedent's rights, as hereinafter detailed, was part of a deliberate pattern of conduct or policy of the Defendant CITY OF LONDON.

3. This is an action at law to redress the deprivation under color of statute, ordinance, regulation, custom, or usage, of rights, privileges, and immunities secured to Decedent and Plaintiffs by the Constitution of the United States and by federal law, particularly the Civil Rights Act, 42 U.S.C. section 1983.

4. The action arises under said Section 1983; under the Fourth, Fifth, Eighth and Fourteenth Amendments to the Constitution of the United States; and under other provisions of federal law. This Court has jurisdiction under and by virtue of 28 U.S.C. section 1331 (the General Federal Question Statute) and 28 U.S.C. section 1343 (the Civil Rights Jurisdiction Statute). All defendants reside, and the claim arose, in the Middle District of West York, London Division.

CLAIM PURSUANT TO 42 U.S.C. SECTION 1983

5. On or about the 21st day of February, 1980, in the early afternoon, Plaintiffs' decedent, WILLIAM DAVID WYTINGER, was accosted by two unidentified London Police Officers. Decedent was a 20 year old man, afflicted with minimal brain damage and heart disease. He was under the almost constant supervision of his mother, Plaintiff PAULA WYTINGER, as his physical and emotional state required constant attention and care. Plaintiffs' decedent had also been under the treatment of a psychiatrist.

6. Defendant UNKNOWN OFFICERS began to question decedent about a burglary which had occurred in the area. Decedent, due to his fragile emotional disposition, became hysterical. On the scene were various neighbors, and Decedent's father, Plaintiff BARRY WYTINGER.

7. The Defendant OFFICERS asked Plaintiff BARRY WYTINGER if Decedent was "all right," and more specifically, whether Decedent had ever "had any sort of nervous breakdown." Decedent's father, pleading that his son not be jailed, answered in the affirmative, and directed the OFFICERS' attention to two bracelets Decedent wore around his wrist. The bracelets read: "MEDICAL WARNING. SEE WALLET CARD" and "HEART PATIENT." Again, Plaintiff BARRY WYTINGER asked that his son not be jailed.

8. Defendant OFFICERS removed the two bracelets and dangled them in front of Decedent's father, telling him that if he would obtain a letter from the boy's psychiatrist, attesting to the boy's condition and to the danger of his being confined, that the boy would in all likelihood be released. Defendant OFFICERS then proceeded to force the hysterical WILLIAM DAVID WYTINGER into their squad car.

9. About an hour later, Plaintiff PAULA WYTINGER spoke to her son over the phone. Decedent was highly distraught at the prospect of confinement in the city jail.

10. Around midnight, PAULA WYTINGER received word that her son had been found hanging from the bars of his jail cell, an apparent suicide.

11. Decedent's death was proximately caused by the acts or omissions of both the TWO UNKNOWN OFFICERS and by the custom or policy in effect at the CITY OF LONDON through its police department. Defendant OFFICERS should have known, in light of Decedent's warning bracelets, his hysterical behavior, and his father's admonitions not to jail him, that to proceed with Decedent's confinement would likely result in some harm or even death to Decedent. Indeed, Plaintiffs allege that Decedent was known at the police department to be a mental patient, by indications on his arrest record.

12. CITY OF LONDON and its police department caused Decedent's death in either or both of the following respects:

a. By allowing a known mental patient, obviously distraught and under unusual stress, to be confined despite exhortations not to by Decedent's father; and

b. By failing to make adequate routine checks of Decedent's cell, which failure of supervision tragically resulted in Decedent's suicide.

13. As a direct and proximate result of the above-detailed conduct of Defendant UNKNOWN POLICE OFFICERS and of Defendant CITY OF LONDON, Plaintiffs and their decedent were deprived of the following rights, privileges, and immunities secured to them by the Constitution of the United States:

a. The right of Decedent to be secure in his person and effects against unreasonable search and seizure under the Fourth and Fourteenth Amendments to the Constitution of the United States;

b. The right of Decedent not to be deprived of life, liberty, or property without due process of law, and the right to equal protection of the laws secured by the Fourteenth Amendment to the Constitution of the United States; and

c. The right to freedom from physical abuse, coercion, and intimidation and from cruel and unusual punishment.

These rights were secured by the provisions of the due process clause of the Fifth and Fourteenth Amendments to the Constitution of the United States, by the Fourth Amendment, by the Eighth Amendment, and by Title 42, United States Code, Section 1983.

14. The acts of Defendants, as described above, were done with callous and reckless indifference to and disregard of Decedent's safety and continued life by reason of which Decedent was, in his lifetime, entitled, by virtue of the West York Wrongful Death statutes, to compensatory damages in the sum of TWENTY THOUSAND and NO/100 ($20,000.00) DOLLARS, and to punitive damages in the sum of ONE HUNDRED THOUSAND and NO/100 ($100,000.00) DOLLARS, and his heirs are now entitled, by virtue of such statute, to an award of such compensatory and punitive damages.

15. Plaintiffs are also entitled to the costs of funeral expenses incurred by their son's death, in the amount of ONE THOUSAND and NO/100 ($1,000.00) DOLLARS, which sum is reasonable and necessary for such costs in Manero County, West York.

16. At the time of his death, Decedent was 20 years of age. By reason of Decedent's wrongful death and the loss to his parents, Plaintiffs BARRY WYTINGER and PAULA WYTINGER, of the aid, association, support, protection, comfort, care and society of the Decedent, and the loss of their respective shares in such estate as the Decedent might reasonably have accumulated in his natural life expectancy, Plaintiffs BARRY WYTINGER and PAULA WYTINGER, as the sole surviving heirs of Decedent, have been damaged in the sum of TWENTY THOUSAND and NO/100 ($20,000.00) DOLLARS.

PRAYER

WHEREFORE, Plaintiffs demand judgment: (a) Awarding Plaintiffs compensatory damages of $20,000; (b) Awarding Plaintiffs punitive damages of $100,000; (c) Awarding Plaintiffs funeral expenses of $1,000; (d) Awarding Plaintiffs loss of future support of $20,000; (e) Awarding Plaintiffs the reasonable costs and expenses of this action, and such other and further relief as may be just.

JURY DEMAND

Plaintiffs respectfully demand trial by jury on all issues so triable.

Respectfully submitted,

DONALD A. PETERS
2200 Linden Avenue, Suite 100
London, West York 77006
(713) 555-6060

The Motion to Dismiss

IN THE UNITED STATES DISTRICT COURT FOR
THE MIDDLE DISTRICT OF WEST YORK
LONDON DIVISION

BARRY WYTINGER and
PAULA WYTINGER, Plaintiffs

v.

TWO UNKNOWN POLICE OFFICERS
and the
CITY OF LONDON, WEST YORK,
Defendants.

CIVIL ACTION NO. CIV-80-2346-G
COMPLAINT FOR DAMAGES
JURY DEMAND

DEFENDANT CITY OF LONDON'S MOTION TO DISMISS

COMES NOW the CITY OF LONDON, named as a defendant in the above styled and numbered action, and would move the Court to dismiss the complaint as to it, and would show as follows:

1. The complaint herein fails to state a claim upon which relief can be granted against this defendant, in that it asserts no facts whatsoever upon which any theory could support a judgment or expose this defendant to liability under 42 U.S.C. Section 1983. *Estelle v. Gamble*, 429 U.S. 97 (1976) (complaint for inadequate medical attention does not state a claim under 1983 unless it alleges "acts or omissions sufficiently harmful to evidence a deliberate indifference to serious medical needs").

2. Further, the complaint fails to state a claim upon which relief can be granted in that it seeks to hold the CITY OF LONDON liable on the theory that it employed individuals who performed the acts complained of. This theory, known in the law as *respondent superior*, is not a theory under which a plaintiff may recover in a suit under 42 U.S.C. section 1983. *Monell v. Department of Social Services*, 436 U.S. 658 (1978) (requiring causation by city's own "official" custom or policy); *Baskin v. Parker*, 602 F.2d 1205 (5th Cir. 1979) (same); *Perry v. Jones*, 506 F.2d 778 (5th Cir. 1975) (same); *Ford v. Byrd*, 544 F.2d 194 (5th Cir. 1976) (same).

WHEREFORE, PREMISES CONSIDERED, the CITY OF LONDON prays that plaintiffs' complaint be dismissed and that it be awarded costs of court.

Respectfully submitted,

J.D. THOMAS, JR.
City Attorney

By: RANDALL PARKS
Assistant City Attorney
P.O. Box 8127
London, West York, 77002
(713) 555-6021

The Court's Order of Dismissal

IN THE UNITED STATES DISTRICT COURT FOR
THE MIDDLE DISTRICT OF WEST YORK
LONDON DIVISION

BARRY WYTINGER and PAULA WYTINGER, Plaintiffs v. TWO UNKNOWN POLICE OFFICERS and the CITY OF LONDON, WEST YORK, Defendants.	CIVIL ACTION NO. CIV-80-2346-G COMPLAINT FOR DAMAGES JURY DEMAND

ORDER

Pending before the court is Defendants' Motion to Dismiss Plaintiffs' claim under 42 U.S.C. § 1983 (1976) for failure to state a claim upon which relief may be granted pursuant to Rule 12(b)(6), Fed. R. Civ. P. . . .

Upon review of the record, Defendants' motion to dismiss, and Plaintiffs' response, it is the opinion of the Court that Plaintiffs' 1983 action is insufficient to state a claim for relief in light of *Estelle v. Gamble*, 429 U.S. 97 (1976) where the Supreme Court concluded that "[i]n order to constitute a cognizable claim, a prisoner must allege acts or omissions sufficiently harmful to evidence deliberate indifference to serious medical needs. . . ."

The allegations in Plaintiffs' complaint, liberally construed and accepted as true, are that decedent was arrested for suspicion of burglary and theft, that he had been diagnosed as suffering from restlessness and anxiety as a result of chronic mild organic brain syndrome, that upon arrest his hysterical and agitated behavior—specifically, striking his head against the windshield and divided glass—alerted Defendants to decedent's condition, that Defendants were aware that decedent was under the care of a psychologist, that the medical-alert bracelets on decedent's wrists and the psychologist's note in his wallet alerted the officers to decedent's condition, and that the conditions of his confinement aggravated his medical needs and led to his suicide.

. . . In light of considerations established by the Court of Appeals for the Fifth Circuit in *Woodall v. Foti*, 648 F.2d 268 (5th Cir. 1981), to determine whether the alleged denial amounts to deliberate indifference to the decedent's medical needs, it is the opinion of the Court that the Plaintiffs' claim is insufficient to state a claim for relief under 42 U.S.C. § 1983 (1976).

Since the Court is of the opinion that Plaintiffs' federal claims are insufficient to state a claim, the Court declines [supplemental] jurisdiction over Plaintiffs' state claims. . . . It is, therefore,

ORDERED that Defendants' motion to dismiss is granted. It is further ordered that Plaintiffs' complaint is dismissed without prejudice. . . .

Signed this day of September, 1983.

GEORGE GILLIAM, JR.
United States District Judge

Notes and Questions

(1) *The Substantive Standard: What Must Plaintiffs Plead and Prove?* Make sure that you understand the required allegations and proof for a prisoner or detainee to prevail on the claim at issue: There must be acts or omissions evidencing (1) "deliberate indifference" to (2) "serious medical needs," and for the city to be liable, they must be caused by (3) an "official custom or policy." This is the required minimum for the civil rights claim asserted here (of course, a separate negligence claim under state law, if available against the city and its officers, would involve a lesser standard of proof). Do you agree with this substantive law standard?

(2) *Evaluating the Dismissal of the Complaint.* Given the substantive legal standard (whether you agree with it or not), do you think the dismissal is correct? You should compare the allegations of the complaint to the required elements of the claim. Also, you should remember the standard for dismissing a complaint.

(3) *Would You Appeal?* The attorneys in a case of this nature typically would operate on a contingent fee basis (*i.e.*, they receive no fee and they pay significant costs unless there is a plaintiff's recovery). Would you have accepted employment in the case on this basis? Would you be willing to represent the client upon appeal, knowing that you must expend more effort and funds for the appeal and will not recover unless you ultimately prevail before a jury?

(4) *The Appeal of the Dismissal: A Cliffhanger.* Plaintiffs' counsel did appeal. Initially, a panel of the court of appeals held for plaintiffs and reversed the dismissal, with one judge dissenting. *Partridge v. Two Unknown Police Officers*, 751 F.2d 1448 (5th Cir. 1985). However, Defendants filed a motion for rehearing. The court then took the unusual step of withdrawing its published opinion, stating that "a new decision and judgment will be entered in due course." 755 F.2d 1126 (5th Cir. 1985). More than six years after plaintiffs' decedent's death, the Fifth Circuit issued another opinion, reversing the dismissal, again with one judge dissenting, 791 F.2d 1182 (5th Cir. 1986); *see also* § 5.03[B] of Chapter 5, below (in which the opinion is summarized). Why do you think this case is such a cliffhanger?

V. Discovery

Read Rule 26(b)(1) of the Federal Rules of Civil Procedure.

Note on Methods of Discovery

What Is "Discovery?" Remember what discovery is: a procedure for obtaining information from opposing parties or non-party witnesses. Discovery is really an aspect of the attorney's investigation. Federal Rule 26(b) defines the scope of discovery as extending to information that is "relevant," "proportional to the needs of the case," and "not privileged."

Methods of Discovery. The methods of discovery include written questions directed to other parties to the suit, document production from other parties, and oral questioning of witnesses before court reporters. Written questions are called "interrogatories," document discovery is done by "requests for production," and witnesses are questioned in "depositions." The case that follows covers each of these discovery types.

Note on the Breadth (or "Scope") of Discovery

Historically, Discovery Was Broader Than It Is Today. During the Twenty-First Century, the consensus of rulemakers was that discovery had become too expensive. At that time, discovery included not only admissible evidence, but also everything that was reasonably likely to lead to the finding of evidence. Attorneys were skillful at writing requests for documents that forced opponents to locate and produce hundreds of thousands or millions of documents.

Narrowing Discovery: The "Proportionality" Standard. In response to this issue, the Supreme Court adopted an amendment to Rule 26 that limits discovery to information that is "proportional to the needs of the case." Make no mistake, however, about this: discovery is still very expensive, and lawyers often disagree about how much information is obtainable. But the following decision cuts some of the cost by applying the requirement of proportionality. Notice that there is a blanket request for "all personnel files" of employees, which is reminiscent of document demands that might have been upheld in the past, but which is handled very differently in this case.

Rollins v. Cone Distributing, Inc.

710 Fed. Appx. 814 (11th Cir. 20117)

PER CURIAM:

Twanetta Rollins sued her former employer, Cone Distributing Inc., for sex discrimination and retaliation under Title VII of the Civil Rights Act of 1964 ("Title VII"), 42 U.S.C. §§ 2000e–2, 3, and the Florida Civil Rights Act of 1992. The district court granted summary judgment in favor of Cone on both claims. Rollins appeals the court's summary judgment ruling as well as several of its discovery rulings. . . . [W]e affirm.

Rollins worked at Cone for 45 days in a probationary capacity as a warehouse worker. Cone is a beverage distribution company, and Rollins was responsible for loading bulk quantities of beer and other beverages onto (and removing them from) Cone trucks. [Other employees complained about Rollins. Dan Yero was a training instructor, and he] reported that Rollins was not receptive and would not listen to his instructions and that she was the most difficult and combative trainee he had ever encountered. . . .

Cone employees within their first 90 days of employment are on probation and subject to close scrutiny. . . . Ultimately, [Director of Human Relations Tim] Null decided to terminate Rollins's employment before the end of her probation. He came to this decision because he concluded that Rollins had difficulty working with others, did not perform tasks as instructed, and failed to follow Yero's instructions during driver training. . . .

[During discovery,] Rollins filed three motions to compel [i.e., to compel Cone to reply to particular discovery requests]. These motions argued that Cone failed to comply with many of Rollins's discovery requests, three of which are relevant on appeal. First, she sought the personnel files of every employee who had ever held Rollins's position at the Tallahassee warehouse to determine if these employees had received more favorable treatment than she did. Second, Rollins asked to conduct a second deposition [i.e., a second questioning session] of Lopez because [allegedly] he was not sufficiently prepared for his first deposition. Third, Rollins insisted that Cone respond to her interrogatories requesting information about the reasons for her termination; any documents related to those reasons, and any policies or procedures she could have utilized to address employment discrimination or harassment.

The district court denied each of these requests as disproportional to the needs of the case and duplicative of items already produced. The court did, however, grant part of one of Rollins's motions to compel and ordered Cone to produce any notes Boyer took during a meeting she held with Rollins and Mitchell. . . .

Cone moved for summary judgment. Rollins opposed the motion. The district court . . . granted summary judgment. This is Rollins's appeal. . . .

A. Discovery Rulings . . .

Rollins challenges the court's denial of her motions to compel. A party may move for an order compelling discovery or disclosure. Discovery may be had as to "any nonprivileged matter that is relevant to any party's claim or defense and proportional to the needs of the case." Fed. R. Civ. P. 26(b)(1). The court must limit the frequency or extent of discovery otherwise permitted if it determines that "the discovery sought is unreasonable cumulative or duplicative," or "the party seeking discovery has had ample opportunity to obtain the information by discovery in the action." Fed. R. Civ. P. 26(b)(2)(C). . . . "Where a significant amount of discovery has been obtained, and it appears that further discovery would not be helpful in resolving the issues, a request for further discovery is properly denied." *Iraola & CIA, S.A. v. Kimberly–Clark Corp.*, 325 F.3d 1274, 1286 (11th Cir. 2003).

The district court did not abuse its discretion in denying Rollins's motion to compel Cone personnel files, a second deposition of Lopez, and responses to several of her interrogatories. . . .

First, the district court did not abuse its discretion in determining that Rollins's requests for personnel files exceeded the proper scope of discovery. Rollins sought the personnel files of every warehouse worker Cone ever employed in the Tallahassee warehouse to determine whether Cone treated any male employee more favorably than Rollins. Cone had already produced the personnel files of Rollins, Mitchell, and another employee whom Rollins specifically identified as a male employee who might have received more favorable treatment, as well as many other documents in response to her discovery requests. Absent any indication that any particular warehouse employee was a comparator who had been treated more favorably, we cannot say that the district court abused its discretion in denying the motion to compel.

Rollins cites a bevy of cases in which other courts have granted Title VII plaintiffs access to personnel files, but an examination of each case reveals that the requests for discovery were more circumscribed and proportional than Rollins's blanket request here. *See, e.g., Coughlin v. Lee,* 946 F.2d 1152, 1159 (11th Cir. 1991) (remanding for district court to consider whether to order production of personnel files of identifiable "employees who had arguably been guilty of a variety of infractions more serious than those committed by plaintiffs, but who nevertheless were not discharged by" the defendant); *Costa v. Remillard,* 160 F.R.D. 434 (D.R.I. 1995) (compelling production of personnel files of two named police officers accused by plaintiff of creating hostile work environment).

Second, it was not an abuse of discretion for the district court to conclude that a second deposition of [Vice President for Administration Joseph] Lopez would have been duplicative or cumulative of other evidence in the record. . . . Rollins deposed Cone's corporate representative, Lopez, for over five hours on a wide variety of topics. Both in her motion to compel and now on appeal, Rollins argues that she [needed a second deposition because] Lopez was unprepared to discuss the topics she identified in her . . . [deposition] notice. Yet the record reflects that Lopez gave responsive answers on all of these topics. For example, Rollins alleges that Lopez was unprepared to discuss the reasons Cone terminated her employment. But Lopez described Yero's difficulty training Rollins, Null's investigation and determination that Rollins was not a good fit for the company, and Null's decision to terminate Rollins on these grounds. Moreover, Rollins deposed Null, Boyer, Verhage, Yero, and at least three other Cone employees. She fails to explain what further evidence Lopez could provide that would be helpful . . . .

Third, the district court did not abuse its discretion when it determined that Rollins's interrogatories were duplicative. Rollins identified three interrogatories to which Cone failed to respond. These interrogatories requested information about the reasons for Rollins's termination, any documents related to those reasons, and any policies or procedures Rollins could have utilized to address employment discrimination or harassment. Although these interrogatories sought relevant information, our review of the record persuades us that Rollins received this same information through her document requests and depositions. "The discovery sought" was therefore "unreasonably cumulative or duplicative" and Rollins "had ample opportunity to obtain the information" she sought. Fed. R. Civ. P. 26(b)(2)(C). The district court's denial of Rollins's motion to compel responses to the three interrogatories was a proper exercise of its discretion. . . .

B. Summary Judgment . . .

We . . . conclude that the district court properly granted summary judgment in Cone's favor because Rollins could not show that Cone's legitimate nondiscriminatory reasons for firing Rollins were pretextual. . . . Rollins was a probationary employee who reportedly had trouble getting along with coworkers, performing her assigned tasks, and following instructions. Each of these was a legitimate nondiscriminatory reason to terminate her employment. [The court similarly finds no basis for Rollins's retaliation claim.] [AFFIRMED.]

Notes and Questions

(1) *Scope of Discovery: "Proportional to the Needs of the Case."* Try to state, briefly, why the court in *Rollins* decided that the personnel files and other discovery sought by the plaintiff were not within the proper scope of discovery.

(2) *"Privilege."* If information is privileged, it cannot be discovered by any means, no matter how relevant or proportional. For example, imagine that, in a case like *Rollins,* the defendant sends an interrogatory to the plaintiff saying, "Describe everything your lawyer has told you about the weaknesses in your case." The requested information is obviously relevant, and it would not be so voluminous that it would exceed proportionality to the needs of the case. But in response, the plaintiff would object by citing the attorney-client privilege.

(3) *The Realities of Discovery: Still Expensive and Still Intrusive.* Rollins took the depositions of at least seven employees of Cone, Cone itself no doubt took depositions, and there were written interrogatories as well as voluminous documents discovered. The process was still expensive, even if "proporional." Another issue: Imagine that you are an employee whose personnel file has been discovered by the plaintiff for comparison purposes. You might dislike hearing that. Proportionality takes some of the edge off, but discovery is expensive and instrusive.

(4) *If You Are a Litigation Lawyer, Discovery Is Where You Live.* Discovery is extremely important to a litigator. In fact, discovery is the activity in which most litigators spend most of their time. In a complex case, documents produced in discovery can easily number in the multiple millions. On the one hand, discovery is the litigant's means of finding "smoking gun" evidence in the opponent's possession.

On the other hand, it can have the effect of harassment, and in the real world, litigants sometimes employ it for that purpose.

VI. Disposition Without Trial: Summary Judgment

Read Rule 56(a) of the Federal Rules of Civil Procedure. Emphasize the second sentence.

Note on the Standards for Summary Judgment

Fed. R. Civ. P. 56(a) says, "The court shall grant summary judgment if the movant shows that there is no genuine dispute as to any material fact and the movant is entitled to judgment as a matter of law." The court decides this question by considering affidavits, discovery products, and other documents. In other words, summary judgment is a kind of "paper trial," but an odd kind. Because this procedure dispenses with the need for an actual trial, the moving party bears a heavy burden. It is not enough for the moving party to show that she is likely to win at trial; she must demonstrate that there are not even any controversies about the facts that could make any difference in the result.

Warren v. Medley

521 S.W.2d 137 (Tex. Civ. App.—Beaumont 1975, writ ref'd n.r.e.)

Keith, Justice.

Plaintiffs appeal from a take nothing judgment entered after defendant's motion for summary judgment had been sustained by the court. . . .

On the evening of the incident in question, plaintiffs were accompanied by a friend to a restaurant where the parties dined. They then went to a nightclub in Dallas where, according to our record, the principal form of entertainment was furnished by . . . "go-go" dancers who performed upon some type of plexiglass covered platform in the club. Having been so entertained, the parties returned to plaintiffs' home but remained there only a very short time. They then went next door to defendant's home where he and his wife were entertaining another couple, Mr. and Mrs. John Reynolds, III. Plaintiffs' arrival interrupted the poker game then in progress and soon the conversation drifted to an account of the performance of the go-go girls at the nightclub. There is a slight but unimportant difference in the testimony of the parties as to exactly what happened next. Defendant and Reynolds said that Mrs. Warren demonstrated the dance which she had seen at the club but this was denied by Mrs. Warren.

Reynolds urged Mrs. Warren to repeat her exhibition but she declined. Reynolds then grabbed her around the waist and placed her upon the top of the table where the poker game had been conducted. This was a glass-topped table with a wrought iron frame and legs with the glass resting entirely within the framework of the table without center support. Defendant knew it would not support the weight of an adult.

A few seconds after being placed on the table and before she had begun any dancing, instead while pleading to be helped down, the glass top broke. Mrs. Warren fell through the broken top and sustained injury to her leg from the broken shards. Plaintiffs sued defendant [Medley, the homeowner,] and Reynolds. The trial court sustained defendant's [Medley's] motion for summary judgment; and plaintiffs, after settling their suit against Reynolds, now appeal from the take nothing judgment. We affirm.

After a careful review of the deposition testimony forming a part of the summary judgment record, we are of the opinion that the defendant successfully negated plaintiffs' right to recover. In arriving at this conclusion we have borne in mind the rules enunciated by our Supreme Court, including, *inter alia*, the following:

> 1. Defendant labored under the burden of establishing as a matter of law that he is not liable under any theory fairly presented by the allegations of plaintiffs' petition. *Kelsey-Seybold Clinic v. Maclay*, 466 S.W.2d 716, 720 (Tex. 1971).
>
> 2. If reasonable minds could differ as to the conclusions to be drawn from the summary judgment facts, the defendant did not discharge the burden placed upon him. *Adam Dante Corporation v. Sharpe*, 483 S.W.2d 452, 455 (Tex. 1972). . . .

Our decision is simplified somewhat by the agreement of the parties that plaintiffs occupied the status of licensees at the time Mrs. Warren received her injuries. Admittedly, the plaintiffs were social guests in defendant's home; and, as such, were licensees. *Weekes v. Kelley*, 433 S.W.2d 769, 771 (Tex. Civ. App.- Eastland 1968, writ ref'd n.r.e.). . . .

The duty owed to a licensee by the owner or licensor has been restated by our Supreme Court in *State v. Tennison*, 509 S.W.2d 560, 562 (Tex. 1974), in these words:

> It is well settled in this State that if the person injured was on the premises as a licensee, the duty that the proprietor or licensor owed him was not to injure him by willful, wanton or gross negligence.

In *McPhearson v. Sullivan*, 463 S.W.2d 174 (Tex. 1971), the Court reaffirmed the earlier definition of gross negligence:

> Gross negligence is "that entire want of care which would raise the belief that the act or omission complained of was the result of a conscious indifference to the right or welfare of the person or persons to be affected by it."

Plaintiffs, citing several out of state cases, argue that the duty of a host to a social guest is in a process of change from the willful and wanton conduct or gross negligence test [as set out in *Tennison, supra*] to one which requires that the host exercise reasonable care to refrain from injuring the guest by "active" negligence.

As an intermediate appellate court, it is our duty to follow the clear decisions of our Supreme Court as to the substantive law when it can be ascertained with certainty.... We will continue to follow *Tennison* until otherwise notified by the Supreme Court.

In the clearest possible language, Mrs. Warren testified that defendant [Medley] did not suggest that she be placed on the table and that he "expressed surprise" at seeing her there. Finally, it was her testimony that "t[h]e [defendant] couldn't have prevented it." From our careful review of the deposition testimony of Mrs. Warren, we conclude that reasonable minds could not differ as to the sequence of events leading up to the accident. It was Reynolds' act in placing her on top of the table—an act in which defendant did not participate—which brought about her injuries.

Defendant has successfully discharged his onerous burden of showing that he was not guilty of any willful or wanton conduct or gross negligence toward Mrs. Warren on the occasion in question. Moreover, he has negated both proximate cause and cause in fact as a matter of law....

The judgment of the trial court is affirmed.

Notes and Questions

(1) *Relationship Between Summary Judgment and the Substantive Law.* In some states (California, for example), distinctions depending upon an injured person's status as a social guest or "licensee" are not controlling in a suit of this kind. In these states, a host may be liable upon a standard of "simple" negligence, rather than the gross negligence standard applied in *Warren v. Medley. E.g., Rowland v. Christian*, 69 Cal. 2d 108, 70 Cal. Rptr. 97, 443 P.2d 561 (1968). If this case had arisen in California, would the result be different? [Note: The summary judgment evidence here may negate even the contention that the incident was caused by simple negligence on defendant Medley's part, and in any event, it disproves proximate causation by him, which is required in California.]

(2) *Denial of Jury Trial as a Consequence of Summary Judgment.* The federal Constitution guarantees a right to jury trial in federal courts (and the constitutions of most states do likewise in their courts). Ms. Warren obviously has not been afforded a jury trial on her claim. How can the granting of summary judgment be considered constitutional? [Note: The judges' decision means that a jury could not reasonably have reached a contrary decision by applying the law to this evidence.]

(3) *Settlement with One Defendant.* Note that the plaintiff, by settlement, has received some compensation from one defendant (the one who seems most clearly to have been causally negligent). This case should remind you of the prevalence of settlement as a means of resolving disputes. The subject of settlement sometimes raises knotty questions. For example, should a claimant be permitted to compromise her claim with the "most guilty" defendant in order to obtain a "war chest" with which to seek a recovery based upon proof of full damages against a "slightly guilty" defendant? (This result can occur.)

VII. Trial: Functions of the Judge and Jury

[A] Jury Selection, Evidence, Verdict, and Judgment

Fein v. Permanente Medical Group

38 Cal. 3d 137, 211 Cal. Rptr. 368, 695 P.2d 665 (1985)

Kaus, Justice.

In this medical malpractice action, both parties appeal from a judgment awarding plaintiff about $1 million in damages. Defendant claims that the trial court committed reversible error during the selection of the jury, in instructions on liability as well as damages, [and in other actions by the court]. . . . We conclude that the judgment should be affirmed in all respects.

I

[Plaintiff Lawrence Fein, an attorney, felt chest pains while exercising. He was unable to see his regular physician at Permanente Medical Group, an affiliate of the Kaiser Health Foundation. However, he obtained a "short appointment" the afternoon he called. He was examined by Cheryl Welch, whom he knew to be a nurse practitioner, and who worked under the supervision of Dr. Wintrop Franz. After consulting Dr. Franz, Nurse Welch advised Fein that she and Dr. Franz believed he had suffered a muscle spasm, and she gave him Dr. Franz's prescription for Valium.

[That night, Fein had severe chest pains, went to the Kaiser emergency room, and was X-rayed by Dr. Lowell Redding, who also diagnosed muscle spasms and administered pain medication. Later, after further pain, Fein returned again, and Dr. Donald Oliver directed an electrocardiogram (EKG). The EKG showed that Fein was suffering a heart attack (acute myocardial infarction). He was transferred to the cardiac care unit and treated without surgery. By the time of trial, he had been permitted to return to virtually all of his prior recreational activities, including jogging, swimming, bicycling, and skiing.

[Fein sued Permanente on the claim that his condition should have been diagnosed earlier and treated to prevent the heart attack or reduce its residual effects.]

At trial, Dr. Harold Swan, the head of cardiology at the Cedars-Sinai Medical Center in Los Angeles, was the principal witness for plaintiff. Dr. Swan testified that an important signal that a heart attack may be imminent is chest pain which can radiate to other parts of the body. Such pain is not relieved by rest or pain medication. . . .

Dr. Swan further testified that in his opinion any patient who appears with chest pains should be given an EKG to rule out the worst possibility, a heart problem. He stated that the symptoms that plaintiff had described to Nurse Welch at the 4 p.m. examination on Thursday, February 26, should have indicated to her that an EKG was in order. He also stated that when plaintiff returned to Kaiser late that same night with his chest pain unrelieved by the medication he had been given, Dr. Redding should also have ordered an EKG. According to Dr. Swan, if an EKG had been ordered at those times it could have revealed plaintiff's imminent heart attack, and treatment could have been administered which might have prevented or minimized the attack.

Dr. Swan also testified to the damage caused by the attack. He stated that as a result of the attack a large portion of the plaintiff's heart muscle had died, reducing plaintiff's future life expectancy by about one-half, to about 16 or 17 years. Although Dr. Swan acknowledged that some of plaintiff's other coronary arteries also suffer from disease, he felt that if plaintiff had been properly treated his future life expectancy would be decreased by only 10 to 15 percent, rather than half.

Nurse Welch and Dr. Redding testified on behalf of the defense, indicating that the symptoms that plaintiff had reported to them at the time of the examinations were not the same symptoms he had described at trial. Defendant also introduced a number of expert witnesses—not employed by Kaiser—who stated that on the basis of the symptoms reported and observed before the heart attack, the medical personnel could not reasonably have determined that a heart attack was imminent. Additional defense evidence indicated (1) that an EKG would not have shown that a heart attack was imminent, (2) that because of the severe disease in the coronary arteries which caused plaintiff's heart attack, the attack could not have been prevented even had it been known that it was about to occur, and finally (3) that, given the deterioration in plaintiff's other coronary arteries, the heart attack had not affected plaintiff's life expectancy to the degree suggested by Dr. Swan.

In the face of this sharply conflicting evidence, the jury found in favor of plaintiff on the issue of liability and, pursuant to the trial court's instructions, returned special verdicts itemizing various elements of damages....

[On appeal,] Defendant maintains that the trial court committed reversible error in ... excusing all Kaiser members from the jury [and in other ways].

II

At the outset of the empanelment of the jury, the court indicated that it would excuse from the jury those prospective jurors who would refuse to go to Kaiser for treatment under any circumstances and also those prospective jurors who were members of the Kaiser medical plan. When defendant noted its objection to the court's exclusion of the Kaiser members without conducting individual voir dire examinations, the court explained to the jury panel: "I am going to excuse you at this time because we've found that we can prolong the jury selection by just such a very long time by going through each and every juror under these circumstances...." On inquiry, it turned out that 24 of the 60 persons on the initial jury panel [i.e., 40% of the panel] were members of Kaiser. They were excused. Voir dire then proceeded in the ordinary fashion, with each party questioning the remaining jurors and exercising challenges for cause and peremptory challenges.

... [Defendant] argues that a potential juror's mere membership in Kaiser does not provide a basis for a challenge for cause under the applicable California statute, Code of Civil Procedure section 602.

Past decisions do not provide a clear-cut answer to the question whether a potential juror's membership in Kaiser would itself render the juror subject to a statutory challenge for cause. Section 602 does not define with precision the degree of "interest" or connection with a party that will support a challenge for cause, and courts in other states have come to different conclusions with respect to the eligibility of potential jurors whose relationship to one of the parties is similar to Kaiser members' relationship to defendant. Some cases have found error when a trial court has failed to excuse such persons for cause (*see, e.g., M & A Electric Power Cooperative v. Georger* (Mo. 1972) 480 S.W.2d 868, 871–874 [members of "consumer" electrical cooperative . . .]). In *McKernan v. Los Angeles Gas etc. Co.* (1911) 16 Cal. App. 280, 283, 116 P. 677—perhaps the closest California case in point—the court indicated that the mere fact that some of the jurors were customers of the defendant utility company would not, in itself, mandate their excusal for cause.

But whether or not under California law membership in Kaiser rendered the prospective jurors excludable for cause under section 602, we believe that it is clear that the trial court's discharge of such members provides no basis for reversing the judgment in this case. To begin with, even if membership in Kaiser is not itself disqualifying, it is not apparent that the trial court abused the broad discretion it retains over the jury selection process (*see, e.g., Rousseau v. West Coast House Movers* (1967) 256 Cal. App. 2d 878, 883–886, 64 Cal. Rptr. 655) by excusing the members in this case. As its comments to the jury suggest, the court had apparently discovered through past experience that in this situation the individual voir dire procedure would prove very time-consuming and unproductive, with a substantial proportion of the Kaiser members ultimately being subject to challenge by one party or the other. Furthermore, the trial court may reasonably have felt that the process of conducting an extensive voir dire of all Kaiser members might itself prejudice prospective jurors who did not belong to Kaiser. From experience, it may have foreseen that such questioning would invariably involve the recounting of specific, potentially prejudicial incidents concerning the prospective jurors and Kaiser, as well as the exploration of the relative satisfaction or dissatisfaction with Kaiser of the particular jurors on this venire. Such matters would, of course, not be admissible in the actual trial of the case, and the court may have feared that such revelations on voir dire might "taint" all of the other prospective jurors in the courtroom. Under these circumstances, it cannot be said that the trial court abused its discretion in excusing the Kaiser members without individual examination.

[Defendant also makes a separate argument, under the Constitution, to the effect that the trial judge excluded a "cognizable group" of potential jurors.] [D]efendant attempts to fit this case within . . . the theory that the removal of the Kaiser members rendered the jury panel unconstitutionally nonrepresentative (*cf. Thiel v. Southern Pacific Co.* (1946) 328 U.S. 217, 66 S. Ct. 984, 90 L. Ed. 1181 [exclusion of daily wage earners]) . . . , but defendant points to no authority which even remotely supports its claim that Kaiser members are a "cognizable class," and the record in this case provides no evidence to suggest that this group has the kind of shared experiences, ideology or background that have been identified as the *sine qua non* of such a class. . . . On this record, we cannot find that the jury that tried this matter was any less a cross-section of the community than it would have been had Kaiser members not been excused.

Accordingly, the manner in which the jury was selected provides no basis for reversing the judgment. [AFFIRMED.]

[Other parts of the court's opinion appear in section [B], below.]

Notes and Questions

(1) *Selecting the Jury.* In jury selection, both sides have an opportunity to ask (or have the judge ask) questions. From the answers, each side may challenge (*i.e.*, remove) a certain number of persons without assigning any reason, as well as an unlimited number of persons "for cause" (such as demonstrable bias or "interest" in the outcome). Could the Kaiser plan members have been properly excluded for financial "interest" in the case? (Perhaps; perhaps not.) If not, why did the trial judge adopt the solution of excusing them as a group?

(2) *Composition of the Jury Venire.* The court's ruling excused 24 of 60 jurors (or 40 percent of the entire panel). As a matter of trial strategy, why were the defendants dissatisfied with this ruling (how did the initial panel differ in bias or lack thereof from the group that remained?). The court holds, however, that the final group was not "any less a cross-section of the community than it would have been had Kaiser members not been excused." Consider whether the case can be distinguished from such decisions as *Thiel v. Southern Pacific Co.*, cited in the opinion, in which the trial judge declined to summon any laborers who were paid by the day, on the ground that jury service would be a hardship to them. In that case, the Supreme Court held that the excusal of this "cognizable group" (day laborers) was improper.

[B] Instructing the Jury

Fein v. Permanente Medical Group

38 Cal. 3d 137, 211 Cal. Rptr. 368, 695 P.2d 665 (1985)

[The facts and holding in this case are given in the preceding section. Briefly, Fein sued Permanente for negligent diagnosis and treatment. The evidence showed relevant actions by both a nurse and a physician employed by Permanente. The facts were hotly contested. The jury found Permanente liable and, by special verdicts, apportioned damages to lost wages, medical expenses, reduced life expectancy, and "noneconomic damages." The judge granted judgment for plaintiff Fein. In this excerpt of the opinion, the court discusses defendant's attacks on the court's instructions to the jury.] . . .

III

Defendant next contends that the trial court misinstructed the jury on the standard of care by which Nurse Welch's conduct should be judged. . . . [T]he court told the jury that "the standard of care required of a nurse practitioner is that of a physician and surgeon . . . when the nurse practitioner is examining a patient or making a diagnosis."

We agree with defendant that this instruction is inconsistent with recent legislation setting forth general guidelines for the services that may properly be performed by registered nurses in this state. Section 2725 of the Business and Professions Code . . . explicitly declares a legislative intent "to recognize the existence of overlapping functions between physicians and registered nurses and to permit additional sharing of functions within organized health care systems which provide for collaboration between physicians and registered nurses." Section 2725 also includes, among the functions that properly fall within "the practice of nursing" in California, the "[o]bservation of signs and symptoms of illness, reactions to treatment, general behavior, or general physical condition, and . . . determination of whether such signs, symptoms, reactions, behavior or general appearance exhibit abnormal characteristics. . . ." In light of these provisions, the "examination" or "diagnosis" of a patient cannot in all circumstances be said—as a matter of law—to be a function reserved to physicians, rather than registered nurses or nurse practitioners. . . . [T]he court should not have told the jury that the nurse's conduct in this case must—as a matter of law—be measured by the standard of care of a physician or surgeon.[In other words, the trial judge should not have told the jury to hold the nurse practitioner to the standard of a physician, and instead, the trial judge should have told the jury to consider the nurse practitioner's alleged negligence by the standard of a reasonable nurse practitioner—Eds.]

But while the instruction was erroneous, it is not reasonably probable that the error affected the judgment in this case. . . . As noted, several hours after Nurse Welch examined plaintiff and gave him the Valium that her supervising doctor had prescribed, plaintiff returned to the medical center with similar complaints and was examined by a physician, Dr. Redding. . . . Dr. Redding—like Nurse Welch—failed to order an EKG. Given these facts, the jury could not reasonably have found Nurse Welch negligent under the physician standard of care without also finding Dr. Redding—who had more information and to whom the physician standard of care was properly applicable—similarly negligent. . . . Accordingly, the erroneous instruction on the standard of care of a nurse practitioner does not warrant reversal. [Thus, the error was harmless—Eds.]

Notes and Questions

(1) *The Judge's Function in Instructing the Jury.* When the jury decides a "fact" such as whether a defendant was "negligent," is it really deciding a question of "fact," a question of "law," or both mixed together? How does the jury find out what the law is?

(2) *"Harmless" Error.* Notice that the court forthrightly agrees with defendant that the instructions were wrong, but it refuses to reverse. Why (and do you agree with the court)?

VIII. Taking the Case Away from the Jury: Motion for Judgment as a Matter of Law or New Trial

Note on Standards and Procedures for Taking the Case Away from the Jury

The jury, as you recall, decides factual disputes. But if, after presentation of the plaintiff's proof, there is no reasonable way that the facts can be construed in the plaintiff's favor, the law controls the case. The judge then has authority to decide the case without the intervention of the jury. (It is usually the defendant who moves for judgment as a matter of law, although this is not always the case.)

Judgment as a Matter of Law. There are two different but very similar procedures for accomplishing this result. During trial, after the opponent has rested his or her case, a party may move for "judgment as a matter of law" (which in some jurisdictions is called a "directed verdict"). The court may grant the motion if indeed the moving party is entitled to judgment as a matter of law (or, in other words, if there are no factual issues in the evidence that could make a difference). In the alternative, after the jury has rendered its verdict, the court may grant a renewed motion for judgment as a matter of law (which in some jurisdictions is called a "motion for judgment notwithstanding the verdict"), so long as the moving party filed the same motion pre-verdict. The standard is essentially the same, except that it takes place after the trial is over.

Motion for New Trial. A "motion for new trial" is a broader device. It seeks to have the court remedy injustices on grounds that may range from trial errors to newly discovered evidence. This procedure, however, does not result in the grant of judgment for the moving party; it merely results in a new trial. A losing party may make both a post-verdict motion for judgment as a matter of law and an alternative motion for new trial.

The following materials include an actual set of motions from a real case. The case that follows it is a different case, in which the Motion for Judgment as a Matter of Law is granted as to one defendant but denied as to another.

Litigation Document Example 1.2

An Example of Post Trial Motions,
from Wilcox Development Co. v. First Interstate Bank of Oregon,
Civil No. 81-1127-RE (D. Ore. Jan. 7, 1985)

IN THE UNITED STATES DISTRICT COURT FOR
THE DISTRICT OF OREGON

WILCOX DEVELOPMENT CO.	
v.	Civil No. 82-754-RE
FIRST INTERSTATE BANK OF OREGON	

MOTION FOR JUDGMENT [AS A MATTER OF LAW]
OR IN THE ALTERNATIVE FOR A NEW TRIAL

1. Defendants having at the close of all the evidence moved for a [judgment as a matter of law], which motion was denied, and the jury having returned a verdict for plaintiffs, defendants move pursuant to Rule 50(b) Fed. R. Civ. P. for an order setting the verdict aside and entering judgment in favor of each defendant in accordance with said motion, on the ground asserted in support thereof that the evidence was insufficient for the jury to find a conspiracy on the part of either defendant in restraint of trade in violation of § 1 of the Sherman Act.

2. If the foregoing motion is denied, defendants move pursuant to Rule 59(a) Fed. R. Civ. P. for an order setting aside the verdict thereon and granting each defendant a new trial, on the following grounds:

a. The court erred in submitting to the jury the issue of a conspiracy between [the defendant banks].

b. The court erred in its instructions to the jury on parallel business conduct and in refusing to give defendants' requested or the court's proposed instruction on that subject.

c. The verdict is contrary to law and against the weight of the evidence.

SPEARS, LUBERSKY,
CAMPBELL, BLEDSOE,
ANDERSON & YOUNG
James H. Clarke

Jordan v. Iverson Mall Ltd. Partnership

2018 U.S. Dist. LEXIS 88542, 2018 WL 2391999 (D. Md.)

George J. Hazel United States District Judge

This case proceeded to trial on a claim of battery against Defendants Iverson Mall Limited Partnership ("IMLP") and Defendant Professional 50 States Protection of DC LLC ("Pro50") and a claim . . . against Prince George's County . . . . The case stemmed, in relevant part, from allegations that while being placed under arrest by officers with the Prince George's County Police Department at Iverson Mall, Plaintiff Byron Jordan was punched in the face by a mall security officer employed by Pro50. . . . [T]he jury returned a verdict finding no liability as to Prince George's County and its officers, but finding Defendants IMLP [the mall owner] and Pro50 [the security company] liable for battery and awarding compensatory and punitive damages against both. Several motions were raised . . . , including Defendants' . . . Motion for Judgment as a Matter of Law. . . .

Federal Rule of Civil Procedure 50(a) provides that "[i]f a party has been fully heard on an issue during a jury trial and the court finds that a reasonable jury would not have a legally sufficient evidentiary basis to find for the party on that issue, the court may . . . grant a motion for judgment as a matter of law against the party." "When the court defers ruling on such a motion, Rule 50(b) allows a party to renew it after the jury returns a verdict." "Judgment as a matter of law is proper when, without weighing the credibility of the evidence, there can be but one reasonable conclusion as to the proper judgment. The movant is entitled to judgment as a matter of law if the nonmoving party failed to make a showing on an essential element of his case with respect to which he had the burden of proof." *Singer v. Dungan*, 45 F.3d 823, 826–27 (4th Cir. 1995).

At the close of Plaintiff's case-in-chief, Defendants made a Motion for Judgment as a Matter of Law . . . . Defendants argued . . . that "there's been no evidence that the people [Mrs. Jordan] saw [punching Mr. Jordan] were actually employed by Pro50" or Iverson Mall Limited Partnership. . . . The Defendants renewed their Motion for Judgment as a Matter of Law at the close of Defendants' case-in-chief. . . . [T]he Court took the Motion under advisement, and reserved ruling. [The jury then rendered verdicts against IMLP and Pro50, and these defendants renewed their Motion for Judgment as a Matter of Law after verdict.] . . .

i. Judgment Against Iverson Mall Limited Partnership

While Plaintiffs alleged that Pro50 and Prince George's County employees were the ones who caused harm to Mr. Jordan, they additionally seek liability from IMLP, arguing that IMLP is vicariously liable under a theory of respondeat superior. ("Iverson Mall is liable for PRO50's battery because PRO50 was acting within the scope of its employment with Iverson Mall."). Under this theory, "an employer may be found liable for torts committed by its employee while acting in the scope of employment." *Asphalt & Concrete Servs., Inc. v. Perry*, 108 A.3d 558, 580 (Md. App. 2015), aff'd, 133 A.3d 1143 (Md. 2016). . . .

Defendants seek judgment as a matter of law in favor of IMLP, arguing that "Plaintiffs introduced no testimony or documents regarding IMLP, the type of organization that it is, the nature of its business, whether it owns any property, how it was connected to the events giving rise to this case, what, if any, relationship it has to the Iverson Mall building, or what, if any, relationship it has with Pro50." Plaintiffs argue that "IMLP cannot argue post-trial that it is not a proper party to this suit, because it waived that argument very early in this litigation." Plaintiffs further argue that "the record powerfully shows that IMLP is synonymous with Iverson Mall," and [they go] on to reference "evidence presented at the damages portion of the trial that IMLP owned and operated Iverson Mall." Finally, Plaintiffs reference IMLP's answers to Plaintiffs' interrogatories as "stipulat[ing]" certain facts about the relationship between Pro50 and Iverson Mall.

Despite Plaintiffs' contentions, the issue here is not whether IMLP was the proper party for Plaintiffs to file suit against; rather, the issue is whether Plaintiffs introduced sufficient evidence at trial in their case-in-chief from which a jury could reasonably determine that IMLP was liable to the Plaintiffs. And the simple fact is that while there was ample discussion about the fact that this incident took place in or around Iverson Mall and involved security guards who worked at the mall, at the conclusion of Plaintiffs' case-in-chief there had not been any reference to IMLP, as an entity. As such, a reasonable jury could not have determined that IMLP was liable to Plaintiffs [even though this jury did—Eds.], as there was no evidence that IMLP had any relationship with the Pro50 guards, or even owned Iverson Mall. Thus, the Court grants IMLP's Motion, and finds [it] not liable as a matter of law.

ii. Judgment Against Pro50

Pro50 argues that "there was insufficient evidence presented by Plaintiff at trial to connect these Pro50 guards to the alleged battery." While Pro50 acknowledges that "Helen Jordan testified that she saw two Pro50 guards punch her husband," it argues that "she did not testify who these guards were or how she knew they were employed by Pro50." Plaintiffs argue that at trial, "Bell admitted that he and Hunt confronted Byron Jordan, Sr. in the mall," and that the jury could—and obviously did—choose to discredit his testimony that no Pro50 guards punched Mr. Jordan. Pro50 responds that "Bell testified unequivocally that he did not punch Mr. Jordan." and that Mrs. Jordan "was unable to identify [the individuals who punched Mr. Jordan] by name."

Here there was sufficient evidence regarding Pro50's liability to send the case to the jury. As Defendants acknowledge, Mrs. Jordan "testified that she saw two Pro50 guards punch her husband." that she described the men, that she identified photographs of the men, and that one of the guards, Antonio Bell, testified. While Defendants complain that "there was no testimony by any witness identifying who these two men in the photographs" identified by Mrs. Jordan were, the jury had the opportunity to review the pictures and see Mr. Bell in person. Thus, a reasonable jury could have credited Mrs. Jordan's testimony that the men in the photographs punched her husband, and concluded based on their own comparison that those men were Mr. Bell and Mr. Hunt. The jury also heard that Bell and Hunt were employed by Pro50, and could have reasonably determined that Pro50 was therefore liable for the actions of its employees. As such, there was sufficient evidence to send the battery claim regarding Pro50 to the jury, and Defendants' Motion on this issue is denied. . . .

[There is no indication of a ruling on a Motion for New Trial. Either Pro50 did not file a Motion for New Trial or its Motion was disposed of in a separate ruling.]

For the foregoing reasons, IMLP and Pro50's Motion and Renewed Motion for Judgment as a Matter of Law, is granted in part and denied in part. . . .

Notes and Questions

(1) *The Standard for Decision.* Does the court grant judgment as a matter of law in favor of IMLP because the judge disagrees with the jury about where the preponderance of the evidence lies? If not, just what is the judge saying about the relationship between the evidence and the jury's verdict?

(2) *The Correctness of the Judge's Decision Here.* The judge makes a point of reference to the jury's verdict. Do you believe that the judge has correctly applied the standard for judgment as a matter of law here? Is the judge saying that he declines to infer that IMLP was responsible, or is he saying that no reasonable person could make the inference that the jury made?

(3) *Grant of Post-Verdict Judgment as a Matter of Law after Denial of Summary Judgment.* If the court had earlier denied summary judgment in this case, what difference would that ruling make in the consideration of the motion for judgment as a matter of law? Actually, it is perfectly consistent to deny summary judgment and then grant a post-verdict judgment as a matter of law because of the different contexts of the two procedures. Can you explain why?

(4) *New Trial.* The judge has broad discretion in granting a new trial on the basis of trial errors even if they would not suffice for appellate reversal, or on the basis of a verdict that he or she considers against the "great weight" of the evidence, even if a judgment as a matter of law could not be granted. The grant of a new trial is not reviewable by an appellate court except on abuse of discretion grounds. Does this procedure give excessive power to the trial judge? (Actually, experienced trial lawyers will tell you that judges rarely use the power to grant new trials. Can you guess why?)

IX. Appeal

Note About the Function of an Appellate Court

A common misconception is that appellate courts decide cases on a clean slate. On the contrary, appellate courts do not have authority to change most of the actions taken in most trials. The appellate courts consider records from the courts below, and then they may reverse only in the event that an error has occurred that has harmed the substantial rights of the complaining party, *if* that party has taken the proper steps to present the issue to both the trial and the appellate courts. It may be helpful to regard the process as resembling an upside-down funnel: At the trial level, issues are diffuse and fact-oriented, but they become more focused and law-oriented in the appeals process.

The funnel image is also useful in visualizing the frequency of appeals as a means of dispute resolution. Most disputes do not result in suits, most suits do not result in trials, and most trials do not result in appeals. The cases that you read in casebooks should not convey the misleading impression that appeal is the norm. Appellate decisions are important because they set standards for trials, but they represent only a small percentage of cases actually litigated.

FEIN v. PERMANENTE MEDICAL GROUP, 38 Cal. 3d 137, 211 Cal. Rptr. 368, 695 P.2d 665 (1985). Reconsider this case, which appears in § VII, above. Fein sued Permanente for negligent diagnosis and treatment. The evidence was hotly contested. The jury found Permanente liable and rendered special verdicts on various damage items. The trial judge granted judgment for Fein. Defendant Permanente appealed and complained that the judge had given wrong instructions to the jury. The California Supreme Court agreed that the instructions were wrong. But the court rejected defendant's attack on the jury instructions because although they were erroneous, it was "not reasonably probable that the instructional error affected the judgment."

Notes and Questions

(1) *Appellate Review of Trial Court Discretion.* Appellate review spreads responsibility among several judges, and our system includes appeals so that a single judge cannot make unexplained decisions on major issues affecting parties' rights. Why, then, did the California Supreme Court uphold the excusing of 40 percent of the panel by deferring to the "broad discretion" of the trial judge? Does the court's decision mean that trial judges can make no errors in excusing groups of jurors (and if not, at what point does a trial judge transgress a limit that can result in appellate reversal)?

(2) *Error That Did Not Have a "Reasonably Probable" Effect.* Should the appellate court refuse to reverse when it does not see a "reasonable probability" that an admitted error affected the judgment? This approach is sometimes called the "harmless error" doctrine. Would it be better to reverse whenever there is any possibility that the error tainted the result? [Note: What is the likelihood of an error-free trial in a case such as *Fein v. Permanente*?]

(3) *Deference to the Jury's Verdict.* Notice that the appellate court simply states the evidence and the jury's holding, without weighing the evidence or commenting on whether the jury was correct. Why? Could the court reverse if it disagreed with the jury? If it disagreed very strongly? If it concluded that there was no reasonable way to justify the jury's verdict based on the evidence?

Chapter 2

The Court's Power Over Persons and Property

I. The Concerns Underlying Personal Jurisdiction and Venue

Your client brings you a copy of a judgment taken against her in a distant state, one where she has never done any business or even visited. She expresses surprise about the judgment and tells you that she thinks it's unfair. In addition, she tells you that she never was informed that any suit had been filed against her, and the judgment was obtained without her knowledge.

The Distant Forum Concern. If you were the client, you would consider this suit abusive because, in the first place, it was brought in a place distant from your home, governed by laws with which you have no connection. This concern for preventing distant forum abuse will be one of the major issues we will consider in this chapter.

The Notice Concern. In the second place, you would be concerned about the absence of notice about the suit. You might have been able to defend against it if you had known about it. This notice concern is also one of the major themes underlying this chapter.

State Laws and the Due Process Clause of the Fourteenth Amendment. Until the adoption of the Fourteenth Amendment, these forum abuse and notice issues were addressed primarily by state law. Now, the Fourteenth Amendment provides that "No State shall . . . deprive any person of life, liberty, or property without due process of law." This concise Due Process Clause is the source of a wide variety of rights and limits on government. In this chapter, we will consider due process as a limit on distant forum abuse and as a requirement for notice. State laws also are still applicable in these areas, and a litigant may be provided with protections against distant forum abuse and lack of notice both by state law and by the Due Process Clause.

A Little History: Territoriality and the Physical Power Concept. Many years ago, civil actions were commenced by seizure of the person or property of the defendant within the territory of the forum. The court obtained jurisdiction by the exercise of raw physical power over persons or property within its territory. This "physical power" method of determining jurisdiction had certain advantages: there were few questions of distant forum abuse, few questions of notice, and few infringements by one sovereign of the rights of another. But seizure also raised problems. The method of having a sheriff or other officer walk up to the defendant and hand him a set of papers commanding the defendant to answer is a more modern invention, signifying that physical power could be asserted, but avoiding the unnecessary use of force. But this history is still relevant today, because the "physical power" notion has influenced the way our jurisdictional concepts have developed.

Problem A: Chapter 2 Summary Problem

VANDIVER v. SMALL ELECTRONICS, INC. (A HYPOTHETICAL CASE OF NATIONWIDE CONTACTS). This problem implicates many of the materials in this chapter and should be "solved" at the end of the chapter (or used as your instructor directs).

Small Electronics, Inc. is a New York corporation that manufactures and sells components to General Systems Corporation, all within New York State. General Systems Corporation, in turn, uses the components to manufacture goods that it sells throughout the entire nation. The result is that these nationwide sales indirectly bring hundreds of thousands of dollars annually to Small Electronics in New York.

Small Electronics knows that its products produce revenue from sales in Florida and that it benefits from that revenue, and it also has a Florida manufacturing plant that is smaller than the New York one, but it makes the same kind of components. Paula Vandiver is a Florida resident who happened to be on vacation in Las Vegas, Nevada. While there, she was injured by a product manufactured by General Systems. An investigation has produced indications that the cause of the injuries was a defect in the components manufactured by Small Electronics.

Vandiver, seeking to sue Small Electronics, consults a Florida lawyer. She would like to file suit in Florida (her residence), where many of General System's products incorporating the Small Electronics components are sold annually, rather than Nevada (even though the accident happened there) or New York. It is impossible to tell whether the component in this case came from New York or Florida. If you were the Florida lawyer, would you take the case on a contingent fee basis? [Adapted from a real case in which one of the authors advised the attorneys for "Vandiver."] You should answer the following questions in this connection:

1. Is it likely that a Florida court would have potential personal jurisdiction over Small Electronics?
2. How can Vandiver have process (*i.e.*, the litigation papers) served upon Small?
3. What result would you expect if Small moves to transfer the suit to Nevada (or to New York)?

II. Jurisdiction Over Persons and Property

[A] The Historical Development of Our Concept of Jurisdiction

[1] Territoriality

How to Read and Understand Pennoyer v. Neff

The case that follows, *Pennoyer v. Neff*, is a venerable landmark. For insight into the characters and the story behind the case, *see* Perdue, *Sin, Scandal and Substantive Due Process: Personal Jurisdiction and* Pennoyer *Reconsidered*, 62 Wash. L. Rev. 479, 480–96 (1987). Some of what the case says is no longer the law today. It would be unthinkable, however, not to include it in this book, because it provides such wonderful insight into the basis of our jurisdictional concepts. In reading this case, you should be alert for several broad themes.

Territoriality and Sovereignty. Each state, according to this case, is a separate entity and is sovereign within its territory. Therefore, the service of process (*i.e.*, of suit papers) is heavily affected (and limited) by territorial boundaries.

The Effect of Service of Process within the Territory. The same notions of territoriality support the exercise of jurisdiction whenever a defendant is physically served with process inside the state. Even if he is present only briefly and for an unrelated purpose, the state obtains power over him, if it can serve him inside its borders, according to this reasoning.

"In Rem" Jurisdiction: Power over Property within the Territory. A state also may exercise what is known as "*in rem*" jurisdiction. "*In rem*" is Latin for "against the thing." If the object of adjudication is a "thing" within the territory of the state, the state has power over it in the same way that it has power over persons served with process inside the state. For example, if there is an issue of title to land located within the state, the state can adjudicate this issue even though it might not be able to obtain personal jurisdiction over the claimants.

Jurisdiction of Persons outside the State. The "flip side" of this notion of territoriality is that the state has little, if any, power over persons located outside the state. The state can, as is indicated above, affect those persons' rights by *in rem* actions against property within the state. But if a nonresident comes into a state and causes a tortious injury, and leaves the state before being served with process, according to *Pennoyer*, the state has no power to render a judgment against the nonresident.

Read U.S. Const. amend. XIV §1 cl. 3 (the Fourteenth Amendment Due Process Clause).

Pennoyer v. Neff

95 U.S. 714 (1877)

[Neff had originally owned a tract of land in Oregon. However, Neff had a contract with one J.H. Mitchell to pay for Mitchell's services as an attorney. When Neff allegedly did not pay, Mitchell sued Neff in an Oregon state court for his fee. Because Neff was a nonresident of Oregon, Mitchell had Neff served with process "by publication." That is, in accordance with governing Oregon statutes, Mitchell published an advertisement in an Oregon newspaper for six successive weeks, containing information about the suit. Neff failed to appear, and Mitchell took a default judgment. Neff's tract of land was sold in a sheriff's sale to satisfy the judgment. Pennoyer acquired title derived from the sheriff's sale.

[When Neff learned of these events, he sued Pennoyer in a federal trial court for the District of Oregon (then called a "Circuit Court") to recover the land. The trial court held for Neff, and Pennoyer took the case to the Supreme Court. But the issue in *Pennoyer v. Neff* really depends upon the earlier suit by Mitchell against Neff. If the court had jurisdiction in *Mitchell v. Neff*, the sheriff's sale was valid, and Pennoyer keeps the land. If it did not have jurisdiction, the sheriff's sale was invalid, and Neff recovers the land. The issue thus depends upon whether the service by publication was effective to give Oregon jurisdiction over the nonresident Neff. The Supreme Court here holds that the service was not effective, and Neff, the original owner, gets the land.]

MR. JUSTICE FIELD delivered the opinion of the Court:

. . . [Plaintiff Neff contends] that the judgment in the State court against the plaintiff was void for want of personal service of process on him, . . . and that the premises in controversy could not be subjected to the payment of the demand of a resident creditor except by a proceeding *in rem*; that is, by a direct proceeding against the property for that purpose. If these positions are sound, the ruling of the Circuit Court as to the invalidity of that judgment must be sustained. . . . And that [the judgment is invalid] would seem to follow from two well-established principles of public law respecting the jurisdiction of an independent State over persons and property. . . . [First], except as restrained and limited by [the Constitution, the states] possess and exercise the authority of independent States. . . . One of these principles is that every State possesses exclusive jurisdiction and sovereignty over persons and property within its territory. . . . The other principle of public law referred to follows from the one mentioned; that is, that no State can exercise direct jurisdiction and authority over persons or property without its territory. Story, *Confl. Laws*, c.2. . . .

Substituted service by publication, or in any other authorized form, may be sufficient to inform parties of the object of proceedings taken where property is once brought under the control of the court by seizure or some equivalent act. . . . Such service may also be sufficient in cases where the object of the action is to reach and dispose of property in the State, . . . by enforcing a contract or a lien respecting the same . . . . In other words, such service may answer in all actions which are substantially proceedings *in rem*. But where the entire object of the action is to determine the personal rights and obligations of the defendants, that is, where the suit is merely *in personam*, constructive service in this form upon a non-resident is ineffectual for any purpose. Process from the tribunals of one State cannot run into another State, and summon parties there domiciled to leave its territory and respond to proceedings against them. [Note: This statement would require revision today—Eds .] . . .

[Here, the Court suggests that Mitchell might have acquired in rem jurisdiction if he had had the court "attach" (or seize) Neff's property within the state, even though the suit had nothing to do with the property. The property would become a kind of "hostage." This part of the opinion has been overruled, as we shall see later.]

Since the adoption of the Fourteenth Amendment to the Federal Constitution, the validity of such judgments may be directly questioned . . . on the ground that proceedings [over which the] court has no jurisdiction do not constitute due process of law. . . . To give such proceedings any validity, there must be a tribunal competent . . . to pass upon the . . . suit; and, if that involves merely a determination of the personal liability of the defendant, he must be brought within its jurisdiction by service of process within the State, or his voluntary appearance. . . .

It follows . . . that the personal judgment recovered in the State court of Oregon against the plaintiff herein, then a non-resident of the State, was without any validity, and did not authorize a sale of the property in controversy.

MUST HAVE SOME RELATION TO STATE IF NON-RESIDANT

To prevent any misapplication of the views expressed in this opinion, it is proper to observe that we do not mean to assert, by any thing we have said, that a State may not authorize proceedings to determine the *status* of one of its citizens towards a non-resident .... The State, for example, has absolute right to prescribe the conditions upon which the marriage relation between its own citizens shall be created, and the causes for which it may be dissolved ....

Neither do we mean to assert that a State may not require a non-resident entering into a partnership or association within its limits, or making contracts enforceable there, to appoint an agent or representative in the State to receive service of process and notice in legal proceedings instituted with respect to such partnership, association, or contracts ... and provide, upon their failure, to make such appointment or to designate such place that service may be made upon a public officer designated for that purpose .... [a judgment based on this kind of service of process on an agent will be valid] ....

Judgment [restoring the property to Neff] affirmed.

Notes and Questions

(1) *Reconsidering Wyman v. Newhouse, supra.* Reconsider *Wyman v. Newhouse*, which appears above in § 1.03. In that case, Wyman lured Newhouse to Florida, a state to which he had no connection, with false messages about her affection for him. When he came, a sheriff was waiting at the airport to serve him with process. In a later action on the resulting default judgment, a court in New York held that Florida had not obtained jurisdiction even though the defendant was served inside the state, because the service was obtained by fraud. Is it clear, now, why Ms. Wyman engaged in her treachery, and what she hoped to gain from it? Is the decision in *Wyman v. Newhouse* consistent with *Pennoyer* (or is it an exception with which *Pennoyer* simply does not deal)?

(2) *"Consent" by Appearance.* Imagine that a nonresident defendant is served with defective process. However, she comes to the forum and makes an appearance in the case. In fact, she files an answer, litigates the case through trial, and loses, without ever raising any question of jurisdiction. After losing, however, she objects on the ground that the court lacks power over her. What result, according to *Pennoyer*?

(3) *"Consent" by Required Appointment of an Agent.* The Court says that a state can condition permission to do business upon a nonresident's appointment of an agent for receipt of service within the state. Explain how this result follows from territorial sovereignty notions. If a nonresident does business in the state without appointing an agent, can the state then appoint one for him, such as the state's Secretary of State?

(4) *"In Rem" Jurisdiction.* Territoriality and sovereignty notions provide strong support for the concept of *in rem* jurisdiction. Remember that "*in rem*" proceedings are proceedings "against a thing." The thing need not be a corporeal object; in fact, it can be something like a debt or an inheritance right under a will. If a decedent is

domiciled in a given state, that state may be able to probate the will notwithstanding the claims of nonresidents under or against the will. Is this result sound? [Note: If not, would there be any state that would be able to probate the will?] On the other hand, is it appropriate for a court to obtain jurisdiction by seizure of property and to use that jurisdiction to adjudicate an issue completely unrelated to the property? [Although *Pennoyer* allows this result, doesn't it amount to using the property as a hostage? This part of *Pennoyer* has been overruled.]

(5) *Actual In-Hand Service on a Person Traveling through the State.* Imagine that a citizen of California is driving to New York, and while he is on an interstate highway in Nebraska, a sheriff stops his car to serve him with summons in a suit in that state. If this defendant has never been to Nebraska before and is just passing through, is it fair for the service to result in jurisdiction? In any event, whether "fair" or not, the service probably would be upheld under the reasoning in *Pennoyer v. Neff.* The governing principle under *Pennoyer* seems to be that, subject to rare exceptions (such as fraudulent enticement as in *Wyman v. Newhouse)*, service within the state creates jurisdiction no matter how briefly the defendant is present and no matter for what purpose. Consider the following case.

GRACE v. MACARTHUR, 170 F. Supp. 442 (E.D. Ark. 1959). Defendant was served with process in a suit in a federal District Court in Arkansas. The service was accomplished while defendant was a passenger over Arkansas airspace on a nonstop flight between Memphis and Dallas on a commercial airliner. (As the court put it, defendant was "physically above the City of Pine Bluff in the Eastern District of Arkansas.") Defendant attacked the service as invalid. The court upheld the service and jurisdiction on the ground that it had taken place while defendant was within the "territorial limits" of the State of Arkansas. [*See also State ex rel. Sivnksty v. Duffield*, 137 W. Va. 112, 71 S.E.2d 113 (1952) (non-resident validly served with process while in jail); *Darrah v. Watson*, 36 Iowa 116 (1872) (non-resident served while in jurisdiction for a few hours); *Peabody v. Hamilton*, 106 Mass. 217 (1870) (non-resident served while on a British ship in Boston harbor).]

Interestingly, the judge in *Grace v. MacArthur* speculated that "a time may come . . . when commercial aircraft will fly at altitudes so high that it would be unrealistic to consider them as being within the territorial limits . . . of any particular State while flying at such altitudes," but concluded that "no such situation is here presented" because defendant was in "an ordinary commercial aircraft." (Or in the space station, perhaps.) Is this reasoning sound?

[2] Implied Consent and Its History in Creating Jurisdiction

HESS v. PAWLOSKI, 274 U.S. 352 (1927). Pawloski sued Hess in a Massachusetts state court for personal injuries received in an automobile accident that occurred in

Massachusetts. The defendant was not personally served with process, nor was his property attached; instead, he was served under the terms of a Massachusetts statute that provided as follows:

> The acceptance by a nonresident of the rights and privileges . . . [of] operating a motor vehicle on a public way in the commonwealth . . . shall be deemed equivalent to an appointment by such nonresident of the registrar or his successor in office, to be his . . . [agent for receipt of service of process in any action] growing out of any accident or collision. . . . Service of process shall be made by leaving a copy of the process with a fee of two dollars in the hands of the registrar . . . ; provided, that notice of such service and a copy of the process are forthwith sent by registered mail by the plaintiff to the defendant, and the defendant's return receipt and the plaintiff's affidavit of compliance herewith are appended to the writ. . . .

The defendant received the required copy of the process sent him by mail. He appeared specially to contest the jurisdiction of the court by filing a motion to dismiss, arguing that the method of service deprived him of due process. The Massachusetts courts upheld the service, and so did the United States Supreme Court. The Court reasoned as follows:

> The process of a court of one State cannot run into another and summon a party there domiciled. . . . *Pennoyer v. Neff* . . . . There must be actual service within the State of notice upon him or upon someone authorized to accept service for him. . . . The power of a State to exclude foreign corporations . . . is the ground upon which [their consent is implied to the appointment of such an agent].
>
> Motor vehicles are dangerous machines; and, even when they are skillfully and carefully operated, their use is attended by serious dangers to persons and property . . . . The measure in question operates to require a non-resident to answer for his conduct in the State where arise causes of action alleged against him. . . . [I]n advance of the operation of a motor vehicle on its highways by a non-resident, the State may require him to appoint one of its officials as his agent on whom process may be served in proceedings growing out of such use. . . .

Judgment affirmed.

Notes and Questions

(1) *Implied (Fictitious?) Consent.* The effect of the Massachusetts statute was that defendant Hess "consented" to the appointment of the registrar as his agent for service. What act of his was it that resulted in this consent? Did he even know he was consenting at the time? Isn't the consent fictitious?

(2) *The Influence of Pennoyer.* Explain why the statute employs this mechanism of consent. Notice that the Court commences its discussion by citing *Pennoyer.* How

does the implication of consent to the appointment of the registrar bring the statute into compliance with *Pennoyer*?

(3) *Criticizing the Reasoning in Hess v. Pawloski: Limited Usefulness.* At least in theory, the law should produce uniform decisions resulting from rules of general applicability. This opinion may not be advantageous from that standpoint. What if the defendant had injured the plaintiff in Massachusetts, but on a private driveway as opposed to a "public way"? What if defendant had injured plaintiff with an airplane, a boat, a gun, or a can opener, used within the State of Massachusetts? Does Massachusetts need to pass separate statutes covering every possible dangerous instrumentality?

(4) *A Better Way.* The Court gives a glimpse of a better rule when it says that the Massachusetts statute "operates to require a non-resident to answer for his conduct in the State wherein arise causes of action alleged against him." See whether you can use this language to articulate a different and better approach that would cover other kinds of injuries (by guns, boats, can openers, or anything else). *See International Shoe Co. v. Washington*, in the next section.

[B] The Modern View of Personal Jurisdiction

[1] The International Shoe *Decision and the "Contacts-Fairness" Test*

Note on the Development of Long-Arm Jurisdiction from Pennoyer *to* International Shoe

Early Rules Against Jurisdiction. The early decisions about jurisdiction focused primarily on corporations. These decisions indicated that a corporation had no existence separate from the jurisdiction that had created it, and it was implied that there could not exist authority to sue it elsewhere. As the Supreme Court put it, "a corporation can have no legal existence out of the boundaries of the sovereignty by which it was created." *Bank of Augusta v. Earle*, 38 U.S. (13 Pet.) 519, 588 (1839). Individuals, of course, were not usually subject to jurisdiction in one state while in another state, as recognized in *Pennoyer.*

"Consent" Implied from "Doing Business." Later, the authority of a state to exclude a corporate business was recognized in a number of decisions, including *Pennoyer*, as a basis for requiring a corporation to designate an agent in the state for service of process. This theory faltered in *Flexner v. Farson*, 248 U.S. 289 (1919), in which the Supreme Court refused to allow implication of consent under a state statute by a partnership that had done business within the state. But *Hess v. Pawloski, supra*, revived the implied consent theory.

"Presence" Implied from "Doing Business." At the same time, a line of cases held that a defendant could be subjected to process if it was "doing business" sufficiently so that it could be said to be "present" in the state. *E.g., Philadelphia & Reading R.R. v. McKibbin*, 243 U.S. 264 (1917).

The International Shoe Holding. The decision that follows, *International Shoe Co. v. Washington*, was the landmark case that rationalized these differing approaches and established the foundations of modern jurisdictional concepts. As you read it, try to concentrate on this question: What is the test that governs whether a state's exercise of jurisdiction over a nonresident is consistent with the Due Process Clause? Notice that the Court emphasizes "minimum contacts" such that the suit does not violate "traditional notions of fair play and substantial justice."

International Shoe Co. v. Washington

326 U.S. 310 (1945)

Mr. Chief Justice Stone delivered the opinion of the Court.

The questions for decision are (1) whether, within the limitations of the due process clause of the Fourteenth Amendment, appellant, a Delaware corporation, has by its activities in the State of Washington rendered itself amenable to proceedings in the courts of that state to recover unpaid contributions to the state unemployment compensation fund exacted by state statutes, . . . and (2) whether the state can exact those contributions consistently with the due process clause of the Fourteenth Amendment.

The statutes in question set up a comprehensive scheme of unemployment compensation, the costs of which are defrayed by contributions required to be made by employers to a state unemployment compensation fund. . . . Section 14 (c) of the Act (Wash. Rev. Stat., 1941 Supp., §9998-114c) authorizes appellee Commissioner to issue an order and notice of assessment of delinquent contributions upon prescribed personal service of the notice upon the employer if found within the state, or, if not so found, by mailing the notice to the employer by registered mail at his last known address. . . .

In this case notice of assessment for the years in question was personally served upon a sales solicitor employed by appellant in the State of Washington, and a copy of the notice was mailed by registered mail to appellant at its address in St. Louis, Missouri. Appellant appeared specially before the office of unemployment and moved to set aside the order and notice of assessment. [The Washington courts upheld jurisdiction, and the Supreme Court here affirms.] . . .

The facts . . . are not in dispute. Appellant is a Delaware corporation, having its principal place of business in St. Louis, Missouri, and is engaged in the manufacture and sale of shoes and other footwear. . . .

Appellant has no office in Washington and makes no contracts either for sale or purchase of merchandise there. It maintains no stock of merchandise in that state and makes there no deliveries of goods in intrastate commerce. During the years from 1937 to 1940, now in question, appellant employed eleven to thirteen salesmen under direct supervision and control of sales managers located in St. Louis. These salesmen resided in Washington; their principal activities were confined to that state; and they were compensated by commissions based upon the amount of their sales. The commissions for each year totaled more than $31,000. Appellant supplies its salesmen with a line of samples, each consisting of one shoe of a pair, which they display to prospective purchasers. On occasion they rent permanent sample rooms, for exhibiting samples, in business buildings, or rent rooms in hotels or business buildings temporarily for that purpose. The cost of such rentals is reimbursed by appellant.

The authority of the salesmen is limited to exhibiting their samples and soliciting orders from prospective buyers, at prices and on terms fixed by appellant. The salesmen transmit the orders to appellant's office in St. Louis for acceptance or rejection, and when accepted the merchandise for filling the orders is shipped f.o.b. ["free on board," meaning that title passes at the place of shipment] from points outside Washington to the purchasers within the state. All the merchandise shipped into Washington is invoiced at the place of shipment from which collections are made. No salesman has authority to enter into contracts or to make collections. . . .

Appellant . . . insists that its activities within the state were not sufficient to manifest its "presence" there and that in its absence the state courts were without jurisdiction, that consequently it was a denial of due process for the state to subject appellant to suit. . . .

Historically the jurisdiction of courts to render judgment *in personam* is grounded on their *de facto* power over the defendant's person. Hence his presence within the territorial jurisdiction of a court was prerequisite to its rendition of a judgment personally binding him. *Pennoyer v. Neff*, 95 U.S. 714, 733. But now that the *capias ad respondendum* [*i.e.*, seizure of the defendant's body] has given way to personal service of summons or other form of notice, due process requires only that in order to subject a defendant to a judgment *in personam*, if he be not present within the territory of the forum, he have certain minimum contacts with it such that the maintenance of the suit does not offend "traditional notions of fair play and substantial justice." *Milliken v. Meyer*, 311 U.S. 457, 463. *See* Holmes, J., in *McDonald v. Mabee*, 243 U.S. 90, 91. . . .

. . . To say that the corporation is so far "present" there as to satisfy due process requirements, for purposes of taxation or the maintenance of suits against it in the courts of the state, is to beg the question to be decided. For the terms "present" or "presence" are used merely to symbolize those activities of the corporation's agent within the state which courts will deem to be sufficient to satisfy the demands of due process. L. Hand, J., in *Hutchinson v. Chase & Gilbert*, 45 F.2d 139, 141. Those demands may be met by such contacts of the corporation with the state of the forum as make it reasonable, in the context of our federal system of government, to require the corporation to defend the particular suit which is brought there. An "estimate of the inconveniences" which would result to the corporation from a trial away from its "home" or principal place of business is relevant in this connection. *Hutchinson v. Chase & Gilbert, supra*, 141.

"Presence" in the state in this sense has never been doubted when the activities of the corporation there have not only been continuous and systematic, but also give rise to the liabilities sued on . . . . *St. Clair v. Cox*, 106 U.S. 350, 355. . . . Conversely it has been generally recognized that the casual presence of the corporate agent or even his conduct of single or isolated [a]ctivities in a state in the corporation's behalf are not enough to subject it to suit on causes of action unconnected with the activities there. *St. Clair v. Cox, supra*, 359, 360. . . .

But to the extent that a corporation exercises the privilege of conducting activities within a state, it enjoys the benefits and protection of the laws of that state. . . .

Applying these standards, the activities carried on in behalf of appellant in the State of Washington were neither irregular nor casual. They were systematic and continuous throughout the years in question . . . . The obligation which is here sued upon arose out of those very activities. It is evident that these operations establish sufficient contacts or ties with the state of the forum to make it reasonable and just, according to our traditional conception of fair play and substantial justice, to permit the state to enforce the obligations which appellant has incurred there. . . .

[The Court also holds, on the merits, that the state has constitutional power to impose and collect the tax.] Affirmed.

Mr. Justice Black delivered the following opinion.

The criteria adopted insofar as they can be identified read as follows: Due Process does permit State courts to "enforce the obligations which appellant has incurred" if it be found "reasonable and just according to our traditional conception of fair play and substantial justice." . . .

I believe that the Federal Constitution leaves to each State, without any "ifs" or "buts," a power to tax and to open the doors of its courts for its citizens to sue corporations whose agents do business in those States. Believing that the Constitution gave the States that power, I think it a judicial deprivation to condition its exercise upon this Court's notion of "fair play," however appealing that term may be . . . .

There is a strong emotional appeal in the words "fair play," "justice," and "reasonableness." But they were not chosen by those who wrote the original Constitution or the Fourteenth Amendment. . . . [A]pplication of this natural law concept, whether under the terms "reasonableness," "justice," or "fair play," makes judges the supreme arbiters of the country's laws and practices. . . .

Notes and Questions

(1) *The International Shoe Test.* In a single sentence, try to articulate the "*International Shoe* test" for the exercise of jurisdiction over a nonresident consistently with due process. The test is not the same as the older notions of "consent," "doing business," or "presence," although it is related to those concepts. As a shorthand rendition, the modern standard is called the "minimum contacts" test. But this is merely the name of the test, and you should be able to articulate the important principle from *International Shoe* in a complete declarative sentence.

(2) *"Minimum Contacts," "Fair Play," and "Substantial Justice."* Almost any relationship of the defendant with a state or with persons inside it can be a contact, including sales to persons in the state, employees in the state, correspondence, contracts, torts, ownership or rental of property, visits to the state, etc. However, a particular contact may or may not make a significant contribution to the court's jurisdiction.

(3) *International Shoe Also Says That in Some Kinds of Cases, the Contacts Must be "Systematic and Continuous."* In a part of the opinion that is not included in the excerpt above, the Court said that in some kinds of cases, the contacts must be "systematic and continuous" to support jurisdiction. In other words, sometimes a one-shot connection between a potential defendant and a state will not allow that state to adjudicate the liability of that defendant. This requirement applies particularly in cases in which the contact is unrelated to the claims. This principle will appear again in greater detail below, in a section about what are called "general jurisdiction" and "specific jurisdiction."

(4) *Justice Black's Criticism; Vagueness.* Justice Black criticizes the Court on the grounds that the standard it creates is not in the Constitution and is so vague that it will make the Justices "supreme arbiters" of state power. Do you agree? In particular, what are the harmful results of a test that is excessively vague? On the other hand, the Constitution doesn't say exactly when distant forum abuse violates due process. Does "due process" have any real meaning in this context if it is not translated into usable standards by court interpretation? And isn't it preferable to have a flexible test, rather than to have one that produces inconsistency—as did the approaches before *International Shoe*?

[2] The "Purposeful Availment" and "Reasonable Anticipation" Requirements

Note on "Purposeful Availment"

The Requirement of "Purposeful Availment." After creating its broad but ambiguous "contacts . . . fair play" test, the Supreme Court found that it needed to limit that test. Fairness, it decided, wasn't the only factor. In the following case, *Hanson v. Denckla*, the Court introduced the requirement that the defendant must have "purposefully availed" itself of the privilege of conducting activities in the forum. "Fairness" isn't enough.

This (Purposeful Availment) Is the Real Limit on Long-Arm Jurisdiction. Pay attention to these cases. In the later cases that follow, purposeful availment will become a more important limit than the contacts-fairness test. Purposeful availment will emerge as the real factor that cuts off long-arm jurisdiction.

How to Read Hanson v. Denckla. Students sometimes find this case difficult, because it involves a trust. But ultimately, the issues are not so difficult. Dora Donner, who has recently died, set up a trust in Delaware during her lifetime. She directed that the trust should benefit certain individuals upon her death. She also left a will in the State of Florida, which benefitted certain other individuals. The recipients under the will ultimately attempted to void the trust, because if the trust were invalidated, its assets would pass to them under the will. But there was a dispute about whether Florida could exercise jurisdiction over the Delaware trustee that administered the trust. It is this question that the Supreme Court decides. It holds that Florida has no jurisdiction over the Delaware trustee, because the trustee never "purposefully availed itself" of the privilege of conducting activities in Florida. And this is the point: the defendant must have "purposely availed" itself.

Hanson v. Denckla

357 U.S. 235 (1958)

[Dora Donner set up a trust in Delaware and named a Delaware bank as trustee. In the trust instrument, she reserved a life estate (*i.e.*, she was entitled to the income for life), and she also reserved a "power of appointment" (which gave her the authority to designate to whom the trust property would pass upon her death). Ms. Donner moved to Florida. There, she received income from the Delaware trustee, communicated regularly with the trustee regarding trust business, and did "several bits of trust administration."

[Before her death in Florida, she exercised the power of appointment, providing that the trust assets would pass to Hanson and others. She also executed a will that gave her property to Denckla and others. In this litigation, the Denckla group sought to invalidate the trust, so that the trust assets would pass to them under the will. The Hanson group, of course, sought to uphold the trust so as to receive the trust assets.

[Two different suits were commenced. One, in Florida, resulted in a holding that the trust was invalid, that the appointment was ineffective, and that the trust assets passed to the Denckla group under the will. The other, in Delaware, came to the opposite result. The Delaware courts refused to give full faith and credit to the Florida judgment and upheld the trust, so that interests in the trust passed by virtue of the power of appointment to the Hanson group. The Supreme Court granted certiorari to resolve the jurisdictional question.

[The key to the case was whether Florida had been justified in exercising jurisdiction over the Delaware trustee, which did not appear in Florida, but which Florida considered an indispensable party. The trustee had no offices, property or business in Florida and had no dealings with that state other than its connection with Ms. Donner. It had corresponded with Ms. Donner, sent her funds from the trust, and cooperated with her in trust business, all while located in Delaware. In addition, the trust was the subject of the power of appointment.

[The Supreme Court here upholds the judgment of the Delaware court and holds that the Florida courts had no jurisdiction over the Delaware trustee. The Court decides that the absent trustee did not have the required kind of contacts with Florida. The Court recognized the trend toward expansion of jurisdiction under such decisions as *International Shoe,* but it said that the defendant must "purposefully avail" itself of activities within the state:]

... [I]t is a mistake to assume that this trend heralds the eventual demise of all restrictions on the personal jurisdiction of state courts.... Those restrictions are more than a guarantee of immunity from inconvenient or distant litigation. They are a consequence of territorial limitations on the power of the ... States [*citing International Shoe* and *Pennoyer*]....

The cause of action in this case is not one that arises out of an act done or transaction consummated in the forum State.... [I]t differs from [other cases].... [T]he record discloses no instance in which the trustee performed any acts in Florida that bear the same relationship to the [forum] as the solicitation in [cases following *International Shoe*]....

... The unilateral activity of those who claim some relationship with a nonresident defendant cannot satisfy the requirement of contact with the forum State.... [I]t is essential in each case that there be some act by which the defendant purposefully avails itself of the privilege of conducting activities within the forum State, thus invoking the benefits and protections of its laws [citing *International Shoe*]. [Mrs. Donner's] execution in Florida of her power of appointment [that is, her designation the trust property for Hanson and others, and her correspondence from Florida with the trustee] cannot remedy the absence of such an act in this case....

[Four Justices dissented from this holding. "[T]here is nothing in the Due Process Clause which denied Florida [jurisdiction]," said Justice Black for three of the dissenters. "Florida had a strong interest in marshalling assets of its domiciliary, distributing them, and winding up her estate." Justice Black concluded:]

It seems to me that where a transaction has as much relationship to a State as Mrs. Donner's appointment had to Florida its courts ought to have power to adjudicate controversies arising out of that transaction, unless litigation there would impose such a heavy and disproportionate burden on a nonresident that it would offend what this Court has referred to as "traditional notions of fair play and substantial justice." ... Florida ... was a reasonably convenient forum for all....

Note on the "Reasonable Anticipation" Requirement

"Reasonable Anticipation." Here, you will see another limit upon the minimum-contacts-fairness test. You have already seen in *Hanson v. Denckla* that the contacts must include some act by which the defendant has "purposely availed" itself of the privilege of conducting activities in the forum. Next, in the following case, you will find that this purposeful availment must rise to such a level such that the defendant could have "reasonably anticipated" being brought into court in the forum state.

WORLD-WIDE VOLKWAGEN CORPORATION v. WOODSON, 444 U.S. 286 (1980). The Robinsons bought a car, an Audi, in New York State. Later, they left

New York on their way to a new residence in Arizona. Unfortunately, while they were traveling through Oklahoma, another car struck the Audi. A fire resulted, severely injuring Mrs. Robinson and her children. The Robinsons, as plaintiffs, filed a product liability suit in Oklahoma, the site of the accident, against Audi, the manufacturer, and against Volkswagen of America, the importer. Both of these entities had many contacts throughout the United States, and they did not contest jurisdiction. But the Robinsons also sued two other defendants—World-Wide Volkswagen Corporation, the wholesaler, and Seaway, the retail dealer that had sold the car to the Robinsons in New York.

These last two defendants, World-Wide and Seaway, did object to jurisdiction, and they moved to dismiss. They pointed out that World-Wide Volkswagen had a contract to distribute cars only in New York, New Jersey and Connecticut, that Seaway was a New York corporation with operations solely in New York, and that there was no showing that any other car sold by them had ever entered Oklahoma. But the Oklahoma trial court held that it had jurisdiction over World-Wide and Seaway. The Oklahoma Supreme Court affirmed. The United States Supreme Court, through Justice White, here reverses and holds that Oklahoma had no jurisdiction over these two New York defendants:

> . . . As has long been settled, and as we reaffirm today, a state court may exercise personal jurisdiction over a nonresident defendant only so long as there exist "minimum contacts" between the defendant and the forum state. *International Shoe Co. v. Washington*. The concept of minimum contacts, in turn, can be seen to perform two related, but distinguishable functions. It protects the defendants against the burdens of litigating in a distant or inconvenient forum. And it acts to insure that the states, through their courts, do not reach out beyond the limits imposed upon them by their status as coequal sovereigns in a federal system. . . .
>
> It is argued, however, that because an automobile is mobile by its very design and purpose it was "foreseeable that the [vehicle] would cause injury in Oklahoma." Yet "foreseeability" alone has never been a sufficient benchmark for personal jurisdiction under the Due Process Clause. *Hanson v. Denckla*. . . .
>
> This is not to say, of course, that foreseeability is wholly irrelevant. But the foreseeability that is critical to due process analysis is not the mere likelihood that a product will find its way into the forum state. Rather, it is that the defendant's conduct and connection with the forum state are such that he should reasonably anticipate being haled into court there . . . .
>
> When a corporation "purposefully avails itself of the privileges of conducting activities within the forum State," *Hanson v. Denckla*, it has clear notice that it is subject to suit there, and can act to alleviate the risk of burdensome litigation by procuring insurance, passing the expected costs on

to consumers, or, if the risks are too great, severing its connection with the State....

...In our view, whatever marginal revenues petitioners may have received by virtue of the fact that their products are capable of use in Oklahoma is far too attenuated a contact to justify that State's exercise of in personam jurisdiction over them.... Reversed.

Note on the "Targeted Effects" Doctrine: Calder v. Jones *and* Keeton v. Hustler Magazine

In *Calder v. Jones,* 465 U.S. 783 (1984), the National Enquirer published a story reporting that actress Shirley Jones drank so heavily as to prevent her from fulfilling her professional obligations. She sued the Enquirer, its editor, and its reporter for defamation. The Enquirer had a circulation of approximately 600,000 in California, where Jones sued; thus, the defendants' "intentional, and allegedly tortious, actions were expressly aimed at California." The defendants, including the reporter, knew that the story would have a "devastating effect" on the plaintiff, "the brunt of [which] would be felt" in California. This reasoning has sometimes been called "the targeted effects doctrine": a defendant is amenable to suit in a forum where that defendant has "targeted the effects" of its actions.

In *Keeton v. Hustler Magazine, Inc.,* 465 U.S. 770 (1984), plaintiff sued in New Hampshire, where between 10,000 and 15,000 copies of a national magazine were distributed monthly. The apparent purpose of the choice of forum was New Hampshire's unusually long statute of limitations (six years in libel cases); an earlier suit in Ohio had been dismissed on limitations grounds. The Supreme Court held that the plaintiff could thus choose the forum: "Petitioner's successful search for a State with a lengthy statute of limitations is no different from the litigation strategy of countless plaintiffs who seek a forum with favorable substantive or procedural rules or sympathetic local populations." The plaintiff was not required to have "minimum contacts" with the forum (by filing suit, the plaintiff had consented to jurisdiction over her). While it was "undoubtedly true that the bulk of the harm done to petitioners occurred outside New Hampshire," that would be true in almost every libel suit brought outside plaintiff's domicile; the defendants had "continuously and deliberately exploited the New Hampshire market," produced a "national publication" of which a "substantial number of copies" regularly were sold there, and could "reasonably anticipate being haled into court there." Thus, the fact that the "targeted effects" are only a fraction of the nationwide effects does not defeat jurisdiction if the contacts are otherwise sufficient.

Problem B

Connolly v. Burt, cert. granted but dismissed as moot, 475 U.S. 1063 (1986). Defendant in this case was a professor at the University of Nebraska. He received a private inquiry from a hospital located in Colorado concerning the performance of the plaintiff, one of his former students, who was seeking an orthopedic residency. He responded to the request by a written communication to the Colorado hospital. Plaintiff later sued him in Colorado, alleging defamation (apparently, the communication was not a positive recommendation). The Colorado Supreme Court held that, under *Calder v. Jones* and *Keeton v. Hustler Magazine*, this single communication was sufficient to support jurisdiction.

The Supreme Court of the United States granted certiorari. But it later ordered the case dismissed as moot (generally, such a dismissal occurs when the dispute has been settled by the parties or otherwise resolved). The question is: If the case had not become moot, how should the Supreme Court have decided it? You should notice the relevance of *Hanson v. Denckla*; the professor perhaps is like the trustee in *Hanson,* who simply corresponded with Ms. Donner in Florida because she happened to be there, not because he had "purposefully availed" himself of opportunities in the forum. Many people would not "reasonably anticipate" suit in another state from sending a response to an inquiry there, to quote *World-Wide Volkswagen.* On the other hand, *Connolly v. Burt* is a specific jurisdiction case, and the Colorado court's citation of *Keeton* and *Calder* seems on point. Finally, does this case call for recognition that the professor is a "little guy" in some sense? The authors had predicted reversal by the Supreme Court—but tentatively.

[3] "General" and "Specific" Jurisdiction

Note: "General" Jurisdiction Versus "Specific" Jurisdiction

In *International Shoe*, the Court noted that the claim asserted by the State of Washington was closely related to the contacts on which the exercise of jurisdiction was based. In fact, Washington's claim for taxes arose out of the same contacts that created jurisdiction. In such a case, the maintenance of a suit might reasonably be deemed fair with fewer contacts than would be required if the contacts had nothing to do with the claim. This situation, in which the claim arises out of or is related to the contacts, is called "specific jurisdiction." The situation in which the claim has arisen in another place, and is unrelated to the contacts with the forum, is referred to as "general jurisdiction." Systematic and continuous contacts (and more, today) are required in a case of general jurisdiction. Consider the following cases.

McGEE v. INTERNATIONAL LIFE INS. CO., 355 U.S. 220 (1957). Petitioner Lulu B. McGee claimed the proceeds of a life insurance policy purchased by her deceased son, Lowell Franklin. Franklin had initially purchased the policy from an Arizona corporation called Empire Mutual, but International Life took over Empire's business. It offered to extend insurance to Franklin by sending him a reinsurance certificate by mail to his home in California. He accepted, and from that date until his death, he sent the required premiums to International Life's office in Texas. When he died, McGee made proof of loss, but International Life refused to pay, stating that Franklin had committed suicide, which voided the policy. McGee then filed suit in a California court and had International Life served under a California statute applicable to nonresident insurers. International Life declined to appear, and McGee obtained a default judgment in the California court. She next brought an action on the judgment in Texas, but the Texas courts refused to enforce the judgment on the ground that California's assertion of jurisdiction violated the Fourteenth Amendment.

International Life had no office, agents, employees, or other business in California. In fact, the striking aspect of the case was that the record showed *no* contact other than the *single* policy of insurance International Life had with McGee's decedent. As the Court put it, "so far as the record before us shows, respondent has never done any insurance business in California apart from the policy involved here." But the Court upheld California's exercise of jurisdiction and ordered the Texas courts to give full faith and credit to the judgment, reasoning as follows:

> ... [I]n *International Shoe Co. v. Washington* ..., the Court decided that "due process requires only that ... a defendant ... have certain minimum contacts with [the forum] such that the maintenance of the suit does not offend 'traditional notions of fair play and substantial justice.'" ...
>
> ... [W]e think it apparent that the Due Process Clause did not preclude the California court from entering a judgment binding on respondent. It is sufficient for purposes of due process that the suit was based on a contract that had substantial connection with that State.... The contract was delivered in California, the premiums were paid from there and the insured was a resident of that State when he died. It cannot be denied that California has a manifest interest in providing effective means of redress to its residents when their insurers refuse to pay claims. These residents would be at a severe disadvantage if they were forced to follow the insurance company to a distant State in order to hold it legally accountable....

PERKINS v. BENGUET CONSOLIDATED MINING CO., 342 U.S. 437 (1952). Plaintiff Perkins filed suit against the Defendant Benguet in a state court in Clermont County, Ohio. Her claim, however, had nothing to do with Ohio; it had arisen in the Philippines, where the company (which was a Philippines corporation) had operated profitable gold and silver mines. The Philippine Islands were occupied by the Japanese (this was during World War II), and operations were halted. The president of the company (who was also its general manager and principal stockholder) then established an office in Clermont County, where he resided. He maintained bank accounts there, and he carried on correspondence, drew salary checks, and supervised the rehabilitation of the company's properties from that location. The Ohio courts held that the exercise of jurisdiction was improper. The Supreme Court disagreed, and it upheld the jurisdiction:

> ... Appropriate tests for [jurisdiction] are discussed in *International Shoe Co. v. Washington*.... [I]f the ... corporation carries on other

continuous and systematic corporate activities as it did here—consisting of directors' meetings, business correspondence, banking, stock transfers, payment of salaries, purchasing of machinery, etc.—those activities are enough....

The instant case takes us one step further to a proceeding *in personam* to enforce a cause of action not arising out of the corporation's activities in the state of the forum. Using the tests mentioned above we find no requirement of federal due process that either *prohibits* Ohio from opening its courts to the cause of action here presented or *compels* Ohio to do so....

Notes and Questions

(1) *General and Specific Jurisdiction.* Remember that "specific" jurisdiction means that the claim is related to the contacts; "general" jurisdiction means that it is not. Is *McGee* a case of specific or general jurisdiction? What about *Perkins*? What difference does it make (for example, if the claim in *McGee* had been unrelated to the insurance policy purchased by McGee's decedent, would the jurisdiction have been upheld)?

(2) *The Relatedness Requirement for Specific Jurisdiction.* The Court has said that specific jurisdiction requires the suit to "arise out of" or be "related to the defendant's contacts with the forum." But that doesn't tell us what kind of kind of connection is required. For example, is a product liability action for personal injury damages sustained in State X, based on a purchase in State Y, "related to" the sale of the same product in State X to other buyers?

(3) *The Test for "Relatedness": But-For, or Relevant-to-an Element, or Something Else?* In trying to define what is "related," some courts have used a "but-for" test that is jurisdictionally expansive because it embraces every event in every jurisdiction that hindsight can logically identify in the but-for causal chain. Others have adopted a restrictive relatedness test requiring the nonresident's contacts to be relevant to an element of the plaintiff's claim, and some have applied a sliding scale of relatedness. Another approach is a "similarity" standard that would allow specific jurisdiction principles to be applied in every state where the nonresident engaged in similar activities. *See generally* Maloney, *Specific Jurisdiction and the "Arise from or Relate to" Requirement... What Does It Mean?,* 50 WASH. & LEE L. REV. 1265, 2176–86, 1299 (1993).

[4] Putting It All Together: Contacts-Fairness, Purposeful Availment, Reasonable Anticipation, and General or Specific

Burger King Corp. v. Rudzewicz

471 U.S. 462 (1985)

[Editors' Note: This case should help you to "put it all together." It involves the major themes considered so far in this section: (1) contacts sufficient for fair play and substantial justice; (2) general and specific jurisdiction; (3) the purposeful availment requirement; and (4) the reasonable anticipation requirement.]

JUSTICE BRENNAN delivered the opinion of the Court.

The State of Florida's long-arm statute extends jurisdiction to "[a]ny person, whether or not a citizen or resident of this state," who, inter alia, "[b]reach[es] a contract in this state by failing to perform acts required by the contract to be performed in this state," so long as the cause of action arises from the alleged contractual breach. Fla. Stat. § 48.193(1)(g) (Supp. 1984). The United States District Court for the Southern District of Florida, sitting in diversity, relied on this provision in exercising personal jurisdiction over a Michigan resident [Rudzewicz] who allegedly had breached a franchise agreement with a Florida corporation by failing to make required payments in Florida. The question presented is whether this exercise of long-arm jurisdiction offended "traditional conception[s] of fair play and substantial justice" embodied in the Due Process Clause of the Fourteenth Amendment. *International Shoe Co. v. Washington*. . . .

I

A

Burger King Corporation is a Florida corporation whose principal offices are in Miami. It is one of the world's largest restaurant organizations, with over 3,000 outlets in the 50 states, the Commonwealth of Puerto Rico, and 8 foreign nations. Burger King conducts approximately 80% of its business through a franchise operation that the company styles the "Burger King System"—"a comprehensive restaurant format and operating system for the sale of uniform and quality food products." . . . Burger King licenses its franchisees to use its trademarks and service marks for a period of 20 years and leases standardized restaurant facilities to them for the same term. In addition, franchisees acquire a variety of proprietary information concerning the "standards, specifications, procedures and methods for operating a Burger King Restaurant." . . . They also receive market research and advertising assistance; ongoing training in restaurant management; and accounting, cost-control, and inventory-control guidance. By permitting franchisees to tap into Burger King's established national reputation and to benefit from proven procedures for dispensing standardized fare, this system enables them to go into the restaurant business with significantly lowered barriers to entry.

Rudzewicz and MacShara jointly applied for a franchise to Burger King's Birmingham, Michigan district office in the autumn of 1978. Their application was forwarded to Burger King's Miami headquarters, which entered into a preliminary agreement with them in February 1979. During the ensuing four months it was agreed that Rudzewicz and MacShara would assume operation of an existing facility in Drayton Plains, Michigan. MacShara attended the prescribed management courses in Miami during this period, . . . and the franchisees purchased $165,000 worth of restaurant equipment from Burger King's Davmor Industries division in Miami. Even before the final agreements were signed, however, the parties began to disagree over site-development fees, building design, computation of monthly rent, and whether the franchisees would be able to assign their liabilities to a corporation they had formed. During these disputes Rudzewicz and MacShara negotiated both with the Birmingham district office and with the Miami headquarters. With some misgivings, Rudzewicz and MacShara finally obtained limited concessions from the Miami headquarters, signed the final agreements, and commenced operations in June 1979. By signing the final agreements, Rudzewicz obligated himself personally to payments exceeding $1 million over the 20-year franchise relationship.

The Drayton Plains facility apparently enjoyed steady business during the summer of 1979, but patronage declined after a recession began later that year. Rudzewicz and MacShara soon fell far behind in their monthly payments to Miami. Headquarters sent notices of default, and an extended period of negotiations began among the franchisees, the Birmingham district office, and the Miami headquarters. After several Burger King officials in Miami had engaged in prolonged but ultimately unsuccessful negotiations with the franchisees by mail and by telephone, headquarters terminated the franchise and ordered Rudzewicz and MacShara to vacate the premises. They refused and continued to occupy and operate the facility as a Burger King restaurant.

B

Burger King commenced the instant action in the United States District Court for the Southern District of Florida .... Burger King alleged that Rudzewicz and MacShara had breached their franchise obligations "within [the jurisdiction of] this district court" by failing to make the required payments "at plaintiff's place of business in Miami, Dade County, Florida" ... and also charged that they were tortiously infringing its trademarks and service marks through their continued unauthorized operation as a Burger King restaurant.... Burger King sought damages, injunctive relief, and costs and attorney's fees. Rudzewicz and MacShara entered special appearances, and argued inter alia, that because they were Michigan residents and because Burger King's claim did not "arise" within the Southern District of Florida, the District Court lacked personal jurisdiction over them. The District Court denied their motions after a hearing....

After a 3-day bench trial, the court again concluded that it had "jurisdiction over the subject matter and the parties to this cause." ... Finding that Rudzewicz and MacShara had breached their franchise agreements with Burger King and had infringed Burger King's trademarks and service marks, the court entered judgment against them, jointly and severally, for $228,875 in contract damages [and granted other relief.] ...

Rudzewicz appealed to the Court of Appeals for the Eleventh Circuit. A divided panel of that Circuit reversed the judgment, concluding that the District Court could not properly exercise personal jurisdiction over Rudzewicz pursuant to Fla. Stat. §48.193(1)(g) (Supp. 1984) because "the circumstances of the Drayton Plains franchise and the negotiations which led to it left Rudzewicz bereft of reasonable notice and financially unprepared for the prospect of franchise litigation in Florida." Accordingly, the panel majority concluded that "[j]urisdiction under these circumstances would offend the fundamental fairness which is the touchstone of due process."

... [W]e ... now reverse.

II

A ...

The Due Process Clause protects an individual's liberty interest in not being subject to the binding judgments of a forum with which he has established no meaningful "contacts, ties, or relations." *International Shoe Co. v. Washington.* ... By requiring that individuals have "fair warning that a particular activity may subject [them] to the jurisdiction of a foreign sovereign," ... the Due Process Clause "gives a degree of predictability to the legal system that allows potential defendants to structure their primary conduct with some minimum assurance as to where that conduct will and will not render them liable to suit," *World-Wide Volkswagen Corp.* ...

Where a forum seeks to assert specific jurisdiction over an out-of-state defendant, who has not consented to suit there, this "fair warning" requirement is satisfied if the defendant has "purposefully directed" his activities at residents of the forum, ... and the litigation results from alleged injuries that "arise out of or relate to" those activities ... Thus "[t]he forum State does not exceed its powers under the Due Process Clause if it asserts personal jurisdiction over a corporation that delivers its products into the stream of commerce with the expectation that they will be purchased by consumers in the forum State" and those products subsequently injure forum consumers. *World-Wide Volkswagen, supra.* Similarly, a publisher who distributes magazines in a distant State may fairly be held accountable in that forum for damages resulting there from an allegedly defamatory story. *Keeton v. Hustler Magazine, Inc., supra; see also Calder v. Jones,* 465 U.S. 783 (1984) (suit against author and editor). ...

[T]he constitutional touchstone remains whether the defendant purposefully established "minimum contacts" in the forum State. *International Shoe.* ... Although it has been argued that foreseeability of causing injury in another State should be sufficient ..., the Court has consistently held that this kind of foreseeability is not a "sufficient benchmark" for exercising personal jurisdiction. *World-Wide Volkswagen.* ... Instead, "the foreseeability that is critical to due process analysis ... is that the defendant's conduct and connection with the forum State are such that he should reasonably anticipate being haled into court there." In defining when it is that a potential defendant should "reasonably anticipate" out-of-state litigation, the Court ... has drawn from ... *Hanson v. Denckla* ... :

> The unilateral activity of those who claim some relationship with a nonresident defendant cannot satisfy the requirement of contact with the forum State .... [I]t is essential in each case that there be some act by which the

> defendant purposefully avails itself of the privilege of conducting activities within the forum State, thus invoking the benefits and protections of its laws . . . .

Jurisdiction in these circumstances may not be avoided merely because the defendant did not physically enter the forum State. . . . So long as a commercial actor's efforts are "purposefully directed" toward residents of another State, we have consistently rejected the notion that an absence of physical contacts can defeat personal jurisdiction there. . . .

Once it has been decided that a defendant purposefully established minimum contacts within the forum State, these contacts may be considered in light of other factors to determine whether the assertion of personal jurisdiction would comport with "fair play and substantial justice." Thus courts in "appropriate case[s]" may evaluate "the burden on the defendant," "the forum State's interest in adjudicating the dispute," "the plaintiff's interest in obtaining convenient and effective relief," "the interstate judicial system's interest in obtaining the most efficient resolution of controversies," and the "shared interest of the several States in furthering fundamental substantive social policies." *World-Wide Volkswagen*. . . . [Specific jurisdiction, that is, when the contacts and the claim are related,] sometimes[s] serve to establish the reasonableness of jurisdiction upon a lesser showing of minimum contacts than would otherwise be required. *See, e.g.*, . . . *McGee v. International Life Insurance Co.* [which was a case of specific jurisdiction]. On the other hand, where a defendant who purposefully has directed his activities at forum residents seeks to defeat jurisdiction, he must present a compelling case that the presence of some other considerations would render jurisdiction unreasonable. . . .

B

(1)

Applying these principles to the case at hand, we believe there is substantial record evidence supporting the District Court's conclusion that the assertion of personal jurisdiction over Rudzewicz in Florida . . . did not offend due process. . . .

In this case, no physical ties to Florida can be attributed to Rudzewicz other than MacShara's brief training course in Miami. Rudzewicz did not maintain offices in Florida and, for all that appears from the record, has never even visited there. Yet this franchise dispute grew directly out of "a contract which had a substantial connection with that State." *McGee v. International Life* . . . . Eschewing the option of operating an independent local enterprise, Rudzewicz deliberately "reach[ed] out beyond" Michigan and negotiated with a Florida corporation for the purchase of a long-term franchise and the manifold benefits that would derive from affiliation with a nationwide organization. Upon approval, he entered into a carefully structured 20-year relationship that envisioned continuing and wide-reaching contacts with Burger King in Florida. In light of Rudzewicz's voluntary acceptance of the long-term and exacting regulation of his business from Burger King's Miami headquarters, the "quality and nature" of his relationship to the company in Florida can in no sense be viewed as "random," "fortuitous," or "attenuated." *Hanson v. Denckla; . . . World-Wide Volkswagen*. Rudzewicz's refusal to make the contractually required payments in Miami, and his continued use of Burger King's trademarks and confidential business information after his termination, caused foreseeable injuries to the corporation in Florida. For these reasons it was, at the very least, presumptively reasonable for Rudzewicz to be called to account there for such injuries.

[The Court rejects the lower court's conclusion that Rudzewicz had no "reason to anticipate a Burger King suit outside of Michigan." The contract documents emphasized the location of the headquarters, required notices and payments there, and specified that agreements were made and enforced from Miami. The course of dealings of the parties emphasized that decision-making authority for Burger King was in Miami.]

[Further, the contract contained an express provision that Florida law would govern the contract. The lower court pointed out that jurisdiction and choice of law are different issues. Nevertheless, an express choice of law provision agreed to by a party is a contact with the state whose law is chosen, and is to be considered in determining whether a party has invoked the protections of the laws of the forum.]

(2)

Nor has Rudzewicz pointed to other factors that can be said persuasively to outweigh the considerations discussed above and to establish the unconstitutionality of Florida's assertion of jurisdiction. We cannot conclude that Florida had no "legitimate interest in holding [Rudzewicz] answerable on a claim related to" the contacts he had established in that State [*i.e.*, a specific jurisdiction claim]. . . .

III

Notwithstanding these considerations, the Court of Appeals apparently believed that it was necessary to reject jurisdiction in this case as a prophylactic measure, reasoning that an affirmance of the District Court's judgment would result in the exercise of jurisdiction over "out-of-state consumers to collect payments due on modest personal purchases" and would "sow the seeds of default judgments against franchisees owing smaller debts." . . . We share the Court of Appeals' broader concerns . . . ; "the facts of each case must [always] be weighed" in determining whether personal jurisdiction would comport with "fair play and substantial justice."

For the reasons set forth above, however, these dangers are not present in the instant case. . . . [W]e conclude that the District Court's exercise of jurisdiction . . . did not offend due process. The judgment of the Court of Appeals is accordingly reversed, and the case is remanded for further proceedings consistent with this opinion.

Justice Stevens, with whom Justice White joins, dissenting.

In my opinion there is a significant element of unfairness in requiring a franchisee to defend a case of this kind in the forum chosen by the franchisor. It is undisputed that respondent maintained no place of business in Florida, that he had no employees in that State, and that he was not licensed to do business there. Respondent did not prepare his french fries, shakes, and hamburgers . . . "with the expectation that they [would] be purchased . . . in" Florida. . . .

Throughout the business relationship, respondent's principal contacts with petitioner were with its Michigan office. . . . [T]he Court seems ultimately to rely on nothing more than standard boilerplate language contained in various documents . . . to establish that respondent "'purposefully availed himself of the benefits and protections of Florida's laws.'" . . . Such superficial analysis creates a potential for unfairness . . . .

Notes and Questions

(1) *Justice Brennan's View Prevails.* The *Burger King* decision might appropriately be called "Justice Brennan's Triumph." *See* Perschbacher, *Minimum Contacts Reapplied: Mr. Justice Brennan Has It His Way, in* Burger King Corp. v. Rudzewicz, 1986 Ariz. St. L.J. 585. After dissenting in *Hanson v. Denckla* and *World-Wide Volkswagen* (as well as *Helicopteros* and *Kulko,* which you will encounter below), he is in the majority and writes the opinion in *Burger King.* Notice that he retains the concept of "purposefully availing," and emphasizes that Rudzewicz purposely established a "long term franchise." In this situation, the scales are tipped against Rudzewicz, who could not make a "compelling" showing that other factors rendered jurisdiction unreasonable.

(2) *Is There a Commercial-Noncommercial Distinction?* Lurking behind Justice Brennan's reasoning, there is an apparent assumption that a commercial defendant that deals with a distant state is more amenable to jurisdiction there than a noncommercial one. A defendant that has purposefully availed itself "must present a compelling case that the presence of some other considerations would render jurisdiction unreasonable." In other words, the burden is on such a defendant to negate jurisdiction, and not just by ordinary evidence, but by a "compelling" case. Is it appropriate to treat a "commercial" defendant differently from a "noncommercial" one? Consider the case of a small business, such as a haberdashery, which was a defendant in one Supreme Court case. Should this sort of defendant be more (or less) amenable to jurisdiction than, say, a gentleman rancher who owns a ranch in another state as a hobby?

[5] The Court Narrows General Jurisdiction

Note on the (Rejected) "Stream-of-Commerce" Theory

The Stream-of-Commerce Theory: What Is It? Often, a manufacturer sells goods to a distributor, who then sells them throughout the United States, and the manufacturer does not know where any individual item is going to go. This practice has been called the placement of goods into the "stream of commerce," and it might be thought, perhaps, to create jurisdiction in each state to which the product ultimately is sent, at least if the case is one of specific jurisdiction. But the decisions in this section seem to reject a generalized stream of commerce theory. Something more than an indiscriminate stream of commerce is required.

The Nicastro and Goodyear Cases, Below, in which the Stream of Commerce Argument Failed. The principal case that follows, *Nicastro,* contains an opinion that severely limits the relevance of the stream of commerce. Even in a case of specific jurisdiction, where the injury comes from the contact, this opinion says, a manufacturer cannot be subjected to jurisdiction merely because it put into the stream of commerce a product that it knew could end up in any state. Instead, the defendant must in some sense have "directed" its efforts at the state in question or even "targeted" the state. Note that *Nicastro* did not produce a majority opinion, and only four Justices joined this restriction of the stream of commerce theory; two other Justices, however, made up a majority that produced the result, and their opinion also takes a limiting view of jurisdiction. Three Justices dissented.

J. McIntyre Machinery, Ltd. v. Nicastro

131 S. Ct. 2780 (2011)

KENNEDY, J., announced the judgment of the Court and delivered an opinion [for a plurality consisting of himself, Chief Justice Roberts, and Justices Scalia and Thomas].

[Plaintiff Nicastro injured his hand while using a scrap-metal machine manufactured in England by an English firm, defendant J. McIntyre Machinery. Nicastro filed this product-liability action in a state court in New Jersey, where the accident happened. Defendant McIntyre moved to dismiss for lack of personal jurisdiction. Nicastro pointed out that an American distributor was engaged in selling McIntyre's products in the U.S., that McIntyre employees appeared at trade shows in the U.S., that at least one McIntyre machine—the one that Nicastro had used—had ended up in New Jersey, and that as many as four McIntyre machines might have ended up in New Jersey at one time or another. He also argued that his case was one of specific jurisdiction, since the McIntyre machine had been involved in the injury in New Jersey. McIntyre countered by showing that it had never had any office, employees, or advertising in New Jersey, and it had neither shipped goods to nor targeted the state in any way, other than shipping this single machine to the distributor.

[The New Jersey courts held that they had jurisdiction. The state supreme court invoked a "stream of commerce" theory, pointing out that McIntyre knew or should have known that its products were distributed through a nationwide system in the United States that might have led to sales in any state, including New Jersey. A fragmented United States Supreme Court, with no majority, but with Justice Kennedy writing a plurality opinion for four Justices, reversed and held that New Jersey had no jurisdiction:]

... Here, the Supreme Court of New Jersey ... held that New Jersey's courts can exercise jurisdiction over a foreign manufacturer of a product so long as the manufacturer "knows or reasonably should know that its products are distributed through a nationwide distribution system that might lead to those products being sold in any of the fifty states." Applying that test, the court concluded that [the defendant] was subject to jurisdiction in New Jersey, even though at no time had it advertised in, sent goods to, or in any relevant sense targeted the State.

That decision cannot be sustained .... [T]he "stream of commerce" metaphor carried the [New Jersey court] far afield. Due process protects the defendant's right not to be coerced except by lawful judicial power. As a general rule, the exercise of judicial power is not lawful unless the defendant "purposefully avails itself of the privilege of conducting activities within the forum State, thus invoking the benefits and protections of its laws." *Hanson v. Denckla*. ... [T]he general rule is applicable in this products-liability case, and the so-called "stream-of-commerce" doctrine cannot displace it. . . .

A court may subject a defendant to judgment only when the defendant has sufficient contacts with the sovereign "such that the maintenance of the suit does not offend 'traditional notions of fair play and substantial justice.'" *International Shoe*. . . . As a general rule, the sovereign's exercise of power requires some act by which the defendant "purposefully avails itself of the privilege of conducting activities within the forum State, thus invoking the benefits and protections of its laws," *Hanson*, In products-liability cases like this one, it is the defendant's purposeful availment that makes jurisdiction consistent with "traditional notions of fair play and substantial justice." . . .

[A defendant submits to] a State's authority for disputes that "arise out of or are connected with the activities within the state," [*i.e.*, specific jurisdiction cases] .... In other words, submission through contact with and activity directed at a sovereign may justify specific jurisdiction "in a suit arising out of or related to the defendant's contacts with the forum." . . .

The stream of commerce, like other metaphors, has its deficiencies as well as its utility. . . . This Court has stated that a defendant's placing goods into the stream of commerce "with the expectation that they will be purchased by consumers within the forum State" may indicate purposeful availment. *World-Wide Volkswagen Corp. v. Woodson*. But that statement does not amend the general rule of personal jurisdiction. It merely observes that a defendant may in an appropriate case be subject to jurisdiction without entering the forum . . . as where manufacturers or distributors "seek to serve" a given State's market. The principal inquiry in cases of this sort is whether the defendant's activities manifest an intention to submit to the power of a sovereign. . . . *Hanson* [*v. Denckla*.] Sometimes a defendant does so by sending its goods rather than its agents. The defendant's transmission of goods permits the exercise of jurisdiction only where the defendant can be said to have targeted the forum; as a general rule, it is not enough that the defendant might have predicted that its goods will reach the forum State ....

Two principles are implicit in the foregoing. First, personal jurisdiction requires a forum-by-forum, or sovereign-by-sovereign, analysis. The question is whether a defendant has followed a course of conduct directed at the society or economy existing within the jurisdiction of a given sovereign, so that the sovereign has the power to subject the defendant to judgment concerning that conduct. . . .

The second principle is a corollary of the first. Because the United States is a distinct sovereign, a defendant may in principle be subject to the jurisdiction of the courts of the United States but not of any particular State . . . . For jurisdiction, a litigant may have the requisite relationship with the United States Government but not with the government of any individual State. That would be an exceptional case, however. If the defendant is a domestic domiciliary, the courts of its home State are available and can exercise general jurisdiction. And if another State were to assert jurisdiction in an inappropriate case, it would upset the federal balance, which posits that each State has a sovereignty that is not subject to unlawful intrusion by other States. Furthermore, foreign corporations will often target or concentrate on particular States, subjecting them to specific jurisdiction in those forums . . . .

[A]lthough this case [involves a] foreign manufacturer[], the undesirable consequences of [a different approach based on fairness and stream of commerce] are no less significant for domestic producers. The owner of a small Florida farm might sell crops to a large nearby distributor, for example, who might then distribute them to grocers across the country. If foreseeability were the controlling criterion, the farmer could be sued in Alaska or any number of other States' courts without ever leaving town. . . . Jurisdictional rules should avoid these costs whenever possible. [Reversed; no jurisdiction.]

[Justice Breyer, joined by Justice Alito, concurred separately, believing that the Court's opinion went too far in denigrating *International Shoe*'s standard of fairness. "I would not work such a change to the law . . . without a better understanding of the relevant contemporary commercial circumstances." Justices Breyer and Alito would have relied upon the scarcity of contacts here, together with *World-Wide Volkswagen* and related cases. "None of our precedents finds that a single isolated sale . . . is sufficient."]

[Justice Ginsburg, joined by Justices Sotomayor and Kagan, dissented. The dissenters saw the commercial dealings of the defendant with the U.S. as more extensive than the other Justices did. They also saw the case as one involving a "local plaintiff" injured locally, *i.e.*, a specific jurisdiction case. Finally, they argued that Justice Kennedy's plurality opinion "would take a giant step away from [*International Shoe*'s] 'notions of fair play and substantial justice.'"]

Notes and Questions

(1) *What Does Nicastro Mean?* One possibility is that it means what the plurality opinion says: that sales of defendant's goods within the state is insufficient unless the defendant has "directed" activities at, or "targeted," the state. At the least, it means that four Justices think so. On the other hand, there are five remaining Justices. Two of them reserve judgment about such a broad rule, but still, they conclude

that there is no jurisdiction in the *Nicastro* situation: no jurisdiction based on a single sale even if the case is one of specific jurisdiction. Only three Justices would find that jurisdiction exists under this fact pattern.

(2) *Does Nicastro Overrule McGee v. International Life, Above?* Recall that in *McGee,* the defendant made an isolated sale of a single life insurance policy to a California resident, and the Court held that this sale was sufficient to create jurisdiction in California. But the concurring opinion in *Nicastro* says that "a single isolated sale" is insufficient, and the concurring opinion seems less restrictive than the plurality opinion. Is it possible that *McGee* is overruled?

(3) *What Amount of Targeting or Directing Is Sufficient?* The plurality says that directing activities at, or targeting, a state is required for jurisdiction. Does this statement apply if the defendant floods the United States with its goods by selling them in every state, through a distributor? If not, what is sufficient? In *McGee, supra,* the defendant did solicit the sale at issue, even though the sale was isolated; maybe this solicitation was sufficient targeting and distinguishes *McGee* from *Nicastro.* But infinitely many situations remain uncertain. If the defendant sells through a distributor, but it itself launches a nationwide television campaign that reaches a state in which an injury from its product occurs, is this enough "targeting"? (Notice that this describes potential cases involving many pharmaceutical manufacturers.)

(4) *Don't Expect Consistency in the Decisions, because It's Unattainable: Arrow's Theorem.* You may be frustrated with the indeterminacy of the decisions, but that's just the way it is. As readers of opinions, you will have to exercise a great deal of patience with the judiciary. Inconsistency isn't just an odd occurrence. It's a natural aspect of public decisionmaking. Inconsistency should be expected among appellate courts, even though the practice is to minimize its appearance with opinion-writing. Here's why.

"Arrow's Theorem" is a construct from game theory, as applied to political science, that explains this strange-sounding conclusion. The best way to explain Arrow's Theorem is to consider an example. Imagine a three-judge appellate court, consisting of Justices First, Second, and Third. In a hypothetical case now before the court, Justice First believes that the decision should be for the plaintiff; if not, this Justice would prefer to hold that there is no jurisdiction (and would resist holding for the defendant). On the other hand, Justice Second's preference is to hold for the defendant, but if not, this Justice would hold for the plaintiff, believing a holding of no jurisdiction is unacceptable because the case must be firmly decided. Justice Third is different still, and believes that the correct holding is that there is no jurisdiction but would hold for the defendant if jurisdiction were to be upheld.

In this situation, the Justices' preferences "cycle," with no resolution. Each outcome has one first-place vote and one second-place vote. To make any decision at all, the Justices will need to find some sort of mechanism for resolution of their impasse, such as designating one of the issues as a "first step." (For example, if the court has a rule that jurisdiction has to be considered before anything else, the holding will be that there is no jurisdiction. Can you see why?) Perhaps this outcome explains why Justice Kennedy's *Nicastro* opinion implies that the "purposeful availment" issue must be considered before the *International Shoe* test!

In general, a three-decisionmaker body (Justices First, Second, and Third), which must make a decision among three choices (vanilla, chocolate, and strawberry) will reach impasse at some point and therefore will produce inconsistency in some decisions—unless, of course, there are no differences of opinion about any decisions, which is unlikely among appellate judges.

WALDEN v. FIORE, 134 S. Ct. 111 (2014). Plaintiffs sued a Georgia police officer in Nevada, alleging that he had violated their Fourth Amendment rights by seizing cash from them in Georgia during their return trip to Nevada and keeping the money after concluding that it did not come from drug-related activity. The District Court dismissed for lack of jurisdiction. The Court of Appeals for the Ninth Circuit reversed. The Supreme Court, per Justice Thomas, here holds that the defendant police officer lacked minimal contacts with Nevada required for exercise of personal jurisdiction, even if the officer knew that his allegedly tortious conduct in Georgia would delay return of funds to passengers with connections to Nevada.

> The inquiry whether a forum State may assert specific jurisdiction over a nonresident defendant "focuses on 'the relationship among the defendant, the forum, and the litigation.'" *Keeton v. Hustler Magazine, Inc.* For a State to exercise jurisdiction consistent with due process, the defendant's suit-related conduct must create a substantial connection with the forum State. Two related aspects of this necessary relationship are relevant in this case.
>
> First, the relationship must arise out of contacts that the "defendant himself" creates with the forum State. *Burger King Corp. v. Rudzewicz.* Due process limits on the State's adjudicative authority principally protect the liberty of the nonresident defendant—not the convenience of plaintiffs or third parties. *See World-Wide Volkswagen Corp.* . . . We have thus rejected a plaintiff's argument that a Florida court could exercise personal jurisdiction over a trustee in Delaware based solely on the contacts of the trust's settlor, who was domiciled in Florida and had executed powers of appointment there. *Hanson v. Denckla* . . . .
>
> . . . Second, our "minimum contacts" analysis looks to the defendant's contacts with the forum State itself, not the defendant's contacts with persons who reside there. *See, e.g., International Shoe* . . . . [REVERSED.]

[6] The "At Home" Limit on General Jurisdiction

Note on the Narrow Scope of General Jurisdiction

(1) *The Defendant Must Be "Essentially at Home" for General Jurisdiction.* The case that follows, *Goodyear,* says that if you intend to assert general jurisdiction (or

so-called "all-purpose jurisdiction"), you must be able to show that the defendant is "essentially at home" in your chosen state. Remember that general jurisdiction is the opposite of specific jurisdiction, in which the contacts and claim are related; thus, in general jurisdiction, the claim and contacts are not connected to each other.

(2) *Narrowing the Scope of General Jurisdiction.* The cases that follow reflect a narrowing trend. Notice that there often will be only one or two forums where general jurisdiction can be found.

GOODYEAR DUNLOP TIRES OPERATIONS, S.A. v. BROWN, 131 S. Ct. 2846 (2011). In this case, the Supreme Court rejected a stream of commerce argument as a basis for general jurisdiction. Two 13-year-old boys from North Carolina died when a bus overturned in France, near Paris. The boys' parents alleged that the cause of the accident was faulty tires. In North Carolina, they sued Goodyear Tire and Rubber Company (Goodyear USA), which was registered to do business in North Carolina and did not contest jurisdiction. They also sued "Goodyear France," "Goodyear Luxembourg," and "Goodyear Turkey," which were foreign subsidiaries of Goodyear USA. The foreign subsidiaries did contest jurisdiction, and the Supreme Court, in an opinion by Justice Ginsburg, here agrees with the foreign subsidiaries and unanimously holds that the claims against the foreign corporations should be dismissed.

The plaintiffs pointed out that Goodyear France and the other foreign subsidiaries made products that were sold in the United States. A small percentage of their tires had been distributed in North Carolina by other companies in a diffuse chain of dealings or "stream of commerce." But the subsidiaries had no place of business, employees, or financial accounts in North Carolina. Furthermore, their products sold there were mostly specialty tires for cement mixers, trailers, and waste haulers; they were not the kind of tires involved in the French accident. The tires involved in the accident had actually been manufactured in Turkey by the Turkish subsidiary. The Court unanimously holds this stream of commerce insufficient to uphold general jurisdiction:

> A court may assert general jurisdiction over foreign (sister-state or foreign-country) corporations to hear any and all claims against them when their affiliations with the State are so "continuous and systematic" as to render them essentially at home in the forum State. Specific jurisdiction, on the other hand, depends on an "affiliatio[n] between the forum and the underlying controversy," principally, activity or an occurrence that takes place in the forum State and is therefore subject to the State's regulation.
>
> HERE Because the episode-in-suit, the bus accident, occurred in France, and the tire alleged to have caused the accident was manufactured and sold abroad, North Carolina courts lacked specific jurisdiction to adjudicate the controversy.... Were the foreign subsidiaries nonetheless amenable to general jurisdiction in North Carolina courts? Confusing or blending general and specific jurisdictional inquiries, the North Carolina courts

answered yes. Some of the tires made abroad by Goodyear's foreign subsidiaries, the North Carolina Court of Appeals stressed, had reached North Carolina through "the stream of commerce . . . ."

A connection so limited between the forum and the foreign corporation, we hold, is an inadequate basis for the exercise of general jurisdiction. Such a connection does not establish the "continuous and systematic" affiliation necessary to empower North Carolina courts to entertain claims unrelated to the foreign corporation's contacts with the State . . . . [REVERSED.]

Daimler AG v. Bauman

571 U.S. 117 (2014)

JUSTICE GINSBURG delivered the opinion of the Court.

[Argentinian residents brought suit in a federal court in California against Daimler AG, a German corporation, under the Alien Tort Statute (ATS), and the Torture Victims Protection Act (TVPA), alleging that its wholly-owned Argentinian subsidiary collaborated with state security forces to kidnap, detain, torture, and kill the plaintiffs or their relatives during Argentina's "Dirty War." The District Court dismissed the case for lack of personal jurisdiction. The Court of Appeals for the Ninth Circuit reversed. The Supreme Court here reverses the reversal and holds that due process does not permit general jurisdiction over the German corporation in California.

[There actually are multiple defendants. Mercedes-Benz USA ("MBUSA") did not contest jurisdiction. A separate corporation, Daimler AG (here called "Daimler"), is the subject of this decision. Personal jurisdiction over Daimler was predicated on the California contacts of Mercedes-Benz USA (MBUSA), a Daimler subsidiary, incorporated in Delaware with its principal place of business in New Jersey. MBUSA distributes Daimler-manufactured vehicles to independent dealerships throughout the United States, including California. Daimler is the successor to MB Argentina, which is the entity that is charged with having actually engaged in the conduct at issue. The Court of Appeals held that MBUSA, which it assumed to fall within the California courts' all-purpose jurisdiction, was Daimler's "agent" for jurisdictional purposes, so that Daimler, too, should be answerable to suit there. The Supreme Court here disagrees.] . . .

The question presented is whether the Due Process Clause of the Fourteenth Amendment precludes the District Court from exercising jurisdiction over Daimler in this case, given the absence of any California connection to the atrocities, perpetrators, or victims described in the complaint. Plaintiffs invoked the court's general or all-purpose jurisdiction. California, they urge, is a place where Daimler may be sued on any and all claims against it, wherever in the world the claims may arise. For example, as plaintiffs' counsel affirmed, under the proffered jurisdictional theory, if a Daimler-manufactured vehicle overturned in Poland, injuring a Polish driver and passenger, the injured parties could maintain a design defect suit in California.

Exercises of personal jurisdiction so exorbitant, we hold, are barred by due process constraints . . . .

II

[The Court points out that California state law includes a statute that allows jurisdiction to extend to the limits of due process. We shall consider state long-arm statues in a later section.] . . .

III

[The Court here traces its jurisdictional decisions from *Pennoyer v. Neff* through *International Shoe* and beyond, most of which are specific jurisdiction cases.] . . .

International Shoe's conception of "fair play and substantial justice" presaged the development of two categories of personal jurisdiction. The first category is represented by *International Shoe* itself, a case in which "the in-state activities of the corporate defendant g[a]ve rise to the liabilities sued on." . . . Adjudicatory authority of this order, in which the suit "aris[es] out of or relate[s] to the defendant's contacts with the forum," is today called "specific jurisdiction."

International Shoe distinguished between, on the one hand, exercises of specific jurisdiction, . . . and on the other, situations where a foreign corporation's "continuous corporate operations within a state [are] so substantial and of such a nature as to justify suit against it on causes of action arising from dealings entirely distinct from those activities." . . .

In *Goodyear Dunlop Tires Operations, S.A. v. Brown*, we addressed the distinction between general or all-purpose jurisdiction, and specific or conduct-linked jurisdiction. As to the former, we held that a court may assert jurisdiction over a foreign corporation "to hear any and all claims against [it]" only when the corporation's affiliations with the State in which suit is brought are so constant and pervasive "as to render [it] essentially at home in the forum State." Instructed by *Goodyear,* we conclude Daimler is not "at home" in California, and cannot be sued there for injuries plaintiffs attribute to MB Argentina's conduct in Argentina. . . .

[*Goodyear*] arose from a bus accident outside Paris that killed two boys from North Carolina. The boys' parents brought a wrongful-death suit in North Carolina state court alleging that the bus's tire was defectively manufactured. . . . A small percentage of tires manufactured by the foreign subsidiaries were distributed in North Carolina . . . , and on that ground, the North Carolina Court of Appeals held the subsidiaries amenable to the general jurisdiction of North Carolina courts.

We reversed, observing that the North Carolina court's analysis "elided the essential difference between case-specific and all-purpose (general) jurisdiction." . . . Because Goodyear's foreign subsidiaries were "in no sense at home in North Carolina," we held, those subsidiaries could not be required to submit to the general jurisdiction of that State's courts.

IV

With this background, we turn directly to the question whether Daimler's affiliations with California are sufficient to subject it to the general (all-purpose) personal jurisdiction of that State's courts.... Plaintiffs have never attempted to fit this case into the specific jurisdiction category. Nor did plaintiffs challenge on appeal the District Court's holding that Daimler's own contacts with California were, by themselves, too sporadic to justify the exercise of general jurisdiction....

Daimler, on the other hand, failed to object below to plaintiffs' assertion that the California courts could exercise all-purpose jurisdiction over MBUSA. We will assume then, for purposes of this decision only, that MBUSA qualifies as at home in California.

A

In sustaining the exercise of general jurisdiction over Daimler, the Ninth Circuit relied on an agency theory, determining that MBUSA acted as Daimler's agent for jurisdictional purposes and then attributing MBUSA's California contacts to Daimler....

The Ninth Circuit's agency finding rested primarily on its observation that MBUSA's services were "important" to Daimler, as gauged by Daimler's hypothetical readiness to perform those services itself if MBUSA did not exist. Formulated this way, the inquiry into importance stacks the deck, for it will always yield a pro-jurisdiction answer: "Anything a corporation does through an independent contractor, subsidiary, or distributor is presumably something that the corporation would do 'by other means' if the independent contractor, subsidiary, or distributor did not exist." The Ninth Circuit's agency theory thus appears to subject foreign corporations to general jurisdiction whenever they have an in-state subsidiary or affiliate, an outcome that would sweep beyond even the "sprawling view of general jurisdiction" we rejected in *Goodyear.*

B

... Even if we were to assume that MBUSA is at home in California, and further to assume MBUSA's contacts are imputable to Daimler, there would still be no basis to subject Daimler to general jurisdiction in California, for Daimler's slim contacts with the State hardly render it at home there....

Goodyear made clear that only a limited set of affiliations with a forum will render a defendant amenable to all-purpose jurisdiction there. "For an individual, the paradigm forum for the exercise of general jurisdiction is the individual's domicile; for a corporation, it is an equivalent place, one in which the corporation is fairly regarded as at home." With respect to a corporation, the place of incorporation and principal place of business are "paradig[m] ... bases for general jurisdiction." Those affiliations have the virtue of being unique—that is, each ordinarily indicates only one place—as well as easily ascertainable. *Cf. Hertz Corp. v. Friend* ("Simple jurisdictional rules ... promote greater predictability."). These bases afford plaintiffs recourse to at least one clear and certain forum in which a corporate defendant may be sued on any and all claims. . . .

Plaintiffs would have us look beyond the exemplar bases *Goodyear* identified, and approve the exercise of general jurisdiction in every State in which a corporation "engages in a substantial, continuous, and systematic course of business."

. . . [T]he inquiry under *Goodyear* is not whether a foreign corporation's in-forum contacts can be said to be in some sense "continuous and systematic," it is whether that corporation's "affiliations with the State are so 'continuous and systematic' as to render [it] essentially at home in the forum State."

Here, neither Daimler nor MBUSA is incorporated in California, nor does either entity have its principal place of business there. If Daimler's California activities sufficed to allow adjudication of this Argentina-rooted case in California, the same global reach would presumably be available in every other State in which MBUSA's sales are sizable. Such exorbitant exercises of all-purpose jurisdiction would scarcely permit out-of-state defendants "to structure their primary conduct with some minimum assurance as to where that conduct will and will not render them liable to suit." . . .

C

Finally, the transnational context of this dispute bears attention. The Court of Appeals emphasized, as supportive of the exercise of general jurisdiction, plaintiffs' assertion of claims under the Alien Tort Statute (ATS) and the Torture Victim Protection Act of 1991 [under which it has been said that American courts have a "strong interest" in "redressing international human rights abuses"]. Recent decisions of this Court, however, have rendered plaintiffs' ATS and TVPA claims infirm. *See Kiobel v. Royal Dutch Petroleum Co.* (presumption against extraterritorial application controls claims under the ATS) . . . .

The Ninth Circuit, moreover, paid little heed to the risks to international comity its expansive view of general jurisdiction posed. Other nations do not share the uninhibited approach to personal jurisdiction advanced by the Court of Appeals in this case. In the European Union, for example, a corporation may generally be sued in the nation in which it is "domiciled," a term defined to refer only to the location of the corporation's "statutory seat," "central administration," or "principal place of business." European Parliament and Council Reg. 1215/2012, Arts. 4(1), and 63(1), 2012 O.J. (L. 351) 7, 18. The Solicitor General [*i.e.*, the United States Department of Justice lawyer for Supreme Court representation] informs us, in this regard, that "foreign governments' objections to some domestic courts' expansive views of general jurisdiction have in the past impeded negotiations of international agreements on the reciprocal recognition and enforcement of judgments." U.S. Brief 2. Considerations of international rapport thus reinforce our determination that subjecting Daimler to the general jurisdiction of courts in California would not accord with the "fair play and substantial justice" due process demands. [REVERSED.]

Justice Sotomayor, concurring in the judgment.

I agree with the Court's conclusion that the Due Process Clause prohibits the exercise of personal jurisdiction over Daimler in light of the unique circumstances of this case. I concur only in the judgment, however, because I cannot agree with the path the Court takes to arrive at that result.

The Court acknowledges that Mercedes-Benz USA, LLC (MBUSA), Daimler's wholly owned subsidiary, has considerable contacts with California. . . .

Are these contacts sufficient to permit the exercise of general jurisdiction over Daimler? The Court holds that they are not, for a reason wholly foreign to our due process jurisprudence. The problem, the Court says, is not that Daimler's contacts with California are too few, but that its contacts with other forums are too many. In other words, the Court does not dispute that the presence of multiple offices, the direct distribution of thousands of products accounting for billions of dollars in sales, and continuous interaction with customers throughout a State would be enough to support the exercise of general jurisdiction over some businesses. Daimler is just not one of those businesses, the Court concludes, because its California contacts must be viewed in the context of its extensive "nationwide and worldwide" operations. In recent years, Americans have grown accustomed to the concept of multinational corporations that are supposedly "too big to fail"; today the Court deems Daimler "too big for general jurisdiction."

. . . [T]he Court's focus on Daimler's operations outside of California ignores the lodestar of our personal jurisdiction jurisprudence: A State may subject a defendant to the burden of suit if the defendant has sufficiently taken advantage of the State's laws and protections through its contacts in the State; whether the defendant has contacts elsewhere is immaterial. . . .

. . . The Court can and should decide this case on the far simpler ground that [California's] exercise of jurisdiction would be unreasonable given that the case involves foreign plaintiffs suing a foreign defendant based on foreign conduct, and given that a more appropriate forum is available. . . .

Notes and Questions

(1) *Is It Unwise to Use a Metaphor ("at Home") as a Legal Standard?* Poets use metaphors precisely because they confuse things. Here is an example: "The moon was a ghostly galleon, tossed upon cloudy seas." That is a great line with a nice metaphor (from *The Highwayman,* by Alfred Noyes),[1] but it wouldn't help a beginning astronomer to understand the moon's size, substance, or surface. When contemplating the concept of a corporation "at home," you don't understand it better by picturing a commercial entity curled up in an easy chair by the fireplace. The

1. Google the words and you will be rewarded if you like a story poem from a more romantic era. You won't expect the ending. It is too bad that this one does not make it into high school English courses.

court says that a corporation can be at home at its principal office or place of incorporation, as well as other places. Well . . . , what other places? "At home" doesn't help much.

(2) *Purchases Are Not Enough to Create General Jurisdiction: Helicopteros Nacionales de Colombia v. Hall,* 466 U.S. 408 (1984). In this case, the United States Supreme Court reversed the exercise of general jurisdiction on federal due process grounds. The facts involved survivors of a helicopter crash in Peru, who sued a Columbian helicopter company in Texas. They based jurisdiction primarily on the defendant's purchases, banking, training, and helicopter servicing in Texas. The Court held that "purchases and related trips, standing alone, are not a sufficient basis for a court's exercise of jurisdiction" in Texas over an incident in Peru. They were not to be considered "systematic and continuous" contacts that could support general jurisdiction.

(3) *The Defendant's Train Tracks Don't Create General Jurisdiction Either: BNSF Railway v. Tyrell,* 137 S. Ct. 1549 (2017). A railroad employee and the estate of another railroad employee sued the railroad (BNSF) in a Montana state court under the Federal Employer's Liability Act ("FELA") for injuries allegedly sustained outside of Montana. (The FELA allows tort claims on terms that are favorable to railroad workers.) BNSF was neither incorporated nor headquartered in Montana, and it maintained less than 5% of its work force and about 6% of its total track mileage in the state. The railroad argued that it was not "at home" in Montana, as required for the exercise of general personal jurisdiction under *Daimler AG v. Bauman,* but the Montana Supreme Court held that Montana courts could exercise general personal jurisdiction over BNSF because FELA § 56 authorizes suits against railroads "doing business" in the state. The Montana court held that *Daimler* did not control, because *Daimler* did not involve a FELA claim or a railroad defendant.

The Supreme Court, per Justice Ginsburg, reversed. It first held that although the FELA provision authorized suits against railroads "doing business" in the state, it was not a jurisdictional grant. The Court then applied the analysis it had set out in *Daimler:*

> BNSF is not so heavily engaged in activity in Montana "as to render [it] essentially at home" in that State. See *Daimler.* . . . "[T]he general jurisdiction inquiry does not focus solely on the magnitude of the defendant's in-state contacts." Rather, the inquiry "calls for an appraisal of a corporation's activities in their entirety"; "[a] corporation that operates in many places can scarcely be deemed at home in all of them." *Ibid.* In short, the business BNSF does in Montana is sufficient to subject the railroad to specific personal jurisdiction in that State on claims related to the business it does in Montana. But in-state business, we clarified in *Daimler* and *Goodyear,* does not suffice to permit the assertion of general jurisdiction over claims like Nelson's and Tyrrell's that are unrelated to any activity occurring in Montana.

[7] Personal Jurisdiction in Family Law Cases

KULKO v. SUPERIOR COURT, 436 U.S. 84 (1978). Ezra and Sharon Kulko were married during Ezra's three-day stopover in California en route from a military base in Texas to a tour of duty in Korea. Both Ezra and Sharon were residents of New York. Sharon returned to New York immediately after the marriage, and Ezra returned, with another stop in California, after his tour of duty. The Kulkos had two children in New York. Later, after thirteen years of marriage, they signed a separation agreement in New York, providing for the children to remain with Ezra during the school year and to spend vacations with Sharon. After a divorce from Ezra in Haiti, Sharon remarried in California.

A year later, the oldest child told Ezra she wanted to live with Sharon, and he bought her a one-way airplane ticket to California. Three years later, Sharon surreptitiously sent a ticket to the younger child, who flew to California to take up residence with her. Less than a month later, Sharon sued Ezra in a California superior court to establish the Haitian decree as a California judgment, to obtain full custody, and to increase Ezra's child-support obligations. Ezra appeared specially to question the jurisdiction of the California courts, which ruled against him.

The Supreme Court reversed, holding that California could not constitutionally exercise jurisdiction over Ezra. If jurisdiction had been based on the marriage ceremony in California thirteen years earlier, said the Court, it would "make a mockery of" the Fourteenth Amendment. Nor could jurisdiction be based on Ezra's cooperation in the oldest child's move, as the California Supreme Court had held. "A father who agrees, in the interests of family harmony and his children's preferences, to allow them to spend more time in California than was required under a separation agreement, can hardly be said to have 'purposefully availed himself' of the 'benefits and protections' of California's laws."

Note on Interstate Jurisdiction in Family Law Cases

Jurisdiction, Full Faith and Credit, and Interstate Conflicts. The "flip side" of *Kulko* is the historical lack of finality in family law judgments. A spouse may obtain a judicial decree in one state only to have it frustrated by the other spouse's act of physically taking the children to another state and there obtaining a different decree. The Supreme Court's decision in *May v. Anderson*, 345 U.S. 528 (1953), provided indirect support for this conduct by confusing the extent to which full faith and credit would apply. The forum's authority to modify existing decrees and to enter emergency orders (such as those pursuant to *habeas corpus* jurisdiction over a child), exacerbated the resulting conflicts and encouraged child snatching.

The UCCJEA and the PKPA. The Uniform Child Custody Jurisdiction and Enforcement Act (a uniform state law commonly called the "UCCJEA") and the Parental Kidnapping Prevention Act (a federal law codified principally in 28 U.S.C. § 1738A and referred to as the "PKPA") constitute an effort to respond to this problem. For example, the UCCJEA creates a preference in child custody cases for jurisdiction in the child's "home state," which generally is the state in which the child has resided for at least six months. The UCCJEA has been adopted, now, in almost all of the states.

A Poor Fit? Family law may have suffered from the application of ill-fitting jurisdictional doctrines that have developed mainly in a commercial context. Students who wish to contribute to legal doctrine that touches the lives of many could do so by thoughtfully researching and writing on these issues.

[8] The Internet and Personal Jurisdiction

CAIAZZO v. AMERICAN ROYAL ARTS, 73 So. 3d 245 (Fla. App. 2011). This case concludes that traditional due process doctrine is sufficient to deal with cases involving internet contacts. A transaction formed by the internet may touch several states (as well as satellites in space) through which its underlying communications passed. Is the state to which a consumer has sent an order a forum that has specific jurisdiction? Or the consumer's state? Or, if the order went through the seller's headquarters in one state to an office in another state, where it was fulfilled, is that the state with specific jurisdiction?

Some early cases adopted special regimes of law for jurisdiction in internet cases as a result of these questions. For example, in *Zippo Mfg. Co. v. Zippo Dot Com,* 952 F. Supp. 1119 (W.D. Pa. 1997), the court adopted a "sliding scale test" that depended upon the degree to which each internet contact was "active" or "passive."

But actually, the internet is like earlier communications methods. Similar questions can arise in transactions completed by telephone or snail mail, and therefore, maybe they are not so puzzling. The court in *Caiazzo* thought so, and it applied the usual principles in deciding personal jurisdiction:

> While the internet's qualities are certainly unique, it is essentially a medium for communication and interaction, much like the telephone and the mail. The United States Supreme Court created the minimum contacts test to determine if jurisdiction is constitutionally proper and no exception to this doctrine has been carved out for situations in which internet activity is part of the mix. In fact, the Supreme Court "long ago rejected the notion that personal jurisdiction might turn on 'mechanical' tests." *Burger King* . . . .
>
> [A] court cannot determine whether personal jurisdiction is appropriate simply by deciding whether a website is "passive" or "interactive" . . . . Even a "passive" website may support a finding of jurisdiction if the defendant used its website intentionally to harm the plaintiff in the forum state. Similarly, an "interactive" or commercial website may not be sufficient to support jurisdiction if it is not aimed at residents in the forum state. [For

general jurisdiction,] ... the contacts through the website [must be] so substantial that they may be considered "systematic and continuous" [and today, must make the defendant "essentially at home"—Eds.] .... Thus, a rigid adherence to the *Zippo* test is likely to lead to erroneous results.

[C] "Long-Arm" Statutes: State Law Restrictions on Jurisdiction

Note on State "Long-Arm" Statutes

Jurisdiction Depends on Both Federal Law and State Law. Remember that the extent of a state's jurisdiction is actually subject to two different kinds of restrictions. First, it must comply with due process. The basic tests for this requirement are the minimum contacts and purposeful availment tests. Second, it must comply with *state* law. Each state has one or more "long-arm" statutes. The reach of long arm jurisdiction depends upon the traditions and values of the people of the state, as expressed by its legislature in its long-arm statute.

Different Kinds of Long-Arm Statutes. There are several different models for long-arm statutes. For example, a state might simply incorporate the due process test in its statute, thereby reaching every defendant it can constitutionally reach. A fundamentally different approach is that of the "laundry list" statute. This type of statute lists the circumstances in which defendants can be subjected to long-arm jurisdiction. The Illinois statute involved in the next case, which has served as the prototype for statutes in several other states, is an example, although it has since been replaced.

A "Laundry List" Long-Arm Statute

Ill. Rev. Stat. ch. 110, § 2-209 (1983) (since repealed and replaced)

§ 2-209. Act submitting to jurisdiction—Process.

(a) Any person, whether or not a citizen or resident of this State, who in person or through an agent does any of the acts hereinafter enumerated, thereby submits such person, and, if an individual, his or her personal representative, to the jurisdiction of the courts of this State as to any cause of action arising from the doing of any of such acts:

(1) The transaction of any business within this State;

(2) The commission of a tortious act within this State;

(3) The ownership, use, or possession of any real estate situated in this State;

(4) Contracting to insure any person, property or risk located within this State at the time of contracting;

(5) With respect to actions of dissolution of marriage and legal separation, the maintenance in this State of a matrimonial domicile at the

> time this cause of action arose or the commission in this State of any act giving rise to the cause of action.
>
> (b) Service of process upon any person who is subject to the jurisdiction of the courts of this State, as provided in this Section, may be made by personally serving the summons upon the defendant outside this State, as provided in this Act, with the same force and effect as though summons had been personally served within this State. . . .

As you read the following case, consider the language that the court quotes from this long-arm statue, and consider what you think the quoted words mean.

Gray v. American Radiator & Standard Sanitary Corp.

22 Ill. 2d 432, 176 N.E.2d 761 (1961)

Klingbiel, Justice.

Phyllis Gray appeals from a judgment of the circuit court of Cook County dismissing her action for damages. The issues are concerned with the construction and validity of our statute providing for [long-arm jurisdiction.] . . .

The suit was brought against the Titan Valve Manufacturing Company and others, on the ground that a certain water heater had exploded and injured the plaintiff. The complaint charges, *inter alia*, that the Titan company, a foreign corporation, had negligently constructed the safety valve; and that the injuries were suffered as a proximate result thereof. [In other words, although the style of the case contains only American Radiator's name, there were several defendants, and Titan Valve is the defendant at issue here.] Summons issued and was duly served on Titan's registered agent in Cleveland, Ohio. The corporation appeared specially, filing a motion to quash on the ground that it had not committed a tortious act in Illinois. Its affidavit stated that it does no business here; that it has no agent physically present in Illinois; and that it sells the completed valves to defendant American Radiator & Standard Sanitary Corporation, outside Illinois . . . . The [trial] court granted Titan's motion, dismissing both the complaint and the crossclaim.

. . . Under section 17(1)(b) a nonresident who, either in person or through an agent, commits a tortious act within this State submits to jurisdiction. (Ill. Rev. Stat. 1959, chap. 110, par. 17.) The questions in this case are (1) whether a tortious act was committed here, within the meaning of the statute, despite the fact that the Titan corporation had no agent in Illinois; and (2) whether the statute, if so construed, violates due process of law.

The first aspect to which we must direct our attention is one of statutory construction. Under section 17(1)(b) jurisdiction is predicated on the committing of a tortious act in this State. It is not disputed, for the purpose of this appeal, that a tortious act was committed. The issue depends on whether it was committed in Illinois, so as to warrant the assertion of personal jurisdiction by service of summons in Ohio.

The wrong in the case at bar did not originate in the conduct of a servant physically present here, but arose instead from acts performed at the place of manufacture. Only the consequences occurred in Illinois. It is well established, however, that in law the place of a wrong is where the last event takes place which is necessary to render the actor liable. Restatement, Conflict of Laws, sec. 377. A second indication that the place of injury is the determining factor is found in rules governing the time within which an action must be brought. In applying statutes of limitation our court has computed the period from the time when the injury is done. [Note: here the court is interpreting "tortious act" by the meaning the words might have in questions of choice of law and limitations.—Eds.]

We think it is clear that the alleged negligence in manufacturing the valve cannot be separated from the resulting injury; and that for present purposes, like those of liability and limitations, the tort was committed in Illinois.

Titan seeks to avoid this result by arguing that instead of using the word "tort," the legislature employed the term "tortious act"; and that the latter refers only to the act or conduct, separate and apart from any consequences thereof. We cannot accept the argument. To be tortious an act must cause injury. The concept of injury is an inseparable part of the phrase. In determining legislative intention courts will read words in their ordinary and popularly understood sense.... We think the intent should be determined less from technicalities of definition than from considerations of general purpose and effect.... As we observed in *Nelson v. Miller*, 11 Ill. 2d 378, 143 N.E.2d 673, the statute contemplates the exertion of jurisdiction over nonresident defendants to the extent permitted by the due-process clause. [Here, the court uses another interpretive method: looking at the legislative intent.—Eds.]

The Titan company contends that if the statute is applied so as to confer jurisdiction in this case it violates the requirement of due process of law. The precise constitutional question thus presented has not heretofore been considered by this court....

Under modern doctrine the power of a State court to enter a binding judgment against one not served with process within the State depends upon ... whether he has certain minimum contacts with the State (*see International Shoe Co. v. State of Washington*....

In *McGee v. International Life Insurance Co.*, 355 U.S. 220, 78 S. Ct. 199, 201, 2 L. Ed. 2d 223, suit was brought in California against a foreign insurance company on a policy issued to a resident of California .... After referring briefly to the *International Shoe* case the court held that "it is sufficient for purposes of due process that the suit was based on *a contract* which had substantial connection" with California. (Emphasis supplied.) ...

In the case at bar defendant does not claim that the present use of its product in Illinois is an isolated instance. While the record does not disclose the volume of Titan's business or the territory in which appliances incorporating its valves are marketed, it is a reasonable inference that its commercial transactions, like those of other manufacturers, result in substantial use and consumption in this State. To the extent that its business may be directly affected by transactions occurring here it enjoys benefits from the laws of this State, and it has undoubtedly benefitted, to a degree, from the protection which our law has given to the marketing of hot water heaters containing its valves. Where the alleged liability arises, as in this case, from the manufacture of products presumably sold in contemplation of use here, it should not matter that the purchase was made from an independent middleman or that someone other than the defendant shipped the product into this State. . . .

We construe section 17(1)(b) [now codified as § 2-209(a)(2), *see* statute preceding this case] as providing for jurisdiction under the circumstances shown in this case, and we hold that as so construed the statute does not violate due process of law. [REVERSED AND REMANDED.]

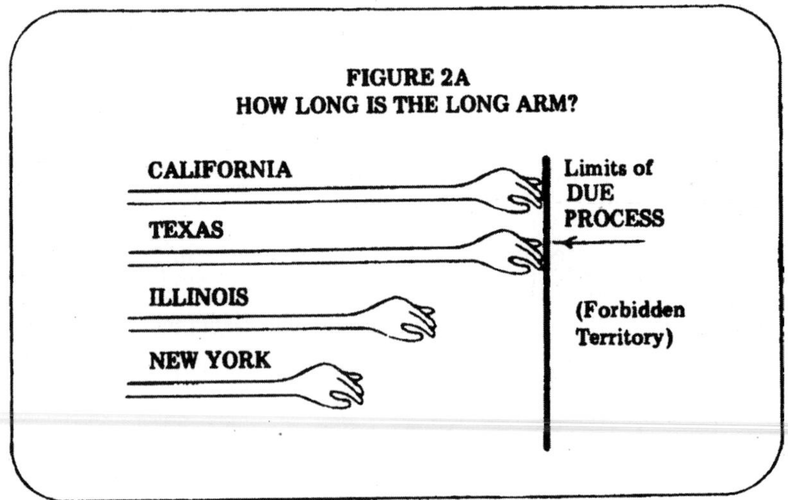

FIGURE 2A
HOW LONG IS THE LONG ARM?

Notes and Questions

(1) *The Two Issues in Gray, State and Federal.* The first step in understanding *Gray* is to formulate the two questions that the court analyzes. One is a question of state law, the other of federal law. Be sure that you can identify the two questions and explain the holding on each. See Figure 2A for a graphic depiction of the two issues, considering the statutes of four different states.

(2) *"Tortious Act."* Had the defendant, Titan, done any "act" in Illinois? Notice, however, that the court, in *Gray*, reaches its result by reading the words "tortious act" to mean "tort." Is this interpretation consistent with the language of the Illinois law (or does it result in the elimination of the requirement of an "act" from the statute)?

(3) *Illinois Lengthens Its Long Arm by Amendment—and Eliminates the Problem Illustrated in Gray.* Following the *Gray* decision, Illinois amended its long arm statute to add the following provision, among others: "A court may also exercise

jurisdiction on any other basis now or hereafter permitted by the Illinois Constitution and the Constitution of the United States." Why do you think Illinois adopted this amendment, and what effect does it have?

(4) *Statutory Construction.* There are many ways to interpret statutes. One is to look to definitions of key terms that would have been available to the legislature (the court in *Gray* does this by considering the concept of a tortious act in conflict-of-laws usages and statutes of limitations). Another is to consider legislative intent, which is discerned by such indications as legislative history or policy considerations (the court in *Gray* infers a legislative intent to reach to the "extent permitted by due process"). Another interpretive approach is to give emphasis to the actual words of the enactment, the text, particularly if they have a "plain" meaning. What would be the result if that (plain meaning) approach were adopted in a case like *Gray*? Consider the decision below. Notice that New York courts probably would have discussed a case like *Gray*, even though New York has its own long arm statute.

FEATHERS v. McLUCAS, 15 N.Y.2d 443, 209 N.E.2d 68 (1965). The Featherses were injured by the explosion in New York of a propane tank manufactured in Kansas. They sued the manufacturer in New York. The manufacturer had no agents or activities in New York, and it moved to dismiss. The New York long-arm statute was closely similar to the Illinois statute at issue in *Gray*; in relevant part, it provided: "A court may exercise personal jurisdiction over any nondomiciliary . . . if, in person or through an agent, he . . . commits a tortious act within the state . . . ."

Speaking through its renowned Judge Fuld, the New York Court of Appeals [which is the state's highest court, analogous to a state supreme court] ordered dismissal for lack of jurisdiction, holding that the New York long-arm statute required a tortious "act" in the state, even if due process did not and even if the Illinois courts did not.

> The language of [the statute]—conferring personal jurisdiction over a nondomiciliary "if, in person or through an agent, he . . . commits a tortious act *within* the state"—is too plain and precise to permit it to be read, as has the Appellate Division, as if it were synonymous with "committing a tortious act *without* the state which causes injury within the state". . . .
>
> Our attention is directed to the broad interpretation accorded in *Gray v. American Radiator & Sanitary Corp.* . . .
>
> We find [*Gray*] unconvincing. It certainly does not follow that, if the "place of the wrong" for purposes of conflict of laws is a particular state, the "place of commission of a tortious act" is also that same state for purposes of interpreting a statute conferring jurisdiction. . . . Moreover, the place of the "tort" is not necessarily the same as the place of the defendant's commission of the "tortious act." In our view, then, the interpretation accorded

the statute by the Illinois courts disregards its plain language and exceeds the bounds of sound statutory construction. . . .

The "Limits-of-Due-Process" Long-Arm Model

A different kind of statutory model simply adopts the limits of due process as the limits of the long arm. By enacting this kind of statute, a legislature authorizes the state courts to exercise jurisdiction over any claim that they can reach under the Constitution. The California statute provides as follows:

Cal. Code Civ. Proc. § 410.10

> § 410.10 Basis [of Jurisdiction]
>
> A court of this state may exercise jurisdiction on any basis not inconsistent with the Constitution of this state or of the United States.

See also R.I. Gen. Laws § 9-5-33 (1985) (which provides, "Every foreign corporation, [individual, or entity] . . . that shall have the necessary minimum contacts with the state of Rhode Island, shall be subject to the jurisdiction of the state . . .").

"Intermediate" Long-Arm Models

Some states adopt neither the "laundry list" nor the "limits of due process" model. For example, the provision of the former Texas statute construed in the case that follows provided that a nonresident doing business within the state was subject to process "in any action . . . *arising out of such business done in this State.*" Former Tex. Rev. Civ. Stat. Ann. art. 2031b (emphasis added). Read literally, this statute would seem to have covered only cases of specific jurisdiction. General jurisdiction cases, such as *Perkins v. Benguet, supra*, would not "arise out of . . . business done in" the state.

However, every state's statutes are subject to interpretation by the courts of that state. The Texas Supreme Court construed that state's long-arm provision in the following case. What did the court do to the statute?

HALL v. HELICOPTEROS NACIONALES DE COLOMBIA, S.A., 638 S.W.2d 870 (Tex. 1982), *rev'd on other grounds*, 466 U.S. 408 (1984). Plaintiffs' decedents were killed in Peru by the crash of a helicopter operated by the defendant. Defendant was a Colombian entity that maintained no office in Texas, though it had purchased helicopters and supplies extensively in that state. The Texas Supreme Court recognized that the claim did not "arise out of" the defendant's "business done in this State," as the literal terms of the statute seemed to require. Nevertheless, a five-member majority of the court, speaking through Justice Wallace, upheld the exercise of jurisdiction. The majority reasoned that the "arising out of" requirement

> . . . is useful in any fact situation in which a jurisdiction question exists; and it is a necessary requirement where the nonresident defendant only maintained single or few contacts with the forum. However, [it] is unnecessary

> when the nonresident defendant's presence in the forum through numerous contacts is of such a nature, as in this case, so as to satisfy the demands of the ultimate test of due process. Accordingly, through the statutory authority of Art. 2031b . . . , there remains a single inquiry: is the exercise of jurisdiction consistent with the requirements of due process of law under the United States Constitution?

Texas' Chief Justice Pope, joined by three other members of the court, dissented on the grounds that both the Texas statute and due process prohibited jurisdiction:

> Article 2031b expressly requires a *nexus* between the helicopter crash and the contacts relied on to justify jurisdiction. The nexus requirement is found in the clear wording of the statute itself. . . .
>
> . . . While the reach of a particular statute could always be coextensive with constitutional confines outlined by the Supreme Court, states were not compelled to assert jurisdiction that far. . . .

The United States Supreme Court later reversed and held that there was no jurisdiction on due process grounds, but its decision left in place the Texas court's construction of the Texas statute, over which the United States Supreme Court had no jurisdiction. However, the Texas Supreme Court subsequently withdrew its opinion in *Hall* (677 S.W.2d 19 (Tex. 1984)), leaving the scope of the statute in controversy.

Notes and Questions

(1) *Helicopteros in the United States Supreme Court: Due Process.* The Texas Supreme Court's decision is the last word on what the Texas long-arm statute means, but it was not the last word on this case. The accident was in Peru, not Texas, and therefore a question remained: even if the Texas long-arm statute is broader than its words seem to imply, does its application in this case comply with due process? The case depends upon general jurisdiction. Therefore, the United States Supreme Court considered whether the defendant's contacts with Texas were sufficiently strong to support general jurisdiction. The Court concluded that they were not and ordered dismissal. *Helicopteros Nacionales de Colombia v. Hall*, 466 U.S. 408 (1984).

(2) *The Effect of the Texas Court's Interpretation.* What has the Texas court done to the Texas statute? Is the majority's interpretation persuasive, or is Chief Justice Pope's dissent correct? Consider whether the effect of the majority's decision is to eliminate the words the legislature chose(!): "arising out of such business done in this state." *See* Richardson, *Hall v. Helicopteros: Clarifying the Limits of Personal Jurisdiction*, 48 Tex. B.J. 651 (1985).

(3) *Choosing Between Long-Arm Models.* If you were a legislator in the newly created hypothetical state of "West York," and you were given the responsibility to draft your state's first long-arm statute, which model would you select—the narrower "laundry list" type, or the broader "limits-of-due process" version? [Note: Which model would give more rights to the constituents who voted for your election? Does this reasoning explain the construction given the statute in Texas,

where judges are elected?] On the other hand, you might consider which kind of statute is "better" philosophically. Can it be argued that the limits-of-due-process approach abdicates the responsibility of the state to set standards for the protection of defendants (or would a narrower approach provide inadequate forum availability for plaintiffs, who might have to go to distant forums for injuries suffered at home)? Auerbach, *General Jurisdiction of Courts — A Critique of the Maryland Law*, 40 Md. L. Rev. 485, 506–07 (1981); Strachan, *In Personam Jurisdiction in Utah*, 1977 Utah L. Rev. 235.

[D] *In Rem* Jurisdiction: Power Over Property

Legitimate Uses of Power Over Property

Title to Property Inside the State and Related Issues. The classic *in rem* case is one involving title to land in the forum. A state has a universally recognized interest in clear titles to land within its borders. Even if claimants to a particular parcel may be scattered among the other forty-nine states and foreign countries, few would disagree with the holding in *Pennoyer v. Neff* affording adjudicatory power to the state where the land is located. Another example is probate jurisdiction; the forum has a strong interest in distributing the estates of its domiciliaries.

Satisfaction of Judgments and Provisional Remedies: "Garnishment," "Attachment," and "Sequestration." A fundamentally different (but equally legitimate) exercise of *in rem* jurisdiction is in securing and enforcing judgments. If the defendant has a debtor in another state, such as a bank in which he has deposited money, this obligation should not be exempt from the satisfaction of a judgment taken against him. The judgment creditor can file an application for a *writ of garnishment* in these circumstances, using what might be called *in rem* jurisdiction. Similarly, *attachment* is a writ used to seize property of a debtor prior to judgment when it may otherwise be wasted, concealed or lost, and *sequestration* is a similar but slightly different procedure, and these too are variations upon *in rem* jurisdiction.

Abuses of In Rem Jurisdiction: Harris v. Balk and Seider v. Roth

But Every "Property" Interest Is Held by a Person. The trouble with power over property is that it is really power to adjudicate the interests of *persons* in the property. Such an exercise of power is fine, if the property interests are really the issue at stake. The difficulty arises when the presence of property is used as a justification for deciding issues *unrelated* to the property. For example, in *Pennoyer v. Neff*, the Supreme Court said that Mitchell could have commenced his Oregon action by seizing Neff's property in that state. The Court did not acknowledge the unfairness of this procedure if, for example, the claim had nothing to do with Oregon or with the land. Unfortunately, this holding gave rise to several cases in which the incidental presence of property was used to justify unrelated (and oppressive) adjudications against persons. The two cases that follow, *Harris v. Balk* and *Seider v. Roth*, are examples.

Harris v. Balk, 198 U.S. 215 (1905). Epstein, a resident of Maryland, claimed that Balk owed him $300. Balk, in turn, was owed $180 by Harris. One day, while Harris was visiting Maryland, Epstein obtained a writ of attachment from a Maryland court and had it served on Harris. What Epstein really wanted, however, was to collect money from Balk without obtaining jurisdiction over Balk, through the expedient of obtaining jurisdiction over Harris and having Harris ordered to pay his debt to Epstein instead of Balk. Using this technique, Epstein obtained a judgment against Harris for Harris's debt to Balk. The United States Supreme Court upheld the Maryland courts' exercise of *in rem* jurisdiction, and it held that it extinguished Harris's debt to Balk. "The obligation of a debtor to pay his debt clings to him ... wherever he goes .... We see no reason why the attachment could not thus be laid." Notice, however, that this holding meant that a right of Balk was destroyed in a distant forum without jurisdiction over Balk(!).

Seider v. Roth, 216 N.E.2d 312 (N.Y. 1966). This more modern case took that holding even farther. Plaintiffs, who resided in New York, were injured in an automobile accident in Vermont. They had no basis for jurisdiction over the Vermont driver, so they obtained a writ of attachment on that driver's insurance company, which also did business in New York, alleging that the Vermont driver was liable to them, that the insurer was liable to the Vermont driver, and that therefore the obligation of the insurer could be seized in New York, under the rule of *Harris v. Balk*. The New York courts upheld this manipulation of *in rem* jurisdiction.

The Questionable Basis of These Decisions ... and Its Ultimate Rejection in Shaffer v. Heitner, which Follows Below. These decisions meant that a creditor's valuable rights could be extinguished in a distant forum to which the creditor had no relationship. Also, an insured driver might be subjected to suit wherever his insurer could be found, and the insurer might have to defend in a forum distant from the witnesses and the events that gave rise to suit. Finally, the Supreme Court decided *Shaffer v. Heitner*, below, which overrules the misuse of *in rem* jurisdiction in *Harris v. Balk*. The Court holds that there must be a "relationship among the defendant, the forum, and the litigation," and property in the state cannot create jurisdiction over an "unrelated" claim. Proper uses of *in rem* jurisdiction still exist, but you will have to find out where the line is drawn.

Shaffer v. Heitner

433 U.S. 186 (1977)

[Plaintiff Heitner brought suit in a Delaware court against Greyhound Corporation, a Delaware corporation, one of its subsidiaries, and 28 present or former officers or directors. Heitner owned one share of Greyhound stock, and his action was a "shareholder's derivative suit," meaning that it sought to force the individuals to pay to the corporation damages they had allegedly caused it. Greyhound's corporate headquarters were in Arizona. The allegedly wrongful actions had occurred in Oregon. (It is common for corporations to be incorporated in Delaware even if they have little connection to that state, because Delaware has pro-business corporate laws.)

[Simultaneously with the suit, Heitner filed a motion for an order of "sequestration," which the court granted. This Delaware procedure allowed for the seizure of a defendant's property. In this case, the sequestration order was directed to holdings of stock and related corporate rights held by the individual defendants, and it was carried out by the use of "stop transfer orders" placed on the company's books, which had an effect similar to seizure of the stock. So far as the record showed, none of the stock certificates was present in Delaware, but the situs of the stock under Delaware law was deemed to be in Delaware because Greyhound was a Delaware corporation.

[Defendant Shaffer was a nonresident of Delaware. Together with other individual defendants, he appeared specially for the purpose of moving to quash service and to vacate the sequestration order. The Delaware trial court rejected the defendants' arguments that the sequestration violated due process. It said,

> The primary purpose of "sequestration" . . . is not to secure possession of property pending a trial. . . . On the contrary, as here employed, "sequestration" is a process used to compel the personal appearance of a nonresident. . . . If the defendant enters a general appearance, the sequestered property is routinely released. . . .

The Delaware Supreme Court affirmed. The United States Supreme Court then accepted the case for review. It reversed, for the following reasons.]

Mr. Justice Marshall delivered the opinion of the Court . . . .

II

The Delaware courts rejected appellants' jurisdictional challenge by noting that this suit was brought as a *quasi in rem* proceeding. Since *quasi in rem* jurisdiction is traditionally based on attachment or seizure of property present in the jurisdiction, not on contacts between the defendant and the State, the courts considered appellants' claimed lack of contacts with Delaware to be unimportant. This categorical analysis assumes the continued soundness of the conceptual structure founded on the century-old case of *Pennoyer v. Neff*, 95 U.S. 714, 24 L. Ed. 565 (1878).

[The Court described the holdings and reasoning of *Pennoyer*.] . . .

From our perspective, the importance of *Pennoyer* is not its result, but the fact that its principles and corollaries derived from them became the basic elements of the constitutional doctrine governing state court jurisdiction. . . . As we have noted, under *Pennoyer* state authority to adjudicate was based on the jurisdiction's power over either persons or property. . . . If a court's jurisdiction is based on its authority over the defendant's person, the action and judgment are denominated "*in personam*" and can impose a personal obligation on the defendant in favor of the plaintiff. If jurisdiction is based on the court's power over property within its territory, the action is called "*in rem*" or "*quasi in rem*." The effect of a judgment in such a case is limited to the property that supports jurisdiction and does not impose a personal liability on the property owner, since he is not before the court.[17] . . .

By concluding that "[t]he authority of every tribunal is necessarily restricted by the territorial limits of the State in which it is established," . . . *Pennoyer* sharply limited the availability of *in personam* jurisdiction over defendants not resident in the forum State. If a nonresident defendant could not be found in a State, he could not be sued there. On the other hand, since the State in which property was located was considered to have exclusive sovereignty over that property, *in rem* actions could proceed regardless of the owner's location. . . .

The *Pennoyer* rules generally favored nonresident defendants by making them harder to sue. This advantage was reduced, however, by the ability of a resident plaintiff to satisfy a claim against a nonresident defendant by bringing into court any property of the defendant located in the plaintiff's State. . . . For example, in the well-known case of *Harris v. Balk*, . . . Epstein, a resident of Maryland, had a claim against Balk, a resident of North Carolina. Harris, another North Carolina resident, owed money to Balk. When Harris happened to visit Maryland, Epstein garnished his debt to Balk. Harris did not contest the debt to Balk and paid it to Epstein's North Carolina attorney. When Balk later sued Harris in North Carolina, this Court held that the Full Faith and Credit Clause, U.S. Const, Art IV, § 1, required that Harris' payment to Epstein be treated as a discharge of his debt to Balk. This Court reasoned that the debt Harris owed Balk was an intangible form of property belonging to Balk, and that the location of that property traveled with the debtor. By obtaining personal jurisdiction over Harris, Epstein had "arrested" his debt to Balk, . . . and brought it into the Maryland court. Under the structure established by *Pennoyer*, Epstein was then entitled to proceed against that debt to vindicate his claim against Balk, even though Balk himself was not subject to the jurisdiction of a Maryland tribunal. . . .

[The Court reviewed the expansion of personal jurisdiction after *Pennoyer* and *Harris v. Balk*, including such decisions as *Hess v. Pawloski* and *International Shoe Co. v. Washington*.]

The question in *International Shoe* was whether the corporation was subject to the judicial and taxing jurisdiction of Washington. Mr. Chief Justice Stone's opinion for the Court began its analysis of that question by noting that the historical basis of *in personam* jurisdiction was a court's power over the defendant's person. That power, however, was no longer the central concern . . . .

(17). "A judgment *in rem* affects the interests of all persons in designated property. A judgment *quasi in rem* affects the interests of particular persons in designated property. . . . As did the Court in *Hanson*, we will for convenience generally use the term "*in rem*" in place of "*in rem* and *quasi in rem*."

Mechanical or quantitative evaluations of the defendant's activities in the forum could not resolve the question of reasonableness:

> Whether due process is satisfied must depend rather upon the quality and nature of the activity in relation to the fair and orderly administration of the laws which it was the purpose of the due process clause to insure. That clause does not contemplate that a state may make binding a judgment *in personam* against an individual or corporate defendant with which the state has no contacts, ties, or relations. . . .

Thus, the relationship among the defendant, the forum, and the litigation, rather than the mutually exclusive sovereignty of the States on which the rules of *Pennoyer* rest, became the central concern of the inquiry into personal jurisdiction. The immediate effect of this departure from *Pennoyer*'s conceptual apparatus was to increase the ability of the state courts to obtain personal jurisdiction over nonresident defendants. . . .

No equally dramatic change has occurred in the law governing jurisdiction *in rem.* There have, however, been intimations that the collapse of the *in personam* wing of *Pennoyer* has not left that decision unweakened as a foundation for *in rem* jurisdiction. Well-reasoned lower court opinions have questioned the proposition that the presence of property in a State gives that State jurisdiction to adjudicate rights to the property regardless of the relationship of the underlying dispute and the property owner to the forum. . . . The overwhelming majority of commentators have also rejected *Pennoyer*'s premise that a proceeding "against" property is not a proceeding against the owners of that property. . . .

. . . We think that the time is ripe to consider whether the standard of fairness and substantial justice set forth in *International Shoe* should be held to govern actions *in rem* as well as *in personam.*

III

The case for applying to jurisdiction *in rem* the same test of "fair play and substantial justice" as governs assertions of jurisdiction *in personam* is simple and straightforward. It is premised on recognition that "[t]he phrase, 'judicial jurisdiction over a thing,' is a customary elliptical way of referring to jurisdiction over the interests of persons in a thing." Restatement (Second) of Conflict of Laws § 56, Introductory Note (1971) (hereafter Restatement). This recognition leads to the conclusion that in order to justify an exercise of jurisdiction *in rem*, the basis for jurisdiction must be sufficient to justify exercising "jurisdiction over the interests of persons in a thing." The standard for determining whether an exercise of jurisdiction over the interests of persons is consistent with the Due Process Clause is the minimum-contacts standard elucidated in *International Shoe.*

This argument, of course, does not ignore the fact that the presence of property in a State may bear on the existence of jurisdiction by providing contacts among the forum State, the defendant, and the litigation. For example, when claims to the property itself are the source of the underlying controversy between the plaintiff and the defendant, it would be unusual for the State where the property is located not to have jurisdiction. In such cases, the defendant's claim to property located in the State would normally indicate that he expected to benefit from the State's protection of his interest. The State's strong interests in assuring the marketability of property within its borders and in providing a procedure for peaceful resolution of disputes about the possession of that property would also support jurisdiction, as would the likelihood that important records and witnesses will be found in the State. . . .

It appears, therefore, that jurisdiction over many types of actions which now are or might be brought *in rem* would not be affected by a holding that any assertion of state-court jurisdiction must satisfy the *International Shoe* standard. For the type of *quasi in rem* action typified by *Harris v. Balk* and the present case, however, accepting the proposed analysis would result in significant change. These are cases where the property which now serves as the basis for state-court jurisdiction is completely unrelated to the plaintiff's cause of action. Thus, although the presence of the defendant's property in a State might suggest the existence of other ties among the defendant, the State, and the litigation, the presence of the property alone would not support the State's jurisdiction. . . .

Since acceptance of the *International Shoe* test would most affect this class of cases, we examine the arguments against adopting that standard as they relate to this category of litigation. . . . For in cases such as *Harris* and this one, the only role played by the property is to provide the basis for bringing the defendant into court. Indeed, the express purpose of the Delaware sequestration procedure is to compel the defendant to enter a personal appearance. In such cases, if a direct assertion of personal jurisdiction over the defendant would violate the Constitution, it would seem that an indirect assertion of that jurisdiction should be equally impermissible.

The primary rationale for treating the presence of property as a sufficient basis for jurisdiction to adjudicate claims over which the State would not have jurisdiction if *International Shoe* applied is that a wrongdoer

> should not be able to avoid payment of his obligations by the expedient of removing his assets to a place where he is not subject to an *in personam* suit.

Restatement § 66, Comment a. . . . This justification, however, does not explain why jurisdiction should be recognized without regard to whether the property is present in the State because of an effort to avoid the owner's obligations. Nor does it support jurisdiction to adjudicate the underlying claim. At most, it suggests that a State in which property is located should have jurisdiction to attach that property, by use of proper procedures, as security for a judgment being sought in a forum where the litigation can be maintained consistently with *International Shoe*. . . .

We therefore conclude that all assertions of state-court jurisdiction must be evaluated according to the standards set forth in *International Shoe* and its progeny.[39]

39. It would not be fruitful for us to reexamine the facts of cases decided on the rationales of *Pennoyer* and *Harris* to determine whether jurisdiction might have been sustained under the

IV

. . . Appellee Heitner did not allege and does not now claim that appellants have ever set foot in Delaware. Nor does he identify any act related to his cause of action as having taken place in Delaware. Nevertheless, he contends that appellants' positions as directors and officers of a corporation chartered in Delaware provide sufficient "contacts, ties, or relations" . . . with that State to give its courts jurisdiction over appellants in this stockholder's derivative action. This argument is based primarily on what Heitner asserts to be the strong interest of Delaware in supervising the management of a Delaware corporation. . . .

This argument is undercut by the failure of the Delaware Legislature to assert the state interest appellee finds so compelling. Delaware law bases jurisdiction, not on appellants' status as corporate fiduciaries, but rather on the presence of their property in the State. . . . If Delaware perceived its interest in securing jurisdiction over corporate fiduciaries . . . to be as great as Heitner suggests, we would expect it to have enacted a statute more clearly designed to protect that interest. . . .

Appellee suggests that by accepting positions as officers or directors of a Delaware corporation, appellants performed the acts required by *Hanson v. Denckla*. He notes that Delaware law provides substantial benefits to corporate officers and directors, and that these benefits were at least in part the incentive for appellants to assume their positions. . . .

But . . . this line of reasoning establishes only that it is appropriate for Delaware law to govern the obligations of appellants to Greyhound and its stockholders. It does not demonstrate that appellants have "purposefully avail[ed themselves] of the privilege of conducting activities within the forum State," *Hanson v. Denckla*, . . . Appellants have simply had nothing to do with the State of Delaware. Moreover, appellants had no reason to expect to be haled before a Delaware court. Delaware, unlike some States, has not enacted a statute that treats acceptance of a directorship as consent to jurisdiction in the State. And "[i]t strains reason . . . to suggest that anyone buying securities in a corporation formed in Delaware 'impliedly consents' to subject himself to Delaware's . . . jurisdiction on any cause of action." . . . Delaware's assertion of jurisdiction over appellants in this case is inconsistent with that constitutional limitation on state power. The judgment of the Delaware Supreme Court must, therefore, be reversed.

Mr. Justice Brennan, concurring in part and dissenting in part.

I join Parts I–III of the Court's opinion. I fully agree that the minimum-contacts analysis developed in *International Shoe Co. v. Washington*, . . . represents a far more sensible construct for the exercise of state-court jurisdiction than the patchwork of legal and factual fictions that has been generated from the decision in *Pennoyer v. Neff*. . . . It is precisely because the inquiry into minimum contacts is now of such

standard we adopt today. To the extent that prior decisions are inconsistent with this standard, they are overruled.

overriding importance, however, that I must respectfully dissent from Part IV of the Court's opinion....

... I am convinced that as a general rule a state forum has jurisdiction to adjudicate a shareholder derivative action centering on the conduct and policies of the directors and officers of a corporation chartered by that State. Unlike the Court, I therefore would not foreclose Delaware from asserting jurisdiction over appellants were it persuaded to do so on the basis of minimum contacts....

I, therefore, would approach the minimum-contacts analysis differently than does the Court. Crucial to me is the fact that appellants voluntarily associated themselves with the State of Delaware, "invoking the benefits and protections of its laws," *Hanson v. Denckla*.... I thus do not believe that it is unfair to insist that appellants make themselves available to suit in a competent forum that Delaware might create for vindication of its important public policies directly pertaining to appellants' fiduciary associations with the State.

[The concurring opinions of Justices Powell and Stevens are omitted.]

Notes and Questions

(1) *Understanding Shaffer: The "Three-Way Relationship" and the "Fairness" Test.* Before you continue reading, make sure that you understand the essential holding in *Shaffer.* It depends upon a "three-way relationship" among the defendant, the forum, and the litigation. The relationship must be sufficient to comply with the "fairness" test.

(2) *Legitimate Uses of In Rem Jurisdiction After Shaffer.* Even after *Shaffer*, a state should have authority to probate wills, to determine real property titles, or to enforce forfeitures, notwithstanding the claims of nonresidents. In fact, these legitimate exercises of state authority are perfectly consistent with *Shaffer.* Can you explain why? [If a state is determining a non-resident's title to property located inside its borders, aren't the requisite "ties among the [person], the state and the litigation" present? And isn't the exercise of jurisdiction consistent with "fair play and substantial justice" precisely because the object of the suit is to determine claims to property located within the forum state?]

(3) *Harris v. Balk and Seider v. Roth After Shaffer.* It is reasonably clear that *Shaffer* overrules *Harris v. Balk.* There were no "ties among" Balk, the State of Maryland, and the litigation that would have satisfied the "fairness" test. But what about *Seider v. Roth*? That case is arguably different, in that the insurer was the "real" target of the suit, and it had clear ties to New York since it did extensive business there. *See* Comment, *The Constitutionality of Seider v. Roth After Shaffer v. Heitner*, 78 Colum. L. Rev. 409 (1978).

(4) *Rush v. Savchuk*, 444 U.S. 320 (1980). In this case, the Supreme Court overruled *Seider v. Roth* and held that attachment of an insurance policy as a means of obtaining jurisdiction to adjudicate a nonresident's liability was unconstitutional. The Court emphasized that the named defendant was the nonresident driver, who

had no contact with the forum. (Is this reasoning persuasive?) *See* Comment, *Seider v. Roth Jurisdiction: A Durable Rule Dies a Slow Death with the Advent of Rush v. Savchuk*, 16 New Eng. L. Rev. (1981). But the New York Court of Appeals has held that quasi-in-rem jurisdiction still survives these decisions in certain circumstances. *Banco Ambrosiano, S.P.A. v. Artoc Bank & Trust Ltd.*, 62 N.Y.2d 65, 476 N.Y.S.2d 64, 464 N.E.2d 432 (1984). A centuries-old concept is hard to subject completely to a "slow death"!

(5) *Enforcement of Judgments After Shaffer.* Assume that plaintiff has a judgment against defendant. Both reside in Pennsylvania, which is also the state where the claim arose and where the judgment was taken. But defendant's only asset is a large bank account in Arizona, a state to which he has no other connections. May plaintiff apply for a writ of garnishment in Arizona as a means of subjecting the Arizona bank account to the satisfaction of his Pennsylvania judgment? [Note: Since the garnishment of defendant's account is the sole issue, isn't the requisite three-way relationship among the defendant, the state and the litigation present?] The result might be different, however, if plaintiff had sought to bring his initial action to determine defendant's liability in Arizona, rather than Pennsylvania. Can you explain why?

(6) *Is In Rem Jurisdiction Abolished After Shaffer?* Since jurisdiction now depends upon the relationship of the defendant to the forum and the litigation, and since the relationship must satisfy the fairness test, doesn't *Shaffer* abolish *in rem* jurisdiction as a distinct basis of adjudicatory power? What, if anything, is the difference between *in rem* and *in personam* jurisdiction after *Shaffer*?

(7) *Can Plaintiff Still Validly Serve, In-Hand, a Defendant Travelling through the State?* Reconsider *Grace v. MacArthur, supra*, § 2.02 (in-hand service valid when made upon defendant in commercial airliner overflying state). Is the holding still viable after *Shaffer* (is the three-way relationship sufficient to satisfy the fairness test?) *Cf. Humphrey v. Langford*, 246 Ga. 732, 273 S.E.2d 22 (1980) (post-*Shaffer* service upheld in analogous situation). Consider the case that follows, in which the Supreme Court revisited this question and decided in favor of very broad jurisdiction.

[E] "Tag" Jurisdiction or In-State Service on a Foreign Defendant: Does "Fairness" Control or Does "Tradition" Control?

Burnham v. Superior Court

495 U.S. 604 (1990)

Justice Scalia announced the judgment of the Court and delivered an opinion in which The Chief Justice and Justice Kennedy join, and in which Justice White joins with respect to Parts I, II-A, II-B, and II-C.

The question presented is whether the Due Process Clause of the Fourteenth Amendment denies California courts jurisdiction over a nonresident, who was personally served with process while temporarily in that State, in a suit unrelated to his activities in the State.

I

[The Burnhams were married in West Virginia in 1976. In 1977, they moved to New Jersey, where their two children were born. In July 1987, the Burnhams decided to separate. They agreed that Mrs. Burnham, who intended to move to California, would take custody of the children. Mrs. Burnham brought suit for divorce in a California state court in early January 1988. In late January, petitioner (Mr. Burnham) visited southern California on business, after which he went north to visit his children in the San Francisco Bay area, where he was served with a California court summons and a copy of Mrs. Burnham's divorce petition. He then returned to New Jersey.]

Later that year, petitioner made a special appearance in the California Superior Court, moving to quash the service of process on the ground that the court lacked personal jurisdiction over him because his only contacts with California were a few short visits to the State for the purposes of conducting business and visiting his children. The Superior Court denied the motion, and the California Court of Appeal denied mandamus relief, rejecting petitioner's contention that the Due Process Clause prohibited California courts from asserting jurisdiction over him because he lacked "minimum contacts" with the State. The court held it to be "a valid jurisdictional predicate for *in personam* jurisdiction" that the "defendant [was] present in the forum state and personally served with process." [Note: this doctrine is sometimes called "tag" jurisdiction. Can you see why?]

II

A

To determine whether the assertion of personal jurisdiction is consistent with due process, we have long relied on the principles traditionally followed by American courts in marking out the territorial limits of each State's authority. That criterion was first announced in *Pennoyer v. Neff*. . . . Since *International Shoe*, we have only been called upon to decide whether these "traditional notions" permit States to exercise jurisdiction over absent defendants in a manner that deviates from the rules of jurisdiction applied in the 19th century. We have held such deviations permissible, but only with respect to suits arising out of the absent defendant's contact with the State. . . . The question we must decide today is whether due process requires a similar connection between the litigation and the defendant's contacts with the State in cases where the defendant is physically present in the State at the time process is served upon him.

B

Among the most firmly established principles of personal jurisdiction in American tradition is that the courts of a State have jurisdiction over nonresidents who are physically present in the State. The view developed early that each State had the power to hale before its courts any individual who could be found within its borders, . . . no matter how fleeting his visit . . . .

This American jurisdictional practice is, moreover, not merely old; it is continuing. It remains the practice of, not only a substantial number of the States, but as far as we are aware *all* the States and the federal government. . . . We do not know of a single State or federal statute, or a single judicial decision resting upon State law, that has abandoned in-State service as a basis of jurisdiction . . . .

C

Despite this formidable body of precedent, petitioner contends, in reliance on our decisions applying the *International Shoe* standard, that in the absence of "continuous and systematic" contacts with the forum . . . a nonresident defendant can be subjected to judgment only as to matters that arise out of or relate to his contacts with the forum. This argument rests on a thorough misunderstanding of our cases. . . .

. . . The short of the matter is that jurisdiction based on physical presence alone constitutes due process because it is one of the continuing traditions of our legal system that define the due process standard of "traditional notions of fair play and substantial justice." That standard was developed by *analogy* to "physical presence," and it would be perverse to say it could now be turned against that touchstone of jurisdiction.

D

Petitioner's strongest argument, though we ultimately reject it, relies upon our decision in *Shaffer v. Heitner*, 433 U.S. 186 (1977). . . . *Shaffer*, like *International Shoe*, involved jurisdiction over an *absent defendant*, and it stands for nothing more than the proposition that when the "minimum contact" that is a substitute for physical presence consists of property ownership it must, like other minimum contacts, be related to the litigation. Petitioner wrenches out of its context our statement in *Shaffer* that "all assertions of state-court jurisdiction must be evaluated according to the standards set forth in *International Shoe* and its progeny," 433 U.S., at 212 . . . . The logic of *Shaffer*'s holding . . . does not compel the conclusion that physically present defendants must be treated identically to absent ones . . . .

It is fair to say, however, that while our holding today does not contradict *Shaffer*, our basic approach to the due process question is different. We have conducted no independent inquiry into the desirability or fairness of the prevailing in-state service rule, leaving that judgment to the legislatures that are free to amend it; for our purposes, its validation is its pedigree, as the phrase "*traditional notions* of fair play and substantial justice" makes clear . . . . Where, . . . as in the present case, a jurisdictional principle is both firmly approved by tradition and still favored, it is impossible to imagine what standard we could appeal to for the judgment that it is "no longer justified." While in no way receding from or casting doubt upon the holding of *Shaffer* or any other case, we reaffirm today our time-honored approach. . . .

III

A few words in response to Justice Brennan's concurrence: It insists that we apply "contemporary notions of due process" to determine the constitutionality of California's assertion of jurisdiction. . . . The "contemporary notions of due process" applicable to personal jurisdiction are the enduring "*traditional* notions of fair play and substantial justice" established as the test by *International Shoe.* By its very language, that test is satisfied if a state court adheres to jurisdictional rules that are generally applied and have always been applied in the United States.

But the concurrence's proposed standard of "contemporary notions of due process" requires more: it measures state-court jurisdiction not only against traditional doctrines in this country, including current state-court practice, but against each Justice's subjective assessment of what is fair and just. Authority for that seductive standard is not to be found in any of our personal jurisdiction cases. It is, indeed, an outright break with the test of "traditional notions of fair play and substantial justice," which would have to be reformulated "*our* notions of fair play and substantial justice. . . ." . . .

Because the Due Process Clause does not prohibit the California courts from exercising jurisdiction over petitioner based on the fact of in-state service of process, the judgment is *Affirmed.*

JUSTICE WHITE, concurring in part and concurring in the judgment.

I join Part I and Parts II-A, II-B, and II-C of Justice Scalia's opinion and concur in the judgment of affirmance. [A]lthough the Court has the authority under the [Fourteenth] Amendment to examine even traditionally accepted procedures and declare them invalid, . . . there has been no showing here or elsewhere that as a general proposition the [rule in question] is so arbitrary and lacking in common sense in so many instances that it should be held violative of Due Process in every case. . . .

JUSTICE BRENNAN, with whom JUSTICE MARSHALL, JUSTICE BLACKMUN, and JUSTICE O'CONNOR join, concurring in the judgment.

I agree with Justice Scalia that the Due Process Clause of the Fourteenth Amendment generally permits a state court to exercise jurisdiction over a defendant if he is served with process while voluntarily present in the forum State. I do not perceive the need, however, to decide that a jurisdictional rule that "has been immemorially the actual law of the land," . . . automatically comports with due process simply by virtue of its "pedigree." . . . I therefore concur [only] in the judgment. . . .

Tradition, though alone not dispositive, is of course *relevant* to the question whether the rule of transient jurisdiction is consistent with due process. Tradition is salient not in the sense that practices of the past are automatically reasonable today. . . .

Rather, I find the historical background relevant because, [t]he fact that American courts have announced the rule for perhaps a century [p]rovides a defendant voluntarily present in a particular State *today* "clear notice that [he] is subject to suit" in the forum. . . .

By visiting the forum State, a transient defendant actually "avail[s]" himself, . . . of significant benefits provided by the State. His health and safety are guaranteed by the State's police, fire, and emergency medical services; he is free to travel on the State's roads and waterways; he likely enjoys the fruits of the State's economy as well. . . .

The potential burdens on a transient defendant are slight. . . . For these reasons, as a rule the exercise of personal jurisdiction over a defendant based on his voluntary presence in the forum will satisfy the requirements of due process. . . .

[The concurring opinion of Justice Stevens is omitted.]

Notes and Questions

(1) *Still a Fragmented Court.* Note that there is no majority opinion for a unanimous Court. Thus, the specific issue—the continuing viability of transient jurisdiction—is resolved, but an articulated basis for the decision is not.

(2) *Is the Court's Due Process Analysis Obsolete*? What is the status of the "minimum contacts" test, today? For 40 years, the court struggled to bring all issues of personal jurisdiction within a coherent body of rules. But the *Burnham* decision restricts the usefulness of the minimum contacts test. What is there in the *Burnham* opinions that could replace minimum contacts? One commentator has suggested that the Court should abandon due process as a basis for regulating personal jurisdiction and let the states and Congress provide legislative direction. *See* Borchers, *The Death of the Constitutional Law of Personal Jurisdiction: From Pennoyer to Burnham and Back Again*, 24 U.C. Davis L. Rev. 19 (1990).

(3) *Maybe Tag Jurisdiction Simply Is a Different Matter from Long-Arm Jurisdiction (but Should It Be, in a General Jurisdiction Case)?* The plurality opinion of Justice Scalia advances the argument that "tag" jurisdiction (when the defendant is served personally while present inside the State's borders) does not require a review of all of the defendant's contacts with the State; it just has to fit within the tradition of what has been accepted. And traditionally, tag jurisdiction has been upheld in nearly all kinds of cases, with few exceptions. Maybe this simple difference distinguishes this tag case from all of the long-arm cases, as Justice Scalia argues. Is this all there is to this case?

[F] Special Bases of Jurisdiction: "Implied Consent," "Contract," and "Nationwide Contacts"

[1] Implied Consent

Hess v. Pawloski

[Reconsider this case, which appears in § II[A][2] earlier in this chapter.]

Notes and Questions

(1) *Consent Before Suit.* The most common situations in which prior consent is required or implied involve (1) corporations doing business within the state, which are typically required to appoint a resident as agent for receipt of service, and (2) implied consent statutes covering nonresident motorists, as in *Hess.* Are there situations in which a state should not be allowed to condition the doing of business on consent to suit in the state? (What about a statute providing that "any person ordering any goods by mail from this State consents to the appointment of the Secretary of State as agent for service of process on any claim against that person"?)

(2) *Using Implied Consent to Make Directors Amenable to Jurisdiction in the State of Incorporation After Shaffer v. Heitner, supra.* "[A]ppellants had no reason to expect to be haled before a Delaware court," said the majority in *Shaffer v. Heitner.* "Delaware, unlike some States, has not enacted a statute that treats acceptance of a directorship as consent to jurisdiction in the State." Delaware acted promptly to remedy this oversight: it adopted a new long-arm statute providing that anyone serving as a corporate director "shall . . . be deemed thereby to have consented to the appointment of the registered agent of such corporation" as his or her agent for service of process.

In *Armstrong v. Pomerance*, 423 A.2d 174 (Del. 1980), neither the corporation nor the directors had done any business in Delaware other than the minimum necessary to maintain Delaware corporate status; nevertheless, the Delaware Supreme Court upheld the exercise of jurisdiction over directors served under this new long-arm provision in a fiduciary duty suit similar to *Shaffer.* The court reasoned that the directors "had purposefully avail[ed] themselves of the privilege of becoming directors of a Delaware corporation," that they had received "benefits and protection" under Delaware law, that they had consented to jurisdiction pursuant to express statutory notice, and that Delaware had "substantial interest" in overseeing the fiduciary duties of directors of its corporations. Is this result correct?

(3) *Consent by Raising the Jurisdictional Issue, Then Failing to Follow the Court's Orders: Insurance Corp. of Ireland v. Compagnie des Bauxites de Guinee*, 456 U.S. 694 (1982). Defendant was a foreign corporation, and it objected to jurisdiction by a properly filed motion to dismiss. The plaintiff then attempted to use discovery to find evidence of the defendant's contacts. Defendant refused to give discovery and disobeyed court orders requiring it to furnish information. The District Court responded to this disobedience by simply holding that jurisdiction existed, under the authority of rules allowing the trial judge to sanction parties disobeying discovery orders. The Supreme Court affirmed. It noted that its decisions repeatedly had upheld jurisdiction by "constructive consent," and it said: "Because the requirement of personal jurisdiction represents first of all an individual right, it can, like other such rights, be waived."

(4) *Consent by "General" (as opposed to "Special") Appearance.* In virtually all common law jurisdictions, a nonresident consents to jurisdiction if he appears in

the action to defend it, even if he has no connection with the forum. Is this rule fair? [If a defendant participates in the trial, loses, and only then raises the jurisdictional issue, is it fair *not* to consider his appearance as consent?] Fed. R. Civ. P. 12(h)(1) embodies an analogous approach; if the defendant files an answer, but does not raise the jurisdictional issue within the time for amendment by right, he "waives" the issue (*i.e.*, he has consented). An appearance in a common-law court solely to raise the jurisdictional issue is called a "special" appearance; any other appearance is a "general" appearance. Consider the following case.

GONZALEZ v. GONZALEZ, 484 S.W.2d 611 (Tex. Civ. App. 1972, writ ref'd n.r.e.). Defendant was not served with process in this divorce case, and he filed no written answer or appearance. The only indication of any action by the defendant in the record was the signature of the defendant's attorney on the judgment of divorce and property division, in a blank below the words: "Approved as to Form." The appellate court held that this action constituted a general appearance sufficient to confer jurisdiction on the trial court.

[2] Private Contracts Fixing Jurisdiction

CARNIVAL CRUISE LINES, INC. v. SHUTE, 499 U.S. 585 (1991). The Shutes, residents of Washington State, purchased passage on a Carnival Cruise Lines ship through their local travel agent. Their tickets, paid for through the agent, each contained a notice generally advising them that the ticket was subject to terms and conditions recited upon the ticket in small print. Among the terms and conditions was a pre-printed agreement that "all disputes and matters whatsoever arising under, in connection with or incident to this Contract shall be litigated, if at all, in and before a Court located in the State of Florida, U.S.A., to the exclusion of the Courts of any other state or country." The Shutes boarded Carnival's ship in Los Angeles. While cruising in international waters off Mexico, Mrs. Shute was injured when she slipped on a deck mat during a guided tour of the ship's galley. The Shutes sued Carnival for the injuries in U.S. District Court in Washington. The District Court dismissed their action on the ground that Carnival had insufficient contacts with Washington to support the exercise of personal jurisdiction. The Court of Appeals reversed, finding sufficient contacts based on Carnival's solicitation of business in Washington, and refused to enforce the forum-selection clause because it was "not freely bargained for" and because there was evidence that the Shutes would be "physically and financially incapable of pursuing [the] litigation in Florida."

The Supreme Court, in an opinion by Justice Blackmun, reversed. The Court decided the case solely on the basis of the forum-selection clause. If they are reasonable, even non-negotiated clauses in a form contract are enforceable under some circumstances. Here the cruise line had a special interest in limiting the fora in which it would be subject to litigation; this clause eliminated any confusion over where such suits could be brought, saving litigants and the courts time and expense and likely passing on reduced fares to the passengers. The Court found an insufficient basis in the record to support a claim that the Shutes could not pursue the case in Florida, and found that even great inconvenience to them would not deny enforcement of the clause when they had sufficient notice. The Court emphasized that form contract clauses are subject to scrutiny for "fundamental fairness," but found no evidence of fraud or overreaching by Carnival.

Justices Stevens and Marshall would have limited enforcement of forum-selection clauses to commercial arrangements between parties with equal bargaining power. They also disputed the Court's claim that the Shutes were fully and fairly notified of the choice of forum clause through the fine print on the back of the ticket by appending a facsimile of the ticket to the opinion. *See* 111 S. Ct. at 1534–38.

Notes and Questions

(1) *Validity of Jurisdictional Contracts Varies with the Jurisdiction.* In some jurisdictions, forum selection agreements are not enforceable on public policy grounds. Is this approach appropriate? Many other jurisdictions, as *Carnival* shows, uphold these contracts fairly freely.

(2) *Invalidity Because of Oppression.* Consider the following possibilities, and analyze whether they would make a difference in the result in *Carnival.* (1) The consent to jurisdiction is written in print so fine and language so complicated that an intelligent consumer could not be expected to comprehend it. [Note: Even if contractual provisions are generally enforceable, might a given provision be unenforceable because it was not really agreed to?] (2) Jurisdiction is fixed in a place that could only have been selected to make defense difficult (*e.g.*, in a state that has no relationship to defendant, plaintiff, or the transaction). (3) Defendant signs a "cognovit" note, consenting not only to waiver of service but also to *confession of judgment* against him in his absence, by an agent chosen by plaintiff. [In *D.H. Overmyer Co. v. Frick Co.*, 405 U.S. 174 (1972), the Supreme Court held that a cognovit note was valid and enforceable, although it might not be if tainted by inequality of bargaining power, etc.]

[3] Rule 4(k) and "Nationwide Contacts"

Note on Rule 4(k) and on Congressional Provisions for Nationwide Service

Rule 4(k) provides that service of a summons or filing a waiver of service is effective to establish personal jurisdiction over a defendant "who is subject to the jurisdiction of a court of general jurisdiction in the state where the district court is located" or "when authorized by a federal statute." Fed. R. Civ. P. 4(k)(1)(A) and (C). In general, therefore, state boundaries are jurisdictional boundaries for federal courts, too. But in some special kinds of cases, there are federal statutes that authorize service more broadly.

Congress has provided for nationwide service of process in a few federal statutes. These provisions cover actions seeking mandamus against federal officials, enforcement suits under the Federal Trade Commission Act, and suits under the securities laws, among other situations. Congress has the apparent power to determine, for example, that when a person issues or sells federally regulated securities, it may be appropriate to dispense with the limitations of state boundaries and to conclude that he has undertaken a nationwide activity that should be subject to nationwide process.

The Courts have generally upheld these provisions. Thus, in *United States v. Union Pacific Railroad*, 98 U.S. 569, 603–04 (1879), the Supreme Court said:

> The jurisdiction of the Supreme Court and the Court of Claims is not confined by geographical boundaries. . . .
>
> There is . . . nothing in the Constitution which forbids Congress to enact that any [federal] court . . . shall, by process served anywhere in the United States, have the power to bring before it all the parties necessary to its decision.

See also Federal Trade Commission v. Jim Walter Corp., 651 F.2d 251 (5th Cir. 1981) (upholding subpoena issued in Texas under FTC Act directed to corporation having all its employees in Florida).

Rule 4(k)(2) also provides further that "[f]or a claim that arises under federal law, serving a summons or filing a waiver of service establishes personal jurisdiction over a defendant if . . . the defendant is not subject to jurisdiction in any state's courts of general jurisdiction; and . . . exercising jurisdiction is consistent with the United States Constitution and laws." Fed. R. Civ. P. 4(k)(2). This paragraph, which operates as a separate federal long-arm provision, allows jurisdiction to be obtained over a person when the claim against that person: (1) arises under federal law, (2) personal jurisdiction is not available in any state or under a situation-specific federal statute, and (3) the person's contacts with the nation as a whole as enough to satisfy applicable constitutional requirements. *See United States v. Swiss Am. Bank Ltd.*, 191 F.3d 30, 39–40 (1st Cir. 1999).

[G] Challenging Personal Jurisdiction

Read Fed. R. Civ. P. 12(b), 12(g), and 12(h)(1).

[1] By Default Followed by Collateral Attack

Wyman v. Newhouse

[Reconsider this case, which appears in § 1.03 above.]

[2] By Special Appearance or Analogous Procedures

Note on Special Appearance and Its Federal Analogue

Collateral Attack Distinguished. The plaintiff is the party who commences the action, and she may select a forum favorable to her. She does this simply by filing suit and having the papers served on the defendant. The defendant may not agree, however, that the forum has jurisdiction, and if he wants to raise the issue, he has two choices. First, he may simply refuse to appear, as in *Wyman v. Newhouse.* If he follows this course, he may later attack the jurisdiction in his home state when an action on the default judgment is brought against him. This attack, made in a court other than the one that rendered judgment, is called a "collateral" attack. Since the default judgment generally cannot be invalidated on any basis other than lack of jurisdiction, a collateral attack is risky. It forecloses the defendant from offering any defenses on the merits. Therefore, default followed by collateral attack is not advisable except in clear-cut cases such as *Wyman.*

Special Appearance, Motion to Dismiss, or Analogous Procedures. Another means of challenging jurisdiction is by "special appearance." A special appearance is made in the court whose jurisdiction is challenged, and it is made solely for the purpose of asserting the challenge. If properly made, it does not subject the defendant to the power of the court. Some states require the defendant to avoid litigating the merits until the jurisdictional issue is resolved. The Federal Rules are more liberal; instead of requiring a strict special appearance, they permit the defendant to assert the issue by motion to dismiss under Rule 12(b) or to include it in the answer. If the defendant makes a Rule 12(b) *motion,* it must include a Rule 12(b)(2) motion to dismiss for lack of personal jurisdiction. Otherwise, the defense is waived. If the defendant responds by filing an *answer,* the answer should include the same defense, but the answer may be amended as permitted by Rule 15(a) within 21 days after service on the plaintiff, assuming the case has not been calendared for trial.

Limits on the Special Appearance. There are a few qualifications to this description of the special appearance, however. First, if the appearance is not properly made—for example, if made late in the case, long after an answer has been filed—the answer will be treated as a general appearance and is a consent to the jurisdiction of the court. Secondly, the special appearance *does consent* to the jurisdiction of the court *for the limited purpose of adjudicating its jurisdiction.* The defendant will be bound by the result. In most jurisdictions, he can defend the case on the merits if he loses the jurisdictional issue, and he then may appeal both the merits and the jurisdictional holding of the trial court. But he is generally foreclosed from collaterally attacking the judgment in another state. In summary, the defendant gets "one bite at the apple": he may either default and collaterally attack the judgment, or he may appear specially and litigate jurisdiction in the trial court chosen by the plaintiff and on appeal, but he cannot do both.

Harkness v. Hyde

98 U.S. 476 (1878)

Mr. Justice Field delivered the opinion of the court.

This was an action . . . brought in September, 1873, in a District Court of the Territory of Idaho for the county of Oneida. The summons, with a copy of the complaint, was soon afterwards served by the sheriff of the county on the defendant, at his place of residence, which was on the Indian reservation, known as the Shoshonee reservation.

The defendant thereupon appeared specially by counsel appointed for the purpose, and moved the court to dismiss the action, on the ground that the service thus made upon him on the Indian reservation was outside of the bailiwick of the sheriff, and without the jurisdiction of the court. Upon stipulation of the parties, the motion was adjourned to the Supreme Court of the Territory, and was there overruled. To the decision an exception was taken. The case was then remanded to the District Court, and the defendant filed an answer to the complaint. Upon the trial which followed, the plaintiff obtained a verdict for $3,500. Upon a motion for a new trial, the amount was reduced to $2,500; for which judgment was entered. On appeal in the Supreme Court of the Territory, the judgment was affirmed. The defendant thereupon brought the case here, and now seeks a reversal of the judgment, for the alleged error of the court in refusing to dismiss the action for want of jurisdiction over him.

The act of Congress of March 3, 1863, organizing the Territory of Idaho, provides that it shall not embrace within its limits or jurisdiction any territory of an Indian tribe without the latter's assent, but that "all such territory shall be excepted out of the boundaries, and constitute no part of the Territory of Idaho," until the tribe shall signify its assent to the President to be included within the Territory. . . . The territory reserved, therefore, was as much beyond the jurisdiction, legislative or judicial, of the government of Idaho, as if it had been set apart within the limits of another country, or of a foreign State. Its lines marked the bounds of that government. . . .

The service was an unlawful act of the sheriff. The court below should, therefore, have set it aside on its attention being called to the fact that it was made upon the defendant on the reservation.

The right of the defendant to insist upon the objection to the illegality of the service was not waived by the special appearance of counsel for him to move the dismissal of the action on that ground, or what we consider as intended, that the service be set aside; nor, when that motion was overruled, by their answering for him to the merits of the action. Illegality in a proceeding by which jurisdiction is to be obtained is in no case waived by the appearance of the defendant for the purpose of calling the attention of the court to such irregularity; nor is the objection waived when being urged it is overruled, and the defendant is thereby compelled to answer.

He is not considered as abandoning his objection because he does not submit to further proceedings without contestation. It is only where he pleads to the merits in the first instance, without insisting upon the illegality, that the objection is deemed to be waived.

The judgment of the Supreme Court of the Territory, therefore, must be reversed, and the case remanded with directions to reverse the judgment of the District Court for Oneida County, and to direct that court to set aside the service made upon the defendant; and it is so ordered.

BALDWIN v. IOWA STATE TRAVELING MEN'S ASSOCIATION, 283 U.S. 522 (1931). Plaintiff sued defendant in a Missouri court. Defendant appeared specially and moved to dismiss. After hearing the evidence about the defendant's contacts with the forum, the court denied the motion and ordered the defendant to answer on the merits within thirty days. When the defendant failed to answer, the Missouri court granted judgment against the defendant.

The plaintiff then filed an action on the judgment in Iowa, where the defendant was incorporated. The defendant again moved to dismiss, claiming that the judgment had been rendered by a court lacking jurisdiction over it. The plaintiff objected to the raising of this issue on the ground that it "constituted a collateral attack and a retrial of an issue settled in the first suit." The Supreme Court agreed, and it held that the judgment must be enforced:

> ... the special appearance gives point to the fact that the respondent entered the Missouri court for the very purpose of litigating the question of jurisdiction. It had the election not to appear at all.... It also had the right to appeal from the decision of the Missouri district court. It elected to follow neither of those courses....
>
> Public policy dictates that there be an end of litigation.... We see no reason why this doctrine should not apply in every case where one voluntarily appears, presents his case, and is fully heard, or why he should not, in the absence of fraud, be concluded by the judgment of the tribunal to which he has submitted his cause....

III. Notice Requirements and Service of Process

[A] Due Process Notice Standards

Mullane v. Central Hanover Bank & Trust Co.

339 U.S. 306 (1950)

[A New York statute permitted trust companies to pool small trusts into a common fund for more efficient administration. The statute also permitted a trust company to petition for judicial approval of its accounts. This procedure had the effect of cutting off potential claims, if any, that beneficiaries of the trusts might have against the trust company. The statute provided that notice to beneficiaries in such a proceeding would be sufficient if given by newspaper advertisement stating merely the name and address of the trust company, the date of establishment of the common trust, and a list of participating estates, trusts, or funds.

[In this portion of its opinion, the Supreme Court interpreted the Due Process Clause as setting minimum standards for notice in legal proceedings.]

. . . Many controversies have raged about the cryptic and abstract words of the Due Process Clause but there can be no doubt that at a minimum they require that deprivation of life, liberty or property by adjudication be preceded by notice and opportunity for hearing appropriate to the nature of the case. . . .

Personal service of written notice within the jurisdiction is the classic form of notice always adequate in any type of proceeding. But the vital interest of the State in bringing any issues as to its fiduciaries to a final settlement can be served only if interests or claims of individuals who are outside of the State can somehow be determined. A construction of the Due Process Clause which would place impossible or impractical obstacles in the way could not be justified . . . .

An elementary and fundamental requirement of due process in any proceeding which is to be accorded finality is notice reasonably calculated, under all the circumstances, to apprise interested parties of the pendency of the action and afford them an opportunity to present their objections. . . . The notice must be of such nature as reasonably to convey the required information, . . . and it must afford a reasonable time for those interested to make their appearance. . . . But if with due regard for the practicalities and peculiarities of the case these conditions are reasonably met, the constitutional requirements are satisfied . . . .

It would be idle to pretend that publication alone, as prescribed here, is a reliable means of acquainting interested parties of the fact that their rights are before the courts. . . . The chance of actual notice is further reduced when, as here, the notice required does not even name those whose attention it is supposed to attract, and does not inform acquaintances who might call it to attention. In weighing its sufficiency on the basis of equivalence with actual notice, we are unable to regard this as more than a feint . . . .

This Court has not hesitated to approve of resort to publication as a customary substitute in another class of cases where it is not reasonably possible or practicable to give more adequate warning. Thus it has been recognized that, in the case of persons missing or unknown, employment of an indirect and even a probably futile means of notification is all that the situation permits and creates no constitutional bar to a final decree foreclosing their rights. . . .

Those beneficiaries represented by appellant whose interests or whereabouts could not with due diligence be ascertained come clearly within this category. As to them the statutory notice is sufficient. However great the odds that publication will never reach the eyes of such unknown parties, it is not in the typical case much more likely to fail than any of the choices open to legislators endeavoring to prescribe the best notice practicable . . . .

Accordingly we overrule appellant's constitutional objections to published notice insofar as they are urged on behalf of any beneficiaries whose interests or addresses are unknown to the trustee.

As to known present beneficiaries of known place of residence, however, notice by publication stands on a different footing. . . .

The trustee has on its books the names and addresses of the income beneficiaries represented by appellant, and we find no tenable ground for dispensing with a serious effort to inform them personally of the accounting, at least by ordinary mail to the record addresses . . . . The trustee periodically remits their income to them, and we think that they might reasonably expect that with or apart from their remittances word might come to them personally that steps were being taken affecting their interests.

The statutory notice to known beneficiaries is inadequate, not because in fact it fails to reach everyone, but because under the circumstances it is not reasonably calculated to reach those who could easily be informed by other means at hand. . . .

In some situation the law requires greater precautions in its proceedings than the business world accepts for its own purposes. In few, if any, will it be satisfied with less. Certainly it is instructive, in determining the reasonableness of the impersonal broadcast notification here used, to ask whether it would satisfy a prudent man of business, counting his pennies but finding it in his interest to convey information to many persons whose names and addresses are in his files. We are not satisfied that it would . . . .

We hold that the notice of judicial settlement of accounts required by the New York Banking Law . . . is incompatible with the requirements of the Fourteenth Amendment as a basis for adjudication depriving known persons whose whereabouts are also known of substantial property rights. Accordingly the judgment is reversed and the cause remanded for further proceedings not inconsistent with this opinion.

[Mr. Justice Burton's dissenting opinion is omitted.]

Notes and Questions

(1) *Notice that Is Never Received: Can It Comply with Due Process?* Remember that the *Mullane* test requires only a method of service that is "reasonably calculated" to fulfill its constitutional purposes. It does not require that the notice actually be received. In fact, the *Mullane* court explicitly recognized that there were "risks" that individual beneficiaries might not receive the notice mailed to them, but it held that the settlement of their accounts would nevertheless be valid.

(2) *Procedures for Reopening Judgments Taken without Notice.* Even though due process may not so require, many jurisdictions do provide procedures by which

judgments taken without actual notice may be reopened after they have become final. *Cf.* Fed. R. Civ. P. 60 (judgment taken by fraud or mistake, etc.). *Texas Industries, Inc. v. Sanchez*, 521 S.W.2d 133, *aff'd per curiam*, 525 S.W.2d 870 (1975), is a striking factual situation: the sheriff set the process on a table near the defendant, a state legislator, who was accompanied by two reporters and talking on the telephone in the press room at the courthouse; he testified that he was unaware anyone had attempted to serve him with process and had no recollection of the event. The appellate court held that he could use a common law procedure called a "bill of review" to set aside the resulting default judgment on the ground that he had not been served. California provides an analogous procedure by statute; *see* CCP § 473.5 (court may set default or default judgment aside on timely motion and on whatever terms "may be just," whenever service of a summons has not resulted in actual notice to a party in time to defend the action).

(3) *"Sewer" Service.* In some jurisdictions, at some times, there have been widespread instances of false returns by process servers who have not served the defendants in question. *Cf.* Comment, *Abuse of Process: "Sewer" Service*, 3 Colum. J.L. & Soc. Prob. 17 (1967) (reporting study showing suspiciously large number of daily summonses served by individual process servers). Ironically, one cause of sewer service is overly stringent requirements that the process server serve the defendant individually, in hand, personally. Should process service that might be slightly less certain to reach the defendant—such as process left with a co-resident of defendant's abode, or service by certified mail, with return receipt, restricted to the addressee only—be permitted, as a means of reducing the cost to the plaintiff and reducing the incentive toward sewer service?

(4) *Service by Publication: When and How?* When is service by publication valid? *Mullane* makes it a last resort but clearly indicates that it is then valid. Can the imperfections of publication be ameliorated by allowance of a lengthy period of time during which defendant has a right to set aside any resulting default judgment? *Cf.* Tex. R. Civ. P. 109, 329, 819 (authorizing publication only when other means are impractical; requiring appointment of attorney *ad litem* to represent absent defendant; prohibiting default judgment, and requiring actual trial; allowing two years after judgment for motion for new trial); *see also* C.C.P. §§ 415.50, 585(c) (special California provisions for default judgments after service by publication).

[B] The Ceremony of Service: Complying with the Rules

[1] Serving Individuals and Corporations: Rule 4(e) and 4(h)

Read Fed. R. Civ. P. 4, with special attention to subdivisions 4(d)(2), (3) (waiver), 4(e) (service on individuals), 4(h) (service on corporations), 4(k) (territorial limits), and 4(m) (time limits). Also, read Rule 5(a), (b), (d).

Leigh v. Lynton

9 F.R.D. 28 (E.D.N.Y. 1949)

[Plaintiff Leigh leased a rent-controlled apartment from Defendant Lynton. He claimed that Lynton had conditioned the lease upon Leigh's purchase of furniture for $5,500, which included disguised rent, and he sued for treble damages under applicable statutes.

[Defendant Lynton was a native of England. During the time of the transaction with Leigh, Lynton resided in the United States, but shortly thereafter, he returned to England and remained there. Lynton's wife, meanwhile, rented an apartment at the Hotel Wyndham in New York City. Leigh had process served upon Lynton by having the deputy marshal leave it with his wife at her apartment in the Hotel Wyndham. Lynton filed a motion to dismiss "or, in lieu thereof, to quash the return of the summons," contending that this service was inadequate under the Federal Rules. The court began by setting forth the relevant provisions of the governing Rule, which is now numbered Rule 4(e)(2), allowing service "[u]pon an individual . . . by delivering a copy of the summons and of the complaint to him personally or by leaving copies thereof at his dwelling house or usual place of abode with some person of suitable age and discretion then residing therein. . . ."]

. . . *Earle v. McVeigh*, 91 U.S. 503, page 508, 23 L. Ed. 398, in defining usual place of abode held:

> . . . the intention evidently is that the person against whom the notice is directed should then be living or have his home in the said house. . . .

In support of the service of process, two cases have been cited, *Rovinski v. Rowe*, 6 Cir., 131 F.2d 687; and *Skidmore v. Green*, D.C.S.D.N.Y., 33 F. Supp. 529, 530. In both cases, service pursuant to [the Rule] had been upheld. They are clearly distinguishable.

In the *Rovinski* case, service of process was effected by delivery to defendant's mother at a house in Menominee, Michigan, and the defendant testified that he always considered and held that place out as his home, that he kept some odds and ends there, and that there was always a bedroom ready for his occupancy when he returned home, and that he invariably occupied it.

In the *Skidmore* case, the facts indicate that the defendant was a retired New York policeman who spent most of his time traveling about the country in an automobile and trailer. The summons and complaint had been delivered to a sister-in-law at the home of defendant's brother in Kingston, New York, which in the application for his New York automobile license, the defendant gave as his address, indicating that this was his home. The court made this comment: ". . . so far as the migratory nature of his life permits of any place of abode or dwelling house, it is the house in Kingston, New York."

As to the defendant, Phillip Lynton, the Hotel Wyndham was not his usual place of abode or dwelling as contemplated in . . . the Federal Rules of Civil Procedure.

Service of the summons and complaint must, therefore, be quashed.

NATIONAL DEVELOPMENT COMPANY v. TRIAD HOLDING CORPORATION, 930 F.2d 253 (2d Cir. 1991). This case involved a motion filed by wealthy, globetrotting Saudi businessman Adnan Khashoggi, to set aside a default judgment for allegedly improper service. Khashoggi claimed twelve different "abodes." The District Court held an evidentiary hearing, which showed that the papers had been served by "leave-with" service on one Aurora DaSilva, the housekeeper residing at a $20–25 million condominium apartment owned by Khashoggi in the Olympic Towers on Fifth Avenue in New York City. Khashoggi claimed he did not get notice until after rendition of the judgment (although the court cited some contrary evidence). He said that he considered his domicile to be a ten-acre compound in Riyadh, Saudi Arabia. The Court of Appeals noted that the cases construing Rule 4 "do not produce consistent results"; some courts, for example, require that "the defendant sought to be served be actually living in the residence at the time service is effected," while others do not. The District Court upheld the service and the default judgment, and the Court of Appeals affirmed:

> There is no dispute that Mrs. DaSilva, with whom the papers were left, is a "person of suitable age and discretion then residing" at the Olympic Tower apartment. We are called upon only to determine whether the Olympic Tower apartment was Khashoggi's "dwelling house or usual place of abode," terms that thus far have eluded "any hard and fast definition." . . . [K]hashoggi testified that the Olympic Tower apartment was only one of twelve locations around the world where he spends his time, including a "home" which he owns in Marabella, Spain, and "houses" in Rome, Paris and Monte Carlo. . . .
>
> There is nothing startling in the conclusion that a person can have two or more "dwelling houses or usual places of abode," provided each contains sufficient indicia of permanence . . . .
>
> It cannot seriously be disputed that the Olympic Tower apartment has sufficient indicia of permanence. Khashoggi owned and furnished the apartment and spent a considerable amount of money remodelling it to fit his lifestyle. [S]ince Khashoggi was actually living in the Olympic Tower apartment on December 22, 1986, service there on that day was . . . reasonably calculated to provide actual notice of the action. *See Mullane v. Central Hanover Bank & Trust Co.*, [above]. . . .
>
> [W]e express no opinion upon the validity of service had Khashoggi not been actually living at the Olympic Tower apartment when service was effected.

Notes and Questions

(1) *Changing the Facts in Leigh v. Lynton.* Would the service on Lynton's wife be valid if he had a tacit or express understanding with her that she would handle all his business in the United States during his absence (would she then be an agent authorized "by appointment")? What if the couple intended that Lynton would stay at the Wyndham apartment if ever he came to New York, and he had visited on two or three occasions and kept a change of clothes there? *See Rovinski v. Rowe*, 131 F.2d 687 (6th Cir. 1942) (rule should be "liberally" construed, in favor of upholding service).

(2) *Valid Service in Lynton?* How could Leigh have procured a valid service upon Lynton under the circumstances? [Note: Lynton is in England; consider Rule 4(f), which provides for "Serving an Individual in a Foreign Country." *See* Weintraub, *The Fifth Circuit Wrestles With the Texas Long Arm*, 14 TEXAS TECH. L. REV. 1 (1983).]

(3) *What to Do about Motions to Quash Service.* In *Leigh v. Lynton*, the defendant (or his attorney) appeared in court with the papers literally in his possession and moved to dismiss the actions on the ground that process was insufficient. If the purpose of service of process is to give the defendant notice (which this defendant obviously received), what purpose is served by dismissal? Some jurisdictions refuse to dismiss in this situation and merely give the defendant an extension of time to answer. *Cf. Butler v. Butler*, in the next section. Isn't this solution better? (In fact, doesn't dismissal hold the legal system up to possible ridicule?)

(4) *Rule Requirements as Opposed to Minimum Due Process Notice Requirements.* These cases should correct a common misconception about service. It is not enough for plaintiff to adopt *some* method of communicating to defendant that might satisfy constitutional requirements. Due process sets a minimum standard, and the forum is free to specify better means of service. For example, if the rules of the forum insist on nothing less than actual in-hand service, plaintiff would not accomplish valid service by mailing process to the defendant. The method of service must comply not only with due process, but also with the governing statute or rule.

(5) *Service on an Agent Authorized by Appointment or by Law.* Both Rule 4(e), pertaining to individuals, and Rule 4(h), pertaining to business organizations, allow service upon an agent authorized by appointment or by law. For an example of an appointed agent, consider *National Equipment Rental, Ltd. v. Szukhent*, discussed above in § 2.02[F][2] (defendant signed promissory note appointing agent within the forum). For an example of an agent authorized by law, consider *Hess v. Pawloski*, in § 2.02[A][2] (state registrar designated by law as agent of nonresident motorist).

(6) *Electronic Service.* Federal Rules 5(b)(2)(E) and 6(d) authorize electronic service of post-complaint filings under certain circumstances, and additional time is given to respond to such filings. Courts are also authorized to institute local rules to "allow" or, under some circumstances, to "require" electronic filing.

Note on Serving Corporations and Other Entities

(1) *Service on Officers, Certain Agents, or by State Law.* Federal Rule 4 provides that a corporation or association can be served by serving (1) an officer, (2) a "managing or general" agent, or (3) according to state law. Can you, for example, serve an assistant treasurer of a corporation? (Only if that person is an officer; not if she is only informally an "assistant" to the treasurer.) If you want to serve a managing or general agent, you cannot deliver the papers to just anyone employed by the defendant; you have to serve someone who "manages" something. Incidentally, a "general" agent is someone who has authority to bind the corporation, as to a contract, for example. Then, there are state law methods, and many allow service by certified mail. Can you use this means, if the state allows it? (Yes, if allowed under state law.)

(2) *How Do You Serve the Palestinian Liberation Organization (PLO)?* That is an issue in the following case. Fortunately for the plaintiffs, the PLO is not a foreign nation (it's just an organization), because if it were a foreign state, service would be more complicated (that is covered in another section, below). And fortunately for the plaintiffs, the PLO had a high-ranking official in the United States.

Waldman v. Palestine Liberation Organization

835 F.3d 317 (2d Cir. 2016)

JOHN G. KOELTL, District Judge:

In this case, eleven American families sued the Palestine Liberation Organization ("PLO") and the Palestinian Authority ("PA") (collectively, "defendants")[1] under the Anti-Terrorism Act ("ATA"), 18 U.S.C. § 2333(a), for various terror attacks in Israel that killed or wounded the plaintiffs-appellees-cross-appellants ("plaintiffs") or their family members.

The defendants repeatedly argued before the District Court . . . that the court lacked personal jurisdiction over them in light of their minimal presence in, and the lack of any nexus between the facts underlying the plaintiffs' claims and, the United States. The district court . . . concluded that it had general personal jurisdiction over the defendants, even after the Supreme Court narrowed the test for general jurisdiction [in] *Daimler AG v. Bauman.* [The method of service of process was also at issue.]

After a seven-week trial, a jury found that the defendants, acting through their employees, perpetrated the attacks and that the defendants knowingly provided material support to organizations designated by the United States State Department as foreign terrorist organizations. The jury awarded the plaintiffs damages of $218.5 million, an amount that was trebled automatically pursuant to the ATA, 18 U.S.C. § 2333(a), bringing the total award to $655.5 million. . . .

1. While other defendants, such as Yasser Arafat, were named as defendants in the case, they did not appear, and the Judgment was entered only against the PLO and the PA.

While the United States does not recognize Palestine or the PA as a sovereign government, . . . the PA is the governing authority in Palestine and employs tens of thousands of security personnel in Palestine. . . .

The district court concluded . . . that the service of process was properly effected by serving the Chief Representative of the PLO and the PA, Hassan Abdel Rahman, at his home in Virginia, pursuant to Federal Rule of Civil Procedure 4(h)(1)(B) (providing that a foreign association "must be served[] . . . in a judicial district of the United States . . . by delivering a copy of the summons and of the complaint to an officer, a managing or general agent . . . ."); see also 18 U.S.C. § 2334(a) (providing for nationwide service of process and venue under the ATA) . . . .

[The court held, however, that there was no personal jurisdiction over the PA and PLO. All of the PA's activities were in Palestine. The PLO operated all over the world as the diplomatic agent of the PA. Neither organization had the kind of systematic and continuous contacts that would make it "essentially at home" in the United States under *Daimler.* Thus, although the service of process was valid, the court lacked personal jurisdiction.] [REVERSED.]

Notes and Questions

(1) *Was the Service Proper in Waldman v. PLO?* The service was on a diplomatic official of the PLO. Was he actually a "managing or general agent" of both the PLO and the PA, as the district court held?

(2) *Service on a Corporation by Mail, as Authorized by State Law: Morton v. F.H. Paschen, Inc.*, 1997 WL 381777 (E.D. Pa. 1997) (unpublished opinion). Plaintiff Morton served the defendant by certified mail in accordance with a Pennsylvania state rule, Rule 402, that authorized mailed service on a Pennsylvania corporation. But this defendant was an out-of-state corporation. The court therefore considered whether the rule for domestic corporations applied equally to out-of-state entities. Another Pennsylvania rule, Rule 424, provided that, generally, service "shall" be performed by in-hand delivery, implying that this was the exclusive method for foreign corporations, since Rule 402 did not explicitly cover them.

But the district court decided that Pennsylvania would not wish to impose more trouble on its citizens in serving an out-of-state corporation than a domestic one. The district court quoted a Pennsylvania court of appeals opinion saying, "the Pennsylvania Supreme Court would . . . reach the same result if it were to consider whether Rule 404(2) permits service of process by mail on foreign corporations despite the apparently conflicting provisions of [R]ule 424." And since Federal Rule 4 authorizes federal service according to state rules, and the state rule thus allowed mailed service, the service was valid.

(3) *Proper Service and Proper Jurisdiction Are Two Different Concepts.* This case, *Waldman v. PLO,* makes this point clear. It is possible for the service of process to be proper but for personal jurisdiction to be lacking.

(4) *Compliance with Due Process Notice Standards Does Not Mean Service Is Proper.* Sometimes, students erroneously conclude that as long as due process is satisfied, you can serve the papers in any way you wish. Not so. On the contrary, the plaintiff must serve process according to the governing rule or statute. That rule or statute must comply with due process, but service is not valid unless is fits the rule.

Note on the Requirement of Exact Compliance

Service of Process Is Technical and Must Be Performed Exactly. If the governing Rule says to deliver two copies of everything, the plaintiff must deliver two copies. If the governing Rule says to mail an extra process to the U.S. Department of Justice, the plaintiff has to do that. Failure to comply means no service.

Some Examples. The reports are full of cases in which the plaintiffs' service of process was not precisely done according to the governing Rules, with results that sometimes include dismissals after statutes of limitations have run. For example, in *Wold v. Robart,* 2018 WL 1135396 (E.D. Wis.), the governing Rule required in-hand service on the defendant plus service on the United States, since the defendant was a federal employee. Service on the United States, in turn, required service on the local United States Attorney plus the mailing of a copy to the U.S. Department of Justice in Washington, D.C. The plaintiff followed instructions given by the court clerk, but they were incomplete, and because of the failure of the plaintiff to accomplish all three steps, the court dismissed. *See, also, e.g., Malcolm v. Honeoye Falls-Lima Education Association,* 684 Fed. Appx. 87 (2d Cir. 2017) (unpublished opinion) (service on an attorney who represented defendant in other matters was not proper service and was invalid, because the attorney was not a "managing or general agent"); *United States ex rel. Miller v. Public Warehousing Corp.,* 636 Fed. Appx. 947 (9th Cir. 2016) (unpublished opinion) (service on subsidiary is not valid as service on parent corporation without showing that subsidiary was managing agent or alter ego).

Can't an attorney count on a subsidiary to pass along lawsuit papers? (No. Compliance with the Rule is required.) Can't an attorney count on the defendant's attorney to pass the papers on to the defendant? (Again, no.) Can't an attorney assume that a U.S. Attorney will pass papers on to the U.S. Department of Justice in Washington? (No.) *See also Newby v. Enron Corporation,* 284 Fed. Appx. 146 (5th Cir. 2008) (unpublished decision) (affirming dismissal because of plaintiff's failure to complete service of process within 120 days allowed by governing Rule despite fact that statute of limitations had run; Rule now allows only 90 days).

[2] The Defendant Who Evades Process: "Substituted Service" and Waiver of Service

Butler v. Butler

577 S.W.2d 501 (Tex. Civ. App. 1978)

RAY, JUSTICE.

This is a divorce case. . . .

Appellant and appellee were married on December 30, 1961. Two children, Billy Joe Butler and Cynthia Kay Butler, were born in Texas during the marriage. . . . On August 12, 1975, Wylie Neal Butler left his wife and moved to Louisiana. Mrs. Butler filed her petition for divorce in Dallas County on August 22, 1975.

When Wylie Neal Butler left, he took his minor daughter, Cynthia Kay, with him. Appellant never told his wife his new location or communicated any information to her concerning the well-being of Cynthia. Appellee was never able to obtain personal service upon her husband, who always eluded service. She enlisted the services of the sheriff's departments of four different counties and parishes and hired a private investigator to locate her husband and daughter. In addition, Mrs. Butler used the Parent Locator Service of the Texas Department of Welfare to try to locate appellant. It was not until she was served with process in a lawsuit instituted by Wylie Neal Butler in Bossier Parish, Louisiana, seeking separation from bed and board and custody of their minor daughter, that Nancy Kay Butler learned the location of her husband and daughter. She obtained a Texas temporary restraining order, hired another private investigator, and went to Louisiana to get temporary custody of her daughter. She was successful in gaining possession of Cynthia Kay while in Louisiana and has retained possession since that time.

On June 24, 1977, the trial court authorized substituted service of citation upon Wylie Neal Butler by delivering the citation to James B. Wells, his attorney of record in the Louisiana divorce proceeding by certified mail, return receipt requested. Service was had on June 27, 1977, and the return was filed with the district clerk of Dallas County on July 1, 1977. . . .

Appellant Butler filed a special appearance in the Texas divorce proceeding on July 1, 1977, asserting that he was not amenable to process issued by the courts of this State. . . . [At the hearing,] [n]o evidence was offered that appellant was not amenable to the jurisdiction of the Texas court. By only raising the issue of defective service, appellant waived his special appearance. On the same day, the trial court . . . entered a decree of divorce, made Nancy Kay the managing conservator of the minor children, ordered child support, and entered a decree for attorney's fees in favor of appellee.

Appellant's main contentions are: (1) that the trial court did not have *in personam* jurisdiction over him; (2) that the manner of substituted service on his attorney of record in the Louisiana proceeding was improper; and (3) that the trial court could not immediately proceed to enter judgment against him. . . .

Appellant contends that the substituted service of process, executed by sending the citation by certified mail, return receipt requested, to his attorney of record in the Louisiana proceeding, was not reasonably calculated to give him notice of the suit. He does not contend that he failed to receive actual notice of the suit.

. . . Tex. R. Civ. P. 106 (Supp. 1978) . . . provides that where it is impractical to secure personal service, then the court, upon motion [supported by sworn evidence], may authorize service in any other manner which will be reasonably effective to give the defendant notice of the suit. In the present case, a hearing was held, and an order was entered directing that service upon Wylie Neal Butler be had by delivering citation to his Louisiana attorney by certified mail, return receipt requested. . . .

. . . Appellant relies upon *Sindorf v. Cen-Tex Supply Co.*, 172 S.W.2d 775 . . . , for the point that personal service can never be effected by service upon a person's attorney. In *Sindorf*, citation was made on Kenneth Slack by delivering a copy . . . to T.F. Slack, "his attorney." [No hearing was held or order sought showing that normal service was impractical in *Sindorf;* the plaintiff simply served the defendant's alleged attorney outright.] *Sindorf* is not a substituted service case under Rule 106 . . . and is not applicable to the present case. [The court proceeded to hold that substituted service upon Wylie Neal Butler, under the special court order allowing service on his attorney after service on him was shown impractical, complied with both due process and with the state rule governing substituted service.]

. . . [I]t was not error for the trial court to immediately proceed to trial in the absence of an answer having been filed by appellant.

[Here, the court considers whether Wylie Neal's failure to file an answer allowed the court to proceed to judgment. The court notes that the "special appearance" was not really a special appearance, since it raised only issues about service of process and not jurisdiction; therefore, the special appearance was waived.] . . . Appellant could have filed his answer along with this sworn special appearance . . . and have forestalled the default judgment which was taken by appellee. Since the court had jurisdiction [and the method of service was proper under both the Constitution and the governing rules], the trial court was authorized to proceed to judgment because no answer had been filed by appellant and the required time for answering had elapsed . . . .

The judgment of the trial court is affirmed.

Note on Waiver of Service

A Simpler, Less Expensive Way: Waiver. Serving process in complex situations can be expensive and can produce delay. Rule 4(d) provides an alternative. The plaintiff can request that the defendant waive service. If the defendant does so, the defendant will be in the same position as if it had been served, without the extra process and expense. The practicality of this procedure depends upon the defendant's recognition that it is pointless to insist on making the plaintiff go through the motions of service if, in fact, service is possible.

Incentives to the Defendant. The defendant who waives service gets additional time to answer. Furthermore, the defendant avoids being assessed the cost of service, which Rule 4(d) provides for. In addition, the Rule makes clear that the defendant retains the right to challenge personal jurisdiction, venue, and every other claim of the plaintiff other than service of process. But the defendant does not have to cooperate. Consider the following case.

HUNSINGER v. GATEWAY MANAGEMENT CORP., 169 F.R.D. 152 (D. Kan. 1996). Before suit, the parties conducted a mediation in which defendant Gateway was represented by a San Francisco law firm. The mediation was unsuccessful in producing a settlement. Plaintiff's counsel then filed this action in a Kansas federal court. Instead of actual service, he sent a request for waiver of service pursuant to Rule 4(d) to the San Francisco attorney who had represented the defendant in the mediation. Later, once 120 days had passed without actual service, defendant Gateway refused to waive service, and represented now by different counsel, moved for dismissal pursuant to Rule 4(m). This Rule provides that the court "must dismiss" if service has not been effected within 120 days [now shortened to 90 days—Eds.]. (The opinion does not indicate whether the requested dismissal would have taken effect after the running of the statute of limitations, but these types of dismissals have occurred, with the result of barring the litigation.)

Plaintiff's counsel countered by relying on the provision in Rule 4(m) that allows an extension of time for "good cause." As basis for a finding of good cause, plaintiff's counsel offered an affidavit stating that the San Francisco lawyer had said he was "considering" the 4(d) waiver request, that there was no reason to believe he lacked authority to waive service, and that actual service now was imminent. Gateway vehemently responded that these assertions were "factual misrepresentations in a desperate attempt to avoid the consequences of [plaintiff's] blatant disregard for proper service procedure in federal court litigation," and it attached an affidavit from the San Francisco lawyer categorically denying the alleged remark about "consideration" of a waiver.

The District Judge denied the motion to dismiss. Rather than infer false representations from either affidavit, the court preferred to "attribute this conflict of recollections to a misunderstanding between counsel." It was clear, nevertheless, that the 4(d) request for waiver had been received by counsel who previously had represented the defendant in this same matter. He did not refuse to waive service until more than 120 days already had passed. Even if these facts did not constitute good cause, Rule 4(m) allows the court, as an alternative to dismissal, to "order that service be made within a specified time," which this court interpreted as granting the judge discretion to allow service after the 120-day [now, 90-day] limit.

Notes and Questions

(1) *What Should Be Done About the Defendant Who Evades Process?* The defendant who deliberately frustrates efforts to serve him is not, unfortunately, uncommon. For an interesting example in addition to *Butler v. Butler*, consider *International Controls Corp. v. Vesco*, 593 F.2d 166 (2d Cir. 1979). After Bahamian counsel was unable to serve the fugitive financier Robert Vesco, the plaintiff obtained an order appointing a process server who was met at the bolted gate by guards who denied entry; she attempted unsuccessfully to serve the guards, then she threw the papers at a young man who identified Vesco as "my father," but he threw the papers back at her. She then telephoned the judge, who authorized further substituted efforts, and effected service by throwing the papers, bound with a blue ribbon, over the fence and onto the lawn, where she photographed them. After accomplishing these acts, she was threatened by armed guards who attempted to enter and then followed her cab. In accordance with the judge's order, the process server also mailed a copy of the summons and complaint to Vesco by ordinary first-class mail (not certified mail, which Vesco could have simply refused). The court later upheld this "blue ribbon" service (but later, a Vesco bodyguard successfully frustrated service of an amended complaint by picking it up from the ground and putting it in the process server's car).

What should be the response of the law to such conduct? Would it be wise or constitutional for the courts to treat evasion as equivalent to notice? To make the defendant liable for expenses of service (or for significant penalties or punitive damages)? To grant default judgment, subject to setting aside on a showing by defendant that he did not know of or deliberately elude service? To enact disciplinary rules sanctioning attorneys who assist in willful evasion? To allow liberal service by mail (including service by plain first-class mail if the defendant refuses to accept certified mail, as often happens)?

(2) *Service by Mail.* Many states allow service by certified mail. Under most state rules, the delivery must be restricted to the addressee only, and the receipt must be filed as part of the return. Federal service may be accomplished by this means if the court is located in one of these states (because Rule 4 adopts state-law means of service). *See* Siegel, *Changes in Federal Summons Service Under Amended Rule 4 of the Federal Rules of Civil Procedure*, 96 F.R.D. 81 (1983). A similar procedure has been suggested as part of the Federal Rules themselves. Should this proposal be adopted? Or is mailed service significantly less likely to communicate to defendants the seriousness of the papers and more subject to fraud than in-hand service?

(3) *The Waiver-of-Service Provision and 120-Day [now 90-Day] Time Limit, as in the Hunsinger Case.* The waiver procedure avoids cost and delay in some instances. If the defendant refuses waiver, however, plaintiffs may suffer disastrous results owing to the 90-day limit and applicable statutes of limitation. It is best to use the waiver procedure early in the 90-day period, if one uses it at all, and then to document one's action, and to act promptly if the defendant is nonresponsive.

(4) *Hunsinger Provides a Mere Glimpse at Discourtesy in Law Practice.* It seems unnecessary for the defense lawyer to have characterized the plaintiff's positions as "mischaracterizations," "desperate," or "blatant disregard for proper service procedure." It apparently didn't impress the judge. But these kinds of remarks make the practice of law unpleasant for the recipient, who is then motivated to retaliate. Bar associations as well as courts have emphatically urged attorneys to practice civility. But the contentious nature of law practice, together with the unfortunate fact that discourteous or even abusive tactics sometimes work, causes uncivility in some instances. *Hunsinger* provides no more than a brief glance at this problem, and you will see much worse conduct on occasion in practice.

IV. Service of Process in International Litigation

"Letters Rogatory," Rule 4(f) and the Hague Convention. International litigation today is more prevalent than ever before. The Hague Convention on the Service Abroad of Judicial and Extrajudicial Documents in Civil or Commercial Matters, 20 U.S.T. 361, T.I.A.S. 6638, is a treaty ratified by 32 nations, providing for means of service with certain reservations by participating nations. Rule 4(f) says that if there is an "internationally agreed" method of service such as the Hague Convention, the service must follow this method. If there is no internationally agreed method, the Rule provides alternative methods, including service "prescribed by the foreign country's law" or "as the foreign authority directs in response to a letter rogatory or letter of request," or by certain other means, including sometimes mail or personal service. A letter of request is explained in the discovery chapter, below. A letter rogatory is "the medium, in effect, whereby one country, speaking through one of its courts, requests another country, acting through its own courts, . . . to assist the administration of justice in the foreign country . . . ." *The Signe*, 37 F. Supp. 819, 820 (E.D. La. 1941).

The Hague Convention provides for flexible means of service—but it is limited by the parties' reservations. Service by a court in the United States upon a person in France or Germany, for example, must be perfected in accordance with the Convention. A litigant may experience serious difficulties if the rules under which she is operating are not compatible with it. *See* Jones, *International Service of Process Requirements in U.S. District Court*, 26 N.H.B.J. 39 (1984).

An Example: Low v. Bayerische Motoren Werke, A.G., 88 A.D.2d 504, 449 N.Y.S.2d 733 (1st Dep't 1982). Low purchased a BMW in Germany. Although he had acted through its subsidiary to initiate the purchase, his first direct contact with the defendant was in Germany. While driving the car in Germany, he was injured. Later, he brought a personal injury action against the defendant in a New York state court. Pursuant to the New York statute, he served the secretary of state and mailed a copy of the summons and complaint to the defendant in Germany. The Appellate Division held this service ineffective. Although article 10 of the Hague Convention allows service by mail, the article is subject to reservation. In its ratification, the

Federal Republic of Germany objected to article 10 and declared that such service should not be effective. The treaty and reservation made under it were held to prevail over the state statute. Plaintiff Low could have obtained service by letter rogatory or by other means provided by the Convention.

Service on a Foreign Subject Inside the United States. In *Volkswagenwerk Aktiengesellschaft v. Schlunk*, 486 U.S. 694 (1988), the Supreme Court interpreted the Hague Service Convention as not applying when process is served on a foreign corporation by serving its domestic subsidiary which, under state law in that case, was the corporation's involuntary agent for service of process. "Where service on a domestic agent is valid and complete under both state law and the Due Process Clause, our inquiry ends and the Convention has no further implications. . . . The only transmittal to which the Convention applies is a transmittal abroad that is required as a necessary part of service." 486 U.S. at 707.

Notes and Questions

(1) *Is E-Mail Service Among the Available Methods of International Service Under Rule 4(f)?* Rule 4(f) contains a "catch-all" provision allowing service upon individuals outside the United States "by other means not prohibited by international agreement, as the court orders." In *Rio Properties, Inc. v. Rio International Interlink*, 284 F.3d 1007 (9th Cir. 2002), the Ninth Circuit had to consider whether a U.S. plaintiff could use e-mail under Rule 4(f)(3) to serve a Costa Rican business entity that was not subject to service in the United States and appeared to be evading the usual means of service. Federal Rule 5(b)(2)(D) authorizes the use of e-mail to serve papers other than the summons and complaint, but there is no explicit authority for the use of e-mail to serve a summons and complaint either within or without the territory of the United States.

Nevertheless, the Ninth Circuit approved the use of e-mail service in this case under an order by the trial court. The court concluded that Rule 4(f)(3) required only that service be directed by the court and not be prohibited by international agreement, even if the method was in contravention of the laws of the foreign country where service was made. Given the Ninth Circuit's grant of broad authority to the district courts, is it likely that domestic plaintiffs will in fact prefer using alternatives to traditional service methods rather than employing the less familiar but more traditional letters rogatory and formal diplomatic methods under the Hague Convention?

(2) *Service by Regular Mail to a Post Office Box?* After initially upholding service of process upon an English defendant by regular mail to a post office box in England, the Ninth Circuit panel changed its mind. In *Brockmeyer v. May*, 383 F.3d 798 (9th Cir. 2004), in a substituted opinion, the Ninth Circuit panel found the service unauthorized. International service of process by regular mail is authorized by Article 10(a) of the Hague Convention when the law of the forum state authorizes such service and the state of destination does not object. Here, however, "the law of

the forum state" did not authorize such service because the plaintiffs did not obtain a waiver of service under Fed. R. Civ. P. 4(d) nor comply with any of the provisions of Rule 4(f). In fact, service by mail has technical requirements in international litigation. Consider the following.

Kumar v. Republic of Sudan

880 F.3d 144 (4th Cir. 2018)

[Family members of victims of terrorism-related bombing of a United States Navy vessel in Yemen filed suit against the Republic of Sudan under the Foreign Sovereign Immunities Act (FSIA). Sudan did not answer and defaulted. The District Court determined an appropriate amount of damages to be awarded to each plaintiff and denied Sudan's motion to vacate entry of judgment. Sudan appealed.]

The Federal Rule of Civil Procedure governing service of process provides that "[a] foreign state . . . must be served in accordance with 28 U.S.C. § 1608," *i.e.*, the FSIA. Fed. R. Civ. P. 4(j)(1). That statute, in turn, describes four methods of serving process on a foreign state, listed in hierarchical order. § 1608(a).

The first method is "in accordance with any special arrangement for service between the plaintiff and the foreign state." § 1608(a)(1). If no such arrangement exists, then service may be made "in accordance with an applicable international convention on service of judicial documents." § 1608(a)(2). And "if service cannot be made under [either of these provisions, the specified documents,] together with a translation of each into the official language of the foreign state, [can be sent] by any form of mail requiring a signed receipt, to be addressed and dispatched by the clerk of the court to the head of the ministry of foreign affairs of the foreign state concerned." § 1608(a)(3). Lastly, [if service by mail under the third method cannot be made within 30 days, the process can be sent to the State Department for delivery through diplomatic channels.]

There is no dispute that the first two methods of service described in § 1608(a) were not available to Kumar. Further, Kumar did not attempt to serve process by delivering the requisite documents through diplomatic channels as set out in subsection (a)(4), in part because failure of subsection (a)(3) service is a prerequisite [and that is what was attempted here] . . . .

The question before the Court, then, is limited to whether Kumar satisfied § 1608(a)(3), which allows service by mail "requiring a signed receipt[] to be addressed and dispatched by the clerk of the court to the head of the ministry of foreign affairs of the foreign state." Specifically, we must decide whether Kumar satisfied the "addressed and dispatched to" requirement when he submitted the packet to be mailed by the clerk of court to the Sudanese embassy in Washington, D.C. . . .

[Sudan] contends that mailing service to the Sudanese embassy in Washington, D.C., does not satisfy 28 U.S.C. § 1608(a)(3) and contravenes the 1961

Vienna Convention on Diplomatic Relations and Optional Protocol on Disputes ("Vienna Convention"), which provides that a foreign state's diplomatic mission is inviolable. . . .

While it is true that subsection (a)(3) does not specify delivery only at the foreign ministry in the foreign state's capital, Kumar's premise that subsection (a)(3) does not require service to be sent there does not lead to his conclusion that service at the embassy satisfies the obligation under subsection (a)(3). The statute is simply ambiguous . . . , given that while the head of a ministry of foreign affairs generally oversees a foreign state's embassies, the foreign minister is rarely—if ever—present there. Serving the foreign minister at a location removed from where he or she actually works is at least in tension with Congress' objective, even if it is not strictly prohibited by the statutory language. . . .

In foreign affairs matters such as we consider here, we afford the view of the Department of State "substantial deference." *See Abbott v. Abbott*, 560 U.S. 1 (2010) . . . . In this case, the State Department contends that service at an embassy does not satisfy subsection (a)(3) and is inconsistent with the United States' obligations under the Vienna Convention. *See* Br. for the United States as Amicus Curiae in Supp. of Reversal 11 ("There is an international consensus that a litigant's service of process through mail or personal delivery to a foreign mission is inconsistent with the inviolability of the mission enshrined in" Article 22 of the Vienna Convention). . . .

Relatedly, the Court properly considers the diplomatic interests of the United States when construing the Vienna Convention and the FSIA. *See Persinger v. Islamic Republic of Iran*, 729 F.2d 835, 841 (D.C. Cir. 1984). The United States has represented that it routinely "refuses to recognize the propriety of a private party's service through mail or personal delivery to a United States embassy." Br. for the United States as Amicus Curiae 13. . . .

Our holding conflicts with the view of the Second Circuit, which has held that serving Sudan's head of the ministry of foreign affairs in a package that was delivered by certified mail to the Sudanese embassy in Washington, D.C., satisfies § 1608(a)(3). *Harrison v. Republic of Sudan* (*Harrison I*), 802 F.3d 399, 402–06 (2d Cir. 2015), *reh'g denied*, 838 F.3d 86 (*Harrison II*) (2d Cir. 2016). The Second Circuit concluded "principles of mission inviolability and diplomatic immunity are [not] implicated" where service is made "*via* the embassy." For the reasons we've already explained, we find the Second Circuit's reasoning weak and unconvincing. [The court also disagrees with other arguments offered by the Second Circuit.]

Because the attempted service of process in this case did not comply with the FSIA's statutory requirements, the district court lacked personal jurisdiction over Sudan and could not enter judgment against it. . . . For that reason, the judgments entered against Sudan are void. . . . *REVERSED IN PART, VACATED IN PART, AND REMANDED WITH INSTRUCTIONS*

V. Venue and *Forum Non Conveniens*

[A] Venue

[1] The Federal Venue Statutes

Note on Venue

What Is "Venue"? Often, there are many federal districts where personal jurisdiction exists. Some of them might be inconvenient. Venue is a separate set of rules that helps to find a convenient place for the suit.

Why Are There Two Separate Sets of Rules about This? Logically, we might prefer to have a single, unified set of rules for jurisdiction and venue. But the law in this area simply evolved this way. And so, you'll have to understand venue as well as jurisdiction.

Read 28 U.S.C. §§ 1390–1391 (general venue provisions); 1400(b) (patent venue); 1404(a) (change of venue); 1406 (cure or waiver of defects).

Problem C

APPLYING THE FEDERAL VENUE STATUTES. Plaintiff A, a resident of San Francisco (in the Northern District of California), has been injured in an automobile collision occurring in Los Angeles (within the Central District of California), as a result of the careless operation of a car driven by Defendant B, a resident of the Boston Division of the District of Massachusetts. The following questions ask you to identify places of proper venue, to discuss tools that parties may use to alter or attack venue, and to analyze their strategies. Figure 2B is a graphic depiction of these problems.

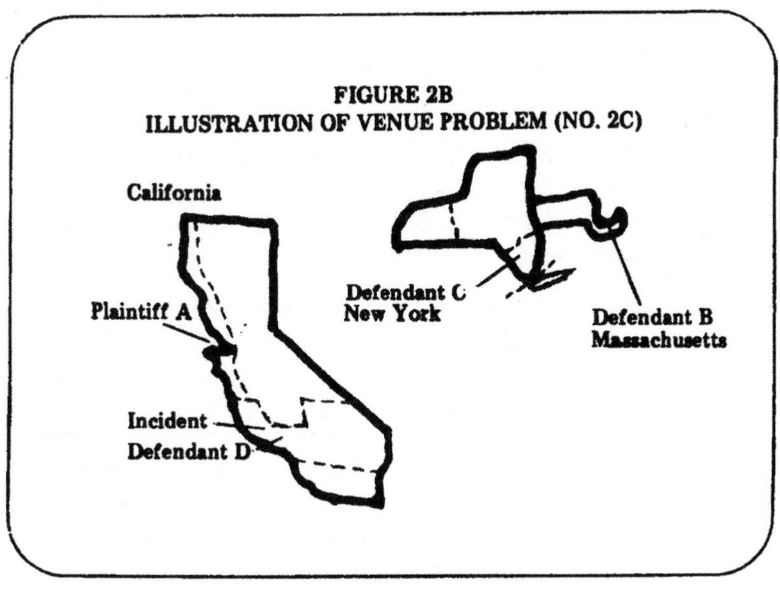

(1) *Venue in Diversity Cases.* Identify the places of proper venue for a diversity action by A against B. [*See* § 1391(a)(1), (b).]

(2) *Multiple Defendants in Different States.* What difference would it make if Plaintiff were to join a second defendant, C, who resides in the Southern District of New York? [Note: § 1391(b)(1) provides that defendants residing in different districts may be sued in either district—but *only* if the two districts are in the same state; and there is now no place where "all" defendants reside. What places are left under the analysis in question 1?]

(3) *Improper Venue.* Imagine that plaintiff files suit only against B—but he files it in a federal court in the Northern District of Illinois, which is no one's residence and is not where any of the "events or omissions giving rise to the claim occurred." If defendant B is dissatisfied with this location and is convinced venue is improper, is there anything he can do? [*See* § 1406: dismissal or transfer in the event of improperly laid venue. Note that if defendant defaults, the resulting default judgment may be valid if personal jurisdiction can be established, because venue rights, unlike lack of jurisdiction, can be waived by nonappearance.]

(4) *Corporations.* Now, imagine that B is a corporation (whose employee carelessly operated B's car) that is incorporated under Massachusetts law with its headquarters in Syracuse, New York (Northern District of New York). B Corporation is licensed to transact business in New York, and has an agent for service of process and a registered office in New York City (Southern District of New York). B Corporation has factories and distribution centers in Houston, Texas (Southern District of Texas) and in San Diego, California (Southern District of California). What are the places of proper venue now? [*See* § 1391(d).]

(5) *Forum Shopping and Venue Choices.* If Plaintiff has many venue choices (as in the case of the suit against the corporation in question 4, above), how is he likely to go about deciding where to sue? [What kinds of considerations influence how one goes about "forum shopping"?]

(6) *Proper but Inconvenient Venue; Transfer.* What is the defendant corporation's remedy if a forum-shopping plaintiff files suit in a district where venue is proper, but one having nothing to do with the parties or the litigation, and distant from all witnesses? [Note: § 1404(a) allows discretionary transfer for the "convenience of parties and witnesses, in the interest of justice."]

(7) *Venue in Federal Question Claims.* Now, imagine that Plaintiff A sues Defendant D, asserting a federal civil rights claim. Defendant D is a citizen of California, as is Plaintiff A. Defendant D resides in, and the claim arose in, the Los Angeles Division of the Central District of California. Now, where is the only proper place of venue? [Note: § 1391(b) controls.]

[2] Transfer of Venue

Note on Transfer of Venue Under Section 1404(a)

A federal statute, 28 U.S.C. § 1404(a), provides for transfer of venue at the discretion of a district court. This statute means that, if the venue is inconvenient, the trial judge can transfer the action to a more convenient location. The decision to transfer depends upon various factors related to "convenience" and "the interest of justice," which are to be weighed in an imprecise way by the district judge, who has broad discretion to grant or refuse transfer. But sometimes there are special factors affecting venue, such as a forum selection clause in a contract. The following case shows how the decision, based on this general statutory language, might be made in that case.

Atlantic Marine Construction Company, Inc. v. District Court

571 U.S. 49 (2013)

[Atlantic Marine Construction Company, a Virginia corporation, entered into a subcontract with respondent J-Crew Management, Inc., a Texas corporation, for work on a construction project. The subcontract included a forum-selection clause, which stated that all disputes between the parties would be litigated in Virginia. When a dispute arose, however, J-Crew filed suit in the Western District of Texas. Atlantic Marine moved to dismiss, arguing that the forum-selection clause rendered venue "wrong" under 28 U.S.C. § 1406(a). In the alternative, Atlantic Marine moved to transfer the case to the Eastern District of Virginia under 28 U.S.C. § 1404(a). The District Court denied both motions. It concluded that § 1404(a) is the exclusive mechanism for enforcing a forum-selection clause; that Atlantic Marine bore the burden of proof; and that the court would consider factors underlying "the convenience of parties and witnesses" and the "interest of justice," only one of which was the forum-selection clause. After weighing those factors, the District Court held that Atlantic Marine had not carried its burden, and it refused the transfer.]

[The Fifth Circuit denied Atlantic Marine's petition for a writ of mandamus. The Court of Appeals agreed with the District Court that § 1404(a) is the exclusive mechanism for enforcing a forum-selection clause and held that the District Court had not abused its discretion in refusing to transfer the case. The Supreme Court here reverses this holding.]

[The Supreme Court holds that Section 1406(a) and Rule 12(b) allow dismissal only when venue is "wrong" or "improper." Whether venue is "wrong" or "improper" depends exclusively on whether the court in which the case was brought satisfies the requirements of federal venue laws. If a case falls within one of § 1391(b)'s districts, venue is proper; if it does not, venue is improper, and the case must be dismissed or transferred under § 1406(a). A forum-selection clause has no bearing. In this case, venue is proper, but still, it can be transferred.]

[Next, the Court concludes that a forum-selection clause may be enforced through a motion to transfer under § 1404(a), which permits transfer to any other district where venue is proper. Section 1404(a), however, governs transfer only within the federal court system. When a forum-selection clause points to a state or foreign forum, the clause may be enforced through the doctrine of *forum non conveniens,* which is discussed in a later section of this book, below.]

In the typical case not involving a forum-selection clause, a district court considering a § 1404(a) motion (or a *forum non conveniens* motion) must evaluate both the convenience of the parties and various public-interest considerations. Ordinarily, the district court would weigh the relevant factors and decide whether, on balance, a transfer would serve "the convenience of parties and witnesses" and otherwise promote "the interest of justice." § 1404(a).

The calculus changes, however, when the parties' contract contains a valid forum-selection clause, which "represents the parties' agreement as to the most proper forum." The "enforcement of valid forum-selection clauses, bargained for by the parties, protects their legitimate expectations and furthers vital interests of the justice system." For that reason, and because the overarching consideration under § 1404(a) is whether a transfer would promote "the interest of justice," "a valid forum-selection clause [should be] given controlling weight in all but the most exceptional cases." The presence of a valid forum-selection clause requires district courts to adjust their usual § 1404(a) analysis in three ways.

First, the plaintiff's choice of forum merits no weight. . . . [W]hen a plaintiff agrees by contract to bring suit only in a specified forum—presumably in exchange for other binding promises by the defendant—the plaintiff has effectively exercised its "venue privilege" before a dispute arises. Only that initial choice deserves deference, and the plaintiff must bear the burden of showing why the court should not transfer the case to the forum to which the parties agreed.

Second, a court evaluating a defendant's § 1404(a) motion to transfer based on a forum-selection clause should not consider arguments about the parties' private interests. When parties agree to a forum-selection clause, they waive the right to challenge the preselected forum as inconvenient or less convenient for themselves or their witnesses . . . . A court accordingly must deem the private-interest factors to weigh entirely in favor of the preselected forum. . . .

As a consequence, a district court may consider arguments about public-interest factors only. Because those factors will rarely defeat a transfer motion, the practical result is that forum-selection clauses should control except in unusual cases. . . .

Third, when a party bound by a forum-selection clause flouts its contractual obligation and files suit in a different forum, a § 1404(a) transfer of venue will not carry with it the original venue's choice-of-law rules . . . . A federal court sitting in diversity ordinarily must follow the choice-of-law rules of the State in which it sits. *See Klaxon Co. v. Stentor Elec. Mfg. Co.,* 313 U.S. 487, 494–496 (1941). However, we previously identified an exception to that principle for § 1404(a) transfers, requiring that the state law applicable in the original court also apply in the transferee court. We deemed that exception necessary to prevent "defendants, properly subjected to suit in the transferor State," from "invok[ing] § 1404(a) to gain the benefits of the laws of another jurisdiction . . . ." [Usually, therefore, the transferee district, upon receiving the case, follows the law of the original transferor court.—Eds.]

The policies motivating our exception to the *Klaxon* rule for § 1404(a) transfers, however, do not support an extension to cases where a defendant's motion is premised on enforcement of a valid forum-selection clause. . . . [A] plaintiff who files suit in violation of a forum-selection clause . . . is entitled to no concomitant "state-law advantages." Not only would it be inequitable to allow the plaintiff to fasten its choice of substantive law to the venue transfer, but it would also encourage gamesmanship. . . . The court in the contractually selected venue should not apply the law of the [original] transferor venue. . . .

The District Court's application of § 1404(a) in this case did not comport with these principles. The District Court improperly placed the burden on Atlantic Marine to prove that transfer to the parties' contractually preselected forum was appropriate. As the party acting in violation of the forum-selection clause, J-Crew must bear the burden of showing that public-interest factors overwhelmingly disfavor a transfer.

The District Court also erred in giving weight to arguments about the parties' private interests, given that all private interests, as expressed in the forum-selection clause, weigh in favor of the transfer. . . . [W]hen J-Crew entered into a contract to litigate all disputes in Virginia, it knew that a distant forum might hinder its ability to call certain witnesses and might impose other burdens on its litigation efforts. . . .

The District Court also held that the public-interest factors weighed in favor of keeping the case in Texas because Texas contract law is more familiar to federal judges in Texas than to their federal colleagues in Virginia. That ruling, however, rested in part on the District Court's belief that the federal court sitting in Virginia would have been required to apply Texas' choice-of-law rules, which in this case pointed to Texas contract law. But for the reasons we have explained, the transferee court would apply Virginia choice-of-law rules. It is true that even these Virginia rules may point to the contract law of Texas, as the State in which the contract was formed. . . . [But] federal judges routinely apply the law of a State other than the State in which they sit. We are not aware of any exceptionally arcane features of Texas contract law that are likely to defy comprehension by a federal judge sitting in Virginia. [REVERSED AND REMANDED.]

Notes and Questions

(1) *A Straightforward Application of the Transfer Provision: Hampton-Muhamed v. James B. Nutter & Co.*, 687 Fed. Appx. 890 11th Cir. 2017) (unpublished decision). This case illustrates § 1404(a) in its usual, simpler application, without a forum selection clause. The trial court granted a convenience-based transfer under § 1404(a) of an action from the Northern District of Georgia to the Middle District of Florida. The action related to debt collection and attempted foreclosure. Plaintiff

argued that she had travel restrictions and that the transfer was inconvenient for her. But the Georgia court lacked jurisdiction over some defendants who were in Florida; the mortgaged property and attempted foreclosure proceedings were in Florida; the majority of witnesses and relevant documents were in Florida; and the plaintiff had traveled to Florida at least twice for hearings relating to foreclosure. The court of appeals held that the transfer was not an abuse of discretion.

(2) *The Deference Usually Granted to Plaintiff's Choice of Forum.* One factor that might influence the outcome of the case above, *Hampton-Muhamed,* is that the courts usually give deference to the plaintiff's choice of forum. That deference was undercut, in *Hampton-Muhamed* by the many convenience factors favoring Florida. A separate question is, why should the courts give deference to the plaintiff's choice, rather than to the defendant's? Consider whether it would be better for the trial judge to begin with a position of neutrality.

Note on Two Kinds of Places to Which Transfer Is Proper: (1) "Where It Might Have Been Brought" or (2) Where All Parties Consent

Two Provisions for Places where an Action May be Transferred: (1) "Where It Might Have Been Brought" or (2) Where All Parties Consent. Historically, there was only one definition provided in the statute for places to which an action could properly be transferred: to "where it might have been brought." This phrase means a venue defined in advance by law, having proper venue and jurisdiction. Later, Congress amended the statute to add another place: where all parties consent. See below.

The Decision in Hoffman v. Blaski, 363 U.S. 335 (1960). This decision of the Supreme Court generated a three-Justice dissent, a great deal of criticism by commentators, and ultimately, Congressional attention. *Hoffman v. Blaski* began with a suit by a patent holder against a defendant that allegedly was infringing the patent. Under the patent venue statute, the suit was filed in the Northern District of Texas, where the defendant resided, and the patent allegedly was infringed. The defendant moved to transfer the action to the Northern District of Illinois, where the plaintiff resided. The trial court granted the transfer. That was not a place designated by the statute as a proper venue, but the defendant addressed that issue by expressly consenting to the venue. The Northern District of Illinois seemed a convenient place for the plaintiff, who was located there; documents and witnesses were located there as well. But the plaintiff objected. Ultimately, the Supreme Court decided that the venue transfer was improper, even though it was to a place convenient to the plaintiff.

The majority reasoned that the language of the statute, allowing transfer of a case only to a location "where it might have been brought," was "plain," and it allowed transfer only to places defined as proper in the statute itself. The majority also decided that allowing transfer anywhere else would be "discriminatory," because a defendant could obtain transfer by consenting to a faraway venue.

The dissenters pointed out that the statutory language was not "plain," because the lower courts had faced the same question many times before, and had decided both ways. The dissenters also rebutted the "discrimination" argument by pointing out that the plaintiff had the right in the first instance to choose the venue, and it could be changed only by order of the court: hardly discriminatory against plaintiffs! Furthermore, the legislative history showed that Congress had based § 1404(a) upon a preexisting common law doctrine called *forum non conveniens*, which allowed transfer in the circumstances of *Hoffman v. Blaski*; and Congress had intended to make transfer under § 1404(a) more flexible, not less flexible, than the common law doctrine.

Commentators have said that the dissent was right and the majority wrong. But the majority's interpretation, of course, has prevailed, and "where it might have been brought" still means a place defined by law, where venue and jurisdiction would have been proper at the time of filing. This interpretation meant that the transfer sought by the defendant in *Hoffman v. Blaski* was improper. The defendant sought to transfer the action to the plaintiff's residence over the plaintiff's objection, and that was not a place of venue defined by statute.

Congress's Action: Does It Provide Only an Incomplete Amendment?! More than 60 years after *Hoffman v. Blaski*, Congress passed the Federal Courts Jurisdiction and Venue Clarification Act of 2011. There, Congress provided a second provision for transfer, saying that transfer also was proper to a venue not specified by statute, but to which all parties consented. This provision is of limited effect; apparently, it applies only if the plaintiff files the action, and then, the plaintiff and the defendant both consent to transfer to a place that otherwise would not be proper. This new provision, therefore, would not reverse the holding in *Hoffman v. Blaski*, because the plaintiff, there, did not consent.

Some Examples. Consider the following situations. Remember that the case can be transferred only to "where it might have been brought" or where all parties consent.

> (1) The plaintiff files an action against the defendant in a division of the Northern District of California, which is the residence of the defendant and is where all of the acts or omissions giving rise to the claim occurred. The defendant moves to transfer to a division of the Southern District of California, where the plaintiff resides (which is not a proper venue: can you explain why?). The plaintiff objects. The transfer would be improper (can you explain why?).
>
> (2) Consider the same suit, but this time, assume that the plaintiff consents. Now, the transfer can properly be granted.

Actually, consider whether it is possible that Congress's treatment of this issue accomplishes very little. The result of *Hoffman v. Blaski* remains, in spite of all the criticism of that decision. The only change is that transfer can be ordered if all parties consent. But does this "change" really change anything important?

Notes and Questions About Transfer Procedure

(1) *What Law Applies After Transfer? Van Dusen v. Barrack*, 376 U.S. 612 (1964). If the case is transferred, the new court follows the law of the original transferring court. Therefore, the basic principle is that the transfer should bring about only a change of courtrooms, and not a change in the governing law. What problems can you see in the implementation of this rule? (For example, if the case is transferred from a court within the Second Circuit to a court within the Ninth, and the two Circuits follow different rules on a given point, will the transferee court be comfortable in expecting that the Ninth Circuit will not reverse if it follows the Second Circuit rule?) *See* Marcus, *Conflicts Among Circuits and Transfers Within the Federal Judicial System*, 93 Yale L.J. 677 (1984). As the *Atlantic Marine* decision shows, above, this rule does not apply when transfer is ordered under a forum clause. The new court follows its own law.

(2) *Transfer When Venue or Jurisdiction Is Improper: Goldlawr v. Heiman*, 369 U.S. 463 (1962). The general rule is that a court lacking jurisdiction should dismiss. However, 28 U.S.C. § 1406 gives federal District Courts authority to dismiss *or transfer* when venue is improper. In *Goldlawr v. Heiman*, the Supreme Court upheld the authority of the court to transfer when personal jurisdiction is lacking. Is this result appropriate? Shouldn't the Court have held that a court lacking jurisdiction has no authority to do anything to affect the action? On the other hand, isn't transfer to an appropriate forum fairer, simpler, and more expeditious than dismissal (particularly if, say, the statute of limitations has run after the action has been pending for some time)?

(3) *Use of the Transfer Provision in Forum Contests.* The transfer provision may be useful to a defendant who contests jurisdiction. In almost every instance, the defendant should make a motion for transfer in the alternative. In a close case, the court may well resolve its dilemma by granting transfer. However, defendants sometimes overlook the transfer provision in this situation.

(4) *Transfer of Venue and Permissive Forum Selection Clauses.* As we have seen in *Atlantic Marine*, a mandatory forum selection clause controls transfer unless the case is exceptional. But what about a permissive venue clause, one that says that a suit "may" be filed in a given venue? In *Almont Ambulatory Surgical Center, LLC v. UnitedHealth Group*, 99 F. Supp. 3d 1110 (C.D. Cal. 2015), the court held that a permissive forum selection clause was among the factors a district court should consider in deciding whether to transfer an action under § 1404(a). Such a clause might not be dispositive of the transfer motion, but it may be weighed as a "significant factor" favoring a transfer.

[B] *Forum Non Conveniens*

Note on the Doctrine of Forum Non Conveniens

Why Do We Have Forum Non Conveniens, in Addition to Venue and Jurisdiction? Sometimes venue and jurisdiction are not enough. Imagine that a lawsuit is brought in the United States, and jurisdiction and venue are technically proper, but everything involved in the suit happened in Singapore, or in Egypt, or in Scotland (as in the *Piper* case, below). American courts cannot transfer venue to Scotland, because it has a separate legal system. Therefore, a judicially created doctrine called *forum non conveniens* addresses this situation.

Applicable When the Other Court Is Not Part of the Same System. An American court sometimes will dismiss or stay the action before it, with the intention of getting the plaintiff to bring it in the other country instead. The same principle can be used if an action is brought in a state court with jurisdiction, but the action really belongs better in the courts of another state (for example, an action that arose in California that is brought in New York or Texas). The proper application of *forum non conveniens*, however, requires a balancing of several factors, as the *Piper* case shows.

Piper Aircraft Co. v. Reyno

454 U.S. 235 (1982)

[Five Scottish subjects were killed in the crash of a small aircraft in the Scottish highlands during a charter flight from Blackpool to Perth. A preliminary British Department of Trade report suggested propeller defects as the cause of the crash. A government hearing, however, found no evidence of defective equipment, and the final investigative report concluded that the inexperienced pilot had caused the accident by pilot error.]

[The decedent's survivors employed counsel in California, whose legal secretary, Reyno, qualified as administrator of the decedents' estates. Reyno then commenced wrongful death actions in California state court against Piper, the manufacturer of the aircraft, and Hartzell Propeller, Inc., the manufacturer of the propellers. The United Kingdom companies that owned, maintained and operated the charter flight were not within the jurisdiction of the court and were not included in the suit. After removal of the case to federal court, and transfer to Pennsylvania, Piper and Hartzell moved for dismissal on the ground of *forum non conveniens*, a discretionary common law doctrine that enables a District Court having jurisdiction to dismiss in deference to a more convenient forum.

[The District Court granted the motion and dismissed. It applied a balancing test set out in *Gulf Oil Corp. v. Gilbert*, 330 U.S. 501 (1947), which required *forum non conveniens* motions to be decided by the weighing of such factors as the availability of proof, compulsory process, and jury view of premises; practical problems of inexpensive and expeditious trial; public interest considerations; and the interest of the plaintiff in his choice of forum. The District Court noted that Piper and Hartzell had agreed to submit to jurisdiction in the Scottish courts, and they had waived any statute of limitations defenses that might be applicable, so that plaintiffs were assured of a Scottish forum.]

[On the other hand, Reyno was a representative of foreign citizens who candidly sought a forum that would apply more favorable substantive tort law to them. Scottish law did not recognize strict liability in tort, permitted only relatives to sue for wrongful death, and limited damages to "loss of support and society." The District Court observed that a plaintiff's choice of forum was usually entitled to substantial deference but concluded that it should be given little weight in this case because it was motivated by efforts to obtain favorable substantive law.]

[The District Court also found "overwhelming" support in the *Gilbert* balancing test for considering Scotland the appropriate forum. The wreckage was there; witnesses to the crash were there and could not be reached in the United States by compulsory process; the charter and maintenance companies could not be made third party defendants in the United States but could only be sued for indemnity later in the United Kingdom, with a "serious risk of inconsistent verdicts"; trial in the United States would require instructing the jury partly in Scottish and partly in American law, creating confusion; and the District Court was unfamiliar with Scottish law and would need to rely upon experts.]

[The Court of Appeals reversed. It held that dismissal was "never appropriate when the law of the alternative forum is less favorable to the plaintiff." It considered the plaintiff's forum choice to be "burdensome" but not "unfair" to the defendants. It also rejected the District Court's "public interest" analysis, holding that American law could be applied and that the States where the propellers and aircraft had been manufactured had greater interest in the suit than did Scotland.]

[The Supreme Court granted certiorari, reversed the decision of the Court of Appeals, and reinstated the trial court's dismissal, for the following reasons.]

II

Justice Marshall delivered the opinion of the Court.

. . . .

The Court of Appeals erred in holding that plaintiffs may defeat a motion to dismiss on the ground of *forum non conveniens* merely by showing that the substantive law that would be applied in the alternative forum is less favorable to the plaintiffs than that of the present forum. The possibility of a change in substantive law should ordinarily not be given conclusive or even substantial weight in the *forum non conveniens* inquiry.

The Court of Appeals' decision is inconsistent with this Court's earlier *forum non conveniens* decisions in another respect. Those decisions have repeatedly emphasized the need to retain flexibility. . . .

In fact, if conclusive or substantial weight were given to the possibility of a change in law, the *forum non conveniens* doctrine would become virtually useless. Jurisdiction and venue requirements are often easily satisfied. As a result, many plaintiffs are able to choose from among several forums. Ordinarily, these plaintiffs will select that forum whose choice-of-law rules are most advantageous. Thus, if the possibility of an unfavorable change in substantive law is given substantial weight in the *forum non conveniens* inquiry, dismissal would rarely be proper. . . .

The Court of Appeals' approach is not only inconsistent with the purpose of the *forum non conveniens* doctrine, but also poses substantial practical problems. If the possibility of a change in law were given substantial weight, deciding motions to dismiss on the ground of *forum non conveniens* would become quite difficult. Choice-of-law analysis would become extremely important, and the courts would frequently be required to interpret the law of foreign jurisdictions. . . .

Upholding the decision of the Court of Appeals would result in other practical problems. . . . The American courts, which are already extremely attractive to foreign plaintiffs, would become even more attractive. The flow of litigation into the United States would increase and further congest already crowded courts.

We do not hold that the possibility of an unfavorable change in law should *never* be a relevant consideration in a *forum non conveniens* inquiry. Of course, if the remedy provided by the alternative forum is so clearly inadequate or unsatisfactory that it is no remedy at all, the unfavorable change in law may be given substantial weight. . . . In these cases, however, the remedies that would be provided by the Scottish courts do not fall within this category . . . .

III

The Court of Appeals also erred in rejecting the District Court's *Gilbert* analysis. . . .

A

The District Court acknowledged that there is ordinarily a strong presumption in favor of the plaintiff's choice of forum, which may be overcome only when the private and public interest factors clearly point towards trial in the alternative forum. It held, however, that the presumption applies with less force when the plaintiff or real parties in interest are foreign.

The District Court's distinction between resident or citizen plaintiffs and foreign plaintiffs is fully justified. . . . When the home forum has been chosen, it is reasonable to assume that this choice is convenient. When the plaintiff is foreign, however, this assumption is much less reasonable. Because the central purpose of any *forum non conveniens* inquiry is to ensure that the trial is convenient, a foreign plaintiff's choice deserves less deference.

B

The *forum non conveniens* determination is committed to the sound discretion of the trial court.... [T]he Court of Appeals seems to have lost sight of this rule, and substituted its own judgment for that of the District Court.

(1)

In analyzing the private interest factors, the District Court stated that the connections with Scotland are "overwhelming." ... This characterization may be somewhat exaggerated. Particularly with respect to the question of relative ease of access to sources of proof, the private interests point in both directions. As respondent emphasizes, records concerning the design, manufacture, and testing of the propeller and plane are located in the United States. [The plaintiff] would have greater access to sources of proof relevant to her strict liability and negligence theories if trial were held here. However, the District Court did not act unreasonably in concluding that fewer evidentiary problems would be posed if the trial were held in Scotland. A large proportion of the relevant evidence is located in Great Britain....

The District Court correctly concluded that the problems posed by the inability to implead potential third-party defendants clearly supported holding the trial in Scotland.... The Court of Appeals rejected this argument. Forcing petitioners to rely on actions for indemnity or contribution would be "burdensome" but not "unfair." ... Finding that trial in the plaintiff's chosen forum would be burdensome, however, is sufficient to support dismissal on grounds of *forum non conveniens.*

(2)

The District Court's review of the factors relating to the public interest was also reasonable....

Scotland has a very strong interest in this litigation. The accident occurred in its airspace. All of the decedents were Scottish. Apart from Piper and Hartzell, all potential plaintiffs and defendants are either Scottish or English .... The American interest in this accident is simply not sufficient to justify the enormous commitment of judicial time and resources that would inevitably be required if the case were to be tried here.

IV

... [The District Court] did not act unreasonably in deciding that the private interests pointed towards trial in Scotland. Nor did it act unreasonably in deciding that the public interests favored trial in Scotland. Thus, the judgment of the Court of Appeals is reversed.

Notes and Questions

(1) *Examining the Factors Underlying Piper Aircraft v. Reyno.* How would the result in *Piper Aircraft v. Reyno* have been influenced if the decedents' survivors

had been American citizens rather than Scots? What if the remedy for wrongful death in the alternative forum was limited by a ceiling of $1,000 or was barred by a non-waivable statute of limitations? What if all of the world's expert witnesses knowledgeable about the propellers resided in the United States? *See* Abbott, *The Emerging Doctrine of Forum Non Conveniens: A Comparison of the English, Scottish, and United States Applications*, 18 VAND. J. TRANSNAT'L L. 111 (1985).

(2) *Dismissal or Stay? California's and New York's Statutes.* CCP § 410.30(a) empowers a California court to stay the litigation—*i.e.*, to cease all proceedings but leave the case pending—in lieu of dismissing. Would this alternative be useful? New York also allows this alternative in CPLR 327.

For a striking example of California doctrine, see *Stangvik v. Shiley, Inc.*, 54 Cal. 3d 744, 1 Cal. Rptr. 2d 556, 819 P.2d 14 (1991). There, Norwegian and Swedish plaintiffs sued a heart valve manufacturer for claimed defects. Even though the defendant itself was located in California, the trial court entered a stay under the *forum non conveniens* doctrine—and the state supreme court upheld it. Citing *Piper Aircraft v. Reyno*, the court emphasized that Norway and Sweden would provide adequate remedies, and it concluded that a nonresident alien is not entitled to deference in forum selection. (But is this reasoning persuasive when the defendant is a forum resident?)

(3) *The Relationship Between Forum Non Conveniens and Venue. Forum non conveniens* preceded modern federal venue provisions. Within the federal system, the proper mechanism is the discretionary venue transfer provision (discussed above) that derives from *forum non conveniens* notions, but does not require dismissal; accordingly, the *forum non conveniens* doctrine is inapplicable insofar as transfer from one federal court to another is concerned. *Forum non conveniens* is, however, still the tool for deference by the courts of one state to another—*e.g.*, a Nebraska court might dismiss so that suit could be brought in Maine—or, as in *Piper Aircraft v. Reyno*, by the federal courts to foreign courts.

[C] Venue in State Courts

In this section, we examine the venue systems of two "benchmark states": California and Texas. As we have previously explained in the Preface, we refer to these states throughout the book, because their systems are well developed, and they provide points of contrast that will enhance your understanding of the federal procedures that are our principal focus.

[1] The California Venue System

California classifies actions as "local" or "transitory" for venue purposes. If the main relief sought relates to real property in certain ways, the action is local and must be brought in the county where the property is located. CCP § 392. All other actions are transitory. For transitory actions, the basic California venue statute is Code of Civil Procedure § 395(a), which provides: "Except as otherwise provided by law and subject to the power of the court to transfer actions or proceedings as provided in this title, the superior court in the county where the defendants or some of them reside at the commencement of the action is the proper court for the trial of the action . . . ." In summary, the California system is organized on a county-by-county basis, and it creates a preference for venue at the defendant's residence. As is implied by the statute, if there are multiple defendants all of whom have been properly joined, venue generally will be proper in the county of residence of any of them. (This latter provision has sometimes led to efforts to join marginal defendants. CCP § 395(a) therefore provides that if a defendant has been improperly joined or joined "solely" for the purpose of supporting venue, "his or her residence shall not be considered.")

There are many exceptions to the rule of venue at defendant's residence. Some of the exceptions depend upon the type of party that is a defendant. For example, a corporation may be sued "where the contract is made or is to be performed, or where the obligation or liability arises, or the breach occurs; or in the county where the principal place of business of such corporation is situated. . . ." CCP § 395.5. There also are exceptions that depend upon the type of action. For example, a contract (other than with a consumer) to perform an obligation in a particular county may be tried in the county in which the obligation is to be performed, or in which the contract was in fact entered into, or in which the defendant resides. CCP § 395(a). Personal injury tort actions based on negligence are triable either in the county in which any defendant resides or the county where the injury occurred. CCP § 395(a).

A defendant may challenge the plaintiff's selection by moving for a change of venue. CCP §§ 396b, 397. The most common grounds are (1) that the court designated in the complaint is not a court of proper venue and (2) that the convenience of witnesses and the ends of justice would be promoted by a change. The propriety of the venue is determined, in general, from the face of the complaint; for example, the nature of the action is determined by the nature of the claims pleaded. There are, however, instances in which the court must be provided with factual information outside the pleadings—*e.g.*, the actual location of a defendant's residence—and these kinds of facts are shown by affidavit. Also, when the motion is based on the convenience of the witnesses, it typically is supported by affidavits or declarations showing the facts bearing on convenience. The motion for change of venue must be timely filed (a "wrong court" motion must be made within the time allowed for the defendant to answer or demur, CCP § 396b, or the objection is waived and the action may be tried where commenced. *See generally* R. Weil & I. Brown, *California Practice Guide: Civil Procedure Before Trial* ¶¶ 3:450–3:606 (The Rutter Group 2000).

CARRUTH v. SUPERIOR COURT, 80 Cal. App. 3d 215, 145 Cal. Rptr. 344 (1978). Plaintiff filed suit against both an individual defendant and a corporate defendant. The suit was filed in a county that was not the residence of either defendant, although it was one of the places in which a corporation or association could properly be sued under CCP § 395.5. The individual defendant filed a motion for change of venue. The court held that, in such a situation, the individual defendant may obtain a change of venue to the county where he or she resides.

WATHEN v. SUPERIOR COURT, 212 Cal. App. 2d 125, 27 Cal. Rptr. 840 (1963), In a contract action, plaintiff filed suit in the alleged county of performance (Santa Clara), which was different both from the county where the contract was made and from defendant's residence. Plaintiff relied on the venue provisions of CCP § 395(a), allowing venue where the obligation was to be performed. Defendant moved for a change of venue, however, because § 395(a) also specifies that the county in which the contract is made is considered the county in which it is to be performed "unless there is a special contract in writing to the contrary." The contract was written on plaintiff's letterhead, and it simply specified performance at plaintiff's place of business without mentioning a county. Nevertheless, because the letterhead showed that plaintiff's office was in Santa Clara County, the court held that the contract was sufficient to support venue in that county.

[2] The Texas Venue System

In conception, the Texas venue scheme is similar to the California scheme. Under the general rule, venue is proper in the county or counties in which all or a substantial party of the events or omissions giving rise to the claim occurred, in the county of a defendant's residence if the defendant is a natural person, and in the county of the defendant's principal office in Texas if the defendant is not a natural person. Tex. Civ. Prac. & Rem. Code § 15.002. As in California, there are additional "permissive" venue provisions covering written contracts specifying a place of performance, negligence, and other special kinds of defendants or actions. Texas law provides for "mandatory" venue in a number of situations, including suits for defamation and for title to land. This type of venue is similar to California's concept of "local" actions.

A venue contest is raised by a motion to transfer venue, which must be filed prior to or concurrently with any other plea (except a special appearance), and which is determined on the basis of the pleadings plus affidavits and discovery products (although the entire record is considered on appeal). *See* Tex. Civ. Prac. & Rem. Code §§ 15.001 *et seq.* Texas venue law also provides that a court may transfer an action from a county of proper venue to any other county of proper venue "for the convenience of the parties and witnesses and in the interest of justice." *See* Tex. Civ. Prac. & Rem. Code § 15.002(b). W. Dorsaneo, D. Crump, E. Carlson & E. Thornburg, *Texas Civil Procedure: Pretrial Litigation*, Ch. 6 (2016–17 ed.).

VI. How to Answer the Chapter Summary Problem: Some Suggestions

Vandiver v. Small Electronics: A Case of Nationwide Contacts.

Important: This section gives only general advice, and you should follow your professor's instructions. For example, in answering most examination questions, you should not start with a conclusion; that goes at the end. But listen to your professor, and if your professor tells you, "Answer first, then state your reasons," do that. Also, in many classes, you will not need to cite case names, statutes or rules. But if your professor tells you to cite cases, do that.

To answer a problem like this one, you should be able to analyze three aspects of it: (1) the applicable law, (2) how the facts fit the law (or don't), and (3) finally, a conclusion.

The Law: make declarative statements that set out rules or principles, in full sentences. Don't make them up or inject what you think "ought to be the law"; they should come from authoritative sources (from cases, rules, or statutes). If it is possible for a given legal principle to be useful in solving the problem, include it, even if you ultimately conclude that there are reasons why it does not apply. In other words, be exhaustive about the legal principles that could be relevant.

The Facts: Use all of the problem facts that bear on the issues. Consider the facts against all of the legal principles.

Conclusion: Express a conclusion, which sometimes can be as short as one sentence.

Vandiver v. Small Electronics. Now, we proceed to analyze this particular problem.

(1) Is There Potential Personal Jurisdiction over Small Electronics?

The Law: Your first step is to set out all of the possibly applicable legal rules or principles, each in a declarative sentence. There are many places to start; let's begin with the first long-arm case you read. Say or write something like this: "Personal jurisdiction requires that the defendant have sufficient contacts with the forum so that the exercise of jurisdiction is consistent with traditional notions of fair play and substantial justice." Next, consider another principle or rule. For example, purposeful availment. But these are only buzz words, so put them into a meaningful sentence that states a rule. Maybe, something like this: "The contacts must show that the defendant has purposefully availed itself of the privilege of conducting activities in the forum." Next, perhaps, consider the reasonable-anticipation principle. Put that into a sentence. And then, go on to state the rest of the rules or principles: define specific jurisdiction, define general or all-purpose jurisdiction, and identify the rules for each (don't forget the "essentially at home" requirement).

The Facts: Identify all of those that are relevant to this jurisdictional issue. Defendant Small's larger office is in New York. It sells product in New York to General

Systems within New York. General Systems then incorporates Small's component into its product and sells large numbers of this product nationwide, bringing money to General and also to Small. But Small also has a Florida manufacturing plant that makes the same product, and it is impossible to tell whether a given component came from New York or Florida. Vandiver, who is a citizen of Florida, was injured in Nevada by a component manufactured by Small. [Is this all of the relevant facts?] Next, you should consider the facts against each rule or principle you've identified. In other words, answer these kinds of questions: Do the facts make jurisdiction in Florida consistent with traditional notions of fair play and substantial justice? Did Small purposefully avail itself of the privilege of conducting activities in Florida? Could Small reasonably anticipate being sued in Florida? And you will probably find it more difficult to answer whether these facts fit general or specific jurisdiction and whether they satisfy the requirements of each (can they possibly fit the "at home" test)?

Conclusion: This, you decide according to what you conclude. "There is no personal jurisdiction over Small." Or, "There is potential personal jurisdiction over Small." Either conclusion could be acceptable if the steps above were followed. What counts is knowledge of the rules and principles and the reasoning method, not the end result.

But Wait: There's another issue in this question of potential personal jurisdiction. Don't forget to consider all of the issues.

Second Issue: The exercise of jurisdiction must be consistent with the forum state's long-arm statute. If jurisdiction here passes the tests listed above and is consistent with the long-arm statute, then there is potential personal jurisdiction. [This may be as far as you can go unless your professor has given you the Florida long-arm statute.]

(2) How Can Vandiver Have Process Served on Small Electronics?

The Law: This question raises fewer issues than the previous one. The Federal Rules create three ways to serve a corporation: by serving an officer, or by serving a managing or general agent, or by serving process in accordance with the law of either state.

The Facts: Therefore, Vandiver can have a process server hand the process over to Small's President, Vice President, or Treasurer (or another officer). Alternatively, she can have process served upon an employee of Small who manages something—perhaps a division manager. Also, she can serve according to state law. For example, many states allow service by certified mail in some circumstances, and if so here, she can do that.

(3) What Result if Small Moves to Transfer Venue to Nevada or New York?

The Law: This issue may be moot if there is no jurisdiction. Assuming jurisdiction, a judge (1) has discretion to transfer a case to another venue (2) where it might have been brought, (3) for the convenience of the parties and witnesses and (4) in the interest of justice. Thus, we must know where the suit might have been brought. Venue for a diversity case can be where a substantial part of the acts or omissions giving rise to the claim occurred or in the residence of any defendant if they all reside in the same state. (There is a default provision for venue, but it is not applicable here.) The residence of a corporation is anywhere that personal jurisdiction exists.

The Facts: As for where the case might have been brought, we must consider the places of proper venue. Nevada is not anyone's residence, but it is a place where a substantial part of the acts or omissions occurred. And assuming jurisdiction exists, both New York and Nevada are places of proper venue, because they both are residences of the defendants. As for convenience factors, most of the witnesses to the event are not in Florida; they are more likely to reside in Nevada. The witnesses to the manufacturing of the product are in New York (or possibly Florida). Vandiver may be the only percipient witness in Florida. But don't let that sway you. Virtually all of Vandiver's damage witnesses will be in Florida. And if she is severely injured, Vandiver may have difficulty traveling cross-country. As for interest-of-justice factors, the usual rule is that the plaintiff's choice of venue is entitled to deference. There is an interest in having local controversies adjudicated locally. The defendant has a substantial presence in Florida. The district judge would have to weigh all of these facts.

Conclusion: Venue would become an issue only if jurisdiction were determined to exist. Then, the court could keep the case in Florida or transfer venue to either of the other states.

VII. Improving Our System of Personal Jurisdiction and Venue: Notes and Questions

(1) *Characteristics of a Good System for Service of Process.* An ideal system for service of process would have the following characteristics. First, it would be simple, expeditious, and inexpensive to use. That is to say, it would allow the plaintiff to obtain quick results, without the expenditure of large amounts of attorney or support personnel time. Secondly, it would allow means for service upon the evasive defendant, also as cheaply and easily as possible. Third, it would guarantee a high probability that the defendants would actually receive notice. Finally, it would have a high probability of communicating to the defendant in a clear-cut way the importance of the process, so that the defendant, even if unsophisticated, would be likely to engage counsel and file an answer rather than default.

It should be apparent that these goals are inconsistent. For example, relatively inexpensive service methods might not be the best means for ensuring that defendant is likely to receive the process or to recognize its importance.

(2) *Toward a Better System for Service of Process.* With these goals in mind (and perhaps with others that might occur to you), you should evaluate the following proposals. Which ones are reasonable? Which are sound?

(a) *Proposal for a Variety of Service Methods, Including Mailed Service.* Each jurisdiction should allow alternative methods that include in-hand service, leave-with service, service on an agent authorized by appointment or by law, and mailed service. So that service by mail does not fail to communicate the relevant information, it should be required to be done by registered or certified mail, restricted to the defendant as addressee. Further, mailed service should be accompanied by a summons advising the defendant that he should consult an attorney and must file an answer by a date certain.

(b) *Proposal for a Waiver-of-Service Procedure.* Each jurisdiction should adopt a waiver procedure, and the defendant should be under an obligation to execute and return the waiver. A defendant who does not do so should be liable for expenses of service. In addition, a defendant who willfully, and with understanding of its character, fails to return the executed acknowledgment should be subject to sanctions (including default judgment in extreme cases).

(c) *Proposal for Substituted Service and Sanctions Against Evasive Defendants.* The court should have broad authority to authorize substituted service by any "reasonably calculated" means upon a showing that the traditional methods of service appear impractical. Proof of impracticality by written affidavit should be authorized, and actual live testimony should not be required. Upon the defendant's appearance, a showing that he has willfully evaded service of process should subject him to sanctions, including default judgment in extreme cases.

(d) *Proposal for Liberal Relief from Default Judgments.* There should be liberal allowance of relief from a default judgment for a relatively long period (*e.g.*, six months or a year) if the defendant has an arguable defense and did not consciously neglect or evade service.

(3) *Characteristics of a Good System of Forum Selection.* A good system of interstate jurisdiction and venue would provide means by which the defendant sued in an inconvenient forum could obtain dismissal or transfer. However, it would also provide a convenient forum to the plaintiff (or at least one as convenient as is consistent with the defendant's rights). It would provide clear and predictable rules so that forum contests were minimized. (This objective may be in competition with the objective of convenience to both parties.) Finally, a good system would minimize forum shopping and distant forum abuse.

(4) *Toward a Better System for Resolving Forum Contests.* Evaluate the following proposals with respect to these objectives:

(a) *Proposal for More Congressional Authorizations of Nationwide Service.* Congress should make more use of its authority to allow nationwide service. A defendant carrying on a large nationwide business should be subject to service in any federal court. The circumstances of this kind of service could be defined by the type of business—*e.g.*, an intercity airline—or its size—any business with assets placing it within the Fortune 500. Provisions for change of venue should then be used to minimize forum shopping or distant forum abuse.

(b) *Proposal for "Laundry List" Statutes Supplemented by a Limited "Catchall" Provision.* Long-arm statutes should conform to the "laundry list" model. This model appears to give greater certainty. There should be a supplementary provision allowing the exercise of jurisdiction under the "limits of due process" model, so that plaintiffs will not be unnecessarily deprived of a convenient forum. However, this "catchall" provision should be subject to invocation only on a showing that the forum is not inconvenient to the defendant and has not been chosen as the result of forum shopping.

(c) *Burden of Proof; Attorneys' Fees and Expenses.* The defendant should have the burden of disproving the existence of minimum contacts. This rule is followed in some state courts; *e.g., Hoppenfeld v. Crook*, 498 S.W.2d 52 (Tex. Civ. App.-Austin 1973, writ ref'd n.r.e.). The rule is based on conclusions that (1) information about the contacts is most readily available to the defendant and (2) an unacceptable percentage of special appearances are brought to impel plaintiffs to make their proof. In addition, the winner of a special appearance should be able to recover reasonable attorneys' fees and expenses from the adversary, whether plaintiff or defendant.

(5) *The Special Problem of Dispersed Defendants.* One problem with the current system of jurisdiction is that it effectively requires the plaintiff to fragment her suit if the defendants she wishes to sue out of a common occurrence are dispersed. For example, in *World-Wide Volkswagen v. Woodson, supra*, if the plaintiffs had wished to sue the local Oklahoma defendant who collided with them in that state, and also to sue World-Wide, they would have found it necessary to file two different suits, one in Oklahoma and one in New York. Shouldn't there be some means of providing a single forum for suits arising out of a common occurrence?

Congress has created a partial solution in a federal statute, but it has application only in rare cases. The solution is complicated and requires an understanding of federal subject matter jurisdiction, which you will study in the next chapter. However, the basic outlines of a broader proposal can be sketched simply:

(a) *Proposal for Congressional Creation of Broader Jurisdiction in Federal Courts When Defendants Are Dispersed.* The proposal would create federal jurisdiction over cases involving dispersed defendants under certain circumstances, even if the jurisdiction could not otherwise exist.

(b) *Related Proposal for Congressional Creation of Nationwide Service of Process to Bring the Dispersed Defendants to a Single Forum.* It would then authorize nationwide service of process upon the defendants, so that they could be compelled to answer in a single forum (such as Oklahoma, in *World-Wide Volkswagen*, § 2.02[C][1], *supra*).

For an excellent discussion of the proposal, *see* Kamp, *The Shrinking Forum: The Supreme Court's Limitation of Jurisdiction—An Argument for a Federal Forum in Multi-Party, Multi-State Litigation*, 21 Wm. & Mary L. Rev. 161 (1979). The original proposal is set forth in ALI, *Study of the Division of Jurisdiction Between State and Federal Courts* 3–4 (1969).

The problem with such a proposal is that one may question the feasibility of reversing *World-Wide Volkswagen*. The Supreme Court reasoned that Oklahoma could not constitutionally exercise jurisdiction over World-Wide. Furthermore, it is difficult to draft such a proposal in *World*-Wide without also making it possible for the plaintiffs to sue all the defendants in New York. Would it be fair for the local Oklahoma defendants to be subjected to suit in New York for an Oklahoma occurrence merely because New York is the residence of the distributor and retailer of the car with which they collided?

Litigation Document Example 2.1: The Anatomy of a Forum Contest: Litigation Documents in *George Miller Co. v. Compudata, Inc.*

[A] Background on the Dispute

On May 1, 2002, George Miller Company contracted with Compudata, Inc., to become a sales representative for Compudata in certain states, including the (imaginary) State of West York. George Miller Company was a West York corporation having its principal place of business in West York, and its activities consisted mainly of soliciting sales for a number of national companies there. Compudata was a manufacturer of disc memory systems for data processing and computing, and it was a corporation created under the laws of, and having its principal place of business in, the "State" of Texafornia.

The sales representation contract provided for a system of commissions to be paid to George Miller Company. It further provided for annual renewal of its terms unless the parties agreed otherwise. It had certain provisions governing termination, including continuation of commissions on a specified basis following notice of termination.

Compudata sent George Miller Company notice of termination on May 22, 2006. Miller later disagreed with Compudata as to (1) the amount of commissions to be paid during the termination notice period and (2) the amount of commission paid during earlier years.

These materials are based upon a real case. The names, dates, places, and events are changed, and the documents are edited or altered for pedagogical purposes. However, the "business" parts of the documents remain close to the originals.

[B] The Pre-Litigation Phase

Demand Letter

To: Compudata Incorporated
6108 Eureka Avenue
Ann Arbor, Texafornia 94304

Dear Sir or Madam:

After your termination of the agreement between Compudata and George Miller Company ("Miller"), Miller undertook to review that agreement to see exactly what rights it had. It found that Compudata owes Miller more commissions than are currently being paid. Also, Miller discovered for the first time that Compudata owes it commissions due in past years but never paid. We believe that you will agree when you consider the following.

First. The contract provides, on page 6, that Compudata will pay an additional amount equal to half of earned commissions for sales made during the termination notice period. "For sales made within the territory covered by this Agreement during the termination notice period, the Company will afford the Representative an additional protection of one-half the regular payable earned commissions to compensate for sales effort during the period of representation." Thus the contract makes it clear that sales during the termination notice period are to be assigned an *additional* half of earned commissions, and there is no reasonable way to interpret the language to make the half commission serve in lieu of regular commissions. However, Miller has been receiving only half of the regular commission on sales made during the termination notice period, and therefore Compudata owes Miller a further full commission on these sales. Our computations show that the amount thus owed is $26,611.95.

Second. In addition to the problem described above, we find that in years past the commissions paid Miller do not conform to what we consider to be the only reasonable interpretation of the contract. The contract, of course, provides on page 3 for a regressive schedule of commissions, ranging downward from 10%, so that as sales increase, Miller's commission on each successive unit decreases. But this is not the whole story. On page 7, the Agreement further provides that:

> The terms of this Agreement are in effect for one (1) year from the date of signing this Agreement. At the end of each anniversary year, the terms and conditions of this Agreement will be reviewed by the Company and the Representative.
>
> This Agreement shall automatically renew for an additional year on each anniversary date so long as no changes or negotiations take place.

Thus, the schedule of commissions was to be renewed each successive twelve-month period, and the first $15,000 of sales for *each* such twelve-month period was to be commissioned at 10%, the next $30,000 at 8% and so forth.

The problem is that commissions paid Miller by Compudata were not computed this way. You did not give the commission schedule renewed effect each year.

You simply reduced the commissions percentage to the minimum after the first $225,000 worth of goods were sold and continued to pay at that rate without regard to the lapse of several year periods. According to our computations, Compudata owes Miller a total of $37,020.28 for commissions thus unpaid over the period from May 1, 2003, to the present. Our computations are set forth on papers enclosed with this letter.

This letter constitutes a request for full payment. We are, of course, prepared to listen reasonably to any opinions you may have to the contrary. We request that you contact us promptly to resolve these matters; otherwise, Miller will pursue its legal remedies without further notice.

Very truly yours,

McINTOSH & WALKER
by *David Stone*

Response to Demand

To: David Stone
McIntosh & Walker
2500 Westar Tower
London, West York 75201

Dear Mr. Stone:

This letter is in response to your letter of November 10, 2006, wherein you made demand upon Compudata, Inc. to pay the George Miller Company certain commissions which you allege are due under a contract dated May 1, 2002.

In the second paragraph of your letter you assert that Miller is entitled to 150 percent of the normal commissions for sales made during the "termination notification period" as provided for in the Contract.

We do not agree with your interpretation of the terms of the Contract governing termination. The text of the relevant provisions is as follows:

> Commissions of orders already on the books . . . are payable in full to the Representative under the terms and conditions of this Agreement upon receipt of payment from the customer.
>
> For sales made within the territory covered by this Agreement during the termination notice period, the Company will forward an additional protection of 1/2 the regular payable earned commissions to compensate for sales effort during the period of representation.

The words "additional protection," when read in context, indicate that the one-half commission rate is in addition to the rights granted under the first paragraph of the above-quoted portion of the Contract; namely, the rights of the Representative to receive full commissions on orders booked as of the date of the termination notice, subject to the other provisions of the Contract governing the payment of commissions. Since the servicing of these orders would occur after termination, the intent of the parties was to reduce the commission. Indeed, it would be ironic to provide for an increase in the commission rate upon notice of termination.

In the second portion of your letter you claim that the Contract should be interpreted so as to renew the schedule of commissions at the beginning of each successive twelve-month period during the term of the Contract. Again, we disagree with your interpretation. The effect of the renewal provisions of the Contract is to renew the obligations of the parties *as they existed* at the end of the preceding year for a renewal term of one year. If the understanding of the parties were otherwise, the bonus provisions contained on page 5 of the contract would not make sense. Furthermore, the conduct of the parties during three renewal years has clearly shown that our interpretation is the correct one.

We hope that our response contained in this letter will persuade you and your client that Compudata has in fact performed all of its obligations to Miller under the Contract. If you feel it will be helpful, we will be happy to discuss this matter with you further. Please be advised, however, that Compudata hereby refuses to comply with your demand for payment.

Very truly yours,

O'HARA, PHILLIPS & STEIN
By *Sarah A. Porter*

Notes and Questions on the Demand Letter and Response

(1) *The Substantive Law: Who Is "Right"?* Each party has traditional maxims of contract interpretation to use in its favor. Compudata relies on the principle that the contract is to be construed as an entire instrument; that the course of dealings between the parties can be used in its interpretation; and that the intent of the parties governs if ascertainable. Miller uses a "plain language" approach, and it has at least one powerful string in its bow: the maxim of "*interpretatio contra proferentem*," or "the language is to be construed against the party who proposed it" (the contract was written entirely by Compudata). Who, then, do you think is "right"? [Note: You will probably have to guess. It is unlikely that there is a reported case directly on point, and the court will be faced with uncertainty in deciding the issue.]

(2) *Characteristics of a Good Demand Letter.* The letter sent by Miller's lawyer is known as a "demand letter" (can you see why it is called that?). What are the characteristics of a good demand letter? (Should it be conciliatory, evenhanded, and candid about any weaknesses in the case, or should it be direct, positive, and confident?) The purpose of such a letter, of course, is to precipitate settlement negotiations. It also may have an important function as a "malpractice preventive." Can you see why?

(3) *Should the Dispute be Settled?* Is this a dispute that "ought" to be settled early? For what amount, and why?

[C] Complaint, Service, and 12(b) Motions

Plaintiff Files Suit: The Complaint

In the United States District Court For
The Middle District of West York
London Division

GEORGE MILLER COMPANY v. COMPUDATA, INCORPORATED	CIVIL ACTION NO. __________

COMPLAINT

COMES NOW, GEORGE MILLER COMPANY, hereinafter referred to as Plaintiff, complaining of COMPUDATA, INCORPORATED, hereinafter referred to as Defendant, and would show the following:

JURISDICTION, PARTIES AND VENUE

1. Plaintiff is a corporation duly incorporated under the laws of the State of West York and having its principal place of business in Manero County, West York. Defendant is a corporation, incorporated under the laws of, and having its principal place of business in, a State other than the State of West York. The matter in controversy herein, exclusive of interest and costs, exceeds the sum of Seventy-Five Thousand Dollars.

2. Defendant, whose address is 6108 Eureka Avenue, Ann Arbor, Texafornia, 94304, is not registered to do business within the State of West York, but it has caused its merchandise to be sold pursuant to the terms of a sales contract with Plaintiff performable within the State, which conduct constitutes doing business in the State according to West York Civ. Prac. & Rem. C. § 17.042 (the West York long-arm statute). Defendant does not maintain a registered agent or a person at a regular place of business upon whom service of process can be had in this State, and therefore service may be had upon Defendant in accordance with Rule 4, Fed. R. Civ. P. and West York Civ. Prac. & Rem. C. § 17.044, by serving the Secretary of State of the State of West York as Defendant's agent.

3. A substantial part of the events or omissions giving rise to the claim occurred in, and the defendant is subject to personal jurisdiction in, this district and division.

FIRST CLAIM

4. On or about May 1, 2002, Plaintiff contracted to become a sales representative of Defendant. The contract was executed on a form written by Defendant in language chosen by Defendant. The contract is attached hereto and incorporated herein for all purposes as Exhibit "A."

5. The contract was renewed annually according to its terms until Defendant sent Plaintiff notice of termination on May 22, 2006. According to the contract, this notice meant that termination would occur seventy-five (75) days thereafter.

6. The contract provides a schedule of sales commissions and further provides, that in the event of termination, "For sales made within the territory covered by

this Agreement during the termination notice period, the Company will afford an additional protection of one-half the regular payable earned commissions to compensate for sales effort during the period of representation." The meaning of this contract language is that Defendant agreed to pay its regular commission to Plaintiff *plus* an additional one-half commission during the termination period.

7. Notwithstanding this language, and in breach of it, Defendant paid only one-half, rather than one and one-half, of regular commissions accrued during the termination notice period. Although Plaintiff has demanded, in addition, payment of the regular commission, which is just, due and owing in the amount of $26,611.95, Defendant has failed and refused, and does fail and refuse, to pay that sum.

8. Further, the commission schedule provided by the contract is based upon the dollar volume of sales to each customer, as follows: "First $15,000—10%; Next $30,000—8%; Next $60,000—6%; Next $120,000—4%; and Over $225,000—A negotiated percent (Rough Guide: 3% down to 1.5% minimum)." The commission thus declined in percentage with increasing dollar volume sold to each customer. However, the contract further provided as follows:

> The terms of this Agreement are in effect for one (1) year from the date of signing this Agreement. At the end of each anniversary year, the terms and conditions of this Agreement will be reviewed by the Company and the Representative.
>
> This Agreement shall automatically renew for an additional year on each anniversary date so long as no changes or negotiations take place.

The meaning of this language was that commissions were to be recomputed separately according to the declining schedule for *each* year period of the existence of the contract.

9. Defendant has failed and refused, and does fail and refuse, to pay Plaintiff's commissions by applying the declining schedule independently to each successive year period. Instead, Defendant has computed and paid commissions by aggregating sales over the entire period of Plaintiff's representation of Defendant, a method resulting in substantially lower commissions. Although Plaintiff has demanded payment of amounts just, due and owing in the sum of $37,020.28, Defendant has failed and refused, and does fail and refuse to pay that sum.

10. The failure and refusal of Defendant to compute commissions properly during the termination notice period, and the failure and refusal of Defendant to make payment according to the declining schedule of commissions applied separately to each successive year period, constitute breach by Defendant of the contract, all to Plaintiff's damage in the amount of $63,632.23. Further, by reason of Defendant's failure to pay this sum, Plaintiff has been required to put the matter in the hands of the undersigned attorneys for collection, and Defendant is thus liable to Plaintiff for a reasonable attorney's fee. Plaintiff would show that a reasonable attorney's fee would be in the amount of $20,000.

SECOND CLAIM

11. Plaintiff incorporates by reference all allegations contained in Paragraphs 1 through 10 above and realleges those allegations as though fully set out at this point.

12. The contract between Plaintiff and Defendant provided expressly that Defendant had the duty to receive purchase money from customers both on its own and on Plaintiff's behalf, to compute commissions, to deduct numerous kinds of charges from said commissions, to divide certain commissions in a discretionary manner "as the Company considers equitable," and to forward monthly and annual statements to Plaintiff justifying its commission computations. By these undertakings, Defendant assumed the duties of a fiduciary toward Plaintiff with respect to the trust fund consisting of monies collected from customers in Plaintiff's area. Plaintiff relied upon proper computation by Defendant.

13. Defendant, without notice to Plaintiff, ignored contract language in failing to pay monies justly due and owing to Plaintiff, and retained said sums instead. Defendant thus breached its fiduciary duties of care and loyalty to Plaintiff. Further, Defendant's failure to render correct monthly and annual statements to Plaintiff constituted a breach of its duty to account and of its duty to identify and segregate Plaintiff's monies. Further, in addition to express contract language creating trust, Plaintiff would show that Defendant's breach of contract and breach of trust caused monies owing to Plaintiff to become impressed with a constructive trust.

14. By reason of these breaches of trust, Defendant has caused damage to Plaintiff in the amount of $63,632.23. Defendant is further liable for exemplary damages in an amount to be set by the court.

WHEREFORE, Plaintiff prays that this Court render judgment for Plaintiff against Defendant for its damages in the amount of $63,632.23, for exemplary damages, for its attorney's fees and costs, and for any other relief to which it may prove itself justly entitled.

Respectfully submitted,

McINTOSH & WALKER
By *David Stone*

Note on Service of Complaint and Summons

David Stone tendered the complaint at the clerk's office, where it was date-stamped and assigned a cause number. The clerk prepared a summons, which contained instructions requiring the defendant to respond.

Stone employed a private process service company which, for a fee, served the summons and complaint on the West York Secretary of State as defendant's agent (paying his fee also). The process server made a return of the service upon the Secretary, which Stone filed among the papers of the case. The Secretary sent the complaint and summons by registered mail, return receipt requested, to the Defendant at the address listed in the complaint, with the following cover letter:

Compudata, Inc.
6108 Eureka
Ann Arbor, Texafornia 94304

Dear Sir or Madam:

Pursuant to the Laws of West York, I forward herewith by Certified Mail, Return Receipt Requested, a copy of process served on the Secretary of State on January 26, 2007.

Very truly yours,

West York Secretary of State
By *Cyrus Vance*
Deputy Secretary

Upon receiving the postal receipt (which was in the form of a green postcard containing the signature of the recipient at Compudata), the Secretary of State prepared a certificate to which the receipt was affixed, to show performance of the Secretary's statutory obligation and receipt by the defendant. Stone then filed this certificate and the receipt. A few days later, the defendant filed the following motion.

Defendant Objects to Jurisdiction: Defendant's Rule 12(B) Motion

In the United States District Court For
The Middle District of West York
London Division

GEORGE MILLER COMPANY
v. } CIVIL ACTION NO. CA-3-5463-C
COMPUDATA, INCORPORATED

DEFENDANT'S MOTION TO DISMISS FOR LACK OF JURISDICTION, TO QUASH SERVICE, AND TO DISMISS FOR IMPROPER VENUE

Pursuant to Fed. R. Civ. P. 12(b), defendant moves the Court as follows:

1. To dismiss the action for lack of jurisdiction of the person of Defendant or, in lieu thereof, to quash the return of service of summons, on the ground that service of a copy of the summons and complaint on the Secretary of State of the State of West York as recited in the return of summons herein is not effective service upon Defendant for the following reasons:

a) Defendant is a corporation organized under the laws of, and having its principal place of business in, the State of Texafornia, and the Secretary of State of West York is not an agent of the defendant authorized by appointment or by law to receive service of process.

b) At the time of the purported service of process and, indeed, at all times prior thereto, Defendant did not maintain any office or warehouse or other place of business in West York, had no bank account in West York, was not listed in any West York telephone directory, was not licensed to do business in West York, did not maintain a registered agent in West York, did not have any directors' or shareholders' meetings in West York, and did not engage in any conduct which constituted doing business in West York.

2. To dismiss the action on the ground that venue is improper, for the reasons stated above.

Respectfully submitted,
WILLIAMS, BEELER & GERSHON
By *Arnold A. Gershon*

Notes and Questions on Pleadings and Service

(1) *The Complaint.* Identify the parts of the complaint that show jurisdiction of the subject-matter, jurisdiction of the person, and venue. Recall the standard for sufficiency of the complaint to state a claim as against a motion to dismiss and analyze whether the complaint meets that standard.

(2) *Service.* Why is the West York long-arm statute used in this federal complaint? Why is the process "served" on the West York Secretary?

(3) *The Rule 12(b) Motion.* From what you know of the underlying facts at this point, do you think the motion is meritorious? Can Defendant even assert it in good faith?

[D] Discovery and Fact Development

Plaintiff's Request for Admissions and Defendant's Answers

In the United States District Court For
The Middle District of West York
London Division

GEORGE MILLER COMPANY		
v.	}	CIVIL ACTION NO. CA-3-5463-C
COMPUDATA, INCORPORATED		

PLAINTIFF'S REQUEST FOR ADMISSIONS

Plaintiff requests that the Defendant admit, for the purpose of this action only and subject to all pertinent objections to admissibility which may be interposed at trial or hearing, the truth of the following facts.

Therefore, you are hereby requested, in accordance with Rule 36 of the Federal Rules of Civil Procedure, to admit the truth of each and all of the following matters, or to deny same, or set forth in detail the reason why you cannot truthfully admit or deny them, within thirty (30) days from the date of receipt hereof; otherwise, they will be taken as admitted. You are further notified that in accordance with

Rule 37 of the Federal Rules of Civil Procedure, if these matters are not admitted and the truth of these facts is proved by Plaintiff, Plaintiff will apply to the Court for an order requiring Defendant to pay Plaintiff the reasonable expenses incurred in making proof, including attorney's fees.

1. That Compudata entered into a written contract with George Miller Company on or about May 1, 2002.

RESPONSE: Admitted

2. That this contract was renewed annually until termination in 2006.

RESPONSE: Admitted.

3. That a true copy of this contract is attached to plaintiff's complaint.

RESPONSE: Admitted.

...

6. That George Miller Company, during the period May 1, 2002, to a date in 2006, or about that period, actively solicited sales orders for goods to be sold by Compudata within the State of West York, with the knowledge and consent of Compudata.

RESPONSE: Defendant objects to Request No. 6 on the ground that the matter set forth therein is not relevant to the subject matter of the pending action, namely the interpretation of the language of certain portions of the contract. Defendant further objects to Request No. 6 on the grounds that the matters therein set forth are not within the personal knowledge of defendant and that said request assumes a conclusion of law, namely that goods of Compudata were sold within the State of West York.

7. That during the period May 1, 2002, to a date in 2006, or about that period, Compudata sold many thousands of dollars worth of goods to buyers within the State of West York.

RESPONSE: Defendant denies that it sold any goods within the State of West York. Defendant admits that it made deliveries, f.o.b. its plant in Texafornia, of many thousands of dollars worth of goods pursuant to purchase orders sent to it by purchasers giving West York addresses and bearing addresses for shipment within West York.

...

9. That during the period May 1, 2002, to a date in 2006, or about that period, Compudata paid many thousands of dollars worth of commissions to George Miller Company.

RESPONSE: Admitted.

10. That such commission payments were made for the purpose of compensating George Miller Company for its performance of the said contract, and for its solicitation of buyers, in whole or in part within the State of West York.

RESPONSE: Defendant cannot truthfully admit or deny the matters set forth in Request No. 10, but defendant must qualify its response and admit that said commissions were paid in part to compensate George Miller Company for soliciting orders prior to May 22, 2006, for Compudata products from organizations located within the State of West York and that said soliciting was done pursuant to said contract.

. . .

12. That Compudata is as of this date still selling thousands of dollars worth of goods to buyers within the State of West York annually.

RESPONSE: Defendant denies that any of its goods are being sold within the State of West York and admits that it is receiving purchase orders from persons giving a West York address for products worth thousands of dollars annually.

13. That Compudata was doing business within the State of West York during the period May 1, 2002, to the present.

RESPONSE: Defendant objects to Request No. 13 on the grounds that it is ambiguous and has no clear meaning which informs the defendant of that to which it is to respond and on the further grounds that it calls for a conclusion of law and that it presents a genuine issue for determination by the trier of fact.

Respectfully submitted,

McINTOSH & WALKER
By: *David Stone . . .*
COMPUDATA, INC.
By: *Andrea G. Dysart,*
Vice President . . .

[The jurat, by which Andrea G. Dysart swore to the answers on behalf of the Defendant before a notary, is omitted here.]

Plaintiff's Interrogatories and Defendant's Answers

In the United States District Court For
The Middle District of West York
London Division

GEORGE MILLER COMPANY

v. CIVIL ACTION NO. CA-3-5463-C

COMPUDATA, INCORPORATED

PLAINTIFF'S INTERROGATORIES TO DEFENDANT

Plaintiff requests the Defendant, by officers or agents thereof, to answer under oath in accordance with Rule 33 of the Federal Rules of Civil Procedure, the following interrogatories as they apply to the Defendant.

These interrogatories are to be deemed continuing interrogatories and the Defendant shall promptly supply, by way of supplemental or amended answer any additional responsive information that may become known to it prior to the trial of this action.

1. State the first date within your knowledge upon which goods of Compudata were sold to any buyer within the State of West York.

ANSWER: All sales of goods of Compudata are consummated within the State of Texafornia pursuant to purchase orders received at its principal office. Deliveries are, and always have been, f.o.b. its plant in Texafornia. Compudata first received a purchase order bearing an address for shipment in West York on or about September 30, 2002.

. . .

4. As to each sale within the past six years of goods of Compudata to any buyer within the State of West York, state the following:

(a) a description of the goods sold.

(b) the quantity of goods sold.

(c) the purchaser.

(d) the location of the purchaser.

(e) the means whereby the purchaser was induced to purchase.

(f) the method of delivery.

(g) the place of delivery.

(h) the date of delivery.

(i) the price of each item sold.

(j) the method of payment.

ANSWER: All sales of goods of Compudata are, and always have been, consummated in the State of Texafornia as described in the answer to Interrogatory No. 1. Purchase orders have been received at Compudata's office in Texafornia from the following organizations showing shipment addresses in West York on their face:

Name	Symbol	Location
Scientific Control Corporation	(SCC)	*Carrollton*
West York Instruments	(WI)	*West City*
University of West York	(UW)	*London*
Tracor	(TRA)	*London*
Space Craft, Int.	(SCI)	*London*
Shell Development Company	(SDC)	*London*
Mobile Research	(MOB)	*West City*
Philco-Ford	(PF)	*London*
NASA	(NAS)	*London*
Camco	(CAM)	*London*
General Computer Systems	(GCS)	*West City*
General Electric	(GE)	*London*
General Electrodynamics Corporation	(GEC)	*Garland*
Infotronics	(INF)	*London*
Ling Temco Vought	(LTV)	*West City*

The goods ordered by such purchasers can be described and identified as follows:

F6, F7 5)

7200 Series) Disc Memory Systems
1737—Disc Memory System plus controller
FPD—"X"—Video Disc Recorder
Video Disc Systems
Spare parts

Data concerning such purchase orders, and the shipments thereunder, as regards interrogatories 4(a), (b), (c), (d), (e), (f), (g), (h), (i), and (j) can be compiled from the information set forth above in this answer and the data contained on the shipment records of Compudata, copies of which are attached and labeled as Exhibit A. In this connection, Defendant relies on Fed. R. Civ. P. 33(d), which provides the "option to produce business records" in response to interrogatories.

5. State whether Compudata has, within the past six years, entered into any contract performable in whole or in part within the State of West York.

ANSWER: Defendant objects to this interrogatory on the grounds that it is ambiguous, that it does not inform the defendant of that to which it is to respond or of the facts sought by plaintiff, and it asks for a legal conclusion.

6. With reference to such contracts, please state:

(a) the duration of contractual relationships;

(b) any and all modifications;

(c) the dates of each performance within West York;

(d) the purchaser upon each such date;

(e) the dollar amount of each such sale;

(f) the amount of any commission paid.

ANSWER: Defendant objects to this interrogatory, which is a continuation of interrogatory number 5, on the same grounds of objection relied on in objecting to said interrogatory number 5.

7. State whether, during the past six years, Compudata has had any salesmen, sales representatives, manufacturer representatives, or agents within the State of West York, whether by independent contract or by employment. Identify such person or persons if any.

ANSWER: Prior to service of the complaint in this action,

(1) George Miller Company—sales representative

(2) Montgomery Industries, Inc.—sales representative—6601 Hillcraft Blvd., London, W.Y.

. . .

11. Please give the dates and contents of any and all written correspondence during the past six years sent by Compudata to any person located within the State of West York concerning any business of Compudata or concerning any contract or sale.

ANSWER: Defendant has had written correspondence with the persons identified in the answer to interrogatory number 4 above, as well as with those sales representatives identified in the answer to interrogatory number 7 above.

Such correspondence is voluminous and may be inspected by plaintiff, except insofar as it pertains to defendant's trade secrets or other proprietary information, in any manner which is reasonable. Defendant relies on Fed. R. Civ. P. 33(d), which provides the "option to produce business records."

12. State the approximate dates, costs and purpose of any long distance calls made by Compudata or its officers, employees or agents to any person within the State of West York during the past six years.

ANSWER: Defendant acknowledges that some such calls have been made. However, defendant has not kept records of such calls and cannot reasonably provide the detailed facts sought by this interrogatory.

16. Please give the dates of any presence within the State of West York of any officer, director or employee of Compudata within the past six years, identifying the officer, director or agent and stating the purpose of his presence.

ANSWER: Defendant has attached as Exhibit F, various documents indicating the presence of employees of Compudata in West York prior to the service of the complaint. The trips indicated in this exhibit were made to lend sales support to plaintiff or to conduct sales effort directly. The present and former employees of Compudata who have visited West York at least once in the six years prior to the date of service of the instant complaint are listed on Exhibit G hereto. These temporary visits were either to conduct sales calls, to demonstrate equipment or to repair or maintain products. At no time during this period was any officer or employee resident in West York. Since approximately July, 2004, Mr. Donald Gaines, who is a resident of West York, has been a director of Compudata. Specific details of activities or trips which may have involved officers, employees or directors being present in West York may be ascertainable from the correspondence made available to plaintiff in the answer to interrogatory number 11.

. . .

[Signature blanks omitted.]

Plaintiff's Motion to Compel Answers and Impose Sanctions

In the United States District Court For
The Middle District of West York
London Division

GEORGE MILLER COMPANY
v. — CIVIL ACTION NO. CA-3-5463-C
COMPUDATA, INCORPORATED

PLAINTIFF'S MOTION FOR RELIEF UNDER RULES 26(g) AND 37

Comes now GEORGE MILLER COMPANY, Plaintiff in the above entitled and numbered cause, and moves that relief under Rules 26(g) and 37 be granted it as against Defendant COMPUDATA, INCORPORATED, and would show the Court as follows:

1. Plaintiff heretofore submitted to Compudata sixteen (16) requests for admissions. Defendant Compudata refused without good reason to answer fully seven (7) of these requests for admissions. The unanswered requests for admissions included the following subjects: That the contract between George Miller Company and Compudata was performable in whole or in part within the State of West York; that George Miller Company solicited sales orders for goods to be sold by Compudata within the State of West York with the knowledge and consent of Compudata; that Compudata was doing business within the State of West York; and that Compudata took purposeful advantage of markets within the State of West York.

2. Compudata had no good reason to object to these requests for admissions and its objections amount to a refusal to answer. As to some such requests, Defendant Compudata objected on the ground that it had no personal knowledge (which is not a permissible reason for refusing to admit). In other cases, Defendant simultaneously objected on the ground that various requests "call for a conclusion of law" and also "present a genuine issue for determination by the trier of fact." These objections are ineffective, because it is permissible to request admission of a fact which the jury might otherwise try, and it is expressly permissible under Rule 36 to request an admission which requires application of a legal standard.

3. Since these requests are not objectionable pursuant to Rule 36(a), the admissions sought were of substantial importance, Defendant Compudata had no reasonable grounds to believe that it might prevail on the matter, and there was no other good reason for the failure to admit, Rule 37(c) provides that the Court "shall" require the opposing party to pay the reasonable expenses incurred in making proof of the matters requested to be admitted, including reasonable attorneys' fees.

4. By virtue of Defendant's conduct, Plaintiff has been required to incur substantial additional expense, in amount equal to at least $5,000.

5. Plaintiff would further show that Defendant refused to answer its interrogatories No. 5, 6, 9 and 19. Defendant's objections were to the effect that Plaintiff's interrogatories were "ambiguous" or "sought a legal conclusion." Such interrogatories are not ambiguous and the objection of "legal conclusion" is invalid under Rule 33(b) as applied to these interrogatories.

WHEREFORE, Plaintiff moves: (1) that requested admissions which Defendant Compudata refused either to admit or deny be taken as admitted; (2) that Plaintiff recover of Defendant Compudata the reasonable expenses incurred in proving the matters sought to be admitted, including reasonable attorneys' fees, in an amount of at least $1,000; and (3) that Defendant Compudata be ordered to answer Plaintiff's interrogatories numbered above.

Respectfully submitted,

McINTOSH & WALKER
By *David Stone*

Note on Fact Development by Stipulation and Affidavit

In addition to these discovery materials, David Stone filed *affidavits* from officers of his client, George Miller Company. These affidavits detailed the contractual relationship between the parties, defendant's sales, the visits by defendant's officers to the State, trade shows in West York, and like matters.

Stone also was informed by his client that Compudata had employed a direct employee in the State of West York since the filing of the suit, who maintained a telephone in the name of Compudata in the City of West City, West York. Stone contacted the opposing lawyer, and in lieu of submitting additional interrogatories, negotiated a *stipulation* to the facts about the employee and telephone. A stipulation is an agreement of counsel that certain facts are to be taken as true for purposes of the proceeding.

Notes and Questions on Discovery and Fact Development

(1) *Nature of the Facts to Be Gathered.* How has plaintiff determined what facts to seek to prove—*i.e.*, what cases guided plaintiff's lawyer in deciding what to ask in his request for admissions and interrogatories?

(2) *How Should the Jurisdictional Issue be Decided?* Explain how you think the District Court should rule, and why. Is the answer doubtful? Or is it clearcut?

(3) *Is Defendant in Compliance with Rules 11 and 26?* Rule 11 provides that when an attorney files a pleading (such as this defendant's motion to dismiss), the attorney's signature constitutes a certification that, to the best of the attorney's "knowledge, information, and belief, formed after an inquiry reasonable under the circumstances," (1) it is not being presented for an improper purpose, such as harassment or delay, (2) the legal claims are warranted by existing law or by a nonfrivolous argument for a change in the law, and (3) the factual claims have evidentiary support or are likely to have evidentiary support after further investigation and discovery. Could defendant's attorney certify properly and in good faith to these matters in the Rule 12 motion? Also, Rule 26 provides an analogous certification for discovery requests or answers. Can the objections and answers of defendant comply with these certifications? (Rules 11 and 26 provide for sanctions in the event of violations, and these issues are further considered in later chapters.)

(4) *Strategy in Drafting and Answering Discovery Requests.* What strategies can you identify with respect to the drafting of the discovery request and answers? (For example, what are the disadvantages of drafting an interrogatory that is very broad and general? One that is very narrow and specific?)

[E] Resolution of the Forum Contest

Court's Order Setting Pretrial Hearing

To: All counsel in No. *CA-3-5463, Geo. Miller Co. v. Compudata*

You are hereby notified that the above titled and numbered cause is set for a pre-trial hearing at 9:00 a.m. on May 9, 2007. Attendance of all counsel is mandatory.

NONCOMPLIANCE WILL SUBJECT PARTIES AND COUNSEL TO SANCTIONS PROVIDED BY THE FEDERAL RULES OF CIVIL PROCEDURE.

G.R. McKay, United States District Judge . . .

Note on Filing of Plaintiff's Brief

Upon receiving the above order, plaintiff's attorney prepared and filed the brief that follows. While the order did not require a brief (and defendant did not file one), plaintiff concluded that it would be wise to file one.

Plaintiff's Brief on the Jurisdictional Issue

In the United States District Court For
The Middle District of West York
London Division

GEORGE MILLER COMPANY
v.   } CIVIL ACTION NO. CA-3-5463-C
COMPUDATA, INCORPORATED

PLAINTIFF'S BRIEF IN OPPOSITION TO MOTION TO DISMISS

Defendant has filed a motion to dismiss and for other relief, alleging that at the time of service Defendant did no business in the State of West York. The Defendant's motion is unfounded. Actually, Plaintiff's claim is for payments due on a contract arising out of Defendant's activities in the forum State, making the case one of specific jurisdiction. Under the constitutional decisions as well as decisions interpreting the West York Long-Arm Statute, Defendant is clearly amenable to service.

I. FACTS CONCERNING JURISDICTION

A. FACTS ADMITTED BY DEFENDANT

Defendant admits that it sold and shipped to purchasers located in West York well in excess of three million dollars worth of goods during the period of the contract between the parties. (The figure is determined from shipping records of Compudata attached to its answer to interrogatory 4.) Further, Compudata currently has a salaried employee, Will Montgomery, in West City. In addition, before service of the complaint, it has had permanent sales representatives located in West York. (Stipulation between counsel; answer to interrogatory 7.)

Defendant also admits that it entered into a contract with Plaintiff and that the attachment to Plaintiff's Complaint is a true copy of this contract (admissions 1–3). This written contract, by its Appendix A, expressly states that Plaintiff is to be the sales representative of Defendant Compudata in West York. The contract refers to Compudata's "products being sold within the confines of the territory outlined in Appendix A" that is, West York and contiguous states (P. 1), "sales within the territory covered by this agreement" (P. 6), and "company products sold in the territory" (P. 7). Thus, the contract forthrightly states that Compudata was selling and intended to sell its goods in West York, and the shipping records show the same thing. The Complaint is for payment under the same Contract, so that the case is one of specific jurisdiction. Complaint, paragraphs 4–14.

Defendant admits that its officers, employees and agents made numerous trips to West York "to conduct sales calls, to demonstrate equipment or to repair or maintain Compudata products" (answer to interrogatory 16). Defendant Compudata has identified 17 of its employees who visited West York during the last six years (attachments to interrogatory 17). Defendant Compudata failed to identify correspondence concerning business with persons located in West York in response to Plaintiff's interrogatories, on the ground that "such correspondence is voluminous." (Answer to interrogatory 11.)

B. PLAINTIFF'S AFFIDAVITS

The affidavits of Bob Wylie and Evans Pitofsky, who are officers of Plaintiff, indicate the vigorous sales efforts that Plaintiff expended on Defendant's behalf and indicate that the sales to West York purchasers were in excess of three million dollars during the period. Furthermore, Bob Wylie's affidavit indicates that Defendant approached Plaintiff at its office in West York, that the contract was negotiated in West York, and that it was signed in West York. They also show that the claims (see Complaint paragraphs 4–14) arise out of the Defendant's contacts with the forum state. (*See* Affidavit of Bob Wylie; Affidavit of Evans Pitofsky.)

C. STIPULATION CONCERNING DEFENDANT'S EMPLOYEE IN WEST YORK

Defendant Compudata has a permanent employee engaged in selling its goods in West York. This employee is permanently residing in West York, works out of an office located in his home, and answers the phone in the name of Defendant. (*See* Stipulation Between Counsel; answer to interrogatory 7.)

II. COMPUDATA IS AMENABLE TO SERVICE IN WEST YORK BECAUSE OF ITS THREE MILLION DOLLARS WORTH OF BUSINESS DONE IN WEST YORK

A. DUE PROCESS REQUIREMENTS ARE CLEARLY MET

These acts of Defendant establish that Defendant has "minimum contacts" with the forum satisfying "traditional notions of fair play and substantial justice." *International Shoe Co. v. Washington*, 326 U.S. 310 (1945). Furthermore, there has been "some act by which the Defendant purposefully avail[ed] itself of the privilege of conducting activities within the forum state" and it could "reasonably anticipate" suit in this forum. *Hanson v. Denckla*, 357 U.S. 235 (1958); *World-Wide Volkswagen Corp. v. Woodson*, 444 U.S. 286 (1980). The case at bar should also be compared to *McGee v. International Life Ins. Co.*, 355 U.S. 220 (1957), in which the Supreme Court held that a single sale of a policy of life insurance made the insurance company amenable to service in a suit brought by the insured in the state where the policy was sold, even though the Defendant insurance company had no other contacts with that forum. This case, like that one, involves specific jurisdiction because the claims and contacts are related, although the contacts here are far more substantial. The case resembles *Burger King Corp. v. Rudzewicz*, 471 U.S. 462 (1985) (upholding jurisdiction in contract case based on contacts less significant than those in this case). This court's jurisdiction is, therefore, consistent with due process.

B. THE WEST YORK LONG-ARM STATUTE AUTHORIZES SERVICE

The West York statute reaches to the limits of due process. *See* West York Civ. Prac. & Rem. C. § 17.041 et seq. Several decisions of the Court of Appeals (following West York state court opinions) have held out-of-state defendants answerable to process served under the West York long-arm statute in fact situations not nearly so strong as those here. One of the more often cited opinions is that by Chief Judge Brown in *Atwood Hatcheries v. Heisdorf & Nelson Farms*, 357 F.2d 847 (5th Cir. 1966). The court unhesitatingly declared that "the legislative purpose [in enacting the long-arm statute] was to exploit to the maximum the fullest permissible reach under Federal Constitutional restraints." 357 F.2d 847 at 852. *See also Eyerly Aircraft Co. v. Killian*, 414 F.2d 591 (5th Cir. 1969); *Coulter v. Sears, Roebuck and Co.*, 426 F.2d 1315 (5th Cir. 1970); *Jim Fox Enterprises, Inc. v. Air France*, 664 F.2d 63 (5th Cir. 1981).

III. CONCLUSION

Defendant's Motion to Dismiss should be overruled.

Respectfully submitted,

McINTOSH & WALKER
By: *David Stone*

Note on Court's Ruling on the Forum Contest

At the pretrial hearing, after short remarks by both counsel, Judge McKay orally overruled the Motion to Dismiss. (As sometimes happens, this ruling was never memorialized in any written document.) Plaintiff's attorney then sent the following letter to his client:

Bob Wylie
Evans Pitofsky
George Miller Company
2018 Kennedy Parkway, Suite 706
London, West York 75260

Re: *George Miller Company v. Compudata, Incorporated*

Dear Bob and Evans:

The Motion of Compudata to dismiss this case on grounds of lack of jurisdiction was overruled today. We will be able to proceed with the case in West York. The judge has set the case for trial in September. I'll keep you posted.

We now have a great deal of work to do. The case has only started. We need to go through all of our records carefully, obtain Compudata's records, take depositions of a number of Compudata personnel, and prepare our case for trial. As I have explained to you, prevailing on the merits of our case will be much more difficult, in this particular instance, than the jurisdictional issue.

Best regards to both of you.

Sincerely yours,

David Stone

Notes and Questions on the Forum Contest

(1) *The 28 U.S.C. § 1404(a) Transfer Provision: A Better Argument?* Might defendant have done better by moving for transfer of venue to Texafornia under 28 U.S.C. § 1404(a)? For example, defendant could have filed a motion reading, in pertinent part, as follows:

> . . . MOTION FOR TRANSFER PURSUANT TO 1404(a)
>
> Defendant moves the court to transfer this action to the District of Texafornia, for the convenience of parties and witnesses, for the following reasons:
>
> 1. At trial, defendant will be required to call numerous witnesses and introduce numerous documents that are located in the State of Texafornia to show the course of dealings between the parties.
>
> 2. Defendant will be required to call witnesses affiliated with other representatives in other States to show how the Agreement has been customarily interpreted. All representatives have close contact with the Texafornia headquarters of Defendant, but few if any have any connection with West York . . . .

Defendants making special appearances sometimes neglect the transfer provision. It should be an alternative argument in most forum contests. Would it have been a better argument here?

(2) *Plaintiff's Brief: Identification of the Issue; Governing Legal Principles; Analysis of the Facts; Conclusion.* Good legal argument (at least when the law is reasonably

well established) often begins with the identification of the issue and statement of the legal rule(s) that govern. Analysis of the facts is next, followed by a conclusion. Indeed, this issue-rule-analysis-conclusion methodology is often advocated as a means of answering law school exam questions. Notice that plaintiff's brief contains these elements, but it puts the facts before the law. Why? [Note: Are the facts particularly persuasive?]

[F] The Merits: Answer and Settlement

Defendant's Answer on the Merits

In the United States District Court For
The Middle District of West York
London Division

GEORGE MILLER COMPANY
v. } CIVIL ACTION NO. CA-3-5463-C
COMPUDATA, INCORPORATED

ANSWER

Defendant Compudata Incorporated, for reply to Complaint filed by plaintiff, George Miller Company, says:

FIRST DEFENSE

1. Defendant is without knowledge or information sufficient to form a belief as to whether plaintiff is incorporated under the laws of the State of West York and has its principal place of business in Manero County, West York. Defendant admits that it is a corporation incorporated under the laws of, and having its principal place of business in, a State other than the State of West York. Defendant admits that the amount in controversy exceeds the sum of seventy-five thousand dollars.

2. Defendant admits that it is not registered to do business within the State of West York and that its address is 6108 Eureka, Ann Arbor, Texafornia 94304. Defendant denies the remaining allegations contained in paragraph 2 of the Complaint.

3. Defendant is without knowledge or information sufficient to form a belief as to whether all plaintiffs reside in this district. Defendant denies all other allegations of paragraph 3 of the Complaint.

4. Defendant admits that on or about May 1, 2002, plaintiff and defendant entered into a written contract, a copy of which is attached to the Complaint labeled Exhibit "A." Defendant denies all the remaining allegations of paragraph 4 of the Complaint.

5. Defendant denies the allegations contained in paragraph 5 of the Complaint.

6. Defendant admits the allegations contained in the first sentence of paragraph 6 of the Complaint. Defendant denies all the remaining allegations contained in paragraph 6 of the Complaint.

7. Defendant admits that it has failed and refused, and does fail and refuse, to pay any sums which may be claimed by plaintiff to be due and owing as commissions, in excess of payments actually made by defendant. Defendant denies all the remaining allegations in paragraph 7 of the Complaint.

8. Defendant denies the allegations contained in the last sentence of paragraph 8 of the Complaint, and admits the balance of the allegations contained in paragraph 8 of the Complaint.

9. Defendant admits that it has refused to pay plaintiff commissions by applying the declining schedule independently to each successive one-year period, and that it has computed and paid commissions by aggregating sales to each individual customer account over the entire period of plaintiff's representation of defendant and then applying the declining commission schedule cumulatively to the resulting aggregate. Defendant denies the remaining allegations contained in paragraph 9 of the Complaint.

10. Defendant denies the allegations contained in paragraph 10 of the Complaint.

11. For reply to the allegations contained in paragraph 11 of the Complaint, defendant hereby incorporates by reference each and every denial and statement contained in paragraphs 1 through 10 hereof, and realleges same as though fully set out at this point.

12. Defendant denies the allegations contained in paragraph 12 of the Complaint.

13. Defendant denies the allegations contained in paragraph 13 of the Complaint.

14. Defendant denies the allegations contained in paragraph 14 of the Complaint.

SECOND DEFENSE

15. As another and further defense, Defendant asserts the applicable statutes of limitations as to any payments alleged by Plaintiff to be due it from Defendant and allegedly accruing more than two years, or, in the alternative, more than four years, before the date of commencement of this action.

WHEREFORE, defendant prays that plaintiff take nothing against it and that defendant have judgment for its costs.

Respectfully submitted,

WILLIAMS, BEELER & GERSHON
By: *Arnold A. Gershon*

Settlement: Release and Agreement

KNOW ALL PERSONS BY THESE PRESENTS:

1. *Consideration and Mutual General Release.* That for and in consideration of the sum of fifteen thousand dollars ($15,000.00) cash paid by Compudata, Inc., the receipt and sufficiency of which is hereby acknowledged and agreed to, and for and in consideration of the dismissal with prejudice by George Miller Company hereinafter referred to, George Miller Company and Compudata, Inc., do hereby compromise, settle and fully release and forever discharge each other and each other's successors and assigns, and each other's related corporations, partnerships,

or business entities, through or with which each, respectively, does business, and also all of each other's present and past officers, directors, employees, representatives, and agents, of and from any and all claims, demands, controversies, contracts, actions or causes of action which either has held or may now or in the future own or hold, or which the heirs, executors, assigns, successors or administrators of either hereafter can, shall or may have, own or hold, for or by any reason for any matter, cause or thing whatsoever occurring or existing prior to the date of this agreement, whether or not now known, including but not limited to any and all claims, demands, controversies, contracts, actions or causes of action alleged in Civil Action No. 3-5463-C, styled *George Miller Company v. Compudata, Inc.*, filed in the United States District Court of the Middle District of West York, or which could have been asserted therein by amendment, counterclaim or other addition.

2. *Agreed Dismissal With Prejudice.* For the aforesaid consideration, George Miller Company agrees to entry of an order in the above-numbered civil action, styled as set forth above, dismissing with prejudice all of the claims, rights and causes of action therein asserted.

3. *No Admission of Liability; Contract, Not Recitals.* It is understood that this settlement agreement is a compromise of a doubtful and disputed claim, and that the payment is not to be construed as an admission of liability on the part of the parties hereby released, by each of whom liability is expressly denied. It is further understood that the terms of this release are contractual and not mere recitals.

4. *No Reliance on Released Parties; Acknowledgement.* In making this agreement and granting this release, the parties hereto acknowledge that they have not relied upon any statement or representation pertaining to this matter made by the parties who are hereby released, or by any person or persons representing them. The signatories further acknowledge that they have carefully read the foregoing release, have consulted with their attorneys concerning the same, know the contents thereof and have signed the same as their own free acts.

WITNESS OUR HANDS THIS *4th* day of *December*, 2007.

GEORGE MILLER COMPANY
By: *Robert E. Wylie*

COMPUDATA, INC.
By: *Andrea G. Dysart*

[The release also contained (1) notarized acknowledgements of the signatures of the parties and (2) signatures of both parties' lawyers approving the release.]

Chapter 3

Subject-Matter Jurisdiction: Power Over the Generic Type of Dispute

I. The Concept of Subject-Matter Jurisdiction

Imagine that you have just been served as defendant in a suit in small claims court. The summons has been properly served, and the complaint has been drafted according to the rules. But when you look at the amount of damages demanded, you notice to your surprise that it exceeds one million dollars.

A Suit for $1 Million in Small Claims Court? In addition to your dismay at being sued in the first place, you legitimately may have strong feelings against being sued for this amount in this particular court. A small claims court has streamlined procedures. It is not equipped to handle large disputes. The state has not authorized small claims courts to make binding orders in million-dollar suits. This is the concept of "subject-matter jurisdiction."

The Different Determinants of Subject-Matter Jurisdiction. Briefly defined, subject-matter jurisdiction is the court's power to act with respect to the generic type of dispute before the court in the posture in which it has been filed. The amount in controversy is a typical determinant of subject-matter jurisdiction, but there are many others. For example, a federal court has jurisdiction to hear claims arising under federal law. (Usually these claims may also be brought in state court: the courts have "concurrent" subject-matter jurisdiction.) Or subject-matter jurisdiction may be based upon the relationship between the parties, such as the federal courts' jurisdiction over diversity cases. But it is with the state courts that we begin, and, as examples, we describe, very briefly, the court systems of California, Texas, and Florida, three large states. First, however, we offer the following "Chapter Summary Problem," which you may read now, but answer at the end of the chapter (or, you should treat it as your instructor tells you).

Problem A: Chapter 3 Summary Problem

SMITH v. HERALD NEWSPAPER COMPANY: A PROBLEM IMPLICATING DIVERSITY, FEDERAL QUESTION, SUPPLEMENTAL AND REMOVAL JURISDICTION. John Smith was a candidate for the West York State legislature. He submitted an advertisement to the Herald Newspaper, advising voters that he was "*not* in favor of increasing the state income tax." Unfortunately, the Herald inadvertently omitted the word "not," so that the advertisement boldly proclaimed that Smith *was* "in favor of increasing the state income tax."

Smith therefore has filed an action in state court against the Herald Newspaper Company. He has stated one claim, for common law libel. The potential application of this claim is affected by the federal Constitution. *See, e.g., New York Times Co. v. Sullivan*, 376 U.S. 254 (1964) (U.S. Const. Amend. I requires a "federal rule that prohibits a public [figure] from recovering damages for defamatory falsehood [u]nless he proves" defendant's knowledge or reckless disregard of falsity). The complaint therefore contains the following allegations, among others:

> In order to comply with the First Amendment to the United States Constitution, plaintiff is required by federal decisions to prove, and plaintiff hereby does allege, that defendant acted with knowledge of the falsity of the publication, or with reckless disregard of whether it was true or false.

Plaintiff Smith is a citizen of West York. Defendant Newspaper Company is a corporation incorporated in Delaware; it owns and operates newspaper businesses throughout the nation, the largest being in West York, and it has its headquarters in California. The newspaper company has concluded that Smith's claim is unmeritorious because Smith actually approved the advertisement copy (apparently, he did not notice the error either), and it plans to counterclaim for the unpaid price of the advertisement in the amount of $10,251.57.

The Newspaper Company wishes to remove the action from state to federal court. Consider the following questions:

1. Does diversity jurisdiction provide a basis?
2. Does federal question jurisdiction provide a basis?
3. Is there a basis for jurisdiction of the counterclaim?
4. Can defendant properly remove?

II. State Courts' Subject-Matter Jurisdiction

[A] The Allocation of Jurisdiction within State Court Systems

Note on the California Trial Court System

California has achieved a system of trial court unification that leaves only a single trial court (the superior court) with full subject-matter jurisdiction.

California's Trial Courts: The Superior Courts. Before 1998 California had a two-tier trial court system. Each county had a superior court with at least one judge and broad subject matter jurisdiction; and each county had at least one municipal court with limited subject matter jurisdiction. Sometimes jurisdiction was unclear, and sometimes counsel made errors by filing in the wrong courts. The result was wasteful use of judicial resources. In 1998, California's voters approved a state constitutional amendment that authorized the superior and municipal court judges of each county to unify the trial courts.

Trial court unification eliminates the municipal courts as separate bodies; each county has only a single unified superior court as the trial court. Nevertheless, many of the distinctive features of the limited jurisdiction municipal courts remain. Cases reflecting the broad jurisdiction of the superior courts are referred to as "unlimited civil cases." Cal. Code Civ. Pro. § 88. Cases previously assigned to the municipal courts—primarily those in which the amount in controversy is $25,000 or less—are now referred to as "limited civil cases." Cal. Code Civ. Pro. § 86. Special discovery rules and rules of court previously governing municipal court cases now govern "limited civil cases." Cal. Rules Ct., Rule 709.

Specialized subject-matter: Different Departments or Divisions of the Unified Superior Court. References to a California "family law court," "probate court," "juvenile court," or the like do not indicate an additional set of trial courts. They merely refer to departments of the superior court that hear cases in these areas for administrative convenience. Superior court judges typically rotate through these departments for limited periods of time. Likewise, "small claims courts" are simply specialized divisions of the municipal courts. Cal. Code Civ. Pro. § 87(a).

But the Size of the Case Still Matters: Different Procedures Apply to "Limited" (Small) Civil Cases. Under the unified superior court system, all civil cases not within the exclusive jurisdiction of the federal courts or other non-judicial tribunals are brought in superior court. However, it still matters whether the case is classified as a limited civil case or not. The caption must state that the case is a limited civil case. Cal. Code Civ. Pro. § 422.30(b). Different filing fees may apply; different discovery and trial testimony rules may be invoked; and a different appeals system applies to limited civil cases. The remedy for misclassifying an action as a limited civil case is a motion for reclassification by the opposing party (or the court on its own motion) and payment of new fees (if higher). Cal. Code Civ. Pro. §§ 403.010–403.090.

LEKSE v. MUNICIPAL COURT, 138 Cal. App. 3d 188, 187 Cal. Rptr. 698 (1982). A landlord filed two separate actions against a tenant for unpaid past due rent, covering two separate months. The actions were both filed in the Small Claims Department. Each of the actions, taken separately, was for an amount within the Small Claims jurisdiction, but if the amounts had been claimed in a single suit, they would have exceeded its jurisdiction. The tenant made no appearance, and the court granted default judgment in both suits. The tenant then retained counsel, who moved to quash efforts to enforce the judgments on the ground that the amount in controversy exceeded the jurisdictional limits of the small claims department. The court denied the motion. Ultimately, the Court of Appeal reversed and held that the Small Claims procedure did not apply.

The landlord contended that it was within the discretion of the court not to consolidate the two claims and that the tenant had waived any error in their separation by failing to appear or object. The court disagreed:

> Our Supreme Court has explained that "[t]he theory behind [the Small Claims Department's] organization is that only by escaping from the complexity and delay of the normal course of litigation could anything be gained in a legal proceeding which may involve a small sum. . . . The chief characteristics of its proceedings are that there are no attorneys, no pleadings and no legal rules of evidence" [citing *Sanderson v. Niemann*, 17 Cal. 2d 563, 110 P.2d 1025 (1941)]. . . .
>
> . . . [A] lay litigant should not have been expected to move the Municipal Court to consolidate the two separate complaints. . . .

The Court then concluded that the two amounts must be added together to determine the amount in controversy. The amount in controversy thus exceeded the power of the Small Claims Department; the consolidated action should have proceeded in the proper system.

Note on the Texas Court System

District, County Level, and Justice Courts. The District Courts are the primary Texas trial courts, and are constitutional courts of general jurisdiction. Tex. Const. Art. 5, § 8; *see also* Tex. Gov. Code §§ 24.007, 24.008, 24.011. As a result of a complex statutory scheme, district courts generally have original civil jurisdiction of cases of divorce, suits for title to land or enforcement of liens on land, election contests, defamation suits, and all civil matters when the amount in controversy is in excess of $500. District Courts share probate and eminent domain jurisdiction with County Level Courts on a county-by-county basis.

The County Level Courts are intermediate trial courts which have civil jurisdiction when the amount in controversy exceeds $200 and does not exceed an upper jurisdictional limit provided by statute. This limit is not uniform for County Level Courts and it may vary from five thousand dollars up to $100,000, or more, depending upon the county. Justice Courts have exclusive jurisdiction of civil cases when the amount in controversy does not exceed $200 and concurrent jurisdiction with County Level and District Courts through $10,000. (Notice that this jurisdictional scheme means that in some cases, two courts have concurrent jurisdiction; in fact, in some cases all three do.) The Justice courts also function as Small Claims courts.

Courts of Appeals and the Texas Supreme Court. Appeals from District and County Level Courts are to the Courts of Appeals. The state's highest civil court is the Texas Supreme Court. *See* Dorsaneo, Crump, Carlson & Thornburg, *Texas Civil Procedure: Pre-Trial Litigation*, Ch. 3 (2018–19 ed.).

CONTINENTAL COFFEE PRODUCTS CO. v. CASAREZ, 937 S.W.2d 444 (Tex. 1996). The plaintiff sued her former employer in a county-court-at-law, which had a jurisdictional limit of $100,000. The plaintiff's original petition sought actual damages of $100,000, but seven months after she filed her original petition, the plaintiff amended her pleadings and claimed actual damages of $250,000, which had accumulated since filing. The defendants filed a plea to the court's subject matter jurisdiction, which the trial court denied. Both the court of appeals and the Texas Supreme Court affirmed the trial court's judgment awarding the plaintiff $150,000 in actual damages.

The Texas Supreme Court ruled that the trial court had jurisdiction to render judgment for an amount in excess of the court's jurisdictional limits, and did not err in overruling the plea to the jurisdiction, under the principle that "[i]f a plaintiff's original petition is properly brought in a particular court, but an amendment increases the amount in controversy above the court's jurisdictional limits, the court will continue to have jurisdiction if the additional damages accrued because of the passage of time." At the hearing on the plea to the jurisdiction plaintiff testified regarding her state of mind and the way she felt about the defendants, as follows: "[i]t's getting worser [sic], every day."

Note on the Florida Court System

Four Principal Levels. The Florida court system has four basic levels: county courts, circuit courts, district courts of appeal, and the Florida Supreme Court.

Trial Courts: The County and Circuit Courts. The lowest rung on the ladder is the county court, sometimes called "the peoples' court." The county courts' jurisdiction includes minor criminal cases and civil suits with less than $15,000 at issue.

Most civil and criminal cases originate in the circuit courts. These are courts of general jurisdiction, handling such matters as domestic relations, major criminal offenses, probate issues, civil cases involving amounts greater than $15,000, and appeals from county courts. *See generally* Pam Childers, Escambia County Clerk, http://www.escambiaclerk.com.

The District Courts of Appeals. Appeal from the circuit courts is usually to the district court of appeals. There are five "DCA's" with jurisdiction over separate geographic parts of the state. Each DCA sits in panels of three judges. This court does not hear witnesses or originate cases; instead, the DCA's consider the record of proceedings below.

The Florida Supreme Court is at the top of the judicial ladder. It has seven justices and sits in Tallahassee, the capital city. The Supreme Court hears both civil and criminal cases. It has mandatory jurisdiction over a few kinds of cases (such as death penalty cases and judgments holding state statutes unconstitutional) and discretionary jurisdiction to review other cases. As a practical matter, a decision by a district court of appeals usually is final, and the state supreme court hears cases of systemic importance. Consider the following case:

ALLEXDEX CORPORATION v. NACHON ENTERPRISES, INC., 641 So. 2d 858 (Fla. 1994). The Florida statutes gave equity jurisdiction to the circuit courts. They gave jurisdiction of monetary claims not exceeding $15,000 to the country courts. Plaintiff filed an action to foreclose a lien on real estate, which the court decided was an equitable proceeding, on property valued at less than $15,000. The question before the Florida Supreme Court was, which court has jurisdiction? The court decided that the answer was both. The circuit and county courts have concurrent jurisdiction:

> We find nothing in [the Florida Constitution] that limits equity jurisdiction exclusively to circuit courts, nor do we find anything that prohibits a county court from also hearing matters of equity. We conclude therefore that the statutes, taken separately, do not conflict with our State Constitution. . . .
>
> . . . [I]n order to give each statute its full effect, we conclude that the legislature intended to provide concurrent equity jurisdiction in circuit and county courts, except that equity cases filed in county courts must fall within the county court's monetary jurisdiction, as set by statute. . . .

Notes and Questions

(1) *Figuring the Amount in Controversy.* In state courts, the most frequent determinant of subject-matter jurisdiction is the amount in controversy. Ordinarily the amount is not difficult to compute, although there can be some ambiguous cases. For example, what if the plaintiff actually recovers less than the jurisdictional limit of the court? If he has made his claim in good faith, most jurisdictions accept this claimed figure; it is the amount "in controversy" that controls. *See, e.g., Rodley v. Curry*, 120 Cal. 541, 543, 52 P. 999, 1000 (1898). What about a non-monetary suit, such as one for an injunction? In that event, valuing the amount in controversy is more complicated. *See* § III[B][3] in this chapter, below.

(2) *The Policy Issue in State Court Jurisdiction: How to Allocate by Amount in Controversy.* Cases depending on jurisdictional issues are, in a sense, illustrations of judicial waste. And while specialization for big cases and little cases may be advantageous, it becomes disadvantageous if it causes waste. Should there, perhaps, be only one trial court, with the authority to invoke different rules for different kinds of cases?

[B] Federal Claims and Defenses in State Courts

Introductory Note

Concurrent State and Federal Jurisdiction. Students occasionally assume, erroneously, that the existence of federal jurisdiction means that state courts are ousted of jurisdiction. On the contrary, there is concurrent state jurisdiction of most federal claims. For example, if the parties are of diverse citizenship and the amount in controversy exceeds $75,000, a suit ordinarily can be brought in either state or federal court. A suit under the federal civil rights laws can generally be brought in federal court, but there is no reason why it cannot instead be brought in state court if the plaintiff chooses. *See* Gordon, *Justiciability of Federal Claims in State Court*, 59 Notre Dame L. Rev. 1145 (1985).

State Judges' Ability and Duty to Apply Federal Law. The truth of the matter is that it is commonplace for state judges to decide federal questions. It is sometimes assumed that a state judge will be less likely than her federal counterpart to enforce federal law accurately, but it is unwarranted to assume that any individual state judge will not accurately enforce federal law. State judges have had legal educations similar to those of their federal counterparts. In fact, might not there be some state trial judges who would read federal law more expansively than some federal judges? Consider the following case.

Testa v. Katt

330 U.S. 386 (1947)

Mr. Justice Black delivered the opinion of the Court.

Section 205(e) of the [Federal] Emergency Price Control Act provides that a buyer of goods at above the prescribed ceiling price may sue the seller "in any court of competent jurisdiction" for not more than three times the amount of the overcharge plus costs and a reasonable attorney's fee. Section 205(c) provides that federal district courts shall have jurisdiction of such suits "concurrently with State and Territorial courts." . . .

The respondent was in the automobile business in Providence, Providence County, Rhode Island. In 1944 he sold an automobile to petitioner Testa, who also resides in Providence, for $1,100, $210 above the ceiling price. The petitioner later filed this suit against respondent in the State District Court in Providence. Recovery was sought under § 205(e). The court awarded a judgment of treble damages and costs to petitioner. On appeal to the State Superior Court, where the trial was *de novo*, the petitioner was again awarded judgment, but only for the amount of the overcharge plus attorney's fees. . . . On appeal, the State Supreme Court reversed, 71 R.I. 472, 47 A.2d 312. It interpreted § 205(e) to be "a penal statute in the international sense." [Eds. Note: A "penal" statute is one that provides a "penalty," unlike a private cause of action; foreign courts often refuse to enforce such laws.] It held that an action for violation of § 205(e) could not be maintained in the courts of that State. . . .

For the purposes of this case, we assume, without deciding, that § 205(e) is a penal statute in the "public international," "private international," or any other sense. So far as the question of whether the Rhode Island courts properly declined to try this action, it makes no difference . . . . For we cannot accept the basic premise on which the Rhode Island Supreme Court [decided this case]. It disregards the purpose and effect of Article VI of the Constitution which provides: "This Constitution, and the Laws of the United States which shall be made in Pursuance thereof; and all Treaties made, or which shall be made, under the Authority of the United States, shall be the supreme Law of the Land; and the Judges in every State shall be bound thereby, any Thing in the Constitution or Laws of any State to the Contrary notwithstanding."

. . . . The first Congress that convened after the Constitution was adopted conferred jurisdiction upon the state courts to enforce important federal civil laws, and succeeding Congresses conferred on the states jurisdiction over federal crimes and actions for penalties and forfeitures.

Enforcement of federal laws by state courts did not go unchallenged. Violent public controversies existed throughout the first part of the Nineteenth Century until the 1860's concerning the extent of the constitutional supremacy of the Federal Government. . . . But after the fundamental issues over the extent of federal supremacy had been resolved by war, this Court took occasion in 1876 to review the phase of the controversy concerning the relationship of state courts to the Federal Government. *Claflin v. Houseman*, 93 U.S. 130. . . . And the Court stated that "If an act of Congress gives a penalty to a party aggrieved, without specifying a remedy for its enforcement, there is no reason why it should not be enforced, if not provided otherwise by some act of Congress, by a proper action in a State court." . . . [REVERSED; jurisdiction ordered.]

HAYWOOD v. DROWN, 556 U.S. 729 (2009). The most interesting part of this case is the dissent by four Justices. The New York legislature set up special jurisdiction for prisoner litigation against correctional officers. For either federal or state claims of this kind, jurisdiction was solely in the New York Court of Claims, and the State of New York was substituted as the defendant. The Supreme Court majority struck down this provision, citing the Supremacy Clause of the Constitution. "Because it regards these suits as too numerous or too frivolous (or both), the State's longstanding policy has been to shield this narrow class of defendants from liability when sued for damages." But "having made the decision to create courts of general jurisdiction that regularly sit to entertain analogous suits, New York is not at liberty to shut the courthouse door to federal claims that it considers at odds with its local policy."

Justice Thomas, joined by three other Justices, dissented in a lengthy opinion. This excerpt contains only a small fraction. The dissenters concluded that the states had power to refuse jurisdiction to any kind of claim because the constitutional history showed that the Founders did not intend to require otherwise. [Note that this argument conflicts with not only the majority's holding, but also with *Testa v. Katt, supra*:]

> . . . [T]here was at least one proposal to expressly require state courts to take original jurisdiction over federal claims [the "New Jersey plan"]. . . . But in light of the failure of this proposal—which was offered before the adoption of the Madisonian Compromise [which resulted in the present federal courts provision]—the assertions by its supporters that state courts would ordinarily entertain federal causes of action cannot reasonably be viewed as an assurance that the States would never alter the subject-matter jurisdiction of their courts. The Framers' decision to empower Congress to create federal courts that could either supplement or displace state-court review of federal claims, as well as the exclusion of any affirmative command requiring the States to consider federal claims in the text of Article III, confirms this understanding.

Notes and Questions

(1) *Plaintiff's and Defendant's Choice in Testa v. Katt.* If the plaintiff, Testa, had wanted to, he could have filed his suit in a federal court. His lawyer apparently felt the state court would more likely view his claim with favor, or preferred state procedures, or had some other reason. Likewise, the defendant, Katt, could have removed the case to federal court but did not do so. State courts are frequently the choices of both parties, even for federal claims.

(2) *Exclusive Federal Jurisdiction.* There are some kinds of claims for which Congress has provided that the federal courts' jurisdiction is exclusive. For example, actions brought under the federal patent or copyright laws must be brought in the federal courts. 28 U.S.C. § 1338(a) (exclusive jurisdiction). Other examples include actions under the federal bankruptcy laws, actions against consuls of foreign states, and actions under federal antitrust laws.

(3) *Exclusive State Jurisdiction Over Federal Issues.* It may surprise you to learn that when the federal Constitution is invoked as a defense to a state-law claim between citizens of the same state, there is no federal jurisdiction. The state court is the exclusive forum. Consider the following section.

III. Federal Subject-Matter Jurisdiction

[A] Federal Question ("Arising Under") Jurisdiction

> Read 28 U.S.C. § 1331 (the "arising under" jurisdiction statute); also, read U.S. Const. art. III, § 2 (the constitutional "arising under" provision).

How to Read the Case of Louisville & Nashville RR. v. Mottley

Jurisdiction Requires a Claim Arising Under Federal Law (Not a Federal Defense). The jurisdictional statute at issue, which is now 28 U.S.C. § 1331, provides that federal District Courts have jurisdiction of "all civil actions arising under the Constitution, laws, or treaties of the United States." This deceptively simple language has been interpreted to mean that the plaintiff's claim (and not the defendant's defense) must "arise under" federal law. One classic statement of the law is set out in *Gully v. First National Bank in Meridian*, 299 U.S. 109, 112–13 (1936): "To bring a case within the statute, a right or immunity created by the Constitution or laws of the United States must be an element, and an essential one, of the plaintiff's cause of action."

"Federal Question Jurisdiction" Is a Misleading Name. The jurisdiction created by section 1331 is commonly called "federal question" jurisdiction. But this label is a misnomer. It might be better to use the term "arising under" jurisdiction. The mere presence of a federal question somewhere in a case does not create federal jurisdiction; it must be in the claim. For example, if the plaintiff sues on a contract under state law, and the defendant defends with a federal law defense, there is no federal jurisdiction. (Students often find this distinction irrational, and there have been many proposals for change.)

"Anticipation" of a Federal Defense by the Plaintiff Also Does Not Create Federal Jurisdiction. Imagine that a plaintiff includes a paragraph in his or her complaint anticipating the federal defense: "I realize that defendant is going to say that the federal statutes destroy my state-law claim, but I don't agree." Does this artful pleading confer jurisdiction on the federal courts? The answer is "No": plaintiff's claim still arises under state law.

Problem B

"ARISING UNDER" JURISDICTION PROBLEMS, IN PREPARATION FOR READING THE MOTTLEY CASE. In each of the following situations, you are required to answer "Yes" or "No" to the question, "Does federal jurisdiction exist?" (Assume that there is no diversity of citizenship.)

(a) *A Contract Claim Under State Law.* Acme Bank sues Joe Blow, alleging that he has failed to pay a promissory note, which he signed upon receiving a loan from the Bank. Does federal jurisdiction exist? [Note: There is nothing in the federal Constitution, laws, or treaties that says a person has to pay a promissory note. The note is a contract, governed by state law.]

(b) *A Federal Defense to the Contract Claim.* In the same suit by Acme Bank, Defendant Joe Blow files an answer alleging as a defense that he is exonerated from having to pay the promissory note because the loan transaction violated the federal banking laws. Now, is there federal jurisdiction?

(c) *An Initial Complaint That Pleads Federal Law to Avoid the Defense.* Now, imagine that Acme Bank knew about Joe's intended defense when it drew up its complaint. It has included in its initial complaint a paragraph alleging, "Any potential defense by Defendant, relying upon the federal banking laws, is inapplicable to this case." Does this pleading create federal jurisdiction?

(d) *A Complaint for Damages Arising Under Federal Law.* Finally, imagine that instead of the Bank suing Joe, Joe sues the Bank. He claims damages because the Bank allegedly violated the federal banking laws in the loan transaction. Do the federal courts have jurisdiction over Joe's claim?

[*The Answers Are:* a. No; b. No; c. No; and d. Yes. Each of the first three situations involves a state-law claim. In the final situation, the plaintiff's claim arises directly under federal law. Now, proceed to read *Mottley.*]

Louisville & Nashville Railroad v. Mottley

211 U.S. 149 (1908)

The appellees (husband and wife), being residents and citizens of Kentucky, brought this suit in equity in the Circuit Court of the United States for the Western District of Kentucky against the appellant, a railroad company and a citizen of the same State. The object of the suit was to compel the specific performance of the following contract:

Louisville, Ky., Oct. 2nd, 1871.

The Louisville & Nashville Railroad Company in consideration that E.L. Mottley and wife, Annie E. Mottley, have this day released Company from all damages or claims for damages for injuries received by them on the 7th of September, 1871, in consequence of a collision of trains on the railroad . . . , hereby agrees to issue free passes on said Railroad . . . , to said

> E.L. & Annie E. Mottley for the remainder of the present year, and thereafter, to renew said passes annually during the lives of said Mottley and wife or either of them.

The [complaint] alleged that in September, 1871, plaintiffs, while passengers upon the defendant railroad, were injured by the defendant's negligence, and released their respective claims for damages in consideration of the agreement for transportation during their lives, expressed in the contract. It is alleged that the contract was performed by the defendant up to January 1, 1907, when the defendant declined to renew the passes. The [complaint] then alleges that the refusal to comply with the contract was based solely upon that part of the act of Congress of June 29, 1906, 34 Stat. 584, which forbids the giving of free passes or free transportation. The bill further alleges: First, that the act of Congress referred to does not prohibit the giving of passes under the circumstances of this case; and, second, that if the law is to be construed as prohibiting such passes, it is in conflict with the Fifth Amendment of the Constitution, because it deprives the plaintiffs of their property without due process of law. The defendant demurred [i.e., it asserted that plaintiffs could not recover on the complaint under the law.] The judge of the Circuit Court overruled the demurrer, entered a decree for the relief prayed for, and the defendant appealed directly to this court.

Mr. Justice Moody, after making the foregoing statement, delivered the opinion of the court.

... [I]n our opinion, the court below was without jurisdiction of the cause. Neither party has questioned that jurisdiction, but it is the duty of this court to see to it that the jurisdiction of the Circuit Court, which is defined and limited by statute, is not exceeded. This duty we have frequently performed of our own motion....

There was no diversity of citizenship and it is not and cannot be suggested that there was any ground of jurisdiction, except that the case was a "suit ... arising under the Constitution and laws of the United States." It is the settled interpretation of these words, as used in this statute, conferring jurisdiction, that a suit arises under the Constitution and laws of the United States only when the plaintiff's statement of his own cause of action shows that it is based upon those laws or that Constitution. It is not enough that the plaintiff alleges some anticipated defense to his cause of action and asserts that the defense is invalidated by some provision of the Constitution of the United States. Although such allegations show that very likely, in the course of the litigation, a question under the Constitution would arise, they do not show that the suit, that is, the plaintiff's original cause of action, arises under the Constitution. [... For example, in] *Boston & Montana Consolidated Copper & Silver Mining Company v. Montana Ore Purchasing Company*, 188 U.S. 632, the plaintiff brought suit in the Circuit Court of the United States for the conversion of copper ore and for an injunction against its continuance. The plaintiff then alleged, for the purpose of showing jurisdiction, in substance, that the defendant would set up in defense certain laws of the United States. The cause was held to be beyond the jurisdiction of the Circuit Court, the court saying, by Mr. Justice Peckham:

> It would be . . . improper in order to prove complainant's cause of action to go into any matters of defence which the defendants might possibly set up and then attempt to reply to such defence, and thus . . . to show that a Federal question might . . . arise in the course of the trial of the case. . . .
>
> . . . The presentation of [plaintiff's] cause of action would not show that it was one arising under the Constitution or laws of the United States . . . .

It is ordered that the judgment be reversed and the case remitted to the Circuit Court with instructions to dismiss the suit for want of jurisdiction.

Notes and Questions

(1) *What Happens Next in the Mottleys' Dispute with the Railroad?* The Supreme Court's decision did not extinguish the Mottleys' claim. After dismissal of their federal suit, the Mottleys brought suit in a Kentucky state court. As could be expected, the Railroad asserted its defense based on the federal statute. The state trial court held for the Mottleys. The Kentucky Supreme Court affirmed. But then the United States Supreme Court accepted the case for review a second time—and held for the Railroad. The Mottleys recovered nothing. *Louisville & Nashville RR. v. Mottley*, 219 U.S. 467 (1911).

(2) *The "Well Pleaded Complaint" Rule: "Claim" or "Defense"?* The *Mottley* case is said to exemplify the "well pleaded complaint" rule: the claim asserted in the plaintiff's well pleaded complaint (meaning a complaint pleaded without anticipation of purely defensive matter) must be founded in federal law.

(3) *Ambiguity in the Jurisdictional Rules: "Claim" or "Defense"?* The trouble is that sometimes the law does not fit into these neat compartments; it may be that a principle of law has a recognized impact upon the claim but has not been clearly categorized as part of the claim or as part of the defense. Furthermore, there can be instances in which federal legislation affecting a state-law claim is not merely a defense, but is so pervasive that the entire area of law is inherently "federalized"—and then, federal question jurisdiction may be applicable. *E.g., Avco Corp. v. Aero Lodge No. 735*, 390 U.S. 557 (1968) (state court action to enforce labor contract removable because federal labor laws pervade field so completely as to federalize state contract law). *Cf.* Hirshman, *Whose Law Is It, Anyway? A Reconsideration of Federal Question Jurisdiction Over Cases of Mixed State and Federal Law*, 60 Ind. L.J. 17 (1985).

(4) *Different Tests for a Federal "Claim": Franchise Tax Bd. v. Construction Laborers Vacation Trust*, 463 U.S. 1 (1983). In this case, the Court articulated two tests for "arising under" jurisdiction: "Either that federal law creates the cause of action [sometimes called the 'creation' test] or that the plaintiff's right to relief necessarily depends upon resolution of a substantial issue of federal law [the 'dependency' or 'substantial ingredient' test]." Are these tests useful? (Note that they may produce different results.)

(5) *Declaratory Judgments: Skelly Oil Co. v. Phillips Petroleum Co.*, 339 U.S. 667 (1950). Would arising-under jurisdiction have existed if the Railroad in the *Mottley* case had sued for a declaration that it was not obligated to issue the railroad passes due to the new federal law? In *Skelly Oil*, Phillips sued in federal court under the federal Declaratory Judgment Act, 28 U.S.C. § 2201, which empowers a court to "declare the rights and other legal relations of any interested party." Specifically, Phillips sought a declaration that certain contracts were in existence and had not been terminated. The validity of an attempted termination by the defendant depended, in turn, upon whether the actions of the Federal Power Commission amounted to issuance of a certificate of public convenience and necessity under federal law. The Court held that there was no jurisdiction. The Declaratory Judgment Act did not create jurisdiction but merely authorized a remedy, and Phillips' claimed rights in the contract were a creature of state law. Whatever federal arguments Phillips might be able to urge based upon the FPC's actions "would in any event be injected into the case only in anticipation of a defense."

In a sense, an action seeking a declaratory judgment of non-liability reverses the parties and transforms a "defense" into a "claim." But a federal court will base jurisdiction on the claim that the declaratory action opposes. Accordingly, if the Railroad in *Mottley* had filed a declaratory judgment action, the jurisdictional outcome would have remained the same: no jurisdiction.

(6) *Policy: Should the Test for Jurisdiction Be Ambiguous? Should It Be Expanded to Authorize Federal Jurisdiction Based Upon Defenses?* It has been suggested that ambiguity in the definition of federal jurisdiction actually may be advantageous(!), because it allows the courts to consider such policy questions as the workload of the federal courts, the likelihood of disposition on state-law questions, and the need for a federal forum to vindicate the rights at issue. Cohen, *The Broken Compass: The Requirement That a Case Arise "Directly" Under Federal Law*, 115 U. Pa. L. Rev. 890, 916 (1967); *see also Gully v. First National Bank*, 299 U.S. 109 (1936).

But shouldn't jurisdictional statutes, like rules of the road, be clear? The waste inherent in ambiguity is illustrated by the two trips the Mottleys made to the Supreme Court.

Another policy issue is whether the denial of jurisdiction to federal defenses is appropriate. A federal law asserted as a defense is presumably of equal dignity, and as much a reflection of federal policy, as a federal law-based claim. Thus, the American Law Institute proposed federal jurisdiction over cases involving federal defenses or counterclaims. ALI, *Study of the Division of Jurisdiction Between State and Federal Courts* 178–80 (1969).

(7) *Implied Claims Under the Constitution: Bivens v. Six Unknown Agents of the Federal Bureau of Narcotics*, 403 U.S. 388 (1971). Another problem arises from federal laws that govern conduct but do not mention claims. If the courts imply a claim, is there federal jurisdiction?

The *Bivens* case illustrates the interplay between jurisdictional issues and implied rights of action. Justice Brennan's opinion begins:

> ... Petitioner's complaint alleged that ... agents of the Federal Bureau of Narcotics ... entered his apartment and arrested him for alleged narcotics violations. The agents manacled petitioner in front of his wife and children, and threatened to arrest the entire family. They searched the apartment from stem to stern. Thereafter, petitioner was ... interrogated, booked, and subjected to a visual strip search.
>
> ... [P]etitioner brought suit in Federal District Court. [H]is complaint asserted that the arrest and search were effected without a warrant, and that unreasonable force was employed in making the arrest; fairly read, it alleges as well that the arrest was made without probable cause. [Petitioner sought damages for violation of the Fourth Amendment to the Constitution.].... The District Court, on respondents' motion, dismissed the complaint on the ground [that it failed to state a claim]....

Before confronting the merits, the Supreme Court considered whether federal question jurisdiction existed over this claim. The defendants argued that the allegations gave rise only to state-law claims, such as trespass and invasion of privacy; that federal law giving them powers of arrest as officers of the FBN would provide them with a defense; and that the sole relevance of federal constitutional law was that it limited the extent of their federal defense. This combination of a state claim, a federal defense, and a federal restriction on the defense would be similar to the situation in *Louisville & Nashville RR. v. Mottley*; in fact, the defendants argued that the claim should be dismissed for want of jurisdiction precisely because it was the equivalent of *Mottley* in civil rights form.

The Supreme Court disagreed. It went on to hold that the Fourth Amendment to the Constitution does imply a right to recover damages for its violation. But consider the following cases, which deal with a different problem: a state law claim with a federal ingredient.

MERRELL DOW PHARMACEUTICALS, INC. v. THOMPSON, 478 U.S. 804 (1986). Plaintiff Thompson brought a product liability case against Merrell Dow under the product liability law of Ohio. The claim thus was based on state law, but the plaintiff asserted that the product defect at issue was that Merrell Dow's drug violated federal law because it lacked adequate warnings and therefore was "misbranded" within the meaning of the federal Pure Food, Drug, and Cosmetic Act. That Act expressly provides that it does not create any private right of action. Merrell Dow removed the case to federal court. The Supreme Court held that there was no federal question jurisdiction:

> We conclude that a complaint alleging a violation of a federal statute as an element of a state cause of action, when Congress has determined that

there should be no private, federal cause of action for the violation, does not state a claim "arising under the Constitution, laws, or treaties of the United States."

Thus, the Supreme Court invoked the "creation test" for arising-under jurisdiction. But consider the next case, in which a "substantial ingredient" of federal law was enough and produced the opposite result.

Grable & Sons Metal Products, Inc. v. Darue Engineering & Manufacturing

545 U.S. 308 (2005)

JUSTICE SOUTER delivered the opinion of the Court.

The question is whether want of a federal cause of action to try claims of title to land obtained at a federal tax sale precludes removal to federal court of a state action . . . raising a disputed issue of federal title law. We answer no, and hold that the national interest in providing a federal forum for federal tax litigation is sufficiently substantial to support the exercise of federal question jurisdiction over the disputed issue . . . .

I

In 1994, the Internal Revenue Service seized Michigan real property belonging to petitioner Grable & Sons Metal Products, Inc., to satisfy Grable's federal tax delinquency. Title 26 U.S.C. § 6335 required the IRS to give notice of the seizure, and there is no dispute that Grable received actual notice by certified mail before the IRS sold the property to respondent Darue Engineering & Manufacturing. Although Grable also received notice of the sale itself, it did not exercise its statutory right to redeem the property within 180 days of the sale, § 6337(b)(1), and after that period had passed, the Government gave Darue a quitclaim deed. § 6339.

Five years later, Grable brought a quiet title action in state court, claiming that Darue's record title was invalid because the IRS had failed to notify Grable of its seizure of the property in the exact manner required by § 6335(a), which provides that written notice must be "given by the Secretary to the owner of the property [or] left at his usual place of abode or business." Grable said that the statute required personal service, not service by certified mail.

Darue removed the case to Federal District Court as presenting a federal question, because the claim of title depended on the interpretation of the notice statute in the federal tax law. The District Court declined to remand the case at Grable's behest after finding that the "claim does pose a significant question of federal law," . . . and ruling that Grable's lack of a federal right of action to enforce its claim against Darue did not bar the exercise of federal jurisdiction. On the merits, the court granted summary judgment to Darue, holding that although § 6335 by its terms required personal service, substantial compliance with the statute was enough. 207 F. Supp. 2d 694 (W.D. Mich. 2002).

The Court of Appeals for the Sixth Circuit affirmed. 377 F.3d 592 (2004). On the jurisdictional question, the panel thought it sufficed that the title claim raised an issue of federal law that had to be resolved, and implicated a substantial federal interest (in construing federal tax law). The court went on to affirm the District Court's judgment on the merits. We granted certiorari on the jurisdictional question alone . . . to resolve a split within the Courts of Appeals on whether *Merrell Dow Pharmaceuticals, Inc. v. Thompson*, 478 U.S. 804 (1986), always requires a federal cause of action as a condition for exercising federal-question jurisdiction. We now affirm.

II

Darue was entitled to remove the quiet title action if Grable could have brought it in federal district court originally, 28 U.S.C. § 1441(a), as a civil action "arising under the Constitution, laws, or treaties of the United States," § 1331. This provision for federal-question jurisdiction is invoked by and large by plaintiffs pleading a cause of action created by federal law (e.g., claims under 42 U.S.C. § 1983). There is, however, another longstanding, if less frequently encountered, variety of federal "arising under" jurisdiction, this Court having recognized for nearly 100 years that in certain cases federal question jurisdiction will lie over state-law claims that implicate significant federal issues. *E.g., Hopkins v. Walker*, 244 U.S. 486, 490–491 (1917). The doctrine captures the commonsense notion that a federal court ought to be able to hear claims recognized under state law that nonetheless turn on substantial questions of federal law, and thus justify resort to the experience, solicitude, and hope of uniformity that a federal forum offers. . . .

[But] the federal issue will ultimately qualify for a federal forum only if federal jurisdiction is consistent with congressional judgment about the sound division of labor between state and federal courts governing the application of § 1331. . . . Because arising-under jurisdiction to hear a state-law claim always raises the possibility of upsetting the state-federal line drawn (or at least assumed) by Congress, . . . there must always be an assessment of any disruptive portent in exercising federal jurisdiction. *See also Merrell Dow, supra*, at 810.

These considerations have kept us from stating a "single, precise, all-embracing" test for jurisdiction over federal issues embedded in state-law claims . . . . We have not kept them out simply because they appeared in state raiment, . . . but neither have we treated "federal issue" as a password opening federal courts to any state action embracing a point of federal law. Instead, the question is, does a state-law claim necessarily raise a stated federal issue, actually disputed and substantial, which a federal forum may entertain without disturbing any congressionally approved balance of federal and state judicial responsibilities.

III

A

This case warrants federal jurisdiction. Grable's state complaint must specify "the facts establishing the superiority of [its] claim," Mich. Ct. Rule 3.411(B)(2)(c)

(2005), and Grable has premised its superior title claim on a failure by the IRS to give it adequate notice, as defined by federal law. Whether Grable was given notice within the meaning of the federal statute is thus an essential element of its quiet title claim, and the meaning of the federal statute is actually in dispute; it appears to be the only legal or factual issue contested in the case. . . . The Government has a strong interest in the "prompt and certain collection of delinquent taxes," *United States v. Rodgers*, 461 U.S. 677, 709 (1983), and the ability of the IRS to satisfy its claims from the property of delinquents requires clear terms of notice to allow buyers like Darue to satisfy themselves that the Service has touched the bases necessary for good title . . . . Finally, because it will be the rare state title case that raises a contested matter of federal law, federal jurisdiction to resolve genuine disagreement over federal tax title provisions will portend only a microscopic effect on the federal-state division of labor. . . .

B

Merrell Dow Pharmaceuticals, Inc. v. Thompson, 478 U.S. 804 (1986), on which Grable rests its position, is not to the contrary. *Merrell Dow* considered a state tort claim resting in part on the allegation that the defendant drug company had violated a federal misbranding prohibition, and was thus presumptively negligent under Ohio law. *Id.*, at 806. [The plaintiff's claim was a state-law product-liability claim for injury by a defective drug, with the plaintiff claiming that the defect arose from the defendant's violation of the federal law by misbranding the drug.] The Court assumed that federal law would have to be applied to resolve the claim, but after closely examining the strength of the federal interest at stake and the implications of opening the federal forum, held federal jurisdiction unavailable. Congress had not provided a private federal cause of action for violation of the federal branding requirement, and the Court found "it would . . . flout, or at least undermine, congressional intent to conclude that federal courts might nevertheless exercise federal-question jurisdiction . . . ."

[Grable argues that there is no federal-law quiet title action. Therefore, it argues, this case is like *Merrell Dow,* where the federal law at issue provided that it did not create a private claim. But the absence of a claim here is not equivalent to the provision in *Merrell Dow* expressly denying a claim. Further, says the Court, "an opinion is to be read as a whole, and *Merrell Dow* cannot be read whole as overturning decades of precedent."]

. . . [T]he Court treated the combination of no federal cause of action and no preemption of state remedies for misbranding as an important clue to Congress's conception of the scope of jurisdiction to be exercised under § 1331 . . . . For if the federal labeling standard without a federal cause of action could get a state claim into federal court, so could any other federal standard without a federal cause of action. And that would have meant a tremendous number of cases. . . .

As already indicated, however, a comparable analysis yields a different jurisdictional conclusion in this case. . . . [J]urisdiction over actions like Grable's would not materially affect, or threaten to affect, the normal currents of litigation.... [Affirmed; federal jurisdiction upheld.]

[The concurring opinion of Justice Thomas is omitted.]

> Read 28 U.S.C. §§ 1330, 1603, 1605(a) (Foreign Sovereign Immunities Act).

Note on the Constitutional Basis of "Arising Under" Jurisdiction: The Example of the Foreign Sovereign Immunities Act

The Breadth of the Constitutional "Arising Under" Provision. The Constitution authorizes federal jurisdiction over actions "arising under" federal law, in language similar to that of § 1331. However, the constitutional provision has been interpreted more broadly than the statute. *See* Chadbourne & Levin, *Original Jurisdiction of Federal Questions*, 90 U. PA. L. REV. 639 (1940). That is to say, Congress has considerable leeway in defining the scope of jurisdiction. Thus, in *Osborne v. Bank of the United States*, 9 Wheat. 738, 6 L. Ed. 204 (1824), Chief Justice Marshall's opinion upheld a statute allowing the Bank of the United States to sue in federal court, even if the claim was based upon state law.

The Foreign Sovereign Immunities Act. The Foreign Sovereign Immunities Act allows foreign nations or their departments or instrumentalities to be sued in federal courts. Before that time, foreign nations had sovereign immunity from suit; the Act codified a narrow version of this immunity, making foreign nations subject to suit on state or federal claims to the extent this immunity did not apply. It also provides that federal District Courts "have original jurisdiction ... of any nonjury civil action against a foreign state ...." 28 U.S.C. § 1330. *See* Note, *Suits by Foreigners Against Foreign States in United States Courts: A Selective Expansion of Jurisdiction*, 90 YALE L.J. 1861 (1981).

Verlinden B.V. v. Central Bank of Nigeria, 461 U.S. 480 (1983), was the case that tested the constitutionality of the Foreign Sovereign Immunities Act. Verlinden, a Dutch corporation, contracted to deliver 240,000 metric tons of cement to the Federal Republic of Nigeria and sued Nigeria's instrumentality, the Central Bank of Nigeria, when it breached the contract. The claim was controlled by Dutch law. Verlinden sued in the United States District Court for the Southern District of New York. The Bank of Nigeria, in addition to defending on the merits, alleged that the grant of jurisdiction in the Foreign Sovereign Immunities Act was unconstitutional. Citing *Osborne*, the Supreme Court upheld the grant of jurisdiction and said: "Congress may confer on the federal courts jurisdiction over any case or controversy that might call for the application of federal law." The District Court necessarily would have to determine whether sovereign immunity existed under the federal Foreign Sovereign Immunities Act. Although this application of federal law, since it did not govern the claim itself, would not be sufficient for jurisdiction under the general federal question statute (§ 1331), it was sufficient to bring the Foreign Sovereign

Immunities Act within the broader scope of the constitutional "arising under" provision. As the Supreme Court put it, "[T]he many limitations which have been placed on jurisdiction under § 1331 are not limitations on the constitutional power of Congress to confer jurisdiction on the federal courts."

Litigation Document Example 3.1: "Arising Under" Jurisdiction

The Complaint in Wytinger v. Two Unknown Police Officers

[Reproduced above in Section IV of Chapter 1, Litigation Document Example 1.1 (Complaint and Dismissal in the *Wytinger* Case).]

For a concrete example of "arising under" jurisdiction, read (or re-read) the complaint in *Wytinger v. Two Unknown Police Officers.* Identify the parts of the complaint that purport to show jurisdiction.

[B] Diversity Jurisdiction

[1] The Requirement of Complete Diversity

> Read 28 U.S.C. § 1332 (the diversity statute); also, reconsider U.S. Const. art. III, § 2 (the constitutional diversity provision).

STRAWBRIDGE v. CURTISS, 7 U.S. (3 Cranch) 267 (1806). The text of this opinion appears above in Chapter 1, § III, and should be read (or re-read) at this point. In essence, Chief Justice Marshall's decision interpreted the diversity statute to require "complete" diversity: "That is, . . . each of the [parties] must be competent to sue, or liable to be sued" by each other party.

Mas v. Perry

489 F.2d 1396 (5th Cir. 1974)

AINSWORTH, CIRCUIT JUDGE:

This case presents questions pertaining to federal diversity jurisdiction under 28 U.S.C. § 1332, which . . . provides for original jurisdiction in federal district courts of all civil actions that are between, *inter alia*, citizens of different States or citizens of a State and citizens of foreign states and in which the amount in controversy is more than $10,000. [Eds. Note: The $10,000 figure later was changed to $75,000.]

Appellees Jean Paul Mas, a citizen of France, and Judy Mas were married at her home in Jackson, Mississippi. Prior to their marriage, the couple were graduate assistants, pursuing coursework as well as performing teaching duties . . . at Louisiana State University in Baton Rouge, Louisiana. Shortly after their marriage, they returned to Baton Rouge to resume their duties as graduate assistants at LSU. They remained in Baton Rouge for approximately two more years, after which they moved to Park Ridge, Illinois. At the time of the trial in this case, it was their intention to return to Baton Rouge while Mr. Mas finished his studies for the degree of Doctor of Philosophy. Mr. and Mrs. Mas were undecided as to where they would reside after that.

Upon their return to Baton Rouge after their marriage, appellees rented an apartment from appellant Oliver H. Perry, a citizen of Louisiana. This appeal arises from a final judgment entered on a jury verdict awarding $5,000 to Mr. Mas and $15,000 to Mrs. Mas for damages incurred by them as a result of the discovery that their bedroom and bathroom contained "two-way" mirrors and that they had been watched through them by the appellant during three of the first four months of their marriage.

At the close of the appellees' case at trial, appellant made an oral motion to dismiss for lack of jurisdiction. The motion was denied by the District Court. Before this Court, appellant challenges the final judgment below solely on jurisdictional grounds, contending that appellees failed to prove diversity of citizenship among the parties and that the requisite jurisdictional amount is lacking with respect to Mr. Mas. Finding no merit to these contentions, we affirm. Under section 1332(a)(2), the federal judicial power extends to the claim of Mr. Mas, a citizen of France, against the appellant, a citizen of Louisiana. [Eds. Note: Now, the courts do not have jurisdiction if a citizen of a state is adverse to a permanent resident alien who is domiciled in the same state. How would this provision affect Mr. Mas today if he were a permanent resident alien?] Since we conclude that Mrs. Mas is a citizen of Mississippi for diversity purposes, the District Court also properly had jurisdiction under § 1332(a)(1) of her claim.

It has long been the general rule that complete diversity of parties is required in order that diversity jurisdiction obtain; that is, no party on one side may be a citizen of the same State as any party on the other side. *Strawbridge v. Curtiss*. . . . As is the case in other areas of federal jurisdiction, the diverse citizenship among adverse parties must be present at the time the complaint is filed. . . . Jurisdiction is unaffected by subsequent changes in the citizenship of the parties. . . .

. . . For diversity purposes, citizenship means domicile; mere residence in the State is not sufficient. . . .

A person's domicile is the place of "his true, fixed, and permanent home and principal establishment, and to which he has the intention of returning whenever he is absent therefrom. . . ." *Stine v. Moore*, 5 Cir., 1954, 213 F.2d 446, 448. A change of domicile may be effected only by a combination of two elements: (a) taking up residence in a different domicile with (b) the intention to remain there. . . .

It is clear that at the time of her marriage, Mrs. Mas was a domiciliary of the State of Mississippi. . . .

Mrs. Mas's Mississippi domicile was disturbed neither by her year in Louisiana prior to her marriage nor as a result of the time she and her husband spent at LSU after their marriage, since for both periods she was a graduate assistant at LSU. . . . Though she testified that after her marriage she had no intention of returning to her parents' home in Mississippi, Mrs. Mas did not effect a change of domicile since she and Mr. Mas were in Louisiana only as students and lacked the requisite intention to remain there. . . . Until she acquires a new domicile, she remains a domiciliary, and thus a citizen, of Mississippi. . . .

Appellant also contends that Mr. Mas's claim should have been dismissed for failure to establish the requisite jurisdictional amount for diversity cases of more than $10,000 [now $75,000]. In their complaint Mr. and Mrs. Mas alleged that they had each been damaged in the amount of $100,000. As we have noted, Mr. Mas ultimately recovered $5,000.

It is well settled that the amount in controversy is determined by the amount claimed by the plaintiff in good faith. . . . Federal jurisdiction is not lost because a judgment of less than the jurisdictional amount is awarded. . . . That Mr. Mas recovered only $5,000 is, therefore, not compelling. As the Supreme Court stated in *St. Paul Mercury Indemnity Co. v. Red Cab Co.*, 303 U.S. 283, 288-290 . . . :

> [T]he sum claimed by the plaintiff controls if the claim is apparently made in good faith.
>
> It must appear to a legal certainty that the claim is really for less than the jurisdictional amount to justify dismissal. The inability of the plaintiff to recover an amount adequate to give the court jurisdiction does not show his bad faith or oust the jurisdiction. . . .

Thus the power of the federal district court to entertain the claims of appellees in this case stands on two separate legs of diversity jurisdiction: a claim by an alien against a State citizen; and an action between citizens of different States. [AFFIRMED.]

Note on the Policy Basis for Diversity Jurisdiction

Concern about Local Prejudice, or Creditor Protection, or Preference for "Better" Courts? The reasons for the diversity provision are shrouded in mystery. There is no indication of the underlying policy in the debates on the Constitution, and the legislative history of the early enactment is of little help. But many commentators infer that the concern is about local prejudice:

> However true the fact may be, that the tribunals of the states will administer justice as impartially as [the federal courts], . . . the Constitution itself either entertains apprehensions on this subject, or views with such indulgence the possible fears and apprehensions of suitors, that it has established . . . national tribunals for the decision of controversies . . . between citizens of different states.

Bank of the United States v. Deveaux, 9 U.S. (5 Cranch) 61, 87 (1809) (Marshall, Ch. J.).

> Many legal scholars who have researched this issue have concluded that [diversity jurisdiction] was based on a fear that State courts would be biased or prejudiced against those from out of State. A minority view is that the Nation's early lawmakers shared misgivings as to whether at least some of the State courts would be fair to the interests of creditors, out-of-staters or in-staters. Another position is that, the Federal courts being better than the State, it was preferable to route as many cases into the former as possible.

Abolition of Diversity of Citizenship Jurisdiction, H.R. Rep. No. 95-893, 95th Cong., 2d Sess. 2 (1978). For a detailed history, see generally D. Bassett, *The Hidden Bias in Diversity Jurisdiction*, 81 Wash. U. L.Q. 119 (2003).

Notes and Questions

(1) *The "Local Prejudice" Rationale: Is It Valid?* As these excerpts indicate, a concern about the possibility of local prejudice is the most commonly asserted justification for diversity jurisdiction. But there is some question today about this theory. Transportation and communication have made the nation more unified than ever before. A Californian and a Nebraskan, for example, may have more in common with each other than they have with other individuals from their respective states.

Furthermore, there is room for doubt whether the addition of federal courts solves the problem of local prejudice, even assuming it exists. If a case is tried in North Carolina, in a federal court, from what state will the federal District judge come? [He or she is likely to have been chosen by one of North Carolina's senators!] From what state will the jurors be summoned? [Obviously, North Carolina!] Therefore, regardless of whether the sign over the courthouse door says "federal" or "state," isn't the case going to be tried by similar kinds of people under closely analogous procedures?

(2) *Is the "Complete Diversity" Requirement Consistent with the "Local Prejudice" Rationale?* If a North Carolinian brings a state-law claim against two defendants—one a fellow North Carolinian, the other a New Yorker—the suit must be in state court, because diversity is destroyed. But isn't the New Yorker just as much in danger of local prejudice as he would be if sued alone? In fact, since he now may have the fingers of both the North Carolina plaintiff and his North Carolina co-defendant pointed at him before a jury of North Carolinians, doesn't the New Yorker need a federal forum even more than if sued alone? This example suggests that the rationale of local prejudice is inconsistent with the requirement of complete diversity.

(3) *Permanent Resident Aliens.* Notice that today, if Mr. Mas happened to be a permanent resident alien, he could not use diversity jurisdiction to sue a citizen domiciled in the same state. Diversity would be destroyed. Is this result consistent with the local prejudice rationale (does an alien suffer prejudice even if he is a permanent resident)?

(4) *Defeating or Preserving Diversity: Games Lawyers Play.* Imagine an influential attorney whose client has a claim against a national corporation, based upon his client's dealings with a local agent. This attorney may be able to choose either to create or to defeat federal jurisdiction. If she prefers a state forum (and attorneys have been known to prefer a given court because of personal relationships with the judge, or even because of having assisted in obtaining the judge's election or appointment), she can sue the corporation and join its local agent, who presumably is of the same citizenship as the local plaintiff. This strategy destroys diversity. On the other hand, if the influential attorney likes the federal court better (perhaps for similar kinds of reasons), she would sue the out-of-state corporation alone in federal court. Should the law facilitate these "games that lawyers play"?

(5) *The Costs of Diversity; Possible Reforms.* Unless diversity is beneficial, it should be abolished, because it has substantial costs: wasteful forum contests, federal-state conflicts, gamesmanship, and impact on the workload of courts that should be hearing federal claims. There have been many proposals for alteration of diversity jurisdiction—or for its outright abolition. *See, e.g.*, Rowe, *Abolishing Diversity Jurisdiction: Positive Side Effects and Potential for Further Reform*, 92 Harv. L. Rev. 963 (1979). We take up some of these arguments at the end of this chapter.

Note on Citizenships of Corporations or Associations

Corporations: Two Kinds of Citizenships. The diversity statute provides that a corporation may have multiple citizenships, including any state in which it is incorporated and the state of its "principal place of business." Although this provision means that a corporation, like an individual, is a citizen for diversity purposes, the existence of two citizenships also means that it destroys diversity more easily.

"Where Is the Principal Place of Business?" Historically, it often was difficult to determine where a corporation's principal place of business was. The Supreme Court has now resolved the issue, by deciding upon the "nerve center" test. (*See* the *Hertz* case, below.)

Partnerships, Associations, and Other Entities. Unincorporated entities do not have a citizenship apart from the citizenship(s) of their members. *United Steelworkers of America v. R.H. Bouligny, Inc.*, 382 U.S. 145 (1965) (Court held that union had citizenships of all members); *cf. Navarro Savings Ass'n v. Lee*, 446 U.S. 458 (1980) (Court held that citizenships of business trust were all citizenships of trustees of business trust). Should this approach be changed by Congress, or does it make sense that a corporation has a distinct citizenship but a partnership does not?

Hybrid Entities. Some entities resemble both corporations and partnerships. "Professional corporations," for example, may resemble a partnership or professional association. For diversity purposes, however, the Seventh Circuit held, in *Hoaglund ex rel. Midwest Transit, Inc. v. Sandberg, Phoenix & von Gontard, P.C.*, 385 F.3d 737 (2004), that a "professional corporation" under state law is a "corporation" within the meaning of the diversity jurisdiction statute, no matter how much the entity may resemble a partnership or other entity. Accordingly, the citizenship of a "professional corporation" will be the place of its incorporation and principal place of business (which typically or usually means its headquarters, as the following case shows).

Hertz Corporation v. Friend

130 S. Ct. 1181 (2010)

Justice Breyer delivered the opinion of the Court.

[California plaintiffs sued Hertz in a state court on state-law claims. Hertz removed the case to federal court, arguing that it was a citizen of New Jersey, where its corporate headquarters were. The plaintiffs, however, wanted the case sent back to state court, and they argued that Hertz's most significant business activities were in California, and therefore Hertz's "principal place of business" was in California. Hertz therefore was a citizen of California, according to the plaintiffs, so that diversity was lacking. The federal court of appeals agreed with the state-court plaintiffs. It applied a test that identified the "principal place of business" as the state in which the corporation's business is "significantly larger" than in other states, or "substantially predominates," and it therefore held that the case must be remanded to state court because diversity jurisdiction was lacking.

[The Supreme Court accepted the case for review because of widespread confusion about the meaning of "principal place of business," and here, it decides that Hertz's principal place of business is to be determined by its nerve center.]

The federal diversity jurisdiction statute provides that "a corporation shall be deemed to be a citizen of any State by which it has been incorporated *and of the State where it has its principal place of business.*" 28 U.S.C. § 1332(c)(1) (emphasis added). We seek here to resolve different interpretations that the Circuits have given this phrase. In doing so, we place primary weight upon the need for judicial administration of a jurisdictional statute to remain as simple as possible. And we conclude that the phrase "principal place of business" refers to the place where the corporation's high level officers direct, control, and coordinate the corporation's activities. [The Courts of Appeals] have often metaphorically called that place the corporation's "nerve center." We believe that the "nerve center" will typically be found at a corporation's headquarters . . . .

The phrase "principal place of business" has proved more difficult to apply than its originators likely expected . . . . *Compare Burdick v. Dillon*, 144 F. 737, 738 (C.A.1 1906) (holding that a corporation's "principal office, rather than a factory, mill, or mine . . . constitutes the 'principal place of business'"), *with Continental Coal Corp. v. Roszelle Bros.*, 242 F. 243, 247 (C.A.6 1917) (identifying the "principal place of business" as the location of mining activities, rather than the "principal office"). Perhaps because corporations come in many different forms, involve many different kinds of business activities, and locate offices and plants for different reasons in different ways in different regions, a general "business activities" approach has proved unusually difficult to apply . . . . This complexity may reflect . . . an effort to find the State where a corporation is least likely to suffer out-of-state prejudice when it is sued in a local court . . . . But, if so, that task seems doomed to failure. . . . At the same time, this approach is at war with administrative simplicity. And it has failed to achieve a nationally uniform interpretation of federal law . . . .

We conclude that "principal place of business" is best read as referring to the place where a corporation's officers direct, control, and coordinate the corporation's activities. It is the place that Courts of Appeals have called the corporation's "nerve center." . . .

Three sets of considerations, taken together, convince us that this approach, while imperfect, is superior to other possibilities. First, the statute's language supports the approach. The statute's text deems a corporation a citizen of the "State where it has its principal place of business." The word "place" is in the singular, not the plural . . . . [The nerve center is a single place, while the "significantly larger general business" approach requires consideration of all of the multiple business activities in the entire state.] . . .

This ["significantly larger general business"] approach invites greater litigation and can lead to strange results, as the Ninth Circuit has since recognized. Namely, if a "corporation may be deemed a citizen of California on th[e] basis" of "activities [that] roughly reflect California's larger population . . . , nearly every national retailer—no matter how far flung its operations—will be deemed a citizen of California for diversity purposes." *Davis v. HSBC Bank Nev., N.A.*, 557 F.3d 1026, 1029–1030 (2009) . . . .

Second, administrative simplicity is a major virtue in a jurisdictional statute. Complex jurisdictional tests complicate a case, eating up time and money as the parties litigate, not the merits of their claims, but which court is the right court to decide those claims. . . .

Third, [the legislative history suggests that simplicity may have been a legislative goal in the adoption of the statutory language.] . . . A "nerve center" test offers such a possibility. A general business activities test does not.

We understand that . . . seeming anomalies will arise. However, in view of the necessity of having a clearer rule, we must accept them . . . . [Vacated and remanded for application of the nerve center test.]

GRUPO DATAFLUX v. ATLAS GLOBAL GROUP, L.P., 541 U.S. 567 (2004). Atlas, a limited partnership, filed a state-law suit against petitioner, a Mexican corporation, in federal court, alleging diversity jurisdiction. After the jury returned a verdict for Atlas, Dataflux moved to dismiss for lack of subject-matter jurisdiction because the parties were not diverse at the time the original complaint was filed. Dataflux argued that, as a partnership, Atlas was a Mexican citizen because two of its partners were Mexican citizens at the time of filing, and petitioner Dataflux was also a Mexican citizen. [An alien suing another alien destroys diversity.—Eds.] But before judgment, the two Mexican citizens exited from the Atlas partnership, leaving complete diversity. The court of appeals affirmed. It held that where, as here, the jurisdictional error was not identified until after the jury's verdict, the postfiling change in the partnership could cure the jurisdictional defect.

The Supreme Court here reverses and holds that a party's change in citizenship cannot cure a lack of subject-matter jurisdiction that existed at the time of filing. Dismissal for lack of subject-matter jurisdiction is the only option:

> Atlas is a citizen of each State or foreign country of which any of its partners is a citizen. *See Carden v. Arkoma Associates,* 494 U.S. 185 (1990). Because Atlas had two partners who were Mexican citizens at the time of filing, the partnership was a Mexican citizen. (It was also a citizen of Delaware and Texas based on the citizenship of its other partners.) And because the defendant, Dataflux, was a Mexican corporation, aliens were on both sides of the case, and the requisite diversity was therefore absent.
>
> It has long been the case that "the jurisdiction of the court depends upon the state of things at the time of the action brought." *Mollan v. Torrance,* 9 Wheat. 537, 539, 6 L.Ed. 154 (1824). This time-of-filing rule is hornbook law . . . taught to first-year law students in any basic course on federal civil procedure. . . .
>
> We have adhered to the time-of-filing rule regardless of the costs it imposes. For example, in *Anderson v. Watt,* 138 U.S. 694 (1891), two executors of an estate, claiming to be New York citizens, had brought a diversity-based suit in federal court against defendants alleged to be Florida citizens. When it later developed that two of the defendants were New York citizens, the plaintiffs sought to save jurisdiction by revoking the letters testamentary for one executor and alleging that the remaining executor was in fact a British citizen. . . . [The Court] dismissed the case for want of jurisdiction, even though the case had been filed about 5½ years earlier, the trial court had entered a decree ordering land to be sold 4 years earlier, the sale had been made, exceptions had been filed and overruled, and the case had come to the Court on appeal from the order confirming the land sale. [REVERSED; no jurisdiction.]

Problem C

PAYNE v. UNITED MOTORS CORP. Plaintiff Paul Payne, a citizen of Ohio, has an alleged wrongful discharge claim for more than $100,000 against United Motors, arising under state law. United Motors is a corporation incorporated under the laws of Delaware. Its corporate headquarters are located in an office building in Detroit, Michigan, but virtually all of its manufacturing operations take place just across the state line, in Ohio. You represent Paul Payne. You would like to have the case heard in a federal court if you can; however, you would like to be certain of the basis for jurisdiction if you obtain a judgment. Question 1: Should you file suit in a federal court? Question 2: How would your answer be affected if you planned to join the United Automobile Workers International Union as a second defendant?

[2] Parties "Improperly or Collusively Made"

> Read 28 U.S.C. § 1359 (the "collusive parties" statute).

KRAMER v. CARIBBEAN MILLS, INC., 394 U.S. 823 (1969). The Panama and Venezuela Finance Company ("Panama"), a Panamanian Corporation, assigned to Kramer a claim it had against Caribbean Mills, a Haitian corporation. Panama would not have been able to sue Caribbean in the federal courts because neither was a citizen of a state, but Kramer (the assignee) was an attorney practicing in Wichita Falls and was a citizen of Texas. Kramer therefore filed an action against Caribbean in a United States District Court. Caribbean moved to dismiss for lack of jurisdiction, arguing that Kramer was "improperly or collusively made" a party for the purpose of creating diversity in violation of 28 U.S.C. § 1359. The Supreme Court agreed, and it upheld the reversal of a judgment for Kramer.

The stated consideration paid by Kramer was one dollar, in exchange for a claim for $165,000 allegedly owed by Caribbean to Panama. Furthermore, by an instrument executed the same day, Kramer had agreed to pay back to Panama 95% of any net recovery on the assigned claim. "When the assignment to Kramer is considered together with his total lack of previous connection with the matter and his simultaneous reassignment of a 95% interest back to Panama, there can be little doubt that the assignment was for purposes of collection, with Kramer to retain 5% of the net proceeds 'for the use of his name and his trouble in collecting,'" said the Court. "If federal jurisdiction could be created by assignments of this kind, . . . then a vast quantity of ordinary contract and tort litigation could be channeled into the federal courts at the will of one of the parties."

Notes and Questions

(1) *Changing the Facts in Kramer: Assignment for Business Reasons.* What if Panama were dissolved by its shareholders and its assets transferred to a New Jersey corporation for independent business and tax reasons, unrelated to the ability to sue in federal court? The courts have sometimes regarded transfer to controlled corporations as "presumptively" ineffective to create diversity, *cf. Prudential Oil Corp. v. Phillips Petroleum Co.*, 546 F.2d 469 (2d Cir. 1976). But wouldn't genuine business reasons make a difference?

(2) *Can the Plaintiff's Own Change of Citizenship Create Diversity?* In *Baker v. Keck*, 13 F. Supp. 486 (1936), the plaintiff was originally a citizen of Illinois—as was the defendant he wanted to sue. Plaintiff moved to Oklahoma, taking his

family and almost all his possessions, produced food crops there, rented property, and registered to vote. The court concluded that one of plaintiff's motives was "to create diversity of citizenship so that he might maintain a suit in the United States courts." However, said the court, "One may change his citizenship for the purpose of enabling himself to maintain a suit in the federal court, but the change must be an actual legal change made with the intention of bringing about actual citizenship. . . ." Since the court credited plaintiff's testimony that his intention was to make Oklahoma his home, it upheld the jurisdiction. Defense witnesses testified that plaintiff had said he was going to move back to Illinois after he got his case settled, but the court said that "a floating intention to return at some indefinite future period" did not affect citizenship. Is *Keck* consistent with *Kramer*?

[3] Amount in Controversy

Note on Ascertaining the Amount in Controversy

Monetary Claims: The Good Faith Complaint. Reconsider *Mas v. Perry*, above. Even though Mr. Mas recovered only $5,000, the amount in controversy was the $100,000 he had prayed for. "It is well settled that the amount in controversy is determined by the amount claimed by the plaintiff in good faith," said the court.

Non-Monetary Claims: The "Value of the Object" and Other Tests. But what if the prayer is not for monetary relief? What if it instead requests an injunction or a declaratory judgment? In that event, the most common test is the so-called "value of the object": The court looks to the value of whatever plaintiff hopes to gain from the suit—or, sometimes, the potential cost to the defendant. Consider the following case.

Williams v. Kleppe

539 F.2d 803 (1st Cir. 1976)

The site of this controversy is a beach known as Brush Hollow on the Atlantic shore of Cape Cod, a three mile expanse between two conventionally operated beaches. For some forty or fifty years this spot, hidden behind some of the highest sand dunes on the Cape, had been used by individuals, couples, and small groups for skinny dipping. . . .

As the popularity of Brush Hollow built up, so did the concern of the owners of residential property [n]ear points of access to the beach. [The concerns included "demonstrable damage to the environment, increasing attendance despite attempts of enforcement, record traffic congestion, litter, and trespassing."] . . .

[The local government], after considering the alternatives, [a]dopted the regulation at issue, which bars public nude bathing within the seashore to all persons over ten years of age. Suit was brought [by plaintiffs, apparently for a declaration of invalidity of the regulation and for an injunction against responsible government officials' enforcement of it] and hearing was had at which affidavits were accepted and evidence taken. The District Court, although finding that "nude bathing at Brush

Hollow is entitled to some constitutional protection," held that the regulation [was valid]. . . .

[Before considering the merits, the Court of Appeals considered whether federal jurisdiction existed to adjudicate the claimed "right" to "skinny dip." Then-existing statutes required an amount in controversy exceeding $10,000, both for diversity and, at that time, for some federal claims. To determine whether the amount exceeded this threshold, the court applied a version of the value of the object test as well as an alternate test, as follows:]

. . . The jurisdictional amount was alleged and has not been made an issue. Applying conventional analysis, we are unwilling to say on this record that the claimed interest of one or more plaintiffs, some being residents of the Seashore area, may not exceed the jurisdictional amount. Perhaps more realistically, we can rely upon the extent of the claimed pecuniary burden on defendants were plaintiffs to prevail. . . .

[On the merits, the court compared the claimed interest to another "protectible, if minor interest, one's desire to wear his hair as he chooses." To the probable disappointment of some readers, the court then proceeded to decide that this "minor" interest in "skinny dipping" was overcome by the "real and substantial interests" supporting the regulation, which it upheld as valid.]

Notes and Questions

(1) *Did the Value of the Object of Plaintiffs' "Minor" Interest Really Exceed the Threshold? The "Legal Certainty" Test.* If the interest truly is "minor," could the government have developed evidence to defeat jurisdiction at the evidentiary hearing? Maybe a "minor" legal interest could have a very high subjective value to a given individual; is this subjective value, rather than the low ranking of the legal interest, the proper focus? Furthermore, remember that the allegation of the jurisdictional amount in good faith is subject to being defeated only if it is shown "to a legal certainty" that plaintiff never had any prospect of recovering any relief in an amount exceeding the threshold. *Cf. Mas v. Perry, supra.* Another technical consideration is that plaintiffs each must individually meet the threshold and may not aggregate the values of their claims to reach it (see below). Did the court "fudge" this aspect of the case?

(2) *The "Loss to the Defendant" Test; Other Approaches.* What if the plaintiff seeks an injunction to protect a right of little monetary value, and so he alleges an amount less than the jurisdictional amount—but the injunction would result in shutting down the defendant's business? In that event, an alternate test considering the defendant's loss may be appropriate. *American Smelting & Refining Co. v. Godfrey,* 158 F. 225 (8th Cir. 1907) (suit for injunction against nuisance); *cf. Oklahoma Retail Grocers Ass'n v. Wal-Mart Stores, Inc.*, 605 F.2d 1155 (10th Cir. 1979) (where suit by association was for injunction to force compliance with statute, it was proper to accept the defendant's allegation that its costs would exceed the jurisdictional amount).

(3) *The "Aggregation" Problem.* What about multiple claims, none of which exceeds the jurisdictional amount if taken by itself, but which do exceed $75,000 in the aggregate? The federal courts allow distinct claims by a single party to be aggregated. Thus, if a plaintiff sues a defendant for two different breaches of contract, causing different injuries and damages, one for $50,000 and the other for $25,001, the amount in controversy exceeds $75,000. But if two alternative claims are made for the same injuries and damages (*e.g.*, negligence and breach of warranty), the alternative claims are not added together. Claims by different plaintiffs also are not added, unless the claims are legally united and indivisible because they involve the enforcement of a joint right by joint owners.

[C] Supplemental Jurisdiction and Exceptions to the Exercise of Jurisdiction

Read 28 U.S.C. § 1367 (supplemental jurisdiction).

Introductory Note

The Need for Supplemental Jurisdiction. Often, real-world disputes involve multiple parties and multiple claims that are partly within a federal court's jurisdiction and partly outside of it. Thus, a plaintiff suing in federal court on a federal claim may want to add closely related state-law claims to the complaint, all in the same suit. The defendant, in turn, may want to place blame upon a third party against whom he asserts a state-law claim, also related to the plaintiff's suit. But a problem arises: unless the plaintiff's state-law claim and the defendant's third-party claim have some basis for federal jurisdiction, they will need to be brought in state court, separately from the federal suit. This result would be wasteful.

How Supplemental Jurisdiction Solves These Problems. Congress passed 28 U.S.C. § 1367 (the supplemental jurisdiction statute) to govern this problem. The statute says that, with certain exceptions in diversity cases, the federal court may hear state law claims if they are "so related to claims in the action within [the court's] original jurisdiction that they form part of the same case or controversy under Article III of the Constitution."

The Relationship of Supplemental Jurisdiction to Two Older Concepts Called "Pendent" and "Ancillary" Jurisdiction. Before Congress passed the supplemental jurisdiction statute, federal judges themselves had invented a solution to the multiple-claim problem. They had created two doctrines called "pendent jurisdiction" and "ancillary jurisdiction." Today, those two doctrines have been replaced in federal court by the supplemental jurisdiction statute; you will need to learn about them, however, so that you can understand the present law. *See also* Mengler, Burbank & Rowe, *Congress Accepts Supreme Court's Invitation to Codify Supplemental*

Jurisdiction, 74 JUDICATURE 213 (1991). These terms are also still used in many state courts.

[1] Supplemental Jurisdiction of the Kind Formerly Called "Pendent Jurisdiction": Joining State and Federal Claims

Note on the Gibbs *Case: The Earlier Doctrine of Pendent Jurisdiction*

Parallel State and Federal Claims. Imagine that you have two closely related claims, one based on federal law and the other based on state law. You want to assert the federal claim in federal court, and you have a right to do so. But you also want to assert the state-law claim in the same suit, and it lacks an independent basis for federal jurisdiction. Unless there is some legal doctrine allowing you to join the non-jurisdictional claim in federal court with the jurisdictional one, you will have to give up the federal forum you want, or else you will need to bring two suits.

Pendent Jurisdiction in the Case of United Mine Workers v. Gibbs, below. This two-claim situation occurred in the *Gibbs* case. The plaintiff asserted a federal claim arising under the federal labor laws for an illegal boycott, and he joined it with a claim, arising under state law, for tortious interference with contract. The Supreme Court applied a judge-created doctrine called "pendent jurisdiction" to allow both claims to be brought together. The word "pendent" comes from a Latin word meaning "to hang"; the state-law claim comes within federal jurisdiction because it piggybacks or figuratively "hangs" on the federal claim.

Supplemental Jurisdiction Replaces the Older Doctrine of Pendent Jurisdiction. Today, pendent jurisdiction has been replaced by the supplemental jurisdiction statute. The *Gibbs* case was decided under the doctrine of pendent jurisdiction, but it is included here because it is an excellent introduction to the supplemental jurisdiction statute.

UNITED MINE WORKERS v. GIBBS, 383 U.S. 715 (1966). The United Mine Workers opposed the opening of a new coal mine operated by workers in a rival union. Therefore, the United Mine Workers picketed the location and undertook other union actions in opposition. As a result, the company made no further efforts to open the mine. Gibbs had a contract to be superintendent of the new mine and to haul the coal, and he lost these rights because of the Mine Workers' actions.

Gibbs filed suit in a federal court, asserting two distinct but related claims against the Mine Workers Union. The first was based on section 303 of the federal Labor Management Relations Act, which prohibits secondary boycotts. (A "secondary boycott" is an effort to coerce persons with whom the union does not have a labor dispute, in order to force them to withdraw their dealings with someone else.) The second claim, involving the same course of conduct by the union, was based on state law: Gibbs alleged that the union had tortiously interfered with his contract in violation of the common law of Tennessee.

The trial court asserted jurisdiction over both claims. The tortious interference claim had no federal ingredient, and there was no diversity, and so jurisdiction over this claim was based on what now would be called supplemental jurisdiction (then called pendent jurisdiction). After a jury trial of the overlapping evidence relevant to both claims, the trial judge refused to grant judgment on the federal claim because the union's actions did not amount to a prohibited secondary boycott under section 303. This holding, however, was not dispositive of the tortious interference claim, and the trial court entered a judgment on the jury's verdict against the union.

Ultimately, the Supreme Court reversed the judgment on the merits. The Court concluded that federal labor legislation had the effect of nullifying Gibbs's tortious interference claim that would limit the union's activities. (In technical language, the federal Labor Management Relations Act "preempted" Gibbs's state common-law claim for tortious interference.)

In the course of reaching this conclusion on the merits, however, the Court necessarily had to address the jurisdictional issue. It upheld the trial court's exercise of jurisdiction:

> Pendent jurisdiction, in the sense of judicial *power*, exists whenever there is a claim 'arising under [the] Constitution, the Laws of the United States, and Treaties made, or which shall be made, under their Authority . . . ,' U.S. Const., Art. III, § 2, and the relationship between that claim and the state claim permits the conclusion that the entire action before the court comprises but one constitutional "case." The federal claim must have substance sufficient to confer subject-matter jurisdiction on the court. The state and federal claims must derive from a common nucleus of operative fact. But if, considered without regard to their federal or state character, a plaintiff's claims are such that he would ordinarily be expected to try them all in one judicial proceeding, then, assuming substantiality of the federal issues, there is *power* in federal courts to hear the whole.

Notes and Questions

(1) *Supplemental Jurisdiction Would Produce the Same Result Today in a Gibbs-Type Situation.* The result would be the same in a *Gibbs*-type case today, under section 1367(a) of the supplemental jurisdiction statute. There are subtle differences between the statute and the older doctrine, but they are closely similar.

(2) *Changing the Facts in UMW v. Gibbs and Applying Supplemental Jurisdiction.* What (if any) difference should it make in *UMW v. Gibbs*, if the following events occurred and if the supplemental jurisdiction statute were applied?

(a) *Early Dismissal of the Federal Claim:* What if the District Court had decided early in the case to dismiss the federal claim, on the theory that it failed to state a basis upon which relief could be granted? [Notice that the statue gives the district court discretion to dismiss the state-law claim.]

(b) *Strong State Governmental Interests; Ambiguous State Law:* What if the state-law claim had been based on an elaborate state statute, recently enacted by the state legislature and never construed by the state courts? [Again, discretion to dismiss.]

(c) *Unrelated State and Federal Claims:* What if the state law claim was not related to Gibbs' loss of the employment and haulage contracts that were the basis of the federal claim, but was instead an effort to collect on a promissory note given by the UMW to Gibbs in an unrelated transaction? [Would jurisdiction even exist in this situation?]

(3) *The Supplemental Jurisdiction Statute Allows the Addition of New Parties.* What happens if a supplemental claim involves the addition of new and different parties? Answer: The last sentence of section 1367(a) expressly permits this addition. Earlier, this question had been controversial. *See Aldinger v. Howard*, 513 F.2d 1257 (9th Cir. 1975) (plaintiff brought civil rights suit against state officials for wrongfully discharging her from a county job, but was disallowed from adding a pendent claim against a different defendant, the county itself). Today, the supplemental jurisdiction statute departs from the *Aldinger* reasoning to promote greater judicial economy by bringing all related parties into one suit.

Litigation Document Example 3.2: Diversity Jurisdiction

Order of Dismissal in Wytinger v. Two Unknown Police Officers

[Reproduced above in Litigation Document Example 1.1, in Section IV of Chapter 1 (Complaint and Dismissal in the *Wytinger* Case).]

For a concrete example of supplemental jurisdiction, read (or re-read) the Order of Dismissal in *Wytinger v. Two Unknown Police Officers*, which appears above in Litigation Document Example 1.1, in Section IV of Chapter 1, Litigation Document Example 1.1. The Amended Complaint attempted to assert a claim under the federal civil rights statute for the plaintiffs' decedent's suicide, and it added a negligence claim arising under state law. The allegation of jurisdiction would have been amended to include an assertion of supplemental jurisdiction over this state-law claim, as follows:

4. The action arises under said [federal] section 1983; . . . AND UNDER THE LAW OF THE STATE OF WEST YORK. This Court has jurisdiction under and by virtue of . . . the General Federal Question Statute . . . AND UNDER 28 U.S.C. § 1367, the Supplemental Jurisdiction Statute.

Note that the court's Order dismisses the federal portion of the complaint for failure to state a claim. The Order also says, "the Court declines jurisdiction over Plaintiffs' state claims under *United Mine Workers v. Gibbs*. . . ." Did supplemental jurisdiction exist, and if so, was the refusal to exercise jurisdiction over the state-law claims appropriate?

[2] Supplemental Jurisdiction over Counterclaims, Third-Party Claims, etc. (and the § 1367(b) Prohibition)

Note on Different Kinds of Supplemental Claims

An Example: Supplemental Jurisdiction over Counterclaims. Imagine that the plaintiff and the defendant have both suffered injuries from a collision between automobiles they were driving. The plaintiff sues the defendant in federal court, basing jurisdiction on diversity of citizenship and claiming damages of $150,000. The defendant thinks that the accident was actually the plaintiff's fault, and he would like to counterclaim. But he can claim only $40,000 in damages. The defendant therefore is lacking an independent basis for federal jurisdiction over his counterclaim, but it would not be appropriate to disallow him from asserting this claim from the same accident in the same suit.

Supplemental Jurisdiction over Different Kinds of Claims. The supplemental jurisdiction statute allows the court to hear counterclaims, third-party claims, cross-claims, or other added claims that lack an independent jurisdictional basis but that should be heard in the same suit as the principal claim. But there is an exception for certain claims by plaintiffs.

Note on the Prohibition of Certain Kinds of Supplemental Claims by Plaintiffs: Owen v. Kroger

The Exception in Section 1367(b): Prohibiting Certain Uses of Supplemental Jurisdiction by Plaintiffs. Section 1367(b) disallows supplemental jurisdiction "over claims by plaintiffs against persons made parties under Rule 14 [*i.e.*, third-party defendants]," as well as certain other claims. In other words, the plaintiff cannot assert a state-law claim in federal court against a co-citizen merely because that party has been brought into the case by the defendant. This provision codifies holdings under the earlier doctrine.

Owen Equipment & Erection Co. v. Kroger, 437 U.S. 365 (1978), illustrates this exception. In that case, Kroger's husband walked next to a steel crane that came too close to electric lines, and he died by electrocution. She sued the local power company. Since she was a citizen of Iowa, and the power company was a citizen of Nebraska, Kroger filed her state-law wrongful death claim as a diversity action in federal court. But the defendant filed a third-party action against the crane operator, Owen, alleging that Owen was solely responsible. Kroger realized that if the power company was correct, her only claim might be against Owen, and she therefore amended her complaint to add a claim directly against Owen. She alleged that

Owen was a citizen of Nebraska and therefore diverse from her, and Owen admitted this allegation in its answer.

The trial resulted in a verdict for Kroger, but it also revealed that as a result of an avulsion of the Missouri River, Owen's jurisdictional admission was mistaken(!) Owen actually was a citizen of Iowa, the same state as Kroger, because the river had shifted. Unless jurisdiction existed, it appeared that Kroger's hard-won verdict would be wiped out.

The Court held that the use of the previous kind of "ancillary" jurisdiction (or what now would be supplemental jurisdiction) was improper. The doctrine of complete diversity meant that jurisdiction under the diversity statute "does not exist unless each defendant is a citizen of a different State from each plaintiff." The federal courts are courts of limited jurisdiction. If supplemental jurisdiction were to be recognized here, a plaintiff could exploit it "by the simple expedient of suing only those defendants who were of diverse citizenship and waiting for them to implead non-diverse defendants." The plaintiff could have achieved the goal of unitary litigation in the state courts, said the Court, but instead "voluntarily chose to bring suit upon a state-law claim in a federal court." The result seems harsh, but it is preserved in the current statute.

The Exception for Plaintiff's Claims Today. The prohibition in section 1367(b) would produce the same result if *Owen Equipment v. Kroger* were to arise today. The statute disallows claims by plaintiffs against third-party defendants. Is this complex exception to supplemental jurisdiction in 1367(b) worth the damage it causes? (On the other hand, note that mistaken admissions of jurisdictional facts probably are rare, and they could be remedied by the usual rule that good faith stipulations to such facts are binding. Perhaps the Supreme Court could have preserved its holding and still avoided a strikingly unjust result by applying this binding-stipulation rule against Owen.)

Situations in Which the Court May Decline Jurisdiction. As noted above, section 1367(c) of the supplemental jurisdiction statute also provides that the court may decline to exercise jurisdiction in certain situations, such as supplemental claims that "predominate."

[3] Interpreting the Supplemental Jurisdiction Statute

Note on Claims to Which the Statute Applies

The supplemental jurisdiction statute has been criticized as being poorly drafted and ambiguous. *See, e.g.*, Thomas Arthur & Richard Freer, *Close Enough for Government Work: What Happens When Congress Doesn't Do Its Job*, 40 Emory L.J. 1007 (1991). The drafters of the statute have answered these critics. They contend that the statute is clear that cross-claims among defendants, compulsory counterclaims by defendants, and impleader claims are expressly authorized by subsection (a) and not prohibited by subsection (b).

Claims by a third-party defendant are authorized by the statute in the same manner. The result does not depend on whether the case is a diversity or federal question case. The drafters also assert that it provides clear guidance in almost all other situations. *See* Thomas Rowe, Jr., Stephen Burbank & Thomas Mengler, *A Coda on Supplemental Jurisdiction*, 40 Emory L.J. 993, 995–96 (1991). But it would be unusual if a statute like this did not create some interpretive issues. Consider the following case.

EXXON MOBIL CORPORATION v. ALLAPATTAH SERVICES, INC., 545 U.S. 546 (2005). Plaintiffs brought a class action based on diversity. Some class members had claims exceeding $75,000, but the class included many plaintiffs whose claims were too small to create jurisdiction independently. The Supreme Court held, however, that the statute allowed supplemental jurisdiction over the smaller claims of these class members:

> *In Finley* [*v. United States,* 490 U.S. 545 (1989),] we emphasized that "[w]hatever we say regarding the scope of jurisdiction conferred by a particular statute can of course be changed by Congress." . . . Congress accepted the invitation. It passed the Judicial Improvements Act, which enacted § 1367 [the supplemental jurisdiction statute], the provision which controls these cases. . . .
>
> Section 1367(a) is a broad grant of supplemental jurisdiction over other claims within the same case or controversy, as long as the action is one in which the district courts would have original jurisdiction. The last sentence of § 1367(a) makes it clear that the grant of supplemental jurisdiction extends to claims involving joinder or intervention of additional parties. . . .
>
> When the well-pleaded complaint in district court includes multiple claims, all part of the same case or controversy, and some, but not all, of the claims are within the court's original jurisdiction, does the court have before it "any civil action of which the district courts have original jurisdiction"? It does. . . .
>
> It follows from this conclusion that the threshold requirement of § 1367(a) is satisfied in cases, like those now before us, where some, but not all, of the plaintiffs in a diversity action allege a sufficient amount in controversy. We hold that § 1367 . . . authorized supplemental jurisdiction over all claims by diverse parties arising out of the same Article III case or controversy, subject only to . . . exceptions not applicable [here] . . . .

The class action was consolidated with another diversity claim by a personal injury plaintiff, joined by her family members. The same principle allowed supplemental jurisdiction over the joined claims even though they were for less than the jurisdictional amount.

Justice Ginsburg dissented, joined by three other Justices:

> . . . [T]his Court has long held that, in determining whether the amount-in-controversy requirement has been satisfied, a single plaintiff may aggregate two or more claims against a single defendant. . . . But in multiparty cases, including class actions, we have unyieldingly adhered to the nonaggregation rule . . . . The rule that each plaintiff must independently satisfy the amount-in-controversy requirement, . . . was thus the solidly established reading of § 1332 [the diversity statute] when Congress . . . added § 1367. . . .
>
> [Section] 1367(a) addresses "civil action[s] of which the district courts have original jurisdiction," a formulation that, in diversity cases, is sensibly read to incorporate the rules on joinder and aggregation tightly tied to § 1332 . . . . In other words, § 1367(a) [should be read to] preserve undiminished, as part and parcel of § 1332 "original jurisdiction" determinations, both the "complete diversity" rule and the decisions restricting aggregation to arrive at the amount in controversy. . . .

Note on Understanding Supplemental Jurisdiction

The following paragraphs illustrate the proper interpretation of the supplemental jurisdiction statute after the Supreme Court's decision in *Exxon Mobil Corp. v. Allapattah Services, Inc.*, 545 U.S. 546 (2005).

(1) *Codification of Gibbs Doctrine in Section 1367(a).* If A sues B and asserts a federal question claim coupled with a state law claim based on the same facts, does the statute provide a basis for supplemental jurisdiction? [Yes, section 1367(a) creates jurisdiction over the related state claims even if A and B are residents of the same state.] It also allows supplemental jurisdiction for compulsory counterclaims under Fed. R. Civ. P. 13(a) and cross-claims under Fed. R. Civ. P. 13(g) because the "same transaction or occurrence" requirement for these claims is the functional equivalent of Section 1367(a)'s "same case or controversy."

(2) *Repeal of Finley's Pendent Party Exception by Section 1367(a).* Section 1367(a)'s last sentence reverses *Finley v. United States*, 490 U.S. 545 (1989). If A has a federal question claim against B as well as a state law claim against C, does the statute provide a basis for supplemental jurisdiction over A's claim against C? [Yes, section 1367(a) creates jurisdiction over the related state claims and the last sentence of section 1367(a) extends this approach to additional parties.]

(3) *Codification of Kroger in Section 1367(b).* Section 1367(b) codifies *Owen Equipment & Erection Co. v. Kroger*, 437 U.S. 365 (1978). Thus, if A sues B in a diversity case and B brings a third-party action against C, there is supplemental jurisdiction over the third-party claim against C even though the third-party claim does not satisfy the statutory amount in controversy requirement and even if B and C are co-citizens. But if A adds a claim against C, is there supplemental jurisdiction over that claim if they are citizens of the same state? [Section 1367(b) allows the

third-party claim, but precludes the plaintiff from using supplemental jurisdiction to sue third party C if that party is a co-citizen of plaintiff A.]

[4] Refusal to Exercise Jurisdiction

[a] The Abstention Doctrines

Justifications for Abstention. In certain circumstances, the federal courts will decline to exercise the jurisdiction given them under the Constitution and statutes. *See generally* Field, *The Abstention Doctrine Today,* 125 U. Pa. L. Rev. 590 (1977). There are at least four situations in which these "abstention doctrines" may apply: (1) when the decision of a constitutional question might be avoided by interpretation of state law; (2) when a federal decision might unnecessarily conflict with a state's governmental affairs; (3) when a significant issue of state law is unsettled; and (4) when there are parallel state and federal proceedings and abstention will reduce the federal workload. *Cf.* C. Wright, *The Law of Federal Courts* 303 (4th ed. 1983).

Abstention Because of Constitutional Issues Involving Pervasive or Ambiguous State Law. Two common abstention doctrines are named after the Supreme Court cases first recognizing them—*Railroad Commission v. Pullman Co.*, 312 U.S. 496 (1941) ("Pullman" abstention), and *Burford v. Sun Oil Co.*, 319 U.S. 315 (1943) ("Burford" abstention). In *Pullman*, the Pullman Company sought to enjoin the enforcement of a state Railroad Commission order. The Supreme Court ordered the trial court to abstain from deciding the case but to retain jurisdiction until a state court decision was obtained on the state issues involved. The Supreme Court reasoned that, in this manner, federal courts could avoid deciding a federal constitutional question prematurely or unnecessarily. In *Burford*, Sun Oil Company attacked the validity of Burford's permit to drill wells in an oil field. The oil field was located in Texas, which had a complicated system for industry regulation. The Supreme Court dismissed the federal proceedings, reasoning that needless conflict with a state's administration of its own affairs should be avoided. Thus, *Burford* abstention avoids the adjudication, by federal courts, of difficult state law questions that threaten to disrupt state policy.

Certification: A Procedure for Federal Courts to Send Difficult Issues of State Law to State Courts. In response to federal abstention, most states have created "certification" procedures. *See* Titze, *Giving Deference to State Law: New South Dakota Certification Statutes Enable Federal Courts to Defer to Supreme Court*, 30 S.D. L. Rev. 299 (1984). In these states, a federal court seeking guidance on a state law question can "certify" the state law question to that state's courts for an answer before proceeding further in the case before it. *Cf. Lehman Bros. v. Schein*, 416 U.S. 386 (1974) (vacating decision of Second Circuit in New York federal diversity action so that court could certify to Florida Supreme Court certain determinative questions of Florida law).

[b] The Domestic Relations and Probate Exceptions

The Domestic Relations Exception. If husband and wife are of diverse citizenship, there is no obvious reason why their divorce action cannot be heard by a federal court—but still, it cannot be. There is a judge-created exception to diversity jurisdiction for "domestic relations" cases. The policy underlying this exception is unclear, since it dates from the decision in *Barber v. Barber*, 62 U.S. (21 How.) 582 (1859), in which the Court did uphold federal enforcement of a divorce decree entered in another state but added, in dictum: "We disclaim altogether any jurisdiction in the courts of the United States upon the subject of divorce, or the allowance of alimony, either as an original proceeding or as incident to a divorce. . . ." The exception was later explained by reference to traditional abstention policies and by the special argument that state child welfare, adoption, or custody agencies do not have established relationships with federal courts. *See* Atwood, *Domestic Relations Cases in Federal Court: Toward a Principled Exercise of Jurisdiction*, 35 HASTINGS L.J. 571 (1984). But there is uncertainty. For example, the federal courts will not exercise jurisdiction to determine alimony—but they usually are able to enforce a contract providing for alimony.

The Probate Exception. A federal court may not probate a will or administer an estate, although it can maintain creditors' actions against executors or administrators so long as the claims do not interfere with the exercise of probate jurisdiction or with control of property by a state court. *See generally* Wright & Kane, *The Law of Federal Courts* 162 (6th ed. 2002). As in the case of the domestic relations exception, the policy basis of this doctrine is unclear (except that it diminishes the workload of the federal courts), and it also can lead to wasteful litigation.

[D] Removal: Defendant's Key to the Federal Courthouse

Read 28 U.S.C. §§ 1441(a), (b), and (c); 1445; 1446; 1447 (the basic removal statutes).

Problem D

APPLYING THE STATUTES DEFINING FEDERAL REMOVAL JURISDICTION. After reading the federal removal jurisdiction statute, 28 U.S.C. § 1441(a)-(c), consider the following cases. All claims are pending in state courts, and all seek damages in excess of $75,000. In each case, answer the question: "Can the defendant remove to federal court?"

(a) *The Straightforward Diversity Situation.* The plaintiff, a citizen of New York, sues defendant, a citizen of Florida, in a New York state trial court, asserting a claim based on state law. [Note: *See* § 1441(a). This one is easy; it boils down to whether the claim is within the federal diversity jurisdiction.]

(b) *A Diversity Case with a Local Defendant.* Now, imagine that the court and suit are the same, but the parties are reversed. That is, the plaintiff is a citizen of Florida, defendant a citizen of New York, and the suit is in a New York State court on state law grounds. [This situation does not call for the same analysis as the first problem!

See § 1441(b)(2). A local citizen lacks the "local prejudice" argument, and Congress wrote § 1441(b) accordingly.]

(c) *The Federal Question Situation.* Next, imagine the same parties in the same court—but this time, the claim arises under federal law. The Florida citizen sues the New York citizen in a New York state court under the federal civil rights statute, 42 U.S.C. § 1983. [Local prejudice is no longer the relevant consideration. The defendant's interest in having a federal court determine a federal claim is the real issue. Therefore, citizenship is irrelevant. *See* § 1441(b)(2).]

Suggested answers: (a) removable; (b) not removable; (c) removable.

Note on Removal Jurisdiction, Procedure, and Policy

The Scope of Removal Jurisdiction. As the problem above demonstrates, the basic thrust of § 1441 is to allow the defendant to remove the case to federal court if it would be suitable for filing there by the plaintiff. However, the statute is slightly more restrictive of removal by defendants than of initial filing by plaintiffs, in that it disallows the use of diversity jurisdiction as a basis for removal by a local defendant. The policy reason is evidently that this defendant can make no argument of local prejudice. The destruction of diversity ordinarily prevents removal, just as it prevents initial filing in federal court by a plaintiff. Notice that this principle enables a plaintiff to structure the suit so that diversity-based removal is prevented, by the expedient of joining a local defendant.

Procedure for Removal. Removal procedure is governed by § 1446. The defendant is required to remove within thirty days of receiving the pleading or other papers upon which removal is based. The statute limits removal in diversity cases to one year after commencement of the action. This statutory provision carries out a policy in favor of prompt determination of which court system is to hear the case. The defendant is required to file a notice of removal in the federal court, stating the grounds. If there are multiple defendants, all must join in the notice, except those who have not been served. The state court is disempowered from further action during the period of removal, even if it later turns out to be improper.

Procedure for Remand. Plaintiff can test the propriety of the removal by a "motion to remand," which is governed by § 1447. As a consequence of the policy in favor of expeditious determination of jurisdiction, § 1447(d) provides that a remand order is not reviewable "by appeal or otherwise" if remand was ordered due to a lack of federal subject matter jurisdiction. *See Carlsbad Technology, Inc. v. HIF Bio, Inc.*, 129 S. Ct. 1862 (2009). Consider the following case.

Caterpillar Inc. v. Lewis

519 U.S. 61 (1996)

Justice Ginsburg delivered the opinion of the Court.

This case, commenced in a state court, involves personal injury claims arising under state law. The case was removed to a federal court at a time when, the

Court of Appeals concluded, complete diversity of citizenship did not exist among the parties. Promptly after the removal, the plaintiff moved to remand the case to the state court, but the District Court denied that motion. Before trial of the case, however, all claims involving the nondiverse defendant were settled, and that defendant was dismissed as a party to the action. Complete diversity thereafter existed. The case proceeded to trial, jury verdict, and judgment for the removing defendant. The Court of Appeals vacated the judgment, concluding that, absent complete diversity at the time of removal, the District Court lacked subject-matter jurisdiction.

The question presented is whether the absence of complete diversity at the time of removal is fatal to federal court adjudication. We hold that a district court's error in failing to remand a case improperly removed is not fatal to the ensuing adjudication if federal jurisdictional requirements are met at the time judgment is entered.

I

[Plaintiff Lewis was injured while operating a bulldozer. He was a citizen of Kentucky, and he filed a Kentucky state court suit for negligence and product defect against two defendants: Whayne Supply Corporation, a Kentucky corporation that had serviced the bulldozer, and Caterpillar, a Delaware corporation, which had manufactured it. Liberty Mutual Insurance Company, a Massachusetts corporation, intervened as a plaintiff to assert what is known as a "subrogation" claim against Whayne and Caterpillar. It had paid workers' compensation benefits to Lewis and was entitled under the law to recover the same amount from the defendants if they were liable. With the suit in this posture, there was no diversity jurisdiction, since Plaintiff Lewis and Defendant Whayne were both citizens of Kentucky.

[A few months later, Lewis settled with Whayne, the Kentucky service company. Caterpillar filed a notice of removal to the federal District Court shortly after learning of the settlement. Caterpillar filed its removal papers less than 30 days after receiving notice of the settlement, and it satisfied, with only one day to spare, the statutory requirement that the removal take place within one year of commencement of the suit. Lewis promptly filed a motion to remand, arguing that Liberty Mutual's claim against Whayne remained in the suit and defeated complete diversity. The District Court denied the motion. The judge evidently reasoned that diversity in Lewis's claim against Caterpillar was sufficient to support jurisdiction.

[Then, shortly before trial, Liberty Mutual also settled with Whayne, so that at last it was clear that diversity was complete. With Caterpillar as the sole defendant adverse to Lewis, the case went to trial in federal court and resulted in a verdict for Caterpillar. The trial judge entered a judgment for the defendant.

[The Court of Appeals accepted Lewis's jurisdictional argument and vacated the judgment. Even though the settlement between Liberty Mutual and Whayne had created complete diversity before entry of judgment, the Court of Appeals concluded that Whayne's continued presence in the case up to that point meant that diversity was not complete at the time of removal. Therefore, denial of Lewis's motion to remand was error. The Supreme Court granted certiorari and here reverses, effectively reinstating the trial court's judgment for the defendant.]

II

. . . When a plaintiff files in state court a civil action over which the federal district courts would have original jurisdiction based on diversity of citizenship, the defendant or defendants may remove the action to federal court, 28 U.S.C. § 1441(a), provided that no defendant "is a citizen of the State in which such action is brought," § 1441(b). In a case not originally removable, a defendant who receives a pleading or other paper indicating the post-commencement satisfaction of federal jurisdictional requirements—for example, by reason of the dismissal of a nondiverse party—may remove the case to federal court within 30 days of receiving such information. § 1446(b). No case, however, may be removed from state to federal court based on diversity of citizenship "more than 1 year after commencement of the action."

Once a defendant has filed a notice of removal in the federal district court, a plaintiff objecting to removal "on the basis of any defect in removal procedure" may, within 30 days, file a motion asking the district court to remand the case to state court. § 1447(c). This 30-day limit does not apply, however, to jurisdictional defects: "If at any time before final judgment it appears that the district court lacks subject matter jurisdiction, the case shall be remanded."

III

We note, initially, two "givens" in this case as we have accepted it for review. First, the District Court, in its decision denying Lewis' timely motion to remand, incorrectly treated Whayne Supply, the nondiverse defendant, as effectively dropped from the case prior to removal. Second, the Sixth Circuit correctly determined that the complete diversity requirement was not satisfied at the time of removal. We accordingly home in on this question: Does the District Court's initial misjudgment still burden and run with the case, or is it overcome by the eventual dismissal of the nondiverse defendant?

Petitioner Caterpillar relies heavily on our decisions in *American Fire & Casualty Co. v. Finn*, 341 U.S. 6 (1951), and *Grubbs v. General Elec. Credit Corp.*, 405 U.S. 699 (1972), urging that these decisions "long ago settled the proposition that remand to the state court is unnecessary even if jurisdiction did not exist at the time of removal, so long as the district court had subject matter jurisdiction at the time of judgment." Caterpillar is right that *Finn* and *Grubbs* are key cases in point and tend in Caterpillar's favor. Each suggests that the existence of subject-matter jurisdiction at time of judgment may shield a judgment against later jurisdictional attack. But neither decision resolves dispositively a controversy of the kind we face, for neither involved a plaintiff who moved promptly, but unsuccessfully, to remand a case improperly removed from state court to federal court, and then challenged on appeal a judgment entered by the federal court. . . .

Beyond question, as Lewis acknowledges, there was in this case complete diversity, and therefore federal subject-matter jurisdiction, at the time of trial and judgment.... Caterpillar maintains that this change cured the threshold statutory misstep, i.e., the removal of a case when diversity was incomplete.

... [C]omplete diversity was established before the trial commenced.... But a statutory flaw—Caterpillar's failure to meet the § 1441(a) requirement that the case be fit for federal adjudication at the time the removal petition is filed—remained in the unerasable history of the case....

Having preserved his objection to an improper removal, Lewis urges that an "all's well that ends well" approach is inappropriate here.... The course Caterpillar advocates, Lewis observes, would disfavor diligent plaintiffs who timely, but unsuccessfully, move to check improper removals in district court. Further, that course would allow improperly removing defendants to profit from their disregard of Congress' instructions, and their ability to lead district judges into error.

Concretely, in this very case, Lewis emphasizes, adherence to the rules Congress prescribed for removal would have kept the case in state court. Only by removing prematurely was Caterpillar able to get to federal court inside the 1-year limitation set in § 1446(b).[12] Had Caterpillar waited until the case was ripe for removal, i.e., until Whayne Supply was dismissed as a defendant, the 1-year limitation would have barred the way, and plaintiff's choice of forum would have been preserved.[14]

These arguments are hardly meritless, but they run up against an overriding consideration. Once a diversity case has been tried in federal court, ... considerations of finality, efficiency, and economy become overwhelming....

... Despite a federal trial court's threshold denial of a motion to remand, if, at the end of the day and case, a jurisdictional defect remains uncured, the judgment must be vacated. In this case, however, no jurisdictional defect lingered through judgment in the District Court. To wipe out the adjudication post-judgment ... would impose an exorbitant cost on our dual court system, a cost incompatible with the fair and unprotracted administration of justice.

Lewis ultimately argues that, if the final judgment against him is allowed to stand, "all of the various procedural requirements for removal will become unenforceable"; therefore, "defendants will have an enormous incentive to attempt wrongful removals." In particular, Lewis suggests that defendants will remove prematurely "in the hope that some subsequent developments, such as the eventual dismissal of nondiverse defendants, will permit th[e] case to be kept in federal court." We do not anticipate the dire consequences Lewis forecasts.

---

12. Congress amended § 1446(b) ... to include the 1-year limitation in order to "reduc[e] the opportunity for removal after substantial progress has been made in state court."

14. Lewis preferred state court to federal court based on differences he perceived in, inter alia, the state and federal jury systems and rules of evidence.

... Lewis' prediction ... rests on an assumption we do not indulge—that district courts generally will not comprehend, or will balk at applying, the rules on removal Congress has prescribed .... The well-advised defendant, we are satisfied, will foresee the likely outcome of an unwarranted removal—a swift, and nonreviewable remand order, attended by the displeasure of a district court whose authority has been improperly invoked. The odds against any gain from a wrongful removal, in sum, render improbable Lewis' projection of increased resort to the maneuver. ... [Reversed and remanded.]

Notes and Questions

(1) *The 30-Day and One-Year Limits on Removal.* Notice what would have happened if Caterpillar had not removed within the 30-day window (after receiving notice of removability) or within the one-year limit (after commencement of suit). The suit then would have been subject to remand. In fact, Lewis argues that the suit really did not become even arguably removable until Whayne's dismissal (as opposed to the private agreement of the parties to settle), and since this dismissal itself occurred more than a year after commencement, Lewis argued that the suit was nonremovable at the time Caterpillar removed, even under Caterpillar's own arguments. Even so, the Supreme Court's holding preserves the judgment. The defendant's time to remove the case to federal court is triggered by simultaneous service of the summons and complaint on the defendant, or by receipt of the complaint by the defendant through service or otherwise, after and apart from service of the summons, but not by receipt of a "courtesy copy" of the complaint without formal service. *Murphy Bros. v. Michetti Pipe Stringing, Inc.*, 526 U.S. 344 (1999).

(2) *The Motion to Remand and the 30-Day Limit for "Procedural" Defects.* The plaintiff must file a motion to remand within 30 days to avoid waiving procedural defects in the removal. What would have happened, then, if Lewis had not made a timely motion to remand? The answer is that he probably would have given up any right to complain about such issues as the one-year limit. But if diversity had not existed at the time of judgment, even the failure to move for remand would not have prevented the plaintiff from raising the issue later.

(3) *Adverse and Non-Adverse Parties: Should the Claim by Liberty Mutual Against Whayne Have Been Disregarded for Diversity and Removal Purposes?* Liberty Mutual's subrogation claim was a peculiar kind of claim against Whayne, and in fact it really could be considered, in practical effect, as a claim against the Plaintiff, Lewis. Whayne's potential liability on the subrogation claim would have extended only to one satisfaction of the damages to Lewis, and if Liberty Mutual prevailed against Whayne, it was entitled to recover the amount it had paid Lewis, whose recovery would be reduced by the same amount. Liberty Mutual's recovery, in other words, came off the top of Lewis's recovery. Caterpillar's argument, then, was that Liberty Mutual's claim against Whayne did not mean that the two co-citizens, Lewis and Whayne, were adverse, especially since they already had settled. Arguably, therefore, the continued presence of Whayne in the suit did not destroy complete diversity,

since no co-citizens were truly diverse (?!). Notice how complex the jurisdictional arguments can become when a case is removed. Consider whether the avoidance of these kinds of ethereal (if not unanswerable) questions indirectly supports the "all's well that ends well" principle created here by the Supreme Court.

(4) *What If a Plaintiff Fraudulently Joins a Nondiverse Party Who Cannot Possibly Be Liable, Merely to Defeat Removal? In re Shell Oil Co.*, 932 F.2d 1518 (5th Cir. 1991). The flip side of the adverse-or-nonadverse-party question raised above arises when the plaintiff, eager to prevent removal, adds a local defendant against whom the plaintiff cannot possibly hope to prove a claim. This situation is said to involve "fraudulent joinder," and the fictitious defendant may be disregarded for jurisdictional purposes so that the removal may be allowed. *Cf.* § 3.03[B][2] above (parties "improperly or collusively" joined). But the proof threshold for the removing defendant is high, and any arguable claim by the plaintiff will defeat it. The removing defendant must show, to a legal certainty, that the plaintiff never had any possibility of recovery against the fraudulently-joined defendant.

In the *Shell Oil* case, above, the defendants removed despite the presence of local citizens, asserting that all were fraudulently joined. The plaintiffs moved to remand but waited until the 34th day after removal to do so. The court held that this untimeliness was a waiver of "defects in removal procedure," which it interpreted to include the removal of a case with a local citizen defendant. It therefore upheld the removal without considering whether the defendants were correct in asserting fraudulent joinder. Is it correct to characterize a possible failure to demonstrate fraudulent joinder as a defect in "procedure," or does the defect really destroy the court's jurisdictional basis instead?

(5) *The Tendencies of Plaintiffs to Prefer State Court and of Defendants to Prefer Removal.* In a footnote, the *Caterpillar* Court explained that Plaintiff Lewis preferred state court because of evidentiary and procedural advantages he perceived. Target defendants in personal injury cases often prefer to remove, and plaintiffs fight to stay in state court. Plaintiffs sometimes join impecunious local individuals even when the noncitizen target corporation is more clearly liable, and sometimes they include express disclaimers of reliance on federal law ("all of the claims herein arise solely under state law"). See whether you can describe some of the differences between state and federal courts that might lead to these strategies by plaintiffs and defendants.

Notes and Questions on Removal Procedure

(1) *Counterclaims: Shamrock Oil & Gas Corp. v. Sheets*, 313 U.S. 100 (1941). As we have already seen, a defendant's answer asserting a federal defense cannot create federal jurisdiction—and it does not allow the defendant to remove. But what if the defendant asserts a federal counter-claim? In this case (*Shamrock Oil & Gas Corp. v. Sheets*), the Supreme Court held that removal was not authorized. Should it be?

(2) *Claims That Are Non-Removable by Statute.* There are certain kinds of claims that are not removable because Congress has expressly provided by statute that they may not be removed. For example, actions under the Federal Employers Liability

Act (providing for claims by injured railroad and sea workers) and actions under worker's compensation laws may be filed in federal court if the plaintiff chooses, but if plaintiff files in state court, the defendant may not remove. 28 U.S.C. §§ 1445(a), (c). These enactments are apparently traceable to a policy of preserving choice of forum for certain favored claimants.

(3) *Removal Procedure: The Twilight Zone Between State and Federal Jurisdiction.* Section 1446 imposes a number of requirements for successful removal. What is the status of the jurisdiction when the defendant has filed the removal notice, but has not accomplished the other steps, such as providing written notice to adverse parties or filing the notice with the state court? Unfortunately, the authorities are divided, with some cases holding that the federal court ousts the state court of power when the notice is filed and others holding that the state court remains in control until all steps have been taken. *Compare, e.g., First National Bank in Little Rock v. Johnson & Johnson*, 455 F. Supp. 361 (E.D. Ark. 1978) (effective on filing of notice), *with Beleos v. Life & Cas. Ins. Co. of Tennessee*, 161 F. Supp. 627 (E.D.S.C. 1956) (effective only after later steps). In addition, *Berberian v. Gibney*, 514 F.2d 790 (1st Cir. 1975), holds that both courts (!) have jurisdiction in this "twilight zone." The most serious problems arise when the state court has entered an order during the twilight period, which the parties then cannot be certain is either valid or invalid.

(4) *Remand Procedure and Appellate Review: Thermtron Prods., Inc. v. Hermansdorfer*, 423 U.S. 336 (1976). Section 1447 provides for remand only if the case was improperly removed. What happens if the federal court remands simply because it wants to reduce its overloaded docket? In *Thermtron*, the District Court expressly remanded for that reason. The Supreme Court held that the usual rule prohibiting review of remand orders does not apply to an order entered on grounds other than the propriety of the removal, and it reversed. But the trial court has authority to make findings about the propriety of the removal, and if it remands on that ground (even if it is subtly affected by docket pressures and even if it is wrong), its order is not reviewable.

(5) *An Exception to the One-Year Limit When the Plaintiff Prevents Removal in Bad Faith.* Sometimes, a plaintiff tries to defeat removal of a diversity suit by tactics that delay the defendant's removal beyond one year. (Remember, diversity removal is limited to one year after commencement of the action.) But Congress counteracted these tactics in a law called the Federal Courts Jurisdiction and Venue Clarification Act, by providing that the one-year limit does not apply if the plaintiff has acted in "bad faith" to "prevent" timely removal. Consider the following examples. Would the exception allow removal?

(a) The plaintiff deliberately delays serving the defendant with process until after the one year has run. (The exception would almost certainly apply then.)

(b) The plaintiff deliberately waits for more than a year after filing to move to dismiss the only defendant who is a co-citizen of the plaintiff.

(c) The plaintiff sends a generic-looking postcard notice that suit has been filed to a remote office of the defendant, which is a huge enterprise such as IBM or Exxon-Mobil (because the 30 days is triggered even by notice other than service of process); then the plaintiff waits a month before serving process.

(6) *Determination of Requisites for Removal; Proof.* In general, the plaintiff's pleading in the state court is the determinant of matters such as the nature of the claim. There are some statements in the cases to the effect that plaintiff's pleading is the only permissible source of removal facts; however, this principle would produce absurd results. For example, most state courts do not require allegations of citizenship, and some state rules do not require specification of an amount in controversy. In that event, plaintiff's pleading will not show diversity, and defendant then must plead the jurisdictional basis in the notice of removal. Proof of these extrinsic facts is required only if they are contested and is usually made by affidavits. Consider the following case.

DART CHEROKEE BASIN OPERATING COMPANY LLC v. OWENS, 135 S. Ct. 547 (2014). This case arises under a different removal statute: the Class Action Fairness Act, or CAFA, which authorizes the removal of certain class actions from state to federal court if the amount in controversy exceeds $5 million. (The Act was intended to allow removal of interstate class actions filed in allegedly unfair venues selected for pro-plaintiff tendencies.) Owens filed an interstate class action against Dart for allegedly underpaying oil and gas royalties. CAFA, like the general removal statute, requires a notice of removal containing a "short and plain statement of the grounds for removal." Dart's notice alleged that the claimed underpayments amounted to more than $8.2 million.

Owens moved to remand on the ground that the notice was "deficient" because it contained no proof of the amount. Dart responded with an executive's detailed declaration showing an amount exceeding $11 million. The district court remanded the case, and the court of appeals denied review. The Supreme Court reversed:

> In remanding the case to state court, the District Court relied, in part, on a purported "presumption" against removal. See, *e.g., Laughlin* [*v. Kmart Corp.*], 50 F.3d, at 873 [(10th Cir. 1995)] ("[T]here is a presumption against removal jurisdiction."). We need not here decide whether such a presumption is proper in mine-run diversity cases. It suffices to point out that no antiremoval presumption attends cases invoking CAFA, which Congress enacted to facilitate adjudication of certain class actions in federal court. . . .
>
> In sum, as specified in § 1446(a), a defendant's notice of removal need include only a plausible allegation that the amount in controversy exceeds the jurisdictional threshold. Evidence establishing the amount is required by § 1446(c)(2)(B) only when the plaintiff contests, or the court questions, the defendant's allegation.

Often, a state-court pleading does not specify an amount in controversy, because an allegation may not be required. What should the defendant do then, to remove? Estimate an amount and make a "plausible" allegation of it.

IV. Real Life as a Lawyer

Note: Financial Judgment About Forum Contests

Imagine that you have just taken on a client whose closely held corporation has been sued in a court in your area. The in-house counsel for your client does not like this particular court. The in-house counsel (who is your client, in effect) would prefer to defend the suit elsewhere than in state court, or in this state, or in this area of the state. Your instinct is that a forum contest will be a long shot, but you think there is a small, outside chance of changing the court by simultaneous attacks upon the court's personal jurisdiction, subject matter jurisdiction, or venue. You explain. Then your client then shocks you by saying, "Would you please prepare me a litigation budget?"

Unfortunately, your law school education never even mentioned how to "prepare a litigation budget" (except in this short note). But one of the most basic principles of litigation is that every activity must be economically sound, even if law school doesn't say so. Everything—depositions, motions, forum contests, and everything else—is done on a budget. This is one of a great many business-of-law subjects that you will need to learn.

The Appendix at the end of this book covers many aspects of "Living a Full Life" as a lawyer. One part of that complex issue is the fact that law is a business. You will need to become adept with financial issues that affect litigation. The Appendix will introduce you at a beginning level to the wide range of business considerations. Specifically, section II[A][5] of the Appendix is titled, "Business Management in the Law Practice." But the Appendix also covers many other Full-Life subjects, ranging from time management to dealing with abusive opponents and from obstreperous clients to relationship difficulties.

V. How to Answer the Chapter Summary Problem: Some Suggestions

Smith v. Herald Newspaper Company: A Problem of Subject-Matter Jurisdiction. (As always, follow your Professor's instructions about how to answer.)

As in Chapter 2, you need to analyze three items for each issue: (1) the law, meaning all potentially helpful rules or principles; (2) the facts, meaning how the facts fit (or don't fit) the law; and (3) your conclusion. What is most important is the method of reasoning, not so much the particular conclusion.

1. Does Diversity Provide a Basis for Jurisdiction?

The Law: Diversity jurisdiction requires that the parties be citizens of different states (or that they have another statutory kind of diversity) and an amount greater than $75,000 in controversy. Diversity must be complete. An individual's citizenship is his/her domicile. The citizenship of a corporation is everywhere that it is incorporated and its principal place of business. The principal place of business is determined by the headquarters or nerve center test: the place where its top officers guide the affairs of the corporation.

The Facts: Plaintiff Smith is a candidate for the West York state legislature, presumably is domiciled there, and thus is a citizen of West York. Defendant Herald is incorporated in Delaware and thus is a citizen of Delaware. Herald also has operations throughout the nation, and it has its biggest operation in West York. But its headquarters is in California, and therefore it is a citizen of California. Diversity is complete. The amount in controversy is not specified, but Smith probably will claim more than $75,000, and if Smith does so in good faith, his claim sets the amount in controversy.

Conclusion: Diversity probably provides jurisdiction.

2. Does Federal Question (Arising Under) Jurisdiction Provide a Basis?

The Law: [Here, state the rules or principles you've learned, using the following ideas:] The claim must arise under federal law, a federal defense is not sufficient, and plaintiff's anticipation of a federal defense is not sufficient. [Explain the substantial ingredient test, the creation test, and their consequences, and the impact of Congress's allocation of state-federal jurisdiction in deciding which test to use.]

The Facts: The claim is for libel. It is arguable that the federal issue is a defense, although it is possible to argue that it is part of the claim, since it is an issue that plaintiff must prove. The creation approach would deny federal question jurisdiction, because the First Amendment does not create a claim for libel; state law does. The substantial ingredient approach could, arguably, support a conclusion that the federal question is a substantial ingredient of the claim. The allocation of jurisdiction intended by Congress can be argued both ways.

Conclusion: arising-under jurisdiction probably does not exist.

3. Is There a Basis for Jurisdiction over the Counterclaim?

The Law: Supplementary jurisdiction creates jurisdiction over a nonjurisdictional claim if it is so related to the plaintiff's claim that it forms part of the same case or controversy. The latter phrase is borrowed from the Constitution and has been interpreted as extending jurisdiction to the limits of the Constitution.

The Facts: The counterclaim here is based on the same basic facts and is part of the same case or controversy as the plaintiff's claim.

Conclusion: There is supplemental jurisdiction over the counterclaim.

4. Can Defendant Properly Remove?

The Law: Arising-under removal is proper if the claim is within the court's original jurisdiction. Diversity removal is proper if the claim is within the court's original jurisdiction, unless there is a defendant who is a co-citizen of the plaintiff. The removal must be within 30 days of defendant's receiving notice of removability and within one year of commencement if based upon diversity.

The Facts: The claim is within the original jurisdiction (see 1 and 2 above) and there is no local-citizen defendant. The facts don't tell us about timing issues.

Conclusion: Defendant can properly remove if within 30 days and one year.

VI. Improving Our Jurisdictional Systems

[A] State Court Reorganization: Notes and Questions

(1) *Goals of a Good Jurisdictional System.* What are the characteristics of good court organization? Consider the following factors, together with others you might think of:

> (a) *Clear Rules for Determining Jurisdiction.* Litigation about where litigation will take place is wasteful. A good court system is like a good traffic code: We should know which side of the road to drive on, and a lawyer ought not to have to guess which court has power to hear his or her suit.
>
> (b) *Specialization.* There should be courts specializing in small disputes with rules that differ from those for million-dollar disputes. There should be courts with domestic relations and probate expertise.
>
> (c) *Avoidance of Overspecialization.* An excess of specialization may lead to narrowness of view and overcomplex jurisprudence. A small specialized bar becomes accustomed to arcane rules that general litigators cannot follow. It is debatable, for example, whether there should be "housing" courts (as there are in some jurisdictions).
>
> (d) *Flexibility.* Docket pressures change faster than the court system can. Rapid development in one county may create sudden demand for more courts. It should be easy to assign underworked judges to help handle the dockets of overworked ones.
>
> (e) *Remedies Against Inappropriate Exercise of Court Authority.* If small claims procedures are used in a case in which they are not authorized, clear means of redress should be readily available.
>
> (f) *Judicial Qualifications Suited to the Jurisdiction.* A judge who is suited to a domestic relations bench may or may not be qualified for another bench. A Small Claims judge arguably must have certain personal qualifications that might not be necessary in a Superior Court judge, and vice versa.

(2) *The Move Toward "Unified" and "Uniform" Court Systems.* These goals have prompted most reformers to call for "unified" or "uniform" systems. Leading legal scholar, Roscoe Pound, advocated one "great court" with three branches: a "county" court with jurisdiction over smaller claims, a "district" court with general jurisdiction, and a "court of appeal." The key to the proposal was that all judges would be judges of the whole court, and they would be assigned by an administrator to various departments as needed. *See* Guittard, *Court Reform, Texas Style*, 21 Sw. L.J. 451 (1967). New Jersey made a pioneer effort toward this model in 1947, and there since have been various degrees of unification elsewhere. The American Bar Association later made a similar proposal, as follows:

> 1.10 Unified Court System: General Principle. The aims of court organization can be most fully realized in a court system that is unified in its structure and administration. . . .
>
> The structure of the court system should be simple, preferably consisting of a trial court and an appellate court, each having divisions or departments as needed. The trial court should have jurisdiction of all cases and proceedings. It should have specialized procedures and divisions to accommodate the various types of criminal and civil matters within its jurisdiction. The judicial functions of the trial court should be performed by a single class of judges, assisted by legally trained judicial officers . . . assigned to such matters as preliminary hearings, non-criminal traffic cases, [and] small claims. . . .

ABA, Commission on Standards of Judicial Administration 2-3 (tent. draft 1973). What do you think would be the advantages and disadvantages of this proposal?

[B] Reform of Federal Jurisdiction

[1] Should Congress Abolish Diversity Jurisdiction?

Abolition of Diversity of Citizenship Jurisdiction

H.R. Rep. No. 95-893, 95th Cong. 2d Sess. (1978)

[House Bill 9622, in 1978, would have abolished diversity jurisdiction between citizens of different states. It would have kept "alienage" jurisdiction (between citizens of states and citizens of foreign countries). It also removed a then-existing requirement in some federal question cases that the amount in controversy exceed $10,000.]

PURPOSE OF THE BILL

. . . Eighteen years ago, in 1959, Chief Justice Earl Warren, in an address to the American Law Institute, observed: "It is essential that we achieve a proper jurisdictional balance between the Federal and State court systems, in the light of the basic principles of federalism." The proposed legislation achieves that goal. As a general proposition, it provides the Federal law questions are to be adjudicated in the

Federal courts, regardless of the amount in controversy; and diversity cases, which involve questions of State law, are to be resolved in the State courts. . . .

. . . The Constitution . . . clearly grants [Congress] power to decide whether, and to what extent, there should be diversity jurisdiction. . . .

NEED FOR THE LEGISLATION

. . . [T]he abolition of diversity jurisdiction is an important step in reducing endemic court congestion and its insidious effects on litigants. During the 1977 judicial year, 31,678 diversity cases were filed in the Federal district courts. These filings comprised almost a quarter of the civil caseload at the trial court level. . . .

The diverting of diversity cases from the Federal courts to the State courts will not impose too great a burden on the latter. Essentially, 32,000 cases pending before 400 Federal district judges will cause few problems when allocated among 6,000 State judges of general jurisdiction. . . . The Conference of State Chief Justices in its Resolution of August 3, 1977, observed that the State courts were "able and willing" to assume all or part of the Federal diversity jurisdiction.

It is the view of the committee that the original reasons for diversity jurisdiction have long since disappeared. At present, there is little evidence that the State courts are less qualified or, due to latent prejudice against out-of-staters, unable to render fair and impartial justice in these cases. Since Federal juries are now drawn from the same registration or voter lists as State jurors, although from a larger area within the State, arguments that Federal juries are less biased than their State counterparts are insubstantial. . . .

Today, the United States is a more mobile society than that of the First Congress or even the 80th Congress. . . . Technological change [and] education . . . [have reduced] the risk of prejudice against out-of-staters. . . .

In conclusion, the proposed legislation recognizes that diversity is an idea whose time has passed. The Federal courts are a scarce resource and should be treated as such. . . . [T]here should be only one court per customer—the choice of forum is a luxury that our judicial system can no longer afford. . . . [T]he Federal courts must be freed from the shackles of congestion to do the job they do best—that of adjudicating disputes in traditional Federal subject-matter areas. . . . In addition, the State court systems must be accorded a respected role in the American judicial systems. . . .

Note on the Defeat of the Diversity Abolition Bill

Passage by the House. The 1978 diversity abolition bill, described above, easily passed the House of Representatives. The Committee vote recommending that it "do pass" actually was unanimous. The House Report chronicled hearings in which professors, lawyers, judges, citizens, and consumer advocates presented testimony. "[T]he vast majority . . . supported abolition of diversity jurisdiction."

The Political Opposition Mobilizes in the Senate. The Senate hearings were different. One of the most effective witnesses was the late Phoenix attorney John P. Frank, who said, "The proposal to abolish the diversity jurisdiction is, from the standpoint of the bar, approximately as popular as tuberculosis in a hospital." Mr. Frank continued:

> These proposals . . . are opposed by the appropriate governing bodies of the State Bars of Arizona, Arkansas, California, Florida, Hawaii, Illinois, Iowa, Kansas, Kentucky, Louisiana, Maine, Michigan, Missouri, New Mexico, New York (Committee on Federal Courts), Ohio, Oregon, Pennsylvania, South Dakota, Texas, Utah, Vermont, West Virginia and Wisconsin . . . ; [they are] supported by not one single state bar. . . .

The Merits of the Opposition. Mr. Frank went on to give three basic reasons for retaining diversity: (1) the disposition of 30,000 cases annually to the general satisfaction of litigants; (2) interaction between the systems with a single, unified bar; and (3) the value of lawyers having a choice:

> The first great value of diversity is its disposition of something on the order of almost 30,000 disputes a year to the general satisfaction of those who need their disposition. . . .
>
> . . . [T]he litigant who loses rarely feels with much conviction that he would have been better off in a different system.
>
> The second great plus is the educational value of having two systems in interaction. . . . The success of the federal rules has led to their widespread emulation in the states. . . .
>
> Those who would drastically cut the diversity jurisdiction . . . think . . . merely that there would be enough federal business left to permit the same effect. . . . I can only say that I do not myself think so. . . . The Federal question cases are more likely to be for specialists in antitrust or FELA or taxes. The inclusion of the full gamut of commercial and tort cases puts the whole litigation bar into federal courts.
>
> Finally, there are elements of prejudice and competence deserving to be taken into account. . . . There are other prejudices than the merely regional, and a litigant may believe that he escapes some of them in federal court. . . . Moreover, interstate prejudice is not dead. . . .
>
> The fact of the matter is that the existence of the option is advantageous to counsel and to litigants wherever it may exist. . . .
>
> [D]uring the period of Judge Ritter's life, lawyers in Salt Lake City tended to move toward the State side where they could to avoid the problems of dealing with Judge Ritter. . . .
>
> . . . The fact is that since Senator Percy had taken over and improved merit selection in Chicago, . . . [t]he Federal district courts in Chicago have been vastly improved. The lawyers want the option, where possible, in getting before those admirable high-quality judges where they can. . . .

Responsive Arguments Favoring Abolition. Professor Charles Alan Wright was one of the principal speakers in response to Mr. Frank's arguments. He explained that his opposition to an earlier abolition bill had been overtaken by events:

> I think the world has changed since 1963. I did support diversity in 1963. I favor its abolition now....
>
> Mr. Frank, if I understood him ... seemed to put his greatest emphasis on the concept of one bar and that we need diversity in order to have lawyers who will be going back and forth between State and Federal courts....
>
> I agree with him. I do not want a Federal bar of specialists or an elitist bar. I do not think that is any longer a problem. I think it may very well have been a problem in 1963....
>
> Mr. Frank talked about people. His concern is with the person who ... will have to wait a long time if the choice is not available....
>
> I am concerned about people also. I am concerned with people who want to take advantage of laws that Congress has passed in the last 15 years, giving rights that did not exist.... I want them to be able to get to trial....
>
> Mr. Frank remembers only one case in his own practice in which there was any serious question about whether there was diversity. But his practice surely must be unique....
>
> I know, as a person who has to read all the cases every year and write about them, that litigants are making mistakes repeatedly on whether or not there is Federal jurisdiction. Even when it turns out there has not been a mistake, judges are having to take the time to [decide] ... whether diversity exists....
>
> Counsel said that we would be reducing the time spent in a civil procedure course. I had two [law students] sitting next to me who are taking a civil procedure course this year here in Washington—and who hope you will pass the bill before the final examination—who said that it gets to the heart of the matter. [Laughter.]

The Senate did not pass the relevant legislation. Since 1978, no bill for the reform or abolition of diversity has passed either House.

David Crump, *The Case for Restricting Diversity Jurisdiction: The Undeveloped Arguments, from the Race to the Bottom to the Substitution Effect*

62 Maine L. Rev. 1 (2010)

[This article is an effort to add to the traditional arguments against diversity contained in the preceding materials. It summarizes the arguments developed there, but it also adds others that the author says are undeveloped by the traditional debate.—Eds.]

. . . Diversity jurisdiction cannot do much to achieve its alleged purposes. As the traditional arguments indicate, the judge is a local citizen, and so are the jurors. The assumption that these local citizens will be differently biased, merely because the courthouse in which they sit is a few blocks from the state courthouse, has little to commend it. Second, the law of diversity defeats its own purposes, because it does not allow for a federal forum when diversity is incomplete. Thus, the federal courthouse closes whenever a local plaintiff joins any local citizen as one of multiple defendants, even if a diverse defendant is the real target. In that situation, if local prejudice really were a valid concern, one would expect that the diverse defendant would need a federal forum even more than in cases with complete diversity, because, by hypothesis, the judge and jury would be infected by xenophobia, and the two local citizens would collaborate strategically to direct all biases at the foreigner. Third, the plaintiff can usually destroy diversity by the simple device of adding superfluous defendants who happen to be local citizens: a strategy that creates its own pathologies. And fourth, communications and mobility today are vastly different than they were at the time of the nation's founding, or even a few years ago; and as a result, an inhabitant of Los Angeles is likely to have more in common with a Bostonian of similar characteristics than either would have with a co-citizen of different social status or lifestyle.

The traditional arguments against diversity also feature the complexity inherent in the jurisprudence of diversity, which involves expenditures of private and judicial resources that do not advance dispute resolution on the merits. Then too, the traditional arguments emphasize the friction between state and federal laws that diversity creates. Furthermore, there is the argument that diversity contributes to delay and crowding in the federal courts, so that litigants with true federal claims cannot have their suits heard promptly.

These arguments have merit, but this Article [seeks] to demonstrate that the traditional debate has left other arguments undeveloped. It has failed adequately to examine the dysfunctional incentives that diversity jurisdiction brings about. For example, there is the Race to the Bottom that results when a litigant with a weak case deliberately selects the more arbitrary forum precisely because arbitrariness is an advantage for the party that anticipates a loss on the merits. [The lawyer who ought to lose, in other words, will file in federal court or file in state court or remove or not remove, all strategically, by selecting the *most dysfunctional* court, with the hope that arbitrariness will enhance the likelihood that the case will not produce the result that it should; i.e., diversity results in a "race to the bottom."]

Then, too, diversity jurisdiction creates a motivation for plaintiffs to add superfluous defendants: parties against which these plaintiffs really have no desire of recovery, but which they add merely to destroy diversity. [Thus, a plaintiff wanting to keep the case in state court, as plaintiffs typically do, will sue the manufacturer, which is a citizen of another state, but will also join a local distributor, even though the manufacturer is probably [a] guilty defendant and is solvent; the local defendant's joinder, then, is motivated solely by the tactic of destroying diversity.] This Article refers to this result as Harassing the Little Guy.

Also, the increased cost of federal litigation gives an edge to obstructionists. This advantage goes to the kind of party that this Article calls the Passive-Aggressive Litigant. [This means that the party who will benefit from the opportunity to impose costs by dragging its feet may be more likely to remove.] And finally, the transition to federal court induces new kinds of bias, so that many lawyers for institutional parties in personal injury or employment litigation routinely remove these cases, believing that the result will be what this Article labels a Tilted Playing Field against individual plaintiffs. [In other words, if defendants usually benefit from greater cost and delay, as they arguably do, they will tend to remove to federal court. The argument, in other words, is that diversity can be anti-plaintiff in some instances.]

In addition, the traditional debate understates how much diversity jurisdiction distorts the substantive law. It increases the number of removals, and removals are inherently prone to distortion. They create what this article refers to as the Twilight Zone Effect, which arises when two different kinds of trial courts handle the same litigation. [The article provides examples of distortion of the issues created in various kinds of cases by removal because of the duality of jurisdiction.] And in spite of the Erie Doctrine [which is the subject of the next Chapter of this Casebook, and which requires federal courts to apply state substantive law in diversity cases], diversity jurisdiction results in frustrating state policy. [The article provides examples of cases in which federal courts did not seriously try to follow state law as they were required to.]

The abolition of general diversity jurisdiction of the kind featured in Section 1332 would not mean the abolition of all jurisdiction founded on diversity. There are reasons other than local prejudice that can support the grant of power to federal courts. [The article gives examples of widely dispersed litigation such as that following a mass disaster, class actions that affect nationwide claims but are concentrated in state forums chosen by plaintiff's lawyers for pro-plaintiff bias, and very large litigation of a kind that can benefit from the judge's having two law clerks and numerous interns, such as a $10 million piece of litigation. Each of these situations is, or has been considered as, the basis for federal jurisdiction based on diversity.]

In suits of average or even modestly large size, however, the dysfunctional incentives and distortions brought about by diversity jurisdiction significantly outweigh any conceivable benefits. The newer arguments developed in this Article show that federal power should be confined to cases in which its exercise serves purposes other than those attributed in the distant past to diversity jurisdiction, and it should be authorized only in situations in which it causes fewer disadvantages. Today, more than ever, there are persuasive arguments for the abolition or retrenchment of the general diversity statute.

[2] Reforming Diversity: Notes and Questions

(1) *"Reform" Rather Than Abolition?* Congress could reduce diversity jurisdiction without abolishing it. *See* Baker, *The History and Tradition of the Amount in Controversy Requirement: A Proposal to Up the Ante in Diversity Jurisdiction*, 102 F.R.D. 299

(1984). One way would be to increase the amount in controversy. This change has a sound historical basis: The original diversity statute required no amount in controversy; later, more than $3,000 was required, then $10,000, then $50,000; and today, the amount is $75,000, although it will be eroded by inflation over the years. Would there be advantages in an increase in the amount in controversy to $100,000 or $250,000, or $1 million (which a sizeable percentage of federal complaints already allege)?

(2) *Disenabling Local Plaintiffs from Using Diversity.* A local defendant is prohibited from removing because the policy of preventing local prejudice does not apply. Should Congress extend the same rule to original filings, by providing that a local plaintiff may not file a diversity suit in a state of which he is a citizen? The ALI has proposed this change.

(3) *Multi-Party, Multi-State Litigation.* There have been numerous proposals for the creation of federal jurisdiction in complex litigation involving multiple litigants scattered throughout the United States or foreign countries. Congress could authorize multi-state, multi-party federal jurisdiction with minimal diversity, perhaps with a significant amount-in-controversy requirement, and provide for nationwide service to avoid fragmented litigation. *See generally* American Law Institute, *Study of the Division of Jurisdiction Between State and Federal Courts* (1969) [hereinafter cited as ALI] for this and other proposals discussed here. [This proposal also addresses problems of personal jurisdiction, and it therefore is discussed in Chapter 2, § VII, above. But it should be reconsidered here, since it concerns the reform of diversity jurisdiction.]

(4) *Congress Has Acted on This Problem in a Limited Way: The Multiparty, Multiforum Jurisdiction Act*, 28 U.S.C. § 1369 (2002). Congress has addressed the problem of diffuse defendants, but only in narrow circumstances. The Multiparty, Multiforum Jurisdiction Act extends federal jurisdiction to a mass accident case with minimal diversity, but only if "at least 75 natural persons have died in the accident at a discrete location." Should Congress broaden this kind of jurisdiction?

[C] Reform of "Arising Under" Jurisdiction: Notes and Questions

(1) *Extending "Arising Under" Jurisdiction to Defenses and Counterclaims.* The ALI also has proposed that removal be authorized on the basis of a federal defense or counterclaim. Does this proposal have merit?

(2) *Reforming Supplemental Jurisdiction by Legislative Reversal of the Result in Owen Equipment & Erection Co. v. Kroger.* Recall that, in *Owen*, the plaintiff asserted a claim against a third-party defendant that all parties believed was diverse. Later, the surprise revelation that it was not diverse led to the reversal of an otherwise legitimate judgment for plaintiff—and to possible destruction of the claim by limitations. Should Congress legislatively reverse the result in *Owen*? (Note that, in § 1367(b), Congress actually carried forward and preserved the *Owen* result.)

Chapter 4

The *Erie* Doctrine

I. State Law in the Federal Courts: The *Erie* Doctrine

[A] State Substantive Law

Note on How to Read the Erie *Case*

The Erie Question. When a federal court hears a diversity case, the claim actually arises under state law. How should a federal court go about deciding a state law claim? Should it follow the decisions of the supreme court of that state? Or should it try to follow the majority rule among the states, or infer the proper rule from principles of federal law? The differences could be significant.

Background: The Rules of Decision Act and the Older Case of Swift v. Tyson, 41 U.S. (16 Pet.) 1 (1842). The first Congress passed the Rules of Decision Act as part of the Judiciary Act of 1789, which provided that "the laws of the several states" would provide the rules of decision except when federal law required otherwise. It might seem that this enactment would solve the problem. But it did not. In *Swift v. Tyson*, the Supreme Court held that state "laws" did not include all of what we today think of as laws. In particular, the decisions of state courts were not "laws." As the Court put it, court decisions "are, at most, only evidence of what the laws are, and are not of themselves laws.... The laws of a state are more usually understood to mean the rules or enactments promulgated by the legislative authority thereof," or laws affecting purely local matters such as property titles. And what was to be the rule of decision in other matters? "General" law, said the Court—meaning that a federal judge would determine what he thought state common law was or should be, by looking to the decisions nationwide.

Tompkins' Suit Against the Erie Railroad. Erie R.R. v. Tompkins, 304 U.S. 64 (1938), which overruled *Swift v. Tyson*, is by far the most celebrated American choice-of-law case. The *Erie* case began sometime after two o'clock in the morning in Hughestown, Pennsylvania, when William Colwell heard a voice shouting that there had been an accident. The story is wonderfully told by Irving Younger, in Younger, *What Happened in Erie*, 56 Texas L. Rev. 1011 (1978):(*)

> "Don't go," said his wife. "Them fellows are crazy." But William Colwell went. He found a man crumpled against the outside rail [of the Erie line]. Between the rails lay the man's severed arm. The man was his neighbor, Harry James Tompkins....
>
> An ambulance soon arrived and took Tompkins to the hospital. The stump of his arm was amputated.... After leaving the hospital, he went in search of a lawyer.

The lawyer Tompkins hired was Bernard Nemeroff, of New York City, whose father had recommended him to Tompkins. Nemeroff learned that Tompkins had been hit by something protruding from a train—"a black object that looked like a door," as Tompkins would later testify at trial—while walking a path that ran parallel to the tracks. Younger continues the story:

> Nemeroff and his colleagues reasoned that it was not enough to prove that the railroad carelessly had permitted a door to swing loose on a moving freight car. The real question was whether the railroad owed a duty to guard against that specific kind of carelessness. Nemeroff's research disclosed that, under the Pennsylvania cases, a traveler, like Tompkins, on a parallel (or "longitudinal") path is regarded as a trespasser, to whom the railroad owes a duty merely to avoid wanton negligence. Since Tompkins could not prove wanton negligence, to sue in the Pennsylvania courts was to invite disaster. Happily, there were alternatives.
>
> Tompkins was a citizen of Pennsylvania. The Erie Railroad was a New York Corporation.... [T]he case would lie in a United States district

> court. . . . More research. More time in the library. More No. 2 pencils worn to a stub on yellow pads. And they found what they were looking for. . . .
>
> "[G]eneral" law supplied the rule of decision in a federal diversity case [according to the then-controlling rule of *Swift v. Tyson*]. And "general" law, Nemeroff and his colleagues found, in the sense of the "majority" rule, was contrary to the rule in Pennsylvania. A railroad, held most cases outside Pennsylvania, owed a duty of ordinary care to a traveler, like Tompkins, on a parallel or "longitudinal" footpath.
>
> Then into a federal court! . . .

Tompkins' lawyers did, indeed, file suit in a federal District Court. At trial, the railroad's lawyer was Theodore Kiendl, of New York's Davis, Polk, Wardwell, Gardiner & Reed. He moved to dismiss after the plaintiff's proof on the ground that "this permissive pathway doctrine is not applicable in this case under the decisions of the highest courts of Pennsylvania." The judge refused. Following "general" law, over Kiendl's objection, he instead instructed the jury that the railroad had a duty to use reasonable care. The jury returned a verdict for Tompkins, finding $30,000 in damages. The Court of Appeals affirmed. Kiendl petitioned for certiorari. Because the Supreme Court takes only a small percentage of cases presented to it (very few of which are negligence cases), it must have been surprising to all concerned when the Court accepted *Erie v. Tompkins* for review.

Erie in the Supreme Court. In his brief in the Supreme Court, Kiendl avoided making a direct attack on *Swift v. Tyson.* It seemed better to argue that *Swift* had been misapplied than to ask the Court to overrule a case that it had reaffirmed repeatedly for almost a century. But the oral argument showed that some members of the Court were considering a change. The rule of *Swift v. Tyson* had a number of disadvantages. First, *Swift v. Tyson* made differences in result depend, unfairly, on whether the parties had diverse citizenship. Secondly, it encouraged people in Tompkins' position to go to extraordinary lengths to shop for forums. And third, it meant that federal decisions unnecessarily frustrated the deliberately chosen policies of the states. These considerations helped to shape the Court's opinion in *Erie.*

Read 28 U.S.C. § 1652 (the Rules of Decision Act).

Erie Railroad v. Tompkins

304 U.S. 64 (1938)

Mr. Justice Brandeis delivered the opinion of the Court.

The question for decision is whether the oft-challenged doctrine of *Swift v. Tyson* shall now be disapproved.

Tompkins, a citizen of Pennsylvania, was injured on a dark night by a passing freight train of the Erie Railroad Company while walking along its right of way at

Hughestown in that State. He claimed that the accident occurred through negligence in the operation, or maintenance, of the train; that he was rightfully on the premises as licensee because on a commonly used beaten footpath which ran for a short distance alongside the tracks; and that he was struck by something which looked like a door projecting from one of the moving cars. To enforce that claim he brought an action in the federal court for southern New York, which had jurisdiction because the company is a corporation of that State. It denied liability; and the case was tried by a jury.

The Erie insisted that its duty to Tompkins was no greater than that owed to a trespasser. It contended, among other things, that its duty to Tompkins, and hence its liability, should be determined in accordance with the Pennsylvania law; that under the law of Pennsylvania, as declared by its highest court, persons who use pathways along the railroad right of way—that is a longitudinal pathway as distinguished from a crossing—are to be deemed trespassers; and that the railroad is not liable for injuries to undiscovered trespassers resulting from its negligence, unless it be wanton or willful. Tompkins . . . contended that . . . the railroad's duty and liability is to be determined in federal courts as a matter of general law.

The trial judge refused to rule that the applicable law precluded recovery. The jury brought in a verdict of $30,000; and the judgment entered thereon was affirmed by the Circuit Court of Appeals, which held that it was unnecessary to consider whether the law of Pennsylvania was [as] contended, because the question was one not of local, but of general, law and that "upon questions of general law the federal courts are free, in the absence of a local statute, to exercise their independent judgment as to what the law is. . . ."

The Erie had contended that application of the Pennsylvania rule was required, among other things, by [the Rules of Decision Act], which provides:

> The laws of the several States, except where the Constitution, treaties, or statutes of the United States otherwise require or provide, shall be regarded as rules of decision in trials at common law, in the courts of the United States, in cases where they apply. . . .

First. Swift v. Tyson, 16 Pet. 1, 18, held that federal courts exercising jurisdiction on the ground of diversity of citizenship need not, in matters of general jurisprudence, apply the unwritten law of the State as declared by its highest court; that they are free to exercise an independent judgment as to what the common law of the State is—or should be. . . .

. . . The federal courts assumed, in the broad field of "general law," the power to declare rules of decision which Congress was confessedly without power to enact as statutes. Doubt was repeatedly expressed as to the correctness of the construction given [the Act] and as to the soundness of the rule which it introduced. But it was the more recent research of a competent scholar, who examined the original document, which established that the construction given to it by the Court was erroneous; and that the purpose of the section was . . . to make certain that . . . the federal courts exercising jurisdiction in diversity of citizenship cases would apply as their rules of decision the law of the State, unwritten as well as written.[(5)]

Criticism of the doctrine became widespread after the decision of *Black & White Taxicab Co. v. Brown & Yellow Taxicab Co.*, 276 U.S. 518. There, Brown and Yellow, a Kentucky corporation owned by Kentuckians, and the Louisville and Nashville Railroad, also a Kentucky corporation, wished that the former should have the exclusive privilege of soliciting passenger and baggage transportation at the Bowling Green, Kentucky, railroad station; and that the Black and White, a competing Kentucky corporation, should be prevented from interfering with that privilege. Knowing that such a contract would be void under the common law of Kentucky [which prohibited monopoly], it was arranged that the Brown and Yellow reincorporate under the law of Tennessee, and that the contract with the railroad should be executed there. The suit was then brought by the Tennessee corporation in the federal court for western Kentucky to enjoin competition by the Black and White; an injunction issued by the District Court was sustained by the Court of Appeals; and this Court, citing many decisions in which the doctrine of *Swift v. Tyson* had been applied, affirmed the decree. [Note that this result frustrated the policy of Kentucky against monopolies—Eds.]

Second. Experience in applying the doctrine of *Swift v. Tyson*, had revealed its defects, political and social; and the benefits expected to flow from the rule did not accrue. Persistence of state courts in their own opinions on questions of common law prevented uniformity; and the impossibility of discovering a satisfactory line of demarcation between the province of general law and that of local law developed a new well of uncertainties.

On the other hand, the mischievous results of the doctrine had become apparent. Diversity of citizenship jurisdiction was conferred in order to prevent apprehended discrimination in state courts against those not citizens of the State. *Swift v. Tyson* introduced grave discrimination by non-citizens against citizens. It made rights enjoyed under the unwritten "general law" vary according to whether enforcement was sought in the state or in the federal court; and the privilege of selecting the court . . . was conferred upon the non-citizen. . . .

In part the discrimination resulted from the wide range of persons held entitled to avail themselves of the federal rule by resort to the diversity of citizenship jurisdiction [*i.e.*, to forum-shop]. Through this jurisdiction individual citizens willing to remove from their own State and become citizens of another might avail themselves of the federal rule. And, without even change of residence, a corporate citizen of the State could avail itself of the federal rule by re-incorporating under the laws of another State, as was done in the *Taxicab* case.

(5) Charles Warren, *New Light on the History of the Federal Judiciary Act of 1789* (1923) 37 Harv. L. Rev. 49, 51-52, 81-88, 108.

. . . If only a question of statutory construction were involved, we should not be prepared to abandon a doctrine so widely applied throughout nearly a century. But the unconstitutionality of the course pursued has now been made clear and compels us to do so.

Third. Except in matters governed by the Federal Constitution or by Acts of Congress, the law to be applied in any case is the law of the State. And whether the law of the State shall be declared by its Legislature in a statute or by its highest court in a decision is not a matter of federal concern. There is no federal general common law. Congress has no power to declare substantive rules of common law applicable in a State whether they be local in their nature or "general," be they commercial law or a part of the law of torts. And no clause in the Constitution purports to confer such a power upon the federal courts. . . .

. . . Thus the doctrine of *Swift v. Tyson* is, as Mr. Justice Holmes said, "an unconstitutional assumption of powers by courts of the United States which no lapse of time or respectable array of opinion should make us hesitate to correct." . . .

Fourth. . . . The Circuit Court of Appeals ruled that the question of liability is one of general law; and on that ground declined to decide the issue of state law. As we hold this was error, the judgment is reversed and the case remanded to it for further proceedings in conformity with our opinion.

Mr. Justice Butler. . . .

No constitutional question was suggested or argued below or here. And as a general rule, this Court will not consider any question not raised below and presented by the petition. . . .

The course pursued by the Court in this case is repugnant to the Act of Congress of August 24, 1937, 50 Stat. 751. It declares:

> That whenever the constitutionality of any Act of Congress affecting the public interest is drawn in question in any court of the United States . . . , the court having jurisdiction of the suit or proceeding shall certify such fact to the Attorney General. In any such case the court shall permit the United States to intervene and become a party. . . .

I am of opinion that the constitutional validity of the rule need not be considered, because under the law, as found by the courts of Pennsylvania and generally throughout the country, it is plain that the evidence required a finding that plaintiff was guilty of negligence that contributed to cause his injuries and that the judgment below should be reversed upon that ground.

Mr. Justice McReynolds concurs in this opinion.

Mr. Justice Reed.

I concur in the conclusion reached in this case, in the disapproval of the doctrine of *Swift v. Tyson*, and in the reasoning of the majority opinion except in so far as it relies upon the unconstitutionality of the "course pursued" by the federal courts.

To decide the case now before us and to "disapprove" the doctrine of *Swift v. Tyson* requires only that we say that the words "the laws" include in their meaning the decisions of the local tribunals. As the majority opinion shows, . . . this Court is now of the view that "laws" includes "decisions," it is unnecessary to go further and declare that the "course pursued" was "unconstitutional," instead of merely erroneous.

. . . If the opinion commits this Court to the position that the Congress is without power to declare what rules of substantive law shall govern the federal courts, that conclusion also seems questionable. The line between procedural and substantive law is hazy but no one doubts federal power over procedure. *Wayman v. Southard*, 10 Wheat. 1. . . .

Notes and Questions

(1) *The Basis of the Erie Decision: The Constitution(?)* Notice that Justice Brandeis purports to base the decision on the Constitution: "[T]he [federal] courts have invaded rights which in our opinion are reserved by the Constitution to the several states." This passage seems to base the decision on the Tenth Amendment, which says that undelegated powers are reserved to the states or to the people. But elsewhere Brandeis says that "Congress has no power to declare substantive rules of common law applicable in a state. . . . And no clause in the Constitution purports to confer such a power upon the federal courts." This language seems to rest the decision on Articles I and III, which create the powers of Congress and of the judiciary. The lack of a citation to the Constitution may reveal a weakness in the opinion. In fact, the constitutional reasoning has been attacked as "dictum" or even "hyperbole." C. Wright & M. Kane, *The Law of Federal Courts* 382-84 (6th ed. 2002) (quoting sources). Note that Justice Reed concurred in the holding but refused to accept its constitutional basis. Is Justice Reed correct?

(2) *The Constitutional Basis: What Difference Does It Make?* Might there be instances in which it would be desirable for Congress to specify rules other than state law as rules of decision in diversity cases? In that event, a constitutional holding could prevent necessary action by Congress. (Of course, that is the purpose of a constitution, but it is also the reason why constitutions should not be read too expansively.) If you have difficulty seeing what problems the constitutional language might cause, see *Sibbach v. Wilson & Co.* and *Hanna v. Plumer*, which appear later in this chapter. *See also* Hill, *The Erie Doctrine and the Constitution*, 53 Nw. U. L. Rev. 427 (1958).

(3) *The Aftermath of Erie: Irving Younger's History.* In *What Happened in Erie*, 56 Texas L. Rev. 1011 (1978), Irving Younger continues his story:(*)

> . . . Chief Justice Hughes[, during the Court's conference after argument,] opened discussion with the comment, "If we wish to overrule *Swift v. Tyson*, here is our opportunity." It quickly appeared that all but Butler and McReynolds agreed the time had come. . . .

Justices Butler and McReynolds, were too well known in history to need introduction by Younger, but we should add a word about them here. They were two of the "Four Horsemen," so called because of their votes against New Deal legislation. Several of the Horsemen were former railroad lawyers, and it is wonderfully ironic to see two of their number passionately arguing that a railroad should be held negligent. They asserted (as Wright puts it, "with what must have been glee") that the Court's decision was illegal, since it was made without notice to the Attorney General. C. Wright, *The Law of Federal Courts* 354-55 (4th ed. 1983). Younger's narrative continues:

> . . . [F]or a time after the Supreme Court's decision on April 25, it seemed that no one outside the profession would ever hear of [*Erie v. Tompkins*]. . . . [N]o general newspaper mentioned it. On Wednesday, April 27, Felix Frankfurter wrote to President Roosevelt:
>
> I certainly didn't expect to live to see the day when the Court would announce, as they did on Monday, that it itself has usurped power for nearly a hundred years. And think of not a single New York paper . . . having a nose for the significance of the decision.
>
> The silence persisted. On May 2, 1938, Justice Stone wrote privately to Arthur Krock of the New York Times. . . . On May 3, Krock devoted his column to *Erie v. Tompkins*, heading it "A Momentous Decision of the Supreme Court." . . . The dam had broken, and the flood has yet to recede. . . .
>
> [Later, it was discovered that the district judge, Judge Samuel Mandelbaum, whose first case on the trial bench had been *Erie v. Tompkins*, had written a marginal note in his copy of volume 304 of the United States reports, adjacent to Justice Brandeis's discussion of the trial court's ruling.] There, . . . in his own unique syntax, Samuel Mandelbaum wrote as follows: "Because the *Swift Tyson* case although before this I never knew of its existence to be truthful and for the confusion the decision brought about, it might have been better to leave it alone and stand by good old Swifty."

See also Note, *Swift v. Tyson Exhumed*, 79 Yale L.J. 284 (1969).

(4) *Why Law Professors Love Erie.* The "confusion" part of Judge Mandelbaum's statement is accurate, as you will see in the next few sections of this chapter. But it is hard to agree with his sentiment for keeping *Swift v. Tyson.* The *Erie* decision, for all its faults, has seemed clearly right to generations of lawyers. It is a case, like *International Shoe*, that you will remember the rest of your life; and it is a case to be savored and enjoyed.

(5) *What Erie Decided.* The *Erie* holding is deceptively simple. In a diversity case, the District Court follows state substantive law. But several problems are concealed

in this formulation of the holding, and they are taken up in the sections of this chapter. In this regard, we offer the following "Chapter Summary Problem," which you may read now but should answer at the end of the chapter (or, as always, you should use it as your instructor directs).

Problem A: Chapter 4 Summary Problem

AN ARGUABLE CONFLICT BETWEEN THE FEDERAL RULES OF CIVIL PROCEDURE AND A STATE MEDICAL MALPRACTICE STATUTE. John Payne sued his physician, Dr. Thomas Manson, for personal injury and medical malpractice in a state court of the (hypothetical) State of West York. Dr. Manson removed the case to federal court. The State of West York has enacted statutes concerning malpractice suits against health care professionals, ostensibly aimed at "curtailing the filing of frivolous lawsuits against health care professionals and thereby curtailing rising medical costs related to malpractice insurance and litigation." One of these provisions requires: "(A) If a claim against a health professional is asserted in a civil action, the claimant shall certify in a written statement that is filed and served with the claim, whether or not expert testimony is necessary to prove the health care professional's standard of care or liability for the claim. (B) If the claimant certifies that expert opinion testimony is necessary, the claimant shall serve a preliminary expert opinion affidavit with the initial disclosures that are required by the State of West York Rules of Civil Procedure."

Under West York law, the preliminary expert opinion affidavit must contain the following information: "(1) The expert's qualifications to express an opinion on the health care professional's standard of care or liability for the claim; (2) The factual basis for each claim against a health care professional; (3) The health care professional's acts, errors, or omissions that the expert considers to be a violation of the applicable standard of care resulting in liability; (4) The manner in which the health care professional's acts, errors, or omissions caused or contributed to the damages or other relief sought by the claimant." West York law further provides that: "The court, on its own motion or the motion of the health care professional, shall dismiss the claim against the health care professional without prejudice if the claimant fails to file and serve a preliminary expert opinion affidavit after the claimant has certified that an affidavit is necessary or the court has ordered the claimant to file and serve an affidavit."

Defendant Manson filed a motion to dismiss the complaint because Plaintiff Payne did not comply with these West York provisions requiring a preliminary expert opinion affidavit. Defendant Manson argues that under the *Erie* doctrine, the federal court, sitting in diversity, must apply state substantive law and federal procedural law. Plaintiff Payne argues that the West York statutes requiring this affidavit do not apply because they are procedural provisions that conflict with federal discovery rules of procedure, specifically Federal Rule of Civil Procedure 26. Fed. R. Civ. P. 26 guides pretrial discovery information gathering. Subdivision (a)(1) requires a party, without making a discovery request, to make initial disclosures of their own supporting evidence. Subsection (a)(2) provides for disclosures of expert testimony. In particular, Rule 26(a)(2) provides that at least 90 days before trial, or when otherwise directed by the court, each party must disclose their expert witnesses who are retained to present expert testimony in the case, accompanied by a written report prepared and signed by the witness containing a complete statement of all opinions to be expressed and the basis and reasons therefor [as well as several other items detailed in the federal Rule].

How should the court rule on Defendant Manson's motion to dismiss? In answering this question, you might consider the following issues:

1. Does state law, or federal law, control the question?
2. How is the answer affected by the existence of Federal Rule of Civil Procedure 26?
3. Is there any incentive for a plaintiff to file in federal court and thereby escape the preliminary expert opinion affidavit that would be required in state court?
4. In the actual case upon which this Summary Problem is based, the court held that the administration of state medical malpractice claims should be the same in both federal and state courts, and therefore, in both courts, a defendant could bring a motion to dismiss the claim as frivolous based on the failure of the plaintiff to file a preliminary expert opinion affidavit. How could the court justify this conclusion in light of *Hanna v. Plumer*?
5. Would the result be the same if the alleged malpractice occurred in another state, the state of Texafornia, although the suit is in West York?
6. What does the federal court do to decide the meaning and importance of the West York statute if there is no decision of the West York Supreme Court interpreting the statute?

[B] Federal Procedural Law

Read 28 U.S.C. §§ 2071, 2072–2074 (the Rules Enabling Act and local rules provision).

Note on the Federal Rules: Their Source and Legitimacy

Federal Procedures: The Federal Rules and the Rules Enabling Act. The Rules Enabling Act, 28 U.S.C. § 2072, provides that the Supreme Court "shall have the power to prescribe general rules of practice and procedure . . . for cases in the [federal courts]." The Act also states, however, that the rules "shall not abridge, enlarge or modify any substantive right." The Supreme Court must transmit proposed rules to Congress by May 1 to allow Congress to act on them, if it chooses, before they take effect, no earlier than December 1 of that year. It is by this process that the Federal Rules of Civil Procedure were adopted in 1938 and are amended.

The Permissible Scope of Federal Procedural Rules: Sibbach v. Wilson & Co., 312 U.S. 1 (1941). The *Erie* doctrine, the Rules Enabling Act, and the substance-procedure distinction all came together shortly after *Erie*, in *Sibbach v. Wilson & Co.* Plaintiff Sibbach brought a diversity suit for personal injuries in a federal court in Illinois. The District Court ordered Sibbach to submit to a medical examination. Although Fed. R. Civ. P. 35 expressly authorized the District Court to make this order, Sibbach refused to comply and pointed out that Illinois state courts had a policy against requiring examinations. She argued that the Rules Enabling Act meant that the court could not change any "substantial" or "important" right that state law gave her, including the right under Illinois law to refuse medical examination.

The Supreme Court disagreed: "The asserted right . . . is no more important than many other [procedural] rights. . . . The test must be whether a rule really regulates procedure. . . ." Four Justices dissented in an opinion written by Justice Frankfurter. The Federal Rule, he said, affected the "inviolability of a person" and was a "drastic change" from previous policy. But the majority ordered the examination.

II. The Substance-Procedure Distinction

Note on the Supreme Court's Varying Approaches to the Substance-Procedure Problem

A Confusing Area of Civil Procedure. The deceptive simplicity of the *Erie* holding contrasts sharply with the confusion in the cases that interpret it. Remember: The court follows state substantive law and federal procedural law. The confusion has arisen primarily when the Supreme Court has tried to tell the difference. The distinction is almost metaphysical, and the Court has contributed to the difficulty by inventing new tests without overruling old ones.

The Approaches. It may be a good idea to sketch some of the approaches in advance, together with the cases in which you will see them at work.

(1) *Outcome Determination:* One early test was based upon whether a given rule was "outcome determinative." If it was likely to make a difference in the result, a rule was probably "substantive"—even if it "looked like" a procedural rule. (This famous test comes from *Guaranty Trust Co. v. York*, which is the next case.)

(2) *"Absolute" Outcome Determination:* A later case confined the outcome determination test to rules that had a "strong" likelihood or even a "certainty" of affecting the outcome (*Byrd v. Blue Ridge Rural Elec. Cooperative Inc.*, below).

(3) *The Interest Balancing Approach:* Several cases classify substance and procedure by the strength of the competing state and federal policies underlying the different rules in question (*Byrd v. Blue Ridge*). For instance, if the

state's policy is definite and important, and the federal interest is slight, this approach would lead to enforcement of the state rule.

(4) *Deference to a Controlling Federal Rule:* Certain other cases say that there should be deference to controlling provisions in the Federal Rules (*Hanna v. Plumer,* below).

(5) *The Policies-of-Erie Approach:* Finally, some cases indicate that the ultimate test really lies in the policies of *Erie.* Thus, if the application of federal law would produce irrational differences in results and encourage forum shopping, the matter is substantive; if not, it is procedural (*Hanna v. Plumer*).

None of these approaches has been clearly overruled. There can be no pretense that the decisions are consistent or predictable.

An Analogy. The will-o'-the-wisp distinction between substance and procedure calls for an analogy. In an elementary physics class, students would be introduced to two apparently inconsistent theories about the phenomenon that we know as "light." The "particle" theory describes light as particles called photons. This theory is useful to describe some characteristics of light (*e.g.*, the "photoelectric effect": the generation of electric current by light). The "wave" theory instead sees light as electromagnetic waves, and it is useful in describing other phenomena (*e.g.*, color). Which theory is the "correct" one? The answer is that both of them are, and yet neither is. In an attempt to describe a unique property of the universe, the physicists have invented crude models. And so, it is with the substance-procedure distinction. The *Erie* doctrine is a complex idea, almost like a unique property of nature, and it cannot be fully described by any single formula.

[A] The "Outcome Determinative" Test

Guaranty Trust Co. v. York

326 U.S. 99 (1945)

[Guaranty was trustee for certain noteholders of Van Swearingen Corporation, including York. In a diversity action brought in a federal court in New York, York sued Guaranty, claiming that Guaranty had breached its fiduciary duties to the noteholders, including York, by cooperating in a plan to rehabilitate the financially troubled Van Swearingen Corporation by permitting the purchase of the notes for 50% of their face value and shares of stock in the Van Swearingen Corporation. The trial court granted summary judgment in favor of Guaranty.]

[On appeal, the Court of Appeals held that the trial court was not required to apply the New York statute of limitations that would govern breach of fiduciary duty cases in New York State courts, because the suit was on the "equity side" of the federal district court (*i.e.*, breach of fiduciary duty was an equitable claim). The Supreme Court granted certiorari to determine whether the New York statute governed the time for bringing the breach of trust claim, rather than equity jurisprudence.]

MR. JUSTICE FRANKFURTER delivered the opinion of the Court. . . .

Our starting point must be the policy of federal jurisdiction which *Erie R. Co. v. Tompkins*, 304 U.S. 64, embodies. In overruling *Swift v. Tyson*, 16 Pet. 1, *Erie R. Co. v. Tompkins* did not merely overrule a venerable case. It overruled a particular way of looking at law . . . . Law was conceived as a "brooding omnipresence" of Reason, of which decisions were merely evidence and not themselves the controlling formulations. Accordingly, federal courts deemed themselves free to ascertain what Reason, and therefore Law, required, wholly independent of authoritatively declared State law, even in cases where a legal right as the basis for relief was created by State authority. . . .

Partly because the States in the early days varied greatly in the manner in which equitable relief was afforded and in the extent to which it was available, . . . Congress provided that "the forms and modes of proceeding in suits . . . of equity" would conform to the settled uses of courts of equity. § 2, 1 Stat. 275, 276, 28 U.S.C. § 723. But this enactment gave the federal courts no power that they would not have had in any event. . . . [C]ongress never gave, nor did the federal courts ever claim, the power to deny substantive rights created by State law or to create substantive rights denied by State law. . . .

Matters of "substance" and matters of "procedure" are much talked about in the books as though they defined a great divide cutting across the whole domain of law. But, of course, "substance" and "procedure" are the same keywords to very different problems. Neither "substance" nor "procedure" represents the same invariants. Each implies different variables depending upon the particular problem for which it is used. . . .

And so the question is not whether a statute of limitations is deemed a matter of "procedure" in some sense. The question is whether such a statute concerns merely the manner and the means by which a right to recover, as recognized by the State, is enforced, or whether such statutory limitation is a matter of substance in the aspect that alone is relevant to our problem, namely, does it significantly affect the result of a litigation . . . ?

It is therefore immaterial whether statutes of limitation are characterized either as "substantive" or "procedural" in State court opinions. . . . *Erie R. Co. v. Tompkins* was not an endeavor to formulate scientific legal terminology. . . . In essence, the intent of that decision was to insure that, in all cases where a federal court is exercising jurisdiction solely because of the diversity of citizenship of the parties, the outcome of the litigation in the federal court should be substantially the same, so far as legal rules determine the outcome of a litigation, as it would be if tried in a State court. The nub of the policy that underlies *Erie R. Co. v. Tompkins* is that for the same transaction the accident of a suit by a non-resident litigant in a federal court instead of in a State court a block away should not lead to a substantially different result. . . .

Plainly enough, a statute that would completely bar recovery in a suit if brought in a State court bears on a State-created right vitally and not merely formally or negligibly. As to consequences that so intimately affect recovery or non-recovery a federal court in a diversity case should follow State law. . . . [I]f a plea of the statute of limitations would bar recovery in a State court, a federal court ought not to afford recovery. [REVERSED AND REMANDED.]

MR. JUSTICE ROBERTS and MR. JUSTICE DOUGLAS took no part in the consideration or decision of this case. [The dissenting opinion of Mr. Justice Rutledge is omitted.]

Notes and Questions

(1) *The Fundamental Flaw in the "Outcome Determinative" Test.* There is a fundamental flaw in testing the extent of the *Erie* doctrine by whether the rule in question is "outcome determinative." Can you see what the flaw is? [Note: Doesn't it destroy the possibility of meaningful rules of "procedure"? By definition, if a procedure ever makes a difference—why, then, it becomes "outcome determinative" and ceases to be procedural!] In *Byrd v. Blue Ridge*, which appears in the next section, you will see the Supreme Court refine the test.

(2) *Does York Overrule Sibbach?* In *Sibbach v. Wilson & Co.*, discussed in the preceding section, the Court held that a federal judge could order a medical examination even if a state judge could not. Is this difference between state and federal rules a difference in "outcome," since it is likely to change the amount of recovery? Does *York*, then, overrule *Sibbach*? Consider the next series of cases.

[B] Balancing State and Federal Interests

RAGAN v. MERCHANTS' TRANSFER & WAREHOUSE CO., 337 U.S. 530 (1949). Ragan filed a diversity action on September 4, 1945, in a federal court in Kansas, but did not serve the complaint on the defendant until December 28 of that year. The vehicular accident that gave rise to the suit had occurred on October 1, 1943, and since the Kansas two-year statute of limitations provided that suit was not deemed commenced until service was accomplished, Ragan's claim would have been barred if brought in the state courts. Fed. R. Civ. P. 3, however, provides: "A civil action is commenced by filing a complaint with the court." If this Rule, rather than the Kansas provision, was controlling, Ragan's suit would have been timely commenced.

The Supreme Court, by an 8 to 1 vote, held that Kansas law was applicable and that Ragan's claim was barred. The Court reasoned that the definition of commencement was "an integral part" of the Kansas statute and therefore should be given effect as a "substantive" law.

Notes and Questions

(1) *"Outcome Determination," or State-Federal "Interest Balancing"?* It is possible to argue that the Kansas rule in *Ragan* was "substantive" because it expressed a

strong state interest in forcing diligent notification of defendants. This state policy was clearly articulated by the Kansas legislature as an "integral part" of the statute of limitations. The federal rule, by contrast, did not clearly advance any distinctly federal interests contrary to the Kansas rule. *See* Leathers, *Erie and Its Progeny as Choice of Law Cases*, 11 Hous. L. Rev. 791 (1974). On the other hand, there were two companion decisions to *Ragan*, and they strengthened the perception that the outcome-determinative test was controlling.

(2) *Woods v. Interstate Realty Co.*, 337 U.S. 535 (1949). In this companion case to *Ragan*, the plaintiff had not qualified to do business in Mississippi (a requirement that included appointing an agent for service of process). A Mississippi statute provided that a foreign corporation that had not qualified "shall not be permitted to bring or maintain any action or suit in any of the courts of this state." Relying on *York*, the Supreme Court held that this law was substantive, and a foreign corporation that was not qualified could not bring a diversity action in a Mississippi federal court either. On the same day, the Court also decided *Cohen v. Beneficial Loan Corp.*, 337 U.S. 541 (1949). There, it held that a New Jersey statute requiring the plaintiff to post bond as security for costs must be applied in a federal action in New Jersey even though the parallel federal rule contained no such requirement.

(3) *The Impact of Ragan, Woods, and Cohen.* After these decisions, the principal drafter of the Federal Rules wrote that "hardly one" of the Rules could be considered safe from attack. "Many observers believed . . . that there was no longer much, if any, room for independent federal regulation of procedure." C. Wright & M. Kane, *The Law of Federal Courts* 403 (6th ed. 2002). But the signals were mixed. The opinions did not articulate a consistent reason for the results. Five members of the Court dissented in at least one of the three cases. And later, in *Byrd v. Blue Ridge Rural Elec. Cooperative, Inc.*, the Court took a different approach.

Byrd v. Blue Ridge Rural Electric Cooperative, Inc.

356 U.S. 525 (1958)

[The plaintiff brought a diversity suit in a federal court in South Carolina for injuries sustained in the course of his employment. The defendant pleaded, as a defense, that it was to be deemed the plaintiff's "statutory employer" for purposes of the South Carolina Workers' Compensation Act. This argument, if accepted, would entitle the plaintiff to workers' compensation benefits but would give the employer immunity from suit for negligence. Under the state law, which was established by the decisions of the South Carolina Supreme Court, this immunity issue was to be decided by the judge alone, without the intervention of a jury, because it was a jurisdictional requirement for the administrative agency that decided compensation claims.]

[The United States Supreme Court therefore had to decide whether South Carolina's "judge-decision only" law was substantive and applicable in federal courts, or whether it was merely procedural. The Court first decided that it should remand

Byrd's suit to enable him to develop evidence rebutting immunity. It then considered whether the immunity issue should be decided on remand in the federal court by the judge alone (as it would be in the state courts), or by a jury.]

Mr. Justice Brennan delivered the opinion of the Court. . . .

First. It was decided in *Erie R. Co. v. Tompkins* that the federal courts in diversity cases must respect the definition of state-created rights and obligations by the state courts. . . . A State may, of course, distribute the functions of its judicial machinery as it sees fit. The [South Carolina state] decisions relied upon, however, furnish no reason for selecting the judge rather than the jury [in a federal court] to decide this . . . affirmative defense in the negligence action. They simply reflect a policy . . . that administrative determination of "jurisdictional facts" should not be final but subject to judicial review. . . . We find nothing to suggest that this rule was announced as an integral part of the special relationship created by the statute. Thus the requirement appears to be merely a form and mode of enforcing the immunity, *Guaranty Trust Co. v. York*, 326 U.S. 99, 108, and not a rule intended to be bound up with the definition of the rights and obligations of the parties. . . .

Second. But cases following *Erie* have evinced a broader policy to the effect that the federal courts should conform as near as may be—in the absence of other considerations—to state rules even of form and mode where the state rules may bear substantially on the question whether the litigation would come out one way in the federal court and another way in the state court if the federal court failed to apply a particular local rule. *E.g., Guaranty Trust Co. v. York, supra.* Concededly the nature of the tribunal which tries issues may be important in the enforcement of the parcel of rights making up a cause of action or defense. . . . Therefore, were "outcome" the only consideration, a strong case might appear for saying that the federal court should follow the state practice.

But there are affirmative countervailing considerations at work here. The federal system is an independent system for administering justice to litigants who properly invoke its jurisdiction. An essential characteristic of that system is the manner in which, in civil common-law actions, it distributes trial functions between judge and jury and, under the influence—if not the command—of the Seventh Amendment, assigns the decisions of disputed questions of fact to the jury. . . . Thus the inquiry here is whether the federal policy favoring jury decisions of disputed fact questions should yield to the state rule in the interest of furthering the objective that the litigation should not come out one way in the federal court and another way in the state court.

We think that in the circumstances of this case the federal court should not follow the state rule. It cannot be gainsaid that there is a strong federal policy against allowing state rules to disrupt the judge-jury relationship in the federal courts. . . . Perhaps even more clearly in light of the influence of the Seventh Amendment, the function assigned to the jury "is an essential factor in the process for which the Federal Constitution provides." . . .

Third. We have discussed the problem upon the assumption that the outcome of the litigation may be substantially affected by whether the issue of immunity is decided by a judge or a jury. But clearly there is not present here the certainty that a different result would follow, *cf. Guaranty Trust Co. v. York, supra,* or even the strong possibility that this would be the case, *cf. Bernhardt v. Polygraphic Co.*, [350 U.S. 198.].... We do not think the likelihood of a different result is so strong as to require the federal practice of jury determination of disputed factual issues to yield to the state rule in the interest of uniformity of outcome. Reversed and remanded.

[The dissenting opinions of Justices Whittaker and Frankfurter are omitted.]

Notes and Questions

(1) *The Interest-Balancing Test: How Does It Work?* This case suggests that an interest-balancing approach determines substance or procedure: if the state's interest in the particular law is stronger, the law is substantive; if not, procedural. But there are several hidden problems in a test distinguishing substance and procedure by balancing state and federal interests. *See* Smith, *Blue Ridge and Beyond: A Byrd's Eye View of Federalism in Diversity Litigation*, 36 Tul. L. Rev. 443 (1962). First, it may be difficult to identify all of the relevant state and federal policies, particularly if they must be derived from a few words in a statute. Also, it may be impossible to compare the competing policies except in a subjective manner. To see why, you might try applying an interest-balancing test to the decisions in *Ragan*, *Woods*, and *Cohen*, and ask yourself whether the results would change.

(2) *Has the Outcome-Determinative Test Become a Requirement That the Law in Question Be "Definitively" Outcome Determinative?* The Court in *Byrd* also contains another test: it says that the substitution of a judge for a jury does not create a "certainty" of a different outcome. Elsewhere it puts the issue in terms of whether "the likelihood of a different result . . . is strong." Has the Court reformulated the outcome determinative test to require that the state rule affect the outcome in a "definitive" way? *Cf. Boggs v. Blue Diamond Coal Co.*, 497 F. Supp. 1105, 1120 (E.D. Ky. 1980) (a substantive state rule is one "which, if all the facts were stipulated, would be meaningful in analyzing the rights and liabilities of parties to a dispute if they were to settle it on the day of filing suit, taking into account the necessity of filing suit, but without actually filing it").

(3) *Bernhardt v. Polygraphic Co. of America*, 350 U.S. 198 (1956). Defendant removed this state-court action to federal court and sought a stay of proceedings pending arbitration, in accordance with a contract between the parties. The state law provided that an agreement to arbitrate was revocable. The Supreme Court relied heavily on the outcome-determinative test in holding that the state law was controlling: "If the federal court allows arbitration where the state court would disallow it, the outcome of litigation might depend on the courthouse where the suit is brought.... The change from a court of law to an arbitration panel might make a radical difference in the ultimate result." Note that *Bernhardt* was decided after *Ragan* and before *Byrd*; the question is, does *Byrd* implicitly overrule *Bernhardt*?

[Note: If the "definitiveness" of outcome determination is the issue, perhaps it does, because the change in fact-finder from jury to arbiter does not seem qualitatively different from changing from jury to judge. But if interest-balancing is the proper approach, perhaps the cases are consistent, because in *Byrd* the result is "influenced" by a strong federal policy expressed in the Seventh Amendment to the Constitution.] Notice that *Byrd* cites the *Bernhardt* holding with apparent approval.

[C] Controlling Federal Rules and the Policies of *Erie*

How to Read Hanna v. Plumer

Hanna v. Plumer involved a service-of-process provision incorporated in a statute of limitations (as did *Ragan*, but of a different kind). The defendant in *Hanna* relied heavily upon the outcome-determination test, which would have resulted in his immediate victory. But the Court rejects an "automatic, 'litmus paper' criterion," and into this area in which you have already seen so much inconsistency, it injects at least two additional approaches. First, deference should be given to a valid and controlling Federal Rule if there is one. Second, the policies underlying *Erie* are important criteria for distinguishing substance and procedure. You will have to determine whether *Hanna* rationalizes or confuses the *Erie* doctrine.

Hanna v. Plumer

380 U.S. 460 (1965)

[Hanna filed a diversity suit in a federal court in Massachusetts, alleging that Louise Plumer Osgood had negligently caused her injuries in an automobile accident. Because Osgood was deceased, Hanna named Plumer, the executor of her estate, as the defendant. Hanna had the complaint and summons served by leaving them at Plumer's residence with his wife. It was undisputed that this service complied with Fed. R. Civ. P. 4, which provides for "leaving [copies at the defendant's] dwelling or usual place of abode. . . ."]

[But Plumer filed an answer asserting a defense under a Massachusetts state statute providing that "an executor or administrator shall not be held to answer to an action by a creditor of the deceased which is not commenced within one year from the time of his giving bond . . . or to such an action which is commenced within said year unless before the expiration thereof the writ in such action has been served by delivery in hand upon such executor or administrator. . . ." The papers in Hanna's suit had been served within the one-year period, but they had not been served on the executor "in hand" within that period, as the Massachusetts statute required.]

[The District Court, citing *York* and *Ragan*, granted summary judgment for defendant Plumer. The Court of Appeals affirmed, finding that "[r]elatively recent amendments to [the Massachusetts statute] evidence a clear legislative purpose to require personal notification within one year." The Supreme Court granted certiorari "[b]ecause of the threat to the goal of uniformity of federal procedure."]

MR. CHIEF JUSTICE WARREN delivered the opinion of the Court. . . .

We conclude that the adoption of Rule 4(d)(1) [now Rule 4(e)(2)], designed to control service of process in diversity actions, neither exceeded the congressional mandate embodied in the Rules Enabling Act nor transgressed constitutional bounds, and that the Rule is therefore the standard against which the District Court should have measured the adequacy of the service. Accordingly, we reverse the decision of the Court of Appeals.

The Rules Enabling Act, 28 U.S.C. § 2072 (1958 ed.), provides, in pertinent part:

> The Supreme Court shall have the power to prescribe, by general rules, the forms of process, writs, pleadings, and motions, and the practice and procedure of the district courts of the United States in civil actions.
>
> Such rules shall not abridge, enlarge or modify any substantive right and shall preserve the right of trial by jury. . . .

Under the cases construing the scope of the Enabling Act, Rule [4] clearly passes muster. . . . [I]t relates to the "practice and procedure of the district courts." . . .

> The test must be whether a rule really regulates procedure,—the judicial process for enforcing rights and duties . . . .

Sibbach v. Wilson & Co. . . .

Thus were there no conflicting state procedure, [Rule 4] would clearly control. . . . However, respondent, focusing on the contrary Massachusetts rule, calls to the Court's attention another line of cases. . . . *Erie R. Co. v. Tompkins*, 304 U.S. 64. . . . [A]s subsequent cases sharpened the distinction between substance and procedure, the line of cases following *Erie* diverged markedly from the line construing the [Rules] Enabling Act. *Guaranty Trust Co. v. York*, 326 U.S. 99, made it clear that *Erie*-type problems were not to be solved by reference to any traditional or common-sense substance-procedure distinction:

> And so the question is not whether a statute of limitations is deemed a matter of "procedure" in some sense. The question is . . . does it significantly affect the result of a litigation for a federal court to disregard a law of a State that would be controlling in an action upon the same claim by the same parties in a State court?

Respondent, by placing primary reliance on *York* and *Ragan*, suggests that the *Erie* doctrine acts as a check on the Federal Rules of Civil Procedure, that despite the clear command of [Rule 4], *Erie* and its progeny demand the application of the Massachusetts rule. Reduced to essentials, the argument is: (1) *Erie*, as refined in *York*, demands that federal courts apply state law whenever application of federal law . . . will alter the outcome of the case. (2) In this case, a determination that the Massachusetts service requirements obtain will result in immediate victory for respondent. If, on the other hand, it should be held that [Rule 4] is applicable, the litigation will continue, with possible victory for petitioner. (3) Therefore, *Erie* demands application of the Massachusetts rule. The syllogism possesses an appealing simplicity, but is for several reasons invalid.

In the first place, it is doubtful that, even if there were no Federal Rule making it clear that in-hand service is not required in diversity actions, the *Erie* rule would have obligated the District Court to follow the Massachusetts procedure. "Outcome-determination" analysis was never intended to serve as a talisman. *Byrd v. Blue Ridge Cooperative*, 356 U.S. 525, 537. Indeed, the message of *York* itself is that choices between state and federal law are to be made not by application of any automatic, "litmus paper" criterion, but rather by reference to the policies underlying the *Erie* rule. . . .

The *Erie* rule is rooted in part in a realization that it would be unfair for the character or result of a litigation materially to differ because the suit had been brought in a federal court. . . . The decision was also in part a reaction to the practice of "forum-shopping" which had grown up in response to the rule of *Swift v. Tyson*. 304 U.S., at 73-74. . . . Not only are nonsubstantial, or trivial, variations not likely to raise the sort of equal protection problems which troubled the Court in *Erie*; they are also unlikely to influence the choice of a forum. The "outcome-determination" test therefore cannot be read without reference to the twin aims of the *Erie* rule: discouragement of forum-shopping and avoidance of inequitable administration of the laws.

The difference between the conclusion that the Massachusetts rule is applicable, and the conclusion that it is not, is of course at this point "outcome-determinative" in the sense that if we hold the state rule to apply, respondent prevails, whereas if we hold that [Rule 4] governs, the litigation will continue. But in this sense *every* procedural variation is "outcome-determinative." For example, having brought suit in a federal court, a plaintiff cannot then insist on the right to file subsequent pleadings in accord with the time limits applicable in the state courts, even though enforcement of the federal timetable will, if he continues to insist that he must meet only the state time limit, result in determination of the controversy against him. So it is here. Though choice of the federal or state rule will at this point have a marked effect upon the outcome of the litigation, the difference between the two rules would be of scant, if any, relevance to the choice of a forum. Petitioner, in choosing her forum, was not presented with a situation where application of the state rule would wholly bar recovery; rather, adherence to the state rule would have resulted only in altering the way in which process was served. Moreover, it is difficult to argue that permitting service of defendant's wife to take the place of in-hand service of defendant himself alters the mode of enforcement of state-created rights in a fashion sufficiently "substantial" to raise the sort of equal protection problems to which the *Erie* opinion alluded.

There is, however, a more fundamental flaw in respondent's syllogism: the incorrect assumption that the rule of *Erie R. Co. v. Tompkins* constitutes the appropriate test of the validity and therefore the applicability of a Federal Rule of Civil Procedure. The *Erie* rule has never been invoked to void a Federal Rule. . . .

... When a situation is covered by one of the Federal Rules, the question facing the court is a far cry from the typical, relatively unguided *Erie* choice: the court has been instructed to apply the Federal Rule, and can refuse to do so only if the Advisory Committee, this Court, and Congress erred in their *prima facie* judgment that the Rule in question transgresses neither the terms of the Enabling Act nor constitutional restrictions....

Erie and its offspring cast no doubt on the long-recognized power of Congress to prescribe housekeeping rules for federal courts even though some of those rules will inevitably differ from comparable state rules.... To hold that a Federal Rule of Civil Procedure must cease to function whenever it alters the mode of enforcing state-created rights would be to disembowel either the Constitution's grant of power over federal procedure or Congress' attempt to exercise that power in the Enabling Act. [Rule 4] is valid and controls the instant case. [REVERSED.]

MR. JUSTICE BLACK concurs in the result.

MR. JUSTICE HARLAN, concurring....

Erie was something more than an opinion which worried about "forum-shopping and avoidance of inequitable administration of the laws," although to be sure these were important elements of the decision. I have always regarded that decision as one of the modern corner-stones of our federalism, expressing policies that profoundly touch the allocation of judicial power between the state and federal systems....

The shorthand formulations which have appeared in some past decisions are prone to carry untoward results that frequently arise from oversimplification. The Court is quite right in stating that the "outcome-determinative" test of *Guaranty Trust Co. v. York*, 326 U.S. 99, if taken literally, proves too much, for any rule, no matter how clearly "procedural," can affect the outcome of litigation if it is not obeyed. In turning from the "outcome" test of *York* back to the unadorned forum-shopping rationale of *Erie*, however, the Court falls prey to like over-simplification, for a simple forum-shopping rule also proves too much; litigants often choose a federal forum merely to obtain what they consider the advantages of the Federal Rules of Civil Procedure or to try their cases before a supposedly more favorable judge. To my mind the proper line of approach in determining whether to apply a state or a federal rule, whether "substantive" or "procedural," is to stay close to basic principles by inquiring if the choice of rule would substantially affect those primary decisions respecting human conduct which our constitutional system leaves to state regulation. If so, *Erie* and the Constitution require that the state rule prevail, even in the face of a conflicting federal rule....

The courts below relied upon this Court's decisions in *Ragan v. Merchants Transfer Co.*, 337 U.S. 530, and *Cohen v. Beneficial Loan Corp.*, 337 U.S. 541. Those cases deserve more attention than this Court has given them, particularly *Ragan* which, if still good law, would in my opinion call for affirmance of the result reached by the Court of Appeals....

In *Ragan* a Kansas statute of limitations provided that an action was deemed commenced when service was made on the defendant. Despite Federal Rule 3 which provides that an action commences with the filing of the complaint, the Court held that for purposes of the Kansas statute of limitations a diversity tort action commenced only when service was made upon the defendant . . . . I think that the decision was wrong. At most, application of the Federal Rule would have meant that potential Kansas tort defendants would have to defer for a few days the satisfaction of knowing that they had not been sued within the limitations period. The choice of the Federal Rule would have had no effect on the primary stages of private activity from which torts arise, and only the most minimal effect on behavior following the commission of the tort. In such circumstances the interest of the federal system in proceeding under its own rules should have prevailed. . . .

It remains to apply what has been said to the present case. . . . If the Federal District Court in Massachusetts applies Rule 4(d)(1) of the Federal Rules of Civil Procedure instead of the Massachusetts service rule, what effect would that have . . . ? As I see it, the effect would not be substantial. It would mean simply that an executor would have to check at his own house or the federal courthouse as well as the registry of probate before he could distribute the estate with impunity. As this does not seem enough to give rise to any real impingement on the vitality of the state policy which the Massachusetts rule is intended to serve, I concur in the judgment of the Court.

Notes and Questions

(1) *Counting and Evaluating the Various "Tests." York* introduced (1) the "outcome determinative" test. Later, *Byrd* arguably redefined the test as (2) a requirement of "absolute" or "definitive" outcome determination. *Byrd* also illustrates (3) the "state-federal interest balancing" approach. *Hanna* relies on (4) a "controlling Federal Rules" analysis, as well as (5) a "policies of *Erie*" test. *See* McCoid, *Hanna v. Plumer: The Erie Doctrine Changes Shape*, 51 Va. L. Rev. 884 (1965). Is there any way to rationalize all of these tests or to say which one is "the best"? *See* Redish & Phillips, *Erie and the Rules of Decision Act: In Search of the Appropriate Dilemma*, 91 Harv. L. Rev. 356 (1977) (arguing for a "refined balancing test").

(2) *Is There Still Hope for Consistency? Walker v. Armco Steel Corp.*, 446 U.S. 740 (1980). In *Hanna*, above, Justice Harlan's concurring opinion implies that *Hanna* overrules *Ragan*. But then, in *Walker*, the Court was faced with another case presenting the *Ragan* problem. The plaintiff's suit was filed before, but service was made after, the running of a state statute of limitations defining commencement by the time of service. The Court unanimously upheld the *Ragan* result. Rule 3 provides only that a civil action "is commenced by filing a complaint. . . ."

As the Court analyzed the matter, "There is no indication that the Rule was intended . . . to displace state tolling rules for purposes of . . . limitations. In our view, in diversity actions Rule 3 governs the date from which various timing requirements of the federal rules begin to run, but does not affect state statutes of limitations." Is this an outcome-determinative analysis, or interest balancing, or a policies-of-*Erie* approach? The court did distinguish the *Hanna* "controlling federal rule" approach by saying that the question was whether the Federal Rule was "sufficiently broad" to control; since it was not, the state and federal rule could "exist side by side, . . . each controlling in its own intended sphere . . . without conflict."

(3) *Dean Ely's Analysis: Focus on the Governing Act of Congress.* In Ely, *The Irrepressible Myth of* Erie, 87 HARV. L. REV. 693 (1974), Dean Ely argues that much of the confusion disappears if one distinguishes between cases controlled by the Rules of Decision Act (*York, Byrd*) and those controlled by the Rules Enabling Act (*Hanna*). In the Rules-of-Decision-Act cases, Congress has directed the federal courts to apply state law (at least when the "policies of *Erie*" are involved) unless it is overridden by significant federal procedural policies, such as the constitutional preference for jury trial. In the Rules-Enabling-Act cases, Congress has directed application of the controlling Federal Rule of Civil Procedure unless it would abridge state substantive rights. The most difficult cases, such as *Walker v. Armco Steel Corp.*, may be read as reflecting efforts to avoid a clash between the two statutes, through narrow interpretation of the Federal Rules. Dean Ely's analysis has proved influential, as the next case shows.

[D] The Two-Step Analysis: First, Follow the Rule

Shady Grove Orthopedic Associates v. Allstate Insurance Co.

130 S. Ct. 1431 (2010)

JUSTICE SCALIA announced the judgment [of a fractured Court, with a majority joining only parts of the opinion and with a four-Justice dissent].

New York law prohibits class actions in suits seeking penalties or statutory minimum damages. We consider whether this precludes a federal district court sitting in diversity from entertaining a class action under Federal Rule of Civil Procedure 23 . . . .

I

The petitioner's complaint alleged the following: Shady Grove Orthopedic Associates, P.A., provided medical care to Sonia E. Galvez for injuries she suffered in an automobile accident. As partial payment for that care, Galvez assigned to Shady Grove her rights to insurance benefits under a policy issued in New York by Allstate Insurance Co. Shady Grove tendered a claim for the assigned benefits to Allstate, which under New York law had 30 days to pay the claim or deny it. Allstate apparently paid, but not on time, and it refused to pay the statutory interest that accrued on the overdue benefits (at two percent per month).

Shady Grove filed this diversity suit in the Eastern District of New York to recover the unpaid statutory interest. Alleging that Allstate routinely refuses to pay interest on overdue benefits, Shady Grove sought relief on behalf of itself and a class of all others to whom Allstate owes interest. The District Court dismissed the suit for lack of jurisdiction. It reasoned that N.Y. Civ. Prac. Law Ann. § 901(b), which precludes a suit to recover a "penalty" from proceeding as a class action, applies in diversity suits in federal court, despite Federal Rule of Civil Procedure 23 [which authorizes class actions without regard to whether they seek penalties]. Concluding that statutory interest is a "penalty" under New York law, it held that § 901(b) prohibited the proposed class action. And, since Shady Grove conceded that its individual claim (worth roughly $500) fell far short of the amount-in-controversy requirement for individual suits under 28 U.S.C. § 1332(a), the suit did not belong in federal court.

The Second Circuit affirmed. . . . We granted certiorari.

II

The framework for our decision is familiar. We must first determine whether Rule 23 answers the question in dispute. . . . If it does, it governs—New York's law notwithstanding—unless it exceeds statutory authorization or Congress's rule-making power. . . . We do not wade into *Erie*'s murky waters unless the federal rule is inapplicable or invalid. . . .

A

The question in dispute is whether Shady Grove's suit may proceed as a class action. Rule 23 provides an answer. It states that "[a] class action may be maintained" if two conditions are met: The suit must satisfy the criteria set forth in subdivision (a) (i.e., numerosity, commonality, typicality, and adequacy of representation), and it also must fit into one of the three categories described in subdivision (b). Fed. Rule Civ. Proc. 23(b). [Note: We shall consider these class action requirements of Rule 23 below, in Chapter 6. For now, just assume that the Rule 23 requirements can be satisfied here—Eds.] By its terms this creates a categorical rule entitling a plaintiff whose suit meets the specified criteria to pursue his claim as a class action. . . . Because [New York's] § 901(b) attempts to answer the same question—i.e., it states that Shady Grove's suit "may *not* be maintained as a class action" (emphasis added) because of the relief it seeks—it cannot apply in diversity suits unless Rule 23 is ultra vires [i.e., unless it was improperly adopted].

The Second Circuit believed that § 901(b) and Rule 23 do not conflict because they address different issues. Rule 23, it said, concerns only the criteria for determining whether a given class can and should be certified; section 901(b), on the other hand, addresses an antecedent question: whether the particular type of claim is eligible for class treatment in the first place—a question on which Rule 23 is silent. . . . Allstate embraces this analysis [because then, no class action]. . . .

We disagree. To begin with, the line between eligibility and certifiability is entirely artificial. Both are preconditions for maintaining a class action. Allstate suggests that eligibility must depend on the "particular cause of action" asserted, instead of some other attribute of the suit. But that is not so. . . . [R]elabeling Rule 23(a)'s prerequisites "eligibility criteria" would obviate Allstate's objection—a sure sign that its eligibility-certifiability distinction is made-to-order.

... Allstate asserts that Rule 23 neither explicitly nor implicitly empowers a federal court "to certify a class in each and every case" where the Rule's criteria are met. But that is *exactly* what Rule 23 does: It says that if the prescribed conditions are satisfied "[a] class action *may be maintained*" (emphasis added)—not "a class action may be permitted." Courts do not maintain actions; litigants do. The discretion suggested by Rule 23's "may" is discretion residing in the plaintiff: He may bring his claim in a class action if he wishes....

We need not decide whether a state law that limits the remedies available in an existing class action would conflict with Rule 23; that is not what § 901(b) does. By its terms, the provision precludes a plaintiff from "maintain[ing]" a class action seeking statutory penalties. Unlike a law that sets a ceiling on damages (or puts other remedies out of reach) in properly filed class actions, § 901(b) says nothing about what remedies a court may award; it prevents the class actions it covers from coming into existence at all. [Note that Justice Scalia seems to be saying that a damage limit might be substantive and require state law; can you see why?—Eds.] ...

B

[Next, the Court must decide whether Rule 23 was properly and constitutionally adopted.] Congress has undoubted power to supplant state law, and undoubted power to prescribe rules for the courts it has created, so long as those rules regulate matters "rationally capable of classification" as procedure.... In the Rules Enabling Act, Congress authorized this Court to promulgate rules of procedure subject to its review, 28 U.S.C. § 2072(a), but with the limitation that those rules "shall not abridge, enlarge or modify any substantive right," § 2072(b).

We have long held that this limitation means that the Rule must "really regulat[e] procedure—the judicial process for enforcing rights and duties recognized by substantive law and for justly administering remedy and redress for disregard or infraction of them." ... The test [for legitimacy of the Rule] is not whether the rule affects a litigant's substantive rights; most procedural rules do.... What matters is what the rule itself regulates: If it governs only "the manner and the means" by which the litigants' rights are "enforced," it is valid; if it alters "the rules of decision by which [the] court will adjudicate [those] rights," it is not....

Applying that test, we have rejected every statutory challenge to a Federal Rule that has come before us. We have found to be in compliance with § 2072(b) rules prescribing methods for serving process, ... and requiring litigants whose mental or physical condition is in dispute to submit to examinations.... Each of these rules had some practical effect on the parties' rights, but each undeniably regulated only the process for enforcing those rights; none altered the rights themselves, the available remedies, or the rules of decision by which the court adjudicated either.

Applying that criterion, we think it obvious that rules allowing multiple claims (and claims by or against multiple parties) to be litigated together are also valid. Such rules neither change plaintiffs' separate entitlements to relief nor abridge defendants' rights; they alter only how the claims are processed. For the same reason, Rule 23—at least insofar as it allows willing plaintiffs to join their separate claims against the same defendants in a class action—falls within §2072(b)'s authorization....

Allstate argues that Rule 23 violates §2072(b) because the state law it displaces, §901(b), creates a right that the Federal Rule abridges—namely, a "substantive right... not to be subjected to aggregated class-action liability" in a single suit. To begin with, we doubt that that is so. Nothing in the text of §901(b) (which is to be found in New York's procedural code) confines it to claims under New York law; and of course New York has no power to alter substantive rights and duties created by other sovereigns.... As a fallback argument, Allstate argues that even if §901(b) is a procedural provision, it was enacted "for substantive reasons." Its end was not to improve "the conduct of the litigation process itself" but to alter "the outcome of that process."

The fundamental difficulty with both these arguments is that the substantive nature of New York's law, or its substantive purpose, *makes no difference.* A Federal Rule of Civil Procedure is not valid in some jurisdictions and invalid in others... depending upon whether its effect is to frustrate a state substantive law (or a state procedural law enacted for substantive purposes)....

Hanna unmistakably expressed the same understanding that compliance of a Federal Rule with the Enabling Act is to be assessed by consulting the Rule itself, and not its effects in individual applications:

> "[T]he court has been instructed to apply the Federal Rule, and can refuse to do so only if the Advisory Committee, this Court, and Congress erred in their prima facie judgment that the Rule in question transgresses neither the terms of the Enabling Act nor constitutional restrictions."

In sum, it is not the substantive or procedural nature or purpose of the affected state law that matters, but the substantive or procedural nature of the Federal Rule....

D

We must acknowledge the reality that keeping the federal-court door open to class actions that cannot proceed in state court will produce forum shopping. That is unacceptable when it comes as a consequence of judge-made rules created to fill supposed "gaps" in positive federal law.... But divergence from state law, with the attendant consequence of forum shopping, is the inevitable (indeed, one might say the intended) result of a uniform system of federal procedure. Congress itself has created the possibility that the same case may follow a different course if filed in federal instead of state court.... [REVERSED AND REMANDED.]

Justice Stevens, concurring in part and concurring in the judgment. [Justice Stevens agreed that Rule 23 applies and does not violate the Rules Enabling Act, but does not concur with Parts IIB, C and D of Justice Scalia's plurality opinion].

Justice Ginsburg, with whom Justice Kennedy, Justice Breyer, and Justice Alito join, dissenting....

The Court, I am convinced, finds conflict where none is necessary. . . . I conclude, as did the Second Circuit and every District Court to have considered the question in any detail, that Rule 23 does not collide with § 901(b). As the Second Circuit well understood, Rule 23 prescribes the considerations relevant to class certification and post-certification proceedings—but it does not command that a particular remedy be available when a party sues in a representative capacity. . . . Section 901(b), in contrast, trains on that latter issue. Sensibly read, Rule 23 governs procedural aspects of class litigation, but allows state law to control the size of a monetary award a class plaintiff may pursue. . . .

In other words, Rule 23 describes a method of enforcing a claim for relief, while § 901(b) defines the dimensions of the claim itself. . . .

I would therefore hold that the New York Legislature's limitation on the recovery of statutory damages applies in this case, and would affirm the Second Circuit's judgment.

Notes and Questions

(1) *A Two-Step Inquiry for Erie Cases? Shady Grove* suggests that there is a two-step inquiry for these cases. First, as *Hanna v. Plumer* suggested, a federal court should ask whether a federal rule (or procedural statute) controls the issue. If so, the court should apply the federal law (provided it is constitutional and does not abridge substantive state law), without any further analysis of the *Erie* question. Second, and only if there is no valid controlling federal rule, the court should use one or more of the other methods to solve the substance-procedure problem. Is this two-step analysis a correct summary of the *Shady Grove* opinion?

(2) *Harmonizing the Two Applicable Statutes.* Arguably, this two-step approach harmonizes the Rules of Decision Act and the Rules Enabling Act. Can you see why this is so?

Problem B: Procedure or Substance? A Difficult Distinction

In *Chieftain Royalty Company v. Enervest Energy Institutional Fund*, 861 F.3d 1182 (10th Cir. 2017), the parties settled a federal class action for underpayments of oil and gas royalties. The claim was determined by Oklahoma state law. The settlement, however, left the amount of attorney's fees for the district court to decide. There were two methods of determination:

> The district court chose [1] the percentage-of-the-fund analysis, explaining that this is "[t]he preferred [federal] method of determining a reasonable attorney fee award in common fund cases." It overruled the objectors' argument that [2] the lodestar approach [used in Oklahoma law] should govern and that the fee is excessive under that analysis. [The "lodestar" approach first determines a reasonable hourly fee in dollars and

> then multiplies that amount by the number of hours worked by claimants' attorneys—Eds.] . . .
>
> . . . [T]he district court ruled that "in fairness and consistent with the best interest of the class," counsel should recover 33 1/3% of the settlement. It stated that an award of that percentage was not unusual, pointing out that "[t]he Tenth Circuit has previously identified the typical fee range as 23.7% to 33.7%."

Thus, the district court followed federal law in deciding that the fee should be determined as a percentage of the total recovery, rather than Oklahoma law, which required the multiplication-of-hourly-fee or "lodestar" method.

What law, state or federal, should determine the amount of an attorney's fee award in a federal court adjudicating a state-law claim? The federal courts would have an interest in applying federal law to see that attorneys adhere to federal standards. But Oklahoma's policy is otherwise. The court of appeals remanded for a determination under Oklahoma law:

> Here, the attorney-fee award was based on the outcome of the litigation, not the district court's power to discipline the litigants. . . . [We must] apply the State's rules on how the amount of the fee is to be calculated because they are "rules of decision by which [the] court will adjudicate [the] right[] [to the fee]."

Was this decision a correct application of *Erie* (was the fee amount substantive or procedural)?

III. Determining What the State Law Is

[A] Which State's Law? Interstate Choice of Law

Note on Interstate Choice of Law

The Erie Case Itself: Choice of New York or Pennsylvania Law. We have omitted one important aspect of *Erie* from our discussion thus far. The *Erie* rule, of course, is that the federal court follows the substantive law of the state where the suit is brought. In *Erie*, that would have been New York. But Justice Brandeis' opinion says that the federal court was not "free to disregard the alleged rule of the *Pennsylvania* common law" making Tompkins a trespasser. Why Pennsylvania, if the court was in New York? The answer is logical: The federal court in New York would have to follow the law that a New York State court would follow, and Justice Brandeis assumed that a New York court would, in this instance, follow the law of Pennsylvania.

Different Approaches to Choice of Law. Every state has principles of law that tell its courts when to follow the law of some other state. This problem is called the "conflict of laws" or "choice of law." For example, if a tort occurs in state *Y*, and suit is brought for damages in state *X*, it may be that the court will follow the "law of the place of the injury" (in Latin, "*lex loci delicti*"). However, another approach is for state *X* to consider which state has the "most significant relationship" to the issue, as is advocated by the Second Restatement of Conflict of Laws. In the *Erie* case, either approach would have given the same result, because Pennsylvania was the place of the injury and also was the state with the most significant relationship to the claim. But consider the following case.

PENNINGTON v. DYE, 456 So. 2d 507 (Fla. App. 1984). A couple from Ohio was vacationing in Florida when they were involved in an automobile accident. The wife sued her husband and his liability insurer for injuries she received due to his alleged negligence. The Ohio doctrine of interspousal immunity would have barred the claim had it been brought in that state. She filed the action in a Florida court, where she argued that there was no such immunity.

The court noted that, historically, Florida had followed the *lex loci delicti* principle (*i.e.*, the law of the place of the injury), which would mean that Florida law would apply to this Florida accident, and the plaintiff might recover. However, in *Bishop v. Florida Specialty Paint Co.*, 389 So. 2d 999 (Fla. 1980), the Florida Supreme Court had adopted the "most significant relationship" test of the Second Restatement. *Bishop* had been a personal injury action arising from the crash of a small aircraft in South Carolina while en route from Florida to North Carolina; the court had applied Florida law because the connections of all parties to Florida were strong. Therefore, the Court in *Pennington v. Dye* concluded that the immunity issue, between two Ohio citizens, must be tested by the most-significant-relationship test.

In deciding whether Florida or Ohio had the most significant relationship to the parties and occurrence, the court recognized that the incident had happened in Florida (which had an interest in regulating drivers within its borders). But the Restatement indicated that the state of domicile (in this case, Ohio) would have the "dominant interest" in the values of marital harmony and prevention of collusive claims against insurers of its citizens that were the basis of the interspousal immunity doctrine. Therefore, the Florida court held that the interspousal immunity question would be governed by the substantive law of Ohio, which barred the claim.

KLAXON CO. v. STENTOR ELECTRIC MFG. CO., 313 U.S. 487 (1941). This case was the first in which the Supreme Court directly addressed the question whether choice of law principles were "substantive" laws controlled by the *Erie* doctrine. Plaintiff brought suit in a federal court in Delaware for damages arising from the breach of a New York contract. The Court of Appeals, without examining Delaware law, held that a New York statute providing for interest in contract actions applied because it represented the "better" rule. The Supreme Court reversed, holding that the court must follow the choice of law principles of Delaware, where the action was brought:

> We are of the opinion that . . . *Erie* . . . extends to the field of conflict of laws. . . . Otherwise, the accident of diversity of citizenship would constantly disturb equal administration of justice in coordinate state and federal courts sitting side by side. Any other ruling would do violence to the principle of uniformity within a state, upon which the *Tompkins* decision is based. . . . [T]he proper function of the Delaware federal court is to determine what the state law is, not what it ought to be.

Notes and Questions

(1) *Which Is Better: Lex Loci or Most Significant Relationship?* Most states that have confronted the question have chosen to replace the older *lex loci* rule with a modern variant of the significant relationship test (or modern "state's interest analysis"). *See* R. Weintraub, *Commentary on the Conflict of Laws* 323-27 (3d ed. 1986). However, some states have chosen to retain the law of the place of the wrong for various reasons, including greater certainty or predictability (although that point is debatable). *Id.* For a hybrid approach, see *Hardly Able Coal Co. v. International Harvester Co.*, 494 F. Supp. 249 (N.D. Ill. 1980) (federal court, applying Illinois conflicts principles, found that significant relationships were equally divided between Illinois and Kentucky, and it therefore followed the law of the situs of the wrong, which was Kentucky).

(2) *Non-Tort Choice of Law.* The preceding discussion, for simplicity, is confined to tort cases. Different kinds of principles apply in cases concerning contracts, property, matrimonial actions, etc. *See generally* R. Weintraub, *supra.*

(3) *Constitutional Limitations on Choice of Law.* What should happen if a state with no legitimate policy interest applies its own law in derogation of a state that has significant interests? In *Phillips Petroleum Co. v. Shutts*, 472 U.S. 797 (1985), the Supreme Court of Kansas applied Kansas law to the claims of all members of a class of royalty owners, notwithstanding the fact that 99 percent of the gas leases in question and 97 percent of the plaintiffs had no connection to Kansas. The Supreme Court reversed. It cited an earlier decision, *Allstate Ins. Co. v. Hague*, 449 U.S. 302 (1981), which held that the Due Process Clause required choice of law to be based on "a significant contact or aggregation of contacts, creating state interests, such that [the] choice . . . is neither arbitrary nor fundamentally unfair."

(4) *A More Complex Case: In re Air Crash Disaster Near Chicago*, 644 F.2d 594 (7th Cir. 1981). One hundred eighteen wrongful death claims, originally filed in six different jurisdictions, were transferred and consolidated in this single federal action against an airline and others arising out of a crash in Illinois. The court held (in accordance with the rule of *Van Dusen v. Barrack*, discussed in Note 2 following *Hoffman v. Blaski* in subsection Chapter 2, § [A][2], above) that the availability of punitive damages would be controlled by choice of law rules of the jurisdictions

in which the various suits were originally filed. Thus, actions filed in New York or Illinois would be governed by the "most significant relationship" test, those filed in California by that state's "comparative impairment" approach, and those in Michigan or Puerto Rico by the law of the place of the injury. As for actions filed in Hawaii, said the court, since the applicable rules were not identified by the parties, the law of the forum would supply the choice of law rule.

In the final analysis, however, the court determined that "under each of the applicable state choice-of-law rules, punitive damages cannot be allowed . . ."(!). Do you suppose the judge decided this way because otherwise figuring out the law would be more complicated than the judge wanted?

(5) *Should Congress Pass a Federal Choice of Law Rule?* For complex or multiple-party cases, or those in which the dispute has such diffuse contacts with so many states that highly refined choice of law may be counterproductive, it has been suggested that Congress should pass a choice of law rule for diversity cases. Would such a law be wise (or constitutional)? In a complex case, might it be that the current approach pressures the court toward "judicial fudging" to produce a uniform choice of law—which often is pragmatically necessary to simplify the dispute and make it manageable? *Cf. In re "Agent Orange" Product Liability Litigation*, 100 F.R.D. 718, 723 (E.D.N.Y. 1983) (rather than apply 50 different sets of state laws, the court simply declared that there was a nationwide "consensus" and that all states thus would apply similar product liability laws (!)).

Problem C: A Three-Way Choice of Law Question

In *Collins v. Mary Kay, Inc.*, 874 F.3d 176 (3d Cir. 2017), Collins brought a federal class action in New Jersey claiming that Mary Kay had underpaid her and other New Jersey workers under the New Jersey Wage Payment Law. Mary Kay moved to dismiss on *forum non conveniens* grounds. It relied on two written documents specifying that Texas law applied to their interpretation and that all legal claims would be submitted to Texas state courts. The district court considered the issue procedural, applied federal common law in considering these agreements, and granted Mary Kay's motion to dismiss. On appeal, Collins argued that New Jersey law should govern. As the court of appeals put it, "This case thus poses a layered choice-of-law question: what law governs the interpretation of a forum selection clause in a written agreement when that agreement also contains a choice of law clause?"

And so, this problem requires you to consider whether federal, New Jersey, or Texas law applies to determine the interpretation of the forum selection clauses (and to analyze the court's decision). The court of appeals held that federal common law covers the "enforceability" of a forum clause: determining whether it is "reasonable," in all of the circumstances, to enforce the clause. But "applying federal common law to interpret a forum selection clause frustrates the principles of *Erie*."

Therefore, the "interpretation" of the clause, or determining what it means, is a matter of state contract law, said the court.

According to *Erie* and *Klaxon,* this holding meant that New Jersey would supply the choice-of-law rule for interpreting the clause. "In diversity cases such as this one, we look to the choice-of-law rules of the forum state—the state in which the District Court sits—in order to decide which body of substantive law to apply to a contract provision, even where the contract contains a choice-of-law clause." The New Jersey Supreme Court had held, "[o]rdinarily, when parties to a contract have agreed to be governed by the laws of a particular state, New Jersey courts will uphold the contractual choice." Thus, New Jersey would apply Texas law to the forum clause. The court of appeals thus applied law of all three jurisdictions to uphold the dismissal. Do you agree with each step?

[B] Unsettled State Law: The "*Erie* Educated Guess"

*Note on "*Erie *Educated Guesses"*

How Does the Federal Court Determine What the State Law Is? The federal court follows the decisions of the state supreme court to determine state law. But what if there is no decision of the state supreme court on point? In that case, the federal court is supposed to consult the decisions of the lower state courts as persuasive although not binding authority, in its effort to decide what the state supreme court probably would decide.

The "Erie Educated Guess(!?)": (Keep Your Sense of Humor Here). But what if there is no decision of any state court that shows what the state law would be? In that case, the federal court consults any source available to make an "*Erie* educated guess" about the state law. This is a not-infrequent occurrence, and it perhaps provides yet another argument for abolishing diversity jurisdiction, because sometimes the federal court does it badly.

*An Example of a Dubious "*Erie *Guess": Elvis Presley's Right of Publicity*

Guessing about Whether Elvis Lives: Federal Treatment of Tennessee's Right-of-Publicity Law. During his lifetime, Elvis Presley formed a Tennessee corporation and assigned to it the exclusive ownership of rights to the commercial use of his likeness and name. This bundle of rights is called the "right of publicity." After Presley's death, a company called Pro Arts sold unauthorized posters of Elvis. Presley's assignee, Factors Etc., Inc., sued for an injunction. Pro Arts defended by arguing that the right of publicity does not survive the death of the subject. The district court granted the injunction, but the court of appeals reversed, holding that the right of publicity did not survive Elvis' death. *Factors Etc., Inc. v. Pro Arts, Inc.*, 652 F.2d 278 (2d Cir. 1981).

Reasoning Based on Utopian Philosophy Rather Than State Law? The federal appeals court asserted that Tennessee law "affords no answer to the question." (This assertion was dubious; see below.) However, another court of appeals had decided the same question by guessing about "practical and policy considerations, the relative weight of the conflicting interests of the parties, and certain moral presuppositions about death, privacy, inheritability, and economic opportunity." These "considerations" and "presuppositions" were not based upon Tennessee authorities, but instead the court had cited such philosophical tracts as John Rawls' *A Theory of Justice.* Rawls' theory has been described as a utopian philosophy and as a philosophy of "radical equality."

The Dissent. Judge Mansfield dissented. He pointed out that the majority had not based its reasoning on Tennessee law. Furthermore, the majority's holding was "inconsistent with that of nearly every other case that has considered the issue" and "contrary to all current views of scholarly commentators." He pointed out that Tennessee probably would instead adopt a policy that advanced the continued growth of Nashville and Memphis as centers for the lives of music personalities.

A Wrong Guess, Without Reliance on Tennessee Law? Tennessee promptly did what the dissenting judge had predicted. Consider the following Tennessee case, which actually considers the Tennessee decisions (as the Second Circuit majority didn't) and comes to the opposite conclusion.

COMMERCE UNION BANK v. COORS, 7 Media L. Rptr. 2204 (Tenn. Chancery Ct. Davidson Co. 1981). Shortly after the Second Circuit's decision in *Factors Etc.*, above, this Tennessee trial court came to the opposite conclusion from the *Factors Etc.* majority. The estate of the late country music giant Lester Flatt sued to prevent Coors' use of his likeness in two beer advertisements. In a thorough opinion, the court discussed the relevant decisions in Tennessee and elsewhere, described the scholarly works on the right of publicity, chronicled the careers of Flatt and Scruggs at the Grand Ole Opry, and granted the injunction. It reasoned, "The Tennessee Supreme Court has recognized that the exclusive right to use a trade name can survive the termination of business by a business entity which used it [citation omitted]. The Tennessee Court of Appeals held that the exclusive right to use the name of a Memphis drugstore passed from the decedent-sole proprietor to his widow who continued to operate the business [citation omitted]."

"Judge Mansfield," said the Tennessee court in closing, "makes a pointedly perceptive comment when he said 'it would be rational for Tennessee courts to adopt a policy enhancing the continued growth of Nashville and Memphis as centers for the lives and activities of music industry personalities.' . . . This Court agrees with Judge Mansfield. It would be unreasonable not to protect the efforts and energies of so many Tennessee artists."

Notes and Questions

(1) *What Should the Second Circuit Now Do?* How much deference must the federal court of appeals give to the Lester Flatt case (*Commerce Union Bank v. Coors*),

and how should it go about deciding whether to reverse itself? *See* Gibbs, *How Does the Federal Judge Determine What Is the Law of the State?* 17 S.C. L. REV. 487 (1965).

Actually, what the court of appeals decided was to do nothing: to leave its decision in place. The court pointed out that another Tennessee chancery court (a trial-level court) had done the opposite: cut off the right of publicity at death.

(2) *The Answer, Today: The Right of Publicity Survives.* Tennessee decisions today answer the question. Elvis lives (or at least, his right of publicity does).

(3) *Do Erie Educated Guesses Furnish an Argument for Abolishing Diversity Jurisdiction?* Consider your response to this question.

(4) *Abstention; State Provisions for Certification of Questions.* As we saw in Chapter 3, the federal courts sometimes abstain so that suits may be re-filed in state court (but abstention is confined to exceptional circumstances). Also, most states have provided mechanisms for federal courts to certify questions to state supreme courts. That procedure would have been helpful in the *Factors Etc.* case. However, it is important to recognize that certification is not a panacea. There simply are too many diversity cases for federal courts to certify every ambiguous issue, and the process effectively adds another layer to an already lengthy appellate process.

IV. Filling the Gaps in Federal Law: Federal Common Law

Note on the Justification for Federal Common Law

Interstate Disputes. In *Erie*, Justice Brandeis flatly said: "There is no general federal common law." In certain selected areas, however, limited versions of "federal common law" unquestionably do exist. In fact, in another case decided the same day as *Erie*, Justice Brandeis wrote that an interstate water rights dispute was "a question of 'federal common law' upon which neither the statutes nor the decisions of either state can be conclusive." *Hinderlider v. La Plata River & Cherry Creek Ditch Co.*, 304 U.S. 92 (1938). Obviously, there is good reason for not deciding a dispute between two states by the laws of either.

Uniquely Federal Interests: Clearfield Trust Co. v. United States, 318 U.S. 363 (1943). In this famous federal common law case, the United States sued a bank that had guaranteed and presented a forged check issued by the United States. The Court decided that it would be inappropriate to apply the law of the state where the transaction took place, which would have placed the loss on the United States because of a delay in notifying the bank. "The issuance of commercial paper by the United States is on a vast scale and transactions in that paper from issuance to payment will ordinarily occur in several states. The application of state law . . . would subject the rights and duties of the United States to exceptional uncertainty. . . . The desirability of a uniform rule is plain."

The Court reached that result by federal common law. *See also Boyle v. United Technologies Corp.*, 487 U.S. 500 (1988) (adopting, as federal common law, a "military contractor" defense, exempting military contractors from tort damages for accidents caused by products produced in conformity with military procurement orders; holding that such a defense implicates two kinds of "uniquely federal interests"—federal obligations, as in *Clearfield Trust*, and federal military procurement).

The (Rare) Conditions for Federal Common Law: Conflict Between Sovereign States, as in Hinderlider, or Between State Law and Federal Law, as in Boyle. In a dispute between two states over water rights, it makes sense that neither sovereign's law should apply. Likewise, if a state's law would hold a federal contractor liable in tort for fulfilling his or her contract, it is apparent that state law should not apply. These are the kinds of conflicts that create the rare phenomenon of federal common law.

V. How to Answer the Chapter Summary Problem: Some Suggestions

Payne v. Manson: A Conflict between Federal Law and a State Malpractice Statute. (As always, follow your Professor's instructions about how to answer.)

1. Does state law, or federal law, control the question? *The Law:* [Consider each applicable principle, including the following:] The court uses federal procedural law and state substantive law. To decide whether the issue is procedural or substantive, consider outcome determination, "absolute" outcome determination, federal-state interest balancing, any controlling federal rule, and the policies of *Erie*. [Explain each in declarative sentences.] *The Facts:* Consider all the relevant facts and apply the principles to them. *Conclusion:* draw your conclusion.

2. How is the answer affected by the existence of Federal Rule of Civil Procedure 26? *The Law:* After *Shady Grove,* it appears that if there is a controlling federal rule that does not unconstitutionally impose on state prerogatives, the rule should be followed. *The Facts:* Rule 26 is about discovery and does not directly eliminate state-imposed preliminary requirements. Defendant's apparent argument is that Rule 26 controls, because the state-law requirement resembles discovery, and Rule 26 contains requirements for disclosure, but this inference does not seem to make it a "controlling" federal rule. The parties can comply with both rules. In that case, we use the other tests for deciding the procedure-substance question. *Conclusion:* Rule 26 probably does not affect the question.

3. Is there any incentive for a plaintiff to file in federal court and thereby escape the preliminary expert opinion affidavit that would be required in state court? On the one hand, a litigant can avoid early costs and can avoid the possibility of an expert statement that contradicts later developments. On the other hand, plaintiff would shortly need an expert and need to make statements about the expert's opinion. There is an incentive, but one can question whether it is large or small.

4. In the actual case upon which this Summary Problem is based, the court held that the administration of state medical malpractice claims should be the same in both federal and state courts, and therefore, in both courts, a defendant could bring a motion to dismiss. How could the court justify this conclusion in light of Hanna v. Plumer? *The Law:* [State the holding of *Hanna* with reference to controlling federal rules.] *The Facts:* [Rule 26 is about discovery and, the state law is analogous to discovery, but is the federal law "controlling"?] *Conclusion:* The court could justify its holding by the reasoning here and in 2., above.

5. Would the result be the same if the alleged malpractice occurred in another state, the state of Texafornia, although the suit is in West York? *The Law:* Substantive law includes the forum state's choice-of-law rules. [Here, set out the lex loci delicti and most significant relationship tests, which are the principal choice-of-law rules covered in the chapter, and explain what they mean.] *The Facts:* The suit is in West York, but the incident of alleged malpractice was in Texafornia. *Conclusion:* The choice-of-law rules of West York apply. Under either approach, however, the court would probably follow the law of Texafornia applicable to the incident. Texaformia is the locus delicti (place of the wrong) and is also the state that has the strongest interest in malpractice occurring in Texafornia.

6. What does the federal court do to decide the meaning and importance of the West York statute if there is no decision of the West York Supreme Court interpreting the statute? The federal court follows the law declared by the West York Supreme Court, but if there is none, it makes an *Erie* educated guess after consulting analogous decisions of that court, decisions of the West York lower courts, and other authorities that the West York Supreme Court would be likely to follow. If the question is sufficiently important and ambiguous, the federal court might certify the question to the West York Supreme Court.

VI. Improving the System of Federal-State Choice of Law: Notes and Questions

(1) *A Federal Choice-of-Law Provision for Complex Diversity Cases?* In 1985, the American Law Institute (ALI) considered the question whether Congress could create federal choice-of-law rules in diversity cases. *See* 7:2 ALI Rep. 1 (Jan. 1985).

Among the proposals before the ALI was one applicable to certain kinds of complex diversity cases, providing that "the [federal] court may make its own determination as to which State rule of decision is applicable." The proposal continued: "In making this determination, the court may consider, among other factors, the following: the law that might have governed if the [federal] jurisdiction . . . did not exist; the forums in which the claims were or might have been brought; the desirability of application of uniform law . . . ; whether a change in applicable law in connection with removal or transfer of the action would cause unfairness; and the danger of creation of unnecessary incentives for forum shopping."

To see why this sort of proposal might be useful, consider *In re Agent Orange Product Liab. Litig.*, 100 F.R.D. 718, 723 (E.D.N.Y. 1983). In this uniquely complex action, brought by scores of thousands of veterans and their families for injuries allegedly caused by defoliants in Vietnam, the application of fifty different sets of laws would have made the case unmanageable. The District Court initially adopted federal common law. Then, when the Court of Appeals reversed this holding, the District Court judge adopted the dubious but pragmatic solution of declaring that there was a nationwide "consensus"—by which all states would apply identical product liability laws to the case. Wouldn't it be better if this kind of policymaking were explicit and authorized by Congress (as per the ALI proposal)?

Note that the quoted choice-of-law proposal would apply only to complex (multiparty, multi-state) cases. In that context, is it desirable?

(2) *Diversity Reform; Uniform Acts.* Abolition or reduction of diversity jurisdiction obviously would reduce the number of *Erie* questions. Does this factor provide another reason for diversity reform? *See* Westen, *Is There Life for Erie After the Death of Diversity?*, 78 Mich. L. Rev. 311 (1980). Similarly, *Erie* issues could be simplified by uniform state laws. The Uniform Commercial Code is an example. Should more uniform laws be adopted by more states? Finally, certification to the state courts sometimes can provide a solution.

Chapter 5

Pleadings

I. How Modern Pleading Developed

[A] Common Law Pleadings

"They Still Rule Us from Their Graves." The great Professor Maitland said that we may think we have buried common law pleadings, but "they still rule us from their graves." Maitland, *Equity* 296 (1909). It is true. Today's affirmative defense is an updated version of common law "confession and avoidance." In some states, litigation over land titles is done by a method resembling the common law action of "ejectment."

Why Study Common Law Pleading? Much of the discussion that follows is adapted from B. Shipman, *Handbook of Common Law Pleading* (Ballantyne 3d ed. 1923). The introduction to Shipman's book points out that the structured logic of the common law system parallels some of our current procedures. And even more significantly, it reveals a persistent policy question: Should pleading rules be tightened, or loosened?

[1] The Plaintiff's Suit: Writ and Declaration

Oral and Written Pleadings; the "Single Issue." Early common law pleadings actually were oral. It was not until the late Fourteenth Century that written pleadings began to replace this procedure. To simplify the dispute, oral pleadings were structured into alternating brief statements by the respective parties. This practice may have been one reason for the extraordinary determination with which the common law judges later insisted upon narrowing the pleadings to a "single issue."

The System of Writs. The plaintiff began his or her suit by obtaining a "writ" from the chancellor, who was the king's representative. The search for the single issue was under way even at this point, for the writ was not a general-purpose device for getting the defendant into court; instead, it was confined to the particular "form of action" that the plaintiff thought his claim might fit. The plaintiff was required to obtain a writ in trespass, for example, if that was the kind of suit she wanted to bring. In its earliest form, the "*capias ad respondendum*," the writ commanded the sheriff to seize the defendant's person. Later, the writ was simply served on the defendant. One of the oddities of the common law practice was that the jurisdiction of the King's Bench sometimes depended upon the custody of the defendant at Marshalsea prison—and therefore, the plaintiff's declaration alleged this confinement even if it was a complete fiction.

Plaintiff's Declaration. The analogue to today's complaint was the "declaration" filed by the plaintiff. But the declaration was full of formal elements, as the example of fictitious custody demonstrates. For example, the following declaration might be used to charge a trespass to the plaintiff's horse:(*)

(*) Reprinted from Shipman, *Common Law Pleading*, with permission of the West Publishing Company.

Declaration in Trespass for Injury to Personalty

In the King's Bench

On ____________________, the ____________________ Day of ____________________, in ____________________ Term, 1 Wm. IV

A.B. (to wit) the plaintiff in this suit, complains of C.D., the defendant in this suit, being in the custody of the marshal of Marshalsea of our said lord the now king, before the king himself, of a plea of trespass, for that the said defendant, on etc. (date of injury, or about it), with force and arms, etc., at etc. (venue; e.g., at ____________________, in the county of ____________________), drove a certain cart, with great force and violence, upon and against a certain horse of the said plaintiff, of great value, to wit, of the value of £ ____________________, there and then being, and there and then with one of the shafts, and other pieces of the said cart of the said defendant, so greatly pierced, cut, hurt, lacerated and wounded the said horse of the said plaintiff that by reason thereof the said horse, being of the value aforesaid, afterwards, to wit, on the day and year aforesaid, died, to wit, at etc. (venue), aforesaid.

And other wrongs to the said plaintiff then and there did, to the great damage of the said plaintiff, against the peace of our said lord the king. Wherefore the said plaintiff saith, that he is injured, and hath sustained damage to the amount of £ ____________________, and therefore brings his suit, etc.

The allegation of "force and arms," like that of imprisonment at Marshalsea, sometimes was "constructive" or fictitious. But it had to be there.

[2] The Defendant's Pleading: Demurrer, Traverse, or Confession and Avoidance

Demurrer. The defendant had several choices. First, if the declaration was insufficient on its face to show a right of action even if the truth of all the facts was admitted, or if it was technically defective in form, the defendant could prevail on a "demurrer." This pleading takes its name from the Latin "demorari" or French "demorrer," meaning to wait or stay; and as the etymology implies, the pleading asserts that defendant need do nothing. Thus, if the plaintiff had omitted the allegation of "force and arms" from the declaration of trespass to his horse, a demurrer would be granted.

Dilatory Pleas: Pleas to the Jurisdiction or in Abatement. These pleadings asserted fundamental defects in the way suit was brought. A "plea to the jurisdiction" attacked subject-matter jurisdiction. A "plea in abatement" was used for a variety of purposes, including attacks on misjoinder or non-joinder of parties.

"Peremptory" Pleas (or Pleas "in Bar"); Traverse and Confession and Avoidance. These were pleas to the merits of the action. A "traverse" was the common law

analogue of today's denials. For example, if the defendant wished to deny that he ran his cart into the plaintiff's horse, he would traverse that allegation. "Confession and avoidance" was the other kind of plea in bar. If the defendant wanted to say that he ran into the horse, but he was acting in self-defense because the plaintiff, while on his horse, was threatening him, he would plead by way of confession and avoidance. The modern analogue is the affirmative defense, sometimes called the "defense of new matter." In essence, the demurrer says: "It's true, but so what?" The traverse says: "It isn't true." A defense in confession and avoidance says: "It's true, but here are some other facts that the plaintiff hasn't told you."

Back to the Plaintiff: Demur, Plead, or Join Issue? The ball was again in the plaintiff's court. He or she could respond with a demurrer; for example, a demurrer to the defendant's plea of self-defense would test its legal sufficiency. It would amount to an assertion that the plea could not avoid liability, even if true. Alternatively, the plaintiff could "join issue": he could signify that he accepted the issue formed by his opponent's traverse.

Replication, Rejoinder, Rebutter, Etc. Or, the plaintiff could continue the paper war by a "replication." This plea would be responsive to the defendant's peremptory plea. Thus, the plaintiff might traverse the self-defense allegations and put their truth in issue, or he could plead in confession and avoidance—*e.g.*, he did threaten the defendant, but acted in defense of a third person. This plea would send the ball back to the defendant, who could demur, plead, or join issue. His plea would be a "rejoinder." The plaintiff could then respond with a "surrejoinder," to which the defendant would in turn file a "rebutter," followed by the plaintiff's "surrebutter." Theoretically, this process could go on indefinitely, but as a practical matter issue usually was joined after the first few exchanges.

[3] The Single Issue: Herein of "Duplicity," "Departure," and the "General Issue"

The "Single Issue" and the Prohibition on "Duplicity" or "Departure." What if the defendant had two different defenses to the merits? For example, it would be quite plausible for him to claim that he acted in self-defense and also that he did not cause the horse's death. But this "duplicity," as the common law labelled it, was strictly prohibited, and the plaintiff could attack it by demurrer. In fact, the system also prohibited a more intricate pleading error called a "departure." Each pleading had to be responsive to the opponent's before it and consistent with the party's own prior pleas. For example, if (1) the plaintiff's declaration was for trespass to his horse, (2) the defendant's peremptory plea was self-defense, (3) the plaintiff's replication was defense of a third person, and (4) the defendant's rejoinder was that the claim had been settled and released, the defendant would have committed the sin of departure. His plea of release would be nonresponsive to the replication and inconsistent with his own peremptory plea. The matter could not be both denied as a matter of self-defense and admitted as being settled with a release. The plaintiff would demur and have judgment.

Demurrer as an Admission. Initially, demurrers were subject to the single issue approach, too. A demurrer was an admission of the facts properly alleged in the declaration. Thus a "general" demurrer was an all-or-nothing proposition: If the declaration was technically defective, the defendant prevailed, but the defendant would lose, whatever the true facts, if the declaration was good on its face. Later, this process was changed by statute; a "special" demurrer, by which the defendant attacked a defect of form by specifically pointing it out, was not an admission, and even the general demurrer, which attacked the substance of the declaration, was permitted to be asserted without binding admission. Still another oddity of the demurrer practice was that the demurrer "opened" or "searched" the record. All errors in previous pleadings were to be sought out, and judgment would be granted against the pleader who made the first error.

The Plea of the "General Issue." In some cases, the common law relaxed completely its insistence on narrow pleadings and permitted the defendant to plead "the general issue." In trespassory actions, the plea was "not guilty"; in assumpsit, it was "non assumpsit" ("he did not promise"). These pleas allowed the defendant to contest most of the allegations that the plaintiff would be required to prove and, in addition, to raise certain affirmative defenses. With characteristic pragmatism, the law appears to have invented this procedure in reaction to the perversion of narrow pleading, which became an obstacle to justice. Ironically, the general issue itself was criticized because it made the issues in controversy less clear.

The Merits and Demerits of this System. You may well have doubts about this system. But its defenders did not. The vigor of their praise has to be read to be believed. Sir Matthew Hale said that common law pleading had reached a "comparatively perfect state" in the reign of Edward I, when it was "methodically formed and cultivated as a science." In 1855, Professor Samuel Tyler called it "the greatest of all judicial inventions." But there was trouble in this paradise. Shipman, who wrote extensively on the subject, put it best: "Competent critics have asserted that common law pleading became a mere game of skill, and, instead of being the servant, became [a]n end in itself, instead of a means to the determination of substantial rights."

Notes and Questions

(1) *Some Examples.* Try your hand at identifying the next proper pleading or the proper result in each of the following cases.

(a) *Plaintiff Responds to a Legally Insufficient Defense.* The plaintiff properly pleads a trespass by assault and battery. The defendant's peremptory plea is by way of confession and avoidance, asserting in effect that the plaintiff was contributorily negligent. This plea cannot furnish a defense to assault and battery as a matter of law. How should the plaintiff plead?

(b) *Departure.* The plaintiff properly pleads an indebtedness on a promissory note. The defendant's peremptory plea is that the action is barred by the statute of limitations. The plaintiff's replication is that the statute is tolled, because the defendant was absent from the jurisdiction during most of the time before suit. The defendant's rejoinder is that the note has been paid. The plaintiff demurs. What result? [Notice that the plea of payment is unresponsive to the limitations and tolling pleas.]

(2) *Advantages of This Pleading System.* Obviously, this system is hypertechnical. But it does have some arguable advantages. What are they?

[4] The Forms of Action

Substance, Remedy, and Procedure Intertwined. The purest essence of the common law was comprised in the "forms of action." Each form defined a substantive theory of recovery, provided idiosyncratic remedies, and even included a system of procedure unique to each form of action. There was no general-usage form or procedure for a civil action, and if the pleader misconceived her case at the outset, she could obtain no relief.

Development of the Forms of Action. Remember that the plaintiff began suit by obtaining a writ from the chancellor. The writ was necessary because no one could use the King's Court without his permission. In the reign of Henry VIII, the Registrum Brevium, or "Register of Writs," was published, organizing this complex field of knowledge. Shipman, at 62, groups the various actions into three groups that still resonate today: actions *ex delicto* (or "for wrongs done"), contractual actions, and real property actions.

Early Torts: The Action of Trespass. Breach of the king's peace was the source of one of the earlier writs, called trespass. It required three elements: first, a wrongful act done with "force"; second, an "immediate" injury (and not merely a "consequential" one); and third, if the injury was to property, actual or constructive possession of it. Mere nonfeasance could not support a trespass because it involved no force; hence the wrongful detention of goods could not be trespass, although a wrongful taking could. But the more intricate requirement was that of immediate injury. As Shipman wrote, at 70, paraphrasing the jurist Sir William Blackstone, "[i]f a person, in the act of throwing a log into the highway hits and injures a passer-by, the injury is immediate and trespass will lie; but if, after a log has been wrongfully thrown onto the highway, a passer-by falls over it, trespass will not lie."

"Trespass on the Case" (or, Simply, "Case"). The example of the passer-by falling over the log shows the need for a later-developed form called trespass on the case, or simply "case." If a plaintiff suffered an injury that should be redressable, but it was not done with "force" or was "consequential" rather than immediate, trespass would not lie—and, slowly, it became recognized that trespass "on the case" was a proper form. The distinctions between trespass and trespass on the case sometimes were almost metaphysical. If a person poured water on another's land, the injury was immediate, and trespass would lie, but if he put a spout on his roof so that water ran from his building, collected, and overflowed onto the plaintiff's land, the injury

was consequential, and the only proper form was trespass on the case. Shipman at 89.

Personal Property: Detinue, Replevin, and Trover. "Detinue" was an early writ used to require the return of personalty. It had serious procedural deficiencies and allowed recovery only of the goods themselves, not of damages. "Replevin," at first, was a narrow remedy that allowed both recovery of the goods and damages for wrongful seizure; it later was extended to most kinds of unlawful takings, but not to cases in which the property was rightfully taken but wrongfully detained. Finally, the action of "trover" (or trover and conversion), which evolved from trespass and trespass on the case, was a damage remedy for the defendant's conversion of personalty to his own use. But if the defendant simply lost property that had been entrusted to his possession, there was no conversion, and no action for trover.

The Early Contract Actions: Debt, Covenant, and Account. The recovery of a "liquidated" (*i.e.*, fixed or certain) sum of money could be accomplished by the action of "debt." This was one of the oldest forms applicable, for example, in the instance of a loan; but it could not be used if the plaintiff sued for general or consequential damages, for installments, or in various other instances. "Covenant" was the action for damages for breach of a covenant under seal (that is, with the defendant's agreement signified by his seal affixed to it). "Account" was a form used in certain circumstances to recover funds from a fiduciary. There were many deficiencies in these actions, and a general-purpose damage remedy for breach of contract did not exist.

Recovery of Real Property: Ejectment. Ancient real property actions were cumbersome to the point of ineffectiveness. Therefore, the genius of the common law invented "ejectment." This form evolved, of all things, out of the action in trespass, through a wonderfully far-fetched fiction. If the plaintiff entered the land and the defendant ejected him by force, trespass would lie. The defendant would plead "not guilty" (not guilty of what? Of the trespass, of course; because he claimed the land and therefore the right to eject the plaintiff). Thus, the trespass action would put the question of title in issue. Later, inventive claimants used "lessees" as stand-ins to be ejected. Fictional assertion of the ejectment became acceptable, and even a plaintiff in undisturbed possession could use this form to quiet title to his property.

[5] Methods of "Trial," Variances, and the Rise of Assumpsit

The Variance Problem. Pleading was not the only stage where there were technicalities. Evidence at trial had to conform to the pleadings with a surprisingly strict kind of accuracy. If the declaration set out a promise made by the defendant, but the proof showed that the promise contained an additional qualification or condition, there was a fatal "variance"—and the plaintiff lost even if he proved that the additional requirement had been satisfied. In one case, an allegation of an absolute contract to deliver "40 bags of wheat" was not sustained by proof of a contract to deliver "40 or 50 bags of wheat." Shipman at 245-46.

Trial by Battle, Ordeal, and Wager of Law. Furthermore, trial by rational development of evidence before a judge or jury was not always available. There was a time when "trial" was by battle between the parties or their champions, or by an "ordeal," in which truth was to be revealed by divine intervention. One method of ordeal was to cast the defendant into water, which would "reject" the guilty; innocent defendants could be rescued by ropes around their waists. A later but only slightly more advanced procedure was "wager of law." If the defendant swore that he did not owe the debt and was supported by twelve "oath helpers" who swore that they believed him, the result was equivalent to a verdict in his favor. This was a "system of licensed perjury," as Shipman puts it. A plaintiff who had loaned money obviously regarded debt as an unattractive remedy since the defaulting debtor could defeat it merely by submitting the requisite thirteen oaths.

Assumpsit Replaces Debt; "General Assumpsit." To avoid wager of law in a debt action, plaintiffs developed a new action called assumpsit. At first, "special assumpsit" was a narrow remedy and could readily be defeated by variances in proof. Eventually, in the Seventeenth Century, a new form called "general assumpsit" was recognized. It allowed recovery for such divergent theories as an unpaid promissory note or money paid over by mistake or even embezzled, in which the "assumpsit" allegation—literally, "he promised"—was fictitious. Its breadth and simplicity made general assumpsit popular with plaintiffs. As in the case of the defense of the general issue, the common law had come full circle: general assumpsit was subject to criticism because, in removing technicalities, it had taken a form that failed to narrow the issues.

Notes and Questions

(1) *Which Form of Action?* Consider which form you would plead if you represented a common law plaintiff in each of these cases.

(a) *The Case of the Purloined Car.* The defendant moves the plaintiff's car outside the garage, so he can get his own car to his parking place. He neglects to move the plaintiff's car back into the garage, and it is stolen. The plaintiff sues in trover; what result?

The answer might be found in *Bushel v. Miller,* 1 Strange 128, 93 Eng. Rep. 428 (K.B. 1718), an analogous case in which the plaintiff lost on a declaration in trover because it was "clear" to the court that the defendant's conduct "could not amount to a conversion." The court added that "there might be a doubt" if trespass had been alleged. Thoughtful readers might conclude that this set of facts instead fits trespass on the case.

(b) *The Case of the Seized Billiard Table.* A thief steals the plaintiff's billiard table and sells it to the defendant. The plaintiff asks for it back, but the defendant refuses; later, when he discovers the true facts, the defendant offers to let the plaintiff take it. But in the meantime, the defendant's landlord has seized the billiard table for the defendant's past-due rent! The plaintiff sues in trover; the defendant pleads the general issue ("not guilty"). What result? In *Burroughs v. Bayne*, 5 Hurlstone & Norman 296 (Exch. 1860), the court discussed (1) trespass, which would not fit because it would require a "taking" by the defendant "out of the possession of the owner"; (2) replevin, which probably would not fit because it was for goods distrained by the defendant but "restored to the owner by process of law"; (3) detinue, which was "a direct remedy . . . where a chattel was detained" but was undesirable because it allowed wager of law; (4) general assumpsit, for a "broken promise," express or implied; and, finally, (5) trover, which was "the action whereby a person entitled to the possession of goods wrongfully detained from him was entitled to recover damages for their detention." The requirement of a "conversion," said the court, was an "unfortunate expression," but it merely signified a detention by the defendant "so as to deprive the [plaintiff] of his dominion over" the property. Held, on trover for the loss of the billiard table, for the plaintiff.

Are the *Bushel* and *Burroughs* decisions consistent?

(2) *Advantages and Disadvantages.* Try to verbalize what is advantageous about the forms of action, if anything. Also, try to enumerate and explain the disadvantages of this system in light of the above cases.

[B] Equity: An Alternative System Develops

During the development of these elaborate forms of action and rules of pleading of the common law, another system was also evolving. The other, radically different, system was called "equity."

The Origins of Equity. The chancellor functioned as a kind of secretary of state to the king. He was keeper of the great seal and supervised the massive amount of writing that had to be done in the king's name. Usually, he was a bishop and was thought of as the king's "conscience." The chancellor also had the duty of issuing writs to commence common law actions; and, in fact, if an aggrieved person could find no established writ for his case, the king remained as a reserve of justice, and in practice the dispensation of that justice by the invention of new writs fell largely to the chancellor. By the Fourteenth Century, the common law courts had become hostile to new forms and would quash writs that differed from those in recognized use. The chancellor developed a more direct route for these cases. He would summon the "defendant" and examine him concerning the "plaintiff's" cause, without referring the matter to a court. The process became formalized, with the petitioner filing a "bill" in Chancery.

"No Adequate Remedy at Law." In the Fourteenth Century, the two systems overlapped, because the chancellors did not perceive any particular restrictions on their authority. But the common law judges were jealous of their jurisdiction, and they used political and judicial power to confine the chancellor to cases in which the law courts did not provide an adequate remedy. For example, if a trustee refused to use the property for the beneficiary, or even if he embezzled it and

took it for himself, the common law would not intervene, because the trustee had legal title and therefore all the title that the law courts recognized. The chancellor therefore took over the enforcement of trusts, which were popular. Furthermore, the common law provided no adequate remedy in various cases of "fraud, accident, or breach of confidence," according to a famous saying. Equity provided redress for these claims. The subjects of equity jurisdiction bore no relationship to each other, because the determinant was that the plaintiff had "no adequate remedy at law."

The Transition from Ecclesiastics to Trained Lawyers: Sir Thomas More. The Lord Chancellor best known today is probably Sir Thomas More, who served from 1529 to 1532. Educated as a lawyer at common law, he marks the shift in administration of equity from ecclesiastics and canons to trained lawyers. His conscience was such that, during the reign of Henry VIII (who needed independence from the papacy to void his marriage), he was executed because he refused to take an oath of the king's supremacy as head of the church. He later was canonized by the Roman Catholic Church.

Equitable Remedies. The common law executed its judgments by seizing property. The chancellors had no such authority, but they did have behind them the power of the king to arrest and imprison the individual before them. Therefore, equity acted "in personam": it would order the respondent to do or refrain from doing an act and imprison him if he disobeyed. This remedy, in fact, was the greatest invention of equity: the injunction. But even today, a claimant seeking an injunction must show the absence of an adequate remedy at law, and if a suit for damages would give complete relief, an injunction cannot issue.

The Chancellor's Discretion and the Absence of Jury Trial. The principles of equity were loose and highly discretionary. The chancellor could refuse relief to a person who had "unclean hands," or who was acting fraudulently himself. Furthermore, the chancellor would balance the equities in deciding on the precise contours of the relief he would tailor to the particular case. In fact, the evolution of new equitable remedies continues to the modern day; the school desegregation cases, in which courts invented zoning, pairing, faculty ratios, and the like, are a prime example. But while the flexibility to meet new needs was desirable, the unpredictability and ostensibly unlimited nature of the power of the chancellor was not. It was said that equity depended on "the length of the chancellor's foot." Given the character of equitable relief, it was clear (and still is clear today) that there was no right to trial by jury in equity. How could the jury draft an injunction? How could it function as the king's conscience in developing new remedies?

Equitable Procedure: Depositions and Discovery. When a bill was filed in Chancery, the pursuit of equitable remedies sometimes required investigation. Equity invented the deposition, and all testimony was presented by deposition. Live witnesses were not used at trial. The investigative power of a bill in Chancery was so significant that litigants in the common law courts filed equitable bills, called "bills of discovery," to aid their suits.

Equity in America. In some but not all of the thirteen American colonies, Courts of Chancery existed alongside the courts at law. There are separate Courts of Chancery in a few states still today, and in many if not most states, the jurisdiction of the courts is partly defined by whether the relief sought is legal or equitable. (California is an example; *see* Chapter 3, § II, above.)

Delay in Chancery: Dickens' Bleak House. Early equity proceedings were efficient, but several problems developed. First, the Chancery's insistence upon trial solely by depositions was slow and very expensive. Secondly, equity insisted upon joining all persons in the suit whose interests might be remotely affected. Numerous parties with contingent interests clogged the proceedings, and settlements were impeded. "This is the Court of Chancery," wrote Charles Dickens in *Bleak House* (1852). "Suffer any wrong that can be done you, rather than come here!":

> [The lawsuit of] Jarndyce and Jarndyce drones on. This scarecrow of a suit has . . . become so complicated that no man alive knows what it means. . . . Innumerable children have been born into the cause: innumerable old people have died out of it. Scores of persons have deliriously found themselves made parties in Jarndyce and Jarndyce without knowing how or why; whole families have inherited legendary hatreds with the suit. . . . [B]ut Jarndyce and Jarndyce still drags its dreary length before the Court. . . .

The litigants and lawyers in *Bleak House* spent so much effort disputing the allocation of a very large inheritance, that the "weary length" of Jarndyce and Jarndyce consumed the entirety of the fund at issue.

[C] "Code" Pleading

[1] Simplification: Pleading "Facts" Constituting a "Cause of Action"

Reform: The Republic of Texas and the New York Commission. The middle of the Nineteenth Century saw serious efforts at reform. In 1840, the Fourth Congress of the Republic of Texas declared that the adoption of the common law "shall not be construed to adopt the common law system of pleading." Texas also abolished the forms of action, merged law and equity, and provided for a simple "petition and answer" based on the Spanish system of pleading. *See* W. Dorsaneo, D. Crump, E. Carlson & E. Thornburg, *Texas Civil Procedure: Pretrial Litigation* § 5.01 (2007–08 ed.).

A few years later, New York's Commission on Practice and Pleading became one of the most influential voices in the reform movement. It proposed a system in which "no action . . . need be designated . . . by any name, form, or distinction of action . . . ; but that the only test of the right of the party complaining, [s]hall be, whether in his complaint he sets forth a sufficient legal right and a violation or withholding of such right by the party complained against." Preliminary Report of the Commissioners on Practice and Pleadings of New York 14–16 (1847).

The "Field Codes." The year after the Commission's preliminary report, New York adopted a new Code known as the Field Code, after the head of the New York Commission, David Dudley Field. The Code became the model for similar reform in other states, whose codes were also loosely called Field codes. The New York Code contained the following provisions:

> § 62. The distinction between actions at law and suits in equity, and the forms of all such actions and suits . . . are abolished; and there shall be in this state, hereafter, but one form of action, . . . which shall be denominated a civil action.
>
> § 120(2). The complaint shall contain . . . [a] statement of the facts constituting the cause of action, in ordinary and concise language, . . . in such a manner as to enable a person of common understanding to know what is intended. . . .
>
> § 132. No other pleading shall be allowed, than the complaint, demurrer, answer, and reply.
>
> § 151. The court shall, at every stage of an action, disregard any error, or defect in the pleadings or proceedings, which shall not affect the substantial rights of the adverse party. . . .

The Field Code represented a dramatic procedural departure from common law traditions. It abolished the forms of action, merged law and equity, limited pleadings to four functional categories, limited the effects of technical errors, and required pleading of "facts constituting the cause of action."

The Hidden Difficulties of Abolishing Common Law Methods: Pleading "the Facts" of the "Cause of Action." The Field Code did not solve all of the problems. First, the forms of action were still the basis of the substantive law. Secondly, there were hidden difficulties in the requirement that the plaintiff plead "the facts constituting the cause of action." For example, a negligence complaint must state the facts giving rise to the defendant's duty, the breach of that duty, proximate causation, the injury to the plaintiff, and the plaintiff's damages. Similarly, a pleading asserting that the defendant "assaulted" the plaintiff would not suffice, because it stated only a conclusion. The courts often found themselves mired in differentiating among "facts," "conclusions," and "evidence," particularly since these conceptions expressed differences only of degree and were inherently difficult to distinguish. *See generally* C. Clark, *Code Pleading* (2d ed. 1947).

Pleading the Absence of Something. Imagine that plaintiff wants to assert a cause of action for malicious prosecution. One of the elements of this tort is that a defendant caused a prosecution to be initiated against the plaintiff without probable cause. A plaintiff cannot plead "facts" showing that there was no probable cause; instead, inevitably, the claim requires a conclusory statement that, "There was no probable cause." But that would be a conclusion, wouldn't it? The emphasis on pleading facts thus failed to cure the historic problem; as with the common law, courts and litigants continued to expend energies on process rather than merits.

[2] The "Theory of the Pleadings" Doctrine

These problems were exacerbated, even under the Field Codes, by an insistence on a single "theory of the pleadings." That is, the plaintiff was confined to one narrow claim. The plaintiff was not permitted to allege, for example, that "Defendant either acted negligently or acted intentionally." Sometimes, a plaintiff might not know which applied, but still, the plaintiff was required to choose just one possibility. Here is an example.

CITY OF UNION CITY v. MURPHY, 176 Ind. 597, 96 N.E. 584 (1911). The City converted a small sanitary sewer into a storm-and-surface-water sewer. The sewer became overloaded and water and sewage backed into Murphy's cellar. At trial, the jury was instructed both that it should find for Murphy if the City had caused his damages by negligence and, also, that it should find for him if the City had willfully created a nuisance. The jury found in Murphy's favor. The appellate court reversed:

> [T]he case must be tried upon a single theory, and plaintiff must recover on that theory or not at all. . . . There is a clear distinction between cases which count on negligence as a ground of action and those which are founded on acts of aggressive wrong or wilfulness, and a pleading should not be tolerated which proceeds upon the idea that it may be good [for either]. . . . If the complaint proceeded on the theory of wilful injury, [Murphy] could not recover for injury caused by the negligence of [the City], even though the court should find facts in his favor showing that he had an action for this cause. Therefore, it was error to give instructions under which [Murphy] could recover either for wilful injury or for injury resulting from negligence. . . .

Notes and Questions

(1) *Problems from Prohibiting Inconsistent Theories and Arguments in the Alternative.* The common law courts, like the Field Codes, were very strict about limiting the dispute to a singular matter. Both systems prevented a plaintiff from arguing in the alternative or joining different claims in a single declaration. In other words, plaintiff had to choose, at the pleadings stage, whether to accuse a defendant of negligence or intentional misconduct, making the procedural characterizations more important than the substantive dispute and resolution. As a practical matter, a large share of the blame for the problems of strict code pleading is due to rules about joinder rather than rules of pleading.

(2) *Permitting Inconsistent Theories.* Modern pleading rules allow inconsistent allegations, for precisely this reason. *See e.g.* Fed. R. Civ. P. 18 (referring to "alternative" claims).

[3] Variances

A variance occurs if there is a fatal difference between the pleadings and the evidence at trial. You should recall that the common law courts were subject to criticism for injustices due to variances. In a system with strict requirements that "facts" rather than conclusions be pleaded, and allowing only a single kind of claim, the variance problem is enhanced, because the lawsuit, as it proceeds, may uncover evidence that disagrees with the "facts" as pled. Consider the following case.

MESSICK v. TURNAGE, 240 N.C. 625, 83 S.E.2d 654 (1954). While the plaintiff was seated as a patron in the defendant's movie theatre, falling plaster and water from the ceiling above her frightened her, so that she involuntarily jumped from her seat, striking the metal seat in front of her and injuring her leg. Her complaint charged the defendant with negligence, in that "the defendant failed to maintain a safe theatre . . . in that the defendant knew or should have known by reasonable observation which was his duty, that [the defendant's] roof was leaking and in bad repair." However, the plaintiff's proof at trial did not show a leaking roof. Instead, it showed that a fixture in the balcony restroom failed to close, the restroom filled with water, the water did not drain because the drainpipe was clogged with cigarette butts and other debris, the water seeped into the balcony carpet, and it loosened the plaster below it, causing it to fall. The trial judge granted judgment for the defendant at the conclusion of the plaintiff's evidence. The appellate court affirmed:

> . . . It was incumbent upon the plaintiff not only to prove negligence proximately causing her injury, but it was her duty to prove negligence substantially as alleged in her complaint. This she failed to do. Proof without allegation is as unavailing as allegation without proof. . . .

[D] Modern State Practice Requiring the Pleading of a "Cause of Action"

One Modern Approach to Pleading: Abolish the Requirement that Plaintiff Plead a Cause of Action. One way to address the problems illustrated by the preceding cases is to remove the requirement that the plaintiff plead a "cause of action." This is the approach adopted by the Federal Rules and, following their example, by many of the states. In these systems, the pleadings are not designed strictly to narrow the issues, nor to separate legal questions from factual ones, and joinder of claims is liberally allowed. While some relationship between the evidence and the pleadings must still exist, pleadings do not have to recite the evidence or contain detail.

Another Modern Approach to Pleading, Followed by Some States: Retain the Requirement That a Cause of Action Be Pleaded, But with Liberalized Rules. Some states have declined to follow the federal model and still require the pleading of a "cause of action." But modern state pleadings do not require narrow fact pleading. The elements of the cause of action must be present in the pleading, but if the pleading gives notice of the plaintiff's factual theory of the elements, it is sufficient. *See, e.g.* Rule 1.110 of the Florida Rules of Civil Procedure (abolishing all "forms of action and technical forms," yet requiring "a short and plain statement of the ultimate facts showing that the pleader is entitled to relief"); Cal. Code. Civ. Proc. § 425.10(a)(the complaint must contain "a statement of the facts constituting the cause of action in ordinary and concise language").

In theory, these rules avoid the disadvantageous baggage of common law or strict code pleading. But they have the advantage of requiring the parties "to recognize the elements of their cause of action and determine whether they have or can develop the facts necessary to support it, which avoids a great deal of wasted expense to the litigants and unnecessary judicial effort." *Continental Baking Co. v. Vincent,* 634 So. 2d 242, 244 (Fla. 5th DCA 1994).

II. The Functions Served by the Pleadings

Shipman, Common Law Pleading

9-10 Ballantyne 3d ed. 1923(*)

... The various possible objects and purposes of pleading may be enumerated somewhat as follows: (1) To separate questions of law from questions of fact and decide them so far as possible prior to the trial of the facts. (2) To reduce questions of fact to clear-cut issues, by eliminating admitted, immaterial, and incidental matters, and narrowing the case to the one or more definite propositions on which the controversy really turns. (3) To notify parties of the claims, defenses, and cross-demands of their adversaries. (4) To serve as the formal basis of the judgment. (5) To place on record the questions raised and give litigants the advantage of a plea of *res judicata*, if the same questions should be raised again in other causes. (6) Lastly, there may be added the function of serving as an index of the points to be proved at the trial and apportioning the burden of proof and rebuttal as between the plaintiff and the defendant.

Notes and Questions

(1) *Ranking the Purposes: Should Notice Come First?* How important are Shipman's first three purposes—those of giving notice, separating law from fact, and defining the issues? Some scholars called for a singular focus on notice. *Cf.* Whittier, *Notice Pleading*, 31 Harv. L. Rev. 501 (1918). Critics, of course, would argue that a focus on notice excludes other valid purposes.

(2) *Missing from the List: Truth?* The Massachusetts commissioners of 1851 stated the purposes of civil pleading as including "(1) that each party may be under the most effectual influences, ... so far as he admits or denies anything, to tell the

(*) Reprinted with permission of the West Publishing Company.

truth; . . . ." Why does Shipman's list not include this purpose? Perhaps the pleadings are not themselves the best device for ascertaining the truth of contested allegations. Then again, an answer to the allegations in a complaint generally requires an "admission" or a "denial." And the ethical rules governing lawyers often state that when representing a client, "a lawyer shall not knowingly . . . make a false statement of material fact or law to a third person . . . ." *See, e.g.*, American Bar Association Model Rules of Professional Conduct, Rule 4.1.

Problem A: Chapter 5 Summary Problem

ALICE DELAGROI'S MEDICAL MALPRACTICE CLAIM. Mrs. Alice Delagroi consults you about alleged malpractice during the removal of her appendix at Singleton Hospital. She emerged from the operation with a severely impaired left arm, in which various injections had been administered by various individuals. Because the impairment of an arm due to an appendix operation is unusual, and you surmise it would not normally occur in the absence of malpractice, you believe you may have a claim against one or more of the following: Mrs. Delagroi's physician; the anesthesiologist; the scrub nurse; various interns; the duty nurse; the hospital; and various other unknown persons or entities. Your suit will be filed in a federal court.

Upon checking, you find that the statute of limitations is two years, and it runs in precisely twenty days. You have a copy of the medical records for this operation, but you have little time to investigate further, and you are uncertain about which substantive law theories—negligence, warranty, strict liability, agency theories, or consumer legislation—might apply to which defendants. You face a dilemma: If you file suit against all the defendants and sort the matter out later, you may violate Rule 11, and these defendants are among those most likely to move for sanctions; but if you leave out any potential defendant, you may find your claim time-barred, especially because the defendants you do sue may point to the absent person as the guilty one. What should you do?

You may read this problem now, but you will need to read the rest of the Chapter to answer it (or, as always, you should treat it as your instructor directs). In analyzing the problem, you might consider the following issues:

1. How solid does your pleading of the claims need to be, in order to avoid the granting of a motion to dismiss?
2. What degree of specificity is required, to avoid the granting of a motion for more definite statement?
3. If you fail to include a given person as a defendant, and if a jury later determines that that person was solely responsible for your client's injuries, what might be the consequences for your client—and for you?
4. If you omit a party now because of uncertain liability, will you be able to amend to include that party after discovery, and have your pleading relate back to a time before the statute of limitations ran? (What can you do to enhance this possibility?)

5. What sanctions are possible under Fed. R. Civ. P. 11 if you carelessly file suit against an innocent party, and what can you do to minimize the likelihood of such sanctions?

[Note: Some jurisdictions follow the rule of *Ybarra v. Spangard*, 25 Cal. 2d 486, 154 P.2d 687, 162 A.L.R. 1258 (1944), which places the burden of "giving an explanation" on the defendants, when the plaintiff shows that she had "unusual" injuries and that the defendants had "control" over her body. This rule affects the plaintiff's dilemma, here—but it does not solve it, because it remains unclear exactly who had "control," and a "reasonable investigation" is still required.]

III. The Complaint in Federal Court

Read Fed. R. Civ. P. 7; 8(a), (d), (e); 10; and 84.

[A] What Kind of Information Must Plaintiff Include?

[1] Earlier Cases with a Looser Standard for Specificity

Note on "Notice Pleading"

Two Related Standards, Often Stated Together. Rule 8 requires that the complaint contain a "short and plain statement of the claim showing that the pleader is entitled to relief." But this standard begs the question. Just how "short"? And what needs to be "plain"? To answer these questions, the Supreme Court has set up two standards, which are related and which often appear together in a single statement:

1. How Much Information? The first standard is about the amount of information that is needed. In early cases, the Court said that the complaint had to give the opposing side "fair notice of the claim and of the grounds" on which it rests. This standard of "notice pleading" might be taken to mean that the complaint must reveal the legal principles on which the claim rests (e.g., negligence) and something about the factual grounds (e.g., that the claim is based on an automobile collision; see former Federal Form 11, cited below). Recently, however, the Court has tightened the idea of notice pleading. The complaint must contain "facts sufficient" to make the inference of a claim "plausible." But early cases did not contain this requirement.

2. If, After the Allegations Are Assumed True, the Plaintiff Cannot Prevail, Dismissal—Even if The Facts Are Specific. There also is a substantive standard. The court must assume that the allegations are true, since there has been no discovery or trial, and there is no evidence; all the court has is the complaint. After assuming the allegations true, if the court can conclude that the plaintiff cannot recover anything under the substantive law, the court can dismiss. This is true even if the factual allegations are highly specific.

In this subsection and in subsection [2] below, we consider principally the first standard—how specific the complaint must be; how much information it must contain—although you will see that the two standards are related. The two requirements are often stated together in a single sentence, by a declaration such as, "The complaint must contain sufficient facts so that if all facts are assumed true, it is plausible to infer that plaintiff has a valid claim." Note that this statement contains the two standards: (1) sufficient facts to make a claim plausible and (2) a valid claim if all of the facts are assumed to be true.

The Standard for Sufficient Information Has Shifted Significantly. Over the years, the courts have struggled to find the appropriate standard for the amount of information that the complaint must contain. There are advantages to a tight pleading standard (fewer unmeritorious cases), but there also are advantages to a more relaxed standard (resolving claims on the merits by trial instead of by technicalities in the pleadings). To understand where we are now, you must understand the tension between these opposing ideas.

Early Cases with Looser Standards about Factual Sufficiency. In the next section, we take up the requirement that there be factual allegations sufficient to allow an inference that the claim is "plausible," which appears in the later cases. But the early cases used a less strict standard. *Dioguardi v. Durning*, the next case, contains no standard except that plaintiff state "a claim," and it has received significant criticism. The case after that, *Conley v. Gibson*, expresses the requirement of notice pleading. It also contains a standard (now overruled) allowing dismissal only if the inadequacy of plaintiff's claim appears "beyond doubt": an approach that probably seemed to judges to discourage dismissals even when they were merited.

Dioguardi v. Durning

139 F.2d 774 (2d Cir. 1944)

CLARK, CIRCUIT JUDGE.

In his complaint, obviously home drawn, plaintiff attempts to assert a series of grievances against the Collector of Customs at the Port of New York growing out of his endeavors to import merchandise from Italy "of great value," consisting of bottles of "tonics." We may pass certain of his claims as either inadequate or inadequately stated and consider only these two: (1) that on the auction day, October 9, 1940, when defendant sold the merchandise at "public custom," "he sold my merchandise to another bidder with my price of $110, and not of his price of $120," and (2) "that three weeks before the sale, two cases, of 19 bottles each case, disappeared." Plaintiff... [alleges that] he made a claim for "refund of merchandise which was two-thirds paid in Milano, Italy," and that the collector denied the claim. These and other circumstances alleged indicate... that the collector, having held [the merchandise] for a year (presumably as unclaimed merchandise under 19 U.S.C.A. § 1491), then sold it, or such part of it as was left, at public auction. For his asserted injuries plaintiff claimed $5,000 damages, together with interest and costs, against the defendant individually and as collector. This complaint was dismissed by the District Court, with leave, however, to plaintiff to amend, on motion of the United States Attorney, appearing for the defendant, on the ground that it "fails to state facts sufficient to constitute a cause of action."

Thereupon plaintiff filed an amended complaint, wherein . . . he vigorously reiterates his claims, including those quoted above and now stated as that his "medicinal extracts" were given to the Springdale Distilling Company "with my betting [bidding?] price of $110: and not their price of $120," and "It isn't so easy to do away with two cases with 37 bottles of one quart. Being protected, they can take this chance." An earlier paragraph suggests that defendant had explained the loss of the two cases by "saying that they had leaked, which could never be true in the manner they were bottled." On defendant's motion for dismissal on the same ground as before, the court made a final judgment dismissing the complaint, and plaintiff now comes to us with increased volubility, if not clarity.

It would seem, however, that he has stated enough to withstand a mere formal motion, directed only to the face of the complaint, and that here is another instance of judicial haste which in the long run makes waste. Under the new rules of civil procedure, there is no pleading requirement of stating "facts sufficient to constitute a cause of action," but only that there be "a short and plain statement of the claim showing that the pleader is entitled to relief," [a]nd the motion for dismissal under Rule 12(b) is for failure to state "a claim upon which relief can be granted." . . .

We think that, however inartistically they may be stated, the plaintiff has disclosed his claims that the collector has converted or otherwise done away with two of his cases of medicinal tonics and has sold the rest in a manner incompatible with the public auction he had announced—and, indeed, required by 19 U.S.C.A. § 1491 . . . . [Reversed and remanded.]

Notes and Questions

(1) *"Filling in the Details" by Discovery.* The premise underlying the Federal Rules is that pleadings can be general because discovery supplies the details. On the other hand, how successful do you think Durning would be in sending interrogatories to Dioguardi asking him to particularize his contentions, and even if he could succeed, is it fair to place the cost of that process on defendant Durning?

(2) *"Claim" and "Cause of Action."* Code pleading required the statement of a "cause of action." A cause-of-action pleading consists of legal and factual notice of each element of the claim. The Federal Rules deliberately avoid that term and require only the statement of a "claim." What is the difference between a "cause of action" and a "claim"? Precise scholars might construe the term "claim" as merely requiring a broad statement that includes a request for monetary, injunctive, or

equitable relief, with notice of the legal theory and the factual context, and the term "cause of action" to require a statement of the elements. In practice, lawyers rarely draw such fine distinctions, and today, the two are hard to distinguish. *See, e.g.*, Oliver McCaskill, *The Elusive Cause of Action*, 4 U. Chi. L. Rev. 281, 285–286 (1937); *Claim or Cause of Action?*, 13 F.R.D. 253 (1952).

(3) *An Attempt to Exemplify a Claim and a Cause of Action.* Recognizing that any distinction is artificial, consider these two examples:

> (a) On [date], the defendant negligently maintained the floor of its store by allowing it to be in a slippery condition. By reason of that negligence, the plaintiff suffered personal injuries, for which the defendant is liable to the plaintiff in the amount of $100,000.
>
> (b) On [date], the plaintiff was a customer in defendant's store and therefore was owed a duty as a business invitee. The defendant negligently maintained its floor by allowing it to be in a slippery condition owing to spillage of liquid. That negligence resulted in plaintiff's slipping and falling and thereby proximately caused the plaintiff to suffer personal injuries, including a broken wrist. The defendant is liable to the plaintiff for those injuries in the amount of $100,000.

To what extent is there a real difference in terms of the proper function of the pleadings?

CONLEY v. GIBSON, 355 U.S. 41 (1957). The complaint in this case alleged that the plaintiffs, who were African-American, had not received "fair representation" by their union, which is one of the duties imposed on unions by federal labor legislation. More specifically, the complaint alleged that plaintiffs were employees of the Texas and New Orleans Railroad; that the railroad purported to abolish their 45 jobs; that all of them were demoted or discharged; that in truth, the jobs were not abolished, but instead were filled by other, newly hired employees who were white; that despite repeated pleas by the plaintiffs, the union did nothing to protect the plaintiffs; that the union refused to provide representation comparable to that given others; and that the union thus had refused to provide plaintiffs with fair representation. (Notice that this was not a civil rights case, but a suit under national labor legislation, although the races of the employees were relevant to the proof.) The District Court granted the union's motion to dismiss, and the Court of Appeals affirmed. The Supreme Court, through Justice Black, reversed:

> In appraising the sufficiency of the complaint we follow, of course, the accepted rule that a complaint should not be dismissed for failure to state a claim unless it appears beyond doubt that the plaintiff can prove no set of facts in support of his claim which would entitle him to relief. Here, the complaint alleged, in part, that petitioners were discharged wrongfully by the Railroad and that the Union, acting according to plan, refused to

> protect their jobs as it did those of white employees or to help them with their grievances all because they were Negroes. If these allegations are proven there has been a manifest breach of the Union's duty to represent fairly....

The [defendants] also argue that the complaint failed to set forth specific facts to support its general allegations of discrimination and that dismissal is therefore proper. The decisive answer to this is that the Federal Rules of Civil Procedure do not require a claimant to set out in detail the facts upon which he bases his claim. To the contrary, all the Rules require is "a short and plain statement of the claim" that will give the defendant fair notice of what the plaintiff's claim is and the grounds upon which it rests.....

[As is indicated above, the "beyond doubt" standard has been overruled. See below—Eds.]

Notes and Questions

(1) *What Does "Notice Pleading" Mean?* The Court says that it is a requirement that the complaint give the defendant "fair notice" of "what the plaintiff's claim is" and "the grounds upon which it rests." But requiring a statement of "the grounds" begs the question. How much does the complaint need to say about "the grounds"?

(2) *Rule 84 and the (Now Abolished) Federal Forms.* For many years, when federal courts invoked *Conley v. Gibson,* above (with its standard of loose notice pleading), Rule 84 of the Federal Rules of Civil Procedure included forms to help lawyers prepare pleadings. Consider Federal Form 11, which was the form alleging negligence in an automobile accident:

> Complaint for Negligence.
>
> 1. [Allegation of jurisdiction.]
>
> 2. On [date], at [place], the defendant negligently drove a motor vehicle against the plaintiff....

This form contained two kinds of information about the claim: (1) the legal theory, in this instance negligence, and (2) the factual context, which in this instance is that the negligence occurred when the defendant drove his automobile and collided with the plaintiff. The factual basis of the negligence allegation was not required by the form. In other words, the form suggests that plaintiff does not need to say whether defendant failed to apply his brakes, or to maintain the brakes, or to steer away, or any of an infinite variety of other possibilities. This approach to pleading seemed sufficient pursuant to *Conley v. Gibson,* which required only notice and allowed dismissal of a case only if the plaintiff's inability to recover was beyond doubt. But this aspect of *Conley v. Gibson* is overruled by the decision below, *Bell Atlantic Corporation v. Twombly.* A few years after that decision, the federal forms codified in Rule 84 were abolished.

[2] The Stricter Cases: Adding a Requirement That Factual Allegations Make the Claim "Plausible"

How to Read the Case of Bell Atlantic v. Twombly

The following case, *Bell Atlantic Corporation v. Twombly*, changes the standards that govern the complaint. It tightens them. It overrules the "beyond doubt" language set out in the earlier case of *Conley v. Gibson*, and it introduces a requirement that the complaint must include enough facts—not mere conclusions, but facts—so that the inference of a claim is "plausible."

The substantive law in this case is the Sherman Antitrust Act, which outlaws any "contract, combination or conspiracy in restraint of trade." This substantive law makes for certain difficulties in reading the opinion. A "contract, combination or conspiracy" obviously will produce parallel behaviors among firms. But so will some kinds of decisions engaged in by each firm individually, even in the absence of a contract, combination or conspiracy. To take a simple example, in the telecommunications industry, it can be expected that the providers will use somewhat similar keypads, because keypads have to be familiar to customers. Also, the prices for given services probably will be at least roughly similar, because if a telecommunications company charges less, it will lose money, and if it charges more, it will lose customers. In other words, parallel behaviors will occur even without a conspiracy.

In *Bell Atlantic v. Twombly*, the allegation is that the competitors have refrained from competing outside of certain territories, or outside their respective regional service areas. But this allegation could simply be explained by independent decisions to avoid risky expenditures in undeveloped regions, just as well as it could be explained by conspiracy theories. And the majority notes that discovery in such a case will be extraordinarily expensive. These costs, it concludes, should not be imposed without a pleading showing that the alleged claim is "plausible."

One of the issues in this case, then, is whether an allegation only of parallel behavior in the form of maintaining regional service areas (or each firm's sticking to its territory), together with a conclusory allegation that a contract, combination, or conspiracy exists, is sufficient. The majority holds that it is not. The parallel behavior may be motivated simply by the independent self-interest of each firm, and the accusatory conclusion charging a conspiracy provides no facts to the contrary. The decision and its application remain controversial, with detractors arguing that it conflicts with the Federal Rules and disenfranchises the plaintiff who is confronted with the unknown motives of defendants.

Bell Atlantic Corp. v. Twombly

127 S. Ct. 1955 (2007)

Justice Souter delivered the opinion of the Court.

Liability under § 1 of the Sherman Act, 15 U.S.C. § 1, requires a "contract, combination . . . , or conspiracy, in restraint of trade or commerce." The question in this putative class action is whether a § 1 complaint can survive a motion to dismiss when it alleges that major telecommunications providers engaged in certain parallel conduct unfavorable to competition, absent some factual context suggesting agreement, as distinct from identical, independent action. We hold that such a complaint should be dismissed.

I

The upshot of the 1984 divestiture of the American Telephone & Telegraph Company's (AT&T) local telephone business was a system of regional service monopolies (variously called "Regional Bell Operating Companies," "Baby Bells," or "Incumbent Local Exchange Carriers" (ILECs)), and a separate, competitive market for long-distance service from which the ILECs were excluded. More than a decade later, Congress withdrew approval of the ILECs' monopolies by enacting the Telecommunications Act of 1996 (1996 Act), . . . which "fundamentally restructure[d] local telephone markets" . . . .

"Central to the [new] scheme [was each ILEC's] obligation . . . to share its network with competitors," . . . which came to be known as "competitive local exchange carriers" (CLECs). . . . A CLEC could make use of an ILEC's network in any of three ways: by (1) "purchas[ing] local telephone services at wholesale rates for resale to end users," (2) "leas[ing] elements of the [ILEC's] network 'on an unbundled basis,'" or (3) "interconnect[ing] its own facilities with the [ILEC's] network." . . .

Respondents William Twombly and Lawrence Marcus (hereinafter plaintiffs) represent a putative class consisting of all "subscribers of local telephone and/or high speed internet services . . . ." . . . In this action against petitioners, a group of ILECs, plaintiffs seek treble damages and declaratory and injunctive relief for claimed violations of § 1 of the Sherman Act, . . . which prohibits "[e]very contract, combination in the form of trust or otherwise, or conspiracy, in restraint of trade . . . ."

The complaint alleges that the ILECs conspired to restrain trade in two ways, each supposedly inflating charges for local telephone and high-speed internet services. Plaintiffs say, first, that the ILECs "engaged in parallel conduct" in their respective service areas to inhibit the growth of upstart CLECs. . . .

Second, the complaint charges agreements by the ILECs to refrain from competing against one another. . . .

The complaint couches its ultimate allegations this way:

> "In the absence of any meaningful competition between the [ILECs] in one another's markets, and in light of the parallel course of conduct that each engaged in to prevent competition from CLECs within their respective . . . markets and the other facts and market circumstances alleged above, Plaintiffs allege upon information and belief that [the ILECs] have entered into a contract, combination or conspiracy to prevent competitive entry in their respective . . . markets and have agreed not to compete with one another and otherwise allocated customers and markets to one another." . . .

not sure but you believe

The United States District Court for the Southern District of New York dismissed the complaint for failure to state a claim upon which relief can be granted. . . . The District Court found plaintiffs' allegations of parallel ILEC actions to discourage competition inadequate because "the behavior of each ILEC . . . is fully explained by the ILEC's own interests in defending its individual territory." . . .

The Court of Appeals for the Second Circuit reversed, holding that the District Court tested the complaint by the wrong standard. It held that "plus factors are not required to be pleaded to permit an antitrust claim based on parallel conduct to survive dismissal." . . .

We granted certiorari to address the proper standard for pleading an antitrust conspiracy through allegations of parallel conduct, . . . and now reverse.

II

A

Because § 1 of the Sherman Act "does not prohibit [all] unreasonable restraints of trade . . . but only restraints effected by a contract, combination, or conspiracy," . . . "[t]he crucial question" is whether the challenged anticompetitive conduct "stem[s] from independent decision or from an agreement, tacit or express". . . . While a showing of parallel "business behavior is admissible circumstantial evidence from which the fact finder may infer agreement," it falls short of "conclusively establish[ing] agreement or . . . itself constitut[ing] a Sherman Act offense." . . . Even "conscious parallelism," a common reaction of "firms in a concentrated market [that] recogniz[e] their shared economic interests and their interdependence with respect to price and output decisions," is "not in itself unlawful." . . .

B

. . . Federal Rule of Civil Procedure 8(a)(2) requires only "a short and plain statement of the claim showing that the pleader is entitled to relief," in order to "give the defendant fair notice of what the . . . claim is and the grounds upon which it rests," *Conley v. Gibson*, 355 U.S. 41, 47 (1957). While a complaint attacked by a Rule 12(b)(6) motion to dismiss does not need detailed factual allegations, . . . a plaintiff's obligation to provide the "grounds" of his "entitle[ment] to relief" requires more than labels and conclusions, and a formulaic recitation of the elements of a cause of action will not do. . . .[1] . . .

In applying these general standards to a § 1 claim, we hold that stating such a claim requires a complaint with enough factual matter (taken as true) to suggest

(1) . . . While, for most types of cases, the Federal Rules eliminated the cumbersome requirement that a claimant "set out *in detail* the facts upon which he bases his claim," *Conley v. Gibson*, 355 U.S. 41, 47 (1957) (emphasis added); Rule 8(a)(2) still requires a "showing," rather than a blanket assertion, of entitlement to relief. Without some factual allegation in the complaint, it is hard to see how a claimant could satisfy the requirement of providing not only "fair notice" of the nature of the claim, but also "grounds" on which the claim rests. . . .

that an agreement was made. Asking for plausible grounds to infer an agreement does not impose a probability requirement at the pleading stage; it simply calls for enough facts to raise a reasonable expectation that discovery will reveal evidence of illegal agreement. . . . And, of course, a well-pleaded complaint may proceed even if it strikes a savvy judge that actual proof of those facts is improbable, and "that a recovery is very remote and unlikely." . . . [But] when allegations of parallel conduct are set out in order to make a § 1 claim, they must be placed in a context that raises a suggestion of a preceding agreement, not merely parallel conduct that could just as well be independent action. . . .

The need . . . for allegations plausibly suggesting (not merely consistent with) agreement reflects [Rule 8's requirement that the complaint] "sho[w] that the pleader is entitled to relief." . . .

. . . As we indicated over 20 years ago in *Associated Gen. Contractors of Cal., Inc. v. Carpenters*, 459 U.S. 519, 528, n.17 (1983), "a district court must retain the power to insist upon some specificity in pleading before allowing a potentially massive factual controversy to proceed." *See also Car Carriers, Inc. v. Ford Motor Co.*, 745 F.2d 1101, 1106 (7th Cir. 1984) ("[T]he costs of modern federal antitrust litigation and the increasing caseload of the federal courts counsel against sending the parties into discovery when there is no reasonable likelihood that the plaintiffs can construct a claim from the events related in the complaint") . . . .

It is no answer to say that a claim just shy of a plausible entitlement to relief can, if groundless, be weeded out early in the discovery process through "careful case management," . . . given the common lament that the success of judicial supervision in checking discovery abuse has been on the modest side. . . . Probably, then, it is only by taking care to require allegations that reach the level suggesting conspiracy that we can hope to avoid the potentially enormous expense of discovery in cases with no "reasonably founded hope [of a]" § 1 claim. . . .

Plaintiffs do not, of course, dispute the requirement of plausibility and the need for something more than merely parallel behavior . . . , and their main argument against the plausibility standard at the pleading stage is its ostensible conflict with an early statement of ours construing Rule 8. Justice Black's opinion for the Court in *Conley v. Gibson* spoke not only of the need for fair notice of the grounds for entitlement to relief but of "the accepted rule that a complaint should not be dismissed for failure to state a claim unless it appears beyond doubt that the plaintiff can prove no set of facts in support of his claim which would entitle him to relief." . . . This "no set of facts" language can be read in isolation as saying that any statement revealing the theory of the claim will suffice unless its factual impossibility may be shown from the face of the pleadings . . . .

. . . *Conley*'s "no set of facts" language has been questioned, criticized, and explained away long enough . . . . [A]fter puzzling the profession for 50 years, this famous observation has earned its retirement. The phrase is best forgotten as an incomplete, negative gloss on an accepted pleading standard: once a claim has been stated adequately, it may be supported by showing any set of facts consistent with the allegations in the complaint. . . .

The judgment of the Court of Appeals for the Second Circuit is reversed, and the cause is remanded for further proceedings consistent with this opinion. . . .

Justice Stevens with whom Justice Ginsburg joins except as to Part IV, dissenting. . . .

. . . I have my doubts about the majority's assessment of the plausibility of this alleged conspiracy. . . . But even if the majority's speculation is correct, its "plausibility" standard is irreconcilable with Rule 8 and with our governing precedents. . . .

. . . This case is a poor vehicle for the Court's new pleading rule, for we have observed that "in antitrust cases, where 'the proof is largely in the hands of the alleged conspirators,' . . . dismissals prior to giving the plaintiff ample opportunity for discovery should be granted very sparingly." . . . Moreover, the fact that the Sherman Act authorizes the recovery of treble damages and attorney's fees for successful plaintiffs indicates that Congress intended to encourage, rather than discourage, private enforcement of the law. . . .

The transparent policy concern that drives the decision is the interest in protecting antitrust defendants—who in this case are some of the wealthiest corporations in our economy—from the burdens of pretrial discovery. . . . That concern [does] not provide an adequate justification for this law-changing decision. . . .

If the allegation of conspiracy happens to be true, today's decision obstructs the congressional policy favoring competition that undergirds both the Telecommunications Act of 1996 and the Sherman Act itself. More importantly, even if there is abundant evidence that the allegation is untrue, directing that the case be dismissed without even looking at any of that evidence marks a fundamental—and unjustified—change in the character of pretrial practice. [I dissent.]

Notes and Questions

(1) *Two Closely Related Standards: Sufficient Information and a Substantively Sufficient Claim.* Remember that the standards governing the complaint actually include two different but closely related requirements, one factually-oriented, and the other legally-oriented.

First, (1) there must be sufficient information in the complaint, including *factual* allegations that make the inference of a claim "plausible," as well as giving notice of the type of claim and grounds. A bare allegation that "defendant owes plaintiff money" is insufficient under this standard, and so is an allegation that "defendants engaged in parallel behavior that shows a contract, combination or conspiracy in restraint of trade."

Second, (2) even if there is a great deal of precise information, the complaint is subject to dismissal if the facts show that the plaintiff cannot recover *under the law.* Thus, a claim with factual detail showing a right to recover money ten years in the future, but adding that "plaintiff wants the money now," is subject to dismissal—not because the claim is unclear, but because it shows that the plaintiff is entitled to nothing even if the allegations are assumed true.

These two standards are often put in a single sentence, as a unified requirement: a requirement of sufficient facts so that, if assumed true, the inference of a claim is plausible. But the situations to which the two standards are addressed are different. In *Bell v. Twombly*, it is conceivable that the plaintiffs might have had an actual claim; the problem was that their factual allegations were not specific enough. This is the standard requiring sufficient information. In another case, a plaintiff may plead factual detail, but the complaint may show that plaintiff has no legal right to recover even if the allegations are taken as true. An example appears later in this chapter, in *Fox v. Lummus Company*, in which the court held that the complaint, though factually detailed enough, alleged claims for which the law provided no remedy.

(2) *Continuing Tension May Follow, because Strict Pleading Has Advantages, and So Does Looser Pleading.* The earlier cases, which allowed looser and more conclusionary pleadings, had advantages. A looser standard means that fewer cases will be decided on the basis of debates about whether the pleadings are sufficient; instead, they will be decided on the merits. On the other hand, stricter pleading standards have advantages too. Discovery can be extraordinarily expensive. Judicial resources are wasted by the need to consider on the merits cases that cannot support factually sufficient pleadings. The tension is likely to continue.

(3) *What Has Happened to "Notice Pleading" under Rule 8? Bell v. Twombly* appears to change the requirement of notice pleading significantly. But the Court does not reject notice pleading; in fact, it mentions it approvingly. The Court explains the apparent change in a footnote, saying that without sufficient factual allegations, it is hard to see how a complaint can give "reasonable notice" not only of the general nature of the claim, but of also the "'grounds' upon which the claim rests," citing *Conley v. Gibson*. Thus, the standard might be stated this way:

> *"The complaint must give fair notice of both the nature of the claim and the grounds upon which it rests, with factual allegations sufficient to make the inference of a claim plausible."—Eds.*

(4) *"Facts," Not "Conclusions."* The factual allegations that show plausibility cannot be supplied by mere "conclusions." But how do we distinguish facts from conclusions? For example, imagine that a negligence complaint alleges that the defendant caused a motor vehicle accident by "driving too fast for the existing conditions." This statement contains a conclusion, but it is difficult to see how a pleader could eliminate this conclusionary element and plead the allegation with pure "facts" (unless the witnesses had radar devices that measured speed exactly).

Ashcroft v. Iqbal

129 S. Ct. 1937 (2009)

[Following the terrorist attacks of September 11, 2001, respondent Iqbal, a Pakistani Muslim, was arrested on criminal charges and detained by federal officials under restrictive conditions. Iqbal sued numerous federal officials, including petitioner Ashcroft, the former Attorney General, and petitioner Mueller, the Director of the FBI.

[Iqbal's complaint alleged that the government defendants had designated Iqbal a person "of high interest" on account of his race, religion, or national origin, in contravention of the First and Fifth Amendments; that the FBI, under Mueller's direction, arrested and detained thousands of Arab Muslim men as part of its September 11th investigation; that petitioners knew of, condoned, and willfully and maliciously agreed to subject Iqbal to harsh conditions of confinement solely on account of the prohibited factors; and that Ashcroft was the policy's "principal architect" and Mueller was "instrumental" in its execution. If these facts had been true, they would have created a claim for well-established constitutional violations. The District Court and Court of Appeals held the complaint sufficient to give "fair notice."

[The Supreme Court recognized that under Rule 8 (requiring a "short and plain statement of the claim showing that the pleader is entitled to relief"), or "notice" pleading, "detailed factual allegations" are not required, citing *Bell v. Twombly.* But the Court added that the Rule calls for sufficient factual matter, accepted as true, to "state a claim to relief that is plausible on its face." A claim has facial plausibility when the pleaded factual content allows the court to "draw the reasonable inference" that the defendant is liable for the misconduct alleged. Mere conclusory statements are not enough.

[The holding in *Twombly* is not limited to antitrust cases, said the Court, because *Twombly* dealt with a pleading standard applicable to all cases. Most claims need not be alleged with "particularity," which is the heightened pleading standard required for fraud claims under Rule 9. Nevertheless, Rule 8 requires a statement about the facts that allows a "plausible" inference that there is a claim, even if the standard is less than that of Rule 8.

[Under the applicable standards, Iqbal's allegation that the defendants acted "on account of his race, religion or national origin" was insufficient. It was a mere conclusion, unsupported by facts making any inference of a claim "plausible." The same was true of his allegations of "knowledge," "condonation," willfulness, and malice:] . . .

We turn to respondent's complaint. Under [Rule] 8(a)(2), a pleading must contain a "short and plain statement of the claim showing that the pleader is entitled to relief." As the Court held in *Twombly*, 550 U.S. 544, the pleading standard Rule 8 announces does not require "detailed factual allegations," but it demands more than an unadorned, the-defendant-unlawfully-harmed-me accusation . . . . A pleading that offers "labels and conclusions" or "a formulaic recitation of the elements of a cause of action will not do." . . . Nor does a complaint suffice if it tenders "naked assertion[s]" devoid of "further factual enhancement." . . .

To survive a motion to dismiss, a complaint must contain sufficient factual matter, accepted as true, to "state a claim to relief that is plausible on its face." A claim has facial plausibility when the plaintiff pleads factual content that allows the court to draw the reasonable inference that the defendant is liable for the misconduct alleged. The plausibility standard is not akin to a "probability requirement," but it asks for more than a sheer possibility that a defendant has acted unlawfully. Where a complaint pleads facts that are "merely consistent with" a defendant's liability, it "stops short of the line between possibility and plausibility of 'entitlement to relief.'"

Respondent pleads that petitioners knew of, "condoned, and willfully and maliciously agreed to subject [him]" to harsh conditions of confinement solely on account of "[his] religion, race, and/or national origin . . . ." . . . These bare assertions, much like the pleading of conspiracy in *Twombly*, amount to nothing more than a "formulaic recitation of the elements" of a discrimination claim, namely, that petitioners adopted the policy "because of, not merely in spite of, its adverse effects upon an identifiable group." As such, the allegations are conclusory and not entitled to be assumed true. To be clear, we do not [reject] these bald allegations on the ground that they are unrealistic or nonsensical . . . . It is the conclusory nature of plaintiff's allegations . . . that disentitles them to the presumption of truth.

. . . Taken as true, these allegations are consistent with petitioners' purposefully designating detainees of "high interest" because of their race, religion, or national origin. But given more likely explanations, they do not plausibly establish this purpose . . . .

The September 11 attacks were perpetrated by 19 Arab Muslim hijackers . . . . It should come as no surprise that a legitimate policy directing law enforcement to arrest and detain individuals because of their suspected link to the attacks would produce a disparate, incidental impact on Arab Muslims, even though the purpose of the policy was to target neither Arabs nor Muslims . . . . As between that "obvious alternative explanation" for the arrests and the purposeful, invidious discrimination respondent asks us to infer, discrimination is not a plausible conclusion . . . .

We hold that respondent's complaint fails to plead sufficient facts to state a claim for purposeful and unlawful discrimination against petitioners. The Court of Appeals should decide in the first instance whether to remand to the District Court so that respondent can seek leave to amend his deficient complaint. [REVERSED AND REMANDED.]

Justice Souter, with whom Justice Stevens, Justice Ginsburg, and Justice Breyer join, dissenting: . . .

. . . The complaint alleges, at a bare minimum, that Ashcroft and Mueller knew of and condoned the discriminatory policy their subordinates carried out. Actually, the complaint goes further in alleging that Ashcroft and Mueller affirmatively acted to create the discriminatory policy. If these factual allegations are true, Ashcroft and Mueller were, at the very least, aware of the discriminatory policy and deliberately indifferent to it . . . .

The allegations singled out by the majority as "conclusory" are no such thing. Iqbal's claim is not that Ashcroft and Mueller "knew of, condoned, and willfully and maliciously agreed to subject" him to a discriminatory practice that is left undefined; his allegation is that "they knew of, condoned, and willfully and maliciously agreed to subject" him to a particular, discrete, discriminatory policy detailed in the complaint. Iqbal does not say merely that Ashcroft was the architect of some amorphous discrimination, or that Mueller was instrumental in an ill-defined constitutional violation; he alleges that they helped to create the discriminatory policy he has described. Taking the complaint as a whole, it gives Ashcroft and Mueller "'fair notice of what the . . . claim is and the grounds upon which it rests.'" *Twombly* . . . . I respectfully dissent.

Notes and Questions

(1) *What Can Iqbal Do on Remand to Salvage His Claim, if Anything?* Ordinarily, the plaintiff is permitted to re-plead the complaint after the grant of a Motion to Dismiss. Assume that Iqbal is allowed to re-plead on remand. What kinds of allegations will he attempt to make, to cure the problem? Suppose that Iqbal adds to his complaint an allegation that "the Attorney General must have approved these actions, because actions of this magnitude customarily require approval by the chief law enforcement officer; and an expert witness, a professor of government, will so testify." Would this kind of allegation be enough? (Probably not. See below.)

(2) *"In Spite of and Not Because of."* It is important to realize that government action causing disparate impact on races is not illegal. If it were, efforts to treat sickle cell anemia would be unlawful, because the disease has disparate impact upon African-Americans. Thus, it was not illegal for the government defendants in *Iqbal* to impose the policy they did with mere *knowledge* that it would impact mostly Arab Muslims, as the majority opinion points out. It would be illegal only if they acted with the *purpose* or *intent* to discriminate against Arab Muslims. They would have to act not "in spite of" racial impact but "because of" that impact. Considering this principle of law, wouldn't the amendment suggested in the note above be insufficient? Consider, also, whether a plaintiff in Iqbal's situation could ever find facts sufficiently showing intentional discrimination.

Consider whether the dissent squarely refutes the majority's argument. The dissent summarizes the complaint as saying that the defendants "maliciously agreed to subject" Iqbal to "a particular, discrete, discriminatory policy detailed in the complaint." But the majority does not focus upon the "particularity" of the policy. Instead, the majority concentrates on the requirement of facts plausibly showing that the defendants acted "because of and not in spite of" the plaintiff's ethnicity. Apparently, the difference between the dissent and the majority is that the dissent would accept allegations that the defendants "maliciously" agreed to a "discriminatory" policy, while the majority regards these statements as insufficiently factual.

(3) *The Other Side of the Issue: Otherwise, Cabinet Officers Would Have No Time for Anything but Lawsuits.* Imagine that the Attorney General were subject to suit, involving discovery and trial, in every case in which a disappointed individual wished to assert, without factual allegations other than conclusory statements of maliciousness, that the individual had been subjected to a denial of due process and that the Attorney General had caused it. Even with substantial pleading rules, there are a great many such suits. In deciding *Twombly* and *Iqbal*, the Supreme Court obviously took account of this problem and attempted to allow potentially meritorious suits but avoid burying public officials under masses of groundless ones.

Justice Breyer disagreed and offered his own solution: "A district court . . . can begin discovery with lower level government defendants before determining whether a case can be made to allow discovery related to higher level government officials." Perhaps the real question, then, is: has the Court charted an appropriate course that avoids either extreme, or has it gone too far in either direction?

(4) *Procedural Rules Have Substantive Effects (on Civil Rights Claims, Here, but also on Other Kinds of Claims).* Civil rights litigators understandably criticize *Ashcroft v. Iqbal.* Sometimes, valid claims cannot be stated in a valid complaint under its standards. The majority recognizes this reality by stating that the plaintiff's claims are not unrealistic. They are merely conclusory. In fact, procedural rules can have substantive effects, and one effect of *Iqbal* may be that some kinds of civil rights claims become impossible to assert.

But the effect isn't only upon civil rights cases. Remember *Twombly*: it's harder now to plead business claims, too. And consider a case in which plaintiff alleges that defendant acted "with intent to cause an assault." The allegation presumably is insufficient. Or imagine a tort claim for malicious prosecution. Plaintiff must show that defendant acted "without probable cause." But how can a pleader allege facts supporting a negative—that is, facts showing action without probable cause?

The problem lies even deeper. The district courts are the enforcers of the pleading standards. Will they, sometimes, react to *Iqbal* by imposing even tighter requirements than that case requires? Yes, because decisions and decisionmakers vary. Consider the case that follows.

[3] Fallout from Twombly-Iqbal: *Unduly Strict Fact Pleading?*

Chapman v. Yellow Cab Cooperative

875 F.3d 846 (7th Cir. 2017)

Easterbrook, Circuit Judge.

[This case shows that *Twombly* and *Iqbal* can produce mistakes that make ordinary claims very difficult to plead, especially if district judges have overly tight expectations.] Dennis Edwards owns a taxicab in Milwaukee. Yellow Cab

Cooperative refers business to his cab; other arrangements between Edwards and Yellow Cab are not in the record. Edwards leased the cab to Parashu Giri, who subleased some of the time to Thomas Chapman. . . . Chapman received fares and tips from passengers, paid rent to Giri, and kept the difference; he did not pay anything to Yellow Cab or receive anything from it.

Chapman contends in this suit under the Fair Labor Standards Act that this arrangement makes him an "employee" of Yellow Cab. He alleges that, after he complained about not receiving the minimum wage, Ali Mohamed, the President of Yellow Cab, told Giri that Chapman was "fired" (in other words, would not be dispatched to passengers who called Yellow Cab seeking a ride). Giri then terminated the sublease. Chapman submits that Mohamed's action violates the Act's antiretaliation clause, 29 U.S.C. § 215(a)(3).

District Judge Randa dismissed all of Chapman's other theories and directed him to file a new complaint. The amended complaint was assigned to Judge Stadtmueller, who concluded that Chapman "must provide more detailed and thorough allegations before the claim can be permitted to proceed." The judge stated that the [new] complaint had not discussed all of the "factors" identified in *Secretary of Labor v. Lauritzen,* 835 F.2d 1529, 1534 (7th Cir. 1987), as potentially relevant to the distinction between an employee and an independent contractor. . . . [Then, t]he judge ordered Chapman to file yet another complaint. The final version was filed and dismissed with prejudice. The judge stated that Chapman still had not addressed all of the factors [that determine whether someone is an "employee"] mentioned in [the cases].

To the extent the district court demanded that complaints plead facts—not only facts that bear on the statutory elements of a claim, but also facts that bear on judicially established standards—it was mistaken. Ever since their adoption in 1938, the Federal Rules of Civil Procedure have required plaintiffs to plead claims rather than facts corresponding to the elements of a legal theory. Old code-pleading and fact-pleading systems were abandoned. Because complaints need not identify the applicable law [citing Supreme Court cases], it is manifestly inappropriate for a district court to demand that complaints contain all legal elements (or factors) plus facts corresponding to each.

It is enough to plead a plausible claim, after which "a plaintiff 'receives the benefit of imagination, so long as the hypotheses are consistent with the complaint.'" *Bell Atlantic Corp. v. Twombly.* A full description of the facts that will prove the plaintiff's claim comes later, at the summary-judgment stage or in the pretrial order. . . .

Perhaps the district court meant to do no more than rely on the plausibility standard of *Twombly* and *Ashcroft v. Iqbal.* . . . Chapman's claim seems implausible . . . . Many decisions . . . hold that one does not become an "employee" of an entity several steps removed in a chain of business relations just because that entity's decisions may have some effect on income.

. . . [But] the district court did not reject it on that [plausibility] ground—and a desire for plausibility would not be enough to require a complaint to contain facts matching all statutory "elements" and judicial "factors," for *Twombly* and its successors disparage such demands. Perhaps, however, we should understand the district court's order as one under Rule 12(e) [authorizing a motion for more definite statement]. . . . Rule 12(e), rather than a judicial demand for fact pleading, is the right way to ask plaintiffs to lay out details . . . . Giving the district court the benefit of the doubt, we treat its order as one under Rule 12(e).

If Chapman had responded to that order with additional details, and the district court still had dismissed the complaint for failure to plead facts matching "elements" or "factors," we would be obliged to reverse. Rule 12(e) cannot be used to turn federal civil procedure into a fact-pleading or code-pleading system. But Chapman did not respond with a plausible claim. . . . Rule 12(e) authorizes the district court to enter any "appropriate order" when the plaintiff does not comply, and after Chapman's multiple failed efforts to frame a plausible claim the most appropriate order was the one the district court employed—dismissal with prejudice. . . .

[The court points out that on appeal, Chapman furnished additional facts that made his "employment" claim seem more plausible, but said that compliance on appeal was too late. Chapman should have obeyed the district court's order, even if it was unduly strict. AFFIRMED.]

Problem B

PAUL PAYNE v. DON DEFENDANT: PLEADING A NEGLIGENCE CLAIM IN COMPLIANCE WITH *TWOMBLY AND IQBAL*. You have just agreed to represent a plaintiff named Paul Payne, who was seriously injured in an automobile collision with a vehicle driven by Don Defendant. Your client tells you, "That guy drove through the light like it wasn't even there, and I had the green, and he got a ticket for that; and he was going like there was a jet behind him, that fast. He didn't even try to stop, just plowed into me. And I think he may have been texting at the time, or something, because he seemed distracted, but I don't know what he was doing, of course, because I couldn't see that." (Your clients will talk this way sometimes.) You have been unable to reach a satisfactory settlement with Don Defendant's insurer, partly because the insurer says that Don denies what your client Payne says. Assume that you have both the jurisdiction and the desire to file suit in a federal court, and you need to prepare a complaint.

You note that Form 11, which was once appended to the Federal Rules, suggests a statement of the claim saying only this: "On [Date], at [Place], the defendant negligently drove a motor vehicle against the plaintiff." You might sensibly worry that this legal conclusion (he drove "negligently"), even though it is in a federal form, may not comply with the Supreme Court's requirement of facts giving rise to a plausible inference of a claim. Now, with Form 11 abolished, and *Twombly* and *Iqbal* as the law of the land, what precise language would you add to Form 11 to be sure of your negligence complaint's sufficiency? Formulate the additional allegations, the exact words that you would write into the statement of the claim, based upon the description of the case above.

[B] Is There Really a "Claim"?: Substantive Sufficiency as Tested by Rule 12 Motions

PARTRIDGE v. TWO UNKNOWN POLICE OFFICERS, 791 F.2d 1182 (5th Cir. 1986). This is the case for which edited pleadings appear in Section IV of Chapter 1, Litigation Document Example 1.1 (Complaint and Dismissal in the *Wytinger* Case), under the name *Wytinger v. Two Unknown Police Officers.* Plaintiffs Ralph and Betty Partridge claimed damages arising from the suicide of their son, Michael, while he was a pretrial detainee in a municipal jail. The District Court dismissed the complaint for failure to state a claim, citing *Estelle v. Gamble*, 429 U.S. 97 (1976), to the effect that only an allegation of "deliberate indifference" to "serious medical need" would suffice in such a case. The Court of Appeals first reversed, with one judge dissenting; it then withdrew its opinion; and finally, it substituted another opinion, with the same judge dissenting. The court upheld the dismissal with respect to one police officer, whom the complaint unambiguously charged only with negligence. But otherwise, it reversed the dismissal:

> . . . We read the complaint as amended as alleging that the defendants had deliberately adopted a policy that constituted indifference to the medical needs of detained persons and, pursuant to policy, failed to render reasonable medical aid to Michael Partridge and to persons similarly subject to suicidal tendencies, that this failure was not the result of an individual act of negligence but was the result of systematic indifference to serious medical needs of pretrial detainees and of a "deliberate pattern of conduct"; that is, of a custom or policy. Those allegations go beyond negligence. . . .
>
> We accept all well-pleaded facts as true and view them in the light most favorable to the plaintiff. . . .
>
> [T]he facts alleged in the complaint are sufficient to support an allegation that the custom of inadequate care was persistent and widespread.

McLAREN v. UNITED STATES INC., 2 F. Supp. 2d 48 (D.D.C. 1998). This odd case provides a clear example of a suit subject to dismissal because even if the plaintiff's factual allegations were taken as true, he was entitled to no relief, as a matter of law. McLaren proclaimed himself the "Chief Ambassador and Consul General" of the "Republic of Texas." He and his followers maintained that Texas never was legitimately annexed by the United States, never became a State, and therefore remained a Republic. So vehement were these separatists' beliefs that they took hostages and engaged in an armed standoff with state law enforcement officers. As part of a "cease fire agreement," McLaren agreed to "commence legal actions in the District Court of the District of Columbia for the rights of the inhabitants on the soil of Texas to by popular vote decide [the] issue of Texas Independence."

McLaren filed the suit. The United States filed a motion to dismiss or for summary judgment. The district judge decided that whether Texas was a State was a pure question of law—and that McLaren's basic legal premise was flawed. The Supreme Court had ruled, in *Texas v. White*, 74 U.S. (7 Wall.) 700 (1868), that "The Republic of Texas was admitted into the Union, as a State, on the 27th of December, 1845. By this act the new State, and the people of the new State, were invested with all the rights, and became subject to all the responsibilities and duties of the original States under the Constitution." The court therefore granted the motion to dismiss.

Read Fed. R. Civ. P. 12(b)-(f). Also, reconsider Rule 8(a).

Note on Rule 12 Motions

Substantive Sufficiency: A Complaint Can Defeat Itself. Consider what should happen if a complaint is crystal clear, but (unlike the one in *Partridge*, above) it shows without question that the law does not allow the plaintiff to recover. For example, the plaintiff may make a statement that on its face concedes the lack of an essential element of its claim. Or the complaint may show on its face that it is unambiguously subject to a complete defense (*e.g.*, statute of limitations or statute of frauds). In these situations, the complaint would be subject to dismissal.

The Rule 12(b)(6) Motion to Dismiss for Failure to State a Claim Upon Which Relief May Be Granted. But a 12(b)(6) motion to dismiss for failure to state a claim has to be judged by a stringent standard. The complaint must be liberally read in the pleader's favor. It must be assumed that the pleader would be able to prove everything asserted in the complaint (because, after all, the court is considering dismissal without hearing any of her proof). Even if there is plenty of factual detail, the court can and should dismiss if the law allows no recovery.

Vague Pleadings and the Rule 12(e) Motion for More Definite Statement. What if the pleading is vague? The court may grant a motion for a more definite statement. This motion is distinct from the standard for substantive sufficiency. A complaint that does not suffice to give notice is sometimes characterized as failing to state a claim, although careful terminology would distinguish that kind of defect.

The Rule 12(f) Motion to Strike. What if the complaint states a claim when read in its entirety, but it contains inappropriate material? For example, what if a suit on a promissory note contains an allegation that "The defendant's spouse has been arrested three times for assault"? In these situations, the opponent may be able to obtain a ruling in response to a motion to strike, which asks the court to remove these allegations.

Understanding the Case of Fox v. Lummus Co., below. The *Fox* case, which follows, is a good illustration of all three of these attacks on a complaint. (1) There is a motion to dismiss directed at some of the claims, and you should bear in mind the relatively stringent standard for this motion and consider whether the court's ruling here is correct. (2) The one remaining claim is attacked by a motion for more definite statement, and the court's ruling on this motion is not carefully explained. (3) Finally, there is a motion to strike one allegation in the remaining count. Thus, this case will give you a "grand tour" of the possible attacks on substance and form of a complaint.

Fox v. Lummus Company

524 F. Supp. 27 (S.D.N.Y. 1981)

Motley, District Judge.

This action arises out of an employment agreement between plaintiff, Ian Fox, . . . and defendant, The Lummus Company. . . . The agreement, entitled "Iraqi Jobsite Agreement" (the Employment Agreement) related to plaintiff's employment as a sub-contract administrator at defendant's construction project in Basrah, Iraq. Plaintiff claims that defendant breached the contract by unjustly withholding salary earned by plaintiff and by denying plaintiff holiday leave and in other ways "harassing" him. Defendant has moved for an order (1) dismissing the first three [claims] of the complaint for failure to state a claim upon which relief can be granted, pursuant to Rule 12(b)(6) . . . ; (2) directing plaintiff to give a more definite statement of the fourth [claim], pursuant to Rule 12(e); and (3) striking allegations of pain and suffering and related requests for relief from the fourth [claim], pursuant to Rule 12(f). For the reasons discussed below, defendant's motions are granted.

[The Employment Agreement contained a provision, Paragraph 5, which was intended to equalize the after-tax salaries of employees of different nationalities, no matter what tax regimes they might be subjected to, so as to avoid discord among them. Plaintiff Fox quoted this Paragraph 5 in his complaint: "The Employee's salary will be reduced by monthly amounts based upon the attached compensation worksheet for theoretical taxes calculated on base pay plus overtime. The Company will hold the Employee harmless for Iraqi and/or home taxes on Company earned income. . . ." Attachment B to the contract, which also was set forth in the plaintiff's complaint, contained exact monthly figures for the "theoretical tax" by which plaintiff's compensation was to be reduced, and it also set forth the precise "net monthly salary" that plaintiff was to receive.

[The complaint also alleged that "the foregoing constituted the entire understanding between the parties," and that the parties had never entered into any subsequent oral or written agreement on the subject. Then, in his first three claims, plaintiff alleged that since no tax ever was levied upon his salary by any governmental authority, defendant's deduction of "theoretical taxes" was improper. Plaintiff's first three claims included implied contract, equitable unjust enrichment, and quasi-contract theories based on this allegation.

[The court first considered the motion to dismiss, by which defendant had attacked these first three claims. You should recall that this motion calls for the complaint to be read liberally in Fox's favor; the court must assume that he would be able to prove all of his assertions and can dismiss only if he would be entitled to none of the requested relief even after making such proof.]

It is clear that the complaint does not allege that defendant breached the express terms of the Employment Agreement. Indeed, plaintiff's claim is that defendant did exactly what the contract stated it would do—reduce plaintiff's salary by a theoretical tax in the amount set forth on the earnings calculation addendum of the agreement. The contract nowhere provided for subsequent payment to plaintiff of the amount deducted, as plaintiff now requests. Plaintiff, however, argues that the court should imply such a payment term. This the court may not do, in light of the express provision of paragraph 5 of the Employment Agreement.

While the fact that a particular provision has not been expressly stated in a contract does not necessarily mean that no such promise exists, "a party who asserts the existence of an implied-in-fact covenant bears a heavy burden, for it is not the function of the courts to remake the contract agreed to by the parties, but rather to enforce it as it exists." *Rowe v. Great Atlantic and Pacific Tea Co., Inc.*, 385 N.E.2d 566 (N.Y. 1978). This burden is met only by proving that the particular unexpressed promise is in fact implicit in the agreement viewed as a whole. *Id.* The additional payment term plaintiff would have this court imply is inconsistent with the provision in paragraph 5 of the Employment Agreement that plaintiff's salary would be reduced each month by a specified amount. It is well established under New York law that, "where the expressed intention of contracting parties is clear, a contrary intent will not be created by implication." *Neuman v. Pike*, 591 F.2d 191, 194 (2d Cir. 1979).

Plaintiff alternatively contends that he is entitled to payment by the defendant under a theory of unjust enrichment or recovery in quasi-contract, which allows the courts to impose a duty to refund money to the person to whom it rightfully belongs. This argument also must fail. A quasi or constructive contract . . . is an obligation created by law only in the absence of an agreement between the parties. *Bradkin v. Leverton*, 257 N.E.2d 643 (N.Y. 1970). As already noted above, where, as here, a written contract does exist, the duty of the courts is to enforce it. Accordingly, defendant's motion to dismiss plaintiff's first three [claims] pertaining to the reduction of plaintiff's salary is granted.

Plaintiff's fourth [claim] alleges that defendant also breached the employment contract by failing to provide plaintiff with back salary and with various leaves and expenses and by "a course of constant harrassment (sic) and pressure the object of which was to make the plaintiff leave his position prematurely. . . ." Defendant claims that the allegation of "harrassment and pressure" is so vague and ambiguous that defendant cannot reasonably be required to frame a responsive pleading and that it warrants a more definite statement in accordance with Rule 12(e) .... The court agrees. Plaintiff, therefore, is directed to amend his complaint to state which acts of defendant constituted the alleged "harrassment and pressure," when such acts occurred, and which persons committed such acts.

Finally, defendant moves for an order striking from paragraph 22 of the complaint plaintiff's allegation that defendant's breach of the employment contract caused him "great mental and physical anguish and suffering" and paragraph 23 which alleges that plaintiff has sustained injuries in the amount of $100,000 as a result of the alleged breach. Defendant argues that such alleged non-economic injury is not cognizable as a matter of law.

The New York rule is that damages for breach of an employment contract are limited to the unpaid salary to which the employee would be entitled under the contract less the amount by which he should have mitigated his damages. *Quinn v. Straus Broadcasting Group, Inc.*, 309 F. Supp. 1208, 1209 (S.D.N.Y. 1970). New York courts have accordingly stricken from the complaint allegations of and demands for damages resulting from mental anguish in breach of employment contract cases. *See Amaducci v. Metropolitan Opera Association*, 33 App. Div. 2d 542, 304 N.Y.S. 2d 322 (1st Dept. 1969). Since, under New York law, plaintiff's damages are limited to his economic injuries, the allegation of mental distress is immaterial and will be stricken pursuant to Rule 12(f). For the same reason, paragraph 23 of the complaint and subparagraph 4 of the *ad damnum* clause demanding $100,000 . . . will also be stricken. . . .

In summary, defendant's motions for an order dismissing the first three [claims], directing plaintiff to state more definitely the fourth [claim], and striking allegations of mental anguish and suffering in paragraph 22, as well as paragraph 23 and subparagraph 24 of the *ad damnum* clause, are all granted. Plaintiff may file an amended complaint in accordance with this opinion within 20 days of the filing of the order which accompanies this opinion.

Notes and Questions

(1) *Changing the Facts in Fox v. Lummus Company.* Would the result have been the same if Fox had claimed an oral modification of the employment agreement, in that his supervisor induced him to stay in Iraq by promising him that he would be docked only the amount of taxes actually paid? (Assuming that the law allows oral modification, which it ordinarily does, this allegation might change the result.)

(2) *Plenty of Facts, Yet Still a Dismissal.* Notice that the dismissal in *Fox* is fundamentally different from the dismissal in *Bell Atlantic v. Twombly.* There, the defect was inadequate information, and the dismissal resulted from the standard requiring sufficient facts to plausibly imply a claim. Here, there are plenty of facts, and the alleged claims are clearly stated, but the complaint fails the second test: even if it is true, the law allows no recovery.

(3) *The Motion for More Definite Statement.* The court does not give much explanation of the reasons for granting the motion for a more definite statement. Some courts have reasoned that a more definite statement can be ordered only if the complaint fails to give notice or to conform to Rule 8(a). On the other hand, some courts have concluded that the motion should be granted if further details will be useful in resolving the case (if addition of the date of the alleged violation might establish a defense of limitations, for example). Here, details might justify a Motion to Dismiss.

(4) *The Motion to Strike.* This motion is like a miniature "motion to dismiss," aimed at a single allegation or set of allegations instead of at the entire complaint. (In fact, a purist might insist that the "motion to dismiss" the first three claims in this case actually was a motion to strike, since it did not seek dismissal of the complaint as a whole.)

[C] Particularized Pleading: Fraud, Damages, and Other Special Matters

Read Fed. R. Civ. P. 9(b), (c), (f), and (g).

Haywood v. Massage Envy Franchising, LLC

887 F.3d 329 (7th Cir. 2018)

Bauer, Circuit Judge.

Kathy Haywood . . . filed this putative class action [under the Illinois Consumer Fraud and Deceptive Business Practices Act (ICFA),] alleging that Massage Envy Franchising, LLC ("Massage Envy"), committed unfair and deceptive business practices by advertising and selling one-hour massages but providing massages that lasted only 50 minutes. [She] now appeal[s] from the district court's order granting Massage Envy's motion to dismiss under Federal Rule of Civil Procedure 12(b)(6) for failure to state a claim. We affirm. . . .

[The district court dismissed the complaint on two Rule 9 grounds: that Haywood's allegations were insufficient to satisfy the "particularity" standard of either (1) the fraud provision or (2) the provision that requires special damages to be "specifically stated."] . . .

We analyze ICFA claims of deception under the heightened pleading standard of Federal Rule of Civil Procedure 9(b). Although Haywood brings one ICFA claim alleging unfair practices, that claim still sounds in fraud because it relies upon the . . . allegation that Massage Envy . . . misled consumers by hiding information on the length of massage time. . . . Rule 9(b) requires the complaint to "state with particularity the circumstances constituting fraud." That means that it must specifically allege the "who, what, when, where, and how of the fraud." . . .

To state a claim under the ICFA as a private party, Haywood must plausibly allege: (1) a deceptive act or promise by Massage Envy; (2) Massage Envy's intent that she rely on the deceptive act; (3) the deceptive act occurred during a course of conduct involving trade or commerce; and (4) actual damage as a result of the deceptive act. "Actual damage" in this context means that Haywood must have suffered actual pecuniary loss. Additionally, the deceptive act must have been the "but-for" cause of the damage. . . .

. . . [T]he [trial] court found that Haywood's allegations failed to establish that the value of the massage she received was "worth less than what [she] actually paid." . . . Haywood argues that the court erred by failing to evaluate her alleged injury under the benefit-of-the-bargain rule, which only requires an allegation that she received something less than what she was promised. However, we need not settle that debate here . . . .

Even had Haywood adequately pleaded actual damages, her allegations fail to establish the requisite causation. . . . There is no allegation in the complaint that her belief about the length of the massage caused Haywood to make the appointment. To the contrary, the only reasonable and plausible inference is that only the receipt of a gift card [which she received from her daughter] caused her to book a massage . . . . Her failure to cite a specific deceptive representation that caused her to pay for something she did not receive is particularly problematic in light of Rule 9(b)'s heightened standard. *See Camasta* [*v. Jos. A. Bank Clothiers, Inc.*, 761 F.3d 732,] at 737 [(7th Cir. 2014)] (plaintiff must plead the "how of the fraud"). She cannot, based on these allegations, establish that Massage Envy's alleged deception was the but-for cause of her injury, and her claims fail as a result. [Dismissal AFFIRMED.]

Notes and Questions

(1) *A Different Case, Holding Plaintiff's Fraud Allegations Sufficient: Davidson v. Kimberly Clark Corporation,* 889 F.3d 956 (9th Cir. 2018). Davidson's complaint alleged that Kimberly Clark's tissues, although advertised as "flushable," were not. The district court dismissed her complaint of violation of a deceptive business practices statute, holding that the fraud element was not stated with the particularity required by Rule 9. The court of appeals reversed:

> Assuming the truth of the allegations and construing them, as we must, in the light most favorable to Davidson, we hold that the FAC [first amended complaint] adequately alleged why the term "flushable" is false. Davidson's theory of fraud is simple: "Unlike truly flushable products, such as toilet paper, which disperse and disintegrate within seconds or minutes, [Kimberly-Clark's flushable wipes] take hours to break down" or disperse, creating a risk that the wipes will damage plumbing systems, septic tanks, and municipal wastewater treatment facilities. Davidson alleged that flushable means "suitable for being flushed," which requires an item to be capable of dispersing within a short amount of time. This definition of flushable

> is supported by multiple allegations in the [complaint], including dictionary definitions.... In contrast to truly flushable or dispersible products, Davidson alleged, Kimberly-Clark's flushable wipes "take hours to begin to break down."

(2) *"Tight" Versus "Loose" Interpretations of Rule 9.* The Rule 9 cases are not consistent. Some are stringent. *Sweeny Co. v. Engineers Constructors, Inc.*, 109 F.R.D. 358 (E.D. Va. 1986), held that plaintiff should have specified not only the mechanism of the fraud, but also "who made the secret plan and approximately when it was conceived," as well as "some or all of the employees or agents of defendants who allegedly carried out such a plan and... who allegedly received and relied on this information," plus "when and why the defendants knew" that their representations were false. (In most fraud cases, plaintiff would be unlikely to find out all of this information before suit.)

On the other hand, there is a line of cases that holds that the "particularity" requirement just extends to the method of committing the alleged fraud, so that the plaintiff need not detail the time, place, person, etc. *E.g., Denny v. Carey,* 72 F.R.D. 574 (E.D. Pa. 1976) (burden of pleading fraud is not a "rigorous" one, and pleading that briefly stated that method of fraud was to underrepresent losses and overrepresent gains on financial statements complied with Rule 9, when harmonized with Rule 8). A court adopting this less rigorous approach might not have dismissed the complaint in *Davidson v. Massage Envy,* above.

(3) *Why Is There a Particularity Requirement?* It is said that the purpose of Rule 9 is to give notice because fraud is a difficult claim to defend, avoid harm to reputation from lightly made claims of moral turpitude, minimize strike suits, and discourage filing of inadequately investigated claims. But why shouldn't these objectives apply to every claim, not just to fraud? *See* Sovern, *Reconsidering Federal Civil Rule 9(b): Do We Need Particularized Pleading Requirements in Fraud Cases?* 104 F.R.D. 143 (1985).

Note: Pleading Requirements for "Special Damages"

Rule 9 says that "special damages" must be "specifically stated." But what kinds of damages are "special," so that the pleader must state them specifically? Unfortunately, the cases do not tell us very specifically. The general idea is conveyed by *Smith v. Debartoli,* 769 F.2d 451 (7th Cir. 1985), in which a vague prayer for "damages" was held insufficient to support recovery for emotional distress. The court said that special damages were "the kinds of injuries that do not *necessarily* flow from" the violation the plaintiff has alleged.

What does this statement mean? If you plead a contract and want consequential damages, you should plead them. If you plead negligence and want lost earnings, you should plead them. If you plead a promissory note and fail to plead attorney's fees, you might not get them. The best advice is to think of all possible types of damages that your claim justifies and plead them.

Notes and Questions

(1) *With What Degree of Specificity Must Special Damages Be Pleaded?* While substantive elements of fraud must be pled with specificity pursuant to Rule 9(b), requests for special damages may not require as much detail pursuant to Rule 9(g). For example, in *Great American Indem. Co. v. Brown*, 307 F.2d 306 (5th Cir. 1962), the complaint lumped the damages together as follows: "For all of his personal injuries, permanent injuries, physical pain and suffering and mental anguish, loss of earnings past and future, and expenses and damages, plaintiff claims the sum of $114,000.00." The court found that to be sufficiently specific, explaining that Rule 9(g) is "designed to inform defending parties as to the nature of the damages claimed in order to avoid surprise and to inform the court of the substance of the complaint."

(2) *Notice Considerations about Pleading Details.* Notice considerations also contributed to the court's ruling in *Great American*, the case in note 1. After the trial was over, the insurance company attempted to argue that the complaint had not adequately detailed the special damages. The court was unsympathetic, observing that "Great American had ample opportunity before trial to file a motion for a more definite statement" and that some of the special damages, including lost earnings, were discussed at the pre-trial conference.

(3) *What to Plead as Special Damages.* Your client's husband was killed in an automobile accident, and you have filed suit against the negligent driver in federal court. Your client has suffered the loss of his earnings, counsel, companionship, and consortium; psychiatric expenses for herself; medical expenses for him before his death; mental and emotional distress; diminished value in the estate she might have expected to recover from him; and possibly other damage elements. State law may permit recovery of attorney's fees and prejudgment interest, and you think the other driver was grossly negligent. How would you plead the damages?

(4) *Congress Can Mandate Other Heightened Pleading Standards.* Of course, statutory schemes can require a plaintiff to include additional details in a complaint. For example, the Private Securities Litigation Reform Act, P.L. 104-67, 109 Stat. 737 (1995), requires a complaint in a securities fraud action, in which the plaintiff alleges that the defendant made an untrue statement of a material fact or material omission, to "specify each statement alleged to have been misleading, the reason or reasons why the statement is misleading, and if an allegation regarding the statement or omission is made on information and belief, the complaint shall state with particularity all facts on which that belief is formed."

(5) *After the Pleadings, Judges Can Still Compel Additional Information.* In certain kinds of complex litigation, under readily-abused statutes, such as the Racketeer Influenced and Corrupt Organizations Act (RICO), several federal district judges have initiated the requirement of a "case statement" to be filed by plaintiffs. *See, e.g., Order Entered by Chief Judge Lucius D. Bunton, Sogelease Corp. v. Farnel*, No. MO-88-CA-87 (W.D. Tex. Jan. 23, 1989). Judge Bunton's order required that the

plaintiff's "case statement" consist of reports on 20 separate items, numbered to correspond to the numbers in the Order. Some of the 20 items had as many as seven subparts, each calling for specific legal or factual information. Although this type of "case statement" might impose an expensive burden on the plaintiff's lawyer, federal judges possess very broad discretion to manage the case, especially through pre-trial and discovery conferences. *See, e.g.* Rule 16(c)(2) and Rule 26(f), FRCP.

(6) *State Legislators Have Created Pre-Suit "Screening" Requirements, Too.* The Illinois Code of Civil Procedure § 2-622 requires that the plaintiff in a medical malpractice action attach to the complaint an affidavit stating that he or she has consulted with a health professional, in whose opinion there is a "reasonable and meritorious cause" for the filing of the action. Plaintiff must also attach a copy of a written report from the health professional, detailing the grounds for his or her opinion. In *DeLuna v. St. Elizabeth's Hospital*, 147 Ill. 2d 57, 588 N.E.2d 1139 (1992), a medical malpractice plaintiff challenged the state and federal constitutionality of this statute, arguing that it violated equal protection, due process, separation of powers, certainty of remedy, and "special legislation" provisions. The court upheld the statute.

[D] Alternate and Inconsistent Allegations

LAMBERT v. SOUTHERN COUNTIES GAS CO., 52 Cal. 2d 347, 340 P.2d 608 (1959). The plaintiffs sought damages for the loss of a bulldozer, which they had rented to certain ranch owners. It was totally destroyed by fire when it struck and punctured a high-pressure gas pipeline less than 15 inches below the surface of the ground. Count one of the complaint alleged negligence on the part of the ranch owners in operating the bulldozer over the pipeline. In the alternative, count two alleged that the gas company was negligent in permitting its pipeline to remain so near the surface.

The gas company, however, filed a general demurrer, arguing that the two counts were inconsistent. Section 402 of the California Vehicle Code provided that negligence in the use of a motor vehicle (including a bulldozer) "shall be imputed to the owner for all purposes of civil damages." Under this provision, any negligence on the part of the ranch owners was attributable to the plaintiffs. Thus, the plaintiffs, in count one, had affirmatively pleaded their own contributory negligence, and California at that time followed the rule that contributory negligence barred any recovery.

The trial court accepted this reasoning and sustained the gas company's demurrer (this holding was analogous to the granting of a motion to dismiss). The California Supreme Court, while agreeing that the negligence of the ranch owners was attributable to the plaintiffs and that the claims were inconsistent, nevertheless reversed the grant of the demurrer:

> But a plaintiff may plead inconsistent causes of action in separate counts of a single complaint. . . . [A] count sufficient within itself may not ordinarily be defeated by importing, from another count, an allegation to which the sufficient count makes no reference. . . .
>
> Here the gas company alone is named defendant in count two, and only its alleged negligence is involved in count two. Count two does not concern the alleged negligence of the ranch owners, which rests on a different premise for the recovery of damages as stated in count one. In short, the two counts in their respective separate statements of alleged negligence—that of the ranch owners, on the one hand, and that of the gas company, on the other—indicate that plaintiffs are in doubt as to which defendants should be held liable. . . . Plaintiffs may do this under the right of joinder of defendants afforded by our system. . . .

Notes and Questions

(1) *Pleading in the Alternative Is a Trap for the Unwary.* Pleading in the alternative, while permissible, can raise credibility issues. Lawyers who plead in the alternative may need to anticipate a motion to dismiss, and must ensure that the complaint, on its face, adequately explains the need for the alternative claims. *Lambert* reveals the importance of keeping the facts supporting each claim separate. "A court need not feel constrained to accept as truth conflicting pleadings that make no sense. . . ." *Haber v. Rabin*, Case: 1:16-cv-00546-KSM (N.D. Ohio, Jun. 10, 2016), *citing Accurate Grading Quality Assur., Inc. v. Thorpe*, No. 12 Civ. 1343(ALC), 2013 WL 1234836 at *8 (S.D. N.Y. Mar. 26, 2013). When pleading alterative claims, keep the facts separate.

(2) . . . *But When Some Facts Are Unknown, Alternative Pleading Is the Best Alternative.* The Federal Rules recognize, however, that not all facts are known at the beginning of a case, and that a plaintiff may need discovery to refine the precise nature of the dispute. Although inconsistent alternative claims may be allowed at the outset, after reviewing the available evidence, counsel may need to make a choice as to which theories to take to trial. But imagine what would happen if alternative pleading were prohibited, but discovery revealed the need for a different theory of the case.

[E] The Form of the Pleadings: No "Magic Words"

FAULKNER v. FORT BEND INDEPENDENT SCHOOL DIST., No. H-85-2281 (S.D. Tex. April 24, 1986). In this case, Judge Lynn N. Hughes entered an order reading in its entirety as follows:

> First, the motion to dismiss by the defendants is denied.
>
> Secondly, the plaintiffs are ordered to replead by May 1, 1986, eliminating from the amended complaint all excessive capitalization, empty

> formalisms, obscure abstractions, and other conceptual and grammatical imbecilities.
>
> Thirdly, at the pretrial conference on May 5, the issues will be narrowly focused.

Notes and Questions

(1) *Should a Pleader Write, "Now Comes" the Plaintiff, or "Comes Now" the Plaintiff?* Beginning attorneys have been known to puzzle over this question. It should be apparent from Rule 8, as well as from the order quoted above, that it makes no difference which of these two forms the plaintiff uses. In fact, it makes no difference if the pleader leaves out this "empty formalism."

(2) *Are There Any "Magic Words"?* The real issue is whether the pleading conveys the substance that is intended. However, there are occasions when small differences in wording can make a difference, and it should be emphasized that the absence of a "magic words" requirement does not mean that any words will do or that the pleader does not need to exercise care. Sometimes, precision is necessary, not because it is "magical," but because it is essential to show that the elements of a claim, or the requirements of jurisdiction, have been properly pled. For example, a plaintiff should not plead that the parties are of diverse "residence," when what is necessary to establish jurisdiction is diversity of "citizenship." The pleading may be insufficient, because the meaning of the words is inadequate to confer jurisdiction. *Robertson v. Cease*, 97 U.S. 646, 648 (1878); *Prescription Plan Serv. Corp. v. Franco*, 552 F.2d 493, 498 n.6 (2d Cir. 1977). The pleading of jurisdiction, in fact, comes as close to a "magic words" approach as is to be found, probably because of the strong policy of limited federal jurisdiction.

(3) *Rule 10: Style, Caption, Paragraphs, Etc.* Rule 10 requires a "caption" containing the names of the parties, etc., or what lawyers often call the "style" of the pleading. Each pleading must be given a "designation" (*e.g.*, "Complaint"). The Rule requires numbered paragraphs, "each limited as far as practicable to a single set of circumstances." It also requires that separate claims or defenses be set out in different "counts" (*e.g.*, "First Claim," etc.). There is nothing in the Rule that requires a specific method of laying out the caption, and indeed defective compliance with Rule 10 is often overlooked. There is some advantage, however, in ensuring that one's pleadings "look right" to the judge and to opposing parties. Before some judges, that concern might even justify "empty formalisms" such as "Now Comes the Plaintiff."

(4) *Spell Check and Edit, Please.* The ease of generating documents has caused typographical and formatting errors to seem commonplace. Some tolerance of minor mistakes, of course, can be expected, but there is a limit. For example, in *Noel v. SDH Services West, LLC et. al*, CASE NO. 17-23078-CIV-ALTONAGA/Goodman (S.D. Fla., Nov. 2, 2017), the Plaintiff sought to file an amended complaint, but Judge Cecilia M. Altonaga simply could not suffer any more:

> The Court notes Plaintiff's proposed Second Amended Complaint is replete with grammatical errors, including improper punctuation, misspelling

> of words, incorrect conjugation of verbs, and lack of apostrophes when required for possessive adjectives; sentence fragments; and nonsensical sentences. The proposed Second Amended Complaint is also an eyesore, with its formatting errors and spaces. . . . Plaintiff's counsel is permitted to file a second amended complaint as a separate docket entry by November 14, 2017, so long as he certifies the pleading has been reviewed and approved by a teacher of the English language—such certification is to be included in the notice of filing the second amended complaint. Should these issues persist in Plaintiff's filings, Plaintiff's counsel will be referred to the Florida Bar for counseling and any other action the Florida Bar deems appropriate.

Litigation Document Example 5.1

Statement of the Claim, George Miller Co. v. Compudata

This Document appears in Litigation Document Example 2.1, in Chapter 2, at the end of the chapter, and is titled "Complaint." Please go to that item. The statement of the claim alleges that Defendant Compudata had a contract with Plaintiff George Miller Company and that it breached the contract by failing to pay as agreed. As you read the statement of the claim, you should consider whether it complies with Rule 8 as interpreted in the Supreme Court's opinions. Specifically, you should decide:

(1) If all of the allegations are assumed true, is there is a possibility that the plaintiff can recover? (You may decide that the answer is yes, but if so, be able to explain why.)

(2) Are there sufficient allegations of fact, not mere conclusions, to allow a plausible inference that a claim exists? (Again, you may decide that the answer is yes, but if so, be able to explain why.)

IV. The Answer in Federal Court

[A] Dilatory Pleas and Attacks on the Complaint

"Dilatory Pleas" and "Demurrers." In common law practice, fundamental defects in the suit were raised by a demurrer, a plea to the jurisdiction (akin to using a motion to dismiss), or a "plea in abatement" (often used to raise improper venue or nonjoinder of parties). Pleas to the jurisdiction or in abatement were known as "dilatory pleas"—in part, because they were often used precisely as the name implies. Dilatory pleas were required to be raised early in the proceedings, in "due order."

The Modern Federal Approach: Rule 12. Today, in the Federal Rules, there is no special category for dilatory pleas or demurrers. The Rules replace these pleadings with the Rule 12(b) motion to dismiss. Personal jurisdiction, subject-matter jurisdiction, venue, process, service, failure to state a claim, and failure to join a party, are all raised in federal practice by the motion to dismiss. Notice that several of these matters will be waived if not timely raised. *See* Rule 12(h). Many states follow the same approach (but there are some states in which demurrers and pleas in abatement are still used). Notice that Rule 12(g) allows the pleader to consolidate multiple defenses or requests in one motion. In fact, Rule 12(g)(2) and (h) also explain that defenses omitted from such a motion may be limited or waived, and cannot be included in any later motion.

Inclusion of Dilatory Pleas in the Answer. The defendant can simply include these matters in the answer, rather than filing a motion. Rule 12(b). Thus, the first paragraph may assert that the complaint fails to state a claim, while later paragraphs may contain admissions and denials and affirmative defenses. However, there are reasons to separate the answer from the motion to dismiss. Some courts require an easier-to-read and self-contained answer. *See, e.g.*, U.S. District Court for the Northern District of Illinois, Local Rule 10.1 ("Responsive pleadings shall be made in numbered paragraphs each corresponding to and stating a concise summary of the paragraph to which it is directed."). In addition, a defendant who wants the court to focus on the jurisdictional issues or other defects in the complaint usually prefers to file a motion to dismiss.

[B] Admissions and Denials

Read Fed. R. Civ. P. 8(b), (c), and (d) and Rule 12(a), (g), and (h).

Note Contrasting the General Denial with Federal Practice

What Is a "General Denial"? Some states permit the defendant to plead a general denial: "The defendant denies each and every, all and singular, the material allegations of the plaintiff's complaint, and demands strict proof thereof before a jury." No particular form of expression is required, so long as the answer makes the point that the defendant is generally denying the plaintiff's allegations, although some kinds of denials must be more specific in some states (see below). This pleading is derived from the common law plea of the "general issue," which allowed the defendant to offer rebuttal evidence without particularizing any positions in the answer.

The Effect of the General Denial. The effect of a general denial is to put in issue all of the ultimate facts required to sustain the plaintiff's claim. Some students perceive this plea as "dishonest," but this perception reflects a misunderstanding. In those states in which it is permitted, the general denial is not literally an assertion that all of the plaintiff's allegations are false; it merely amounts to a demand that the plaintiff "prove it."

Strategy and Desirability of the General Denial. A defendant would prefer to assert a general denial, if it is available. In those jurisdictions in which it is permitted, a defendant often files an answer that consists of a single sentence. By not offering specific responses early in the case, the defendant minimizes the probability of variances between pleading and the evidence revealed in discovery or at trial. States that permit general denials often make exceptions that require more specific pleading of some kinds of denials, such as denial of execution of a written instrument or denial of the existence of a corporation.

The Federal Approach: Admissions and Denials. The Federal Rules require a more detailed approach. The defendant is required to sift through the complaint and address the truth or falsehood of each allegation. Rule 8(b) says that denials "must fairly respond to the substance of the allegation." Furthermore, "[a] party that intends in good faith to deny only part of an allegation must admit the part that is true and deny the rest." Don't be confused by the reference in Rule 8(b) to a "general denial"; the rule also says that defendant "must admit" the allegations that are true. In other words, the denial can be worded to deny everything "except the following, which are admitted . . . ." Some federal practitioners begin their answers with a general denial, and then provide itemized answers to all paragraphs.

White v. Smith

91 F.R.D. 607 (W.D.N.Y. 1981)

Elfvin, District Judge.

Plaintiff in this *pro se* civil rights action was granted permission to proceed *in forma pauperis* January 26, 1981. In my Memorandum and Order I outlined plaintiff's allegations and cited legal authority to the effect that, as presented, plaintiff's contentions pose tenable constitutional claims.

. . . By their attorney, New York State Assistant Attorney General Douglas S. Cream, defendants moved for additional time to answer. . . .

[The defendants obtained an extension of time to answer.] . . . [T]wo months after they were served, all four defendants jointly filed their Answer, recounted in full below.[(1)]

---

(1) The body of defendants' Answer is as follows:

Defendants, HAROLD SMITH, DORIS BEITZ, CHARLES SCULLY, EDITH ALMETER, as and for their answer to the complaint, by their attorney, Robert Abrams, Attorney General of the State of New York, Douglas S. Cream, Assistant Attorney General, of counsel, set forth as follows:

1. DENY each and every allegation of the complaint which allege [sic] or tends to allege that they violated any of plaintiff's constitutionally protected rights.

AS AND FOR AN ADDITIONAL AND FURTHER DEFENSE:

2. The complaint fails to state a claim upon which relief can be granted.

AS AND FOR AN ADDITIONAL AND FURTHER DEFENSE:

3. The defendants are immune from liability.

AS AND FOR AN ADDITIONAL AND FURTHER DEFENSE:

4. At all times herein relevant, the defendants were employed by the New York State Department of Correctional Services.

As a general rule, federal court pleadings need not be extensive or detailed. On the contrary, Fed. R. Civ. P. Rule 8(b) requires only that defenses shall be stated "in short and plain terms." For the most part, denials are to be "specific denials of designated averments or paragraphs." . . .

. . . The federal rule does not contemplate an elaborate reply to every allegation of a complaint. . . . It does not even condemn averments of insufficient information or knowledge upon which to form a belief as to the truth of the complainant's allegations. . . . Nonetheless, the "form answer" submitted by defendants in this action does not come close to complying . . . .

Although plaintiff is proceeding *pro se*, his claims are plainly and cogently presented. Admittedly, there is no numbering or other denomination of his separate allegations; but, essentially, he alleges that, despite the pendency of a state habeas corpus challenge to his extradition to North Carolina, defendants delivered him to the North Carolina authorities before the hearing.

Unlike many other *pro se* complaints filed in this court, this Complaint raises allegations which do not hinge solely on plaintiff's word against the defendants' words. . . .

On the contrary, plaintiff's description of the events surrounding his extradition are meticulously detailed and quite specific. He includes all critical names and dates. Finally, attached to the Complaint are various documents pertaining to his detainer, state habeas corpus petition, and subsequent extradition which, in the court's view, tend to support his claim.

Surely it would not have been an onerous burden for defendants' attorney to compare plaintiff's averments and attached documents to defendants' own records [*i.e.*, the records of another department and of another state] to enable him to frame meaningful and responsible answers to plaintiff's charges. . . .

The absurdity of defendants' general denial appears all the more flagrant when the answer is compared to plaintiff's claims. Three examples will suffice, though many more are obvious. If defendants' general denial is to be believed, then notwithstanding the Complaint and its Exhibit B, the District Attorney of North Carolina did not request a detainer against plaintiff; notwithstanding the Complaint and its Exhibit F, Acting Superintendent Scully did not sign and send an "Offer to Deliver Temporary Custody" of plaintiff; and notwithstanding the Complaint and its Exhibit I, Doris Beitz neither was informed that plaintiff's petition for habeas corpus was [pending] nor informed plaintiff of the hearing date in an inter-office communication . . . .

---

5. All acts performed by the defendants were performed by them within the scope of their duties.

6. All acts performed by defendants were performed in the reasonable and good faith belief that those acts would not violate any of plaintiff's constitutionally protected rights.

On the basis of defendants' wholly inadequate response to plaintiff's clearly framed allegations, I can only conclude that defendants' general denial is neither offered in "good faith," Fed. R. Civ. P. rule 8(b), nor complies with Fed. R. Civ. P. rule 11. For all the reasons discussed above, I would be stretching attorney Cream's credibility far beyond the realm of rationality were I to find that "to the best of his knowledge, information, and belief there is good ground to support [his general denial]." Fed. R. Civ. P. rule 11. . . .

Under the circumstances of this case, appropriate sanctions are more than justified. [A] pleading filed in violation of Fed. R. Civ. P. rule 11 may be stricken as sham and false and the action may proceed as though the pleading had not been served. I am satisfied that such a penalty is fully warranted in this matter . . . .

Nevertheless, because counsel for defendants has been permitted in the past to use this same type of unresponsive answer and because he and his office should have some advance warning prior to the imposition of the ultimate sanction of entry of a default and the proving up of a default judgment—and this Memorandum and Order is such a warning that such will occur in future similar situations—it is hereby

ORDERED that the defendants' Answer is stricken; and it is further hereby

ORDERED that defendants shall file an answer or answers to the Complaint not later than twenty (20) days after the entry of this Order.

Notes and Questions

(1) *Plaintiff's Strategy in Pleading a Federal Complaint.* Federal plaintiffs often plead in greater detail than the Rules require, since the defendants must respond to each allegation. By using separate paragraphs to set out each individual allegation of fact that the defendant in good faith must admit, the plaintiff may be able to pressure the defendant, whose answer time is short, and obtain more admissions. However, plaintiffs usually stay with broad and general language in pleading allegations that are at the heart of the claim (*e.g.*, allegations of the defendant's actions in a negligence case). This latter strategy helps to avoid variances between allegations and proof.

(2) *Is There Justification for the General Denial?* The defendant, after all, has only 21 days to answer the complaint under the Rules, and therefore may not have had time to investigate the claims fully. The plaintiff has a strategic motivation to press the defendant with a complaint containing a large array of facts that should be admitted. If the plaintiff amends the complaint (as happens in a large percentage of cases), the defendant will be required to answer again. In any event, the particulars of the defendant's contentions can be specified through discovery or a pretrial order. The general denial, when allowed in state courts, avoids these difficulties.

[C] Affirmative Defenses

Note: What Is an Affirmative Defense?

The affirmative defense is a modern version of the common law plea in confession and avoidance. It is also sometimes called the "defense of new matter." Rather than denying or rebutting an element of the plaintiff's claim, the affirmative defense adds a new set of facts that defeats the claim even if the plaintiff proves all of the elements. Rule 8(c) lists certain affirmative defenses, of which contributory negligence, estoppel, fraud, limitations, and waiver are among the most common. By definition, a denial is insufficient to raise an affirmative defense; it must be set forth affirmatively. In general, the burden of proving the elements of the affirmative defense is also assigned to the defendant. Consider the following case.

Jones v. Department of Corrections

429 F.3d 276 (D.C. Cir. 2005)

Appellant Angela R. Jones brought this action against her employer, the District of Columbia Department of Corrections ("Department"), and various individuals, alleging sexual harassment, retaliation, and common law claims. We reverse the judgment of the district court.

I

In September 1997, Jones began work as a correctional officer at the Department's Occoquan prison facility. Sergeant Darryl Ellison supervised one of the zones in which Jones worked. Jones claims Ellison's statements and conduct gave rise to a hostile work environment and the Department retaliated against her after she submitted harassment complaints against Ellison. Jones's allegations focus on three primary incidents. First, . . . Ellison allegedly went into the gym with Jones, shut the door, and told Jones, "I want to kiss you." He also allegedly grabbed her, pulled her toward him, and held her face, telling her she was "sexy" and commenting about her lips. Second, . . . Ellison allegedly called Jones into his office for a work evaluation and told her he wanted to kiss her. He also commented about her breasts and panty line. Third, . . . Ellison allegedly approached Jones in the mess hall, commented about Jones's breasts and panty line, and brushed himself up against Jones "with his whole body."

Jones asserts that, after the gym incident, she reported Ellison's behavior to a Sergeant Armstrong, who said he would talk to Ellison, but the harassment continued nonetheless. Jones filed an internal harassment complaint. . . . The warden immediately issued cease-and-desist orders to both Jones and Ellison, instructing them to "avoid unnecessary contact." Department personnel then conducted an investigation, taking recorded statements from fourteen witnesses and issuing a thirty-one-page investigation report. The report's summary noted that several witnesses had denied or contradicted Jones's allegations and concluded there was "insufficient evidence to support a finding of Probable Cause." Jones, however, alleges the investigation was perfunctory and biased.

Jones asserts that she was transferred to the night shift "almost immediately" after filing her internal harassment complaint [and she alleges other actions that she claimed were retaliatory. Ultimately, she filed this suit.].

II

In *Faragher v. Boca Raton*, 524 U.S. 775 (1998) and *Burlington Industries, Inc. v. Ellerth*, 524 U.S. 742 (1998), the Supreme Court delineated the circumstances in which an employer may be held vicariously liable for a supervisor's harassment of a subordinate. If the harassment takes the form of a tangible employment action—that is, a "significant change in employment status, such as hiring, firing, failing to promote [or other, similar changes,]" . . . then the supervisor has unquestionably exercised authority on behalf of the employing enterprise in furtherance of the harassment, and the employer is therefore liable. Vicarious liability is less certain, however, where the harassment does not result in a change in status amounting to a tangible employment action. In such cases, "a defending employer may raise an affirmative defense to liability or damages, subject to proof by a preponderance of the evidence. The defense comprises two necessary elements: (a) that the employer exercised reasonable care to prevent and correct promptly any sexually harassing behavior, and (b) that the plaintiff employee unreasonably failed to take advantage of any preventive or corrective opportunities provided by the employer or to avoid harm otherwise."

[T[he *Faragher-Ellerth* defense is explicitly an "affirmative defense" as to which the employer has the burden of proof. Federal Rule of Civil Procedure 8(c) states: "In pleading to a preceding pleading, a party shall set forth affirmatively . . . any . . . matter constituting an . . . affirmative defense." In *Harris v. Secretary, United States Department of Veterans Affairs*, 126 F.3d 339, 345 (D.C. Cir. 1997), we construed Rule 8(c) strictly:

> . . . [W]e hold that Rule 8(c) means what it says: a party must first raise its affirmative defenses in a responsive pleading before it can raise them in a dispositive motion. . . .

Here, the Department concedes that it failed to raise the *Faragher-Ellerth* defense in its answer to the amended complaint, and it presents this court with no argument as to why our holding in *Harris* should not apply, arguing instead that Jones suffered no prejudice from its failure to plead the defense. However, in *Harris*, we were very clear that lack of prejudice is not determinative: ". . . Rule 8(c) requires that a party actually plead its affirmative defenses, not that it plead them only in those cases where failure to plead would result in prejudice to the opposing party." . . .

We conclude the district court erred in granting summary judgment based on the *Faragher-Ellerth* defense in a case in which the defense had not been raised in the pleadings. As described in *Harris*, the Department may move to amend its answer on remand. If the trial court permits the amendment, then the Department may renew its motion for summary judgment or attempt to prove the elements of its *Faragher-Ellerth* defense at trial. [REVERSED.]

Problem C

DEFENSIVE THEORIES NOT LISTED IN RULE 8(c)—WHICH ONES ARE AFFIRMATIVE DEFENSES? Rule 8(c) does not purport to be an exhaustive list of affirmative defenses. In fact, whether a defensive theory is an affirmative defense is usually determined by reference to the substantive law governing the claim. *Jicarilla Apache Tribe v. Andrus*, 687 F.2d 1324 (10th Cir. 1982). Consider the following examples:

(a) *Novation.* A "novation," in the law of contracts, is "a mutual agreement . . . for the discharge of a valid existing obligation by the substitution of a new valid obligation on the part of the debtor. . . ." Is novation an affirmative defense? *See Charles Kahn & Co. v. Sobery*, 355 F. Supp. 156 (E.D. Mo. 1972) ("The burden of establishing that a novation occurred is upon the party claiming" it, "and in this regard [it] is an affirmative defense under Rule 8(c)").

(b) *Unavoidable Accident.* The doctrine of unavoidable accident provides that if a natural occurrence that could not be avoided was the actual and sole cause of the plaintiff's injuries, then the defendant cannot have been guilty of negligence proximately causing those injuries. Is unavoidable accident an affirmative defense? *Sanden v. Mayo Clinic*, 495 F.2d 221 (8th Cir. 1974) said no: "a defense that merely negates some element of plaintiff's *prima facie* case is not a true affirmative defense and need not be pleaded." The defendant may introduce evidence of unavoidable accident, and obtain jury instructions if provided by law on that subject, without pleading the doctrine.

Notes and Questions

(1) *Which Defenses Should Be Treated as Affirmative Defenses? Gomez v. Toledo*, 446 U.S. 635 (1980). An officer sued for an alleged violation of civil rights under section 1983 can defend by showing that the officer's action was reasonable and in good faith. In *Gomez v. Toledo*, the Supreme Court decided that this defense of good faith was an affirmative defense that must be pled by the defendant.

The Court gave two reasons for recognizing an affirmative defense. First, if the claim does not include an element requiring negation of the defense, it probably is an affirmative defense. Second, if the defendant is likely to have greater knowledge of the controlling facts, the defense is probably an affirmative defense. These factors convinced the Court in *Gomez v. Toledo* to treat good faith as an affirmative defense. First, absence of good faith is not an element in section 1983, and second, the defendant is likely to have greater knowledge about his alleged good faith. (It should be added, however, that a series of later cases has adjusted burdens of pleading and proof of this defense, and it is a more complex subject than can be covered here.)

(2) *State Law Conflicting with Rule 8(c).* In a diversity case, what happens if Rule 8(c) lists an "affirmative defense" that is not an affirmative defense under state law?

The cases are inconsistent. In *Amelio v. Yazoo Mfg. Co.*, 98 F.R.D. 691 (N.D. Ill. 1983), the court struck the defendant's pleading of contributory negligence. Although this defense is listed in Rule 8(c) as an affirmative one, Illinois law made it only a partial defense, and therefore the court concluded that it could be raised in federal court without being pleaded. But the majority view appears to be that Rule 8(c) is a procedural requirement, governing which party must plead a given defensive theory, even though state law may allocate the burden of proof to the other party, and even though the court will follow the state burden of proof at trial. *Gilmore v. Witschorek*, 411 F. Supp. 491 (E.D. Ill. 1976) (where state law requires plaintiff to prove freedom from contributory negligence, that burden is governed by state law under the *Erie* doctrine, but 8(c) requires defendant to plead the defense).

(3) *Sufficiency of Pleading.* The question remains whether adequacy of the defendant's pleadings to raise a given affirmative defense is tested by standards similar to those governing the complaint. *E.g., Barnwell & Hays, Inc. v. Sloan*, 564 F.2d 254 (8th Cir. 1977) (plea of waiver, even though it did not use the word "waiver" but instead alleged the existence of an oral agreement relied on by the defendant, was adequate because it "apprised" the plaintiff of the defense). The cases are inconsistent, with some holding that the *Twombly-Iqbal* requirement of factual plausibility applies to affirmative defenses and others that it does not.

(4) *What Do You Do When You Are Unsure Whether Your Theory Is an Affirmative Defense?* If in doubt, plead the defensive theory affirmatively. As the above materials make clear, there is often room for doubt. The paper on which you type the defense is cheap, but paying a malpractice judgment because your client was precluded from offering evidence of the defense at trial is expensive.

[D] The Plaintiff's Reply

What Is a Reply? A reply is the modern derivative of the plaintiff's replication in common law pleading. Under Federal Rule 7, a plaintiff is required to file a reply "to a counterclaim designated as a counterclaim"; this kind of reply resembles an answer to a complaint. Rule 7 refers to this pleading as "an answer to a counterclaim" but otherwise does not require or allow the filing of a reply unless "the court orders one." Courts are unlikely to order one, however, because a plaintiff's reply to an answer is "likely to be self-serving and not based on any legitimate need." *Fort Independence Indian Cmty. v. California*, 2008 U.S. Dist. LEXIS 109356 (E.D. Cal. 2008), *citing* 5 Charles A. Wright & Arthur R. Miller, Federal Practice and Procedure § 1185 (3d ed. 2004). Instead, in the absence of a reply, Rule 8(b)(6) explains that the allegations of the answer automatically will be "considered denied or avoided."

Replies as Avoidance of Matters in the Answer. Still, courts can and do order replies to answers. Say that the plaintiff has pleaded a contract claim; the defendant has responded with an answer stating the affirmative defense of limitations; and the plaintiff avoids the defense by arguing that the limitations period is tolled by the absence of the defendant from the jurisdiction. This "tolling" argument is a kind of "affirmative defense to the affirmative defense," and if the plaintiff is not required to plead it, how will the defendant find out about it? Possibly through discovery; but it seems inappropriate to require the defendant to conduct discovery on every basic legal theory that the plaintiff might invoke at trial. A requirement of a reply would place the same duty of pleading upon the plaintiff that is placed on the defendant.

Litigation Document Example 5.2

Answer in George Miller Co. v. Compudata

This Document appears in Litigation Document Example 2.1 in Chapter 2, at the end of the chapter, and is headed "Answer." It contains numbered paragraphs that either admit, deny, or state that the defendant lacks sufficient information to answer, and it also pleads a defense of limitations. As you read the answer, you should consider whether it is consistent with the Rules. Specifically, you should consider whether this pleading complies with Rule 8, meaning:

(1) Whether the first defense (admissions and denials, etc.) is properly pleaded (whether it is responsive to every allegation in an appropriate way); and

(2) Why the defense of limitations is separately pleaded and whether it is pleaded in a proper manner.

V. Devices for Deterring Abuse of Liberal Pleading Rules

Read Fed. R. Civ. P. 23.1 and Rule 11.

[A] Older Approaches: Verification, etc.

Note on Verification: A Dubious Solution?

State and federal civil procedure rules require pleadings on certain subjects to be "verified." "Verification" means that someone signs the particular pleading allegation under oath. Federal Rule 23.1 requires verification of stockholder's derivative suits, which are claims by shareholders accusing officers or directors of a corporation of malfeasance. Some states' rules contain lists of subjects requiring sworn statements, ranging from denial of a partnership or corporation to pleas of usury to lack or failure of consideration. The reason for the federal Rule: suits of this kind are sometimes thought to be "strike" suits—easy to bring even if unmeritorious, expensive to defend, and capable of creating inordinate settlement pressure. But the deterrent value of verification remains questionable.

SUROWITZ V. HILTON HOTELS CORP., 383 U.S. 363 (1966). Dora Surowitz, an immigrant with little education, used her earnings as a seamstress to invest in Hilton. One day, she received a communication from the corporation that alarmed her, and she consulted her son-in-law, an attorney with a wonderful name: Irving Brilliant. Mr. Brilliant investigated, and he concluded that the company's managers had engaged in fraudulent activities. Brilliant explained all of this to Surowitz, who agreed to file a shareholder's derivative suit. She swore to (that is, she "verified") the allegations, as is required by Rule 23.1. But the defendant's lawyers promptly took Surowitz's deposition, which demonstrated that she did not understand the allegations or the underlying facts. The District Court therefore dismissed the suit as a "sham," and the Court of Appeals affirmed. The Supreme Court reversed and ordered the suit reinstated. Surowitz had trusted her attorneys and had sworn to "grave charges of fraud . . . based on reasonable beliefs growing out of careful investigation." The verification requirement "was written to further, not defeat the ends of justice."

Notes and Questions

(1) *Back to the Future, Yet More of the Same.* At one time, a huge backlog of real estate collection cases grew because banks could not provide evidence that they held the mortgage note after electronic transactions. The Supreme Court of Florida accepted a task force recommendation and adopted a new rule that embraced old methods. *In re Amendments to the Florida Rules of Civil Procedure*, Case No. SC09–1460 (2010). Complaints seeking to foreclose on a mortgage for residential real property must "allege with specificity the factual basis by which the claimant is a person entitled to enforce the note," and must be verified, as follows: "Under penalties of perjury, I declare that I have read the foregoing, and the facts alleged therein are true and correct to the best of my knowledge and belief." Rules 1.115(a) and (e), Florida Rules of Civil Procedure. Fifteen months later, a special investigation by Reuters revealed that many banks were "still taking the same shortcuts they promised to shun," including "robo-signing" foreclosure complaints without possessing the supporting documentation. Scot J. Paltrow, *Special Report: Banks Still Robo-Signing*, Reuters Business News (July 18, 2011).

(2) *Why Verification Is a Dubious Solution.* The result in *Surowitz* may be sensible, but it means that the verifier does not need to know or understand what is verified. Even if the result is sensible, doesn't it mean that verification is unlikely to work effectively? Perhaps the Florida experience with mortgage loan verification supports this conclusion, too.

(3) *Another Reason Verification Is a Dubious Solution:* David Siegel, *New York Practice* 281 (1978). Professor Siegel points out that although false verification is

"technically a perjury," district attorneys have more pressing problems. And although at one time, fear of one's fate in the afterlife may have encouraged truthfulness in verification, today, the fear of "hell has little effect on New York Practice." Verification, Siegel concludes, "has nothing more to recommend it than the legislature."

[B] Rule 11: Certifications and Sanctions

Note on the Modern Approach: Rule 11

The "Oldest" Rule 11 and the Early Certification Requirement. Before 1983, an earlier version of Rule 11 ("oldest" Rule 11) was applicable. That rule provided that the attorney's signature on a pleading automatically constituted a "certification" that, among other things, the attorney believed there was "good ground to support it." That standard was vague and subjective, and it was rare that violations could be established. The standard required proof that the pleading had been filed in bad faith, and this proof was impossible in most cases, no matter how bad the pleading was.

The "Old" Rule 11 Certifications, the Objective Test, and Mandatory Sanctions. In 1983, Rule 11 was amended, and the revisions created a duty to investigate. An attorney's signature constituted an implied, automatic certification of several matters. The most important is that "to the best of the person's knowledge, information, and belief, formed after an inquiry reasonable under the circumstances," the allegations have "evidentiary support" (or are likely to, after discovery), and "are warranted by existing law" (or by a nonfrivolous argument for a change in existing law). The requirement of "reasonable" inquiry made Rule 11 a potent force. It set forth an objective standard: an attorney acting in ignorance of facts and law could not take refuge in good faith or purity of heart. Additionally, the court's imposition of "an appropriate sanction" was mandatory.

"Old" Rule 11 and Its Replacement by "New" Rule 11. The provision for mandatory sanctions in old Rule 11 was perceived as discouraging new legal theories, raising costs, and imposing unfair penalties. Rule drafters changed it again in 1993, and now we have "new" Rule 11.

"An Appropriate Sanction," Discretionary Imposition, and the "Safe Harbor." New Rule 11 has removed the mandatory sanction requirement by replacing language saying that the court "shall" impose a sanction with the permissive statement that "the court may . . . impose an appropriate sanction . . . ," thus giving the judge discretion. The amendments also introduced a requirement of notice and time to cure an offending pleading, as a "safe harbor" or protection for the pleader. Whether Rule 11 sanctions are too loosely allowed, or too narrowly restricted, is a matter of continuing controversy. *See* Edward D. Cavanagh, *Mandating Rule 11 Sanctions? Here We Go Again!*, 74 WASH. & LEE L. REV. 31 (2017).

[1] An Objective Standard Requiring a "Reasonable Inquiry": Mandatory Sanctions under "Old" Rule 11

EASTWAY CONSTRUCTION CORP. v. CITY OF NEW YORK, 762 F.2d 243 (2d Cir. 1985). This was one of the early influential decisions under "old" Rule 11 (after the 1983 amendments) which defined violations objectively and prescribed mandatory sanctions. Eastway Construction Corporation was excluded from contracts on New York City construction projects after conduct of its officers involving bribes and defaults. This exclusion put Eastway out of business. Eastway then brought an action, "[s]omewhat desperately, perhaps," alleging that the City and other defendants had committed antitrust and civil rights violations. Judge Weinstein granted summary judgment for the defendants because (1) there was no basis for Eastway to claim the type of marketplace injury required for an antitrust claim (namely injury to the competitive market, as opposed to injury to an individual firm such as Eastway) and (2) a company merely hoping to obtain public contracts could not claim a property interest that could give rise to a due process or civil rights violation. The City, which had expended public funds defending against this groundless suit, moved for Rule 11 sanctions. But Judge Weinstein refused to impose sanctions on Eastway, explaining that "I can't say this was a frivolous case."

The Court of Appeals reversed and remanded the case to Judge Weinstein with orders to impose an "appropriate sanction." The court reasoned that Rule 11 (at that time) required objective reasonableness, not the more lax, subjective good faith standard that had applied earlier (based on the oldest versions of Rule 11 that predated the 1983 amendments). Therefore, sanctions were mandatory:

> The addition [to Rule 11] of the words "formed after reasonable inquiry" demand that we revise our inquiry. . . . No longer is it enough for an attorney to claim that he acted in good faith, or that he personally was unaware of the groundless nature of an argument or claim. For the language of the new Rule explicitly and unambiguously imposes an affirmative duty on each attorney to conduct a reasonable inquiry into the viability of a pleading before it is signed. Simply put, good faith no longer provides the safe harbor it once did. . . .
>
> [Moreover,] sanctions shall be imposed against an attorney and on his client [for any violation]. [Note: This mandatory-sanctions feature was a consequence of the wording of the old version, and it has since been changed by new Rule 11].
>
> In framing this [objective] standard, we do not intend to stifle the enthusiasm or chill the creativity that is the very lifeblood of the law. . . . But where it is patently clear that the claim has absolutely no chance of success under the existing precedents, and where no reasonable argument can

> be advanced to extend, modify or reverse the law as it stands, Rule 11 has been violated....
>
> ... [Eastway's] claim of an antitrust violation, ... without any allegation of an antitrust injury, was destined to fail. [Separately, the court analyzed the civil rights claim, which similarly was unfounded.] Moreover, a competent attorney, after reasonable inquiry, would have had to reach the same conclusion.

On remand, the City showed that a reasonable attorney's fee for responding to Eastway's unfounded claims was $58,550, and it sought recovery of this sum as a sanction. Judge Weinstein, however, regarded Eastway's suit as only "marginally frivolous," and so he imposed a sanction of only $1,000, requiring the City to bear the rest of its $58,500 loss. The Court of Appeals again reversed. It held that this $1,000 sanction was an abuse of discretion, and it ordered Judge Weinstein to impose a sanction of $10,000 "to serve the ... purpose of the rule." *Eastway Construction Corp. v. City of New York*, 821 F.2d 121 (2d Cir. 1987).

BUSINESS GUIDES, INC. v. CHROMATIC COMMUNICATIONS ENTERPRISES, INC., 498 U.S. 533 (1991). This case caused widespread concern, because it showed that an honest error in pleadings could lead to a mandatory penalty for the pleader. Business Guides sought injunctive relief against Chromatic for allegedly copying its business directory. The company claimed that its directory included bits of false information, called "seeds," and that ten entries in Chromatic's directory were copies of these seeds. The District Court's law clerk, however, verified the information in Chromatic's directory: the alleged "seeds" were not seeds, and the businesses existed. Business Guides had made a serious mistake, but in the meanwhile, Chromatic had spent $13,865.66 opposing Business Guides's unfounded allegations. The magistrate recommended this amount as a sanction against both Business Guides and its lawyers. The Supreme Court affirmed the party sanctions (and showed that an honest mistake could invoke serious penalties under Rule 11).

Four Justices dissented: "[P]atience ... must be an attribute of the judicial system .... Our annoyance at spurious and frivolous claims ... must not drive us to adopt interpretations of the rules that make honest litigants fear to petition the courts."

Notes and Questions

(1) *What Is a "Reasonable" Inquiry?* The rule does not tell us just how much information a litigant must have to comply with Rule 11. *Business Guides*, above, raises serious questions about the extent to which an attorney may believe the client without obtaining further information. In *General Accident Ins. Co. of America v. Fidelity & Deposit Co. of Md.*, 598 F. Supp. 1223 (E.D. Pa. 1984), the defendant filed a third-party complaint that incorporated the allegations made in the plaintiff's original

complaint. The court denied sanctions on the ground that the defendant had not merely pleaded the third-party allegations in sole reliance on the original complaint but had at least minimally discussed those allegations with officials of the plaintiff before filing the third-party complaint.

On the other hand, in *Florida Monument Builders v. All Faiths Memorial Gardens*, 605 F. Supp. 1324 (S.D. Fla. 1984), the plaintiffs filed an antitrust complaint with no independent investigation, basing allegations of conspiracy solely upon the beliefs and experience of one of the plaintiff's attorneys derived from similar litigation in other parts of the country. The court upheld a sanction in the amount of $25,000 assessed against the plaintiff and its attorneys jointly.

(2) *The Pleader Should Document the "Reasonable Inquiry."* Consider the following advice:

> ... Before signing any pleading that you have reason to believe ... may subject you to a motion for sanctions, specifically take Rule 11 into account and review it. This is important ... so that [you] can file an affidavit when resisting Rule 11 sanctions. ...
>
> In this regard you should determine the steps taken to make the reasonable inquiry required by the rule. ... Consider the source of the information you are relying upon in filing a certain pleading. In many instances the information must come from the client. What other sources of information besides the client are there, and, as a practical matter, is any additional inquiry necessary or fruitful? Be sure ... to lay out in detail the nature of the inquiry or the reason that the inquiry was limited. ...

Dombroff, *Attorneys in Affirming Pleadings Risk Sanctions,* NAT. L.J., Jan. 27, 1986, at 15, col. 3.

(3) *Important: What Should I Do to Conduct a Reasonable Inquiry?* In general, attorneys should consider documenting the following steps as part of the reasonable inquiry. (1) First, before filing suit, a plaintiff's lawyer should write a demand letter to the opponent, inviting a response. It's not just an overture to settlement. It's also a malpractice prevention device. (2) Second, the attorney should thoroughly cross-examine the client and seek to verify the information thus received. (3) Third, if appropriate, the attorney should employ an expert whose credentials have been examined. (4) Fourth, the attorney should undertake at least minimal legal research. (5) Fifth, if the subject requires expertise, the attorney should associate with another attorney who knows the subject. (6) Sixth, the attorney should promptly undertake discovery and react to information revealing the inaccuracy of any allegations or denials. *See generally Shaffer, Rule 11 and the Prefiling Duty,* NAT. L.J. Aug. 18, 1986, at 28.

(4) *The Side Effects of Mandatory Sanctions, Part I: Increased Cost and Discouragement of New Claims.* Mandatory sanctions made lawyers much more cautious. To avoid being blindsided by the effects of their own innocent misapprehensions, lawyers redundantly investigated even facts that were not likely to be disputed and

law that seemed well established, driving up costs for their clients and pricing some clients out of their cases. By discouraging frivolous claims, Rule 11 also discouraged attorneys from bringing claims that were difficult, novel, or ambiguous but that ought to have been aired in the courts. *See* Note, *Reasonable Inquiry Under Rule 11—Is the Stop, Look and Investigate Requirement a Litigant's Roadblock?*, 18 Ind. L. Rev. 751 (1982).

Sometimes, because of factual nuances and limitations of counsel in particular cases, judges could find reasons to relieve a party from sanctions. *See, e.g., Mohammed v. Union Carbide Corp.*, 606 F. Supp. 252 (E.D. Mich. 1985) (difficulty of investigating conspiracy and monopolization lessens the effort required for "reasonable" inquiry); *Anderson v. Cryovac, Inc.*, 96 F.R.D. 431 (D. Mass. 1983) (no sanctions where plaintiff's attorney testified that he checked the complex complaint line by line with his retained expert and was advised that each line was justified); *but cf. Duncan v. WJLA-TV, Inc.*, 106 F.R.D. 4 (D.D.C. 1984) (sanctions assessed where pleading was based on information from unqualified expert and where plaintiff and her counsel had failed to investigate the "expert's" qualifications).

(5) *Side Effects of Mandatory Sanctions, Part II: An Explosion of Litigation about Sanctions.* It is impossible to say precisely how much Rule 11 discouraged litigation. However, the Rule certainly became a new weapon in the adversary system, leading to more than 700 reported decisions in the five years after its amendment (and undoubtedly many more that were unreported). Margolick, *At the Bar*, N.Y. Times, Mar. 11, 1988. There were many commentaries on old Rule 11 and its side effects. *See* Miller, *The New Certification Standard under Rule 11*, 130 F.R.D. 479 (1990).

The incentive to litigate sanctions could be high. Consider, *e.g., Dayan v. McDonald's Corp.*, 126 Ill. App. 3d 11, 466 N.E.2d 945 (1984) (assessing over $1.8 million sanction under Illinois state rule, after 65-day trial with 1,072 photographs showed plaintiff's allegations to be baseless). The award of over $1.8 million is unusual in amount, but the appellate court emphasized that it was justified by proof of attorney's fees and expenses incurred by McDonald's.

[2] The 21-Day Safe Harbor and Limited, Discretionary Sanctions: "New" Rule 11

Note on the 1993 Amendments to Rule 11: Is It Better—or Toothless?

Re-visiting the Prior Versions of Rule 11. As noted earlier, Rule 11 has undergone various revisions. To understand the ongoing controversy about sanctions, remember the three phases. First, in the earlier years, Rule 11 required proof of subjective bad faith. This subjective standard meant that the rule rarely could be enforced. In the second phase, the rule was amended so that an attorney whose improper pleading was not based on a "reasonable investigation" was subject to a mandatory sanction. This version of Rule 11 was an objective, negligence-like standard. But later, the mandatory sanction was thought to be too draconian. Finally, Rule 11 was amended again. Sanctions became discretionary, and the Rule created a safe harbor process.

New Rule 11: Safe Harbor; Discretionary. The most significant change was to make Rule 11 sanctions discretionary with the court. Fed. R. Civ. P. 11(c)(1). The amended rule also provided a "safe harbor." Once a motion for sanctions is served (but not yet filed), the alleged offender has 21 days to withdraw or correct the challenged paper or representation with no adverse consequences. Only if no corrective action is taken may the motion be filed with the court for further action. Fed. R. Civ. P. 11(c)(2). Justice Scalia dissented from these amendments, saying that they made Rule 11 "toothless."

The Court's Power to Sanction without the Safe Harbor. The Rule also provides that the judge may impose sanctions—without the 21-day notice-and-cure warning. But since this power is exercised without warning, it requires more serious misconduct. *See* the *Hadges v. Yonkers Racing Corp.* and *Muhammad v. Wal-Mart Stores East, L.P.* cases below.

Who Can Be Sanctioned, and When? Other changes in the rule mean that sanctions may be imposed for later advocating a position without sufficient basis although there was a sufficient basis for the position when the paper was filed. Fed. R. Civ. P. 11(b). Sanctions are limited to "what suffices to deter repetition of the conduct or comparable conduct by others," and ordinarily monetary sanctions will be paid to the court, not the other party. Fed. R. Civ. P. 11(c)(4). Law firms will ordinarily be held jointly responsible for violations of individual attorneys. Fed. R. Civ. P. 11(c)(1). However, there is now a limitation on sanctioning represented parties for frivolous legal arguments, in Fed. R. Civ. P. 11(c)(5)(A), that could have affected the outcome of *Business Guides, Inc. v. Chromatic Communications Enterprises, Inc.*, 498 U.S. 533 (1991). The result of the amendments has been a decrease in Rule 11 motions and sanction awards. Consider the following decisions.

HADGES v. YONKERS RACING CORP. 48 F.3d 1320 (2d Cir. 1995). The District Court imposed sanctions against the plaintiff, George Hadges, and his well-known lawyer, the late William M. Kunstler. Hadges's lawsuit sought "to compel various racetracks and state agencies to permit him to pursue his career as a harness racehorse driver, trainer and owner." The lawsuit alleged a boycott and secret agreement among all the racetracks. In a sworn statement, Hadges alleged that he had spent his "fifth year . . . out of work," and Kunstler submitted a signed memorandum of law asserting that Hadges "has not worked for more than four years."

But after Yonkers Racing Corp. (YRC) produced documents revealing that Hadges had in fact raced five times in 1991 and seven times in 1993, YRC requested sanctions. Hadges admitted he had raced, but said he considered the races insignificant since he had earned less than $100 total over the two years. The trial judge imposed Rule 11 sanctions of $2,000 on Hadges and censured Kunstler for failing to make adequate inquiry as to the truth of Hadges' affidavits.

The appellate court, however, pointed out that YRC had not served Hadges with the request for sanctions 21 days before filing it, as the "safe harbor" provision of Rule 11 required. The court reversed the sanctions against both Hadges and Kunstler.

Muhammad v. Wal-Mart Stores East, L.P.

732 F.3d 104 (2d Cir. 2013)

Per Curiam:

Christina Agola is an attorney practicing primarily employment law in the Western District of New York. She has a long disciplinary history in the courts of this Circuit.... [In this case,] at summary judgment, Agola represented to the court that Muhammad [the plaintiff, acting pro se] had clearly pled a gender discrimination claim which he had not. Sua sponte, the court ordered Agola to show cause why she should not be sanctioned under Federal Rule of Civil Procedure 11. Agola insisted that the liberal pleading standard afforded pro se complaints meant that Muhammad's complaint should be read to include a gender discrimination claim. The court rejected this argument as frivolous, reprimanded Agola, and imposed a $7,500 sanction.... Because the district court misapplied the relevant legal standard, we vacate the sanction order and reverse....

... On the district court's pro se discrimination complaint form, Muhammad checked the box for Title VII and ADA discrimination, indicating that he intended to sue pursuant to "Title VII of the Civil Rights Act of 1964 ... (race, color, gender, religion, national origin)" and the "Americans with Disabilities Act of 1990." ...

In response to the prompt "Defendant's conduct is discriminatory with respect to which of the following (check all that apply):" Muhammad did not check the boxes for "a. Race b. Color. c. Sex." Instead, he checked only the box for "h. disability." In the narrative portion of the form, Muhammad discussed only Wal-Mart's actions related to his alleged disability. He made no mention of race or gender discrimination....

[Defendant Wal-Mart moved for summary judgment after discovery.] Agola filed Muhammad's opposition to summary judgment .... She claimed that Muhammad "clearly" pled gender discrimination and suggested that unless the complaint "limited the ground(s) upon which Plaintiff seeks relief" a plaintiff may seek relief for any wrong he believes the defendant has done him. According to Agola, Walmart should have anticipated a gender discrimination claim from Muhammad's deposition responses.

The district court was understandably displeased by Agola's last-minute introduction of an unpled gender-discrimination claim. After disposing of the suit's merits, the district court, sua sponte, ordered Agola to show cause why she should not be sanctioned .... Agola filed a lengthy response ... but did not attend the hearing; rather, she sent an associate .... The court rejected her arguments and imposed a reprimand and a $7,500 sanction. Agola appeals ....

Rule 11 contemplates that "ordinarily" opposing counsel will initiate sanctions proceedings. In those situations opposing counsel must serve a notice of the sanctions claim on the accused attorney 21 days before moving for sanctions to give an opportunity to correct the asserted misconduct. Rule 11 also gives the court the power to initiate sanctions proceedings, sua sponte. In these rarer cases, however, the 21–day safe harbor does not apply and the court may impose sanctions without providing opportunity to withdraw the misstatement.

For sanctions issued pursuant to a motion by opposing counsel, courts have long held that an attorney could be sanctioned for conduct that was objectively unreasonable [i.e., by a negligence-like standard—Eds.]. [But in] *In re Pennie & Edmonds LLP,* we considered . . . the appropriate standard for sua sponte sanctions. 323 F.3d 86, 90 (2d Cir.2003). In *Pennie,* we determined that the power of the court under Rule 11 to issue sanctions sua sponte without affording the offender the opportunity to withdraw the challenged document . . . is akin to the court's inherent power of contempt. We reasoned that, like contempt, sua sponte sanctions in those circumstances should issue only upon a finding of subjective bad faith [resembling the standard under "oldest Rule 11 before the 1983 Amendments—Eds.]. The only question for this court is whether the record . . . could sustain a finding that Agola was in bad faith . . . . [W]e find that it could not.

. . . [T]he district court did not apply the correct legal standard. . . . [I]ts analysis . . . indicates that it was applying an objective reasonableness test. The court couched its conclusion in terms of what "any competent attorney" would have done and extensively discussed Agola's admittedly incompetent practice in other areas. This is not enough to demonstrate subjective bad faith. [REVERSED.]

Notes and Questions

(1) *The 21-Day "Safe Harbor' Notice Provision in New Rule 11: Does It Protect Good-but-Mistaken Attorneys or Does It Encourage Reckless Ones?* Amended Rule 11 has the effect of requiring the opposing attorney, before filing a motion for sanctions, to serve the motion first on the alleged offender, describing the specific conduct alleged as a violation. This change nullifies the sanctions motion if the violation is corrected within 21 days. The process allows an attorney to avoid sanctions if he or she acts diligently to minimize the harm after being notified of a mistake. In cases like *Hadges,* some people would think this might make sense, because advocacy sometimes involves guesses in understanding the facts and shaping the legal theories. However, another perspective is that it allows bad actors to escape responsibility. As is indicated above, when the Supreme Court adopted the rule amendments, Justice Scalia filed a dissenting statement asserting that making sanctions discretionary and providing the safe harbor would "render the Rule toothless." Groundless litigation can be catastrophic, even ruinous, for its victims. Some litigants may rightly consider that the safe harbor shifts to them the costs generated by the reckless Rambo who doesn't conduct a reasonable inquiry.

(2) *When the Court, Rather than Counsel, Initiates Rule 11 Sanctions. Hadges* shows that a judge generally does not have discretion to grant sanctions when Rule 11 procedures have not been followed. Under Rule 11(c)(3), a court may initiate a Rule 11 sanction proceeding on its own motion. However, as the Advisory Committee Notes explain, no "safe harbor" opportunity exists to withdraw or correct a submission challenged in such a court-initiated proceeding. In *In re Pennie & Edmonds, LLP*, 323 F.3d 86 (2d Cir. 2003), the Second Circuit held that although the mental state generally applicable to liability for Rule 11 sanctions is objective unreasonableness, a different standard applies to court-initiated Rule 11 proceedings: they require the use of a subjective "bad faith" standard. In contrast, the Fifth Circuit, in *Jenkins v. Methodist Hospitals of Dallas, Inc.*, 478 F.3d 255 (5th Cir. 2007), rejected this proposition, instead concluding that the same objective standard applies regardless of whether it is the court or counsel that initiates the sanction process.

(3) *A Safe-Harbor Nightmare: The Clever, Persistent Bad-Faith Litigant.* Imagine that a litigant files an unfounded pleading with numerous complex factual allegations and issues of law. The opponent, at great expense, documents the errors in a 21-day notice. On the 20th day, the bad-faith litigant withdraws the offending pleading. But the same litigant immediately files an amended pleading containing new, equally groundless allegations. Now the innocent opponent must begin the costly process of investigating the errors all over again (and perhaps this is exactly what the bad-faith litigant intended). Does Rule 11 provide a practical solution? [See the next section for other sanction doctrines.]

(4) *Sanctions Still Are Mandatory in Securities Litigation.* The Private Securities Litigation Reform Act of 1995 was intended to reduce the volume of securities litigation perceived as unwarranted. In addition to other provisions tightening pleading standards, the Act makes certain sanctions mandatory, somewhat as did earlier Rule 11. See the Heightened Pleading Requirements coverage in § III[C] above.

(5) *Severity of the Sanction: Is the Shift from Compensatory Standards to Minimal Deterrence Justified?: Bergeron v. Northwest Publications, Inc.*, 165 F.R.D. 518 (D. Minn. 1996). Applying amended Rule 11's emphasis on deterrence rather than compensation, the district court in this case made the following sanction order:

> [The sanctioned lawyer] is required, at his own expense, to successfully complete a course in the Federal Rules of Civil Procedure, and the Local Rules of this Court. . . . The course shall be taught by a professor at an accredited law school . . . .

Now aren't you glad you paid attention in class? (But you may feel that the opponent who didn't should pay the resulting costs, rather than your client, who will pay an increased fee under a minimalist-sanctions rule.)

Problem D

"BLACKWELL v. CARSON"— Adapted from *"Mr. Blackwell: Fashion Critic's Suit Clogs Courts and Costs Public,"* HOUSTON CHRONICLE, Mar. 21, 1992, at 10B. This

editorial began by observing, "Over the years [the fashion critic who calls himself Mr. Blackwell] has gained international attention by putting celebrities on his 10 worst-dressed list and savaging them with vitriolic comments." But then, it relates, the then-host of the Tonight Show on NBC made fun of Mr. Blackwell by joking that Blackwell had criticized Nobel Prize winner Mother Teresa as a "nerdy nun" and a "fashion no-no." Blackwell promptly filed suit in a California state court for defamation, saying (correctly) that he had made no such statements and alleging that the humorous monologue had subjected him to "hatred, contempt, and ridicule."

The editorial called Blackwell's suit "frivolous," saying that it would "add another little clog to the court system and cost taxpayers a few dollars more." And indeed, the suit does seem to be flatly unmeritorious, because the Supreme Court has held that parody, even if outrageous and even if intended to cause emotional distress, is protected from suit under the First Amendment to the Constitution. *See Hustler Magazine v. Falwell*, 485 U.S. 46 (1988).

The editorial concluded that the California court "should [impose] whatever sanctions it can if it deems the lawsuit frivolous. The courts should not be part of show biz." *Questions:* If it had been filed in a federal court, could Mr. Blackwell's suit properly have invoked sanctions? If so, what kind, against whom, and under what procedures?

[C] Beyond Rule 11: "Inherent" Power and Other Sanction Powers

Note on Sanctions for Conduct Other than Filing or Advocating Pleadings

Other Federal Sanction Powers: "Vexatious" Proceedings and More. Rule 11 is not the only source of federal sanctions; there are other devices that can deter litigation misconduct. After all, Rule 11 is limited to papers filed. Section 1927 of Title 28 authorizes sanctions against any attorney who "multiplies the proceedings in any case unreasonably and vexatiously," whether by pleadings or otherwise. Sanctions for frivolous appeals also are available through 28 U.S.C. § 1912 and Federal Rule of Appellate Procedure 38.

"Inherent Power" to Sanction. Federal courts also claim an "inherent power" to sanction attorneys for misconduct in any proceedings. *Roadway Express Inc. v. Piper*, 447 U.S. 752 (1980). (Consider, also, the case below.) Further, we will see in Chapter 7 that there are separate rules (Rules 26(g) and 37), governing sanctions for discovery abuse, and in Chapter 9 we will revisit the concept of sanctions in connection with Rule 41 (governing dismissals). *See* Joseph, *Rule 11 Is Only the Beginning*, ABA Journal, May 1, 1988, at 62.

State Analogues of Rule 11. Sanctions are also available in state courts under many state statutes. *See, e.g.*, Cal. Code Civ. Pro. § 128.5 (similar to current Rule 11); *see also* Tex. R. Civ. P. 13 (similar in effect to the 1993 version of Rule 11 though differently phrased).

CHAMBERS v. NASCO, INC., 501 U.S. 32 (1991). Do courts have inherent power to impose sanctions when Rule 11 is unavailable? In *Chambers*, the Supreme Court answered this question in the affirmative. The District Court relied on its inherent power to shift nearly $1 million in sanctions in the form of attorney's fees and expenses to Chambers. The alleged sanctionable conduct occurred both in and out of court and included even conduct occurring before suit was filed, by which the defendant fraudulently attempted to defeat jurisdiction. The Court deemed Rule 11 insufficient to support the sanction against Chambers, since the rule does not reach conduct other than the filing or advocacy of pleadings or motions.

Chambers entered into a written contract to sell a television license and station facilities to Nasco. He changed his mind and so informed Nasco. Nasco gave Chambers notice, required by federal rules, that it intended to file suit and seek a restraining order to prevent Chambers from otherwise transferring the contracted-for property. Then, Chambers and his attorney quickly acted to transfer the property to relatives for the purpose of placing it beyond the reach of the court before the restraining order could be issued. They determined that a recorded sale to a third party would have this effect under applicable law because the contract with Nasco was not recorded.

The District Court rendered judgment for Nasco on the merits, and it imposed sanctions on Chambers of approximately $1 million—representing Nasco's entire attorney's fee. The court relied on its "inherent power" to sanction bad-faith litigation conduct, not on any federal or state rules or statutes. It based sanctions on Chambers' attempt to deprive the court of jurisdiction by acts of fraud, as well as other conduct that occurred both in and out of court (including the filing of false and frivolous pleadings and using tactics of delay and expense to "reduce [Nasco] to exhausted compliance"). The Court of Appeals affirmed the sanctions.

The Supreme Court also upheld the sanction, holding that federal courts have the discretionary, inherent power to punish bad-faith litigation conduct. The Court rejected the argument that 28 U.S.C. § 1927, Rule 11, and other express sanctioning authority displace courts' inherent power to impose attorney's fees as a sanction for bad faith conduct.

Justice Kennedy, in dissent, characterized the decision as a "vast expansion of the power of federal courts, unauthorized by rule or statute." He would require federal district courts to exhaust their express sanctioning authority before resorting to inherent power.

Notes and Questions

(1) *What Due Process Protections Should Accompany a Court's Use of Its Inherent Sanction Powers?* In its current version, Rule 11 requires notice and a reasonable opportunity to respond before the court can impose sanctions. In *F.J. Hanshaw Enterprises, Inc. v. Emerald River Development, Inc.*, 244 F.3d 1128 (9th Cir. 2001), the district court imposed a $500,000 monetary sanction payable to the United

States on a party found to have offered a bribe to the court-appointed receiver, but the Ninth Circuit held that the sanction should have been treated as equivalent to criminal contempt, requiring "the procedural protections appropriate to a criminal case." 244 F.3d at 1139. Because the sanctioned conduct occurred outside the court's presence, these protections require the use of an independent prosecutor, a jury trial, and a standard of proof beyond a reasonable doubt. According to the appellate court, "[t]he more punitive the nature of the sanction, the greater the protection to which an individual is entitled."

(2) *Sanctions Awarded Under Court's Inherent Power Must Consider Ability to Pay.* In *Martin v. Automobili Lamborghini Exclusive, Inc.*, 307 F.3d 1332 (11th Cir. 2002), the Eleventh Circuit vacated a $1.5 million sanction awarded jointly and severally against a plaintiff, his counsel, and a paralegal under the court's inherent power because the district court judge failed to consider each individual's financial circumstances. "[W]hen exercising its discretion to sanction under its inherent power, a court must take into consideration the financial circumstances of the party being sanctioned." Accordingly, the Eleventh Circuit vacated the sanctions award and remanded the matter to the district court to assess an appropriate sanction based on the individual resources of each party.

Note: How Does the Lawyer Pay the Sanctions?

The Nightmare: Personal Liability for a Large Sanction Soon after the Lawyer Begins Practice. A student of one of the authors (before Rule 11 was amended) was required to pay more than $200,000 as a sanction under amended Rule 11 a short time after he started practice. He and his partners underwent several difficult years while they personally paid the sanction.

Will or Should Offending Lawyers' Malpractice Insurance Pay Their Sanctions (And What Effect Would That Rule Have Upon the Cost of Your Own Insurance)?: Bar Plan v. Campbell, No. 57946, 1991 Mo. App. LEXIS 1429, 60 U.S.L.W. 2225 (Mo. App. Sept. 17, 1991). The answer depends upon (1) the insurance policy, (2) the violation and (3) state law. In this Missouri case, the "pay all sums" clause of the policy required the insurer to "pay [a]ll sums [w]hich the Insured shall become legally obligated to pay as damages as a result of [claims made during the policy period] by reason of any fact or omission by the Insured [in his] professional capacity providing legal services." "Damages," in turn, was defined in the policy as "a monetary judgment award [not including] fines or statutory penalties." The policy excluded "fraudulent" or "maliciously or deliberately wrongful acts."

The Missouri court concluded that Rule 11 imposed a standard "similar to [n]egligence," that the sanctions were not a "statutory penalty" or a "fine," and that they met the policy definition of "damages" even though they might be imposed as a deterrent. Therefore, insurance covered the sanction. But if malpractice insurance must cover mischievous behavior like the conduct in *Chambers v. Nasco*, then the costs of malpractice insurance become more expensive for everyone else too.

Note that some lawyers elect to "go bare," or practice without insurance, because they find the cost already prohibitive.

VI. Amendment of Pleadings

Read Fed. R. Civ. P. 15.

[A] Amendment by Right or by Leave

Beeck v. Aquaslide 'n' Dive Corp.

562 F.2d 537 (8th Cir. 1977)

BENSON, DISTRICT JUDGE.

This case is an appeal from the trial court's exercise of discretion on procedural matters in a diversity personal injury action.

Jerry A. Beeck was severely injured on July 15, 1972, while using a water slide. He and his wife, Judy A. Beeck, sued Aquaslide 'N' Dive Corporation (Aquaslide), a Texas corporation, alleging it manufactured the slide involved in the accident, and sought to recover substantial damages on theories of negligence, strict liability and breach of implied warranty.

Aquaslide initially admitted manufacture of the slide, but later moved to amend its answer to deny manufacture; the motion was resisted. The district court granted leave to amend. On motion of the defendant, a separate trial was held on the issue of "whether the defendant designed, manufactured or sold the slide in question." This motion was also resisted by the plaintiffs. The issue was tried to a jury, which returned a verdict for the defendant, after which the trial court entered summary judgment of dismissal of the case. Plaintiffs took this appeal, and stated the issues presented for review to be: [first, whether the trial court abused its discretion in permitting an amendment that denied manufacture after the statute of limitations had run, and second, whether the separate trial was an abuse of discretion].

I. Facts....

In 1971 Kimberly Village Home Association of Davenport, Iowa, ordered an Aquaslide product. A slide was delivered to Kimberly Village, and was installed by Kimberly employees. On July 15, 1972, Jerry A. Beeck was injured while using the slide at a social gathering sponsored at Kimberly Village by his employer, Harker Wholesale Meats, Inc. Soon after the accident investigations were undertaken by representatives of the separate insurers of Harker and Kimberly Village. On October 31, 1972, Aquaslide first learned of the accident through a letter sent by a representative of Kimberly's insurer to Aquaslide, advising that "one of your Queen

Model # Q-3D slides" was involved in the accident. Aquaslide forwarded this notification to its insurer. Aquaslide's insurance adjuster made an on-site investigation of the slide in May, 1973, and also interviewed persons connected with the ordering and assembly of the slide. An inter-office letter dated September 23, 1973, indicates that Aquaslide's insurer was of the opinion the "Aquaslide in question was definitely manufactured by our insured." The complaint was filed October 15, 1973. Investigators for three different insurance companies, representing Harker, Kimberly and the defendant, had concluded that the slide had been manufactured by Aquaslide, and the defendant, with no information to the contrary, answered the complaint on December 12, 1973, and admitted that it "designed, manufactured, assembled and sold" the slide in question.

The statute of limitations on plaintiff's personal injury claim expired on July 15, 1974. About six and one-half months later Carl Meyer, president and owner of Aquaslide, visited the site of the accident prior to the taking of his deposition by the plaintiff. From his on-site inspection of the slide, he determined it was not a product of the defendant. Thereafter, Aquaslide moved the court for leave to amend its answer to deny manufacture of the slide.

II. Leave to Amend

Amendment of pleadings in civil actions is governed by Rule 15(a), Fed. R. Civ. P., which provides in part that once issue is joined in a lawsuit, a party may amend his pleading ["only with the opposing party's written consent or the court's leave. The court should freely give leave when justice so requires"].

In *Foman v. Davis*, 371 U.S. 178, 83 S. Ct. 227, 9 L. Ed. 2d 222 (1962), the Supreme Court had occasion to construe that portion of Rule 15(a) set out above:

> Rule 15(a) declares that leave to amend "shall be freely given when justice so requires," this mandate is to be heeded.... In the absence of any apparent or declared reason—such as undue delay, bad faith or dilatory motive on the part of the movant, repeated failure to cure deficiencies by amendments previously allowed, undue prejudice to the opposing party by virtue of allowance of the amendment, futility of amendment, etc.—the leave sought should, as the rules require, be "freely given." Of course, the grant or denial of an opportunity to amend is within the discretion of the District Court....

This Court in *Hanson v. Hunt Oil Co.*, 398 F.2d 578, 582 (8th Cir. 1968), held that "[p]rejudice *must be shown*." (Emphasis added). The burden is on the party opposing the amendment to show such prejudice....

It is evident from the order of the district court that in the exercise of its discretion in ruling on defendant's motion for leave to amend, it searched the record for evidence of bad faith, prejudice and undue delay which might be sufficient to overbalance the mandate of Rule 15(a), F.R. Civ. P., and *Foman v. Davis*, that leave to amend should be "freely given." Plaintiff had not at any time conceded that the slide in question had not been manufactured by the defendant, and ... the court had to decide whether the defendant should be permitted to litigate a material factual issue on its merits.

[The Defendant's] reliance upon investigations of three insurance companies, and the fact that "no contention has been made by anyone that the defendant influenced this possibly erroneous conclusion," persuaded the court that "defendant has not acted in such bad faith as to be precluded from contesting the issue of manufacture at trial." The court further found "[t]o the extent that 'blame' is to be spread regarding the original identification, the record indicates that it should be shared equally."

In considering the issue of prejudice that might result to the plaintiffs from the granting of the motion for leave to amend, the trial court held that the facts presented to it did not support plaintiffs' assertion that, because of the running of the two year Iowa statute of limitations on personal injury claims, the allowance of the amendment would sound the "death knell" of the litigation. In order to accept plaintiffs' argument, the court would have had to assume that the defendant would prevail at trial on the factual issue of manufacture of the slide, and further that plaintiffs would be foreclosed, should the amendment be allowed, from proceeding against other parties if they were unsuccessful in pressing their claim against Aquaslide. On the state of the record before it, the trial court was unwilling to make such assumptions, and concluded "[u]nder these circumstances, the Court deems that the possible prejudice to the plaintiffs is an insufficient basis on which to deny the proposed amendment." The court reasoned . . . further that it would be prejudicial to the defendant to deny the amendment. . . .

On this record we hold that the trial court did not abuse its discretion in allowing the defendant to amend its answer.

III. Separate Trials

[Aquaslide had moved for separate trial of the issue of manufacture on the ground that it would "save considerable trial time" and would "protect Aquaslide from substantial prejudice." The court granted the motion under Fed. R. Civ. P. 42, which allows the trial judge discretion. The Court of Appeals held that the separate trial was not an abuse of discretion because the issue of manufacture was a substantial one, other issues would require lengthy trial, and evidence about the severe injuries of plaintiff Beeck could prejudice the defendant's claim of non-manufacture.] [Affirmed.]

Notes and Questions

(1) *Serious Prejudice to Plaintiff?* Assuming plaintiff now finds a truly guilty manufacturer, won't the statute of limitations severely prejudice the plaintiff? It would seem that the answer is yes. Notice that the court does not say otherwise; it says only that the "possible" prejudice did not compel the district judge to deny the amendment, where defendant was in good faith and diligent.

(2) *Suing the Wrong Defendant: A Real Problem!* In the real world, defendants do not come labeled as such. We shall consider this problem in the next section in the case of *Krupski v. Costa Crociere, S.p.A.*

(3) *Amendment as of Right.* Rule 15(a) provides that a party may amend "once as a matter of course" at a time that is early in the case but determined by other pleadings. This provision creates a limited right to amend without consent or leave. Most amendments, however, occur later, so amendment of right does not furnish a major source of amendments.

(4) *Leave "Freely Given"; Discretion to Deny.* The Rule is written so as to support liberal granting of leave to amend. For example, the mere passage of time between the complaint and its amendment is not ground by itself for denying leave. *Chitimacha Tribe v. Harry L. Laws Co., Inc.*, 690 F.2d 1157 (5th Cir. 1982). The amendment may assert a wholly new theory, and there are cases in which leave has been granted although the court recognized that the amendment might be insufficient to state a claim as a matter of law. *Harper v. Holiday Inns, Inc.*, 498 F. Supp. 910 (E.D. Tenn.), *aff'd*, 633 F.2d 215 (1978). However, this "liberal allowance" approach should not be taken too expansively. There still is good reason not to rely upon the ability to amend. The trial judge has considerable discretion in taking into account the counterweights of delay, insubstantiality, number of previous amendments, prejudice to the opponent, and other factors. *E.g., Chitimacha Tribe v. Harry L. Laws Co., supra* (trial court should consider whether amendment would cause undue delay or other disadvantages). In addition, a trial court may enter a scheduling or docket control order imposing a cutoff date for amendment.

[B] Amendment and the Statute of Limitations: Rule 15(c)

Note on "Relation Back" to Avoid the Limitations Bar

"Relation Back": Treating a Late Amendment as if Filed before the Limitations Period Expired. As the case in the previous section shows (*Beeck v. Aquaslide 'N Dive)*, a plaintiff can be diligent and still may sue the wrong defendant. Then, a treacherous result may occur: the expiration of the statute of limitations period, which may exonerate a truly responsible defendant. As the *Beeck* case shows, the outcome can be harsh. It may be appropriate to have rules that avoid this result in some cases.

Rule 15(c): A Limited Relation-Back Provision. To address this situation, Rule 15(c) provides that in limited circumstances, an amendment "relates back to the date of the original pleading," allowing it sometimes to avoid the limitations bar. This relation-back provision applies if two requirements are satisfied. (1) The added defendant received notice of the suit in some manner, so that it is not prejudiced by the delay; and (2) the defendant knew or should have known that the suit would have been brought against it except for the mistake. (Relation back is also available if the limitations law itself allows it or if the added claim arose from the same facts as the original claim and adds no new parties.)

A Limited Provision, upon Which Reliance Should Be Minimized. Notice that this escape valve is narrow. In many cases (perhaps in *Beeck*, for example), the two conditions will not be satisfied. Even if there is some evidence that the conditions are met, the late-added defendant often will advance evidence showing that it is indeed prejudiced and that it did not (and should not have been expected to) know.

KRUPSKI v. COSTA CROCIERE, S.p.A., 130 S. Ct. 2485 (2010). Krupski sued "Costa Cruise Lines" after she broke her leg on a cruise ship. Costa Cruise informed Krupski that the actual carrier was "Costa Crociere, S.p.A.," and Costa Crociere, S.p.A. was identified as the carrier on Krupski's cruise ticket, along with information regarding submitting claims. However, Krupski did not amend her complaint until after the statute of limitations had expired. Costa Crociere subsequently moved to dismiss, arguing that the amended complaint did not satisfy Rule 15(c).

The district court and the Eleventh Circuit found relation back improper, noting that Krupski either knew or should have known Costa Crociere's identity because of its mention on her ticket. The Supreme Court reversed, holding that the lower courts had improperly focused on Krupski's knowledge rather than the defendant's knowledge:

> By focusing on Krupski's knowledge, the Court of Appeals chose the wrong starting point. The question under Rule 15(c)(1)(C) is not whether Krupski knew or should have known the identity of Costa Crociere as the proper defendant, but whether Costa Crociere knew or should have known that it would have been named as a defendant but for an error. Rule 15(c)(1)(C) asks what the prospective *defendant* knew or should have known during the Rule 4(m) period, not what the *plaintiff* knew or should have known at the time of filing her original complaint. . . .
>
> The District Court held that Costa Crociere had "constructive notice" of Krupski's complaint within the Rule 4(m) period. . . . Costa Crociere should have known, within the Rule 4(m) period, that it was not named as a defendant in that complaint only because of Krupski's misunderstanding about which "Costa" entity was in charge of the ship—clearly a "mistake concerning the proper party's identity."

The Supreme Court also observed that Costa Cruise and Costa Crociere were "related corporate entities with very similar names; 'crociera' even means 'cruise' in Italian. . . . This interrelationship and similarity heighten the expectation that Costa Crociere" should have known of the mistake.

Notes and Questions

(1) *Suing the Wrong Defendant: A Common Problem!* The problem disclosed by this case is much more common than you might surmise. It arises frequently when interrelated businesses are involved. For example, you have claimed against Jones & Smith (a partnership), but the true entity against which your client has a valid claim is Jones & Smith, Inc. (a corporation controlled by the same individuals). In that situation, would Rule 15(c) make your later amendment to correct the party "relate

back" to the original filing? Quite possibly, but of course it would be preferable not to have to find out.

Alternatively, in a complex transaction in which the actors undertook various roles, one or more may have negligently injured your client, but sorting out the roles takes longer than the limitations period. Finally, consider the case in which your client may have a claim against the operators of an establishment called Temple's Fried Chicken; you sue Temple Corporation only to discover, after limitations has run, that the store was actually owned and operated by the Acme Company, which is unrelated to Temple except that it is licensed to use the Temple name. (Does 15(c) apply in this last case? Unless there is more to it, relation back seems doubtful.)

(2) *How Do You Avoid Suing the Wrong Defendant?* The uniform use of careful steps to minimize errors is a part of professionalism. There is good reason for using a demand letter in every case, whether the case seems likely to settle or not. Further, a skillful and diligent plaintiff's attorney would promptly take steps, after filing suit, to verify that the defendant sued is really the right defendant. For example, the use of discovery, including a request that the defendant admit that it operated the Temple Fried Chicken establishment at the time and place in question and that the personnel were within its employ, would be appropriate.

Of course, there remain extraordinary cases—*Beeck v. Aquaslide 'N' Dive Corp.*, above, is an excellent example—in which even these steps will not suffice. It should go without saying that a plaintiff's attorney should immediately ascertain and calendar the limitations date for every claim in the office "tickler" system. *Cf.* Note, *Amendments That Add Plaintiffs Under Federal Rule of Civil Procedure 15(c)*, 50 GEO. WASH. L. REV. 671 (1982).

[C] Trial and Post-Trial Amendments

Note on Rule 15(b)

Even after a trial has ended, parties may seek to amend the pleadings to conform to the evidence. In cases where the parties actually have raised the issues, modifications may be allowed. But post-trial efforts to strategically remake the case might not fare as well.

CUNNINGHAM v. QUAKER OATS COMPANY, FISHER-PRICE DIVISION, 107 F.R.D. 66 (W.D.N.Y. 1985). This action was brought by the father of a child who had suffered severe brain damage when he ingested a small toy manufactured by defendant, causing blockage of oxygen to his brain. A jury found the product defective owing to its size and ingestibility. By its verdict, the jury found damages for the child, for the father, and for the mother. The problem was that the mother was not named as a plaintiff in the complaint. Plaintiff sought to make an amendment under Rule 15(b) to conform to the evidence.

The court granted the motion, as follows: "[T]he issue of Mrs. Cunningham's damages was actually tried before the jury in this case [w]ith defendant's knowledge. Mr. and Mrs. Cunningham were cross-examined in the same way. The proof elicited from Mrs. Cunningham in the questions relating to value of services and loss of guidance and companionship was no less a matter of concern for the defendant than the proof elicited from Mr. Cunningham on these same points. [T]his case would not have been defended in a substantially different manner if Mrs. Cunningham's name appeared on the complaint. . . ." The court added that Rule 15(b) of the Federal Rules of Civil Procedure provides that ["[w]hen an issue not raised by the pleadings is tried by the parties' express or implied consent, it must be treated in all respects as if raised in the pleadings"]. Amending the pleadings to conform to the proof at trial may be done "at any time, even after judgment."

Notes and Questions

(1) *Amendment after Trial Is Not Always Successful and Is Always Risky: Ross v. American Red Cross,* 567 Fed. Appx. 296 (6th Cir. 2014). Ross claimed that during blood donation, a Red Cross worker injured a nerve and caused her to develop a chronic pain condition. The jury rejected her negligence claim. After trial, she sought to amend to add a strict liability claim based on inherently dangerous activity. The district court denied the amendment. The court of appeals affirmed the denial, saying that Rule 15(c) "was not designed to allow parties to change theories in mid-stream." The Rule allows post-trial amendment after trial of an issue "by consent," which the court said requires "considerable litigation" of the issue.

(2) *How Can This Kind of Pleading Error Occur?* It can occur easily. Before trial, the facts are not well known, and sometimes pleading errors are hidden. One of the authors of this casebook tried a case in which the pleadings alleged fraud in the obtaining of a loan, whereas the fraud was committed in connection with the renewal of the loan. The pleading had been filed years before by another lawyer in the firm before the facts were fully developed, and through trial, no one noticed. But the judge did. An amendment under 15(c) allowed the pleadings to conform to issues tried by consent.

VII. State-Court Pleadings Today: Stating a "Cause of Action" Under Modern Rules

[A] Texas: Fair Notice of Factual Contentions

Plaintiff's Petition in Texas. A plaintiff's complaint in Texas must state a cause of action and give fair notice of the plaintiff's factual contentions as well as the plaintiff's legal theories. Dorsaneo, Crump, Carlson and Thornburg, *Texas Civil Procedure: Pretrial Litigation*, Ch. 5 (2007–08 ed.). The fair notice requirement requires a statement of the factual bases of the plaintiff's claim, but it is not necessary that the plaintiff plead the evidence on which the plaintiff places reliance. Thus, a general allegation of "negligence" is not sufficient to give fair notice of the plaintiff's factual claim. Older cases seem to require an identification of specific acts or omissions. *See, e.g., White v. Jackson*, 358 S.W.2d 174 (Tex. Civ. App.-Waco 1962, writ ref'd n.r.e.). Modern Texas cases interpret the fair notice standard to require roughly the same degree of factual specificity as Federal Form 9. *See, e.g., Willock v. Bui*, 734 S.W.2d 390 (Tex. App.-Houston [1st Dist.] 1987, no writ).

Defendant's Pleadings: Preliminary Matters ("Dilatory Pleas") and Special Exceptions. The defendant asserts that the court lacks subject matter jurisdiction by a plea to the jurisdiction; that it lacks personal jurisdiction by a special appearance; and that venue is improper or inconvenient by a motion to transfer venue. Most other matters not involving the merits (*e.g.*, failure to join a person needed for just adjudication) are raised by a plea in abatement (which, you should recall, is a common law legacy). Texas has abolished the general demurrer. A party's attack on the formal or substantive sufficiency of another party's pleadings in Texas is called a "special exception" and is related to the common law special demurrer. The special exception is used to attack vagueness, inappropriate matter, or legal insufficiency, and thus, this single type of pleading performs the functions fulfilled by the motion to dismiss for failure to state a claim, the motion to strike, and the motion for more definite statement in federal court.

General Denial and Other Defensive Pleadings on the Merits. Texas permits the defendant to assert a general denial in most instances. There are many kinds of denials that must be specific. Many of these denials must be "verified" (*i.e.*, supported by affidavit). Affirmative defenses must be "set forth affirmatively" under Tex. R. Civ. P. 94, which is modeled on Rule 8(c) of the Federal Rules.

WILLOCK v. BUI, 724 S.W.2d 390 (Tex. App.-Houston [1st Dist.] 1987, no writ). The plaintiff obtained a default judgment which the defendant challenged on appeal asserting, among other things, that the petition was inadequate to support a default judgment.

The pertinent part of Plaintiff Bui's petition reads as follows:

> III.
>
> On January 9, 1985 at approximately 8:00 a.m., Toan Viet Bui sustained serious personal injuries while driving a 1985 Toyota pickup truck which was involved in a rear-end collision, which forced his vehicle into the car in front of him. The automobile which Toan Viet Bui was operating was struck from behind during the collision which involved a Pontiac, Texas license number 3232-ADH, driven by George Michael Willock. The collision occured at 130 Hays Road, Houston Texas.
>
> IV.
>
> The collision described in paragraph III above and made the basis of this suit was directly and proximately caused by the negligence of George

> Michael Willock. On the occasion in question, George Michael Willock was guilty of acts of negligence each of which were a proximate cause of the collision made the basis of this suit.

A majority of the three-judge court of appeals' panel determined that the petition, though "inartfully drawn," gave the defendant fair notice of the claim involved. "A fair interpretation of the petition is that the appellee claims that he and the appellant were involved in an automobile collision, and that he was injured as a result of the appellant's negligence. The petition adequately informed appellant of the nature of the claim against him in compliance with Tex. R. Civ. P. 45 and 47." Another member of the panel dissented, reasoning that "the pleading fails to apprise the appellant of what his specific involvement was in the collision. Appellee's assertion that the appellant's vehicle was 'involved' in a collision with him, that also involved several other vehicles, does not assert a violation of any duty or responsibility owed by the appellant to the appellee."

[B] California: Pre-Printed Official Complaints, Common Counts, and Fictitious "Doe" Defendants

Official Pre-Printed Forms; Pleading a Cause of Action. Under the authority of CCP § 425.12, the California Judicial Council has promulgated officially approved forms for the "drafting" of the complaint. A plaintiff actually files two different kinds of documents—a "complaint," which contains fill-in-the-blank-and-check-the-box designations of parties, jurisdiction, damages, and type of claim, supplemented by an "attachment," stating the particularized cause of action, and also containing blanks and boxes. Plaintiff uses these forms to comply with the rules, which require that the cause of action be stated in terms of the "ultimate facts," not conclusions or evidence—although the cases interpret this requirement more liberally than the common law or Code pleading requirements. The pleading forms are optional, not mandatory.

Fictitious Defendants. One interesting aspect of California practice is the treatment of "Doe" defendants. *See* J. Hogan, *California's Unique Doe Defendant Practice: A Fiction Stranger than Truth*, 30 Stan. L. Rev. 51 (1977). If the complaint states that the name of a defendant is unknown to plaintiff, the defendant may be designated by this fictitious name, and, if the complaint is properly filed, plaintiff thus may avoid the bar of the statute of limitations. Doe defendants are used in situations in which plaintiff believes that certain individuals are liable but does not know their names, as well as in cases in which plaintiff is not sure whether the unknown defendants even exist (or whether they acted together with known defendants). Most of the cases indicate that the plaintiff's ignorance of the Doe defendants' identities must be real and not feigned, and the plaintiff must act promptly to identify them in the pleading when their true identities are learned. *Id.*

"Common Counts." As a holdover from the common law action of general assumpsit, California allows the pleading of common counts, in which it is sufficient to

allege in a general way that the defendant "became indebted to the plaintiff" upon an open account (or a written account, or in some other manner, or for money had and received, etc.).

Defendant's Pleadings. The defendant may attack the form or legal sufficiency of the complaint by demurrer. (Certain kinds of motions are also available; *e.g.*, the motion for judgment on the pleadings, motion to strike, and motion to dismiss.) The answer is roughly analogous to that in federal practice, in that the defendant is required to sift the complaint and deny specific allegations; however, the defendant need not state expressly which allegations are admitted, in that those that are not denied are admitted. Also, denials must be more specific in form, in that the defendant must identify those allegations that are denied outright, those that are denied on "information and belief," and those that are denied "because of lack of sufficient information or belief." Again, the Judicial Council has promulgated Official Forms, which provide space for each variation in their truth and therefore denies them. Affirmative defenses must be separately pleaded. One interesting exception to these requirements: If the plaintiff's demand does not exceed $1,000, the defendant may use a general denial rather than admissions and denials. Cal. Code Civ. Pro. §§ 431.30 & 431.40.

SCHERER v. MARK, 64 Cal. App. 3d 834, 135 Cal. Rptr. 90 (1976). The plaintiff's original complaint alleged that defendant Memorial Hospital and "Does I through XXX, inclusive" were "each . . . responsible for the events and happenings hereinafter alleged." The complaint charged that all the defendants had "negligently and carelessly treated the plaintiff in that they failed to follow a standard of care in common practice," including watching over her while she was taking a bath and providing her with a safe place to bathe while handicapped and under medication, and that as a result she fell and was injured. After the running of the statute of limitations, she amended the complaint to insert the name of her physician, Howard Mark, in place of Doe I. Defendant Mark filed a demurrer, which was sustained evidently on the theory that the complaint stated no cause of action against him because, unlike the hospital, he had no duty with respect to the events in question. The plaintiff was given leave to amend.

The plaintiff's second amended complaint contained, first, the same cause of action in the original complaint. Second, it added a cause of action against Mark and Does 26, 27 and 28, to the effect that these "defendants . . . so negligently prescribed instructions and drugs and bathroom privileges and related treatment . . . that plaintiff was caused to" suffer injury. This time, Mark filed an answer containing denials as well as the affirmative defenses of contributory negligence and statute of limitations. The trial court granted summary judgment on the limitations defense, because the second cause of action was pleaded after limitations had run, and the appellate court affirmed. First, assuming the plaintiff was entitled to use John Doe practice as to her doctor, whose name she knew, "Ignorance of the facts giving rise to a cause of action, like ignorance of the true name, should be real and not feigned." Here, "plaintiff knew all of the basic facts" at the outset. Furthermore, the pleading against Mark could not relate back to the original filing because the cause of action alleged against him had been itself added after limitations had run. "[A]n amendment purporting to state a new cause of action against such Doe defendant in his true name will be barred if filed after the expiration of the statute of limitations."

[C] Florida: A Complaint Stating Operative Facts of a Cause of Action

What Is a Cause of Action in Florida? Florida litigation is started with a complaint, which must state a cause of action. Fla. Rule Civ. P. 1.110(b). A "cause of action," in turn, is "[a] group of operative facts giving rise to one or more bases for suing; a factual situation that entitles one person to obtain a remedy in court from another person." *Roden v. R.J. Reynolds Tobacco Co.,* 145 S.2d 183 (Fla. 4th DCA 2014) (court concluded that a personal injury suit that developed into a wrongful death suit stated one cause of action because both claims were based on the same operative facts, and thus it avoided a statute of limitations defense).

But the Pleading of the Operative Facts Need Not Be Technical. The Florida Rule generally follows the Federal Rule, except that it requires a cause of action. Rule 1.110(b). The standard appears to be that the complaint must provide "notice of the operative facts." *Ron's Quality Towing, Inc. v. Southeastern Bank,* 765 So. 2d 123 (Fla. 1st DCA 2000). The court there quoted *Cabot v. Clearwater Constr. Co.,* 89 So. 2d 662, 664 (Fla.1956), in which the Florida Supreme Court said, "[T]he objective of all pleading is merely to provide a method for setting out the opposing contentions of the parties. No longer are we concerned with the 'tricks and technicalities of the trade' . . . . It is no longer a game of chess in which the technique of the maneuver captures the prize."

Admissions, Denials and Affirmative Defenses. Florida's rules for defensive pleadings resemble the Federal Rules for the most part. The defendant is required to answer each allegation in good faith, and affirmative defenses must be pleaded affirmatively. Rule 1.110(c)–(d). Some kinds of denials must be specific. For example, according to Rule 1.120(c), a denial of performance or occurrence must be made specifically and with particularity. *See Godschalk v. Countrywide Home Loan Servicing L.P,* 81 So. 3d 626 (Fla. 5th DCA 2012) (defendant sued by lender cannot merely deny that defendant complied with all requirements but must specifically identify what was not done).

VIII. How to Answer the Chapter Summary Problem: Some Suggestions

Alice Delagroi's Medical Malpractice Claim: A Pleadings Problem. (As usual, follow your Professor's instructions about how to answer.)

1. How solid does your pleading of the claims need to be to avoid dismissal? Law: A complaint can be dismissed if, after all allegations and inferences from them are assumed true, there is no recovery for plaintiff under the law. The possibility of recovery is sufficient even if it is doubtful. *Facts and Conclusion:* For example, if the basis of recovery is negligence, the allegations in the complaint must be enough so that dismissal is not possible after the allegations are assumed true, or in other words, so that there is at least some prospect of recovery.

2. What degree of specificity is required? Law: The complaint must give notice of the legal and factual basis of the claim and must provide sufficient facts, not mere conclusions, to support a plausible inference that the claim exists. It need not show a probability that the claim exists. *The Facts:* Assuming a claim based on negligence, the allegations should provide notice that this is the claim, and sufficient facts must be alleged to support the required plausible inference. This probably means that plaintiff must factually describe the act or omission of negligence and proximate causation. *Conclusion:* The pleading probably will have to say something like this: "Defendant XX or Defendant YY injected a substance into plaintiff's arm and, contrary to the practice of a reasonable medical professional, did so in a manner such that the needle severed or otherwise proximately caused damage to a nerve . . . ."

3. If you fail to include a given person as a defendant, and if a jury later determines that that person was solely responsible for your client's injuries, what might be the consequences for your client—and for you? Limitations is about to expire, at least on some claims. Any later suit against persons left out of the list of defendants may be subject to the defense of limitations and, unless this defense can be overcome, the plaintiff will not be able to recover anything. But the plaintiff may be able to recover against you if she can prove that your failure to include the person was negligent.

4. If you omit a party now because of uncertain liability, will you be able to amend to include that party after discovery, and have your pleading relate back to a time before the statute of limitations ran? (What can you do to enhance this possibility?) Law: Relation back requires that (1) The added defendant received notice of the suit, so that it is not prejudiced by the delay; and (2) the defendant knew or should have known that the suit would have been brought against it except for the mistake. *Facts:* Perhaps you can increase the likelihood of relation back if you send each person who conceivably could be liable a copy of the complaint with a message saying, "(1) You now have notice of this suit and cannot be prejudiced by a delay if you are sued later, and (2) if you are liable and plaintiff's leaving you out of the suit as a defendant is a mistake, you are notified that except for the mistake, the suit would be brought against you." *Conclusion:* You cannot know whether this tactic will be successful. Alternatively, sometimes a particular defendant will agree to extend the limitations period to avoid suit.

5. What sanctions are possible under Fed. R. Civ. P. 11 if you carelessly file suit against an innocent party, and what can you do to minimize the likelihood of such sanctions? *Law:* You must, based upon a reasonable investigation, have evidence of each allegation, or in the alternative, you can designate any allegation and state that you expect to have evidence to support it after discovery. If you violate the rule, your opponent will be able to seek sanctions sufficient to deter such violations after giving you 21 days' notice to correct the violation, or the court can sanction you, with the standards varying among the courts of appeals from willfulness as in contempt proceedings to negligence. *Facts:* You don't know very much and cannot know very much in the short time remaining. 21 days does not leave you enough time, either, so you cannot rely excessively on the safe harbor. Your potential allegations are prone to error. These are precisely the kind of defendants who are likely to seek sanctions.

Conclusions: Take steps set out in this chapter to avoid Rule 11 violations: documenting your reasonable investigation, including reasons for steps not taken; sending demand letters; employing an expert witness; associating an expert lawyer; doing sufficient legal research; using discovery to verify your allegations; reacting by correcting any allegation found erroneous; and carefully interviewing your client.

IX. Improving the Rules of Pleading: Notes and Questions

(1) *Should We Require Pleading of a "Claim" or of a "Cause of Action"?* This question is an important issue raised by this chapter. One can validly object to the narrow kind of "fact" pleading required under the common law and Field Codes, but no such objection can be leveled at modern state rules governing the pleading of a cause of action. Those rules probably result in somewhat earlier definition of issues and screening of inappropriate claims, but might also result in a higher number of variances (although this effect can be reduced by liberal allowance of trial and post-trial amendments) than federal "notice" pleading would. Which approach is better?

(2) *Should Federal Pleadings Really Require "Facts" That Make the Inference of a Claim "Plausible"?* In imposing this requirement, the Supreme Court moved the federal courts closer to cause-of-action pleading. This change, which discarded decades of federal practice, avoids judicial waste and party expense in some cases. But won't it increase costs through hearings of disputes about pleadings and won't it make some valid claims impossible to plead when plaintiff doesn't know key facts known to defendants, without discovery (as may have happened in *Iqbal*)?

(3) *Amendments; Limitations.* Under some state systems (*e.g.*, Texas), amendments are allowed without leave of court until a certain number of days before trial

unless the opponent objects and shows prejudice. Might this approach be preferable to requiring judges to rule on each motion to amend, particularly since the leave is supposed to be "freely given"? Meanwhile, California's use of the unknown "Doe Defendant" helps plaintiffs avoid misnaming defendants and having the statute of limitations expire. On the one hand, this tool can be disadvantageous to some defendants, who would experience delay in their investigations of claims against them, and might dilute the purposes of the statute of limitations in avoiding stale claims; on the other hand, it would protect a plaintiff who has a genuine claim if, and only if, the plaintiff was genuinely unable to name the defendant at the time of suit.

(4) *Sanctions.* Rule 11 in its current form requires notice and an opportunity to cure (the 21-day safe harbor). Controversy continues over whether this provision avoids discouraging innovation, or results unfairly in putting the burden of investigation on innocent opponents.

In 2017, Congress considered, and the House of Representatives passed, the Lawsuit Abuse Reduction Act of 2017. The proposed legislation would strike the discretionary "may" and replace it with a mandate that the judge "shall" award sanctions, including reasonable attorney's fees, "to compensate the parties that were injured by such conduct." But in other ways, it would expand judicial discretion, stating that "The court may also impose additional appropriate sanctions, such as striking the pleadings, dismissing the suit, or other directives of a non-monetary nature, or, if warranted for effective deterrence, an order directing payment of a penalty into the court." Should sanctions be mandatory on the initial violation; if so, how much?

(5) *The Form of Denials.* Should the general denial be permissible as it is in Texas's practice? [Note: its use can better be appreciated when one considers that the plaintiff has the limitations period in which to plead, but the defendant has only a few days (unless the time is extended by agreement of the parties or order of the court); furthermore, the defendant can be compelled to admit or deny facts through a request for admissions.] In the alternative, should the federal courts consider California's compromise, which allows the general denial to be used in small cases?

(6) *Coordination Among Pleadings, Discovery, and Pretrial Conferences and Orders.* In considering a system of pleading rules, one must keep in mind the relationship between pleadings, discovery, and pretrial conferences and orders. The federal system allows "notice" pleading, in part because it assumes that the opponent can obtain sufficient definition of facts and issues from discovery, and the court can narrow the issues at pretrial. At what stage in the lawsuit should the judge attempt to narrow the issues?

Litigation Document Example 5.3

Pleadings from Three Jurisdictions

This material is like the earlier Litigation Document Examples in Chapters 1 and 2, but it is online. You will need to go to https://caplaw.com/sites/cp7 to view these documents.

There, you will find pleading examples from three states: New York, Texas, and California. The New York pleadings are from *Palsgraf v. Long Island R.R.*, which is one of the most famous cases in the field of Torts and which you probably will read in your Torts course. The Texas case is *Pennzoil Co. v. Texaco Inc.*, which produced the then-biggest jury verdict in history at that time (more than $11 billion). The California example is a blank form for pleading a product liability case. There are also Notes and Questions in connection with each of these sets of examples, and you should also read and try to answer them. Please go to https://caplaw.com/sites/cp7, then click on Litigation Document Example 5.3: Sample Pleadings from Three Jurisdictions.

Chapter 6

Multiple Parties and Claims

I. An Overview of the Devices for Joining Multiple Parties or Claims

A Simplified Introduction. In this chapter, we take up procedural devices for combining (or separating) multiple parties or claims. These devices arise in litigation situations that are abstractly defined and hard to visualize. In addition, they create their own knotty procedural problems. Students sometimes find parts of this material difficult, and accordingly, this overview is designed to give you a simplified introduction.

Perhaps the best way to visualize these concepts is to consider them simply as different ways of putting together or taking apart the parties and claims that make up a lawsuit. The various rules complement each other, and they are designed to allow the suit to have as large a number of parties or claims, or as few a number, as conveniently fits the factual situation in dispute. This overview will give you an idea of the purpose of each of these devices.

Third-Party Practice ("Impleader") (Rule 14). Assume that Paul Plaintiff is driving his car, begins to stop for a stop sign, and is rear-ended by Dan Defendant. Paul sues Dan for his injuries. But Dan, upon receiving the complaint, recalls that an instant before hitting Paul, he, Dan, was struck from the rear by an automobile driven by Tom Thirdparty. It was this impact which caused him to be propelled into Paul's vehicle. For a diagram of this accident, see Figure 6A, below.

If you represented Dan Defendant, you of course would want to defend him against Paul's claim. But is there anything else that you might want to do to represent Dan?

Of course there is! Tom Thirdparty is conspicuously left out. The device for bringing Tom into the suit is called a "third-party claim." More formally, it is known as "impleader": We say that Dan "impleads" Tom. For a diagram of impleader or third-party joinder, see Figure 6B.

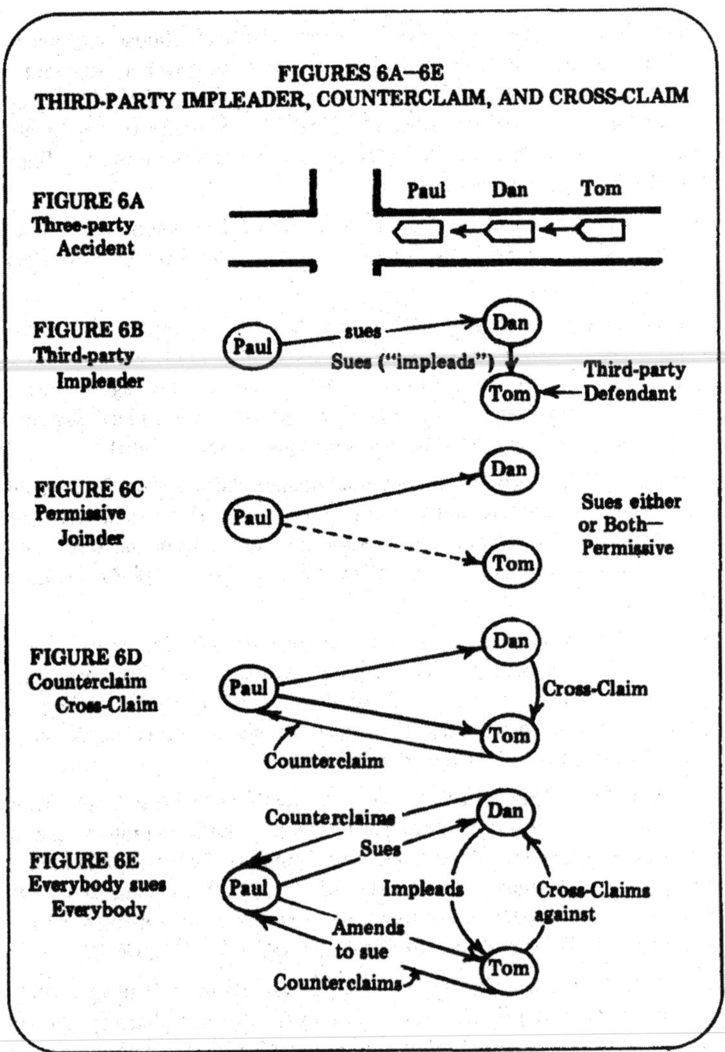

Why might Dan Defendant decide to implead Tom Thirdparty? Because if Dan is found liable to Paul, he may still be able to recover part or all of that liability from Tom if he can show that Tom was at fault. Of course, Dan is not required to implead Tom; that is a question of tactics.

Permissive Joinder of Parties (Rule 20). In the situation above, involving Paul, Dan, and Tom, what would you do if you represented Paul Plaintiff from the beginning, and you were trying to decide whom to sue?

If there were a basis for saying that either or both Dan and Tom were negligent, you could (and probably should) join both of them in one suit. You might do well to claim a right to relief against them severally (*i.e.*, they are both liable for the full judgment); jointly (*i.e.*, they are each liable for portions of the judgment); and in the alternative (*i.e.*, if it wasn't Dan's fault, it was Tom's, and vice versa).

Figure 6C is a diagram of this type of joinder, called "permissive joinder."

What if you wanted to sue one or the other (that is, either Dan or Tom), but not both? The rules allow you to do that, too, if you prefer.

That is why this procedure is called "permissive" joinder. Paul can choose whether to sue one, sue the other, or sue both. If Paul thinks that Dan has sufficient assets to cover a judgment and was guilty of negligence, and if Tom was relatively free from negligence and his addition would only complicate matters, Paul may decide to sue Dan only. On the other hand, if Tom is guilty of negligence, while Dan has cooperated and settled his claim with Paul, Paul may decide to sue Tom only. Or, finally, if both appear to have been responsible, he may join both of them.

What if Dan Defendant is sued alone, and Dan doesn't like it? That's too bad; he can't complain about the non-joinder of Tom. His remedy is to file his own claim, in the form of a third-party action against Tom, if he wants to do so.

Counterclaims and Cross-Claims (Rule 13). The next two claim-joinder devices are diagrammed in Figure 6D. The simplest example of a "cross-claim" is an action by one defendant against another defendant. Thus, if Paul has sued both Dan and Tom, Dan may assert a cross-claim against his co-defendant, Tom. For example, Dan could file a cross-claim seeking to recover for damages to his person or property. Alternatively, Dan might seek contribution to any liability to Paul, in case Dan is found liable to Paul.

The simplest example of a counterclaim (also illustrated in Figure 6D) is a suit by the defendant against the plaintiff. Dan Defendant thinks Paul Plaintiff actually was the one at fault, so he sues Paul in a counterclaim.

Everybody Claims Against Everybody Else. These devices—impleader, permissive joinder, counterclaims, and cross-claims—were invented so that the litigation between and among multiple parties can be efficiently resolved. Legal terminology should not prevent all of their related claims from being heard in a single suit, if that is the most efficient procedure. These devices allow this flexibility, no matter who sues whom—and regardless of who is nominally called the plaintiff. The lawsuit could result in claims by all parties against all other parties, as Figure 6E shows.

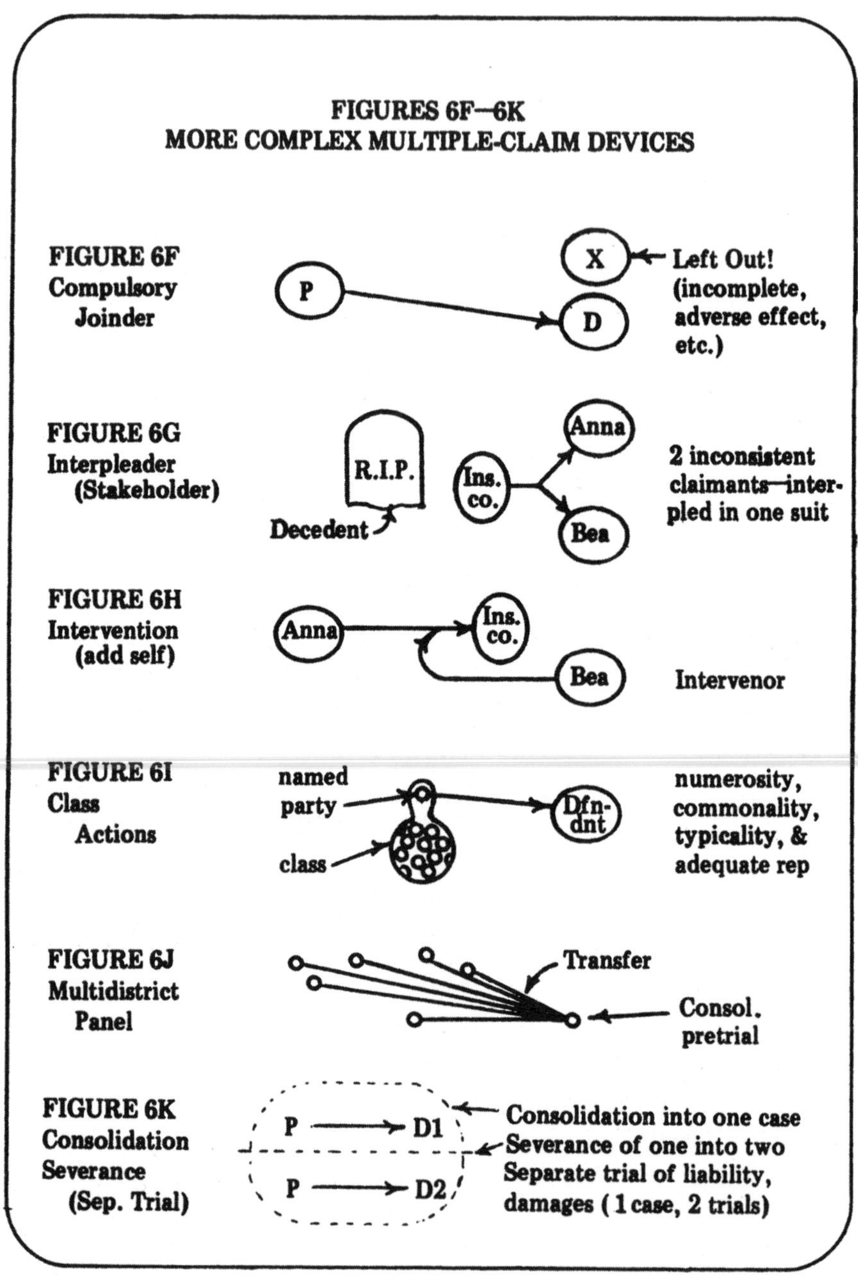

Compulsory Joinder: Persons Needed for Just Adjudication (Rule 19). Most situations involving multiple parties are permissive joinder situations, because there is no harm in allowing the plaintiff to have a choice of whom to sue. But there are some situations in which someone could be harmed because a potential party is left out. Also, there are some situations in which the lawsuit cannot effectively serve its purpose because someone is left out. We say that the absent person is a "person[] required to be joined if feasible," in the terminology of Rule 19. This situation is diagrammed in Figure 6F.

Here is one simple example of compulsory joinder. Assume that a decedent, *D*, has just died, leaving a will that gives his estate to certain persons. One of *D*'s relatives is left out of the will. He sues to contest the will, claiming that it is invalid. But the only person who this disgruntled relative sues is the executor named in the will. The persons who would receive property under the will are not parties. Obviously, there is something wrong here. The action should not proceed unless the disgruntled relative names all the other potential recipients as plaintiffs or defendants in the suit, assuming it is feasible to do so.

Figure 6F illustrates this situation. *X* is left out of the suit. This omission means that complete relief cannot be granted to the existing parties, or the interests of the omitted party will be affected.

Interpleader (Rule 22; 28 U.S.C. § 1335). Interpleader is designed to solve the problem of a "stakeholder" faced with conflicting demands. This device is illustrated by Figure 6G.

Assume that a life insurance company has issued a policy to an insured who is now deceased. The insured had designated as the beneficiary "my wife, Anna." But before he died, he and Anna divorced, and he married his second wife, Bea. He never changed the designation of the beneficiary as "my wife Anna," and now he can't, because he is dead.

Anna says to the insurance company, "Pay me the $100,000 policy amount! I'm the named beneficiary." But Bea says, "No! Pay ME the $100,000. I'm his wife!"

Now, the insurer has several options. First, it could simply pay out the money to the one it thinks is entitled to it. But that course of action may be unwise because, if it guesses wrong, it may be liable for another $100,000 to the claimant it didn't pay. Second, it could wait until it is sued by one of the claimants. It runs the risk, however, of being sued in two separate actions by the two different claimants, and it could be subjected to two judgments for $100,000.

The device of interpleader was invented to handle this kind of "stakeholder's dilemma." The insurance company can file a complaint for interpleader and have both Bea and Anna served as defendants (or interpleader claimants). This procedure will, in effect, say to Anna and Bea, "The insurance company is faced with conflicting demands from you two. Come into this lawsuit and litigate your entitlement against each other."

Intervention (Rule 24). What if there is someone who might have an interest in a lawsuit, but who has not been made a party? Is there anything that this person can do to get into the lawsuit to protect her interests—*i.e.*, to intervene in the lawsuit?

Yes, there is. It is a procedure that is called, appropriately enough, "intervention."

Take the situation of Anna, Bea, and the life insurance company, which we have already discussed. Assume that the insurer refuses to pay out the $100,000, but does not file an interpleader action. Instead, Anna files suit against the insurer. This turn of events might disturb Bea, because she is left out of the suit. If she wants, Bea can file a motion to intervene under Rule 24.

Class Actions (Rule 23). This device is illustrated by Figure 6I. Although Rule 23 is sometimes difficult to apply, the justification for class actions is relatively simple. A class action is a way of disposing of a case expeditiously when there are a very large number of plaintiffs or defendants, by combining all their claims in one case and having representative parties litigate.

For instance, assume that a corporation called the Superhuge Holding Company has issued a large number of shares of stock to the public. Something goes wrong, and Superhuge stock becomes worthless. It then develops that the brokerage firm that sold Superhuge stock made a number of fraudulent representations. Each of the stock purchasers has a potential claim against the brokerage firm. One or more of the purchasers might file a class action on behalf of themselves and all other purchasers.

The Judicial Panel on Multidistrict Litigation (28 U.S.C. § 1407). In theory, a class action can allow the resolution of claims from all over the country in one case. But in practice, matters involving large numbers of injured people often begin with multiple lawsuits in multiple places. Let's continue to consider the situation of the brokerage firm that has allegedly defrauded tens of thousands of buyers of Superhuge Holding Company stock.

A class action is not the only possible result. It can, and probably will, happen that people all over the country will sue the brokerage firm in their respective districts. The brokerage firm may be sued in every district of every state. If that happens, the brokerage firm may go broke just from having to defend hundreds of different suits in different locations, even if it wins every suit.

The brokerage firm's lawyers may say to themselves, in effect, "We don't like class actions very much, but we sure wish there was some way to put all these lawsuits in one case! Is there anything we, as the defendant's lawyers, can do to protect our client?"

Yes, there is, and it is illustrated in Figure 6J. There is a statute, 28 U.S.C. § 1407, that sets up a "Judicial Panel on Multidistrict Litigation." The brokerage firm may apply to the Panel to transfer all the federal cases to one place for consolidated and coordinated pretrial proceedings.

Consolidation, Severance, and Separate Trial (Rules 42, 21, 13(i), 14(a), and 20(b)). Typically, the pleadings and the decisions of the parties shape the disputes. However, the courts also have broad discretion to modify the parties and the issues. Judges can consolidate multiple lawsuits into a single action if they share common questions. In addition, judges have broad discretion to order separate trials. In this respect, it may separate combined claims, or it may even order multiple trials for a single claim (*e.g.*, a first trial on liability, and if liability is established, a second trial on damages).

Rules 14(a) and 21 mention, in addition, a "severance." Although the rules do not make the distinction, a severance is generally understood as the separation of different claims into different suits, as opposed to separate trials for a single claim.

II. Adding or Subtracting Single Claims or Parties

[A] Counterclaims

Read Fed. R. Civ. P. 13 (counterclaim and cross-claim).

Cavanaugh v. Western Maryland Railway Co.

729 F.2d 289 (4th Cir. 1984)

DONALD RUSSELL, CIRCUIT JUDGE.

... Western Maryland Railway Company (Western) and Baltimore & Ohio Railroad Company (B & O) appeal from an order of the district court dismissing their counterclaim for property damage in an action brought by Robert M. Cavanaugh (Cavanaugh) under the Federal Employers' Liability Act (FELA), 45 U.S.C. §§ 51 *et seq.* [This Act creates a special kind of negligence claim for railroad workers.—Eds.] The district court held that the maintenance of the railroads' counterclaim would violate §§ 5 and 10 of the FELA, 45 U.S.C. §§ 55 and 60, and thus would be contrary to the public policy reflected in such Act. We disagree and reverse.

Cavanaugh was employed by Western or B & O as a railroad engineer.... [T]he B & O train on which Cavanaugh was serving as engineer collided head-on with another B & O train proceeding in the opposite direction on tracks owned and controlled by B & O.... Cavanaugh instituted this FELA action to recover one and a half million ($1,500,000) dollars for personal injuries sustained by him as a result of the collision. The railroads answered and counterclaimed under state law for property damage in the amount of one million, seven hundred thousand ($1,700,000) dollars, sustained by them as a result of the same accident. Cavanaugh moved to dismiss this counterclaim. The district court granted the motion....

In determining whether the railroads have a right of action which they can assert as a counterclaim in an FELA action begun by a railroad employee, we begin by recognizing that there is a well accepted common law principle that a master or employer has a right of action against his employee for property damages suffered by him "arising out of ordinary acts of negligence committed within the scope of [his] employment" by the offending employee....

Moreover, this right of action in favor of the employer or master may be asserted either in an independent action by the employer against the offending employee or by a counterclaim filed by the employer in the employee's action to recover for injuries sustained by him in the same occurrence. But, if the employee sues the employer in federal court for injuries sustained in the occurrence the employer has no option; federal practice compels the employer-master to assert by way of a counterclaim his claim against the employee for damages caused by the employee's negligence to his (employer's) property under penalty of loss of his right of action.(4) . . . It follows that if the railroads in this case are denied the right to assert their claim against the plaintiff by way of a counterclaim, they could be denied any right of action ever to recover for the damages to their property suffered as a result exclusively of plaintiff's negligence and the plaintiff in turn could be given absolute immunity from any liability for his negligence both in this action and in any other action begun after judgment in the present action.

It is difficult to believe that such an unfair result is compelled. However, the plaintiff argues that the railroads are foreclosed by the terms of the FELA from asserting their claim against him by way of a counterclaim in his FELA action. The plaintiff does not point to any explicit language in the Act which could be said to require, or even suggest, such a sacrifice of the railroads' rights. . . . He would find the basis for such implication of a prohibition against a counterclaim by the railroads in the language of Sections 5 and 10 of the Act. . . .

Section 5 of the Act provides in pertinent part that "[a]ny contract, rule, regulation, or device whatsoever, the purpose or intent of which shall be to enable any common carrier to exempt itself from any liability created by this chapter, shall to that extent be void. . . ." The plaintiff [argues] that . . . the present counterclaim under review constituted a device contrived in violation of Section 5 "to deprive plaintiffs [in FELA actions] of their right to an adequate recovery" and "to chill justifiable FELA claims." We do not find the argument persuasive.

. . . The term "device" is defined in the section. It is [any] "contract, rule, regulation, or device whatsoever, *the purpose or intent of which shall be to enable any common carrier to exempt itself from any liability created by this chapter* (Italics added)."

. . . It is only when the "contract . . . or device" qualifies as an "exempt[ion] itself from any liability" that it is "void[ed]" under Section 5. But a counterclaim by the railroad for its own damages is plainly not an "exempt[ion] . . . from any liability" and is thus not a "device" within the contemplation of Congress.

The second section from which the plaintiff would deduce a basis for implying a statutory bar against the railroads' counterclaim is section 10 of the Act. Section 10 proscribes any "device" the "purpose, intent, or effect" of which would "prevent employees of any common carrier from furnishing voluntarily information to a

---

(4) This result is a consequence of Rule 13(a), Fed. R. Civ. P., which defines a compulsory counterclaim under federal practice. Claims which must be asserted by counterclaim are ["any claim that—at the time of its service—the pleader has against an opposing party if the claim: (A) arises out of the transaction or occurrence that is the subject matter of the opposing party's claim; and (B) does not require adding another party over whom the court cannot acquire jurisdiction]."

person in interest as to the facts incident to the injury or death of any employee. . . ." As the language plainly indicates, this section was intended to prevent the railroad from making inaccessible to an injured employee other railroad employees whose testimony might be helpful to the injured employee if he chose to sue the railroad. . . .

The plaintiff, however, finds lurking obscurely in the language of Sections 5 and 10 a legislative purpose to interdict counterclaims by defending railroads in FELA suits because the filing of such counterclaims will unfairly coerce or intimidate the injured employee from filing and pursuing his FELA action. [T]here is nothing in the language of the Act or its legislative history that supports this reasoning. . . .

We would pose this hypothetical situation: The ruling of the district court would not prevent the railroads in this case from filing an independent action against the plaintiff-employee herein as a defendant to recover damages to its property as a result of his negligence. Assuming that the railroads can maintain such action, is the plaintiff-employee required under Rule 13(a), to assert his FELA claim as a counterclaim? If he is, we have substantially the same situation as we would have if the right of the railroads to counterclaim in the plaintiff's FELA action is recognized. If, however, the plaintiff-employee is not required to assert his FELA claim as a counterclaim in the railroads' independent action, will the plaintiff be barred by Rule 13(a) from asserting such claim in an action under FELA against the railroads after judgment in the railroads' independent action? We do not seek to answer these questions but pose them simply to emphasize the illogic of the ruling denying the railroads the right to counterclaim in the FELA action for their damages to their property resulting from the accident. . . .

. . . [W]e reverse the ruling of the district court dismissing the defendant-railroads' counterclaim and remand the cause for further proceedings not inconsistent with this decision. In remanding, however, we direct that, the district court shall, on remand, order the FELA case and the counterclaim be tried separately. This has been the manner in which similar cases seem to have been handled. . . .

K.K. Hall, Circuit Judge, dissenting. . . .

Contrary to the majority's assertion, the language of the FELA supports the conclusion that Congress intended to prohibit counterclaims, such as the one filed by the railroad here,[1] because the filing of such counterclaims will unfairly coerce or intimidate the injured employee . . . .

---

(1) At oral argument before the district court, counsel for the railroads acknowledged that railroads generally do not bring actions against their employees for property damage because they have no reasonable expectation of recovery and because their employees may in fact be judgment proof. . . . In fact, counsel for the railroads admitted to the district court that:

> In this case, [Cavanaugh] is not going to be judgment proof when he recovers a vast sum of money, which he is attempting to recover from the Railroads.
>
> As a matter of fact, he is going to be a rich man once he recovers, and can establish a right to recovery. And that is why this [counterclaim] has been asserted. . . .

In my view, the railroads' counterclaim is a "device" calculated to intimidate and exert economic pressure upon Cavanaugh, to curtail and chill his rights, and ultimately to exempt the railroads from liability under the FELA. "[T]he railroads' counterclaim violates 45 U.S.C. § 55 . . . ." . . .

Notes and Questions

(1) *The Strategic Use of Counterclaims.* Counterclaims are frequently used strategically based on the logic that "the best defense is a good offense." A plaintiff encountering a counterclaim must take it into account in settlement negotiations even if it is of marginal validity, because the discovery and other procedures necessary to defeat it will entail significant cost—and because there is always the chance that the trier of fact may give more credit to its validity than the plaintiff does.

The majority's reasoning in *Cavanaugh*, however, also has logical merit. The FELA certainly doesn't say that a railroad is deprived of its right of action for property damage. Nor does it prohibit railroad counterclaims. In fact, it often occurs that the "real" plaintiff is the counterclaimant; a potential defendant, knowing that suit is imminent, beats the "plaintiff" to the punch by filing suit as the plaintiff, leaving that party to counterclaim. As the court points out, if the railroad sued first, Cavanaugh could be the one to file a counterclaim.

(2) *"Compulsory" Counterclaims: Is the Rule Too Harsh?* The majority's reasoning in *Cavanaugh* is strengthened because the counterclaim is a "compulsory" counterclaim. As the court says, if the railroad does not assert the claim in this same suit, it will be forever barred. The courts have not been consistent in the theories they have used to justify the bar in a subsequent suit. Some reason that the failure to counterclaim operates as a waiver, while some say that it works as estoppel of the later claim; an apparently greater number of courts reason that the previous judgment is *res judicata* of any compulsory counterclaim. But the simplest rationale is just to say that Rule 13 bars the subsequent claim. This is the reasoning in *Cavanaugh. See* C. Wright, *Estoppel by Rule: The Compulsory Counterclaim Under Modern Pleading*, 39 Iowa. L. Rev. 255 (1954). Critics of Rule 13, however, have argued that the compulsory bar is an excessively harsh penalty for mere omission to make the counterclaim and that it would make more sense to require the relitigator to pay the opponent's added court costs and attorney's fees. *See* Kennedy, *Counterclaims under Rule 13*, 11 Hous. L. Rev. 255 (1974).

(3) *Examples of the Compulsory Counterclaim Bar.* In *J. Aron & Co., Inc. v. Service Transp. Co.*, 515 F. Supp. 428 (D. Md. 1981), an insurer sued for a declaratory judgment of noncoverage, in other words, seeking a ruling that stated that the insurer had no duty to pay. In a subsequent suit, the insured claimed that the insurer had failed to provide appropriate insurance coverage to it. The court held that the subsequent

---

Thus, it is clear to me that the railroads filed their counterclaim either to coerce Cavanaugh into settling his claim or, if his FELA action proceeded to trial, to strip him of any damages by means of an offset. . . .

suit arose out of the same transaction or occurrence as that in the initial suit; it was therefore barred by the compulsory counterclaim rule. In *Smith v. McDaniel*, 503 F. Supp. 13 (N.D. Ga. 1980), *aff'd*, 633 F.2d 581 (11th Cir. 1981), the plaintiff initially sued a professional wrestler for injuring him in a scuffle at a public match at which the plaintiff was a spectator. The plaintiff-spectator obtained a judgment on this suit, which was in Virginia; he then brought an action on the judgment in Georgia, where the wrestler's assets were. In that suit, the wrestler asserted a counterclaim to the effect that the plaintiff-spectator had instead assaulted the wrestler as he sought to enter the ring. The court held that this claim was "inextricably" intertwined with the plaintiff's Virginia suit and was barred by the wrestler's failure to assert it there.

(4) *Permissive Counterclaims.* Any other kind of counterclaim, not a compulsory one, is termed "permissive." It "may" be asserted in the same action, *see* Rule 13(b), but it is not barred in a subsequent suit. For example, in *Meinrath v. Singer Co.*, 87 F.R.D. 422 (S.D.N.Y. 1980), a broker sued for "bonus" commissions allegedly due him under a compensation agreement. The defendant asserted a counterclaim alleging that, on prior occasions, it had paid "bonus" commissions exceeding what was due under the agreement, and demanding repayment of those amounts. The court held that this counterclaim was merely permissive, not compulsory, and that ancillary jurisdiction could not extend to it. [Is this decision correct? Can't it be said that the previous excess payments have a logical relationship to the currently claimed underpayment?]

(5) *Compulsory Counterclaims Involve Existing Parties.* Claims against different persons who are not named as parties to the case are not compulsory counterclaims. For example, in *Pace v. Timmermann's Ranch & Saddle Shop, Inc.*, 795 F.3d 748 (7th Cir. 2014), the employer alleged, in a civil complaint, that Ms. Pace, their bookkeeper, had embezzled funds, stolen merchandise, sold stolen articles on eBay for her personal benefit, and improperly used the company's business credit card to make personal purchases. In 2011, the Sheriff took Ms. Pace into custody overnight. In 2012, the State's Attorney charged Ms. Pace with theft, forgery, and unlawful use of a credit card. Refuting the accusations, Ms. Pace and Dan Pace, her husband, sued Timmermann's and four of its employees in 2013. Ms. Pace alleged that she suffered extreme emotional distress because the employees had conspired to facilitate Ms. Pace's false arrest, and Mr. Pace claimed a loss of consortium. The district court dismissed the Paces' complaint as an untimely compulsory counterclaim, but was reversed on appeal. The Circuit Court carefully distinguished the concept of joining claims from joining parties, and explained how Rule 13 was different from Rule 19:

> Although Rule 13(a)(1)(B), like Rule 19, encourages that all claims be resolved in one action with all the interested parties before the court, Rule 13 fulfils this objective by allowing, not mandating, that a defendant bring counterclaims that require additional parties. Whether a party must be joined in an action continues to be governed only by Rule 19. Rule 13 does not provide for compulsory joinder [of counterclaims that are not

> compulsory, but permissive]. Requiring Ms. Pace to bring the claims against the individual defendants as a counterclaim in the initial action might well serve judicial economy, but the Federal Rules of Civil Procedure do not require such a result. The rules generally allow for a plaintiff to decide who to join in an action.

(6) *Cross-Claims against Other Existing Parties.* A counterclaim is exemplified by a suit by a defendant against a plaintiff, while a cross-claim is a suit by one coparty against another (*e.g.*, one defendant demands contribution or indemnity from another defendant). Rule 13(g) says that a cross-claim is permitted if it arises out of the same transaction or occurrence as the principal action. As is indicated by the Supreme Court in *United Mine Workers v. Gibbs*, found in Chapter 3, these types of claims are within the court's supplemental jurisdiction. Consider the following case.

[B] Cross-Claims

ABRAMCO, INC. v. BOSSCLIP B.V., 570 F.2d 233 (5th Cir. 2009). This is an admiralty action for a damaged shipment against the shippers and their vessel (here called the "Vessel Interests") and also against a stevedoring company, Pacorini Holdings, Inc. The Vessel Interests asserted a forum selection clause requiring suit in England and obtained a dismissal of the claim against them. This dismissal left only Pacorini, the stevedore company, as the defendant.

Pacorini wanted to assert a claim against the Vessel Interests, asserting that they had inflicted the damage, and did so under Rule 14 (covered in the next section), which allows a defendant to assert some kinds of claims against a person who is not a party to the suit. The district court dismissed Pacorini's Rule 14 claim on the (erroneous) ground that a third party claim could not be asserted against a person who was once a party to the suit. Instead, said the district court (erroneously), Pacorini's claim should have been asserted as a "cross-claim" under Rule 13, which allows a claim against a coparty to the suit. Pacorini appealed the dismissal.

> The district court held that Pacorini could have brought its claims against the Vessel Interests by asserting a cross-claim under Rule 13(g). Rule 13(g) provides,
>
> > A pleading may state as a crossclaim any claim by one party against a coparty if the claim arises out of the transaction or occurrence that is the subject matter of the original action or of a counterclaim....
>
> Fed. R. Civ. P. 13(g). By its terms, Rule 13(g) requires the cross-claimant to be a party to the lawsuit at the time the cross-claim is asserted. However, by the time Pacorini asserted its claims against the Vessel Interests, the Vessel Interests had already been dismissed from the suit and were no longer a party to the underlying suit; thus, a cross-claim under Rule 13(g) was no

longer an available mechanism for asserting Pacorini's claims against the Vessel Interests. The district court therefore erred in holding that Pacorini's claims could have been properly brought under Rule 13(g).

Instead, Pacorini properly brought its claims pursuant to Rule 14, [which allows the defendant to bring in a third-party defendant (see the next section of this chapter), and the district court erred in dismissing that third-party claim]. . . .

We do, however, recognize that it would be the height of judicial inefficiency to conduct two separate [trials about the same issues]. For this reason, the district court, on remand, may consider staying Pacorini's claims pending a resolution of the English court's adjudication of Ambraco's claims against the Vessel Interests. . . .

Notes and Questions

(1) *Should Cross-Claims Be Made Compulsory?* By definition, a cross-claim arises out of the same transaction or occurrence as the plaintiff's claim. Its assertion in the same suit would normally serve judicial economy. Rule 13(g) could be rewritten to make cross-claims compulsory. Adding claims, however, can complicate cases and evidence.

(2) *Can Cross-Claims Be Compulsory Under Rule 13(g)?* Although a cross-claim is not normally compulsory, it can sometimes become a compulsory counterclaim. For example, if Pacorini succeeds in bringing the Vessel Interests into the suit and asserting claims against them, then any claim held by the Vessel Interests against Pacorini for the same damage would not only be a cross-claim, but also would fit the definition of a compulsory counterclaim under Rule 13(a).

[C] Third-Party Practice ("Impleader")

Read Fed. R. Civ. P. 14.

Mitchell v. Hood

614 Fed. Appx. 137 (5th Cir. 2015) (unpublished opinion)

[This is a dispute about election tactics in a judicial race. Judge Anderson-Trahan defeated Kiana Mitchell by 263 votes. Shortly before election day, 3,000 households had received a dirty-trick postcard falsely alleging that Mitchell had violently attacked an "innocent pregnant woman." The postcard said that it had been "Paid for by B. Hood." Mitchell therefore sued Brett Hood on four claims of "abuse of right." Defendant Hood then impleaded Judge Anderson-Trahan (that is, he filed a third-party claim against her), alleging that she was responsible for the postcard.

Hood asserted claims "under Rule 14" for fraud, misrepresentation, abuse of right, and injury to personal and professional reputation.

[Thus, the claim that is important here is the attempted third-party suit by Hood against Anderson-Trahan. Hood's claim was for Hood's own personal damages. He alleged that he had no involvement in the offensive postcard and that it had been perpetrated instead by Anderson-Trahan and her supporters. Crucially, however, Hood did not assert claims against Anderson-Trahan for indemnity or contribution. ("Indemnity" means payment of the liability of another person. Insurance is an example, and so is the liability of a manufacturer of a defective product to a distributor. "Contribution" means payment of a share of the liability among tortfeasors.) In other words, instead of seeking repayment for any damages he might have to pay to Mitchell, Hood asserted his own separate claims, although they arose from the same election campaign.]

... Because we conclude that Judge Anderson-Trahan was not properly impleaded under Rule 14, she is not a proper party to this case....

Federal Rule of Civil Procedure 14 permits a defending party to, "as third-party plaintiff, [bring a claim against] a nonparty who *is or may be liable to It for all or part of the claim against it.*" Fed.R.Civ.P. 14(a)(1) (emphasis added). Impleader under Rule 14 is only proper if the claims asserted by the third party are derivative of the main claim—if the impleaded party is or may be liable for part of "the claim against [the original defendant.]" Impleader is *not* permitted because a third party may be liable to the original defendant for some other, independent reason. In other words, it is not enough that the impleaded claims arise from the same facts and events as the original claim; rather, ... the potential liability of the third-party defendant must be contingent upon the outcome of the original claim. *See, e.g., United States v. Joe Grasso & Son, Inc.,* 380 F.2d 749, 752 (5th Cir.1967).

Hood's claims against Judge Anderson-Trahan are not contingent upon Mitchell's claims against Hood....

... [W]hether Mitchell proves that Hood made defamatory statements in the postcard does not govern Hood's claims against Judge Anderson-Trahan. Hood's claims against Judge Anderson-Trahan for putting Hood's name on the postcard may succeed or fail in a scenario where Mitchell's claims against Hood succeed or a scenario where Mitchell's claims against Hood fail. Judge Anderson-Trahan is no more or less liable to Hood based upon Hood's liability to Mitchell.

Furthermore, Hood has not asserted that his claims against Judge Anderson-Trahan are derivative of Mitchell's claims against Hood. Hood does not seek damages from Judge Anderson-Trahan contingent upon his liability on Mitchell's claims.... Hood's amended complaint does not limit his claims to mitigating any damages that he may need to pay to Mitchell. [REMANDED FOR DISMISSAL of the third-party complaint.]

Notes and Questions

(1) *A Claim for Indemnity or Contribution Would Have Been Different.* If Hood had sued Anderson-Trahan for indemnity or contribution, the result would have been different. Can you explain why?

(2) *If Your Only Assertion Is That You Are Innocent, You Can't Use a Third-Party Claim: Barab v. Menford,* 98 F.R.D. 455 (E.D. Pa. 1983). Menford sued Channel Home Centers, Inc. for selling an allegedly defective doormat upon which a customer slipped. Channel alleged that it had not sold the mat at all; instead, it claimed, the at-fault seller was Joy Plastics, Inc. Therefore, Channel attempted to assert a third-party claim against Joy. The court denied leave to file the third-party suit because Channel's claim was not derivative. Channel was not attempting to recover from Joy anything that it might have to pay to Menford; it merely wanted to substitute Channel for Joy because allegedly Joy was the "real" liable party. Therefore, the claim failed the requirement of Rule 14 that it must seek recovery from someone who is or may be liable to the *defendant* for all or part of the *plaintiff's* recovery. If your only claim is that you're innocent, you can't third-party the alleged "real" defendant.

(3) *There Is a Reason for This Seemingly Odd Result.* Denying an innocent party the right to bring in an at-fault party may seem illogical. But maybe it's not. In the first place, Menford could have sued Joy if it had thought Joy was the guilty party (and presumably it still can do so). But Menford didn't. Menford may think that it sued the right party, that Channel is at fault, and that it does not want another party brought in because addition of parties complicates the suit. Furthermore, Channel can still defend itself perfectly well if Joy is left out of the suit by showing the jury that Joy did it. Channel can use the old "empty chair demonstration": pushing a chair in front of the jury and saying, "This empty defendant's chair should be occupied by Joy Plastics, because that's the real defendant."

(4) *Third Party's Answer.* The third-party defendant may set up in its answer any defense it has against the third-party claim and, in addition, "may assert against the plaintiff any defense that the third-party plaintiff has to the plaintiff's claim." Rule 14(a). This provision enables the third party adequately to defend in the event that the defendant refuses or neglects to assert a given theory of defense. For example, if there is an argument that the plaintiff's claim is barred by limitations, but the defendant decides that this defense is too tenuous to plead, the third party, if it disagrees, may plead it.

(5) *The Court's Discretion to Deny Impleader after 14 Days.* Unless the third-party claim is asserted within 14 days after answer, the claimant must obtain leave of court, which the court has discretion to grant or deny. In *Barab v. Menford,* the court first held that the third-party claim was improper under the rule, and then, as a second reason for the dismissal, explained that it would have exercised its discretion to deny leave anyway, because the claim was asserted late and would have interfered with the discovery schedule.

[D] Permissive Joinder of Parties and Claims by Plaintiff

> Read Fed. R. Civ. P. 20 (permissive joinder), 18 (joinder of claims).

Grogan v. Babson Brothers Co.

101 F.R.D. 697 (N.D.N.Y. 1984)

MUNSON, CHIEF JUDGE . . . .

This action was commenced in the Supreme Court of the State of New York, Oneida County, by service of the summons and complaint. . . . [T]he action was removed to this court . . . . [Thereafter, Plaintiff] filed a new motion seeking to amend his complaint to join two additional non-diverse defendants pursuant to Rules 15 [governing amendment] and 20 [governing joinder], Fed. R. Civ. P. For the reasons hereinafter stated the plaintiff's motion to amend his complaint joining the additional non-diverse defendants is granted. Because such joinder will divest this court of diversity jurisdiction, this case must be remanded to state court.

FACTS

Plaintiff initiated the present action against Babson Brothers Co. of Illinois alleging, *inter alia*, negligence and breach of warranty. Plaintiff's claims relate to certain livestock milking equipment manufactured by Babson Brothers Co. of Illinois, distributed by Surge Inc. of Babson Brothers Co., and retailed . . . [and installed on plaintiff's premises] by Don Carrier Surge Inc. [Don Carrier]. Plaintiff alleges that the equipment caused electric current to come into contact with the livestock during the milking operations. Don Carrier undertook to modify and correct the defect but allegedly abandoned its efforts without having corrected the problem.

Plaintiff seeks to amend his complaint [by] joining Surge Inc. of Babson Brothers Co. [the distributor]and Don Carrier [the installer] to the present action. Plaintiff had previously commenced a separate action in state court against these two proposed defendants. Plaintiff argues that by granting the instant motion the court will preserve precious judicial resources and avoid multiplicity of litigation. Defendant contends that the motion should be denied because plaintiff's sole motive in seeking joinder is to destroy diversity of citizenship thereby subverting the defendant's right to defend this litigation in a federal forum.

DISCUSSION

. . . As a threshold matter, however, the court must determine whether joinder under Rule 20 is permissible in the first instance. . . .

Rule 20(a) imposes two specific requisites for the joinder of parties: (1) a right to relief must be asserted by, or against, each plaintiff or defendant [with respect] to or arising out of the same transaction or occurrence; and (2) some question of law or fact common to all the parties will arise in the action. . . . Joinder is to be construed liberally "in order to promote trial convenience and to expedite the final determination of disputes, thereby preventing multiple lawsuits." . . . Moreover, under the federal rules "the impulse is toward the broadest possible scope of action consistent with fairness to the parties; joinder of claims, parties and remedies is strongly encouraged." *United Mine Workers of America v. Gibbs* . . . .

In the case at bar these requisites are clearly satisfied. Plaintiff's action arises out of the defective nature of certain milking equipment, liability for which may rest with one or more of the proposed defendants. Questions of law and fact are common to all these parties. There is no question that the joinder of these parties will promote trial convenience and will prevent the possibility, if not likelihood, of multiple litigation.

In opposition to plaintiff's motions the defendant has pointed to the oft-stated general rule that the plaintiff cannot act so as to divest a court of jurisdiction over a case that has been properly removed. However, the majority of federal courts which have addressed this issue have concluded that when there is no showing that the plaintiff seeks to join the additional defendants *solely* to effectuate a remand, "in the exercise of . . . sound discretion the court may permit a new party to be added, although his citizenship destroys diversity and requires a remand." . . .

In the present case there is no evidence to suggest that plaintiff seeks to join additional defendants solely to effectuate a remand to state court. When plaintiff filed his original complaint he was apparently under the impression that Surge Inc. . . . was the exclusive manufacturer of the defective equipment. He subsequently discovered that Babson Brothers Co. . . . of Illinois was the manufacturer of the defective product and thus the instant lawsuit was commenced. The plaintiff's motive in bringing this [amended] suit is simply to consolidate the pending [federal] suit with the state court action. . . . If this motion were denied it would necessitate the continuance of parallel cases resulting in a great waste of judicial resources. Moreover, granting the motion will not prejudice the defendant because both lawsuits are in their infancy.

Having concluded that the reasons for bringing this motion are legitimate, the court grants the plaintiff's motion to amend its complaint adding the two nondiverse defendants. Because their joinder destroys this court's jurisdiction over the lawsuit, the case must be remanded to the New York State Supreme Court, Oneida County, pursuant to 28 U.S.C. § 1447(c).

Notes and Questions

(1) *"Same . . . Series of Transactions or Occurrences."* Notice that the three defendants technically engaged in different transactions: Babson Illinois manufactured the equipment; Surge Inc. distributed it; and Don Carrier installed it. Since these acts technically were different, isn't the court wrong in saying that each defendant's potential liability arose from the "same transaction or occurrence"? Technically, perhaps, but the court's holding on this point is justified anyway. The court did not

quote the entire rule, which includes not only the same transaction or occurrence, but the same "series" of transactions or occurrences. The chain of manufacture, distribution and installation has the sort of sequential relationship that constitutes a "series" of transactions.

(2) *How Different May Events Be and Still Be Part of the Same "Series" of Transactions or Occurrences?* In *King v. Ralston Purina Co.*, 97 F.R.D. 477 (W.D.N.C. 1983), the three plaintiffs worked in different places and different divisions of the company. They sued under the Age Discrimination in Employment Act. But because they alleged a companywide policy of discrimination, they were permitted to join as plaintiffs in a single suit. But if they had alleged independent discrimination by three separate supervisors, they would not have been able to join the claims. Can you explain why?

(3) *The Discretion of the Court, Again: What Is a "Common Question" of Law or Fact?* It has been said that "common questions must be of substantial importance as compared with all of the issues, and . . . the question of the comparative weight and importance of common and separate issues . . . is quite largely a matter of judgment" for the trial court. *Akely v. Kinnicutt*, 238 N.Y. 466, 473, 144 N.E. 682, 684 (1924). In *Akely*, nearly 200 investors joined to sue the promoters of a sham corporation. Although each plaintiff's case included separate issues such as whether he received and relied on the fraudulent representations, the common question whether the scheme itself was fraudulent outweighed those separate questions and justified joinder. *Akely* has been explained as requiring the showing of "evidence common to all plaintiffs." *See, e.g., Park Club, Inc. v. Resolution Trust Corp.*, 967 F.2d 1053, 1058 (5th Cir. 1992). But in truth, courts use a variety of approaches: for example, by considering the "similarity in the factual background of a claim," *Coughlin v. Rogers*, 130 F.3d 1348, 1350 (9th Cir. 1997), or by looking for a "logical relationship between the separate causes of action," *In re EMC Corp.*, 677 F.3d 1351, 1358 (Fed. Cir. 2012).

[E] Consolidation, Separate Trial, and Severance

Read Fed. R. Civ. P. 42 (consolidation; separate trials). Also, read Rules 21 (misjoinder, nonjoinder, and severance) and 25 (substitution of parties).

GITTENS v. SCHOOL BOARD OF LEE COUNTY, 2018 WL 839242 (M.D. Fla. 2018). This case demonstrates the discretionary nature of severance but also suggests some of the criteria that guide discretion. The motion to sever was unopposed, but the court still denied it. Plaintiffs, who were African-American, alleged that they had applied but were not chosen for various positions with the administration of the School Board. Plaintiffs claimed that the School Board had a pattern and practice of refusing to hire well-qualified African-American employees to administrative positions. One plaintiff (Dr. Thompson) moved to sever his claim. Although the motion was unopposed, the court still denied it, for the following reasons:

> Dr. Thompson's new counsel argues that Plaintiffs only initially joined in one action to establish a class action, which has been denied, and [now are] proceeding as a group of four individuals .... He states that the claims of each Plaintiff are factually distinct from those of all other plaintiffs, and do not arise out of the same ... series of transactions or occurrences so that there was initially a misjoinder of parties that can be remedied only by severance. Dr. Thompson also asserts that Plaintiffs' claims ... will require the testimony of different witnesses and documents and counsel have different strategies for presenting their cases, which would cause prejudice.
>
> Here, the Amended Complaint cites a district-wide policy designed to discriminate against well-qualified African American employees to administrative positions, and that each Plaintiff was allegedly subjected to such a policy. Thus, the Court finds that the claims of each Plaintiff arise out of the same series of transactions or occurrences.... Dr. Thompson ... fails to explain how prejudice would outweigh the convenience and judicial economy of keeping all Plaintiffs in one case and proceeding through discovery in one case. There is no doubt [of the existence of] an overlap of witnesses common to all parties .... Dr. Thompson may always move to sever one or more issues or claims from his case for trial under Federal Rule of Civil Procedure 42(b). [Severance DENIED.]

Notes and Questions

(1) *Severance Is Discretionary: Granted in Campbell-McCormick, Inc. v. Oliver,* 874 F.3d 390 (4th Cir. 2017). In *Gittens*, above, the court exercised discretion to deny a severance when one could have been justified. In *Campbell-McCormick v. Oliver,* the court exercised discretion to grant a severance that could have been denied. The plaintiff's claim was a straightforward asbestos claim in state court against one defendant for causing plaintiff's mesothelioma. Defendant Campbell-McCormick impleaded a number of third parties seeking contribution; and then, the third parties asserted a complex federal defense available to government contractors and used a special statute to remove to federal court. Plaintiff moved to sever his much simpler claims, so that they would be remanded to the state courts. Although it is unusual to sever a main claim from a third-party claim, the district court granted the plaintiff's motion to sever, in part because, this way, plaintiff could get to trial while he was healthy enough to do so and still living.

(2) *Consolidation, or Putting Two Lawsuits Together: Does v. Boy Scouts of America,* 2017 LEXIS 193013 (D. Idaho 2018). The first plaintiff here filed suit alleging constructive and actual fraud by the Boy Scouts in concealing from the plaintiff the dangers of being a Boy Scout, which allegedly caused him to suffer abuse from his Scoutmasters that caused physical, mental, and emotional injury. Then, a second plaintiff, represented by the same attorney, filed a nearly identical suit, although it

alleged only constructive fraud. The plaintiffs moved to consolidate the two suits to conserve judicial and private resources. The court exercised discretion to deny consolidation, mainly on the ground that the first suit had progressed to the point that adding the second suit would interfere with scheduling deadlines already underway. The court pointed out that it could issue orders to minimize waste (e.g., by combining some discovery processes).

By way of contrast, courts do sometimes consolidate cases involving similar claims of multiple plaintiffs, or even dissimilar but related claims. For example, in *Hall v. Hall,* 138 S. Ct. 1118 (2018), the Supreme Court upheld and explained an order in which the trial court had consolidated a claim for breach of trust by a sister against her brother with a claim by the brother for intentional infliction of emotional distress against the sister. The combining of these two disparate types of claims is unusual, but the court has wide discretion, and the interconnection of the two suits justified consolidation (all claims involved the siblings' feud).

(3) *Separate Trial: Beeck v. Aquaslide 'n Dive Corp.,* in Chapter 5, Pleadings, above. While a "severance" separates two distinct claims into two lawsuits, a "separate trial" is a mechanism for splitting a single claim so that one issue is tried before other issues in the same case. In the *Aquaslide* case, as we saw, the court allowed the defendant to amend its answer to deny manufacture of the allegedly dangerous product, which it earlier had admitted. The court also ordered a separate trial of one issue: whether the defendant had manufactured the product. If the jury found that the slide was not Aquaslide's product, there would be no need for any further proceedings. (The jury exonerated Aquaslide.)

(4) *Disadvantage to One Party or Another from These Devices.* A party may argue that it is disadvantaged by a severance, consolidation, or separate trial. One can foresee that the plaintiff in *Aquaslide* would prefer to show to the jury the dangerousness of the slide and the severity of his injuries, rather than be limited to an antiseptic inquiry into who manufactured the product, with the fear that the jury may not appreciate the seriousness of the case in such a bloodless hearing.

[F] Compulsory Joinder

Read Fed. R. Civ. P. 19 (compulsory joinder).

How to Understand Rule 19

"Persons Needed for Just Adjudication." Rule 19(a) defines "persons required to be joined if feasible." The terminology of the Rule is complex, but in simple terms, some cases present circumstances where the existing suit cannot properly accomplish its purpose (give "complete relief") or in which there may be unfair repercussions to the absent person or to the parties.

What If Joinder Isn't Feasible? Sometimes the joinder of a particular new party isn't feasible. (For example, no one may have thought about the absent person until after the court has granted judgment, and ordinarily it isn't feasible to join a new party at that point.) Rule 19(b) then tells the judge to decide whether, "in equity and good conscience," the judgment should stand. The Rule identifies four factors the court should consider.

How to Read the Provident Tradesmens *Case, Including Information About Insurance Law*

(1) *How an Insurance Policy Works: The Background to This Case.* An insurance policy has to define who is covered. An automobile policy may have an "omnibus clause," which covers the named insured, members of his household, and also anyone driving the covered automobile with the named insured's permission. Here, the named insured, Dutcher, loaned his car to a man named Cionci, who had a multiple-fatality accident with it. Dutcher had a policy of insurance with Lumbermen's Casualty Company. The question remained whether Cionci was driving with Dutcher's permission. Lumberman's claimed that Cionci had deviated from the original errand for which he had permission, and therefore, Cionci was not insured.

(2) *The Covered Liability and Liability Limits.* An insurance policy also usually defines the kind of liability it will cover. For an automobile policy, the "pay all sums" clause usually requires the insurer to pay damages for which the insured persons are liable, with certain exceptions. The policy usually contains a "policy limit" clause, too, which sets the maximum amount payable from any accident; in this case the limit was $100,000. Thus, Lumberman's could have been liable for damages assessed against Cionci for his negligence (assuming that Cionci was driving with permission and was therefore a covered insured), up to $100,000. In addition, Lumberman's could have been liable to pay damages assessed against Dutcher, the owner and named insured.

(3) *Why Is Dutcher a "Person Necessary for Just Adjudication"?* But Lumberman's total liability was limited to $100,000. If Cionci were found liable for damages and if the policy covered him, the amount available to cover Dutcher's liability would be reduced accordingly. Dutcher might be liable for damages on the theory that Cionci was his agent, or Dutcher could be liable on the theory that he had "negligently entrusted" the vehicle to Cionci. And then, if the fund had been exhausted from paying for Cionci's liability, Dutcher would be effectively uninsured.

(4) *The Litigation: First, Liability Suits against Accident Participants, and Second, This Suit against the Insurance Company.* The estates of persons killed in the accident, as well as one person who was injured, brought three suits. One suit was brought against Cionci by Provident Tradesmens as administrator of one of the estates; that case settled for $50,000, which remained unpaid because Cionci's estate was penniless. The other plaintiffs sued not only Cionci, but also others, including Dutcher. Provident Tradesmens [the executor] then sued Lumbermen's, the insurer,

for a declaratory judgment that Cionci was driving with permission and therefore was a covered insured. Provident joined the other tort plaintiffs as parties, but it did not join Dutcher in this federal declaratory judgment action because Dutcher would have destroyed diversity. In the trial court, Provident obtained a judgment that Cionci was driving with permission and was insured. This, in turn, meant that the insurance policy furnished a source of funds to pay damages on behalf of Cionci's estate.

(5) *The Problem of Dutcher's Absence from the Suit.* Then, for the first time on appeal, the appellate court focused on the questions whether Dutcher was a "person required for just adjudication" and whether the suit could proceed in his absence. Why? Because, again, the judgment for Provident, which required Lumbermen's to pay Cionci's liability, would have reduced available funds to pay Dutcher's potential liability. Suits against Dutcher were still pending. Now, with the case in this posture, and with Dutcher being a person "who should [have been] joined if feasible," the Supreme Court must decide whether the litigation against Lumbermen's can continue to proceed, or whether it must be dismissed because of Dutcher's absence.

Provident Tradesmens Bank & Trust Co. v. Patterson

390 U.S. 102 (1968)

Mr. Justice Harlan delivered the opinion of the Court.

This controversy, involving in its present posture the dismissal of a declaratory judgment action for nonjoinder of an "indispensable" party, began nearly 10 years ago with a traffic accident. An automobile owned by Edward Dutcher, who was not present when the accident occurred, was being driven by Donald Cionci, to whom Dutcher had given the keys. John Lynch and John Harris were passengers. The automobile crossed the median strip of the highway and collided with a truck being driven by Thomas Smith. Cionci, Lynch, and Smith were killed and Harris was severely injured.

Three tort actions were brought. Provident Tradesmens Bank, the administrator of the estate of passenger Lynch and petitioner here, sued the estate of the driver, Cionci, in a diversity action. Smith's administratrix, and Harris in person, each brought a state-court action against the estate of Cionci, Dutcher the owner, and the estate of Lynch. These Smith and Harris actions, for unknown reasons, have never gone to trial and are still pending. The Lynch action against Cionci's estate was settled for $50,000, which the estate of Cionci, being penniless, has never paid.

Dutcher, the owner of the automobile and a defendant in the as yet untried tort actions, had an automobile liability insurance policy with Lumbermens Mutual Casualty Company, a respondent here. That policy had an upper limit of $100,000 for all claims arising out of a single accident. This fund was potentially subject to two different sorts of claims by the tort plaintiffs. First, Dutcher himself might be held vicariously liable as Cionci's "principal"; the likelihood of such a judgment against Dutcher is a matter of considerable doubt and dispute. Second, the policy by its terms covered the direct liability of any person driving Dutcher's car with Dutcher's "permission."

The insurance company [asserted] that Cionci had not had permission and hence was not covered by the policy. The facts allegedly were that Dutcher had entrusted his car to Cionci, but that Cionci had made a detour from the errand for which Dutcher allowed his car to be taken. The estate of Lynch brought the present diversity action for a declaration that Cionci's use of the car had been "with permission" of Dutcher. The only named defendants were the [insurance] company and the estate of Cionci. The other two tort plaintiffs were joined as plaintiffs. Dutcher, a resident of the State of Pennsylvania as were all the plaintiffs, was not joined either as plaintiff or defendant....

[The district court rendered a declaratory judgment that the plaintiffs' claims were covered by Lumbermens' policy. The defendant insurance company appealed, raising questions of state law only.

[Without reaching the state law questions, the Court of Appeals for the Third Circuit reversed on grounds not raised at all in the trial court. It noted that Dutcher had interests adverse to the claimants. Specifically, he had a potential need to call on the insurance fund to pay any judgments that might be taken against him, and therefore he had an interest in not having the $100,000 fund depleted by payment of Cionci's liability.]

[Thus, the Court of Appeals concluded] that Dutcher was an indispensable party. The court held that [Dutcher's] "adverse interests" ... required him to be made a party. The court did not consider whether the fact that a verdict had already been rendered, without objection to the nonjoinder of Dutcher, affected the matter. Nor did it follow the provision of Rule 19 of the Rules of Civil Procedure that findings of "indispensability" must be based on stated pragmatic considerations. [Note: Rule 19(b) formerly referred to "indispensable" parties, but no longer does so—Eds.] It held, to the contrary, that the right of a person who "may be affected" by the judgment to be joined is a "substantive" right, unaffected by the Federal Rules; that a trial court "may not proceed" in the absence of such a person; and that since Dutcher could not be joined as a defendant without destroying diversity jurisdiction the action had to be dismissed.

Since this ruling presented a serious challenge to the scope of the newly amended Rule 19, we granted certiorari.... Concluding that the inflexible approach adopted by the Court of Appeals in this case exemplifies the kind of reasoning that the Rule was designed to avoid, we reverse....

... We may assume, at the outset, that Dutcher falls within the category of persons who, under § (a), should be "joined if feasible." The action was for an adjudication of the validity of certain claims against a fund. Dutcher, faced with the possibility of judgments against him, had an interest in having the fund preserved to cover that potential liability....

The optimum solution, an adjudication of the permission question that would be binding on all interested persons, was not "feasible," however, for Dutcher could not be made a defendant without destroying diversity. Hence the problem was the one to which Rule 19(b) appears to address itself: in the absence of a person who "should be joined if feasible," should the court dismiss the action or proceed without him? Since this problem emerged for the first time in the Court of Appeals, there were also two subsidiary questions. First, what was the effect, if any, of the failure of the defendants to raise the matter in the District Court? Second, what was the importance, if any, of the fact that a judgment, binding on the parties although not binding on Dutcher, had already been reached after extensive litigation? The three questions prove, on examination, to be interwoven.

We conclude, upon consideration of the record and applying the "equity and good conscience" test of Rule 19(b), that the Court of Appeals erred in not allowing the judgment to stand.

Rule 19(b) suggests four "interests" that must be examined in each case to determine whether, in equity and good conscience, the court should proceed without a [person whom it is not feasible to join]. . . . First, the plaintiff has an interest in having a forum. . . . Second, the defendant may properly wish to avoid multiple litigation, or inconsistent relief, or sole responsibility for a liability he shares with another. . . . Third, there is the interest of the outsider whom it would have been desirable to join. . . . [A]s Rule 19(a) expresses it, the court must consider the extent to which the judgment may "as a practical matter impair or impede [the person's] ability to protect" his interest in the subject matter. . . . Fourth, there remains the interest of the courts and the public in complete, consistent, and efficient settlement of controversies. . . .

Rule 19(b) also directs a district court to consider the possibility of shaping relief to accommodate these four interests. . . . [A] court should consider modification of a judgment as an alternative to dismissal. . . .

Had the Court of Appeals applied Rule 19's criteria to the facts of the present case, it could hardly have reached the conclusion it did. We begin with the plaintiffs' viewpoint. It is difficult to decide at this stage whether they would have had an "adequate" remedy had the action been dismissed before trial for nonjoinder: we cannot here determine whether the plaintiffs could have brought the same action, against the same parties plus Dutcher, in a state court. After trial, however, the "adequacy" of this hypothetical alternative, from the plaintiffs' point of view, was obviously greatly diminished. . . .

Opposing considerations in this case are hard to find. The defendants had no stake, either asserted or real, in the joinder of Dutcher. They showed no interest in joinder until the Court of Appeals took the matter into its own hands. This properly forecloses any interest of theirs, but for purposes of clarity we note that the insurance company, whose liability was limited to $100,000, had or will have full opportunity to litigate each claim on that fund against the claimant involved. Its only concern with the absence of Dutcher was and is to obtain a windfall escape from its defeat at trial.

The interest of the outsider, Dutcher, is more difficult to reckon . . . . The only possible threat to him is that if the fund is used to pay judgments against Cionci the money may in fact have disappeared before Dutcher has an opportunity to assert his interest. Upon examination, we find this supposed threat neither large nor unavoidable.

. . . Petitioner asserts here that under the applicable Pennsylvania vicarious liability law there is virtually no chance of recovery against Dutcher . . . . Furthermore, even in the event of tort judgments against Dutcher, it is unlikely that he will be prejudiced by the outcome here. . . . If the Court of Appeals was unconvinced that the threat to Dutcher was trivial, it could nevertheless have avoided all difficulties by proper phrasing of the decree. . . . Payment could have been withheld pending the suits against Dutcher and relitigation (if that became necessary) by him. In this Court, furthermore, counsel for petitioner represented orally that the tort plaintiffs would accept a limitation of all claims to the amount of the insurance policy . . . . [This stipulation removed any adverse interest of Dutcher—Eds.]

The suggestion of potential relitigation of the question of "permission" raises the fourth "interest" at stake in joinder cases—efficiency. It might have been preferable, at the trial level, if there were a forum available in which both the company and Dutcher could have been made defendants, to dismiss the action and force the plaintiffs to go elsewhere. Even this preference would have been highly problematical. . . . By the time the case reached the Court of Appeals, however, the problematical preference on efficiency grounds had entirely disappeared: there was no reason then to throw away a valid judgment just because it did not theoretically settle the whole controversy. . . .

The majority of the Court of Appeals read *Shields v. Barrow* [58 U.S. (17 How.) 130 (1854)] to say that a person whose interests "may be affected" by the decree of the court is an indispensable party, and that all indispensable parties have a "substantive right" to have suits dismissed in their absence. We are unable to read *Shields* as saying either. . . . Rule 19(b), which the Court of Appeals dismissed as an ineffective attempt to change the substantive rights stated in *Shields*, is, on the contrary, a valid statement of the criteria for determining whether to proceed [without] an interested person. It takes . . . adequate account of the . . . substantive claims to fairness on the part of outsiders that may arise in some cases. This, however, simply is not such a case. [Vacated and remanded.]

Republic of the Philippines v. Pimentel

553 U.S. 851 (2008)

Justice Kennedy delivered the opinion of the Court.

[Ferdinand Marcos was a past President of the Republic of The Phillipines. His tenure prompted many claims of human rights abuses and of stolen public funds, and he eventually was overthrown. During his time in office, Marcos had incorporated a company called Arelma, S.A., whose assets were held by the Merrill Lynch brokerage firm in New York. Also during his time in office, a group of human rights victims (the Pimentel group) had filed a class action against Marcos and obtained a $2 billion judgment. The Pimentel group then sought to attach the assets of Arelma to satisfy their judgment. However, the Phillipines Commission on Good Governance (which was empowered by the Republic to collect misappropriated assets) claimed title to the assets under a Phillipine statute authorizing forfeiture of property "unlawfully acquired" by a public servant. The Commission therefore applied to a court in the Phillipines for entitlement to the assets.

[Faced with conflicting demands for the same assets, Merrill Lynch used a procedure called an "interpleader," which is a type of action to determine rival claims. Specifically, Merrill Lynch filed a federal suit in which it "interpleaded" the Pimentel group, the Commission, and the Republic, and asked that they litigate their entitlement out against each other. The Republic and the Commission, however, asserted sovereign immunity, which allows a sovereign country to avoid a claim against it in some circumstances. The Republic and the Commission also moved for dismissal under Rule 19, asserting that the action could not proceed without them. The District Court denied the motion because it found that the interests of the Republic and the Commission had so little chance of success that the action could proceed without them, and it awarded the assets to the Pimentel class. The Court of Appeals affirmed. The Supreme Court here reverses and orders dismissal under Rule 19.] . . .

This case turns on the interpretation and proper application of Rule 19 of the Federal Rules of Civil Procedure and requires us to address the Rule's operation in the context of foreign sovereign immunity.

This interpleader action was commenced to determine the ownership of property allegedly stolen by Ferdinand Marcos when he was the President of the Republic of the Philippines. Two entities named in the suit invoked sovereign immunity. They are the Republic of the Philippines and the Philippine Presidential Commission on Good Governance, referred to in turn as the Republic and the Commission.

The United States Court of Appeals for the Ninth Circuit, agreeing with the District Court, held the action could proceed without the Republic and the Commission as parties. Among the reasons the Court of Appeals gave was that the absent, sovereign entities would not prevail on their claims. We conclude the Court of Appeals gave insufficient weight to the foreign sovereign status of the Republic and the Commission, and that the court further erred in reaching and discounting the merits of their claims.

[The parties all agreed that the Republic and the Commission were "parties required to be joined if feasible" under Rule 19(a). They claimed an interest in the subject of the action and thus were "persons required to be joined if feasible" under 19(a). But if such a person cannot be joined, as the Republic and the Commission could not because of their sovereign immunity, Rule 19(b) sets out a four-factor balancing test to determine whether the action can proceed without that party, "in equity and good conscience." The Supreme Court applied the four-factor test.]

A . . .

[The first balancing factor in Rule 19(b) is the prejudice to absent persons and parties from a judgment if the court proceeds. The lower courts gave insufficient weight to the harm that would affect the Republic and the Commission, given their sovereign status.] . . . [This] Court has observed that [sovereign immunity] is designed to "give foreign states and their instrumentalities some protection from the inconvenience of suit." . . .

. . . The claims of the Republic and the Commission arise from events of historical and political significance for the Republic and its people. The Republic and the Commission have a unique interest in resolving the ownership of or claims to the Arelma assets and in determining if, and how, the assets should be used to compensate those persons who suffered grievous injury under Marcos. There is a comity interest in allowing a foreign state to use its own courts for a dispute if it has a right to do so . . . .

. . . As to existing parties, we do not discount the Pimentel class' interest in recovering damages it was awarded pursuant to a judgment. Furthermore, combating public corruption is a significant international policy . . . . This policy does support the interest of the Pimentel class in recovering damages awarded to it. But it also underscores the important comity concerns implicated by the Republic and the Commission in asserting foreign sovereign immunity . . . . [T]he District Court and the Court of Appeals did not accord proper weight to the compelling claim of sovereign immunity . . . .

B

As to the second Rule 19(b) factor—the extent to which any prejudice could be lessened or avoided by relief or measures alternative to dismissal—there is no substantial argument to allow the action to proceed. No alternative remedies or forms of relief have been proposed to us or appear to be available . . . .

C

As to the third Rule 19(b) factor—whether a judgment rendered without the absent party would be adequate—the Court of Appeals understood "adequacy" to refer to satisfaction of the Pimentel class' claims. But adequacy refers to the "public stake in settling disputes by wholes, whenever possible." . . . Going forward with the action without the Republic and the Commission would not further the public interest in settling the dispute as a whole because the Republic and the Commission would not be bound by the judgment in an action where they were not parties.

D

As to the fourth Rule 19(b) factor—whether the plaintiff would have an adequate remedy if the action were dismissed for nonjoinder—the Court of Appeals made much of what it considered the tort victims' lack of an alternative forum should this action be dismissed. This seems to assume the plaintiff in this interpleader action was the Pimentel class. It is Merrill Lynch, however, that has the statutory status of plaintiff as the stakeholder in the interpleader action.

[The Court observes that the class claimants are somewhat "comparable" to plaintiffs, but they are not plaintiffs, and their interests are considered in the first part of the Rule, "prejudice to parties," analyzed in Part A above.]

Merrill Lynch, as the stakeholder, makes the point that if the action is dismissed it loses the benefit of a judgment allowing it to disburse the assets and be done with the matter .... [But a]ny prejudice to Merrill Lynch in this regard is outweighed by prejudice to the absent entities invoking sovereign immunity ....

... The balance of equities may change in due course. One relevant change may occur if it appears that the [Phillipines court] cannot or will not issue its ruling within a reasonable period of time. Other changes could result when and if there is a ruling .... The present action, however, may not proceed .... The judgment of the Court of Appeals for the Ninth Circuit is reversed, and the case is remanded with instructions to order the District Court to dismiss the interpleader action.

Notes and Questions

(1) *The Old Approach—Rigid Categories of "Indispensable" Parties.* The older, now discredited, approach to compulsory joinder was to classify parties rigidly, depending upon the kinds of substantive rights they asserted. Based on prior versions of the Federal Rules, persons who owned joint interests in the subject of the action (or who claimed joint interests) had to be joined, and if they were not, the court did not have jurisdiction. This rule was particularly disadvantageous when non-joinder became an issue after judgment (as in *Provident Tradesmens*). But the rule was amended in 1966, becoming less rigid. The modern rule contains a broad grant of judicial discretion: Rule 19(a)(1) mandates that required parties "must be joined *if feasible*," and Rule 19(b) then allows the court to use "equity and good conscience" to determine whether a case should proceed without such a party.

(2) *"Bleak House": The Historical Problem of Compulsory Joinder Returns.* From our discussion of equity (Chapter 5, § I[B], above), you should recall that the overdeveloped law of compulsory joinder was a principal factor underlying the advice of Charles Dickens in *Bleak House*: Suffer any wrong, rather than come to the Court of Chancery! But sometimes, history repeats, and *Republic of the Philippines v. Pimentel* seems like a return to the days of Dickens. Seventeen years after a class action was certified, and despite 9,539 human rights victims, the U.S. Supreme Court held that the U.S. courts could not hear a case involving assets in the U.S. Instead, the parties must wait and see whether a Philippine court would "issue its ruling within a reasonable period of time," an opinion that triggered predictably harsh criticisms:

> Elevating pragmatism over dogmatism is, even at its worst, a net beneficial approach to Rule 19 and sovereign immunity.... Dismissal in the face of

> no alternate forum and no outlet for relief, i.e., the Pimentel "solution," is a solution in name only . . . .

Compulsory [Mis]Joinder: The Untenable Intersection of Sovereign Immunity and Federal Rule of Civil Procedure 19, EMORY L.J. 60.5 (2011).

[G] Intervention and the Real-Party-in-Interest Requirement

Read Fed. R. Civ. P. 24 (intervention). Also, read Rule 17(a) (real party in interest).

Understanding Intervention Under Rule 24

Intervention "of Right" Versus "Permissive" Intervention. Rule 24 sets out two different kinds of intervention. In the absence of a federal statute covering the precise situation, Rule 24(a) provides for intervention "of right" when the intervenor claims a legally protectable "interest" in the case that may be impaired and is not adequately represented by any existing party. "Permissive" intervention, on the other hand, is discretionary with the court and may be granted pursuant to Rule 24(b) whenever the claim or defense presented by the applicant for intervention has a question of law or fact in common with the existing action. *See* Kennedy, *Let's All Join In: Intervention under Federal Rule 24*, 57 KY. L.J. 329 (1969).

Intervention in the Case That Follows: Pennsylvania v. United States. Intervention decisions sometimes are confusing because there are multiple positions to consider. Here, the United States has created certain regulations under the Affordable Care Act. Pennsylvania has sued the United States to prevent the alleged loss of insurance benefits to some people, which it says might result from the regulations. The claim at issue, however, is asserted by the Little Sisters of the Poor, a Catholic charitable organization. The Little Sisters seek to intervene to argue against a result in Pennsylvania's suit that might force them to act in ways that violate their religious beliefs. The issue is not whether the Little Sisters are correct in their position on the merits but whether they should be heard at all, by a claim in intervention.

Commonwealth of Pennsylvania v. President [of the] United States of America

888 F.3d 52 (3d Cir. 2018)

HARDIMAN, Circuit Judge.

In this appeal, we review an order of the United States District Court . . . denying a motion to intervene filed by the Little Sisters of the Poor . . . . The Little Sisters sought to intervene in litigation challenging regulations promulgated under the Patient Protection and Affordable Care Act [sometimes referred to as Obamacare]. The District Court denied the motion, finding that the Little Sisters lacked a significantly protectable interest in the case and that their interests were adequately represented by the federal government. We will reverse.

The Little Sisters of the Poor are an international Roman Catholic congregation whose mission is to serve the elderly poor of all backgrounds. They operate more than 25 homes for the elderly in the United States . . . .

[The Affordable Care Act mandates that employers obtain employee insurance coverage of contraceptive methods, without copayment by the patient, and it imposes daily penalties of $100 for noncompliance (the "contraception mandate"). To accommodate religious objections, the Department of Human Services (HHS) created regulations that allowed insured employers to "self-certify" their religious concerns, after which their insurers would provide the coverage without the employers' further intervention. The Little Sisters took the position that the self-certification accommodation would force them to "take actions that directly cause others to provide contraception or appear to participate in the Departments' delivery scheme," both of which would violate their religious conviction. They claimed that the regulations violated the Constitution, the Religious Freedom Restoration Act (RFRA), and the Administrative Procedure Act. RFRA, in turn, requires certain kinds of religious accommodation.

[In an earlier case, *Zubik v. Burwell*, — U.S. —, 136 S. Ct. 1557 (2016) (per curiam), the Supreme Court had addressed Affordable Care Act issues about contraception and indicated that RFRA protected certain of the parties' rights. But the Court had assumed, based on the parties' representations, that then-existing regulations protected all interests. It had stayed the contraception mandate, directing the parties to attempt "to arrive at an approach going forward that accommodates petitioners' religious exercise while at the same time ensuring that women covered by petitioners' health plans receive full and equal health coverage, including contraceptive coverage." But the "*Zubik* compromise" failed to protect all interests. When the United States promulgated new regulations, there were heavily divided groups.

[This case arose when the Commonwealth of Pennsylvania sued the United States for a declaration that the new regulations were illegal — but for a very different reason from the Little Sisters' concerns. Pennsylvania asserted that the regulations would result in loss of contraception insurance to some people, in violation of the Affordable Care Act. The Little Sisters moved to intervene in this suit.] . . .

The Little Sisters moved to intervene either as of right under Rule 24(a) of the Federal Rules of Civil Procedure or alternatively for permissive intervention under Rule 24(b). The District Court . . . found intervention under Rule 24(a) inappropriate after concluding that the Little Sisters did not have a significantly protectable interest in the litigation and that their interests were adequately represented by the federal government. And it determined that [permissive] intervention under Rule 24(b) would delay the litigation and "prejudice the interest of the parties in securing an efficient resolution" of the case. The Little Sisters appealed [the denial of their intervention], and a week later the District Court issued an opinion and order granting Pennsylvania's request for preliminary injunctive relief. The federal government appealed the order granting the preliminary injunction, and this Court stayed that case pending the outcome of our decision in this appeal. . . .

A party that has filed a timely motion has a right to intervene under Rule 24(a) if it can show three things: (1) a sufficient interest in the litigation; (2) "a threat that the interest will be impaired or affected, as a practical matter, by the disposition of the action"; and (3) that its interest is not adequately represented by the existing parties to the litigation. Since there is no dispute that the Little Sisters' motion was timely, we consider these three elements in turn. . . .

A

Did the Little Sisters demonstrate a sufficient interest in the litigation? To meet this prong, the Supreme Court has held that an applicant must assert an interest that is "significantly protectable." *Donaldson v. United States,* 400 U.S. 517, 531 (1971). We have interpreted this to mean "a cognizable legal interest, and not simply an interest of a general and indefinite character." An applicant must therefore demonstrate that its interest is "specific to [it], is capable of definition, and will be directly affected in a substantially concrete fashion by the relief sought." . . .

First, the Little Sisters have a significantly protectable interest in the continued protection afforded by [the earlier Supreme Court decision in] *Zubik* [i.e., the application of RFRA's protection of religious exercise to the contraception mandate]. This litigation has the potential to reopen issues that turn on the meaning of RFRA as it bears on self-certification, potentially influencing any substantive outcome. The Commonwealth's APA [Administrative Procedure Act] challenge calls into question whether the new religious exemption is required by RFRA and therefore justifies bypassing notice-and-comment rulemaking to issue the [regulations] quickly. If this Court were to reach the RFRA issue, we would be answering the very question the Supreme Court chose not to address in *Zubik,* i.e., whether the self-certification process imposes a substantial burden on the Little Sisters' sincerely held religious beliefs. . . .

Second, the Little Sisters have a significantly protectable interest in the [new] religious exemption [regulation], since it constitutes the very "approach" contemplated by *Zubik*. . . .

B

Having concluded that the Little Sisters have a sufficient interest in the litigation, we now consider whether that interest "is in jeopardy in the lawsuit." To meet this requirement, an applicant "must demonstrate that [its] legal interests may be affected or impaired[] as a practical matter by the disposition of the action."

Far from providing permanent protection, *Zubik* afforded the parties merely "an opportunity" to arrive at a suitable compromise. Furthermore, the Supreme Court instructed the courts of appeals to provide the parties with "sufficient time" to settle their differences. But what if the parties are unable to settle their differences within what the courts of appeals deem "sufficient time"? In that event, the appellate courts will have no choice but to revisit the merits of the RFRA questions . . . .

And, as already discussed, the pending litigation poses a tangible threat to the Little Sisters' regulatory protection because it has the potential to declare that exemptions from the self-certification accommodation are not required by RFRA. . . . This, in turn, could affect whether the Little Sisters will remain exempt from the mandate. . . .

C

Finally, we evaluate whether the Little Sisters have established that their interests are not adequately represented by the federal government. We have held that an applicant's interests are not adequately represented if they diverge sufficiently from the interests of the existing party, such that "the existing party cannot devote proper attention to the applicant's interests." *United States v. Territory of the Virgin Islands,* 748 F.3d 514, 520 (3d Cir. 2014). This burden is generally "treated as minimal" and requires the applicant to show "that representation of his interest 'may be' inadequate."

The parties dispute the degree of divergence between the interests of the Little Sisters on the one hand and those of the federal government on the other. The Commonwealth [of Pennsylvania] contends that the Little Sisters and the government are in "lockstep" because they both seek to defend the validity of the [regulations]. . . . The Little Sisters argue that . . . the government must defend "numerous complex and conflicting interests," including the rights of nonprofit and for-profit religious objectors, moral objectors, and women seeking access to contraceptive services. Without the right to intervene, the Little Sisters contend that their "straightforward" interests "may become lost in [this] thicket of sometimes inconsistent governmental policies." . . .

. . . [T]he unique position in which *Zubik* has placed the federal government renders this case sufficiently similar to [decisions allowing intervention] for us to conclude that the Little Sisters carry a "comparatively light" burden here . . . .

For the reasons stated, we will reverse the District Court's order denying the Little Sisters' motion to intervene under Rule 24(a), and we will remand the case to permit intervention for the purpose of defending the portions of the religious exemption [regulation] that apply to religious nonprofit entities. [REVERSED.]

Notes and Questions

(1) *Sufficiency of the Claimed Interest.* In *South Carolina v. North Carolina,* 558 U.S. 256 (2010), two states engaged in a water rights dispute with original jurisdiction in the Supreme Court of the United States pursuant to Article III, Section 2 of the Constitution. In these cases, the Federal Rules of Civil Procedure, including Rule 24, were taken as "guides" to the court's procedure. The states disagreed over the apportionment of waters in the Catawba River, which crossed their boundaries.

The Court noted that "[r]espect for state sovereignty also calls for a high threshold to intervention by nonstate parties in a sovereign dispute committed to this Court's original jurisdiction." Nevertheless, Duke Energy Carolinas, LLC sought to intervene, because it operated 11 dams and reservoirs in both states that generated electricity for the region and controlled the flow of the river. Obviously, as a private company delivering power to both regions, Duke had very different interests from the states. Although not directly invoking the language of Rule 24, the court focused on critical factual issues to explain why Duke's interests were sufficient to warrant intervention:

> It is likely that any equitable apportionment of the river will need to take into account the amount of water that Duke Energy needs to sustain its operations and provide electricity to the region . . . Just as important, Duke Energy has a unique and compelling interest in protecting the terms of its existing [Federal Energy Regulatory Commission] license . . . which regulates the very subject matter in dispute: the river's minimum flow into South Carolina.

(2) *Adequate Representation by Existing Parties.* In the same case of *South Carolina v. North Carolina,* both the Catawba River Water Supply Project (hereinafter CRWSP) and the City of Charlotte, North Carolina, also sought to intervene. The Supreme Court treated these two entities very differently.

The CRWSP is an unusual municipal entity that serves the water needs of Union County, North Carolina, and Lancaster County, South Carolina. It has an advisory board consisting of representatives from both counties, draws its revenues from its bistate sales, and operates infrastructure and assets that are owned by both counties as tenants-in-common. The Court recognized that the CRWSP had a compelling interest in protecting the viability of its operations, and that neither state could properly represent the interests of the CRWSP in this litigation. The motion to intervene was granted.

The City of Charlotte, North Carolina, also had rights to transfer waters from the Catawba River basin. South Carolina's complaint actually named Charlotte, but did not seek relief against the city directly, and the Supreme Court noted that Charlotte's water use constituted part of North Carolina's equitable share. Applying Rule 24, the Court rejected Charlotte's motion to intervene.

> Charlotte's interest falls squarely within the category of interests with respect to which a State, based on the concept of *parens patriae,* must be deemed to represent all of its citizens. Indeed, North Carolina has said that it will defend Charlotte's authorized water transfers.

(3) *Permissive Intervention.* In situations where proposed intervenors seek permissive intervention, the two same factors—"sufficiency of interests" and "adequacy of existing representation"—are considerations, but courts have also considered such factors as whether the intervention will prejudice existing parties by undue delay or by complicating the action; whether the intervenor will benefit from intervention;

and whether the intervenor will contribute to the development of the issues. *See, e.g., United States Postal Service v. Brennan*, 579 F.2d 188 (2d Cir. 1978).

III. Devices for Handling Numerous Parties

[A] Interpleader: The "Stakeholder's Remedy"

Read Fed. R. Civ. P. 22 and 28 U.S.C. '§ 1335, 1397 and 2361 (interpleader);

Note on Interpleader: A "Stakeholder's Remedy"

What Is Interpleader? Interpleader is an equitable proceeding that allows a stakeholder to require rival claimants to the same rights to join in a single action to determine who is entitled to those rights. Otherwise, the claimants might sue in multiple forums, and the stakeholder might be liable multiple times when it should be liable only once. The *State Farm* case that follows is an example. The essence of interpleader is that the stakeholder faces *inconsistent claims.*

Rule 22 Versus Statutory Interpleader. The interpleader statute, 28 U.S.C. § 1335, has several bells and whistles that are not present in Rule 22 alone. For example, federal courts have interpleader jurisdiction on "minimal" diversity—that is, if any one claimant is diverse from any other. Furthermore, interpleader is available even if the claims are merely potential and not yet matured, because the statute covers persons who "may" claim (the Rule probably does too, but is less clear). Both of these threshold issues arose in the following case, *State Farm v. Tashire.*

The Accident and the Interpleader Action in State Farm v. Tashire. A Greyhound bus and a truck collided in California, killing two people and injuring many more. State Farm insured the truck driver. It therefore had two obligations: (1) to pay its insured's liability up to policy limits (in this case, $20,000) and (2) to furnish its insured with a defense in suits or claims irrespective of cost. In this case, in which suits in multiple forums were likely, the defense obligation probably would cost much more than $20,000. State Farm filed an interpleader action in Oregon concerning the $20,000 policy limits. It sought to use the interpleader action to bring not only all claims against this fund, but all claims against its insured, into this one forum. It hoped to reduce litigation costs.

Why an interpleader? The $20,000 fund could not satisfy all claimants, who might be entitled to millions. If State Farm paid any one claimant, it might face multiple liability to others.

The Equitable Origins of Interpleader; the Injunction. It should not surprise you to learn that interpleader is a creature of equity. Furthermore, the equity courts help the interpleader plaintiff by issuing an injunction to prevent the interpleader defendants from suing in multiple forums. In *State Farm v. Tashire*, State Farm sought, and the trial court granted, a very broad injunction: In effect, it required all claims from the accident—not just those against the $20,000 fund—to be prosecuted in the same suit. That result was efficient.

The question, in *State Farm v. Tashire*, was: Is it lawful?

"Inconsistency" or Adverse Claims Between Rival Claimants, as the Key to Interpleader. A person cannot interplead anyone and everyone merely to obtain a convenient forum. The key requirement is that the claims must be inconsistent. The claims against State Farm's $20,000 were potentially inconsistent, because they would probably total many millions and far exceed this limited fund. But is there any inconsistency if Greyhound is held liable to every claimant? Or, for that matter, if State Farm's insured is held liable many times in different forums? The answer is No, there is no inconsistency in these claims at all. In *State Farm v. Tashire*, the Supreme Court confined the scope of the interpleader, and the scope of the injunction, for these reasons.

State Farm Fire & Cas. Co. v. Tashire

386 U.S. 523 (1967)

Mr. Justice Fortas delivered the opinion of the Court.

Early one September morning, a Greyhound bus proceeding northward through Shasta County, California, collided with a southbound pickup truck. Two of the passengers aboard the bus were killed. Thirty-three others were injured, as were the bus driver, the driver of the truck and its lone passenger. One of the dead and 10 of the injured passengers were Canadians; the rest of the individuals involved were citizens of five American States. The ensuing litigation led to the present case, which raises important questions concerning administration of the interpleader remedy....

The litigation began when four of the injured passengers filed suit in California state courts, seeking damages in excess of $1,000,000. Named as defendants were Greyhound Lines, Inc., a California corporation; Theron Nauta, the bus driver; Ellis Clark, who drove the truck; and Kenneth Glasgow, the passenger in the truck who was apparently its owner as well. Each of the individual defendants was a citizen and resident of Oregon. Before these cases could come to trial and before other suits were filed in California or elsewhere, petitioner State Farm Fire & Casualty Company, an Illinois corporation, brought this action in the nature of interpleader in the United States District Court for the District of Oregon.

In its complaint State Farm asserted that at the time of the Shasta County collision it had in force an insurance policy with respect to Ellis Clark, driver of the truck, providing for bodily injury liability up to $10,000 per person and $20,000 per occurrence and for legal representation of Clark in actions covered by the policy. It asserted that actions already filed in California and others which it anticipated would be filed far exceeded in aggregate damages sought the amount of its maximum liability under the policy. Accordingly, it paid into court the sum of $20,000 and asked the court (1) to require all claimants to establish their claims against Clark and his insurer in this single proceeding and in no other, and (2) to discharge State Farm from all further obligations under its policy—including its duty to defend Clark in lawsuits arising from the accident. Alternatively, State Farm expressed its conviction that the policy issued to Clark excluded from coverage accidents resulting from his operation of a truck which belonged to another and was being used in the business of another.

Joined as defendants were Clark, Glasgow, Nauta, Greyhound Lines, and each of the prospective claimants. Jurisdiction was predicated upon 28 U.S.C. § 1335, the federal interpleader statute, and upon general diversity of citizenship, there being diversity between two or more of the claimants to the fund and between State Farm and all of the named defendants.

An order issued, requiring the defendants to show cause why they should not be restrained from filing or prosecuting "any proceeding in any state or United States Court affecting the property or obligation involved in this interpleader action, and specifically against the plaintiff and the defendant Ellis D. Clark." . . . Defendants Nauta, Greyhound, and several of the injured passengers responded, contending that the policy did cover this accident and advancing various arguments for the position that interpleader was either impermissible or inappropriate in the present circumstances. Greyhound, however, soon switched sides and moved that the court broaden any injunction to include Nauta and Greyhound among those who could not be sued except within the confines of the interpleader proceeding.

[A] temporary injunction along the lines sought by State Farm was issued by the United States District Court for the District of Oregon. . . . The injunction was later broadened to include the protection sought by Greyhound, but modified to permit the filing—although not the prosecution—of suits. The injunction, therefore, provided that all suits against Clark, State Farm, Greyhound, and Nauta be prosecuted in the interpleader proceeding.

On interlocutory appeal, the Court of Appeals for the Ninth Circuit reversed . . . The court . . . concluded that interpleader was not available in the circumstances of this case. It held that . . . the insurance companies may not invoke federal interpleader until the claims against the insured, the alleged tortfeasor, have been reduced to judgment. Until that is done, said the court, claimants with unliquidated tort claims are not "claimants" within the meaning of § 1335, nor are they "persons [with] claims [that may expose a plaintiff to double or multiple liability]" within the meaning of Rule 22 of the Federal Rules of Civil Procedure. . . . Although we reverse the decision of the Court of Appeals upon the jurisdictional question, we direct a substantial modification of the District Court's injunction for reasons which will appear.

I. [Jurisdiction]

Before considering the issues presented by the petition for certiorari, we find it necessary to dispose of a question neither raised by the parties nor passed upon by the courts below. Since the matter concerns our jurisdiction, we raise it on our own motion.... The interpleader statute, 28 U.S.C. § 1335, applies where there are "[t]wo or more adverse claimants, of diverse citizenship...." This provision has been uniformly construed to require only "minimal diversity," that is, diversity of citizenship between two or more claimants, without regard to the circumstance that other rival claimants may be co-citizens. There remains, however, the question whether such a statutory construction is consistent with Article III of our Constitution, which extends the federal judicial power to "Controversies ... between Citizens of different States ... and between a State, or the Citizens thereof, and foreign States, Citizens or Subjects." In *Strawbridge v. Curtiss*, 3 Cranch 267 (1806), this Court held that the diversity of citizenship statute required "complete diversity": where co-citizens appeared on both sides of a dispute, jurisdiction was lost. But Chief Justice Marshall there purported to construe only "[t]he words of the act of Congress," not the Constitution itself. And in a variety of contexts this Court and the lower courts have concluded that Article III poses no obstacle to the legislative extension of federal jurisdiction, founded on diversity, so long as any two adverse parties are not co-citizens. Accordingly, we conclude that the present case is properly in the federal courts.

II. [Ripeness of Claims]

We do not agree with the Court of Appeals that ... the company must wait until persons asserting claims against its insured have reduced those claims to judgment before seeking to invoke the benefits of federal interpleader. [The interpleader statute includes claimants who "may claim" in the future.] Until the decision below, every court confronted by the question has concluded that the ["may claim" language] removed whatever requirement there might previously have been that the insurance company wait until at least two claimants reduced their claims to judgments....

... Were an insurance company required to await reduction of claims to judgment, the first claimant to obtain such a judgment or to negotiate a settlement might appropriate all or a disproportionate slice of the fund before his fellow claimants were able to establish their claims. The difficulties such a race to judgment pose for the insurer, and the unfairness which may result to some claimants, were among the principal evils the interpleader device was intended to remedy.

III. [Narrowing the Injunction]

The fact that State Farm had properly invoked the interpleader jurisdiction under § 1335 did not, however, entitle it to an order both enjoining prosecution of suits against it *outside* the confines of the interpleader proceeding and also extending such protection to its insured [Ellis Clark], the alleged tortfeasor. Still less was Greyhound Lines entitled to have that order expanded so as to protect itself and its driver, also alleged to be tortfeasors, from suits brought by its passengers in various state or federal courts....

... [A]n insurance company whose maximum interest in the case cannot exceed $20,000, should not be allowed to determine that dozens of tort plaintiffs must be compelled to press their claims—even those claims which are not against the insured and which in no event could be satisfied out of the meager insurance fund—in a single forum of the insurance company's choosing. There is nothing in the statutory scheme, and very little in the judicial and academic commentary upon that scheme, which requires that the tail be allowed to wag the dog in this fashion.

State Farm's interest in this case, which is the fulcrum of the interpleader procedure, is confined to its $20,000 fund. That interest receives full vindication when the court restrains claimants from seeking to enforce against the insurance company any judgment obtained against its insured, except in the interpleader proceeding itself. To the extent that the District Court sought to control claimants' lawsuits against the insured and other alleged tortfeasors, it exceeded the powers granted to it by the statutory scheme.

We recognize, of course, that our view of interpleader means that it cannot be used to solve all the vexing problems of multiparty litigation arising out of a mass tort. But interpleader was never intended to perform such a function, to be an all-purpose "bill of peace." None of the legislative and academic sponsors of a modern federal interpleader device viewed their accomplishment as a "bill of peace," capable of sweeping dozens of lawsuits out of the various state and federal courts in which they were brought and into a single interpleader proceeding. . . .

[W]e hold that the interpleader statute did not authorize the injunction entered in the present case. Upon remand, the injunction is to be modified consistently with this opinion. [REVERSED.]

[The dissent in part of Justice Douglas is omitted. He argued that the litigants were not "claimants," and that "neither are they in the category of those who 'are claiming' or who 'may claim' to be entitled to" the $20,000 fund. Therefore, interpleader is not available here, he said.]

Notes and Questions

(1) *The Requirement of Inconsistency: A Plaintiff Who "May Be Exposed to Double or Multiple Liability" on a Single Obligation.* Since interpleader is not an all-purpose "bill of peace," a potential debtor cannot interplead claimants if they all have rights to recovery that are not inconsistent. *See* Ilsen & Sardell, *Interpleader in the Federal Courts*, 35 St. John's L. Rev. 1 (1960). If, for example, a careless driver injures two people in one accident, the driver cannot use interpleader to prevent them from suing her in separate suits. There is no reason why both of them cannot recover from her, so interpleader is not available. In fact, that is why Greyhound cannot interplead the claimants in *State Farm v. Tashire* and cannot be protected by an injunction.

Consider the case of *Charles H. Tompkins Co. v. Lloyd E. Mitchell, Inc.*, 259 F.2d 177 (D.C. Cir. 1958). A general contractor, despite two adverse awards in arbitration proceedings that had become final, claimed that either its electrical subcontractor or its mechanical subcontractor had failed to perform certain disputed work that it, the general contractor, had therefore been required to do. From the subcontract payments, it withheld a "fund" covering the value of the disputed work and sought to interplead the two subcontractors. The Court of Appeals held that interpleader was not available because the claim of inconsistent "double or multiple" liability was fictitious. Is this holding correct? *See also Metropolitan Life Ins. Co. v. Prater*, 508 F. Supp. 667 (E.D. Ky. 1981) (where only potential claimant disclaimed fund, and where state statute absolved insurer for paying fund to sole claimant, there was no "substantial" prospect of multiple liability, and insurer could not interplead fund).

(2) *"Rule 22 Interpleader" Versus "Statutory Interpleader."* In reality, there are two different interpleader provisions in federal practice: Rule 22 interpleader and statutory interpleader. In addition to the jurisdictional differences pointed out above, there are other distinctions. Statutory interpleader pursuant to 28 U.S.C. § 1335 requires only $500 in controversy, while Rule 22 requires ordinary diversity jurisdiction (in excess of $75,000). The statutory version has a special venue provision allowing suit at the residence of one or more claimants; Rule 22 does not cover the matter, and the ordinary venue provisions control in a Rule 22 case. You may be tempted to conclude that statutory interpleader has all the advantages and that Rule 22 has no place, but that conclusion would be erroneous. Diversity under Rule 22 is determined by traditional plaintiff-defendant distinctions, so Rule 22 interpleader comes within diversity jurisdiction if the claimants are all of the same citizenship, so long as the stakeholder is diverse from them. *Aetna Life & Cas. Co. v. Spain*, 556 F.2d 747 (5th Cir. 1977). Statutory interpleader requires diversity between adverse claimants, or between the claimants and an interested stakeholder. But it requires only "minimal diversity," not complete diversity, meaning that one set of adverse parties with different citizenship is required.

Statutory interpleader also provides for nationwide service of process, which is discussed below.

(3) *A Missed Opportunity for Efficiency?* Because of the Supreme Court opinion, State Farm was protected by the interpleader action against inconsistent claims to the $20,000 fund, and the injunction prevented claims against this fund in other forums. But State Farm still is faced with the prospect of having to defend claims against its insured in multiple, scattered forums, possibly at great (and from its point of view, unnecessary) expense.

In this regard, the Court in *State Farm v. Tashire* says that interpleader is not an "all-purpose bill of peace." The "bill of peace" was an equitable proceeding, related to interpleader, that allowed a person subject to vexatious multiple litigation to require consolidation of the claims in certain circumstances. The decision in *State Farm v. Tashire* does not seem consistent with other rules emphasizing judicial efficiency. *See* Comment, *Promoting Judicial Economy Through the Extension of Interpleader to the Tortfeasor in the Mass Tort Area*, 17 WAYNE L. REV. 1241 (1971).

(4) *Consolidation Possibilities in the Federal System.* State Farm may be able to use other tools in the Federal Rules and statutes to obtain at least some consolidation.

For example, it can seek transfers of venue to a single venue based on 28 U.S.C. § 1404 and the "convenience of parties and witnesses" and "interest of justice." Or it can try to use a device that we shall see later in this Chapter: a motion pursuant to 28 U.S.C. § 1407 seeking to manage the pretrial stages of multi-district litigation in a single district. These devices will provide only limited help, however, because they apply to federal claims, not state claims.

(5) *Attorney's Fees?* Ordinarily, an interpleader plaintiff is entitled to recover attorney's fees, at least if she is a disinterested stakeholder who seeks only to be discharged from the risks of liability. *United States v. Browne Elec. Co.*, 168 F. Supp. 806 (E.D. Va. 1959). This relief is within the equitable discretion of the court. *Cf. Murphy v. Travelers Ins. Co.*, 534 F.2d 1155 (5th Cir. 1976) (abuse of discretion found when court required disinterested stakeholder, which was neither dilatory nor in bad faith, to shoulder its own costs and attorney's fees). The usual procedure is to award costs and fees against the losing party—*i.e.*, the one whose claim made the interpleader necessary—although this principle, too, is within the court's discretion.

(6) *Nationwide Service, "Minimal" Diversity, and the Reduction of Jurisdictional Restrictions.* Congress passed the Federal Interpleader Act, 28 U.S.C. §§ 1335, 1397, 2361, partly as a response to *New York Life Ins. Co. v. Dunlevy*, 241 U.S. 518 (1916). There, the stakeholder was unable to use interpleader because it could not obtain personal jurisdiction of one claimant in the forum where it had been sued by the other claimant. *See* Chafee, *Modernizing Interpleader*, 30 Yale L.J. 814 (1921). The Federal Interpleader Act provides for nationwide service, so that personal jurisdiction no longer is an impediment to impleader in the *Dunlevy* situation. Furthermore, to prevent restrictions on subject matter jurisdiction from interfering with federal remedies in a multi-state situation, the Act provides for jurisdiction in cases of "minimal" diversity (as *State Farm v. Tashire* illustrates).

[B] Class Actions

> Read Fed. R. Civ. P. 23 (class actions).

Note on Understanding Rule 23

Rule 23 is carefully structured. Its first two sections define the conditions under which class actions are permitted, and the remaining sections govern procedural matters.

(a) Prerequisites: "Numerosity," "Commonality," "Typicality," and "Adequate Representation." Rule 23(a) sets out the basic requirements that every class action must satisfy. The most obvious is (1) that the members must be "so numerous" that their joinder is "impracticable." If all of the members could be normal parties to a suit, a class action is unnecessary. This first element is often called "numerosity"

by class action lawyers. (2) There must be "questions of law or fact common to the class." Class action lawyers call this element "commonality." (3) The entire class will be represented by the named parties. These representatives will do a better job, perhaps, if they have the same interests as the rest of the class. To ensure this incentive, the third requirement is that the representatives' claims or defenses must be "typical" of the class. This element, as you probably can predict, is called "typicality." (4) Finally, the court must satisfy itself that the named parties "will fairly and adequately protect the interests" of the class—the "adequate representation" requirement.

(b) The Three Types of Class Actions. But these four universal prerequisites are not all of the requirements. Once they are satisfied, the class action also must be shown to fall within one of the three types of class actions that section (b) says are "maintainable." These are:

> *(b)(1): Inconsistent Results.* If there is a risk that individual suits would create inconsistent results, a class action is maintainable. The prototypical case under this subsection is one involving a limited fund with numerous claimants. If all members of the class are not brought into the litigation, the party opposing them might face court orders in separate suits that would require it to pay out more than the fund limits. Or early individual victors would obtain amounts greater than their proportional shares of the fund. (It should be clear to you that a "subsection (b)(1) class action" is analogous to a big interpleader action.)
>
> *(b)(2): Uniform Injunctive or Declaratory Relief.* The prototype "(b)(2) class action" is the civil rights class action, in which class representatives sue to have a statute declared unconstitutional. The relief is granted with respect to the class as a whole.
>
> *(b)(3): Common Questions "Predominate" and a Class Action Is the "Superior" Means of Managing the Case.* The "(b)(3) class action" is the type that we usually visualize when we think of a class action. The claims can be independent, so long as they arise in a context of sufficiently common questions. Consumer class actions, antitrust class actions, and securities fraud class actions are examples. There are two requirements: The common questions must "predominate" over questions that are individual to each member, and the class format must be the "superior" means of managing their resolution.
>
> *The Four-Factor Test for (b)(3) Class Actions.* Subsection (b)(3) is slightly more complex than this review would indicate, however, because it goes on to specify four factors that are "pertinent" to the determination. Briefly put, the factors are: (A) class members' interest in "individually controlling" their own actions; (B) other pending litigation, if any; (C) the appropriateness of the forum; and (D) the "likely difficulties in managing" a class action.

Remember, a class action must clear each of the hurdles set out in subsection (a)—the prerequisites—and, in addition, it must conform to at least one of the three types of actions described in subsection (b).

(c) Certification and Notice. Section (c) of the Rule requires the court to conduct a hearing "[a]t an early practicable time" to determine whether the class action may be maintained. This determination is called "certification" of the class action. At the hearing, the court determines whether the four prerequisites of Rule 23(a) are met and, in addition, whether the action fits one of the three types set out in Rule 23(b). In addition, subsection (c) requires the court to direct notice to class members in a (b)(3) action. The notice must be "the best . . . practicable under the circumstances." This section also provides for members to request "exclusion" (to "opt out") if they desire.

(d) Flexible Orders in Conduct of Actions. Section (d) of the Rule is intended to give the court flexible authority to tailor the notice, pleadings, and pretrial orders to the shape of the particular class action, as well as ability to deal with "similar procedural matters." Class actions are different from ordinary litigation, and they sometimes require creativity on the part of the judge. In the case that you will read next, the court attempts to structure both the notice and the possible relief in novel ways.

(e) Settlement, Voluntary Dismissal, or Compromise. Since the representative parties have obligations to the class, section (e) requires that the court approve any settlement, voluntary dismissal, or compromise of a certified class, that notice be given to class members of these events, and that the court may refuse to approve a class settlement unless class members are provided with a second opportunity to opt out of the class once they know the terms of the settlement.

(f) The Class Action Fairness Act of 2005 (CAFA). The Class Action Fairness Act (CAFA) expanded federal court jurisdiction over large, multi-state class actions. This legislation was a response to concerns about the bringing of nationwide class actions in state courts chosen by class action lawyers because they were perceived as favorable to plaintiffs (and unfavorable to defendants). The Act amended 28 U.S.C. § 1332, the diversity jurisdiction statute, to permit federal subject-matter jurisdiction of class actions in which the aggregated amount-in-controversy exceeds $5 million and at least one plaintiff is a citizen of a State different from a defendant, subject to limited exceptions. *See* 28 U.S.C. § 1332(d). The Act also liberalized removal procedures in such class actions, authorizing the removal of a CAFA class action (1) by any defendant, even if one or more other defendants do not consent, (2) even if one of the defendants is a citizen of the State in which the lawsuit was filed, and (3) without regard to the one-year limit imposed by section 1446. *See* 28 U.S.C. § 1453(b).

Problem A

STAR DEALERSHIP, INC. v. CONTINENTAL MOTORS COMPANY. This problem is designed to take you through each of the steps required for certification of a class action. Your client owns Star Dealership, which is one of the authorized dealers of automobiles manufactured by Continental Motors—one of the largest corporations in the world, which has a large share of the national automobile market.

Your client has a complaint about the way that Continental Motors distributes advertising allowances to dealers. He says that the distribution violates the antitrust laws, and, after looking into the matter, you determine that he may have a point (then again, he may not—that's the way antitrust cases are). It appears that Star may be able to prove something on the order of $50,000 in damages. That amount may sound large, but you determine that for an expensive, uncertain kind of claim such as one under the antitrust laws, you would not be willing to bring suit with damages of such size.

Your client tells you, however, that there are about fifty to a hundred other Continental dealers who are adversely affected by the advertising distribution scheme. They are located throughout the country, but there are many in your state. Each one has a separate contract with Continental, and therefore, the proof of the claim will entail slight differences from dealer to dealer. Of course, each one has different damage amounts. Upon checking, you learn that two individual dealers have brought suits in distant states already. Your client would like to see the present method of distribution stopped by an injunction or by declaratory relief, if possible, and a uniform, lawful method adopted; he would also like to see Star Dealership obtain damages if that is possible.

Answer the following questions:

(a) Are the four prerequisites—numerosity, commonality, typicality, and adequate representation—present?

(b)(1) Can the action be maintained as a (b)(1) action? This subsection requires a "risk" of inconsistent results.

(b)(2) Can it be maintained as a (b)(2) action? This subsection requires that the thrust of the action be for "injunctive or declaratory relief" applicable to the class as a whole. No other relief can be sought unless it is "incidental."

(b)(3) Can it be maintained as a (b)(3) action? This subsection requires that common questions predominate and that a class action be the superior means of management. You must evaluate the four factors of (A) the members' interest in individually controlling their own actions, (B) the relevance of pending litigation, (C) the desirability of concentrating all the litigation in your district, and (D) the "manageability" of this particular action.

(c) Will notice be a problem? What about the cohesiveness of the class? Might it be necessary to define subclasses for the different categories of claims that the dealers might have because of their different treatment by Continental?

(d) Will you take the case for your client and the class? The court must set your fee, as to the class, if (and only if) you prevail.

Eisen v. Carlisle & Jacquelin

417 U.S. 156 (1974)

Mr. Justice Powell delivered the opinion of the Court.

[Eisen brought a class action on behalf of himself and other traders on the New York Stock Exchange. The suit alleged that Carlisle & Jacquelin and DeCoppet & Doremus, two brokerage firms that together handled 99% of the Exchange's odd-lot business [trading in increments less than 100 shares], had engaged in monopolistic pricing. The case underwent three stages. In "Eisen I," the District Court dismissed the suit as a class action, but the Court of Appeals ultimately determined that a class action was proper. In "Eisen II," the Court of Appeals reversed the dismissal of the class action in an "exhaustive but ultimately inconclusive analysis of Rule 23." The District Court had held that the Petitioners met the first three requirements of a class action—numerosity, commonality, and typicality—but on the fourth factor, concluded that petitioner might not "fairly and adequately protect the interests of the class." The Court of Appeals disagreed with the reasoning behind the latter conclusion and directed the District Court to reconsider the point, but it did not resolve another contested issue related to the notice requirement.

[Next, in "Eisen III" (this case), the Court of Appeals disagreed with the District Court again, rejecting the use of publication notice, finding that the petitioners must bear the costs of individual notice, and dismissing the matter because of the likely difficulties in managing a class action. This defect meant that a class action was not a "superior" method of resolving the case, pursuant to Rule 23(b)(3)(D). The Supreme Court then granted certiorari, with the majority opinion focused on the notice issues.]

A critical fact in this litigation is that petitioner's individual stake in the damages award he seeks is only $70. No competent attorney would undertake this complex antitrust action to recover so inconsequential an amount. Economic reality dictates that petitioner's suit proceed as a class action or not at all. Opposing counsel have therefore engaged in prolonged combat over the various requirements of Rule 23.... Thus, after six and one-half years and three published decisions, the Court of Appeals endorsed the conclusion reached by the District Court in its original order... —that petitioner's suit could not proceed as a class action. In its procedural history, at least, this litigation has lived up to Judge Lumbard's characterization of it as a "Frankenstein monster posing as a class action."

Turning to the merits of the case, we find that the District Court's resolution of the notice problems was erroneous in two respects....

A

Rule 23(c)(2) provides that, in any class action maintained under subdivision (b)(3), each class member shall be advised that he has the right to exclude himself from the action on request or to enter an appearance through counsel, and further that the judgment, whether favorable or not, will bind all class members not requesting exclusion. To this end, the court is required to direct to class members "the best notice [that is] practicable under the circumstances, including individual notice to all members who can be identified through reasonable effort." We think the import of this language is unmistakable. Individual notice must be sent to all class members whose names and addresses may be ascertained through reasonable effort.

The Advisory Committee's Note to Rule 23 reinforces this conclusion. . . . The Committee explicated its incorporation of due process standards by citation to *Mullane v. Central Hanover Bank & Trust Co.*, 339 U.S. 306 (1950) and like cases.

In *Mullane*, the Court addressed the constitutional sufficiency of publication notice, rather than mailed individual notice, to known beneficiaries of a common trust fund as part of a judicial settlement of accounts. . . . It further stated that notice must be "reasonably calculated, under all the circumstances, to apprise interested parties of the pendency of the action and afford them an opportunity to present their objections." [And it required individual notice to persons who could reasonably be identified.]

B

We also agree with the Court of Appeals that petitioner must bear the cost of notice to the members of his class. The District Court reached the contrary conclusion and imposed 90% of the notice cost on respondents. . . .

We find nothing in either the language or history of Rule 23 that gives a court any authority to conduct a preliminary inquiry into the merits of a suit in order to determine whether it may be maintained as a class action. . . . The court's tentative findings, made in the absence of established safeguards, may color the subsequent proceedings and place an unfair burden on the defendant. . . .

We therefore remand the cause with instructions to dismiss the class action as so defined.

Notes and Questions

(1) *A Frankenstein Monster — Or a Means to Vindicate the Little Guy?* Class actions invite emotional reactions from many people. *See generally* A. Miller, *Of Frankenstein Monsters and Shining Knights: Myth, Reality, and the "Class Action Problem,"* 92 Harv. L. Rev. 664 (1979). At different times in the modern history of Rule 23, the courts have viewed it with great favor; at other times, they have been gloomy about it. This latter attitude seems to surface in *Eisen*. The Court almost appears to be using the requirement of notice as a restraint on overly exuberant uses of class actions — as a means to "chain down" the "Frankenstein monster."

For a different perspective, see *Phillips Petroleum Co. v. Shutts*, 472 U.S. 797 (1985) ("Class actions . . . permit the plaintiffs to pool claims which would be uneconomical to litigate individually. [T]his lawsuit involves claims averaging about $100 per plaintiff; most of the plaintiffs would have no realistic day in court if a class action were not available"). *See also* A. Miller & D. Crump, *Jurisdiction and Choice of Law in*

Multistate Class Actions After Phillips Petroleum Co. v. Shutts, 96 YALE L.J. 1 (1986); D. Bassett, *Constructing Class Action Reality,* 2006 BYU L. REV. 1415.

(2) *Did Practicality Arguments Lose or Does Frankenstein Yet Live?* Eisen unsuccessfully argued that sending individual notice to 2,250,000 class members created prohibitively high costs that effectively frustrated petitioner's attempt to vindicate the policies underlying the antitrust and securities laws. An earlier lower court opinion, however, suggested that the class might be divided into much smaller subclasses, and perhaps a subclass treated as a test case, with the other subclasses held in abeyance. "Individual notice at what would probably be a reasonable cost could then be given to all members of the particular small subclass who can be easily identified." Addressing that point, the Supreme Court majority opinion noted that "The record does not reveal whether a smaller class of odd-lot traders could be defined." In a concurring opinion, Justice Douglas emphasized this point, explaining how the notice issues overlapped with the other practical and manageability concerns:

> The power to create a subclass is clear and unambiguous. Who should be included and how large it should be are questions that only the District Court should resolve. Notice to each member of the subclass would be essential under Rule 23(c)(2); and under Rule 23(c)(2)(A), any notified member may opt out. There would remain the question whether the subclass suit is manageable. But since the subclass could be chosen in light of the nonmanageability of the size of the class whose claims are presently before us, there is no apparent difficulty in that sense.

(3) *Do New Technologies Change the Notice (and Manageability) Issues?* The case that follows cites *Eisen,* but it allows lesser notice. Is it consistent with *Eisen?* Perhaps; perhaps not.

MULLINS v. DIRECT DIGITAL, LLC, 795 F.3d 654 (7th Cir. 2015). Plaintiffs were representatives of a class of consumers who bought a dietary supplement for body joints. They alleged that the seller, Direct Digital, made false representations in advertising and marketing materials. The most significant problem in class certification involved the amorphous nature of the class. This issue raised manageability questions about how notice to class members, damage measurement, and payment of damages could be handled.

In spite of citing *Eisen v. Carlisle & Jacquelin,* the court affirmed the trial court's finding that the proposed class action was the superior means of handling the dispute. It did so by dispensing with the individualized (mailed) notice that was emphasized in *Eisen,* and instead, by using creative means:

> Direct Digital asserts that the only method of identifying class members here is by affidavits from the putative class members themselves.... We assume for purposes of this decision that Direct Digital will have no

records for a large number of retail customers. We also assume that many consumers of Instaflex [the dietary supplement] are unlikely to have kept their receipts since it's a relatively inexpensive consumer good.

Some courts have argued that imposing a stringent version of ascertainability [i.e., of identifying class members] "eliminates serious administrative burdens that are incongruous with the efficiencies expected in a class action by insisting on the easy identification of class members." . . .

. . . [But i]mposing a stringent version of [class member identification] because of concerns about administrative inconvenience renders the manageability criterion of the superiority requirement superfluous. It also conflicts with the well-settled presumption that courts should not refuse to certify a class merely on the basis of manageability concerns. . . .

When class members' names and addresses are known or knowable with reasonable effort, notice can be accomplished by first-class mail. *See, e.g., Eisen v. Carlisle & Jacquelin,* 417 U.S. 156, 174–75 (1974). When that is not possible, courts may use alternative means such as notice through third parties, paid advertising, and/or posting in places frequented by class members, all without offending due process. *See Hughes v. Kore of Indiana Enterprise, Inc.,* 731 F.3d 672, 676–77 (7th Cir.2013). . . .

. . . In these cases, "only a lunatic or a fanatic" would litigate the claim individually, so opt-out rights are not likely to be exercised by anyone planning a separate individual lawsuit. . . . That is why in *Hughes,* for example, where each plaintiff's claim was valued at approximately $1,000 or less, we approved a notice plan consisting of sticker notices on the defendant's two ATMs, publication of a notice in the primary local newspaper, and notice on a website. We did not insist on first-class mail . . . . We approved the plan because the notice plan was "commensurate with the stakes." . . . [AFFIRMED.]

Notes and Questions

(1) *Does This Holding, in Mullins, Violate the Requirements Set Out by the Supreme Court in Eisen?* The Supreme Court in *Eisen* held that individual notice was not discretionary for class members who were reasonably identifiable. If there are any in *Mullins* who are easily identified, as surely there must be, doesn't the court have to require individual notice to them? But in *Mullins* and the other cases it discusses, courts show a willingness to consider alternatives. The notice demands of due process, it seems, remain flexible after all.

(2) *Certification Is the Critical Step.* The *Mullins* case, with its emphasis on a practical approach to class action management, shows judicial awareness of just how important the certification issue is. If the action is certified, it becomes viable; if not certified, it is not viable. As a result, the parties expend considerable energy arguing about certification.

(3) *Damages for an Amorphous Class?* The *Mullins* court will need to know the individual class members to convey damages to them. Or will it? Could the court create a "fluid class" and allow future discounts on merchandise to people who are possible or probable class members? (That solution might violate several Supreme Court cases holding that it is illegal to compensate non-injured persons.)

[C] The Judicial Panel on Multidistrict Litigation

Notes and Questions

Read 28 U.S.C. § 1407 (multidistrict litigation).

(1) *Purpose of the Multidistrict Litigation Statute.* 28 U.S.C. § 1407 addresses the problem of scattered, duplicative litigation that would waste judicial and private resources unless consolidated. *See* Herndon & Higginbotham, *Complex Multidistrict Litigation—An Overview of 28 U.S.C.A. § 1407,* 31 Baylor L. Rev. 33 (1979).

(2) *Procedure.* Section 1407 sets up a "Judicial Panel on Multidistrict Litigation," consisting of seven Circuit and District judges designated by the Chief Justice of the United States. Either on its own initiative or upon the motion of a party in any action, the Panel may order actions "involving one or more common questions of fact," pending in different Districts, transferred for "coordinated or consolidated pretrial proceedings." The Panel takes action on the vote of four members, pursuant to "a record of [a] hearing at which material evidence may be offered by any party. . . ." The standard for transfer is very general: The panel need only determine that transfer "will be for the convenience of parties and witnesses and will promote the just and efficient conduct of [the] actions." Multidistrict consolidation is used in antitrust, mass tort, securities, patent, and civil rights cases, and indeed it can be used in any type of dispute that generates dispersed but overlapping litigation.

(3) *Perspective of the Attorney for the Individual Litigant; Of the Defendant.* To an attorney pursuing an individual claim, multidistrict consolidation is often undesirable. She perceives the Panel as having "yanked" "her" case away from her, sending it to a distant place where it will not be heard from again for a long time. The individual attorney frequently perceives the Panel's procedures as cumbersome; for example, motion papers may be required to be sent to a mailing list of hundreds of other lawyers. To the defendant, however, the procedure may be a godsend. The defendant can avoid the duplication of expense it would otherwise incur (and, not incidentally, is spared the leverage in settlement negotiations that this expense otherwise gives the individual litigant). Some plaintiffs' counsel may share this favorable view, particularly class action counsel or attorneys likely to play prominent roles in the platoon system that will be devised to handle the litigation.

(4) *Restrictions on Multidistrict Consolidation.* Section 1407 allows consolidation only of federal litigation. Scattered litigation in courts of different states cannot

be consolidated by this procedure (unless, of course, the individual cases can be removed to federal courts). Furthermore, multidistrict consolidation is for pretrial proceedings only; the panel is required to remand each case for trial to the district from which it was transferred (unless it is settled or otherwise terminated in pretrial proceedings, as happens in the great majority of cases). Would it be appropriate for Congress to create a mechanism for consolidating scattered state and federal litigation?

Additionally, the Class Action Fairness Act (CAFA) provides that class actions removed to federal court "may not thereafter be transferred to any court." CAFA means that these class actions may remain as dispersed litigation.

(5) *The Presiding Judge Cannot Keep the Case for Trial, but Must Transfer It Back.* For many years, there was a practice by which the presiding judge sometimes would receive (or solicit) a motion for transfer under § 1404(a) of the entire case in all the consolidated suits. Since this was a pretrial matter, the judge might grant the motion, transferring all trials to the consolidated court as well. Was this an impermissible "end run" around the limits of § 1407? Yes, said the Supreme Court in *Lexecon v. Milberg Weiss Bershad Hynes & Lerach*, 523 U.S. 26 (1998). The language of § 1407 says that "[e]ach action so transferred *shall* be remanded" to the initial district for trial (emphasis added). This "plain command," said the Court, means that the district court cannot transfer all the actions to itself, but must transfer back all that are not settled—in spite of the "longstanding practice" to the contrary.

GELBOIM v. BANK OF AMERICA CORPORATION, 135 S. Ct. 897 (2015). This decision of the Supreme Court shows how multidistrict consolidation works under section 1407, but it also shows that the separate nature of the claims remains after consolidation. Bondholder plaintiffs brought a putative class antitrust action alleging that numerous banks had conspired to artificially suppress the daily interest rate benchmark on their bonds, the London InterBank Offered Rate (LIBOR), by understating their borrowing costs, thereby depressing LIBOR and enabling banks to pay lower interest rates on financial instruments sold to investors. The Multidistrict Panel consolidated this case for pretrial proceedings with more than sixty other cases brought by plaintiffs asserting additional federal and state claims, in addition to antitrust claims. Under section 1407, the Multidistrict Panel transferred all of these cases to the United States District Court for the Southern District of New York, which was chosen, presumably, for its location and expertise in the subject area.

The district court dismissed all of the antitrust claims, meaning that this class action was dismissed, but it left open other cases that had been consolidated with it. The court of appeals dismissed the bondholder plaintiffs' appeal for want of appellate jurisdiction, because the judgment left open all other cases and therefore allegedly was not final. The Supreme Court reversed, holding that each consolidated and transferred case was its own case, and therefore the judgment was final and appealable.

[D] The Multiparty, Multiforum Trial Jurisdiction Act of 2002

The Multiparty, Multiforum Trial Jurisdiction Act of 2002 added section 1369 to title 28 of the United States Code. Section 1369 authorizes original jurisdiction in mass tort cases involving 75 or more deaths at a single location when minimal diversity exists between adverse parties. Special provisions govern venue, removal, service of process, and subpoenas in section 1369 actions. The Act also indicates a preference for remand to state courts for individual damage determinations after common liability determinations. The legislative history behind the Act is sparse, and the Act has been criticized as reflecting haste. What advantages does the Act serve procedurally? Should the Act be broadened to encompass mass torts involving fewer victims—or restricted to actions involving more victims?

[E] Global Settlement Class Actions: May a Court Manage an Intractable Dispute by Cutting the Gordian Knot?

Amchem Products, Inc. v. Windsor

521 U.S. 591 (1997)

Justice Ginsburg delivered the opinion of the Court.

This case concerns the legitimacy under Rule 23 of the Federal Rules of Civil Procedure of a class-action certification sought to achieve global settlement of current and future asbestos-related claims. The class proposed for certification potentially encompasses hundreds of thousands, perhaps millions, of individuals tied together by this commonality: each was, or some day may be, adversely affected by past exposure to asbestos products manufactured by one or more of 20 companies....

The United States District Court for the Eastern District of Pennsylvania certified the class for settlement only, finding that the proposed settlement was fair and that representation and notice had been adequate. The Court of Appeals for the Third Circuit vacated the District Court's orders, holding that the class certification failed to satisfy Rule 23's requirements in several critical respects. We affirm the Court of Appeals' judgment.

I

A

The settlement-class certification we confront evolved in response to an asbestos-litigation crisis. A United States Judicial Conference Ad Hoc Committee on Asbestos Litigation ... described facets of the problem ...:

> "The most objectionable aspects of asbestos litigation can be briefly summarized: dockets in both federal and state courts continue to grow; long delays are routine; trials are too long; the same issues are litigated over and over; transaction costs exceed the victims' recovery by nearly two to one;

> exhaustion of assets threatens and distorts the process; and future claimants may lose altogether."

Real reform, the report concluded, required federal legislation creating a national asbestos dispute-resolution scheme.... To this date, however, no congressional response has emerged.

In the face of legislative inaction, the federal courts ... endeavored to work with the procedural tools available to improve management of federal asbestos litigation .... [T]he MDL Panel transferred all asbestos cases then filed, but not yet on trial in federal courts to a single district, the United States District Court for the Eastern District of Pennsylvania; pursuant to the transfer order, the collected cases were consolidated for pretrial proceedings before Judge Weiner. *See In re Asbestos Products Liability Litigation (No. VI)* [above]. The order aggregated pending cases only; no authority resides in the MDL Panel to license for consolidated proceedings claims not yet filed.

B

After the consolidation, attorneys for plaintiffs and defendants formed separate steering committees and began settlement negotiations .... Although the MDL order collected, transferred, and consolidated only cases already commenced in federal courts, settlement negotiations included efforts to find a "means of resolving ... future cases." ...

To that end, [Defendants'] counsel approached the lawyers who had headed the Plaintiffs' Steering Committee in the [initial] unsuccessful negotiations, and a new round of negotiations began; that round yielded the mass settlement agreement now in controversy. At the time, the former heads of the Plaintiffs' Steering Committee represented thousands of plaintiffs with then-pending asbestos-related claims—claimants the parties to this suit call "inventory" plaintiffs. [Defendants] indicated in these discussions that it would resist settlement of inventory cases absent "some kind of protection for the future." ...

Settlement talks thus concentrated on devising an administrative scheme for disposition of asbestos claims not yet in litigation. In these negotiations, counsel for masses of inventory plaintiffs endeavored to represent the interests of the anticipated future claimants, although those lawyers then had no attorney-client relationship with such claimants.

Once negotiations seemed likely to produce an agreement purporting to bind potential plaintiffs, [Defendants] agreed to settle, through separate agreements, the claims of plaintiffs who had already filed asbestos-related lawsuits. In one such agreement, ... defendants promised to pay more than $200 million to gain release of the claims of numerous inventory plaintiffs....

C

[To implement the settlement, the settling parties presented the District Court with a package consisting of a class action complaint, an answer, a proposed settlement agreement, and a joint motion for conditional class certification, all on the same day. They had no intent to litigate the class complaint, which was a vehicle for settlement only. The complaint identified nine plaintiffs and their families, all as representatives of the entire class. The class was defined as all persons (and certain of their family members) who had ever been exposed to asbestos products manufactured by one of the defendants, but who had never filed suit.

[The settlement agreement proposed to determine all claims of the class members and preclude all other litigation by them. It set up an administrative mechanism for distributing designated payments to class members who had met defined medical and exposure qualifications. It also fixed the range of damages for four types of cancers and other conditions. It denied compensation, however, for numerous conditions even if state law otherwise allowed it, including loss of consortium, emotional distress based on exposure alone, enhanced risk, medical monitoring, and pleural claims related to lung plaques without physical impairment. The compensation categories were not adjusted for inflation.]

D

[The trial judge conditionally certified the class and appointed . . . class counsel. No subclasses were created. The judge then assigned another judge to conduct "fairness proceedings" regarding the settlement. This judge approved elaborate plans for notice to class members by media and otherwise. The notice informed class members of a three-month period in which they could opt out.]

Objectors raised numerous challenges to the settlement. They urged that the settlement unfairly disadvantaged those without currently compensable conditions in that it failed to adjust for inflation or to account for changes, over time, in medical understanding. They maintained that compensation levels were intolerably low in comparison to awards available in tort litigation or payments received by the inventory plaintiffs. And they objected to the absence of any compensation for certain claims, for example, medical monitoring, compensable under the tort law of several States. . . .

Strenuous objections had been asserted regarding the adequacy of representation, a Rule 23(a)(4) requirement. Objectors maintained that class counsel and class representatives had disqualifying conflicts of interests. In particular, objectors urged, claimants whose injuries had become manifest and claimants without manifest injuries should not have common counsel and should not be aggregated in a single class. Furthermore, objectors argued, lawyers representing inventory plaintiffs should not represent the newly-formed class.

Satisfied that class counsel had ably negotiated the settlement in the best interests of all concerned, and that the named parties served as adequate representatives, the District Court rejected these objections . . . . [T]he District Court found "no antagonism of interest between class members with various medical conditions, or between persons with and without currently manifest asbestos impairment." Declaring class certification appropriate and the settlement fair, the District Court preliminarily enjoined all class members from commencing any asbestos-related suit against the . . . defendants in any state or federal court. . . . The United States Court of Appeals for the Third Circuit vacated the certification, holding that the requirements of Rule 23 had not been satisfied. . . .

We granted certiorari and now affirm [the Court of Appeals decision decertifying the class].

II

Objectors assert in this Court, as they did in the District Court and Court of Appeals, an array of jurisdictional barriers. [The Court declines to consider these jurisdictional issues because they "would not exist but for the [class action] certification," and decertification thus avoids them.]

III

To place this controversy in context, we briefly describe the characteristics of class actions for which the Federal Rules provide. [The opinion here examines the history and provisions of Rule 23.]

A proposed amendment to Rule 23 would expressly authorize settlement class certification, in conjunction with a motion by the settling parties for Rule 23(b)(3) certification, "even though the requirements of subdivision (b)(3) might not be met for purposes of trial." [This amendment would have changed the analysis, but it was not adopted.—Eds.] We consider the certification at issue under the rule as it is currently framed.

IV

We granted review to decide the role settlement may play, under existing Rule 23, in determining the propriety of class certification. The Third Circuit's opinion stated that each of the requirements of Rule 23(a) and (b)(3) "must be satisfied without taking into account the settlement." That statement, petitioners urge, is incorrect.

We agree with petitioners to this limited extent: settlement is relevant to a class certification. The Third Circuit's opinion bears modification in that respect. But . . . the Court of Appeals in fact did not ignore the settlement; instead, that court homed in on settlement terms in explaining why it found the absentees' interests inadequately represented. The Third Circuit's close inspection of the settlement in that regard was altogether proper.

Confronted with a request for settlement-only class certification, a district court need not inquire whether the case, if tried, would present intractable management problems, *see* Fed. R. Civ. Proc. 23(b)(3)(D), for the proposal is that there be no trial. But other specifications of the rule—those designed to protect absentees by blocking unwarranted or overbroad class definitions—demand undiluted, even heightened, attention in the settlement context. . . .

Rule 23(e) [requires court approval of settlement, as well as notice to class members.] Subdivisions (a) and (b) focus court attention on whether a proposed class has sufficient unity so that absent members can fairly be bound by decisions of class representatives. That dominant concern persists when settlement, rather than trial, is proposed. . . .

Federal courts, in any case, lack authority to substitute for Rule 23's certification criteria a standard never adopted—that if a settlement is "fair," then certification is proper. . . .

A

We address first the requirement of Rule 23(b)(3) that "[common] questions of law or fact . . . predominate over any questions affecting only individual members." The District Court concluded that predominance was satisfied based on two factors: class members' shared experience of asbestos exposure and their common "interest in receiving prompt and fair compensation for their claims, while minimizing the risks and transaction costs inherent in the asbestos litigation process as it occurs presently in the tort system." . . .

The predominance requirement stated in Rule 23(b)(3), we hold, is not met by the factors on which the District Court relied. The benefits asbestos-exposed persons might gain from the establishment of a grand-scale compensation scheme is a matter fit for legislative consideration, but it is not pertinent to the predominance inquiry. That inquiry trains on the legal or factual questions that qualify each class member's case as a genuine controversy, questions that preexist any settlement. . . .

The Third Circuit highlighted the disparate questions undermining class cohesion in this case: "Class members were exposed to different asbestos-containing products, for different amounts of time, in different ways, and over different periods. Some class members suffer no physical injury or have only asymptomatic pleural changes, while others suffer from lung cancer, disabling asbestosis, or from mesothelioma. . . . Each has a different history of cigarette smoking, a factor that complicates the causation inquiry . . . ."

Differences in state law, the Court of Appeals observed, compound these disparities. No settlement class called to our attention is as sprawling as this one. . . . [This] certification cannot be upheld, . . . for it rests on a conception of Rule 23(b)(3)'s predominance requirement irreconcilable with the rule's design.

B

Nor can the class approved by the District Court satisfy Rule 23(a)(4)'s requirement that the named parties "will fairly and adequately protect the interests of the class." The adequacy inquiry under Rule 23(a)(4) serves to uncover conflicts of interest between named parties and the class they seek to represent. . . .

As the Third Circuit pointed out, named parties with diverse medical conditions sought to act on behalf of a single giant class rather than on behalf of discrete subclasses. . . .

The Third Circuit found no assurance here . . . that the named plaintiffs operated under a proper understanding of their representational responsibilities. That assessment, we conclude, is on the mark.

C

Impediments to the provision of adequate notice, the Third Circuit emphasized, rendered highly problematic any endeavor to tie to a settlement class persons with no perceptible asbestos-related disease at the time of the settlement. . . .

Because we have concluded that the class in this case cannot satisfy the requirements of common issue predominance and adequacy of representation, we need not rule, definitively, on the notice given here. In accord with the Third Circuit, however, we recognize the gravity of the question whether class action notice sufficient under the Constitution and Rule 23 could ever be given to legions so unselfconscious and amorphous.

V

The argument is sensibly made that a nationwide administrative claims processing regime would provide the most secure, fair, and efficient means of compensating victims of asbestos exposure. Congress, however, has not adopted such a solution. And Rule 23 . . . cannot carry the large load [the defendants], class counsel, and the District Court heaped upon it. [Affirmed.]

Justice Breyer, with whom Justice Stevens joins, concurring in part and dissenting in part.

Although I agree with the Court's basic holding that "settlement is relevant to a class certification," I find several problems in its approach that lead me to a different conclusion. First, I believe that the need for settlement in this mass tort case, with hundreds of thousands of lawsuits, is greater than the Court's opinion suggests. Second, I would give more weight than would the majority to settlement-related issues for purposes of determining whether common issues predominate. Third, I am uncertain about the Court's determination of adequacy of representation, and do not believe it appropriate for this Court to second-guess the District Court on the matter without first having the Court of Appeals consider it. Fourth, I am uncertain about the tenor of an opinion that seems to suggest the settlement is unfair. And fifth, in the absence of further review by the Court of Appeals, I cannot accept the majority's suggestions that "notice" is inadequate. . . .

These difficulties flow from the majority's review of what are highly fact-based, complex, and difficult matters, matters that are inappropriate for initial review before this Court. The law gives broad leeway to district courts in making class certification decisions, and their judgments are to be reviewed by the Court of Appeals only for abuse of discretion. . . .

Notes and Questions

(1) *Should the Supreme Court Have Been More Accommodating of Settlement Classes? Comparing the Amchem Majority and Dissent.* Every Justice in *Amchem* seems to agree that the asbestos claims at issue are intractable without either congressional action or novel interpretation of Rule 23. In fact, they all seem to agree that asbestos claims are a "crisis." Given this consensus, perhaps the dissent should

have been more persuasive. Should the majority have "followed the law," as it purports to do, or should it have tried harder instead to "make sense of" the law in Rule 23 by "cutting the Gordian knot"?

(2) *The Supreme Court Revisits the Amchem Issue, But with a Twist: Ortiz v. Fibreboard Corp.*, 527 U.S. 815 (1999). In 1993, before the *Amchem* decision, Fibreboard, another former asbestos products manufacturer, reached a $1.5 billion "global" settlement of asbestos claims (including past, present, and future claims) against it in a nationwide, mandatory, non-opt-out, Rule 23(b)(1)(B) class action. In 1995, the settlement was approved in federal district court and affirmed by the Fifth Circuit Court of Appeals. Following the *Amchem* decision, the Supreme Court remanded the case to the Fifth Circuit for reconsideration in light of *Amchem*, but the Fifth Circuit again upheld the settlement.

The Supreme Court reversed. The seven-Justice majority rejected the Fifth Circuit's use of a "limited fund" theory under Rule 23(b)(1)(B) to craft the mandatory settlement. According to Justice Souter's opinion, the limited fund concept should stay close to the historical model of a "fund" with a definitely ascertained limit that is inadequate to pay all claims against it.

Chapter 7

Discovery and Disclosure

I. The Objectives, Policies, and Planning of Discovery

[A] Objectives of Discovery

The Importance of Discovery to a Trial Lawyer. The discovery phase of a lawsuit consumes more time, effort, expense and energy than any other phase. In an adversary system, the purposes for which attorneys use discovery may include some or all of the following:

Purpose No. 1: Finding Out about the Lawsuit. The most obvious purpose of discovery is to find out everything possible about the transaction or occurrence that is at the heart of the lawsuit. If an attorney finds out that the opposing party admits to having driven ten miles per hour in excess of the speed limit, the attorney probably has advanced toward winning the suit. But the strategy is not limited to the discovery of helpful information. If the opposing party's contention is that the client ran a red light, the attorney will try to discover this claimed fact also. Having discovered it, he or she can consider how to limit the contention.

Purpose No. 2: "Freezing" the Harmful Evidence. A second function of discovery is to "freeze" the testimony of harmful witnesses. Does the opposing party claim that the plaintiff was traveling at ten miles per hour in excess of the 30-mile-per-hour speed limit? In that event, the opponent will have difficulty if she testifies at trial that the plaintiff was going "at least seventy." The deposition does not prevent a change in testimony, but it can be used to impeach the credibility of the witness if she testifies contrary to it. For this reason, skillful litigators are adept at getting deposition witnesses to give detailed answers.

Purpose No. 3: Preserving Evidence or Putting It in Usable Form. A third purpose of discovery is to put useful evidence in a form admissible at trial or in pretrial hearings. Let us say that the plaintiff's principal expert witness has written the plaintiff's attorney a letter summarizing the findings made after examining the product that is the subject of the action. The expert's schedule is such that she will not be available for trial, and it may be permissible under applicable law to use a deposition as a substitute for the expert's live testimony. The letter itself is not admissible in evidence (it would be excluded as hearsay). The plaintiff may wish to take the expert's deposition—not to discover information this time, but simply because the deposition, unlike the letter, may be admissible at trial.

Purpose No. 4: Deliberately Abusive Discovery. Discovery may also be used in an abusive manner. In the right kind of case, most skillful litigators would be able to write interrogatories within an hour that could cost tens of thousands of dollars to answer. Or the discovering party's objective may be to expose sensitive information or to impose unnecessary costs. By the same token, various methods can be used to hide information or to increase the cost of obtaining it. This conduct generally is improper, but you must recognize that discovery sometimes is used or resisted for abusive reasons.

Problem A: Chapter 7 Summary Problem

PAYNE v. WEST YORK HERALD-TRIBUNE: A PROBLEM RELATING TO DISCOVERY SCOPE, METHODOLOGY, SANCTIONS AND USAGE. Plaintiff John Payne has filed a diversity suit against the *West York Herald-Tribune*, alleging that the newspaper libeled him. His complaint alleges that the newspaper carried a story falsely reporting that Payne "acted as a bribe collector for certain West York politicians." The story was written by a reporter named Rob Woodwind, who relied upon statements by two individuals to whom he promised anonymity. The newspaper company's answer asserts that the report was true, denies its falsity, and denies that the newspaper acted negligently, with knowledge of the statement's falsity or reckless disregard for its falsity.

After the Rule 26(f) conference was conducted, Payne sought to discover "the identities of any persons who furnished information upon which the story about Payne allegedly was based." Payne also has requested production of "any written statement of or concerning any person who allegedly supplied any fact tending to show that Payne acted as a bribe collector, whether obtained before or after the filing of suit." The newspaper company desires to avoid producing any of these items, and reporter Woodwind states that he "never" will disclose his confidential sources, "no matter what happens to me or to the newspaper." Consider the following questions:

1. Is the requested information within the scope of discovery? (Don't forget to consider electronic materials, such as emails.)
2. Is any of the information covered by provisions codifying the "work product" doctrine, and if so, can the plaintiff satisfy the conditions for obtaining it?
3. What other methods or doctrines can the newspaper company invoke in an effort to obtain protection, and what are its chances of success?
4. What sanctions might be imposed if the *Herald-Tribune* refuses to disclose any of the information requested: (1) before being ordered to do so by the court, or (2) after the court has ordered full responses?
5. Formulate a full plan for all discovery by the plaintiff in such a case. (Assume, for this purpose, that the interrogatory and the request quoted here have not yet been propounded.)
6. Describe the initial and expert disclosures that would be required by each party and compute the latest possible date for filing the initial ones (not easy to do—you will need to cross-reference Rules 26(a), 26(f), and 16(b)). Assume that the suit was filed less than a month ago and was answered on the first day of the month in which you solve this problem.

[B] The Policies behind Broad Discovery—and the Limits

Modern Discovery Is Broad in Scope. Federal Rule 26 generally extends to any matter that is "relevant" and "proportional to the needs of the case." Rule 26 also provides that discoverable information "need not be admissible at the trial." It may be permissible, for example, for a party to discover hearsay information or witness speculation, even if it will be excluded at trial.

The Purposes of Broad Discovery. Broad discovery, it is often said, makes the adversary process a better instrument for arriving at the truth. It discourages trial by ambush. It provides each party with greater knowledge about the case, and thus it arguably leads to fairer trials and perhaps to a higher proportion of disputes settled without trial. The latter result is sometimes said to be reflected in a more efficient system of justice, although this point is debatable.

Other Limits on the Scope of Discovery. The most important limit on discovery is probably the requirement that it be "proportional to the needs of the case," as is shown above. Second, the information may be privileged, in which event it is exempted from discovery. For example, the attorney-client privilege shields most confidential communications between attorney and client from discovery, even though they are highly relevant to the action. Third, the trial judge has discretion to impose limits on discovery to shield a person from embarrassment or undue expense. *See* Fed. R. Civ. P. 26(c) (protective orders). And finally, material prepared in anticipation of litigation is usually immune from discovery.

The expense, burden, and intrusiveness of discovery have led to other kinds of limits, too. The Federal Rules now limit the number of written interrogatories and the length of depositions. *See* Fed. R. Civ. P. 30(d)(1) ("a deposition is limited to 1 day of 7 hours") and 33 (written interrogatories ordinarily may not exceed 25). The rules require discovery conferences and plans early in the case.

The "Broad-versus-Narrow-Discovery" Controversy has a long history and is still ongoing. Ironically, in criminal cases, there is far less formal discovery than in civil cases—yet this fact does not seem to decrease the incidence of settlement without trial in criminal cases, and it is difficult to assert that criminal trials are less fair or accurate than civil ones as a result. The aims of discovery, then, are simply ultimate goals that the rules may, or may not, actually achieve. *See* G. Hazard, *Discovery Vices and Trans-Substantive Virtues in the Federal Rules of Civil Procedure*, in *Symposium*, 137 U. Pa. L. Rev. 1873 (1989).

[C] The Discovery Tools and the Concept of Required Disclosures

The following discovery mechanisms are provided for in the Federal Rules of Civil Procedure. Similar mechanisms have been adopted in the states.

The Concept of Required, Self-Initiated Disclosures. Rule 26 requires all parties to make (1) "Initial Disclosures" of persons, documents, damages, and insurance early in the case, without any demand or question. This duty is serious, and the court has power to impose sanctions for inadequate disclosures. Then, there must be (2) "Disclosure of Expert Testimony" containing information about expert witnesses. Finally, there are (3) "Pretrial Disclosures" of fact witnesses and exhibits. These disclosure requirements are automatically imposed on each party, without the need for any request. *See generally* W. Brazil, *The Adversary Character of Civil Discovery: A Critique and Proposals for Change*, 31 Vand. L. Rev. 1348 (1978).

Written Interrogatories to Parties. Interrogatories are written questions directed by one party to another, to be answered under oath. Because this discovery device allows the opponent leisure to consider her response, and because opposing counsel generally determines the form of the answers, responses are frequently evasive, and thus interrogatories are not an effective method for obtaining controversial information. But interrogatories may be a way to acquire background information, to establish the positions of opposing parties, and to identify dates, documents, witnesses, and similar information. Interrogatories may be directed to parties only.

Requests to Produce or Inspect (for Discovering Documents, Tangible Things or Realty). The request to produce is the method for obtaining documents and other tangible things from other parties. A party sends to another party a request listing the documents, tangible things or realty she wishes to copy or inspect. For nonparties, the appropriate device is called a "subpoena duces tecum."

Interrogatories and requests for production can create significant costs for voluminous information, and the rules attempt to limit this problem, although not always successfully.

Requests for Admission. A party opponent may be requested to admit or deny factual propositions submitted to her. This kind of discovery is useful for eliminating issues about which there is no real dispute.

Oral Depositions (and Other Kinds of Depositions). Depositions are questions asked of a witness before trial, answered under oath in the presence of a court reporter, with opposing parties having the right to be present and ask questions also. This type of discovery may be used both as to party and non-party witnesses. It is set up by a written notice to all other parties and, for a non-party witness, issuance of a subpoena. Depositions are the most effective means for obtaining information from adverse witnesses because the examiner may ask follow-up questions in the event of evasion.

As an alternative to the oral deposition, a party may send written questions to a person authorized to administer a written deposition to the deponent. But the "deposition on written questions" is a weak form of discovery, because the deposition taker cannot ask follow-up questions. Its most frequent use is for authentication of documents.

Motions for Physical or Mental Examinations. Upon a motion showing good cause, the court may order the physical or mental examination of a person whose condition is in controversy.

Opposing Discovery: Objections and Motions for Protective Orders. A person who is the target of a discovery effort, and who thinks the requests are not allowed by the Rules, can object and obtain a court ruling on the issue. And even if the Rules do not prohibit the discovery request, the discoveree may invoke the court's discretion by a motion for a protective order. Upon motion by the person from whom discovery is sought, the court may protect the movant from harassment, embarrassment, oppression or undue burden or expense by limiting discovery.

[D] Basics of Discovery Planning

"Waves" of Discovery: First, Disclosures. The discovery phase of the litigation usually begins after the parties conduct a Rule 26(f) conference in order to develop a proposed discovery plan and to make or arrange for the disclosures required by Rule 26(a)(1). These disclosures include the name, address, and telephone number of each individual likely to have discoverable information that supports the claims or defenses of the disclosing party; a copy or description by category and location of all documents, electronically stored information, and tangible things in the control of the disclosing party that may be used to support the disclosing party's claims and defenses; the computation of any category of damages claimed; and a copy of any liability insurance policy that may be available. Disclosures are the first step.

The Second Wave: Interrogatories. Typically, the discovery plan developed by the parties at the Rule 26(f) conference will not go into great detail concerning the use of the discovery tools or the sequence in which they will be used by the parties, and neither will disclosures. The "second wave" of discovery will usually consist of interrogatories to obtain basic information not covered by the Rule 26(a)(1) disclosures. For example, interrogatories may be used to ask the other party to identify persons having knowledge of relevant facts; the identity and location of documents; other potential parties to the suit; and whether the defendant has been sued in the correct name. Interrogatories also may ask the other party to explain contentions alleged generally in the party's pleadings.

The Third Wave: Requests for Production. Once the basics are established by disclosures and answers to interrogatories, the next or "third wave" of discovery, frequently consisting of requests for document production, will be conducted. While human testimony may vary, documents contain what they contain, and they are useful to have available when one takes depositions.

The Fourth Wave: Depositions. The "fourth wave" may be depositions of witnesses or parties who know about the transaction at issue. These depositions may lead to a fifth or sixth wave of discovery, consisting of additional interrogatories, document requests, or other depositions. Finally, a request for admissions may be used as a last step in the discovery process to eliminate issues that the discovery process has shown to be undisputed and to authenticate documents to be introduced at trial.

Fitting the Discovery to the Case. These "waves" are not always as described. They vary with the case. Cost considerations limit discovery in every suit. An automobile accident with minor injuries may justify only a brief deposition or two. An antitrust case may call for the expenditure of hundreds of thousands of dollars in attorneys' fees for discovery.

Problem B

USING THE DISCOVERY DEVICES. What device or devices might enable you to obtain each of the following items or information? Which of the following items or information would be disclosed in self-initiated disclosures? Explain.

(a) Information related to the plaintiff's medical expenses in a personal injury suit for personal injuries, including such matters as the doctors she consulted, the amount of money she paid and the treatment she underwent. You represent the defendant.

(b) The bank statements or cancelled checks of the plaintiff for these expenditures.

(c) In an action on a contract, the genuineness of the copy of the contract in your client's possession, which you wish to establish for trial.

(d) In a suit over an automobile accident, the opposing party's version of facts surrounding the accident.

(e) Records maintained by an automobile repair shop, which is not a party to the suit, concerning the condition of the brakes of the automobile driven by the opposing party.

Problem C

RESPONDING TO DISCOVERY REQUESTS. What would you consider doing in each of the following situations?

(a) In an antitrust case, your opponent subjects your client to interrogatories which, although relevant to the issue of damages, would require disclosure of the names and addresses of all your client's customers, your client's method of doing business, and the process by which your client's product is made.

(b) In a contract action for loss of profits, your opponent seeks production of all your client's income tax records, claiming that they are relevant to the issue of damages.

(c) Your opponent seeks production from your client of "all documents produced as a result of any investigation by you or your attorneys of the accident upon which this suit is founded."

Morris, *Strategy of Discovery*

18 For the Defense 83 (1977)(*)

[The following outline gives the author's suggestions for the planning of discovery in the defense of a medical malpractice case. You should consider the extent to

(*) Copyright 1969. Reprinted with the permission of the Practicing Law Institute and the author. The format has been changed in some respects to fit this book better.

which it is applicable to other kinds of cases and whether it is "proportional to the needs" of those cases. How, for example, would these approaches have to be adapted if you represented the plaintiff in a medical malpractice case? What about an automobile negligence case in which the damages are small? What about an antitrust case?—Eds.]

I. INTRODUCTION

Discovery for the defense begins with the defense—not with the plaintiff

For it is the law that determines

(1) What facts are needed

(2) What form these facts must take to be admissible

Ideally—defense counsel should know as much about the law of his case before starting discovery as after conclusion of the appeal

II. THE LAW OF THE CASE

A. *Ways to achieve*

(1) Review the petition and the file and resolve—in your own mind—the legal issues

(2) Review your experiences re trials of similar cases—what were the issues. . . .

(3) Review the experience of others in similar cases

(a) *Reported cases* [Morris suggests reading not only the opinions, but also such sources as briefs and records.]

(b) *Unreported cases* [Morris suggests talking to lawyers and judges in such cases.]

B. *Purpose*

(1) *Define the issues*

(a) *re negligence. . . .*

(b) *re responsibility*

Who else involved

By what legal route:

[Morris suggests consideration of such diverse theories as the "captain of the ship" doctrine, administrative negligence, joint venture, etc.]

(2) *Delineate proof needed*

(a) *re substance*

Contractual relationships between the parties

Actual relationship between the parties

Representations to the patient

(b) *re form. . . .*

III. DISCOVERY OF DEFENSE

"Know thyself"

- as completely as possible

Rules of Thumb

Rule 1: Assume nothing—Take nothing for granted; cross-check everything and everyone including time-honored assumptions

Rule 2: Be resourceful. . . .

Rule 3: Be thorough. . . .

Rule 4: Preserve evidence—As you go, record: identifying information, serial numbers, etc.

A. *Primary sources* (of the fact)

(1) *Records involved*

1. *The hospital record (patient's medical chart)* covering the event in question

(a) Is your copy *complete*—*Caveat*: You must know the format for any hospital records: admission sheet, admitting history and physical, doctor order sheets, lab sheets, nurse's notes, etc.

(b) Is your copy *legible*—*Caveat*: What you can't read may be vital.

(c) *Understanding your copy*

1. Lay out chronologically—not easy to do

2. Get doctor to explain significance—of all recorded events; of all missing events

2. *Accessory Records* [These include Emergency Room, Out-Patient, Physiotherapy, Clinic, Pathology, and Autopsy Records.]

3. *Records behind the records*

Original entries in original books from which hospital records are made up:

(a) *Laboratory*: [including work notebooks, logs, and routing slips]

(b) *Pathology*: [including work notebooks, slides, paraffin blocks, and amputated parts]

(c) *Operating Room*: [including log schedules, material schedules, and financial charges]

(d) *Equipment & Supplies*: [including purchase orders, maintenance and service, and financial charges]

(e) *Financial records*: [oxygen given, R.N. service, etc.]

(f) *X-ray*: [films, therapy dosage, and charts]

(g) *Doctors' notes*: [Summaries, etc. (if any)]

4. *Legal records*

Caveat: Probably privileged from discovery by plaintiffs. *Sierra Vista Hospital v. Superior Court of California* (Ct. App. 1967), 56 Cal. Rptr. 387 [Hospital's incident report privileged from plaintiff's discovery]; *Brown v. Superior Court* (Dist. Ct. App. 1963) 32 Cal. Rptr. 527 [Malpractice Committee Review of case privileged from plaintiff's discovery.]

(a) Incident report

(b) Correspondence and file, etc.

5. *Medical investigating records reviewing case*—*Caveat*: Probably privileged from discovery by plaintiffs. *Judd v. Park Avenue Hospital* (Sup. Ct. N.Y.), 235 N.Y.S.2d 843, *aff'd*, 235 N.Y.S.2d 1023 ["any and all medical staff discussions and meetings of committees" privileged from plaintiff's discovery.]

(a) *Hospital review committees* [Tissue, Disciplinary, and Mortality committees, etc.]

(b) *Outside committees. . . .*

Comment: Probably privileged from discovery by anyone but may have been published anonymously and can be recognized from factual situation [citations omitted].

(c) *Medical literature*

Comment: Occasionally a doctor will have published (before suit filed) an article on the case at bar itself because of its scientific interest. Check medical literature under authors for doctors' names involved and under subject matter involved from year of incident to date. [*E.g.*,] *Rizzo, Admrx, etc. v. American Cyanamid Co. et al.*, (Common Pleas Ct., Cuyahoga County, Ohio, Docket No. 748722) [Death from allergic reaction to Kynex; prior to suit being filed one of defendant doctors published article about the very case: JAMA, 172: 155–57 (1-9-60) *Fatal Thrombocytopenic Purpura after Administration of Sulfamethoxpyridazine*].

6. *Regulations applicable*

(a) *Joint Commission on Accreditation*—Was hospital accredited; If so, when last inspected; report on inspection and recommendations; Compliance by hospital with recommendations

(b) *Hospital's own regulations* [including Constitution, Bylaws, Minutes of Trustees meetings or Medical Counsel, departmental rules, nursing rules]

(c) *Handbooks* [Nursing and operating procedures]

(d) *Standing orders of doctors*—especially defendant doctor

(2) *Personnel involved*

Each must be identified; each must be interviewed

1. *Identify*

   (a) *Operating room*

   - Everyone present at any time

   Prima facie: Surgeon, 1st Asst. Surgeon (resident), 2nd Asst. Surgeon (intern), Anesthesiologist (including all replacement doctors), Asst. Anesthesiologist . . . , Instrument or scrub nurse, Circulating nurse. *Perhaps also present*: Family doctor, Teams of specialists [heart-lung specialists, etc.], Observers [including doctors, students, and patient's family]

   (b) *Laboratories*: Head of department, all technicians doing the lab work, all who had personal contact with the patient.

   (c) *Nursing and Room Care*

   (1) *Hospital Personnel*

   Registered Nurses: Supervisor of floor, all R.N.'s on duty, all R.N.'s seeing patient

   Licensed Practical Nurses: All seeing patient

   Nurse's aides: All seeing patient

   Orderlies: Any involved

   (2) *Non-hospital Personnel*: Registered nurse, licensed practical nurses, friends and relatives rendering aid

   (3) *Roommates*: Get addresses from financial records. . . .

   (4) *Visitors*: Family, friends, relations, priest, social workers, etc.

   Comment: Check hospital nurse's notes, financial records, and registry of nurses, etc. to locate above

   (d) *Medical Care*: Attending physician [including replacement attending physician]; consultants; family doctor; specialists; residents; interns; Any doctor anywhere in hospital records, including nurse's notes, doctor's order sheets, etc.

   (e) *Special Departments*: Check all personnel on duty or seeing patient Examples: Physiotherapy Department, X-ray Department, Emergency Room, Out-Patient Clinics, etc.

2. *Interview*

   (a) Refresh their recollections—from hospital records, etc.

   (b) Commit to writing—even if negative statement

   (c) Inquire re collateral sources—which may lead to other evidence

(d) Get permanent address—for later location, including future plans

(e) Ask if they ever gave statement to plaintiffs

(f) Advise need not talk to plaintiff's side if don't want to and contact you if approached

(g) Qualifications: All education, all positions held, professional associations, honors, Board-certified in specialty

(h) All scientific writings by each

(i) Who they recommend to you as expert in their field

(j) Medical theories of case—theirs; others they know about

(k) Make them "level" with you re unpleasant facts about case or about themselves you should know

- "cross-examine" them on this

- any colleagues who hate them

3. *Investigate*

(a) *Personnel file*

- Review re each employee of hospital in question

- Review re each doctor on staff. . . .

(b) *Talk to colleagues*

- re general reputation of personnel in question

- re specific incident

4. *Equipment involved*

(a) *Identify*: locate, examine, get copy of instructional manual

Record: Serial number, model number, type number, manufacturer's name

(b) *Preserve* (for trial): perhaps photograph; allow no changes

(c) *Investigate*: Purchase records, maintenance records, outside service records, adaptations and changes records, performance records, installation records

(d) *Collateral Investigation*

- State of art of manufacturer at time installed

- Safety features on other makes not on this one

- Later safety features for this one since manufacture but before incident which might have been installed before incident

(e) *Testing*: Have expert examine and test re alleged incident and re its maintenance status

(f) *Scene of Accident*: Operating room, etc. (1) Inspect it yourself; (2) Prepare scale diagram, etc.; (3) Photograph

(g) *Third-party suits*: Discovery may reveal others owing hospital indemnity (1) Manufacturers of defective equipment; (2) Suppliers of drugs; (3) Independent contractor actors [anesthesiologists, etc.]

B. *Secondary Sources* (before the fact; after the fact)

(1) *Before the fact*

1. Hospital's experience re this type of incident: re legal "notice" to hospital; re causes

2. Hospital's experience re this type of equipment: re notice; re modifications

3. Hospital experience re this personnel

- *quality*—prior training, prior experience, record in general, colleagues' opinions

- *quantity*—how much experience with this operation, etc. (a) Has hospital had; (b) Has this surgeon had. . . .

(2) *After the fact*

What changes have occurred since this incident which bear on this incident—In practice, in procedure, in rules and regulations, in personnel, in equipment, etc.

C. *Collateral Sources*

Comment: All versions must be checked against independent expert sources to ascertain probable medical truth of matter.

(1) *Experts*

(a) *Quality*—the best obtainable

(b) *Quantity*—at least two in each specialty to check on each other

(c) *Review*—Careful review of all important known data and full hospital records by each expert

(2) *Medical and Scientific literature*: Check it yourself

(a) *Re medicine*—medical library articles and texts

(b) *Re drugs*—Manufacturer's brochure; Physician's Desk Reference; Pharmacology texts; pharmacologist; medical literature

(c) *Re equipment*—manufacturer's brochure, scientific texts and journals, scientific experts

IV. DISCOVERY OF THE PLAINTIFF

Comment: Now that you "know thyself" you are ready for discovery into plaintiff's case

A. *Discovery is discovery*—no magic; same as any other lawsuit

(1) *Interrogatories*

Cover all hospital admissions birth to date. Include hospital of birth and all doctors, medications, illnesses, etc.

(2) *Depositions*

(a) Plaintiff-patient especially re alleged verbal admissions by defendants and others and (b) All relatives and friends seeing patient in the hospital

(3) *All Hospital Records*—a gold mine

to death whether relevant or not

All admissions—all Emergency and Out-patient Departments

B. *Check on plaintiff's version*

(1) With all doctors and hospital personnel

(2) Investigators: Neighborhood checks, etc.

C. *Ascertain plaintiff's experts and their theory of case*

(1) *Discovery*

(a) interrogatories

(b) motions to produce [citation omitted]

(c) snooping—gossip

(d) ask your doctors who likely

(e) pre-trial hearings

(2) *Check on plaintiff's expert*

(a) ask other doctors

(b) research literature for his articles

(c) ask local academy re his qualifications

(d) text of medical specialists

D. *Physical examinations of plaintiff*

(a) Re recovery and present status

(b) Re causation and etiology

(c) Thorough: all experts necessary; all tests necessary—chromosome studies, allergy studies, X-ray studies, physical exam, laboratory studies, etc.

Comment: Generally, plaintiff's deposition should wait until after defense's discovery of defense is complete. *Reason*: Operative facts are highly medical and beyond knowledge of plaintiff and within knowledge of defendants—unlike auto accident case, etc.

However: Occasionally, defendant's discovery must begin with plaintiff and plaintiff's witnesses. *Examples*: (1) Plaintiff's claim Emergency Room treatment—yet defendant hospital has no record of same [citation omitted]. (2) Plaintiff claims an R.N. injured his sciatic nerve with I-M injection of medicine and hospital records shows many shots—which does he blame [citation omitted]?

V. CONCLUSION

Suits against hospitals fall into two main categories

(1) Complicated medical situations—operating room accidents, etc.

(2) Very simple factual situations—fall out of bed; hot water bottle burns, etc.

Above format especially important re category (1); category (2) may proceed with discovery of plaintiff first

But in both (1) and (2) No substitute for full discovery of defendant and of plaintiff

Thorough and painstaking discovery and preparation is [the] keynote of success. . . .

Notes and Questions

(1) *Beginning the Discovery Plan.* Why should discovery by the defense "begin with the defense"? What is the reason for beginning "not with the facts, but the law"?

(2) *"Proportionality to the Needs of the Case."* Would this outline be appropriate for a case in which damages, if recoverable, will be less than $50,000—or may be as much as $10 million? Notice that a plaintiff probably could use this outline productively by focusing on the "know thyself" advice directed to the defendant.

(3) *The Volume of Paper Discovery.* In a suit involving a "complicated medical situation," as the author puts it, how many documents would you guess might be generated by discovery? Note that the number might be increased by the existence of multiple defendants, cross-claims, addition of claims based on products liability, etc. What problems would be created by the sheer number of documents, and how would the lawyers solve these problems?

(4) *Interviewing (Versus Deposing) Cooperative Witnesses.* The author says, "persons involved . . . each must be interviewed." Why "interviewed," rather than deposed?

(5) *The Breadth of the "Relevance" Concept in Discovery.* Why should interrogatories to the plaintiff "cover all hospital admissions, birth to date"? Will a plaintiff

willingly comply with this request? What does the author mean by suggesting that the plaintiff's hospital records, which he calls a "gold mine," be sought "birth to death whether relevant or not"? (It has to be relevant to be discoverable. The author may be referring to the standard for admissible evidence at trial, which is narrower than the discovery standard.)

(6) *Verifying the Client's Version.* Why must "all versions"—including, presumably, your client's version and those of friendly witnesses—be "checked against independent expert sources to ascertain probable medical truth"? Can't a lawyer assume that her client is truthful?

(7) *The Cost of Discovery.* What would be the cost of investigation and discovery in a case involving a "complicated medical situation"? What sort of financial resources would the plaintiff's lawyers have to possess in such a case, and why? Consider whether discovery this thorough can be done if the injuries are minor (a case in which potential damages are perhaps $50,000). The defense might engage in discovery that would cause the plaintiff to expend many times the $50,000 at stake. What does this possibility suggest about the way that discovery rules should be written or interpreted?

(8) *Privileges and Discovery Limits.* Note the reference to defense material that may be "privileged," such as internal incident reports, review committee documents and the like. Why would the plaintiff want to obtain such documents? [Note: the plaintiff will want them irrespective of whether they contain admissible evidence.] What sort of financial difference might it make to the plaintiff's attorney if such documents are privileged? Why should they be privileged?

II. The Scope of Discovery

Read Fed. R. Civ. P. 26(b)(1)-(2) (basic scope of discovery).

[A] The Discovery Standard: Information That Is "Relevant" and "Proportional"

Note on the Breadth (or "Scope") of Discovery

How Broad Is Discovery? Some History, Exemplified by Kerr v. District Court, 511 F.2d 192 (9th Cir.), *aff'd,* 426 U.S. 394 (1976). In the not-too-distant past, discovery extended to anything that was "reasonably calculated to lead to admissible evidence." This standard led to what was generally seen as overly broad discovery. In the *Kerr* case, California prison inmates sued the state parole board on the ground that its rules denied them due process of law. During discovery, they demanded production of enormous amounts of information, including the personnel files of every parole hearing examiner, "all written proposals for any change whatsoever in . . . substantive criteria or procedures," and "all memoranda written by the Chairman of the [Parole Board], no matter to whom sent."

There were dozens of requests, each calling for numerous documents. How could these kinds of documents lead to admissible evidence, when the issue was not about any particular hearing or set of hearings or proposals or actions of the Chairman, but only about the rules the Board followed? Well, the inmates explained, if the hearing examiners were ignorant and biased, special rules might be required, and that was why they needed the personnel files. The court held that the documents were "reasonably calculated to lead to admissible evidence," and therefore they were relevant and discoverable, even if the cost of producing them might be hundreds of thousands of dollars. The only remaining question was whether privilege laws covered any documents. This was the old style of discovery.

The Current Rule: Discovery Must Be "Proportional to the Needs of the Case." This kind of broad discovery drew a reaction. The current Rule provides that discovery must be relevant, but it does not extend to everything that might lead to evidence; instead, it must be "proportional to the needs of the case." The following decision reflects the change. For example, a request for "all personnel files," as in the *Kerr* case, above, would be harder to justify today.

Cain v. Wal-Mart Stores, Inc.

2018 WL 1434819, 2018 U.S. Dist. LEXIS 47160 (E.D.N.C. March 22, 2018)

James E. Gates United States Magistrate Judge

I. BACKGROUND

This personal injury case arises out of an incident occurring in a Wal-Mart store in Hope Mills, North Carolina . . . . Plaintiff entered the store to purchase, among other things, a 50-pound bag of Ol' Roy Dog Food. The 50-pound bags of dog food were piled in stacks and one stack was approximately 3 feet high. When plaintiff bent down to pick up a bag from the 3-foot-high stack, another 50-pound bag of dog food fell from an adjacent 8-foot-high stack and landed on plaintiff's head, neck, and back, causing severe and permanent injury.

In his complaint, plaintiff asserted claims for negligence . . . . Plaintiff seeks punitive damages and compensatory damages.

. . . [P]laintiff served on Wal-Mart his first set of interrogatories and requests for production of documents. . . . Wal-Mart served its responses . . . , asserting a number of objections to most of plaintiff's requests [and answering others only partially]. Despite numerous requests by plaintiff that Wal-Mart reconsider its objections, Wal-Mart stands by them. [There also were disagreements about other discovery issues and about Plaintiff's motions to compel responses.]

II. APPLICABLE LEGAL PRINCIPLES

The Federal Rules of Civil Procedure enable parties to obtain information by serving requests for discovery on each other, including interrogatories and requests for production of documents. Rule 26 provides for a broad scope of discovery:

> Parties may obtain discovery regarding any non-privileged matter that is relevant to any party's claim or defense and proportional to the needs of the case, considering the importance of the issues at stake in the action, the amount in controversy, the parties' relative access to relevant information, the parties' resources, the importance of the discovery in resolving the issues, and whether the burden or expense of the proposed discovery outweighs its likely benefit. Information within this scope of discovery need not be admissible in evidence to be discoverable. Fed. R. Civ. P. 26(b)(1).

The district court has broad discretion in determining relevance for discovery purposes. *Seaside Farm, Inc. v. United States,* 842 F.3d 853, 860 (4th Cir. 2016). The party resisting discovery bears the burden of establishing the legitimacy of its objections. *Eramo v. Rolling Stone LLC,* 314 F.R.D. 205, 209 (W.D. Va. 2016) . . . .

III. PLAINTIFF'S MOTIONS TO COMPEL

A. Written Discovery Requests

The information and documents sought by the interrogatories and production requests in dispute can be divided into three broad categories: (1) the incident itself and investigation of it; (2) Wal-Mart's policies and procedures regarding stacking of merchandise; and (3) other claims arising from merchandise stacking incidents.

1. The Incident Itself and Investigation of It . . . .

a. Interrogatory No. 1

Interrogatory No. 1 seeks identifying information [about] all Wal-Mart employees who were working in the store at the time of the incident. Wal-Mart objects on grounds [of] . . . the attorney-client privilege and work-product doctrine.

Wal-Mart's objection based on the attorney-client privilege and work-product doctrine is unfounded. [Among other reasons, the attorney-client privilege applies only to confidential communications, and the work product doctrine applies only to items prepared for litigation; neither applies to underlying facts. The objection is far off base.—Eds.] Indeed, the notion that [these objections would] protect from disclosure . . . the names of potential witnesses would gut the fact-finding principles envisioned by the discovery process.

Wal-Mart also objects on grounds that the interrogatory is overbroad [i.e., that it is not "proportional to the needs of the case"]. . . . Again, the court disagrees. The identity of store employees present at the time of the incident is a defined set of individuals and as potential witnesses to the incident, is [discoverable].

Finally, Wal-Mart states that without waiving the objections, it will identify "the following individuals who may have had contact with the plaintiff after the subject incident" and then provides only the name of the store assistant manager. Wal-Mart's answer is not responsive to the interrogatory....

Plaintiff's first motion is therefore allowed as to Interrogatory No. 1. Wal-Mart shall serve on plaintiff by 12 April ... a supplemental answer to this interrogatory "[i]dentify[ing] all employees ... who were working at the store ... at the time of [the incident]." ... Wal-Mart shall not assert any objections in its supplemental answer.

> b.-d. [In similar fashion, the court considers ten more interrogatories and requests for production, granting some and ordering supplemental answers.] ...
>
> e. Production Request No. 3

Production Request No. 3 seeks photographs and videotapes of the stacks of dog food in the area where the incident occurred during [the] calendar year [of the incident]. Wal-Mart objected to this production request on the grounds that it is overbroad [i.e., not proportional.] Without waiving those objections, Wal-Mart produced a surveillance videotape of the incident and indicates that any incidental videotape capture of the incident would have since been destroyed.

The court agrees with Wal-Mart that this production request is overbroad. The record does not ... establish the [discoverability] of the photographs and videotape requested for the entire year in which the incident occurred. However, photographs and videotape of the stack of dog food on the day of the incident have been shown to be [discoverable]....

2. Stacking Policies (Interr. No. 3; Prod. Req. No. 1)

Interrogatory No. 3 and Production Request No. 1 seek information and documents ... relating to Wal-Mart policies and procedures for stacking merchandise. While the interrogatory is limited to policies and procedures as of the date of the incident, it is not expressly limited to policies and procedures applicable to [this store]. Conversely, the production request is not limited temporally, but is limited to [this store].... [The court limits both types of discovery accordingly.]

3. Other Claims Arising from Stacking Incidents (Interrs. Nos. 4, 5, and 8)

Interrogatories Nos. 4 and 5 seek information about any other claims ... [about] the stacking of merchandise above eye level in the customer area of a store, including the forum in which each claim was brought and the identity of the attorneys representing each claimant. Interrogatory No. 8 seeks the number of customers who claim they were injured as a result of merchandise being stacked at or above eye level "at any [Wal-Mart store]," the date of the event underlying each claim, and the amount, if any, paid to each claimant. [Wal-Mart objects that these interrogatories are overbroad, i.e., not proportional.]

The court agrees that the interrogatories are overbroad. . . . [T]he interrogatories appear to apply to all Wal-Mart brand stores [anywhere]. The interrogatories are appropriately limited to stores in the State of North Carolina because . . . the same North Carolina law standard for negligence and other claims would apply . . . . Further, the interrogatories are overbroad because of lack of a temporal limitation. An appropriate temporal limitation is, as Wal-Mart proposes, the three-year period up to the date of the incident. Lastly, Interrogatory No. 8 is not limited to stacking in the customer area of the store. [The court limits the discovery accordingly.]

[Other issues. The court here deals with questions regarding depositions, disclosures, and other discovery issues.]

V. CONCLUSION

In summary . . . , IT IS ORDERED as follows: 1. Plaintiffs first motion [to compel responses] is allowed in part and denied in part. 2. Plaintiffs second motion to compel [which was similar to the first] is denied as moot. 3. Plaintiffs third motion is allowed in part and denied in part . . . . 4. The court finding that the award of expenses would be unjust, each party shall bear its own expenses incurred on the motions. SO ORDERED.

Notes and Questions

(1) *How Could the District Judge Get Anything Done (Such as Trials) if Every Case Involved This Many Discovery Disputes?* Wal-Mart created a large number of issues, but to have this number of disputed issues is atypical. In many cases, discovery proceeds without intervention by the court. It is done by agreements among attorneys, and that is the way it is supposed to work.

(2) *Magistrate Judges Make Discovery Rulings, as Assigned by District Judges.* Another way that district judges get their work done is by referring disputes to magistrate judges. If you look on the internet for discovery decisions, you will find that many are by magistrate judges, including this one (*Cain v. Wal-Mart*). Magistrate judges are appointed by the district judges and are not nominated by the President or confirmed by the Senate, and they have fewer powers. Their rulings are subject to review by district judges. But they have a great deal of authority (including authority for sanctions) and usually are not overturned by district judges.

(3) *What Does "Proportional to the Needs of the Case" Mean?* In most cases, the proportionality standard is the main determinant of discovery. Rule 26(b) lists six factors for the court to consider, but few opinions really apply the six factors (other than to quote them as a list). The courts tend to describe the discovery request and then to pronounce it either proportional or not. An article by one of the authors here, David Crump, *Goodbye, Reasonably Calculated; You're Replaced by Proportionality: Deciphering the New Federal Scope of Discovery*, 23 Geo. Mason L. Rev.

1093 (2016), analyzes the six factors and shows what they might mean in given cases but concludes that the courts are simply using a general concept of proportionality rather than the factors.

(4) *Limiting Requests by Time, Geography, and Subject.* One takeaway from *Cain v. Wal-Mart* is that you are unlikely to get the court to approve a request for "all documents" of a given type if the request covers everything ever generated at any time, anywhere, on any subject. A request is more likely to earn approval if it is limited by time (the court limited one request in *Cain* to three years' duration), place (another request is limited to North Carolina), and subject (another request is limited to coverage of stacking in the customer area).

(5) *It Doesn't Have to Be Admissible to Be Discoverable.* The information the plaintiff is seeking includes a great deal that will not be admissible at trial. For example, some information about other claims against Wal-Mart will be excluded under the Rules of Evidence. But that is not the issue, because Rule 26 says that the information does not have to be admissible.

(6) *Why Does the Plaintiff's Lawyer Want So Much Information?* This is investigation, and the lawyer never knows which lead will turn up helpful information. The lawyer suspects that the opponent will answer discovery requests narrowly, if possible. And no one can guess what particular evidence will impress a jury. It might be that showing the videotape of the accident, together with an expert witness on retail management, would be enough, but maybe not. And the complaint asks for punitive damages, which require another level of proof. In addition, there is the tendency to leave no stone unturned. Finally, a lawyer often adapts "form" interrogatories created over many cases and designed to seek the broadest discoverable information possible.

(7) *Discovery of Other Claims against Wal-Mart.* The plaintiff's attorney's request for claims by other plaintiffs may lead to contacts with attorneys who have found effective evidence, as well as other helpful leads. Does the plaintiff's attorney seem to have used discovery strategy well?

(8) *Why Did the Magistrate Judge Not Impose Expenses on Wal-Mart?* Most lawyers would not make an objection to identities of potential witnesses, especially not one based on attorney-client privilege. And Wal-Mart's answer providing only the name of the store assistant manager was unquestionably improper. Why did the magistrate judge not require payment of expenses?

The answer is that judges sometimes are hesitant to impose sanctions. First, the necessary inquiries take the judge ever farther from resolving the merits of the case. Second, it is difficult to assess overall fault (one can also ask, why did the plaintiff's lawyer ask broad questions that the judge had to narrow). Finally, judges want to be perceived as impartial enough to preside over continuing proceedings, and imposing sanctions compromises this appearance. On the other hand, judges definitely will impose sanctions, sometimes.

[B] Self-Initiated Disclosures

Note on the Standard for Disclosures

Rule 26(a)(1) says that "a party must, without awaiting a discovery request," disclose persons or documents likely to have information "that the disclosing party may use to support its claims or defenses, unless the use would be solely for impeachment. . . ." This provision differs from other forms of discovery in that no request is necessary, and it is discussed in more detail later in this Chapter.

[C] Information That Is "Not Privileged"

Certain confidential communications are privileged in the sense that their disclosure cannot be compelled either at trial or during the discovery process. Privileges at common law include, among others, the attorney-client privilege, the physician-patient privilege, the psychotherapist-patient privilege, and a privilege for spousal communications. In civil actions where state law governs, as in diversity cases, privilege is a matter of state law. Fed. R. Evid. 501.

Upjohn Company v. United States

449 U.S. 383 (1981)

Justice Rehnquist delivered the opinion of the Court.

[This case involved the scope of the attorney-client privilege in the corporate context. Upjohn discovered that one of its subsidiaries had made "questionable payments" for the benefit of foreign officials to gain business abroad. Upjohn's General Counsel undertook a "highly confidential" investigation, during which he and outside counsel sent out written questionnaires and interviewed 33 employees. The company had to report certain information about the payments to the Securities and Exchange Commission and to the IRS. The IRS then undertook an investigation in which it demanded production of the answered questionnaires and interview notes. Upjohn refused, claiming attorney-client privilege.

[The court of appeals rejected the privilege. It adopted the so-called "control group" test, by which only those officers who were able to decide upon policy in response to legal advice were covered. It reasoned that the privilege did not apply to "communications . . . made by officers and agents not responsible for directing Upjohn's actions in response to legal advice . . . for the simple reason that the communications were not the 'client's.'" Communications with lower-level employees were not privileged. Only communications with the "control group" were covered.

[The Supreme Court reversed. It disapproved the control group test, because that test destroyed the privilege when an attorney needed to obtain facts from lower level employees, who might be the individuals who best knew them. Also, the control group test inhibited legal advice to employees outside the control group, who might be the implementers of the advice.] . . .

The attorney-client privilege is the oldest of the privileges for confidential communications known to the common law. Its purpose is to encourage full and frank communication between attorneys and their clients and thereby promote broader public interests in the observance of law and administration of justice. . . .

The communications in issue were made by Upjohn employees for Upjohn acting as such to secure legal counsel. . . . The communications concerned matters within the scope of the employees' corporate duties, and the employees themselves were sufficiently aware that they were being questioned in order that the corporation could obtain legal advice . . . . Pursuant to explicit instructions from the Chairman of the Board, the communications were considered "highly confidential" when made, and have been kept confidential by the company. . . .

The privilege only protects disclosure of communications; it does not protect disclosure of the underlying facts by those who communicated with the attorney. . . . Here the Government was free to question the employees who communicated with Thomas and outside counsel. Upjohn has provided the IRS with a list of such employees, and the IRS has already interviewed some 25 of them. . . . [REVERSED AND REMANDED.]

Notes and Questions

(1) *Waiver.* The protections afforded by a particular statutory or common law privilege can be waived by a client in appropriate circumstances. As a general rule, the law will imply a waiver whenever the holder of the privilege voluntarily discloses or allows to be disclosed any significant part of the privileged matter. But what if the disclosure is inadvertent? If a party produces hundreds of thousands (or even millions) of documents (and e-mails), it can easily include a privileged one by mistake. Rule 26(b)(5)(B) now addresses this issue, permitting a party who has produced information in discovery that is subject to a claim of privilege or work product to notify the recipient of this claim. Upon notice of such a claim, the recipient "must promptly return, sequester, or destroy the specified information and any copies it has."

(2) *Assistants and Investigators.* The privilege extends to representatives of both the client (as in *Upjohn*) and the attorney. For example, in *Ballew v. State*, 640 S.W.2d 237 (Tex. Crim. App. 1982), the court recognized that confidential communications to a psychiatrist retained by an attorney were within the protection of the privilege because they were used to render legal services.

(3) *Other Statutory Privileges.* As is indicated above, many states have statutory provisions for husband-wife, clergy-penitent, physician-patient, and psychotherapist-patient privileges. The privilege against self-incrimination is protected by the Constitution and has been asserted successfully in civil cases. Other possible privileges include an accountant-client privilege, a news reporter's privilege, a social worker-client privilege,

a privilege for trade secrets, and a privilege for professional peer review committees (such as those operating in hospitals). The existence and scope of these privileges vary from state to state.

(4) *How Do the Federal Courts Find Privileges? The Common Law.* Congress has been unable to agree on the text of rules to define privileges. Therefore, the federal courts find privileges in the common law, by "reason and experience." (Does that standard sound as though it would produce consistent or predictable results?) Consider the following case.

Doe v. Old Dominion University

289 F. Supp. 3d 744 (E.D. Va. 2018)

[A student brought an action under the pseudonym "Jane Doe" against the university, alleging discrimination in violation of Title IX on basis of sex, by subjecting her to an ongoing hostile educational environment after an on-campus sexual assault, and other claims. The university moved to compel production of documents.]

During discovery, Defendant requested that Plaintiff produce . . . all emails between Plaintiff . . . and her victim advocate. Plaintiff's privilege log indicates that there are more than one hundred fifty (150) such emails. Plaintiff objected to producing these emails, on the grounds that communications between sexual assault victims and their advocates are privileged. . . .

Plaintiff asserts the victim-advocate privilege, "whether by statute or otherwise, including, but not limited to," Section 63.2–104.1 of the Virginia Code." [This statute requires victim advocates to "protect the privacy and confidentiality of persons receiving services." The duty of nondisclosure, however, exists only if not "compelled by statutory or court mandate."]

Defendant argues that no such privilege exists, and that the Court should not create one in this case. Defendant argues that Plaintiff's citation to the Virginia Code is misplaced, because "this Title IX action involves a federal, not a state, claim . . . ." Defendant further argues that, even if state law did apply, the provision Plaintiff cited does not create a victim-advocate privilege. . . .

. . . [T]his Court has the authority "to define a new privilege by interpreting common law principles in light of reason and experience." Fed. R. Evid. 501; *Jaffee v. Redmond*, 518 U.S. 1, 8 (1996). Plaintiff argues that the Court should recognize a victim-advocate privilege in this case, for the same reasons the Supreme Court recognized a psychotherapist-patient privilege in *Jaffee v. Redmond.* In *Jaffee,* the Supreme Court articulated four (4) reasons for recognizing the privilege:

> 1. Successful psychotherapy "depends upon an atmosphere of confidence and trust in which the patient is willing to make a frank and complete disclosure . . . 2. The privilege "serves the public interest by facilitating the provision of appropriate treatment for individuals suffering the effects

of a mental or emotional problem" . . . . 3. "[T]he likely evidentiary benefit that would result from the denial of the privilege is modest. . . . Without a privilege, much of the desirable evidence to which litigants . . . seek access— for example, admissions . . . —is unlikely to come into being. . . . 4. "All 50 States and the District of Columbia have enacted into law some form of psychotherapist privilege."

[The court holds that all four conditions are met in the survivor's relationship with a victim advocate. There is a need for confidence and trust, the privilege serves the public interest by helping survivors to recover, the likely evidentiary benefit of denial of the privilege would be slight because survivors then would not confide in an advocate, and all states have adopted some form of confidentiality for victim advocates. However, the privilege, said the court, is not absolute but "qualified." The qualified nature of the privilege means that "communications otherwise protected . . . may be released, if the Court determines that their theoretical relevance outweighs the public policy in favor of keeping them confidential."

[The district judge next reviewed the emails between Doe and Dunn one by one, in camera, and ordered the disclosure of ten of them. Other emails, the court ruled, were privileged and nondiscoverable.]

Problem D

DISCOVERY RELEVANCE AND PRIVILEGE QUESTIONS RAISED IN SHAW v. SHOPPING CENTER ASSOCIATES, INC. Shaw brought suit to recover a brokerage commission allegedly due him in a case concerning a complex transaction to purchase an existing shopping center. During the deposition of Dr. Phillip Moskwitz, one of the limited partners in the venture, the plaintiff's attorney asked a number of questions concerning the witness' interpretation, as a layperson, of the legal meanings of several documents related to the transaction. He also asked about conversations with the deponent's attorney, undertaken in the presence of all the joint venturers, all of whom the attorney represented, as well as about the deponent's personal attorneys in matters unrelated to the subject of the suit. The following materials are adapted from a real case and fairly reflect the nature and substance of the actual questions, although the names have been changed and the questions have been altered for simplicity and continuity.

Excerpts from Certified Questions in the Deposition of Dr. Phillip Moskwitz:

Q: (by Mr. Jensen [plaintiff Shaw's attorney]): Now, doctor, you can read this little management and consulting agreement, which is just a little one-page form, right?

A: Yes, sir.

Q: It doesn't contain any legal terminology, does it?

Mr. Stone [defendant's attorney]: Just a minute. Whether or not a management agreement contains legal terminology and the meaning of it would be a legal question, and it obviously does contain legal terminology, because it's a contract.

Q: [ignoring defendant's counsel]: Why don't you just read that contract, doctor, and tell me what you think it means?

A: I don't understand what it means.

Q: Why don't you read it, first? And then tell me what you think it means, or what you understand it to mean, as a layman.

A: I frankly don't have any idea what it is. I've never seen it before, and I don't know how it relates to this lawsuit, if it does.

Mr. Stone: I don't think that asking a witness to interpret a legal document for counsel is a proper question.

Mr. Jensen: I am asking him what it means to him. It is a one-page, double spaced document that he can read in about 20 seconds.

Mr. Stone: I am going to instruct the witness not to do that.

Q: [ignoring defendant's attorney]: Now that the objection is on the record, you can go ahead and answer, if you would, sir.

Mr. Stone: Just a minute. [to the witness]: I am instructing you not to answer that question.

A: I'm going to follow my attorney's advice.

Mr. Stone: He is not going to answer that question. Ask him another one.

Mr. Jensen [to the court reporter]: Certify the question [*i.e.*, "Transcribe that series of questions separately for use in connection with a motion to the court to compel answers"].

Q: [by Mr. Jensen]: Now, doctor, do you presently have a lawyer or lawyers with whom you consult on business other than what's related to this suit?

The Witness: I personally feel it's a private matter, because I consult attorneys about all kinds of matters, in all kinds of firms. I don't think that has to be brought out in this lawsuit.

Mr. Stone: Well, I will instruct the witness not to answer about what matters he may have consulted whatever other attorneys on, in matters unrelated to this lawsuit or to the shopping center deal that is at issue here.

Q: [by Mr. Jensen]: Are you going to answer my question, sir?

A: Absolutely not.

Mr. Jensen: Certify the question.

Q: Now, have you had any lawyers whom you have consulted on your personal matters since the date of this shopping center matter?

A: That's the same question as before!

Mr. Stone: I will instruct the witness not to answer.

Q: Are you going to answer my question, sir?

A: No, sir.

Mr. Jensen: Certify the question.

Q: Now, I want to talk to you about a meeting that took place after my client, Mr. Shaw, contacted Shopping Center Associates about his brokerage fee, with you and Mr. Williamson and possibly other people. Please tell me what the conversation was at that meeting.

Mr. Stone: Just a minute. Mr. Williamson was your lawyer then?

The Witness: Yes. And he served as the business manager and accountant for the venture.

Mr. Stone: And the other people present, did he represent them? Were they the other people in the venture with you?

The Witness: Yes, to my knowledge.

Mr. Stone: And did he give you legal advice, or did you discuss legal matters confidentially?

The Witness: Yes, sir.

Mr. Stone: I object to the question on grounds it is privileged, and I'm going to instruct the witness not to answer.

Q: But now that the objection is on the record, you can go ahead and answer the question, doctor.

Mr. Stone: Just a minute. [To the witness:] Don't answer the question. Just say, I'm not going to answer.

A [The Witness]: I'm not going to answer.

Q: Now, what was the subject of the discussions?

Mr. Stone: Just a minute. He's not going to answer that.

Mr. Jensen: Certify the question.

---

(1) *Relevance.* Consider the relevance, in discovery terms, of (a) asking a lay witness to interpret the meaning of a contract that forms a part of the transaction, but that she has never seen; (b) asking the witness to name her personal lawyers in unrelated matters; (c) asking the witness to detail discussions with her attorney-business manager-accountant.

(2) *Privilege.* Is the claim of privilege well taken? [What if the discussion at the "meeting" concerned accounting or business matters that, although confidential, were relevant to the suit?]

(3) *Persistent Questions, Objections, and Instructions to the Witness.* Why does Mr. Jensen ignore the objections and continue to urge the witness to answer? [Suggestion: What would be the result if Mr. Stone was asleep at the switch, and the witness happened to answer a general question about the discussions at the meeting?] Why does Mr. Stone not merely object, but also specifically instruct the witness not to answer? Notice that some of the questions—including those dealing with the witness' lay interpretation of legal questions and the identities of his other lawyers—probably wouldn't be harmful to the substance of the lawsuit if the witness answered. And answering would remove the controversy over those items. Why shouldn't Mr. Stone just tell his client to answer them? And—perhaps the most puzzling question—why did the real "Mr. Jensen" ask these questions? [Suggestion: There is a fair amount of gamesmanship in some lawsuits.]

[D] Work Product and Related Exceptions

[1] Trial Preparation Materials

The Problem. Imagine that, in the course of discovery, one party serves upon the other a request for production of "the entire file maintained by your attorney relating to this case, and all documents that are included in it, except those that are covered by the attorney-client privilege." This request would cover the attorney's investigation and research, including notes of witness interviews, diagrams, written statements by anyone other than the client, legal memoranda, etc. The contents of the lawyer's file clearly would be "relevant" in the discovery sense, and they would not be "privileged" except insofar as they embodied confidential communications between attorney and client (as opposed to information obtained from other sources).

The Invention of the "Work Product" Doctrine: Hickman v. Taylor. At the time the following case (*Hickman v. Taylor*) arose, the Rules did not address this kind of discovery request. It presumably would be possible to set up a fair system of procedure in which discovery this broad would be allowed, but our system, by deliberate design, is maintained as an "adversary" system. *Cf.* Waits, *Work Product Protection for Witness Statements: Time for Abolition*, 1985 Wis. L. Rev. 305. In *Hickman*, the courts invented the phrase "work product of the lawyer" to describe this kind of information. Today, Rule 26(b)(3) codifies a conditional protection for attorneys' "trial preparation" materials.

Read Fed. R. Civ. P. 26(b)(3) (trial preparation materials or "work product").

Hickman v. Taylor

329 U.S. 495 (1947)

Mr. Justice Murphy delivered the opinion of the Court.

[This case arose out of the sinking of the tugboat "J.M. Taylor." Five of the nine crew members drowned. Three days after the tug sank, the owners and their insurers hired a law firm to investigate potential claims. Fortenbaugh, one of the members of the defendants' law firm, interviewed the survivors and took signed witness statements from them "with an eye toward the anticipated litigation." Fortenbaugh also interviewed other persons, and in some cases he made memoranda of what they told him. Later, a public hearing was held, at which most of these witnesses testified, and their testimony was publicly available.

[Ultimately, one of the survivors' representatives brought suit in federal court. The claimant's attorney made a discovery request for "copies of all statements of the [witnesses] if in writing, and if oral ... the exact provisions of any such oral statements or reports."

[The tug owners resisted discovery of the written statements and refused to summarize or set forth the contents of the oral communications on the ground that "such requests called for 'privileged matter obtained in preparation for litigation.'"]

[The District Court ordered discovery. The Third Circuit reversed. The Supreme Court granted certiorari.] ...

In urging that he has a right to inquire into the materials secured and prepared by Fortenbaugh, petitioner emphasizes that the deposition-discovery portions of the Federal Rules of Civil Procedure are designed to enable the parties to discover the true facts and to compel their disclosure wherever they may be found.... [S]ince the discovery provisions are to be applied as broadly and liberally as possible, the [attorney-client] privilege limitation must be restricted to its narrowest bounds.... And since the materials here in issue were secured by Fortenbaugh from third persons rather than from his clients, the tug owners, the conclusion is reached that these materials are proper subjects for discovery under Rule 26....

We agree, of course, that the deposition-discovery rules are to be accorded a broad and liberal treatment. No longer can the time-honored cry of "fishing expedition" serve to preclude a party from inquiring into the facts underlying his opponent's case.... But discovery, like all matters of procedure, has ultimate and necessary boundaries....

We also agree that the memoranda, statements and mental impressions in issue in this case fall outside the scope of the attorney-client privilege and hence are not protected from discovery on that basis....

... [But p]etitioner has made more than an ordinary request for relevant, non-privileged facts.... He has sought discovery as of right of oral and written statements of witnesses whose identity is well known and whose availability to petitioner appears unimpaired. . . . Interrogatories were directed toward all the events prior to, during and subsequent to the sinking of the tug. Full and honest answers to such broad inquiries would necessarily have included all pertinent information gleaned by Fortenbaugh through his interviews with the witnesses . . . . We are thus dealing with an attempt to secure the production of written statements and mental impressions contained in the files and the mind of the attorney Fortenbaugh . . . .

In our opinion, neither Rule 26 nor any other rule dealing with discovery contemplates production under such circumstances. That is not because the subject matter is privileged or irrelevant . . . . It falls outside the arena of discovery and contravenes the public policy underlying the orderly prosecution and defense of legal claims. . . .

. . . [These materials were] aptly though roughly termed by the Circuit Court of Appeals in this case as the "work product of the lawyer." Were such materials open to opposing counsel on mere demand, much of what is now put down in writing would remain unwritten. An attorney's thoughts, heretofore inviolate, would not be his own. Inefficiency, unfairness and sharp practices would inevitably develop in the giving of legal advice and in the preparation of cases for trial. The effect on the legal profession would be demoralizing. And the interests of the clients and the cause of justice would be poorly served.

We do not mean to say that all written materials obtained or prepared by an adversary's counsel with an eye toward litigation are necessarily free from discovery in all cases. Where relevant and non-privileged facts remain hidden in an attorney's file and where production of those facts is essential to the preparation of one's case, discovery may properly be had . . . . And production might be justified where the witnesses are no longer available or can be reached only with difficulty. . . . But the general policy against invading the privacy of an attorney's course of preparation is . . . well recognized . . . . [A] burden rests on the one who would invade that privacy to establish adequate reasons to justify production through a subpoena or court order. . . .

But as to oral statements made by witnesses to Fortenbaugh, whether presently in the form of his mental impressions or memoranda, we do not believe that any showing of necessity can be made under the circumstances of this case so as to justify production. . . . Such testimony could not qualify as evidence; and to use it for impeachment or corroborative purposes would make the attorney much less an officer of the court and much more an ordinary witness. The standards of the profession would thereby suffer.

Denial of production of this nature does not mean that any material, non-privileged facts can be hidden from the petitioner in this case. . . . Searching interrogatories directed to Fortenbaugh and the tug owners, production of written documents and statements upon a proper showing, and direct interviews with the witnesses themselves all serve to reveal the facts in Fortenbaugh's possession to the fullest possible extent consistent with public policy. Petitioner's counsel frankly admits that he wants the oral statements only to help prepare himself to examine witnesses and to make sure that he has overlooked nothing. That is insufficient.... [AFFIRMED.] ...

MR. JUSTICE JACKSON, concurring.

[Justice Jackson pointed out that the demand for counsel's recollection of oral statements was particularly troublesome. "I can conceive of no practice more demoralizing to the Bar than to require a lawyer to write out and deliver to his adversary an account of what witnesses have told him.... [T]he statement would be his language permeated with his inferences. Everyone who has tried it knows it is almost impossible so fairly to record the expressions and emphasis of a witness that when he testifies in the environment of the court and under the influence of the leading question there will not be departures in some respects." And whenever the witness varied from the lawyer's account, the lawyer would be called by the adversary as an impeaching witness. "Counsel producing his adversary's 'inexact' statement could lose nothing by saying, 'Here is a contradiction, ladies and gentlemen of the jury. I do not know whether it is my adversary or his witness who is not telling the truth, but one is not.'"

[But above all, Justice Jackson emphasized that "a common law trial is and always should be an adversary proceeding. Discovery was hardly intended to enable a learned profession to perform its functions either without wits or on wits borrowed from the adversary."]

Bank of the Orient v. Superior Court

67 Cal. App. 3d 588, 136 Cal. Rptr. 741 (1977).

TAYLOR, Presiding Justice.

[San Francisco Federal Savings Association sued Bank of the Orient, claiming that the Bank had permitted one of San Francisco Federal's branch managers to deposit unauthorized checks in his personal account at the Bank and, further, had negligently permitted him to withdraw, and thereby embezzle, the funds. During the course of discovery, the Bank sought to obtain production of a report by an accounting firm (the "Coopers & Lybrand report") commissioned by San Francisco Federal's board of directors two days after the discovery of the embezzlement, as well as a special audit committee report entitled "Suggestions for Improvement to Our System of Internal Control." Both reports contained details of the manner in which the embezzlement occurred and discussed weaknesses in the Association's internal auditing procedures.

[San Francisco Federal claimed that the reports were not discoverable. First, section 1151 of the California Evidence Code provided that subsequent remedial measures are not admissible in evidence to prove fault: "When ... remedial or precautionary measures are taken, which ... would have tended to make the event less likely to occur, evidence of such subsequent remedial measures is inadmissible to prove negligence or culpable conduct." The reports were subsequent remedial measures and not discoverable, said San Francisco Federal.

[Second, San Francisco Federal argued that the reports were work product or "trial preparation materials" and therefore exempt from discovery.

[The court of appeal, however, here holds that the reports are discoverable. As to the first objection, even though they might not be admissible in evidence themselves, the reports obviously were likely to lead to admissible evidence (and by today's standards, they would have been proportional: just two documents). As to the second objection, the reports were not work product or trial preparation materials:]

Evidence Code section 1151 [does not] provide support for [San Francisco Federal's] refusal to produce documents or to answer questions related thereto.... [T]he section is a prohibition on the admissibility of evidence at trial. It does not purport to limit the scope of discovery....

We conclude that the refusal of the [trial] court to compel production of the Coopers & Lybrand report and the document entitled "Suggestions for Improvement to Our System of Internal Control" was an abuse of discretion....

[Also, the reports were not trial preparation materials.] [T]he Coopers & Lybrand report was requested by the board of directors of plaintiff.... Thus, as [the Bank] points out, the report was commissioned not by an attorney but by the board of directors, some four months prior to the time the complaint was filed. A report which is not the product of the attorney or his agents or employees is not work product, and an attorney "cannot, by retroactive adoption, convert the independent work of another, already performed, into his own." ... [Ed. Note: The result may be correct, but is this really the reason the reports are not work product or trial preparation materials?]

SPORCK v. PEIL, 759 F.2d 312 (3d Cir. 1985). This case concerned so-called "opinion work product," or discovery invading the mental impressions of an attorney. During pretrial discovery in a securities fraud action, plaintiff Peil served numerous sets of combined interrogatory and document requests on the defendants. Defendants produced hundreds of thousands of documents. Thereafter, counsel for defendant Sporck prepared him for deposition by showing him "an unknown quantity of the numerous documents produced by defendants in response to plaintiff's discovery requests." These documents had been "selected" and "compiled" by defense counsel and "the selected documents represented, as a group, counsel's legal opinion as to the evidence relevant both to the allegations in the case and the possible legal defenses." None of the individual documents contained work product.

At Sporck's deposition and later by written motion pursuant to Federal Rule 34, Peil's counsel requested production of "[a]ll documents examined, reviewed or referred to by Charles E. Sporck in preparation for the session of his deposition."

Defense counsel objected because the documents had already been produced and because the selection and grouping of the documents constituted work product, even if the documents, taken individually, did not. Peil filed a motion to compel production of the selected documents. The district judge granted the motion. Sporck sought a writ of mandamus. The Third Circuit concluded that the district judge had committed an error in ordering production because "the selection and compilation of documents by counsel in this case in preparation for pretrial discovery falls within the highly protected category of opinion work product."

After noting that Federal Rule 26(b)(3) recognizes the distinction between "ordinary" work product which can be invaded on the moving party's "showing of substantial need and undue hardship" and "opinion" work product which remains entitled to protection despite "need" and "hardship," the Circuit Court explained that:

> [o]pinion work product includes such items as an attorney's legal strategy, his intended lines of proof, his evaluation of the strengths and weaknesses of his case, and the inferences he draws from interviews of witnesses. . . . Such material is accorded almost absolute protection from discovery because any slight factual content that such items may have is generally outweighed by the adversary system's interest in maintaining the privacy of an attorney's thought processes and in ensuring that each side relies on its own wit in preparing their respective cases.

Notes and Questions

(1) *Materials Prepared by Agents of an Attorney: United States v. Nobles*, 422 U.S. 225, 238–39 (1975). One of the aspects of the work product doctrine left unanswered by *Hickman v. Taylor* was whether materials prepared by an attorney's agent in anticipation of litigation were likewise entitled to a qualified immunity from discovery. In *United States v. Nobles*, the Supreme Court answered the question affirmatively:

> One of the realities is that attorneys often must rely on the assistance of investigators and other agents in the compilation of materials in preparation for trial. It is therefore necessary that the doctrine protect material prepared by agents for the attorney as well as those prepared by the attorney himself.

See generally Special Project, *The Work Product Doctrine*, 68 Cornell L. Rev. 760 (1983). *See also* E. Thornburg, *Rethinking Work Product*, 77 Va. L. Rev. 1515 (1991).

(2) *Materials Prepared by a Party or Its Agents in Anticipation of Litigation.* The *Bank of the Orient* case holds that "A report which is not the product of the attorney or of his agents or employees is not an attorney work product, and an attorney 'cannot, by retroactive adoption, convert the independent work of another, already performed, into his own.'" This view is too narrow. Imagine that the party, in that case, had undertaken to investigate the matter using its own employees, and it did so precisely because it expected a lawsuit but had not had time to hire an attorney.

The text of the Rule protects the findings. Can the *Bank of the Orient* case better be rationalized by observing that the reports were not prepared in anticipation of litigation, but instead were intended to improve the plaintiff's compliance systems and internal controls?

(3) *Anticipation of Litigation.* When is a report prepared in anticipation of litigation or in preparation for trial? Consider an accident report prepared by a bus driver, and required by the company every time there is an accident, or a hospital "incident report" if hospital employees are directed to prepare one every time an accident occurs. Work product does not apply (although a hospital privilege might). *See* Note, *The Work Product Doctrine: Why Have an Ordinary Course of Business Exception?*, 1988 COLUM. BUS. L. REV. 587.

[2] Testifying Experts and Consultants

> Read Fed. R. Civ. P. 26(b)(4) (trial preparation—experts).

Ager v. Jane C. Stormont Hospital & Training, Etc.

622 F.2d 496 (10th Cir. 1980)

[Emily Ager filed a medical malpractice case in which she alleged that the negligence of Dr. Dan L. Tappen, together with that of the Hospital, "joined and concurred in causing plaintiff's mother's death and plaintiff's bodily injuries and damages and resultant disability." Dr. Tappen propounded the following interrogatories to the plaintiff:]

1. Have you contacted any person or persons, whether they are going to testify or not, in regard to the care and treatment rendered by Dr. Dan Tappen involved herein?
2. If the answer to the question immediately above is in the affirmative, please set forth the name of said person or persons and their present residential and/or business addresses.
3. If the answer to question #1 is in the affirmative, do you have any statements or written reports from said person or persons?

[The plaintiff objected to the interrogatories. Dr. Tappen sought relief in the form of an order compelling discovery. The United States Magistrate ordered the plaintiff to answer the interrogatories but ruled that the plaintiff need not identify "an expert who was informally consulted in preparation for trial, but who was never retained or specially employed and will not be called as a witness."]

[The plaintiff's counsel answered the interrogatories in part, but failed to provide any information concerning experts not expected to testify. Ultimately, the District

Court held the plaintiff's lawyer in contempt because of his refusal to comply. Execution of the order was stayed pending appeal.]

[After determining that the viability of the order of contempt depended upon the validity of the underlying discovery order, the Court of Appeals considered the subject of expert discovery in detail. It set forth the provisions of Rule 26(b)(4), which the court said separates experts into four categories: (1) experts expected to testify at trial; (2) consultants "retained or specially employed" for the litigation, but not expected to testify; (3) experts consulted informally, and not "retained or specially employed"; and (4) experts contacted for purposes unrelated to the litigation. "We are here concerned," said the court, "only with the second and third category of experts"—experts retained or informally consulted by a party, but not expected to testify at trial.]

A. Discovery of Experts Informally Consulted, but Not Retained or Specially Employed

No provision in . . . Rule 26(b)(4) . . . expressly deals with non-witness experts who are informally consulted by a party in preparation for trial, but not retained or specially employed in anticipation of litigation. The advisory committee notes to the rule indicate, however, that subdivision (b)(4)(B) "precludes discovery against experts who [are] informally consulted in preparation for trial, but not retained or specially employed." We agree with the District Court that this preclusion not only encompasses information and opinions developed in anticipation of litigation, but also insulates discovery of the identity and other collateral information concerning experts consulted informally. . . .

Ager urges that "an 'expert' would be considered informally consulted if, for any reason, the consulting party did not consider the expert of any assistance," and that "[a] consulting party may consider the expert of no assistance because of his insufficient credentials, his unattractive demeanor, or his excessive fees.'" . . . This view is, of course, at odds with the Trial Court's ruling that:

> If one makes an appointment with a medical expert to discuss a case or examine records and give advice or opinion for which a charge is made and the charge is paid or promised—what is informal about such consultation? On the other hand, [if] an attorney meets a doctor friend at a social occasion or on the golf course and a discussion occurs concerning the case—no charge is made or contemplated—no written report rendered—such could clearly . . . be an "informal consultation." . . .

We decline to embrace either approach in its entirety. In our view, the status for each expert must be determined on an *ad hoc* basis. Several factors should be considered: (1) the manner in which the consultation was initiated; (2) the nature, type and extent of information or material provided to, or determined by, the expert in connection with his review; (3) the duration and intensity of the consultative relationship; and (4) the terms of the consultation, if any (*e.g.*, payment, confidentiality of test data or opinions, etc.). Of course, additional factors bearing on this determination may be examined if relevant. . . .

. . . If the expert is considered to have been only informally consulted in anticipation of litigation, discovery is barred.

B. Discovery of the Identities of Experts Retained or Specially Employed

Subdivision (b)(4)(B) of Rule 26 specifically deals with non-witness experts who have been retained or specially employed by a party in anticipation of litigation. The text of that subdivision provides that "facts [known] or opinions [held]" by non-witness experts retained or specially employed may only be discovered upon a showing of "exceptional circumstances under which it is impracticable for the party to obtain facts or opinions on the same subject by other means." Inasmuch as discovery of the identities of these experts, absent a showing of exceptional circumstances, was not expressly precluded by the text of subdivision (b)(4)(B), the District Court found the general provisions of Rule 26(b)(1) controlling. . . .

The advisory committee notes indicate that the structure of Rule 26 was largely developed around the doctrine of unfairness—designed to prevent a party from building his own case by means of his opponent's financial resources, superior diligence and more aggressive preparation. Dr. Tappen contends that "[d]iscoverability of the identity of an expert [h]ardly gives the discovering party a material advantage or benefit at the expense of the opposing party's preparation. Once those identities are disclosed, the discovering party is left to his own diligence and resourcefulness in contacting such experts and seeking to enlist whatever assistance they may be both able and willing to offer." The drafters of Rule 26 did not contemplate such a result:

> [A]s an ancillary procedure, a party may *on a proper showing* require the other party to *name* experts retained or specially employed, but not those informally consulted. [Emphasis supplied.] . . .

There are several policy considerations supporting our view. Contrary to Dr. Tappen's view, once the identities of retained or specially employed experts are disclosed, the protective provisions of the rule concerning facts known or opinions held by such experts are subverted. The expert may be contacted or his records obtained and information normally non-discoverable, under Rule 26(b)(4)(B), revealed. Similarly, although perhaps rarer, the opponent may attempt to compel an expert retained or specially employed by an adverse party in anticipation of trial, but whom the adverse party does not intend to call, to testify at trial. *Kaufman v. Edelstein*, 539 F.2d 811 (2d Cir. 1976). . . . Finally, we agree with Ager's view that "[d]isclosure of the identities of [medical] consultative experts would inevitably lessen the number of candid opinions available as well as the number of consultants willing to even discuss a potential medical malpractice claim with counsel. . . . If one assumes that access to informed opinions is desirable in both prosecuting valid claims and eliminating groundless ones, a discovery practice that would do harm to these objectives should not be condoned."

In sum, we hold that the identity, and other collateral information concerning an expert who is retained or specially employed in anticipation of litigation, but not expected to be called as a witness at trial, is not discoverable except as "provided in Rule 35(b) or [on showing] exceptional circumstances under which it is impracticable for the party . . . to obtain facts or opinions on the same subject by other means."(8) . . .

Disposition

. . . On remand, the status of the non-witness experts against whom discovery is sought should be undertaken as a two-step process. First, was the expert informally consulted in anticipation of litigation but not retained or specially employed? If so, no discovery may be had . . . . Second, if the expert *was not* informally consulted, but rather retained or specially employed in anticipation of litigation, but not expected to testify at trial, do exceptional circumstances exist justifying disclosure of the expert's identity, opinions or other collateral information?

Problem E

DISCOVERY FROM EXPERTS. How would the following experts be treated under the current Federal Rule? (a) Expert A, consulted over the telephone by Ms. Ager's counsel about Dr. Tappen's general reputation, who will not testify at trial and who has not helped in the preparation of the case; (b) Expert B, consulted in connection with the case and who will testify at a hearing or trial; (c) Expert C, consulted in connection with the case for compensation and to prepare Expert B for cross-examination; (d) Expert D, who was not consulted in connection with any litigation, but who has assisted the defendant in complying with health and safety regulations before the event giving rise to the litigation occurred. *See generally* Day, *Expert Discovery in the Eighth Circuit: An Empirical Study*, 122 F.R.D. 35 (1988); Note, *Blind Man's Bluff: An Analysis of the Discovery of Expert Witnesses Under Federal Rule of Civil Procedure 26(b)(4) and a Proposed Amendment*, 64 IND. L.J. 925 (1989); Note, *Gimme Shelter? Not If You Are a Non-Witness Expert Under Rule 26(b)(4)(B)*, 56 U. CIN. L. REV. 1027 (1988).

---

(8) Professor Albert Sacks, reporter to the advisory committee, listed two examples of exceptional circumstances at a Practicing Law Institute Seminar on Discovery held in Atlanta, Georgia, September 25–26, 1970:

> (a) Circumstances in which an expert employed by the party seeking discovery could not conduct important experiments and test[s] because an item of equipment, etc., needed for the test[s] has been destroyed or is otherwise no longer available. If the party from whom discovery is sought had been able to have its experts test the item before its destruction or nonavailability, then information obtained from those tests might be discoverable.
>
> (b) Circumstances in which it might be impossible for a party to obtain its own expert. Such circumstances would occur when the number of experts in a field is small and their time is already fully retained by others.

See: ALI-ABA, *Civil Trial Manual* p. 189.

Notes and Questions

(1) *State Rules with Broader or Narrower Coverage.* The subject of discovery from experts is extremely important. *See* Note, *Discovery of Retained Nontestifying Experts' Identities under the Federal Rules of Civil Procedure*, 80 MICH. L. REV. 513 (1982). The subject therefore is given elaborate treatment in the Federal Rules and in many state provisions regarding discovery. Rule 193.3 of the Texas Rules of Civil Procedure appears to allow broader discovery than the Federal Rules because it authorizes discovery from a non-testifying consultant "whose mental impressions or opinions have been reviewed by a testifying expert." New York State's CPLR 3101(d) appears somewhat more restrictive of discovery than both the Texas and Federal Rules.

(2) *Expert Used in the Party's Ordinary Business: Marine Petroleum Co. v. Champlin Petroleum Co.*, 641 F.2d 984 (D.C. Cir. 1979). An expert who was not contacted in connection with existing or expected litigation—such as a staff engineer or intern at a hospital that is a party—is not ordinarily shielded from discovery. But suppose the expert is hired initially in an operational capacity, not in anticipation of litigation, and that the expert later is asked to provide consultation in defending against a particular claim, but without testifying. In *Marine Petroleum Co.*, the court held that the discovering party could obtain discovery of facts known or opinions held by the expert before his role changed, but not with respect to information developed thereafter, absent exceptional circumstances. *See also* Note, *The In-House Expert Witness: Discovery Under the Federal Rules of Civil Procedure*, 33 S.D. L. REV. 283 (1988).

(3) *Determination of Expert's Status: "Gamesmanship."* Attorneys often are motivated to engage in "gamesmanship" about identities of experts. By delaying disclosure, they may hope to react to their opponents' designations, keep their adversaries in the dark, or hold their own options open. Thus, it often happens that an interrogatory, asking a party to identify experts whom that party anticipates calling at trial, is answered by the sentence: "This has not been determined." When does the matter have to be determined? *See* Fed. R. Civ. P. 26(e) (party has duty to supplement answers regarding experts "by the time the party's pretrial disclosures under Rule 26(a)(3) are due"); *see also* Fed. R. Civ. P. 26(a)(2) (party must disclose identity of expert witnesses "at least 90 days before the date set for trial or for the case to be ready for trial"). *Compare Washington Hospital Center v. Cheeks*, 394 F.2d 964 (D.C. Cir. 1968) (trial recess granted to take deposition of undisclosed expert), *with Tabatchnick v. G.D. Searle & Co.*, 67 F.R.D. 49 (1975) (excluding testimony of expert). *See* Day, *Discovery Standards for the Testimonial Expert Under Federal Rule of Civil Procedure 26(b)(4): A Twentieth Anniversary Assessment*, 133 F.R.D. 209 (1991).

[E] Protective Orders

Read Fed. R. Civ. P. 26(b)(2), (c)-(d) (limitations on discovery scope; protective orders; sequence and timing of discovery); Fed. R. Civ. P. 30(a)(2) and 30(d)(4) (limits on taking oral depositions).

Note on Standards for Protective Orders

A Three-Stage Balancing Test? Centurion Industries, Inc. v. Warren Steurer & Assoc., 665 F.2d 323 (10th Cir. 1981). A protective order is issued to protect a party or witness from otherwise valid discovery that, under the circumstances, would cause annoyance, embarrassment, or an undue burden. But all litigation is annoying and burdensome, so more than generalities are required. *Centurion* suggests a three-step process: (1) the movant shows the amount of specific harm that would result from the discovery, (2) the opponent shows the magnitude of particularized need for the information, and (3) the district judge balances the two. (Your clients will be shocked to learn that their rights depend upon an unorganized balancing by the judge.)

Balancing: An Ad Hoc Process. But the test is often stated with less exactness than in *Centurion.* The court may simply balance without articulating what it is balancing. Or the court may require specific harm from the movant and balance without identifying the values on the other side. Or the court may emphasize the thoroughness of judicial inquiry into the movant's showing, as the court in the following case does, no doubt because of the issues involved.

In re Ohio Execution Protocol Litigation

845 F.3d 231 (6th Cir. 2016)

Siler, Circuit Judge.

Plaintiffs are Ohio death-row inmates challenging Ohio's execution protocol and practice. Defendants include Ohio officials as well as anonymous drug manufacturers, compounders, intermediaries, and others involved in Ohio's execution process. Plaintiffs appeal from a district court's entry of a protective order precluding the disclosure of any information that could reveal the identity of suppliers or manufacturers of Ohio's legal-injection drugs. . . . During the pendency of this appeal, we affirmed a related appeal from an order dismissing certain constitutional challenges to Ohio's execution protocol. *Phillips v. DeWine,* 841 F.3d 405 (6th Cir.2016). We now AFFIRM the entry of the protective order. . . .

I.

Ohio enacted legislation . . . to address confidentiality of information about lethal injection in Ohio. The secrecy statute precludes the release of information that would identify the manufacturer or supplier of drugs for use in Ohio's lethal-injection protocol. . . . [The state statute is not dispositive in this federal case but is a relevant consideration.]

. . . Defendants moved for a protective order to prevent the release of any information in their possession that could identify the sources of Ohio's lethal-injection drugs. After hearing evidence and testimony from four witnesses, the district court granted the motion and issued the following protective order:

> The Court therefore ORDERS that any information . . . in Defendants' . . . control that identifies . . . any person or entity who participates in the acquisition or use of the specific drugs . . . that Ohio indicates in its execution protocol it will use . . . to carry out executions, is protected and not subject to discovery. . . .

Plaintiffs moved for a modification that would permit limited disclosures to counsel only under the designation "attorney's eyes only." The district court denied the motion, noting that "disclosure of identities subjects the disclosed persons or entities to suit."

. . . [T]he parties notified the court that Ohio plans to move forward with three scheduled executions . . . . Defendants represented that they intend to use a new three-drug protocol: midazolam hydrochloride, potassium chloride, and one of the following drugs: procuronium bromide, vecuronium bromide, or pancuronium bromide. The new protocol mirrors the Oklahoma protocol [approved] by the Supreme Court. . . .

II.

Under Federal Rule of Civil Procedure 26(c)(1), a district court may grant a protective order preventing the production of discovery to protect a party or entity from "annoyance, embarrassment, oppression, or undue burden or expense." Fed. R. Civ. P. 26(c)(1). We review the grant of a protective order for abuse of discretion. *Serrano v. Cintas Corp.*, 699 F.3d 884, 899–900 (6th Cir. 2012). . . .

III.

Plaintiffs argue that the protective order prevents the prosecution of their federal and state causes of action. Plaintiffs maintain that the protective order is contrary to law because the order cuts off all discovery on Ohio's execution procedures . . . .

[Plaintiffs also argue that t]he protective order runs afoul with Rule 26(c) . . . because Defendants failed to make particular and specific demonstrations of harm. . . . Plaintiffs suggest that the district court . . . rel[ied] on generalized . . . harm suffered from the risk of threats, intimidation, and harassment. . . . According to Plaintiffs, the record is devoid of evidence that, but for the protective order, Ohio could not carry out executions because of harm to drug manufacturers upon discovery of their identities. . . . But even so, according to Plaintiffs, Defendants failed to produce or point to any credible, specific evidence in the record to demonstrate an inability to obtain lethal-injection drugs or to carry out executions in the absence of a protective order.

Plaintiffs posit that even if evidence exists of harm to Defendants, the harm caused by cutting off discovery in this case outweighs the harms attributed to Defendants.... We disagree and conclude that the district court did not abuse its discretion when entering the protective order.

A.

To sustain a protective order under Rule 26(c), the moving party must show "good cause" for protection from one (or more) harms identified in Rule 26(c)(1)(A) "with a particular and specific demonstration of fact, as distinguished from stereotyped and conclusory statements." *Serrano*..... Good cause exists if "specific prejudice or harm will result" from the absence of a protective order. *Father M. v. Various Tort Claimants (In re Roman Catholic Archbishop)*, 661 F.3d 417, 424 (9th Cir. 2011). [Note: as in this cited case, litigation involving priests sexually abusing children generated several protective orders; can you see why?—Eds.] A court must balance the "right to discovery with the need to prevent 'fishing expeditions.'" *Serrano*.

B.

... [T]he district court found that the disclosures would cause an undue burden on and prejudice Defendants by subjecting them to the risk of harm, violence, and harassment and by making it difficult for them to obtain lethal-injection drugs.... True, the record lacks an affidavit from an Ohio manufacturer under duress or direct evidence from one of Ohio's drug sources; still, the accumulation of evidence favors a protective order....

The district court scrutinized with care Ohio's representations, probing whether Defendants (either directly or derivatively) suffered a burden or prejudice from identifying certain entities in association with lethal injection. For example, Defendants produced a privilege log on the eve of the evidentiary hearing, which identified persons or entities that have applied for statutory protection from disclosure.... Without legitimate dispute, the district court was appraised of how Ohio has been hobbled in its efforts to perform executions. Amid the stalled status of executions in Ohio, the district court observed, "[i]f execution by lethal injection is legal, and the United States Supreme Court has repeatedly said it is, then it follows that there must be some manner of carrying it out." ... In view of witness testimony and other evidence about Ohio's execution history, the district court found that "[i]f the question is whether a reasonable pharmacy owner or compounder would feel burdened by [receiving threats,] the answer is likely if not certainly yes."

Record evidence supports the district court's finding of "a particular and specific demonstration of fact, as distinguished from stereotyped and conclusory statements," of Defendants' burden and prejudice in the absence of the protective order. *Serrano*.... It is as if Plaintiffs seek to impose a summary-judgment evidentiary standard when Rule 26(c) merely requires the district court to weigh evidence against the movant's burden.... To ignore Defendants' interest in a capability to perform executions is to ignore the elephant in the room....

C.

. . . That Defendants could have provided more evidence by offering execution team members behind a screen or affidavits from drug sources has no moment. Plaintiffs fail to cite case law compelling Defendants to submit for screened inquisition individuals for which they seek protection. . . . In addition, the district court did not err in rejecting Plaintiffs' request to designate certain information subject to the protective order as "attorney's eyes only." Taken to an extreme, all protective orders could be circumvented by requesting that otherwise undiscoverable information be made available for use by counsel only.

. . . [T]he protective order does not stonewall Plaintiffs' efforts to obtain relief. Should Plaintiffs seek to obtain samples of the drugs and their independent testing reveal irregularities (or if salient information from other sources comes to light), such events could generate cause for greater investigation and modification of the protective order.

IV.

. . . We therefore AFFIRM because the district court did not abuse its discretion in entering the protective order.

[The dissenting opinion of Judge Stranch, which concludes that the Defendants failed to make a sufficient showing of harm and that the harm to the plaintiffs in impairment of their ability to discover their claims outweighed any harm to Defendants, is omitted here.]

Problem F

VARIETIES AND METHODS OF PROTECTIVE ORDERS: CONSIDERING A TRADE SECRET CASE. Protective orders are important in cases involving trade secrets (like the *Centurion* case cited above). Trade secrets need protection, but they are so pervasive that business disputes often cannot be litigated without discovery of them. Would the trial court abuse its discretion, in a case like *Centurion,* involving computer software: (1) If it entered a protective order absolutely prohibiting discovery of software trade secrets that were important to the case? (2) If it appointed a "neutral" expert to receive the information from the affected party, and to convey it to the discovering party, in such quantity and form as to maximize knowledge of the facts relevant to the lawsuit while minimizing the competitive disadvantage created? *Cf. Triangle Mfg. Co. v. Paramount Bag Mfg. Co.*, 35 F.R.D. 540 (E.D.N.Y. 1964) (trial judge ordered "impartial third party" to give discoverer "the maximum amount of information while at the same time maintaining the secrecy of the actual" underlying trade secrets). (3) If it had limited discovery to written questions, rather than document production or depositions, in the hope that unnecessary invasion of trade secrets thus could be minimized? And, (4), a final question: Assuming that various alternatives might be within the court's discretion, how should the court go about deciding which alternative to choose (*i.e.*, which approach is "best")?

Notes and Questions

(1) *"Good Cause": When Does a Trial Judge Abuse His or Her Discretion by Denying a Protective Order? Silkwood v. Kerr-McGee Corp.*, 563 F.2d 433 (10th Cir. 1977). The trial judge in this case denied a protective order sought by a news reporter who sought to avoid disclosing confidential sources. The Court of Appeals reversed and remanded on the ground that the trial judge had not considered the nature of the evidence sought, the discoveror's efforts to obtain it from other sources, or the necessity or relevance of the evidence. *See also Automatic Drilling Machines, Inc. v. Miller*, 515 S.W.2d 256 (Tex. 1974) (trial judge's summary denial of motion for protective order, sought by non-party inventor, reversed, where proof supporting motion showed that discoverer was in direct competition with inventor, information was highly confidential, and it probably would be the subject of an application for letters patent). *See also* Smith, *A Practical Approach to Rule 26(c) Protective Orders in Aviation Litigation*, 56 J. Air L. & Com. 765 (1991); Campbell, *The Protective Order in Products Liability Litigation: Safeguard or Misnomer?*, 31 B.C.L. Rev. 771 (1990).

A related question is, when does a trial judge abuse his or her discretion by *granting* a protective order removing information from discovery? *Cf. Williams v. City of Dothan*, 745 F.2d 1406 (11th Cir. 1984) (District Court erred in granting protective order shielding from discovery the City's earlier payments for municipal projects, where the plaintiffs alleged racial discrimination in such payments, where the pattern in earlier years was relevant to the issue of discriminatory intent, and where the potential harm from disclosure was slight).

(2) *The Type of Protection Granted; The Broad Range of Alternatives.* Rule 26(c) lists a wide range of options available to the court, including curtailing discovery, specifying conditions or methods, protecting confidentiality, etc. Consider the following cases and questions:

(a) *Curtailing Discovery of Relevant Information: Farnsworth v. Procter & Gamble Co.*, 758 F.2d 1545 (11th Cir. 1985). In a product liability claim for a death allegedly due to toxic shock syndrome resulting from use of the defendant's tampons, the plaintiff sought extensive discovery from the Center for Disease Control, a non-party and agency of the United States government. The District Court granted a protective order disallowing the plaintiff from discovering the names of individual tampon users who participated in a study conducted by the Center, principally on the ground that such disclosure would damage the Center's ability to obtain survey participants in the future. The Court of Appeals affirmed.

(b) *Staying All Discovery: Crown Central Petroleum Co. v. Department of Energy*, 102 F.R.D. 95 (D. Md. 1984). The defendant Department sought and obtained a protective order staying all discovery in an action for declaratory relief by a petroleum products marketer, upon the Department's showing that there was a pending administrative proceeding presenting overlapping issues in which the plaintiff was seeking many of the same items in discovery.

(c) *Specifying a Different Method of Discovery Than That Used by the Party Seeking Discovery: Fishman v. A.H. Riise Gift Shop, Inc.*, 68 F.R.D. 704 (D.V.I. 1975). The party that was the target of discovery sought a protective order requiring the use of depositions rather than interrogatories. The court granted the motion, observing that the discoverer had attempted to misuse interrogatories.

(d) *Conditions for Discovery—Prepayment of Expenses: In re Coordinated Proceedings in Petroleum Products Antitrust Litig.*, 669 F.2d 620 (10th Cir. 1982). The plaintiff, the State of Florida, sought discovery from a nonparty. The discovery was time-consuming and could not inure to the benefit of the nonparty, and therefore, the trial court required the plaintiff to advance the costs of the requested document production. The Court of Appeals affirmed.

(e) *Designation of Time and Place: Detweiler Bros., Inc. v. John Graham & Co.*, 412 F. Supp. 416 (E.D. Wash. 1976). The plaintiff sought to prohibit the taking of its employee's deposition on the ground that he lacked knowledge of the subject of inquiry and was out of state. The court refused to prohibit the taking of the deposition, but held that the plaintiff could properly seek to control the time and place of the deposition by protective order. Also, consider the following materials.

[F] "Umbrella" Confidentiality Agreements and Orders

SCRANTON PRODUCTS, INC. v. BOBRICK WASHROOM EQUIPMENT, 190 F. Supp. 3d 419 (M.D. Pa. 2016). In many business disputes, both parties foresee that sensitive information is going to be disclosed in discovery. The parties may stipulate to a so-called "umbrella (or blanket) confidentiality agreement" and have the court enter it as a protective order. This order will allow the parties to designate information or documents as confidential. Sometimes the order imposes conditions for items that can be designated and contains mechanisms for resolving disputes. Designation is done by stamps or legends on documents.

The present case might be called "The Battle of the Bathroom Builders." The complaint filed by Scranton Products ("SP") alleged that Defendant Bobrick had "carefully orchestrated a campaign to scare architects, product specifiers, procurement representatives, building owners, and others in the construction industry into believing that Scranton Products' toilet partitions are fire hazards, are unsafe and pose health and safety risks." The parties managed to stipulate to an umbrella confidentiality agreement, but "the parties have engaged in protracted . . . discovery disputes, filing motion after motion requesting the Court's intervention."

The relevant dispute here concerns Bobrick's' challenges to certain "Confidential" and "Attorneys Eyes Only" ("AEO") designations by SP under the Modified Stipulated Protective Order (the "Protective Order"). These designations make it harder to use the information, and Bobrick tried to get the court to remove them:

Under the Protective Order, a producing party may designate certain documents and information as "Confidential" when the information sought to be designated is "comprised of technical, financial, customer, or other commercial information. . . ." For documents and information "comprised of trade secrets, confidential research and development, or other confidential technical information," the producing party may designate such documents and information as AEO [Attorneys' Eyes Only]. Once a designation has been challenged, . . . the producing party must demonstrate . . . that [removal of the] designation "will result in a clearly defined, specific and serious injury."

Bobrick asserts that SP failed to demonstrate "good cause" in connection with 557 "Confidential" designations under the Protective Order. . . . [T]he documents and information at issue "concern an extensive and multifaceted research and development process executed by SP to ensure that its HDPE toilet partitions comply with [regulations]." . . . SP implemented this process with the assistance of various technical consultants and fire performance experts. . . . The information . . . includes raw test data, test notes, draft test notes, photographs, videos, quotations and invoices and correspondences regarding fire performance testing. . . . [D]e-designation would result in a specific and concrete harm, because [it] "will permit SP's competitors . . . to learn how SP developed its partitions [and other information]."

Bobrick next requests that the Court de-designate two categories of information SP has designated as AEO (attorneys' eyes only): "(1) specific pricing information . . . ; and (2) information disclosing the manner in which the . . . partitions . . . are made." The Court declines Bobrick's requests to de-designate this information. . . . "[C]ourts have found 'trade secrets' to include '. . . marketing information including . . . costing and pricing information. . . .'" Here, SP has demonstrated that . . . its pricing information qualifies for trade secret protection and . . . has established "good cause" to support its designations.

For these reasons, . . . [t]he Court denies [Bobrick's] requests to de-designate certain documents and information as "Confidential" and/or "Attorneys Eyes Only."

Notes and Questions

(1) *The Practical Issues.* If there is a breach of an agreement such as that in *Scranton Products v. Bobrick* by unauthorized disclosure (perhaps years after disposition of the litigation), how is the agreement or the order resulting from it to be enforced? For that matter, how does the aggrieved party even detect a violation? It also is entirely possible that the parties may engage in inadvertent or unintended "leaks" of sensitive information, or that designated contact employees may use the

information in later assignments. On the other hand, there probably is no better alternative. *See* Joslin, *Confidentiality Orders in Complex Litigation*, 4 Rev. Litigation 109 (1985).

(2) *Rule Amendment Governing Protective Agreements.* An amendment legitimizes umbrella agreements by eliminating the requirement of "good cause" when confidentiality is agreed to. But it also contemplates that any "person" may be "allowed to intervene to seek modification or dissolution"—*e.g.*, a news reporter in a high profile case.

III. The Mechanics of Discovery

[A] Mandatory Self-Initiated Disclosures

(1) *An Overview: Three Kinds of Required Disclosures.* Fed. R. Civ. P. 26 requires mandatory disclosure of core information, including initial disclosure without any formal request of (1) the names, addresses and telephone numbers (if known) of any persons "likely to have discoverable information—along with the subjects of that information—that the disclosing party may use to support its claims or defenses . . ."; (2) copies or descriptions of documents that may be used; (3) a computation of any category of damages claimed; and (4) copies of insurance agreements that may be liable to satisfy any judgment [Rule 26(a)(1)(A)]. The rule also requires disclosure of expert testimony [Rule 26(a)(2)] and pretrial disclosure of witnesses who may be called to testify [Rule 26(a)(3)].

(2) *The Discovery Meeting and Plan.* The rule requires the parties to meet to discuss and arrange disclosures before the Rule 16(b) judicial scheduling conference [Rule 26(f)]. The rule also contains a separate certification and signing requirement [Rule 26(g)].

(3) *Sanctions.* The rules also enable the court to sanction a party for inadequate disclosures, most frequently by excluding testimony by witnesses not properly disclosed or excluding other kinds of proof. Sanctions can be avoided if the failure was "substantially justified" or "harmless." Rule 37(c)(1). Note that this means that an inadvertent nondisclosure (of something you overlooked) can mean that you will not be able to use crucial evidence that you need. The possibility of unfair results is there, along with the hope of more efficiency.

Harriman v. Hancock County

627 F.3d 22 (1st Cir. 2010)

Howard, Circuit Judge.

This civil rights action involves competing accounts of an arrestee's weekend stay in Maine's Hancock County Jail. Plaintiff David Harriman, although he remembers virtually nothing that occurred over the entire weekend, contends that one or more correctional officers beat him until he sustained a lasting brain injury. Defendants Hancock County, its sheriff and several correctional officers assert that Harriman fell on his head. Harriman appeals the district court's preclusion of two affidavits [because of delayed disclosure supplementation] and entry of summary judgment in defendants' favor. After careful review, we affirm.

I. BACKGROUND

We recount the facts in the light most favorable to Harriman as the party opposing summary judgment. *Statchen v. Palmer*, 623 F.3d 15, 16 (1st Cir. 2010).

A. *The Weekend*

On a Friday evening in October 2006, Maine State Trooper Gregory Mitchell responded to a disturbance at the Blue Hill Hospital involving a disorderly emergency room patient later identified as Harriman.... [Harriman ran away but was caught.] Harriman appeared to be drunk. [The court adds that a blood test showed that Harriman's blood alcohol was at least .3 percent, which is unusually high.—Eds.] Because Harriman was prohibited from consuming alcohol in connection with a previous infraction, Mitchell arrested him.

Mitchell escorted Harriman outside to the police cruiser and searched him. Harriman launched a stream of epithets against Mitchell, including threats to Mitchell and his children. As Mitchell guided Harriman into the cruiser, Harriman resisted and fell to the ground, pulling Mitchell down with him. Mitchell got back on his feet and hoisted Harriman up and into the cruiser. Once in the cruiser, Harriman spit at Mitchell and then fell asleep.

At about 8 p.m., the pair arrived at the jail. Mitchell escorted Harriman into the intoxilyzer room. Harriman leveled several new expletives against Mitchell and struggled against Mitchell's hold until correctional officers Ryan Haines and Michael Pileski arrived to take custody....

What happened next is the subject of some dispute. According to the defendants, Haines and Pileski escorted Harriman directly to the nurse's station where Haines asked him several questions in order to evaluate whether he was a suicide risk. Harriman did not respond. In accordance with jail protocol, Harriman was determined to be a suicide risk until he could respond in a manner that showed otherwise. With some assistance from Haines, Harriman changed into an anti-suicide smock [which the court explains is a stiff, tear-resistant gown that prevents a detainee from fashioning a noose]. At about 8:30 p.m., Haines and Pileski moved Harriman to HD-1, which is a holding cell further inside the jail and adjacent to the jail's control room. Correctional officers began monitoring Harriman at successive fifteen-minute intervals. Harriman then lay down and went to sleep.

A little after 10 p.m., Sergeant Heather Sullivan, from her position in or around the control room, heard Harriman "yelling" and "hollering" in his cell. When Sullivan looked over, she saw Harriman "banging around" his cell naked; she also noticed blood on the bridge of his nose. Sullivan radioed Haines and instructed him to investigate. Harriman greeted Haines with shouted expletives and, from behind the glass partition, drew his fist back as though he would punch Haines. Sullivan soon arrived outside Harriman's cell. While she and Haines were deciding on a course of action, they both heard a loud "thump" or "thud" from inside Harriman's cell. Although neither Sullivan nor Haines saw what happened in Harriman's cell, Pileski and another correctional officer, Crystal Hobbs, from their vantage point in the control room, saw Harriman fall to the floor in a leftward motion. Pileski further saw Harriman strike his head as he fell against the lefthand concrete wall of his cell.

Haines entered the cell and saw Harriman lying on the floor in his own urine, apparently unconscious. Harriman then had what appeared to be two seizures, each lasting a matter of seconds. At Sullivan's request, Hobbs called an ambulance from the control room at about 10:20 p.m. . . . Haines accompanied Harriman in the ambulance and stayed with him at the hospital until relieved by another correctional officer later that evening.

Harriman remembers next to nothing about his jail stay. From his arrest on Friday until he woke up at home on Monday or Tuesday night, Harriman remembers only the following: "a lot of hollering"; "echoes from hollering"; "flashes of light"; "somebody saying he's had enough or I think that's enough or maybe even that's enough"; "seeing my wife's cousin [Foster Kane, another jail detainee] but just barely"; "somebody telling me that they were going to take me to Augusta"; and "the smell . . . [of] urine mixed with cleaning fluid."

Given his anamnestic difficulties, Harriman relies on Mitchell's deposition testimony and affidavits from two other witnesses to contradict the defendants' version of events.

Mitchell testified at deposition that he spent roughly an hour in the booking room finishing up paperwork . . . . When Mitchell exited the booking room at about 9 p.m., he noticed Harriman through a glass partition in a room known as secure holding, not in HD-1, which was further inside the jail. . . . Harriman appeared to be unaccompanied and was wearing civilian clothes.

Foster Kane, the detainee who Harriman vaguely remembers seeing, stated in an affidavit that, from his cell near the booking room, he "heard yelling and screaming and loud thuds of someone hitting a wall." He further stated that the "commotion went on for approximately 45 minutes before I saw the correctional officers dragging David Harriman into my cell block." And, "David had two black eyes, a cut on his nose, and a cut on his forehead over his right eye."

Jenny Sheriff, the emergency medical technician who responded to the jail's call for an ambulance, stated in an affidavit that she "picked Mr. Harriman up in [secure holding]." Sheriff noticed dried blood on Harriman's nose, and was "certain that I did not receive the call to respond to the Jail immediately after the injuries occurred." She also stated that Harriman was naked and that there was "no robe or suicide smock in his cell."

The rest of the weekend is materially undisputed.... Later that day, a family member bailed him out and drove him home. The next thing Harriman remembers is waking up at home on Monday or Tuesday night.

B. *The Lawsuit*

... Harriman ... asserted five claims premised on constitutional violations (excessive force, false arrest, conspiracy under both §§ 1983 and 1985, and deprivation of due process) and three claims premised on state tort law (negligence, intentional infliction of emotional distress, and punitive damages). In due course, the magistrate judge assigned to the case entered a scheduling order setting dates for, among other things, initial disclosures ..., close of discovery [and a trial date]....

Harriman's initial disclosure identified fourteen individuals likely to have discoverable information; critically, however, it did not identify either Kane or Sheriff. *See* Fed.R.Civ.P. 26(a)(1)(A)(i) (requiring identification of individuals "likely to have discoverable information"). Discovery proceeded over the next several months, during which the parties exchanged written discovery and deposed almost all individuals that Harriman had identified in his initial disclosure.

... [T]he defendants moved for summary judgment.... [T]wo days before Harriman's response to the defendants' motion was due and more than two months after discovery had closed, Harriman's attorney sent the defendants a "supplemental" initial disclosure that identified Kane and Sheriff as two additional individuals likely to have discoverable information. In a cover letter to the amended disclosure, Harriman's attorney explained that he had retained a private investigator, that the investigator had located Kane and Sheriff, and that Harriman intended to submit affidavits from Kane and Sheriff in opposition to summary judgment.... [Then,] Harriman filed his opposition papers, which drew heavily from the Kane and Sheriff affidavits in contesting the defendants' motion.

In their reply, the defendants requested that the magistrate judge strike these affidavits as a sanction pursuant to Fed.R.Civ.P. 37(c)(1). The magistrate judge held a telephone conference with counsel to discuss this request. Following the conference, ... Harriman submitted a memorandum and supporting affidavits addressing the failure to identify Kane and Sheriff earlier. Those affidavits revealed that Harriman's attorney had not retained the investigator until ... ten days before the defendants' summary judgment motion was due and more than a month after the close of discovery.

The magistrate judge issued an order that precluded the Kane and Sheriff affidavits as a sanction, and recommended summary judgment in favor of the defendants on all remaining claims.... Nevertheless, the magistrate judge stated that summary judgment was appropriate even if one considered the Kane and Sheriff affidavits, and so purported to analyze Harriman's claims under the full record. When the magistrate judge analyzed Harriman's excessive force claim, however, she disregarded the Kane affidavit on the basis of her earlier decision precluding that affidavit:

> Clearly *if* Harriman has met his burden of creating a genuine dispute of material fact on his theory that he was deliberately beaten by the guards by providing competent evidence of his theory, a trial would be necessary on this count. However, I have determined that the Kane Affidavit must be stricken because Harriman has in no way demonstrated a justification for his late disclosure (and tardy efforts to investigate). The Sheriff Affidavit also is stricken, but even if it were not, this evidence would not be sufficient to carry Harriman's burden of providing a dispute of fact that justifies sending this count to trial.

(Emphasis in original.) The district court adopted in full the magistrate judge's report and recommendation and entered judgment . . . .

II . . . .

B. *Preclusion of the Kane and Sheriff Affidavits.*

Harriman challenges the magistrate judge's decision precluding the Kane and Sheriff affidavits. . . .

. . . Rule 26 requires a party, without awaiting a discovery request, to "provide to the other parties . . . the name . . . of each individual likely to have discoverable information—along with the subjects of that information—that the disclosing party may use to support its claims or defenses." Fed.R.Civ.P. 26(a)(1)(A)(i). That obligation is a continuing one. *See* Fed.R.Civ.P. 26(e)(1)(A) (requiring a party to supplement its disclosure promptly "if the party learns that in some material respect the disclosure or response is incomplete or incorrect.").

Failure to comply with disclosure obligations can have severe consequences. Rule 37 authorizes district courts to sanction noncomplying parties; although sanctions can vary depending on the circumstances, "[t]he baseline rule is that 'the required sanction in the ordinary case is mandatory preclusion.'" Fed.R.Civ.P. 37(c)(1) (providing that if a party fails to disclose . . . , that "party is not allowed to use that information or witness to supply evidence on a motion").

We consult an array of factors when reviewing preclusion decisions. They include the sanctioned party's justification for the late disclosure; the opponent-party's ability to overcome its adverse effects (*i.e.*, harmlessness); the history of the litigation; the late disclosure's impact on the district court's docket; and the sanctioned party's need for the precluded evidence. [T]he sanctioned party shoulders a "heavy burden" to show that an abuse [of discretion] has occurred . . . .

Harriman's justification for the late disclosure is nonexistent. He argues on appeal that "had Defendants written truthful reports, or testified truthfully in deposition, Plaintiff would have learned far earlier that Plaintiff was kept in the Secure Holding Cell throughout the evening. . . . But these statements only pound the table. They do not explain, let alone justify, Harriman's late disclosure or his decision to begin looking for Kane and Sheriff in earnest only after discovery closed.

The record shows . . . that Harriman knew very early on that Kane and Sheriff could help his case. . . . Harriman knew that Kane was in jail with him over the weekend [and Kane was a relative of Harriman's] . . . . So, too, with Sheriff. Harriman may not have remembered Sheriff, but multiple witnesses testified at their depositions that an EMT responded to the jail . . . . But the salient point is that Harriman knew during discovery that an EMT existed who had information that could support his claims, and yet he did nothing whatsoever to find that individual until after discovery closed.

As for the next factor, Harriman's late disclosure was not a harmless inconvenience. The defendants prepared and filed a summary judgment motion premised on evidence submitted before the discovery deadline. Harriman opposed the motion with affidavits obtained after that deadline . . . . [T]he prejudice to defendants was real.

Furthermore, Harriman took no steps to minimize the harm caused by the late disclosure. Harriman's attorney retained an investigator ten days before the defendants' summary judgment motion was due, but did not put the defendants or the court on notice that he was attempting to locate Kane and Sheriff. And . . . he sought and received an extension to file an opposition to summary judgment—not in order to find additional witnesses—but on the ground that he was busy with other cases and had been sick. . . .

The history of the litigation also cuts against Harriman's position. This was not the first time Harriman missed a deadline. He failed previously to designate an expert by the deadline set by the court, and he requested an extension five days later. . . . Harriman also failed timely to respond to the defendants' request to strike the Kane and Sheriff affidavits. Here again the magistrate judge gave Harriman one last extension. Although these infractions may not rise to the level of dereliction displayed in other cases, *see, e.g., Santiago-Diaz v.* [*Laboratorio Clinico y de Referencia del Este*], 456 F.3d [272] at 277 [(1st Cir. 2006)] (referencing the plaintiff's "obvious and repeated" disregard for the court's deadlines), they do place the court's preclusion decision in context. . . .

The only factor that favors Harriman is his need for the affidavits. Reversals based on a sanctioned party's need for precluded evidence are rare, and seldom based on that factor alone. In one recherché case, *Esposito* [*v. Home Depot U.S.A.*], we reviewed an order that had precluded the plaintiff's only expert because he failed to designate him in time. 590 F.3d 72 [(1st Cir. 2009)]. We reversed, with one judge dissenting, because the parties agreed that preclusion was tantamount to dismissal, and there was no evidence that the plaintiff had disregarded other deadlines or sought to gain a calculated advantage by delay. . . .

In sum, given the above, we cannot fault the district court for precluding the affidavits. Another judge faced with the same facts might have selected a lesser sanction. But preclusion was not "so wide of the mark as to constitute an abuse of discretion." [Summary judgment for defendants affirmed.]

Notes and Questions

(1) *Reduction of Cost and Delay—or Encouragement of Waste and Gamesmanship?* One of the most hotly debated issues about initial disclosures is whether they reduce cost and delay—or increase it. The possibility of exclusion of essential proof because of accidental nondisclosures means that lawyers over prepare these documents in many cases.

(2) *Limiting Disclosure to the Party's Own Claims or Defenses (as Opposed to Requiring Each Party to Figure Out the Opponent's Theories).* The disclosure requirements generally are restricted to information "that the disclosing party may use to support its claims or defenses, unless the use would be solely for impeachment." The earlier rule covered "every individual likely to have discoverable information relevant to disputed facts," whether the facts concerned the discloser's theories or the opponent's. The discloser, arguably, was required to adopt the opponent's frame of mind, to figure out what would help the opponent's case. The current language lets the discloser limit its search to "its claims or defenses." Perhaps this change lightens the burden. But then again, the improvement may not be as great as it seems, because one's own claims and defenses are closely related to the opponent's; they are the flip side of the opponent's, in a way.

(3) *Time Management and Scheduling of Events: A Big, Big Problem.* The clock and the calendar create a real shock for beginning lawyers, as the *Harriman* case suggests. While we are law students, we do not have to keep a schedule, because our class times and examination dates are well established. Then, in practice, we suddenly find ourselves in a maze of shifting dates numbering perhaps in the hundreds in a docket full of different cases, and the awful thing about it is that missing dates creates disaster. Then, there is the problem of keeping time records by quarter-hours during the day and realization that these concerns are elbowing out our personal lives. The solutions are attention to time management, careful use of scheduling devices and methods, and (sometimes) assistants who can back up our own efforts. Some experienced attorneys say that time management is *the* key ability in law practice, more important than legal abilities.

(4) *Sanctions for Failing to Disclose Obvious Witnesses: An Example.* The language of Rule 26(a)(1) would indicate that disclosures are still required even if the information is known to the adversary. One of the problems is that of the undisclosed witness who is overlooked because she is obvious. Imagine that you have filed a claim on a promissory note for principal, interest, and attorney's fees, and your opponent answers with defenses of fraud, usury, and the like. Can you begin to make a list of the categories of witnesses and documents that you would disclose? [Note: If you didn't think of disclosing *yourself* as a witness, you may be precluded from supplying testimony necessary to recover attorney's fees! The complexity of the other issues, combined with the obviousness of the required testimony for

attorney's fees, might lull a lawyer into nondisclosure—but how useful will it be to point out that the opponent "must have known" this testimony would be offered?]

(5) *"Good Faith" Is Not Enough.* Consider the situation of a party who finds, at trial, that an important piece of information has not been disclosed, but who has acted in good faith, in that the party simply did not realize that the information was relevant. Is such a party protected from the sanction of exclusion by an argument that the disclosures were made in good faith? The lawyer in *Harriman* probably acted in good faith. Isn't the answer, "probably not"?

(6) *Disclosure of Damage Computations.* Rule 26 requires that a party disclose the "computation" of any category of claimed damages. This rule is a significant source of court opinions about sanctions. Does the term "computation" connote the specification of a figure, mathematical formula, or calculation? Consider *Dynegy Marketing and Trade v. Multiut Corp.*, 648 F.3d 506 (7th Cir. 2011), in which the claimant's disclosures included specific dollar figures as estimates of damages, but did not give the mathematics by which the dollar figures were derived, saying that it would "supplement" according to "further discovery." The court of appeals upheld the trial court's exclusion of the claimant's damage affidavit in response to a motion for summary judgment.

Consider an attorney who has filed suit on behalf of a plaintiff with paraplegic injuries and who seeks to comply fully with this Rule with respect to such damages as future medical expenses, future pain and suffering, loss of consortium, and like categories. How would the initial disclosures be written to cover the "computation" of these damages? (It isn't always easy.)

NGUYEN v. IBP, INC., 162 F.R.D. 675 (D. Kan. 1995). A second set of disclosure requirements covers expert witnesses. These disclosures, too, can create difficult issues. In addition to information about opinions, bases of opinions, personal information, and payments, the expert must provide a list of cases in which the expert has testified during the last four years. What if the expert has not kept detailed enough records to give, for example, case numbers (who records those)? Here, the court's response is essentially, "You shouldn't have hired this expert, and the plaintiff shouldn't have used him as his doctor":

> [Dr. Schechter set] forth a summary of his physical examination and medical opinions. . . . Plaintiff also supplied [his] curriculum vitae and a list of patients about whom Dr. Shechter had given deposition testimony. . . . Plaintiff also served a supplemental answer to [an] interrogatory [stating] that Dr. Shechter was to be paid the sum of $750.00 . . . .
>
> . . . Plaintiff states that, while the witness has testified in hundreds of cases over the years, the only information retained by him related to his previous testimony is "the patient's name, the attorney's name who scheduled the deposition, the attorney's phone number and the date the deposition

was given." Plaintiff's counsel states that he, personally, spent approximately eight hours compiling the information provided from the records retained by the witness for the preceding three years. He alleges that no record of deposition testimony beyond three years has been retained by the witness. Plaintiff argues that since all "reasonably available information listing the cases in which Dr. Shechter has testified" has been provided, the testimony of the witness should not be excluded. . . .

. . . The court will allow the plaintiff to provide a supplemental disclosure which corrects the deficiencies identified herein within 40 days from the date of the filing of this order, otherwise, Dr. Shechter will not be permitted to testify at the trial of the action. . . .

Notes and Questions

(1) *Cost and Delay Reduction—Or Cost and Delay Increase?* Assembly of the information required by the court here will require large expenditures of time and money by the party offering the witness, if it even is possible at all. The market value of this fruitless effort almost certainly exceeds the entire $750 fee charged by the expert witness. The value of the information and the likelihood that this is the most efficient form for discovering it are doubtful. Does this judge's application of the disclosure rule reduce cost and delay or increase them?

(2) *What if the Information Simply Is Unavailable? Considering the Court's Holding That the Rule Is "Mandatory."* The expert has not kept records for all of the past four years and has kept only partial records in any event. People who are not attorneys often do not retain their documentation according to categories responsive to possible future litigation. Consider what should happen if the records simply do not permit a full listing of all prior cases with the precision that this opinion demands. (The judge holds that the disclosures are "mandatory." Is this holding appropriate, given that the rule expressly empowers the court to order that disclosures are not required in a particular case?)

(3) *What Kinds of "Experts" Are Subject to the Disclosure Requirements?—The Example of Treating Physicians: Salas v. United States*, 165 F.R.D. 31 (W.D.N.Y. 1995). In contrast to the strictness of the case above, several cases have held that treating physicians, like Dr. Schechter, are not subject to the disclosure requirement, even though they are experts whose testimony fits the terms of the disclosure rule. The reasoning is that treating physicians are not "specially retained" within the meaning of the rule but instead are "viewers" or "actors" who testify to what they observed or did—even though they also testify to diagnosis, causation, indicated treatment, prognosis, etc. In *Salas*, the judge exempted five different physicians from disclosure requirements.

Litigation Document Example 7.1

Plaintiff's Initial Disclosures in Dynatech Corp. v. American Aerospace Partnership LLP

This document is available at https://caplaw.com/sites/cp7. *Dynatech Corporation v. American Aerospace* was a suit by one NASA contractor against another. The defendant removed the case from state to federal court on the (dubious) ground that the claims, although based on state law, "became federal" because the United States had an "interest" in space exploration. The court ultimately remanded, but the plaintiff's initial disclosures were due before the remand. This Litigation Document Example shows the disclosures, with names and identifying features removed.

Notice the items covered: identification of individuals knowing facts, documents relevant to the facts, damages, and insurance—as the Rule requires. Consider the cost for attorneys' time: probably well into six figures (obtaining the remand cost over $130,000). Please go to https://caplaw.com/sites/cp7, then click on Litigation Document Example 7.1: Plaintiff's Initial Disclosures in *Dynatech Corp. v. American Aerospace Partnership LLP.*

[B] The Discovery Devices

[1] Oral Depositions

> Read Fed. R. Civ. P. 28(a), 29, 30, 31, 32 (depositions), and 45 (subpoenas).

Sun Capital Partners, Inc. v. Twin City Fire Ins. Co.

310 F.R.D. 523 (S.D. Fla. 2015)

William Matthewman, United States Magistrate Judge.

[Sun Capital here sues its excess insurer, Twin City, for breach of its insurance policy. The suit involves a large dispute that was settled by the primary insurer, leaving unpaid loss for Sun Capital, which here looks to its second ("excess") insurer for payment. The insurer, Twin City, has issued notices for taking depositions of Sun City's co-founders and co-chief executive officers and general counsel. Sun City moves to quash and for a protective order prohibiting these depositions on the ground that these personnel have no special knowledge of the events in question and did not participate in them in any unique way.

[The court characterizes the attempted discovery as "apex depositions," which are efforts to depose top executives. Apex depositions often result in harassment and may be undertaken for that purpose. Therefore, courts have set requirements for this kind of discovery.]

"[A] party seeking to depose a high ranking corporate officer [by an apex deposition] must first establish that the executive: (1) has unique, non-repetitive, firsthand knowledge of the facts at issue; and (2) that other less intrusive means of discovery, such as interrogatories and depositions of other employees, have been exhausted without success." *Hickey v. North Broward Hosp. Dist.*, 2014 WL 7495780 (S.D.Fla. Dec. 17, 2014). . . . .

Here, although Twin City lists several reasons why it wishes to depose [the executives], . . . Twin City fails to adequately demonstrate that [the executives] have any unique, non-repetitive firsthand knowledge about the matters at issue in this case. Sun has offered Thomas Clare, who was Sun's defense counsel in the underlying litigation, as a corporate representative to be deposed regarding the facts at issue. Twin City has not shown that Clare, or any other person, cannot adequately testify to the facts at issue. Twin City merely asserts that "Sun's proposed lower level depositions will reveal what Twin City already knows—Sun's executives played an integral and unique role in the settlement process, and their depositions cannot be avoided."

Twin City also fails to carry its burden of showing that the information . . . cannot be obtained from any other source. In certain cases, even when a high-ranking official of a corporation does have direct knowledge of the facts, it is inappropriate to compel his or her deposition without first deposing lesser-ranking employees who have more direct knowledge of the facts at issue. *Stelor Productions, Inc. v. Google, Inc.*,2008 WL 4218107 (S.D.Fla. Sept. 15, 2008) (holding that although plaintiff claimed that Google's two top executives did have direct, unique, and personal knowledge of the facts at issue, it made sense to require plaintiff to seek the information from other sources first). [The court quashes the deposition notices, but without prejudice to re-issue them if conditions change.]

Notes and Questions: Setup of the Deposition

(1) *"Apex" Depositions.* Plaintiff sometimes notices what is called an "apex" deposition: a deposition of the CEO or other high officer, even though the case concerns a strictly local incident. For example, imagine that a plaintiff slips and falls in a Wal-Mart store and then seeks to depose Wal-Mart's president and all members of the Walton family (the founders). Slip-and-falls at Wal-Mart must be daily occurrences, and testifying about them would quickly occupy all of the executives' waking hours. On the other hand, the effort may be legitimate; for example, the plaintiff may be trying to discover company-wide policies related to the dispute that originated with the CEO. Apex depositions are not favored, because they may simply amount to harassment in the hope of increasing difficulties for the opponent that will precipitate settlement. The effort here to depose multiple executives and founders increases the skepticism.

(2) *Setting up the Deposition: Notice and Timing.* The process of taking a deposition is begun by a deposition notice to every other party to the action. Fed. R. Civ. P. 30(b)(1). The notice must be "reasonable," although no fixed rule can be laid down as to what constitutes a reasonable time. *Compare Stover v. Universal Moulded Prod. Corp.*,

11 F.R.D. 90 (E.D. Pa. 1950) (two days' notice unreasonable in absence of showing of special need), *with Radio Corp. of America v. Rauland Corp.*, 21 F.R.D. 113 (N.D. Ill. 1957) (one day's notice not unreasonable when counsel were all in a foreign city for the taking of depositions at that time.) The notice is required to include the name and address, if known, of the witness, the time and place of the deposition, and a description of the documents or tangible things to be produced by the witness.

(3) *An Inconvenient, Distant Location.* The idea of apex depositions suggests another issue. Imagine that a party notices many of another party's employees' depositions (or those of nonparty witnesses) in the forum, or at another place that is located a thousand miles from them. Under the Federal Rules, a non-party witness who resides in a place that is far distant from the place in which the action is pending normally cannot be deposed in the forum; however, the court has broad discretion in this regard. *See* Fed. R. Civ. P. 45(c); *see also Baker v. Standard Indus., Inc.*, 55 F.R.D. 178 (D. P.R. 1972) (defendant could not avoid depositions in Puerto Rico by protective order, when its officers often travelled there, and it had operations there). *But see Salter v. Upjohn Co.*, 593 F.2d 649 (5th Cir. 1979) (refusing to require defendant's CEO to travel to forum to be deposed and refusing to order defendant to reimburse plaintiff for expenses in traveling to CEO's location).

(4) *Compelling Appearance: Parties (Notice Is Enough) and Nonparties (Subpoena).* A subpoena is necessary to compel the appearance of a non-party witness. Fed. R. Civ. P. 45(a)(2). When the witness is a party to the action, service of notice on the party's counsel has the same effect as a subpoena for the purpose of compelling attendance; thus, a subpoena is not needed for a party-witness. *See* Fed. R. Civ. P. 37(d). Rule 45 requires the trial court to quash or modify a deposition subpoena that requires a person who is not a party or an officer of a party to travel more than 100 miles from the place where that person resides, is employed, or regularly transacts business. Fed. R. Civ. P. 45(c)(3)(A).

(5) *Compelling Production.* When production of documents is desired from a non-party, the notice and subpoena must set forth the documents to be produced. When information is withheld because it is privileged, the response must "expressly make [this] claim, and . . . describe the nature of the withheld" items sufficiently to "enable the parties to assess the claim." Fed. R. Civ. P. 45(d). A person who is served with a subpoena duces tecum must produce the subpoenaed documents "as they are kept in the ordinary course of business or . . . organize and label them to correspond to the categories in the demand." Fed. R. Civ. P. 45(d). Likewise, the notice of deposition to a party may be accompanied by a request for production of documents made in compliance with Rule 34, which governs production. Fed. R. Civ. P. 30(b)(2).

Notes and Questions: Taking the Deposition

(1) *Manner of Taking the Deposition.* In federal practice, persons authorized by the laws of the United States to preside at depositions, as well as persons authorized by state law to so preside, may record the testimony. Thus, a state-certified court

reporter may perform the task. Fed. R. Civ. P. 28. The witness is required to be placed under oath by the deposition officer. Fed. R. Civ. P. 30(c). A party may also take a deposition by nonstenographic means (*i.e.,* by recording or videotape) by so stating in the notice. Fed. R. Civ. P. 30(b)(3). The Federal Rules also provide that the parties may stipulate in writing, or the court on motion may order, that a deposition be taken by telephone or other remote means. Fed. R. Civ. P. 30(b)(4).

(2) *Objections to Procedural Defects.* Rule 32(d) requires prompt objection to certain types of procedural defects, such as irregularities in the notice, disqualification of the reporter, and deficiencies in the form of questions or answers. An objection will allow the deposer to address the alleged defect by restating the question. If not made promptly, these objections are waived. Most evidentiary objections, on the other hand, can be made at the time the deposition is offered in evidence (except objections to the form of questions or answers or other matters that could be cured on timely objection during the deposition). Thus, for example, the opponent does not need to object to preserve her right to exclude inadmissible prejudicial testimony in a deposition. She probably does need to object during the deposition, however, to a leading question directed to a non-adversary witness, if she wants to exclude the answer on that basis at trial—because it concerns the "form" of the question and because it could have been cured on timely objection.

(3) *Signature, Certification, Return, and Filing.* A party or deponent may request, before the completion of the deposition, review of the transcript or recording. If this request is made, the deponent has 30 days after the transcript or recording is available to review it. If there are changes in form or substance, the deponent must make a statement regarding the changes and sign the statement. Fed. R. Civ. P. 30(e). (Sometimes court reporters garble words or sentences.)

(4) *Stipulations Regarding Discovery Procedure Under Rule 29: The "Usual Agreements."* Rule 29 allows the parties to make stipulations about the taking of depositions and to modify most other discovery procedures. For example, attorneys frequently agree to waive the requirement that the witness sign the deposition or, more likely, they agree that it may be signed before any notary, rather than before the court reporter. Agreements concerning the taking of the deposition by a non-certified court reporter, or concerning the allocation of deposition expenses, also sometimes occur. Indeed, the parties sometimes unnecessarily stipulate to matters already provided for by Rule, such as agreeing to waive notice defects (provided for by Rule 32(d)(1)).

(5) *Stipulating that "All Objections May Be Made at Trial."* But perhaps the most frequent stipulation is that all objections to admissibility may be made at the time of trial, even if they otherwise would be required to be made contemporaneously under Rule 32. If you propose to offer the deposition at trial, you must consider carefully whether to enter into this stipulation. If you agree to the stipulation, your opponent's objections to the form of questions and answers can be postponed until trial, rather than made during the deposition when you can cure them. But the stipulation still may be useful, since it avoids the need for the opponent to interrupt

the deposition frequently. Without such a stipulation, many opposing attorneys will interpose lengthy objections to all questions, just to protect the record.

Therefore, you probably should agree to allow all objections at trial for an adverse witness such as an opposing party or person closely identified with a party. At trial, leading questions are allowed for these witnesses, so there usually will not be any valid objections to form at trial. By agreeing to allow objections at the time of trial, you avoid unnecessary interruptions.

(6) *"The Usual Agreements?" ("But What Are They?").* So widespread is the use of Rule 29 stipulations that attorneys often begin a deposition by directing the court reporter to insert "the usual agreements." This shorthand may be acceptable if all parties have the same "usual agreements" in mind, but local custom does vary. If there is any doubt, you should ask: "And what do you understand the 'usual agreements' to be?" For a discussion of deposition strategy, see Blumenkopk, *Deposition Strategy and Tactics*, 5 AM. J. TRIAL ADVOCACY 231 (1981).

(7) *Presumptive Limits of Ten Depositions and Time Limits on Depositions.* Rule 30(a) places a presumptive limit of ten depositions upon the parties (subject to stipulation otherwise by the parties, and to the court's authority to modify the limit for a particular case). Is such a rule a good idea? In addition, Rule 30(d) limits each deposition to no more than "1 day of 7 hours."

Litigation Document Example 7.2

Deposition Practice, Including Sample Checklist, Advice to a Client About to Be Deposed, and Sample Deposition in Pringle v. Jim Dandy Fast Foods

These documents are online at https://caplaw.com/sites/cp7. The first item here is a general-purpose checklist for the taking of a plaintiff's deposition in a personal injury case by the defendant. The second is a handout to a client in preparation for the client's testifying in a deposition.

Then, the third item is a sample deposition transcript. The case is *Pringle v. Jim Dandy Fast Foods, Inc.*, which is a relatively simple product liability suit in which the plaintiff bit into a piece of fried chicken from a fast food outlet and was injured by a bone cut in an unusual way. The deposition is of the plaintiff, taken by the defense lawyer. In reading this document, notice the subjects covered (typically, these are: assurance that the plaintiff understands what the deposition is about, to help with impeachment at trial; her background; the liability-producing events; and all damages claimed). Also, notice how the defense lawyer starts asking about the event (with a very general question, inviting narrative). So, please go to https://caplaw.com/sites/cp7, then click on Litigation Document Example 7.2: Deposition Practice, Including Sample Checklist, Advice to a Client About to Be Deposed, and Sample Deposition in *Pringle v. Jim Dandy Fast Foods.*

Note on Depositions on Written Questions

Most procedural systems provide for taking depositions on written questions. This discovery device bears a stronger resemblance to written interrogatories than to oral depositions. The questions are prepared in advance and served with the deposition notice. The deposition officer propounds the questions and takes the answers. *See* Fed. R. Civ. P. 31.

The deposition on written questions is a weak form of discovery in comparison to an oral deposition because there is no opportunity to follow a witness' response with more probing questions. The written deposition can be useful, however, to authenticate documents, such as non-party business records, or for a friendly witness in a small case who is located at a distance.

[2] Interrogatories

> Read Fed. R. Civ. P. 26(b)(2) and (c) (limitations on discovery scope; protective orders), and 33 (interrogatories).

Jackson v. Willoughby Eastlake School District

2018 WL 1468666, 2018 U.S. Dist. LEXIS 49508 (N.D. Ohio March 23, 2018)

David A Ruiz, United States Magistrate Judge.

[Jackson sued the District, other governmental units, and several individuals for allegedly inadequate responses to the bullying of his daughter ("C.J.") at school. His complaint alleged claims under the Due Process Clause, the Equal Protection Clause, and Title IX of the Civil Rights Act of 1968, which imposes duties upon educational institutions. During discovery, Plaintiff Jackson requested information covering various investigations of bullying incidents, including information about students allegedly involved. Significant parts of the information were confidential under the Family Educational Rights and Privacy Act ("FERPA"), 20 U.S.C. § 1232g. Relying on FERPA, and asserting that a fire had destroyed documents containing some of the information, the defendants filed an opposition to the plaintiffs' motion to compel and a motion for protective order.]

Plaintiffs' supplemental motion to compel moves that the court order defendants to provide, under a protective order, "all individual personnel records as identified in interrogatory Nos. 7, 16, 17, 22, 23, and 25" and requested student disciplinary records. No. 7 requests specific information concerning any "follow-up action" taken in response to allegations of bullying, harassment, or physical assault of C.J. by fellow students.... Interrogatory Nos. 16 and 17 request specific information concerning "the investigation of any allegations made against [student D.H.,]" including any documents or reports created as part of the investigation. Defendants' response indicates David Miller [a school official] was involved in the investigation, but otherwise objects that each of the interrogatories "seeks information which is confidential in nature and protected by FERPA."

Similarly, Nos. 22 and 23 request specific information concerning "the investigation of any allegations made against [student H.S.,]" including any documents or reports created as part of the investigation. Defendants' response identifies Jason Wilson [again, a school official] as involved in the investigation.... Interrogatory 25 seeks information regarding documents or reports created as part of "the investigation of any allegations made against [student H.J.] Defendants object that [each interrogatory] "seeks information which is confidential in nature and protected by FERPA." ...

The purpose of written interrogatories, permitted under Rule 33, is "to focus the fundamental issues between the parties and to enable the parties to learn what the facts are and where they may be found before trial, to the end that the parties may prepare their case in the light of all the available facts." *United States v. A.B. Dick Co.*, 7 F.R.D. 442, 443 (N.D. Ohio 1947)....

[Here, the court undertakes analysis of the federal confidentiality statue, FERPA, which protects students' educational records, including disciplinary investigations, as confidential.] ... FERPA, however, "does not ..., by its express terms, prevent discovery of relevant school records under the Federal Rules of Civil Procedure." *Richardson* [*v. Board of Educ.*], 2014 WL 8619228 [(S.D. Ohio 2014)]. In other words, records that are considered protected under a statute are not necessarily privileged for discovery purposes, and FERPA does not provide such a privilege.... [But] "the party seeking the information is required to demonstrate a genuine need for the information that outweighs the privacy interests of the students."*Jones* [*v. Espanola Mun. Sch. Dist.*], 2016 WL 10257481 [(D. N.M. 2016)]....

In this case, plaintiffs' complaint identifies three specific students accused of engaging in abuse, assault, bullying, and intimidation against plaintiff C.J. Plaintiffs claim that the individual records of T.H., D.H. and H.J., specifically, and other reports against individual students made by C.J., are not merely relevant but are "critical in either proving or disproving the portion of her claims supported by these allegations." ... Conversely, aside from claiming the requested discovery seeks confidential information protected from disclosure by FERPA, Defendants have not asserted any other pertinent objection or argued that the requested information lacks relevance.

... The court finds that the Plaintiffs' need for the discovery outweighs the students' privacy interests, and the motion to compel is granted, as to the production sought, namely requested student disciplinary records and "all individual personnel records as identified in interrogatory Nos. 7, 16, 17, 22, 23, and 25." ...

[The court next considers the defendants' motions for protective orders.] ... Documents and information produced by defendants pursuant to this order or otherwise that include student information shall be marked "Confidential." All such records will be produced subject to a protective order limiting the use of such information to this litigation only, for attorneys' eyes only, and preventing the filing of such individual student records except under seal.

[Then, the court considers the plaintiffs' motion for sanctions because of the destroyed documents. There is no dispute that the destruction was by an accidental fire, but even negligent spoliation of evidence can be subject to sanctions.] ... The court finds that plaintiffs have failed to carry their burden to establish that defendants destroyed the evidence at issue "with a culpable state of mind." ... The motion for sanctions is denied....

[In summary, the court grants the motion to compel with respect to the contested interrogatories and production requests, grants a protective order, and denies sanctions.]

Note on Effects of the Proportionality Requirement

The Burdensome Nature of Interrogatories and Document Requests: Burns v. Thiokol Chemical Corp, 483 F.2d 300 (5th Cir. 1973). *Burns v. Thiokol* shows how extensive interrogatory discovery can be. Plaintiff alleged racial discrimination in employment. He directed interrogatories to the defendant requesting voluminous information. For example, here is just one sample interrogatory: "9. List the name, age, address, sex, and school years completed by/of each white person hired by the Company at its Huntsville plant since January 1, 1960 and presently employed by the Company and with respect to each such employee state (a) date of initial employment: (b) all job classifications held since date of initial employment, including present job classification; (c) date of each job classification change; (d) plant age; (e) department age; and (f) line of promotion age."

The Changed Rules. This single interrogatory might take a team of researchers weeks to answer, given that the defendant was unlikely to have arranged its records to allow easy correlation of these disparate issues. But the court held, under the then-existing standard, that the requests were relevant and discoverable. Interrogatories and production requests can be exceedingly burdensome to answer. The current requirement that the information be "proportional to the needs of the case" was directed at this problem, and it would probably cut off the interrogatories in *Burns v. Thiokol.*

SARGENT-WELCH SCIENTIFIC CO. v. VENTRON CORP., 59 F.R.D. 500 (N.D. Ill. 1973). "Contention" interrogatories are an important discovery tool. Here, in language complying with the "notice pleading" requirements of the Federal Rules governing pleadings, the plaintiff charged the defendants with "monopolization" and certain other violations of the antitrust laws. The defendants served four interrogatories on the plaintiff, of the kind sometimes called "contention interrogatories" because they seek to discover the opponent's contentions. Specifically, the defendants asked the plaintiff to state the factual basis of the plaintiff's allegations that the defendants possessed "market power and dominance," which, according to the complaint, had been "maintained, strengthened and enhanced" and had "created substantial competitive advantages for" the defendants. Similar "contention interrogatories" asked the plaintiff to specify the factual basis for the plaintiff's allegations of competitive injury and of generally stated violations by the defendants. The plaintiff objected to these interrogatories on the ground that they sought to elicit the plaintiff's legal theories and extended to issues of "pure law" not properly the subject of interrogatories. The court ordered the plaintiff to answer, pointing out that Rule 33(b) [now Rule 33(a)(2)—Eds.] specifically permitted interrogatories of this kind:

> It is well settled that an interrogatory is not objectionable merely because it calls for an opinion or contention that relates to fact or the application of law to fact.... [Citing Advisory Committee Note to Rule 33(b).] [now Rule 33(a)(2)—Eds.]
>
> The clear trend of recent cases has been to require "factual opinions" or opinions calling for the application of law to fact since this type of discovery can be most useful in narrowing and sharpening the issues, which is a major purpose of discovery.... An interrogatory which inquires into the facts upon which certain vague and general allegations of a complaint are founded and the claimed relationship between such facts is not objectionable on the ground that it calls for a legal conclusion....
>
> [Motion to compel answers granted.]

Notes and Questions

(1) *Time and Expense; Corporation's "Composite" Knowledge Required.* How much time and expense would it take the defendants to answer Plaintiff Jackson's interrogatories? What persons will actually prepare the answers? *See* Haydock & Herr, *Interrogatories: Questions and Answers*, 1 Rev. Litigation 263 (1981). The answers of corporate parties to interrogatories call for the "composite" knowledge of the corporation. *General Dynamics Corp. v. Selb Manufacturing Co.*, 481 F.2d 1204 (8th Cir. 1973), *cert. den.*, 414 U.S. 1162 (1974) (interpreting Fed. R. Civ. P. 33). This characteristic of interrogatories is significant because an attempt to force a corporation to give its corporate knowledge by a deposition is not easy to accomplish when that knowledge is possessed by numerous different persons. With interrogatories, the party must instead collect all of the necessary information itself.

(2) *Rules Limiting the Number of Interrogatories.* Certain District Courts have adopted local rules limiting the number of interrogatories, including subparts. Rule 33 creates a presumptive limit of 25 interrogatories (subject to stipulation and to the court's power to modify the limit). The number 25 reflects the Rule requiring self-initiated disclosures, which would cover similar subjects.

(3) *Self-Initiated "Disclosures" as a Substitute for Interrogatories.* The Rules adopt a system of automatic disclosures, which are required to be made without request. *See* § I[C], above. This mechanism substitutes for some of the function of interrogatories. Therefore, fewer interrogatories may be sufficient.

(4) *Opinions, Contentions and Legal Theories.* As indicated in the *Sargent-Welch Scientific Co.* case, an interrogatory is not objectionable under the Federal Rules merely because the interrogatory "asks for an opinion or contention that relates to fact or the application of law to fact," although "pure" questions of law remain objectionable. This rule allows so-called "contention interrogatories." What advantages does this approach have (as versus limiting discovery to "facts")?

(5) *Business Records; Protective Orders; Judicial Management.* Notice that, under Federal Rule 33, it is permissible to produce business records as an answer to interrogatories if the questioning party can find answers "as readily as the responding party could." But the Rule is rarely used. Can you see why? (First, consider whether an organization would want an adversary to comb through its records. Second, an organization can usually find answers in its own records more easily than an outsider, so an opponent cannot ordinarily locate them "as readily as the responding party.")

Note on Interrogatories in Practice: *George Miller Co. v. Compudata, Inc.*

[This Document appears in Litigation Document Example 2.1 in Chapter 2, at the end of the chapter, and is headed "Plaintiff's Interrogatories."]

For a concrete example of interrogatories, answers, and objections, read (or re-read) the documents in *George Miller Co. v. Compudata, Inc.*, in § [D] of Litigation Document Example 2.1 in Chapter 2. You should particularly note: (1) the specificity of the questions that get useful answers; (2) the kinds of objections (note that objections based on applications of legal conclusions, as in interrogatory 5, are inappropriate); and (3) use of the option to produce business records (interrogatory 11).

Seitz, *Get More Information and Less Indigestion from Your Interrogatories*

71 A.B.A.J. 74 (1985)(*)

Do you feel you're doing more for your interrogatories than they're doing for you? . . .

Do you dream of force-feeding the last lecturer who convinced you that "the interrogatory is THE effective, cheap discovery device" with the last set you slaved over, which not only got zip for answers but also had the judge jumping all over you for sending [them]? . . .

Here's the secret

Despair not—there is hope. [T]he secret is to throw out the hyperbole and harassment mind-set that made interrogatories synonymous with the Black Death. The days of intimidation through tons of paper are over, thanks to Rules 11 and 26(e) [a]nd the outbreak of rules controlling the maximum number of questions. . . .

The most important thing to remember when you prepare interrogatories is that your opposing counsel, not the party, writes the final answers . . . . Remember this so you won't have dashed expectations of spontaneous true confessions.

There are four more things that those of us with short attention spans need to tattoo on a ready reference spot. One, there is no way for a quick follow-up to an answer. If you need a follow-up, save the question for a deposition. Two, expect the answer to be "more of less." Attorneys like to play hide and seek with information, giving the least amount possible. Three, do not ask questions to which you already know the answer. Instead, serve a request for admissions to tie the fact down. Four, keep interrogatories simple. Deliver yourself from drafting drudgery.

Why do we bother?

Why do we bother with interrogatories? Because they are frequently our best first line of discovery . . . . They are the most efficient way to learn: (1) who knows the facts supporting the claims [or] defenses, (2) what documents exist pertaining to the claims or defenses, (3) the when and where as relevant to each claim or defense, (4) the areas meriting deposition discovery and (5) general background details.

Note there isn't a "why" in the list. If you want subjective or interpretive information—information that depends on the credibility or demeanor of the answering party, or complex or confusing types of information—use depositions.

Here is a checklist of the information that interrogatories can deliver:

- The identity of all lay witnesses who have knowledge of the facts of the case (claims or defenses). If the responding party doesn't know these names, however, it does not have to conduct an investigation beyond the scope of Rule 26 to uncover them. [Also, disclosures may supply this.]
- The identity of the persons from whom the other side obtained statements or interviewed in the course of trial preparation. [T]he caveat is you can obtain attorney work product information [o]nly if you can show good cause, but sometimes the other side will give them to you.
- Greater factual particularity of the claims or defenses. . . .
- The identity of expert witnesses the opposition will call at trial, the subject matter and substance of facts and opinions about which each will testify and a summary of the grounds of each opinion. [Again, disclosures may supply this.]
- The identity of others allegedly liable to the opposition and the basis of that liability.
- Information regarding relevant insurance coverage (either liability or collateral source). [Disclosures may supply this.]
- A detailed description of injuries or damages, including the elements of damages and the measure by which the opposition claims they should be computed. [Disclosures may partially supply this.] . . .

- The existence, description, custody, condition and location of documents and tangible things relating to the subject matter, including items that a party or witness has written, signed, read or composed; contracts or transactions between or relating to the parties before and after the events of the case; similar incidents, complaints or problems the party or third persons has encountered relating to the subject matter of the case; financial information relevant to the case; and governmental licenses that affect a party's conduct. [Disclosures may supply some of this.]
- Business entity background, the nature of the business, principal place of business, state of incorporation and so forth.
- Personal background, including family history, work and school experience, other litigation or claims and criminal records.
- Facts pertaining to the court's jurisdiction.
- The identity of persons who were consulted or assisted in the preparation of the answers.

When to send them . . .

Ask clear, precise, direct questions. Brief questions requiring brief answers are winners because they are downright difficult to dodge. Stay away from vague, broad or overconclusive questions. They not only produce zero answers but also give your opponent a chance to strike them, which often is accompanied by a judge's verbal thrashing and an awkward explanation to the client. If you send out cumbersome, complex interrogatories, don't be surprised if the other side just photocopies them, adds a new cover sheet and sends them back to you. When you draft questions, ask yourself:

- Could each question be simpler?
- Could some be eliminated or consolidated?
- What helpful information will I get from each answer?
- What loophole will my opponent find to avoid a complete answer? . . .

[3] Requests for Admissions

Read Fed. R. Civ. P. 36.

Trevino v. Central Freight Lines, Inc.

613 S.W.2d 356 (Tex. Civ. App.-Waco 1981, no writ)

[Central Freight sued J. Trevino "d/b/a Academy Surplus No. 5" claiming that it sold merchandise to Trevino that was accepted by Trevino's agent, Billy Brooks, at Trevino's Academy Surplus store. Central Freight also alleged that Trevino had provided Brooks "written authorization" to make purchases but that the check that Brooks gave Central Freight was drawn against insufficient funds to Central Freight's damage in the amount of $989.50. Central Freight also sought recovery of attorney's fees.

[Trevino filed an answer that denied Central Freight's allegations. Central Freight then served a request for admissions.]

The requested admissions were these:

1. The attached exhibit "A" is a genuine copy of a letter presented to Central Freight Lines, Inc., on September 28, 1976, by or on behalf of J. TREVINO, Defendant herein.

2. The original of the attached exhibit "A" is written on stationery of Academy Surplus.

3. The original of the attached exhibit "A" is written on paper on which the Academy Surplus logo is printed along with the address and phone number of Academy Surplus No. 5 Store.

4. J. TREVINO personally wrote the following on the original of the attached exhibit "A":

Dear Jerry Please Let Bill Brooks Purchase Any Merchandise He Wishes For Us Here At Academy Surplus. My Tax Exempt # is 1-74-1707803-1 Thanks

5. J. TREVINO personally signed the original of the attached exhibit "A."

6. J. TREVINO has never, personally, or through any agent, servant or employee withdrawn, amended or contradicted the statement quoted in request for admission number four.

7. J. TREVINO is the sole owner of Academy Surplus No. 5.

8. J. TREVINO is the manager and operator of Academy Surplus No. 5.

9. On September 28, 1976, Bill Brooks purchased each item listed in the attached exhibit "B" from Central Freight Lines, Inc.

10. On September 28, 1976, Bill Brooks agreed to pay the prices listed in the attached exhibit "B" for each item listed in the attached exhibit "B."

11. The items listed in the attached exhibit "B" were delivered into the custody of Bill Brooks by Central Freight Lines, Inc.

12. Prior to the delivery referred to in request for admission number eleven, the items listed in the attached exhibit "B" were owned by Central Freight Lines, Inc.

13. The total purchase price of the items listed in the attached exhibit "B" was $989.50.

14. Bill Brooks delivered a check to Central Freight Lines, Inc. to pay the purchase price referred to in request for admission number thirteen.

> 15. The attached exhibit "C" is a genuine copy of the check referred to in request for admission number fourteen.
>
> 16. The check referred to in request for admission number fourteen was not paid due to insufficient funds.
>
> 17. Bill Brooks paid Central Freight Lines, Inc. $50.00 towards the check referred to in request for admission number fourteen.
>
> 18. Other than the $50.00 payment referred to in request for admission number seventeen, no payment has been made on the purchase price of $989.50.

It is undisputed that defendant did not respond to plaintiff's request for admissions. . . .

. . . [D]efendant filed, under oath, his first amended original answer. In addition to a general denial [which is permitted in this state], defendant pleaded that at the time of the "alleged execution" by defendant of the written authorization relied upon by plaintiff, defendant was vice-president of Killeen Surplus, Inc., "and any acts alleged by Plaintiff to have been committed by Defendant in the execution of said instrument would have been done on behalf of Killeen Surplus, Inc., and not on behalf of Defendant individually"; that defendant did not, either orally or in writing, authorize the purchase of merchandise upon which this suit is based; and that he did not authorize anyone to make the purchase for him or for Killeen Surplus, Inc.

The case was called for trial . . . . On that day, immediately prior to the trial, defendant filed a motion for extension of time for filing answers to plaintiff's request for admissions. Defendant alleged that . . . he furnished his attorney handwritten answers to the requested admissions; that he relied upon the attorney to answer the request; that he "did not know until now" the request was not answered; that his failure to answer was not the result of conscious indifference or disregard; that his amended original answer sets forth his position, and, therefore, the granting of the extension of time would not operate as a surprise to plaintiff; that the request for admissions was "overly broad" . . . in that it inquired into all elements of plaintiff's case, and also included matters outside defendant's personal knowledge; and that if all of the requested admissions should be deemed admitted because of defendant's failure to answer, then "Defendant would be required to stand mute at his own trial." . . .

After [a] hearing, the court denied the motion and adjudged that all eighteen matters of which admissions were requested by plaintiff were "deemed admitted." The case was then tried on its merits without a jury.

On the merits, plaintiff rested upon the introduction of its request for admissions and evidence supporting its plea for attorney's fees. Defendant then attempted to testify that he was not the sole owner of Academy Surplus No. 5, and was not doing business as Academy Surplus No. 5, . . . [at] the time in question in this case. Plaintiff objected to this testimony on the ground that it contradicted the request for admissions, specifically requested admissions seven and eight. The objection was sustained. Defendant then sought and received permission of the court "to make a Bill of Exception as to what we would like to prove regarding the sole ownership of the store." Defendant testified on the Bill that Academy Surplus No. 5 was owned by Killeen Surplus, Inc. [and that he was acting only on behalf of that entity as its manager and not himself in this transaction]....

After defendant perfected his bill of exception, judgment was rendered that plaintiff recover from defendant $939.50 plus $450.00 attorney's fees, and costs.

Defendant brought this appeal on two points of error, asserting the court erred (1) in overruling his motion for extension of time for answering the request for admissions, and (2) in granting plaintiff's motion to deem the requested admissions admitted. We overrule these contentions....

Defendant's uncontradicted testimony established that his failure to timely answer the request for admissions was due solely to the neglect of his attorney. Under the agency relationship of attorney and client, the neglect of the attorney is attributable to the client.... In the light of this rule, and the facts, the trial court did not abuse its discretion in overruling defendant's motion for extension of time to answer the request for admissions.

Under his second point, defendant contends the court erred in deeming admitted requested admissions nine through eighteen. He asserts that these requests dealt with facts not known to him, and which plaintiff would have the burden of proving at the trial. He cites several decisions in which it is stated that the purpose of [admissions] "is to simplify the trial by eliminating matters that really are not in controversy" and that the Rule "was not intended to be used as a demand upon a plaintiff or defendant to admit that he had no cause of action or ground of defense." ...

... In our case, if defendant did not have personal knowledge of the matters in question, he should have ascertained their accuracy if that could have been done without cost or considerable burden. If that could not have been done, then defendant should have filed a sworn statement setting forth in detail why he could not truthfully admit or deny without assuming a costly and unreasonable burden.... [AFFIRMED.]

Notes and Questions

(1) *Scope of Admissions: They Can Include Matters of Opinion.* The Rule provides that requests requiring the application of law to fact, or requiring opinions or conclusions, are not objectionable. The basis for these amendments was to eliminate discovery gamesmanship. *See* Advisory Committee Notes on Amendments to Federal Rule 36:

> Not only is it difficult as a practical matter to separate "fact" from "opinion," ... but an admission on a matter of opinion may facilitate proof or narrow the issues or both. An admission of a matter involving the application of law to fact may, in a given case, even more clearly narrow the issues. For example, an admission that an employee acted in the scope of his employment may remove a major issue from the trial.

(2) *Effect of Failure to Answer.* On its face, Fed. R. Civ. P. 36 is self-enforcing. When answers are not made, the requests are deemed admitted merely by the operation of the rule. Nonetheless, courts have broad discretion to allow late responses. *See French v. United States*, 416 F.2d 1149 (9th Cir. 1969). Hence in districts where judges are lenient, as a practical matter, the requesting party cannot safely consider the matters deemed admitted unless a motion to deem has been granted. *See* Garner & Wolfe, *Late Responses to Requests to Admit: When Should Courts Allow Them?*, 78 ILL. B.J. 502 (1990).

(3) *Proof After Inappropriate Denial Authorizes Recovery of Expenses of Making Proof.* There is another way in which admissions are ostensibly self-enforcing. If a party denies a request and the requesting party later proves the requested matter, the answering party may be taxed the costs of such proof, including reasonable attorneys' fees, unless the court finds that one of several good faith reasons exists for the failure to admit. Fed. R. Civ. P. 37(c). But this Rule may or may not be strictly enforced, as a practical matter.

(4) *Effect of Admissions.* Unlike answers to interrogatories and to deposition questions, admissions have conclusive effect and cannot be contradicted by the admitting party. *See* Fed. R. Civ. P. 36(b) (procedure for withdrawing an admission).

Note on Requests for Admissions in Practice: *George Miller Co. v. Compudata, Inc.*

[This Document appears in Litigation Document Example 2.1 in Chapter 2, at the end of the chapter, and is headed "Answer."]

For a concrete example of requests for admission and responses to them, see the admissions and responses in *George Miller Co. v. Compudata, Inc.*, in § [D] of Litigation Document Example 2.1 in Chapter 2. Note the wording of the requests; are the objections valid?

[4] Production of Documents (Including Electronic Documents) and Tangible Things

Read Fed. R. Civ. P. 34. Also, read Rule 26(b)(2).

Judge Lee H. Rosenthal, *Electronic Discovery: Is the System Broken? Can It Be Fixed?*

51 THE ADVOCATE 8 (2010)

The [electronic] discovery amendments to the Civil Rules resulted from recognizing that the existing rules were not adequate to accommodate the distinctive features of electronic discovery, features like volume, broad dispersal, difficulty of review, and difficulty of preservation .... But [c]hanging what the rules say can only go so far and only do so much. To begin with, rules apply once a case is filed; there is much that happens before then that may affect the case (think about preservation, retention, and destruction policies and decisions). And rules are not self-executing; they need to be invoked and applied. In addition to rules, litigation behaviors affect the amount, type, costs, and burdens of discovery. Many of the lawyers' and litigants' practices and habits that worked in a paper age do not work well in an electronic world. Electronically stored information has made us all think about the need for changing not only what the rules say but how they are applied by judges and lawyers and how lawyers and litigants approach their discovery rights and obligations . . . .

Note on How to Read the Major Tours *Case*

The Structure of Rule 26(b)(2), Governing Electronic Information. Rule 26 presupposes that a party must produce "electronically stored information" (such as emails or audio recordings), but the party need not do so if the information is "not reasonably accessible because of undue burden or cost." In the case that follows, the requested information is available only on backup tapes, and the estimated cost of retrieving it is $1.5 million. But even if the information is not reasonably accessible, the court may order retrieval and discovery if the requesting party shows "good cause." The application of these standards is at issue in this case.

Rule 34: Production of Documents, Electronic Information, Tangible Things, Etc. The overarching Rule, however, is Rule 34, which governs discovery not merely of electronic items, but also of traditional documents, tangible things, and inspection of realty. This Rule requires that a request for production "describe [the items requested] with reasonable particularity." But because discovery often concerns finding out about matters as yet unknown, a request for production often covers broad categories of documents.

The Rise of a Cottage Industry: Computer Experts in Litigation. Unfortunately, one outgrowth of these Rules is that lawyers are dependent upon computer consultants. Experts sometimes can retrieve information that seems to have been lost, and they can give opinions about the relative difficulty of doing so. An unusual battle of experts sometimes results, between a requesting party's computer expert who says that the information can reasonably be retrieved and an opponent whose expert estimates that the cost and effort will be excessive. Lawyers and judges have been forced to learn about electronic information management.

"Spoliation" and "Litigation Holds." Rule 37 provides sanctions for nondisclosure, unless the failure was "substantially justified" or is "harmless." This Rule creates especially difficult questions with electronic records, because they are evanescent. "Spoliation" of electronic information by deletion or burying can invoke sanctions, but the Rule provides that absent exceptional circumstances, sanctions cannot be assessed if electronic records are "lost as a result of the routine, good-faith operation" of a system. But what if the party knows that particular information that might otherwise be destroyed is relevant to a threatened or planned litigation? The party

may be subject to sanctions or other adverse orders if relevant information is not preserved. Litigants often provide notification to their opponents to trigger the duty to preserve, and a party that knows of upcoming litigation is wise to put in place a "litigation hold": an order to agents and employees to preserve electronic information.

The Case That Follows (Major Tours) involves a party that did not properly set up a litigation hold and is at fault for not preserving certain electronic records, even though it did not act intentionally in doing so. The court must decide what to do under these circumstances, where the information now is difficult and expensive to retrieve.

Major Tours, Inc. v. Colorel

720 F. Supp. 2d 587 (D.N.J. 2010)

Simandle, District Judge . . .

I. INTRODUCTION

This civil rights case involves allegations of racial discrimination in New Jersey's system of commercial bus safety inspections. Plaintiffs bring this action against two groups of defendants, the state agencies and officials who operate the inspection system ("State Defendants") and a repair shop and its owner who Plaintiffs allege are involved in the discrimination ("Garage Defendants"). [In addition to other issues,] Plaintiffs . . . appeal a decision of Magistrate Judge Schneider regarding preservation of government emails and discovery of email backup tapes . . . .

[The greater part of the court's opinion is taken up by analysis of dismissal and amendment issues. The discovery issue, which involves electronically stored information, appears in Part V, as follows:] . . .

V. APPEAL OF MAGISTRATE JUDGE ORDER

A. Background of the E-mail Discovery Dispute

On March 9, 2009 the State Defendants moved for a Protective Order to avoid production of emails that had been deleted from the active server and now were available only on backup tapes. [The plaintiffs claim that these emails include some that might help them to prove discrimination.] [But] Defendants maintain that restoring emails from Defendant's system of backup tapes is complicated and expensive because the backup tapes are designed to reproduce the entire network environment in the event of a crash, and not for retrieval of particular documents. [They would have to be searched one by one, visually.] Rule 26(b)(2)(B) provides that a party need not produce electronically stored information from sources that are not reasonably accessible because of the undue cost of retrieval. Fed.R.Civ.P. 26(b)(2)(B). [Here, the court quotes the relevant parts of Rule 26.] The rule allows for discovery of difficult-to-access data when the requesting party shows good cause. *Id.* Defendants argued that the high cost of the retrieval from the backup tapes meets this "undue burden" exception, and that Plaintiffs cannot demonstrate good cause.

Plaintiffs argued, among other things, that Defendants' failure to maintain the emails in an accessible format should not provide a basis upon which to avoid having to produce them, because Defendants had an obligation to preserve them for litigation. [The emails at issue were in various categories defined by Plaintiffs in an effort to uncover evidence of discrimination.] This appeal involves Judge Schneider's treatment of this argument. [The orders of a Magistrate Judge are reviewable by the District Judge, and this opinion results from that review.—Eds.]

On August 4, 2009 Judge Schneider ordered the production of Defendants' litigation hold letters, finding that Plaintiffs had made a preliminary showing of spoliation of evidence. Judge Schneider also found that September 11, 2003 was the date Defendants' duty to preserve relevant evidence was triggered by a letter threatening litigation regarding racial profiling in bus inspections. Judge Schneider found that an informal and probably inadequate hold letter was not issued until November 5, 2005, and that the first formal hold letter was not sent until March 22, 2007.

Judge Schneider's opinion of October 20, 2009, begins by determining whether the emails on the backup tapes are reasonably accessible under Rule 26(b)(2)(B). Relying in large part on *Zubulake v. UBS Warburg LLC*, 217 F.R.D. 309, 319–20 (S.D.N.Y. 2003), Judge Schneider determined that they were not reasonably accessible. Plaintiffs offered no evidence rebutting Defendants' affidavit estimating the cost of recovery at $1.5 million.

Judge Schneider then turned to the question of whether Plaintiffs have nevertheless demonstrated good cause for the production of the emails, examining the seven factors stated in the Advisory Committee Notes to Fed.R.Civ.P. 26(b)(2)(B). These include:

> (1) the specificity of the discovery request; (2) the quantity of information available from other and more easily accessed sources; (3) the failure to produce relevant information that seems likely to have existed but is no longer available on more easily accessed sources; (4) the likelihood of finding relevant, responsive information that cannot be obtained from other, more easily accessed sources; (5) predictions as to the importance and usefulness of further information; (6) the importance of the issues at stake in the litigation; and (7) the parties' resources.

Id. Judge Schneider found that most of these factors tilted in Defendants' favor [and thus against discovery]. Although Judge Schneider found the request to be reasonably specific and the issues at stake very important, he also found that substantial information was available from other discovery sources, that the likelihood of finding critical information was largely speculative, that the emails are likely to be cumulative of evidence already produced, and that the resources of the State of New Jersey, while vast, are not unlimited.

Judge Schneider examined Defendants' culpability for the present inaccessibility of previously accessible emails under the third factor. Judge Schneider found that because most of the emails of the key individuals had been produced, there was a relatively small likelihood that the failure to preserve the emails had resulted in relevant emails becoming archived. To the extent that any relevant emails were improperly deleted and archived, he found that there was no evidence that Defendants intentionally did so.

Finding that, overall, the factors favored Defendants and that Plaintiffs had not demonstrated good cause, Judge Schneider ordered that the State Defendants were not required to fully review their backup tapes for responsive documents. Judge Schneider provided that if Plaintiffs requested that the State Defendants search their December 2007 backup tapes, then Plaintiffs and the State Defendants had to equally share the retrieval costs, but that if Plaintiffs wanted to search the March 2006 tapes, they had to pay all costs. The remainder of the tapes did not have to be produced at all . . . .

The question upon this appeal is whether Judge Schneider gave appropriate weight to Defendants' culpability for the emails being inaccessible, given that the reason for the increased costs of recovery was Defendants' failure to institute a timely and effective litigation hold. [Plaintiffs do not challenge Judge Schneider's finding that there was no evidence of intentional spoliation.]

B. Standard of Review

To the extent that Plaintiffs frame their appeal as an argument that no matter the other circumstances, as a matter of law, a defendant cannot be granted a protective order under 26(b)(2)(B) if the failure to institute a proper litigation hold was the cause of the inaccessibility, then the Court reviews this question of law de novo. To the extent that Plaintiffs are not arguing for such a bright line rule, and instead are arguing that, in this particular case, Judge Schneider gave insufficient weight to Defendants' culpability as one of several factors, then this argument would be a challenge to the exercise of discretion. Magistrate judges are given great deference in such decisions, and they will be reversed only for an abuse of discretion.

C. Analysis

1. De Novo Review

The first question is whether, as a matter of law, a protective order under Rule 26(b)(2)(B) can ever be granted to a party when the evidence is inaccessible because of that party's failure to institute a litigation hold. The Court examines this question de novo, and concludes that no such bright line rule exists.

Nothing in the plain language of Rule 26(b)(2)(B) requires such a threshold determination of who is at fault for the data having become inaccessible . . . . The Advisory Committee notes point to a multi-factored balancing test for assessing good cause.

Both of the parties and Judge Schneider rely heavily on a line of cases from the Southern District of New York known as the *Zubulake* cases. *See Zubulake v. UBS Warburg LLC ("Zubulake IV")*, 220 F.R.D. 212 (S.D.N.Y. 2003) (Scheindlin, J.). These cases address the questions of when a duty to preserve evidence begins, what must be preserved in the context of electronic data, what is meant by inaccessible data, and what the proper remedies are for spoliation of this evidence.

... [N]one of the *Zubulake* cases ... address[es] the question of whether a party can be granted a protective order under Rule 26(b)(2)(B) when the inaccessibility of evidence is that party's fault. Instead, these cases speak to the question of when spoliation sanctions are warranted ....

This need for case-by-case discretionary balancing of factors also applies to the analysis under Rule 26(b)(2)(B) [to decide whether good cause exists to discover information that is not reasonably accessible]. *See Disability Rights Council of Greater Washington v. Washington Metropolitan Transit*, 242 F.R.D. 139 (D.D.C. 2007). In *Disability Rights Council*, Magistrate Judge Facciola considered the argument raised by Plaintiffs here, but concluded that the proper approach was to balance Defendants' culpability as one factor in the seven-factor analysis. Only after considering the seven factors suggested by the Advisory Committee did Judge Facciola find that discovery of the backup tapes was warranted. The Rules compel exactly this discretionary balancing of costs and benefits of discovery, not a bright line requirement of production....

Plaintiffs object that unless there is a prophylactic bright line rule, future parties will have a road map to avoiding discovery obligations. This Court disagrees ....

2. Abuse of Discretion

Having found that there is no bright line rule preventing a party from invoking Rule 26(b)(2)(B) when that party's negligence is responsible for the inaccessibility of the data, the Court next examines whether Judge Schneider abused his discretion in his application of the good cause factors to the facts of this case. He did not, and so the Court will affirm his decision.

Judge Schneider found that the amount of evidence produced by Defendants (including depositions of the key individuals and tens of thousands of emails) meant that the backup tapes were likely to produce evidence of only marginal, cumulative benefit, and at great expense. He found that this outweighed the slim likelihood of the discovery of non-cumulative evidence even if there was some unknown degree of negligent spoliation.

While the undersigned might have weighed the evidence of negligent spoliation more heavily in deciding whether to order discovery of the pre-2007 backup tapes, it is not clear that this re-weighing would result in a different outcome, much less that Judge Schneider's weighing was so far afield as to constitute an abuse of discretion .... This Court will not order the state to perform over a million dollars worth of discovery on the off chance that it might add to the five year's worth of discovery already obtained .... [Magistrate Judge Schneider's] Orders ... will be affirmed ....

Note on Sanctions for Nondisclosure of Electronic Records

Sanctions Generally: Rule 37. Rule 37 provides for sanctions in cases of misconduct during discovery. It covers all kinds of discovery, not just electronic records. We shall consider discovery sanctions in a later part of this chapter, but we discuss them briefly here because electronic discovery has produced a number of interesting cases and variations on sanctions.

The Range of Sanctions for Electronic Evidence Spoliation. In some instances, courts have sanctioned parties that have lost or suppressed electronic evidence by shifting costs of retrieval to the misbehaving party. This has included conduct involving inadequate litigation holds. *See IWOI, LLC v. Monaco Coach Corp.*, 2011 U.S. Dist. LEXIS 55333 (N.D. Ill. 2011). In other cases, courts have ordered "spoliation instructions": instructions to juries, to the effect that the missing evidence should be considered to have been adverse to the party that suppressed it. (Obviously, this kind of instruction to a jury is devastating.) *See Ogin v. Ahmed*, 563 F. Supp. 2d 539 (M.D. Pa. 2008). In still other cases, when evidence simply cannot be retrieved, courts have determined that even a spoliation instruction cannot sufficiently address the violation, because the evidence in question would have been central to the other party's proof of the case and now is completely lost. In this situation, courts have struck pleadings, granted default judgments, or concluded that issues are to be considered as found against the offending party. *See Victor Stanley, Inc. v. Creative Pipe, Inc.*, 269 F.R.D. 497 (D. Md. 2010).

But Amendments Make Sanctions Less Scary. Rule 37 has been amended to decrease the burden of preservation a little. The worst sanctions are available only for intentional spoliation. Rule 37(e)(2) now provides that severe sanctions such as adverse jury instructions, default, or dismissal can be imposed only if the at-fault party has acted "with the intent to deprive another party of the information's use." This amendment makes the litigation hold issue a little less scary. But remember, the court can still impose the duty to produce high-expense data.

Notes and Questions

(1) *Electronic Data and the Federal Rules.* Rule 34 governs production of documents generally, including electronic documents. But notice that Rule 26 includes a reference to "electronically stored information" within its initial disclosures provision, imposes a duty to preserve electronic data (but creates a "safe harbor" for data destroyed as part of a regular purging process), and includes electronically stored information within the definition of what is discoverable. The Rule creates two tiers of discovery for electronically stored information. (1) Electronically stored information that is "reasonably accessible" must be searched and produced; but (2) if it is not reasonably accessible, the court still may order discovery for good cause and with conditions, including cost-shifting.

Rule 34 now specifically includes "electronically stored information" within the purview of requests for production of documents and requires that if the request does not specify a form for producing electronically stored information, the party responding to such a request "must produce [the information] in a form or forms in which it is ordinarily maintained or in a reasonably usable form or forms."

Absent exceptional circumstances, Rule 37 precludes the imposition of sanctions for "failing to provide electronically stored information lost as a result of the routine, good-faith operation of an electronic information system." Rule 45, dealing with subpoenas, also now contains provisions referring to "electronically stored information."

(2) *Non-Electronic Documents, Paper Records, and Warehouses.* Rule 34 covers traditional paper documents too, of course. Some of the same issues apply, such as spoliation and destruction. And there are separate issues as well. Sometimes records are so voluminous that setting up a warehouse may be necessary. The adequacy of the producing party's filing system becomes an issue, and so does the length of time during which the producing party must keep the documents accessible.

(3) *Scope of Request: Description of Documents with "Reasonable Particularity."* Fed. R. Civ. P. 34(b) provides that "The request . . . must describe with reasonable particularity each item or category of items to be inspected." *See Robbins v. Camden City Bd. of Educ.*, 105 F.R.D. 49 (D.N.J. 1985) (holding that request for production of documents that "relate or refer to" plaintiff, in employment discrimination suit, was not "reasonably particular" since every document in the defendant's possession could be said to relate to the plaintiff's employment).

(4) *Necessity of Providing Requested Documents in Usable Form.* Courts have held that an inadequate or unwieldy filing system does not excuse a party from producing requested documents in a usable form. *See, e.g., Rowlin v. Alabama Dep't of Public Safety*, 200 F.R.D. 459, 461 (M.D. Ala. 2001) ("To allow a [party] whose business generates massive records to frustrate discovery by creating an inadequate filing system, and then claim undue burden, would defeat the purposes of the discovery rules"); *Northern Natural Gas Co. v. Teksystems Global Applications, Outsourcing, LLC*, 2006 U.S. Dist. Lexis 64149 (D. Neb. 2006) (concluding that the responding party "must produce the responsive data in a form usable by [the requesting party]," including providing the requesting party with access to the software necessary to access the responding party's data systems).

(5) *Choice in Organizing the Response.* Rule 34(b) states that "A party must produce documents as they are kept in the usual course of business or must organize and label them to correspond to the categories in the request." Is this choice—between organizing the documents "as they are kept in the usual course of business" or organizing the documents "to correspond to the categories in the request"—a decision made by the requesting party or by the responding party? *See Board of Educ. v. Admiral Heating and Ventilating, Inc.*, 104 F.R.D. 23 (N.D. Ill. 1984) (permitting the requesting party to make the choice); *but see American Int'l Specialty Lines Ins. Co. v. NWI-I, Inc.*, 2007 U.S. Dist. LEXIS 3025 (N.D. Ill. 2007) (suggesting that the responding party has the choice). The majority view seems to give the choice to the responding party. *See, e.g., CP Solutions PTE, Ltd. v. General Elec. Co.*, 2006 U.S. Dist. LEXIS 27053 (D. Conn. 2006) ("Defendants, having chosen to produce the documents as kept in the ordinary course of business, do not need to

categorize them or label and organize them to correspond to specific requests for production.").

(6) *Possession, Custody or Control.* Under federal practice, inspection can be required if the party to whom the request is made has the right to obtain physical possession of the document, even though in fact the party has no copy. *Schwartz v. Travelers Ins. Co.*, 17 F.R.D. 330 (S.D.N.Y. 1954); *In re Ruppert*, 309 F.2d 97 (6th Cir. 1962) (document previously given to attorney).

Problem G

THE "LOUSY, CRUMMY MACHINE" AND THE MISSING E-MAILS. You represent a manufacturer and seller of a particular kind of machinery. One of your client's customers claims that a machine bought from your client malfunctioned because of a defect and that it caused damage to that customer in an amount exceeding $10 million. Your defensive theory is that the machine was not defective under the contract of sale, that it had characteristics that were fully understood by the buyer at the outset, and that even if it might otherwise be defective to another customer with particular needs, the buyer here accepted the product, thus waiving its alleged claim of defect, ratifying the condition in which it was received, and creating a novation. The buyer, of course, claims that its management was clueless about the characteristics constituting the alleged defect until the malfunction and that the alleged defect was in fact a defect, and a very serious one. Both sides have conducted extensive discovery, consisting of interrogatories, production of paper documents, and depositions of all parties. They also have requested from each other all internal e-mails that concern the product or that took place within two years after shipment of the product.

The problem is this. The paper and oral discovery provides some indications that some members of management of the buyer may have known of the characteristics of the product that are at issue, but those indications are ambiguous, and there also are portions of the documents that tend to support the buyer's position. The buyer preserved e-mails of management from the time of shipment, in spite of its usual electronic deletion policy, because by the time its destruction policy would have been in effect, it knew about the dispute and preserved them because of it. These e-mails contain candid expression between upper management, including sharp reprimands, occasional profanity, and blunt assessments of performance. Most of the exchanges about the machine, however, center upon whether the buyer even needed such a machine at all. One manager's e-mail calls it a "lousy, crummy machine" and incidentally mentions the specific characteristic that now is alleged to constitute the defect, but it is doubtful that it provides sufficient evidence to support your case, because its thrust is that the machine was not needed in the first place.

But although it preserved management e-mails, the buyer did not preserve the e-mails among lesser ranking employees, the ones who actually used the machines. Depositions of some of these employees indicate that they possibly knew of the defect and complained about it, but probably, they were countermanded by management.

But the depositions provide oral testimony only, and the employees are loyal to their company and they hedge all of their remarks. You expect that their e-mails would contain more compelling, raw statements uttered at the key times, if you had those e-mails. But you don't, because the buyer deleted them. The buyer's explanation is that its information technology department did not understand the preservation request, applied it to management e-mails only, would have experienced great expense anyway in applying it to all lesser employees because there are so many, probably acted reasonably in not retaining that huge volume of communications, and if it had retained those e-mails, they probably would not have turned up anything useful anyway. Your expert tells you that the buyer might be able to retrieve these e-mails, but it might cost anywhere from $100,000 to $1 million to retrieve them, and there is no assurance that all, or even any, could in fact be retrieved.

(1) *The Transformation of Evidence Brought about by E-mail, in Cases in General—Not Just This One.* E-mail is pervasive in business as a substitute for what was once done by face-to-face communications or telephone. Like those media, it often includes raw expression of a kind unlikely to surface in a business memorandum or letter. Why do you suppose that this is so, and what effect do you think discovery of e-mails will have in changing the nature of proof offered in business or personal disputes, in general, in the future?

(2) *Your Options for Obtaining Discovery or Other Relief with Respect to the Employee E-mails.* What are your options for seeking discovery or other relief with respect to the lower-employee e-mails, how would you develop them, and what would you need to supply to the court to show your entitlement to them? This question will require you to generate and understand the arguments that the opposing party, the buyer, may make, as well as your own arguments.

(3) *The Strange New World of Data Preservation or "Legal Holds": See the Following Article.* Actually, the process of electronic discovery begins long before the situation arises that is assumed in this problem. Even before suit, a potential party has duties of data preservation and must set up a "legal hold" of electronically stored information. The task is burdensome, and the penalties for failure can be severe. Consider the following article.

Brad Harris & Craig Ball, *What's There to Hold Onto?: An Enlightened Approach to Data Preservation in the Era of the Legal Hold*

Corporate Counsel, Feb. 14, 2011 (Online Version)

... All too often, we see half-hearted attempts at data preservation undertaken with little understanding of an organization's information resources. A generic hold directive dispatched en masse to custodians carries high risks. Many will ignore it as incomprehensible or dismiss it as impractical. Worse, it may trigger absurd Herculean preservation efforts crippling productivity and budgets.

The [court] decisions tip the scales toward:

- *Higher standards*—practices once thought acceptable or perhaps merely negligent are now understood to be sufficient to touch off sanctions;
- *Higher stakes*— [the rules can put] litigants at risk of the most severe sanctions, even dispositive sanction; and
- *New vulnerabilities*—adversaries in litigation have greater incentive to challenge an opponent's preservation efforts when a flawed legal hold becomes a shortcut to victory.

Take a Fresh Look at Legal Holds

. . . It is important to note what a legal hold is not. It is not just a letter, memo or e-mail. It is not a rote exercise. It is not a perfect process. There is no "one-size-fits-all" solution. A legal hold is an organic, bespoke process.

1. Know where you're going, then construct your legal hold to get there.

. . . Begin the process by anticipating the evidence that your side will require and the other side will seek. Who are the most likely witnesses? What did they rely upon in decision-making? What are the issues before the court and the records that bear on them?

Anticipate as well the changes that are likely to occur between the times the preservation obligation attaches and the collection or processing of relevant data is performed. Employees leave or change positions. Systems are replaced and updated. Content is purged. Tapes are rotated. Hard drives fail.

2. Have a legal hold process—and execute it.

Demonstrating that you had routine policies, procedures, tools, personnel, and lines of communication in operation, ones that were likely to promote sound preservation, goes a long way to deflecting the evidence of bad faith at the heart of most sanctions. To meet the threshold that courts expect, consider the following as key elements of a sound legal hold process:

1. Issue timely, written legal hold directives;
2. Ensure custodians understand what's required and how to comply;
3. Follow up (e.g., confirmation and clarity);
4. Provide for periodic updates and reminders;
5. Account for employee mobility and turnover;
6. Consider third-party custodians;
7. Thoroughly document actions and the bases for decisions;
8. Develop procedures, recordkeeping and training materials that leverage past preservation efforts; and
9. Remember that legal hold is a process, not simply a document.

Often, the process can be greatly aided using software tools designed to manage the legal hold . . . .

3. Know that spoliation occurs even when you do your best.

. . . Implementing a legal hold is not about scooping up all of the ESI and responsive data and locking it in a vault; it's taking reasonable steps to assure that data will be there when needed.

4. Don't over-preserve.

Over-preservation saddles litigants with a real, immediate cost that must be weighed against the potential for responsive information being lost. A hold notice goes too far when it compels an organization to "preserve everything." That's gross negligence, too—except that the "sanction" is immediate and self-inflicted . . . .

5. Create a detailed written record of legal hold efforts.

. . . Extensive, lucid documentation shows the court that you took your preservation duties seriously: absent, incomplete or confusing documentation proves you didn't. Clear, thorough documentation doesn't just happen. It has to be someone's responsibility. Be sure that a person "in-the-loop" with the skills to do the job well is tasked to serve as your "Boswell," to document the effort.

6. Create targeted hold notifications for specific custodians.

. . . In *Samsung v. Rambus* the instructions were "to save all relevant documents." The court said that this was the "sort of token effort [that] will hardly ever suffice." Consider different functional teams and tailor your hold notifications to their functions. A database administrator needs to know that he should archive back-up tapes for an enterprise resource planning software system, but if a sales manager received the same notice, it would only lead to confusion.

7. Understanding that "self-preservation" has two meanings.

. . . Sometimes clients or employees lie. When preservation boils down to employees searching their own files for relevant material they become the sole arbiter of relevance—a task for which they are often ill-equipped or conflicted. Counsel cannot ignore the potential for custodians to act in their self-interest and "overlook," alter or delete information that could compromise or embarrass them or the company . . . .

Final Thoughts

. . . The elements of a successful legal hold are straightforward and not difficult to execute; but they demand organization, diligence, thought, and care . . . .

[5] Physical and Mental Examinations

Read Fed. R. Civ. P. 35 (physical and mental examinations).

Schlagenhauf v. Holder

379 U.S. 104 (1964)

MR. JUSTICE GOLDBERG delivered the opinion of the Court.

This case involves the validity and construction of Rule 35(a) of the Federal Rules of Civil Procedure as applied to the examination of a defendant in a negligence action....

An action based on diversity of citizenship was brought in the District Court seeking damages arising from personal injuries suffered by passengers of a bus which collided with the rear of a tractor-trailer. The named defendants were The Greyhound Corporation, owner of the bus; petitioner, Robert L. Schlagenhauf, the bus driver; Contract Carriers, Inc., owner of the tractor; Joseph L. McCorkhill, driver of the tractor; and National Lead Company, owner of the trailer. Answers were filed by each of the defendants denying negligence, as well as cross-claims....

Pursuant to a pretrial order, Contract Carriers filed [an answer] ... alleging that Schlagenhauf was "not mentally or physically capable" of driving a bus at the time of the accident.

Contract Carriers and National Lead then petitioned the District Court for an order directing petitioner Schlagenhauf [the bus driver] to submit to both mental and physical examinations by one specialist in each of the following fields: (1) Internal medicine; (2) Ophthalmology; (3) Neurology; and (4) Psychiatry. For the purpose of offering a choice to the District Court of one specialist in each field, the petition recommended two specialists in internal medicine, ophthalmology, and psychiatry, respectively, and three specialists in neurology—a total of nine physicians. The petition alleged that the mental and physical condition of Schlagenhauf was "in controversy," as it had been raised by Contract Carriers' answer to Greyhound's cross-claim. This was supported by a brief of legal authorities and an affidavit of Contract Carriers' attorney stating that Schlagenhauf had seen red lights 10 to 15 seconds before the accident, that another witness had seen the rear lights of the trailer from a distance of three-quarters to one-half mile, and that Schlagenhauf had been involved in a prior accident [in which he had similarly rear-ended another vehicle]....

While disposition of this petition was pending, National Lead filed its answer to Greyhound's cross-claim and itself "cross-claimed" against Greyhound and Schlagenhauf for damage to its trailer. The answer asserted generally that Schlagenhauf's negligence proximately caused the accident. The cross-claim additionally alleged that Greyhound and Schlagenhauf were negligent

> [b]y permitting said bus to be operated over and upon said public highway ... when both the said Greyhound Corporation and said Robert L. Schlagenhauf knew that the eyes and vision of the said Robert L. Schlagenhauf was [sic] impaired and deficient.

The District Court, on the basis of the petition filed by Contract Carriers, and without any hearing, ordered Schlagenhauf to submit to nine examinations—one by each of the recommended specialists—despite the fact that the petition clearly requested a total of only four examinations. [The trial judge later issued a "corrected" order that required only four examinations.] . . .

Petitioner . . . contends that his mental or physical condition was not "in controversy" and "good cause" was not shown for the examinations, both as required by the express terms of Rule 35. . . .

It is notable . . . that in none of the other discovery provisions is there a restriction that the matter be "in controversy," and only in Rule 34 is there Rule 35's requirement that the movant affirmatively demonstrate "good cause." . . .

The "good cause" and "in controversy" requirements are not met by mere conclusory allegations of the pleadings—nor by mere relevance to the case—but require an affirmative showing by the movant that each condition as to which the examination is sought is really and genuinely in controversy and that good cause exists for ordering each particular examination. Obviously, what may be good cause for one type of examination may not be so for another. The ability of the movant to obtain the desired information by other means is also relevant. . . .

Of course, there are situations where the pleadings alone are sufficient to meet these requirements. A plaintiff in a negligence action who asserts mental or physical injury, *cf. Sibbach v. Wilson & Co., supra*, places that mental or physical injury clearly in controversy and provides the defendant with good cause for an examination to determine the existence and extent of such asserted injury. . . .

Here, however, Schlagenhauf did not assert his mental or physical condition either in support of or in defense of a claim. His condition was sought to be placed in issue by other parties. Thus, under the principles discussed above, Rule 35 required that these parties make an affirmative showing that petitioner's mental or physical condition was in controversy and that there was good cause for the examinations requested. This, the record plainly shows, they failed to do.

The only allegations in the pleadings relating to this subject were the general conclusory statement in Contract Carriers' answer to the cross-claim that "Schlagenhauf was not mentally or physically capable of operating" the bus at the time of the accident and the limited allegation in National Lead's cross-claim that, at the time of the accident, "the eyes and vision of . . . Schlagenhauf was [sic] impaired and deficient."

The attorney's affidavit attached to the petition for the examinations provided:

> That . . . Schlagenhauf, in his deposition . . . admitted that he saw red lights for 10 to 15 seconds prior to a collision with a semi-tractor trailer unit and yet drove his vehicle on without reducing speed and without altering the course thereof. . . .
>
> . . . Schlagenhauf has admitted in his deposition . . . that he was involved in a [prior] similar type rear end collision. . . .

This record cannot support even the corrected order which required one examination in each of the four specialties of internal medicine, ophthalmology, neurology, and psychiatry. Nothing in the pleadings or affidavit would afford a basis for a belief that Schlagenhauf was suffering from a mental or neurological illness warranting wide-ranging psychiatric or neurological examinations. Nor is there anything stated justifying the broad internal medicine examination.

The only specific allegation made in support of the four examinations ordered was that the "eyes and vision" of Schlagenhauf were impaired. Considering this in conjunction with the affidavit, we would be hesitant to set aside a visual examination if it had been the only one ordered. However, as the case must be remanded to the District Court because of the other examinations ordered, it would be appropriate for the District Judge to reconsider also this order in light of the guidelines set forth in this opinion. . . .

Mr. Justice Black, with whom Mr. Justice Clark joins, concurring in part and dissenting in part.

[Justice Black regarded evidence that might bear on Schlagenhauf's ability to drive as "of the highest relevance." He would have allowed broader examination, including Schlagenhauf's "mental or physical health." As he put it, when a driver twice rear-ends a visible moving truck on an open road, "one is . . . likely to ask, 'What is the matter with that driver? Is he blind or crazy?'"]

Mr. Justice Douglas, dissenting in part.

[Justice Douglas feared that the plaintiff's doctors would "go on a fishing expedition in search of anything which will tend to prove that the defendant was unfit." And "a doctor for a fee can easily discover something wrong with any patient." Thus "the real trial will be held there and not before the jury. . . . The doctor has a holiday in the privacy of his office." As Justice Douglas saw the matter, Congress and the Court had authorized medical examinations when the party had claimed a medical condition, as a personal injury plaintiff, but not otherwise, and the "right to keep one's person inviolate" should therefore prevail.]

[The dissenting opinion of Justice Harlan is omitted.]

Notes and Questions

(1) *Persons under Party's "Control."* Rule 35 states that "The court has the same authority to order a party to produce for examination a person who is in its custody or under its legal control." Some courts have held that this does not include a party's agents or employees. *See Kropp v. General Dynamics Corp.*, 202 F. Supp. 207 (E.D. Mich. 1962).

(2) *Who Chooses the Examining Physician?* As a general rule, the examining party has been the one to choose the examining physician, but it is within the trial court's discretion to select a neutral physician. *See Postell v. Amana Refrigeration, Inc.*, 87 F.R.D. 706 (N.D. Ga. 1980). *See also Employers Mut. Cas. Co. v. Street*, 702 S.W.2d

779 (Tex. App.-Ft. Worth 1986) (interpreting Tex. R. Civ. P. 167a, which is substantially identical to Fed. R. Civ. P. 35).

[6] "Discovery That Is Not Discovery": Freedom of Information Laws

Note on FOIA

Federal and state freedom of information laws were not enacted for the primary purpose of giving litigators another method for discovering facts. Nonetheless, it is permissible to take advantage of them for that purpose, and many lawyers do so. *See* Tomlinson, *Use of the Freedom of Information Act for Discovery Purposes*, 43 Md. L. Rev. 119 (1984). The federal Freedom of Information Act, 5 U.S.C. §552 (1982), requires federal agencies and departments to make their records available for inspection and copying upon request. The government's obligation to provide the records is subject to several exceptions.

[7] Discovery in International Litigation: The Hague Evidence Convention

Note on the Hague Convention

Importance of International Litigation; The Hague Evidence Convention. The Hague Evidence Convention is an international agreement among certain "Contracting States" to provide for litigation that is not confined to one nation's borders. In Chapter 2, we described the Hague Convention as a method of obtaining international service of process; this related Evidence Convention provides mechanisms for international discovery.

How Discovery Under the Hague Evidence Convention Can Be Used to Obtain Information Abroad, from Persons Not Present in the United States: "Letters Rogatory." Discovery under the Hague Evidence Convention most commonly begins with a "Letter of Request" or "Letter Rogatory." (The best way to prepare such a letter probably is to work backwards; that is, begin with a form that is familiar to the Central Authority in the foreign jurisdiction, adapt it to case details in the foreign language, and then translate it into English.) The discoverer then moves the trial court in the United States to enter an Order approving the Letter of Request. The discoveror then sends the Order and Letter of Request, together with a certified official-language translation (that's why it is best to work backwards), to a "Central Authority," which the foreign jurisdiction is required under the Convention to designate. That authority forwards the Request to the "Competent Authority" that will execute it and then returns the responsive documents through the same channels.

Other Nations Disfavor U.S.-Style Discovery: "Blocking Statutes." But because extensive pretrial discovery is not favored outside the United States, it is difficult to obtain full responses. In fact, some nations have adopted "blocking" statutes designed to prevent American-style discovery. *E.g.*, French Penal Code Law

No. 80-538, Art. 1A. *See generally* Alonso, *International Business Litigation*, in University of Houston, Advanced Business Litigation D1, D13-D16 (D. Crump ed. 1991). Consider the following case, which allows the discoveror to avoid these strictures.

SOCIETE NATIONALE INDUSTRIELLE AEROSPATIALE v. UNITED STATES DISTRICT COURT, 482 U.S. 522 (1987). When the suit is against a foreign national (or even a foreign government) that is present or doing business in the United States, must the claimant use the Hague Evidence Convention—or can the broader mechanisms of the Federal Rules be used? In the *Aerospatiale* case, the defendants were French corporations, owned by and operated as instrumentalities of the French government. Plaintiffs were persons injured by a crash of one of defendants' airplanes in Iowa. When the plaintiffs sued in a federal District Court and sought broad Federal-Rules-style discovery from the French defendants of documents and information located on French soil, the French defendants sought a protective order. The Supreme Court affirmed the denial of the protective order, holding that the Convention was "optional":

> [T]he text of the Evidence Convention, as well as the history of its proposal and ratification by the United States, unambiguously supports the conclusion that it was intended to establish optional procedures that would facilitate the taking of evidence abroad. [It] did not deprive the District Court of jurisdiction [t]o order a foreign national party before it to produce evidence physically located within a signatory nation. . . .

Four Justices joined in a separate opinion that would have called for a "general presumption" of first resort to the Convention.

Notes and Questions

(1) *Is the Aerospatiale Decision Appropriate—Or Is It Merely Ethnocentric?* On the one hand, it can be argued that the court in this case is appropriately solicitous of the litigant's need for information. But on the other hand, maybe deference to other sovereign nations means that treaties ought to define the method of first resort. Might other nations have good reasons for not adopting the intrusiveness and expense that is unique to American discovery?

(2) *Be Careful Doing Discovery Abroad.* In some countries, the taking of evidence is a governmental function, and privately conducted depositions on such a nation's soil can be a criminal act even if done in conjunction with litigation centered in the United States.

[C] The Duty to Supplement Responses

> Read Fed. R. Civ. P. 26(e) (duty to supplement responses).

RIGBY v. PHILIP MORRIS USA INC, 717 Fed. Appx. 834 (11th Cir. 2017) (unpublished opinion). Plaintiffs Rigby and Georgia Florida Tobacco Exchange brought suit against Phillip Morris after disputes arose regarding grading, buying, and selling tobacco. The District Court excluded affidavits of four out of five fellow growers who were plaintiffs' witnesses and granted defendants' motion for summary judgment. The court of appeals here affirms, because plaintiffs failed to fulfill their mandatory duty under Rule 26(e) to supplement discovery responses that were "incomplete or incorrect":

> [T]he disclosing party has a continuing duty to supplement its disclosure [or answers] upon learning that a previous disclosure was incomplete or incorrect. Fed. R. Civ. P. 26(e)(1)(A).
>
> In the event a party fails to disclose a witness as required by Rule 26, that "party is not allowed to use that information or witness . . . , *unless the failure was substantially justified or is harmless.*" Fed. R. Civ. P. 37(c)(1) (emphasis added). [In other words, failure to supplement creates a *mandatory* sanction of exclusion, unless justified. — Eds.]
>
> In their initial Rule 26(a) disclosure, Plaintiffs listed only Roger Davis — one of the five growers and graders — as a person likely to have discoverable information, but they did so by name only. Plaintiffs thus failed to describe "the subjects of that information" or the means of contacting Davis. Fed. R. Civ. P. 26(a)(1)(A)(i). Plaintiffs' failure to disclose the contact information was perhaps excusable, but the failure to include a description of the witness's discoverable information was not. Defendants were not required to blindly search for suit-related information that Plaintiffs possessed . . . .
>
> Although Plaintiffs supplemented their disclosure and identified the other four growers and graders as possible witnesses, they did so only after the discovery period had ended and Defendants had filed their motion for summary judgment. When Plaintiffs offered affidavits from all five in opposition to the summary judgment motion, Defendants moved to exclude the proffered affidavits. . . . Plaintiffs failed to offer a reason why they could not have discovered earlier and timely disclosed the identities of the affiants and the subjects of the information they possessed. Thus, the failure to disclose was not substantially justified. Nor was the nondisclosure harmless: Even if, as Plaintiffs argue, Defendants knew Plaintiffs' witnesses from prior dealings in the tobacco business, Defendants did not know that Plaintiffs intended to use information they possessed. [Summary judgment AFFIRMED.]

[D] The Use of Discovery in Hearings or Trials

Read Fed. R. Civ. P. 32(a) (use of discovery in court proceedings).

Frechette v. Welch

621 F.2d 11 (1st Cir. 1980)

LEVIN H. CAMPBELL, CIRCUIT JUDGE.

In this diversity tort action, plaintiffs' major contention on appeal is that the district court committed reversible error by admitting into evidence two depositions where the conditions for their use, as set forth in Fed. R. Civ. P. 32(a), were not satisfied.

Plaintiffs were seriously injured when defendant's automobile crossed the center line of a highway and struck, head on, the car in which they were riding. Defendant's defense was that the loss of control over his vehicle was the result of a sudden, unexpected, and unforeseeable blackout and therefore he was not negligent. *Savard v. Randall*, 103 N.H. 234, 169 A.2d 276 (1961). At trial, the defendant sought to substantiate his blackout defense with the testimony of three physicians, Drs. Blacklow, Zuckerman, and Turner. The jury, accepting this defense, returned a verdict for defendant. The depositions admitted into evidence that form the basis for this appeal were those of Drs. Blacklow and Zuckerman . . . .

[W]ith respect to the videotape deposition of Dr. Zuckerman there was no exploration whether any of the conditions in Rule 32(a)(3) [pertaining to the witness' unavailability] were met. [Today this provision is found in Rule 32(a)(4)—Eds.] Rather, in accordance with the apparently standard practice of the federal district court of New Hampshire, the court stated in a pre-trial order that the videotape deposition was admissible "as a matter of course." With respect to two other non-videotape depositions of Drs. Turner and Blacklow the court ruled, in the same pre-trial order, that defendant was "to make every attempt to have [the doctors'] testimony live," but in the event the doctors were not available their depositions could be used. At trial only Dr. Turner was present, and a different judge admitted, over plaintiffs' objection, the deposition of Dr. Blacklow, without requiring defendant to establish the existence of any of the Rule 32(a)(3) [now Rule 32(a)(4)] conditions.(1)

The defendant now argues (1) that plaintiff agreed to the use of the depositions, and (2) that defendant's use of the depositions is sanctioned by New Hampshire state law which, under *Erie R.R. Co. v. Tompkins*, 304 U.S. 64, 58 S. Ct. 817, 82 L. Ed. 1188 (1938), should prevail in a federal diversity action.

---

(1) A colloquy directed to Rule 32(a)(3) [now Rule 32(a)(4)] preceded the admittance of Dr. Blacklow's deposition. The court took judicial notice that Dr. Blacklow's residence was within 100 miles of the court. Defense counsel then stated that he had been told, but had no firsthand knowledge, that Dr. Blacklow had just been through open heart surgery. Subsequent to the admission of Dr. Blacklow's deposition, defendant filed a statement from Dr. Blacklow mentioning two operations undergone six to seven months before trial. This was insufficient to establish that Dr. Blacklow was, at the time of trial, unable "[to] attend or testify because of . . . illness. . . ." Fed. R. Civ. P. 32(a)(3)(C) [now Fed. R. Civ. P. 32(a)(4)(C)]. No exceptional circumstances within the meaning of Rule 32(a)(3)(E) [now Rule 32(a)(4)(E)] were otherwise brought forward, and the court did not purport to rest its ruling on that basis.

We are unable to find that plaintiffs agreed to the use of the depositions in lieu of live witnesses. At the commencement of Dr. Zuckerman's videotape deposition, plaintiffs recorded their opposition to the use of the videotape as a substitute for Dr. Zuckerman's actual presence unless the strictures of Fed. R. Civ. P. 32(a)(3) [now Rule 32(a)(4)] were met. This objection was renewed in a pre-trial memorandum and was repeated at the trial. Plaintiffs similarly objected, on the basis of Rule 32, when defendant offered Dr. Blacklow's deposition. Defendant would now rely upon a stipulation which prefaces Dr. Blacklow's deposition providing,

> It is stipulated and agreed that the deposition . . . when transcribed, may be used for all purposes for which depositions are competent under the laws of the State of New Hampshire.

The Blacklow deposition, as evidenced by the caption on its title page, was taken in conjunction not only with the present action but also with the case of Ernest Record (the driver of another car involved in the accident) versus defendant which was filed in the New Hampshire Superior Court. The stipulation, then made, relating to the purposes for which the deposition could be used, is insufficiently explicit to constitute a waiver of plaintiffs' federal rights under Rule 32.

A New Hampshire State statute, 5 N.H.R.S.A. 517:1, allows a deposition to be used in lieu of live testimony unless the party objecting to the use of the deposition procures the attendance at trial of the deponent. The statute provides:

> The deposition of any witness in a civil cause may be taken and used at the trial, unless the adverse party procures him to attend so that he may be called to testify when the deposition is offered.

Unlike federal practice under Fed. R. Civ. P. 32(a)(3) [now Rule 32(a)(4)], New Hampshire practice does not restrict the substantive use of deposition testimony to only those instances where a witness is unavailable for a particular reason such as death, illness, or the like. *Taylor v. Thomas*, 77 N.H. 410, 413, 92 A. 740 (1940). In New Hampshire, a sufficient reason for the use of a deposition is the adverse party's failure to produce the deponent in court. *Id.*, 413, 92 A. 740.

Rule 32(a)(3) [now Rule 32(a)(4)], however, prevails over the conflicting New Hampshire practice. . . . "When a situation is covered by one of the Federal Rules, . . . the court . . . can refuse [to apply the federal rule] only . . . [if] the Rule in question transgresses . . . the terms of the Enabling Act [or] constitutional restrictions." *Hanna v. Plumer*. . . .

We therefore conclude that the district court erred in allowing defendant, over objection, to use the depositions of Drs. Zuckerman and Blacklow without an adequate showing that any of the conditions of Fed. R. Civ. P. 32(a)(3) [now Rule 32(a)(4)] were met. We further conclude, however, that the error was harmless, Fed. R. Civ. P. 61, and does not warrant reversal or a new trial.

[The court pointed out that Dr. Turner, who testified in person, had cared for defendant very soon after the accident, unlike the two doctors whose depositions were used. Therefore, the factors on which plaintiff cross-examined Dr. Turner, although they could also have furnished possible grounds for cross-examination of the other two physicians, were unlikely to make a difference if the others had testified in person too; as the court said, "we think it a remote possibility at best that such cross-examination could have affected the weight of their testimony."] Affirmed.

Notes and Questions

(1) *Unavailability: Should it Really Be Required?* Which approach to the admission of deposition evidence is preferable? The so-called unavailability requirements of Fed. R. Civ. P. 32(a)(4) are explainable in terms of a preference for live testimony. Note that the 100-mile distance in Rule 32(a)(4) corresponds with the scope of subpoenas under Rule 45. Fed. R. Civ. P. 45(c)(3)(A). This preference is shared by jurors, who generally are suspicious of or unimpressed by evidence read by counsel from a deposition that looks like a little book. (This jury suspicion does not seem to extend to videotaped depositions.) On the other hand, states that admit depositions irrespective of witness availability may reason that the proponent of the evidence takes the risk of this suspicion, and the opponent can bring the live witness if she considers it important. In other words, New Hampshire's rule is unlikely to harm the opponent. Furthermore, frequent resets of cases often make efforts to produce live witnesses chaotic. Aren't these considerations valid?

(2) *Should Experts Be Exempted from an Unavailability Requirement?* Federal amendments proposed for 1992 but not adopted would have exempted expert witnesses from the unavailability requirement. Given that experts are costly and often difficult to make available, does this proposal make sense?

(3) *Objections to the Reading of Inadmissible Parts of Depositions.* Because discovery relevance is broader than trial admissibility, it often happens that parts of a deposition, though properly taken, are inadmissible. Rule 32 enables the opponent to interpose most kinds of evidentiary objections at trial. Notice, however, that the Rule provides that objections to matters of form, or matters that could have been cured, are waived if not asserted during the deposition.

IV. Discovery Abuse and Sanctions

Note on Rules 26 and 37

Certifications and Conferences. Upon sending or answering discovery requests, an attorney automatically makes certain "certifications." The certifications are roughly analogous to those in Rule 11 for pleadings. In addition, the rule provides for a discovery "conference" and for sanctions upon violation. Sherman, *The Judge's Role in Discovery*, 3 Rev. Litig. 89 (1982).

Sanctions. Rule 37 provides a range of sanctions for discovery abuse, ranging from simply ordering the discovery to very severe sanctions such as dismissal or default. Within limits, the choice of sanctions is within the discretion of the court. To understand the nature of discovery abuse, consider the following. (*See also* Note, *Discovery Abuse under the Federal Rules: Causes and Cures*, 92 YALE L.J. 352 (1982).)

Read Fed. R. Civ. P. 26(f)-(g) (discovery conference, automatic certifications, sanctions); also, read Rule 37 (sanctions).

[A] "Pushing" and "Tripping"

ROESBERG v. JOHNS-MANVILLE CORP., 85 F.R.D. 292 (E.D. Pa. 1980). In this asbestos personal injury case, the plaintiffs served fifty-seven interrogatories on each of several defendants. One defendant, GAF Corporation, answered six interrogatories but objected to the others as overly broad, burdensome, oppressive, not reasonably calculated to lead to admissible evidence, and privileged. The District Court granted a motion to compel answers to all fifty-seven. It noted, at the outset, that GAF had labelled virtually every interrogatory as "overly broad, burdensome, oppressive and irrelevant," but the court said: ". . . GAF cannot simply intone this familiar litany. Rather, GAF must show specifically how, despite the broad and liberal construction afforded by the federal discovery rules, each interrogatory is not relevant or how each question is overly broad, burdensome or oppressive . . . by submitting affidavits or offering evidence revealing the nature of the burden." The court then went on to give examples of cases in which interrogatories had been held unduly burdensome, as follows:

> . . . *Cf. In re United States Financial Securities Litigations*, [74 F.R.D. 497 (S.D. Cal. 1975)] (interrogatories three hundred eighty-one pages long and two inches high containing almost three thousand questions and costing over twenty-four thousand dollars to answer held unduly oppressive); *Alexander v. Rizzo*, 50 F.R.D. 374 (E.D. Pa. 1970) (objections to interrogatories denied even though answering would require hundreds of employees many years and hours, to "unearth" answers); *Krantz v. United States*, 56 F.R.D. 555 (W.D. Va. 1972) (fifteen hundred interrogatories held oppressive); *Frost v. Williams*, 46 F.R.D. 484 (D. Md. 1969) (two hundred interrogatories held oppressive); *Breeland v. Yale and Towne Manufacturing Co.*, 26 F.R.D. 119 (E.D.N.Y. 1960) (two hundred interrogatories held oppressive). . . .

[Note that, today, these numbers of interrogatories would exceed the limit of 25 questions imposed by the Federal Rules, and the burden would exceed the proportionality limit.—Eds.]

Notes and Questions

(1) *Objecting to Unreasonable Requests (i.e., to "Pushing") Slatnick v. Leadership Housing Systems*, 368 So. 2d 78 (Fla. App. 1979). Is it reasonable for the court to take the position that a party always must object specifically to each individual interrogatory or other discovery request, and must show that each individually is oppressive? Or can the court consider the cumulative weight of the discovery requests? The use of unreasonable discovery requests is sometimes referred to as "pushing." Perhaps the world's champion reported case of "pushing" in discovery is *Slatnick v. Leadership Housing Systems.* The court described the interrogatories, there, as "composed of 2,300 legal size pages in small type (without excessive space between questions)." The court quoted one "choice sample" question, which called for detailed information about the load carried by each steel pipe column in each of eighteen condominium buildings. The court estimated that this single question (which occupied part of one of the 2,300 pages) "might take a week to answer" by itself. The discovering party argued that objections to the interrogatories must be overruled, because they were not particularized, question by question; the appellate court disagreed on the ground that the judge could not possibly review and hear argument on each individual interrogatory "unless he were to accept it as an exclusive line of work for weeks."

(2) *"Tripping": Unreasonable Noncompliance.* Another form of discovery abuse is to hinder the discovery of relevant non-privileged information by means ranging from delay to concealment to destruction of evidence. This practice is euphemistically called "tripping." Consider the conduct of GAF in *Roesberg v. Johns-Manville Corp.* GAF answered only six of the interrogatories. In other parts of its opinion, the court pointed out that GAF had objected to one interrogatory on the ground that it contained the allegedly "vague and ambiguous" word "associated" (the court held that this term had a "clear" meaning in the context of the question); GAF claimed that a question calling for safety claims in advertising was "irrelevant" (the court held the relevancy of this interrogatory to be "obvious" in an asbestos products liability case); and there were similarly dubious objections throughout. Is this conduct properly characterized as "tripping"? Might it be difficult in some cases to tell the difference between tripping and *bona fide* objections with which a court simply disagrees?

(3) *"Canned" Interrogatories: SCM Societa Commerciale S.P.A. v. Industrial and Commercial Research Corp.*, 72 F.R.D. 110 (N.D. Tex. 1976). Some kinds of cases, with recurring issues or fact patterns, may lend themselves to standardized interrogatories. In the *SCM* case, however, the court described the indiscriminate use of canned interrogatories as "an unprofessional and insulting practice." Would this statement be true, say, of a personal injury defense lawyer who sent interrogatories inquiring about the incident and the damages in similar form, with minor tailoring, in each intersectional collision case she handled?

(4) *Remedial Measures: Limits in the Federal Rules on the Numbers of Depositions and Interrogatories.* What is the best solution to the type of problem presented by the *Slatnick* case? Obviously, this type of problem led to the general limits on the

number of depositions and interrogatories and to the proportionality standard. Should similar limits be placed on requests for production of documents, or should the trial judge play a more active managerial role in regulating the timing and extent of discovery? *See also* Sherman, *Federal Court Discovery in the 80's: Making the Rules Work*, 2 REV. LITIG. 10 (1981).

[B] Discovery Certifications and the Discovery Conference

ASSOCIATED RADIO SERVICE COMPANY v. PAGE AIRWAYS, INC., 73 F.R.D. 633 (D.C. Tex. 1977). In an antitrust case characterized by the district judge as one in which "Plaintiffs' allegations of antitrust have spilled over to the discovery process where nobody trusts anybody," the trial judge called a discovery conference and ordered counsel to attempt informal resolution of their discovery disputes and to submit a Discovery Conference Report. After both sides could not agree on what had been resolved at the discovery conference, two different reports were filed and the trial judge was required to conduct a hearing "in light of the disparity between the two conference report drafts." Then, because of the "failure to comply with my order concerning the discovery conference and the filing of the discovery conference report," the trial judge, pursuant to Fed. R. Civ. P. 37(b)(2), "decided to award expenses caused by the failure to comply with my order only against the attorneys."

The trial judge determined the amount of the monetary sanctions by considering the extent to which unnecessary legal expenses were incurred in preparation for and attendance at the hearing that itself was made necessary by the two conference reports. He ordered the respective law firms to pay the opposing clients this sum and further ordered that the law firms "shall not be indemnified or compensated in any other way by [their] clients or any party to this suit for the amount of this assessment."

Notes and Questions

(1) *The Rules Require a Discovery Conference. See* Rule 26, which requires the parties to meet and confer about discovery at the beginning of each case.

(2) *The Discovery Plan and the Federal Form for It.* The Rule also requires a written plan. Question: if the case is small and relatively routine—say, an intersection collision or a slip-and-fall case—does this requirement enhance efficiency, or does it merely increase the costs?

[C] Sanctions

Lew v. Kona Hospital

754 F.2d 1420 (9th Cir. 1985)

PREGERSON, CIRCUIT JUDGE.

Appellant Barry G. Lew, M.D., appeals a decision of the district court granting summary judgment to defendants on his claim of civil rights violations, unfair trade practices, and defamation. In addition, Dr. Lew challenges the district court's order that he pay costs and attorneys' fees incurred by defendants in connection with his deposition at which he failed to appear. We affirm the district court's grant of summary judgment and its award of costs and attorney's fees.

FACTS AND PROCEDURE

[Dr. Lew sued the Kona State Hospital and various individuals because his probationary staff privileges were terminated. After a series of interim orders, the defendants moved for summary judgment. The trial court granted summary judgment for all defendants.]

Defendants also filed a Motion to Dismiss for Dr. Lew's failure to appear for his deposition . . . . Dr. Lew filed an opposition, claiming that he was unable to attend his deposition because of economic difficulties and because of the withdrawal of local counsel. . . . [T]he district judge denied the motion to dismiss, but ordered that Dr. Lew pay the attorneys' fees and costs that defendants incurred in connection with the scheduled deposition. Dr. Lew [appealed]. . . .

I. *Summary Judgment*

[The court affirms the summary judgment. The court then turns to the issue of the sanctions assessed against Dr. Lew.]

II. *Imposition of Sanctions*

A. *Standard of Review*

The district court has great latitude in imposing sanctions under Fed. R. Civ. P. 37. We review the imposition of sanctions for failure to comply with discovery orders under an abuse of discretion standard. . . .

B. *Merits*

Rule 37(d) allows the district court to impose sanctions, including payment of expenses, on a party who fails to appear for his own deposition after receiving proper notice. Pursuant to his authority under the rule, the district judge ordered Dr. Lew to pay $1,203.55 in costs and attorneys' fees for failure to appear at his deposition . . . . Dr. Lew admits that the deposition was properly noticed, but argues that his failure to appear was "substantially justified" under the rule because he was not represented by local counsel at the time and his appearance at the deposition would therefore have been "futile."

The district judge was plainly acting within his discretion in ordering the payment of attorneys' fees and costs. The Advisory Committee Notes to Rule 37(d) themselves indicate that the failure to appear need not be willful. Rather, the Notes emphasize the discretion of the trial judge in deciding which sanctions to impose:

> In addition, in view of the possibility of light sanctions, even a negligent failure should come within Rule 37(d) ....

See also Marquis v. Chrysler Corp., 577 F.2d 624, 642 (9th Cir. 1978) (even negligent failure to allow reasonable discovery may be punished). This circuit has upheld a sanction as severe as dismissal for failure to comply with discovery orders. *See, e.g., Sigliano v. Mendoza*, 642 F.2d 309, 310 (9th Cir. 1981) (dismissal for failure to answer interrogatories); *Pioche Mines Consolidated, Inc. v. Dolman*, 333 F.2d 257, 269 (9th Cir. 1964) (dismissal for willful failure to attend deposition) ... ; *Fong v. United States*, 300 F.2d 400, 409 (9th Cir.) (entry of default judgment for failure to resume depositions), ... *See also Al Barnett & Son, Inc. v. Outboard Marine Corp.*, 611 F.2d 32, 35 (3d Cir. 1979) (dismissal for failure to attend deposition)....

Dr. Lew's failure to attend his deposition could be characterized as "willful." Although he and his attorney received proper notice of the deposition, they concluded that appearance would be futile because Dr. Lew was not then represented by local counsel. After reaching this conclusion, however, neither Dr. Lew nor his attorney notified opposing counsel of their decision not to attend. In light of this "willful failure," the sanction the district court imposed was a light one. [Affirmed.]

Notes and Questions

(1) *Is "Gross Negligence" Enough for Severe Sanctions or Is "Willfulness" Required?: Cine Forty-Second Street Theatre Corp. v. Allied Artists Picture Corp.*, 602 F.2d 1062 (2d Cir. 1979). Although the Ninth Circuit, in *Lew v. Kona Hospital*, above, implied that "willful" misconduct might be required for severe sanctions such as dismissal or default judgment, the Second Circuit in *Cine Forty-Second Street* concluded that "gross negligence" could suffice. In an antitrust case, the plaintiff, Cine, failed to answer interrogatories through a series of intermediate orders, which included several warnings by the magistrate. The magistrate ultimately entered a "preclusion order," precluding the plaintiff from making any proof of damages, since that was the subject of the interrogatories. This order had the same effect as a dismissal, since the plaintiff could recover nothing if it could not offer evidence of damages. The District Court, however, concluded that Cine's counsel could have been confused by the magistrate's oral orders, and it "regretfully" declined to uphold the magistrate's severe sanction. The Court of Appeals reversed and reinstated the sanction:

> ... Cine's action was, at the very least, grossly negligent....
>
> [S]anctions serve a threefold purpose. Preclusionary orders ensure that a party will not be able to profit from its own failure to comply.... Rule 37 strictures are also specific deterrents and, like civil contempt, they seek to secure compliance with the particular order at hand.... Finally, although

> the most drastic sanctions may not be imposed as "mere penalties," . . . courts are free to consider the general deterrent effect their orders may have . . . .
>
> [The court discussed the *Societe Internationale* case, 357 U.S. 197 (1958), which indicated that dismissal could be authorized against a party who engaged in "willfulness, bad faith, or . . . fault."]
>
> Unless we are to assume that the Court chose its words carelessly, we must accord the term "fault" a meaning of its own within the *Societe Internationale* triad. And plainly, if "fault" has any meaning not subsumed by "willfulness" and "bad faith," it must at least cover gross negligence of the type present in this case.

The courts have continued to struggle with the precise level of "fault" that should be required to justify severe sanctions.

(2) *The Relevance of the Rule 26(g) Certifications: An Objective Standard of "Reasonable Inquiry" Analogous to Rule 11.* You should remember that Rule 26(g) attributes to every attorney signing a discovery request, response, or objection an automatic certification based upon a standard of "reasonable inquiry." This standard probably provides further support for the "negligence" standard adopted in *Lew v. Kona Hospital,* since both are objective standards of similar meaning (although 26(g) is not directly applicable to *Lew v. Kona* since it did not concern the signing of discovery requests). Does Rule 26(g) also support the result in such cases as *Cine Forty-Second Street*, which imposes a severe sanction for unintentional conduct? Rule 26(g) apparently provides separate authority for sanctions, in addition to Rule 37, although the purposes of the two Rules overlap. *See* George, DeSalvo & Grose, *Rule 26(g)—The "Undiscovered Rule,"* 24 Trial 33 (1988).

(3) *Procedural Considerations: Fjelstad v. American Honda Motor Co.*, 762 F.2d 1334 (9th Cir. 1985). When the court contemplates imposing sanctions, what procedures must it follow? In *Fjelstad*, the sanctioned party made the following attacks: first, the order compelling discovery was so vague that sanctions based on its violation would not comply with due process; second, there was not sufficient notice given by the opponent's motion for sanctions; and third, the hearing held by the court on sanctions was inadequate. The court rejected these arguments because the underlying order made clear the party's duty to answer the questioned interrogatories completely, the motion clearly drew attention to the failure to do so, and the hearing transcript showed that the party had an adequate opportunity to address the issue.

(4) *The Range of Sanctions. Cine Forty-Second Street*, in Note 1 above, gives a short summary of the range of sanctions, from ordering expenses at the milder end of the range; through taking facts as established, precluding evidence, or striking pleadings as intermediate sanctions; to dismissal, default, or contempt at the more severe end. For violation of a court order regarding discovery, however, these sanctions are merely examples, and the court actually has broad authority to "issue further just

orders." Rule 37(b)(2). *See also* Note, *The Misuse of Inherent Powers When Imposing Sanctions for Discovery Abuse: The Exclusivity of Rule 37*, 9 CARDOZO L. REV. 1779 (1988).

Note on Sanctions in Practice: Rule 37 Motion in *George Miller Co. v. Compudata, Inc.*

[This Document appears in Litigation Document Example 2.1 in Chapter 2, at the end of the chapter, and is headed "Plaintiff's Motion."]

For a concrete example of the use of sanctions, read (or re-read) the Rule 37 Motion in *George Miller Co. v. Compudata, Inc.*, in § [D] of Litigation Document Example 2.1 in Chapter 2. Note that the respondent had refused to answer some questions and requests for admissions on "legal conclusion" grounds, in circumstances wherein the Rules clearly preclude this objection. What sanctions, if any, would be appropriate? In the real cases the court assessed no sanctions—but that was before the 1983 and 1993 amendments to Rule 11, the certification requirements in Rule 26, and the current "get tough" attitude on sanctions.

V. Discovery Under State Rules

Variations on the Federal Theme. Many of the states follow the federal discovery model closely. To a greater or lesser degree, so do the states whose laws are discussed here. These notes are not complete descriptions of any of the systems discussed; they bring out a few interesting differences from the federal system.

California's Discovery Provisions. California's system is often closely analogous to the federal system. CCP § 2017.010. Protective orders, however, are not confined to a single, central provision as in Federal Rule 26(c); instead, there are protective order and sanction provisions tailored to each of the discovery devices. For example, sixteen different oral deposition protective orders are specified in § 2025.420, plus a catchall provision. Some of the other California provisions that differ significantly from federal practice are § 2033.280, which requires the requesting party to seek a court order providing that unanswered requests for admission are deemed admitted (but requires the court to make the order unless the opposing party substantially complies before the hearing); and §§ 2025.340 and 2025.620, which contain detailed provisions for videotaped depositions and allow videotaped experts' depositions to be used at trial irrespective of availability.

In addition, California has presumptive limits upon discovery. Under § 2025.610, only one deposition of any natural person is allowed, unless the court orders otherwise after a showing of good cause. And §§ 2030.030 and 2033.030 limit each party to 35 interrogatories and 35 requests for admission, although a party may exceed these limits by filing appropriate declarations.

California's Economic Litigation Act for Limited Civil Cases, CCP §§90–100. When the amount in controversy is $25,000 or less, this California Act prescribes a standard-form "case questionnaire"—and, beyond that, confines the parties to one (1) deposition plus any combination of thirty-five (35) interrogatories ("with no subparts"), demands to produce, and requests for admission. There are other provisions more generally applicable. [Is this a good idea?]

Texas: A Few Significant Differences from the Federal Rules. The Texas discovery rules set up a three-tiered discovery scheme in an effort to tailor the amount of discovery to the complexity of the case. Level 1 applies to small cases (monetary recovery of $50,000 or less). Level 2 applies to most cases and Level 3, which requires a tailored discovery control plan, comparable to a Rule 16 scheduling order, is applicable to complex cases. Tex. R. Civ. P. 190.

In Level 1 cases, each party may have no more than six hours to examine all witnesses in oral depositions. The parties may agree to expand this limit to ten hours, but cannot agree to more than ten hours without a court order. In Level 2, each side is entitled to no more than 50 hours in oral depositions to examine opposing parties, experts and persons subject to the control of opposing parties. Other witnesses are not subject to the 50 hour limit. In Level 3, the court determines the amount of deposition discovery. *See* Tex. R. Civ. P. 190. In any event, unless otherwise agreed, no side may examine an individual witness for more than six hours. *See* Tex. R. Civ. P. 199.5.

Texas discovery also provides a "request for disclosure" of basic information. Tex. R. Civ. P. 194. This procedural device replaces the use of interrogatories for certain commonly relevant factual matters and for information regarding testifying experts. Tex R. Civ. P. 195.1. Interrogatories are limited to no more than 25 under level 1 and level 2. Tex. R. Civ. P. 190. Depositions may be used at trial without any showing of unavailability, as in California. Tex. R. Civ. P. 203. Expert witnesses are covered differently than they are by the Federal Rules. Texas expressly provides for discovery of consultants' opinions if their work is reviewed by a testifying expert, but not otherwise. Tex. R. Civ. P. 192.3(e). Also the Texas version of work product, which otherwise resembles Federal Rule 26(b), does not protect witness statements from discovery. Tex. R. Civ. P. 192.5. A statement taken from a client may, however, be protected by the attorney-client privilege. Tex. R. Civ. P. 192, cmt. 9.

VI. Real Life as a Lawyer

What Do You Do in Discovery Against a So-Called "Rambo" Lawyer?

Imagine that you have filed a lawsuit based on a claim that you know is going to be difficult to prove. Now, you receive an answer signed by Ed R. Hardcastle. Everyone knows that Hardcastle is a "Rambo lawyer": one who will harass, insult, and bully, while breaking both rules and customs. And you realize that you won't get help from the court, because the judge vehemently avoids what she calls "squabbles between lawyers" (as many judges do). If you file a motion for sanctions, you can bet that Hardcastle will file a counter-motion for sanctions against you and back it up with a good story. Hardcastle's answer is full of defenses that probably don't exist, but it will take many hours of investigation to sort them out.

In discovery, Hardcastle knows how to send innocent-looking interrogatories and document requests that will take weeks or months to answer. He will refuse to answer legitimate discovery by asserting invented rules. He will push and insult your client and witnesses in depositions. He will schedule depositions and then, without notice, not show up for them, causing you and your client to waste whole afternoons. Then, his secretary will call with a lame excuse.

Actually, this is only one of many types of difficult people that you will encounter occasionally in law practice. Judges may unexpectedly embarrass you in front of clients, your clients may in turn disappoint and criticize you, co-counsel may let you down, and rules of law may produce unexpected, unjust results. Most of the time, these things don't happen, and law practice is rewarding, but they happen enough so that you will need to learn to deal with them. (Incidentally don't say, "I'm not going into litigation, so it won't happen to me" because these things happen to transactional lawyers too.) The Appendix at the end of this book tells more. *See Appendix* Parts II[2]–[4]; *see* Part II [4] for advice about the Rambo litigator.

VII. How to Answer the Chapter Summary Problem: Some Suggestions

Payne v. West York Herald Tribune: A Problem Relating to Discovery. (As always, you should follow your Professor's instructions about how to answer.)

1. Is the requested information within the scope of discovery? (Don't forget to consider electronic materials, such as emails.) Law: Legal principles include relevance, proportionality to the needs of the case (which is subject to six factors set out in the rule), and not privileged. [Explain each.] The items need not be admissible in evidence. Some states have reporter-source privileges, but they usually do not cover claims for libel. Electronically stored information is discoverable if reasonably accessible, or if not, if there is good cause. *Facts:* The request seeks the identities of two important witnesses and seeks "any written statement of or concerning any person" who supplied any facts. The discovery is relevant, but is it proportional? This statement could be read to include any writing done by or about the reporter or editor in their entire lives, and to that extent, it is not proportional. *Conclusion:* Reporters have learned not to promise anonymity. Some requested information here is not within discovery because it is not proportional.

2. Is any of the information covered by provisions codifying the "work product" doctrine, and if so, can the plaintiff satisfy the conditions for obtaining it? *Law:* Legal principles include coverage of materials prepared in anticipation of litigation or for trial, unless there is undue hardship and substantial need, which do not apply to opinion work product. [Explain all.] *Facts:* Since the request includes documents obtained "before or after" suit, it could cover such items as memoranda expressing timelines or the like, and these would be protected assuming they were prepared for purposes of the litigation. Plaintiff will have a heavy burden proving recklessness about truth, which might provide undue hardship, but would have difficulty showing substantial need, given other available material. And many such writings will contain opinion work product. *Conclusion:* The request will undoubtedly cover non-discoverable items of work product, which will be hard to separate from discoverable material.

3. What other methods or doctrines can the newspaper company invoke in an effort to obtain protection, and what are its chances of success? *Law:* The court can protect a person from annoyance, hardship, etc. The methods are discretionary with the court but range from denying the discovery altogether to imposing confidentiality limits. The movant for protection shows harm, the nonmovant shows need, and the court balances. *Facts:* For some information, the newspaper will be harmed by disclosure, but the plaintiff needs the information. The court will have to consider differing protective methods and the balance of harm and need. For example, the court could require disclosure of the sources' identities but disallow transmission to anyone but the plaintiff's attorney. *Conclusion:* Some kinds of information probably should be subject to protective orders.

4. What sanctions might be imposed if the Herald-Tribune refuses to disclose any of the information requested: (1) before being ordered to do so by the court, or (2) after the court has ordered full responses? *Law:* Objecting reasonably to discovery is not sanctionable. After a court order, the court may impose sanctions. Minor offenses require fault, but merits sanctions require something akin to willfulness. Sanctions range from monetary impositions to striking pleadings, establishment-preclusion, dismissal or default, and contempt. *Facts and Conclusion:* The court will have to determine the degree of the Herald-Tribune's fault, if any. If, for example, the newspaper is willing to make disclosure but the reporter refuses, it may be that the court cannot sanction the newspaper but only the reporter.

5. Formulate a full plan for all discovery by the plaintiff in such a case. (Assume, for this purpose, that the interrogatory and the request quoted here have not yet been propounded.) After giving and receiving disclosures, plaintiff should use discovery to ensure that the right defendants have been sued, perhaps by requests for admission. Then, the first wave may be interrogatories to find who, what, when, and where. Then, requests for production of documents. Then, depositions of parties and witnesses. Finally, another set of requests for admission.

6. Describe the initial and expert disclosures that would be required by each party and compute the latest possible date for filing the initial ones (not easy to do—you will need to cross-reference Rules 26(a), 26(f), and 16(b)). Assume that the suit was filed less than a month ago and was answered on the first day of the month in which you solve this problem. *Law:* Initial disclosure is required of information about persons who could support a party's claims or defenses; about documents that support the claims or defenses; about damage calculations; and about the existence and contents of applicable liability insurance. Expert disclosures include identities of experts whom the party may use to testify at trial, with reports including a long list of items including opinions, the bases and reasons, facts or data considered, etc. The time for initial disclosures depends on Rules 26(a), 26(f), and 16(b). *Facts and Conclusions:* initial disclosures for the newspaper will extend to numerous witnesses, including the reporter, the editor, anyone else who contributed to the story, witnesses about journalistic standards, etc., documents, damage calculations, and existence and contents of insurance. The newspaper should specifically object to disclosure of the sources and move for protection from it.

VIII. Improving the Discovery Rules: Notes and Questions

(1) *Small Cases.* One of the issues in cases without a large amount in controversy is conducting discovery without the cost exceeding the probable worth of plaintiff's claim. Consider the following proposals. Which ones, if any, would be worth adoption?

(a) *Standardized Bill of Particulars Practice as a Substitute for Individually Drafted Interrogatories.* New York has a bill of particulars practice, which actually is part of the pleading system in that state and which is standardized in terms of items that can be demanded, at least in personal injury cases. Texas has an analogous request for disclosure. A defendant need not draft interrogatories from scratch, and a plaintiff can know, at the time of the initial client interview, that there is a certain laundry list of information that will likely be required to be particularized. Would widespread adoption of this practice be wise?

(b) *Informal "Meetings," Perhaps Conducted by Telephone, as Partial Substitutes for Depositions.* In some kinds of proceedings, unrecorded meetings could be a substitute for discovery. In very small cases, might it not make sense for the attorneys to have the right to request a four-person meeting of the parties and attorneys, and to have it conducted by telephone, and not reported by a reporter, as a substitute for the more expensive deposition?

(c) *California's Economic Litigation Act; How to Tell the Difference Between a Big Case and a Small One—And Whether to Treat Them Differently.* One problem with big-case-small-case distinctions is that the *ad damnum* may not show the real value of the case. Consider whether California's use of amount in controversy of $25,000 or less, to limit each party to one deposition and 35 written discovery requests, makes sense. If you object to different treatment of "large" and "small" cases, would it make sense to have the limited procedure be the norm in a small case, but allow either party to invoke more expansive procedures by motion to the court?

(2) *General Cost-Reduction Devices.* Evaluate the following proposals:

(a) *Required Disclosures; Limiting the Number of Interrogatories (or Required Answers).* Consider the required disclosures contained in the rules. Is this a useful device? Also, the rules create a "presumptive" limit of 25 interrogatories. What advantages or disadvantages would such a rule have? [Can't a single question be written so as to call for large amounts of information? *Cf. Slatnick v. Leadership Housing, supra.*] The parties could use more interrogatories by motion to the court, which the court should grant liberally, particularly in large cases.

(b) *Limiting the Number of Required Answers.* An alternative means of limiting interrogatory costs is to limit the number of answers. One problem is that, just as it is difficult to tell when one has twenty or thirty "questions," there can be varying judgments as to what is an "answer" (*e.g.*, plaintiff's attorney, with questionable ethics, answers a question about treating physicians with multiple names, treating each physician's first, middle and last name as a separate "answer").

(c) *Do Admissions Need to Be Limited?* Some, but many fewer, courts limit admission requests. This discovery device calls only for an "admitted" or "denied" and is less onerous to answer.

(d) *Limiting Production.* Document production is one of the more expensive aspects of discovery. It is difficult to limit, because two different cases with similar damages might require radically different numbers of documents. Might it make sense to provide that a production request may not call for more than 500 separate documents without a motion to the court? Indeed, might it make sense to require the discoverer to show "good cause" to obtain documents beyond a certain point? (Note that this proposal resurrects a form of Rule 34 that was discarded in 1970.)

(e) *Limiting the Number of Depositions.* Should a provision limit the number of depositions that either side could take in a case? Note California's Economic Litigation Act and the Federal Rules (10 depositions). Would it make sense to impose a limit of, say, five depositions when the amount in controversy does not exceed

$50,000, subject to court authority to allow further depositions upon motion showing need? Also, the presumptive seven-hour limit on each deposition protects witnesses and allows any deposition to be completed in one day. A good idea?

(3) *Privileges and Work Product.* One of the problems with respect to items such as trade secrets and work product is that the contours of the protection are vague, and it is readily subject to being breached. As a result, there is a disproportionate amount of litigation over these items. Would the following proposals make sense?

(a) *A "Trade Secret" Privilege.* Some jurisdictions (*e.g.*, California) provide a privilege for trade secrets. The difficulty with this idea is that anything known to a firm and not shared with competitors arguably is a "trade secret," including most information relevant to a lawsuit, and so definition is difficult. Furthermore, even "hard core" trade secrets such as confidential information on advances in the state of the art can be highly relevant to litigation. A trade secret privilege cannot be absolute. Nevertheless, would it be useful?

(b) *Express, and Absolute, Immunity from Discovery as a Partial Substitute for the Work Product Doctrine.* Some jurisdictions (*e.g.*, Texas) historically have had absolute exemptions from discovery for some items that the Federal Rules would treat as work product. Would it make sense, in order to enhance predictability and reduce litigation, to supplement the general work product doctrine with specific provisions of this kind?

(4) *Experts.* Should it be easier to discover "consulting" experts, on the theory that witnesses whom one side decides not to call are likely to be good witnesses for the other side?

(5) *Use of Discovery at Trial.* Given the unpredictable nature of trial scheduling in most courts (*see* Chapter 8, *infra*), and given that the proponent usually takes the risk of jury skepticism, shouldn't Rule 32 be revised to allow the free use of depositions as evidence at trial, as California and Texas do?

(6) *Discovery Plans, Conference, and Sanctions.* Would the following proposals be wise to adopt?

(a) *Model Discovery Plans.* Just as there are forms of pleadings appended to the Rules, might it make sense for the Rules Advisory Committee to promulgate model forms of discovery plans for different kinds of cases and to incorporate them into the Rules? What disadvantages would such a proposal entail?

(b) *Automatic (or "Semi-Automatic") Sanctions.* One alleged deficiency in discovery sanctions is the lack of uniformity and predictability in their imposition. Would it make sense for District Courts, by local rule, to experiment with "automatic" sanction amounts in given situations? For example, a failure timely to answer interrogatories, in the absence of a showing of good cause, might invoke the imposition of a $500 sanction (unless the actual costs or losses of the opponent were greater). This idea has a great deal in common with the enactments in some states of determinate sentencing laws in criminal cases. What disadvantages would such a proposal have?

Chapter 8

Pretrial Conferences and Case Management

I. Pretrial Conferences and Pretrial Orders

> Read Fed. R. Civ. P. 16 (pretrial conference; scheduling; management).

[A] The Purposes of Pretrial Conferences

BELL ATLANTIC CORPORATION v. TWOMBLY, 550 U.S. 544, 593 & n.13 (2007) (dissenting opinion). We first encountered this case in connection with pleadings. The Supreme Court majority held that the plaintiffs' complaint was insufficient. It lacked fact allegations demonstrating plausibility. Here, in dissent, Justice Stevens argues that instead, courts should manage litigation by using pretrial conferences and other devices rather than requiring detail in pleading. He maintains that a federal court can use Rule 16 to simplify "sprawling, costly, and hugely time-consuming discovery." This opinion describes some of the purposes of pretrial conferences:

> . . . Rule 16 [the pretrial conference rule] invests a trial judge with the power, backed by sanctions, to regulate pretrial proceedings via conferences and scheduling orders, at which the parties may discuss, *inter alia,* "the elimination of frivolous claims or defenses," Rule 16(c)(1); "the necessity or desirability of amendments to the pleadings," Rule 16(c)(2); "the control and scheduling of discovery," Rule 16(c)(6); and "the need for adopting special procedures for managing potentially difficult or protracted actions that may involve complex issues, multiple parties, difficult legal questions, or unusual proof problems," Rule 16(c)(12). [Together with the discovery rules, it] confers broad discretion to control the combination of interrogatories, requests for admissions, production requests, and depositions permitted in a given case; the sequence in which such discovery devices may be deployed; and the limitations imposed upon them. [Rule 26, which operates in conjunction with Rule 16,] specifically permits a court to take actions "to protect a party or person from annoyance, embarrassment, oppression, or undue burden or expense" by, for example, disallowing a particular discovery request, setting appropriate terms and conditions, or limiting its scope.
>
> In short, the Federal Rules contemplate that pretrial matters will be settled through a flexible process of give and take, of proffers [and] stipulations, . . . not by having trial judges screen allegations for their plausibility *vel non* without requiring an answer from the defendant.

Notes and Questions

(1) *The Breadth the of the Rule 16 List of Purposes: Chevrette v. Marks,* 558 F. Supp. 1133 (M.D. Pa. 1983). Notice the broad list of purposes contained in Rule 16. *Chevrette* states the general purpose of "sharpening the genuine questions involved in the dispute," and it also indicates that the court may have an alternate purpose: to create a record that would justify dismissal if the complaint indeed is not supportable. The case was a pro se prisoner complaint that had swelled to eighty-nine documents and was pending before the District Court on ten recommendations by

the magistrate relating to pending motions. Many of the plaintiff's motions were "inane," and the court suspected that the claim was groundless, but could not be certain. The District Court suggested that, in these circumstances, the magistrate could use a pretrial conference under Rule 16 to dispose of the entire case:

> [A] conference might very well have resolved the entire action. . . . Thus, if the Magistrate had held a pretrial conference and concluded that the plaintiff had no proof to support his nonfrivolous claims, [summary judgment] might have been appropriate. . . .

Is this purpose proper? [Note: Can you think of any purpose related to the disposition of the action that, in fact, would not be covered by the broad purposes of Rule 16?]

(2) *But There Is a Limit to the Value of Pretrial Conferences.* The Rule 16 list of purposes may seem to suggest a judicial philosophy of "getting the attorneys in early and often." But will that really work? At a certain point, efforts to obtain concessions, narrow issues, and remove dubious positions through what Justice Stevens calls "a flexible process of give and take" will collide with the parties' positions, which after all, oppose each other. Would the *Twombly* dispute really have been possible to "simplify" without requiring plausible facts, as Justice Stevens said, or is his opinion just a triumph of hope over experience that would lead to more expense and delay?

(3) *Flexibility: No Conferences in Some Cases; Series of Conferences in Others.* Rule 16 does not require the court to hold a pretrial conference, and many cases may be resolved more expeditiously with none at all. Would that have been the case in *Chevrette v. Marks* if the case had not grown so complex?

On the other hand, a "big" case may require a whole series of pretrial conferences, perhaps held for different purposes. The *Manual for Complex Litigation* suggests multiple conferences: (1) an initial conference to begin the structuring of a case-management plan and scheduling order; (2) recurring conferences, the necessity of which is determined by the judge, to monitor the litigation and resolve problems as they arise; and (3) a final pretrial conference once discovery is complete and a firm trial date has been set. *See Manual for Complex Litigation* (Fourth), §§ 11.21–11.22 (2004).

[B] The Effects of Pretrial Orders

United States v. First National Bank of Circle

652 F.2d 882 (9th Cir. 1981)

SCHWARZER, DISTRICT JUDGE:

The United States brought this action under Section 3505(b) of the Internal Revenue Code, 26 U.S.C. § 3505(b), to collect from the First National Bank of Circle (Bank) the unpaid withholding and Federal Insurance Contribution Act (F.I.C.A.)

taxes owed by Fort Belknap Builders, Inc. (Builders). The District Court granted the Bank's motion for summary judgment, and the United States appeals. We reverse, having determined that the court's actions were not in conformity with Rule 16, Fed. R. Civ. P. . . .

Factual and Procedural Background

. . . In order to finance the purchase of a contract with the Department of Housing and Urban Development (H.U.D.) for the erection of 50 houses, Builders borrowed funds from the Bank and one of its affiliates in 1970. . . .

During the latter part of 1971, Builders' account with Bank was substantially overdrawn. Beginning in the fourth quarter of 1970 and through 1971, Builders paid its employees but failed to pay withholding and F.I.C.A. taxes.

This action was filed on July 18, 1974, to recover from the Bank under Section 3505(b) unpaid withholding and F.I.C.A. taxes owed by Builders for the fourth quarter of 1970 and all four quarters of 1971. That section imposes liability for federal withholding taxes on a person who supplies funds to an employer for the payment of wages, knowing that the employer does not intend or will not be able to pay those taxes.(1) The complaint alleged that during the relevant period the Bank supplied funds to Builders or for its account with knowledge that Builders did not intend or was not able to pay federal withholding taxes. . . .

. . . [A]ppellant and the Bank entered into a pretrial order which included a statement of agreed facts and a summary of each party's contentions. Paragraph 20 of the agreed facts stated:

> Numerous loans and advances were made by the [Bank] together with various participating Banks or other affiliated entities [during the relevant time].

The Bank's contentions set forth in the pretrial order were in substance that (1) it did not have the requisite knowledge, (2) Builders was always able to pay the taxes, (3) the loans it made were ordinary working capital loans not for the specific purpose of paying wages, (4) the taxes owing by Builders had been paid, and (5) the action was barred by the statute of limitations and laches.

On the first day of trial the Bank moved for summary judgment on the ground that it had not been a supplier of funds. After appellant submitted an offer of proof as directed by the trial court, the court granted the motion. It held that the Bank, having only acted as agent for the participating banks in arranging for loans to Builders, had not supplied funds. It further held that the Bank had not supplied

---

(1) Section 3505(b) provides:

(b) Personal liability where funds are supplied.—If a lender . . . supplies funds to . . . an employer for the specific purpose of paying wages . . . , with actual notice or knowledge . . . that such employer does not intend to or will not be able to make timely payment . . . of tax . . . , such lender . . . shall be liable in his own . . . to the United States in a sum equal to the taxes (together with interest). . . .

funds by honoring Builders' temporary overdrafts. The government now appeals from the judgment entered for the Bank.

Effect of the Pretrial Order

Appellant argues that it was error for the trial court to award judgment to the Bank on a theory which was not included among the Bank's contentions in the pretrial order and was at variance with the agreed facts stated in that order.

Rule 16, Fed. R. Civ. P., states in relevant part:

> The court shall make an order which recites the action taken at the [pretrial] conference . . . ; and such order when entered controls the subsequent course of the action, unless modified at the trial to prevent manifest injustice. [Rule 16 was later restyled without change to this standard.—Eds.]

. . . Unless pretrial orders are honored and enforced, the objectives of the pretrial conference to simplify issues and avoid unnecessary proof by obtaining admissions of fact will be jeopardized if not entirely nullified. Accordingly, a party need offer no proof at trial as to matters agreed to in the order, nor may a party offer evidence or advance theories at the trial which are not included in the order or which contradict its terms. Disregard of these principles would bring back the days of trial by ambush and discourage timely preparation by the parties for trial.

That is not to say that a pretrial order should not be liberally construed to permit evidence and theories at trial that can fairly be said to be embraced within its language. But particular evidence or theories which are not at least implicitly included in the order are barred unless the order is first "modified to prevent manifest injustice." Fed. R. Civ. P. 16.

Neither evidence that the loans to Builders during the relevant period were made by others than the Bank nor the contention that the Bank did not supply funds to Builders could be said to be included in the pretrial order even under the most liberal construction; in fact, that evidence and that contention are plainly contrary to the terms of the order.

Under Rule 16, the trial court had authority to modify the pretrial order if in the court's discretion modification was determined to be necessary "to prevent manifest injustice." The court, however, did not purport to make a modification of the order before granting the Bank's motion for summary judgment. For the court to have properly exercised its discretion to modify the order, it would have had to consider such factors as (1) the degree of prejudice to the Bank resulting from a failure to modify; (2) the degree of prejudice to plaintiff from a modification; (3) the impact of a modification at that stage of the litigation on the orderly and efficient conduct of the case; and (4) the degree of willfulness, bad faith or inexcusable neglect on the part of the Bank.

. . . [W]here as here the court departs substantially from the order to the prejudice of a party without exercise of its discretion informed by consideration of the relevant factors, the judgment must be reversed. . . .

Notes and Questions

(1) *Preparation of the Pretrial Order: Drafts, Cooperation, and Burdens on Counsel and Parties.* It is typical for a pretrial order to specify all contested issues of fact, all contested issues of law, all agreed propositions of fact and law, all witnesses and the substance of their testimony, all exhibits (with designation of those objected to), all pending motions, and all requested charges to the jury. While there can be little question that an order containing these items, in detail, would simplify trial, it should be obvious that the drafting of the order can result in significant burdens on counsel and the parties. First, the sheer number of issues or exhibits can be a problem. In an antitrust case, for example, the parties may have produced documents numbering in the millions and may offer thousands before the jury. Given the possibilities of settlement, resolution on other issues, and other trial developments, might the judicial and private resources expended in attempting to catalogue all documents before trial be counterproductive?

Second, the specification of the issues requires cooperation between the parties outside court; since they disagree about the dispute, they may well disagree about the specification of the issues. In many courts, the plaintiff is given primary responsibility for ensuring that the pretrial order is prepared; is this allocation of the burden reasonable? [Note: What happens if the plaintiff's attorney has difficulty reaching the opponent by telephone, e-mail or otherwise, as often happens with busy (or nonresponsive) attorneys?]

(2) *Burdens on the Parties (Particularly the Plaintiff). Padovani v. Bruchhausen*, 293 F.2d 546 (2d Cir. 1961), is a classic example of the pressure that pretrial order drafts sometimes place on the parties. The plaintiff sued the Liggett & Myers Tobacco Company for negligence and breach of warranty that allegedly caused him to develop cancer of the larynx after smoking the defendant's products. The defendant demanded, and the judge issued an order requiring, a statement from the plaintiff of (1) "the facts," including those admitted and contested; (2) "plaintiff's legal theories of recovery"; (3) what facts the plaintiff intended to prove in support of each theory; (4) the "details" of the plaintiff's damage; (5) all proposed exhibits; (6) names, areas of specialization, and substance of the testimony of all expert witnesses; (7) names, addresses and substance of the testimony of all lay witnesses; and (8) any further discovery required. The plaintiff prepared these items, but the judge considered the plaintiff's statement too general. The plaintiff filed a second draft, then a third; finally, the judge entered a "preclusion order," which effectively prevented the plaintiff from offering evidence to prove his case. The Second Circuit reversed and said:

> [Rule 16] calls for a conference of counsel to prepare for, not to avert, trial.... It is subordinate and conciliatory, rather than compulsive, in character. Nothing in the Rule affords any basis for clubbing the parties into admissions they do not willingly make....

Today there is a greater emphasis on management of cases by trial judges. Do you think this emphasis might change the result in *Padovani* today?

(3) *Construction of the Pretrial Order; Modification to Prevent "Manifest Injustice"; Court's Discretion.* Notice the way in which deviations from the letter of the pretrial order are to be evaluated. First, the court is to construe the order liberally. It is a general plan, not a straitjacket. *See Jones v. Nabisco, Inc.*, 95 F.R.D. 24 (E.D. Tenn. 1982) (parties are not bound by "precise" language of order). Question: in *First National Bank of Circle*, the principal case above, could the Bank have attempted to uphold its judgment successfully on this ground? (The appellate court said no; it seems probably correct.)

Secondly, if a party deviates so that it is outside even a liberal construction of the pretrial order, the trial court is called upon to exercise its discretion in considering whether to modify the order. Note that in the *First Bank of Circle* case, the appellate court did not hold that a modification would be improper. Question: If the trial judge had expressly modified the order to allow First Bank of Circle to deny that it had supplied funds, would this action have been upheld on appeal? [Remember that this standard is to be evaluated on abuse-of-discretion grounds.]

(4) *Relationship between Pleadings and Pretrial Order.* The pretrial order might be viewed as a kind of extension of the pleadings. The federal system engages in heavy use of pretrial conferences and orders to narrow the issues. *See* Rule 16(d). Some state pleading systems instead use slightly more rigorous pleadings, coupled with discovery, to achieve similar purposes. At some point, the process must result in a narrowing of issues; perhaps the principal difference in these approaches depends on which stage, pleading or pretrial, does the narrowing.

Litigation Document Example 8.1

Pretrial Order in Bordelon v. Triangle J Company

This document is available online at https://caplaw.com/sites/cp7. It contains excerpts from a typical draft of a pretrial order assembled from inputs by the parties and filed as a proposal to the judge. Notice that this document includes statements related to jurisdiction, motions, contentions, admissions, contested and agreed issues of law, witnesses, exhibits and trial scheduling. The actual draft included attachments containing each party's suggested voir dire questions, exhibit lists, experts, and proposed charges to the jury. This kind of document may cost scores of thousands of dollars in attorney preparation time. See it at https://caplaw.com/sites/cp7, then click on Litigation Document Example 8.1: Final Pretrial Order in *Bordelon v. Triangle J Co.*

II. The Trend Toward Judges as "Managers"

[A] How the Rules Encourage Judges to Manage Cases

Note on the Case Management Controversy: What the Opposing Advocates Say

The Case Management Controversy: Should Judges Interrogate Lawyers, Set Time Deadlines, Limit Issues, Etc.? There is no question that federal judges, today, "manage" cases in a tighter manner than historically they might have. For example, judges often set time deadlines for the many steps that must be undertaken before resolution of the cases before them. They limit discovery, streamline issues, and perform other types of managerial tasks. For decades, there have been two sides to the debate over whether judges ought to be doing these types of management.

Resnik's View: Intrusive Management Ought to Be Avoided. One of the most visible early critics was Professor Judith Resnik. Her concerns include the possibility that judicial management will not be neutral; instead, it may have a tendency to influence the outcome on the merits. A simple example might involve a judge who is skeptical about a given aspect of the plaintiff's claim and who therefore limits discovery in a way that disenables the plaintiff from finding evidence to support that part of the claim. Resnik also is concerned about wasteful consumption of resources in responding to judges' inquiries about managerial issues, in complying with orders that may not advance resolution on the merits, and in preparing answers to judges' inquiries. Judith Resnik, *Managerial Judges*, 96 Harv. L. Rev. 374 (1982). As she puts it, "I want to take away trial judges' roving commission and to bring back the blindfold. I want judges to balance the scales, not abandon them altogether in the press to dispose of cases quickly."

Flanders' View: But Some Methods of Judicial Management Help Resolve Disputes Promptly and at Lesser Cost. The most visible early opponent of Resnik's arguments contended that management brings about prompt resolution and reduces litigation costs. Steven Flanders, *Case Management and Court Management in the United States District Courts* (1977). Flanders did not argue for a "roving commission" or for every type of management, as Resnik feared; he instead cited data that showed that some managerial practices produced faster disposition. In "highly productive courts," he explained, the following management techniques prevailed:

> *An automatic procedure* ensures, for every civil case, that pleadings are strictly monitored, discovery begins quickly and is completed within a reasonable time, and a prompt trial follows if needed. . . .
>
> *Procedures minimize or eliminate* judges' investment of time through the early stages of a case, until discovery is complete. Docket control, attorney contacts, and most conferences are delegated. . . .
>
> *The role of the court* in settlement is minimized; judges are highly selective in initiating settlement negotiations, and normally do so only when a

> case is ready, or nearly ready, for trial. Some judges also arrange to raise the [settlement] issue early . . . .

On the other hand, Flanders's data also showed that certain other procedures were not useful. "[S]trong case management is not determinative since both fast and slow courts exhibited it; nor is a comprehensive pretrial order requirement determinative; and getting the lawyers in 'early and often' seems 'a poor use of time.'" In summary, Flanders argued that some forms of judicial management produced positive results, but that expenditure of large amounts of judicial and attorney time was counterproductive.

Notes and Questions

(1) *Resnik's Doubts about Conclusions from Flanders's Study.* Resnik cites Flanders but questions reliance on his study for conclusions about cost savings (because Flanders did not directly measure parties' costs or court costs) or about management without diminution of decisional quality (because Flanders provides no measurement of quality; instead he assumes a "close positive relationship between speed and quality"). In fact, Resnik concludes, "Little empirical evidence supports the claim that judicial management 'works' either to settle cases or to provide cheaper, quicker, or fairer dispositions." Resnik, *supra*, at 380, 417-24. But isn't it probable that shortened disposition times, which Flanders's data do correlate with certain management techniques such as early initial pretrial, are correlated with lower costs—and isn't prompt resolution an ingredient of the quality of justice?

(2) *Flanders's Response to Resnik.* For Flanders's answer, see Flanders, *Blind Umpires—A Response to Professor Resnik*, 35 Hastings L.J. 505 (1984). Flanders concludes that Resnik does "a modest service by reminding [readers] of certain well-known problems" such as the dangers of "energetic judicial involvement in settlement negotiations," but that she "does her readers a remarkable disservice by overstating one problem and lumping together all forms of judicial case management." Further, he says, Resnik "is far more radical than she imagines in suggesting so thorough a reassertion of an 'umpireal' role, or what I call a system of blind umpires." Are these conclusions valid (*i.e.*, is Resnik's work indeed only marginally useful)?

(3) *Flanders's View, Calling for Judicial Management of an Empirically Efficient Type, Has Won Out: Current Rule 16.* Several of the Federal Rules, including Rule 16, were amended to authorize more judicial management. *See also* Doerfer, *Why Judicial Case Management Pays Off at Trial*, 29 Judges' J. 12 (1990). Consider, also, the following article.

Steven S. Gensler, *Judicial Case Management: Caught in the Crossfire*

60 Duke L.J. 669 (2010) [footnotes omitted]

. . . Judging changed thirty years ago. That was when everyday federal pretrial practice evolved to assimilate the active case-management approach originally developed for use in cases that were protracted or complex. No longer do federal judges sit back passively and let the lawyers manage their cases unless and until they encounter a problem that requires judicial attention. Rather, federal judges now take control of their cases from the start. The process of taking control typically begins with the judge issuing a case-management order that sets a detailed schedule based on the particular needs of the case. As the case goes forward, the federal judge can continue to exercise control by, among other things, closely managing the scope, timing, and sequence of discovery and dispositive motions. . . . [A] series of amendments have enshrined active judicial case management into the Federal Rules of Civil Procedure (Civil Rules), formally validating it as a favored practice . . .

But . . . many practical questions about the real-world effectiveness of judicial case management remain at least partly unanswered. Does judicial case management really work? Does it actually reduce expense and delay? Do judges have the right tools at their disposal? Do judges have the resources they need? Are judges sufficiently and properly using the tools and resources they do have? If judges are not using those tools and resources effectively, why is that occurring and what can be done to change it? . . .

Not everyone [has] jumped on the bandwagon. . . . The leading critic is Professor Judith Resnik. According to Professor Resnik's critique, active case management creates a heightened risk that judges would exert activist or ideological pressures in ways that would elude appellate oversight. More simply stated, the concern is that judges, through unreviewable case-management techniques, could help parties or positions they favor and impede parties or positions they disfavor. At a more pragmatic level, Professor Resnik also questions whether case management . . . really [does] reduce cost or speed up the process. . . . [O]ther commentators share these doubts and concerns. Perhaps the most influential of them is Judge Frank Easterbrook, who, in a widely cited article, argues that case management cannot work as intended because the judges do not have the information they need to manage effectively. . . .

By the mid-1990s, active judicial case management had been a central feature of federal pretrial practice for over a decade. Yet cost and delay—concerns that case management was intended to address—still existed, and may have grown worse, raising again the question of whether the purported benefits of case management were real. In response, a first wave of empirical studies . . . attempted to determine whether case-management techniques really do reduce expense and delay. The results from these studies have been called inconclusive. A study by the RAND Institute suggested that early case management might actually increase costs unless the court also imposes a shortened period for discovery. A follow-up report by RAND massaged the point, concluding that, although early case management does increase costs up front, it pays dividends later so long as the court requires the parties to develop and submit a discovery plan. . . .

The empirical studies of that era, however, showed one thing clearly: that lawyers were convinced of the net benefits of judicial case management. . . . Moreover, when asked what reform they thought held the most promise for reducing discovery problems, their "clear choice [was] increased judicial case management." . . .

A second wave of empirical studies on discovery and case management has attempted to provide [further] answers. Though I do not intend to thoroughly canvass or analyze the new data . . . [,] I think it fair to say that the results this time around are more consistently and convincingly encouraging. . . . The American Bar Association (ABA) Section of Litigation Survey respondents overwhelmingly agreed that early intervention by judges helps to narrow the issues and control discovery. The ABA Survey also reported that client satisfaction increased when the judge was actively involved in managing the case. The joint survey by the Institute for the Advancement of the American Legal System (IAALS) and the American College of Trial Lawyers (ACTL) showed similarly strong support for active judicial case management among its respondents. Any doubts about the bar's craving for case management were erased at the Duke Conference [on Judicial Case Management] itself. In reporting on the Conference, Judge Mark Kravitz, the current Chair of the Advisory Committee on Civil Rules, remarked, "Pleas for universalized case management achieved virtual, perhaps absolute, unanimity."

So, how should . . . judges spend their time? Deciding merits issues? Managing their cases? The federal judiciary's answer is "both." . . .

. . . Good case managers work with the parties and their lawyers to identify the real issues in dispute and to identify how best to proceed to resolve those issues. . . . Good case managers interact with the parties and welcome—if not invite or even require—client participation. Practiced that way, case management provides the parties not just with an opportunity to be heard but also with an opportunity to see (and feel) that justice is being done.

Consider the type of Rule 16 conference suggested by Judge [Lee H.] Rosenthal. In one of these live conferences, the lawyers (and sometimes also the parties) would be in the same room as the judge. [In some instances, the conference might be conducted by other means, such as by telephone.] Some or all of the following might take place:

- The lawyers and the judge might engage in a genuine exchange about the case so that the judge can learn critical information about the needs of the case. [And the judge may do better at ruling on motions as a result.—Eds.]
- The judge might learn whether the parties have had a meaningful Rule 26(f) [discovery planning] conference or whether they have just gone through the motions and therefore are not truly in a position to discuss their pretrial needs. [The judge may therefore ask input and set particularized limits: ten depositions per side in a case of a given size, for example, and other kinds of limits.—Eds.]
- The judge might learn whether there are threshold issues to be resolved and might consider having the parties conduct discovery or make dispositive motions in stages. [E.g., the judge may carve out an issue such as whether

limitations has run or whether the plaintiff in fact was exposed to the allegedly defective product and order that this dispositive issue is to be decided first.]

- The judge might discuss e-discovery issues with the parties, exploring ways to focus the process and address potential problems before they mushroom.

The overriding theme is that judges who take the time to talk with the lawyers and involve the parties at the Rule 16 stage are in a much better position to tailor the pretrial process to achieve the "just, speedy, and inexpensive" determination of the claims. Moreover, these types of activities . . . strike me as being just as "judicial" as deciding motions or presiding over a trial. But not everyone agrees, and I certainly respect the views of those who see things differently. . . .

[B] Sanctions for Failure to Participate "in Good Faith" in Conferences and Settlement Negotiations

Kothe v. Smith

771 F.2d 667 (2d Cir. 1985)

Van Graafeiland, Circuit Judge:

Dr. James Smith appeals from a judgment of the United States District Court for the Southern District of New York (Sweet, J.), which directed him to pay $1,000 to plaintiff-appellee's attorney, $1,000 to plaintiff-appellee's medical witness, and $480 to the Clerk of the Court. For the reasons hereinafter discussed, we direct that the judgment be vacated.

Patricia Kothe brought this suit for medical malpractice against four defendants, [including] Dr. Smith, . . . seeking $2 million in damages. . . .

Three weeks prior thereto, Judge Sweet held a pretrial conference, during which he directed counsel for the parties to conduct settlement negotiations. Although it is not clear from the record, it appears that Judge Sweet recommended that the case be settled for between $20,000 and $30,000. He also warned the parties that, if they settled for a comparable figure after trial had begun, he would impose sanctions against the dilatory party. Smith, whose defense has been conducted throughout this litigation by his malpractice insurer, offered $5,000 on the day before trial, but it was rejected.

Although Kothe's attorney had indicated to Judge Sweet that his client would settle for $20,000, he had requested that the figure not be disclosed to Smith. Kothe's counsel conceded at oral argument that the lowest pretrial settlement demand communicated to Smith was $50,000. Nevertheless, when the case was settled for $20,000 after one day of trial, the district court proceeded to penalize Smith alone. In imposing the penalty, the court stated that it was "determined to get the attention of the carrier" and that "the carriers are going to have to wake up when a judge tells them that they want [sic] to settle a case and they don't want to settle it." Under the circumstances of this case, we believe that the district court's imposition of a penalty against Smith was an abuse of the sanction power given it by Fed. R. Civ. P. 16(f). . . .

Rule 16 of the Fed. R. Civ. P. was not designed as a means for clubbing the parties—or one of them—into an involuntary compromise. *See Padovani v. Bruchhausen*, 293 F.2d 546, 548 (2d Cir. 1961). . . .

We find the coercion in the instant case especially troublesome because the district court imposed sanctions on Smith alone. . . . Smith never received a demand of less than $50,000. Having received no indication from Kothe that an offer somewhere in the vicinity of $20,000 would at least be given careful consideration, Smith should not have been required to make an offer in this amount simply because the court wanted him to.

Smith's attorney should not be condemned for changing his evaluation of the case after listening to Kothe's testimony during the first day of trial. [I]t is not at all unusual [f]or a defendant to change his perception of a case based on the plaintiff's performance on the witness stand . . . .

Although we commend Judge Sweet for his efforts to encourage settlement negotiations, his excessive zeal leaves us no recourse but to remand the matter with instructions to vacate the judgment.

Notes and Questions

(1) *Permissible Sanctions Regarding Settlement Efforts: G. Heileman Brewing Co., Inc. v. Joseph Oat Corp.*, 871 F.2d 648 (7th Cir. 1989) (en banc). Are there circumstances in which a settlement arrived at after trial has begun could, properly, lead to sanctions? What if, for example, the defendant had contemptuously refused even to consider talking to the plaintiff in *Kothe v. Smith*, even after the judge's order to negotiate—and then, as in *Kothe v. Smith*, had agreed to settle for $20,000 after the beginning of trial?

In the *Heileman* case, the magistrate ordered all parties to attend a pretrial conference not only through counsel, but also through a party representative with "full authority to settle." Three parties complied—but one defendant, which earlier had indicated its unwillingness to settle, sent only its attorneys, who the defendant said had "authority to settle," provided that they were not to agree to pay any money! The magistrate ultimately recommended sanctions in the amount of the opposing party's costs—and the Seventh Circuit, en banc, upheld these sanctions. The decision has been the subject of much commentary; *compare, e.g.*, Tozer, *The Heileman Power: Well-Honed Tool or Blunt Instrument?*, 66 Ind. L.J. 977 (1991) (decision "threatens the traditional role of American courts"), *with* Note, *Expanding the Federal Court's Power to Encourage Settlement Under Rule 16*, 1990 Wis. L. Rev. 1397 (1990) (recommending guidelines to prevent coercion). Current Rule 16 authorizes the imposition of sanctions under these circumstances.

(2) *Proper "Persuasion" Versus "Coercion."* Rule 16 obviously allows for the trial judge to have powers of persuasion that will make the parties behave more

accommodatingly than they would otherwise. *See* Wall & Schiller, *Judicial Involvement in Pretrial Settlement: A Judge Is Not a Bump on a Log*, 6 AM. J. TRIAL ADVOC. 27 (1982). How is this "persuasion" to be distinguished from prohibited "coercion"? Imagine a party whose attorney refuses to make any concession whatsoever at pretrial, even in narrowing issues or conceding unmeritorious ones. Can the judge make a show of exasperation, with the implication that discretionary rulings may take this background of uncooperative behavior into account? *Cf. Hess v. New Jersey Transit Rail Operations*, 846 F.2d 114 (2d Cir. 1988) (reversing sanctions imposed where defendant failed to make any offer after District Court's order to "make a *bona fide* offer").

(3) *Sanctions for Failure to Participate "in Good Faith"; Inducing Settlement.* Rule 16(f) authorizes the use of sanctions in connection with pretrial matters. Also, there should remain no question that inducing settlement negotiations is now "part of the job description" for federal judges. Note that the court in *Kothe v. Smith* makes a point of commending the trial judge's efforts even as it reverses his methods. But can the trial judge exercise this authority without adversely affecting the adjudication of cases that "need to be tried"?

[C] Reference to Magistrate Judges or Masters

> Read Fed. R. Civ. P. 53 (masters); 72-73 (magistrate judges); 28 U.S.C. §636(a), (b), (c)(1) (magistrate judges).

MATHEWS v. WEBER, 423 U.S. 261 (1976). The United States District Court for the Central District of California promulgated a local rule called General Order 104-D, which directed the clerk of the court to refer all Social Security review cases to magistrates [now called magistrate judges]. The magistrates were required to conduct "such factual hearings and legal argument as may be appropriate," to prepare a "proposed written order or decision" together with "proposed findings of fact and conclusions of law," and to send the file to the responsible district judge, together with any objections of the parties. The Secretary of Health, Education and Welfare argued that reference under General Order 104-D was illegal because it authorized magistrates to exercise decision-making authority in excess of that given by the Federal Magistrates Act. The Supreme Court, however, upheld the order of reference:

> After several years of study, Congress . . . enacted the Federal Magistrates Act . . . .
>
> [The Act] outlines a procedure by which the district courts may call upon magistrates to perform other functions, in both civil and criminal cases. It provides:

> Any district court . . . may establish rules pursuant to which any . . . magistrate . . . may be assigned . . . such additional duties as are not inconsistent with the Constitution and laws of the United States. The additional duties authorized by rule may include, but are not restricted to—
>
> (1) service as a special master in an appropriate civil action, pursuant to the applicable provisions of this title and the Federal Rules of Civil Procedure . . . ; [and]
>
> (2) assistance to a district judge in the conduct of pretrial or discovery proceedings in civil or criminal matters; . . .

. . . Under the part of [General Order 104-D] at issue, the magistrates perform a limited function which falls well within the range of duties Congress empowered the district courts to assign to them. . . . The magistrate gives only a recommendation to the judge, and only on the single, narrow issue: is there in the record substantial evidence to support the Secretary's decision? . . . The district judge is free to follow it or wholly ignore it . . . .

Notes and Questions

(1) *Magistrate Judges' Authority and Typical Duties.* The Court in *Mathews v. Weber* implies that a closed record [e.g., a suit to set aside an administrative ruling] is an appropriate matter to refer to a magistrate judge. Would a District Court violate the Magistrates Act if it referred to the magistrate judge a fact-finding matter in which the magistrate was required to hear evidence from live witnesses? No. The Act expressly allows the magistrate judge to "hear and determine any pretrial matter" (with exceptions for dispositive motions and certain other matters, and even as to the exceptions, the magistrate judge may "conduct hearings, including evidentiary hearings," from which he submits proposed findings and recommendations to the district judge). *See* 28 U.S.C. § 636(b). Does this procedure conform to the Constitution's requirement of an Article III judge appointed for life term? *See* Weinstein & Wiener, *Of Sailing Ships and Seeking Facts: Brief Reflections on Magistrates and the Federal Rules of Civil Procedure*, in *Symposium*, 62 St. John's L. Rev. 429 (1988).

(2) *Submission by Agreement to the Magistrate Judge (Including Jury Trials).* Section 636(c) of the Magistrates Act also provides that the parties may agree to have the magistrate judge perform functions that would otherwise be carried out by the district judge, including presiding at jury or non-jury trials. In some districts substantial percentages of actual trials are conducted in this manner by magistrate judges.

III. Docket Control and Case Flow Management

Read Fed. R. Civ. P. 6, 40, 78-79 (scheduling and time computation).

[A] Trial Settings and Continuances

OATES v. OATES, 533 S.W.2d 107 (Tex. Civ. App. 1976, no writ). Paul Oates's attorney was forced to trial in a federal case on the same day that Oates's divorce case was set. Oates's attorney sent a telegram to the divorce trial judge, as follows: "RE: NO. 74 CI-8328 OATES V. OATES PLEASE CONSIDER THIS AS RESPONDENT'S FIRST MOTION FOR CONTINUANCE REASON: RECORD ATTORNEY FOR PAUL OATES HAS PREVIOUS COMMITMENT FOR TRIAL IN U.S. DISTRICT COURT SHERMAN TEXAS ON APRIL 7 1975 STYLED EARL WATSON VS MKT RAILROAD. THIS MOTION IS NOT MADE FOR PURPOSES OF DELAY BUT THAT JUSTICE MAY BE DONE." The telegram concluded with a request for confirmation of the court's order by return wire.

The trial judge, however, denied the continuance and proceeded to hear the divorce case in the absence of Oates and his attorney. The appellate court affirmed for two reasons. First, the motion for continuance was not in the proper form; among other defects, it was not supported by an affidavit. Secondly, continuance for absence of counsel is particularly within the discretion of the court, and the trial judge was not required to reschedule the trial merely because Oates's attorney was trying a case somewhere else.

Notes and Questions

(1) *The Federal Approach Is Similar.* Federal district judges have "broad discretion in supervision of the [time of] trial," and denial of continuance "will not be disturbed on appeal absent an abuse of discretion." *E.g., Sturgeon v. Airborne Freight Corp.*, 778 F.2d 1154 (5th Cir. 1985).

(2) *Why Perry Mason Should Read the Oates Case and Weep.* Full-time trial lawyers often have multiple, overlapping settings for trials, hearings, or other events. *See* Dorsaneo & Crump, *Texas Civil Procedure: Trial and Appellate Practice* 23 (Matthew Bender 2d ed. 1989) (reproducing actual calendar of typical metropolitan litigator, showing fifteen different events set during two-week period, including seven trial settings, one a "preferential" setting). The ability to manage one's time, in a schedule in which many of these events fail to take place, is crucial to success as a litigator. Many trial judges, understanding the trial lawyer's plight, willingly reschedule trials upon learning, even informally, that counsel is in trial elsewhere; however, as *Oates* indicates, trial judges in most jurisdictions are not required to reschedule. Although statistics are unavailable, the authors' experience is that federal judges are less flexible in this regard than state judges.

(3) *Getting the Case to Trial: Delays and Repeated Settings.* The flip side of the continuance problem is the difficulty that counsel sometimes experiences in getting a prompt trial setting. A related, but perhaps more serious, problem is that sometimes cases are repeatedly rescheduled with long intervening periods, making

preparation difficult. *See, e.g.*, Dorsaneo & Crump, *supra*, at 12–15 (documenting five different trial settings in prototypical personal injury case in metropolitan courts, with intervals ranging from less than a week to several months, resulting in trial four years after event).

(4) *The Disruptions and Burdens that Resettings Create.* It may be difficult to appreciate the effect that repeated settings of this kind can have. Clients fail to understand the need for repeated subpoenas and often think their lawyer is incompetent. Witnesses become less cooperative. Trial preparation suffers when the trial may or may not take place. Students might consider the analogy of a final examination that is rescheduled without advance warning for a date six months in the future, only to be rescheduled on that date for a date when it is again rescheduled! For most attorneys, trials require a similar kind of preparation (and are at least as nerve-wracking) as their law school examinations. Modern docket management, which seeks to reduce the number of resettings and the intervals between them, provides only a partial solution.

[B] The Scheduling Order and Its Amendment

Kantsevoy v. LumenR LLC

301 F. Supp. 3d 577 (D. Md. 2018)

Ellen Lipton Hollander, United States District Judge.

[Rule 16 requires the court in most cases to issue a "scheduling order" early in the proceedings. The scheduling order sets deadlines for such processes as amendment of pleadings, adding parties, discovery, and trial. The present case is one of a great many that deny amendment of a scheduling order, deny amendment of pleadings after a scheduled date, and thus destroy claims because of missed deadlines.]

[Dr. Kantsevoy sued LumenR, a medical device manufacturer, over a contract for compensation for work in developing a tissue retractor. LumenR counterclaimed on various contract and tort claims. The court describes the litigation as "scorched-earth style" with "thousands of pages of vitriolic submissions."]

The court [set a deadline] . . . for joinder of additional parties and amendment of pleadings . . . [, a] deadline . . . for completion of discovery, and . . . [a] dispositive pretrial motions deadline. . . . Three times, upon motions agreed to by both parties, the court extended deadlines briefly.

[Later, after the deadline for amending pleadings, LumenR moved to amend its counterclaim to assert a third-party-beneficiary contract claim. Kantsevoy opposed the motion and argued that it did not show "good cause," which is not ordinarily required for amendment of pleadings under Rule 15 but is required for amendment of a Rule 16 deadline. The court here explains the structure of the rules:]

. . . [Under Rule 15, the amendment of pleadings Rule,] the court "should freely give leave to amend when justice so requires."

At this juncture, however, LumenR must do more than satisfy the liberal standard for amendments set forth in Fed. R. Civ. P. 15(a). When, as here, a party seeks to amend a pleading after the expiration of a deadline set forth in a scheduling order, Rule 16(b)(4) is implicated. Rule 16(b)(4) states that a scheduling order may be modified to amend a pleading "only for good cause and with the judge's consent." . . .

In determining whether the moving party has met its burden to show good cause, a court may consider "whether the moving party acted in good faith, the length of the delay and its effects, and whether the delay will prejudice the non-moving party." *Elat* [*Ngoubene*], 993 F.Supp.2d at 520. If the movant "'was not diligent, the inquiry should end.'" . . .

In its Motion to Amend, LumenR merely gestures at the "good cause" standard . . . . [LumenR said,] "Here, there can be no real question that good cause exists to move the Court to permit LumenR to amend its Answer after the scheduling order deadline has passed because, as stated above, the relevant facts were not fully developed until late in 2017." . . .

By all accounts, LumenR was aware of the "core operative facts" of its proposed counterclaim before the deadline to amend the pleadings had passed, and "the fact that [LumenR] may not have had sufficient evidence to *prove* [its] claim before the deadline for the amendment of pleadings had no bearing on his ability to *plead* [its] claim in a timely manner." This suggests a lack of diligence on LumenR's part, and diligence is the focus of the Rule 16(b) inquiry. [AMENDMENT DENIED.]

Notes and Questions

(1) *What about Rule 11 as Good Cause when Proof Is Lacking?* The court says that the defendant could have proceeded to assert a cause of action without yet having proof of the cause of action(!?), and it negates good cause for delay for this reason. But Rule 11 requires a reasonable inquiry that finds evidence or the pleading of likelihood of discovery of evidence. Theoretically, one can hypothesize a situation in which a litigant might be able to plead a claim that it cannot yet prove. But that requires risky guessing for counsel and may create dubious claims, which it seems unlikely that the courts would want to encourage. Should the court have found good cause?

(2) *What Does It Take to Amend a Scheduling Order? De La Torre v. Ryan,* 2018 WL 1664179 (D. Ariz.). Plaintiff in this case was an inmate who sued the prison system for failure to provide him with a diet he claimed was required by his religion. The court explained, "Plaintiff seeks an extension of all case deadlines because his papers were confiscated by the F.B.I. in June and were 'only recently' returned to him." The court granted an amendment of the scheduling order because, under these conditions, plaintiff was able to show diligence.

(3) *The Increasing Occurrence of "Adjudication by Deadline."* In *Kantsevoy,* the principal case above, a partial judgment on the pleadings against LumenR followed

the denial of its motion to amend. The proliferation of deadlines means that more will be missed, and, in turn, it means that increasingly, rights will be lost through "adjudication by deadline." Has the management movement progressed too far?

(4) *The Result Is Like a Proliferation of Statutes of Limitations.* Law practice today requires an effective calendaring system more than almost anything else. The effect of scheduling orders on you is that you suddenly have a dozen or more "statutes of limitation" to observe in every federal case (and in some states, every state case).

(5) *Effectiveness of Scheduling Orders.* In spite of (or perhaps because of?) their tendency to cause the loss of rights, studies show that scheduling orders produce quicker and less expensive disposition of cases.

(6) *What Does a Scheduling Order Look Like?* Rule 16 provides, "The scheduling order must limit the time to join other parties, amend the pleadings, complete discovery, and file motions." In addition, it can include an indefinite variety of other requirements. Here is an example of a blank scheduling order form:

Scheduling Order

Issue having been joined herein, it is Ordered pursuant to Rule 16, Fed. R. Civ. P. and Local Rule 300-6, that:

1. Joining of other parties and the amending of the pleadings shall be on or before ____________________ unless an extension is granted on good cause shown.

2. Filing of all motions shall be on or before ____________________ unless an extension is granted on good cause shown.

3. Discovery shall be completed by the parties on or before ____________________ unless an extension is granted on good cause shown.

4. A conference of attorneys shall be held on or before ____________________ unless an extension is granted on good cause shown.

5. Counsel for the parties shall submit their proposed agreed pre-trial order to the Court on or before ____________________ unless an extension is granted on good cause shown. The proposed order shall supply information required by Local Rule 300-6 and the pre-trial order check-list (Form PT-1), which is enclosed.

6. In the event counsel are unable to agree on the form of a proposed agreed pre-trial order, then counsel for each party is directed to submit his version of an approximate pre-trial order within ten (10) days after the expiration of the date set in paragraph 5 . . . .

[The form contains five additional paragraphs of orders, including the setting of a date for trial.]

[C] Rules Giving Judges Statistical Incentives

State Administrative Rules. Consider the following set of "Administrative Rules," which were proposed in one state but not adopted and which were designed to accomplish some of the same results as the Scheduling Order requirement under Federal Rule 16. This proposal was considered in one state, but the concept could be applied in any state. As is indicated below, attorneys' opposition defeated adoption of these particular rules.

> Rule 1. The courts and bar of [this state] will manage their work to achieve the disposition of cases within the periods of time listed:

	50%	90%	98%
Domestic Actions and Actions for Liquidated Damages	90 days	180 days	360 days
All Other Civil Actions	180 days	360 days	540 days

> Rule 2. [Requires each clerk of a trial court to report statistics to the administrative judge of the court district, including the ages of all disposed cases and "a report on the percentage of cases exceeding the designated limits. . . ."]
>
> Rule 3. [Requires the judge to enter an order establishing a "plan" for completion of discovery and preparation for trial in every case, "as soon as practicable" after the lapse of certain deadlines for the parties to propose such "plans."]

Notes and Questions

(1) *Unified, Vociferous Opposition by Attorneys Defeated this Proposal.* As might be expected, attorneys vigorously opposed the adoption of these administrative rules. Their opposition was so united and so strong that it overwhelmed rule proponents, and the proposals were resoundingly rejected by the state supreme court. The objections to such rules typically include the assertion that they unnecessarily channel energy into adversary proceedings over the collateral matter of scheduling when attorneys would otherwise arrive at the result by accommodation; that no harm is done if cases are allowed to remain pending on the docket for periods of time; and that the result will be a more high-handed attitude necessarily adopted by the trial judges. Are these arguments meritorious? [But might the result actually be reductions in judicial time, earlier settlement, and less wasted motion for attorneys?]

(2) *Statistical Pressure on the Judge to Clear the Docket.* Notice that the state administrative rules above contain a feature that makes them different from the Federal Rules: a statistical target, in the form of percentages of cases disposed of within certain periods of time. The rules contemplate that the trial judge will improve case dispositions, upon pain of having poor statistics (and possibly receiving reassignments or losing the vote of the electorate as a result). Will these rules have the undesirable effect of making judges excessively disposition-minded and

high handed? [On the other hand, if they don't keep current dockets, can the judges perform their usual judging tasks adequately?]

[D] "Differential Case Management," "Fast Tracking," "Staging," and Other Docket-Management Techniques

Note on Docket Management Techniques

Differential Case Management. This complex-sounding term refers to a simple idea: categorizing cases for different kinds of treatment. One might conclude that under traditional methods, all cases will be handled the same way, with the same sequence of pleadings, motions, and conferences. But differential case management instead assigns different categories of cases to different "tracks" with different amounts of discovery, different time limits for different events, and the like. Numerous jurisdictions have adopted systems for differential management. Bakke & Solomon, *Case Differentiation: An Approach to Individualized Case Management,* 73 JUDICATURE 17 (1989).

Specifically, these authors describe one particular differential management system in New Jersey in which every case is assigned to one of three "tracks." The assignment is based on such factors as the amount of damages, the type of case, and attorneys' estimates of the required time to dispose of the case. The attorneys begin the assignment process by filing an information statement with their complaint or answer. The court then assigns the case to one of three categories: "expedited, standard, or complex." This assignment, in turn, brings to bear a number of rules designed for the case category, including a case management plan, various cutoff dates for processes such as discovery, different kinds of judicial monitoring, and a trial schedule. Bakke and Solomon claim that attorney disagreement with case categorization is rare in New Jersey and that that differential case management has dramatically reduced resolution times.

Case Plans, Time Limits, and Fast Tracking: Early Setting of a Trial Date. Even in the absence of a tracking system, there have long been recommendations for courts to develop case management plans that control discovery and impose time limits. *See* Litan, *Speeding Up Civil Justice,* 89 JUDICATURE 162 (1989). "[T]he most important deadline that should be set early . . . is the trial date. Nothing does more to convince the parties and their lawyers to move expeditiously toward a resolution than . . . knowing at the outset when they are scheduled for trial."

Staging. Some disputes can be divided into separate issues that can be disposed of in sequence, so that later issues need not be litigated if early issues prove to be dispositive. Imagine that there is a serious issue about a statute of limitations defense. If that defense prevails, the rest of the dispute becomes moot, and therefore, the court might "stage" the case so that the limitations issue is considered first in a separate trial. Another example appears in the chapter of this book on pleadings, in the case of *Beeck v. Aquaslide 'N' Dive Corporation.* There, the court ordered a separate initial trial on the question whether the defendant had manufactured the allegedly defective product that had injured the plaintiff. The jury answered, No. The result enabled the court to avoid all of the other issues.

Fast Tracking. Some jurisdictions have adopted practices that strongly encourage or force cases to be resolved within certain numbers of years. California's deadline for trial is an example; it creates a virtual statute of limitations, having the effect of prohibiting the claim if five years pass without resolution or trial. There are other systems that encourage prompt resolution by setting deadlines for judges to observe or by requiring and having presiding judges react to statistics showing the number or percentage of cases pending before each judge for more than certain lengths of time.

Undesirable Byproducts of These Approaches, Including Adjudications by Deadline. These management techniques undoubtedly have good effects. But consider the possibility that they may have some undesirable effects too. For example, could staging isolate an issue so that its full context is lost? How often might discovery limits prevent the finding of evidence? Will the proliferation of deadlines result in at least a few "adjudications by deadline": the loss of claims, defenses, or access to needed processes because of the passage of a date, when many dates control the case?

Kakalik, et al., *Just, Speedy and Inexpensive? An Evaluation of Judicial Case Management Under the Civil Justice Reform Act*

49 Ala. L. Rev. 17, 18–19 (1997)(*)

The Judicial Conference and the Administrative Office of the U.S. Courts asked RAND's Institute for Civil Justice to evaluate the implementation and the effects of [case management programs] in . . . [pilot] districts . . . .

To preview the main findings of the evaluation:

1. [Many kinds of programs] had little effect on time to disposition, litigation costs, and attorneys' satisfaction and views of the fairness of case management.
2. But our analysis of case management as practiced across districts and judges shows that what judges do to manage cases matters:
    - Early judicial case management, setting the trial schedule early, shortened time to discovery cutoff, and having litigants at or available for settlement conferences are associated with a significantly reduced time to disposition. Early judicial case management also is associated with significantly increased costs to litigants, as measured by attorney work hours.

(*) Copyright 1997. Originally published in 49 Ala. L. Rev. 17 (1997). Reprinted with permission.

- Shortened time to discovery cutoff is associated with significantly decreased attorney work hours.
- None of these policies significantly affect attorneys' satisfaction or views of fairness, either positively or negatively.

3. If early case management and early setting of the trial schedule are combined with shortened discovery cutoff, the increase in costs associated with the former can be offset by the decrease in costs associated with the latter. . . .

Notes and Questions

(1) *The Trouble with Tracking, Part 1: Attorneys' Expectations and Disputes about Assignment.* An attorney might say, "I think my civil rights suit against the city and its officers for beating my client should be on the 'complex case' track, but the tracking coordinator and the defendant persuaded the judge to put it on the 'expedited' track!" Early assignment to the expedited or standard track will reduce available discovery time and methods (in fact, that's the point of tracking). If the attorneys disagree, ultimately the judge must resolve the track assignment dispute (in yet another hearing that does not concern the merits).

(2) *The Trouble with Tracking, Part 2: Enforcing "Fast Track" Deadlines by Sanctions or Dismissals—Gorman v. City of Phoenix*, 152 Ariz. 179, 731 P.2d 74 (1987). To solve a serious backlog, Maricopa County, Arizona adopted a "fast track" system with deadlines enforceable by dismissal under local Rule V(e). The Arizona Supreme Court observed in *Gorman* that "[l]awyers who fail to comply with [R]ule V(e) do so at their peril," even though the trial court should allow reinstatement in circumstances involving diligence and prejudice. *See also Flynn v. Cornoyer-Hedrick Architects & Planners, Inc.*, 160 Ariz. 187, 772 P.2d 10 (Ariz. App. 1988) (no reinstatement where initial delay in obtaining service caused plaintiff to get off-track). Won't "tracking" inevitably produce more of these kinds of dispositions based on deadlines?

(3) *The Trouble with Tracking, Part 3: Increases in Attorney's Own Docket-Control Costs.* When Harris County [Houston, Texas] family court judges adopted case management strategies to reduce backlogs, divorce lawyers said that "inflexible judges with strict deadlines . . . increase the cost of an uncontested divorce by as much as 25 percent . . . ." TEXAS LAWYER, June 16, 1997, at 1. It takes effort, and therefore it costs money, to monitor and comply with tracking requirements. Tracking may also save money elsewhere, but the question is whether it costs more than it gains.

(4) *The Benefits of Tracking.* Perhaps, however, these "troubles" merely reflect the fact that the world is imperfect. Do the benefits outweigh the costs? Can the costs be minimized by employment of skillful coordinators, liberal reinstatement of dismissed cases, and experience with track assignments?

(5) *"Staging" as Compared to "Tracking."* Note that "staging" is at least somewhat incompatible with an early plan setting deadlines (since it implies that deadlines

will depend on intervening events). Can the two coexist, and if so, will staging contribute to prompt and fair dispositions?

(6) *California's "Fast Track" Seeks a Two (2) Year Limit: The Trial Court Delay Reduction Act*, Cal. Gov. Code §§68600 et seq. (1991). California adopted a proposal known colloquially as "Fast Track," requiring each Superior Court to adopt a "plan" that will result in trial or disposition of civil cases within two years of filing, enforced by a reporting requirement. (Is this a good idea? If so, why did lawyers generally oppose it?)

(7) *The Texas System: Administrative Rules.* Although Texas did not initially adopt administrative rules mandating case "plans" for all cases (*see* §IV[B]), it did adopt time standards for the handling of civil litigation. Any case not disposed of within the time standards in the Texas Supreme Court's Administrative Rules "may be placed on a dismissal docket," which will mandate prompt action by the attorneys and will thereafter require strict deadlines. Tex. R. Civ. P. 165a. In addition, Texas adopted discovery rules which require "discovery control plans," creating three "discovery levels" according to case types, and by establishing a nine-month discovery period for each case and limiting the amount of pretrial discovery that may be conducted during the discovery period. Tex. R. Civ. P. 190. Are these managerial techniques a good idea?

IV. The Dismal Phenomenon of "Adjudication by Deadline"

Karubian v. Security Pacific National Bank

152 Cal. App. 3d 134 (1984)

[This case shows that time limits created as part of judicial management can cause "adjudications by deadline." Plaintiffs filed an action for negligent damage to real property. The trial court ultimately dismissed the action for plaintiffs' failure to comply with a provision of the California Code of Civil Procedure, section 583(b), which required a plaintiff to bring a case to trial within five years after its filing. The decision results from a complicated system for calendaring trials in Los Angeles. The court here describes the process as follows:]

... [T]he California Rules of Court basically establish a three-step procedure for setting cases for trial in Los Angeles County. That procedure is set in motion by the filing of an "at-issue memorandum." A "civil active list" of cases in which the "at-issue memorandum" has been filed is periodically created by the superior court. The moving of a case from the "civil active list" to the "trial ready list" requires the filing, by a party, of a Certificate of Readiness.

Since the state of the calendar in Los Angeles County is such that a case cannot be brought to trial within 6 months after the filing of a Certificate of Readiness, the rules provide that the Certificate of Readiness cannot be filed before receipt of notification from the clerk of eligibility to do so. . . .

[The complaint in this case was filed in Los Angeles. The next year, plaintiffs' lawyer filed an "at issue" memorandum, which was a required to start the process for calendaring the case for trial. Then, another law firm was substituted as counsel, which was substituted for by yet another attorney. Approximately 18 months before the five-year deadline, the Los Angeles clerk issued the "notice of eligibility," which was necessary before the "Certificate of Readiness" could be filed. The notice of eligibility, in essence, meant that the case was close enough to the head of the line of cases, in age, to be eligible to be set for trial. But the clerk erroneously mailed the notice of eligibility (and a second notice) to the plaintiffs' original attorney, who had long since been removed from the case. That attorney did not forward the notice.

[As a result, plaintiffs' attorneys received no notice of eligibility. They did not file a Certificate of Readiness, and when no Certificate of Readiness was filed, the clerk removed the case from the "civil active list." Plaintiffs' lawyers happened to file a motion to specially set the case for trial, and it was not until shortly after the hearing that plaintiffs' lawyers discovered these facts. The trial court denied the motion and denied a motion to reconsider. Only forty days remained of the five years at this point, and the calendar did not permit additions. Therefore, the trial court dismissed the case. The court of appeals, here, affirms.

[The court of appeals first notes that there is a court-created exception to the five-year rule if bringing the case to trial within that time would be "impractical, impossible, or futile." But the court adds that this exception applies only if the plaintiff has been "diligent." And in the case at bar, this condition was not met, says the court:]

[This case presents] the question . . . whether a plaintiff, or his or her counsel, can be considered diligent in continuing to rely on official duty being performed after the passage of an amount of time sufficient to indicate to a reasonably knowledgeable attorney that official duty was not going to be performed and that the public official had obviously "goofed." . . .

. . . [E]ven under circumstances where reliance on the performance of official duty is initially justified, there comes a time when plaintiff can no longer be considered to be "diligent," . . . without at least taking some action to call the matter to someone's attention. . . .

. . . The rule, which requires notification by the clerk as a condition precedent to the filing of a Certificate of Readiness, operates in Los Angeles County for the very reason that a case cannot get to trial within 6 months after the filing of such certificate. Thus an attorney who has not received such notification by the end of the fourth year after the filing of a complaint, has to know that the case, if it is to come to trial, can only come to trial in the last six months available before the running of the 5 year period. . . . [Dismissal affirmed.]

Notes and Questions

(1) *Adjudication by Deadline: The Burden on Today's Attorneys.* The *Karubian* case illustrates "adjudication by deadline." The passage of time, together with the absence of a particular step taken during that time, can result in a decision of the case just as surely as a judgment founded on a jury verdict. Unfortunately, deadlines increase with active judicial management. Scheduling orders, timetables under rules, and similar requirements create multiple deadlines in many cases. To add to the difficulty, deadlines shift, owing to other events. Attorneys who practice law today need effective systems (very effective) for keeping deadlines.

(2) *Forgiveness Doctrines, Allowing Courts to Extend Time or Alter Deadlines.* Sometimes, a court has power to extend time so as to avoid adjudication by deadline. In certain kinds of cases, this dispensation is relatively liberally granted. The case of *Butner v. Neustadter*, in the next chapter, shows an example: relief from default judgments. On the other hand, there are occasions when the decision whether to extend is within the wide discretion of a trial court, which has power to extend a deadline but is not required to. (No attorney wants to be in the position of having to ask for this, however; it might not be granted.) Sometimes, there are strict conditions for extension, as in *Karubian*, and in some circumstances, there is no possibility of extension at all, as we shall see in a case in Chapter 12 *(Bowles v. Russell)*, which involves certain kinds of appellate deadlines.

(3) *Updating Karubian: California Still Apparently Regards It as Good Law.* The details of the trial-calendaring laws that brought about the result in *Karubian* have changed, which is not surprising after many years. But *Karubian* has continued to be cited. *Robert's Drywall v. N.T. Hill, Inc.*, 2006 Cal. App. Unpub. LEXIS 445 at *6 (unpublished opinion).

(4) *Were the Trial-Calendaring Rules in Karubian Really an Undercover Way to "Ration Trials"?* A court cannot try every case that is filed with it. In fact, judges work hard at trying to minimize trials, by encouraging settlement or making other dispositions. Notice that Los Angeles County, at the time of *Karubian*, had a system designed to delay trial settings, owing to the "state of the calendar"—i.e., docket congestion—by delaying cases for years until they could even be scheduled for trial. Is it possible that the system in Los Angeles also served an underground function, namely, discouraging trials in order to "ration" them, in a system that could not offer enough trials?

V. Real Life as a Lawyer

How Can I Manage This Chaotic Schedule?

Imagine yourself working on an answer to a motion for summary judgment that is due tomorrow. You have a hearing in the morning at 8:30 on a discovery motion that you have yet to prepare for, a new client meeting at noon, and a deposition to take at 2 p.m. across town. You realize that you have several more deadlines this week, although you can't remember what they are without consulting your calendar. In real life, events clump together and crises cumulate. How can you possibly manage this chaotic schedule?

Time management, many lawyers will say, is the most important capability for a lawyer. More so than argument, briefing, or document preparation. The chaos produced by deadlines is a shock to lawyers just out of law school, where the daily schedule doesn't vary. In practice, you may have 50 (or even hundreds of) cases, all with deadlines. And the deadlines change with events. You need a method for reliably keeping all your deadlines, and it needs to be mistake-proof, because this chapter shows how missing deadlines can hurt your clients. You also need a method for keeping time precisely and billing it promptly. You need to plan each day, and you need to have alternative work in case something falls through.

Fortunately, it can be done. There are commercially available systems for keeping time and deadlines, and there are even reliable pencil-and-paper ways of doing it. But then too, you've got to manage your practice so that work doesn't swallow you up. You may have to schedule, actually schedule(!), time in which to have a life. And it all has to be done reliably. The Appendix at the end of this book has more information about time management. *See* section II [A][1], which includes the observation that time management is the most important variable over which you have at least partial control.

VI. Improving Pretrial Conferences and Case Management: Notes and Questions

(1) *Exemptions from Scheduling Orders.* Rule 16 contemplates that the District Courts, by local rules, will exempt given categories of cases from the requirements of scheduling orders. Which categories of cases should be exempted? One court with a long laundry list is the Western District of Texas, which exempts Social Security, habeas corpus, forfeiture, IRS summonses, bankruptcy, land condemnation, interpleader, pro se prisoner § 1983, student loan, VA overpayment, and certain other cases. Do these categories make sense? There is little consistency in these rules from district to district. Should the exempted categories be set forth in Rule 16 itself to ensure nationwide uniformity? (To some extent, they have been.)

(2) *Should Scheduling Orders Be Required? Should Uniform Pretrial Orders Be Required?* Some judges have opposed a requirement of case management in every case. Should the scheduling order requirement (which requires at least a little bit of management in every non-exempted case) be repealed?

(3) *Settlement Conferences.* There are several ways in which settlement could be treated in the pretrial process. One is to remove it from the list of factors to be considered in Rule 16 (but this approach has the arguable disadvantage that the trial

judge's docket will increase rapidly, and the parties may settle the case later with greater expense). A second idea is to separate the function of settlement mediation from that of ruling on the merits, such as by having a settlement conference presided over by a person otherwise not involved in the case (but this mediator will have less influence with the parties, the approach will require additional hearings and additional personnel usage, and it will be difficult to prevent the discussion of settlement at other hearings). A final approach is that of the current rules, which allow the judge to combine settlement mediation and adjudication. Which approach is most appropriate?

(4) *Trial-Setting Mechanisms.* Should setting for trial be initiated by action on the part of the attorneys, as it is in some states? Or should the court have a major scheduling function in initiating the trial setting process, as it does in most federal courts?

(5) *"Individual" Dockets Versus "Unified" Dockets or "Master Calendar."* Individual dockets involve the assignment of cases at random to individual judges, who preside over all pretrial matters as well as trials. "Unified" dockets, on the other hand, involve assignment of a trial judge immediately before trial. (In California, this method is referred to as a "master calendar system.") The theory is that a unified docket uses the court's resources fully because if a judge's docket for a given week "washes out" due to settlement or continuances, the individual docket would leave her with no cases to try. What disadvantages, however, can you perceive in the unified docket? Would it decrease judicial responsibility?

(6) *Encouraging Early Disposition.* The federal courts' scheduling order, California's "Fast-Track," and Texas' administrative rules all are different means of encouraging early disposition. Which is the best way of achieving this objective?

(7) *"Differential Case Management," "Staging," and Discovery Plans.* What is the utility of these management techniques? How can we avoid the disadvantages of tracking (*i.e.*, disputes about track assignment and dismissals for missed deadlines)?

Chapter 9

Adjudication Without Trial: Summary Judgment, Dismissal, Default, and Related Procedures

I. Judgment on the Pleadings

Note on Judgment on the Pleadings

When Judgment on the Pleadings Can Be Granted. Suppose that the pleadings of both parties have been filed and the time for amendment has expired. Suppose, also, that the pleadings show that the parties agree on all of the factual issues. The case therefore depends solely on questions of law. Rule 12(c) provides a procedure, called a "judgment on the pleadings," that is proper in these circumstances.

Defendant's Motion for Judgment on the Pleadings (Equivalent to a Motion to Dismiss). After the pleadings are closed, the defendant may move for judgment on the pleadings on the theory that the plaintiff's complaint fails to state a claim. As a practical matter, this procedure is similar to a motion to dismiss for failure to state a claim under Rule 12(b)(6); to be technical, however, the motion to dismiss is proper before the pleadings are closed and the motion for judgment on the pleadings is proper after.

Plaintiff's Motion for Judgment on the Pleadings. Imagine the following scenario. The plaintiff files a complaint that validly states a claim. A trial would be required if the defendant denied material allegations of the complaint, but instead, the defendant files an answer admitting all allegations of the complaint. The plaintiff now can obtain judgment by filing a Rule 12(c) motion for judgment on the pleadings. (This procedure is a kind of analogue to the defendant's motion to dismiss for failure to state a claim, but the plaintiff doesn't want a dismissal, of course.)

Example. Consider the following case as an example of the successful use by the plaintiff of the motion for judgment on the pleadings.

UNITE HERE LOCAL 1 v. HYATT CORPORATION, 862 F.3d 588 (7th Cir. 2017). The union's contract with Hyatt prohibited managers from performing tasks ordinarily done by lower level employees. The union won two arbitration awards ordering Hyatt to cease and desist from violating this provision of the contract. The union, as plaintiff, sued to confirm the awards ("confirmation" of an arbitral award simply means that a court incorporates the award into a judgment). The union wanted a court judgment, because it would be enforceable by contempt of court proceedings, whereas an arbitral award would not.

Hyatt's defense was that enforcement of the award would violate principles of equity, since it might interfere with arbitration of other alleged violations that were still pending. The union responded that this defense was invalid as a matter of law and moved for judgment on the pleadings for plaintiff. The trial court agreed and entered a judgment on the pleadings for the union. The court of appeals here affirms:

> Judgment on the pleadings is appropriate when there are no disputed issues of material fact and it is clear that the moving party, in this case Local 1, is entitled to judgment as a matter of law.... In reviewing the judgment, we, like the district court, are confined to the matters presented in the pleadings, and we must consider those pleadings in the light most favorable to Hyatt....
>
> The union agrees that any unresolved disputes must wend their way through the contractual dispute resolution process, and that any request for contempt sanctions will be premised on future arbitration awards....

[T]herefore, . . . we can discern no concrete impact that confirmation of these two awards will have on . . . that process. . . .

The district court committed no error in granting [plaintiff's] motion for judgment on the pleadings. . . . [AFFIRMED.]

II. Summary Judgment

[A] The Standard for Granting Summary Judgment

Read Fed. R. Civ. P. 56 (summary judgment).

WARREN v. MEDLEY, 521 S.W.2d 137 (Tex. Civ. App. 1975, writ ref'd n.r.e.). The text of this opinion appears above at § VI of Chapter 1 and should be read, or reread, at this point. After an evening at a nightclub with topless dancers as entertainment, Ms. Warren, Mr. Reynolds, and others went to Mr. Medley's home. There, Reynolds lifted Warren onto a glass-topped table against her wishes, urging her to demonstrate the dance. The table broke and Warren was injured. She sued Medley, the homeowner.

After pointing out that summary judgment is not available "[i]f reasonable minds could differ as to the conclusions to be drawn from the summary judgment facts," the court affirmed the trial judge's grant of summary judgment in defendant Medley's favor. Under the controlling law, the defendant could be liable only if he was grossly negligent. Warren's own deposition admitted that Medley "expressed surprise" at her plight, "couldn't have prevented it," and had nothing to do with it. Thus, the summary judgment materials negated gross negligence and causation on Medley's part, unequivocally and as a matter of law.

Notes and Questions

(1) *The Relationship Between Summary Judgment and Other Dispositive Procedures.* You may have noted a similarity among various procedures for disposition as a "matter of law," including (1) the Rule 12(b)(6) motion to dismiss for failure to state a claim; (2) the Rule 12(c) motion for judgment on the pleadings; (3) the motion for summary judgment; (4) the motion for judgment as a matter of law during trial ("directed verdict"); and (5) the motion for judgment as a matter of law after trial ("judgment notwithstanding the verdict"). What are the similarities, and what are the distinctions, among these procedures? See Figure 9A for a summary.

FIGURE 9A:
SUMMARY JUDGMENT AND OTHER DEVICES FOR DECIDING A CASE "AS A MATTER OF LAW"

1. **DISMISSAL FOR FAILURE TO STATE A CLAIM (when court can say that the plaintiff would not be able to obtain relief on any theory fairly encompassed within the complaint, even if supported by evidence; done before any evidence is received, so court must assume all of plaintiff's plausible, non-conclusory allegations are true.)**

2. **JUDGMENT ON THE PLEADINGS (when pleadings leave no material fact to be decided, and the movant is entitled to judgment as a matter of law; done after the pleadings are closed, with no evidence yet received.)**

3. **SUMMARY JUDGMENT (when pleadings, affidavits, and discovery products demonstrate that there is no genuine issue of material fact, so that a reasonable juror properly applying the law could only find in favor of the movant; done on the basis of a paper record, so the judge must assume all inferences and credibility determinations would be made in favor of the non-movant.)**

4. **JUDGMENT AS A MATTER OF LAW DURING TRIAL ("DIRECTED VERDICT") (when the evidence that has been received, viewed in light most favorable to the non-movant, permits only one reasonable inference, in favor of the movant; done when the opponent rests or closes or at close of all evidence.)**

5. **JUDGMENT AS A MATTER OF LAW AFTER TRIAL ("JUDGMENT NOTWITHSTANDING THE VERDICT") (standard same as for judgment as a matter of law during trial, but done after the verdict has been received.)**

6. **APPELLATE REVERSAL BECAUSE EVIDENCE DOESN'T SUPPORT VERDICT (standard same as for judgment as a matter of law in trial court, but done by the appellate court.)**

(2) *The Basic Standard for Summary Judgment.* Rule 56 says that the summary judgment materials must show that there is no genuine dispute as to any material fact and that the moving party is entitled to prevail "as a matter of law." This language begs the question as to what conditions remove all genuine disputes about material fact or what entitles the movant to judgment "as a matter of law." *See* Schwarzer, *Summary Judgment under the Federal Rules: Defining Genuine Issues of Material Fact*, 99 F.R.D. 465 (1984). It may help to think of the standard as a requirement that a reasonable juror correctly applying the governing law could come to only one conclusion.

(3) *The Movant's Burden to Establish Entitlement to Summary Judgment.* As *Warren v. Medley* demonstrates, the movant has the burden to demonstrate the absence of genuine fact disputes about the elements of the non-movant's claims. The non-movant has no burden until and unless the state of the record is such that

the movant would otherwise be entitled to summary judgment. Once the movant's burden is carried, then (and only then) the non-movant must show that there is a genuine issue for trial. *See* Louis, *Federal Summary Judgment Doctrine: A Critical Analysis*, 83 YALE L.J. 745 (1974).

At this point, we offer the following "Chapter Summary Problem." As usual, you should read it at this point but analyze it at the end of the Chapter (or, treat it as your instructor directs).

Problem A: Chapter 9 Summary Problem

BROWNE v. SMITH: A PROBLEM INVOLVING SUMMARY JUDGMENT, DISMISSAL, AND DEFAULT. In this case, defendant Thomas Smith is a lawyer. Plaintiff David Browne is his former client. The complaint alleges that Browne at one time was employed by the City of London, in the hypothetical State of West York, as an airport police officer. On October 13, 2003, he was fired. Browne's complaint further alleges that he retained Smith to represent him in an appeal of his suspension to the City Civil Service Commission, but that Smith negligently failed to perfect the appeal in a timely manner and thereby proximately caused the loss of Browne's right to reinstatement.

The answer contains a defense of limitations. Browne sustained a legal injury on October 23, 2003, when Smith did not file the appeal within 10 days. But suit was not filed until October 30, 2005, apparently after the running of the applicable statute, which provides a two-year limit. West York follows the "discovery" rule in legal malpractice cases, which means that the claim does not accrue, and the limitations period does not begin to run until the plaintiff "knew or should have known" in the exercise of reasonable diligence of the wrongful act and the resulting injury. Also, limitations can be "tolled" during any period of "fraudulent concealment" of the claim by the defendant.

The affidavits and discovery products on file show that Smith and Browne received a letter from the city on October 29, 2003, unequivocally advising them that the 10-day limit had passed and that no appeal would lie. But plaintiff Browne testified in his deposition that when he raised this issue with Smith, Smith said that "we would take them [the city] to court and sue them," and he believed Smith still could win him reinstatement. (For more detail, see Litigation Document Example 9.2, found at https://caplaw.com/sites/cp7, which reproduces the relevant documents from *Browne v. Smith*.)

1. Can the defendant successfully argue for summary judgment?
2. Can the plaintiff obtain voluntary dismissal of the claim if he senses that an adverse summary judgment is imminent?
3. If plaintiff Browne had obtained a default judgment because defendant Smith's lawyer had inadvertently misplaced the complaint and failed to answer it, would the defendant be able to set aside the default judgment?

[B] The Relevance of the Ultimate Burden of Proof: Summary Judgment Because the Opponent "Can't Prove Her Case"

DYER v. McDOUGALL, 201 F.2d 265 (2d Cir. 1952). Dyer sued McDougall for slander. The complaint alleged that McDougall had published the slanders by uttering them to two people, Mr. Almirall and Mrs. Hope. McDougall moved for summary judgment, supported by his own affidavit that he never uttered the alleged slander and by the affidavit of Mr. Almirall and the deposition of Mrs. Hope, both of whom stated that they had never heard the slander uttered. The court affirmed summary judgment for the defendants.

The court reasoned that, to obtain summary judgment, "The defendants had the burden of proving that there was no [genuine] issue" of material fact. "[O]n the other hand, at a trial the plaintiff would have the burden of proving the utterances; and therefore, if the defendants [s]ucceeded in proving that the plaintiff would not have enough evidence to go to the jury on the issue, the [summary] judgment was right." A jury would not be permitted to find slander from testimony that uniformly denied it. Thus, the defendant affirmatively had foreclosed all possible avenues of proof. Summary judgment AFFIRMED.

Note on How to Read the Case of Celotex Corp. v. Catrett

Showing that Plaintiff Cannot Have Sufficient Evidence. Dyer v. McDougall shows one way a defendant can obtain summary judgment: by affidavits that affirmatively foreclose all possible sources of the plaintiff's proof. But there is another way. Rule 56 does not require the movant to produce affidavits; it just requires the movant to carry the burden of showing that there are no genuine disputes about the material facts. And so, if the defendant can show by inference that the plaintiff wouldn't be able to produce any evidence at a trial that would carry her burden to prove her case, the defendant may be entitled to summary judgment. That is what the following case is about.

Understanding the Celotex Case, Below. But remember: the threshold question isn't whether the opponent has come forward with evidence to raise a fact dispute; instead, it's whether the movant has shown that there are no fact disputes. In the case that follows, the defendant propounded interrogatories asking for all of the plaintiff's witnesses, and the plaintiff never gave the name of a single witness even after two years had passed. Does that fact justify an inference that the plaintiff "can't prove it"? (The majority and dissent disagree about the possible answers to that question.)

Ambiguities in Celotex. This case may appear difficult because some of its language is ambiguous. For instance, the Court never tells us exactly what the defendant has to do, to show that the plaintiff "can't prove it"; instead, it remands so that the Court of Appeals can consider that issue. Remember, the movant's burden still remains. The movant must demonstrate—either directly or by inference—the absence of genuine disputes about the material facts.

The Need for Discovery to Show That the Opponent "Can't Prove It." The movant must have some way to demonstrate what proof the opponent will have. In the absence of clairvoyance, the movant can't do this by its own affidavits; instead it will have to ask the opponent. The movant will first need to use discovery to get the opponent to specify all of its proof.

Celotex Corp. v. Catrett

477 U.S. 317 (1986)

Justice Rehnquist delivered the opinion of the Court.

The United States District Court for the District of Columbia granted the motion of petitioner Celotex Corporation for summary judgment against respondent Catrett because the latter was unable to produce evidence [showing] that the decedent had been exposed to petitioner's asbestos products. A divided panel of the Court of Appeals . . . reversed, however, holding that petitioner's failure to support its motion with evidence tending to *negate* such exposure precluded the entry of summary judgment in its favor . . . . This view conflicted with that of the Third Circuit in [another case]. We granted certiorari to resolve the conflict . . . .

[Catrett filed suit in 1980 seeking damages against 15 named asbestos manufacturers on negligence, warranty, and strict liability theories for the death of her husband. Defendant Celotex's motion argued that summary judgment was proper because Catrett had "failed to produce evidence that any [Celotex] product . . . was the proximate cause of the injuries alleged . . . ." In particular, Celotex noted that Catrett had been asked in interrogatories about witnesses who could testify to the decedent's exposure to Celotex's products, and in answering, had failed to identify any. In opposing summary judgment, plaintiff Catrett relied on a hearsay transcript of the deposition of the decedent in a separate workers' compensation case, saying he had been exposed; an unsworn hearsay letter from another defendant's insurance company about the decedent's exposure; and an unsworn hearsay letter from the decedent's former supervisor describing the products to which he had been exposed. Celotex argued that none of these documents could be considered because all were inadmissible hearsay, not in affidavit form.

[In July 1982, almost two years after the filing of the suit, the District Court granted the motion on the stated ground that "there [was] no showing" of the decedent's exposure. A divided panel of the Court of Appeals reversed in reliance on *Adickes v. S.H. Kress & Co.*, [398 U.S. 144 (1979)], which held that "the party opposing the motion for summary judgment bears the burden of responding *only after* the moving party has met its burden of coming forward with proof of the absence of any genuine issues of material fact." Judge Bork dissented, arguing that there was no requirement that a summary judgment movant "must always make an affirmative evidentiary showing . . ." and that the majority's holding "undermined the traditional authority of trial judges to grant summary judgment in meritless cases."]

We think that the position taken by the majority of the Court of Appeals is inconsistent with the standard for summary judgment set forth in Rule 56(c) [now Rule 56(a)—Eds.] of the Federal Rules of Civil Procedure. Under Rule 56(c), summary judgment is proper "if the pleadings, depositions, answers to interrogatories, and admissions on file, together with the affidavits, if any, show that there is no genuine issue as to any material fact and that the moving party is entitled to a judgment as a matter of law." [The 2007 and 2010 "restyling" amendments to the Federal Rules of Civil Procedure made minor changes to the wording of Rule 56(c) and moved the standard to Rule 56(a).—Eds.] In our view, the plain language of Rule 56(c) [now 56(a)—Eds.] mandates the entry of summary judgment, after adequate time for discovery and upon motion, against a party who fails to make a showing sufficient to establish the existence of an element essential to that party's case, and on which that party will bear the burden of proof at trial. In such a situation, there can be "no genuine issue as to any material fact," since a complete failure of proof concerning an essential element of the nonmoving party's case necessarily renders all other facts immaterial. The moving party is "entitled to judgment as a matter of law" because the nonmoving party has failed to make a sufficient showing on an essential element of her case with respect to which she has the burden of proof. "[T]h[e] standard [for granting summary judgment] mirrors the standard for a directed verdict under Federal Rule of Civil Procedure 50(a). . . ." *Anderson v. Liberty Lobby, Inc.*, 477 U.S. 242, 250 (1986).

Of course, a party seeking summary judgment always bears the initial responsibility of informing the district court of the basis for its motion, and identifying those portions of "the pleadings, depositions, answers to interrogatories, and admissions on file, together with the affidavits, if any," which it believes demonstrate the absence of a genuine issue of material fact. But unlike the Court of Appeals, we find no express or implied requirement in Rule 56 that the moving party support its motion with affidavits or other similar materials *negating* the opponent's claim. On the contrary, Rule 56(c), which refers to "the affidavits, *if any*" (emphasis added), suggests the absence of such a requirement. [This language has been dropped from Rule 56.—Eds.] And if there were any doubt about the meaning of Rule 56(c) in this regard, such doubt is clearly removed by Rules 56(a) and (b), which provide that claimants and defendants, respectively, may move for summary judgment "*with or without supporting affidavits*" (emphasis added). [This language has been dropped from Rule 56.—Eds.] The import of these subsections is that, regardless of whether the moving party accompanies its summary judgment motion with affidavits, the motion may, and should, be granted so long as whatever is before the district court demonstrates that the standard for the entry of summary judgment, as set forth in Rule 56(c) [now Rule 56(a).—Eds.], is satisfied. One of the principal purposes of the summary judgment rule is to isolate and dispose of factually unsupported claims or defenses, and we think it should be interpreted in a way that allows it to accomplish this purpose.

[I]n cases like the instant one, where the nonmoving party will bear the burden of proof at trial on a dispositive issue, a summary judgment motion may properly be made in reliance solely on the "pleadings, depositions, answers to interrogatories, and admissions on file." Such a motion, whether or not accompanied by affidavits, will be "made and supported as provided in this rule," and Rule 56(e) therefore requires the nonmoving party to go beyond the pleadings and by her own affidavits, or by the "depositions, answers to interrogatories, and admissions on file," designate "specific facts showing that there is a genuine issue for trial." [The 2007 "restyling" amendments to the Federal Rules of Civil Procedure also made minor changes to the wording of Rule 56(e).—Eds.]

We do not mean that the nonmoving party must produce evidence in a form that would be admissible at trial in order to avoid summary judgment. Obviously, Rule 56 does not require the nonmoving party to depose her own witnesses. Rule 56(e) permits a proper summary judgment motion to be opposed by any of the kinds of evidentiary materials listed in Rule 56(c), except the mere pleadings themselves, and it is from this list that one would normally expect the nonmoving party to make the showing to which we have referred. [Today, see Rule 56(c)-(e).—Eds.]

The Court of Appeals in this case felt itself constrained, however, by language in our decision in *Adickes v. S.H. Kress & Co.*, 398 U.S. 144 (1970). [T]he *Adickes* Court said that "[t]he 1963 Amendment [w]as not intended to modify the burden of the moving party . . . to show initially the absence of a genuine issue concerning any material fact." . . . But we do not think the *Adickes* language . . . . should be construed to mean that the burden is on the party moving for summary judgment to produce evidence showing the absence of a genuine issue of material fact, even with respect to an issue on which the nonmoving party bears the burden of proof. Instead, as we have explained, the burden on the moving party may be discharged by "showing"—that is, pointing out to the District Court—that there is an absence of evidence to support the nonmoving party's case . . . . [See Rule 56(c)(1)(B).—Eds.]

Respondent commenced this action in September 1980, and petitioner's motion was filed in September 1981. The parties had conducted discovery, and no serious claim can be made that respondent was in any sense "railroaded" by a premature motion for summary judgment. Any potential problem with such premature motions can be adequately dealt with under Rule 56(f), which allows a summary judgment motion to be denied, or the hearing on the motion to be continued, if the nonmoving party has not had an opportunity to make full discovery. . . . [Today, see Rule 56(d).—Eds.]

[T]he Court of Appeals declined to address either the adequacy of the showing made by respondent . . . or the question whether such a showing would be sufficient to carry respondent's burden of proof at trial. We think the Court of Appeals with its superior knowledge of local law is better suited than we are to make these determinations in the first instance.

The Federal Rules of Civil Procedure have for more than 50 years authorized motions for summary judgment upon proper showings of the lack of a genuine, triable issue of material fact. Summary judgment procedure is properly regarded not as a disfavored procedural shortcut, but rather as an integral part of the Federal Rules as a whole, which are designed "to secure the just, speedy and inexpensive determination of every action." . . .

The judgment of the Court of Appeals is accordingly reversed, and the case is remanded for further proceedings consistent with this opinion.

Justice White, concurring.

I agree that the Court of Appeals was wrong in holding that the moving defendant must always support his motion with evidence or affidavits showing the absence of a genuine dispute about a material fact. I also agree that the movant may rely on depositions, answers to interrogatories, and the like, to demonstrate that the plaintiff has no evidence to prove his case and hence that there can be no factual dispute. But the movant must discharge the burden the Rules place upon him: It is not enough to move for summary judgment without supporting the motion in any way or with a conclusory assertion that the plaintiff has no evidence to prove his case. . . .

Petitioner Celotex does not dispute that, if respondent has named a witness to support her claim, summary judgment should not be granted without Celotex somehow showing that the named witness' possible testimony raises no genuine issue of material fact. . . . It asserts, however, that respondent has failed on request to produce any basis for her case. Respondent, on the other hand, does not contend that she was not obligated to reveal her witnesses and evidence but insists that she has revealed enough to defeat the motion for summary judgment. Because the Court of Appeals found it unnecessary to address this aspect of the case, I agree that the case should be remanded for further proceedings.

Justice Brennan, with whom The Chief Justice and Justice Blackmun join, dissenting.

[The dissenters "[did] not disagree with the Court's legal analysis" rejecting the requirement that the movant present affirmative evidence. But the dissenters believed that Celotex had not met its burden of production under Rule 56 and therefore they did not join in the remand to the Court of Appeals, concluding that the summary judgment should simply be reversed outright.]

[Justice Brennan delineates two types of defendants' summary judgments: the type in which the defendant makes an affirmative showing by uncontested evidence that destroys the claim, and the different type, at issue here, in which the defendant relies on the plaintiff's lack of evidence.]

Where the moving party [s]eeks summary judgment on the ground that the nonmoving party—who will bear the burden of persuasion at trial—has no evidence, the mechanics of discharging Rule 56's burden of production are somewhat trickier. . . . [As] the Court confirms, a party who moves for summary judgment on the ground that the nonmoving party has no evidence must affirmatively show the absence of evidence in the record . . . . This may require the moving party to depose the nonmoving party's witnesses or to establish the inadequacy of documentary evidence. If there is literally no evidence in the record, the moving party may demonstrate this by reviewing for the court the admissions, interrogatories and other exchanges between the parties that are in the record. Either way, however, the moving party must affirmatively demonstrate that there is no evidence in the record to support a judgment for the nonmoving party. . . .

I do not read the Court's opinion to say anything inconsistent with or different than the preceding discussion. My disagreement with the Court concerns the application of these principles to the facts of this case.

[The dissent points out that the three items produced by Catrett, although themselves inadmissible, included (1) a letter from an insurance representative of another defendant describing asbestos products to which the decedent had been exposed, (2) a letter from a former supervisor of decedent—whom Catrett indicated she intended to call as a witness at trial—describing asbestos products to which decedent had been exposed, and (3) a copy of decedent's deposition in an earlier workers' compensation hearing. Since the record thus did contain evidence—including at least one witness—that arguably supported plaintiff's claim, "there simply is no question that Celotex failed to discharge its initial burden of production."

[The dissenting opinion of Justice Stevens is omitted.]

Notes and Questions

(1) *Celotex on Remand: The Court of Appeals Repeats Its Reversal.* On remand from the Supreme Court, the Court of Appeals decided that Celotex's motion for summary judgment must still be denied, because the record before the District Court regarding decedent's exposure to a Celotex product was not so one-sided that Celotex was entitled to judgment as a matter of law. The record included hearsay documents that left open the possibility that relevant witnesses might exist, the court concluded, even though the documents might not themselves be admissible. Judge Bork again dissented. *Catrett v. Johns-Manville Sales Corp.*, 826 F.2d 33 (D.C. Cir. 1987).

(2) *When Can Defendant Obtain Summary Judgment on the Ground that "Plaintiff Can't Prove It"? Comparing Dyer and Celotex.* What is the difference between the situation in *Dyer*, where the defendant affirmatively showed that the plaintiff could not prove the case, and *Celotex*? Notice that *Celotex* expresses a general agreement by the Justices that affirmative proof of the *Dyer* variety is not required. See whether you can state, briefly, just what is (or should be) required of a defendant

in Celotex's position to prevail on its motion for summary judgment. (Doesn't this movant need to use discovery to require the opponent to show all of its evidence?) *See* G. Miller, *The Pretrial Rush to Judgment: Are the "Litigation Explosion," "Liability Crisis," and Efficiency Cliches Eroding Our Day in Court and Jury Trial Commitments?*, 18 N.Y.U. L. Rev. 982 (2003).

(3) *"When [Evidence Is] Unavailable": Rule 56(d).* The non-movant may be able to prevent summary judgment through the mechanism of Rule 56(d), which allows the opponent to prevent summary judgment by an affidavit of inability to obtain evidence that may be obtainable in the future. Notice that the nonavailability of evidence must be shown by the non-movant through "affidavits" or "declarations," according to the Rule. *See* Note, *Summary Judgment Before the Completion of Discovery: A Proposed Revision of Federal Rule of Civil Procedure 56(f)* [now 56(d)], 24 U. Mich. J.L. Ref. 253 (1990).

Note on Wider Acceptance of Summary Judgment

The Supreme Court's encouragement of summary judgment in the *Celotex* and *Matsushita* cases has had an effect. Even before these decisions, the courts were headed in the same direction. In *Knight v. U.S. Fire Insurance Co.*, 804 F.2d 9, 12 (2d Cir. 1986), Chief Judge Feinberg stated:

> It appears that in this circuit some litigants are reluctant to make full use of the summary judgment process because of their perception that this court is unsympathetic to such motions and frequently reverses grants of summary judgment. Whatever may have been the accuracy of this view in years gone by, it is decidedly inaccurate at the present time, as borne out by a recent study by the Second Circuit Committee on the Pretrial Phase of Civil Litigation . . . . The Committee . . . found that the affirmance rate on appeals from orders granting summary judgment was 79%. That figure is comparable to this circuit's 84% affirmance rate for appeals in civil cases generally.

For an excellent treatment of a broader thesis, see A. Kamp, *Federal Adjudication of Facts: The New Regime*, 12 Am. J. Trial Ad. 437 (1989). Professor Kamp persuasively argues that pretrial fact adjudication has expanded through a variety of procedural devices that include not only summary judgment but also rules governing pleading specificity and fact-oriented dismissals, among others.

Litigation Document Example 9.1

Summary Judgment Motion in Jones v. [President] Clinton

This document is available online at https://caplaw.com/sites/cp7. Paula Jones sued President Bill Clinton under the civil rights remedy statute (42 U.S.C. § 1983) and other claims, with allegations that he had her brought to a hotel room, exposed himself to her, and made crude remarks. This response shows how lawyers can use existing evidence from the discovery process, coupled with relevant legal standards, to argue against summary judgment. Notice how the response is worded to meet the summary judgment standard (no genuine issue of material fact) and how every claim is covered. Please go to https://caplaw.com/sites/cp7, then click on Litigation Document Example 9.1: Summary Judgment Motion in *Jones v. Clinton*.

[C] The "Summary Judgment Evidence"

McNEIL v. SONOCO PRODUCTS COMPANY, 2017 WL 3725360 (6th Cir.) (unreported decision). This opinion repeats the often-stated principle that a litigant who says in an affidavit that it is based upon "information and belief" automatically destroys the affidavit for use in a summary judgment proceeding. Affidavits must be based upon personal knowledge, cannot be merely conclusory, and must show admissibility in evidence. The principle is so well established that most recent holdings to this effect are unpublished.

McNeil claimed that Sonoco had refused to hire him because of his race. Sonoco filed properly sworn affidavits by personnel asserting that the decision was not based on race and that they had not hired any less qualified person of another race. McNeil responded with affidavits refuting Sonoco's summary judgment affidavits, but they stated that they were based on "information and belief." The district court granted summary judgment, and the court of appeals affirmed:

> McNeil's affidavits state, based upon information and belief, that no African-Americans have ever been rehired by Sonoco. "Affidavits defeat summary judgment only if they are 'made on personal knowledge, set out facts that would be admissible in evidence, and show that the affiant or declarant is competent to testify on the matters stated.'" *Ondo v. City of Cleveland,* 795 F.3d 597, 604 (6th Cir. 2015) (quoting Fed. R. Civ. P. 56(c)(4)); *see also Lopez-Carrasquillo v. Rubianes,* 230 F.3d 409, 414 (1st Cir. 2000) (rejecting affidavit where affiant's assertions made "to the best of my knowledge" were not based on personal knowledge). Because [McNeil's] affidavits are not based upon specific facts arising out of the affiants' personal knowledge, there is no genuine dispute as to whether Sonoco hired a person not belonging to McNeil's protected class who was not more qualified than McNeil. [AFFIRMED.]

Notes and Questions

(1) *Affidavits and Discovery Materials as a Substitute for Evidence in the Summary Judgment Hearing.* In a summary judgment proceeding, the question is whether there are factual disputes that would require a trial. It makes sense, therefore, to test the affidavits and discovery materials by asking whether they show that the proponent could offer admissible evidence at the trial. In fact, the phrase

"summary judgment evidence" is often used to describe the materials that the court considers.

(2) *After Celotex, Do the Summary Judgment Materials Need to Conform to the Rules of Evidence?* For affidavits and discovery products offered by the movant, the answer to this question is probably still "yes," even after *Celotex*. But for the non-movant, *Celotex* seems to set a more relaxed standard. "We do not mean that the non-moving party must produce evidence in a form that would be admissible at trial in order to avoid a summary judgment," says the Court. This issue probably should be clarified by a Rule amendment.

Litigation Document Example 9.2

Summary Judgment Motion, Response, and Briefs in Browne v. Smith

These documents are online at https://caplaw.com/sites/cp7. They concern a malpractice suit by a client, David Browne, against his attorney, Thomas Smith, for letting an administrative deadline pass so as to defeat Browne's claim. Ironically, lawyer Smith's defense is that Browne's new lawyer also missed a deadline by filing this claim after the statute of limitations had run. The documents include defendant Smith's motion for summary judgment, plaintiff Browne's response, and affidavits and briefs from both parties.

In reading these documents, keep in mind the standard for summary judgment (no genuine issue of material fact). The key issue upon which the movant must eliminate factual disputes is the date when the so-called "discovery" rule allowed the limitations period to begin running: i.e., when the plaintiff knew or should have known of the facts giving rise to the malpractice cause of action. Also note that this material is part of the Chapter Summary Problem. Please go to https://caplaw.com/sites/cp7, then click on Litigation Document Example 9.2: Summary Judgment Documents in *Browne v. Smith*.

III. Voluntary Dismissal

Read Fed. R. Civ. P. 41 (dismissal).

ARIAS v. CAMERON, 776 F.3d 1262 (2015). Arias sued Cameron and his employer, The Dow Chemical Company, for injuries sustained in a traffic accident. Cameron had provided a driver's license from another state, with a past address, and Arias attempted to serve him under the nonresident motorist statute. Arias filed suit within the limitations period, but it turned out that Cameron resided in-state, and when Arias finally discovered this fact and properly served Cameron, the limitations period had ended. The defendants filed a motion for summary judgment on the claimed ground that Arias had not been diligent in serving Cameron. Arias then moved to be allowed to dismiss the action voluntarily, without prejudice. A state statute provided that in such a situation, Arias could refile and serve process within six months. The defendants opposed dismissal without prejudice.

Arias had attempted service in three different ways over a 27-day period, finally succeeding by instructing the process server to remain at Cameron's home until he appeared. She seemed to have been diligent. The court of appeals concluded that the balance of equities favored Arias: . . .

> The district court granted Arias's motion to voluntarily dismiss her case and denied as moot Defendants' motion for summary judgment. But the court nonetheless directed that if Arias chose to refile her claims, she must first pay Defendants' attorneys' fees and costs incurred in this action . . . . [The court has power to impose conditions and often requires costs and fees as a condition.—Eds.] . . .
>
> . . . [W]e conclude that the district court acted well within its discretion when it granted Arias's motion for voluntary dismissal. First, . . . Arias filed her lawsuit in Georgia state court before the two-year statute of limitations ran. Second, . . . Arias acted diligently . . . . Third, none of the facts of this case demonstrate bad faith on the part of Arias's counsel . . . . Fourth, Defendants' claimed statute-of-limitations defense is weak, at best. And, finally, the only reason that Defendants even arguably have a statute-of-limitations defense is because they removed the case to federal court. Had the case stayed in Georgia court, where Arias chose to file it, there would have been no question that she would have been able to voluntarily dismiss the case and take advantage of Georgia's six-month refiling provision. . . . [Dismissal without prejudice AFFIRMED.]

Notes and Questions

(1) *Is There Prejudice to the Defendant?* An important question is, will the conditions (including compensation) actually remove any prejudice to the defendant? On the one hand, in *Arias v. Cameron,* the defendant loses a viable (but weak) defense. On the other hand, it is placed in the same position as if the plaintiff had known how to make proper service in the first place. For a different prejudice dilemma, see *McCants v. Ford Motor Co.,* 781 F.2d 855 (11th Cir. 1986), which is cited in *Arias.* There, the defendant had a solid limitations defense, but the plaintiff moved for dismissal without prejudice so that he could refile in another state with a longer limitations period. Even in this case, the court upheld a dismissal without prejudice.

(2) *The Court's Discretion in Attaching Conditions.* Another question is, how should the trial court go about deciding how much of Cameron and Dow's litigation

costs to charge to the plaintiff? Some of the costs here may reduce costs in the refiled litigation.

IV. Involuntary Dismissal for Want of Prosecution: The Court's Inherent Power

LEE v. BERRYHILL, 719 Fed. Appx. 729 (9th Cir. 2018) (unpublished opinion). Local Rule 41.1(a) in the Southern District of California provides that a case that has been pending "for more than six months, without any proceeding or discovery having been taken . . . , may, after notice, be dismissed by the court for want of prosecution." But even if such a dismissal is ordered without prejudice, it can be a harsh sanction, because limitations or other deadlines may run, and the effects of discovery and rulings may be lost. In this case, the court of appeals affirmed a dismissal ordered under the local six-month rule:

> Lee's counsel stated that she did not take any action for six months because she was waiting for the magistrate judge to issue a Report and Recommendation after the judge denied her requests for an extension of time to file Lee's motion for summary judgment. That explanation did not justify counsel's lengthy period of inaction. Under Rule 72 of the Federal Rules of Civil Procedure, a magistrate judge must issue a Report and Recommendation only for rulings on case-dispositive motions. A motion for an extension of time to file a motion for summary judgment is not a case-dispositive motion . . . . If counsel intended to seek review of the magistrate judge's order by the district judge, she was required to file objections within 14 days. [Rule] 72(a). Counsel failed to do so . . . .
>
> The district court did not abuse its discretion in determining that dismissal of the action without prejudice, rather than some less drastic sanction, was the appropriate response to counsel's inactivity. . . . The district court properly provided notice to Lee's counsel that it was contemplating dismissal of the action and conducted a telephonic hearing on the matter. The court permissibly concluded that the explanation offered by Lee's counsel for allowing the case to languish for six months was inadequate to avoid dismissal under Local Rule 41.1(a). [AFFIRMED.]

Notes and Questions

(1) *"Dismissal Dockets."* In many courts, it is common practice to set up "dismissal dockets," consisting of cases that have been on file for lengthy periods without recent action. The court may then provide notice to the plaintiffs that their cases will be dismissed unless they undertake a given step (*e.g.*, filing a request for trial setting, or even filing a "Motion to Retain on the Docket"). Dismissal dockets

are useful because there typically are many cases on a busy court's docket in which counsel have withdrawn, clients have disappeared, etc., and the parties are unlikely to resolve them. *See* Note, *Dismissal with Prejudice for Failure to Prosecute: Visiting the Sins of the Attorney Upon the Client*, 22 GA. L. REV. 195 (1987).

(2) *Other Dismissals: For Failure to State a Claim, for Want of Jurisdiction, as a Discovery Sanction, Etc.* Notice that Rule 41(b) provides, "Unless the dismissal order states otherwise, a dismissal under this subdivision (b) and any dismissal not under this rule—except one for lack of jurisdiction, improper venue, or failure to join a party under Rule 19—operates as an adjudication on the merits," *i.e.*, it is "with prejudice" to any future litigation. Thus, a dismissal for want of jurisdiction would not bar the plaintiff from refiling in a proper court—but a dismissal for failure to state a claim would, unless it "otherwise specifies." *See* Note, *Res Judicata Effects of Involuntary Dismissals: When Involuntary Dismissal Based Upon Prematurity or Failure to Satisfy a Precondition to Suit Should Bar a Second Action,* 70 CORNELL L. REV. 667 (1985). As to general sanctioning authority under the court's inherent power, see Chapter 5, above.

V. Default Judgment

Read Fed. R. Civ. P. 55 (default).

Butner v. Neustadter

324 F.2d 783 (9th Cir. 1963)

HAMLIN, CIRCUIT JUDGE.

This is an appeal from an order of the United States District Court for the Southern District of California denying appellant's motion to set aside a default judgment....

[The defendant was served with process in a California state suit while he was in Los Angeles temporarily. At that time, California rules required an answer within ten days. The defendant sent the papers to his attorney in Little Rock, Arkansas, where defendant resided; he enclosed the name of Los Angeles attorney Samuel Reisman. By the time his Little Rock lawyer contacted Reisman's office to secure California counsel, answer time had nearly expired under the California state rules, and Reisman then was out of town. An associate of Reisman left messages with the plaintiff's attorney seeking an extension of time, but the plaintiff's attorney ultimately responded that he had already secured a default judgment on the day after answer day, which he refused to set aside.]

[The defendant's attorneys then removed the case to federal court, where they (1) filed an answer, which they claimed superseded the default, since it was filed within the twenty-day period provided under the federal rules; and (2) moved in the alternative to have the federal court set aside the state default judgment, pursuant to Federal Rule 60(b). The district court refused to set aside the default. The Court of Appeals, in this opinion, reversed.]

The issues presented are: (1) Is defendant entitled to have the default judgment vacated as a matter of law upon removal to federal district court; and (2) if not, did the trial court abuse its discretion in not granting the motion to set aside?

Appellant contends that he is entitled to have the default judgment set aside as a matter of law upon removal to federal district court. His reasoning is as follows: section 1446(b) gives a defendant the right to remove within twenty days after service of process. Fed. R. Civ. P. 12 gives him twenty days within which to appear and plead. If a default judgment entered in a state court within ten days after service of process is allowed to take precedence over the removal statute which allows him twenty days to remove, then, he contends, the whole purpose of the removal statute is defeated. Appellee maintains, on the other hand, that although the removal after the default judgment is perfectly proper, it cannot be taken to supersede the default judgment which must be regarded as valid until set aside. We agree.

... The federal court takes the case as it finds it on removal and treats everything that occurred in the state court as if it had taken place in federal court. Therefore, this default judgment should be treated as though it had been validly rendered in the federal proceeding. Appellant's argument that state law cannot prevent removal or defeat its effects is quite correct. That does not mean that the default judgment must be vacated as a matter of law. Instead, a motion to set aside a default may be made in the district court under Fed. R. Civ. P. 60(b) because of mistake, inadvertence, surprise, or excusable neglect.

Appellant argues that the trial court abused its discretion in denying the motion to vacate .... In *Karlein v. Karlein* [103 Cal. App. 2d 496, 229 P.2d 831 (1951)], the district court of appeal said:

> An appellate court listens more readily to an appeal from an order denying relief [from default]. ... [A]ny doubt as to the propriety of setting aside a default should be resolved in favor of the application, even in a case where the showing ... is not strong .... Neither party should be deprived of a hearing except when guilty of inexcusable neglect, and doubts should be resolved in favor of an application to set aside a default judgment.

These statements are a good guide to action in this case. Appellant contends he has a good defense on the merits, namely that the note in question was obtained by means of fraud and that appellee is not a holder in due course. Whether or not this is true, if he is not guilty of inexcusable neglect, he should have a hearing on the merits.

Appellee maintains that appellant was guilty of inexcusable neglect in that he sent the summons and complaint to his attorney in Arkansas with directions to contact Mr. Reisman in Los Angeles, that he was acquainted with lawyers in Los Angeles, and that he was an astute businessman and should have simply contacted Mr. Reisman himself. Then the fact that Mr. Reisman was out of town would not have made any difference, for appellant would have been aware of that circumstance and could have made appropriate arrangements to get another attorney. While there may be some doubt as to the wisdom of appellant's actions in this case, there are several possible explanations of his conduct. Having been a resident of Little Rock for more than a year, he might quite naturally wish to send all his legal business to his Little Rock attorney, and merely in this one instance have sent the name of Mr. Reisman along as a convenience to the Little Rock attorney. . . .

There is a possibility of a meritorious defense. An attempt was made to take action on the complaint within the allotted ten days but was frustrated by certain events. There is doubt as to whether the circumstances which frustrated the attempt could amount to inexcusable neglect. . . . We hold that the order by the district court [refusing to set aside the default judgment] was an abuse of discretion. [REVERSED.]

Notes and Questions

(1) *Standards for Setting Aside Defaults upon "Excusable Neglect": Changing the Facts in Butner v. Neustadter.* Would (or should) relief have been available in *Butner v. Neustadter* if default had resulted simply because the defendant had mislaid the summons and complaint and forgotten it? (Yes, probably.) Or if it resulted because the defendant sent the papers to his attorney and the Post Office delayed for several weeks in delivery? (Yes, probably.) Or if the defendant ignored the suit because he was "too busy" to deal with them? (Probably not; this situation is different.)

Getting a default judgment set aside is not always easy. Many court of appeals decisions refuse to set aside defaults in short unpublished opinions. *E.g., Hodson v. Kroll,* 712 Fed. Appx. 831 (10th Cir. 2018).

(2) *Technical Scrutiny of Default Judgments on Timely Direct Attack.* There can be little question that default judgments are more readily subject to setting aside than judgments after defense. Areas of attack may include: (1) inadequacy of the summons or return (e.g., the return fails to describe the service properly); (2) absence of jurisdiction; (3) failure to make an adequate record at the default hearing; (4) in some jurisdictions, failure to have a reporter record the default hearing (on the theory that the defaulting defendant is entitled to appeal); (5) in some jurisdictions, lack of specificity in the complaint; and (6) lack of notice of default or misleading instructions from the opposing party or court personnel.

(3) *Proof Requirements for Damages in Default Judgments.* If the claim is "liquidated" (*i.e.*, if it is for "a sum certain or for a sum which by mathematical calculation can be made certain," as in the case of a promissory note), Rule 55(b)(1) says that the clerk shall enter judgment on proper application. But application must be made to the court if the sum is unliquidated. The court may order a hearing and evidence. Ordinarily, the damages must be proved by competent evidence, and the

court may require liability facts to be proved under Rule 55(b)(2) when needed "to enter or effectuate judgment."

ORGANIZACION MISS AMERICA LATINA, INC. v. URQUIDI, 712 Fed. Appx. 945 (11th Cir. 2017) (unpublished opinion). Ordinarily, the district court must receive evidence establishing damages after default. Sometimes written affidavits may suffice as evidence, but the court may need to hold a hearing with live testimony. In the *Organizacion Latina* case, however, the claim was for trademark infringement, for which there are statutory damages in fixed amounts, and for breach of a contract that provided a calculable amount that was to be paid. The district court relied on Rule 55(b)(1), which allows a judgment on a liquidated claim without a damages hearing. The court of appeals affirmed:

> . . . [W]e agree with [plaintiff] that the damages in this case were capable of mathematical calculation. The statutory damages chosen by the judge were an ascertainable value per violation, simply multiplied by the number of violations. Appellants challenge neither number even on appeal. Additionally, the damages for breach of contract were ascertainable—i.e., the money not paid by Appellants or wrongly collected by Appellants. In both of these damage awards the amounts were capable of mathematical calculation. The lower court did not abuse its discretion in refusing to hold an evidentiary hearing on damages.

VI. How to Answer the Chapter Summary Problem: Some Suggestions

Browne v. Smith: A Problem Involving Summary Judgment, Dismissal, and Default. (As always, follow your Professor's instructions about how to answer.)

1. Can the defendant successfully argue for summary judgment? *Law:* Summary judgment can be granted when there are no genuine disputes of material fact and the movant is entitled to judgment as a matter of law. *Facts:* Receipt of the letter that the city sent to Browne occurred more than two years before suit, creating a limitations defense. He pleads the discovery rule, but arguably, the letter should have given him notice of the facts giving rise to his cause of action. Browne also relies on the fraudulent concealment rule to avoid limitations, but the statement by Smith to the effect that we will file suit and get your job back does not seem to be fraudulent or to conceal anything. *Conclusion:* Summary judgment for defendant.

2. Can the plaintiff obtain voluntary dismissal of the claim if he senses that an adverse summary judgment is imminent? *Law:* The court has discretion over voluntary dismissal without prejudice. It can set conditions. *Facts:* If the court finds that plaintiff seeks dismissal to avoid an adverse summary judgment and perhaps to refile in another jurisdiction, the court might refuse to dismiss without prejudice or attach conditions such as that the record remains the same or that plaintiff pays the costs of defendant's defense. *Conclusion:* These events could mean that the dismissal without prejudice may be denied or become meaningless.

3. If plaintiff Browne had obtained a default judgment because defendant Smith's lawyer had inadvertently misplaced the complaint and failed to answer it, would the defendant be able to set aside the default judgment? *Law:* The Rules include a provision allowing relief from a final judgment caused by "excusable neglect," provided that the proper motion is made within one year. *Facts:* Inadvertent misplacement of the complaint is probably excusable neglect. (Notice that the rule does not preclude relief from judgment because of fault; it's applicable in a negligence-like situation.) *Conclusion:* Smith could probably obtain relief from the default judgment.

VII. Improving Summary Judgment and Other Non-Trial Disposition Methods: Notes and Questions

(1) *Clarifying the Standard for Summary Judgment Against the Party with the Burden of Proof.* After *Celotex*, it is clear that the party without the burden of proof can obtain summary judgment without putting her own evidence in the record. However, a comparison of the opinion of the Court with the separate opinion of Mr. Justice Brennan makes it clear that the standard remains ambiguous. Should the Rule be amended to make clear that summary judgment can be granted if the movant's interrogatories asking the non-movant to particularize her evidentiary basis for her contentions remain unanswered after the non-movant has had adequate time for discovery? Or should amendment limit considerations only to materials admissible in evidence?

(2) *Conditions on Voluntary Dismissal.* If the plaintiff has subjected the defendant to suit in a given forum and wishes to dismiss without prejudice, it seems only fair that the plaintiff should pay the expenses that this choice has occasioned for the defendant and that the issues actually determined in the defendant's favor should carry over to other litigation, absent reason to the contrary. Would it make sense to amend Rule 41 to provide that the plaintiff must pay the defendant's reasonable expenses and that the dismissal preserves rulings favorable to the defendant unless the court otherwise provides in its order?

(3) *Default.* Would it make sense to provide for the manner of making proof to support default judgment (*e.g.*, by expressly providing in the Rule that affidavits are satisfactory proof)? Should the time for setting aside default be enlarged so that it is longer than time limits for setting aside other kinds of judgments? Since setting aside defaults is *sui generis*—it really is a different kind of issue than setting aside other kinds of judgments based on fraud, newly discovered evidence, etc.—would it make sense to govern the process of setting aside default by a liberal provision contained in its own separate Rule?

Chapter 10

Trial

I. The Order of Events in a Jury Trial

Although there are some jurisdictional variations, the events in a jury trial usually follow this sequence:

Trial Setting and Final Pretrial Conference. The trial may have been set for years, or it may have been set for a few weeks or months only. The federal system contemplates a final pretrial conference close in time to the trial, although practice varies. This process is covered in detail in Chapter 8, *supra*, but it is important to remember its relationship to the trial.

Motions on the Eve of Trial. These motions may include requests for particular orders relating to jury selection (*e.g.*, for individual examination of jurors), for evidence rulings, etc. A "motion in limine" is frequently asserted at this stage in some jurisdictions. "*In limine*" is Latin, meaning "at the threshold." The motion asks the court to exclude potentially prejudicial evidence in advance, unless the proponent of the evidence raises the issue outside the presence of the jury first. In jurisdictions without extensive use of pretrial conferences, these motions may be presented and ruled upon the day trial begins.

Voir Dire Examination of Jurors. The trial itself begins with a panel of potential jurors in the courtroom. The judge, or the attorneys, or both—depending upon the jurisdiction and the court—question the panel members about their qualifications.

Challenges to Potential Jurors ("Jury Selection"). During the examination, attorneys may challenge disqualified jurors, and each side is allowed to remove a certain number of potential jurors without giving reasons. The first twelve (or, in some courts, a different number of) panel members who remain are impaneled and sworn.

Opening Statements. The plaintiff's attorney gives an opening statement, followed by the defendant's attorney. In some jurisdictions, the defendant may choose to give an opening statement after the plaintiff rests, right before defendant's case begins.

Invoking "the Rule" (Sequestering Witnesses). At this stage (or sometimes earlier), many jurisdictions permit either attorney to demand that the court sequester the witnesses (*i.e.*, order them to refrain from listening to the evidence or discussing the case with persons other than the attorneys). This procedure is often called "invoking 'the rule'" ("Your honor, I invoke the rule.").

The Right to Open and Close. The party with the burden of proof on the whole case (usually the plaintiff) has the right to open and close the evidence and jury arguments.

Plaintiff's Evidence. The plaintiff calls her first witness. The evidence for the plaintiff must be submitted in accordance with the Rules of Evidence, which govern what is admissible. The plaintiff's evidence also may include stipulations, discovery products, or facts judicially noticed by the court. The plaintiff ends this phase of trial by saying, "plaintiff rests."

Motion for Judgment as a Matter of Law or "Directed Verdict." The defendant may move to have the case taken from the jury and decided by the judge on the ground that the plaintiff's evidence cannot support a verdict.

Defendant's Evidence. The defendant may choose to submit evidence. The same kinds of evidentiary rules control. At the conclusion, the defendant rests.

Rebuttal and Surrebuttal Evidence. The plaintiff now may move for judgment against the defendant. In addition, the plaintiff may offer evidence in rebuttal to the defendant's evidence. The defendant may offer surrebuttal, to which the plaintiff may again respond, etc.

Motion for Judgment as a Matter of Law or "Directed Verdict" at the Close of the Evidence. Either party may move for judgment as a matter of law (also called a "directed verdict") when all parties close.

The Charge Conference: Requests and Rulings. The attorneys must be given an opportunity to make requests for jury charges. In many federal courts, the requests must be made before trial; in some state courts, they may be made during trial. Typically, the court confers with the parties about the charge. The Federal Rules require that the judge inform the parties of its rulings on requested charges before the attorneys give their jury arguments.

Objections to the Charge. The attorneys must be given an opportunity to place their objections to the charge on the record. Many jurisdictions prohibit appellate consideration of errors in the charge unless they were objected to before the jury retired.

Jury Argument (or "Summation"). The attorneys argue the law and the evidence to the jury, giving their explanations of the way in which the jurors should resolve the issues. The party with the burden of proof on the whole case (usually the plaintiff) opens the jury argument. The defendant gives the second jury argument. The plaintiff gives the final (rebuttal) argument.

The Court's Charge and Submission of the Case to the Jury (Verdict Forms). The court then instructs the jury on the applicable law and submits a question, or series of questions, to the jury, together with a form for its verdict. In some courts, the court charges the jury before the arguments of counsel.

Jury Deliberations; Further Charges or Questions; Verdict. The jury retires to deliberate. In certain circumstances, the court may give further charges after the jury retires. The jury returns written answers, in the form of a verdict, to the questions asked. The judge receives the verdict if it is in order. Either side may demand that the jury be "polled" (that is, that each juror be asked whether the verdict is his or her verdict). The jurors then may be discharged.

Post-Trial Motions and Judgment. These steps are not part of the trial proper, although they are related closely to it. The verdict loser may move for judgment as a matter of law (also known as a "judgment notwithstanding the verdict") and for a new trial. Under the federal rules, the verdict loser can make both motions after judgment. The court has the responsibility of applying the law to the jury's verdict to produce a judgment, which is an order granting or denying the requested relief.

The Subjects in This Chapter. Here, we take up these events (with some omissions and some additions) in roughly the order in which they occur in a trial. We also will briefly consider trial before the court. First, however, we offer the following Chapter Summary Problem, which you should read now but analyze at the end of the chapter (or you should treat it as your instructor directs).

Problem A: Chapter 10 Summary Problem

JUDGE OR JURY TRIAL IN STONE v. CRESTVIEW APARTMENT CO. You represent Myron and Charlotte Stone. While both were away at their jobs, their three-year-old daughter—who was in the care of her usual babysitter—wandered off, fell into the apartment swimming pool, and suffered severe brain damage. She will require extensive medical and custodial care for the rest of her life. Your complaint charges Crestview Apartment Company with negligence for failing to keep the gate in the fence surrounding the pool locked. Consider the following questions:

1. *Right to Trial by Jury?* To what extent could you have a right to trial by jury in a federal court if the negligence claim is joined with a claim for an injunction against a fraudulent transfer (because you fear that Crestview may shift its assets to a newly formed entity)?

2. *Should You Challenge the Array?* You are convinced that jury venires in the county of suit are underinclusive of young people, ages 18 to 25, because jury summonses are based on voter registration lists. Should you make a challenge to the array on these grounds (and if so, when and how)?

3. *Should You Demand a Jury—Or Waive It?* There are some cases in which you would be better off trying your case before a judge without a jury. Is this one of those cases—or would you demand a jury (and if so, when and how)?

4. *Examination by the Judge or by the Attorneys.* The state courts in your jurisdiction give the parties the right to question the potential jurors, through their attorneys. The federal judges in the region, however, usually exercise the option to conduct the examination themselves alone. The attorney opposing you is much more experienced in jury trials than you are. If diversity of citizenship gave you the choice, would you file suit in state court or federal court?

5. *Insurance Questions During Voir Dire.* Assuming you are in federal court, you have the opportunity to file written requests for questions to be asked by the judge. The probability exists that you will want to have the jurors questioned about their insurance affiliations, both because (1) you believe that insurance-affiliated persons will be unfavorable jurors and because (2) Crestview is a small family business, and you would not want the jurors to assume that your suit would make it insolvent. But there is a strict prohibition in this jurisdiction upon introducing before the jury the fact that the defendant is, or is not, covered by liability insurance. How would you word the requested questions so as to maximize the probability of obtaining

information, obtaining a basis for challenges for cause if they exist, and counteracting the possibility of prejudice in favor of the defendant as a "little guys" corporation?

6. *The "Ideal Juror."* Try to construct a profile of the kinds of jurors you would want. Would you want young people or old people? Rich or poor? College-educated jurors or high-school dropouts? Professional people or blue-collar workers? Law students?

7. *Peremptory Challenges Based upon Ethnicity or Gender.* Assume that a survey indicates that Asian-Americans are strongly disposed to favor the defendant in this case, and that women are much more favorable to the plaintiff than men. [In fact, a survey did show these predispositions; this problem is based on a real case—*see* Litigation Document Example 10.1, available online at https://caplaw.com/sites/cp7.] Is a strike illegal or unethical if it is influenced by these considerations? What steps should you take if 100% of defendant's peremptory challenges are against women?

8. *Court's Charge and Verdict.* Assume that the jury returns a general verdict for $2 million, but it also returns special verdicts on each of the permissible elements of damage, adding up to only $1 million. What would you urge the judge to do?

[Ed. Note: A jury in a state court delivered a verdict for $84 million in a case in which a baby drowned and her young sister suffered brain damage after entering an apartment pool area through an unlocked gate. *See Jury Delivers $84 Million Verdict in Drowning Case*, Houston Chronicle, April 12, 1991, at A-21, col.2. What performance by the plaintiff's and defendant's lawyers do you think made the difference between this verdict and one for $100,000—or for that matter, between this verdict and a defendant's verdict? Consider the New Dublin Jury Study, reproduced below in the Litigation Document Example 10.1, available online at https://caplaw.com/sites/cp7.]

II. The Right to Trial by Jury

[A] In Federal "Suits at Common Law"

Read U.S. Const. amend. VII and Fed. R. Civ. P. 38 (right to jury trial).

Note on the Kinds of Claims that Carry the Right to Trial by Jury

The Federal Rules and the Seventh Amendment. So accustomed are we to thinking of the right to trial by jury as fundamental, that it may surprise you to learn that the right does not exist in all federal suits. The Seventh Amendment provides, "in suits at common law, . . . the right of trial by jury shall be preserved. . . ." From Chapter 5, you should remember that "suits at common law" are distinct from suits in equity. The equity courts did not try cases by jury before the adoption of the

Seventh Amendment in 1791; therefore, it follows that the Seventh Amendment does not preserve a right to trial by jury in these cases. There are certain other areas (*e.g.*, admiralty cases) in which no right to jury trial historically was recognized and to which the right does not extend today. Federal Rule 38 does not create any additional rights, but only states that the right exists "as declared by the Seventh Amendment to the Constitution or as provided by a federal statute."

Claims that Evolved Since Adoption of the Constitution; Statutory Claims. Another question is that of the right to jury trial for claims that did not exist when the Seventh Amendment was adopted. For example, strict product liability claims as we know them today did not exist before the twentieth century. Also, modern statutes create new causes of action. Does the Seventh Amendment "preserve" a right to trial by jury in an employment discrimination claim based upon the Civil Rights Act of 1964? What about statutes giving rise to complex litigation, so that a jury would be required to sit for two to five years? The materials that follow address these questions as well. *See also* James, *Right to a Jury Trial in Civil Actions*, 72 Yale L.J. 655 (1963).

[1] Effects of the Nonexistence of the Right in Equity Cases

How to Read the Case of Beacon Theatres v. Westover

In the case that follows, the action is complicated because the plaintiff sued for two kinds of relief: an injunction and a declaratory judgment. The injunction is equitable. The declaratory judgment is harder to characterize—but if it relates to a claim that is legal in origin, the Supreme Court apparently would treat it as legal. The problem, therefore, is that the case includes both legal issues, which carry the right to jury trial, and equitable issues, which do not. But similar facts control both kinds of issues. How, then, should the district court decide these facts—with a jury, or without? The district judge adopted a solution by which he, alone, effectively would decide them. In this decision, however, the Court holds that the right to a jury trial does apply. Is the decision faithful to the "preservation" language of the Seventh Amendment?

Beacon Theatres, Inc. v. Westover

359 U.S. 500 (1959)

Mr. Justice Black delivered the opinion of the Court.

Petitioner, Beacon Theatres, Inc., sought by mandamus to require a district judge in the Southern District of California to vacate certain orders alleged to deprive it of a jury trial of issues arising in a suit brought against it by Fox West Coast Theatres, Inc. The Court of Appeals for the Ninth Circuit refused the writ, holding that the trial judge had acted within his proper discretion in denying petitioner's request for a jury. . . . We granted certiorari. . . .

[Fox had contracts giving it exclusive rights of distribution of motion pictures in a certain geographic area. Beacon notified Fox that it considered these contracts to be in violation of the antitrust laws. Fox then filed suit against Beacon, alleging that the contracts were valid under the antitrust laws. Fox prayed for declaratory relief, under the Declaratory Judgment Act, that the contracts were not in violation of the antitrust laws. However, Fox also sought "an injunction . . . to prevent Beacon from instituting any action against Fox and its distributors" on the ground that Beacon had made alleged threats of treble damage suits against Fox and its distributors which, Fox alleged, subjected Fox to "duress and coercion" and deprived it of a valuable property right (the right to negotiate for exclusive distribution contracts). This latter claim, for an injunction, was ostensibly equitable.]

[Beacon answered and counterclaimed. The counterclaim raised many of the same legal and factual issues as the complaint, in reverse. Specifically, Beacon alleged that the exclusive distribution contracts violated the antitrust laws, and it prayed for the treble damages allowed by those laws. Beacon also demanded a jury trial of all factual issues.]

[The district judge concluded that the claims presented by Fox's complaint were "essentially equitable." Acting under the authority of Rule 42 (which allows separate trial of any claim or issue) and Rule 57 (which empowers the judge to order a speedy trial of a declaratory judgment action and to advance it on the docket), the district judge held that these "equitable" claims would be tried first. Further, since he thus considered plaintiff Fox's claims to be "equitable," the judge planned to determine them himself, without a jury. This order of trial probably would effectively deprive Beacon of the right to have fact issues determined by a jury, since any fact findings made by the judge probably would be binding, under the principle of collateral estoppel, in a later trial of the issues raised by Beacon's counterclaim. Beacon sought mandamus as a means of having the appellate court order the trial judge not to determine the "equitable" issues first and, more importantly, to preserve the right to jury trial. The Supreme Court, in this opinion, accepts Beacon's arguments.]

The District Court's finding that the Complaint for Declaratory Relief presented basically equitable issues draws no support from the Declaratory Judgment Act, 28 U.S.C. §§ 2201, 2202. . . . That statute, while allowing prospective defendants to sue to establish their nonliability, specifically preserves the right to jury trial for both parties. It follows that [Beacon] cannot be deprived of that right merely because Fox took advantage of the availability of declaratory relief to sue Beacon first. Since the right to trial by jury applies to treble damage suits under the antitrust laws, . . . the Sherman and Clayton Act issues on which Fox sought a declaration were essentially jury questions.

Nevertheless the Court of Appeals refused to upset the order of the district judge. . . . A party who is entitled to maintain a suit in equity for an injunction, said the court, may have all the issues in his suit determined by the judge without a jury regardless of whether legal rights are involved. . . .

[T]he Court of Appeals [then] held it was not an abuse of discretion of the district judge, acting under Federal Rule of Civil Procedure 42(b) [separate trial], to try the equitable cause first even though this might, through collateral estoppel, prevent a full jury trial of the counterclaim and cross-claim which were as effectively stopped as by an equity injunction. . . .

Viewed in this manner, the use of discretion by the trial court under Rule 42(b) to deprive Beacon of a full jury trial on its counterclaim and cross-claim, as well as on Fox's plea for declaratory relief, cannot be justified. Under the Federal Rules the same court may try both legal and equitable causes in the same action. . . . [The court can preserve the status quo if necessary by issuing a temporary injunction, which does not have collateral estoppel effect.] Whatever permanent injunctive relief Fox might be entitled to on the basis of the decision in this case could, of course, be given by the court after the jury renders its verdict. In this way the issues between these parties could be settled in one suit giving Beacon a full jury trial of every antitrust issue. . . .

If there should be cases where the availability of declaratory judgment or joinder in one suit of legal and equitable causes would not in all respects protect the plaintiff seeking equitable relief from irreparable harm while affording a jury trial in the legal cause, the trial court will necessarily have to use its discretion in deciding whether the legal or equitable cause should be tried first. Since the right to jury trial is a constitutional one, however, . . . that discretion is very narrowly limited and must, wherever possible, be exercised to preserve jury trial. . . . [O]nly under the most imperative circumstances, circumstances which in view of the flexible procedures of the Federal Rules we cannot now anticipate, can the right to a jury trial of legal issues be lost through prior determination of equitable claims. . . .

Reversed.

Mr. Justice Stewart, with whom Mr. Justice Harlan and Mr. Justice Whittaker concur, dissenting.

. . . The district judge simply exercised his inherent discretion, now explicitly confirmed by the Federal Rules of Civil Procedure, to schedule the trial of an equitable claim in advance of an action at law. . . .

The Court's opinion does not, of course, hold or even suggest that a court of equity may never determine "legal rights." For indeed it is precisely such rights which the Chancellor, when his jurisdiction has been properly invoked, has often been called upon to decide. Issues of fact are rarely either "legal" or "equitable." All depends upon the context in which they arise.

. . . It has also been long settled that the District Court in its discretion may order the trial of a suit in equity in advance of an action at law between the same parties, even if there is a factual issue common to both. . . .

For these reasons I think the petition for a writ of mandamus should have been dismissed.

Notes and Questions

(1) *Is Beacon Theatres Consistent with the Historical Approach of the Seventh Amendment "Preservation" Requirement?* It repeatedly has been held that the

Seventh Amendment adopts a historical approach. *Curtis v. Loether*, 415 U.S. 189 (1974); *cf. Parsons v. Bedford*, 28 U.S. (3 Pet.) 433 (1830). The language of the amendment "preserves" the right as it existed in England at the time of adoption of the Bill of Rights in 1791; it does not purport to create a broader right than then existed. There is little question, however, that *Beacon Theatres* extends a right to trial by jury to a case in which, at the time of adoption of the Bill of Rights, it would not have existed. Is *Beacon Theatres*, therefore, inconsistent with the historical approach of the Seventh Amendment, as Justice Stewart's dissent implies?

(2) *"Suits at Common Law" as an Evolving Concept.* Perhaps the historical view of the Seventh Amendment has flexibility built into it, since the common law itself is evolutionary. Consider the following language from *Parsons v. Bedford, supra*, 28 U.S. (3 Pet.) at 447:

> [The drafters of the Constitution understood the "common law" to include] suits in which legal rights were to be ascertained and determined, in contradistinction to those where equitable rights [or other nonlegal rights] alone were recognized.... Probably, there were few, if any, states in the union, in which some new legal remedies, differing from the old common-law forms, were not in use; but in which, however, the trial by jury intervened.... [T]he amendment then may well be construed to embrace all suits, which are not of equity and admiralty jurisdiction, whatever may be the peculiar form which they may assume to settle legal rights.

Is *Beacon Theatres* consistent with an historical view of the Seventh Amendment when viewed in light of this "evolution" argument? *See* Rothstein, *Beacon Theatres and the Constitutional Right to Jury Trial*, 51 A.B.A.J. 1145 (1965).

(3) *The Disadvantages of a Jury Trial, and Advantages of Equity, in Beacon Theatres.* Fox, the plaintiff in *Beacon Theatres*, may well have been in a quandary and in need of a very rapid declaration of its rights. If it continued to use exclusive contracts, it might be in continued violation of the antitrust laws, and its conduct could make it liable for damages—treble damages, in fact, under the antitrust laws. But if it ceased to rely upon exclusive contracts, it might later find that these arrangements were perfectly legal and gave an advantage in the meantime to its competitors. One of the serious disadvantages of jury trial is that it often entails lengthy delay. Has the Court, in fact, deprived Fox of the adaptability, flexibility, and accommodation to the needs of the lawsuit that are the principal characteristics of equitable remedies?

DAIRY QUEEN, INC. v. WOOD, 369 U.S. 469 (1962). The respondents licensed petitioner to use the trademark "Dairy Queen" in certain parts of Pennsylvania, in exchange for contractual payments, which varied over time with the petitioner's receipts. The respondents claimed that the petitioner had failed to make the required payments and filed suit asking for three kinds of relief: (1) temporary and permanent injunctions against the petitioner's use of the trademark; (2) an accounting to determine the exact amount of money owed by the petitioner; and

(3) an injunction against the petitioner's collecting any money from Dairy Queen stores during the accounting.

The requested injunctions were equitable claims. The request for an "accounting" also ostensibly invoked an equitable remedy. (An equitable "accounting" is available when the accounts between the parties are of such a "complicated nature" that they can satisfactorily be unraveled only by a court of equity.) The respondents had thus structured the complaint so that it appeared to seek purely equitable relief, apparently in an attempt to avoid jury trial; indeed, when the petitioner demanded a trial by jury, the respondents moved to strike the demand. The District Court granted the motion, struck the jury demand, and explained that the action was "purely equitable" or, if it was not purely equitable, that whatever legal issues were raised were "incidental" to equitable issues and therefore triable before the Court without a jury.

The Supreme Court reversed, holding that the petitioner had the right to jury trial. It first rejected the argument that jury trial could be denied as to legal issues that were "incidental" to equitable issues. "[O]ur previous decisions make it plain that no such rule may be applied in the federal courts," said the Court. "The holding in *Beacon Theatres* was that where both legal and equitable issues are presented in a single case, 'only under the most imperative circumstances . . . can the right to a jury trial of legal issues be lost through prior determination of equitable claims.'" The Court then went on to hold that the claim for an "accounting" was really a legal claim rather than an equitable one because it was "an action on a debt allegedly due under a contract, seeking a 'money judgment'":

> Petitioner's contention . . . is that insofar as the complaint requests a money judgment it presents a claim which is unquestionably legal. We agree with that contention. The most natural construction of the respondents' claim for a money judgment would seem to be that it is a claim that they are entitled to recover whatever was owed them under the contract as of the date of its purported termination plus damages for infringement of their trade-mark since that date. . . . As an action on a debt allegedly due under a contract, it would be difficult to conceive of an action of a more traditionally legal character. And as an action for damages based upon a charge of trademark infringement, it would be no less subject to cognizance by a court of law.
>
> The respondents' contention that this money claim is "purely equitable" is based primarily upon the fact that their complaint is cast in terms of an "accounting," rather than in terms of an action for "debt" or "damages." But the constitutional right to trial by jury cannot be made to depend upon the choice of words used in the pleadings. The necessary prerequisite to the right to maintain a suit for an equitable accounting, like all other equitable remedies, is, as we pointed out in *Beacon Theatres*, the absence of an adequate remedy at law. Consequently, in order to maintain such a suit on a cause of action cognizable at law, as this one is, the plaintiff must be able

> to show that the "accounts between the parties" are of such a "complicated nature" that only a court of equity can satisfactorily unravel them.... [T]his is certainly not such a case.... The legal remedy cannot be characterized as inadequate merely because the measure of damages may necessitate a look into petitioner's business records....

Notes and Questions

(1) *Bankruptcy: Katchen v. Landy*, 382 U.S. 323 (1966). In *Katchen*, the petitioner filed a claim in a bankruptcy proceeding for debts allegedly due him by the bankrupt. The trustee in bankruptcy promptly sued the petitioner to recover payments made by the bankrupt to the petitioner as "voidable preferences" (a voidable preference is a transfer on the eve of bankruptcy that preferentially benefits an individual creditor at the expense of other creditors, and it is subject to being set aside). The petitioner demanded a jury trial of the voidable preference issue. He pointed out that he would have been entitled to a jury trial on that issue if sued in District Court, and therefore, to deny him a jury trial simply because he had filed a bankruptcy claim would be inconsistent with *Beacon Theatres* and *Dairy Queen*. The Supreme Court rejected the argument and denied the petitioner a jury trial. The Court admitted that petitioner might be entitled to a jury trial if he had presented no claim and had awaited a federal district court action by the trustee, but "when the same issue arises as part of the process of allowance and disallowance of [bankruptcy] claims, it is triable in equity. The Bankruptcy Act ... converts the creditor's legal claim into an equitable claim...." The Court also pointed out that the "delay and expense" of jury trials would be inconsistent "with the equitable purposes of the Bankruptcy Act" because "petitioner's argument would require that in every case where a jury trial is demanded the proceeding on allowance of claims must be suspended." Is *Katchen v. Landy* consistent with *Beacon Theatres* and *Dairy Queen*? *See* Sabino, *Jury Trials in the Bankruptcy Court: A Continuing Controversy*, 90 Com. L.J. 342 (1985).

(2) *Ross v. Bernhard*, 396 U.S. 531 (1970). The petitioners brought a shareholders' derivative suit against corporate managers for allegedly paying excessive brokerage commissions to a firm with which they were affiliated. The trial court granted the petitioners' demand for jury trial; the Second Circuit reversed; and, finally, the Supreme Court reversed the reversal, upholding the right to jury trial. The Supreme Court admitted that a shareholders' derivative suit is a creature of equity, since the common law provided no remedy by which shareholders could make corporate officers and directors accountable. However, the Court noted that the shareholders' suit was simply an equitable device to allow shareholders to assert claims, including legal claims, owned by the corporation against corporate managers, and the legal claims included trial by jury. Justice Stewart dissented, arguing that the shareholders' derivative suit historically could be brought only in equity.

(3) *The "Ross Footnote": A Three-Part Test for the Right to Jury Trial.* In a famous footnote, the majority opinion in *Ross v. Bernhard* sets out three factors for distinguishing legal from equitable claims. 396 U.S. at 538 n. 10. "[T]he 'legal' nature

of an issue is determined by considering, first, the . . . custom of reference to such questions [before the merger of law and equity]; second, the remedy sought; and third, the practical abilities and limitations of juries." The first factor in this "*Ross* Footnote Test" is the familiar historical approach supported by the language of the Seventh Amendment. The second factor, which looks to the remedy as well as the claim, may also be viewed historically. The third factor, "the practical abilities and limitations of juries," is new; it seems to imply an approach oriented more toward policy considerations. How should the "*Ross* footnote" affect a huge, complex case—one that might take several years to try, include hundreds of thousands of documents as evidence, and require resolution of fact issues inseparable from legal questions? *See* subsection II[B], below.

(4) *Equitable Fact Findings That Collaterally Estop Later Legal Issues: Parklane Hosiery Co. v. Shore*, 439 U.S. 322 (1979). The Securities and Exchange Commission sued Parklane and twelve of its personnel for an injunction against the distribution of a proxy statement that the SEC alleged was materially false and misleading. After a four-day trial, the District Court found, as a fact, that the proxy statement was indeed materially false and misleading. Then, in a separate suit filed as a shareholders' derivative suit against the same defendants, the plaintiffs moved for partial summary judgment on the ground that the findings in the injunction action were binding against these defendants in the derivative suit also, under the doctrine of collateral estoppel. The lower courts denied the motion on the ground that it would violate the Seventh Amendment. The Supreme Court reversed, holding that collateral estoppel could apply. Justice Stewart (who had dissented in *Beacon Theatres* and *Ross*) wrote the opinion.

Justice Rehnquist dissented, in part because of a "nagging sense of unfairness as to the way petitioners have been treated." More importantly, the majority reduced the jury trial right, "which Blackstone praised as 'the glory of English law,' to a mere 'neutral' factor . . . in the name of procedural reform." Thus, Justice Rehnquist's solitary dissent would have extended the Bill of Rights where the other eight Justices would not. Are his arguments persuasive?

Problem B

C & K ENGINEERING CONTRACTORS v. AMBER STEEL CO. (*see* § 10.02[D], below). The plaintiff sues under the terms of a contract. A contract action is a classic common law claim. However, in this case, the plaintiff attempts to base the action on the equitable doctrine of promissory estoppel (under which a party may be bound by a promise if it induces injurious reliance by the other). You may assume that state law would recognize such a claim as an equitable claim and would hold the defendant bound to perform the promise; further, state law grants a right to monetary damages in such actions. You may also assume that the state courts, following a decision of the state supreme court interpreting the state constitution, would deny a jury trial (in fact, the California Supreme Court did, on the theory that the "gist of the action" was equitable; *see* § II[D]).

If defendant removes the case to federal court and demands a jury trial, should the court grant it? Incidentally, you should not be unduly influenced by what the state courts would do; federal law presumably controls. [Why?]

[2] Statutory Actions

Tull v. United States

481 U.S. 412 (1987)

JUSTICE BRENNAN delivered the opinion of the Court.

[Section 1913 of The Federal Clean Water Act subjects a violator to an injunction as well as to "a civil penalty not to exceed $10,000 per day" in some cases. The Government sued Tull, a real estate developer, for dumping fill on certain wetlands, and it sought both an injunction and a large civil penalty—in excess of $22 million. The District Court denied Tull's timely demand for a jury trial. Sitting without a jury, the trial judge found that Tull had committed violations of the Act, but he limited the civil penalty to a drastically reduced amount of no more than $325,000.

[The Clean Water Act, of course, did not exist at the time of adoption of the Seventh Amendment. The Supreme Court nevertheless holds that the jury trial right can apply to statutory claims, and that Tull is entitled to a jury trial on liability—but not on the amount of the penalty.]

II

... The Court has construed [the Seventh Amendment] to require a jury trial on the merits in those actions that are analogous to "Suits at common law." ... This analysis applies not only to common law forms of action, but also to causes of action created by congressional enactment.

To determine whether a statutory action is more similar to cases that were tried in courts of law than to suits tried in courts of equity or admiralty, the Court must examine both the nature of the action and of the remedy sought. First, we compare the statutory action to 18th-century actions brought in the courts of England prior to the merger of the courts of law and equity.... Second, we examine the remedy sought and determine whether it is legal or equitable in nature....

The petitioner analogizes this Government suit under § 1319(d) to an action in debt within the jurisdiction of English courts of law. Prior to the enactment of the Seventh Amendment, English courts had held that a civil penalty suit was a particular species of an action in debt that was within the jurisdiction of the courts of law....

After the adoption of the Seventh Amendment, federal courts followed this English common law in treating the civil penalty suit as a particular type of an action in debt, requiring a jury trial.... Actions by the Government to recover civil penalties under statutory provisions therefore historically have been viewed as one type of action in debt requiring trial by jury....

The Government argues, however, that [t]he closer historical analogue is an [equitable] action to abate a public nuisance. . . .

Whether . . . a public nuisance action is a better analogy than an action in debt is debatable. But we need not decide the question. . . . It suffices that we conclude that both the public nuisance action and the action in debt are appropriate analogies to the instant statutory action. . . .

We reiterate our previously expressed view that characterizing the relief sought is "[m]ore important" than finding a precisely analogous common law cause of action in determining whether the Seventh Amendment guarantees a jury trial.

A civil penalty was a type of remedy at common law that could only be enforced in courts of law. . . . Subsection (d) does not direct that the "civil penalty" imposed be calculated solely on the basis of equitable determinations, such as the profits gained from violations of the statute, but simply imposes a maximum penalty of $10,000 per day of violation. . . .

Thus, the petitioner has a constitutional right to a jury trial to determine his liability on the legal claims.

III

The remaining issue is whether the petitioner additionally has a Seventh Amendment right to a jury assessment of the civil penalties. The legislative history of the 1977 Amendments to the Clean Water Act shows [t]hat Congress intended that trial judges perform the highly discretionary calculations necessary to award civil penalties after liability is found. . . .

The answer must depend on whether the jury must shoulder this responsibility as necessary to preserve the "substance of the common-law right of trial by jury. . . ." Is a jury role necessary for that purpose? We do not think so. "Only those incidents which are regarded as fundamental, as inherent in and of the essence of the system of trial by jury, are placed beyond the reach of the legislature." The assessment of a civil penalty is not one of the "most fundamental elements." Congress' authority to fix the penalty by statute has not been questioned, and it was also the British practice. . . .

Since Congress itself may fix the civil penalties, it may delegate that determination to trial judges. In this case, highly discretionary calculations that take into account multiple factors are necessary in order to set civil penalties under the Clean Water Act. These are the kinds of calculations traditionally performed by judges. . . .

IV

We conclude that the Seventh Amendment required that the petitioner's demand for a jury trial be granted to determine his liability, but that the trial court and not the jury should determine the amount of penalties, if any. . . .

Chauffeurs, Teamsters and Helpers, Local No. 391 v. Terry

494 U.S. 558 (1990)

JUSTICE MARSHALL delivered the opinion of the Court except as to Part III-A.

This case presents the question whether an employee who seeks relief in the form of backpay for a union's alleged breach of its duty of fair representation has a right to trial by jury. We hold that the Seventh Amendment entitles such a plaintiff to a jury trial.

[Terry and other employees of McLean Trucking Company sued McLean and their union, alleging that McLean had breached its collective-bargaining agreement with the union in violation of § 301 of the Labor Management Relations Act and that the union had violated the duty of fair representation it owed to them by not pressing their grievances as a result of a series of transfers, layoffs and recalls by McLean. Terry requested a jury trial. The union moved to strike the jury demand on the ground that no right to a jury trial exists in a duty-of-fair-representation suit. The District Court denied the union's motion and the Court of Appeals affirmed.]

[The Supreme Court first holds that "[w]hether the employee sues both the labor union and the employer or only one of those entities, he must prove the same two facts to recover money damages: that the employer's action violated the terms of the collective bargaining agreement and that the union breached its duty of fair representation."]

III.

We turn now to the constitutional issue presented in this case—whether respondents are entitled to a jury trial.... The right to a jury trial included more than the common-law forms of action recognized in 1791; the phrase "suits at common-law" refers to "suits in which *legal* rights [are] to be ascertained and determined, in contradistinction to those where equitable rights alone [are] recognized, and equitable remedies [are] administered." *Parsons v. Bedford*, 3 Pet. 433, 447 (1830) ... The right extends to causes of action created by Congress. *Tull v. United States.*

To determine whether a particular action will resolve legal rights, we examine both the nature of the issues involved and the remedy sought. *Tull.* The second inquiry is the more important in our analysis. *Grandfinanciera, S.A. v. Nordberg*, 492 U.S. 33, 42 (1989).

A

An action for breach of a union's duty of fair representation was unknown in 18th-century England; in fact, collective-bargaining was unlawful. We must therefore look for an analogous cause of action that existed in the 18th century to determine whether the nature of this duty of fair representation suit is legal or equitable.

The Union contends that this duty of fair representation action resembles a suit brought to vacate an arbitration award because respondents seek to set aside the result of the grievance process. In the 18th Century, an action to set aside an arbitration award was considered equitable....

The arbitration analogy is inapposite, however, to . . . this case. No grievance committee has considered respondents' claim that the Union violated its duty of fair representation; the grievance process was concerned only with the employer's alleged breach of the collective-bargaining agreement. . . .

The Union next argues that respondents' duty of fair representation action is comparable to an action by a trust beneficiary against a trustee for breach of fiduciary duty. Such actions were within the exclusive jurisdiction of courts of equity. This analogy is far more persuasive than the arbitration analogy. Just as a trustee must act in the best interests of the beneficiaries, a union, as the exclusive representative of the workers, must exercise its power to act on behalf of the employees in good faith. . . .

Respondents contend that their duty of fair representation suit is less like a trust action than an attorney malpractice action, which was historically an action at law. . . .

[But] [u]nlike employees represented by a union, a client controls the significant decisions concerning his representation. Moreover, a client can fire his attorney if he is dissatisfied with his attorney's performance. . . . Thus, we find the malpractice analogy less convincing than the trust analogy.

Nevertheless, the trust analogy does not persuade us to characterize respondents' claim as wholly equitable. . . . To recover from the Union here, respondents must prove both that McLean violated § 301 by breaching the collective bargaining agreement and that the Union breached its duty of fair representation. When viewed in isolation, the duty of fair representation is analogous to a claim against a trustee for breach of fiduciary duty. The § 301 issue [i.e., whether the employer breached the agreement], however, is comparable to a breach of contract claim—a legal issue.

Respondents' action against the Union thus encompasses both equitable and legal issues. The first part of our Seventh Amendment inquiry, then, leaves us in equipoise as to whether respondents are entitled to a jury trial.

[The Court here proceeds to the second part of the inquiry: whether the remedy is legal or equitable in nature.] [I]n this case, the only remedy sought is a request for compensatory damages representing backpay and benefits. Generally, an action for money damages was "the traditional form of relief offered in the courts of law." [B]ecause we conclude that the remedy respondents seek has none of the attributes that must be present before we will find an exception to the general rule and characterize damages as equitable, we find that the remedy sought by respondents is legal. . . .

. . . Considering both parts of the Seventh Amendment inquiry, we find that respondents are entitled to a jury trial on all issues presented in their suit . . . .

Justice Brennan, concurring in part and concurring in the judgment.

I agree with the Court that respondents seek a remedy that is legal in nature and that the Seventh Amendment entitles respondents to a jury trial on their duty of fair representation claims. I do not join that part of the opinion which reprises the particular historical analysis this Court has employed to determine whether a claim is a "Suit at common law" under the Seventh Amendment, because I believe the historical test can and should be simplified.

I would decide Seventh Amendment questions on the basis of the relief sought. If the relief is legal in nature, I would hold that the parties have a constitutional right to trial by jury—unless Congress has permissibly delegated the particular dispute to a non-Article III decisionmaker and jury trials would frustrate Congress' purposes in enacting a particular statutory scheme....

Indeed, ... it is unlikely that the simplified Seventh Amendment analysis I propose will result in different decision than the analysis in current use. In the unusual circumstance that the nature of the remedy could be characterized equally as legal or equitable, [t]he comparison of a contemporary statutory action [t]o some ill-fitting ancient writ is too shaky a basis for the resolution of an issue as significant as the availability of a trial by jury. If, in the rare case, a tie-breaker is needed, let us break the tie in favor of a jury trial.

[The concurring opinion of Justice Stevens, and the dissenting opinion of Justice Kennedy, joined by Justices O'Connor and Scalia, are omitted.]

Notes and Questions

(1) *Tension Among Tests Emphasizing the Right, or the Remedy, or Functional (Practical) Concerns.* The views of the Justices illustrate the tension that exists between the traditional historical approach and modern, more functional approaches. Should the focus be on remedies rather than analogies to 18th century forms of action? (Do we need a simpler test—is Justice Brennan correct?)

(2) *Is the Court "Fudging" the Issue by Preferring Juries Even When the Constitution Doesn't?* Given *Granfinanciera, Lytle, Tull,* and *Terry,* hasn't the Court returned to an approach that prefers juries as factfinders "except under the most imperative circumstances," one that selectively uses the historical test only when it clearly supports the right to trial by jury?

(3) *No Right to Jury Trial in Administrative Proceedings—A "Public Rights" Exception: Atlas Roofing Co. v. Occupational Safety & Health Review Commission,* 430 U.S. 442 (1977). Petitioners claimed the right to trial by jury in Occupational Safety & Health Act ("OSHA") proceedings, but the Commission's administrative law judges rejected this argument and imposed fines on petitioners in accordance with the administrative scheme of the Act. The Supreme Court upheld the denial of jury trial:

> At least in cases in which "public rights" are being litigated—*e.g.,* cases in which the government sues in its sovereign capacity to enforce public rights ... —the Seventh Amendment does not prohibit Congress from assigning the fact finding function ... to an administrative forum with which the jury would be incompatible.

(4) *The Court Zigzags Between the Functional Test and the Historical Approach.* In *Markman v. Westview Instruments, Inc.*, 517 U.S. 370 (1996), the Supreme Court appeared to opt for the functional test. In this patent infringement case, the Court considered whether the issue of interpretation of a patent claim is properly within the province of the judge or jury. Justice Souter first performed a detailed historical analysis and, finding no clear answers and no governing precedent, moved directly to the functional test. The Court examined who was better suited to construe the patent, the judge or jury. Due to the judge's experience and background, the Court reasoned that the judge could more aptly give the patent terms the proper interpretation: "Where history and precedent provide no clear answers, functional considerations also play their part in the choice between judge and jury to define terms of art."

Then, however, in *Feltner v. Columbia Pictures Television, Inc.*, 523 U.S. 340 (1998), the Court considered the Copyright Act, which provides for "statutory damages" of "not less than $500 nor more than $20,000, as the Court considers just." This flexible range might seem to call for a functional approach, and one might expect, after *Tull*, that the judge would set the amount of damages, just as the judge sets the flexible penalty in a pollution case. But the Supreme Court followed a strict historical approach: Because the Act provided for damages, and because damages traditionally are a legal remedy, the jury must determine the amount.

And in *City of Monterey v. Del Monte Dunes at Monterey, Ltd.*, 526 U.S. 687 (1999), the Court again used a historical approach. The suit was for damages for a taking of property, brought under the civil rights statute, § 1983. The City argued that the better analogy was eminent domain, which does not carry the right to jury trial. The Court concluded that the better analogy was a suit for monetary relief or damages, and this historical link required a jury trial.

Perhaps one can sum these cases by saying that an historical approach dominates, but when the historical analysis is unclear, a functional test can tip the scales.

[B] Changing the Size or Function of the Jury

Read Fed. R. Civ. P. 48 (number of jurors).

COLGROVE v. BATTIN, 413 U.S. 149 (1973). Many district courts, by local rule, have provided for six-member juries in civil cases. In this case, petitioner demanded, instead, to have a twelve-member jury, which the common law courts would have provided. The Supreme Court upheld the use of the six-member jury. The Court said, "We . . . conclude . . . that by referring to the 'common law,' the framers of the Seventh Amendment were concerned with preserving the right of trial by jury . . . , rather than the various incidents of trial by jury. . . ." The Court also relied upon studies of the operations of juries to conclude that different size made "no discernible difference" in the results reached.

Notes and Questions

(1) *Changing the "Incidents": The Size and Function of the Jury.* How much of a change in the size or function of the jury can be made without violating the Seventh Amendment? Specifically, would a statute or rule violate the Constitution if it resulted in: (a) Making the jury responsible for deciding what the law is, as well as the facts? [Note: The common law provided a judge as decider of the law. *Patton v. United States*, below.] (b) Accepting non-unanimous verdicts, such as by the vote of a majority of jurors? [Note: The common law required unanimity. *Patton*, below.] (c) Changing the size of the jury to three members? [Note: *See Ballew v. Georgia*, below.] *See also* Bieger & Varrin, *Six-Member Juries in the Federal Courts*, 58 JUDICATURE 425 (1975); *cf. Tull v. United States*, above (determination of penalty amount is not a "fundamental" incident of jury trial).

(2) *Criminal Jury Incidents: Patton v. United States*, 281 U.S. 276 (1930). In this criminal case, the Supreme Court held that the Sixth Amendment right to trial by jury included the "essential elements" recognized in England and the United States when the Constitution was adopted and that it specifically included (1) a twelve-person jury, (2) superintendence by a judge having power to instruct on the law and advise on the facts, and (3) a unanimous verdict. Later, however, in *Williams v. Florida*, 399 U.S. 78 (1970), the Court held that a six-person jury was constitutionally acceptable in state or federal criminal cases. In *Ballew v. Georgia*, 435 U.S. 223 (1978), the Court held that the use of five-person juries in state criminal cases was unconstitutional.

(3) *The Seventh Amendment Has Not Been Applied to State (as Opposed to Federal) Trials.* The Supreme Court has never applied the Seventh Amendment directly to the states. The states, are, of course, bound by the Fourteenth Amendment's Due Process Clause. What difference would this (presumably) less stringent standard mean in the freedom of the states to change the nature of jury trial in civil cases?

[C] Demand and Waiver of the Right

> Read Fed. R. Civ. P. 38, 39, 81(c) (trial by jury or by the court).

Note on Waiver in the Absence of Timely Demand

A Person Who has the Right to Jury Trial Can Lose It, without a Timely Demand. Rule 38 requires a demand within 14 days of the last pleading to preserve the right to jury trial. Failure to make this demand is generally a waiver of the right.

However, in a removed case (such as *Lewis v. Time Inc.*, the case that follows), the rules governing demand are more complicated. Rule 81(c) provides that an "express demand" in state court obviates the need for further demand after removal, and if no express demand is required in state court, the Rule dispenses with the requirement in federal court also. In any event, unless Rule 81(c) is satisfied, a litigant must make demand after the removal, within the fourteen-day period provided by Rule 38 to preserve the right. *See* Note, *Demanding a Jury Trial in the Federal Court System: Federal Rules of Civil Procedure 38 and 39*, 37 FED'N INS. & CORP. COUNS. Q. 299 (1987).

Discretionary Relief from Waiver; Advisory Juries. If the jury right does not exist or has been waived, all may not be lost. Rule 39(c) allows the court to impanel an "advisory" jury (whose findings the court has authority to accept or reject) or the parties may consent to trial by jury. Under Rule 39(b), in the absence of timely demand, the court may also grant a motion for jury trial in the exercise of its discretion. The following case limits that discretion narrowly. Is the reasoning correct?

Lewis v. Time Inc.

710 F.2d 549 (9th Cir. 1983)

DUNIWAY, CIRCUIT JUDGE:

Lawyer Jerome Lewis appeals from a judgment against him in his action against TIME Inc. for defamation. We affirm.

I. *Facts.*

The cover story of TIME magazine's April 10, 1978 issue was a 10-page article entitled "Those #*X§!!! Lawyers." This case is about one subsection of that article, titled "Ethics Enforcement." In relevant part, it stated:

> If the legal profession has been reluctant to discipline its shadier practitioners, it has been swift to crack down on anyone threatening to cut fees or reduce business....
>
> Under these circumstances, it is hardly surprising that some Americans have grown cynical about lawyers—and the law.... Thanks to painfully slow bar discipline, a northern California lawyer named Jerome Lewis is still practicing law despite a $100,000 malpractice judgment against him in 1970 and a $60,000 judgment including punitive damages in 1974 for defrauding clients of money....

Lewis, the only lawyer criticized by name in this section of the article, sued in California state court on March 2, 1979. He alleged libel, slander, invasion of privacy, and intentional infliction of emotional distress....

A month after TIME was served on April 30, it removed the case to the United States District Court for the Eastern District of California....

... The court also granted a partial summary judgment in favor of TIME. First, it found that Lewis's libel, slander, invasion of privacy, and intentional infliction of emotional distress claims were all bound up into one claim for relief for defamation. Lewis does not contest the finding.

Second, the district court took judicial notice of two state court judgments entered against Lewis. In one of the cases, a jury had awarded damages of $100,000 to a client who had sued Lewis for malpractice.... In the other case, another client had won $60,000, including punitive damages, on a counterclaim against Lewis for fraud. The district court held that TIME's statements about the money judgments against Lewis were protected because they were truthful statements of matters of public record. With respect therefore to any of the article's clearly factual statements about Lewis, the court found that the only remaining question of fact was whether the assertion that Lewis defrauded "*clients*," when the fraud judgment against him was in favor of only a single *client*, was a material variance from the truth, and therefore a basis for liability for defamation as a derogatory falsehood....

After the grant of partial summary judgment, the only remaining issue to be tried was the significance of the plural "clients." The district court granted Lewis's motion for relief from his untimely demand for a jury trial, but then on its own motion reconsidered and denied the motion. After trial to the court, the district judge found that the addition of the "s" in "clients" was not a material variance from the truth. Judgment for TIME was entered on December 15, 1981....

IV. *Demand for Jury Trial.*

Finally, Lewis argues that the district judge incorrectly denied his motion for a jury trial on the issue of whether the word "clients" was a material variance from the truth.

Under F.R. Civ. P. 81(c), the federal "rules apply to civil actions removed to the United States district courts from the state courts and govern procedure after removal." The rule further states in relevant part:

> A party who, prior to removal, has made an express demand for trial by jury in accordance with state law, need not make a demand after removal. If state law applicable in the court from which the case is removed does not require the parties to make express demands in order to claim trial by jury, they need not make demands after removal unless the court directs that they do so.... [The 2007 "restyling" amendments to the Federal Rules of Civil Procedure slightly changed this language.—Eds.]

Lewis did not request a jury trial before his case was removed from California state court. Under California law, a litigant waives trial by jury by, *inter alia*, failing to "announce that one is required" when the trial is set. Cal. Civ. Proc. Code §§631, 631.01. (1982 Supp.). We understand that to mean that an "express demand" is required. Therefore, Fed. R. Civ. P. 38(d), made applicable by Rule 81(c), required Lewis to file a demand "not later than 10 days after the service of the last pleading directed to such issue [to be tried]." [The time limit has been changed to 14 days.—Eds.] Failure to file within the time provided constituted a waiver of the right to trial by jury. Rule 38(d).

Lewis did not request a jury trial until March 17, 1980, nine months after TIME filed its answer, the last pleading on the issue to be tried. Lewis then filed a motion for relief from failure to make a timely demand for jury trial.

The district court, in its discretion, may order a jury trial on a motion by a party who has not filed a timely demand for one. Fed. R. Civ. P. 39(b). That discretion is narrow, however, and does not permit a court to grant relief when the failure to make a timely demand results from an oversight or inadvertence. *Chandler Supply Co. v. GAF Corp.*, 9 Cir., 1980, 650 F.2d 983, 987; *Mardesich v. Marciel*, 9 Cir., 1976, 538 F.2d 848, 849 . . . .

Therefore, because Rule 39(b) does not permit relief where the waiver was caused by oversight or inadvertence, *see Chandler Supply* and *Mardesich, supra*, the district court correctly denied Lewis's motion for a jury trial . . . .

Affirmed.

Notes and Questions

(1) *Sufficiency of the Demand: Pinemont Bank v. Belk*, 722 F.2d 232 (5th Cir. 1984). Rule 38 does not prescribe any formal language for the demand. The most frequent practice is to endorse the demand at the bottom of the pleading: "Plaintiff/Defendant demands trial by jury of all issues triable of right by jury." In *Pinemont Bank v. Belk*, local rules prescribed a cover sheet with a preprinted notation: "Jury Demand: Check 'Yes' only if demanded in complaint. Yes _______ No _______." The plaintiff checked the box marked "Yes," although in fact he had made no demand in the complaint. At the time of trial, the defendant claimed that he had relied in good faith upon the indication of jury demand on the cover sheet. The Fifth Circuit reversed the District Court's denial of jury trial. Although criticizing reliance upon the cover sheet as dangerous and "not the preferred method of compliance," it held that the right was preserved. Note that the defendant effectively may rely upon the plaintiff's demand because Rule 38(d) prohibits withdrawal without consent of the parties.

(2) *Liberal Allowance of Discretion.* Frequently, appellate courts say trial courts have "broad" discretion to allow a jury trial after waiver. The narrow scope of discretion allowed by the Ninth Circuit in *Lewis* differs sharply from the approach of some other courts. In fact, many of the decisions indicate narrow discretion to deny jury trial, rather than narrow discretion to grant it. *E.g., United States v. Unum, Inc.*, 658 F.2d 300 (5th Cir. 1981). The Rule itself does not prevent a discretionary jury trial in the event of inadvertent or mistaken waiver; is the Ninth Circuit's implication of an exclusion in cases of inadvertence justified?

(3) *Discretionary Denial of Jury Trial.* Of course, jury trials are more time-consuming than trials to the court. Judge Posner has estimated that the average jury trial lasts 4.48 days compared to 2.21 days for the average non-jury trial. R. Posner, *The Federal Courts* 130 n.1 (1985). The court is likely to consider this fact. *See In re N-500L Cases*, 517 F. Supp. 821 (D.P.R. 1981) (district court considered issues to be tried, expenses to be incurred, time elapsed, possibility of prejudice resulting

from trial without jury as opposed to trial by jury, as well as congestion of docket, and concluded that these factors did not weigh in favor of relieving movant of its waiver).

(4) *Should the Trial Judge Encourage Waiver After Demand of Jury Trial? Black, Sivalls & Bryson, Inc. v. Keystone Steel Fabrication, Inc.*, 584 F.2d 946 (10th Cir. 1978). In this patent case, the plaintiff's counsel stated that an infringement question could properly be decided by the court since it was primarily technical, and the defendant's counsel responded to an inquiry by the court that he was "certainly more than happy" to have the court decide the issue in spite of an earlier jury demand. The Court of Appeals held that this oral stipulation, entered on the record, was sufficient to waive a jury in spite of an earlier demand. Should trial judges use pretrial conferences to attempt to persuade counsel to waive juries in complex cases?

[D] The Jury Trial Right in State Courts: Notes and Questions

(1) *California—The "Gist" of the Action: C & K Engineering Contractors v. Amber Steel Co.*, 23 Cal. 3d 1, 151 Cal. Rptr. 323, 587 P.2d 1136 (1978). Cal. Const. Art. I sec. 16 preserves the right to jury trial as it existed at common law in 1850, when the state constitution was adopted. "[A]nd what that right is," said the California Supreme Court in *C & K Engineering*, "is a purely historical question, a fact which is to be ascertained like any other social, political or legal fact." In *C & K Engineering*, the plaintiff's damage suit for breach of contract was based entirely upon the equitable doctrine of promissory estoppel. Since promissory estoppel is an equitable doctrine, said the court, there was no right to jury trial. The court refused to look to whether legal questions might be involved in the case or to protect the jury trial right for those issues (as federal courts would do under the *Beacon Theatres* approach). Instead, Justice Richardson's opinion held that the right depended upon the "gist" of the action. Because, in this case, the "gist" was equitable, trial would be held before the court alone.

(2) *Texas—Extension of the Right to Equity Cases: State v. Texas Pet Foods, Inc.*, 591 S.W.2d 800, 803 (Tex. 1979). The right to trial by jury in Texas is more extensive than in most jurisdictions, because Tex. Const. Art. 5, § 10 extends it to "all causes in the District Courts." The term "cause" has been given a broad construction and includes suits in equity as well as actions at law. Although a litigant has the right to trial by jury in an equitable action, only ultimate issues of fact are submitted for jury determination. The jury does not determine the propriety of equitable relief, and the determination whether to grant an injunction, as well as its scope, is for the trial court, exercising chancery powers. In *Texas Pet Foods*, the jury found numerous violations of pollution control statutes. Then, predicated on the past violations found by the jury, the trial court determined that future violations were likely to occur and granted injunctive relief. Texas also is liberal in allowing late demand for a jury, which can be made at any reasonable time, not less than 30 days before trial. *See* Tex. R. Civ. P. 216.

(3) *Florida*— The Florida Constitution provides, "The right of trial by jury shall be secure to all and remain inviolate." The right is "is not to be narrowly construed." *O'Neal v. Florida A & M Univ. ex rel. Bd. of Trustees for Florida A & M Univ.*, 989 So. 2d 6, 9 (Fla. 1st DCA 2008). But Florida, like the federal jurisdiction, follows a primarily historical approach, depending on the right that existed in 1845 when Florida became a state. Therefore, the right to trial by jury in Florida does not extend to equitable or admiralty claims. *See In re Forfeiture of [a] 1978 Chevrolet Van*, 493 So. 2d 433 Fla. (1986).

The mechanism for demanding a jury trial is also similar to the federal method. The demand must be made "not later than ten days after" the last relevant pleading. Fla. R. Civ. P. 1.430(b). The judge "may allow an amendment in the proceedings to demand a trial by jury or order a trial by jury on its own motion." Fla. R. Civ. P. 1.430(d). There is authority to the effect that a late demand should be granted, provided that it "would impose neither an injustice upon the adversary nor an unreasonable inconvenience upon the court." *Herrera v. Wee Care of Flagler County, Inc.*, 615 So. 2d 233, 224 (Fla. 5th DCA 1993).

III. Jury Selection

[A] The "Fair Cross-Section" Requirement

Thiel v. Southern Pacific Co.

328 U.S. 217 (1946)

[Plaintiff Thiel's complaint alleged that the defendant railroad was liable to him for damages for its negligence, in that its agents knew that he was "out of his normal mind" and should not have been accepted as a passenger or should have been guarded. He jumped out of the window of a moving train and was injured.]

[After demanding a jury trial, Thiel moved to strike the entire panel, alleging that it consisted of "mostly business executives or those having the employer's viewpoint" and that "poorer classes" were discriminated against. The judge denied this challenge to the jury array, and the trial resulted in a verdict for the railroad.]

[The evidence in Thiel's challenge to the array included testimony of the clerk and the jury commissioner that they "deliberately and intentionally excluded from the jury list all persons who worked for a daily wage." They worked from the city directory. In the words of the clerk, "If I see in the directory the name of John Jones and it says he is a longshoreman, I do not put his name in, because I have found by experience that that man will not serve as a juror, and I will not get people who will qualify. The minute that a juror is called into court on a venire and says that he is working for $10 a day and cannot afford to work for four, the judge has never made one of those men serve. . . ." The evidence indicated, however, that laborers who were paid weekly or monthly wages were placed on the jury list, as well as the wives of daily wage earners, and the judge in Thiel's trial specifically found that five of the twelve jurors "belong more closely and intimately with the working man and employee class than they do with any other class."]

[In an opinion by Justice Murphy, the Supreme Court reversed and remanded for the following reasons:]

The American tradition of trial by jury, considered in connection with either criminal or civil proceedings, necessarily contemplates an impartial jury drawn from a cross-section of the community. . . . This does not mean, of course, that every jury must contain representatives of all the economic, social, religious, racial, political and geographical groups of the community; frequently such complete representation would be impossible. But it does mean that prospective jurors shall be selected by court officials without systematic and intentional exclusion of any of these groups. . . .

This exclusion of all those who earn a daily wage cannot be justified by federal or state law. Certainly nothing in the federal statutes warrants such an exclusion. . . .

It is clear that a federal judge would be justified in excusing a daily wage earner for whom jury service would entail an undue financial hardship. But that fact cannot support the complete exclusion of all daily wage earners regardless of whether there is actual hardship involved. Here there was no effort, no intention, to determine in advance which individual members of the daily wage earning class would suffer an undue hardship by serving on a jury at the rate of $4 a day. All were systematically and automatically excluded. . . .

It is likewise immaterial that the jury which actually decided the factual issue in the case was found to contain at least five members of the laboring class. The evil lies in the admitted wholesale exclusion of a large class of wage earners in disregard of the high standards of jury selection. To reassert those standards, to guard against the subtle undermining of the jury system, requires a new trial by a jury drawn from a panel properly and fairly chosen. Reversed.

MR. JUSTICE FRANKFURTER, with whom MR. JUSTICE REED concurs, dissenting. . . .

Trial by jury presupposes a jury drawn from a pool broadly representative of the community as well as impartial in a specific case. Since the color of a man's skin is unrelated to his fitness as a juror, [African Americans] cannot be excluded from jury service because they are [African Americans]. *E.g., Carter v. Texas*, 177 U.S. 442. A group may be excluded for reasons that are relevant not to their fitness but to competing considerations of public interest, as is true of the exclusion of doctors, ministers, lawyers, and the like. *Rawlins v. Georgia*, 201 U.S. 638. . . .

Obviously these accepted general considerations must have much leeway in application. In the abstract the Court acknowledges this. . . . But it is not without illumination that under California law all those belonging to this long string of occupations are exempted from jury service: judicial, civil, naval, and military officers of the United States or California; local government officials; attorneys, their clerks, secretaries, and stenographers; ministers; teachers; physicians, dentists, chiropodists, optometrists, and druggists; officers, keepers, and attendants at hospitals or other charitable institutions; officers in attendance at prisons and jails; employees on boats and ships in navigable waters; express agents, mail carriers, employees of telephone and telegraph companies; keepers of ferries or tollgates; national guardsmen and firemen; superintendents, engineers, firemen, brakemen, motormen, or conductors of railroads; practitioners treating the sick by prayer. California Code of Civil Procedure, § 200 . . . .

It is difficult to believe that this judgment would have been reversed if the trial judge had excused, one by one, all those wage earners whom the jury commissioner, acting on the practice of trial judges of San Francisco, excluded. . . .

FEIN v. PERMANENTE MEDICAL GROUP, 38 Cal. 3d 137, 211 Cal. Rptr. 368, 695 P.2d 665 (1985). The text of this case appears in § 1.08 of Chapter 1, above, and should be read (or re-read) at this point. In this medical malpractice case, in which the evidence "sharply conflict[ed]," the trial judge ordered a blanket exclusion of all prospective jurors who were members of the Kaiser medical plan. The defendant, Permanente, was an affiliate of the Kaiser Health Foundation, and the judge explained: "I am going to excuse you at this time because we've found that we can prolong the jury selection by just such a very long time by going through each and every juror under these circumstances." The court's ruling excused twenty-four of sixty jurors (or forty percent of the entire panel), and Kaiser objected to the exclusion. While conceding that "past decisions do not provide a clearcut answer," the California Supreme Court affirmed a judgment for the plaintiff. The court held, first, that the trial judge had broad discretion which he had not abused by his ruling, and second, that Kaiser members "were not a cognizable class" with the kind of "shared experiences, ideology or background" that prior cases had protected against "systematic exclusion."

Notes and Questions

(1) *Is the Requirement Really a "Fair Cross-Section" (Or Is There Only a Prohibition Upon "Systematic Exclusion" of "Cognizable Groups")?* In the *Thiel* case, the Supreme Court began its analysis by saying that trial by jury "necessarily contemplates an impartial jury drawn from a cross-section of the community." But is there really a requirement that the panel from which the jury is drawn be a "cross-section"? As the dissent points out, all government officials, attorneys, ministers, teachers, physicians, and members of certain other occupations were exempted from *Thiel*'s jury. And if a "cross-section" is required, how can *Thiel* be distinguished from *Fein v. Permanente*? The answer may be that the requirement is not one of a "cross-section" at all, but instead is a prohibition upon the "systematic exclusion" of "cognizable groups." It is on that basis that the California court distinguished *Thiel;* it reasoned that the Kaiser plan members were not a "cognizable group." Is the distinction persuasive? *See* Druff, *The Cross-Section Requirement and Jury Impartiality*, 73 Calif. L. Rev. 1555 (1985).

(2) *The Jury Selection and Service Act of 1968.* The federal Jury Selection and Service Act, 28 U.S.C. § 1861 et seq., was passed since the *Thiel* decision. It requires selection at random from a "fair cross-section" and a "fair opportunity" to serve, as well and prohibits invidious discrimination. Each district court is to devise a "plan for random jury selection" with the following features: Management by a jury commission or by the court clerk; use of voter registration lists, lists of actual voters, or these lists plus supplementation from other sources; random selection of names for placement into a jury wheel; specification of exemptions by individual request and exemptions barring service; and other features. There are minimum qualifications (including citizenship, ability to read and write English, freedom from certain criminal charges or convictions, etc.). Furthermore, the Act provides a cutoff date for asserting a challenge to the array (*i.e.*, to the manner of summons). The challenge must be made before examination of the jury begins, or within seven days of the time when defects in the array should have been discovered, whichever is earlier.

(3) *Do "No-Shows" Who Distort Jury Composition Negate a "Fair Cross-Section"? United States v. Carter,* 483 Fed. Appx. 70 (6th Cir. 2012). The defendant argued that the court should pursue summoned black venirepersons who did not appear. Otherwise, he argued, the panel from which the jury would be selected would not be a fair cross-section. The trial court denied this challenge, and the court of appeals disposed of it quickly, saying "The district court is under no obligation to compel no-shows." But what if the jury panel is distorted by "widespread juror apathy" that court officials make no effort to combat? In *United States v. Gometz*, 730 F.2d 475 (7th Cir. 1984) (*en banc*), the court rejected such a challenge.

(4) *Is the Use of Voter Registration Lists Unconstitutionally Underinclusive? People v. Harris*, 36 Cal. 3d 36, 201 Cal. Rptr. 782, 679 P.2d 433 (1984). In this criminal case, the California Supreme Court held unconstitutional a jury pool randomly selected from a voter registration list. The defendant offered total population figures showing a statistically significant underrepresentation of Blacks and Hispanics, compared to their proportions in the community. The court held that a "party is constitutionally entitled to a petit jury that is as near an approximation of the ideal cross section of the community as the process of random draw permits." Voter registration lists could have been supplemented by drivers' license records. Is this reasoning correct? Authority in other state and federal courts that have considered the question is to the contrary, with many decisions holding that the argument presents no constitutional issue. *E.g., United States v. Clifford*, 640 F.2d 150 (8th Cir. 1981); *United States v. Lewis*, 472 F.2d 252 (3d Cir. 1973); *Davis v. Zant*, 721 F.2d 1478 (11th Cir. 1984). Today, many jurisdictions supplement voter registrations with driver's license records.

(5) *Disqualifications and Exemptions.* In addition to statutory disqualifications, such as noncitizenship and inability to read, write, or speak English (*see* 28 U.S.C. § 1865), a prospective juror may be excluded on the ground that the juror "may be unable to render impartial jury service or that his service as a juror would be likely to disrupt the proceedings, or . . . for good cause shown." 28 U.S.C. § 1866(c). The

district court has wide discretion regarding challenges for cause and, on appeal, is reviewed on an abuse of discretion standard. *Vanskike v. ACF Indus., Inc.*, 665 F.2d 188, 207 (1981), *cert. denied*, 455 U.S. 1000. Regarding impartiality, the Supreme Court has said the following (in a criminal case although the same is no doubt true for civil cases): ". . . It is not required, however, that the jurors be totally ignorant of the facts and issues involved. . . . It is sufficient if the juror can lay aside his impression or opinion and render a verdict based on the evidence presented in court." *Irvin v. Dowd*, 366 U.S. 712, 722–23 (1961).

[B] *Voir Dire* Examination and Challenges

Note on How Jurors Are "Selected": Previewing Flowers v. Flowers

The Voir Dire Examination. The jury venire is seated in the courtroom, usually in the public seats. The venire generally consists of many more individuals than will ultimately serve on the jury, since some—perhaps most—of them will be removed by challenges. The process called "*voir dire* examination," or examination of the jurors to determine their qualifications or undesirability to either side, then begins. ("*Voir dire*" is taken from French words meaning "to see" and "to speak.") *See* Hittner, *Federal Voir Dire and Jury Selection*, 25 Trial 85 (March 1989).

"Peremptory" Challenges and Challenges "for Cause." The *voir dire* may show that some venire members do not meet the general requirements for service (*e.g.*, non-citizenship or illiteracy) or disqualification from serving in the particular case (most commonly, by an unavoidable bias against a party or against a principle of law at issue). Then, a party may remove this person by a challenge "for cause." In addition, each party is entitled to a number of "peremptory" challenges set by rule or statute; in the federal courts, the Jury Selection and Service Act allows three peremptory challenges to each side. 28 U.S.C. § 1870. These three "strikes" can be exercised without the assignment of any reason. The idea is that both sides are more likely to appreciate that the jury is impartial if each party is allowed to remove a few potential jurors who seem most likely to be unfavorable. *See Symposium, The Selection and Function of the Modern Jury*, 40 Am. U. L. Rev. 541 (1991).

Procedure for Examination and Challenges. Rule 47 allows a federal judge discretion to conduct the *voir dire* examination herself, or to allow the attorneys to do it, or to conduct it herself with supplemental examination by the attorneys. (One question you should consider in this section is, what difference does the exercise of this discretion make?) When an individual subject to challenge for cause is identified, the attorney usually raises it at the time; the judge has responsibility for ruling on the challenge. The attorneys in some jurisdictions exercise peremptory challenges at the conclusion of the *voir dire*, customarily by drawing lines through the names of the challenged jurors on a list compiled by the clerk, but the practice varies.

Tactics. The process seeks to impanel a fair and impartial jury, but the parties certainly don't. The adversary system very definitely is in effect at this stage. Each lawyer is alert even to small cues about possibly unfavorable thoughts among venire members, so as best to use peremptory challenges. If the attorneys conduct the *voir dire*, they inevitably use it to prepare jurors for the proof; sometimes they test the limits of propriety. And if it appears that a venire member is biased and subject to a party's challenge for cause—well, that may mean that the venire member is highly desirable to the opponent, who will attempt to "rehabilitate" this individual with questions designed to minimize the appearance of bias. *See* Fulero & Penrod, *The Myths and Realities of Attorney Jury Selection Folklore and Scientific Jury Selection: What Works?*, 17 OHIO N.U. L. REV. 229 (1990).

The Judge's Function in Ruling on Challenges for Cause: A Preview of the Flowers Case. The judge applies the governing law of disqualification and, simultaneously, makes a fact finding (which often is implicit) about the individual venire member. The judge may have "wiggle room" in making this fact determination. Because every juror has opinions, a mere feeling about the issues is not sufficient basis for disqualification. (For example, in a negligence case, many potential jurors may have heard about the tort reform debate, but it would make no sense to remove all of those who have any thoughts about the subject.) The ultimate question is whether the putative bias or prejudice will unfairly affect the juror's decision or whether she is capable of deciding the case from the law and evidence. Often, judges are understandably reluctant to allow marginal challenges, for fear of distorting the balance of the jury pool or depleting it. Consider the following case, and also see the case that follows (that effectively overrules) it.

[1] Challenges "For Cause" Versus "Peremptory" Challenges

Flowers v. Flowers

397 S.W.2d 121 (Tex. Civ. App.-Amarillo 1965, no writ)

CHAPMAN, JUSTICE.

[This decision has been overruled *sub silentio.* See below.] The subject matter of this suit involves a question of the disqualification of a juror in a child custody contest tried to a jury. . . .

This case was tried in a town and county of very small population where the record shows many members of the jury panel had heard what they referred to as gossip or rumors concerning the case. The parties to the suit are Billie Charlene Flowers, plaintiff below, the mother; and R.A. Flowers, Jr., the father. The victims of the unfortunate broken home are three little girls ranging in ages from two to ten at the time of the filing of divorce by their mother in January 1964. . . .

The jurors were told on voir dire examination that the evidence would show that plaintiff drank some socially and on one or two occasions had consumed alcoholic beverages to excess. They were questioned as to whether that fact standing alone would prejudice them against her as a fit and proper person to have custody of the children.

The record preserved upon examination of Mrs. Schmidt as a prospective juror shows that she first testified she was well acquainted with the Flowers family, belonged to the same Baptist church they did in the little town of Miami, and that she had no opinion formed in the case at all. Then when counsel said to her the evidence will show "that Billie does drink upon social occasions with the crowd at a dance, or something of that sort, she would have a highball or cocktail, and it will show on one occasion that she had too much, or two times had too much, what is your attitude—" she answered:

> A: I am against drinking in any manner, any kind.
>
> Q: Any way or any fashion at all?
>
> A: Any type.
>
> Q: Mrs. Schmidt, that would definitely affect your judgment in the case, wouldn't it?
>
> A: If the evidence was true . . . .
>
> Q: If the evidence shows Billie has had one drink or two—drinks at a social occasion, you would hold that against her?
>
> A: I don't approve.

The court then took over the examination and asked her a number of questions, one of which was:

> Q: Well, are you saying by that, Mrs. Schmidt, that you wouldn't grant either party to this law suit custody of the children if they drank?
>
> A: I am. [Note that the law did not permit a juror to disqualify a parent automatically if she drank.—Eds.]

The court then turned to leading questions to the juror as to her attitude about passing upon whether the mother was a fit person to have the custody of the girls, saying:

> Q: Dependent upon the testimony you hear in a trial; the mere fact that she got drunk a few times and threw a conniption fit or something, you wouldn't hold that against her and think she wasn't—
>
> A: Not especially.

The court then overruled the challenge of the juror for cause. . . .

Article 1, Section 15 of the Texas Constitution, Vernon's Ann. St., guarantees the right to trial by jury, which our courts have held to be an impartial jury. . . .

Article 2134, Vernon's Ann. Tex. Civ. St., provides as one of the disqualifications: "Any person who has a bias or prejudice in favor of or against either of the parties."

This disqualification for bias or prejudice extends not only to the parties personally, but also to the subject matter of the litigation. . . . *Compton v. Henrie*, Tex., 364 S.W.2d. 179.

In defining the terms "bias" and "prejudice" as used in Article 2134 our Supreme Court in the *Henrie* case just cited has said:

> Bias, in its usual meaning, is an inclination toward one side of an issue rather than to the other, but to disqualify, it must appear that the state of mind of the juror leads to the natural inference that he will not or did not act with impartiality. Prejudice is more easily defined for it means prejudgment, and consequently embraces bias....

Mrs. Schmidt's statements indicate to us both bias and prejudice factually and such a prejudgment of the case as to indicate she could not have acted with impartiality. If we are correct in this factual conclusion then under the authorities just cited her disqualification is not a matter of discretion with the trial court but a matter of law. We believe the record compels such holding on our part....

Even if we are in error in our pronouncements in the preceding paragraphs, it cannot be gainsaid that the record shows bias and prejudice on the part of Mrs. Schmidt toward plaintiff and toward her alcoholic consumption her attorney admitted would be shown before the examination of the jury on voir dire. From the viewpoint of this writer, such feelings on the part of Mrs. Schmidt are to her credit even if it did disqualify her as a juror. But even if under the facts of this case bias or prejudice was a fact to be determined by the trial court, those feelings having been clearly established, her answer of "Yes, sir" to a leading question to the effect that she would be able to decide the case on the evidence submitted, should be disregarded.... [Reversed.]

CORTEZ ex rel. ESTATE OF PUENTES v. HCCI-SAN ANTONIO, INC., 159 S.W.3d 87 (2005). This case appears to have overruled *Flowers v. Flowers*, although it does not mention that decision. The plaintiff sued for injuries allegedly caused by the defendants' negligence. During voir dire, plaintiff's attorney questioned veniremember Snider, who had handled automobile claims as an insurance adjuster. Snider said that his experience might give him "preconceived notions." "I would feel bias," he said, "but I mean, I can't answer anything for certain." When the trial judge asked him to explain his bias, he said that he had seen "lawsuit abuse ... so many times." He said that "in a way," the defendant was "starting out ahead." He explained: "This type [of] case I'm not familiar with whatsoever, so that's not a bias I should have. It's just there." Upon further questioning, he agreed that at times when he evaluated automobile claims, he found that they had merit, and that he was "willing to try" to listen to the case and decide it on the law and the evidence. The trial judge denied the plaintiff's challenge for cause; plaintiff used a peremptory challenge to remove Snider; plaintiff then did not have sufficient remaining peremptory challenges to remove another undesired juror; and the trial resulted in a verdict for plaintiff, but with damages significantly less than the plaintiff wished.

Plaintiff appealed on the ground that the trial court should have removed Snider for cause. Consistently with *Flowers*, plaintiff argued that after a clear statement of bias, a potential juror should not be rehabilitated by general statements of intent to be fair. The state supreme court held that the trial judge had not committed error and upheld the judgment:

> Cortez . . . argues . . . that veniremembers cannot be "rehabilitated"—that once a veniremember has expressed "bias," further questioning is not permitted and the veniremember must be excused. We disagree that there is such a rule, and to the extent [earlier] decisions conflict with our opinion here, we disapprove those cases . . .
>
> [V]oir dire examination is largely within the sound discretion of the trial judge and that broad latitude is allowed for examination. *Babcock v. N.W. Memorial Hosp.*, 767 S.W.2d 705, 709 (Tex.1989). Both of these principles are completely inconsistent with the assertion that voir dire must stop at the moment a veniremember gives any answer that might be disqualifying . . . .
>
> Nor do challenges for cause turn on the use of "magic words." Cortez argues, and we do not disagree, that veniremembers may be disqualified even if they say they can be "fair and impartial," so long as the rest of the record shows they cannot. By the same token, veniremembers are not necessarily disqualified when they confess "bias," so long as the rest of the record shows that is not the case . . . .
>
> . . . [Snider's] answers to the trial judge's questions revealed that any initial apparent bias he expressed was actually against lawsuit abuse . . . . Snider said he was willing to listen to all the evidence and to withhold judgment until the entire case had been presented. He never indicated any inability to find for Cortez, if Cortez proved his case. More significantly, he said he was "willing to try" to make his decision based on the evidence and the law. That is all we can ask of any juror.

Notes and Questions

(1) *Why Do Judges Try to Keep Opinionated Jurors?* Notice that in *Flowers v. Flowers*, the trial judge seems to be trying hard to keep the potential juror, Mrs. Schmidt, even though she seems excessively opinionated. Why didn't the judge just sustain a challenge for cause to this potential juror? The answer is that it probably would have been better to have done so, and many judges would have done exactly that. But the question remains: why would a judge want to keep a potential juror who is opinionated? There are several reasons.

> (a) *To keep a balanced panel, with a range of views, and avoid skewing the jury.* For any given controversy, there are potential jurors who hold one view, and potential jurors who hold the opposite. There are people who oppose drinking, and there are people who drink every day or support drinking—including employees of bars (who probably like for people to drink!). If the judge cuts off either end of this spectrum, the result is a distorted jury panel, favorable to one side or the other.

(b) *In an effort to consider the arguments and positions of both lawyers.* Just as one side may wish that the judge would excuse a given potential juror, the other side may want that juror retained, and if the particular juror has opinions that fall short of disqualification, that side has a sound argument for retention. . . .

(c) *To avoid a "run" on the jury panel.* If the entire panel sees one potential juror successfully answer questions so as to get excused, others may imitate that potential juror's behavior, just to avoid serving as jurors. The result may be what sometimes is called a "run" on the panel, with so few citizens left in the courtroom that a jury cannot be formed.

Again, these considerations probably do not justify the retention of the potential juror in *Flowers*, but they may explain why the judge did what he did, and in many instances these concerns can be valid.

(2) *The Result of the Cortez Case, Following Flowers.* Notice that the reasoning in *Cortez* (the case after *Flowers*) probably would change the result. It probably would have meant that the trial judge in *Flowers* would have been affirmed after retaining the potential juror there, Mrs. Schmidt. The state supreme court, in *Cortez*, simply affords the trial judge much more discretion, more room to make a fact finding about the potential juror's lack of bias, than the court had allowed in *Flowers*. The trial judge in *Cortez* could have excused that potential juror (Mr. Snider). Many lawyers would think so. Do the considerations given in the note immediately above explain the holding in *Cortez*?

McDONOUGH POWER EQUIPMENT, INC. v. GREENWOOD, 464 U.S 548 (1984). Greenwood's son was seriously injured in an accident with a riding lawnmower manufactured by McDonough. After a three-week trial, the jury returned a verdict for the defendant McDonough. One of Greenwood's grounds for a new trial concerned questioning on *voir dire* asking whether there had been "injuries . . . that resulted in any disability or prolonged pain or suffering" to members of any potential juror's immediate family. One venire member named Payton, who actually served on the jury, failed to respond to this question, although his son had sustained a broken leg as a result of an exploding tire. The District Court denied a motion for new trial and entered judgment for McDonough. The Court of Appeals reversed, holding that juror Payton's failure to respond had prejudiced Greenwood's right of peremptory challenge. The court concluded that the "unrevealed information" indicated probable bias "because it revealed a particularly narrow concept of what constitutes a serious injury." The Court assumed that the juror had answered in good faith, but said, "Good faith . . . is irrelevant to our inquiry."

In an opinion by Justice Rehnquist, the Supreme Court reversed. It began with the principle of harmless error, pointing out that "[a] litigant is entitled to a fair trial but not a perfect one." The Court then reasoned as follows:

> Voir dire examination serves to protect [the right to an impartial jury] by exposing possible biases, both known and unknown, on the part of potential jurors. Demonstrated bias in the response to questions on voir dire may result in a juror being excused for cause; hints of bias not sufficient to warrant challenge for cause may assist parties in exercising their peremptory challenges....
>
> ... Juror Payton apparently believed that his son's broken leg sustained as a result of an exploding tire was not [a disabling or prolonged] injury. In response to a similar question from petitioner's counsel, however, another juror related such a minor incident as the fact that his six year old son once caught his finger in a bike chain....
>
> To invalidate the result of a three-week trial because of a juror's mistaken, though honest response to a question, is to insist on something closer to perfection than our judicial system can be expected to give.... We hold that to obtain a new trial in such a situation, a party must first demonstrate that a juror failed to answer honestly a material question on voir dire, and then further show that a correct response would have provided a valid basis for a challenge for cause. The motives for concealing information may vary, but only those reasons that affect a juror's impartiality can truly be said to affect the fairness of a trial....

Justice Blackmun (joined by Justices Stevens and O'Connor) concurred on the ground that the Court's opinion did not "foreclose the normal avenue of relief available to a party who is asserting that he did not have the benefit of an impartial jury." Justice Brennan (joined by Justice Marshall) concurred only in the judgment: "I cannot join ... in the legal standard asserted by the Court's opinion. In my view, the proper focus when ruling on a motion for new trial in this situation should be on the bias of the juror and the resulting prejudice to the litigant."

Notes and Questions

(1) *The Attorney's Burden in Setting Up Challenges for Cause.* In *Flowers v. Flowers*, what would have been the outcome: (a) If Mrs. Flowers' attorney, through inadvertence or deliberate choice, had refrained from asking about juror attitudes toward drinking during the voir dire examination? (b) If he had asked the whole panel whether any member automatically would refuse custody to a parent who drank, and Mrs. Schmidt remained silent? (c) If he had succeeded in identifying Mrs. Schmidt but failed to pin her down, beyond the expression of a general opposition to drinking? *See also* Note, *Juror Bias Undiscovered During Voir Dire: Reviewing Claims of a Denial of the Constitutional Right to an Impartial Jury*, 39 Drake L. Rev. 201 (1990).

(2) *The Difficulty of the "Bias" Inquiry.* Examining venire members like Mrs. Schmidt is a difficult art form. First, the attorney must succeed in causing these individuals to identify themselves. The general question, "Is anybody biased?" is unlikely to produce appropriate responses, since few of us place ourselves in that

category and even if we did, we might be reluctant to stand up in a courtroom and say so. Furthermore, a general attribution of bias may be insufficient; the question is whether the bias is severe enough to prevent the juror from deciding the case on the law and facts. Finally, some members of the venire ultimately will decide the lawyer's case, as jurors, and so heavy-handed efforts to pin a potential juror down may be counterproductive. In fact, the task calls for extreme diplomacy.

(3) *Peremptory Challenges: Are They Adequately Protected by the McDonough Holding?* Greenwood's principal argument, in *McDonough v. Greenwood*, was that he was denied a fair opportunity to make a peremptory challenge against juror Payton. But the Court's holding is that "to obtain a new trial . . . , [Greenwood] must . . . show that a correct response would have provided a valid basis for a challenge for cause." Notice that, if a correct answer would clearly indicate a peremptory challenge that any reasonable lawyer would have exercised, the standard in *McDonough* provides no protection of the right to make it. To take a concrete example, imagine that a venire member flatly and falsely denies being an insurance adjuster. As a result, the plaintiff's attorney withholds a peremptory challenge in circumstances in which any plaintiff's attorney in possession of accurate information would have exercised it. But since mere employment as an insurance adjuster is not alone sufficient to make "a valid basis for a challenge for cause," the literal language of *McDonough* would deny a new trial. Is this result appropriate? Why is the Court so restrictive of new trials based on jury challenges? *See* Crump, *Peremptory Challenges After McDonough Power Equipment, Inc. v. Greenwood: A Problem of Fairness, Finality, and Falsehood*, 69 Ore. L. Rev. 741 (1990).

[2] Prohibited Grounds for Peremptory Challenges

Note on Batson *Issues: Not Race or Gender*

Can the Reasons for Exercising Peremptory Challenges Be Illegal? Racially Motivated Strikes and Batson v. Kentucky, 476 U.S. 79 (1986). In *Batson*, a criminal case, the Court held that it would be unconstitutional for a prosecutor to exercise racially motivated peremptory challenges. A *prima facie* showing by the defendant (such as disproportionate removal of African-Americans from the panel) would place upon the prosecutor the burden of justifying the challenges by reference to non-racial factors. The Supreme Court extended this holding to civil cases in *Edmonson v. Leesville Concrete Co.*, 500 U.S. 614 (1991). And the Court has applied the same rule to prohibit challenges based on gender.

Race and Gender Are Prohibited Grounds. Thus, it is illegal to exercise a peremptory challenge against persons because they are black or white or because they are men or women. There is a temptation to do so, because sometimes gross statistical studies show differences among these kinds of groups. In a later section of this chapter, we excerpt a jury study that showed significant differences of this kind. Attorneys are required to ignore those group differences.

You should be aware that "label" characteristics—such as age, wealth, occupation, and social class—are frequent selection factors, and many attorneys probably would agree that at least some of these factors are legitimate. In an employment discrimination suit in which the plaintiff alleges a racially motivated discharge, won't both parties be considering these "label" characteristics in exercising peremptories—but will they be considering race as a factor, too? It is illegal to do so. But enforcing this rule is difficult. Consider the following decision.

Hines v. City of Columbus

676 Fed. Appx. 546 (6th Cir. 2017) (unpublished decision)

Suhrheinrich, Circuit Judge.

Plaintiff Joseph Hines (Plaintiff) seeks a new trial following a jury verdict in this civil rights action alleging excessive use of force by several City of Columbus, Ohio police officers. . . .

[A jury awarded Hines $30,000 in compensatory damages for injuries received in an arrest that the jurors decided was completed with excessive force. The court awarded attorney's fees of over $75,000. Plaintiff seeks a greater amount of damages.]

On appeal, Plaintiff contends that he was denied a fair trial and is entitled to a new one because the district court erred in denying his *Batson* challenge during jury selection. . . . [The *Batson* decision establishes that it is illegal to remove jurors with peremptory challenges on the basis of race.—Eds.]

Plaintiff, who is African American, complains that the district court erred in denying his *Batson* challenge because Defendants did not offer a race-neutral explanation for excluding one of the African-American jurors. "The 'Constitution forbids striking even a single prospective juror for a discriminatory purpose.'" *Foster v. Chatman,* 136 S.Ct. 1737, 1747 (2016). *Batson* set up a three-step process for determining whether a juror has been struck for a discriminatory purpose. First, the party asserting the *Batson* violation must make a prima facie showing that a peremptory challenge is based on race. [The prima facie showing is made statistically, by an attorney's reciting into the record the numbers of jurors struck and their races, if the strikes of a particular race are disproportionate.—Eds.] If that showing is made, the party who exercised the strike must offer a race-neutral explanation. That explanation need not rise to the level of a challenge for cause, but instead need only be a plausible, race-neutral reason for peremptorily striking the juror. *Purkett v. Elem,* 514 U.S. 765, 767–68 (1995). Third, the trial court must determine whether the opposing party has shown purposeful discrimination [i.e., that the neutral explanation is not pretextual]. *Foster,* 136 S.Ct. at 1747.

Defendants exercised their first peremptory challenge to remove Juror #78, an African American. Plaintiff did not contemporaneously object to Juror #78's removal. [At that point, there was no disproportion in strikes.—Eds.] However, when Defendants used their third peremptory challenge to strike Juror #37, also an African American, Plaintiff argued that Defendants were "systematically excusing members of ethnicity. The first excused was somebody of African-American descent. . . . And the individual that he has just proposed to be excused, Number 37, is African-American." Plaintiff noted again that "Two of the three peremptories were African-American challenges." Later he reiterated that "there were only two African-Americans in the entire venire, and the defense has struck them both. And with a *Batson* objection, I'm arguing that, one; they can't do this because they're systematically excluding African-Americans." In response, the district court said, "Well, they have excused one without any objection. And, okay, go ahead now. Do you wish to respond, Mr. Mangan [counsel for Defendants]?" At that point, defense counsel offered a race-neutral explanation for striking Juror #37, which the district court accepted, and then overruled the objection. Plaintiff does not challenge this ruling on appeal. However, defense counsel did not offer any explanation for peremptorily striking Juror #78, the district court did not ask defense counsel to give one, and Plaintiff did not insist that defense counsel provide one. The question on appeal is whether Plaintiff can assert a *Batson* challenge regarding Juror #78 where Plaintiff did not make a *Batson* challenge when Juror #78 was peremptorily dismissed, but before any perceptible "pattern" of race-based challenges had emerged.

Plaintiff's *Batson* challenge regarding Juror #78 was timely under our precedent. In *United States v. Tomlinson,* we held that "a strictly contemporaneous objection is not required and that a party's *Batson* objection is timely if it is made before the jury is sworn and the trial commences." *United States v. Tomlinson,* 764 F.3d 535, 537 (6th Cir. 2014). Plaintiff timely made the *Batson* challenge regarding Juror #78 as soon as he perceived what he thought to be "a pattern of strikes against African American jurors."

Nonetheless, because Plaintiff failed to demand that defense counsel give a race-neutral explanation for peremptorily striking Juror #78 once Plaintiff perceived a pattern, he forfeited his right to seek one for the first time on appeal. Plaintiff's counsel was a highly experienced trial attorney who did not hesitate when it came to making a record for appeal on other matters. Yet he inexplicably made no effort to have the district court follow the second and third *Batson* steps to ensure a proper record for appeal as to Juror #78. While not exactly "invited error," Plaintiff should not be allowed to use the appellate process "to profit from the legal consequences of having the ruling set aside" when he could have corrected the error contemporaneously. Thus, we hold that although Plaintiff properly raised the *Batson* issue with respect to Juror #78 once the purported pattern of race-based peremptory challenges occurred (even though the challenge was not made at the time Juror #78 was struck), Plaintiff failed to make a record in the district court sufficient to preserve the issue for appeal. [AFFIRMED.]

Notes and Questions

(1) *The "Fog of Trial": Was the Plaintiff's Attorney's Action "Inexplicable"?* Carl von Clausewitz, in his landmark volume *On War,* laid the foundation for modern warfare. One of his observations is that there is a "fog of war" ("die Nebels des Krieges") that causes confusion so deep that it is impossible to understand unless

one has experienced war. And experienced trial lawyers know that there is a "fog of trial" that has similar effects. During trial, complexities pile on each other at a speed that is impossible completely to keep up with. In other words, it is not "inexplicable" that the plaintiff's attorney did not object again after making the several points he did with the judge about his *Batson* challenge. Should it be easier to make this kind of objection?

(2) *Extending the Batson-Edmonson Reasoning—Will Extension Wipe Out the Peremptory Challenge?: Gender, Age, Social Status, Etc.* Do *Batson* and *Edmonson* implicitly outlaw peremptories exercised on the basis of gender? Age? Religion? Social status? Wealth? Any and every unexplainable basis? (See below.) If so, doesn't it eliminate peremptories, since the nature of peremptories is that they are exercised on the basis of generalizations or "hunches," and without cause? For an argument that the Supreme Court's reasoning really requires abolition of peremptories, see Garcia, *Strike Three and It's Out: There Goes the Peremptory*, HOUS. LAWYER, Nov.-Dec. 1991, at 22.

(3) *The Batson/Edmonson Rule Extends to Prohibit Gender-Based Strikes: J.E.B. v. Alabama ex rel. T.B.*, 511 U.S. 127 (1994). In this paternity/child support case, the state court empaneled an all-female jury after rejecting the father's *Batson* claim that the State's peremptory challenges to remove male jurors violated the Equal Protection Clause. The United States Supreme Court reversed the decision, holding that the Equal Protection Clause forbids using gender as a proxy for juror competence and impartiality. The majority also ruled that gender-based peremptory challenges did not substantially further the State's legitimate interest in achieving a fair and impartial trial.

Interestingly, about one month after *J.E.B.* was decided, prohibiting gender-based peremptory challenges and opening the door to challenges based on other suspect categories, the Court denied certiorari in a Minnesota Supreme Court case allowing religion-based peremptory challenges, even though the opinion's reasoning arguably was contrary to the J.E.B. extension of *Batson (Minnesota v. Davis*, 504 N.W.2d 767 (1993), *cert. denied*, 511 U.S. 1115 (1994)). Is religion different, since it defines beliefs and attitudes?

Notes on How to Present a Batson-Edmonson *Objection*

(1) *The "Complex" Matter of Making or Rebutting an Edmonson Challenge: How Do You Do It?* The progeny of *Batson* suggest that the objector must, in a timely fashion, make out a *prima facie* case, usually by statistics (*e.g.*, the opponent has exercised his peremptories disproportionately on persons of one race or ethnicity). The burden then shifts to the opponent to make a "neutral" explanation (*i.e.*, one not based on race). Many of the cases depend upon determining whether the race-neutral explanation is "pretextual," or in other words whether it is offered as a cover-up. But sometimes it may be difficult for the opponent to offer an articulate "explanation" even if she genuinely is *not* racially motivated, since peremptory challenges are supposed to include strikes exercised, quite properly, by mere

"hunches." *See, e.g., Hernandez v. New York*, 498 U.S. 1065 (1991) (explanation held race-neutral, where trial court found that exercise of peremptories against Hispanic venirepersons was motivated by concern that, as Spanish-speakers, they would not be able to rely solely upon English translation by interpreter).

(2) *What Is a "Race-Neutral" Explanation for Striking a Potential Juror?* Imagine that the defense lawyer in Hines had explained his peremptory challenge to the second black juror by saying, "When I talked to him, he crossed his arms and glared at me, and I could tell he was against me." Would this be sufficient as a race-neutral explanation, if credited by the trial judge? Notice that the explanation need not be the basis of a challenge for cause; it just has to be a credible reason for exercising a peremptory. It can even be a strange or foolish reason, if the judge finds that it is the real reason. In other words, this explanation, if accepted by the trial judge, would be sufficient. In fact, real peremptory challenges sometimes depend upon much less than a conclusion that a potential juror is "against me." This is one of the difficulties in enforcing the *Batson* principle.

(3) *Has the Supreme Court Eased the Burden for the Proponent of a Peremptory Challenge?* In *Purkett v. Elem*, 514 U.S. 765 (1995), in a per curiam opinion with Justices Stevens and Breyer dissenting, the Court reversed the Eighth Circuit Court of Appeals's habeas corpus determination that a prosecutor had not sufficiently justified the peremptory strike of two black men from a jury panel. The prosecutor had explained that he struck one juror because he had long, unkempt hair, a mustache, and a beard. The Court emphasized that the proponent of a peremptory strike need not offer a reason that "makes sense," only one that "does not deny equal protection." It then becomes the trial judge's burden to determine as a matter of fact whether or not the strike was racially motivated.

[3] The Conduct of the Voir Dire *Examination*

> Read Fed. R. Civ. P. 47 (jury examination and selection); also, read 28 U.S.C. § 1861 et seq. (the Jury Selection and Service Act).

Simmons v. Napier

626 Fed. Appx. 129 (6th Cir. 2015) (unpublished opinion)

Boggs, Circuit Judge. . . .

Mario Simmons was arrested by Wayne State University Police Officers Dianna Napier and Musa Mahoi . . . after Simmons had an argument with the clerks at a Mobil gas station. The officers responded to a call from dispatch stating that there was an armed man threatening to shoot the clerks. According to the officers, they encountered Simmons near the gas station and, at gunpoint, commanded him to stop. After Simmons refused their commands, Officer Napier took Simmons to the ground. Officers Napier and Mahoi then handcuffed Simmons and patted him down, finding a boxcutter. The officers used verbal warnings, physical force, and ultimately pepper spray to complete the arrest when Simmons refused to get into the police car.

... Simmons ... [was transported to a hospital and] was released without charge the following day.

After he was released from police custody, Simmons went to Henry Ford Hospital, where he was diagnosed with numerous bulging and herniated discs in his spine. Simmons underwent a spinal fusion soon after.

Simmons alleged that he was cooperative throughout the encounter. . . .

... Simmons filed a complaint under 42 U.S.C. § 1983 and Michigan law . . . , alleging that Defendants . . . deprived him of his rights by using excessive force that caused physical injuries and psychological trauma. . . .

... [T]he jury found in favor of the officers on all counts. . . . Simmons raised seven grounds for relief [in a motion for new trial and on appeal, including] the failure of the district court to conduct meaningful voir dire of the jury. . . . *Cf. Fifth Third Mortg. Co. v. Chi.Title Ins. Co.*, 692 F.3d 507, 509 (6th Cir.2012) ("When a party comes to us with nine grounds for reversing the district court, that usually means there are none."); *Gagan v. Am. Cablevision, Inc.*, 77 F.3d 951, 955 (7th Cir.1996) ("Losers in a trial can go hunting for relief on appeal with a rifle or a shotgun. The rifle is better. . . .") . . .

Simmons argues that the district court erred by conducting its own voir dire of the jury and by failing "to ask numerous questions [that were] specifically requested." This argument is easily rejected. . . .

1

Federal Rule of Civil Procedure 47(a) provides that a "court may permit the parties or their attorneys to examine prospective jurors *or may itself do so.*" (emphasis added). The Rule thus places the decision as to whether to have the parties or the judge conduct voir dire firmly in the discretion of the district court. Rule 47(a) further provides that, "[i]f the court examines the jurors, it must permit the parties or their attorneys to make any further inquiry it considers proper, or must itself ask any of their additional questions it considers proper." *See also Eisenhauer v. Burger*, 29 Ohio Misc. 138, 431 F.2d 833, 836 (6th Cir.1970) ("The scope of questions permitted to be asked on voir dire examination is generally a matter addressed to the sound discretion of the court.").

In this case, the district court allowed the parties to suggest questions and asked the prospective jurors many of those questions. [Note that the Rule requires the requests for questions to be in writing, and prescribing an examination in writing in advance is difficult.—Eds.] The court did "declin[e] to ask certain questions offered by both parties because the questions were argumentative and improper," and Simmons raised no arguments challenging that determination. Indeed, even on appeal, Simmons fails to identify any specific questions that the district court failed to ask during voir dire that caused him prejudice. Moreover, in making the bald assertion that "voir dire was effectively useless" because, for example, it did not "delve into the natural bias of persons" in favor of police officers, Simmons simply ignores the extensive questioning conducted by the district court on that very topic, which resulted in at least one potential juror being dismissed for cause.

2

Simmons cites the Fifth Circuit's 1977 decision in *United States v. Ledee* and alludes to various legal scholarship in support of the argument that refusing attorneys "the right" to conduct voir dire harms "the judicial system" because it leaves attorneys and their clients "feeling helpless and disenfranchised" and because attorneys are better able to expose potential juror bias than judges. These arguments, which would more appropriately be presented to legislators or in a law journal, do not change the outcome.

In *Ledee*, the Fifth Circuit did observe that "voir dire examination in both civil and criminal cases has little meaning if it is not conducted by counsel for the parties" because "[a] judge cannot have the same grasp of the facts, the complexities and nuances as the trial attorneys entrusted with the preparation of the case." 549 F.2d 990, 993 (5th Cir.1977). Despite this observation made in dictum, however, the *Ledee* court itself made clear that "[i]n the federal courts questioning is generally done by the judge and counsel may submit questions for the jury which the judge may or may not use." *Ibid.* (contrasting the "'federal' method" of "having the judge carry the burden of questioning" with the "'state' method" of "affording counsel reasonable opportunity for direct questioning of jurors individually"). Indeed, the Fifth Circuit ultimately found no error. . . . .

Simmons's conclusory assertion that the district court's "failure to allow counsel to conduct voir dire" and "refus[al] to ask numerous questions" denied him "a full opportunity to determine the biases of the possible jurors," is simply insufficient to demonstrate prejudice in this context. The district court here "conducted voir dire in accordance with Rule 47 and within the bounds of its broad discretion." [AFFIRMED.]

Notes and Questions

(1) *A Possible Trend Toward Judges' Allowing Attorneys to Conduct State-Style Voir Dire Examinations? Taylor v. Stratton Corp.*, 514 Fed. Appx. 68 (2d Cir. 2013). Some district judges do allow attorney *voir dire*, either as main examinations or as supplementations of the judge's questions, and perhaps there is a trend in this direction. In *Taylor,* the court allowed the attorneys to conduct *voir dire* examination, although limited to thirty minutes of questioning.

(2) *The Opposite Problem: When the Judge or Lawyer Asks Too Much — Wichmann v. United Disposal Co.*, 553 F.2d 1104 (8th Cir. 1977). Here, the defendant argued that the trial court had committed reversible error by *voir dire* questions to the jury that

had improperly injected the inadmissible issue of insurance coverage into the case. First, the trial judge asked the entire panel: "Do you or does anyone in your family or do any of your close friends have any connection with the insurance business as an officer, employee, stockholder, claims adjuster or otherwise . . . ?" Secondly, the judge asked whether "The suspicion that one or more of the parties to this suit were or were not covered . . . by insurance" would affect the impartiality of any panel member. The appellate court affirmed, but it criticized the second question:

> . . . Although the sensitive issue of insurance must be treated circumspectly in voir dire, it is permissible to determine whether any prospective juror harbors some bias due to direct or indirect involvement with an insurance company. . . . However, the second question overemphasizes the element of insurance. Upon establishing that prospective jurors maintain no direct or indirect ties with the business of insurance, the district court should not question them concerning their abstract feelings about insurance coverage. Such a question, by implication, injects the specter of insurance into the case to an unnecessary and undesirable degree.

Some other cases have upheld the judge's discretionary decision to refuse asking about insurance affiliation at all. *E.g., Smith v. Vicorp., Inc.*, 107 F.3d 816 (10th Cir. 1997). But shouldn't a personal injury plaintiff know if a prospective juror is an insurance adjuster, for example?

(3) *The District Court's Duty—and the Discretion to Omit or Include Voir Dire Questions: Fietzer v. Ford Motor Co.*, 622 F.2d 281 (7th Cir. 1980). In this products liability suit, arising out of a rear-end collision involving a Mercury Comet which burst into flames, the trial judge chose to conduct a limited *voir dire* examination, consisting of six very general questions, none of which focused on the nature of the claim. Ford requested the trial court to ask several additional questions, including whether any juror had been in a rear-end collision, whether any juror had been a witness to an accident involving fire, whether any juror or member of his or her family had ever suffered burn injuries, and like inquiries. The trial judge refused to inquire into these matters.

The Court of Appeals reversed, stating that the issue was "whether the procedure used for testing impartiality created a reasonable assurance that prejudice would be discovered if present." It concluded, "[N]o such assurance could be found from the voir dire examination in this case." However, the cases generally disclose a wide discretion in the court to define the manner of examination and the subjects of inquiry. *E.g., Darbin v. Nourse*, 664 F.2d 1109 (9th Cir. 1981) (court need not follow questions submitted by parties if it covers substance of important areas); *Stephan v. Marlin Firearms Co.*, 353 F.2d 819 (2d Cir. 1965) (in suit for injuries sustained in hunting accident, trial judge's refusal to permit plaintiff to inquire into experience of prospective jurors with guns was not abuse of discretion); *Jamestown Farmers Elevator, Inc. v. General Mills, Inc.*, 413 F. Supp. 764 (D.N.D. 1976) (failure to ask whether jurors might own stock in or work for corporate defendant not abuse of discretion).

Note on Broader State Protection of Attorney Voir Dire

California and Texas, among other states, differ sharply from federal practice in *voir dire* examination. By rule or by custom, these states allow attorneys to conduct the bulk of the examination of jurors in civil cases (although California has sharply restricted it in criminal cases). The result is deeper inquiry into possible disqualification, but the disadvantages of attorney *voir dire* also are present.

The Discretionary Federal Practice prompts many federal judges to conduct the *voir dire* examination themselves, alone. This approach undoubtedly conserves valuable time and avoids some of the abuses of *voir dire*. *See* Strand & Hart, *The Best Method of Selecting Jurors*, 29 JUDGES' J. 8 (1990). Why have state courts come to such a different resolution of the issue?

Litigation Document Example 10.1

Jury Selection Materials, Including an Article about Attorney Tactics, Excerpts from the Voir Dire *in* Pennzoil Co. v. Texaco Inc., *and a Jury Study in Preparation for Trial*

These materials are online at https://caplaw.com/sites/cp7. *Pennzoil Co. v. Texaco Inc.* produced the then-biggest jury verdict in history (exceeding $ 11 billion for plaintiff Pennzoil), in part because of the plaintiff's *voir dire* examination, which is excerpted here. These materials also include an article that explains the tactics that attorneys may use during *voir dire* examination. The effort is not only to find out about the jurors for the purpose of peremptory challenges and challenges for cause, but also to persuade jurors. You may want to compare the tactics described in the article with the actual *voir dire*.

Finally, there is a pollster's report of a survey of potential jurors in the location where a toddler suffered brain damage because an apartment owner left the gate surrounding a swimming pool unlocked. This survey was a great help to the plaintiff's lawyers during jury selection in the trial of their case against the apartment owner. As you read it, consider: what are the characteristics of an ideal juror—and of a juror you'd want to strike? (Note that race and gender, although dealt with in are the report, are prohibited considerations.) Please go to https://caplaw.com/sites/cp7, then click on Litigation Document Example 10.1: Jury Selection Materials, Including an Article about Attorney Tactics, Excerpts from the Voir Dire in *Pennzoil Co. v. Texaco Inc.*, and a Jury Study in Preparation for Trial.

IV. Opening Statements

Note on the Opening Statement

Purposes. The opening statement has been likened to the table of contents or introduction to a book. It is designed to let the jury know what to expect: What proof will be offered and how it fits with the legal issues. Depending on the case, for example, counsel might outline the testimony witness by witness. But it may be best to outline themes first: "We will show you three things. First, the defendant was driving way too fast; this was careless. Second, the plaintiff was unaware of the danger. Third, it would take more than $5 million dollars to compensate any reasonable person for this loss." Some courts prohibit "argumentative" statements about legal propositions (but this approach tends to diminish the usefulness of the opening statement in relating the facts to the legal theories, if it is too strict). In some jurisdictions, the opening statement may not be important, because of wide latitude in the *voir dire* examination.

Tactics. A good opening statement should be clear, direct, and positive. It should be expressed in laypersons' language. It should preview the evidence so that jurors can understand how it fits with the legal theory, and it should make the jurors interested in hearing the case. It should avoid overstating the case, however. Some of the opponent's best final arguments may take the form of: "They told you they would show you thus-and-so, and they did not keep that promise." *See* Shrager, *The Opening Statement*, 21 Trial 102 (Oct. 1985).

The Importance of Establishing Themes in Opening Statements: Major Impact on Juror Decisions. Jury research has shown that jurors form tentative judgments very early in the case—at the voir dire or opening statement stage—and, in fact, they usually do not vary from those early judgments when they reach the verdict stage. This research suggests that close cases, at least, can be "won" in voir dire and opening statement. It also suggests that a chronological preview of the witnesses may be less effective than a thematic, or scenario, approach. "The defense will bring you three major themes: First, we will show you that the defendant was driving carefully; secondly, we will show that the child darted out so that he couldn't avoid hitting her; and third, we will show you that this tragic accident wouldn't have happened if her parents had showed her the proper way to cross the street."

This approach works, not because jurors confuse the opening statement with the evidence, but because their reasoning is deductive rather than inductive: that is, they start with certain hypotheses and then seek support from the evidence, rather than building to a conclusion by weighing bits and pieces of evidence. The lawyer who most persuasively establishes these themes thus has established a "filtering system" for the jurors—or a lens through which they will look at all the evidence. *See* Vinson, *Jury Trials: The Psychology of Winning Strategy* (1986).

Legal Problems. In some jurisdictions, it is possible for the defendant to move for nonsuit at the conclusion of the opening statement, on the theory that the proof outlined in the statement would not support a verdict even if all received and believed. *Hurn v. Woods*, 132 Cal. App. 3d 896, 183 Cal. Rptr. 495 (1982). Another issue concerns opening statements telling the jury about evidence that turns out, later, to be inadmissible. What should be done then? In *Smith v. Covell*, 100 Cal. App. 3d 947, 161 Cal. Rptr. 377 (4th Dist. 1980), the court held that reversal should follow when an attorney makes harmful remarks in the opening statement, and when she knows that evidence to support them will not be admitted. [Question:

This formulation hints that an appellate court would affirm if the attorney disclosed prejudicial inadmissible information believing in good faith that it possibly might be admissible. Why?]

V. Presenting the Case: Evidence and "Proof"

[A] The Rules of Evidence

Read Fed. R. Civ. P. 43, 45. Also, if your instructor assigns them, read Fed. R. Evid. 103, 401-403, 602, 701-702, 801(c), and 803(1), (2), (6), and (8).

What the Rules of Evidence Are About. The Anglo-American judicial system does not permit the parties to present to the jury any and every item of information they might choose. Instead, the form and content of the evidence is controlled by rules, which have a number of purposes. First, these rules are designed to focus inquiry on matters relevant to the issues, rather than matters that are collateral or prejudicial. Second, they are designed to screen out information that is particularly unreliable or incapable of verification. Third, they seek to allow each party a balanced opportunity to develop and test the evidence. Fourth, they insure the making of an organized and reproducible record. Like all rules, however, the principles of evidence are imperfect, and they can result in the exclusion of arguably useful information. Furthermore, they leave a great deal to the discretion of the judge, and therefore they depend heavily upon reasonable interpretation on the spur of the moment, during trial. *See generally* Comment, *A Practitioner's Guide to the Federal Rules of Evidence*, 10 U. Rich. L. Rev. 169 (1975).

An Example to Work With: The Evidence in a Simple Automobile Accident. To illustrate the operation of the rules of evidence, let us take an example. Imagine a common, ordinary automobile-pedestrian accident. Paul Plaintiff alleges that he was injured by the negligence of Dan Defendant, who he alleges ran a red light after becoming intoxicated. Dan denies intoxication, claims that his brakes failed suddenly, and attributes the accident to Paul's negligence in walking outside the pedestrian crosswalk (which Paul denies). A passerby named Bill Bystander saw some of the relevant events. Let us use this example to see what kinds of evidence would likely be received if offered, and what items of information the court would probably exclude.

The Basic Rule of Admissibility: "Relevant" Evidence. Federal Rules of Evidence 401-402 express a general principle of admissibility. "Relevant" evidence is admissible at trial, unless it is excluded by a particular exclusionary rule. "Relevant" evidence, in turn, is defined as evidence having "any tendency" to make a fact that is of consequence to the determination of the action more probable or less probable than it would be without the evidence. This rule is, and should be, liberal; there is no requirement of certainty, and no requirement that the ultimate fact follow inevitably from the evidence, but only a requirement that it have some tendency—"any" tendency—to support the inference. For example, imagine that Paul offers testimony that he saw several empty beer cans in Dan's car immediately after the accident. There is no proof that beer from these cans contributed to Dan's alleged intoxication, or even that he drank them. Nevertheless, many courts would admit this evidence, because it does have a "tendency" to support an ultimate inference that is of consequence to the determination of the action. Therefore, the evidence is "relevant."

The Hearsay Rule of Exclusion. Given the broad rule of admissibility contained in Rules 401-402, it should not surprise you that many of the rules of evidence are rules of exclusion. One of the best known exclusionary rules is the hearsay rule, set forth in Federal Rules of Evidence 801-802. For example, if Dan attempted to show that Paul was outside the crosswalk by testifying that Bill Bystander told him so, the evidence would be relevant, but it would be excluded by the hearsay rule.

However, the definition of hearsay is more complex than this simple example might imply. Rule 801 says that hearsay is "a statement, other than the one made by the declarant while testifying at the trial or hearing, offered in evidence to prove the truth of the matter asserted." Thus, it sometimes is proper to offer testimony including someone else's statement, if that statement is part of what happened and therefore not offered to prove "the truth of the matter asserted." Furthermore, certain admissions of a party opponent are specifically excluded from the definition of hearsay. For example, imagine that Paul offers testimony that at the scene, Dan said: "I just ran into a train, didn't I?" Paul offers this testimony to show Dan's intoxication. This evidence would not be excluded by the hearsay rule for at least two reasons. First, it is an admission of a party opponent. Secondly, it is not offered to prove the truth of the matter asserted (because Paul is offering it to show intoxication, not to show that Dan "ran into a train").

Exceptions to the Hearsay Rule: From "Excited Utterances" to Business Records. The rule excluding hearsay exists because hearsay evidence is hard to test for reliability and is usually unnecessary. There are, however, some kinds of hearsay that should be admitted. Some categories of hearsay have indications of trustworthiness that substitute for the usual manner of testing by cross-examination, and also, certain forms of hearsay are likely to be the best available evidence. Therefore, there is a long list of exceptions to the hearsay rule. For example, Rule 803 allows reception of hearsay statements relating "present sense impressions" as well as hearsay in the form of "excited utterances." For example, if Paul Plaintiff were to testify that Bill Bystander shouted, "That driver's not going to stop!" an instant before the accident, the repetition of this statement would be hearsay—but it probably would be admissible, under both of these exceptions.

Another common pair of exceptions admits business records and public records or reports. For example, imagine that Paul offers the repair records kept by Dan's automobile mechanic, which contain the mechanic's statement the day before the accident: "Checked brakes—working fine." This evidence, properly predicated, would be admissible. If courts excluded business records of this sort merely because they contained some hearsay assertions, the jury would be deprived of valuable evidence that might provide the only available means of proving crucial facts. Paul might also attempt to offer the police report compiled by officers who investigated the accident.

Balancing Relevancy and Prejudice. As we have seen, the definition of relevant evidence is broad. However, a piece of evidence might have relevance so slight, in comparison to its prejudicial impact, that it should not be admitted. For example, suppose that Paul attempted to show that ten years ago, Dan got drunk and fell into the swimming pool at his high school prom. This information may have some tendency to show that Dan has an inclination toward intoxication in the present, but its probative value is slight. Rule 403 says that, if the relevance of a piece of evidence is "substantially outweighed" by unfair prejudice, confusion, misleading tendencies, delay, or inquiry into collateral issues, the judge has discretion to exclude it.

The Requirement of Personal Knowledge and Limits on Opinion Testimony from Lay Witnesses. Rule 602 requires a showing that the witness has "personal knowledge" of the matter she is testifying about. But verbal expression is complicated, and it would not do to exclude testimony merely because it contains some element of "opinion." Therefore, Rule 701 says that opinion evidence is admissible if it is "rationally based on the perception of the witness" and is "helpful to a clear understanding" of her testimony. To take an example, if Paul Plaintiff calls Bill Bystander as a witness, Bill of course would be permitted to testify to what he observed. He could testify about Dan's "glassy-eyed stare" and about his inability to walk without stumbling. He even could give an opinion in the form of an estimate of the speed Dan was driving or a statement that Dan was intoxicated (these matters are clearly based on perception and are helpful to clear understanding). But the court is much less likely to receive Bill's generalized opinion testimony that "Dan handled the situation badly."

Expert Witnesses and Scientific Evidence: Greater Allowance of Opinion Testimony. A separate set of rules applies to expert witnesses. Rule 702 provides that an expert, qualified by "knowledge, skill, experience, training, or education," may testify in the form of an opinion that may encompass information not observed by the witness. The court probably would not allow Bill Bystander, if he is a lay person, to testify that "Paul has a Colles fracture with causalgia for which the prognosis is permanent twenty percent disability," but an expert witness (most likely a physician) could provide this testimony.

Procedure: The Manner of Examination and Enforcement of the Rules. The Rules provide that leading questions ordinarily should not be used on direct examination. A leading question is one that suggests its own answer. The court has discretion to make exceptions, however, for such matters as background testimony, child witnesses, etc. Furthermore, testimonial evidence customarily is received in question-and-answer form, rather than as a free-flow narrative from the witness (to which objections would be difficult).

Another procedural principle imbedded in the evidence rules is that the attorneys have important responsibilities in the enforcement of the rules. Rule 103 provides that error may not be predicated upon the admission of evidence unless the opponent has timely objected, stating a specific ground. And if the proponent of evidence claims error in its exclusion, she must make an "offer of proof": either by explaining it, or by putting it in the record outside the presence of the jury. Thus, for example, if Paul's lawyer were to ask him, "You were crossing the street inside the crosswalk, weren't you?" Dan could object and should state his ground: The question is leading. On the other hand, if Paul believes that the judge has made an error in excluding evidence—for example, the judge did not permit Bill Bystander to say that Dan was "intoxicated"—Paul must get the substance of this evidence on the record, either by a verbal statement or by questions and answers, if he wants to be able subsequently to claim error.

Cross-Examination and Impeachment. There is no prohibition of leading questions in cross-examination. "You were outside the crosswalk in the street, weren't you?" is a proper question for Dan's lawyer to put to Paul. (In fact, some skilled lawyers maintain that every single question a cross-examiner asks should be a leading question.) And greater latitude is allowed in admitting evidence to impeach the opponent's witnesses. For example, Federal Rules of Evidence 608-611 allow the use of prior inconsistent statements, reputation for untruthfulness, and even convictions for certain crimes. Thus, Paul's lawyer (assuming he has a good-faith basis in information for each question) may ask Dan: "Even though your testimony here is that you were sober, isn't it a fact that last week you told your bartender that you were drunk at the time of the accident?" or "You have a reputation for untruthfulness, don't you?" or "Two years ago, you were convicted of aggravated perjury, weren't you?"

Documents, Objects, Photographs, etc. Unlike TV's Perry Mason, Paul's lawyer would not be successful if he offered an exhibit by standing up and simply saying: "This is a whiskey bottle, your honor, and we offer it into evidence." The exhibit first must be numbered (because it must be made a part of the record). It must be identified, shown to be relevant, and "authenticated"—that is, it must be shown to be "what its proponent claims." The whiskey bottle would become admissible upon testimony from Bill Bystander, for example, as follows: "Exhibit 1 is a whiskey bottle. I saw it fall out of Dan's car immediately after the accident, and I recognize it because of markings on the label, the level of contents, and its general appearance." For similar reasons, photographs must be shown to "fairly and accurately depict" matters relevant to the suit. Finally, documents also must be supported by authentication and a showing of relevance. Thus, if Dan claims to have received a written release from Paul, he must have it marked, identify it, show its relationship to the case, authenticate it ("that's Paul's signature"), offer it, and have it received in evidence.

An Example: Owens v. Republic of Sudan, Below. For an example of the Rules of Evidence in actual operation, consider the *Owens* case, which follows. The case decides issues about expert qualification, expert opinions, hearsay, and public reports as an exception to the hearsay rule. As you read the case, notice the importance that the Rules of Evidence have for a trial lawyer. There is a separate, upper-level course in Evidence at every law school, in which you will study the subject in detail. Here, our objective is more modest: to demonstrate how the Rules fit into the overall scheme of civil procedure.

Owens v. Republic of Sudan

864 F.3d 751 (D.C. Cir. 2017)

Ginsburg, Senior Circuit Judge:

On August 7, 1998, truck bombs exploded outside the United States embassies in Nairobi, Kenya and in Dar es Salaam, Tanzania. The explosions killed more than 200 people and injured more than a thousand. Many of the victims of the attacks were U.S. citizens, government employees, or contractors.

As would later be discovered, the bombings were the work of al Qaeda, and only the first of several successful attacks against U.S. interests culminating in the September 11, 2001, attack on the United States itself.

[This lengthy opinion affirms a judgment against the government of Sudan for providing "material support" to al-Qaeda, a terrorist organization, in activities that caused the bombings. The laws violated included the Foreign Sovereign Immunities Act (FSIA), which withdraws sovereign immunity upon proof of state action in extrajudicial killings. The alleged support consisted of the government's providing to al Qaeda free passage, safe space in which to operate, contacts with other organizations, and assistance in purchasing properties. The district court also found that Sudan "had provided financial, governmental, military, and intelligence support to al Qaeda."]

[Sudan refused to appear at or before trial, although it attacked the judgment and now appeals the overruling of its arguments. This tactic meant that the plaintiffs were required to prove their case without discovery or defendant's pleadings. How does a plaintiff prove a case of this nature, including the activities of al Qaeda, the support provided, and the participation of the official government in providing this support, without any information from inside the government?]

[The sources of evidence included three expert witnesses, three former al-Qaeda operatives, videos produced by al Qaeda, and public documents produced by the State Department, among others. Here, we excerpt certain parts of the court's discussion pertaining to expert witnesses and hearsay evidence, including the public documents. The discussion covers admissibility of these kinds of evidence.]

1. The expert testimony

Sudan ... attacks the reliability of the experts' opinions in this case as inconsistent with the underlying facts. In other words, Sudan asks this court to hold the expert opinions are inadmissible because the plaintiffs' witnesses have not "reliably applied [their] principles and methods to the facts of the case." See Fed. R. Evid. 702(d). . . .

[Usually, these questions would be answered by reference to Supreme Court interpretations of the Federal Rules of Evidence in *Daubert v. Merrell Dow Pharmaceuticals, Inc.,* 509 U.S. 579 (1993), and *Kumho Tire Co. Ltd. v. Carmichael,* 526 U.S. 1373 (1999). These cases set standards for the relevance of underlying principles to asserted opinions, reliability of those principles, and application of the principles to underlying facts and data. But the analysis is truncated here because of the nonappearance of the defendant at trial. — Eds.]

The problem with this argument is that Sudan has not explained — either at the evidentiary hearing or on appeal — why these expert opinions are unreliable or clearly erroneous. By refusing to participate in the evidentiary hearing, Sudan gave up its opportunity to challenge the fit between the experts' opinions and the underlying facts. At the hearing, the witnesses described the general bases of their expertise, and the district court found them qualified to give opinions on Sudan's material support for al Qaeda. In doing so, the experts said they had relied upon multiple sources of information, including but not limited to those presented at the hearing. But the experts did not — and did not need to — provide the specific basis for their knowledge for each factual proposition they advanced. See Fed. R. Evid. 705 ("an expert may state an opinion — and give the reasons for it — without first testifying to the underlying facts or data"). Therefore, we cannot know with certainty whether the experts' opinions were consistent or in conflict with the underlying facts upon which they relied. Had Sudan participated in the hearing, it could have challenged the experts to substantiate each and every factual proposition they asserted.

2. The State Department reports

[The State Department reports are hearsay, but fit an exception to the hearsay rule of exclusion. — Eds.]

Of course, the district court did not rely solely upon expert testimony to establish jurisdiction and liability. Of particular importance, the plaintiffs marshaled nearly a decade of State Department reports that speak directly to Sudan's support for terrorist groups, including al Qaeda. See, e.g., U.S. Dep't of State, Patterns of Global Terrorism: 1993 ("Despite several warnings to cease supporting radical extremists the Sudanese government continued to harbor international terrorist groups in Sudan"); U.S. Dep't of State, Patterns of Global Terrorism : 1998 ("Sudan provides safe haven to some of the world's most violent terrorist groups, including Usama Bin Ladin's al-Qaida"); U.S. Dep't of State, Patterns of Global Terrorism : 2000 (2001) ("Sudan . . . continued to be used as a safe haven by members of various groups, including associates of Osama bin Laden's al-Qaeda organization"). These reports both bolster the experts' conclusions about Sudan's material support for the al Qaeda embassy bombings and independently show the plaintiffs' claims "ha[ve] some factual basis," as required by § 1608(e).

As with the expert testimony, Sudan contends these reports are inadmissible hearsay. [Note that written statements can be hearsay, just as oral statements can be.—Eds.] The plaintiffs urge the State Department reports were admissible under the hearsay exception for public records. See Fed. R. Evid. 803(8). That exception allows the admission of "a record or statement of a public office if" it: (1) contains factual findings (2) from a legally authorized investigation. Id at 803(8)(iii). Pursuant to the "broad approach to admissibility" under Rule 803(8), a court may also admit "conclusion[s] or opinion[s]" contained within a public record. *Beech Aircraft Corp. v. Rainey*, 488 U.S. 153, 170 (1988). Once proffered, a public record is presumptively admissible, and the opponent bears the burden of showing it is unreliable.

The State Department's Patterns of Global Terrorism reports fit squarely within the public records exception. First, the reports contain both factual findings and conclusions on Sudan's support for terrorism in general and al Qaeda in particular. Second, the reports were created pursuant to statute, see 22 U.S.C. § 2656f(a) (requiring annual reports on terrorism), and are therefore the product of a "legally authorized investigation." *See Bridgeway* [*Corp. v. Citibank*], 201 F.3d at 143 [(2d Cir. 2000)] (holding State Department reports required by statute are public records). Indeed, in contested FSIA proceedings we have previously approved admission of the very reports Sudan challenges.

Sudan objects on appeal to the "trustworthiness" of these reports, but that objection should have been made in the district court. See Fed. R. Evid. 803(8)(B) (providing for the admission of public records if "the opponent does not show that the possible source of the information or other circumstances indicate a lack of trustworthiness"). Even now, Sudan does not present any reason, beyond their reliance upon hearsay, to deem these reports unreliable. See *Kehm v. Procter & Gamble Mfg. Co.*, 724 F.2d 613, 618 (8th Cir. 1983) (holding inclusion of hearsay is not a sufficient ground for excluding a public record as unreliable). Although the reports lack the details that the expert witnesses provided concerning Sudan's material support, they are competent, admissible evidence, which together with the plaintiffs' admissible opinion evidence satisfy the burden of production on material support and jurisdictional causation.... [AFFIRMED except for a question about applicability of emotional damages in one claim that is certified to the state supreme court.]

Notes and Questions

(1) *The Exclusion of Unreliable Expert Testimony.* The trial judge acts as a "gatekeeper" for expert opinions, using multilayered requirements set out by the Rules of Evidence and court interpretations of those rules. First, the expert must be "qualified" under the rules, which allow expertise based upon various sources, ranging from experience to education. Also, an expert opinion must be capable of "assisting" the jury, meaning that it must be based upon principles that are relevant to the issue. And further, the principles upon which it is based must have a minimum

degree of reliability, which implies testability, peer review, error rates, breadth of acceptance, and other factors.

Given these requirements, imagine two potential expert witnesses who offer expert opinions on the participation of a particular country's government in terrorism. One is a Ph.D. in foreign Affairs and a professor at the Kennedy School of Government at Harvard who specializes in terrorism-related issues and regularly visits the relevant country. She will testify based upon study and experience in the country that high government officials provide financial support and tactical assistance to terrorists. This expert resembles one who testified in *Owens*, above. The other is a newspaper columnist who writes about international politics and will testify on the basis of his reading and study of news sources that the country is well known as a sponsor of terrorism. How will the courts go about evaluating these two witnesses?

(2) *The Hearsay Rule and Hearsay Exceptions.* The State Department reports received in *Owens* are hearsay. The label has nothing to do with whether they are valuable or authoritative; it means that they include statements that are not current testimony and that are used to prove case facts. Specifically, hearsay is defined as a statement, that is not current testimony, and that is offered to prove the truth of the matter asserted. Hearsay includes written as well as oral statements. But public reports are an exception to the hearsay rule of exclusion, including factual findings made with publicly delegated authority. Is it clear to you why the State Department documents here are hearsay, and can you see why they nevertheless are admissible?

[B] Making the Record

GUETERSLOH v. C.I.T. CORP., 451 S.W.2d 759 (Tex. Civ. App.-Amarillo 1970, writ ref'd n.r.e.). This was a suit on a promissory note by C.I.T. Corporation as plaintiff against M.F. Guetersloh, as maker of the note, and Herman Guetersloh, as co-maker and guarantor. The Court granted judgment for the plaintiff. On appeal, the defendant's first point of error was that plaintiff C.I.T. Corporation failed to introduce the note into evidence. It appears that, during the trial, plaintiff produced the original document; it was inspected by defendant's trial counsel; it was marked by the court reporter as "plaintiff's exhibit 1"; it was handed to the judge, and it was included by the court reporter among the exhibits that were part of the proceeding. However, plaintiff never offered it into evidence, and the judge never made a ruling ordering that it be received or admitted. Therefore, the defendant argued, neither it nor its contents could properly have been considered by the trial court. Without the note as an exhibit, the trial record was inadequate to sustain a finding of the existence, possession, or terms of the note.

The appellate court affirmed. There is a requirement that a party offer the exhibit and that the court rule on its admittance. But the court reasoned that the precise word "offer" was not required, nor did the court's ruling have to take any particular form. Here, there was an *implied* offer and admittance:

> During the trial . . . the original document . . . was handed to and received by the Court, and it was placed in the [record of evidence received] by the court reporter. The defendant's trial counsel treated the note as though it were in evidence. In fact, during the testimony the defendant's counsel objected to a question on the ground that it would "vary the terms of the contract which is already in evidence." The circumstances here . . . indicate that the note was introduced in evidence.

Notes and Questions

(1) *A Scary Situation for the Plaintiff's Lawyer!* The Court of Appeals easily could have reached the opposite result. A plaintiff's lawyer in this situation needs to notify her malpractice insurance carrier. It's best if the record is made correctly.

(2) *Desirability of a Clear Record of Evidence to Support a Favorable Judgment.* Although the plaintiff prevailed and the decision leaves a sense that justice was done, it would have been better if this appellate issue had never arisen. The plaintiff could not be certain of victory, because there have been numerous cases in which courts have refused to consider evidence that was not a part of the record. *See, e.g., Celotex Corp. v. Catrett,* in § II[B] in Chapter 9, above (Supreme Court refused to consider summary judgment evidence that was not in proper form, although included in record). An attorney should (1) prepare a proof outline before trial (it is surprising in some relatively simple cases how many discrete facts plaintiff must prove) and (2) consider it as a checklist before resting.

(3) *The Record as Including Both Admitted and Excluded Evidence.* The trial judge's ruling admitting an exhibit is necessary because the record includes both evidence that has been received for the jury's consideration and information that has been excluded (*e.g.*, offers of proof received outside the jury's presence).

(4) *Necessary Steps for Admitting an Exhibit.* In federal courts, exhibits may be marked and admitted in a pretrial conference. Some local rules admit all exhibits not objected to before trial. But in courts in which pretrial admission is not customary, the following is a list of steps that may be necessary: (1) Have the exhibit marked by the court reporter or courtroom deputy. "May I have this marked as plaintiff's exhibit 1, please?" (2) Have the sponsoring witness identify it. "It's a photograph of the accident scene." (3) Lay the predicate to authenticate and show relevancy. "And does plaintiff's exhibit 1 fairly and accurately depict the accident scene as you saw it?" "Yes." (4) Tender it to opposing counsel, who may object to its admission. (5) Formally offer it into evidence. "I offer plaintiff's exhibit 1 into evidence, Your Honor, after having tendered it to opposing counsel." (6) Be ready to argue its admissibility against an objection, if necessary. (7) Take affirmative steps to obtain a ruling from the court to the effect that the exhibit is "admitted" or "received" in evidence. "Is plaintiff's exhibit 1 admitted, Your Honor?" "Yes." (8) Take steps to have the exhibit communicated to the jury. "May the bailiff pass plaintiff's exhibit

1 to the jurors, Your Honor?" [Note: Custom varies; for example, in some jurisdictions an exhibit should be shown to opposing counsel before the witness speaks about it, and in some jurisdictions, most documentary evidence is admitted before trial.]

[C] The "Burden of Proof"

Note on the Burdens of Production and of Persuasion

The "Burden of Production." The phrase "burden of proof" actually refers to two distinct concepts: the "burden of production" and the "burden of persuasion." The burden of production is the burden to introduce some evidence that is minimally sufficient to support a jury finding on a given issue. It sometimes is described as the burden to "make out a *prima facie* case" or the burden to introduce "sufficient evidence to get to the jury." In practical terms, the party who bears the burden of production is the one that would lose if neither side introduced any evidence.

The "Burden of Persuasion." The burden of persuasion, on the other hand, is the requirement that a party introduce evidence that persuades the trier of fact on a given issue. Usually, in a civil case, the preponderance of the evidence standard defines the burden of persuasion. Thus, the party with the burden of persuasion is the one that would lose if the jury viewed the evidence as precisely balanced.

Allocating the Burdens Between the Parties. On some issues, the plaintiff may have both the burden of production and the burden of persuasion; on others, the defendant may have both burdens. Sometimes, one party has the burden of production, the other the burden of persuasion; and there are some cases in which it can be said that one burden or the other "shifts" when one party makes out a *prima facie* case.

A Simple Example: Proof of Agency by a Presumption Based on the Defendant's Placement of Its Trade Name on Its Vehicle. In some jurisdictions, proof that a vehicle carries the defendant's trade name creates a "mandatory, rebuttable presumption" that the defendant's agent was operating the vehicle and that he was acting within the scope of his agency. In other words, proof of the trade name automatically establishes the responsibility of the defendant, unless the defendant offers evidence of non-agency. Thus, if the plaintiff meets her initial burden of production—by showing that the truck that struck her carried the defendant's trade name—she has presumptively established the defendant's responsibility, even if she can prove nothing else about the driver. That is so, unless the defendant responds by carrying his own burden of production (by offering some evidence, for example, from which a jury could conclude that the truck was stolen and missing at the time of the accident). In that event (*i.e.*, where both parties at least minimally have met their burdens of production), some jurisdictions would submit the case to the jury with the ultimate burden of persuasion placed on the plaintiff. *See* C. McCormick, Evidence §§ 343–344 (3d ed. 1984). The following case is a more complex application of the same principles.

Young v. United Parcel Service, Inc.

135 S. Ct. 1338 (2015)

Justice BREYER delivered the opinion of the Court.

[The Pregnancy Discrimination Act broadened Title VII of the Civil Rights Act of 1964, which covers employment discrimination. It states that illegal discrimination includes actions "because of or on the basis of pregnancy, childbirth, or related medical conditions." The Act also provides that employers must treat "women affected by pregnancy . . . the same for all employment-related purposes . . . as other persons not so affected but similar in their ability or inability to work." In this case, the employer's policy accommodated many, but not all, workers with nonpregnancy-related disabilities.]

[Petitioner Young was a part-time driver for respondent United Parcel Service (UPS). When she became pregnant, her doctor advised her that she should not lift more than 20 pounds. UPS, however, required drivers like Young to be able to lift up to 70 pounds. UPS told Young that she could not work while under a lifting restriction. Young subsequently filed this federal lawsuit, claiming that UPS acted unlawfully in refusing to accommodate her pregnancy-related lifting restriction. She brought only a disparate-treatment claim of discrimination, which a plaintiff can prove by using the three-step burden-shifting framework set forth in *McDonnell Douglas Corp. v. Green,* 411 U.S. 792 (1973).]

[Under the *McDonnell Douglas* framework, (1) the plaintiff has "the initial burden" of "establishing a prima facie case" of discrimination. If she carries her burden, (2) the employer must have an opportunity "to articulate some legitimate, non-discriminatory reason[s] for" the difference in treatment. If the employer articulates a non-discriminatory reason, (3) the plaintiff then has "an opportunity to prove by a preponderance of the evidence that the reasons . . . were a pretext for discrimination." *Texas Dept. of Community Affairs v. Burdine,* 450 U.S. 248, 253 (1981).]

[After discovery, UPS sought summary judgment. In reply, Young presented several favorable facts that she believed she could prove. In particular, she pointed to UPS policies that accommodated workers who were injured on the job, had disabilities covered by the Americans with Disabilities Act of 1990 (ADA), or had lost Department of Transportation (DOT) certifications. Pursuant to these policies, Young contended, UPS had accommodated several individuals whose disabilities created work restrictions similar to hers. She argued that these policies showed that UPS discriminated against its pregnant employees because it had a light-duty-for-injury policy for numerous "other persons," but not for pregnant workers.]

[UPS responded that, since Young did not fall within the on-the-job injury, ADA, or DOT categories, it had not discriminated against Young on the basis of pregnancy, but had treated her just as it treated all "other" relevant "persons." The District Court granted UPS summary judgment. The court found that those with whom

Young had compared herself—those falling within the on-the-job, DOT, or ADA categories—were too different to qualify as "similarly situated comparator[s]." The Fourth Circuit affirmed. In this opinion, the Supreme Court reverses.] . . .

Thus, a plaintiff alleging that the denial of an accommodation constituted disparate treatment under the Pregnancy Discrimination Act's second clause may make out a prima facie case by showing, as in *McDonnell Douglas*, that she belongs to the protected class, that she sought accommodation, that the employer did not accommodate her, and that the employer did accommodate others "similar in their ability or inability to work."

The employer may then seek to justify its refusal to accommodate the plaintiff by relying on "legitimate, nondiscriminatory" reasons for denying her accommodation. 411 U.S., at 802, 93 S.Ct. 1817. But, consistent with the Act's basic objective, that reason normally cannot consist simply of a claim that it is more expensive or less convenient to add pregnant women to the category of those ("similar in their ability or inability to work") whom the employer accommodates. . . .

If the employer offers an apparently "legitimate, non-discriminatory" reason for its actions, the plaintiff may in turn show that the employer's proffered reasons are in fact pretextual. We believe that the plaintiff may reach a jury on this issue by providing sufficient evidence that the employer's policies impose a significant burden on pregnant workers, and that the employer's "legitimate, nondiscriminatory" reasons are not sufficiently strong to justify the burden, but rather—when considered along with the burden imposed—give rise to an inference of intentional discrimination.

The plaintiff can create a genuine issue of material fact as to whether a significant burden exists by providing evidence that the employer accommodates a large percentage of nonpregnant workers while failing to accommodate a large percentage of pregnant workers. Here, for example, if the facts are as Young says they are, she can show that UPS accommodates most nonpregnant employees with lifting limitations while categorically failing to accommodate pregnant employees with lifting limitations. Young might also add that the fact that UPS has multiple policies that accommodate nonpregnant employees with lifting restrictions suggests that its reasons for failing to accommodate pregnant employees with lifting restrictions are not sufficiently strong—to the point that a jury could find that its reasons for failing to accommodate pregnant employees give rise to an inference of intentional discrimination.

Under this interpretation of the Act, the judgment of the Fourth Circuit must be vacated. . . . Viewing the record in the light most favorable to Young, there is a genuine dispute as to whether UPS provided more favorable treatment to at least some employees whose situation cannot reasonably be distinguished from Young's. In other words, Young created a genuine dispute of material fact as to the fourth prong of the *McDonnell Douglas* analysis. . . . The Fourth Circuit did not consider the combined effects of these policies (accommodating on-the-job, ADA, and DOT limited workers), nor did it consider the strength of UPS' justifications for each when combined. That is, why, when the employer accommodated so many, could it not accommodate pregnant women as well? . . . [VACATED AND REMANDED.]

[The concurring opinion of Justice Alito is omitted, as are the dissenting opinions of Justice Kennedy and of Justice Scalia, joined by Justices Kennedy and Thomas.]

Notes and Questions

(1) *Burdens of Production and Persuasion in Employment Discrimination Cases.* The Court's holding can be stated this way: The plaintiff has the initial burden of production. When that burden is satisfied, the defendant has the burden of production of a non-discriminatory explanation. If both burdens of production are met, the plaintiff has the burden of persuasion, that is, of showing that the reason is pretextual. Given this explanation, what should be the result if: (a) The plaintiff makes out a *prima facie* case sufficient to meet her burden of production, and the defendant offers no explanation whatever? (b) Both parties meet their burdens of production, and neither party offers any further evidence? (c) Both parties meet their burdens of production, and the plaintiff then offers further evidence, but the trier of fact is not persuaded by the plaintiff's evidence taken as a whole?

(2) *Presumptions: What Are They?* A "presumption" is a factual conclusion that the law permits or requires the factfinder to make if other specified facts (sometimes called the "base facts" or "trigger facts") are proved. In many jurisdictions, proof of the base facts compels a finding of the presumed fact, unless the opponent rebuts the proof. For example, evidence that a letter was mailed (with proper address and postage) creates a presumption that the letter was received by the addressee. Thus, if the defendant offers no contrary evidence, the plaintiff would be entitled to have the court instruct the jury that it must find that the defendant received it.

[D] Judgment as a Matter of Law (or "Directed Verdict")

Read U.S. Const. amend. VII (right to jury trial) and Fed. R. Civ. P. 50.

Reeves v. Sanderson Plumbing Co.

530 U.S. 133 (2000)

Justice O'Connor delivered the opinion of the Court.

This case concerns the kind and amount of evidence necessary to sustain a jury's verdict that an employer has unlawfully discriminated on the basis of age. . . . We must also decide whether the employer was entitled to judgment as a matter of law under the particular circumstances presented here.

I

[This was an age discrimination suit under the federal Age Discrimination in Employment Act (ADEA). Roger Reeves, age 57, was a supervisor of Sanderson Plumbing's "Hinge Room," as it was called. Joe Oswalt, in his mid-thirties, also was a supervisor, and Russell Caldwell, age 45, was the manager of the Hinge Room. Powe Chesnut, who was company's director of manufacturing, ordered an audit of the Hinge Room's timesheets. The audit showed that unauthorized absenteeism was frequent in the Hinge Room, and it revealed numerous timekeeping errors and misrepresentations by Reeves, Caldwell, and Oswalt. Chesnut recommended that Reeves and Caldwell, age 57 and 45 respectively, be fired, but he did not recommend firing Oswalt, the one in his mid-thirties. Sandra Sanderson, the company's president, followed this recommendation and discharged Reeves and Caldwell.]

[In his suit, plaintiff Reeves claimed that his age was a motivating factor for his discharge, in violation of the ADEA. Defendant Sanderson Plumbing countered by contending that it had fired Reeves due to his failure to maintain adequate attendance records. But Reeves offered testimony tending to show that the company's explanation was a pretext. Reeve's evidence, if believed, would have shown that he accurately recorded attendance and that Chesnut, the man who had recommended Reeves's firing, had demonstrated age-based animus toward Reeves by making derogatory age-related remarks.]

During the trial, the District Court twice denied oral motions by respondent for judgment as a matter of law under Rule 50 of the Federal Rules of Civil Procedure, and the case went to the jury.... [T]he jury returned a verdict in favor of [plaintiff Reeves].... Respondent [later] renewed its motion for judgment as a matter of law and alternatively moved for a new trial.... The District Court denied respondent's motions and [entered judgment for nearly $100,000 in favor of Reeves].

The Court of Appeals for the Fifth Circuit reversed, holding that petitioner [Reeves] had not introduced sufficient evidence to sustain the jury's finding of unlawful discrimination.... Specifically, the court noted that Chesnut's age-based comments "were not made in the direct context of Reeves's termination"; there was no allegation that the two other individuals who had recommended that petitioner be fired (Jester and Whitaker) were motivated by age; two of the decisionmakers involved in petitioner's discharge (Jester and Sanderson) were over the age of 50; all three of the Hinge Room supervisors were accused of inaccurate recordkeeping; and several of respondent's management positions were filled by persons over age 50 when petitioner was fired. On this basis, the court concluded that petitioner had not introduced sufficient evidence for a rational jury to conclude that he had been discharged because of his age. [In performing this "weighing" of the evidence, the Fifth Circuit followed its previous decision in *Boeing Co. v. Shipman*, 411 F.2d 365 (5th Cir, 1969) (*en banc*), which held that a motion for judgment as a matter of law required review of the entire record, as opposed to consideration of only the evidence favoring the nonmovant.] ...

[Part II of the Court's opinion, dealing with the text and proof structure of the ADEA, is omitted here. After its discussion of the ADEA, the Court turned to the general issue of motions for judgment as a matter of law, in Part III, as follows.]

III A

... Under Rule 50, a court should render judgment as a matter of law when "a party has been fully heard on an issue and there is no legally sufficient evidentiary basis for a reasonable jury to find for that party on that issue." Fed. R. Civ. Proc. 50(a). [The 2007 "restyling" amendments to the Federal Rules of Civil Procedure have changed this language slightly.—Eds.] The Courts of Appeals have articulated differing formulations as to what evidence a court is to consider in ruling on a Rule 50 motion. Some decisions have stated that review is limited to that evidence favorable to the non-moving party, *see, e.g., Aparicio v. Norfolk & Western R. Co.*, 84 F.3d 803, 807 (6th Cir. 1996); *Simpson v. Skelly Oil Co.*, 371 F.2d 563, 566 (8th Cir. 1967), while most have held that review extends to the entire record, drawing all reasonable inferences in favor of the nonmovant, *see, e.g., Tate v. Government Employees Ins. Co.*, 997 F.2d 1433, 1436 (11th Cir. 1993); *Boeing Co. v. Shipman*, 411 F.2d 365, 374 (5th Cir. 1969) (*en banc*).

On closer examination, this conflict seems more semantic than real. Those decisions holding that review under Rule 50 should be limited to evidence favorable to the nonmovant appear to have their genesis in *Wilkerson v. McCarthy*, 336 U.S. 53 (1949). *See* 9A C. Wright & A. Miller, Federal Practice and Procedure § 2529, pp. 297–301 (2d ed. 1995) (hereinafter Wright & Miller). In *Wilkerson*, we stated that "in passing upon whether there is sufficient evidence to submit an issue to the jury we need look only to the evidence and reasonable inferences which tend to support the case of" the nonmoving party. But subsequent decisions have clarified that this passage was referring to the evidence to which the trial court should give credence, not the evidence that the court should review. In the analogous context of summary judgment under Rule 56, we have stated that the court must review the record "taken as a whole." And the standard for granting summary judgment "mirrors" the standard for judgment as a matter of law, such that "the inquiry under each is the same." ... *Celotex Corp. v. Catrett.* It therefore follows that, in entertaining a motion for judgment as a matter of law, the court should review all of the evidence in the record.

In doing so, however, the court must draw all reasonable inferences in favor of the nonmoving party, and it may not make credibility determinations or weigh the evidence. "Credibility determinations, the weighing of the evidence, and the drawing of legitimate inferences from the facts are jury functions, not those of a judge." Thus, although the court should review the record as a whole, it must disregard all evidence favorable to the moving party that the jury is not required to believe. *See* Wright & Miller 299. That is, the court should give credence to the evidence favoring the nonmovant as well as that "evidence supporting the moving party that is uncontradicted and unimpeached, at least to the extent that that evidence comes from disinterested witnesses."

B

Applying this standard here, it is apparent that respondent was not entitled to judgment as a matter of law. In this case, in addition to establishing a prima facie case of discrimination and creating a jury issue as to the falsity of the employer's explanation, petitioner introduced additional evidence that Chesnut was motivated by age-based animus and was principally responsible for petitioner's firing. Petitioner testified that Chesnut had told him that he "was so old [he] must have come over on the Mayflower" and, on one occasion when petitioner was having difficulty starting a machine, that he "was too damn old to do [his] job." According to petitioner, Chesnut would regularly "cuss at me and shake his finger in my face." Oswalt, roughly 24 years younger than petitioner, corroborated that there was an "obvious difference" in how Chesnut treated them. He stated that, although he and Chesnut "had [their] differences," "it was nothing compared to the way [Chesnut] treated Roger." Oswalt explained that Chesnut "tolerated quite a bit" from him even though he "defied" Chesnut "quite often," but that Chesnut treated petitioner "in a manner, as you would . . . treat . . . a child when . . . you're angry with [him]." Petitioner also demonstrated that, according to company records, he and Oswalt had nearly identical rates of productivity in 1993. Yet respondent conducted an efficiency study of only the regular line, supervised by petitioner, and placed only petitioner on probation. Chesnut conducted that efficiency study and, after having testified to the contrary on direct examination, acknowledged on cross-examination that he had recommended that petitioner be placed on probation following the study.

Further, petitioner introduced evidence that Chesnut was the actual decisionmaker behind his firing. Chesnut was married to Sanderson, who made the formal decision to discharge petitioner. Although Sanderson testified that she fired petitioner because he had "intentionally falsified company pay records," respondent only introduced evidence concerning the inaccuracy of the records, not their falsification. A 1994 letter authored by Chesnut indicated that he berated other company directors, who were supposedly his co-equals, about how to do their jobs. Moreover, Oswalt testified that all of respondent's employees feared Chesnut, and that Chesnut had exercised "absolute power" within the company for "as long as [he] can remember."

In holding that the record contained insufficient evidence to sustain the jury's verdict, the Court of Appeals misapplied the standard of review dictated by Rule 50. Again, the court disregarded critical evidence favorable to petitioner—namely, the evidence supporting petitioner's prima facie case and undermining respondent's nondiscriminatory explanation. The court also failed to draw all reasonable inferences in favor of petitioner. For instance, while acknowledging "the potentially damning nature" of Chesnut's age-related comments, the court discounted them on the ground that they "were not made in the direct context of Reeves's termination." And the court discredited petitioner's evidence that Chesnut was the actual decisionmaker by giving weight to the fact that there was "no evidence to suggest that any of the other decision makers were motivated by age." Moreover, the other evidence on which the court relied—that Caldwell and Oswalt were also cited for poor recordkeeping, and that respondent employed many managers over age 50—although relevant, is certainly not dispositive. . . . [T]he Court of Appeals impermissibly substituted its judgment concerning the weight of the evidence for the jury's. [Reversed.]

[The concurring opinion of Justice Ginsburg is omitted.]

W. Dorsaneo, *Reexamining the Right to Jury Trial*

54 SMU L. Rev. 1695 (2001)(*)

[In this article, Professor Dorsaneo explains the impact of the *Reeves* case and the meaning of its holding.] . . .

[T]he *Reeves* Court addressed, and for the most part resolved, longstanding differences among the courts of appeals on the issue of the scope and standard of appellate review of fact findings. The Court explained that some decisions "have stated that review is limited to the evidence favorable to the nonmoving party while most hold that review extends to the entire record." But the Court regarded this distinction as "more semantic than real" and explained that while review of all of the evidence is required to determine a motion for judgment as a matter of law, the trial judge is required to give credence only to the evidence and reasonable inferences that tend to support the finding and to disregard all contrary evidence the jury was not required to believe. This means that the reasonableness of inferences involves a consideration of the evidence as a whole, but not that a reviewing court may make credibility determinations or weigh the evidence . . . .

A clear understanding of the Court's opinion in *Reeves* dictates how whole-record review is properly conducted. First, the whole record is reviewed to identify the direct and circumstantial evidence favoring the party with the burden of proving a particular issue as well as the limited range of evidence the fact finder is required to believe or credit. In the context of circumstantial evidence, this means that a reviewing court must determine from the evidence as a whole whether reasonable inferences can be drawn from the circumstantial evidence in support of the proponent's issue and what those inferences are.

Second, . . . a reviewing court must test the sufficiency of the evidence by "giving credence" only to the evidence that supports an affirmative finding on the proponent's issue and the undisputed evidence the jury was required to believe. By definition, this means that evidence contrary to the finding that the jury was not required to credit, and even reasonable inferences in derogation of the finding are not given credence and otherwise should not be part of the second step in the evaluative process.

The primary reason for this two-step method of whole-record review is for reviewing courts to avoid the temptation to weigh the evidence and make credibility determinations in cases involving conflicts in the direct evidence. . . .

The better view . . . is that if the circumstantial evidence will support more than one reasonable inference, it is for the jury to decide which one is more convincing or more reasonable. The reviewing court's focus should be restricted to an evaluation of the reasonableness of the favorable inference, a matter that does not require the consideration of competing reasonable inferences. . . .

[I]n *Pennsylvania R.R. v. Chamberlain*, [288 U.S. 333,] a Federal Employers' Liability Act (FELA) case decided in 1933, the Supreme Court stated that "where proven facts give equal support to each of two inconsistent inferences; in which event, neither of them being established, judgment, as a matter of law, must go against the party upon whom rests the necessity of sustaining one of these inferences." . . .

[T]he "equal inferences rule" [of *Chamberlain*] is not merely unnecessary, it is actually quite harmful. In the hands of a reviewing judge who wants to violate the jury's province so as to impose his or her own idiosyncratic preferences on the case, the "equal inferences rule" provides an ideal tool. The abuse-of-power demons on the judge's shoulder need only whisper, "Just declare that the inferences are 'equal,' even if to do so requires an application of experience that our system entrusts to the jury." This is, in fact, what the Fifth Circuit panel did in *Reeves* . . . .

VI. Jury Argument

Note on Legitimate Functions of Jury Argument

When the evidence is concluded, the case must be submitted to the jury. Jury argument by the opposing lawyers is a part of that process. Before considering jury argument, it will be useful to consider why it is included in a trial. What purposes does it serve?

Rational Analysis of Evidence in Light of the Law. The rational component of jury argument implies at least three separate functions. (1) Argument should help the jury better understand the court's charge, which may contain such confusing concepts as "proximate cause" or "promissory estoppel," by illustrating it with simple examples. (2) Counsel on both sides may legitimately use argument to select, arrange, and interpret those portions of the evidence that are relevant to their theories. (3) Counsel may guide the jury in judging the credibility of witnesses. *Cf.* Crump, *The Function and Limits of Prosecution Jury Argument*, 28 Sw. L.J. 505, 506-09 (1974).

Emotional or Social Policy Arguments. Emotionally based argument creates more difficult problems, but there are instances in which it is appropriate. (1) It can legitimately give the jury the determination to ignore prejudicial distractions, which may themselves be emotionally rooted and incapable of removal by logic. (2) It may properly remind the jury to take both sides of the case seriously. (3) It can assist the jury in setting community and social standards by which to resolve questions of degree that are at the heart of virtually every case. When a jury is asked whether the defendant's conduct was "negligent" or whether a contractual breach was "substantial," it is required to combine legal and factual elements with issues of policy that cannot be answered without exploration of societal values. *Id.*

The Pressures Toward Improper Argument. In an adversary context, these legitimate functions do not always prevail. Attorneys may perceive advantage in misrepresenting the law, injecting prejudicial matter, arguing matters outside of the evidence, or making inflammatory personal attacks. Striking a balance between these abuses and the beneficial effects of sound adversary argument has long been a difficult problem for the courts. *See* Carlson, *Argument to the Jury: Passion, Persuasion, and Legal Controls*, 33 St. Louis U. L.J. 787 (1989).

Tran v. Arellano

2011 WL 1548344, 2011 Cal. App. Unpub. LEXIS 3004
(Cal. App. April 21, 2011) (unpublished non-citable opinion)

McIntyre, J.

Defendant Leonel Arellano appeals from a judgment on special verdict awarding plaintiff Bun Bun Tran damages of $23,370,747 for severe brain injuries he suffered in a collision between his car and Arellano's truck. The accident occurred when Arellano ran a stop sign while speeding and driving intoxicated and struck the driver's door of Tran's car. Arellano contends the jury's verdict was the result of passion and prejudice resulting from erroneous evidentiary rulings, erroneous jury instructions, and improper closing argument by Tran's counsel. We affirm.

[The court first rejects Arellano's complaints based on evidence and instruction issues, finding each one either not error or not reversible error. It then turns to Arellano's arguments based upon Tran's final arguments to the jury.]

III. *Closing Argument*

A. *"Golden Rule" argument*

Arellano contends he was prejudiced when Tran's counsel twice made a prohibited "golden rule" argument during his closing statement. Prohibited golden rule argument is argument "by which counsel asks the jurors to place themselves in the plaintiff's shoes and to award such damages as they would 'charge' to undergo equivalent pain and suffering." (*Beagle v. Vasold* (1966) 65 Cal.2d 166, 182, fn. 11.) ...

Arellano claims Tran's counsel first violated the prohibition against golden rule argument by stating the following: "I think we've all heard this passage. [¶] First they came for the Jews, and I did not speak out because I was not a Jew. Then they came for the Communists, and I did not speak out because I was not a Communist. Then they came for the trade unions, and I did not speak out because I was not a trade union. Then they came for me, and there was no one left to speak out for me.

[¶] If you accept that this man is vegetative, and no work should be done to teach him how to communicate again, the same insensitivity some day will be visited upon you and your loved ones, because our society accepts what we tolerate."

This portion of counsel's closing argument is not a ground for reversal because Arellano's counsel did not object to it or request an admonition. (*Brokopp v. Ford Motor Co.* (1977) 71 Cal.App.3d 841, 860 [golden rule argument was not preserved for appeal because counsel failed to object to the argument or request an admonition].) . . . Curing misconduct error by admonishing a jury is possible when the "'error is isolated and unemphasized, [but] an attempt to rectify repeated and resounding misconduct by admonition is . . . like trying to unring a bell.'" (*Neumann v. Bishop* (1976) 59 Cal.App.3d 451, 469, fn. 5.)

Arellano contends that Tran's counsel committed a second golden rule violation by stating: "Would anyone, anyone put—exchange life with Bun Tran?" Arellano's counsel immediately objected stating, "Golden Rule" as the ground for the objection. The court sustained the objection and Arellano's counsel immediately moved to strike the improper argument. The court granted the motion to strike. Arellano's counsel did not request an admonition.

Counsel's rhetorical question whether anyone would exchange life with Tran was a single isolated and unemphasized remark; it was not repeated and was not sufficiently egregious to constitute "resounding misconduct" as to which an admonishment would have been ineffective. . . .

B. *Insurance reference*

Finally, Arellano contends that Tran's counsel committed prejudicial misconduct by implying in closing argument that Arellano was financially able to pay a multimillion dollar verdict through insurance. Tran's counsel stated: "My client needs compensation for the rest of his dear human life. Arellano is the most appropriate and the best source. [¶] You cannot speculate, as the Court said, on funding. But we are here, I am here, because I know who the real cause is, and I know my client needs compensation." Arellano did not object to these statements at the time Tran's counsel made them. However, the next day, outside of the jury's presence, he moved for a mistrial based Tran's counsel's reference to "funding." The court denied the motion.

Putting aside Arellano's failure to immediately object to the statements in question and request an admonition, we conclude that the statements by Tran's counsel, although ill-advised, were not prejudicial. Counsel did not expressly state that Arellano had insurance coverage that would cover the jury's award of damages; he merely hinted at the existence of such coverage.

We believe that jurors ordinarily would assume that a driver with the financial means to pay for insurance is insured even if there is no explicit mention of insurance at trial. Absent aggravating circumstances, the brief mention of [insurance] . . . is very unlikely to cause the jury to conclude either that the plaintiff will be fully compensated for his injuries by insurance or that the defendant should be relieved of liability for any reason. Considering the evidence of the permanency and extent of Tran's injury, we conclude it is not reasonably probable that Arellano would have obtained a more favorable verdict absent the alleged misconduct of Tran's counsel. . . .

Brokopp v. Ford Motor Co.

71 Cal. App. 3d 841, 139 Cal. Rptr. 888 (4th Dist. 1977)

KAUFMAN, ASSOCIATE JUSTICE.

In this action to recover damages for personal injuries sustained in a single-vehicle accident, defendant Ford Motor Company ("Ford") appeals from a judgment entered upon a jury verdict in favor of plaintiffs Robert and Carol Brokopp ("plaintiffs") in the amount of $3,010,000. . . .

Misconduct of Counsel

Ford contends that, in arguing to the jury, counsel for plaintiffs was guilty of several acts of prejudicial misconduct, to wit: (1) he made a variant of the "golden rule" argument; (2) he made an appeal to the sympathy of the jury based on Ford's size and corporate status; (3) he expressed his personal opinion on the credibility of several of Ford's expert witnesses; (4) he made an appeal to the self-interest of the jurors as taxpayers; and (5) he argued a matter not in evidence and, indeed, contrary to all of the pertinent expert testimony. Although in all but one instance we agree that the substance of Ford's charges is correct, Ford is foreclosed from asserting these defects as grounds for reversal because it failed to make an adequate record below. Misconduct of counsel may not be urged as a ground for reversal absent both timely objection and request for admonition in the trial court. . . .

In his opening argument plaintiff's counsel made a number of statements from which the jury might have inferred it was proper in calculating damages to place themselves in Mr. Brokopp's shoes and award the amount they would "charge" to undergo equivalent disability, pain and suffering. This so-called "golden rule" argument . . . is impermissible.

But Ford's counsel neither objected to the statements nor requested any admonition. . . .

Counsel for plaintiffs also argued: "Save a buck, and that is the only reason I can think of why they would handle things the way they do. These large corporations, in effect, crippled Bob; they took his manhood away from him; they took his privacy from him; they took his body away from him; and they left him in pain. . . ."

Appeals to the sympathy of the jury based on the size or corporate status of a defendant are improper. However, Ford failed to object to this argument and requested no admonition.

In argument, counsel for plaintiffs also stated: "You know, in this trial, I never have had more evasive witnesses than Mr. Valant and Mr. Brink. I just never have seen witnesses as Mr. Valant and Mr. Brink who just would not answer a question."

Ford characterizes this as a statement of counsel's personal opinion on the credibility of these witnesses. We believe not. An attorney is permitted to argue all reasonable inferences from the evidence, and may with propriety comment on the demeanor of a witness indicating recalcitrance.

Moreover, again, Ford lodged no objection and requested no admonition with respect to this statement.

Counsel for plaintiffs also told the jury: "Bob doesn't have to stay at the V.A. hospital. I don't think that we, the taxpayers, ought to pay for Bob in preference to Ford, if they are liable." An appeal to the jurors' self-interest as taxpayers constitutes misconduct. . . . Although Ford objected to this statement, it failed to secure a definitive ruling and requested no admonition. Any impropriety could easily have been remedied by a prompt and proper admonition.

Ford's contention that plaintiff's counsel argued a matter not in evidence arises out of the following situation. It was important to plaintiffs' theory that the power steering belt came off its pulley while the pulley was in motion and not as a result of the crash. All the experts, including those called by plaintiffs, agreed that there were no marks on the belt from which it could be determined that the belt came off a moving pulley. Nevertheless, in his argument, counsel for plaintiffs insisted that he could see marks on the belt, implied that these marks indicated the belt had come off a moving pulley, and started to mark the belt with a yellow crayon. . . . Ford's counsel [objected]. The judge thereupon removed the crayon marks from the belt and ordered plaintiffs' counsel not to mark any exhibits. Proceedings were then resumed before the jury, and plaintiffs' counsel proceeded with his argument during which he told the jury that, if they would hold the belt down in the light, they would see two faint lines. No further objection, motion to strike, or request for admonition was interposed by the defense.

Ford urges that, although the belt was in evidence, there was no evidence whatever that any marks on the belt indicated the belt came off a moving pulley. Ford is correct. The belt was in evidence and counsel could argue that there were marks visible on it. It was improper, however, to suggest to the jury that these marks indicated the belt came off a moving pulley. While an attorney may argue all reasonable inferences from the evidence . . . it is misconduct to argue matters not in evidence or to assert as fact matters allegedly within counsel's personal knowledge. . . .

However, that was not the thrust of the defense objection. Although this particular portion of the argument covers several pages of transcript, it was not until plaintiffs' counsel started marking the belt with yellow crayon that the defense objected, and the trial court justifiably understood the objection as being against counsel's marking the exhibit. This impropriety the trial court corrected. Argument thereafter resumed without further objection or any request for admonition by defense counsel. The impropriety now asserted was waived. . . . [Affirmed.]

Notes and Questions

(1) *The Varieties of Improper Jury Argument.* Improper argument usually falls into one or more of the following categories:

(a) *Appeals to Improper Prejudice: Texas Employers Ins. Ass'n v. Haywood*, 266 S.W.2d 856 (Tex. 1954). In this case, reversal resulted because the defendant's attorney argued that witnesses were not credible because they were African-American and said, "Why then didn't they . . . bring some white fellow that you could see and know was telling the truth?" Even without objection, the Court reversed, holding the argument "incurable." Similar kinds of arguments, based upon race, religion, national origin, or other invidious distinctions, can be found in the digests of decisions in every state. *Cf. Cherry Creek National Bank v. Fidelity & Cas. Co.*, 207 A.D. 787, 202 N.Y.S. 611 (4th Dep't 1924). Generally, arguments against a party because of wealth, or because it is a corporation, are similarly improper; *but see Wayte v. Rollins International, Inc.*, 169 Cal. App. 3d 1, 215 Cal. Rptr. 59, (2d Dist. 1985) (defendant could argue about wealth of defendant corporations because it was relevant to punitive damages).

But argument is not improper merely because it is hard-hitting or emotional, provided that it is related to the issues and is not based upon invidious categories. *See Leonard & Harral Packing Co. v. Hahn*, 571 S.W.2d 201 (Tex. Civ. App.-San Antonio 1978, writ ref'd n.r.e.) (in suit for wrongful death of young wife, plaintiff's attorney's argument on damages, including recitation of marriage vows and reference to popular song titles such as "Just Me and My Shadow" and "Little Things Mean a Lot," were not improper appeals to prejudice; attorney not required to be "apathetic").

(b) *Diverting the Jury from Following the Law: Wank v. Richman & Garrett*, 165 Cal. App. 3d 1103, 211 Cal. Rptr. 919 (2d Dist. 1985). In this case, the court had ordered separate trials on liability and damages. Defendant's attorney made several remarks suggesting to jurors that they should decide the liability trial against the plaintiff so they could avoid the separate damage trial, including the remark that jurors would have to come back and "sit for eight weeks" to decide the damage issues. The court concluded that these remarks were error, but declined to reverse. Such an argument (like the "golden rule" argument, disapproved in *Tran v. Arellano,* above) is improper because it urges the jury to decide the case on a different standard than the legal standard contained in the court's instructions.

A similar, but more controversial, issue is presented by "per diem" arguments, in which the plaintiff's attorney breaks down units of time and multiplies them by dollar figures to obtain very large amounts as suggested pain-and-suffering verdicts. Some states (*e.g.*, California) rigidly confine these arguments, but other states (*e.g.*, Texas) permit them. In any event, it is not improper for counsel to explain the law to the jury, by using simple examples or translations into everyday language. *E.g., State v. Haire*, 334 S.W.2d 488 (Tex. Civ. App.-Austin 1960, writ ref'd n.r.e.) (explanation of definition of market value, in jury argument in which attorney constructed hypothetical situation for jury, not improper).

(c) *Remarks Outside the Record and Not Inferable from It: Howard v. Faberge, Inc.*, 679 S.W.2d 644 (Tex. App.-Houston [1st Dist.] 1984 writ ref'd n.r.e.). In this product liability suit, the plaintiff claimed to have been burned by the defendant's product. In order to show that the plaintiff's theory was impossible, the defendant's attorney, during his jury argument, poured the product on his arm and attempted to light it, saying, "God, if I am wrong, burn me," adding that he had "tried a hundred times" without it burning. The court reversed without an objection, holding the argument incurable, since it injected facts not in evidence or subject to cross-examination.

But attorneys are given very broad latitude in making any reasonable inference from the evidence, even if it is not the only possible inference. Credibility arguments are an example. Counsel can properly state that a witness is not believable based upon the evidence, including such support as conflicting witnesses, conflicts within the witness's own testimony, demeanor, motive, or other factors. The attorney is even allowed some degree of poetic license—for hyperbole or literary allusion. Thus, in *Standard Fire Ins. Co. v. Reese*, 584 S.W.2d 835 (Tex. 1979), the Court held that the evidence authorized the defendant's lawyer's inference that the plaintiff's lawyer had sent him to a particular physician to inflate the damages and that the plaintiff had "driven past a thousand doctors." The court quoted Shakespeare (*Romeo and Juliet*: "A thousand times good night!") and John Milton ("Thousands at his bidding speed, and post o'er land and ocean without rest") to hold that counsel's figure of speech was legitimate argument, even though "a thousand doctors" might have been an exaggeration. *See* Levitt, *Rhetoric in Closing Argument*, 17 Litigation 25 (Winter 1991).

(d) *Invective and Arguments Ad Hominem: Wetherbee v. United Ins. Co. of America*, 265 Cal. App. 2d 921, 71 Cal. Rptr. 764 (1968). Harsh rhetoric about credibility and conduct is not inappropriate if it is supported by the evidence. When it lacks support in the evidence, however, harsh invective is likely to be error. In *Wetherbee*, the insured's counsel argued that the case was one of "mass fraud." The court held this remark unwarranted by the fact that a letter received by the insured was a form letter, in the absence of a showing that similar letters went to other policyholders or were relied upon by them. *See also Fortenberry v. Fortenberry*, 582 S.W.2d 188 (Tex. Civ. App.-Beaumont 1979, writ ref'd n.r.e.) (reference to will proponents as "vultures circling in the air" above the testatrix, held improper).

(2) *"Preservation" of Error in Jury Argument Is Difficult, and Reversal Is Not Common.* To preserve error in jury argument for appeal requires extraordinary diligence, because an objection, followed by a request for admonition (an instruction to disregard), must be made at the time. Furthermore, frequent objection may be tactically unwise in some jurisdictions, because objections may be required to be done in the jury's presence. The doctrines of "cured" or "harmless" error probably result in the affirmance of the majority of cases in which argument is held improper, as *Tran v. Arellano* shows.

(3) *The Timing of Jury Argument: Before or After Court's Charge.* In some jurisdictions, jury argument by counsel is first and the court's charge follows afterward.

Perhaps this order of proceeding puts the cart before the horse. How can counsel effectively argue to the jury how the court's instructions should be applied, if the court hasn't given the instructions yet? The Federal Rules address this problem by requiring the judge to rule on counsel's objections and requested charges to the jury before argument, even though the court's charge may be given after counsel's argument. This provision does not completely solve the problem, however, because counsel may be required to argue the case without quite knowing what the court is going to say to the jury. Thus, some courts allow counsel to address argument to the jury after the court's charge. Current Federal Rules give the judge discretion to do this. Is this approach better, or does it have its own disadvantages?

(4) *The Right to Open and Close the Final Jury Arguments: A Powerful Plaintiff's Advantage.* It is customary in most jurisdictions for the party with the burden of proof on the whole case (usually the plaintiff) to open and close the argument. In other words, the plaintiff argues first; the defendant argues next; and the plaintiff, finally, is allowed time for rebuttal. This sequence gives the plaintiff a powerful forensic advantage. The plaintiff can unleash her most emotional argument as the last word the jury hears before retiring. Also, the plaintiff has the opportunity to rebut the defendant's last argument, but the defendant does not have that right with respect to the plaintiff's final argument. Is there a better way? (Many jurisdictions theoretically confine the plaintiff's rebuttal argument to matters raised in the preceding two arguments, but that is not much of a limitation in most cases.)

VII. Jury Instructions and Verdicts

[A] The General Charge versus Special Interrogatories

Read Fed. R. Civ. P. 49 (special verdicts and interrogatories).

Note on the Two Basic Forms of Verdicts

The General Charge. There are two distinct methods of submitting a case to the jury. One is the "general charge," which involves instructing the jury on all applicable principles of law and asking it a single question: Who wins? If the verdict is for the plaintiff, a second finding may be necessary, for the amount of damages. It might be said that a general charge involves one single, long question. In a negligence case, for example, the jury might be instructed on such principles as the significance of negligence and proximate causation, the treatment of contributory negligence, the proper measure of damages, and the proof standard. But the jury would make no discrete fact findings.

The Charge with Special Verdicts. The other method of submission is by "special verdicts." The judge asks the jury factual questions: who was negligent, was the negligence a proximate cause of the occurrence, etc. The jury must be given definitions of terms (such as negligence or proximate cause), but it need not be told the significance of its answers, and it need not consider who is to win. The special verdict system is virtually the exclusive method of submission in some states. It sometimes happens that the jury does not even know who has won after it renders its verdict.

Discretionary, Mixed Systems (California; Federal). In some jurisdictions, both methods are in use. California, for example, affords the trial judge discretion. The federal system does also; Rule 49 effectively allows the judge to choose between special verdicts, the general charge, or both together.

The Advantages and Disadvantages of Each System. As is often the case with choices among procedural alternatives, both types of charge have advantages and disadvantages. Special verdicts are said to impose a logical structure on the jury's responses, requiring the jurors to "think with their heads rather than with their hearts." Prejudicial distractions, such as which party is more attractive personally, are reduced by the focus of the charge on factual issues, rather than upon who wins. Also, the special-verdict charge gives a record of the jury's fact findings. The trial judge renders judgment in accordance with the law, and if some of the findings are unsupported on the evidence, that outcome is not concealed as it would be with the general charge. If one of the claims or defenses is invalid as a matter of law, but others are valid, the appellate court may not need to reverse (as it would in the case of a general charge).

On the other hand, the special-verdict charge can be criticized because, in some cases, it makes too much depend upon a single word or set of words in a single question. It has great potential for misleading the jury about what is being asked. As a result, attorneys haggle over every nuance—sometimes over every comma—in the questions. And there are some kinds of claims that are difficult to split into a series of questions about the "elements," because they are made up of different factors that have to be weighed against each other. Finally, the champions of the general charge point out that the jury is not a mere factual computer. The general charge permits "play in the joints" so that the jury can round out the rough edges of the substantive law and temper its unfairness—which is a traditional function ascribed to the jury.

Broad Special Verdicts, Blending into a General Charge. The above discussion treats these two approaches as though they were polar opposites. But with special verdicts, it is possible to break the case down into fine, discrete parts—or it is possible to ask broad, general questions, each combining several elements. For example, if the first interrogatory is "Whose negligence, if any, proximately caused the occurrence in question," and the second is, "In what percentage did each party's causal negligence, if any, contribute to the occurrence?" and the third interrogatory inquires about damages, the charge technically may be a "special verdict" charge—but it is very close to a general charge, in effect. Different jurisdictions have different approaches to the breadth or narrowness of the submissions that customarily are used.

How to Read the Case of McLaughlin v. Fellows Gear Shaper Co.

In the case that follows, the trial judge used both a general verdict and a verdict on special interrogatories, in combination. But the answers the jury returns are inconsistent. What is to be done when that happens? If the special verdict answers are consistent with each other, Rule 49 says that the judge can (1) ignore the general verdict and grant judgment on the special verdicts. Alternatively, she can (2) send the jury back to deliberate further or (3) grant a new trial. If the special verdicts are inconsistent with each other, the court is supposed to send the jury back to deliberate or grant a new trial. Here, the trial judge instead sent the jury back with more questions—and the result, including the trial judge's treatment of it, is confusing (and, even in the final analysis, a little unclear). In the process of comparing the analyses done by the majority and the dissent of this aberrational conduct by the trial judge, you will learn something about the advantages and disadvantages of both kinds of charges.

McLaughlin v. Fellows Gear Shaper Co.

786 F.2d 592 (3d Cir. 1986)

Mansmann, Circuit Judge.

I.

This is a Pennsylvania diversity action in which plaintiffs were successful in recovering damages under the strict liability theory of Section 402A of the Restatement of Torts for personal injury caused by defectively designed machinery. On appeal, defendants have raised several trial errors, chiefly, that the district court erred in resubmitting the foreseeability issue to the jury and in *sua sponte* setting aside the jury's finding of assumption of the risk. Finding no merit in any of the allegations raised, we affirm.

II.

[Plaintiff Wilbur McLaughlin was manually doing "setup" on a hobbing machine (a machine that cuts indentations in metal to make gears) by standing on top of it and rotating it. When he engaged the machinery by lowering the "collar" of the device onto the workpiece, it amputated his left thumb.]

[Plaintiffs' theory of liability was that the machine should have had an "interlock" or automatic shutoff. The defendant had two theories of defense. First, it claimed that the absence of an automatic shutoff did not make it responsible for McLaughlin's injuries, since the law required only that it make its product safe for foreseeable uses, whereas McLaughlin's injury had been caused by his standing on the machine, which the defendant claimed was unforeseeable misuse. Secondly, defendant argued that McLaughlin had assumed the risk, which would provide an affirmative defense to liability.]

[The court, in the exercise of its discretion under Rule 49, determined that it should submit both a general charge and special interrogatories to the jury. The verdict sheet consisted of four interrogatories on liability, plus an interrogatory on damages. The effect of the trial judge's instructions was that a positive answer to the damage interrogatory would be both a finding of the amount of damages and, also, a general verdict for plaintiff on liability.]

... The [five] interrogatories and the jury's answers [to them] were as follows:

> **1.** When the hobbing machine was delivered [from Defendant] . . . , was it in a defective condition rendering it unsafe for its intended use?
>
> Yes X No ____________________
>
> **2.** If so, was the defective condition of the hobbing machine a proximate cause of the accident and plaintiff's injury?
>
> Yes X No ____________________
>
> **3.** Was it foreseeable to the manufacturer that operators would, on occasion, stand on the machine while carrying out the setting-up process?
>
> Yes ____________________ No X
>
> **4.** Did plaintiff assume the risk?
>
> Yes X No ____________________
>
> **5.** (To be completed only if your verdict is in favor of plaintiffs.)
>
> We, the jury, award damages as follows:
>
> Mr. McLaughlin $100,000
>
> Mrs. McLaughlin $20,000

Upon learning the jury's answers, defendants moved for entry of judgment in their favor, and plaintiffs moved for a mistrial. The district court denied both requests. Instead, the court submitted two additional questions to the jury to clarify the foreseeability question, in particular, to determine the effect of McLaughlin's standing on the machine during the time it was being set up for operation. The supplemental interrogatories and answers were as follows:

> **3(a)** Was the fact that plaintiff stood on the machine a substantial factor in causing the accident?
>
> Yes ____________________ No X
>
> **(b)** Was it the sole cause of the accident?
>
> Yes ____________________ No X

After ascertaining that the jury was unanimous in its answers to these supplemental interrogatories, the district court asked the following questions of the jury in open court and received the following responses:

> THE COURT: Finally, members of the jury, by the answers that you have given, is it your intention to find in favor of the plaintiffs or in favor of the defendant? Can somebody state what you have in mind?
>
> [THE FOREPERSON]: Plaintiff.

> THE COURT: You all agree you intend to find in favor of the plaintiffs in the sum of $120,000?
>
> (The jury answered in the affirmative.)

Subsequently, the district court set aside the jury's finding of assumption of the risk and entered judgment in favor of the plaintiffs in the amount of $135,879.45, including delay damages. Defendants' subsequent motions for judgment notwithstanding the verdict and for a new trial were denied by the district court.

III.

Defendants' first argument faults the procedural course of the case. Specifically, defendants contend that the district court erred when it determined that the answers to the special interrogatories were inconsistent and when it set aside the jury's finding of assumption of the risk and entered judgment for plaintiffs, which defendants characterize as an entry of judgment n.o.v. in favor of plaintiffs on this issue. Given the record in this case, two things are clear: first, the district court followed the procedure for general verdicts and interrogatories outlined in Federal Rule of Civil Procedure 49(b) and second, this case does not involve a judgment n.o.v. and so does not turn upon the procedural dictates of Federal Rule of Civil Procedure 50 which governs motions for directed verdict and for judgment notwithstanding the verdict. For these reasons, we find defendants' first argument to be unpersuasive.

A. Rule 49(b)

When assessing [the] jury findings, the district court observed in its . . . opinion:

> Obviously, these answers were inconsistent with each other. Under the instructions of the court, the jury could not have found in favor of the plaintiffs and thus awarded them damages, while at the same time finding that plaintiff had assumed the risk. And it was equally apparent that the true import of the jury's answer to the third question could not be determined, because of the unfortunate incompleteness in the wording of the question. The finding that plaintiff's "misuse" of the machine was not foreseeable would absolve the defendants from liability if, but only if, there was a causal connection between the manner in which plaintiff was conducting the set-up operation, (*i.e.*, the misuse of the product) and the happening of the accident—and the jury had not been asked to make a finding on that subject.

Accordingly, at the time of trial, the district court submitted to the jury two supplemental interrogatories in order to clarify the effect of McLaughlin's standing on the hobbing machine while he was preparing it for operation. On this point the district court offered the following explanation:

> . . . If they find it was the sole cause of the accident, and it was not foreseeable, then I think certainly it is a defendants' verdict. And obviously if their finding of assumption of risk stands up that would be a defendants' verdict. . . .

Defendants complain that the district court was required by the Seventh Amendment to reconcile the inconsistencies in the original five jury interrogatories. Moreover, defendants contend that the answers to these five interrogatories were not inconsistent, that they could be reconciled and that a defense verdict was mandated.

In *Atlantic & Gulf Stevedores, Inc. v. Ellerman Lines, Ltd.*, 369 U.S. 355 (1962), the Supreme Court of the United States held:

> Where there is a view of the case that makes the jury's answers to special interrogatories consistent, they must be resolved that way. For a search for one possible view of the case which will make the jury's finding inconsistent results in a collision with the Seventh Amendment [which prohibits "reexamination" by the Court of a jury verdict except as allowed at common law.] . . .

In the case before us, however, the answers are inconsistent on their face and cannot be read to be consistent. Answers to the first and second questions are inconsistent with the answers to the third and fourth* questions. Moreover, the answers to the third and fourth questions are inconsistent with the general verdict in favor of plaintiffs. Recognizing this, the district court gave the jury further instructions and two supplemental questions and asked it to return for further deliberations. The district court did not redetermine the facts as found by the jury but rather asked the jury to reconsider its decision. In this there can be no Seventh Amendment violation.

Moreover, the decision to seek clarification from the jury in order to resolve the apparent conflict in the answers to the five original interrogatories is precisely what Rule 49(b) of the Federal Rules of Civil Procedure prescribes in such a situation, and the district court cannot be faulted for having followed it. In relevant part Rule 49(b) states [that the court] "*may return the jury for further consideration* of its answers and verdict or may order a new trial." (emphasis supplied). . . .

B. Judgment N.O.V.

[The defendant argues that the jury's initial finding of assumption of the risk should have been controlling, and that in refusing to follow it, the trial court granted an improper "judgment notwithstanding the verdict," or "judgment n.o.v.," for the plaintiff. The rules require that a party must move for directed verdict during trial before being entitled to move for judgment notwithstanding the verdict after. But the plaintiff did not move for directed verdict.]

[The appellate court rejects this argument. It holds that the trial judge did not grant a "judgment notwithstanding the verdict" at all. At the time the judge received the final verdict of the jury, what he received was the general verdict. The plaintiff,

---

* [Eds. Note: Is the majority wrong about the fourth question? Couldn't a jury conclude that a defective product (question 1) was a cause of the accident (question 2), but that a given plaintiff assumed the risk (question 4)?]

under this verdict, had prevailed. The plaintiff had no need to file a motion for judgment notwithstanding the verdict to get the judge to set aside the assumption-of-the-risk finding. In fact, he would have had no right to have the trial judge consider such a motion if he filed it, because the assumption-of-the-risk finding no longer was any part of the case—the jury impliedly had invalidated it. The trial judge therefore was correct in ignoring the assumption of the risk finding, because it no longer existed, and what the judge actually did was to render judgment on the verdict.]

[The appellate court bolsters this reasoning by analyzing the evidence of assumption of the risk. The evidence showed only that McLaughlin engaged the machine through inattention and inadvertence. There was no evidence from which the jury could have concluded that he "consciously or willingly accepted the risk of having his thumb amputated." As a matter of law, this evidence would not have supported a finding of assumption of risk. The court concludes:]

We have reviewed the district court's entire charge to the jury, especially that portion dealing with assumption of risk, and conclude that the court fully explained the legal principles which the jury was to apply in rendering its decision. We must only assume that the jury, hearing all of this, understood the charge and accordingly rendered a [general] verdict for plaintiffs. Having received a verdict in their favor, plaintiffs were not in a position to be seeking judgment n.o.v. . . .

The finding by the jury on the assumption of the risk issue was contrary to the evidence, and it was, therefore, appropriately set aside by the district court. Moreover, it was appropriate for the district court to enter judgment in favor of plaintiffs. . . . [Affirmed.]

ADAMS, CIRCUIT JUDGE, dissenting.

I respectfully dissent because the majority in affirming the district court has sanctioned a violation of Rule 49(b) of the Federal Rules of Civil Procedure as well as a transgression of the time-honored rule of this Court, bottomed largely on the Seventh Amendment to the Constitution, that before judgment notwithstanding the verdict may be granted there must be a motion for a directed verdict. . . .

[The majority] reasons that the "resubmission" of additional special interrogatories was permissible under Federal Rule of Civil Procedure 49(b) [s]ince the jury's initial answers to special interrogatories were inconsistent with each other and with the general verdict. It further concludes that the trial judge did not err in setting aside the jury's finding of assumption of risk because that action did not amount to granting a judgment notwithstanding the verdict and thus was not governed by the procedural strictures of Federal Rule of Civil Procedure 50(b). . . .

I disagree that this case involves a matter of resubmission to the jury of inconsistent answers to special interrogatories. The special findings of the jury, both before and after the trial court submitted the supplemental questions, were reconcilable with one another. Although the findings by the jury were plainly inconsistent with the general verdict for plaintiffs, both the Seventh Amendment and Fed. R. Civ.

P. 49(b) prohibit a federal court from choosing from among a jury's findings those that will be set aside and those that will be given effect. Under Fed. R. Civ. P. 49(b), when a jury's answers to special interrogatories are consistent with each other but inconsistent with the general verdict, the court may either request the jury to reconsider all of its answers, enter a judgment consistent with the jury's special findings, or grant a new trial. Even if the special findings of the jury in this case were inconsistent with one another, the appropriate course of action under Rule 49(b) was to order a new trial or to resubmit *all* of the answers to the jury to allow it to reconcile them itself.

Furthermore, the procedure employed in the district court violated the clear-cut requirement stated in Federal Rule of Civil Procedure 50(b) and emphasized in numerous opinions by this Court that a grant of judgment n.o.v. must be preceded by a motion for a directed verdict specifically identifying the ground upon which judgment n.o.v. is requested. This rule serves important practical purposes in ensuring that neither party is precluded from presenting the most persuasive case possible and in preventing unfair surprise after a matter has been submitted to the jury. More importantly, the rule has constitutional underpinnings in the Seventh Amendment's guarantee that "no fact tried by a jury, shall be otherwise re-examined in any court of the United States, than according to the rules of the common law."

. . . I would vacate the judgment for plaintiffs and order . . . a new trial. . . .

Notes and Questions

(1) *Does the Dissent Have It Right (And if so, Is There any Way to Defend the Majority's Affirmance)?* In terms of hard analysis of the Rules, the dissent seems very persuasive. First, isn't the dissent right in concluding that the special verdicts were not inconsistent? Isn't it entirely possible that the machine was defective, and that the defect was a proximate cause of the occurrence, but, at the same time, the plaintiff's assumption of the risk was a cause too? Secondly, wasn't the trial judge precluded from "setting aside" the assumption of risk finding, since he could only do that by granting a motion for judgment n.o.v., which the plaintiff was not entitled to make since he had not made a motion for directed verdict?

But perhaps the majority's opinion can be defended thus: After they were sent back to deliberate, the jurors agreed once again on the general verdict in the plaintiff's favor, and that was the verdict they reported (orally) at the end of the proceedings, tacitly reversing their assumption-of-the-risk finding. The trouble is, first, the jury never changed its written finding that the plaintiff assumed the risk, and second, the majority repeatedly refers to the trial judge's action as "setting aside" the finding. Certainly, the trial judge couldn't set it aside just because he wanted to, could he? *See* Comment, *Special Verdicts: Rule 49 of the Federal Rules of Civil Procedure*, 74 Yale L.J. 483 (1965).

(2) *Did the Jury Understand the Charge?* The jury returned a special verdict of assumption of risk that the majority says cannot be reasonably inferred from the

evidence. And it returned a general verdict that obviously was inconsistent with the finding of assumption of risk. Isn't it clear that the jury misunderstood the charge? For an excellent treatment of the problem of jury misunderstanding of the charge, see Tanford, *The Law and Psychology of Jury Instructions*, 69 NEB. L. REV. 71 (1990).

(3) *General Verdict, Special Verdicts, or Both—Which Is Best?* What does this case tell you about the relative advantages of the various types of verdicts? It might be argued that the jury's inconsistent actions support the use of special verdicts, because they make the jury focus on the facts rather than jumping to conclusions that may be at variance with the facts. But it also might be argued that if the judge had submitted only a general verdict, he would have kept the jury from getting bogged down in minutiae that they were unlikely to understand. *See* Sunderland, *Verdicts, General and Special*, 29 YALE L.J. 253 (1920).

Problem C

SPECIAL INTERROGATORIES AND VERDICTS IN HOWARD v. BACHMAN. In this intersection collision case, the court's charge and the verdict included the following:

> QUESTION NO. 1: On the occasion in question, did Bruce F. Bachman:
>
> (a) Fail to keep such a lookout as a person using ordinary care would have done? Answer: No.
>
> (b) Drive at a greater rate of speed than a person using ordinary care would have driven? Answer: Yes. . . .
>
> If you have answered any subdivision of Question No. 1 "yes," and only in that event, then answer the corresponding subdivision of Question No. 2.
>
> QUESTION NO. 2: Was such act or omission a proximate cause of the occurrence in question with respect to:
>
> (a) Failure to keep . . . a lookout . . . ? Answer: [Unanswered.]
>
> (b) Driving at a greater rate of speed than a person using ordinary care would have driven? Answer: No. . . .
>
> QUESTION NO. 3: On the occasion in question, did Ollie B. Howard:
>
> (a) Fail to keep such a lookout as a person using ordinary care would have kept? Answer: Yes.
>
> (b) Fail to yield the right of way to the vehicle driven by Bruce Bachman? Answer: Yes.
>
> [An instruction setting forth and explaining a state statute requiring observance of the right of way is omitted here.]
>
> If you have answered any subdivision of Question 3 "yes," and only in that event, then answer the corresponding subdivision of Question No. 4.

QUESTION NO. 4: Was such act or omission a proximate cause of the occurrence with respect to:

(a) Failure to keep . . . a lookout . . . ? Answer: No.

(b) Failure to yield the right of way to Bruce Bachman as that term is above defined? Answer: Yes.

QUESTION NO. 5: What percentage of the negligence that caused the occurrence do you find from a preponderance of the evidence to be attributable to each of the parties found by you to have been negligent? . . . [Answer:] Bruce F. Bachman, 40%; Ollie B. Howard, 60%.

QUESTION NO. 6: Find from a preponderance of the evidence the reasonable cost in Manero County, West York, of repairs, if any, necessary to restore Bruce Bachman's vehicle to the condition in which it was immediately before the occurrence in question. . . . Answer: $1271.30.

(a) *Is the Verdict Complete?* Notice that at least one question, No. 2(a), remains unanswered. Yet the trial judge treated the verdict as complete, and this treatment was correct. Why?

(b) *The Wording of Question 3(b).* Question 3(b) asks whether Ollie Howard "failed to yield the right of way," but it doesn't ask whether this conduct was negligent or whether it violated a standard of ordinary care. Why not? Is there a factual issue omitted here that the jury should decide? [Note: From your Torts course, what is the consequence in a negligence action of proof of a statutory violation?]

(c) *Are the Answers Inconsistent, or Can They Be Reconciled?* Notice that the jury finds that Howard's negligence proximately caused the occurrence, but Bachman's didn't. Then, however, the jury attributes to Bachman 40 percent of the negligence "that caused" the occurrence. Are these findings reconcilable? [Note: The court in *Howard v. Bachman*, 524 S.W.2d 414 (Tex. Civ. App.-Eastland 1975, no writ) ruled that there was no conflict between them, as precedent had established the principle that the specific findings on liability control over the general findings apportioning percentages of liability to the parties. Therefore, the failure to find Bachman's action a proximate cause rendered the comparative apportionment finding immaterial. In addition, because the comparative causation question didn't result in a finding that Bachman "proximately" caused the occurrence, and because "proximate" causation, not merely cause-in-fact, is required before a causation finding has any significance, the percentage causation question had no significance to the outcome whatsoever. Do you agree?]

(d) *Who Wins, and How Much?* The court in *Howard v. Bachman, supra*, held that Bachman recovered 100% of his damages. Correct?

(e) *Is This a Good Way to Submit a Jury Charge?* It seems doubtful that the jury focused on the difference between "cause" and "proximate cause." One might speculate that the jury may not have understood the consequences; it may have thought it was awarding Bachman only 60% of his damages. Assuming it didn't understand, is that factor irrelevant on the theory that it shouldn't have been able to "fudge" its answers anyway? Is this charge a good method of submitting a case to a jury?

(f) *Broad-Form Questions Are Different (They're Closer to a General Verdict.)* Since that case, Texas has repudiated the proliferation of narrow questions illustrated by *Howard v. Bachman*, and its rules now call for "broad form" questions. Today, questions 1 through 4 (with all of their subparts) would be compressed into a single interrogatory asking, in essence, "Whose negligence, if any, proximately caused the occurrence in question?" *See Lemos v. Montez*, 680 S.W.2d 798 (Tex. 1984). The verdict form would look like this:

> Question 1. Whose negligence, if any do you find from a preponderance of the evidence proximately caused the occurrence in question?
>
> Answer "Yes" or "No" for each of the following:

	Yes	No
(a) John Doe	______	______
(b) Sally Smith	______	______

This question would be followed by one asking the jury to attribute to each party a percentage of the negligence (if any) (*i.e.*, a comparative negligence question). Finally, the third and last question would inquire about damages.

Is this approach preferable, or does it give up the advantages attributed to special verdicts? *See generally* William V. Dorsaneo, III, *Broad-Form Submission of Jury Questions and the Standard of Review*, 46 S.M.U. L. Rev. 601 (1992).

[B] Instructions to the Jury

> Read Fed. R. Civ. P. 51 (instructions to jury; objections).

[1] Explanation of the Law by the Judge

Meagher v. Long Island R.R. Co.

27 N.Y.2d 39, 313 N.Y.S.2d 378, 261 N.E.2d 384 (1970)

Jasen, Judge.

This is an action to recover for the death of plaintiff's testator alleged to have been caused through the negligence of the defendant. For a number of years, the decedent regularly used the Long Island Rail Road in commuting between his Williston Park home and his place of employment in New York City.

On July 20, 1966, the decedent called his wife to inform her that he had "missed his East Williston train" and was instead taking a train to the Mineola station. Although the train was not scheduled to stop at Mineola, it was customary for the train to travel slowly in the vicinity of the Mineola station, pending clearance to proceed through the crossover switch and onto the Oyster Bay Line. The decedent was fatally injured while disembarking from the train in the Mineola station. There is a conflict of evidence as to whether the train had stopped or was moving at the time of the accident, and also, whether the decedent was fatally injured as a result of his riding on the platform (vestibule) of the car in violation of section 83 of the Railroad Law.

A reversal and new trial is required here solely upon the ground that the trial court's instructions to the jury, with regard to the applicability of section 83 of the Railroad Law Consol. Laws, c. 49 and the issue of contributory negligence, were erroneous.

Section 83 of the Railroad Law provides in pertinent part:

> No railroad corporation shall be liable for any injury to any passenger while on the platform [vestibule] of a car . . . in violation of the printed regulations of the corporation, posted up at the time in a conspicuous place inside of the passenger cars, then in the train, if there shall be at the time sufficient room for the proper accommodation of the passenger inside such passenger cars.

Undisputed testimony indicated that on this train signs appeared in the front and rear vestibules of each car and inside each car, stating: "Please keep off the platform until the train stops." Also, it is undisputed that there were empty seats in the car from which the decedent exited. Thus, there was testimony that both prerequisites of section 83 were satisfied.

In a written request, defendant asked the court to instruct the jury that if the decedent went upon the car platform while the car was in motion, in violation of section 83 of the Railroad Law, and such act on the part of the decedent was the proximate cause of his injuries, the plaintiff could not recover. Instead, the court instructed the jury that section 83 does not apply "to a passenger preparing to leave the train at a station who enters upon the platform as the train enters the station."

There can be little dispute that the statute clearly relieves the railroad of liability if the passenger rides on the platform in violation of the posted regulations of the railroad. . . .

In addition to incorrectly instructing the jury with regard to the applicability of section 83 of the Railroad Law, the trial court improperly charged the jury as to the standard of contributory negligence.

In its written requests to charge, the defendant asked the court to charge that if the jury found decedent stepped or jumped off a moving train, then the jury must find for the defendant. Instead, the court instructed the jury:

> While a railroad is under a duty to allow its passengers a reasonable time in which to board or alight from a train, a passenger is guilty of contributory negligence, as a matter of law, if he attempts to get off a train that is moving

> at *other than* an exceedingly slow rate of speed, for example, not more than two or three miles per hour. (Emphasis added.)

The well-established rule of law in this State is that boarding or alighting from a moving train is negligence per se . . . .

Although the instructions to the jury were erroneous, a question is raised as to whether each of these issues has been preserved for our review.

As mentioned, the defendant submitted proper written requests to charge with regard to the applicability of section 83 of the Railroad Law and the issue of contributory negligence. The trial court did not so charge. Immediately after the instruction to the jury, the following colloquy took place in open court:

[The Court]: If there are any exceptions or requests to charge I will hear them in chambers. Are there any? Are there some?

> Mr. Donnelly [Defendant's attorney]: I have no exceptions, your Honor.
>
> The Court: Do you have any exceptions?
>
> Mr. Donnelly: I have no exceptions.
>
> Mr. Halpern: No, your Honor.
>
> The Court: Do you have requests to charge?
>
> Mr. Donnelly: Judge, it is not a request—
>
> The Court: If you have, I will hear it in chambers.
>
> Mr. Donnelly: It isn't a request, your Honor—
>
> Mr. Halpern: May we step inside, sir?
>
> Mr. Donnelly: It isn't a request.
>
> The Court: All right.
>
> Mr. Halpern: I have no requests, Judge.
>
> Mr. Donnelly: Can we come up to the bench, Judge? It isn't a request, actually.

There followed a discussion off the record at the bench and then the jury was sent to begin their deliberations. Immediately thereafter, a conference was held in the Judge's chambers and defense counsel requested the Judge to charge the jury in a manner similar to the written requests earlier submitted. The court declined to so charge and noted: "Let the record show that defendant's attorney requested the following charges to the jury be made by the Court and that any of the requests to charge as hereinafter indicated that were not included in the Court's charge may be considered as having been declined by the Court to so charge."

CPLR 4017 provides:

> [A]t any time before the jury retires to consider its verdict, a party shall make known his objection to a charge to the jury or a failure or refusal to charge as requested. Failure to so make known objections may restrict

> review upon appeal in accordance with paragraphs three and four of subdivision (a) of section 5501. . . .

While the defendant herein did not object to the failure to charge as requested until after the jury had retired, we are of the opinion that the issue of the charge was adequately preserved for our review.

The trial court had indicated to counsel that it did not desire to have the exceptions and requests to charge heard before the jury, and instructed counsel that such be brought up in chambers. Counsel was entitled to rely upon this instruction of the court in withholding his exception until the conference in chambers. Moreover, the objection was raised in chambers immediately following submission of the case to the jury. Had the court accepted counsel's requests, the deleterious effect on the jury's deliberative process in recalling the jury and recharging them would have been *de minimis*. Furthermore, the response of the court in chambers to counsel's requests clearly indicates that the court had considered the earlier written requests and had made an irrevocable decision not to charge in accordance with those requests. In such a situation, it would exalt useless formalism over substance to hold that the issue of the charge had not adequately been preserved for review.

Accordingly, the order of the Appellate Division [which had affirmed the trial court] is reversed and the action remitted to the Supreme Court for a new trial. . . .

Gibson, Judge (dissenting): . . .

[T]here was not, in my view, an adequate and timely exception to the trial court's omission to charge in accordance with either of the requests now argued; and, in fact, when the jury some time later returned for further instructions, the court, without objection or exception on the part of either party, reread its charge in respect of negligence and contributory negligence, including the interpretation of section 83 of which appellant now complains. To excuse noncompliance with CPLR 4017 is to deny effect to the salutary and well-recognized purpose underlying its enactment; and that purpose was not served by the blanket exception which defendant sought to make, after the jury had retired, to the court's disposition of a series of written requests.

Scileppi, Bergan and Breitel, JJ., concur with Jasen, J.

Gibson, J., dissents and votes to affirm in a separate opinion in which Fuld, C.J., and Burke, J., concur.

Notes and Questions

(1) *The Requirement of Contemporaneous Objection to the Charge: Federal Rule 51; Pogo Holding Corp. v. New York Property Ins. Underwriters Ass'n*, 62 N.Y.2d 969, 479 N.Y.S.2d 336, 468 N.E.2d 291 (1984). Federal Rule 51 provides that if the trial court has informed a party of its proposed instructions before instructing the jury and before final jury arguments, the party is required to object "before the instructions and arguments are delivered." Fed. R. Civ. P. 51(b), (c). The New York law construed in *Meagher* is similar. In the *Pogo* case, the insurance company's defense was

that the plaintiff had made fraudulently inflated claims, and the court erroneously instructed the jury that the defendant should prevail if the claim was "knowingly" false. This statement of the law was seriously misleading, because the defendant was required to prove an "intent to deceive" on plaintiff's part. The Court of Appeals, however, held that since the plaintiff had not objected before the jury retired, the erroneous instruction "is the law governing this case." Is this procedure unnecessarily harsh?

(2) *The Charge Conference, Requests by Attorneys, and Objections.* It is typical for the court to hold a "charge conference" in the presence of the attorneys at the conclusion of the evidence, at which requested instructions and questions are received and discussed. The conference may be very short (if the case is "plain vanilla" and the attorneys are in substantial agreement about the proper charge) or it may last days, in unusual circumstances. In some federal courts, the attorneys are required to submit requested charges before trial, but the charge conference still may be necessary. The charge conference typically is informal and may be unreported; the court often is seeking to hear opposing views on how the charge should be given. The objections to the charge, on the other hand, must be made a part of the record, because their purpose is to preserve error. Note that, in the *Meagher* case, the trial judge told the attorneys that they could make objections in chambers; the jury already had begun to deliberate when the judge ruled on them. What would be the result under Federal Rule 51? (Perhaps this attorney was "saved by the bell." The decision is by a four-to-three majority.)

(3) *The Format and Drafting of the Instructions: Sprague v. Equifax Inc.*, 166 Cal. App. 3d 1012, 213 Cal. Rptr. 69 (2d Dist. 1985). This California case illustrates the range of objections that can be addressed to the format, sources, and substance of the instructions in that state. The jury rendered special verdict findings that resulted in a judgment holding the defendants liable for conspiring to defraud the plaintiff of insurance benefits to which he was entitled, with actual damages of $100,000 and punitive damages of $5 million assessed. The first objection was that the instructions on conspiracy were repetitious and excessive in number. Although the instructions occupied a major portion of the charge and were repetitious, the appellate court noted that when taken as a whole, the instructions on conspiracy did not "unfairly emphasize" the plaintiff's theory of the case. Furthermore, "repetition of a correct instruction rarely constitutes reversible error." [Does this principle make sense? If you were the plaintiff in a conspiracy case, wouldn't you request a lengthy charge on the subject?]

Secondly, the defendants argued that the instructions were vague. The court concluded that again, the question was whether the charge as a whole was inadequate. Many otherwise vague phrases were understandable if viewed in the context of instructions at other points in the charge. [Does this holding make sense? Will the jury cross-reference all of the legal concepts in a charge that may be twenty-five or more pages long?] Third, the defendants objected that the conspiracy instructions were "argumentative." An argumentative instruction "is one which embodies detailed recitals of fact drawn from the evidence in such a manner as to constitute an argument to the jury in the guise of a statement of law." The charge did include the instruction that "direct evidence of a conspiracy is rare," imbedded in discussions of how the jury should treat the evidence; the court agreed that this remark "might better have been left for argument [by counsel]," but it was not reversible when the charge was read as a whole. [Is this analysis persuasive?] [Note: The search for perfection in jury charges would result in a 100 percent reversal rate if unduly emphasized. Was this consideration behind the court's consideration of this case?]

(4) *The Impact of Substantively Erroneous or Misleading Instructions: Henderson v. United States Fidelity & Guaranty Co.*, 695 F.2d 109 (5th Cir. 1983). The federal approach to instruction errors is deferential. The trial court has discretion in choosing the form of the charge and the method of conveying required information to the jury. Substantive error in the charge, however, may lead to reversal. The charge is to be read as a whole in the context of the evidence and pleadings, and only if the charge remains misleading is reversal required, even after objection. In *Henderson*, above, the trial judge instructed the jury that the sending of notice of cancellation of insurance would not result in cancellation if the insured did not receive it. This charge was contrary to the governing state law, but since the court elsewhere in the charge corrected it, and since the whole was not misleading, the appellate court held that the error was not reversible. Apparently, only very serious distortions of the law, which persist after the entire charge is understood and absorbed, will result in reversal. *E.g., Brewer v. Jeep Corp.*, 724 F.2d 653 (8th Cir. 1983) (instruction that allowed plaintiff benefit only of strict liability claim, and denied plaintiff opportunity to have breach of warranty claim carrying lesser proof requirements, held reversible error). *See generally* Steven A. Childress, *Federal Standard of Review* (2d ed. Salem 1992). Is the federal approach appropriate? It might lead to sloppiness by judges giving instructions and to "brinkmanship" by attorneys requesting them.

[2] Comments by the Judge on the Evidence

LEWIS v. BILL ROBERTSON & SONS, INC., 162 Cal. App. 3d 650, 208 Cal. Rptr. 699 (2d Dist. 1984). In this personal injury suit, in which the plaintiff claimed that he had slipped and fallen due to the defendant's negligent maintenance of his premises, the trial judge informed the jury after the attorney's arguments that he would exercise his authority, under Cal. Const. art. VI, § 10, to comment "on the evidence and the testimony and the credibility of any witness." He began his summary by telling the jurors that they had just heard an impassioned plea based upon prejudice from the plaintiff's attorney that was in no way based on the evidence.

The judge then told the jurors that (1) ninety percent of automobile lots had chains around them like the one plaintiff had tripped over and anyone over eight years of age knew they were meant to keep people out; (2) the plaintiff's argument that he could not have used a safer entrance was a smokescreen to cloud over the elements of negligence that the plaintiff was required to prove; (3) there was no horrendous pain and suffering in a broken arm that had healed perfectly; and (4) the plaintiff's doctor had not testified that he would have any permanent pain. The judge went on to say that the plaintiff's method of calculating damages was a false method, although the jurors were "perfectly free" to ignore the judge's opinion. He told the jurors that "no defect in these premises had anything to do with this fall." He repeated this statement but told the jurors they could ignore his comments and tell him to "go jump in the lake" if they thought the court was wrong. The plaintiff moved for an instruction to the jury that it disregard these comments, or for a mistrial; the judge refused. After beginning its deliberations, the jury asked to have the judge's comments read again; the judge refused this request on the ground that it was "[c]ompletely irrelevant to the jury's duties." The jury returned a 9–3 verdict for the defendant. The appellate court reversed:

> [The constitutional provision] allows the trial judge to use his experience and training in evaluating the evidence, so as to aid the jury in reaching a just verdict. . . . The court's function . . . goes well beyond a colorless recital of the evidence. A judge may analyze all or part of the testimony and express his views with respect to its credibility. . . .
>
> Nevertheless, a judge's power to comment on the evidence is not unlimited. He cannot withdraw material evidence . . . or distort the testimony, and he must inform the jurors that they are the exclusive judges of fact and of the credibility of the witnesses. . . .
>
> The record here discloses that the trial judge failed to comply with the limitations suggested in other cases. . . . [Those cases hold that the judge should avoid] commenting on the crucial issues of proximate causation, damages or credibility. . . .
>
> Not only did the trial judge in this case comment on the crucial issue of proximate cause, but he distorted the testimony. . . . [Uncontroverted testimony showed that plaintiff sustained permanent damage from the fall.] . . . [Reversed.]

Notes and Questions

(1) *The Scope of Proper Comments.* Notice that the judge's authority to comment, in this state, is broad, and the judge need not confine the comments to "colorless" summation. The federal law is generally similar. *E.g., Bass v. International Brotherhood of Boilermakers*, 630 F.2d 1058 (5th Cir. 1980) (judge has great discretion, but must be fair and impartial when commenting substantively on evidence).

(2) *The Texas View: Prohibiting Comment by the Trial Judge on the Weight of the Evidence.* Why should the judge be permitted to comment directly on the evidence to the jury at all? The Texas view is that the judge should not be. In fact, Tex. R. Civ.

P. 277 expressly prohibits the judge from commenting directly on the weight of the evidence. One criticism of this approach is that it leads to large numbers of reversals, since it is difficult for the court to charge the jury meaningfully without commenting, at least indirectly, on the evidence. For this reason, the modern Texas rule relaxes the prohibition, outlawing only "direct" comments. *Cf. Brown v. Russell*, 703 S.W.2d 843 (Tex. App.-Fort Worth 1986, no writ) (reversal of child custody case where judge criticized former wife's failure to submit expert psychological evidence about second husband). Another possible objection to the Texas approach is that it deprives the jury of the judge's expertise. Does the Texas approach have advantages, however? *Cf.* Note, *Deadlocked Juries and the Allen Charge*, 37 MAINE L. REV. 167 (1985).

(3) *Should the Jury Be Told the Effects of Its Answers to a Special Verdict Charge?* Some jurisdictions prohibit the court from telling the jurors the legal effects of their answers to special verdict questions on the judgment. *Cf. Gulf Coast State Bank v. Emenhiser*, 562 S.W.2d 449 (Tex. 1978) (instruction that if jury found certain facts, it should "find for" defendants held error). The prohibition is based on the notion that telling the jurors might make them "fudge" their answers. On the other hand, many jurisdictions (including the federal courts) have no such prohibition, and there are some jurisdictions that actually require the judge to inform the jury. *See* Comment, *Informing the Jury of the Legal Effect of Special Verdict Answers in Comparative Negligence Actions*, 1981 DUKE L.J. 824 (1981).

Litigation Document Example 10.2

Jury Argument, Charge, and Objections, Featuring the Litigation in Pennzoil Co. v. Texaco Inc.

These materials are online at https://caplaw.com/sites/cp7. They are taken from *Pennzoil Co. v. Texaco Inc.*, which produced the then-biggest jury verdict in history. The first item is the court's charge to the jury. The second item is objections to the charge. Texaco vigorously objected to the charge on the ground that it favored Texaco, and you should try to understand why. The third item is an article explaining attorneys' tactics in jury argument. You may wish to compare these tactics to the jury argument in *Pennzoil.* That argument is excerpted in the fourth item. Please go to https://caplaw.com/sites/cp7, then click on Litigation Document Example 10.2: Jury Argument, Charge, and Objections, Featuring the Litigation in *Pennzoil Co. v. Texaco Inc.*

VIII. Trial to the Court Without a Jury

Read Fed. R. Civ. P. 52 (findings by the court); also, read 28 U.S.C. §§ 144, 455 (bias of judge; disqualification).

Note on Trial to the Court

If you understand trial by jury, then, in general, you understand trial to the court. It is simpler in many respects—it is not necessary, obviously, to select or to charge the jury. There are, however, some important differences, and there are a few respects in which trial to the court involves complexities not present in jury trials.

Relaxation of Formalities in Evidence and Proof: Eagle-Picher Indus., Inc. v. Liberty Mut. Ins. Co., 682 F.2d 12 (1st Cir. 1982). In the absence of indications to the contrary, it will be assumed that the trial judge disregarded inadmissible evidence and based her fact findings on admissible evidence. In the *Eagle-Picher* case, which involved interpretation of contract language, the appellate court advised trial judges to admit "provisionally" all extrinsic evidence of the parties' intent, unless it is clearly inadmissible, privileged, or too time-consuming—to guard against reversal for failure to admit evidence. In a jury trial, receipt of harmful inadmissible evidence over objection brings about a quite different result (reversible error). Is the relaxation of this approach in trials to the court appropriate?

Findings of Fact and Conclusions of Law. Probably the most complex difference between jury and judge trials involves the means of establishing the factual basis of the judgment. Knowing the "facts" that were found may be important in the appellate court, since a given legal theory may be viable or not, depending on how controverted facts were decided in the trial court. In a trial to the court, however, there are no instructions or verdicts. Federal Rule 52 fills this need by providing that the trial judge shall make findings of fact (or write an opinion or memorandum of decision) for purposes of review.

IX. How to Answer the Chapter Summary Problem: Some Suggestions

Stone v. Crestview Apartment Company: Judge or Jury Trial? (As usual, follow your Professor's instructions about how to answer.)

1. Right to Trial by Jury? To what extent could you have a right to trial by jury in a federal court if the negligence claim is joined with a claim for an injunction against a fraudulent transfer (because you fear that Crestview may shift its assets to a newly formed entity)? *Law:* The right to jury trial is preserved for claims at common law. *Facts:* A claim for damages for negligence is solidly a legal claim. But an injunction against fraudulent transfer is equitable. *Conclusion:* The trial court should consider a preliminary and permanent injunction. But the plaintiff has the right to have the jury decide the negligence claim and damages.

2. Should You Challenge the Array? You are convinced that jury venires in the county of suit are underinclusive of young people, ages 18 to 25, because jury summonses are based on voter registration lists. Should you make a challenge to the

array on these grounds (and if so, when and how)? *Law:* The Constitution requires a "fair cross section," but what is required is that there be no systemic exclusion of a "cognizable group." This concept is difficult to define, except to say that it means a classification like race or gender. *Facts:* It is doubtful that young people are of this character—the classification is not immutable or permanent, for example—and it can be correlated with attitudes that would be of concern to given parties in litigation. The use of voter registration lists complies with the Jury Selection and Service Act. The Act says that a challenge must be made "before the voir dire examination begins, or within seven days after the party discovered or could have discovered, by the exercise of diligence, the grounds therefore."

3. *Should You Demand a Jury—Or Waive It?* ***There are some cases in which you would be better off trying your case before a judge without a jury. Is this one of those cases—or would you demand a jury (and if so, when and how)?*** It depends in part on who the judge is. If the judge is like what can be described as an ideal juror, you might be better off with that judge. Studies show that the judge prefers the plaintiff or defendant about as often as vice versa, and most of the time they agree. The jury is shown to find greater damages on average.

4. *Examination by the Judge or by the Attorneys.* ***The state courts in your jurisdiction give the parties the right to question the potential jurors, through their attorneys. The federal judges in the region, however, usually exercise the option to conduct the examination themselves alone. The attorney opposing you is much more experienced in jury trials than you are. If diversity of citizenship gave you the choice, would you file suit in state court or federal court?*** Often, plaintiffs want state courts, because they tend to make the process less complicated. But in this case, the difference in attorney experience might be a factor nudging you in the direction of a trial by the judge. The voir dire is an important example of a process in which experience makes a big difference, and there are others. The advantage given to the other lawyer is reduced in a trial before a judge.

5. *Insurance Questions During Voir Dire.* ***Assuming you are in federal court, you have the opportunity to file written requests for questions to be asked by the judge. The probability exists that you will want to have the jurors questioned about their insurance affiliations. But there is a strict prohibition in this jurisdiction upon introducing before the jury the fact of insurance. How would you word the requested questions so as to maximize the probability of obtaining information, obtaining a basis for challenges for cause if they exist, and counteracting the possibility of prejudice in favor of the defendant as a "little guy" corporation?*** *Law:* The judge has discretion about exactly what to ask but must consider your written suggestions (which are very difficult to write in advance). The judge's duty is to conduct a voir dire that gives reasonable assurance that any bias would be detected. *Facts:* It is a real art. The plaintiff would want to know about jurors who are employed by or otherwise affiliated with insurers, because they might have anti-plaintiff bias. The key is to ask about jurors' possible insurance affiliations without suggesting that the defendant in this particular case has relevant insurance.

6. The "Ideal Juror." Try to construct a profile of the kinds of jurors you would want. Would you want young people or old people? Rich or poor? College-educated jurors or high-school dropouts? Professional people or blue-collar workers? Law students? The New Dublin jury study in Litigation Document Example 10.1, available at https://caplaw.com/sites/cp7, suggests that if you are in a district that resembles New Dublin, the ideal plaintiff's juror may be an uneducated, lower-or-middle income woman, in her fifties, Anglo or black, working (perhaps as a secretary) outside the home, with children, of Baptist religion. The study suggests that highly educated jurors would be worse for the plaintiff than high school dropouts, and rich people worse than poor (however, some "gambling" with including wealthier people may be necessary to obtain significant damages). Remember, though, that race and gender are prohibited considerations.

7. Peremptory Challenges Based upon Ethnicity or Gender. Assume that a survey indicates that Asian-Americans are strongly disposed to favor the defendant in this case, and that women are much more favorable to the plaintiff than men. Is a strike illegal or unethical if it is influenced by these considerations? What steps should you take if 100% of defendant's peremptory challenges are against women? The Law: The Supreme Court has been clear in saying that race and gender are prohibited considerations. Sometimes people assume that if they have a statistical study showing different attitudes, they have a loophole allowing them to consider these illegal grounds—which is wrong. The objector to these kinds of strikes can make prima facie proof statistically, and the violator's invocation of statistical differences among races or genders is irrelevant. *The Facts:* 100% of defendant's strikes are against women. *Conclusion:* This fact can be used to make a prima facie proof of violation. The movant must timely object, state into the record the identities or numbers of the stricken jurors, and state that they are women (don't overlook the obvious). The movant should insist on a "neutral explanation," and if a reason is proffered, be prepared to argue that it is not neutral or is pretextual.

8. Court's Charge and Verdict. Assume that the jury returns a general verdict for $2 million, but it also returns special verdicts on each of the permissible elements of damage, adding up to only $1 million. What would you urge the judge to do? The Law: First, the judge has the duty to "harmonize" the findings if possible. Second, if the findings cannot be harmonized, the issue is covered by Rule 49(b). When the special verdicts are consistent with each other but inconsistent with the general verdict, the judge may (1) enter judgment on the special verdicts and disregard the general verdict, (2) return the jury for further consideration of its answers and verdict, or (3) order a new trial. *The Facts:* Sometimes the special verdicts do not cover literally "each" of the permissible elements of damage, and sometimes there is enough "play in the joints" so that the special verdicts may not *compel* a $1 million judgment because there are other factors than can support the $2 million judgment. *Conclusion:* Plaintiff should argue vigorously for harmonizing and for accepting the general verdict. If the conflict is irreconcilable, the plaintiff should move the judge to return the jury for further consideration if the jury is still available. The plaintiff presumably does not want a verdict based on the special verdicts (a lesser amount) or a new trial (unless sure of obtaining another liability verdict).

X. Improving Trial Processes: Notes and Questions

(1) *Providing Jury Trial in the Right Cases (and Not in the Wrong Ones?)* Jury trials seem most important in cases in which citizens' perceptions of the balance of interests might diverge from the views of government, and when the issues are related to those in common experience. To the extent that there is constitutional room not to provide a jury, however, it may be appropriate to consider the fact that jury trials are more unpredictable, much more expensive for all concerned, and more likely to produce delay. Consider the following proposals:

(a) *Congress Should Expressly Consider Whether the Jury Trial Right Applies when Passing Legislation.* In cases in which the right might not otherwise attach under the Constitution and Rule 38, yet in which the arguments for jury trial are strong, Congress should provide for jury trial (*e.g.*, in enacting a civil rights law providing for a straightforward damage remedy). But in cases in which these policies are inapplicable, should Congress structure the legislation so that the right does not attach? *Compare Tull v. United States*, above (court followed Congress' intent that judge, not jury, should assess amount of penalty).

(b) *Should Legislatures Avoid Unnecessary Provision for Jury Trial in Complex Cases Requiring Special Experience?* For example, some states provide juries in child custody cases—but other states do not. The custody decision is one in which a judge's longer experience, including the experience of seeing how one's decisions in earlier cases have turned out, might be most valuable. Is this the kind of case in which a legislature should refrain from providing for jury trial? [On the other hand, family practitioners have observed that custody decisions of judges tend to be more influenced by gender bias than those of juries!]

(2) *Improving the Process of Voir Dire Examination and Jury Selection.* If the jury examination is done by the attorneys, the trial starts with a personality contest. If, on the other hand, voir dire is done exclusively by the judge, it is much less likely to ferret out unconscious prejudices. Neither method is perfect. Might we improve the system if we amended the rules to provide that the judge may conduct the bulk of the examination, but that she must provide a reasonable time for supplementary questioning of the venire by the attorneys? In the alternative, should the rules be amended to give the trial judge discretion to examine the jury herself about sensitive subjects such as insurance, and allow the attorneys to conduct the bulk of the examination?

(3) *Presentation of Evidence.* The rules of evidence are in large measure premised on the notion that juries will misuse many kinds of information and that this information must be kept from them. Both because these rules sometimes hide facts that are relevant and true, and because their enforcement is itself a factor that makes the

trial more complex, there have sometimes been suggestions for streamlining the rules. Might it be better simply to place before the jury all facts of any kind that the attorneys wish to bring them (perhaps subject to a reasonable limit on the length of presentation) and to let the jurors sort out this information?

(4) *Jury Argument.* Improper jury argument is frequent. The contemporaneous objection requirement clearly is one reason; the application of harmless error principles is another. Would it be better to provide that an attorney may properly object at the end of the opponent's jury argument, rather than during it, and to provide for reversal in the event of clear violations whether or not they are harmful?

(5) *The Court's Authority to Comment to the Jury on the Evidence.* As you have seen, some jurisdictions (*e.g.*, California; the federal system) allow judges to comment liberally on the evidence, so long as the comments are not excessively one-sided. Other jurisdictions (*e.g.*, Texas) prohibit this practice. Which approach is better? Might judicial comment cure some of the deficiencies in overzealous argument by counsel (or is it likely itself to invade the jury's function)?

(6) *Submitting the Case to the Jury.* One of the more profound questions raised by this chapter is whether the general charge or special interrogatories should be the basic model for jury submission. What is your conclusion at this point? Also, consider the following possibilities:

(a) *"Broad" Special Interrogatories.* Perhaps a compromise between general and special interrogatories is possible. The court could be required or encouraged to submit the case on special interrogatories, but permitted to submit them broadly and generally. For example, a negligence case could consist of three questions: One asking the jury to decide whose negligence proximately caused the occurrence, one asking the jury to assign percentages of responsibility to the parties for comparative negligence purposes, and one inquiring about the amount of damages. Does this approach preserve the advantages of both verdict types?

(b) *Plain Language.* There may be room for skepticism about the "plain language" movement in some kinds of legal documents, but not in the area of jury instructions. Section 10.07, above, shows the difficulty jurors sometimes have in understanding the court's charge. *See generally* Tanford, *The Law and Psychology of Jury Instructions*, 69 NEB. L. REV. 71 (1990). *See also* Sand & Reiss, *A Report on Seven Experiments Conducted by District Court Judges in the Second Circuit*, 60 N.Y.U. L. REV. 423, 456 (1985) (efforts to ensure comprehension, including recording); Note, *Improving Jury Comprehension in Complex Civil Litigation*, 62 ST. JOHN'S L. REV. 549 (1988). But there is a major difficulty with "plain language" efforts: it is very difficult to draft complete and accurate instructions without using complex terminology. Thus, a readily comprehensible explanation in plain words may be subject to attack as inaccurate, and a fully accurate explanation may be difficult to comprehend.

(c) *Pattern Jury Instructions.* In some jurisdictions, official charge form books are available. California's "BAJI" (Book of Approved Jury Instructions) is a notable example. In other jurisdictions, there are unofficial but authoritative sources, such as the State Bar of Texas' Pattern Jury Charges. *See also* E. Devitt & C. Blackmar, *Federal Jury Practice and Instructions* vols. 1–3 (3d ed. 1977). Would it be preferable for each jurisdiction to adopt official charge forms and encourage their use?

(7) *The Vanishing Trial?* Various studies have documented the decreasing numbers of cases that proceed all the way to trial. One study, reported in the December 14, 2003 issue of The New York Times, noted that in 1962, 11.5 percent of all civil cases filed in federal court proceeded to trial. By 2002, that number had dropped to 1.8 percent. The decrease is reflected in the raw numbers as well: In 1985, 12,529 civil trials were conducted in federal court; in 2002, only 4,569 civil cases were tried in federal court. Is this reduction in civil trials a good or a bad thing? *See* R. Perschbacher & D. Bassett, *The End of Law*, 84 B.U. L. Rev. 1 (2004) (noting the resultant privatized law, distorted norms, diminished case resolution and explanation, and other effects due to efforts to reduce trials), *see also* Chapter 15, below.

Chapter 11

Post-Trial Motions

I. Judicial Power to Take the Case Away from the Jury

Taking the Case Away from the Jury. The right to trial by jury does not mean that the jury makes all decisions. At several points in the process—some of which we have already seen, including summary judgment and dismissal—the judge may be called upon to withdraw the case from the jury's decision.

The Procedures: Judgment on the Verdict, Judgment as a Matter of Law, New Trial, and Relief from Judgments. First, the judge may have a complex task in granting judgment on the verdict. In some cases, that step is clearcut; in others, it is not, and it may require the application of the law to the verdict in non-obvious ways. Secondly, the judge may be called upon, by a motion for judgment as a matter of law during trial (also called a "directed verdict") or after trial (also called a "judgment notwithstanding the verdict"), to countermand a verdict that is unsupportable by the record evidence. Third, the judge may be called upon to determine whether the trial has included procedural errors, misconduct, or lopsided results so serious as to constitute a miscarriage of justice. If so, the judge has discretionary authority to grant a new trial. Finally, there is the possibility that a final judgment, as to which all time limits for the usual kinds of attacks have expired, may be so egregiously unjust that the court should have narrow authority to set it aside. This authority is given the court by the Rule 60 Motion for Relief from Judgment. Consider the following Chapter Summary Problem, which you should analyze at the end of the chapter (or otherwise treat as your instructor directs).

Problem A: Chapter 11 Summary Problem

THE AUTOMOBILE ACCIDENT BETWEEN PAULA GREEN AND THE WEST YORK BUS COMPANY: A POST-TRIAL MOTIONS PROBLEM. This case concerns a collision between an automobile driven by plaintiff Paula Green and a bus operated by the West York Bus Company. At trial, there was only one hotly contested issue related to Paula's negligence claim:

> The bus driver testified that plaintiff Paula drove across the median and collided with the bus on its side of the road, while Paula testified that she was in her proper lane a few seconds before the collision, when she suffered a heart attack that rendered her unconscious, and she woke up with her vehicle still in her lane. The trial judge excluded the testimony of an accident-reconstruction expert called by Paula. No other testimony on this issue was submitted. At the conclusion of all evidence, the defendant moved for "judgment as a matter of law" on the ground that there was no legally sufficient evidence of negligence.

The judge instead submitted the case to the jury. But he erroneously instructed the jurors that the defendant had the burden of showing contributory negligence "by clear and convincing evidence." The defendant did not object to this instruction. After a verdict for the plaintiff, the defendant learned that plaintiff Paula had said in a live television interview broadcast at the scene of the accident, "I have no idea how the accident happened, but maybe I crossed the median." Paula's pretrial deposition contained her testimony that she was "unaware of any testimony or evidence that even remotely supports the bus driver's version."

1. If the defendant now (post-verdict) moves for "judgment as a matter of law," should the court grant the motion?
2. What are the defendant's chances of obtaining relief through a motion for new trial?
3. What should the plaintiff do if the Court of Appeals reverses the judgment for the plaintiff and, for the first time, grants judgment for the defendant on the ground that the plaintiff's evidence was legally insufficient?
4. What recourse would the defendant have had if it learned of the plaintiff's broadcast statement six months after the trial court had granted a judgment for the plaintiff? What if it learned two years after?

II. Judgment on the Verdict

The Judge's Duty with Respect to the Verdict. If the jury has rendered a general verdict that is supported by the evidence and can be the basis for judgment in accordance with the law, the entry of judgment on the verdict is straightforward. But special verdicts may present complex questions of law. If there are many interrogatories, it may not be obvious to a neutral observer who has won. For a simple example, consider a case in which the jury finds that a defective product caused the occurrence and that the plaintiff concurred in causing it by her contributory negligence. But assume further that there is no statute or decision that makes clear whether contributory negligence is a defense to a strict product liability claim. It is entirely likely that both sides will claim to have "won" the right to judgment on the jury's verdict. The trial judge will face the decision of a case of first impression.

An Example: Fein v. Permanente Medical Group, 38 Cal. 3d 137, 211 Cal. Rptr. 368, 695 P.2d 665 (1985). In § VII[A] of Chapter 1, we considered the case of *Fein v. Permanente Medical Group.* The California Medical Injury Compensation Reform Act ("MICRA") placed a $250,000 "cap" on noneconomic damages (*i.e.*, pain and suffering) in medical malpractice cases. The jury's verdict fixed the plaintiff's noneconomic loss at $500,000. The verdict was not a determination that the plaintiff was entitled to recover that amount; it merely was a fact finding that the judge was required to use in rendering a final judgment.

The judge determined that correct application of the law to the jury's findings resulted in a judgment for $250,000 (not $500,000) in noneconomic damages. In so deciding, the judge had to face several complex legal questions, including the question whether the cap was unconstitutional. Technically, however, the trial judge's decision did not set aside the jury's verdict. It was a judgment entered on the verdict, because the legal consequence of the jury's finding was the judgment actually rendered.

III. Judgment as a Matter of Law

[A] During Trial

Problem B

EVALUATING PLAINTIFF'S EVIDENCE IN WEBER v. JARNIGAN. The law of the (hypothetical) State of West York is that in medical malpractice cases, other than those involving negligence of a kind that laypersons are capable of evaluating clearly, the plaintiff must offer expert testimony to set the standard of care that the allegedly negligent physician should have observed. (This is the law in most states.) In his trial in a West York district court, plaintiff Weber testifies that he engaged Dr. Jarnigan to remove his appendix; that Dr. Jarnigan performed the operation; that after the operation, he, Weber, experienced pain in the area of his appendix;

that Dr. Jarnigan informed him that infection had set in and that a second operation would be necessary; and that, as a result, he, Weber, experienced pain and discomfort. Weber also testifies that in his opinion as a layperson, Dr. Jarnigan was extremely sloppy and negligent in letting the infection set in. Weber then rests without submitting any other testimony.

If you represented Dr. Jarnigan, what motion would you make to the court at this point? How should the court rule? [And, finally, here is a slightly more difficult question: Would your conclusions be the same if Weber also testified that Dr. Jarnigan admitted that his inadvertence in leaving a sponge inside the sutured wound probably was the source of the infection?]

Note on "Directed Verdict," "Judgment Notwithstanding the Verdict," and "Judgment as a Matter of Law"

Earlier Terminology: Directed Verdict (During Trial) and Judgment Notwithstanding the Verdict (After Trial). Long before the present rules, the judge had authority to grant a "directed verdict" in favor of a party that was entitled as a matter of law to prevail. A directed verdict aborted the trial after the nonmovant had rested, on the ground that reasonable minds could not differ with the position of the movant, i.e., that no legally sufficient evidence supported the finding or verdict sought by the nonmovant. There was also a motion for "judgment notwithstanding the verdict," which actually amounted to a renewal of a motion for directed verdict, but which was urged after the trial. In the federal courts, the motion literally was the same motion renewed after the trial, and it was considered by the same standard. (A judgment notwithstanding the verdict sometimes was called a "judgment non obstante veredicto" or "judgment N.O.V.," which means the same thing.)

The Federal Rules: Designating Both Motions by the Single Phrase, "Judgment as a Matter of Law." Rule 50 jettisoned both "directed verdict" and "judgment notwithstanding the verdict" and instead adopted the term, "judgment as a matter of law" to describe both processes. The purposes were to modernize the nomenclature and to emphasize the identity of the two motions. It is debatable whether this change was necessary or even beneficial.

The Legal Standard for Judgment as a Matter of Law. Rule 50 provides that a court should render judgment as a matter of law when "a party has been fully heard on an issue during a jury trial and the court finds that a reasonable jury would not have a legally sufficient evidentiary basis to find for the party on that issue." As you might expect, however, the concept cannot be fully conveyed by this one sentence. Consider the Rule and the following decision.

> Read Fed. R. Civ. P. 50(a) (judgment as a matter of law during trial).

Lavender v. Kurn

327 U.S. 645 (1946)

MR. JUSTICE MURPHY delivered the opinion of the Court.

The Federal Employers' Liability Act permits recovery for personal injuries to an employee of a railroad engaged in interstate commerce if such injuries result "in whole or in part from the negligence of [the railroad]." 45 U.S.C. § 51.

Petitioner, the administrator of the estate of L.E. Haney, brought this suit under the Act against the respondent trustees of the St. Louis-San Francisco Railway Company (Frisco) and the respondent Illinois Central Railroad Company. It was charged that Haney, while employed as a switch-tender by the respondents in the switchyard of the Grand Central Station in Memphis, Tennessee, was killed as a result of respondents' negligence. Following a trial in the Circuit Court of the City of St. Louis, Missouri, the jury returned a verdict in favor of petitioner and awarded damages in the amount of $30,000. Judgment was entered accordingly. On appeal, however, the Supreme Court of Missouri reversed the judgment, holding that there was no substantial evidence of negligence to support the submission of the case to the jury. . . . We granted certiorari to review the propriety of the [Missouri] Court's action under the circumstances of this case. . . .

The Illinois Central tracks run north and south directly past and into the Grand Central Station. About 2,700 feet south of the station the Frisco tracks cross at right angles to the Illinois Central tracks. A west-bound Frisco train wishing to use the station must stop some 250 feet or more west of this crossing and back into the station over a switch line curving east and north. . . .

It was very dark on the evening of December 21, 1939. At about 7:30 p.m. a west-bound interstate Frisco passenger train stopped on the Frisco main line, its rear some 20 or 30 feet west of the switch. Haney, in the performance of his duties, threw or opened the switch to permit the train to back into the station. The respondents claimed that Haney was then required to cross to the south side of the track before the train passed the switch; and the conductor of the train testified that he saw Haney so cross. But there was also evidence that Haney's duties required him to wait at the switch north of the track until the train had cleared, close the switch, return to his shanty near the crossing and change the signals from red to green to permit trains on the Illinois Central tracks to use the crossing. The Frisco train cleared the switch, backing at the rate of 8 or 10 miles per hour. But the switch remained open and the signals still were red. Upon investigation Haney was found north of the track near the switch lying face down on the ground, unconscious. An ambulance was called, but he was dead upon arrival at the hospital.

Haney had been struck in the back of the head, causing a fractured skull from which he died. There were no known eyewitnesses to the fatal blow. Although it is not clear, there is evidence that his body was extended north and south, the head to the south. Apparently he had fallen forward to the south; his face was bruised on the left side from hitting the ground and there were marks indicating that his toes had dragged a few inches southward as he fell. His head was about 5 1/2 feet north of the Frisco tracks. Estimates ranged from 2 feet to 14 feet as to how far west of the switch he lay.

The injury to Haney's head was evidenced by a gash about two inches long from which blood flowed. The back of Haney's white cap had a corresponding black mark about an inch and a half long and an inch wide, running at an angle downward to the right of the center of the back of the head. A spot of blood was later found at a point 3 or 4 feet north of the tracks. The conclusion following an autopsy was that Haney's skull was fractured by "some fast moving small round object." One of the examining doctors testified that such an object might have been attached to a train backing at the rate of 8 or 10 miles per hour. But he also admitted that the fracture might have resulted from a blow from a pipe or club or some similar round object in the hands of an individual.

Petitioner's theory is that Haney was struck by the curled end or tip of a mail hook hanging down loosely on the outside of the mail car of the backing train. This curled end was 73 inches above the top of the rail, which was 7 inches high. The overhang of the mail car in relation to the rails was about 2 to 2 1/2 feet. The evidence indicated that when the mail car swayed or moved around a curve the mail hook might pivot, its curled end swinging out as much as 12 to 14 inches. The curled end could thus be swung out to a point 3 to 3 1/2 feet from the rail and about 73 inches above the top of the rail. Both east and west of the switch, however, was an uneven mound of cinders and dirt rising at its highest points 18 to 24 inches above the top of the rails. Witnesses differed as to how close the mound approached the rails, the estimates varying from 3 to 15 feet. But taking the figures most favorable to the petitioner, the mound extended to a point 6 to 12 inches north of the overhanging side of the mail car. If the mail hook end swung out 12 to 14 inches it would be 49 to 55 inches above the highest parts of the mound. Haney was 67 1/2 inches tall. If he had been standing on the mound about a foot from the side of the mail car he could have been hit by the end of the mail hook, the exact point of contact depending upon the height of the mound at the particular point. His wound was about 4 inches below the top of his head, or 63 1/2 inches above the point where he stood on the mound—well within the possible range of the mail hook end.

Respondents' theory is that Haney was murdered. They point to the estimates that the mound was 10 to 15 feet north of the rail, making it impossible for the mail hook end to reach a point of contact with Haney's head. Photographs were placed in the record to support the claim that the ground was level north of the rail for at least 10 feet. Moreover, it appears that the area immediately surrounding the switch was quite dark. Witnesses stated that it was so dark that it was impossible to see a 3-inch pipe 25 feet away. It also appears that many hoboes and tramps frequented the area at night in order to get rides on freight trains. Haney carried a pistol to protect himself. This pistol was found loose under his body by those who came to his rescue. It was testified, however, that the pistol had apparently slipped out of his pocket or scabbard as he fell. Haney's clothes were not disarranged and there was no evidence of a struggle or fight. No rods, pipes or weapons of any kind, except Haney's own pistol, were found near the scene. Moreover, his gold watch and diamond ring were still on him after he was struck. Six days later his unsoiled billfold was found on a high board fence about a block from the place where Haney was struck and near the point where he had been placed in an ambulance. It contained his social security card and other effects, but no money. His wife testified that he "never carried very much money, not very much more than $10." Such were the facts in relation to respondents' theory of murder.

Finally, one of the Frisco foremen testified that he arrived at the scene shortly after Haney was found injured. He later examined the fireman's side of the train very carefully and found nothing sticking out or in disorder. In explaining why he examined this side of the train so carefully he stated that while he was at the scene of the accident "someone said they thought that train No. 106 backing into Grand Central Station is what struck this man" and that Haney "was supposed to have been struck by something protruding on the side of this train." The foreman testified that these statements were made by an unknown Illinois Central switchman standing near the fallen body of Haney. The foreman admitted that the switchman "didn't see the accident. . . ." This testimony was admitted by the trial court over the strenuous objections of respondents' counsel that it was mere hearsay falling outside the *res gestae* rule.[(*)]

The jury was instructed that Frisco's trustees were liable if it was found that they negligently permitted a rod or other object to extend out from the side of the train as it backed past Haney and that Haney was killed as the direct result of such negligence, if any. The jury was further told that Illinois Central was liable if it was found that the company negligently maintained an unsafe and dangerous place for Haney to work, in that the ground was high and uneven and the light insufficient and inadequate, and that Haney was injured and killed as a direct result of the said place being unsafe and dangerous. This latter instruction as to Illinois Central did not require the jury to find that Haney was killed by something protruding from the train.

The [Missouri] Court, in upsetting the jury's verdict against both the Frisco trustees and the Illinois Central, admitted that "It could be inferred from the facts that Haney could have been struck by the mail hook knob *if* he were standing on the south side of the mound and the mail hook extended out as far as 12 or 14 inches." But it held that "all reasonable minds would agree that it would be mere speculation and conjecture to say that Haney was struck by the mail hook" and that "plaintiff failed to make a submissible case on the question." . . .

(*) [In the terminology of today's Rules of Evidence, we would say that the declaration was hearsay and did not fit either the exception for present sense impressions or the exception for excited utterances. *See* § V of Chapter 10, *supra*.—Eds.]

We hold, however, that there was sufficient evidence of negligence on the part of both the Frisco trustees and the Illinois Central to justify the submission of the case to the jury and to require appellate courts to abide by the verdict rendered by the jury.

The evidence we have already detailed demonstrates that there was evidence from which it might be inferred that the end of the mail hook struck Haney in the back of the head, an inference that the Supreme Court admitted could be drawn. That inference is not rendered unreasonable by the fact that Haney apparently fell forward toward the main Frisco track so that his head was 5 1/2 feet north of the rail. He may well have been struck and then wandered in a daze to the point where he fell forward. . . .

It is true that there is evidence tending to show that it was physically and mathematically impossible for the hook to strike Haney. And there are facts from which it might reasonably be inferred that Haney was murdered. But such evidence has become irrelevant upon appeal, there being a reasonable basis in the record for inferring that the hook struck Haney. . . . Under these circumstances it would be an undue invasion of the jury's historic function for an appellate court to weigh the conflicting evidence, judge the credibility of witnesses and arrive at a conclusion opposite from the one reached by the jury. . . .

It is no answer to say that the jury's verdict involved speculation and conjecture. Whenever facts are in dispute or the evidence is such that fair-minded [people] may draw different inferences, a measure of speculation and conjecture is required on the part of those whose duty it is to settle the dispute by choosing what seems to them to be the most reasonable inference. Only when there is a complete absence of probative facts to support the conclusion reached does a reversible error appear. [Reversed.]

McLAUGHLIN v. FELLOWS GEAR SHAPER CO., 786 F.2d 592 (3d Cir. 1986). This case appears in Chapter 10 above and should be reconsidered at this point. The plaintiff sued on the theory that a defective machine had amputated his thumb. The jury rendered a special verdict of "Yes" to the question, "Did plaintiff assume the risk?" But the appellate court concluded, as a matter of law, that there was no evidence to support any finding of assumption of risk. Nevertheless, both the district judge and the appellate court were unable to grant the plaintiff a judgment as a matter of law *after* trial—because the plaintiff's lawyer had not specified the absence of evidence of assumption of risk as a ground for judgment as a matter of law *during* the trial. The court of appeals found other grounds for disregarding the assumption-of-risk finding, over the dissent of one judge who accused the court of violating Rule 50(b).

Notes and Questions

(1) *The Standard for Judgment as a Matter of Law.* Briefly put, a judgment as a matter of law is proper if there is no reasonable way that a jury, properly applying the

law, could find the facts so as to return a verdict for the non-movant. This standard is sometimes expressed in terms of the non-movant's having introduced "no evidence" (which does not mean literally no evidence, but evidence insufficient to make a case). The judge is required to draw all reasonable inferences in favor of the non-movant and may not make credibility determinations or weigh the evidence. *See Reeves v. Sanderson Plumbing Co.*, 530 U.S. 133 (2000). *See also* Cooper, *Directions for Directed Verdicts: A Compass for Federal Courts*, 55 MINN. L. REV. 903 (1971).

(2) *Is a Judgment as a Matter of Law a Violation of the Seventh Amendment Right to Jury Trial? Galloway v. United States*, 319 U.S. 372 (1943). Galloway sued for disability benefits owing to his insanity, claiming that it originated during his service in the Army in World War I. But the evidence failed to account for lengthy periods of years between his service and the present. The Supreme Court therefore upheld a judgment as a matter of law for the government. The Court emphasized that the insanity needed to have been continuous to the present. "Insanity so long and continuously sustained does not hide itself from the eyes and ears of witnesses."

The more interesting issue in the case, however, was Galloway's argument that the judgment as a matter of law, in the form granted against him, was unknown to the common law at the time of the Seventh Amendment. The common law did provide a procedure called a "demurrer to the evidence," but it required that the defendant "conced[e] the full scope of the [plaintiff's] evidence," *i.e.*, if the ruling did not favor the defendant, the automatic result was judgment for the plaintiff. The Court rejected Galloway's argument. First, his argument denied a jury trial to the defendant: "To force this choice . . . would be to embed in the Constitution the hypertechnicality of common-law pleading and procedure. . . ." In addition, "[t]he Amendment did not bind the federal courts to the exact procedural incidents or details of jury trial . . . in 1791." . . .

(3) *Evidence Amounting to a "Mere Scintilla."* Most courts state that a "mere scintilla" is not legally sufficient evidence from which a reasonable factfinder can draw a legitimate inference. For example, in *Boeing Co. v. Shipman*, 411 F.2d 365, 374 (5th Cir. 1969) (en banc), the court of appeals explained that a "mere scintilla" is insufficient to present a question for the jury. But "if there is . . . evidence of such quality and weight that reasonable and fair-minded [people] in the exercise of impartial judgment might reach different conclusions . . . the case [must be] submitted to the jury."

(4) *Circumstantial Evidence.* Many, if not most, cases require the factfinder, whether judge or jury, to draw inferences from the circumstantial evidence in reaching a verdict on broader issues, such as whether the defendant's conduct proximately caused the occurrence, whether the applicable standard of care was violated, or about other so-called mixed questions of law and fact that are within the jury's province. In this respect, *Lavender v. Kurn* is a typical case in which the Court held that "there was [circumstantial] evidence from which it might be inferred that the end of the mail hook struck the decedent," and therefore judgment as a matter of law was improper. The Court devised a "reasonable basis in the record standard"

under which the jury performs the important function of drawing reasonable inferences from the circumstantial evidence.

(5) *If a Fact Issue Can Be Resolved by the Exercise of Logic—If It Doesn't Require Some Degree of "Speculation" and "Conjecture"—Then Paradoxically, It Isn't a Jury Issue!* An interesting paradox lies hidden in *Lavender v. Kurn*. The Court says:

> It is no answer to say that the jury's verdict involved speculation and conjecture. Whenever facts are in dispute or the evidence is such that fair-minded [people] may draw different inferences, a measure of speculation and conjecture is required on the part of those whose duty it is to settle the dispute....

And, conversely, if the case can be resolved by deductive logic, there is no need for a jury decision of the facts, because there is no jury issue! A paradox thus arises: If there is no speculation and conjecture required, then judgment as a matter of law is proper; but if the reviewing court thinks that too much speculation and conjecture is required, then judgment as a matter of law also is proper. The resolution of the paradox lies in the recognition that reasonableness is the standard: If different people, using a "reasonable" kind of "speculation and conjecture," could arrive at different inferences, then a jury issue is presented; otherwise, it is not.

(6) *Evidence that Contradicts Itself.* Internal inconsistencies in the plaintiff's evidence do not necessarily destroy its probative value. The jury may be able to reconcile the conflict in favor of the plaintiff in a reasonable way. *Cf. Wilson v. Bailey*, 257 F.2d 352 (10th Cir. 1958). On the other hand, when the contradiction means that no reasonable juror could credit the plaintiff's theory, a judgment as a matter of law is proper.

Procedural Aspects of Judgment as a Matter of Law: Notes and Questions

Read Rule 50(a) (judgment during trial).

(1) *Statement of Grounds for the Motion.* Rule 50 says that the motion must "specify... the law and facts that entitle the movant to the judgment." How specific does it have to be? *Cf. United States Industries, Inc. v. Semco Mfg. Co.*, 562 F.2d 1061 (8th Cir. 1977), in which the plaintiff moved for judgment as a matter of law in a contract case simply by saying that there was a legally enforceable contract and overwhelming evidence of the defendant's breach; the court held the statement sufficient. The main reason for the requirement is to enable the opponent to correct the deficiency, if she can, while the jury still is present. Presumably, that purpose should be considered in judging the sufficiency of the statement.

(2) *Timing of the Motion.* The motion is proper when the opponent rests or closes, or when all parties close. *Compare Rocco v. Johns-Manville Corp.*, 754 F.2d

110 (3d Cir. 1985) (motion was clearly untimely and could not be considered when asserted for the first time after the jury had rendered its verdict), *with Panotex Pipe Line Co. v. Phillips Petroleum Co.*, 457 F.2d 1279 (5th Cir. 1972) (grant of motion in favor of defendants during defense testimony, even though not immediately after plaintiff's having rested, not improper).

(3) *Making the Motion Outside the Jury's Presence.* A defendant usually should make the motion outside the presence of the jury. If the motion is overruled, the jury otherwise would hear the judge reject the defendant's arguments and may infer that the plaintiff's claim is meritorious. *But cf. Womble v. J.C. Penney & Co.*, 47 F.R.D. 350 (E.D. Tenn.), *aff'd*, 431 F.2d 985 (6th Cir. 1970) (failure to excuse jury during hearing before the bench on motion for judgment as a matter of law not improper).

[B] After Trial

> Read Rule 50(b) (judgment after trial).

Note on Requirements for Post-Trial Judgment as a Matter of Law

Reserving Decision of the Motion. If a Rule 50(a) motion is not granted, the trial judge is deemed to have submitted the action to the jury subject to a later determination of the motion. In other words, the trial judge can decide the motion after trial, even though it was initially made during trial. For one thing, the jury might decide the case the "right" way and thus might avoid the need to decide the legal question. If not, the court can grant the motion under the same legal standard after the verdict is in—and, if the appellate court disagrees, it can reinstate the verdict without the necessity of a retrial. Note, *Rule 50(b), Judgment Notwithstanding the Verdict*, 58 Colum. L. Rev. 517 (1958). Arguably, this is the careful course of action in a close case, and it allows for briefing and deliberation rather than quick decision in the heat of trial.

The Motion During Trial as a Prerequisite. As a consequence of this reasoning, a motion during trial is a prerequisite for moving for judgment as a matter of law after trial. Indeed, under a prior version of Rule 50, a Rule 50(a) motion made *before* the close of all the evidence had to be renewed at the *close* of all the evidence in order to preserve the ability to bring a Rule 50(b) motion. Under the current version of Rule 50, however, any Rule 50(a) motion may be renewed in a Rule 50(b) motion after trial.

The Legal Standard After Trial Is the Same as that During Trial. It follows that a post-trial judgment as a matter of law "is nothing more than a directed verdict granted after, rather than before, the jury has had an opportunity to bring in its verdict." *Lester v. Dunn*, 475 F.2d 983 (D.C. Cir. 1973). The same legal standard is applicable to both, because both are the same motion. In fact, the same standard also applies to the issue in an appellate court.

Notes and Questions

(1) *Motion During Trial as a Prerequisite to a Post-Trial Motion—A Trap for the Unwary: Guglielmo v. Scotti & Sons, Inc.*, 58 F.R.D. 413 (W.D. Pa. 1973). Rule 50(b) confines the granting of a judgment as a matter of law to parties who have moved during trial. The theory is that, if the jury still is present, the opponent may be able to supply the missing element in her proof if apprised of the problem by the "specific statement of the grounds." In the *Gugliemo* case, *supra*, the defense attorney approached the bench after the last witness in the case and informed the trial judge that he "did not have a motion" to make, but did have a written "point for binding instructions" to the jury. He then proceeded to make arguments about the contents of the jury instructions, including remarks about the standard of care, the gist of which was that the jury should be bound to hold for the defendant. Post-verdict, the defense attorney attempted to assert a motion for judgment as a matter of law on related grounds; the court held, however, that he had waived the motion, because his remarks to the court did not amount to a motion for a Rule 50(a) judgment as a matter of law.

Actually, Rule 50(b) issues can arise in several ways. For example, what if the movant requests a "dismissal" when she should request a judgment as a matter of law? *Cf. Peterson v. Hager*, 724 F.2d 851 (10th Cir. 1984) (held, although not proper in a jury trial, a "motion to dismiss" at the close of evidence will be treated as a motion for judgment as a matter of law). What if the grounds for the later motion for judgment after trial were not contained in the motion during trial? *Compare, e.g., Moran v. Raymond Corp.*, 484 F.2d 1008 (7th Cir. 1973) (written motion was insufficient by itself to preserve right to make later Rule 50(b) motion for judgment as a matter of law, because it contained no grounds; but since movant's oral argument made the grounds clear, no waiver), *with Western Oil Fields, Inc. v. Pennzoil United, Inc.*, 421 F.2d 387 (5th Cir. 1970) (where Rule 50(a) motion for judgment as a matter of law was filed but did not raise issue of damages, that issue could not later be urged as basis after trial for a Rule 50(b) judgment as a matter of law or as basis for appellate reversal). For a particularly poignant case, consider *Wegner v. Rodeo Cowboys Ass'n*, 417 F.2d 881 (10th Cir. 1969), in which the defendant said, "We have a motion in addition, if your honor please; a renewal of it," and clearly alluded to a previous motion stating specific grounds. But the judge said he would hear and consider the motion later, outside the jury's presence, and the defendant never presented it further nor obtained a definitive ruling from the judge. Held, a waiver: The defendant should have insisted on a ruling.

(2) *Should the Prerequisite of a Motion During Trial Be Abolished? (If So, Is Its Abolition Constitutionally Permissible?): Slocum v. New York Life Ins. Co.*, 228 U.S. 364 (1913). The frequency of procedural default, by which a party wins a judgment to which it is clearly not entitled on the merits, may be an argument for abolishing the

prerequisite. In fact, many states allow a motion for judgment notwithstanding the verdict, without the necessity of an earlier motion for directed verdict. *See, e.g.*, California CCP § 629; N.Y. CPLR § 4404; Tex. R. Civ. P. 301. Perhaps the approach followed by California, New York, and Texas can be criticized for failing to notify the non-movant of the defect during trial; but the justification is that the non-movant has the obligation of making a case to go to the jury, and instances in which that party would be able to remedy defects in the evidence must be very rare.

If you conclude that the federal courts also should abolish the prerequisite, you must consider whether the change would be constitutionally permissible. The Seventh Amendment not only preserves jury trial but also contains the "reexamination" clause, which prohibits facts found by the jury to be reexamined other than in the ways provided by the common law. The common law did not allow bare post-trial motions for judgment as a matter of law; it only allowed the judge to take the directed verdict motion under advisement, to be decided after trial. Certain older cases, such as *Slocum*, above, suggest that the Seventh Amendment requires this procedure. The decisions have been criticized, and it is possible that they may not indicate what the Court would decide today.

(3) *Motions Both During and After Trial Are Prerequisites to Appellate Consideration, Too.* Note that a motion during trial is also a prerequisite to an appellate attack on the sufficiency of the evidence to support the verdict. And also, the appellant must have filed a motion after trial, renewing the earlier motion. If no attack has been made in the trial court, there is no error to assign on appeal; and if there has been no attack by motion during trial, there can be no attack by post-trial motion for judgment as a matter of law—and hence the trial court has not committed any error that can be the basis of a reversal. In other words, if the motion is not made twice, there is no appeal on grounds of insufficient evidence. *E.g., Coughlin v. Capitol Cement Co.*, 571 F.2d 290 (5th Cir. 1978) (in absence of motion for directed verdict, sufficiency of evidence not reviewable on appeal).

UNITHERM FOOD SYSTEMS, INC. v. SWIFT-ECKRICH, INC., 546 U.S. 394 (2006). The losing defendant in this case made a Rule 50(a) Motion for Judgment as a Matter of Law during trial. The trial judge denied it. After trial, however, the defendant failed to renew its Motion for Judgment as a Matter of Law. The defendant also did not file a Motion for New Trial. The trial court therefore granted judgment for the plaintiff. The court of appeals, however, vacated the trial court's judgment. It held that the plaintiff had not produced legally sufficient evidence and that the state of the record would have allowed the trial judge to grant a Judgment as a Matter of Law (although under the circumstances, it remanded the case to the trial court for new proceedings).

The Supreme Court reversed the reversal and reinstated the judgment for the plaintiff, even though it did not disagree with the court of appeals holding that the plaintiff had not produced legally sufficient evidence. (Notice that this holding means that the judgment for plaintiff was upheld, in spite of the court of appeals holding that plaintiff had failed to prove its claim.) The case law had long since established that a post-verdict Motion for Judgment as a Matter of Law could not be granted, nor could an appellate court reverse for lack of evidence, unless there had been a Motion for Judgment as a Matter of Law during trial. (In fact, they are the same motion; the post-verdict motion is deemed a renewal of the motion during trial.) In this case, the Supreme Court held that a Motion for Judgment as a Matter of Law after trial is also a prerequisite to appellate reversal. Both motions are required for an appeal based on evidentiary sufficiency.

The Supreme Court reasoned that it is not error for the trial court to deny even a correct Motion for Judgment as a Matter of Law during trial, because the careful procedure is to obtain the jury's verdict. In summary, the Court's holding means that a party seeking appellate reversal on the ground that there is legally insufficient evidence must have filed *both* a Motion for Judgment as a Matter of Law during Trial, and a Motion for Judgment as a Matter of Law after trial, renewing the earlier motion; otherwise, the evidence will be treated as though it were sufficient even if it is not:

> . . . [W]hile a district court is permitted to enter judgment as a matter of law [during trial] when it concludes that the evidence is legally insufficient, it is not required to do so. To the contrary, the district courts are, if anything, encouraged to submit the case to the jury, rather than granting such motions. As Wright and Miller explain:
>
> "Even at the close of all the evidence it may be desirable to refrain from granting a motion for judgment as a matter of law. . . . If judgment as a matter of law is granted and the appellate court holds that the evidence in fact was sufficient to go to the jury, an entire new trial must be had. If, on the other hand, the trial court submits the case to the jury, though it thinks the evidence insufficient, final determination of the case is expedited greatly. . . ." 9A Federal Practice § 2533, at 319.
>
> Thus, the District Court's denial of respondent's preverdict motion cannot form the basis of respondent's appeal, because the denial of that motion was not error. . . . The only error here was counsel's failure to file a postverdict motion pursuant to Rule 50(b).

[C] Judgment as a Matter of Law in Favor of the Party with the Burden of Persuasion

Relevance of the Burden of Persuasion. Assume that the plaintiff is the only living person who knows how the accident occurred. The plaintiff testifies in a manner that, if believed, shows the defendant to have been negligent in the extreme. The defendant's attorney cross-examines the plaintiff; but the defendant never is able to offer evidence that contradicts the plaintiff's evidence. Since it remains undisputed, does the plaintiff's evidence entitle her to a judgment as a matter of law? The answer is, not necessarily. The plaintiff still has the burden of persuading the jury.

The Standard for Granting Judgment as a Matter of Law for the Party with the Burden of Proof. Theis means that it is harder for the party with the burden of proof to get a judgment as a matter of law. Some courts express the standard in terms of "conclusive" proof (which probably overstates the requirement). Fundamentally, the standard is the same as that applicable to the party without the burden: is the plaintiff's proof so definitive that no reasonable person could come to any other conclusion? Consider the following case.

GHALEB v. AMERICAN STEAMSHIP COMPANY, 684 Fed. Appx. 545 (6th Cir. 2017) (unpublished opinion). Ghaleb sued his ship's owner under the Jones Act, which is a federal statute providing a favorable negligence claim for sea workers. He charged negligence per se, because his employer had him work hours over a statutory maximum, and the work fatigued him and caused him to be injured. Ghaleb testified that he dropped a cable, which hit him, and he fell and was injured. During trial, Ghaleb made a Motion for Judgment as a Matter of Law (JMOL).

But the jury rendered a verdict for Defendant American Steamship. Ghaleb then renewed his Motion for JMOL. The trial court granted the motion, even though Ghaleb had the burden of proof as plaintiff. The court held that a reasonable jury could find only that Ghaleb and the chief had "worked more than the hours permitted by the statute in the days leading up to Plaintiff's accident." Also, there was "no explanation except for a lack of 'immediate and wakeful readiness' for why Plaintiff . . . did not extricate himself from the area . . . when he recognized he would be hit by the power cable and possibly killed." But the court of appeals reversed:

> . . . [C]ourts have recognized that granting the motion for a party with the burden of persuasion should happen only in "extreme cases." 9B Wright & Miller, Fed. Prac. & Proc. Civ. § 2535. The court must determine that the "effect of the evidence is not only sufficient to meet [the] burden of proof, but is overwhelming, leaving no room for the jury to draw significant inferences in favor of the other party." . . .
>
> Assuming American Steamship violated the [work hours] statute—a rather safe assumption from the evidence—this case requires us to apply the demanding JMOL standard in conjunction with the Jones Act's . . . relaxed proximate cause standard. As Ghaleb correctly asserts, the Act lessens his burden on the causation element—he must prove only "that employer negligence played any part, even the slightest, in producing the injury . . . ." But Ghaleb conflates this relaxed causation standard with a relaxed JMOL standard. He asserted . . . at oral argument that he needed only to show "any evidence" that a violation played a role in his accident to prevail on his JMOL motion.

> [T]his is wrong. . . . Because Ghaleb predicates negligence . . . on work-hours violations, this essentially means that if the jury could find that . . . fatigue [did not play a] causal role in his accident, Ghaleb is not entitled to JMOL. Here, the evidence allowed a reasonable jury to conclude that this was either a faultless accident or an accident unrelated to . . . fatigue.
>
> The district court stated that there was "no explanation except for a lack of immediate and wakeful readiness" for why Ghaleb stayed in the cable's path when throwing the heaving line down to the dock. . . .
>
> [But] a jury could find Ghaleb acted as a reasonable, wakeful person would. And in fact, Ghaleb touted testimony by Chief Warren that Ghaleb "did nothing wrong" during the rope maneuver. . . . Moreover, even if the jury believed that Ghaleb put himself at risk, it did not need to accept that he did so due to fatigue. . . .

One judge dissented: "The majority opinion lays out the governing legal principles clearly and accurately . . . . I respectfully dissent, however, because viewing the evidence in the light most favorable to defendant, . . . no reasonable jury could fail to conclude that crew fatigue played some part in the accident, however slight."

Notes and Questions

(1) *Did the Court Apply the Standard Correctly?* It is understandable that this case is unpublished, because it contributes no new principle of law. In a case like this one, the issue is one of judging the facts. Whether the court's decision is right depends, on the one hand, on whether a review of the inferences makes it reasonable to conclude that the sailors' fatigue had absolutely nothing to do with the accident—nothing at all. On the other hand, it seems difficult to conclude that fatigue had no role whatever, and perhaps the court of appeals is wrong.

(2) *The Same Principle Applies if the Defendant Has the Burden of Proof: Arbegast v. Board of Education.* 480 N.E.2d 365 (N.Y. 1985). Apparently, "donkey ball" is common in some areas of New York, because the court in this case mentioned a game of donkey ball without explanation, as if the case were about a car or a bus. Your authors here, who are not from New York, infer that donkey ball is basketball, but with the difference that the participants ride donkeys: evidently a New York custom. Arbegast, a teacher in the school district, played in a donkey ball game as a fund-raiser for the senior class. Her donkey threw her. She sued the Buckeye Donkey Ball Company (apparently, such enterprises exist) and the district for negligence because the donkey was not gentle enough.

The donkey ball company's defense was assumption of the risk. Only express assumption of the risk was recognized under New York law. But the evidence showed, and Arbegast agreed, that participants had been warned that "the donkeys do buck and put their heads down causing people to fall off and . . . if injuries happened the participants were at their own risk." The appellate court held that the trial court should have granted a directed verdict for defendant, even though the defendant had the burden of proof on the affirmative defense of assumption of the risk, because the plaintiff's own testimony to the controlling facts had established the defense as a matter of law.

IV. New Trial

Read Rule 50(b) (alternative motion for new trial) and Rule 59 (new trials and amendment of judgments).

Standard for the Motion for New Trial; Uses. Unlike the motion for judgment as a matter of law (which serves only a single purpose and is subject to a mechanical standard), the motion for new trial is a multi-purpose device and is highly discretionary. Although these two post-trial motions are often asserted simultaneously, they have very different functions.

Addressing a Broad Range of Miscarriages of Justice: Trial Error, Newly Discovered Evidence, Misconduct, Result Contrary to the Weight of the Evidence, Etc. While the purpose of a judgment as a matter of law is to give judgment to the party entitled to it, the purpose of a new trial is to start the process over again because the current result reflects a possible miscarriage of justice. That purpose encompasses a wide variety of potential grounds. The most common, probably, is trial or pre-trial error. The trial judge can order a new trial because of error in the charge, admittance of inadmissible evidence, erroneous rulings during jury selection, etc.

Furthermore, a trial judge can grant a new trial upon a showing of newly discovered evidence, under certain narrow circumstances. Also, misconduct of jurors, parties, or attorneys can be grounds for a new trial. And the motion for new trial even invokes the judge's authority to set aside the result because the judge believes the jury's verdict is against the "great weight" of the evidence—an idea that would be heresy in a judgment as a matter of law. The trial judge also has authority to grant a new trial because the amount of damages is excessive or inadequate when compared to the record—which also is a weight-of-the-evidence concept.

Reversible Error Is Not Required; Discretion. The trial judge can grant a new trial even if an appellate court could not. The reason need not amount to reversible error. For example, an error in the charge that was not objected to, still can be a ground for new trial if the judge decides to grant it. In theory, the judge should confine such a ruling to miscarriages that had a probable effect on the outcome, and Fed. R. Civ. P. 61 requires the disregard of any defects "that do not affect any party's substantial rights"; but usually, the trial judge's grant of a new trial in the federal system is final because it is reviewable on appeal only under the deferential standard of abuse of discretion. *See* Case Comment, *Appellate Review of Trial Court's Ruling on a Motion for New Trial*, 9 Memphis St. U. L. Rev. 535 (1979).

[A] New Trial Based on Procedural Errors

Conway v. Chemical Leaman Tank Lines, Inc.

687 F.2d 108 (5th Cir. 1982)

Johnson, Circuit Judge:

This is the fourth time this diversity action has been before this Court on appeal. This case has been tried before a jury on three different occasions.... The issue in the instant appeal is whether the district court abused its discretion in granting a new trial because the defendant, Chemical Leaman Tank Lines, Inc. (Chemical Leaman), introduced a surprise expert witness in the second trial. We hold that the district court did not abuse its discretion.

I. *Background*

This tort action arose when two heavy tank trucks sideswiped each other near the centerline of a highway ... at approximately 4:00 a.m.... The westbound truck, owned by Dixie Transport of Texas, Inc. (Dixie Transport), lost its left front tire at impact, veered off the road to the left, and overturned, killing its driver, Robert Eugene Conway. Conway's widow, sons, and Dixie Transport brought this action against Chemical Leaman, owner of the eastbound truck involved in the collision. The essence of plaintiffs' contention is that the Chemical Leaman truck negligently crossed over the centerline of the highway, striking the oncoming Dixie Transport truck driven by Conway.

The only living eyewitness to the collision was Chemical Leaman's driver, John Johnson, who testified that Conway suddenly turned onto Johnson's side of the road when the vehicles were about a truck-length apart, both traveling about fifty miles per hour. Crucial to Johnson's credibility before the jury was the expert witness testimony concerning the various marks made by the trucks at the site of the collision. The expert witness testimony involved the tire marks in Dixie Transport's (Conway's) westbound lane, in Chemical Leaman's (Johnson's) eastbound lane, the gouge marks, and the physical dimensions of the trucks and the road.

[*The First Trial: Judgment for Plaintiff Reversed on Appeal on Evidence Grounds.*] At the first jury trial..., Dixie Transport's safety director and an accident reconstruction expert testified that the tire marks were skid marks which indicated that Conway was properly in his right hand lane just before the collision, while Johnson's left wheels were over the centerline in Conway's lane. Expert witnesses for the defendant, Charles Ruble and Dr. William Tonn, testified, however, that it was Conway's truck which was driven on the wrong side of the roadway at the time of the collision, while Johnson's truck was in its proper lane. After hearing this testimony, the jury returned its verdict which was favorable to the plaintiffs. On appeal, this Court reversed and remanded on the grounds that the district court failed to admit certain impeachment evidence. *Conway v. Chemical Leaman, Inc., (Conway I)*, 525 F.2d 927 (5th Cir.), *modified on petition for rehearing*, 540 F.2d 837 (5th Cir. 1976).

[*The Second Trial: A Surprise Witness and a Confusing Verdict.*] At the second jury trial . . . , the plaintiffs' witnesses again testified that tire marks indicated Chemical Leaman's truck had crossed the centerline and caused the collision. After the plaintiffs had rested their case, the defendant's counsel failed to call to the stand the two expert witnesses it had called in the previous trial, Ruble and Tonn. Instead, Chemical Leaman's safety director, Arnold Hay, was called to testify.

Hay had been designated as the representative for Chemical Leaman at the beginning of the first trial and occupied that position throughout all of that proceeding. Hay's name was not placed on the list of witnesses in the court's pre-trial order and such order specifically required notification of any further witnesses to the other party five days prior to the trial. [H]ay sat at the defendant's counsel table as the representative of Chemical Leaman, assisting defendant's counsel throughout the entire trial.

. . . [T]he time at which Hay was called is of particular note: It was [a]fter the plaintiffs' witnesses had been excused, and it was near the end of the second jury trial of the case. When Hay was called to take the stand plaintiffs' counsel immediately objected that he was a surprise witness, and the district court granted a running or continuing objection to all of his testimony.

Hay's testimony at this second trial included his opinion that the Chemical Leaman truck was not the source of the questioned eastbound tire marks. Rather, Hay testified that the eastbound marks were made when a vehicle of a different type later tracked asphalt from the asphalt spill left by Conway's overturned truck. Hay also testified that what he claimed to be Chemical Leaman tire marks were not skid or brake marks; he asserted they would have been lighter than the westbound tire marks. [H]ay's analysis allowed the jury to determine that both vehicles came so close to the centerline that they clipped mirrors as the cabs of the tractors passed on the highway, causing Conway to lose control of his vehicle.

Hay's testimony failed to point out that differences in weight between Conway's asphalt-loaded truck and the Chemical Leaman truck might explain the lighter tire marks in the eastbound lane. [I]n any event, the jury's response to the court's interrogatories in the second trial clearly imply that they were influenced by Hay's testimony.(2) The jury returned a verdict favorable to the defendant.

---

(2) [Note that under then-existing law, contributory negligence in any degree, however slight, was a complete defense in this jurisdiction.—Eds.] The jury verdict in the second trial recites in pertinent part, as follows:

> INTERROGATORY NO. 1
>
> Do you find from a preponderance of the evidence that the Defendant, Chemical Leaman Tank Lines, Inc., its agents, servants or employees, committed some act or omission of negligence which was a proximate cause of the injuries and death of the deceased, Robert Eugene Conway?
>
> Answer: "Yes" or "No".
>
> ANSWER: Yes.

[*The Motion for New Trial: Erroneously Granted on the First Stated Ground of an Allegedly "Defective" Verdict.*] The plaintiffs thereafter filed a motion to set aside the verdict of the jury and to grant a new trial. The motions were based on two grounds: (1) the answers of the jury to the interrogatories did not support a judgment favorable to any party [this assertion was erroneous]; and (2) the district court erred in permitting the surprise witness, Hay, to testify for the defendant. The district court granted the motion for a new trial [erroneously] on the first ground only [i.e., on the ground that the verdict did not support any judgment; but at the time, contributory negligence in any degree was a complete defense, and the verdict in fact supported a judgment for defendant in this jurisdiction—Eds.]. The court did not address the plaintiffs' second ground concerning the surprise witness feature. No judgment was entered in this second jury trial.

[*The Third Trial: Judgment for Plaintiff Reversed on Appeal Because the "Defective Verdict" Ground for New Trial (After the Second Trial) Was Erroneous.*] ... [In the third trial,] the jury returned a verdict favorable to the plaintiffs. Upon appeal this Court determined that [after the second trial,] the trial court erred in ordering a new trial (the third trial) because the jury's answers in the second trial supported a judgment for the defendant, Chemical Leaman. *Conway v. Chemical Leaman Tank Lines, Inc., Conway II*, 610 F.2d 360 (5th Cir. 1980). The case was reversed and remanded with instructions that the trial court enter judgment for Chemical Leaman based on the jury's answers in the second trial. The trial court complied and entered judgment for Chemical Leaman. 487 F. Supp. 647.

[*The Trial Court Re-Grants the New Trial—On the Other Ground, "Unfair Surprise."*] Plaintiffs once again filed a motion for new trial, reasserting the ground—previously urged but not ruled upon—set forth in plaintiffs' motion to set aside the verdict of the jury and to grant a new trial: that the trial court erred in allowing Hay to testify as [a surprise] expert witness for defendant at the second trial. The trial court granted this motion for new trial, 87 F.R.D. 712, and entered judgment in favor of plaintiffs upon the jury verdict returned at the third trial. The trial court's

---

If you have answered interrogatory No. 1 "Yes" and only in that event, list below the acts or omissions of negligence you have so found.

We have decided the defendant was too close to center line, as was the plaintiff, causing the collision of mirrors, after which uncontrollable acts by both drivers caused the final collision.

INTERROGATORY NO. 2

Do you find from a preponderance of the evidence that the deceased, Robert Eugene Conway, committed some act or omission of negligence which was a proximate cause of the injuries and death of the deceased?

Answer: "Yes" or "No".

ANSWER: Yes.

If you have answered interrogatory No. 2 "Yes", and only in that event, list below the acts or omissions of negligence you have so found.

We have decided the plaintiff was also too close to the center line, causing the collision of mirrors, after which uncontrollable acts by both drivers caused the final collision.

power to consider the second ground of Conway's motion for new trial, and its order granting a new trial, were affirmed by this Court. In this Court's opinion, *Conway v. Chemical Leaman Tank Lines, Inc.* (*Conway III*), 644 F.2d 1059, 1062 (5th Cir. 1981), it was suggested that, instead of ordering a fourth trial, judgment might be rendered for Conway on the third trial, absent any errors in that trial. [The trial court did enter judgment on the third trial, and defendant brought this fourth and last appeal, attacking the Unfair Surprise ground for setting aside the second judgment.]

II. *The Unfair Surprise Claim*

Rule 59(a) of the Fed. R. Civ. P. states that a "new trial may be granted to . . . any of the parties . . . in an action in which there has been a trial by a jury, for any of the reasons for which new trials have heretofore been granted in actions at law in courts of the United States." It is well settled that Rule 59 provides a means of relief in cases in which a party has been unfairly made the victim of surprise. 11 Wright & Miller, *Federal Practice and Procedure* § 2805 at 38 (1973). The surprise, however, must be "inconsistent with substantial justice" in order to justify a grant of a new trial. Fed. R. Civ. P. 61. The district court is therefore entitled to grant a new trial only if the admission of the surprise testimony actually prejudiced the plaintiffs' case. . . . This Court has limited reversible error from unfair surprise to situations where a completely new issue is suddenly raised or a previously unidentified expert witness is suddenly called to testify. . . .

The determination of a trial judge to either grant or deny a motion for a new trial is reviewable under an abuse of discretion standard. . . .

In the instant case, Hay was a previously unidentified witness who was called without any forewarning to testify as an expert at the second trial. Hay's testimony was not cumulative; rather, it introduced the theory that the questioned eastbound tire marks were asphalt marks from another vehicle. No other party—plaintiff or defendant—had presented this theory. Under the circumstances, plaintiffs had no time or opportunity to prepare a response to this unexpected turn of events. The interrogatories answered by the jury in the second trial leave no doubt that the jury was influenced by Hay's testimony.

Even assuming the testimony was unfair and prejudicial, Chemical Leaman nevertheless contends that the plaintiffs should have moved for a continuance rather than a new trial. Indeed, the granting of a continuance is a generally more appropriate remedy than exclusion of evidence when claims of unfair surprise are raised. *See* Advisory Committee's Note to Rule 403, Fed. R. Evid. The granting or denial of a continuance, however, is a procedural matter of the kind that this Court has repeatedly said is subject to the discretion of the trial judge. . . . At the time that Hay's testimony was admitted, the trial was almost completed. A continuance at this point may have been, from the vantage of the district court judge, impractical and inefficient. Although this Court has acknowledged that continuance is a preferable remedy for prejudicial error from unfair surprise, there is no ironclad rule requiring it. . . .

Accordingly, the district court did not abuse its discretion in granting a new trial on grounds of unfair surprise. . . . [AFFIRMED.]

Note: Understanding the Sequence in Conway

First Trial: Plaintiff Conway wins verdict and judgment.

First Appeal: Reversed on evidentiary grounds (not relevant to this decision).

Second Trial: Defendant Chemical Leaman uses surprise witness; obtains verdict that both drivers negligent. New trial granted on defective verdict ground; no ruling on surprise ground.

Third Trial: Verdict for plaintiff.

Second Appeal: Reversed. Verdict not defective; it supports judgment for defendant.

Judge Grants New Trial on still-pending surprise ground.

Third Appeal: Upholds power for new trial; suggests granting judgment on third trial.

Trial Judge Grants Judgment for plaintiff on verdict in third trial.

Fourth Appeal: Affirms surprise-ground new trial and judgment for plaintiff.

Notes and Questions

(1) *Why Do We Have Juries? Are Their Verdicts Accurate?* People sometimes think that jury verdicts are "accurate" and predictable. As this case shows, they vary unpredictably, at least in close cases. Some experienced lawyers believe that the reason for jury trials is that they bring about authority and acceptance of judgments due to public participation, rather than enhanced accuracy. In some circles, insisting on a jury trial is referred to as "rolling the dice." Does this case bear out that description?

(2) *Don't Let this Case Mislead You into Thinking that New Trials Are Easily Obtained.* The trial judge's behavior in *Conway,* in granting repeated new trials after jury verdicts, is quite unusual. A judge is cognizant of the backlog in her docket, including many cases in which the parties have not yet had a single trial, let alone two or three. Furthermore, perfect trials are rare. Thus, trial judges have a natural resistance to granting new trials. *See* SACRAMENTO BEE, April 8, 1984, at B-8, col. 1 (reporting on retirement of California Judge Warren K. Taylor, who stated that his respect for juries was so strong that he set aside only two (2) jury verdicts in 21 years).

(3) *Reversible Error in Granting a New Trial.* The judge has broad discretion. Notice, however, that (after the third trial) the court of appeals held that ordering the third trial was a reversible abuse of discretion because the jury's answers in

the second trial were not insufficient to support a judgment, as the trial judge had thought. Whether the verdict will support a judgment is a pure question of law, and so "abuse" of discretion is easier to find.

Note that this attack, which actually concerned the second trial, occurred after the third trial—because the grant of a new trial is not a final judgment, and therefore it ordinarily is not appealable. Thus, attacks on the third judgment included allegations of error in the third trial and, also, allegations that the third trial never should have been held because the second verdict should not have been set aside.

(4) *What Should Conway Jr. Do Now? Go to Law School!* Having finally prevailed, Conway's son went to law school. He ended up in a procedure class taught by one of the authors of this book. From his experience in the case against Chemical Leaman, he already knew a great deal.

[B] New Trial Based Upon the "Great Weight" of the Evidence

Note on "Great Weight" of the Evidence

What Does the "Great Weight of the Evidence" Mean? Imagine that the winning party's evidence is weak, but it still presents a jury question, and the judge cannot grant a judgment as a matter of law (JMOL). Nevertheless, the judge thinks that the jury's verdict is not only wrong, but terribly wrong. The judge can grant a new trial based on the "great weight" of the evidence even though a JMOL is impossible.

The Judge Can "Weigh" the Evidence for a MNT But Not a JMOL. Notice that weighing the evidence is improper on a motion for JMOL. On a MNT, however, the judge does weigh the evidence. But the judge is confined to granting a new trial only if the verdict offends the "great" weight of the evidence. The judge does not use a preponderance standard; that's for the jury.

Experience Hendrix, LLC v. Hendrixlicensing.Com, Ltd.

762 F.3d 829 (9th Cir. 2013)

Ebel, Circuit Judge:

This litigation stems from a dispute over the commercial use of a deceased celebrity's image, likeness, and name.... Experience Hendrix owns trademarks that it uses to sell and license products related to [legendary rock star] Jimi Hendrix.... Experience Hendrix succeeded [in obtaining a jury verdict] on its claims alleging that Defendants Andrew Pitsicalis and his company, Hendrixlicensing.com, L.L.C. (collectively "Pitsicalis"), were licensing Hendrix-related merchandise that infringed Experience Hendrix's trademarks. The district court, however, significantly reduced the jury's award by granting a judgment as a matter of law (JMOL) and, alternatively, granted defendant's motion for new trial (MNT) on damages [on the ground that the verdict was against the "great weight" of the evidence. The court of appeals here vacates the damage reduction (the JMOL) but affirms the new trial on great weight grounds.] ...

Pitsicalis owns, or has licenses to use, photographs and original pieces of art depicting Hendrix, as well as visual artwork created by Hendrix himself.... Pitsicalis began licensing the right to use these images to ... sell Hendrix-related merchandise .... Pitsicalis placed marks on his licensed products that used the names "Hendrix" and "Jimi Hendrix," as well as Jimi Hendrix's signature and a logo of Hendrix's headshot with a guitar.... Pitsicalis also used two websites with the domain names hendrixlicensing.com and hendrixartwork.com.

... At trial, a jury found that Pitsicalis's trademark infringement also amounted to an unfair or deceptive trade practice under [state law].... Although the jury awarded Experience Hendrix damages ... totaling $1,723,300, the district court [granted a JMOL and] reduced the jury's award to $60,000. [In the alternative, in the event this ruling should be reversed, the district court granted a new trial because the damages were against the great weight of the evidence.]

[The damages verdict included $60,000 consisting of profits made by Pitscalis. To that amount, the jury added questionable items: damages for lost profits and damages to Experience Hendrix's image and goodwill. The lost profits arguably were duplicative of Pitscalis's profits, and it was arguable that the image-and-goodwill damages were unsupported by evidence. The district court therefore resolved these latter items by granting a JMOL and, in case the JMOL should be reversed, an alternative new trial based on great weight of the evidence. Thus, the district court granted judgment for only $60,000.]

[The court of appeals held that the evidence of these damages was at least minimally sufficient, enough to survive a Motion for JMOL. For example, the court observed,] There was undisputed evidence that, at the same time that Pitsicalis was licensing his infringing goods, Experience Hendrix suffered a significant decline in its own licensing revenue earned from products similar to Pitsicalis's infringing merchandise.

In considering a Rule 50(b)(3) motion for judgment as a matter of law, the district court must uphold the jury's award if there was any "legally sufficient basis" to support it. [It must draw] all reasonable inferences in favor of the nonmoving party, Experience Hendrix; the court may not make any credibility decisions or weigh the evidence. [Therefore, the JMOL is reversed.] ...

[A motion for new trial is sharply different.] The district court can grant a new trial under Rule 59 on any ground necessary to prevent a miscarriage of justice. In this case, the district court specifically concluded that a new trial was warranted because the damages awards were "against the clear weight of the evidence and the product of speculation, error, and disregard of the Court's instructions." ... Our standard of review of the district court's ruling [on a new trial] also differs from the de novo standard governing our review of a district court's [JMOL] decision. The district court's decision on a Rule 59 motion for a new trial "will be overturned on appeal only for abuse of discretion." For the following reasons, we conclude the district court's reasons are sufficient to warrant a new trial on both Experience Hendrix's lost profits and damages for its loss of reputation and goodwill....

Experience Hendrix's supporting evidence underlying each of these measures of damages, while providing a legally sufficient basis to survive a [JMOL], was minimal and, in the eyes of the district court, not very credible.... [New trial AFFIRMED on great-weight-of-the-evidence grounds.]

Notes and Questions

(1) *Why Is the Trial Judge Restricted to Considering the "Great" Weight of the Evidence, Not Merely the Preponderance?* If the judge sets aside the jury's verdict based merely on her opinion of the "weight" of the evidence, doesn't she thereby substitute her judgment of the preponderance of the evidence for the jury's? Shouldn't the judge be required to say that the verdict is based upon "grossly" insufficient evidence, or is against the "great" weight of the evidence? For a decision expressing the prevailing federal view that the judge may grant a new trial based upon the "great" weight—but not merely on the "greater" weight, or preponderance—see *Eyre v. McDonough Power Equip., Inc.*, 755 F.2d 416 (5th Cir. 1985). *See also* Figure 11A.

Note that the *Hendrix* case also deals with the standard for appellate reversal: abuse of discretion. Thus, we have a trial court standard requiring the judge to consider the "great" weight, but an appellate standard upholding the trial judge's discretion according to a looser test. In any event, "[t]he holding... means that it will be a rare case in which the trial judge will not have authority to grant a new trial because of factual disagreement with the jury." Crump & Crump, *The Year's Developments in Civil Procedure*, 16 Texas Tech. L. Rev. 115, 137 (1985).

(2) *Not Enough that Judge Disagrees with Jury: Foster v. Continental Can Corp.*, 101 F.R.D. 710 (E.D. Ind. 1984). In this vehicular accident case, the judge concluded that the verdict, which was for the defendant, came "very close" to being contrary to the weight of the evidence, and that the judge himself would have decided the case differently, but these conclusions were "not enough" to compel the granting of a new trial. *See also, e.g., Brown v. McGraw-Edison Co.*, 736 F.2d 609 (10th Cir. 1984) (new trial not warranted because verdict not "clearly, decidedly, or overwhelmingly" against evidence).

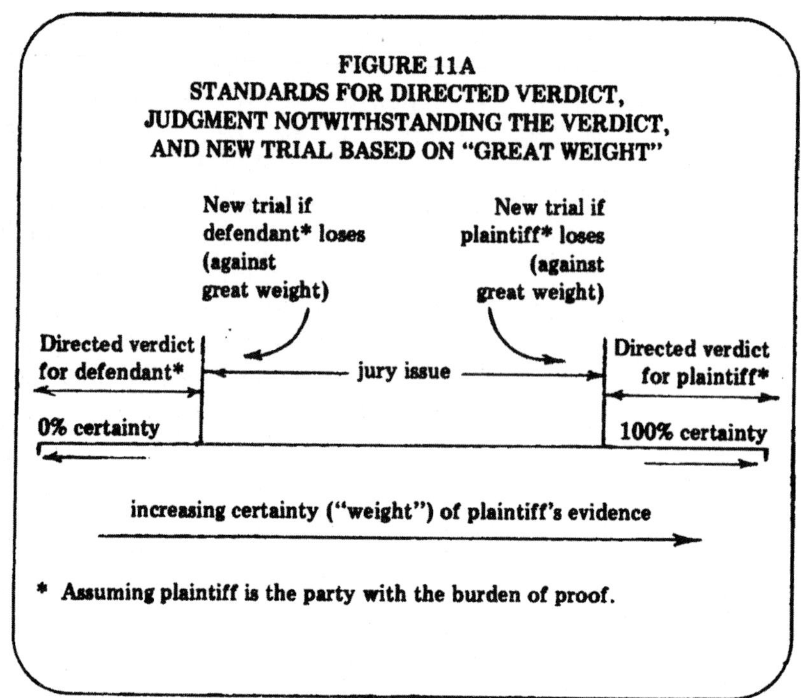

[C] New Trial Based on the Amount of Damages: "Remittitur" and "Additur"

Remittitur. The trial judge also can grant a new trial because the damage verdict is excessive or inadequate. Actually, this kind of new trial is really just a special case of a new trial based on the great weight of the evidence. When the trial judge concludes that the damage award is so high that it is against the great weight of the evidence, she may grant a "conditional" new trial; that is, she may order that the verdict will be set aside and a new trial held unless the plaintiff agrees to a judgment for a lesser amount specified by the judge. Such a conditional new trial is called a "remittitur." *See, e.g., United States v. 158. 24 Acres of Land*, 696 F.2d 559 (8th Cir. 1982).

The issue is sometimes put in terms of whether the jury's award "shocked the conscience of the court" or must have been influenced by "passion or prejudice." *See Gasperini v. Center for Humanities, Inc.*, 518 U.S. 415, 422 (1996); *see also Norfin, Inc. v. International Business Machines Corp.*, 81 F.R.D. 614 (D. Colo. 1979) (jury award of $7.5 million as lost profits in patent infringement action was not so high that it could "shock the conscience of the court"). Review is confined to an abuse of discretion standard.

A High Rate of Damages Reductions. In 1987, the RAND Corporation's Institute for Civil Justice published a study of tort litigation in the United States, "Trends in Tort Litigation." Among its many interesting findings were that 20% of all jury awards are reduced by the court or through negotiations; that the higher the award, the more likely it will be cut; and that awards including punitive damages are cut an average 43%. *See also* Schnapper, *Judges Against Juries—Appellate Review of Federal Civil Jury Verdicts*, 1989 WISC. L. REV. 237.

Additur. The trial judge lacks authority, in the federal system, a grant a new trial conditioned upon "additur," or upon a defendant's agreement to an increase in damages. However, the trial judge can grant the plaintiff a new trial because the damages are inadequate. For a state court opinion upholding the use of additur, see *Jehl v. Southern Pacific Co.*, 66 Cal. 2d 821, 427 P.2d 988, 95 Cal. Rptr. 276 (1967) (where jury award of $100,000 was exceeded by clearly proved economic damages even without pain and suffering, trial judge could grant new trial, but also could consider additur).

[D] New Trial Based on Newly Discovered Evidence

HENLEY v. FMC CORPORATION, 20 Fed. Appx. 108 (4th Cir. 2001) (unpublished opinion). Plaintifffs brought this action on behalf of a class who they claimed had been injured by FMC's accidental release of phosphorous trichloride. FMC's defensive theory, testified to by its expert, Eggleston, was that winds had blown the cloud away from the class and into an uninhabited area. The plaintiffs then offered an unannounced surprise witness, Drake, from the state Department of Environmental Protection (DEP), who contradicted Eggleston. The jury returned a $3.8 million verdict for plaintiffs.

FMC moved for a new trial based upon newly discovered evidence and offered the affidavits of Spann, who was Drake's supervisor at DEP and who pointed out errors in Drake's testimony. The court granted the new trial. The second trial resulted in a verdict for FMC. The plaintiffs appealed. The case shows the stringent standards for a new trial based on newly discovered evidence, for which the two most difficult requirements may be (1) evidence that could not have been discovered with diligence and (2) evidence that would probably change the result. In spite of this high barrier, the court of appeals affirmed the grant of new trial:

> The first two elements of the newly discovered evidence test are whether the evidence is, "in fact, newly discovered," and whether there are facts alleged "from which the court may infer diligence on the part of the movant." The Appellants argue that "FMC could have taken Mr. Spann's deposition at any time before trial, but chose not to do so," and that FMC "had access to Spann before trial...." [But] the district court found that the Appellants "waited until the waning days of a lengthy trial to spring a surprise witness and unexpected evidence upon FMC's lawyers and then only after Dr. Eggleston left town." Accordingly, the district court found that "FMC was excusably ignorant and exercised appropriate diligence

> upon Spann's return to expose Plaintiff's calculated, late, surprise and successful effort to crush the cornerstone of its defense." . . .
>
> The third element of the newly-discovered-evidence standard is whether the evidence is "not [] merely cumulative or impeaching." The Appellants contend that Spann's testimony "was offered for no other purpose than to contradict the testimony of Mark Drake," and, therefore, it was merely impeachment evidence. The district court found that "[t]he new evidence here . . . is much more than . . . impeachment" because "[i]t not only serves to seriously deprecate Drake's trial testimony and his interpretation of the documents, but also supplants that testimony entirely, replacing it with his supervisor's contrary account of the critical wind direction evidence." We agree. . . .
>
> The fourth and fifth elements of the test for newly discovered evidence are whether it is "material to the issues involved," and whether the "evidence is such that it is likely to produce a new outcome if the case were retried . . . ." The district court found that the timing and nature of Drake's testimony were crucial to the case because Drake's testimony undermined Eggleston's testimony, which formed the backbone of FMC's defense . . . .

The court of appeals thus held that the district court had not abused its discretion in granting the new trial. But it decided to reverse for yet a third trial, because of other errors.

Notes and Questions

(1) *The Restrictions on New Trials for Newly Discovered Evidence.* Notice that new trial for newly discovered evidence is narrowly circumscribed. A showing of non-discovery and diligence prior to trial is required, as this opinion shows. *See also Moore v. Rosecliff Realty Corp.*, 88 F. Supp. 956 (D.N.J. 1950) (where attorney attempted to find witness during three weeks preceding trial, diligence not sufficiently shown). But even these factors are not sufficient unless the evidence is itself very significant. *Cf. Pioneer Paper Stock Co. v. Miller Transport Co.*, 109 F. Supp. 502 (D.N.J. 1953) (photograph showing that vehicle lights were on, contrary to trial court finding, was merely cumulative and related to subordinate fact and probably would not have changed result). The law is restrictive of new trials on newly discovered evidence, because it is usually easy to find another piece of evidence after trial, and for many lawyers, losing a jury trial is a painful personal rejection. If it were easy, newly discovered evidence motions would be filed frequently.

(2) *Henley's Diligence Argument: Was It Better than the Courts Thought?* The plaintiffs say that FMC was not diligent because they could easily have taken Spann's deposition but didn't. Did this show lack of diligence? (On the other hand, FMC had no reason to take Spann's deposition until Drake surprised them, and the courts would not want to encourage unnecessary discovery.)

V. The Interplay Between Motion for Judgment as a Matter of Law (or Notwithstanding the Verdict) and Motion for New Trial

Read Rule 50(c)-(e) (interplay between motion for judgment as a matter of law and motion for new trial).

The Verdict Loser Often Files Both a Motion for Judgment as a Matter of Law (or Notwithstanding the Verdict) and a Motion for New Trial. Remember, the two motions serve different, and complementary, purposes. The first motion (MJMOL) serves the narrow purpose of giving judgment to a party unambiguously entitled to it on the basis of the evidence. The second motion (for new trial, MNT) ensures the fairness of the process and result. If you have lost the jury verdict, you may very well want to file both kinds of motions.

Rule 50(c)-(e): A Confusing, but Logical, Procedure for Considering both Motions, with Only One Appeal. Subsections (c) through (e) of Rule 50 may confuse you at first. But they are ultimately logical. They are premised upon two policy considerations. First, (1) all parties should have the benefit of making both kinds of motions. Second, (2) there should be only one appeal from both motions.

The Simplest Case: The Trial Judge Denies Both Motions. Overwhelmingly, the most frequent pattern is that the judge denies the motion for judgment as a matter of law (or notwithstanding the verdict), because the jury's verdict does have some support in the evidence, and also denies the motion for new trial, because the process and result are not unfair. The losing party has had the opportunity to make both motions, and a single appeal can be taken from both rulings.

A More Difficult Case: The Trial Judge Grants the Motion for Judgment as a Matter of Law (or Notwithstanding the Verdict) and Then Must Rule Conditionally on the Same Party's Motion for New Trial (And Also on the Opponent's Motion for New Trial). Here, the process becomes confusing, but we ask the gentle reader to persevere, with the promise that there is a kind of logic to the Rule. If the trial judge grants the Motion for Judgment as a Matter of Law (or Notwithstanding the Verdict) ("MJMOL"), the verdict loser is now the (satisfied) judgment winner. But the opponent (the verdict winner, now the judgment loser) isn't, and may appeal. If the appellate court reverses and reinstates the verdict, the Rules contemplate a single appeal, and that result could not be accomplished if the appellate court had to remand for a ruling on the pending Motion for New Trial ("MNT").

Therefore, immediately after granting the MJN, the trial judge must rule conditionally on the MNT. In other words, she must say in advance what ruling she would make on the MNT, in case the MJN is reversed. *See* Rule 50(c)(1). And, finally, the verdict winner, who is now the judgment loser, also must have the opportunity to file a MNT, since this party, too, is entitled to the benefit of both motions. Although having lost the judgment, this party may take the position that rulings of the trial court unfairly forced that result (*e.g.*, the trial judge erroneously excluded evidence that would have proved the case, so that a new trial is appropriate). *See* Rule 50(d).

A Third Case: Appellate Reversal on Sufficiency-of-Evidence Grounds. Now, imagine that the verdict winner receives judgment, and has no dissatisfaction with the trial court's disposition of the case. But the court of appeals, for the first time, rules that the evidence did not support the verdict—and that the opponent's MJN should have been granted. The verdict winner is now the judgment loser, but has not had the benefit of a motion for new trial. As the following case, *Neely v. Martin K. Eby Constr. Co.*, indicates, the policy in favor of a single appeal has led to a strange requirement: that the losing appellee must move for new trial in the court of appeals. (Notice that this is one of the few instances in which action in the appellate court is not predicated on action in the trial court.) *See* Rule 50(e). In *Neely*, the trouble was that this requirement, which today is reasonably clear, was not at all clear at that time.

Neely v. Martin K. Eby Construction Co., Inc.

386 U.S. 317 (1967)

Mr. Justice White delivered the opinion of the Court.

Petitioner brought this diversity action . . . alleging that respondent's negligent construction, maintenance, and supervision of a scaffold platform used in the construction of a missile silo . . . had proximately caused her father's fatal plunge from the platform during the course of his employment as Night Silo Captain for . . . an engineering firm engaged in the construction of a missile launcher system in the silo. At the close of the petitioner's evidence and again at the close of all the evidence, respondent moved for a directed verdict. The trial judge denied both motions and submitted the case to a jury, which returned a verdict for petitioner for $25,000.

Respondent then moved for judgment notwithstanding the jury's verdict or, in the alternative, for a new trial, in accordance with Rule 50(b), Federal Rules of Civil Procedure. The trial court denied the motions and entered judgment for petitioner on the jury's verdict. Respondent appealed, claiming that its motion for judgment *n.o.v.* should have been granted. Petitioner, as appellee, urged only that the jury's verdict should be upheld.

The Court of Appeals held that the evidence at trial was insufficient to establish either negligence by respondent or proximate cause and reversed the judgment of the District Court "with instructions to dismiss the action." Without filing a petition for rehearing in the Court of Appeals, petitioner then sought a writ of certiorari, presenting the question whether the Court of Appeals could, consistent with . . . Rule 50 of the Federal Rules and with the Seventh Amendment's guarantee of a right to jury trial, direct the trial court to dismiss the action. Our order allowing certiorari directed the parties' attention to whether Rule 50(d) [now Rule 50(e)—Eds.] and our decisions . . . permit this disposition by a court of appeals despite Rule 50(c)(2) [now Rule 50(d)—Eds.], which gives a party whose jury verdict is set aside by a trial court 10 days in which to invoke the trial court's discretion to order a new trial. We affirm. . . .

The question here is whether the Court of Appeals, after reversing the denial of a defendant's Rule 50(b) motion for judgment notwithstanding the verdict, may itself order dismissal or direct entry of judgment for defendant. As far as the Seventh Amendment's right to jury trial is concerned, there is no greater restriction on the province of the jury when an appellate court enters judgment *n.o.v.* than when a trial court does; consequently, there is no constitutional bar to an appellate court granting judgment *n.o.v.*. . . .

This brings us to Federal Rules 50(c) and 50(d), which were added to Rule 50 . . . to clarify the proper practice under this Rule. Though Rule 50(d) is more pertinent to the facts of this case, it is useful to examine these interrelated provisions together. Rule 50(c) [now Rule 50(c)(2)—Eds.] governs the case where a trial court has granted a motion for judgment *n.o.v.* Rule 50(c)(1) explains that, if the verdict loser has joined a motion for new trial with his motion for judgment *n.o.v.*, the trial judge should rule conditionally on the new trial motion when he grants judgment *n.o.v.* If he conditionally grants a new trial, and if the court of appeals reverses his grant of judgment *n.o.v.*, Rule 50(c)(1) provides that "the new trial shall proceed unless the appellate court has otherwise ordered." On the other hand, if the trial judge conditionally denies the motion for new trial, and if his grant of judgment *n.o.v.* is reversed on appeal, "subsequent proceedings shall be in accordance with the order of the appellate court." [T]he appellate court [then] will review on appeal both the grant of judgment *n.o.v.*, and, if necessary, the trial court's conditional disposition of the motion for new trial. . . .

Rule 50(d) [now Rule 50(e)] is applicable to cases such as this one where the trial court has denied a motion for judgment *n.o.v.* Rule 50(d) [now Rule 50(e)] expressly preserves to the party who prevailed in the district court the right to urge that the court of appeals grant a new trial should the jury's verdict be set aside on appeal. Rule 50(d) also emphasizes that "nothing in this rule precludes" the court of appeals "from determining that the appellee is entitled to a new trial, or from directing the trial court to determine whether a new trial shall be granted." [Similar language today appears in Rule 50(e).] Quite properly, this Rule recognizes that the appellate court may prefer that the trial judge pass first upon the appellee's new trial suggestion. Nevertheless, consideration of the new trial question "in the first instance" is lodged with the court of appeals. . . .

In our view, therefore, Rule 50(d) [now Rule 50(e)] makes express and adequate provision for the opportunity—which the plaintiff-appellee had without this rule—to present his grounds for a new trial in the event his verdict is set aside by the court of appeals. [He may do so] in his brief—or in a petition for rehearing. . . .

[In the case before us,] Petitioner, as appellee, suggested no grounds for a new trial in the event her judgment was reversed, nor did she petition for rehearing in the Court of Appeals, even though that court had directed a dismissal of her case. . . . Indeed, in her brief in the Court of Appeals, petitioner stated, "This law suit was fairly tried and the jury was properly instructed." . . . [Affirmed.]

Petitioner's case in this Court is pitched on the total lack of power in the Court of Appeals to direct entry of judgment for respondent. We have rejected that argument and therefore affirm.

Mr. Justice Douglas and Mr. Justice Fortas, while agreeing with the Court's construction of Rule 50, would reverse the judgment because in their view the evidence of negligence and proximate cause was sufficient to go to the jury.

Mr. Justice Black, dissenting.

I dissent from the Court's decision in this case for three reasons: First, I think the evidence in this case was clearly sufficient to go to the jury on the issues of both negligence and proximate cause. Second, I think that under our prior decisions and Rule 50, a court of appeals, in reversing a trial court's refusal to enter judgment *n.o.v.* on the ground of insufficiency of the evidence, is entirely powerless to order the trial court to dismiss the case, thus depriving the verdict winner of any opportunity to present a motion for new trial to the trial judge who is thoroughly familiar with the case. Third, even if a court of appeals has that power, I find it manifestly unfair to affirm the Court of Appeals' judgment here without giving this petitioner a chance to present her grounds for a new trial to the Court of Appeals as the Court today for the first time holds she must. . . .

Notes and Questions

(1) *The Clairvoyance Required of the Trial Judge in Making a Conditional Ruling on the MNT.* After granting a MJN, the trial judge must rule conditionally on the same party's MNT (in case the MJN is reversed). Can you perceive any difficulty in this task? [Note: The trial judge must respond, in advance, to the reasoning of an opinion of the court of appeals that she can only imagine, reversing another ruling that she believes to be correct.]

(2) *The Omniscience Required of the Court of Appeals in Ruling on the Losing Appellee's Motion for New Trial.* If it grants judgment on the theory a MJN should have been granted against the appellee, Rule 50(d) (and the *Neely v. Martin K. Eby* case) tell us that the appellate court must consider the MNT in the first instance. Can you see any difficulty in this task? [Note: What if the characteristics of live witnesses' testimony are such that the trial judge would have granted a new trial, but those characteristics do not appear in the printed record? The Supreme Court points out, of course, that the Court of Appeals can remand to the trial court. But by definition, it would remand so that the trial court can take account of matters unknown to the Court of Appeals, and if the matters are unknown to the Court of Appeals, how can it know to remand?]

We told you, at the beginning of this subsection, that the structure of Rule 50(c)-(d) is logical, and it is; we didn't say it was workable or sound policy. In fact, to the extent that we have had personal experience with the presentation of new trial grounds to appellate courts in the *Neely v. Martin K. Eby* situation, we have gained the impression that the process is both unfamiliar and unworkable from their viewpoint.

Litigation Document Example 11.1

Post-Trial Motions in Wilcox Development Co. v. First Interstate Bank

Read (or re-read) the post-trial motions from *Wilcox Development Co. v. First Interstate Bank of Oregon*, which appear in Litigation Document Example 1.2 in §VIII of Chapter 1, above. Notice that the defendant has asserted in the same instrument both a Rule 50(b) motion for judgment as a matter of law and a motion for new trial. The motion for new trial is conditioned on denial of the motion for judgment as a matter of law. Notice, also, that the motion for new trial contains several different grounds, including attacks on the instructions (trial error) and attacks on the weight of the evidence.

In the actual case, the court granted the motion for judgment as a matter of law and then, as Rule 50 requires, conditionally ruled on the motion for new trial—by saying that, if the JMOL were reversed, a new trial would be granted on the ground that the verdict was against the great weight of the evidence.

VI. Relief from Final Judgments

[A] The Rule 60 Motion

Read Rule 60 (relief from judgments).

Reopening a Final Judgment. Imagine that a final judgment has been rendered against your client. You are not happy with it, but your client is resigned to it and is convinced that the process that led to it was fair. But suddenly one day, you discover that the written draft of the judgment entered with the clerk does not match the judgment rendered because the draft added two zeros—so that now, instead of liability for $10,000, your client faces liability for $1 million. (In the alternative, imagine that you learn, after all time limits for a new trial or appeal have run, that the opposing attorney obtained a default judgment by forging the return of service.) In these kinds of cases, there should be a narrow escape valve from the doctrine of finality.

Rule 60: Clerical Mistakes, Other Mistakes, Inadvertence, Excusable Neglect, Newly Discovered Evidence, Fraud, Etc. Rule 60(a) allows the court to correct clerical errors *sua sponte* at any time and, on motion made at a reasonable time not more than a year after entry, Rule 60(b) authorizes relief from judgments in cases of mistake, fraud, etc. Relief under Rule 60(b) is narrowly circumscribed, because of the strong policy favoring repose of final judgments. But it does exist, as the following case shows.

Rembrandt Vision Technologies, L.P. v. Johnson & Johnson Vision Care, Inc.

818 F.3d 1320 (Fed. Cir. 2016)

Stoll, Circuit Judge.

Rembrandt Vision Technologies, L.P. ("Rembrandt") appeals from the district court's denial of Rembrandt's motion for [relief from final judgment] under Federal Rules of Civil Procedure 60(b)(2) [covering newly discovered evidence] and (3) [covering fraud, misrepresentation, and other misconduct]. Because the district court abused its discretion in denying Rembrandt's Rule 60(b)(3) motion [for misconduct], we reverse and remand for a new trial.

BACKGROUND

Rembrandt sued Johnson & Johnson Vision Care, Inc. ("JJVC"), alleging that its Acuvue Advance® and Oasys® contact lenses infringed . . . [Rembrandt's patent]. At trial, the parties disputed whether JJVC's accused lenses met the "surface layer" and "soft" limitations of the asserted claim [i.e., whether differences in either of these factors avoided infringement]. Following trial, the jury returned a verdict of noninfringement. The district court, in the alternative, granted judgment as a matter of law that Rembrandt failed to prove that the accused lenses were "soft." We affirmed the district court's grant of JMOL. . . .

At trial, Rembrandt relied on expert testimony from Dr. Thomas Beebe to prove that the accused lenses met both the "surface layer" and "soft" claim limitations. During his direct examination regarding the "soft" limitation, Dr. Beebe presented test results to show that the accused lenses met this limitation. During cross-examination, however, Dr. Beebe drastically changed his testimony regarding the testing methodology he used. Because his testimony on cross-examination significantly conflicted with both his testimony during his direct examination and the testing methodology disclosed in his expert report, the district court ultimately struck Dr. Beebe's trial testimony regarding this testing. After noting that Dr. Beebe's stricken testimony was the only evidence that Rembrandt advanced to prove the accused lenses were "soft" in opposing JJVC's motion, the district court granted JMOL that JJVC did not infringe.

In turn, JJVC relied on expert testimony from Dr. Christopher Bielawski to support its position that its accused lenses did not meet the "surface layer" limitation, but did not present expert testimony with respect to the "soft" limitation. During the course of his trial testimony, Dr. Bielawski took advantage of several opportunities to impugn Dr. Beebe's credibility.... During his closing argument, JJVC's counsel urged that "... You should not trust Dr. Beebe."

After trial, Rembrandt received information suggesting that Dr. Bielawski [had] testified falsely at trial. Although the district court denied Rembrandt's request for post-trial discovery, Rembrandt received much of the discovery it sought from Dr. Bielawski's employer, the University of Texas, through an open records request and state court litigation. In light of that discovery, the parties do not dispute that Dr. Bielawski testified falsely during trial.

Specifically, Dr. Bielawski repeatedly testified that he personally conducted ... laboratory testing on JJVC's accused lenses when, in fact, the testing was conducted by Dr. Bielawski's graduate students and various lab supervisors. The post-trial discovery suggests that Dr. Bielawski was not even in the country when some of the testing was done. Moreover, the post-trial discovery suggests that Dr. Bielawski overstated his qualifications and experience with these testing methodologies. Whereas Dr. Bielawski was presented to the jury as an expert in TOF-SIMS testing, he actually "had no TOF-SIMS experience whatsoever." As such, for the purpose of considering the Rule 60(b) motions, the district court "assume[d] ... that Dr. Bielawski testified falsely ...."

In addition to showing Dr. Bielawski's false testimony, the post-trial discovery revealed that Dr. Bielawski withheld test results and data analysis that would have undermined his opinions and trial testimony ....

In light of this post-trial discovery, Rembrandt moved for a new trial under Rules 60(b)(2) and (3), which state:

> On motion and just terms, the court may relieve a party ... from a final judgment ... for the following reasons: ... (2) newly discovered evidence, that with reasonable diligence, could not have been discovered in time to move to a new trial under Rule 59(b); [or] (3) fraud ..., misrepresentation, or misconduct by an opposing party.

Following a lengthy hearing on the issue, the district court denied Rembrandt's motion. With little discussion, the district court dismissed Rembrandt's argument that the withheld documents prevented it from fully and fairly presenting its case.... Rembrandt appeals....

DISCUSSION

We first consider Rembrandt's motion for a new trial under Rule 60(b)(3), which permits a district court to grant a new trial in cases involving "fraud ..., misrepresentation, or misconduct by an opposing party." Fed.R.Civ.P. 60(b)(3). To prevail on a motion under Rule 60(b)(3) in the Eleventh Circuit, the movant must establish that: (1) the adverse party engaged in fraud or other misconduct; and (2) this conduct prevented the moving party from fully and fairly presenting its case. Proof that the result of the case would have been different but for the fraud or misconduct is not required; instead, Rule 60(b)(3) "is aimed at judgments which were unfairly obtained, not at those which are factually incorrect." *Rozier v. Ford Motor Co.*, 573 F.2d 1332, 1339 (5th Cir.1978) . . . .

I.

We start with the easier question of whether Rembrandt had a full and fair opportunity to present its case given Dr. Bielawski's false testimony and withholding of relevant documents. . . . [T]he district court concluded that "even accounting for Dr. Bielawski's misconduct, Rembrandt was not prevented from making its case," and explained that this holds true "even without considering that JJVC was entitled to judgment as a matter of law because Rembrandt failed to present evidence on an essential element of its case." . . . We conclude that the district court clearly erred in finding that Rembrandt had a full and fair opportunity to present its infringement case.

Dr. Bielawski testified on a central infringement issue at trial—whether JJVC's accused lenses met the "surface layer" claim limitation. . . . The verdict was irretrievably tainted by Dr. Bielawski's false testimony and Dr. Bielawski's and JJVC's withholding of relevant documents. While we do not know the exact impact the false testimony would have had on the jury, the false testimony may well have been critical to the noninfringement verdict and the jury may well have been impacted upon learning that Dr. Bielawski committed an act at least as egregious as Dr. Beebe's.

JJVC and the dissent nonetheless assert that the district court did not abuse its discretion, relying on a rationale different from that of the district court. Specifically, JJVC argues that Rembrandt had a full and fair trial because Dr. Bielawski did not testify regarding the "soft" limitation and Rembrandt cannot show that the false testimony and improperly withheld documents resulted in substantial impairment of its ability to present its case on the "soft" limitation. We are not convinced by JJVC's argument. . . .

The district court granted JMOL, not because of the merits of JJVC's noninfringement position, but because its exclusion of Dr. Beebe's unreliable testimony compelled that result. The district court judge acknowledged that he may well have responded differently [about excluding Dr. Beebe] had he been aware at the time of Dr. Bielawski's false testimony. . . .

II.

We next look to whether Rembrandt established that "the adverse party engaged in fraud or other misconduct." We conclude that the district court abused its discretion in concluding otherwise. Specifically, the district court erred by . . . requiring proof that JJVC or its counsel was complicit in Dr. Bielawski's false testimony. . . .

. . . As used in Rule 60(b)(3), "'[m]isconduct' does not demand proof of nefarious intent or purpose as a prerequisite to redress. . . . The term can cover even accidental omissions—elsewise . . . , 'fraud' and 'misrepresentation' would likely subsume it." *Anderson v. Cryovac, Inc.*, 862 F.2d 910, 923 (1st Cir.1988) . . . .

. . . [W]e have previously affirmed a grant of a new trial under Rule 60(b)(3) in view of an expert's perjured testimony, even when it was undisputed that the party was unaware of the perjury. *See Viskase Corp. v. Am. Nat'l Can Co.,* 261 F.3d 1316, 1324 (Fed.Cir.2001). In *Viskase,* an expert witness lied about his personal involvement in laboratory testing concerning alleged infringement. Although there was no evidence that the sponsoring party or its counsel was aware of the expert's perjury, the district court had determined that the party's counsel "surely knew there must have been additional documents and that there were additional tests conducted" that had not been produced, and, as a result, "conclude[d] that [the party] cannot escape responsibility for [the expert's] testimony." . . . We are presented with very similar facts here. Although JJVC may have been unaware of Dr. Bielawski's false testimony, JJVC should have known that additional tests were conducted and additional documents were generated. Indeed, it provided samples of the third-party lenses to Dr. Bielawski, requested that he conduct initial testing on those lenses, and questioned Dr. Bielawski on the same subject matter during trial. . . .

III.

Because we reverse the district court's denial of Rembrandt's motion for a new trial under 60(b)(3), we do not consider whether the district court abused its discretion in denying Rembrandt's Rule 60(b)(2) [newly discovered evidence] and discovery motions. . . . [REVERSED AND REMANDED.]

Dyk, Circuit Judge, dissenting.

This case presents two important questions about the interpretation of Rule 60(b)(3) . . . in the context of false testimony by an expert witness. The first is whether a showing by a movant that it lacked a "full and fair" opportunity to present its case requires some showing that the result could have been affected by the false testimony. The second is whether false testimony by an expert witness can be attributed "to the opposing party" (as required by the rule) without a showing of knowledge or reason to know that the testimony was false. I respectfully suggest that the majority is wrong on both counts. . . .

The [first question concerns] whether Dr. Bielawski's later-discovered false testimony about the "surface layer" limitation should result in re-opening the district court's JMOL of non-infringement based on the plaintiff's failure to produce any evidence in response to the JMOL motion (absent Dr. Beebe's stricken testimony) that the accused lenses met the "soft" limitation. The district court correctly concluded that the JMOL should not be reopened because Rembrandt was not deprived of a full and fair opportunity to present its case on the "soft" limitation—an issue which was dispositive of non-infringement [and resolved by JMOL]. . . .

There is also, in my view, a second error in the majority opinion. Under Rule 60(b)(3), "the court may relieve a party or its legal representative from a final judgment, order, or proceeding" if there was "fraud . . . , misrepresentation, or misconduct by an opposing party." I also disagree with the majority's conclusion . . . that the rule does not require any evidence that the misconduct was attributable to "the opposing party" as required by the text of Rule 60(b)(3). The two other circuits that have confronted the issue have reached the opposite conclusion. As the Seventh Circuit explained, "[e]xpert witnesses . . . are free agents. Parties and counsel have an obligation not to deceive the court about the witness and to correct statements they know to be false, but they are not responsible for the details of the witness's testimony." *Metlyn Realty Corp. v. Esmark, Inc.*, 763 F.2d 826, 833 (7th Cir.1985). . . . I respectfully dissent.

Notes and Questions

(1) *Fraud, Misrepresentation and Other Misconduct: Metlyn Realty Corp. v. Esmark, Inc.*, 763 F.2d 826 (7th Cir. 1985). Notice that this standard is easier to meet than it might appear, although Rule 60 is never really "easy." It does not require actual "fraud." Mere "misconduct" will do, and the misconduct can even be "accidental." In *Metlyn Realty*, an expert witness made "misstatements," and the parties settled the case, entering a final judgment on the basis of the record including those misstatements. Afterward, one party moved for relief under the Rule 60 "fraud, misrepresentation and other misconduct" provision on this basis. The court held that where counsel were unaware of witness misconduct, but they should have been aware, the misconduct standard can be met. Garden-variety injustice is not enough, however, and the movant must show substantial danger that an unjust result actually was produced. Notice that Rule 60 may apply to settlements as well as judgments resulting from trial (which, after all, are a small minority of judgments).

(2) *Rule 60's Coverage of Mistake, Inadvertence, Surprise, Excusable Neglect: Murray v. Ford Motor Co.*, 770 F.2d 461 (5th Cir. 1985). A separate section of Rule 60 covers these grounds for relief. Obviously, many kinds of "mistakes" must remain unredressable (*e.g.*, one party or the other did not prepare properly for the trial because of a mistake in interpreting the law). What kind of "mistake," etc., qualifies? In *Murray*, the plaintiff initially obtained a default judgment in a state court action. The defendant moved, in state court, to set aside the default, and then removed the case. The state court entered an order setting aside the default, which both parties mistakenly believed was effective. When the defendant realized, more than a year later, that the state court order was not effective because it had been entered after the removal was effectuated, it moved for relief under Rule 60. The court granted relief under the mistake, inadvertence, etc. subdivision, using the original state court motion to avoid the bar of the one-year limit for 60(b)(1) motions. The court concluded that the state-court motion, which had been filed within one year of the default judgment and still was pending in the removed action, was sufficient for this purpose. *See* Note, *Relief from Final Judgment Under Rule 60(b)(1) Due to Judicial Errors of Law*, 83 MICH. L. REV. 1571 (1985).

(3) *Newly Discovered Evidence: Bradley Bank v. Hartford Acc. & Indem. Co.*, 562 F. Supp. 241 (W.D. Wis. 1983). Since newly discovered evidence is a ground for a motion for new trial, and since the requirements there are stringent, it is reasonable to assume that the courts would be even more restrictive of newly discovered evidence as a ground for Rule 60 relief—and that is the case. In *Bradley Bank*, for example, the insurance company belatedly discovered evidence that showed that the policy in question had been redrafted in its present form for the very purpose of clarifying an ambiguous term. The bank had exploited this now-irrelevant ambiguity in obtaining judgment. The insurance company also satisfied the court that it could not have learned of this evidence earlier by the exercise of due diligence. The court denied relief under Rule 60 on the ground that the evidence was not sufficiently significant to change the result.

(4) *Void Judgments, Satisfied Judgments, Etc.* Rule 60(b)(4)–(5) provides for relief from a variety of judgments that are not themselves substantively defective but that should not be enforced. If, for example, the court had no subject-matter jurisdiction—a small claims court entered a judgment for $1 million—the mechanism for setting it aside after time limits have run is the Rule 60(b)(4) attack on a void judgment. Also, if the judgment is paid, it is customary to reflect that fact in the record (*e.g.*, by the filing of a Release of Judgment); if, however, that is not done, and the judgment remains as a cloud on title or even as a basis for enforcement efforts, the Rule 60(b)(5) attack on a satisfied or discharged judgment is appropriate. Rule 60(b)(6) contains a "catchall" provision for "other" reasons. Rule 60(b)(4)–(6) motions must be made "within a reasonable time," but, unlike motions under Rule 60(b)(1)–(3), are not subject to the outer limit of "no more than a year after the entry of the judgment or order or the date of the proceeding." *See McCorvey v. Hill*, 385 F.3d 846, 849–50 (5th Cir. [Tex.] 2004), *cert. denied*, 543 U.S. 1154 (2004) (Norma McCorvey a/k/a Jane Roe's attack on *Roe v. Wade* was not too late "as a matter of law" despite 30-year delay in making Rule 60(b)(6) motion, but mootness doctrine precluded review).

(5) *Clerical Errors Are Correctable at Any Time, but Errors of Law or Fact Ordinarily Are Not.* Rule 60 ordinarily is not a means of correcting errors of fact or law that the court has made in rendering judgment. *Cf. McKnight v. U.S. Steel Corp.*, 726 F.2d 333 (7th Cir. 1984) (review should be sought, instead, by timely appeal). *But see Parks v. U.S. Life & Credit Corp.*, 677 F.2d 838 (11th Cir. 1982) (Rule 60 can encompass "mistakes in the application of the law"). On the other hand, "clerical" mistakes are subject to correction at any time, and the court may act on its own motion. *E.g., Chavez v. Balesh*, 704 F.2d 774 (5th Cir. 1983) (where judge inadvertently failed to include liquidated damages in signed judgment, although findings of fact entered same day unambiguously entitled plaintiff to them, later correction was clerical in nature). Sometimes it is difficult to distinguish "legal" errors, which are harder to correct, from "clerical" errors. *Scola v. Boat Frances R.*,

Inc., 618 F.2d 147 (1st Cir. 1980) (where "error" consisted in choosing wrong interest provision, it was not "clerical" in nature and was subject to correction only in timely fashion).

[1] Rule 60 as a Mechanism for Setting Aside Default

The Excusable Neglect Standard: Butner v. Neustadter, 324 F.2d 783 (9th Cir. 1963) (reproduced in §V of Chapter 9, above). If a default judgment is discovered within 10 days, the defendant can obtain relief by a motion for new trial, but after that time, the mechanism is the Rule 60 motion. The "excusable neglect" standard is often used for this purpose. In *Butner v. Neustadter*, which appears above in Chapter 8, illustrates a Rule 60 setting aside of default. This uisee of Rule 60, at least when the defendant has not deliberately ignored the suit and there is no prejudice to the plaintiff, is more liberally granted than most other kinds of Rule 60 motions. *See* Project, *Relief from Default Judgments Under Rule 60(b)—A Study of Federal Case Law*, 49 Fordham L. Rev. 956 (1981).

[2] The Independent Action for Relief from Judgment

The One-Year Time Limit for Rule 60(b)(1)–(3) Motions. In *Rozier v. Ford Motor Co.*, cited above, the court explains the one-year limit. It quotes the Supreme Court in *Hazel-Atlas Glass Co. v. Hartford-Empire Co.*, 322 U.S. 238, 244 (1944):

> Federal courts . . . long ago established the general rule that they would not alter or set aside their judgments after the expiration of the term at which the judgments were finally entered. This salutary general rule springs from the belief that in most instances society is best served by putting an end to litigation after a case has been tried and judgment entered. . . .

"Rule 60 substitutes a general one year limitations period for the earlier 'term rule,'" but it "continues to reflect a strong policy favoring an end to litigation by severely restricting the relief available after the one year limit has run." *Rozier*, 573 F.2d at 1338. Subsections (4) and (5) are not limited, nor is section (a).

The More Stringent Standard for the Independent Action. An "independent action" to set aside a final judgment is all that is available after one year on some of the Rule 60 grounds, and it requires "extrinsic fraud" on the court: that is, fraud of a kind that the judicial system is not set up to detect. *Rozier* points out that "only the most egregious misconduct, such as bribery of a judge or members of a jury, or the fabrication of evidence by a party in which an attorney is implicated, will constitute a fraud on the court." 573 F.2d at 1338. Question: If the plaintiff's counsel, in the *Rembrandt Vision* case, above, had learned of the misconduct of the opposing expert witness several months later, so that his motion was not filed within one year, would the requested relief have been granted? [Probably not. *Rozier* points out that "[l]ess egregious misconduct, such as nondisclosure to the court of facts allegedly pertinent to the matter before it, will not ordinarily rise to the level of fraud on the court" for purposes of an independent action.]

VII. How to Answer the Chapter Summary Problem: Some Suggestions

Paula Green v. West York Bus Company: A Problem about Post-Trial Motions. (As always, follow your Professor's instructions about how to answer.)

1. If the defendant now (post-verdict) moves for "judgment as a matter of law," should the court grant the motion? *Law:* The standard is that a JMOL can be granted if there is no reasonable way, under the governing substantive law, to evaluate the evidence in favor of the verdict winner to maintain a judgment in favor of that party. But a motion after trial cannot be granted except on grounds contained in a motion during trial (it's the same motion). *Facts:* First, identify the relevant facts. Then, explain why they do (or don't) reasonably support a judgment for Paula Green. *Conclusion:* The Bus Company is (or is not) entitled to a JMOL.

2. What are the defendant's chances of obtaining relief through a motion for new trial? *Law:* A court has discretion to grant a new trial on such grounds as procedural errors, a verdict against the great weight, and newly discovered evidence. Procedural errors must be serious enough to have impaired substantial rights, not harmless errors. Against the great weight means much more than a preponderance: something akin to a verdict against overwhelming evidence. Newly discovered evidence must be evidence that could not have been discovered earlier by diligence and that would probably change the result, not merely impeaching or cumulative evidence. *Facts:* First, identify the relevant facts. The erroneous instruction may have affected the outcome and is a serious violation of the law. Even if it was not objected to, the court may grant a new trial (but is less likely to, without an objection). Or the court can decide that the verdict is against the great weight by deciding that Paula's waking up in her lane is really, really weak evidence to show that the Bus Company was negligent. Or Paula's statement might be sufficiently important evidence if diligence can be shown (probably). *Conclusion:* A new trial is a reasonable prospect on one of the three grounds. [Identify the ground and explain.]

3. What should the plaintiff do if the Court of Appeals reverses the judgment for the plaintiff and, for the first time, grants judgment for the defendant on the ground that the plaintiff's evidence was legally insufficient? *Law:* The law is set up to serve two policies: each litigant is entitled to both the MJMOL and the MNT, and there is to be only one appeal. Paula should move for rehearing (both to seek relief from the adverse rendition of judgment and to assert a motion for new trial). The appellate court can either decide the MNT or remand for consideration by the trial judge. *Facts:* The exclusion of Paula's accident reconstruction expert is the kind of event for which a new trial might be granted, but the outcome depends upon evidence law and proper preservation of the issue by Paula during trial. *Conclusion:* Paula may have a chance for a new trial if she follows these steps.

4. What recourse would the defendant have had if it learned of the plaintiff's broadcast statement six months after the trial court had granted a judgment for the

plaintiff? What if it learned two years after? *Law:* The Rule 60 motion for relief from judgment includes newly discovered evidence as a ground if the motion is asserted within one year. This ground requires diligence and evidence that is not merely cumulative or impeaching. After that time limit, the movant is limited to the common law action to set aside the judgment for extrinsic fraud. *Facts:* [Identify the relevant facts.] The evidence is important enough and may not have been capable of discovery by diligence. *Conclusion:* Plaintiff may be entitled to relief if the motion is within one year, but the common law motion seems difficult, because there is no indication of extrinsic fraud.

Chapter 12

Appeals

I. The Scope of Appellate Review

[A] Errors of Law and Avoidance Doctrines

Read Fed. R. Civ. P. Rule 61 (harmless error) and 28 U.S.C. § 2111.

[1] Harmless Error Principles

McDONOUGH POWER EQUIPMENT, INC. v. GREENWOOD, 464 U.S. 548 (1984). This case appears in § III[B][1] of Chapter 10, above, and should be considered again at this point. Plaintiff Greenwood had first appealed from the trial court's refusal to grant a new trial, which had been sought on the basis that one of the jurors had concealed material information during the jury selection process. After the Court of Appeals ordered a new trial, Defendant McDonough sought review in the U.S. Supreme Court. In reversing the Court of Appeals, the Court held that under principles of "harmless error," a new trial is only appropriate when a juror is shown to have been dishonest in failing to answer a material question on voir dire *and* it also is shown that a correct (honest) response would have provided a valid basis for a challenge for cause. The Court's explanation of "harmless error" is set forth in the following excerpt:

> We have also come a long way from the time when all trial error was presumed prejudicial and reviewing courts were considered "citadels of technicality." . . . [T]he general rule governing motions for a new trial in the district courts is contained in Federal Rule of Civil Procedure 61, which provides:
>
>> No error . . . is ground for granting a new trial or for setting aside a verdict . . . unless refusal to take such action appears to the court inconsistent with substantial justice. The court at every stage of the proceeding *must* disregard any error or defect in the proceeding which does not affect the substantial rights of the parties (emphasis added). [The 2007 "restyling" amendments changed this language slightly.—Eds.]
>
> . . . Congress has further reinforced the application of Rule 61 by enacting the harmless error statute, 28 U.S.C. § 2111, which applies directly to appellate courts and which incorporates the same principle as that found in Rule 61.

Notes and Questions

(1) *The Harmless Error Principle.* As the case indicates, a litigant is entitled to a "fair trial but not a perfect one." States follow this principle, as well. For example, Tex. R. App. P. 44 provides that "[n]o judgment may be reversed on appeal on the ground that the trial court made an error of law unless the court of appeals concludes that the error complained of: (a) probably caused the rendition of an improper judgment; or (b) probably prevented the appellant from properly presenting the case to the court of appeals." Similarly, Florida law provides that "No judgment shall be set aside or reversed . . . unless . . . the error complained of has resulted in a miscarriage of justice." § 59.041, Fla. Stat. (2017). California has held that even instructional errors do not warrant reversal of the judgment unless they cause actual prejudice. *Soule v. General Motors Corp.*, 8 Cal. 4th 548, 34 Cal. Rptr. 2d 607, 882 P.2d 298 (1994).

(2) *Applying Harmless Error Principles.* How should the broad principle of "substantial justice" be applied to protect a party's "substantial rights"? Should harm ever be presumed because of the nature of the error? Imagine, for example, that the appellant claims that the trial judge erroneously denied him a trial by jury, but the appellee responds that even if the denial was error, it was harmless, because the

evidence is so overwhelming that neither a judge nor a jury was likely to find in the appellant's favor.

Problem A: Chapter 12 Summary Problem

DOBSON v. JONES: APPEALABILITY, GROUNDS, SUSPENSION AND APPELLATE STEPS. A federal district court has just entered what it labels a "Judgment Final Except for Periodic Reporting and Adjustment" against the City of New Dublin and in favor of a named plaintiff (Patrick Dobson) and a class consisting of all pretrial detainees arrested during the last four years. The judgment requires extensive changes in the management of the city police department in order to prevent a "pattern of violence . . . perpetrated by police officers on arrested or detained suspects," according to the Findings of Fact filed by the judge. Mayor Sandra Jones, publicly has complained that the judge was biased, made "unbelievable" findings, and relied on experts who simply had no credentials or expertise. The order requires Jones to make monthly reports and provides for certain specified "adjustments" to the judgment, depending on future court findings that will be based on further evidence. The judgment also requires payment of more than $20 million by the city to the class members, but it leaves open the amount of attorneys' fees.

Mayor Jones wishes to appeal because the judgment is "destroying officers' morale, keeping us from responding to crime victims, and ruining the city's bond rating." She plaintively adds: "We actually have a better police department than most other cities our size, even though we all have problems." You have concluded that the findings involve extremely broad inferences from the evidence, and the intrusiveness of the order is unusual.

Assume that you represent Mayor Jones or, in the alternative, consider that you represent Patrick Dobson. Dobson believes that the trial judge erred in refusing to adopt certain findings tendered by him, awarded inadequate damages, and entered an order that "won't even begin to make a dent in the problem." Dobson bitterly denounces what he sees as an "out-of-control police department," and he points out that his own claim is enhanced by a citizen's videotape of two officers injuring him during his arrest.

1. Is this "final" judgment wholly or partly appealable?
2. What appellate steps are required next, and when?
3. Has the trial judge committed reversible error?
4. Can the city avoid complying with the judgment during the appeal?

[2] The Preservation Requirement; "Plain" Error

Read Fed. R. Civ. P. Rule 46, 50, 51, and 59.

Neu v. Grant

548 F.2d 281 (10th Cir. 1977)

[Nina Neu brought a negligence action against Frank and Lorna Grant as a result of injuries she sustained in a car wreck as a passenger in a 1967 Plymouth Fury owned by the Grants and driven by Lorna. The accident was the result of a "speed contest" between a pickup truck operated by Frank and the Plymouth operated by Lorna on Poison Spider Road in Casper, Wyoming.]

Neu contends that the jury verdict resulted from an "unlawful" instruction, *i.e.*, that Neu was a guest in the Plymouth Fury and that, in light of the Wyoming Guest Statute, W.S. 31-233,(1) it was obligatory that Neu prove that Lorna Marie Grant was grossly negligent. Following a pre-trial conference, Neu filed a Motion to Strike Paragraph 6 of Grant's Answer to her Amended Complaint, which alleged that the Wyoming Guest Statute barred recovery, "upon the grounds that Wyoming's guest statute is unconstitutional, denies equal protection of law under the Constitution of the State of Wyoming and the Constitution of the United States of America and should be stricken." [The trial court overruled the Motion to Strike.]

On appeal Neu attacks the judgment-verdict on the basis that the Wyoming Guest Statute is constitutionally infirm [under both the state and federal constitutions]....

Neu did not adequately preserve her objections to the Wyoming Guest Statute for appellate consideration....

Critically, insofar as Neu's appeal is concerned, this record *does not* evidence (1) any objection following the Court's denial of Neu's Motion to Strike or Motion for Partial Summary Judgment, (2) any objection to the court's instructions on the applicability of the Wyoming Guest Statute and (3) any motions by Neu following the jury verdict or the court's judgment to set them aside or for a new trial. In fact, after the jury was discharged the trial court inquired if there were any motions. Counsel for Neu responded "No motions, your Honor." ...

... Fed. Rules Civ. Proc., Rule 46 requires that "... a party, at the time of the ruling or order of the court is made or sought, makes known to the court the action which he desires the court to take or his objection to the action of the court and his grounds therefore; and, if a party has no opportunity to object to a ruling or order at the time it is made, the absence of an objection does not thereafter prejudice him." [The 2007 "restyling" amendments have streamlined this language—Eds.] The purpose for timely objection or motion as a precedent to review on appeal is two-fold. It provides the trial court with the opportunity to know the *specific*

---

(1) W.S. § 31-233. *Liability of owner to guest.*—No person transported by the owner or operator of a motor vehicle as his guest without payment for such transportation shall have a cause of action for damages against such owner or operator for injury, death or loss, in case of accident, unless such accident shall have been caused by the gross negligence or wilful and wanton misconduct of the owner or operator of such motor vehicle and unless such gross negligence or wilful and wanton misconduct contributed to the injury, death or loss for which the action is brought.

contentions and to take corrective action, if required. And—more importantly for appellate review—it *does not* permit a party to sit idly by, watching error being committed, and then take a "first" shot at the claimed error without having accorded the trial court the opportunity to correct its action. . . . [AFFIRMED.]

Notes and Questions

(1) *Preservation of Objections; Waiver.* As a general rule, a party must promptly make known to the court the action which the party desires the court to take or the objection to the court's action, state the grounds for objection, and obtain a ruling. Fed. R. Civ. P. 46; *see also* Fed. R. Civ. P. 51; Fed. R. Evid. 103. Otherwise, no complaint can be made about the court's action on appeal. The principal case points out that the purpose for a timely complaint is twofold: (1) to advise the trial court so that the judge can take corrective action, and (2) to prevent litigants from "riding the verdict," protected by apparently reversible error. A similar approach applies to the preservation of appellate complaints about the sufficiency of the evidence. *See Unitherm Food Systems, Inc. v. Swift-Eckrich, Inc.*, 126 S. Ct. 980 (2006), in Chapter 11, *supra*.

(2) *The Concept of "Plain" Error.* In many procedural systems, there is a concept called "plain" or "fundamental" error. *See, e.g.*, Fed. R. Civ. P. 51(d)(2). When this type of error has been committed, the failure to make an objection or obtain a ruling may be excused. Some states take a strict view that limits the scope of the doctrine to errors that go to the jurisdiction of the trial court. Others take a more relaxed approach that treats serious denial of a party's rights as plain error when it is apparent on the face of the appellate record. *See, e.g.,Morreale v. Downing*, 630 F.2d 286 (5th Cir. 1980); *see also Miley v. Delta Marine Drilling Co.*, 473 F.2d 856, 857–58 (5th Cir. 1973) (excusing counsel's failure to object to trial judge's comments during trial on basis that "[w]here a trial judge's comments were so prejudicial as to deny a party an opportunity for a fair and impartial trial, the absence of objections will not preclude our review since counsel will be loath to challenge the propriety of a trial judge's utterances for fear of antagonizing him and thereby prejudicing a client's case").

[B] Standards of Review: Deference to Trial Court Discretion

DOE v. UNIVERSITY OF CINCINNATI, 872 F.3d 393 (6th Cir. 2017). "University of Cincinnati students John Doe and Jane Roe engaged in sex at John Doe's apartment. John contends that the sex was consensual; Jane claims it was not." Ultimately, "defendant University of Cincinnati ('UC') held a disciplinary hearing on Jane Roe's sexual assault charges against . . . Doe. Despite Jane Roe's failure to appear at the hearing, the University found John Doe 'responsible' for sexually assaulting Roe based upon her previous hearsay statements to investigators."

The University suspended Doe for a year. Doe sued, claiming that the University had denied him due process by denying him the right to confront his accuser. The district court agreed and issued a preliminary injunction preventing the University from enforcing the suspension. The appellate court here affirms, concluding that the district court had discretion that it did not abuse:

> In reviewing a district court's decision to grant a preliminary injunction, "we evaluate the same four factors that the district court does": (1) whether the movant has demonstrated a strong likelihood of success on the merits; (2) whether he would suffer irreparable injury without the injunction; (3) whether the injunction would cause substantial harm to others; and (4) whether issuing the injunction would serve the public interest. . . .
>
> We review a district court's legal conclusions de novo, its factual findings for clear error, and its ultimate decision to grant preliminary relief for abuse of discretion. Practically speaking, this means "when we look at likelihood of success on the merits, we independently apply the Constitution [or whatever law controls], but we still defer to the district court's overall balancing of the four preliminary-injunction factors."
>
> [The court here analyzed the due process issue and concluded that the defendant had a right to confront Jane Roe at the disciplinary hearing. It then examined whether the district court acted within its discretion in issuing the preliminary injunction. It ended its opinion by saying,] "we conclude that the district court did not abuse its discretion in enjoining John Doe's suspension." [AFFIRMED.]

[C] Review of Determinations of Fact

> Read Fed. R. Civ. P. 52(a) (the "clearly erroneous" standard).

Anderson v. City of Bessemer City

470 U.S. 564 (1985)

Justice White delivered the opinion of the Court . . . .

[Anderson, a 39-year-old female schoolteacher with college degrees in social studies and education, applied for the position of Recreational Director. A City committee instead hired Kincaid, a 24-year-old man who had recently obtained a physical education degree. Anderson filed an action alleging that the City's decision was affected by gender discrimination in violation of Title VII of the Civil Rights Act of 1964. The District Court heard evidence at trial and issued a memorandum announcing its holding in favor of Anderson and requesting that she propose findings of fact and conclusions of law. The court also requested a response from the City. When the court issued its findings and conclusions, its finding that Anderson had been denied employment because of gender discrimination was based upon

Anderson's proposed findings to some degree but also differed from those proposed findings. The court found that Anderson was the most qualified candidate for certain specified reasons, that she had been asked questions about her spouse's feelings that other candidates had not been asked, and that the male committee members were biased against hiring a woman.

[The Court of Appeals reversed. It held that the District Court's controlling findings of fact were "clearly erroneous" within the meaning of Rule 52(a). The Supreme Court granted certiorari and, in this opinion, reversed the Court of Appeals' decision.]

II

We must deal at the outset with the Fourth Circuit's suggestion that "close scrutiny of the record in this case [was] justified by the manner in which the opinion was prepared," . . . that is, by the District Court's adoption of petitioner's proposed findings of fact . . . .

We, too, have criticized courts for their verbatim adoption of findings of fact prepared by prevailing parties, particularly when those findings have taken the form of conclusory statements unsupported by citation to the record. . . .

. . . Nonetheless, our previous discussions of the subject suggest that even when the trial judge adopts proposed findings verbatim, the findings are those of the court and may be reversed only if clearly erroneous.

In any event, the District Court in this case does not appear to have uncritically accepted findings prepared without judicial guidance by the prevailing party. . . .

III

Because a finding of intentional discrimination is a finding of fact, the standard governing appellate review of a district court's finding of discrimination is that set forth in Federal Rule of Civil Procedure 52(a): "Findings of fact shall not be set aside unless clearly erroneous, and due regard shall be given to the opportunity of the trial court to judge of the credibility of the witnesses." . . .(*)

Although the meaning of the phrase "clearly erroneous" is not immediately apparent, certain general principles governing the exercise of the appellate court's power to overturn findings of a district court may be derived from our cases. The foremost of these principles . . . is that "a finding is 'clearly erroneous' when although there is evidence to support it, the reviewing court on the entire evidence is left with the definite and firm conviction that a mistake has been committed." *United States v. United States Gypsum Co.*, 333 U.S. 364 (1948). This standard plainly does not entitle a reviewing court to reverse the finding of the trier of fact

---

(*) As a result of the 2007 "restyling" amendments, the applicable subsection of Rule 52(a) provides: "Findings of fact, whether based on oral or other evidence, must not be set aside unless clearly erroneous, and the reviewing court must give due regard to the trial court's opportunity to judge the witnesses' credibility." Fed. R. Civ. P. 52(a)(6).

simply because it is convinced that it would have decided the case differently.... If the district court's account of the evidence is plausible in light of the record viewed in its entirety, the court of appeals may not reverse it even though convinced that ... it would have weighed the evidence differently. Where there are two permissible views of the evidence, the fact-finder's choice between them cannot be clearly erroneous. ...

This is so even when the district court's findings do not rest on credibility determinations, but are based instead on physical or documentary evidence or inferences from other facts. To be sure, various Courts of Appeals have on occasion asserted the theory that an appellate court may exercise *de novo* review over findings not based on credibility determinations. *See, e.g., Orvis v. Higgins*, 180 F.2d 537 (2d Cir. 1950).... This theory has an impressive genealogy ... but it is impossible to trace the theory's lineage back to the text of Rule 52, which states straightforwardly that "findings of fact shall not be set aside unless clearly erroneous." ...

The rationale for deference to the original finder of fact is not limited to the superiority of the trial judge's position to make determinations of credibility. The trial judge's major role is the determination of fact, and with experience in fulfilling that role comes expertise. Duplication of the trial judge's efforts in the court of appeals would very likely contribute only negligibly to the accuracy of fact determination at a huge cost in diversion of judicial resources. In addition, the parties to a case on appeal have already been forced to concentrate their energies and resources on persuading the trial judge ... ; requiring them to persuade three more judges at the appellate level is requiring too much. As the Court has stated in a different context, the trial on the merits should be "the 'main event' ... rather than a 'tryout on the road.'" *Wainwright v. Sykes*, 433 U.S. 72, 90 (1977)....

When findings are based on determinations regarding the credibility of witnesses, Rule 52 demands even greater deference to the trial court's findings; for only the trial judge can be aware of the variations in demeanor and tone of voice that bear so heavily on the listener's understanding of and belief in what is said. ...

IV

Application of the foregoing principles to the facts of the case lays bare the errors committed by the Fourth Circuit in its employment of the clearly-erroneous standard. In detecting clear error in the District Court's finding that petitioner was better qualified than Mr. Kincaid, the Fourth Circuit improperly conducted what amounted to a *de novo* weighing of the evidence in the record.... The District Court, after considering the evidence, concluded that the position of Recreation Director in Bessemer City carried with it broad responsibilities for ... a recreation program involving not only athletics, but also other activities for citizens of all ages and interests. The court determined that petitioner's more varied educational and employment background and her extensive involvement in a variety of civic activities left her better qualified to implement such a rounded program than Mr. Kincaid, whose background was more narrowly focused on athletics.

The Fourth Circuit, reading the same record, concluded that the basic duty of the Recreation Director was to implement an athletic program . . . . Accordingly, it seemed evident to the Court of Appeals that Mr. Kincaid was in fact better qualified than petitioner.

Based on our own reading of the record, we cannot say that either interpretation of the facts is illogical or implausible. . . . When the record is examined in light of the appropriately deferential standard, it is apparent that it contains nothing that mandates a finding that the District Court's conclusion was clearly erroneous. . . . Reversed.

[The concurring opinions of Justices Powell and Blackmun are omitted.]

Notes and Questions

(1) *Applying the "Clearly Erroneous" Rule to a Mixed Question of Law and Fact: Commissioner v. Duberstein*, 363 U.S. 278 (1960). The "clearly erroneous" standard does not apply to questions of law, such as the interpretation of a statute or an unambiguous contract. "Law," as opposed to fact, questions are reversible by a Court of Appeals even if they are subject to differing interpretations. But what about a District Court finding that "mixes" law and fact? An example would be an ultimate factual conclusion that a person was "negligent" or that a particular transaction amounted to a "gift" for tax purposes. These findings do involve facts—but they may also contain implicit decisions about knotty legal questions, such as the definition of "negligence" or of a "gift."

In *Commissioner v. Duberstein, supra*, the Supreme Court held that a trial judge's determination that a payment to a taxpayer was a "gift" was reviewable under the clearly erroneous standard, and it analyzed the evidence in accordance with Rule 52(a). But what if the Court had reason to suspect that the "finding of fact" was influenced by an erroneous view of the law defining "gifts" in the mind of the trial judge? *See* Nangle, *The Ever Widening Scope of Fact Review in Appellate Courts—Is the "Clearly Erroneous Rule" Being Avoided*?, 59 Wash U. L.Q. 409 (1981).

(2) *A Different Approach to Constitutional Cases: Fiske v. Kansas*, 274 U.S. 380 (1927). Many cases hold that fact findings governing an ultimate question of constitutionality are treated differently. Where the constitutional issues are intertwined with the facts found, *Fiske* and subsequent cases require a review by the appellate court of the entire record to decide those issues. Is this approach justifiable?

(3) *Comparing the "Clearly Erroneous" Standard to the Standard for Review of Jury Verdicts: Reconsidering Reeves v. Sanderson Plumbing, supra, Chapter 10, and Lavender v. Kurn, supra, Chapter 11.* You should recall that a jury verdict is subject to being disregarded upon a motion for judgment as a matter of law only if reasonable persons properly applying the law could not differ as to the result. This standard is highly deferential. The weight of authority appears to favor the proposition that, under the "clearly erroneous" standard, appellate courts may review findings by judges more freely than findings by juries.

II. Appellate Procedure

> Read Fed. R. App. P. 3, 4(a) (notice of appeal); 7 (cost bond); 10(a)-(b), 11, 12(a) (record); 28, 30(a), 31(a), 32(a)-(b) (briefs and appendix).

[A] Time Limits: Notice of Appeal, Record Preparation, and Briefs

Bowles v. Russell

551 U.S. 205 (2007)

JUSTICE THOMAS delivered the opinion of the Court.

In this case, a District Court purported to extend a party's time for filing an appeal beyond the period allowed by statute. We must decide whether the Court of Appeals had jurisdiction to entertain an appeal filed after the statutory period but within the period allowed by the District Court's order. We have long and repeatedly held that the time limits for filing a notice of appeal are jurisdictional in nature. Accordingly, we hold that petitioner's untimely notice—even though filed in reliance upon a District Court's order—deprived the Court of Appeals of jurisdiction.

I

... [A]n Ohio jury convicted petitioner Keith Bowles of murder for his involvement in the beating death of Ollie Gipson. The jury sentenced Bowles to 15-years-to-life imprisonment. Bowles unsuccessfully challenged his conviction and sentence on direct appeal.

Bowles then filed a federal habeas corpus application on September 5, 2002. [Note that habeas litigation is partly controlled by the Rules of Civil Procedure.—Eds.] On September 9, 2003, the District Court denied Bowles habeas relief. After the entry of final judgment, Bowles had 30 days to file a notice of appeal. Fed. Rule App. Proc. 4(a)(1)(A); 28 U.S.C. §2107(a). He failed to do so. On December 12, 2003, Bowles moved to reopen the period during which he could file his notice of appeal pursuant to Rule 4(a)(6), which allows district courts to extend the filing period for 14 days from the day the district court grants the order to reopen, provided certain conditions are met. See §2107(c).

On February 10, 2004, the District Court granted Bowles' motion. But rather than extending the time period by 14 days, as Rule 4(a)(6) and §2107(c) allow, the District Court inexplicably gave Bowles 17 days—until February 27—to file his notice of appeal. Bowles filed his notice on February 26—within the 17 days allowed by the District Court's order, but after the 14-day period allowed by Rule 4(a)(6) and §2107(c).

On appeal, respondent Russell argued that Bowles' notice was untimely and that the Court of Appeals therefore lacked jurisdiction to hear the case. The Court of Appeals agreed. . . . The court . . . noted that courts of appeals have uniformly held that Rule 4(a)(6)'s 180-day period for filing a motion to reopen is . . . mandatory and not susceptible to equitable modification. Concluding that "the fourteen-day period in Rule 4(a)(6) should be treated as strictly as the 180-day period in that same Rule," the Court of Appeals held that it was without jurisdiction. We granted certiorari and now affirm.

II

According to 28 U.S.C. § 2107(a), parties must file notices of appeal within 30 days of the entry of the judgment being appealed. . . . [I]f certain conditions are met, district courts have the statutory authority to grant motions to reopen the time for filing an appeal for 14 additional days. . . . Rule 4(a)(6) describes the district court's authority to reopen and extend the time for filing a notice of appeal after the lapse of the usual 30 days:

> "(6) Reopening the Time to File an Appeal.
>
> "The district court may reopen the time to file an appeal for a period of 14 days after the date when its order to reopen is entered, but only if all the following conditions are satisfied:
>
> "(A) the motion is filed within 180 days after the judgment or order is entered or within 7 days after the moving party receives notice of the entry, whichever is earlier;
>
> "(B) the court finds that the moving party was entitled to notice of the entry of the judgment or order sought to be appealed but did not receive the notice from the district court or any party within 21 days after entry; and
>
> "(C) the court finds that no party would be prejudiced." [The rule has been amended in ways not relevant here.—Eds.]

. . . Thus, the question before us is whether the Court of Appeals lacked jurisdiction to entertain an appeal filed outside the 14-day window allowed by § 2107(c) but within the longer period granted by the District Court.

A

This Court has long held that the taking of an appeal within the prescribed time is "mandatory and jurisdictional." *Griggs v. Provident Consumer Discount Co.*, 459 U.S. 56, 61 (1982) [and other cited cases]. . . . Reflecting the consistency of this Court's holdings, the courts of appeals routinely and uniformly dismiss untimely appeals for lack of jurisdiction. . . .

Like the initial 30-day period for filing a notice of appeal, the limit on how long a district court may reopen that period is set forth in a statute, 28 U.S.C. § 2107(c). Because Congress specifically limited the amount of time by which district courts can extend the notice-of-appeal period in § 2107(c), that limitation is more than a simple "claim-processing rule." . . . Bowles' failure to file his notice of appeal in accordance with the statute therefore deprived the Court of Appeals of jurisdiction. And because Bowles' error is one of jurisdictional magnitude, he cannot rely on forfeiture or waiver to excuse his lack of compliance with the statute's time limitations.

B

... [T]his Court has no authority to create equitable exceptions to jurisdictional requirements.... Accordingly, we reject Bowles' reliance on the [equitable] doctrine, and we overrule [previous cases] to the extent they purport to authorize an exception to a jurisdictional rule....

C

If rigorous rules like the one applied today are thought to be inequitable, Congress may authorize courts to promulgate rules that excuse compliance with the statutory time limits. Even narrow rules to this effect would give rise to litigation testing their reach and would no doubt detract from the clarity of the rule. However, congressionally authorized rulemaking would likely lead to less litigation than court-created exceptions without authorization. And in all events, for the reasons discussed above, we lack present authority to make the exception petitioner seeks. [Dismissal of appeal affirmed.]

Justice Souter, with whom Justice Stevens, Justice Ginsburg, and Justice Breyer join, dissenting.

... It is intolerable for the judicial system to treat people this way, and there is not even a technical justification for condoning this bait and switch. I respectfully dissent....

[A]n exception to the time limit in 28 U.S.C. § 2107(c) should be available when there is a good justification for one, for reasons we recognized years ago. In *Harris Truck Lines, Inc. v. Cherry Meat Packers, Inc.*, 371 U.S. 215, 217 (1962) (per curiam), and *Thompson v. INS*, 375 U.S. 384, 387 (1964) (per curiam), we found that "unique circumstances" excused failures to comply with the time limit. In fact, much like this case, *Harris* and *Thompson* [which are the cases the majority overruled] involved district court errors that misled litigants into believing they had more time to file notices of appeal than a statute actually provided....

... [I]t was reasonable to rely on a facially plausible date provided by a federal judge.... I would vacate the decision of the Court of Appeals and remand for consideration of the merits.

Notes and Questions

(1) *Federal Rules of Appellate Procedure.* The contents of a notice of appeal are set forth in Fed. R. App. P. 3(c); *see also* Official Form 1 of the Appellate Rules. In addition to the notice of appeal, an appellant in a civil case may be required to file a cost bond (Fed. R. App. P. 7), will be required to file the record (Fed. R. App. P. 10, 11, 12(b)), and should file a brief and an appendix (Fed. R. App. P. 28, 28.1, 30–32) in

compliance with the appellate timing requirements contained in those rules. None of the latter steps is jurisdictional, but failure to accomplish them can result in dismissal of the appeal.

(2) *Computing Time.* Appellate Rule 4(a)(4) defines the time for filing a notice of appeal in civil cases if any party files a motion for judgment as a matter of law, a motion for new trial, and certain other post-trial motions. The time "runs for all parties from the entry of the order disposing of the last such remaining motion." Fed. R. App. P. 4(a)(4).

(3) *Extension for Excusable Neglect or Good Cause.* The rule that authorizes the district court to extend the time for the notice of appeal requires "excusable neglect or good cause" in most instances. Rule 4(a)(5).

(4) *Paralegal's Misreading of Rule May Constitute "Excusable Neglect."* In *Pincay v. Andrews*, 389 F.3d 853 (9th Cir. 2004), the en banc Ninth Circuit held that a lawyer's reliance on a paralegal, who miscalculated the deadline for filing an appeal, could constitute "excusable neglect" that would permit an extension of the filing deadline under Rule 4(a)(5) of the Federal Rules of Appellate Procedure. Note that no lawyer wants to have to rely on a rule about excusable neglect, which offers only unreliable relief. Great care is warranted about the appellate timetable.

[B] Suspending Enforcement Pending Appeal: Supersedeas Bonds

> Read Fed. R. Civ. P. 62(a)-(d) (stay of enforcement of judgment; security requirements) and Fed. R. App. P. 8 (stay or injunction pending appeal).

TEXACO INC. v. PENNZOIL COMPANY, 784 F.2d 1133 (2d Cir. 1986). Pennzoil obtained a judgment for $11.12 billion from Texaco in a Texas state court. Under Texas law, the filing of a cost bond (usually for a small amount) did not suspend execution or enforcement of a judgment. In order to stay enforcement of the judgment pending appeal, under Texas law, Texaco was required to post another bond, called a supersedeas bond, "in at least the amount of the judgment, interest and costs," which amounted to more than $12 billion. The first bond (cost bond) covers the costs of appeal, but the second (the supersedeas bond) secures the winning plaintiff's ability to recover.

Next, Texaco filed a federal suit seeking a preliminary injunction against Pennzoil's enforcement of the Texas judgment. Among other arguments, Texaco claimed that the Texas provisions for supersedeas bonds effectively denied it the right of appeal and therefore denied it due process and equal protection of the laws under the United States Constitution.

The federal district judge granted the injunctive relief requested by Texaco, but he conditioned relief on the posting by Texaco of a $1 billion bond in order to protect Pennzoil against Texaco's transferring or encumbering assets. Texaco promptly posted the $1 billion bond. Pennzoil, however, appealed the preliminary injunction. In its opinion, the Second Circuit considered the allegedly irreparable harm that Texaco would suffer without the injunction, as well as other requisites of injunctive relief, and affirmed the trial judge's decision:

> It is beyond dispute that, absent injunctive relief, enforcement of Texas' lien and supersedeas bond provisions would rapidly produce a catastrophe of major proportions, causing substantial harm to Texaco itself and to thousands of others throughout the United States, including stockholders, customers, and suppliers. Pennzoil concedes that Texaco, although it has a liquidation value of $22 billion and a net worth of about $23 billion, could not possibly post a bond or security in the sum of the approximately $12 billion that is mandated by Tex. R. Civ. P. 362(b). [The supersedeas bonding capacity of the entire free world is not that big.—Eds.] The simultaneous attachment of a lien pursuant to Tex. Prop. Code Ann. §§ 52.001 *et seq.* on Texaco's real property in Texas, valued at $5 billion, would seal the company's fate. [It would be an event of default under many lending agreements.—Eds.] Unable to finance its operations or obtain credit lines needed for its continued existence, Texaco, the fifth largest business organization in the United States, would be forced into bankruptcy or liquidation. . . .
>
> [T]he district court was required to balance [these issues against] the threat to Pennzoil's interests caused by granting the stay. A judgment creditor's primary concern when a judgment in his favor is stayed pending appeal is that he be "secure . . . from loss resulting from the stay of execution." . . .
>
> . . . Texaco's financial statement shows that . . . it had an appraised net worth of $22.622 billion. . . . [The] Chairman of Pennzoil's Board stated that . . . "he did not doubt Texaco's ability to pay the damages." . . .

Notes and Questions

(1) *The Supreme Court Reversed This Decision: Pennzoil Co. v. Texaco, Inc.*, 481 U.S. 1 (1987). The Supreme Court overturned Texaco's injunction. The Court's unanimous decision said, "Both the District Court and the Court of Appeals failed to recognize the significant interests harmed by their unprecedented intrusion into the Texas judicial system. Similarly, neither of those courts applied the appropriate standard in determining whether adequate relief was available in the Texas courts. . . ." Texaco immediately requested a stay from a Texas Court—which granted a temporary stay for one week until a full hearing could be held. On the sixth day, however, pressure from creditors and vendors was so strong that Texaco obtained a stay by filing a bankruptcy petition.

(2) *Pennzoil's Potential Interests in the Supersedeas Bond.* Does the Second Circuit's approach fully protect Pennzoil's legitimate interests? Imagine a litigant in

Texaco's position that might be willing to take steps during the several years of pendency of appeals to frustrate recovery of the judgment. Hypothetically, such a litigant could arrange its affairs so as to favor other creditors (including suppliers who contracted with it after the plaintiff obtained judgment). It also might seek the protection of the bankruptcy courts, years after the judgment.

(3) *The Merits of the Texas Supersedeas Approach Compared to Those of Federal Rule 62; Amendment of the Texas Rule.* The ostensible virtue of the federal approach under Rule 62 is that it is more flexible. On the other hand, doesn't the Texas approach have merit? It provides better assurance that the appellee—who, after all, has gone through all of the steps necessary to obtain a jury verdict and the judgment of a district court, often many years after the claimed injury—will find its judgment effectively collectible. [After this decision, Texas amended its rule to allow reduction of the bond. *See* Tex. R. App. P. 24.2(b).]

[C] The Record, Briefs, and Submission

The Record. After the notice and cost bond have been filed, the appellant has the responsibility for getting the trial court record prepared and filed. As a general proposition, any error that is raised on appeal must appear in the record. The record also must show that the error is reversible under the appropriate standard of review. In federal practice, Appellate Rules 10 and 11 indicate how the record is prepared and forwarded to the appellate court. *See* Fed. R. App. P. 10, 11.

Briefs, Submission, and (If Allowed) Oral Argument. After the record is filed the appellant is required to file a brief "within 40 days" unless this time is extended by court order "for good cause shown." *See* Fed. R. App. P. 31(a); Fed. R. App. P. 26 (Computation and Extension of Time). The appellee is required to file a brief within 30 days after service of the appellant's brief or "the appellee will not be heard at oral argument except by permission of the court." Fed. R. App. P. 31(a), (c). The appellant may serve and file a reply brief within 14 days after service of the appellee's brief. Fed. R. App. P. 31(a).

Submission may involve oral argument, but when the facts and legal arguments are adequately presented in the briefs, it is not uncommon for oral argument to be eliminated. *See* Fed. R. App. P. 34. In fact, although oral argument may seem more dramatic, experienced appellate advocates agree that in a well-prepared court, the brief is more important.

Form of the Brief. The form and contents of briefs are set out in Fed. R. App. P. 28.

III. Appealable Orders

Read 28 U.S.C. § 1291 (the final decision rule).

[A] The Final Judgment Rule

Note on Authorization of Supreme Court Rules

The "Judicial Improvements Act of 1990" amended 28 U.S.C. § 2072 (The Rules Enabling Act) to give the Supreme Court rulemaking authority to specify the terms and conditions under which District Court decisions should be treated as "final" for purposes of 28 U.S.C. § 1291.

Coopers & Lybrand v. Livesay

437 U.S. 463 (1978)

Mr. Justice Stevens delivered the opinion of the Court.

[Plaintiffs filed a putative class action based upon alleged securities law violations. Plaintiffs themselves had a total loss of only $2,650. The trial court first certified the class, then decertified it. Plaintiffs filed a notice of appeal of the decertification order. The court of appeals held that it had jurisdiction, but the Supreme Court, in this case, held that the court of appeals did not have jurisdiction, because the order was not a "final judgment."]

... The Court of Appeals regarded its appellate jurisdiction as depending on whether the decertification order had sounded the "death knell" of the action. After examining the amount of respondents' claims in relation to their financial resources and the probable cost of the litigation, the court concluded that they would not pursue their claims individually. The Court of Appeals therefore held that it had jurisdiction to hear the appeal and, on the merits, reversed the order decertifying the class.

... Federal appellate jurisdiction generally depends on the existence of a decision by the District Court that "ends the litigation on the merits and leaves nothing for the court to do but execute the judgment." An order refusing to certify, or decertifying, a class does not of its own force terminate the entire litigation because the plaintiff is free to proceed on his individual claim. Such an order is appealable, therefore, only if it comes within an appropriate exception to the final-judgment rule....

[The Court first concluded that the denial of certification was not appealable under what is known as the "collateral order doctrine," which is discussed in a later section of this chapter, below.]

[T]he "death knell" doctrine assumes that without the incentive of a possible group recovery the individual plaintiff may find it economically imprudent to pursue his lawsuit to a final judgment and then seek appellate review of an adverse class determination. Without questioning this assumption, we hold that orders relating to class certification are not independently appealable under § 1291 prior to judgment....

The potential waste of judicial resources is plain. The district court must take evidence, entertain argument, and make findings; and the court of appeals must review that record and those findings simply to determine whether a discretionary class determination is subject to appellate review. And if the record provides an inadequate basis for this determination, a remand for further factual development may be required. . . . And since other kinds of interlocutory orders may also create the risk of a premature demise, the potential for multiple appeals in every complex case is apparent and serious. . . .

[Next, the Court discussed appeals by permission under § 1292(b), which are referred to as "discretionary" appeals and which are considered later in this chapter. The present appeal had not been taken in compliance with § 1292(b), because the appellants did not get the trial judge or court of appeals to "certify" the appeal. Moreover, the Court points out that "Congress carefully confined the availability of such review" by requiring certain conditions and providing for "screening," in the form of discretion at both the trial and appellate court levels, governing whether the appeal may be taken. The death knell doctrine "circumvents these restrictions," the Court concludes.]

Accordingly, we hold that the fact that an interlocutory order may induce a party to abandon his claim before final judgment is not a sufficient reason for considering it a "final decision" . . . . The judgment of the Court of Appeals is reversed with directions to dismiss the appeal.

Note on Amendment of Rule 23

An amendment in 1998 added a new subdivision (f) to Rule 23. Rule 23(f) provides that a court of appeals "may permit an appeal from an order granting or denying class-action certification." This amendment changes the holding in *Coopers & Lybrand* in the narrow context of class actions. The certification decision, whichever way it is made, is so important to the viability of the action that a discretionary immediate appeal makes sense.

In other contexts, however, the *Coopers & Lybrand* holding remains viable. The general rule is that non-final orders, also called interlocutory orders, are not appealable.

Note on the Final Judgment Rule

(1) *What the Rule Means: The Judgment Generally Must Be Final as to All Parties, All Claims, and All Requested Grounds of Relief.* The final judgment rule means that a judgment must dispose of the claim, not merely of some aspect of the claim. But it also means a great deal more than that; as the Supreme Court says in *Coopers & Lybrand v. Livesay*, a final judgment generally is one that "terminate[s] the entire litigation." Thus, as a general rule, the judgment must dispose of all claims and defenses in the case, must be final as to all parties, and must adjudicate all grounds for relief. *See generally* Note, *Appealability in the Federal Courts*, 75 Harv. L. Rev. 351 (1961).

(2) *Some Examples.* Imagine that Plaintiff P sues two defendants, D1 and D2. Imagine further that Defendant D1 moves for summary judgment, and the trial

court grants the motion. Is there a final judgment? The answer: No, because P's claim against D2 remains pending, and so the judgment is not final as to the "entire" litigation. For another example, imagine that P sues a single defendant D, asserting four different claims. The trial court dismisses the first two claims on the ground that they fail to state any basis upon which relief can be granted. Is the dismissal order a final judgment? Again, the answer is "No."

(3) *The Policy Reasons for the Final Judgment Rule.* As the Supreme Court indicated in *Coopers & Lybrand*, the foremost policy underlying the final judgment rule is that of efficiency. Piecemeal appeals are wasteful. If P were to appeal the summary judgment granted to D1, and later appeal the outcome of his claim against D2, judicial and private resources would twice be devoted to the same factual context and perhaps to overlapping issues of law. Moreover, piecemeal appeals may cause delay, as final disposition awaits appellate decision of the correctness of some intermediate step. Finally, there is the more subtle matter of what *Coopers & Lybrand*, in another part of the opinion, calls "the appropriate relationship between the respective courts." If a case is partly in the trial court and partly in the appellate court, conflicts may arise, or there may be ambiguities as to which court has authority to decide an issue.

(4) *Difficult Questions of Finality; Brown Shoe Co. v. United States*, 370 U.S. 294 (1962). Occasionally there are cases in which it is difficult to decide whether a judgment should be called "final." Consider a case in which a trial court dismisses on *forum non conveniens* grounds but retains limited jurisdiction to ensure that the foreign forum is adequate. Is the judgment final? An issue remains open, but it is remote and speculative, and the practical termination of the action may effectively be unreviewable if the judgment is not considered final. In the *Brown Shoe* case, the District Court ordered divestiture of a company acquired in a merger attacked under the antitrust laws, but ongoing issues required continuing negotiations and determinations in response to future changing conditions. The Court held the order final and appealable in spite of these concerns. (Otherwise, it might never have become appealable!)

Likewise, some claims that are consolidated may be disposed of in ways that leave other claims open but still amount to final judgments. In *Hall v. Hall*, 138 S. Ct. 1118 (2018), the trial court consolidated two cases involving claims by two parties against each other. When the court disposed of one party's case but not the other's, the losing party filed a notice of appeal. The Supreme Court held that the two cases were really separate, and the judgment was appealable. "[The history of the consolidation Rule] makes clear that one of multiple cases consolidated under the Rule retains its independent character, at least to the extent it is appealable when finally resolved, regardless of any ongoing proceedings in the other cases."

(5) *Exceptions to the Finality Requirement.* A more significant concern arises in the case of orders that ought to be immediately appealable even though it is clear they are not final. (Non-final orders are called "interlocutory" orders.) For example, a preliminary injunction may irreparably alter the status quo, causing ongoing

harm if not appealed until the end of the case. As *Coopers & Lybrand* points out, there are special appeal mechanisms for just such cases. These mechanisms are considered in the later sections of this chapter.

(6) *Rule 54(b) and Sears v. Mackey.* In the case that follows, the trial court dismisses two of four claims, leaving the other two pending. The dismissal order, obviously, would normally not be final. But this case—*Sears Roebuck & Co. v. Mackey*—involves a special procedure. In effect, Rule 54(b) gives the trial judge the power artificially to make some non-final orders into final judgments by including certain recitations in them.

[B] Rule 54(b) Certification and Appealable Interlocutory Orders

> Read 28 U.S.C. § 1292(a)-(b) (appealable interlocutory orders); also, read Fed. R. Civ. P. 54(b) (final judgment in cases involving multiple claims).

[1] Rule 54(b): Making the Judgment Final

SEARS, ROEBUCK & CO. v. MACKEY, 351 U.S. 427 (1956). The plaintiffs brought suit against Sears on four distinct claims. The district judge dismissed two of the claims without leave to amend. Pursuant to Rule 54(b) of the Federal Rules of Civil Procedure, the order of dismissal expressly directed that judgment be "entered" for Sears on the two dismissed claims and also expressly determined that there was "no just reason for delay" in entering judgment. These provisions ostensibly made the order into a "final judgment" under Rule 54(b). However, when plaintiff Mackey appealed, Sears moved to dismiss the appeal, contending that the trial court's order was not a "final decision" and could not be appealed under 28 U.S.C. § 1291, which provides that "The courts of appeals shall have jurisdiction of appeals from all final decisions of the district courts. . . ." The Supreme Court allowed the appeal, on the ground that the district court's action under 54(b) made the judgment "final":

> [Rule 54(b)] does not relax the finality required of each decision, . . . but it does provide a practical means of permitting an appeal to be taken from one or more final decisions on individual claims . . . .
>
> To meet the demonstrated need for flexibility, the District Court is used as a "dispatcher." It is permitted to determine, in the first instance, the appropriate *time when each "final decision"* . . . in a multiple claims action is ready for appeal. This arrangement already has lent welcome certainty to the appellate procedure. . . . [T]he District Court must make both "an

express determination that there is no just reason for delay" and "an express direction for the entry of judgment." . . .

Accordingly, the appellate jurisdiction of the Court of Appeals is sustained, and its judgment denying the motion to dismiss the appeal for lack of appellate jurisdiction is affirmed.

Notes and Questions

(1) *The "One Final Judgment" Rule.* Recall the social policies that support the general "one final judgment" rule. Is current Rule 54(b) consistent with those policies?

(2) *Defining a Claim.* For Rule 54(b) purposes, what is a claim? Can an order determining liability be appealed if the District Court "dispatches" it to the Court of Appeals, even though damages have not been determined?

[2] The "Collateral Order" Doctrine

COHEN v. BENEFICIAL INDUSTRIAL LOAN CORP., 337 U.S. 541 (1949). In a stockholder's derivative action brought in a federal District Court in New Jersey on diversity grounds, the trial judge denied the defendant's motion to require the plaintiff to give security for costs. The defendant's motion was based on a New Jersey statute that required a bond for costs in a derivative action against a corporation. The trial judge held that the statute did not apply in federal court. The Court of Appeals reversed. The Supreme Court affirmed the reversal, but first it considered whether the order denying security, which obviously was an interlocutory (non-final) order, properly could be appealed:

> . . . When [the final judgment] comes, it will be too late effectively to review the present order and the rights conferred by the statute, if it is applicable, will have been lost, probably irreparably. We conclude that the matters embraced in the decision appealed from are not of such an interlocutory nature as to affect, or to be affected by, decision of the merits of this case.
>
> This decision appears to fall in that small class which finally determine claims of right separable from, and collateral to, rights asserted in the action, too important to be denied review and too independent of the cause itself to require that appellate consideration be deferred until the whole case is adjudicated. . . . [This "collateral" order therefore is appealable.]

Notes and Questions

(1) *What Isn't a Collateral Order: Coopers & Lybrand, Above; Stringfellow v. Concerned Neighbors in Action*, 480 U.S. 370 (1987). "Concerned Neighbors" sought to intervene in litigation about a nearby toxic waste dump. The District Court allowed only very limited intervention, and Concerned Neighbors attempted to appeal. The

Supreme Court held that the collateral order rule was not applicable because the denial of intervention was completely redressable in the main appeal (*i.e.*, if Concerned Neighbors could show error that affected the result, it could obtain reversal and a new trial). Remember that, in *Coopers & Lybrand*, above, the Court held that the collateral order doctrine did not allow appeal of the denial of class certification. Why not? [Note: What factors govern class certification, and are they unrelated to the merits?] Today, by rule amendment, there is an appeal in class certification decisions (see the Note following the cases above).

(2) *Civil Rights Immunity Determinations as Collateral Orders: Williams v. Collins*, 728 F.2d 721 (5th Cir. 1984). A defense of immunity to a civil rights claim not only prevents a public official's liability; it is designed to prevent an innocent official from even the requirement of defending an unmeritorious suit beyond the earliest stages. In the *Williams* case, the court held that denial of immunity was an appealable collateral order. Does this holding seem correct?

[3] Injunctions and Receiverships: Section 1292(a)

NORTHEAST OHIO COALITION FOR THE HOMELESS v. BLACKWELL, 467 F.3d 999, 1002 (6th Cir. 2006). The Ohio Secretary of State moved the court of appeals to stay or vacate a temporary restraining order ("TRO") that prohibited enforcement of newly enacted absentee voter identification provisions. The Plaintiffs-appellees argued that 28 U.S.C. § 1292(a)(1) did not permit interlocutory appeals of TROs. The court recognized that this was the general rule but concluded that it did have jurisdiction in this case. It first noted that under section 1292(a)(1), the court has jurisdiction of appeals from "[i]nterlocutory orders of the district courts of the United States . . . granting, continuing, modifying, refusing or dissolving injunctions" and recognized that the court of appeals "generally lacks jurisdiction to hear an appeal of the district court's decision to grant or deny a TRO." It explained:

> The rationale for this rule is that TROs are of short duration and usually terminate with a prompt ruling on a preliminary injunction, from which the losing party has an immediate right of appeal. *See Vuitton v. White,* 945 F.2d 569, 573 (3d Cir.1991). Therefore, an appeal of the TRO is not necessary to protect the rights of the parties, and practical reasons favor waiting for an appeal of the preliminary injunction . . . .
>
> [But] the label attached to an order by the trial court is not decisive, and the court looks to the nature of the order and the substance of the proceeding below to determine whether the rationale for denying appeal applies. . . .
>
> An order may be appealed under section 1292(a)(1) if it has the practical effect of an injunction and [if appeal] "further[s] the statutory purpose of 'permit[ting] litigants to effectually challenge interlocutory orders

> of serious, perhaps irreparable, consequence.'" *Carson v. Am. Brands, Inc.*, 450 U.S. 79, 84 (1981).... Accordingly, courts have allowed interlocutory appeal of TROs which threatened to inflict irretrievable harms before the TRO expired.... Furthermore, courts have allowed interlocutory appeal of TROs that do not preserve the status quo but rather act as a mandatory injunction requiring affirmative action. [*C*]*f. Summit County Democratic Cent. and Executive Comm. v. Blackwell*, 388 F.3d 547 (6th Cir.2004) (issuing a stay of a TRO affecting election day requirements).

The court found that the TRO under review "both threatens to inflict irretrievable harm before it expires and acts as a mandatory injunction that does not preserve the status quo" because it "will be difficult, if not impossible, to equitably enforce the voter identification requirements retroactively for these ballots." Therefore, "[t]he nature and effect of this TRO necessitate an immediate interlocutory appeal, and the court has subject matter jurisdiction over it." The court went on to conclude that the district court had abused its discretion by granting the TRO.

[4] "Discretionary" Appeals: Section 1292(b)

Drummond Company, Inc. v. Conrad & Scherer, LLP

885 F.3d 1324 (11th Cir. 2018)

Jill Pryor, Circuit Judge:

Drummond, Inc., sued Conrad & Scherer, LLP ("C&S"), a law firm, and its partner, Terrence Collingsworth, for defamation [in connection with certain complex litigations referred to here as "alien tort actions"]. In this appeal, C&S seeks interlocutory review of the district court's order concluding that the crime-fraud exception could defeat the firm's and Collingsworth's assertions ... of attorney-client privilege and attorney work product protection. The district court made a preliminary determination that the crime-fraud exception may apply to overcome their assertions of privilege and attorney work product protection and ordered a special master to perform an in camera review to determine whether the crime-fraud exception does apply. Although non-final orders generally are not immediately appealable, the district court certified its order for immediate appeal ... under 28 U.S.C. § 1292(b).

... [W]e conclude that interlocutory review is appropriate to address only one aspect of the district court's order [namely, whether an attorney's crime or fraud can destroy the attorney-client privilege and work-product protection if the client is not involved in the crime or fraud]. We ... elect not to exercise our discretion to review [another question]: whether the district court erred in applying agency principles to conclude that C&S [through Collingsworth] [acted] in furtherance of the crime or fraud. We decline to review this issue because it does not present a pure question of law suitable for review ... under § 1292(b)....

The federal courts of appeals "have jurisdiction of appeals from all final decisions of the district courts of the United States." 28 U.S.C. § 1291. "A final decision is one by which a district court disassociates itself from the case ...." *Doe No. 1 v. United States*, 749 F.3d 999, 1004 (11th Cir. 2014). It "ends the litigation on the merits and leaves nothing more for the court to do but execute the judgment." "Discovery orders are ordinarily not final orders that are immediately appealable." *Id.*

There are, however, exceptions .... We have discretion to hear interlocutory appeals from district court orders under the certification procedure in 28 U.S.C. § 1292(b):

> When [1] a district judge, in making in a civil action an order not otherwise appealable under this section, shall be of the opinion that such order involves a controlling question of law as to which there is substantial ground for difference of opinion and that an immediate appeal from the order may materially advance the ultimate termination of the litigation, he shall so state in writing in such order. [2] The Court of Appeals which would have jurisdiction of an appeal of such action may thereupon, in its discretion, permit an appeal to be taken from such order ....

Our precedent identifies several principles to guide us when deciding whether to exercise our discretion under § 1292(b) to allow for a rare interlocutory appeal. In general, we exercise our discretion only when (1) the appeal presents a pure question of law, (2) the question is controlling of at least a substantial part of the case, (3) the district court identifies the question in its order, (4) there are substantial grounds for differences of opinion on the question, and (5) resolution of the question may reduce the amount of litigation necessary on remand. But even if all of these factors are present, we still have discretion to disallow the appeal.

After considering these guiding principles, we ... decline to exercise our discretion to decide the first question presented in this appeal. Paraphrased, the first question asks whether a court may apply the crime-fraud exception to a partnership by imputing to the partnership the actions and knowledge of a partner. C&S argues that the district court improperly used agency principles to impute Collingsworth's intent to commit a fraud or crime to C&S ....

[This] question ... requires a fact-specific inquiry into whether the evidence in this case—which showed, at a minimum, that Collingsworth was the C&S partner to whom Scherer, the managing partner, had delegated responsibility for the alien tort cases ... —is sufficient to support the application of agency principles in the crime-fraud context. To answer it would require the court to apply law to the particular facts of the case and thus to take a deep dive into this case's voluminous record. The purpose of § 1292(b) is not to provide interlocutory appellate review of such fact-driven issues.... Accordingly, ... we decline to exercise our discretion to hear an interlocutory appeal related to the first question.

We now turn to the second question raised in this appeal, which we do exercise our discretion to answer. To clarify the question, we rephrase it slightly as follows:

> Can the crime-fraud exception be applied to overcome attorney work product protection when the attorney or law firm was engaged in the crime or fraud but the client was not?

With this question, C&S in effect seeks to bar the disclosure of work product materials created in the alien tort actions, claiming that because its clients in those cases were innocent of any wrongdoing, work product protection is maintained despite the firm's participation in the wrongdoing. . . .

[On the merits, the court proceeds to decide that the answer is Yes.] Regarding the second question certified on appeal, we conclude that the crime-fraud exception may in appropriate cases be applied to overcome work product protection based on attorney misconduct, even if the attorney's client is innocent of any wrongdoing. Accordingly, we affirm the district court's order on the crime-fraud exception.

Notes and Questions

(1) *Procedure.* There has been concern that discretionary appeals will be attempted too frequently. Consider the exact procedure that must be followed under 28 U.S.C. § 1292(b). Given the facts that: (1) the trial judge must certify that the interlocutory order "involves a controlling question of law as to which there is substantial ground for difference of opinion and that an immediate appeal from the order may materially advance the ultimate termination of the litigation"; and (2) the Court of Appeals has "discretion" to "permit [or deny] an appeal," is there any real likelihood that § 1292(b) will be abused? *See generally* Note, *Interlocutory Appeals in the Federal Courts Under 28 U.S.C.A. § 1292(b)*, 88 Harv. L. Rev. 607 (1975).

(2) *Other Approaches to Interlocutory Review.* Section 1292 reflects two fundamentally different approaches to the problem of interim review of interlocutory orders. Subsection (a) identifies particular interlocutory orders and makes them appealable all of the time. Subsection (b) does not restrict itself to particular orders but its provisions are only available when both the trial and appellate judges believe that an interlocutory appeal is appropriate.

[C] Mandamus and Other Writs

> Read 28 U.S.C. § 1651 (the "All Writs Act," which authorizes issuance of mandamus and other writs by trial and appellate courts).

KERR v. UNITED STATES DISTRICT COURT, 511 F.2d 192 (9th Cir.), *aff'd*, 426 U.S. 394 (1976). The case was a class action brought by prisoners in the custody of the California Department of Corrections in which the plaintiffs sought to discover documents over the defendants' objection that the documents were privileged. The District Court ordered production of the documents. The defendants filed two petitions for a writ of mandamus under 28 U.S.C. § 1651(a), requesting the Court of Appeals to vacate the District Court's discovery order. The Court of

Appeals denied both requests. On certiorari, the Supreme Court affirmed the Court of Appeals and explained why the remedy of mandamus was unavailable:

> The remedy of mandamus is a drastic one, to be invoked only in extraordinary situations. . . .
>
> As we have recognized before, mandamus actions such as the one involved in the instant case "have the unfortunate consequence of making the [District Court] judge a litigant, obliged to obtain personal counsel or to leave his defense to one of the litigants [appearing] before him" in the underlying case. . . .
>
> . . . More importantly, particularly in an era of excessively crowded lower court dockets, it is in the interest of the fair and prompt administration of justice to discourage piecemeal litigation. . . . As a means of implementing the rule that the writ will issue only in extraordinary circumstances, we have set forth various conditions for its issuance. Among these are that the party seeking issuance of the writ have no other adequate means to attain the relief he desires, . . . and that he satisfy "the burden of showing that [his] right to issuance of the writ is 'clear and indisputable.'" . . .
>
> When looked at in the framework of these factors, it would appear that the actions of the Court of Appeals in this case should be affirmed. . . . [P]etitioners request only that "production of the confidential documents not be compelled without a prior informed determination by the district court that plaintiffs' need for them in the action below outweighs their confidentiality." . . . Petitioners ask in essence only that the District Court review the challenged documents in camera before passing on whether each one individually should or should not be disclosed. But the Court of Appeals' opinion dealing with the Adult Authority files did not foreclose the possible necessity of such in camera review. . . .
>
> . . . Accordingly the orders of the Court of Appeals are affirmed.

Notes and Questions

(1) *Availability of Mandamus: La Buy v. Howes Leather Co.*, 352 U.S. 249 (1957). As the principal case shows, the federal courts are reluctant to issue writs of mandamus in discovery matters, which generally involve highly discretionary interest balancing. The absence (or abuse) of discretion must be clear. For an example of the successful use of mandamus, consider *La Buy v. Howes Leather Co.*, in which the District Court referred a garden-variety antitrust case to a master. The Supreme Court upheld the appellate court's writ of mandamus, because reference to a master is confined to "extraordinary" cases, and thus, the abuse of discretion was clear. *See also* Ward, *Can the Federal Courts Keep Order in Their Own House? Appellate Supervision Through Mandamus and Orders of Judicial Councils*, 1980 B.Y.U. L. Rev. 233.

(2) *Habeas Corpus.* One method of testing a pretrial order compelling conduct such as the production of documents is by temporarily refusing to obey the order

and being held in (civil) contempt. The lawfulness of the order of contempt depends, in these circumstances, on the lawfulness of the order that is being enforced. Thus, once the trial court has adjudicated the attorney in contempt, he may seek a writ of habeas corpus in the Court of Appeals (usually after being admitted to bail pending the outcome). If the underlying order is invalid, the contempt adjudication is reversed; if not, the attorney usually can purge himself of the contempt by complying with the order. This method was used in *Hickman v. Taylor* (the "work product" case), which appears in Chapter 7, above.

IV. The Supreme Court

Note on the Jurisdiction of the Supreme Court

Read 28 U.S.C. §§ 1251–1254, 1257 (jurisdiction of the Supreme Court).

Review by Writ of Certiorari. A writ of certiorari (literally, "to be made more certain") is a discretionary order allowing review of a lower court's decision. In the Supreme Court, 28 U.S.C. § 1254(1) provides broad authority for review by writ of certiorari, "before or after rendition of judgment or decree." Review extends to decisions of both federal and state courts, provided the issue is one of federal law. Today, almost all of the cases reviewed by the Supreme Court are reviewed by certiorari. But the Court receives thousands of petitions for certiorari annually, and it must deny most of them. The percentage granted varies from year to year, but generally has been considerably less than 5 percent. For example, in 2016, the Court considered close to 6300 petitions for certiorari and accepted review in 75 cases, which means the Court only granted review in 1.2 % of the cases. *See* https://harvardlawreview.org/2017/11/supreme-court-2016-term-statistics/.

Late in 1988, Congress passed and the President signed legislation giving the Supreme Court almost total discretionary control over its docket. In all cases except direct appeals (see below), review must now proceed by writ of certiorari.

Direct Appeal from District Courts. There is a very narrow class of cases in which appeal to the Supreme Court lies directly from the District Courts, bypassing the Courts of Appeals.

Original Jurisdiction: The Supreme Court as the "Trial" Court. The Supreme Court has original jurisdiction in a narrow class of cases defined by the Constitution, particularly those "in which a State shall be a Party." U.S. Const. art. III, § 2. Typical examples would include suits by one state against another concerning boundaries, water rights, or the right to tax. *Cf. Ohio v. Wyandotte Chemicals Corp.*, 401 U.S. 493 (1971) (Court had, but declined to exercise, original jurisdiction of suit by state against alleged polluters of Lake Erie); *Kansas v. Nebraska,* 135 S. Ct. 1042, 1052 (2015) (recognizing "its inherent authority, as part of the Constitution's grant of original jurisdiction, to equitably apportion interstate streams between States.").

Procedure for Review by Certiorari or Appeal

The Petition for Certiorari. Invocation of the Supreme Court's discretionary jurisdiction is an esoteric art. The applicant files a petition for certiorari. The purpose of this document is not to argue the merits; instead, it is to convince the Court that there are "special and important reasons" (in the language of Supreme Court Rule 17.1) why the Court should make the case one of the very few it hears. *See* Prettyman, *Petitioning the United States Supreme Court—A Primer for Hopeful Neophytes*, 51 VA. L. REV. 582 (1965). Paradoxically, a demonstration that the case is unique, or that it is an aberration, or even that it is opposed by unanimous contrary authority, may actually be counterproductive(!). Instead, citations showing that the issue has been considered by many courts, and that some have decided for the petitioner and some the other way, are likely to be more persuasive.

Grant or Denial of Certiorari; The "Rule of Four." Affirmative votes by four members of the Court suffice to grant certiorari. This convention is known as the "rule of four." *See Rogers v. Missouri Pac. R. Co.*, 352 U.S. 521, 529 (1957) (Frankfurter, J., dissenting). Denial of certiorari is of no precedential value, and the principle is well established that it means only that there were not four members of the Court who chose to hear this particular case at this time. *See Hughes Tool Co. v. Trans World Airlines*, 409 U.S. 363 (1973); Linzer, *The Meaning of Certiorari Denials*, 79 COLUM. L. REV. 1227 (1979).

Principles Guiding the Certiorari Decision. Ironically, justice to the individual parties is *not* the concern underlying a grant of certiorari. That is the purpose of intermediate appellate review; contrary to popular conception, however, it is not the purpose of certiorari. Supreme Court Rule 17.1 sets out certain circumstances in which certiorari is indicated. Among the most important are those in which there are conflicts between Courts of Appeals, or between a Court of Appeals and a state court of last resort, or those in which substantial issues of federal law have not been, but should be, decided by the Supreme Court. Thus, review by certiorari addresses systemic problems, rather than problems of individual justice.

Adequate State Grounds. Review of state court decisions is limited to federal questions, and the Court will decline to review even important issues of federal law if the lower court's decision rests upon an "adequate state ground" (*i.e.*, if it could be upheld without reference to the federal issue). However, the Court has indicated a greater willingness to consider cases in which state and federal grounds are interwoven and the basis for decision is ambiguous. *Michigan v. Long*, 463 U.S. 1032 (1983).

V. How to Answer the Chapter Summary Problem: Some Suggestions

Dobson v. Jones: A Problem about Appeals. (As always, follow your Professor's instructions about how to answer.)

1. Is this "final" judgment wholly or partly appealable? *Law:* A final judgment is one that is final as to all parties, all issues, and all requested grounds of relief. Generally, only final judgments are appealable. There is an exception if the judgment will never be "final" in this way but operates now. In addition, the court can make part of the judgment final by declaring under Rule 54(b) that there is a novel question upon which there is substantial ground for difference of opinion whose prompt decision will enhance termination and, also, directing entry of judgment now. Further in addition, the court can certify an appeal, and if the court of appeals concurs, appeal can result. Finally, injunctions are appealable, whether "final" or not. *Facts:* [Identify the relevant facts and compare them to each part of the law.] *Conclusion:* [Make a conclusion as to each method of appeal.]

2. What appellate steps are required next, and when? *Law:* First, the city must file a notice of appeal within 30 days (which is extendable for a short period, but don't rely on that). *Facts and Conclusion:* [Identify the next steps: requesting the record and transcript, docketing, briefs, etc.]

3. Has the trial judge committed reversible error? *Law:* Reversible errors of law must have been harmful (affecting substantial rights, usually meaning that they probably changed the outcome), preserved, not cured, and not within the trial court's discretion. Errors of fact must have been "clearly erroneous," meaning implausible. *Facts:* If the mayor is right, some fact findings may be clearly erroneous. There also may be harmful, preserved, and uncured applications of law (although the cited facts do not disclose any), but the trial court has great discretion in weighing the factors for an injunction. *Conclusion:* If the mayor is right, there may be reversible fact findings, but no reversible error is otherwise shown by the facts.

4. Can the city avoid complying with the judgment during the appeal? For the damages judgment, the city may be required to post a supersedeas bond in addition to the bond for costs (the usual rule: amount of the judgment plus costs). It may seek a stay, which is decided similarly to an injunction. As for the orders revising the police department, the city will need to move for a stay. If the trial court refuses, the city can seek a stay in the court of appeals.

Chapter 13

Res Judicata, Collateral Estoppel, and Related Preclusion Doctrines

I. Res Judicata: Claim Preclusion

[A] The Elements: "Same" Claim, "Same" Parties, Final Judgment

The Effect of Judgments. The doctrine of *res judicata* deals generally with the conclusive effect of judgments. The term itself (*res judicata*, meaning "the subject has been adjudicated") is sometimes used broadly to encompass the separate doctrines of (1) "claim" preclusion, or merger and bar (precluding relitigation when a subsequent suit is brought on the same claim), and (2) "issue" preclusion, or collateral estoppel (precluding relitigation of an issue settled in a prior suit, even if on a different claim). Here, we deal with the broader doctrine of *res judicata* as "claim" preclusion; a later section of this book deals with "issue" preclusion, or collateral estoppel.

The Restatement View of Res Judicata. Sections 18 and 19 of the Restatement (Second) of Judgments set out the principles of claim preclusion in the following manner:

> § 18. Judgment for Plaintiff—The General Rule of Merger
>
> When a valid and final personal judgment is rendered in favor of the plaintiff: (1) The plaintiff cannot thereafter maintain an action on the original claim or any part thereof, but he may be able to maintain an action upon the judgment; and (2) In an action upon the judgment, the defendant cannot avail himself of defenses he might have interposed, or did interpose, in the first action.
>
> § 19. Judgment for Defendant—The General Rule of Bar
>
> A valid and final personal judgment rendered in favor of the defendant bars another action by the plaintiff on the same claim.

Policies Served by Res Judicata. These rules are said to rest upon the policy of protecting a party from being twice vexed for the same cause, together with that of achieving judicial economy. Other policy considerations include the prevention of double recovery and the promotion of the stability or finality of decisions. *See generally* Cleary, *Res Judicata Reexamined*, 57 Yale L.J. 339, 344-49 (1948).

The Elements of Res Judicata or Claim Preclusion. It is impossible accurately to summarize the doctrine of *res judicata* in a few words. Nevertheless, it may be useful to outline the doctrine by referring to three "elements." With these thoughts in mind, one might say that *res judicata* requires:

1. An existing, valid, final judgment on the merits;
2. Between the "same" parties (or, in some cases, parties sufficiently closely related to the present parties);
3. Concerning the "same claim" (or same cause of action, or a cause of action sufficiently closely related to the present one).

Cf. Ray v. Tennessee Valley Authority, 677 F.2d 818, 821 (11th Cir. 1982).

Different Approaches. As this statement of the "elements" implies, different jurisdictions vary in the breadth of the preclusive effects that they afford to judgments. Some preclude only claims that are very closely similar to the prior claim. Here, we call this approach the "individualized" or "same evidence" approach. Other jurisdictions have adopted broader preclusive doctrines, which we call the "transactional analysis" or "broad procedural duty" approaches.

Problem A: Chapter 13 Summary Problem

FIRST BANK v. DONALDSON CORPORATION: A PROBLEM OF RES JUDICATA AND COLLATERAL ESTOPPEL. The Donaldson Corporation executed a guaranty agreement that guaranteed two different promissory notes of The Alpha Company. Both of the notes were in default, and Alpha was completely insolvent. Therefore, the holder of the notes, The First Bank and Trust Co., filed suit against

Donaldson in a state court in the (hypothetical) State of West York, to enforce the guaranty and make the Donaldson Corporation pay Alpha's debt.

But for some unknown business or tactical reason, the Bank included the amount of only *one* of the notes in this suit—the older one, which was longer in default. Donaldson Corporation alleged a defensive theory of "economic duress" in an attempt to avoid the guaranty, but the court granted summary judgment rejecting this defense without giving a reason (although the record showed that Donaldson Corporation had not properly responded to the summary judgment motion under state procedural law). Plaintiff Bank obtained a final state court judgment on the guaranty, awarding it the amount of the older note.

Later, the bank filed a second suit on the same guaranty, seeking to enforce it for the amount of the second note—the one omitted from the first suit. This time the Bank also joined James Donaldson personally as an additional defendant. James Donaldson had also signed the guaranty personally, and at all times he was president and sole shareholder of the Donaldson Corporation. The defendants again alleged the "economic duress" defense. All parties then alleged various theories of preclusion in the second suit.

1. Can the defendants successfully assert that the second claim is barred by *res judicata*?
2. Can the plaintiff collaterally estop either the Donaldson Corporation, or James Donaldson personally, from asserting economic duress again as a defense in the second suit?
3. If the second suit were to be brought in a federal court in a different state, could the result be different?

[B] The "Same Claim" Requirement: How Broad Is a "Claim"?

[1] The "Individualized/Same Evidence" Approach

SMITH v. KIRKPATRICK, 111 N.E. 2d 209 (N.Y. 1953). The plaintiff filed suit on an employment contract and later added an action to establish a partnership. The judge dismissed the contract claim and found against the partnership claim after trial. The plaintiff then commenced a second suit in which he asserted a claim in quantum meruit (or implied contract) involving the same background facts. The court used a same-evidence approach to hold that res judicata did not bar the second suit:

> By his [first suit] the plaintiff sought to enforce a right which arose out of an express agreement and from defendant's asserted ownership of accounts procured by him [in partnership]. . . . In the present action plaintiff's alleged right rests upon an implied contract. . . . The wrong alleged is defendant's acceptance and retention of benefits, conferred upon him by plaintiff, without payment in return of fair compensation. . . .

> The two actions involve different "rights" and "wrongs." The requisite elements of proof and hence the evidence necessary to sustain recovery vary materially. The causes of action are different and distinct and the rights and interests established by the previous adjudication will not be impaired by a recovery [in the second suit]. . . .

Notes and Questions

(1) *Scope of Preclusion.* As the principal case indicates, under the "individualized/same evidence" approach, even a minimal alteration of material facts may give rise to a new cause of action if the alteration makes available a new rule of substantive law. When a new rule of substantive law becomes involved, the cases are said to involve different "rights" and "wrongs." The doctrine of merger and bar is restricted and causes of action are "small sized." The approach has been criticized as being too narrow and oblivious to important policy considerations. *See* Steakley & Howell, *Ruminations on Res Judicata*, 28 Sw. L.J. 355, 361-62 (1974).

(2) *Diligence and Tactics.* Why wasn't the *quantum meruit* claim included in the second complaint? Is there a tactical reason why the claim was not included?

[2] The "Transactional Analysis" Approach

Note on Overruling of Smith v. Kirkpatrick, *Above*

The case above, *Smith v. Kirkpatrick,* was expressly overruled in *O'Brien v. City of Syracuse,* 429 N.E.2d 1158 (N.Y. 1981), in which New York replaced its "same evidence" approach with a transactional approach. Plaintiff O'Brien's first suit alleged that the city, through its urban rehabilitation regulations, had *de facto* taken a parcel of his land without just compensation. A nonjury trial resulted in a judgment for the city. O'Brien then filed a second suit, alleging that the city had taken the property by tax deed and had damaged it by trespass. O'Brien pointed out that the claims and wrongs were different in the second suit from those in the first suit, and he relied on *Smith v. Kirkpatrick.*

But the court applied a different test. "This state has adopted the transactional analysis approach in deciding *res judicata* issues." If a later suit asserting an alternate theory is based on "what is essentially the same relief for harm arising out of the same or related facts" as an earlier suit, such that they "would constitute a single 'factual grouping,'" then the "circumstance that the two theories involve . . . different elements of proof" will not avoid *res judicata.*

Williams v. City of Yonkers

60 A.2d 1017 (N.Y. App. 2018)

The plaintiff began his employment with the defendant, City of Yonkers, . . . as an "environmental maintenance worker." The position required him to possess a valid New York State class B commercial driver license to operate a City-owned sanitation truck, and the plaintiff obtained that license . . . .

By letter . . . , the City [later] informed the plaintiff that he no longer possessed a valid New York State class B commercial driver license and advised him that, unless he obtained such a license . . . , his employment would be terminated. [He did not, and the City terminated him.]

. . . [Eventually,] the plaintiff, acting pro se, commenced a CPLR article 78 proceeding against the City, alleging that he was wrongfully terminated from his position and that his union failed to grieve his termination or obtain a hearing prior to his termination. [An article 78 proceeding is a suit to review an action of a public body such as a city.—Eds.] In his petition, the plaintiff alleged that he was unable to renew his class B commercial driver license due to a learning disability and that the City had helped him obtain his prior license. The plaintiff also alleged that other people who worked for the City's Sanitation Department did not have the required commercial driver license and were not terminated. In his petition, the plaintiff sought reinstatement to his former position and back-pay.

The City opposed the petition. . . . [The trial court denied the petition and dismissed the case on the ground that it was barred by limitations.] . . . .

Through counsel, . . . the plaintiff commenced this action against the City to recover damages and reinstatement to his prior position as a result of his wrongful termination stemming from a breach of the collective bargaining agreement . . . . [Notice that this cause of action requires proof of different fact elements and asserts different rights and wrongs from those in plaintiff's first suit.—Eds.]

. . . [A] party may move to dismiss a cause of action based on the doctrine of res judicata. . . . "Typically, principles of res judicata require that once a claim is brought to a final conclusion, all other claims arising out of the same transaction or series of transactions are barred, even if based upon different theories or if seeking a different remedy" (*Xiao Yang Chen v. Fischer*, 6 N.Y.3d at 100 . . . .)

"[W]here a plaintiff in a later action brings a claim for damages that could have been presented in a prior CPLR article 78 proceeding against the same party, based upon the same harm and arising out of the same or related facts, the claim is barred by res judicata" (*Parker v. Blauvelt Volunteer Fire Co.*, 93 N.Y.2d 343, 347–348 "[A] dismissal on the ground of the statute of limitations is considered to be on the merits for res judicata purposes" (*Webb v. Greater N.Y. Auto. Dealers Assn., Inc.*, 144 A.D.3d 1134, 1135, 42 N.Y.S.3d 324). . . . Consequently, the court properly granted . . . the City's motion . . . to dismiss . . . [based on res judicata]. . . . [Dismissal AFFIRMED.]

Notes and Questions

(1) *Scope of Preclusion: The Transactional Approach.* The transactional approach defines the breadth of a "claim" or "cause of action" for *res judicata* purposes to embrace all the remedial rights of a plaintiff growing out of the relevant transaction or series of transactions. The unit or entity that may not be split is "coterminous with the transaction regardless of the number of substantive theories or

variant forms of relief flowing from those theories . . . ." *Restatement (Second) of Judgments*, § 24, comment a. The expression "transaction or series of transactions" is one that "connotes a natural grouping or common nucleus of operative facts." *Id.* comment b. The idea is similar to the compulsory counterclaim concept in Rule 13(a).

(2) *"Broad Procedural Duty" Analysis.* Some court opinions and commentators have asserted that the entire problem of claim preclusion could be dealt with more effectively by imposing a broad procedural duty on the plaintiff to join all related claims. *See* Schopflocher, *What is a Single Cause of Action for the Purpose of the Doctrine of Res Judicata?*, 21 Ore. L. Rev. 319, 320-23 (1942); *see also Griffin v. Holiday Inns of America*, 496 S.W.2d 535, 538 n.1 (Tex. 1973), expressly overruled in *Barr v. Resolution Trust Corp.*, 837 S.W.2d 627, 630-31 (Tex. 1992), which adopted the Restatement's "transactional approach." Of course, if the procedural duty is defined in terms of an obligation to join all claims arising out of the same transaction, the procedural duty analysis becomes identical to the transactional analysis approach at least in terms of defining the duty. It should be noted, however, that the procedural duty approach probably is more complex than transactional analysis. *See, e.g., Ogletree v. Crates*, 363 S.W.2d 431 (Tex. 1963) (focusing on external policy considerations involved in child custody cases).

(3) *Does Williams v. City of Yonkers Use All Three Approaches: Same Evidence, Transactional, and Broad Procedural Duty, Combined?* The *Williams* case hints at (1) the "broad procedural duty" approach when it says that a claim "that could have been presented" in an earlier suit is barred. But in the preceding paragraph, the opinion says that "claims arising out of the same transaction or series of transactions are barred, even if based upon different theories," and thus it seems to adopt (2) the "transactional" approach. Then, yet another part of the opinion says that a second claim is barred if it is "based upon the same harm and aris[es] out of the same or related facts." This statement suggests (3) the "same evidence/same wrong" test. So: which approach did the court adopt? (Perhaps the opinion is so confused that the answer is "all three.")

[3] Public Policy Exceptions to Preclusion

CANONSBURG GENERAL HOSPITAL v. BURWELL, 807 F.3d 295 (D.C. Cir. 2015). In this case, the court recognized the possibility of public policy exceptions or equitable exceptions to res judicata. The court began by pointing out that the exception, if it exists, is narrow: "There is no general public policy exception to the operation of res judicata." We limit equitable exceptions to issue preclusion to certain limited circumstances, none of which applies here.

> First, we have explained that issue preclusion is inappropriate if there has been an intervening "change in controlling legal principles." Second, we

> have recognized that issue preclusion would be unfair "if the party to be bound lacked an incentive to litigate in the first trial, especially in comparison to the stakes of the second trial." . . . [W]e [have also] clarified that, in weighing a party's incentive to litigate, we should be concerned with whether "the losing party clearly lacked any incentive to litigate the point in the first trial, but the stakes of the second trial are of a vastly greater magnitude." Similarly, application of issue preclusion is inappropriate if the "prior proceedings were seriously defective." [Citing cases.] . . .

BOGARD v. COOK, 586 F.2d 399 (5th Cir. 1978). This case shows one of the rare kinds of situations in which the courts will recognize public policy exceptions to res judicata. Bogard, a former prisoner at the Mississippi State Penitentiary, brought suit for personal injuries against various supervisory officials, employees, and inmates based on 42 U.S.C. § 1983 and pendent state tort claims. While he was an inmate, Bogard was subjected to corporal punishment and suffered two incidents of prison violence. The first incident occurred when Bogard was struck in the foot by a rifle bullet fired by a prisoner who had been made a "trusty shooter" by prison officials. Trusty shooters were inmate-guards armed with rifles and charged with guarding other inmates. The second was when another inmate knifed Bogard when Bogard was sent to get a sewing machine from the other inmate by a prison official. The knife wound rendered Bogard a permanent paraplegic because the blade severed his spine. Bogard alleged that both incidents were caused by the negligence of prison officials.

Prior to Bogard's damage suit, Bogard participated (as a class member, meaning that he was subject to preclusion simply because of his not having opted out) in *Gates v. Collier*, 349 F. Supp. 881 (N.D. Miss. 1972), *aff'd*, 501 F.2d 1291 (5th Cir. 1974). The *Gates* case sought declaratory and equitable relief for inmates, including Bogard, from violations of civil rights. The District Court granted sweeping declaratory and injunctive relief. Consequently, because Bogard could have brought his damage claims in the *Gates* litigation, the defendants asserted that the claims were barred.

The Court of Appeals concluded that "[p]rinciples of res judicata are not ironclad . . . res judicata will not be applied when it contravenes an important public policy." Holding that the inmates were not given any indication that they could assert damage claims in *Gates* by the class action notice, the Court stated that "[i]t would be a harsh and improper application of res judicata to hold, on the basis of the notice sent out in *Gates*, that prisoners forfeited their rights to personal redress [of constitutional rights] for lack of knowledge that federal law . . . required that injunctive and monetary relief be sought in one action."

[C] The Other Elements—Identity of Parties and a Judgment That Should Be Given Preclusive Effect: Notes and Questions

(1) *What Kind of Judgment Is Sufficient? Restatement § 20.* The *Restatement (Second) of Judgments* provides a list of situations in which a valid judgment, even if final, should not be given preclusive effect. Examples include a dismissal on grounds such as jurisdiction, venue, misjoinder or nonjoinder; a nonsuit without prejudice; or a judgment to which preclusive effect is denied by statute. Many jurisdictions have statutes denying preclusive effect to small claims (and certain other) judgments. *See, e.g.*, Tex. Civ. Prac. & Rem. C. §§ 31.004–31.005; *Gilberg v. Barbieri*, in § II[C][1], below (New York). Likewise, most take-nothing judgments based on prematurity or failure to satisfy a precondition to recovery are not preclusive of a later suit brought after the condition is satisfied. *See generally Restatement (Second) of Judgments* § 20 (1982). *Res judicata* may be based upon a judgment that still is subject to appeal, in some jurisdictions—although a judgment based upon preclusion is subject to being set aside if the earlier judgment ultimately is reversed. *See id.* §§ 13–16.

(2) *What Kinds of Persons Are Bound Though Not Themselves Parties to the Action? Restatement §§ 34–42.* The basic rule is that parties to the action and subject to the court's jurisdiction are bound. The more interesting question, however, concerns persons who are subject to the preclusive effect of the judgment although they are not parties to the action. For example, a person who "controls or substantially participates in the control of the presentation on behalf of a party" may be bound as though he were a party. *Id.* § 39. Persons "represented by" parties—such as trust beneficiaries represented by a trustee, estate beneficiaries represented by an executor, principals who authorize their agents to sue in their behalf, class members represented by named parties in a class action, and certain other kinds of nonparties—may be bound by a judgment to which they were not parties, with certain exceptions (based upon, *e.g.*, noncompliance with notice requirements). *Id.* §§ 41–42.

II. Collateral Estoppel: Issue Preclusion

[A] The Basic Elements

The branch of the doctrine of *res judicata* that is termed "collateral estoppel" (or "estoppel by judgment" by traditionalists and "issue preclusion" by modernists) is applied when one of the parties to a civil action argues that preclusive effect should be given to one or more issues determined in an earlier civil action. *Restatement (Second) of Judgments*, introduction at 2, 263-265 (1982). Collateral estoppel is like "res judicata for one issue."

The elements of the doctrine are explained by Professor Rex Perschbacher as follows:

> . . . Collateral estoppel has changed from a precisely defined and narrowly applied doctrine to a vaguely defined idea widely used by harried courts. Originally, collateral estoppel prevented relitigation only of factual issues that were *actually litigated* and *essential* to an earlier judgment on a *different cause of action* binding the *same parties.* In comparison, *res judicata* prevented relitigation of issues that might have been raised, but were not. . . .
>
> Recently a refashioned and broadened doctrine of collateral estoppel has emerged with simplified formal requirements, best expressed in the *Restatement (Second) of Judgments.* Issues of either law or fact can be the basis of collateral estoppel. Mutuality is no longer necessary; only the estopped party need be bound by the prior determination. Nonjudicial bodies, particularly administrative agencies, can make this prior determination provided they operate "in a judicial capacity." Only a party who lacked a "full and fair opportunity" to litigate the issue . . . is excepted from the doctrine's operation.

R. Perschbacher, *Rethinking Collateral Estoppel: Limiting the Preclusive Effect of Administrative Determinations in Judicial Proceedings*, 35 U. FLA. L. REV. 422, 423-24 (1983).

Section 27 of the *Restatement (Second) of Judgments* contains the following general rule:

> § 27. Issue Preclusion—General Rule. When an issue of fact or law is actually litigated and determined by a valid and final judgment, and the determination is essential to the judgment, the determination is conclusive in a subsequent action between the parties, whether on the same or a different claim.

[B] The Requirement of "Actual Litigation" of the "Same" Issue, Which Was "Essential to" the Prior Judgment

CROMWELL v. COUNTY OF SAC, 94 U.S. 351 (1876). As in all collateral estoppel situations, this case involved two different actions. The first action was brought on Cromwell's behalf against Sac County, Iowa, for recovery of interest on twenty-five bond coupons. This action ended in a judgment for Sac County. The court found that the County had issued a number of bonds to raise money for the construction of a courthouse; but the contractor had given one of the bonds as a "gratuity" to the county executive, and the courthouse was never constructed. The court found the transaction to have been so tainted with fraud and illegality that only a *bona fide* purchaser for value could recover on any of the bonds or coupons. Since it was not shown in the first suit that Cromwell had paid value for the twenty-five coupons, the court rendered judgment against Cromwell.

Later, in the second action, Cromwell sued upon certain *other* bonds and coupons from the same transaction. The defendant, Sac County, pleaded the doctrine of collateral estoppel. The lower courts agreed with the defendant and held that Cromwell's right to recover in the second action was estopped by the prior judgment. The Supreme Court noted that the issue of fraud and illegality had been actually litigated in the prior suit. The issue was identical for all bonds, since if the transaction was fraudulent and illegal it affected all of them. Thus, collateral estoppel did apply to this issue, and consequently, Cromwell would be required to prove in the second action that he had purchased the bonds and coupons for value. But the second suit involved *different* bonds and coupons than the first, and so the question whether Cromwell had been a *bona fide* purchaser for value in the second suit had not been decided in the first. Therefore, the payment-of-value issue was not subject to collateral estoppel, and the Supreme Court reversed the lower court's judgment for defendant. The Court reasoned as follows:

> [I]t should be borne in mind . . . that there is a difference between the effect of a judgment as a bar [i.e., res judicata] . . . and its effect as an estoppel in another action between the same parties upon a different claim or cause of action. In the former case, the judgment, if rendered upon the merits, constitutes an absolute bar to a subsequent action. It is a finality . . . not only as to every matter which was offered . . . but [also] as to any other admissible matter which might have been offered . . . .
>
> But where the second action . . . is upon a different claim or demand, the judgment in the prior action operates as an estoppel only as to those matters . . . , upon the determination of which the finding or verdict was rendered. . . . [T]he inquiry must always be as to the point or question actually litigated and determined in the original action; not what might have been thus litigated and determined. . . .
>
> . . . [T]he matters adjudged in [the first] case were these: that the bonds were void as against the County in the hands of parties who did not . . . give value for them, and that plaintiff, not having proved that he gave such value, was not entitled to recover upon the coupons. . . . If, therefore, the plaintiff received the [different] bond and coupons in [the second] suit . . . for value, as he offered to prove, he should have been permitted to show that fact. . . . [Reversed and remanded.]

Notes and Questions

(1) *Different Cause of Action.* A principal distinction between the doctrine of claim preclusion (merger and bar) and the doctrine of issue preclusion (collateral estoppel) is that under the latter doctrine, the prior lawsuit can involve a different

cause of action than the second action. In other words, even though claim preclusion or res judicata principles are inapplicable, the prior adjudication can preclude relitigation of an issue in a subsequent suit if the issue was already litigated. To test your understanding of this basic difference between claim preclusion and issue preclusion, why wasn't the second action against Sac County barred altogether? Notice that the prior adjudication had no effect on the subsequent lawsuit.

The Requirement that the Finding Be "Essential" to the Prior Judgment: Rios v. Davis, 373 S.W.2d 386 (Tex. Civ. App.-Eastland 1963, writ ref'd). Even though an issue is "actually litigated" and made the subject of jury findings, it will not affect the judgment if the judgment rests on other findings. Thus, collateral estoppel is limited to issues that were "essential to" the prior judgment. For example, in *Rios v. Davis*, a truck owned by Popular Dry Goods and driven by Rios collided with a vehicle driven by Davis. In the first suit, which was filed in a county-level court with an amount-in-controversy jurisdiction not exceeding $1,000, Popular sued Davis for damage to its truck, and Davis filed a "third-party" claim against Rios for damages to Davis's car. The jury found all three parties guilty of negligence proximately causing the collision, and since contributory negligence was then a complete bar under the governing law, neither Popular nor Davis recovered anything. Later, in the second suit brought in a district court, Rios sought to recover approximately $20,000 from Davis for his personal injuries. Davis pleaded that the jury's finding of Rios's causal negligence in the first suit collaterally estopped his recovery in the second suit. The lower courts applied the collateral estoppel doctrine as Davis requested, but the appellate court—correctly—held that collateral estoppel was inapplicable. Can you see why?

[In the first suit, the finding that Rios was causally negligent was not "essential"; in fact, it was immaterial to the first judgment. Davis did not recover from Rios, because of his own contributory negligence. Thus, it made no difference whether Rios was found negligent or not negligent in the first suit. Furthermore, Rios was not adversely affected by the first judgment, since it was in his favor. He would not have been allowed to complain about the finding of his negligence on appeal, and in fact he could not appeal the judgment at all on that ground.]

Ryan v. New York Telephone Co.

62 N.Y.2d 494, 478 N.Y.S.2d 823, 467 N.E.2d 487 (1984)

Jasen, J. . . .

[Ed. Note: In New York, this decision has been reversed legislatively. (See the Note that follows the case). It nevertheless illustrates common law reasoning of more general application, and your reading of it is essential to your understanding of the legislation.]

Plaintiff, Edward Ryan, was discharged from his employ with defendant New York Telephone Company for theft of company property. Defendants Lauriano and Perrino, company security investigators, had observed Ryan removing what appeared to be company property from the workplace. They stopped him and called the police who arrested Ryan and charged him with petit larceny and criminal possession of stolen property.

Following his discharge from work, Ryan applied for unemployment insurance benefits, but his application was rejected by a claims examiner of the Department of Labor on the ground that the discharge was the result of his own misconduct. . . . This determination was subsequently affirmed by the Unemployment Insurance Appeal Board whose decision was, in turn, upheld by the Appellate Division.

During the pendency of the foregoing administrative proceedings and judicial review, the criminal action in which Ryan was represented by counsel resulted in . . . dismissal. . . .

. . . [P]laintiffs commenced this action asserting claims for false arrest, malicious prosecution, slander and wrongful discharge, and an additional claim for the resultant injuries to Ryan's wife. Defendants pleaded an affirmative defense of *res judicata* and collateral estoppel on the basis of the prior administrative determination denying Ryan's claim for unemployment benefits. [P]laintiffs moved to dismiss the affirmative defense. . . . [The lower courts granted plaintiff's motion and dismissed the affirmative defense, but the Appellate Division certified to the Court of Appeals the question whether this ruling was correct.] We now reverse, grant defendants' cross motion to dismiss, and answer the certified question in the negative. . . .

The doctrine of collateral estoppel, a narrower species of *res judicata*, precludes a party from relitigating in a subsequent action or proceeding an issue clearly raised in a prior action or proceeding and decided against that party or those in privity, whether or not the tribunals or causes of action are the same.

. . . What is controlling is the identity of the issue which has necessarily been decided in the prior action or proceeding.

Of course, the issue must have been material to the first action or proceeding and essential to the decision rendered therein . . . and it must be the point actually to be determined in the second action or proceeding such that "a different judgment in the second would destroy or impair rights or interests established by the first" . . . .

Applying the foregoing rules of law to this case demonstrates clearly that collateral estoppel bars plaintiffs from litigating the subject claims . . . .

The critical issue in the prior administrative proceeding was whether Ryan was discharged by reason of misconduct and, therefore, not entitled to unemployment benefits. The Administrative Law Judge's specific findings, essential to the disallowance of benefits to Ryan, was that the latter was guilty of unauthorized removal and possession of company property, and that he was discharged for that reason. . . .

The first cause of action [in Ryan's complaint] alleges false arrest resulting from the defendants' complaints against Ryan to the police. The lack of legal justification is an essential element of the tort of false arrest, but the administrative determination of criminally chargeable misconduct is dispositive of the presence of such justification and, consequently, grounds for dismissal of the cause of action.... [Here, the court proceeds to decide that the Administrative Law Judge's findings precludes each of Ryan's other claims, too.] ... [REVERSED; claims are collaterally estopped.]

Note on Legislative Reversal of Ryan v. New York Telephone Co.

Ryan v. New York Telephone Co. has been legislatively overruled. New York Labor Law § 623, as amended, provides (in essence) that no finding of fact or law in a decision rendered on a claim for unemployment insurance may be given preclusive effect in subsequent litigation, unless the subsequent litigation also involves unemployment insurance.

[C] Parties Who Had "Full and Fair Opportunity" to Litigate the Issue

[1] When the First Action Is Minor or Informal

GILBERG v. BARBIERI, 423 N.E.2d 807 (1981). Gilberg and Barbieri were involved in an altercation. Gilberg filed a criminal complaint, charging Barbieri with "harassment," a petty offense designated as a "violation" by the New York Penal Law. After a brief non-jury trial, which was to be followed by a felony trial, the judge of the City Court of Mount Vernon, New York, immediately found Barbieri guilty and sentenced him to a one-year "conditional discharge," saying, "You're not found guilty of a crime, it's a violation...." The day following the conviction, a summons was issued in Gilberg's civil suit against Barbieri for assault, in which Gilberg sought a quarter of a million dollars in damages. Gilberg moved for summary judgment, arguing that the City Court finding on the harassment charge collaterally estopped Barbieri's denial of liability. The trial court granted summary judgment, noting that the conviction was based on a finding that Barbieri had used "physical force against" Gilberg. The Appellate Division affirmed. The Court of Appeals, however, reversed because it found that Barbieri had not had a "full and fair opportunity" to litigate the issue in the prior proceeding:

> The doctrine of collateral estoppel is based on the notion that it is not fair to permit a party to relitigate an issue which has previously been decided against him in a proceeding in which he had a fair opportunity to fully litigate the point.
>
> Because of the relative insignificance of the charge, the defendant had no constitutional or statutory right to a jury trial, as he would have ... in the subsequently initiated civil action for damages.... Nor could he expect or be expected to defend with the same vigor. The brisk, often informal, way in which these matters must be tried, as well as the relative insignificance

> of the outcome, afford the party neither opportunity nor incentive to litigate . . . as thoroughly as he might if more were at stake. . . . [*Reversed.*]

Notes and Questions

(1) *"Criminal-Civil" Estoppel; "Non-Mutual" Estoppel.* New York allows collateral estoppel to be based on a criminal judgment in a proper case. Furthermore, it applies the collateral estoppel doctrine even if the non-estopped party was not a party to the prior suit, so that he could not have suffered estoppel (as was true of Gilberg, since he was not a party to the harassment action). The court recognized these principles in *Gilberg v. Barbieri*. However, the nature of the prior action obviously may affect the application of the "full and fair opportunity" doctrine. (For coverage of the "mutuality" issue, see § II[D] below.)

(2) *Gilberg v. Barbieri as a Case of "Offensive" (Rather than "Defensive") Collateral Estoppel.* The distinction between offensive and defensive use of collateral estoppel is based on the relative positions of the parties as defendants or plaintiffs in the second action. When a litigant seeks to impose liability on a defending party in the second suit, the use of collateral estoppel is "offensive." When a litigant seeks to avoid liability to a claimant in the second action, the use of collateral estoppel is "defensive." *Gilberg v. Barbieri* involved an attempted use of offensive collateral estoppel; should this feature of the action have affected the outcome? *See Restatement (Second) of Judgments* § 29, comment d (pointing out that it may be relevant that the party "had no choice, or restricted choice, as to the forum" in the prior action, particularly in offensive collateral estoppel cases).

[2] When the Parties Are Not Identical

MONTANA v. UNITED STATES, 440 U.S. 147 (1979). This case concerns the proper use of collateral estoppel against a person who "controlled" the earlier litigation. Montana imposed a tax on contractors who worked on public (but not private) construction projects. The United States, whose contractors were subject to this tax, considered that the tax was unconstitutionally discriminatory. Therefore, the federal government recruited one of its contractors (Peter Kiewit Sons' Co., which had worked on a federal dam project in Montana and had paid the tax) to sue Montana in a Montana state court. The United States was not a party to the state litigation, but "[t]he litigation was directed and financed by the United States." The state litigation terminated in a unanimous decision of the Montana Supreme Court upholding the Montana tax. The contractor at first sought review in the United States Supreme Court, but it then abandoned this effort—at the request of the United States.

Despite this loss, the United States pursued a separate suit against Montana, this time in the name of the United States, and in a United States District Court. The District Court rejected Montana's defense of collateral estoppel and struck down the tax. The Supreme Court reversed:

> [The purposes underlying collateral estoppel] are similarly implicated when nonparties assume control over litigation in which they have a direct financial [i]interest and then seek to redetermine issues previously resolved. [These litigants] cannot be said to be "strangers to the [earlier] cause." . . .
>
> That the United States exercised control over the [Kiewit] litigation is not in dispute. [T]hus, although not a party, the United States plainly had a sufficient "laboring oar" in the conduct of the state-court litigation to actuate principles of [collateral] estoppel.

Weinberger v. Tucker

510 F.3d 486 (4th Cir. 2007)

Gregory, Circuit Judge:

. . . [This case considers whether collateral estoppel can apply when the relevant issue was decided in the first suit only in response to a motion rather than decided by a final judgment. In the second suit,] Alan D. Weinberger ("Weinberger") and ASCII Group, Inc. ("ASCII") sued their former lawyer, Stefan F. Tucker ("Tucker"), for fraud, breach of fiduciary duty, and professional negligence. For the reasons outlined below, we affirm the district court's finding that collateral estoppel bars this lawsuit.

[The claims of Tucker's malpractice arose from his earlier representation of both ASCII and a party named Voltfsun. Tucker had introduced these two parties, and the relationship grew into an investment by ASCII in TechNet, in which Voltfsun also invested. ASCII signed a guaranty protecting Volftsun in connection with the transaction, and the guaranty later became the subject of this litigation. Before negotiations over that investment, attorney Tucker specifically sent ASCII a waiver-of-conflict letter, to the effect that he represented only Voltfsun, not ASCII.

[The investment in Technet went bad, and Voltfsun sued ASCII and TechNet. In the course of that litigation, ASCII moved to disqualify Tucker and his law firm from representing Voltfsun. The issues in that motion, which was vigorously litigated, concerned the alleged conflict of interest of Tucker. ASCII lost that motion because of the conflict-waiver letter, and Tucker's firm continued as Voltfsun's lawyer. It was this finding on the motion to disqualify that became the basis of collateral estoppel in the present case.] . . .

A. Voltfsun v. ASCII Group (ASCII I). Volftsun, represented by Venable [Tucker's law firm], sued ASCII . . . and TechNet (collectively "ASCII") in the Eastern District of Virginia to enforce the guarantee ("the underlying case"). ASCII filed a motion to disqualify counsel, alleging a conflict of interest. Volftsun filed a brief in opposition. . . . The court held a hearing . . . and denied the motion to disqualify, based on [Tucker's] waiver letter. Ultimately, the court found the guarantee binding on ASCII and entered a final judgment in favor of Volftsun.

B. Weinberger v. Tucker (ASCII II). [Then], Weinberger and ASCII (collectively "Weinberger" with respect to this action) filed a suit against Tucker for fraud, breach of fiduciary duty, and professional negligence. Tucker moved to dismiss, based on collateral estoppel. . . . The district court held a hearing on Tucker's motion, dismissed Weinberger's claim based on collateral estoppel, and entered a judgment for Tucker . . . . Weinberger appeals to this Court. . . .

[To sustain the decision based on collateral estoppel, the court examines (1) whether Weinberger, the party in the second suit, was in privity with and represented by ASCII in the first suit, and also, (2) whether Tucker was in privity with Voltfsun in the motion to disqualify Tucker in the first suit.]

Collateral estoppel, or issue preclusion, provides that once a court of competent jurisdiction actually and necessarily determines an issue, that determination remains conclusive in subsequent suits, based on a different cause of action but involving the same parties, or privies, to the previous litigation. . . .

. . . Weinberger argues that the parties are not the same . . . . Tucker responds that even though Tucker and Weinberger were not parties to the original proceedings, privity exists between Weinberger, as the founder and CEO of ASCII, and the company itself, as well as between Volftsun and Tucker, as his lawyer.

"Under both Fourth Circuit and Virginia decisions, the test for privity is [] the same: whether the interests of one party are so identified with the interests of another that representation by one party is representation of the other's legal right." . . . According to the Virginia Supreme Court in *State Water Control Board v. Smithfield Foods, Inc.*, 542 S.E.2d at 769,

> There is no single fixed definition of privity for purposes of res judicata. Whether privity exists is determined on a case by case examination of the relationship and interests of the parties. The touchstone of privity . . . is that a party's interest is so identical with another that representation by one party is representation of the other's legal right. . . .

[1. *Weinberger's Privity to ASCII.*] Weinberger argues that his interests are distinct from ASCII's in the underlying action. He maintains that he was personally represented by Tucker and is bringing the action not only on behalf of ASCII but on behalf of himself in his individual capacity. Tucker responds that the damages Weinberger alleges stem from his shared economic identity with ASCII. He is correct.

As the chairman of both ASCII and the holding company and as the owner of a majority of ASCII's stock, Weinberger is the real party of interest when ASCII incurs damages. Weinberger's interests are so in line with those of ASCII that representation by ASCII in the underlying action effectively represented Weinberger's legal rights in the present case. We, therefore, hold that there is privity between Weinberger and ASCII. . . .

[2. *Tucker's Privity to Volftsun.*] According to Weinberger, Tucker is not in privity with Volftsun. Weinberger argues that the attorney-client relationship is not sufficient to establish privity. Furthermore, Weinberger points out that Tucker did not represent Volftsun in ASCII I [although his law firm did] and that Tucker never testified or presented any evidence that he had a personal stake in the ASCII I litigation. Tucker responds that he and Volftsun shared identical interests with respect to the motion to disqualify Venable [Tucker's law firm] and the validity of the guarantee. Tucker argues that he had a particularly strong interest, as the enforcement of the guarantee rested on his conduct and he faced the possibility of a legal malpractice suit by Volftsun had the defendants in ASCII I succeeded in their defenses that the guarantee had expired or that the guarantee was fraudulently induced. We again agree with Tucker. . . .

Tucker's professional conduct, in fact, was validated by the court's honoring the waiver and enforcing the guarantee. Accordingly, we hold that Volftsun and Tucker were privies. [Collateral estoppel holding AFFIRMED.]

Notes and Questions

(1) *Should Collateral Estoppel Rest on a Holding About Privity on a Motion, as Opposed to a Judgment?* Litigation over a motion to disqualify may not be supported as vigorously by the client (here *Volftsun*) as the fight over a final judgment would be. The client's case is not destroyed by a disqualification of plaintiff's counsel, and plaintiff can get other counsel and proceed with the case. But in this situation, in which the lawyers were concerned about malpractice and the alleged malpractice is said to have affected the guaranty upon which the client sues, the identity of interests might be stronger.

(2) *The Restatement Approach.* Both §§ 28 and 29 of the *Restatement (Second) of Judgments* recognize that a party is not precluded from relitigating an issue when the party "lacked full and fair opportunity to litigate the issue in the first action or other circumstances justify affording him an opportunity to relitigate the issue." *Restatement (Second) of Judgments* § 29 (1982). Neither section contemplates that a person who was not a party can be bound *unless* she is represented by a party or has interests that are derived from a party. The "Reporter's Note" to § 29 identifies this principle as "a rule of Constitutional law." Notice that the "identity of parties" concept overlaps the concept of a party who had a "full and fair opportunity to litigate" in the first action.

[D] Mutuality: Is It (or Should It Be) Required?

Parklane Hosiery Company, Inc. v. Shore

439 U.S. 322 (1979)

MR. JUSTICE STEWART delivered the opinion of the Court.

[In the first lawsuit, the Securities and Exchange Commission ("SEC") obtained injunctive and declaratory relief against Parklane Hosiery Co. and others after a four-day nonjury trial. The basis for the judgment was that a proxy statement was materially false and misleading to shareholders.]

[In the second lawsuit, individual shareholders, including Leo Shore, brought a stockholders' derivative suit for damages against the same defendants for damages on the ground that the proxy statement was materially false and misleading in essentially the same respects. Shore and the other shareholders were not parties to the SEC's earlier suit against Parklane.]

[Leo Shore moved for partial summary judgment on the basis that the defendants were collaterally estopped from relitigating the issues that had been resolved against them in the action brought by the SEC. The motion was denied by the district judge on the theory that such an estoppel would deny the defendants' Seventh Amendment right to a jury trial. The Second Circuit reversed. The Supreme Court granted certiorari.]

I

The threshold question to be considered is whether, quite apart from the right to a jury trial under the Seventh Amendment, the petitioners can be precluded from religating facts resolved adversely to them in a prior equitable proceeding with another party under the general law of collateral estoppel. Specifically, we must determine whether a litigant who was not a party to a prior judgment may nevertheless use that judgment "offensively" to prevent a defendant from relitigating issues resolved in the earlier proceeding.

A

Collateral estoppel, like the related doctrine of res judicata, has the dual purpose of protecting litigants from the burden of relitigating an identical issue with the same party or his privy and of promoting judicial economy by preventing needless litigation. *Blonder-Tongue Laboratories, Inc. v. University of Illinois Foundation*, 402 U.S. 313, 328-329. . . . Until relatively recently, however, the scope of collateral estoppel was limited by the doctrine of mutuality of parties. Under this [older] mutuality doctrine, neither party could use a prior judgment as an estoppel against the other unless both parties were bound by the judgment. Based on the premise that it is somehow unfair to allow a party to use a prior judgment when he himself would not be so bound, the mutuality requirement provided a party who had litigated and lost in a previous action an opportunity to relitigate identical issues with new parties.

By failing to recognize the obvious difference in position between a party who has never litigated an issue and one who has fully litigated and lost, the mutuality requirement was criticized almost from its inception. Recognizing the validity of this criticism, the Court in *Blonder-Tongue Laboratories, Inc. v. University of Illinois Foundation, supra*, abandoned the mutuality requirement, at least in cases where a patentee seeks to relitigate the validity of a patent after a federal court in a previous lawsuit has already declared it invalid. The "broader question" before the Court, however, was "whether it is any longer tenable to afford a litigant more than one full and fair opportunity for judicial resolution of the same issue." . . . The Court strongly suggested a negative answer to that question:

> In any lawsuit where a defendant, because of the mutuality principle, is forced to present a complete defense on the merits to a claim which the plaintiff has fully litigated and lost in a prior action, there is an arguable misallocation of resources. . . . Permitting repeated litigation of the same issue as long as the supply of unrelated defendants holds out reflects either the aura of the gaming table or "a lack of discipline and of disinterestedness on the part of the lower courts, hardly a worthy or wise basis for fashioning rules of procedure." . . .

B

The *Blonder-Tongue* case involved defensive use of collateral estoppel—a plaintiff was estopped from asserting a claim that the plaintiff had previously litigated and lost against another defendant. The present case, by contrast, involves offensive use of collateral estoppel—a plaintiff is seeking to estop a defendant from relitigating the issues which the defendant previously litigated and lost against another plaintiff. In both the offensive and defensive use situations, the party against whom estoppel is asserted has litigated and lost in an earlier action. Nevertheless, several reasons have been advanced why the two situations should be treated differently.

First, offensive use of collateral estoppel does not promote judicial economy in the same manner as defensive use does. . . . Since a plaintiff will be able to rely on a previous judgment against a defendant but will not be bound by that judgment if the defendant wins, the plaintiff has every incentive to adopt a "wait and see" attitude, in the hope that the first action by another plaintiff will result in a favorable judgment. Thus offensive use of collateral estoppel will likely increase rather than decrease the total amount of litigation, since potential plaintiffs will have everything to gain and nothing to lose by not intervening in the first action.

A second argument against offensive use of collateral estoppel is that it may be unfair to a defendant. If a defendant in the first action is sued for small or nominal damages, he may have little incentive to defend vigorously, particularly if future suits are not foreseeable. . . . Allowing offensive collateral estoppel may also be unfair to a defendant if the judgment relied upon as a basis for the estoppel is itself inconsistent with one or more previous judgments in favor of the defendant.[(14)] Still another situation where it might be unfair to apply offensive estoppel is where the second action affords the defendant procedural opportunities unavailable in the first action that could readily cause a different result.

C

We have concluded that the preferable approach for dealing with these problems in the federal courts is not to preclude the use of offensive collateral estoppel, but

---

(14) In Professor Currie's familiar example, a railroad collision injures 50 passengers all of whom bring separate actions . . . . [If the first ten plaintiffs lose, but the eleventh wins a judgment against the railroad, may the remaining thirty-nine claimants use the judgment in the eleventh case to collaterally estop the railroad from denying its negligence?]

to grant trial courts broad discretion to determine when it should be applied. The general rule should be that in cases where a plaintiff could easily have joined in the earlier action or where, either for the reasons discussed above or for other reasons, the application of offensive estoppel would be unfair to a defendant, a trial judge should not allow the use of offensive collateral estoppel.

In the present case, however, none of the circumstances that might justify reluctance to allow the offensive use of collateral estoppel is present. [T]he respondent probably could not have joined in the injunctive action brought by the SEC even had he so desired. Similarly, there is no unfairness to the petitioners in applying offensive collateral estoppel in this case. . . .

II

The question that remains is whether, notwithstanding the law of collateral estoppel, the use of offensive collateral estoppel in this case would violate the petitioners' Seventh Amendment right to a jury trial. . . .

[The Court held that application of collateral estoppel under the circumstances did not violate the Seventh Amendment, even though the prior judgment had been rendered in a proceeding to which the right to a jury trial did not attach. REVERSED AND REMANDED for application of collateral estoppel.]

[The dissenting opinion of Mr. Justice Rehnquist is here omitted.]

Notes and Questions

(1) *New York's "Aggressive" Application of Offensive Collateral Estoppel: Kaufman v. Eli Lilly & Co.*, 482 N.E.2d 63 (N.Y. 1985). Lilly was held liable in one of fifteen pending cases alleging damages sustained by the plaintiff's daughters from their mothers' ingestion of diethylsilbestrol (DES). Kaufman, the plaintiff in another of the fifteen cases, promptly moved for partial summary judgment based on offensive collateral estoppel. The New York Court of Appeals applied offensive collateral estoppel to a number of issues, including Lilly's negligence in testing DES. The court said: "[The case] fits the example described by James and Hazard of an instance in which there are several similar cases and the first tried is 'roughly typical' of the rest. In that situation, the professors noted, it is not unfair to preclude the defendant from retrying the issues previously litigated and decided adversely to it (James & Hazard, *Civil Procedure* § 11.24, at 581 [2d ed.])." Is this approach sensible?

(2) *Non-Mutual Use of Defensive Collateral Estoppel: Hardy v. Fleming*, 553 S.W.2d 790 (Tex. Civ. App.-El Paso 1977, writ ref'd n.r.e.). Hardy suffered what he claimed was a heart attack on the job and filed a worker's compensation claim. The jury found that Hardy had suffered no injury, and the court rendered judgment that he take nothing. In a second suit, Hardy alleged that his physician, Dr. Fleming, had negligently caused him to suffer the same "heart attack." The Court of Appeals affirmed a summary judgment for defendant Fleming, based upon collateral estoppel. Defensive collateral estoppel, as in *Hardy v. Fleming*, poses fewer problems than

the offensive variety when mutuality is lacking. *See also Ryan v. New York Telephone Co.*, § II[B], above.

III. Interjurisdictional Preclusion: State-State and State-Federal Effects

Read 28 U.S.C. §§ 1738, 1738A (full faith and credit).

MARRESE v. AMERICAN ACADEMY OF ORTHOPAEDIC SURGEONS, 470 U.S. 373 (1985). So far in this chapter, we have considered cases in which there was no issue raised about two jurisdictions with different preclusion doctrines. But what if the two cases are in different jurisdictions that treat res judicata differently? Then, the question arises, which jurisdiction's law of preclusion applies? In the *Marrese* case, the first suit asserted a state-law antitrust claim in an Illinois state court, and the second was a federal antitrust claim in a federal court. The federal antitrust claims could not have been brought in the first (state court) suit, because the federal courts have exclusive jurisdiction over federal antitrust claims. The lower court held that the state court judgment precluded the later federal claims, even though they could not have been brought in the state court. In so holding, the lower court relied on federal law of preclusion.

The Supreme Court looked to section 1738, the "Full Faith and Credit" statute, which provides that the law of the forum state determines the preclusive effect of a federal judgment. *Marrese,* therefore, holds that the first step is that the forum state's law normally determines the preclusive effect of a federal judgment, and the second step is to determine whether another principle of law requires otherwise. The Court remanded the case for consideration, first, of Illinois state law of preclusion, and second, for a determination whether an overriding reason required application of some other principle of law:

> In this case the Court of Appeals should have first referred to Illinois law to determine the preclusive effect of the state judgment. Only if state law indicates that a particular claim or issue would be barred, is it necessary to determine if an exception to § 1738 should apply [because of the state court's inability to consider federal antitrust claims]. Although for purposes of this case, we need not decide if such an exception exists for federal antitrust claims, we observe that the more general question is whether the concerns underlying a particular grant of exclusive jurisdiction justify a finding of an implied partial repeal of § 1738 [which is the "Full Faith and Credit" statute, requiring federal courts to follow state court judgments].

> Resolution of this question will depend on the particular federal statute as well as the nature of the claim or issue involved in the subsequent federal action. Our previous decisions indicate that the primary consideration must be the intent of Congress.... [REVERSED AND REMANDED for a determination of these questions.]

Matsushita Electric Industries Co., Ltd. v. Epstein

516 U.S. 367 (1996)

Justice THOMAS delivered the opinion of the Court.

[This case partially answers the question left open in *Marrese,* above: when a state's laws would give preclusive effect to an earlier judgment, how does a later federal court decide whether to depart from the state's res judicata law? Matsushita acquired MCA, Inc. by a tender offer (a tender offer is an offer to the public to buy shares of the target company). A number of shareholders claimed that the acquisition violated securities laws. The tender offer therefore precipitated two suits. The first was a Delaware state-court action based solely on state-law claims, and the second was a federal suit based on federal securities laws claims (which cannot be brought in state court, because federal courts have exclusive jurisdiction).]

[The Delaware state-court action resulted in a global settlement. In exchange for $2 million to be distributed to class members, the class released all claims of class members who did not opt out, including federal claims. The Delaware state court entered a judgment that approved the settlement, and the Delaware Supreme Court affirmed. Then, however, the federal court of appeals held that the Delaware judgment did not have res judicata effect over the federal action because the absence of jurisdiction over the federal claims required an exception to section 1738 (the "Full Faith and Credit" Act, which requires federal deference to state-court judgments). In this opinion, the Supreme Court reverses and holds that the Delaware judgment has preclusive effect.] ...

The Full Faith and Credit Act mandates that the "judicial proceedings" of any State "shall have the same full faith and credit in every court within the United States ... as they have by law or usage in the courts of such State ... from which they are taken." 28 U.S.C. § 1738. The Act thus directs all courts to treat a state court judgment with the same respect that it would receive in the courts of the rendering state. Federal courts may not "employ their own rules ... in determining the effect of state judgments," but must "accept the rules chosen by the State from which the judgment is taken." Because the Court of Appeals failed to follow the dictates of the Act, we reverse....

Marrese provides the analytical framework for deciding whether the Delaware court's judgment precludes this exclusively federal action. When faced with a state court judgment relating to an exclusively federal claim, a federal court must first look to the law of the rendering State to ascertain the effect of the judgment. If state law indicates that the particular claim or issue would be barred from litigation in a court of that state, then the federal court must next decide whether, "as an exception to § 1738," it "should refuse to give preclusive effect to [the] state court judgment." "[I]n the absence of federal law modifying the operation of § 1738, the preclusive effect in federal court of [a] state-court judgment is determined by [state] law." . . .

Perhaps the clearest statement of the Delaware Chancery Court's view on this matter [is] . . . , "When a state court settlement of a class action releases all claims which arise out of the challenged transaction and is determined to be fair and to have met all due process requirements, the class members are bound by the release or the doctrine of issue preclusion. Class members cannot subsequently relitigate the claims barred by the settlement in a federal court." *In re MCA, Inc. Shareholders Litigation,* 598 A.2d 687, 691 (1991). We are aware of no Delaware case that suggests otherwise. . . .

Because it appears that the settlement judgment would be res judicata under Delaware law, we proceed to the second step of the *Marrese* analysis and ask whether § 27 of the Exchange Act, which confers exclusive jurisdiction upon the federal courts for [securities] suits arising under the Act, partially repealed § 1738. Section 27 contains no express language regarding its relationship with § 1738 or the preclusive effect of related state court proceedings. Thus, any modification of § 1738 by § 27 must be implied. In deciding whether § 27 impliedly created an exception to § 1738, the "general question is whether the concerns underlying a particular grant of exclusive jurisdiction justify a finding of an implied partial repeal of § 1738." *Marrese.* "[T]he primary consideration must be the intent of Congress."

As an historical matter, we have seldom, if ever, held that a federal statute impliedly repealed § 1738. [Here the Court cites a number of cases refusing to impliedly override the Full Faith and Credit Act]. There is no suggestion in § 27 that Congress meant for plaintiffs with Exchange Act claims to have more than one day in court to challenge the legality of a securities transaction. . . .

The legislative history of the Exchange Act elucidates no specific purpose on the part of Congress in enacting § 27. We may presume, however, that Congress intended § 27 to serve at least the general purposes underlying most grants of exclusive jurisdiction: "to achieve greater uniformity of construction and more effective and expert application of that law." When a state court upholds a settlement that releases claims under the Exchange Act, it threatens neither of these policies. There is no danger that state court judges who are not fully expert in federal securities law will say definitively what the Exchange Act means and enforce legal liabilities and duties thereunder. And the uniform construction of the Act is unaffected by a state court's approval of a proposed settlement because the state court does not adjudicate the Exchange Act claims but only evaluates the overall fairness of the settlement, generally by applying its own business judgment to the facts of the case. . . .

The Court of Appeals did not engage in any analysis of Delaware law pursuant to § 1738. Rather, the Court of Appeals declined to apply § 1738 on the ground that where the rendering forum lacked jurisdiction over the subject matter or the parties, full faith and credit is not required.... [REVERSED AND REMANDED.]

Notes and Questions

(1) *State-to-State Preclusion: Riley v. New York Trust Co.*, 315 U.S. 343, 349 (1942). Consider what preclusive effect a state court should give to another state's judgment. (For example, what should happen if Marrese next files an action in the courts of another state, asserting that state's antitrust laws?) Notice how § 1738 is written: It requires "every court within the United States" to give the same effect to a judgment as it would have under the law of the state that rendered it. The *Riley* case, cited in *Marrese*, discusses the general issue.

(2) *State Administrative Agency Decisions—Can They Preclude Federal Claims?: University of Tennessee v. Eliot*, 478 U.S. 788 (1986). In this case, an unreviewed state administrative hearing resulted in a finding of no discrimination. The plaintiff later brought a federal employment discrimination claim under Title VII of the Civil Rights Act of 1968. The Supreme Court held that the federal court must apply state preclusion law, under which an administrative finding did have preclusive effect that barred the Title VII action. Does this holding go too far? *See also* Shreve, *Preclusion and Federal Choice of Law*, 64 TEX. L. REV. 1209 (1986).

(3) *Preclusive Effect of Federal Judgments.* Federal common law governs the preclusive effect of federal judgments in both federal question and diversity cases. If the federal judgment is rendered in a case based on diversity of citizenship jurisdiction, the claim preclusive effect of the federal judgment is determined by the law of the state in which the federal court was sitting, unless the state law is incompatible with federal interests. *Semtek Int'l v. Lockheed Martin*, 531 U.S. 497, 506-09 (2001). In contrast, federal judgments in federal question cases have the preclusive effect prescribed by federal law, without reference to state law. The same approach is probably applicable to the preclusive effect of federal judgments in connection with issue preclusion.

IV. The "Law of the Case" Doctrine

UNITED STATES v. HATTER, 532 U.S. 557 (2001). This case began when Congress extended Medicare to federal employees and required most judges to participate, meaning that they were subject to Medicare taxes and saw a reduction in their after-tax pay. A number of judges sued, asserting that the Compensation Clause of the Constitution, which guarantees federal judges "a Compensation which shall not be diminished during their Continuance in Office," made collection of the tax from them illegal. The court of appeals agreed, holding that the Compensation Clause prohibited collection of the tax. On petition for certiorari, because some

Justices were disqualified and the Supreme Court failed to find a quorum, the court of appeals judgment was affirmed "with the same effect as upon affirmance by an equally divided court."

On remand, the court of appeals again held that the Compensation Clause prevented the Government from collecting the tax. The Supreme Court now had sufficient Justices to make a quorum, and it granted review. The questions presented included whether the Compensation Clause barred collection of the tax, which was the same question that had already been decided once in the judges' favor by a Supreme Court that lacked a quorum.

The plaintiff judges argued that their earlier victory on the Compensation Clause issue was the law of the case. The "law of the case" doctrine says that when a court decides an issue of law in a final order, that decision continues to govern the same issues in subsequent stages in the same case. Although the doctrine is discretionary, it usually means that the decision of an issue in a first appeal is binding in a second appeal of the same issue. In this case, however, the Supreme Court decided that the law of the case doctrine did not make its earlier affirmance binding:

> At the outset, the [plaintiff] judges claim that the "law of the case" doctrine prevents us from now considering the first question presented, namely, the scope of the Compensation Clause. They note that the Government presented that same question in its petition from the Court of Appeals' earlier ruling on liability. They point out that our earlier denial of that petition for lack of a quorum had the "same effect as" an "affirmance by an equally divided court." And they add that this Court has said that an affirmance by an equally divided Court is "conclusive and binding upon the parties as respects that controversy." *United States v. Pink,* 315 U.S. 203, 216 (1942).
>
> *Pink,* however, concerned [an earlier decision in the same] case, *United States v. Moscow Fire Ins. Co.,* 309 U.S. 624 (1940), in which this Court had heard oral argument and apparently considered the merits prior to concluding that affirmance by an equally divided Court was appropriate. The law of the case doctrine presumes a hearing on the merits. This case does not involve a previous consideration of the merits. Indeed, when this case previously was before us, due to absence of a quorum, we could not consider either the merits or whether to . . . grant . . . a writ of certiorari. This fact . . . convinces us that *Pink* 's statement does not control the outcome here [and] that the "law of the case" doctrine does not prevent our considering [the Compensation Clause] issue . . . .

On the merits, the Supreme Court said, "There is no good reason why a judge should not share the tax burdens borne by all citizens." It held against the judges and decided that the Compensation Clause did not prohibit collection of the tax.

V. How to Answer the Chapter Summary Problem: Some Suggestions

First Bank v. Donaldson Corporation: A Problem about Res Judicata and Collateral Estoppel. (As usual, follow your Professor's instructions about how to answer.)

1. Can the defendants successfully assert that the second claim is barred by res judicata? *Law:* Identify and explain at least these three approaches: individualized/ same evidence, transactional, and broad procedural duty. In general, there must be a previous final judgment, on the "same claim," between the "same parties" or their privies [and explain these concepts]. *Facts:* There are two promissory notes but one guaranty. Donaldson controls the Donaldson Corporation and had every incentive to defend the first suit. He is probably in privity with the Corporation. Both suits probably concern the same transaction but may not fit the individualized/same evidence test if it is narrowly applied. *Conclusion:* The first judgment is probably res judicata of the second suit under both the transactional and broad procedural duty approaches but may not be res judicata under a narrow interpretation of the individualized/same evidence theory.

2. Can the plaintiff collaterally estop either the Donaldson Corporation, or James Donaldson personally, from asserting economic duress again as a defense in the second suit? *Law:* Explain the elements of collateral estoppel, including the material-to-both-judgments requirement, actually-adjudicated requirement, final judgment, and same parties or privies. Mututality may or may not be required, depending on the jurisdiction, and the opponent must have had a full and fair opportunity to litigate the issue. There are few public policy or equitable exceptions, and none appears to exist here. *Facts:* Donaldson appears to be in privity to the Donaldson Corporation for the reasons stated in response to (1), above. There is a previous final judgment. The "economic duress" defense is material to both judgments, but the question whether it was actually adjudicated in the first suit is open—if the procedural default adjudicated it, then it was. No reason appears that shows that Donaldson lacked a full and fair opportunity. There is mutuality, if required. *Conclusion:* There probably is collateral estoppel.

3. If the second suit were to be brought in a federal court in a different state, could the result be different? *Law:* Section 1738 requires the federal court (or for that matter, the sister state, under the Full Faith and Credit Clause) to follow West York's (the first state's) law of preclusion, meaning that the scope of preclusion probably will be precisely the same as the scope in a West York state court. This is so, unless "a later statute contains an express or implied repeal" of § 1738. *Facts:* Repeal is unlikely unless federal law governs the second suit or heavily impacts it. *Conclusion:* The result probably would not be different.

Chapter 14

Remedies, Judgments, and Their Enforcement

I. Prejudgment Emergency and Temporary Relief

[A] Seizure of Assets Before Hearing on the Merits: Attachment, Garnishment, Sequestration, Replevin, etc.

Read Fed. R. Civ. P. 64 (provisional remedies).

Kheel, *New York's Amended Attachment Statute: A Prejudgment Remedy in Need of Further Revision*

44 Brooklyn L. Rev. 199, 202 (1978)(*)

Consider . . . the situation of a businessman in financial trouble who fails to pay for goods purchased or consigned. If his creditor brings suit for payment, the debtor can rely on the fact that it will be months and—given the usual reluctance of the courts to grant summary judgment—perhaps years before he will be required to pay. . . . But if the creditor can obtain an attachment of the debtor's bank account, the debtor will no longer be able to use or control the creditor's money prior to judgment. . . . In this way attachment often motivates a defendant to settle a claim which he might not otherwise be willing to settle—at least at that time. For the same reason, an order of attachment could provide a swift and effective remedy against fraud or conversion and may even serve to deter a defendant from such acts. . . .

Attachment . . . also can cause a devastating impact on a defendant. Since orders of attachment often are granted *ex parte*, a defendant does not have notice and cannot protect himself against the unexpected disruptions they bring. Attachment of a bank account may cause checks to bounce, enrage employees who cannot be paid, or otherwise disrupt ongoing business relations. Under most lending agreements the entry of an order of attachment against the borrower's property constitutes an act of default; consequently, a defendant's obligations to his lenders may be accelerated. The disruption of business and acceleration of debts exert powerful pressure on the defendant to settle prior to any adjudication of the dispute.

On the other hand, to many a plaintiff who seeks the prompt return of property owed by a defendant, an early settlement may be the only solution. A court "victory" ordering the return of plaintiff's property after years or even months may be as bad as losing the battle. The pressure that a plaintiff can exert with an order of attachment is thus the countervailing force which can get him a prompt and meaningful remedy, through the courts.

(*) Reprinted with permission of Brooklyn Law Review.

Problem A: Chapter 14 Summary Problem

THE EMBEZZLEMENT FROM ACME COMPANY AND EFFORTS TO RECOVER FROM ROBERT BAILEY: PROBLEMS OF PREJUDGMENT SEIZURE, TEMPORARY RELIEF, DAMAGES, EQUITABLE REMEDIES AND ENFORCEMENT. The Vice President for Finance of Acme Company is worried. He tells you that he has just detected a very large embezzlement, exceeding $2 million. He believes that a single individual, whom he identifies as Robert Bailey, committed the embezzlement over a period of some four years, and although he has no direct proof, the circumstantial evidence is such that "it couldn't have been anyone else." Bailey left the company's employment a few months ago.

Bailey is known to have extensive holdings of valuable business equipment, precious metals, and stocks; these items (or the certificates) are held partly by Bailey and partly by others. The Vice President believes that the value of Bailey's holdings has increased tremendously over the last few years. In effect, Bailey has invested the apparently stolen funds in a way that has enriched him handsomely. But the Vice President confides that Bailey has "underworld connections, and he once bragged to me that he could disappear in a day by going to a foreign country where there's no extradition treaty." [These facts are a dramatization of several more mundane (and frustrating) cases in which some of the authors of this casebook have from time to time been involved.]

Consider what possibilities exist of using the following collection tools or remedies, what conditions you would need to show for each, and what advantages or disadvantages each might entail:

1. Devices to secure property before suit, or to prevent Bailey's disappearance or transfer of property either before, during or after suit;
2. Damage and damage-related remedies;
3. Equitable remedies (might there be some such remedies that would afford greater recovery than damages?); and
4. Means of collecting or enforcing a judgment against Bailey at the post-judgment stage, if suit is successful.

Fuentes v. Shevin

407 U.S. 67 (1972)

MR. JUSTICE STEWART delivered the opinion of the Court.

We here review the decisions of two . . . federal District Courts that upheld the constitutionality of Florida and Pennsylvania laws authorizing the summary seizure of goods or chattels in a person's possession under a writ of replevin. Both statutes provide for the issuance of writs ordering state agents to seize a person's possessions, simply upon the *ex parte* application of any other person who claims a right to them and posts a security bond. Neither statute provides for notice to be given to the possessor of the property, and neither statute gives the possessor an opportunity to challenge the seizure at any kind of prior hearing. The question is whether these statutory procedures violate the Fourteenth Amendment's guarantee that no State shall deprive any person of property without due process of law.

I

[The appellants each had been subjected to seizures in dubious circumstances. For example, appellant Margarita Fuentes had bought certain appliances on a conditional sales contract for about $600, but she refused to pay approximately the last $200 because of a dispute about a related service agreement. Under the governing Florida law, the vendor had only to file an unsworn fill-in-the-blank form with the clerk of the small claims court to cause issuance of a writ of replevin that resulted in the seizure of the appliances the same day. Mrs. Fuentes filed this federal action shortly thereafter, attacking the Florida replevin procedure under the Due Process Clause. The Pennsylvania appellants, likewise, included three who had purchased goods on installment only to have them seized by replevin, plus one appellant whose experience was more bizarre: Her ex-husband, a deputy sheriff who was litigating the custody of their son with her and who was familiar with the procedures, obtained the seizure of the boy's toys, furniture and clothes.]

II

Under the Florida statute challenged here, "[a]ny person whose goods or chattels are wrongfully detained by any other person . . . may have a writ of replevin to recover them. . . ." Fla. Stat. Ann. § 78.01 (Supp. 1972–1973). There is no requirement that the applicant make a convincing showing before the seizure that the goods are, in fact, "wrongfully detained." . . . It requires only that the applicant file a complaint, [r]eciting in conclusory fashion that he is "lawfully entitled to the possession" of the property, and that he file a security bond. . . .

Thus, at the same moment that the defendant receives the complaint seeking repossession of property through court action, the property is seized from him. He is provided no prior notice and allowed no opportunity whatever to challenge the issues of the writ. *After* the property has been seized, he will eventually have an opportunity for a hearing, as the defendant in the trial of the court action for repossession, which the plaintiff is required to pursue. And he is also not wholly without recourse in the meantime. For under the Florida statute, the officer who seizes the property must keep it for three days, and during that period the defendant may reclaim possession of the property by posting his own security bond in double its value. . . .

The Pennsylvania law differs, though not in its essential nature, from that of Florida. . . . [A] private party may obtain a prejudgment writ of replevin through a summary process of *ex parte* application to a prothonotary. . . . Unlike the Florida statute, however, the Pennsylvania law does not require that there *ever* be opportunity for a hearing on the merits of the conflicting claims to possession of the replevied property. . . .

III

[The Court acknowledged that these replevin statutes were "descended from the common-law replevin action of six centuries ago," but it said, "they bear little resemblance to it." Common law replevin was used by tenants to recover property wrongfully distrained from them by their landlords; these statutes "are most commonly used by creditors to seize goods allegedly wrongfully detained . . . by debtors."]

IV

For more than a century the central meaning of procedural due process has been clear: "Parties whose rights are to be affected are entitled to be heard; and in order that they may enjoy that right they must first be notified." *Baldwin v. Hale*, 1 Wall. 223, 233. . . .

The Florida and Pennsylvania prejudgment replevin statutes fly in the face of this principle. To be sure, the requirements that a party seeking a writ must first post a bond, allege conclusorily that he is entitled to specific goods, and open himself to possible liability in damages if he is wrong, serve to deter wholly unfounded applications for a writ. But those requirements are hardly a substitute for a prior hearing, for they test no more than the strength of the applicant's own belief in his rights. . . .

V

The right to a prior hearing, of course, attaches only to the deprivation of an interest encompassed within the Fourteenth Amendment's protection. . . .

A deprivation of a person's possessions under a prejudgment writ of replevin, at least in theory, may be only temporary. [B]ut it is now well settled that a temporary nonfinal deprivation of property is nonetheless a "deprivation" in the terms of the Fourteenth Amendment. *Sniadach v. Family Finance Corp.*, 395 U.S. 337; *Bell v. Burson*, 402 U.S. 535. . . .

The present cases are no different. . . . The Fourteenth Amendment draws no bright lines around three-day, 10-day or 50-day deprivations of property. Any significant taking of property by the State is within the purview of the Due Process Clause. . . .

The appellants who signed conditional sales contracts lacked full legal title to the replevied goods. The Fourteenth Amendment's protection of "property," however, has never been interpreted to safeguard only the rights of undisputed ownership. Rather, it has been read broadly to extend protection to "any significant property interest". . . .

VI

There are "extraordinary situations" that justify postponing notice and opportunity for a hearing. *Boddie v. Connecticut*, 401 U.S., at 379. . . . Only in a few limited situations has this Court allowed outright seizure without opportunity for a prior hearing. [T]hus, the Court has allowed summary seizure of property to collect the internal revenue of the United States, to meet the needs of a national war effort, to protect against the economic disaster of a bank failure, and to protect the public from misbranded drugs and contaminated food.

The Florida and Pennsylvania prejudgment replevin statutes serve no such important governmental or general public interest. . . .

VIII

We hold that the Florida and Pennsylvania prejudgment replevin provisions work a deprivation of property without due process of law insofar as they deny the right to a prior opportunity to be heard before chattels are taken from their possessor. Our holding, however, is a narrow one. We do not question the power of a State to seize goods before a final judgment in order to protect the security interests of creditors so long as those creditors have tested their claim to the goods through the process of a fair prior hearing. . . . [Vacated and remanded.]

MR. JUSTICE POWELL and MR. JUSTICE REHNQUIST did not participate in the consideration or decision of these cases.

MR. JUSTICE WHITE, with whom THE CHIEF JUSTICE and MR. JUSTICE BLACKMUN join, dissenting. . . .

. . . It goes without saying that in the typical installment sale of personal property both seller and buyer have interests in the property until the purchase price is fully paid, the seller early in the transaction often having more at stake than the buyer. . . .

. . . The interests of the buyer and seller are obviously antagonistic during this interim period: the buyer wants the use of the property pending final judgment; the seller's interest is to prevent further use and deterioration of his security. By the Florida and Pennsylvania laws the property is to all intents and purposes placed in custody and immobilized during this time. The buyer loses use of the property temporarily but is protected against loss; the seller is protected against deterioration of the property but must undertake by bond to make the buyer whole in the event the latter prevails. . . .

. . . Surely under the Court's own definition, the creditor has a "property" interest as deserving of protection as that of the debtor. At least the debtor, who is very likely uninterested in a speedy resolution that could terminate his use of the property, should be required to make those payments, into court or otherwise, upon which his right to possession is conditioned. . . .

. . . The Court's rhetoric is seductive, but in end analysis, the result it reaches will have little impact and represents no more than ideological tinkering with state law. It would appear that creditors could withstand attack under today's opinion simply by making clear in the controlling credit instruments that they may retake possession without a hearing, or, for that matter, without resort to judicial process at all. Alternatively, they need only give a few days' notice of a hearing, take possession if hearing is waived or if there is default; and if hearing is necessary merely establish probable cause for asserting that default has occurred. It is very doubtful in my mind that such a hearing would in fact result in protections for the debtor substantially different from those the present laws provide. On the contrary, the availability of credit may well be diminished or, in any event, the expense of securing it increased. . . .

Notes and Questions

(1) *Ironic Results of Fuentes v. Shevin, Part I: What Protection Is Left for Property Interests of Persons Not in Possession?* The creditor who seeks a provisional remedy may have a property interest in the chattel at issue, just as the purported debtor may. In some instances, the creditor may have title; in others, he may have a security interest; in many other instances, he may be entitled to immediate possession. In fact, consider the case of a person whose property has been taken by force or fraud and is now in the possession of a thief. *Fuentes v. Shevin* provides protection of the interest of the alleged debtor in the first instance, and of the thief in the second; what, if any, protection does it provide for the creditor or true owner not in possession?

(2) *Ironic Results of Fuentes v. Shevin, Part II: Effects on Credit Costs.* Ironically, might the *Fuentes* decision also harm the interests of some future buyers on credit? Prices of goods sold on credit in a market economy, of course, must reflect the losses attributable to bad debts and to costs of collection. If you were a purchaser on credit who intended to pay for the purchase as agreed, wouldn't you prefer to be in a jurisdiction where your creditor had expeditious remedies against defaulting parties, so that your own payments would not include costs attributable to them?

(3) *Ironic Results of Fuentes v. Shevin, Part III: Private Repossession Is Not State Action and Is Not Subject to the Due Process Clause.* What happens if, instead of using the sheriff and the mechanisms of the law, the creditor employs an army of private "repo men," and they simply take chattels away from debtors whom the creditor considers to be in default? Note that the dissenters argue that the creditor can accomplish this result by putting provisions in an installment sales contract. Actually, it's easier than that, because §9-609 of the Uniform Commercial Code provides, "Unless otherwise agreed a secured party has on default the right to take possession of the collateral. . . ." In general, self-help remedies do not invoke the protection of the Fourteenth Amendment, because it provides that "no State" shall deny due process, and self-help does not involve state action. *See Flagg Bros., Inc. v. Brooks*, 436 U.S. 149 (1978). Is it desirable to prohibit use of legal remedies and to substitute purely private conduct in this situation?

(4) *Is There a Middle Ground?* In *Fuentes*, the provisional remedies at issue lacked appropriate protections. Criticism of *Fuentes* might better be directed at its rhetoric and reasoning than at its holding. Is there a middle ground that can use the law to protect interests both of possessors and non-possessors? [Note that *Fuentes* is a four-to-three decision, in which neither Justice Rehnquist nor Justice Powell participated.] Consider the following decision, rendered a year and a half after *Fuentes*.

MITCHELL v. W.T. GRANT CO., 416 U.S. 600 (1974). Mitchell bought a refrigerator, range, stereo, and washing machine on an installment credit contract with W.T. Grant Co. On Grant's application showing that Mitchell was in default, and without a prior adversary hearing, a state court in New Orleans issued a writ of sequestration in conformity with a Louisiana statute, authorizing the seizure of the merchandise. Stressing the differences between the Louisiana procedure for seizure and the processes at issue in *Fuentes v. Shevin*, the Supreme Court upheld the sequestration order:

> Petitioner [Mitchell] no doubt "owned" the goods he had purchased under an installment sales contract, but his title was heavily encumbered. The seller, W.T. Grant Co., also had an interest in the property, for state law provided it with a vendor's lien to secure the unpaid balance of the purchase price. Because of the lien, Mitchell's right to possession and his title were subject to defeasance in the event of default in paying the installments due from him....
>
> ... The reality is that both seller and buyer had current, real interests in the property.... Resolution of the due process question must take account not only of the interests of the buyer of the property but those of the seller as well....
>
> The Louisiana sequestration statute followed in this case mandates a considerably different procedure. A writ of sequestration is available ... to forestall waste or alienation of the property, but, different from the Florida and Pennsylvania systems, bare, conclusory claims of ownership or lien will not suffice under the Louisiana statute. Article 3501 authorizes the writ "only when the nature of the claim and the amount thereof, if any, and the grounds relied upon for the issuance of the writ clearly appear from specific facts" shown by verified affidavit. Moreover, in the parish where this case arose, the requisite showing must be made to a judge, and judicial authorization obtained. Mitchell was not at the unsupervised mercy of the creditor and court functionaries.... [S]hould the writ be dissolved there are "damages for the wrongful issuance of a writ" and for attorneys' fees "whether the writ is dissolved on motion or after trial on the merits." ...
>
> ... Louisiana law expressly provides for an immediate hearing and dissolution of the writ "unless the plaintiff proves the grounds upon which the writ was issued." ... [As in *Fuentes*, Louisiana also required the creditor to post security and allowed the debtor to obtain return of the property by posting security.]
>
> To summarize, the Louisiana system seeks to minimize the risk of error of a wrongful interim possession by the creditor. The system protects the debtor's interest in every conceivable way, except allowing him to have the property to start with, and this is done [t]o put the property in the

possession of the party who furnishes protection against loss or damage to the other pending trial on the merits. . . .

Justice Powell concurred separately. Justices Brennan, Stewart, Douglas and Marshall dissented. Justice Stewart's opinion argued that an *ex parte* hearing did not adequately protect the debtor's interest and that the case was "identical to" *Fuentes.*

Notes and Questions

(1) *Is Mitchell Sufficiently Different from Fuentes to Make a Difference (or Is It the Result of Personnel Changes on the Court)?* The factors "protecting" the debtor in *Mitchell* include requirements of (a) sworn testimony by the creditor (b) showing specific facts (c) conforming to narrow grounds authorizing the writ (d) before a judicial officer (e) supported by a bond posted by the creditor, (f) subject to an "immediate" post-seizure hearing on the debtor's demand (g) at which the creditor must prove entitlement to the writ, with (h) the debtor having a right to possession on posting security and (i) to damages if the writ is dissolved. Justice Stewart claimed that the Court had ignored the principle of *stare decisis*; is he right? [This question, in turn, depends both upon whether the case is sufficiently distinguishable and upon whether the broad language of *Fuentes*, requiring a prior adversary hearing for even a "temporary" deprivation, is controlling.]

(2) *The Debtor's Interest After Mitchell: Is It Adequately Protected?* Isn't it possible, after *Mitchell*, that a plaintiff could obtain a writ of sequestration in bad faith and avoid paying very large damages caused to the possessor because the plaintiff is judgment-proof? Is there a better way?

(3) *Reaffirming the Fuentes Holding after Mitchell: North Georgia Finishing, Inc. v. Di-Chem, Inc.*, 419 U.S. 601 (1975). In this case, the creditor used a Georgia statute that allowed *ex parte* garnishment upon a sworn application before a judge or clerk, showing that the creditor "has reason to apprehend the loss" of the amount claimed, and supported by a bond. "The Georgia garnishment statute ha[d] none of the saving characteristics of the Louisiana statute" upheld in *Mitchell*, said the Court, and therefore it was unconstitutional.

(4) *The Limits of Fuentes's Reach: Property Interests Only—Town of Castle Rock v. Gonzales,* 545 U.S. 748 (2005). The police department of this Town had a policy of not responding to violations of domestic abuse restraining orders. Gonzales obtained a restraining order, which her husband repeatedly violated, with no intervention by the Town or its officers. The husband abducted their three daughters. He went to the police department and opened fire with a semi-automatic pistol, whereupon officers returned fire, killing him. The police then discovered the three murdered daughters in his vehicle.

Gonzales sued the Town under the civil rights remedy statute, 42 U.S.C. § 1983. The Tenth Circuit held that she had stated a claim, but the Supreme Court reversed, holding that Gonzales had no "property interest" in the restraining order, in spite of the "horrible facts." Therefore, the principle of *Fuentes v. Shevin* did not apply.

But Justice Stevens, joined by Justice Ginsburg, dissented. He found a "property interest" in the fact that the police had no discretion but to act upon Gonzales's restraining order, because the relevant statute said that they "*shall* use every reasonable means to enforce a restraining order" and "*shall* arrest" a violator. Citing *Fuentes v. Shevin,* the dissenters said:

> Because respondent had a property interest in the enforcement of the restraining order, state officials could not deprive her of that interest without observing fair procedures. Her description of the police behavior in this case and the department's callous policy of failing to respond properly to reports of restraining order violations clearly alleges a due process violation. At the very least, due process requires that the relevant state decision-maker *listen* to the claimant and then *apply the relevant criteria* in reaching his decision. The failure to observe these minimal procedural safeguards creates an unacceptable risk of arbitrary and "erroneous deprivation[s]."

Note on the Use of Provisional Remedies Today

Replevin, Sequestration, or Other Seizure of Specific Chattels. Most jurisdictions provide a pre-judgment remedy involving seizure of a chattel on application of a person entitled to its possession, when it may be subjected to waste, removal, destruction, etc. The remedy may be named, variously, "replevin" (as in Florida and Pennsylvania), or "claim and delivery" (as in California) or "sequestration" (as in Louisiana and Texas), or merely "seizure" (New York). Of course, the statute and the procedure actually used must conform to the *Fuentes-Mitchell* requirements. This remedy is most often used by sellers of goods, although it is open to use by others in proper circumstances.

Self-Help Repossession Under the UCC. As is pointed out in the preceding text, the UCC provides for the repossession of collateral by a secured party upon default. One important condition is that the repossession must be undertaken without a "breach of the peace." Force, threats, or unauthorized entry into a building are examples of the kinds of private actions that may be breaches of the peace and may subject the repossessor to liability for damages. In the event of resistance, the creditor should withdraw and use a judicial remedy. *See also* Del Duca, *Pre-Notice, Pre-Hearing, Pre-Judgment Seizure of Assets—Self-Help Repossession Under UCC § 9-503, Its Antecedents and Future,* 79 Dick. L. Rev. 211 (1975).

Attachment. In many states, a separate remedy is provided to unsecured creditors allowing seizure of a debtor's property, even if the creditor does not have a specific security or other ownership interest, provided that the creditor makes a satisfactory showing of emergency need under the appropriate statute. For example, imagine that Bank B loans funds to Debtor D in exchange for her promissory note. Debtor D is in default and the Bank is concerned because she is frittering away the assets she has purchased with the loan (or is transferring them to related persons so as to place them beyond the Bank's reach). Note that one problem the Bank will have is in demonstrating, by particularized facts satisfying the *Fuentes-Mitchell* criteria, the probable loss of its debt, since often the creditor does not have access to evidence that would support such a demonstration (and the mere fact of default is unlikely to be enough).

Pre-Judgment Garnishment. As the case of *North Georgia Finishing, Inc. v. Di-Chem, Inc.*, above, shows, many jurisdictions provide a pre-judgment remedy allowing seizure of property in the hands of a third person. The most common situation, as in *Di-Chem*, is that in which Debtor D is in default and has funds on deposit in a bank. The plaintiff files suit against the bank as garnishee, with notice to Debtor D. Pre-judgment garnishment, today, requires conformity to the *Fuentes-Mitchell* protections.

Real Property: Notice of Lis Pendens. A dispute over real estate title may give rise to the need for this procedure. A claimant, to prevent the possessory party's transfer of property to a *bona fide* purchaser without notice, may file a notice of pending dispute over title—or notice of lis pendens—in the real property records maintained by the local county clerk or other authorized officer. Strictly speaking, this notice may not be a "provisional remedy" but arguably is a form of self-help. It effectively discourages the transfer of title unless the purchaser is able to satisfy herself that it is safe to ignore the dispute.

Real Property: Forcible Entry and Detainer; Eviction; Writ of Possession. Most jurisdictions provide expeditious remedies for possession of real property. The common law writ of possession obtained at the conclusion of a suit for eviction (also called forcible entry or forcible detainer) is an example. The usual pattern is for the service of process to notify the possessor of a prompt hearing (not for ex parte seizure).

Note on Damages for Wrongful Use of Provisional Remedies

One aspect of provisional remedies that should be stressed is that they should not be lightly used. Most jurisdictions provide serious remedies for wrongful process. In some jurisdictions, fault is not required; all that is necessary is that the issuance of the order be wrongful. Consider the following cases.

BARFIELD v. BROGDON, 560 S.W.2d 787 (Tex. Civ. App.-Amarillo 1978, no writ). Barfield, an attorney, took his lawnmower for repairs to Brogdon. He disputed the price, refused to pay, and was met with Brogdon's retention of the lawnmower. Barfield then sued for, and obtained, a writ of sequestration, despite his lack of entitlement because he had no right to possession (Brogdon had a possessory lien for the price of repairs under state law). Brogdon answered and claimed damages for wrongful sequestration. The court awarded Brogdon actual damages. It also awarded exemplary damages. The original repair bill had been $24.32; Barfield became liable on a judgment for $74.32 actual damages and $3,000 exemplary damages, or $3,074.32 total.

RICHMAN v. RICHMAN, 52 A.D.2d 393, 384 N.Y.S.2d 220 (1976). After determining that the defendant was liable for wrongful attachment of certain savings accounts and stock of the plaintiff, the trial court granted (and the appellate court affirmed) judgment for $5,799.80 in damages and $4,500 in attorney's fees.

[B] Temporary Restraining Orders

Read Fed. R. Civ. P. 65 (injunctions).

Weber, *So You Need a Temporary Restraining Order?*

41 Tex. B.J. 728 (1978)(*)

Imagine this situation:

> You are sitting at your desk at 2:00 p.m. on Friday. The telephone rings. One of your better clients, Sam Successful, is frantic! Sam has recently purchased a beautiful 50-acre tract of woodlands on which he and his wife plan to build a summer home. Today Sam received word from an adjoining landowner that Landeater Lumber Company has cut his fence and begun cutting the timber on his homesite. Landeater has a timber deed by which it claims the right to cut the timber. Landeater refuses to cease operations and hopes to have the land cleared before the weekend is over. Sam wants you to stop Landeater immediately, before the entire tract is ruined. You need a temporary restraining order!

The facts always differ, but two things are always the same: there is a crisis, and both you and your client are in a hurry. . . .

I. What Papers Do We Need?

These are the items the lawyer must have ready when he or she applies for a temporary restraining order:

A. The petition or complaint.

B. The temporary restraining order itself.

C. The restraining order bond.

D. The filing fee.

These items will be discussed in detail, but remember—by now it is 2:30 on Friday afternoon. You must make the practical arrangements to see that the necessary people are available to issue and serve the writ. This is "greasing the skids."

(*) Copyright 1978. Reprinted with permission.

II. Greasing the Skids

You cannot issue and serve the temporary restraining order yourself. You will need the cooperation of the district judge (state or federal), the district clerk (state or federal), and the county sheriff or federal marshal. Each of these persons has a role to play and each must be available.(a)

A. *Call the District Clerk:* A personal call to the clerk's office and a conversation with the deputy who will be handling the application for the TRO is a must. Give the clerk an estimate of when the papers will be prepared and the application filed. In counties with multiple judges, one judge may be designated the injunction judge. The clerk can give you this information....

B. *Contact the Judge:* You should immediately contact the injunction judge to determine his availability. Has he or she left for the weekend? Where can he or she be reached? Can another judge hear the matter? ... The judge may want you to advise Landeater or his lawyer to be present. [Note that Rule 65(b) requires the applicant to certify in writing the reasons for dispensing with notice, if that is the case, and also requires that the reasons appear in the order.—Eds.] ... Also, the judge might be asked the amount of the bond he or she is inclined to set so you can have it prepared in advance.

C. *Contact the Marshal or Sheriff:* The TRO is worthless to the lawyer unless he can get it served on Landeater and its employees....

III. Preparing the Papers

A. *The Bond.* The bond is the last instrument you will need, but the first you need to prepare. [Federal Rule 65(c) requires] posting of a bond in almost all cases before issuance of a restraining order.

If you intend to post a corporate surety bond, you should contact the bonding or insurance agent immediately. By now it is 3:30 p.m. and the bond must be prepared quickly, before the bonding company closes....

B. *Prepare the Facts.* Who and where are the parties? Sam must supply you with basic information concerning Landeater Lumber Company, including some address where the sheriff or marshall can find its management, in order to serve the TRO.

Get a good factual summary of the events giving rise to your case. Hard, specific facts are needed for the application for temporary restraining order, to show that Sam owns the property in question, that Landeater has actually begun cutting the timber without permission, and that, unless Landeater is restrained, Sam will suffer irreparable harm for which there is no adequate remedy at law. Remember you or your client must swear to the factual allegations (... Rule 65(b), F.R.C.P.) ...

(a) [Amendments to Fed. R. Civ. P. 4 now provide for the use of private process servers in lieu of the marshal.—Eds.]

C. *The Petition or Complaint.* The petition or complaint will contain [several] parts, many of which are common to any original petition or original complaint:

(1) *The names of the parties* and places where the defendant can be served with [process];

(2) *The factual allegations* giving rise to your right to relief, *i.e.*, that Sam owns the land and that Landeater is cutting the timber without right or authority. Sam must further allege and show that irreparable harm will result if the temporary restraining order is not granted, to wit: that the land upon which he is hoping to build his summer home is being ruined by the cutting of the timber, that his remedy at law of money damages is not adequate to protect him, and that Landeater is unable to respond in money damages anyway. These allegations must be of specific facts—pleading legal conclusions is not sufficient.

(3) *The prayer* should ask for not only a temporary restraining order but also that Landeater be cited to appear and show cause why the restraining order should not be converted into a [preliminary] injunction. The prayer should further request a permanent injunction upon final hearing on the merits.

(4) *The affidavit:* [The Rules] require verified pleading, or alternatively, in the federal court, supporting affidavits. . . .

D. *Temporary Restraining Order.* The requirements of the order itself are set out in . . . Rules 65(b) and (d), F.R.C.P. The order should track the complaint. . . .

(1) defining the injury in specific factual terms;

(2) stating specifically why the injury is irreparable; mere conclusory statements will not suffice;

(3) stating why the order was granted without notice;

(4) providing for the posting of a bond as a prerequisite to the clerk's issuing writs of injunction (Note: the amount of the bond can be left blank to be filled in by the judge when the order is signed);

(5) *specifically* setting out the act or acts being enjoined;

(6) specifically stating the order is binding on the parties, their officers, agents, servants, employees, attorneys, and those persons in active concert with them who receive actual notice of the order by personal service or otherwise;

(7) setting a date, within ten days, for a hearing on application for temporary injunction.

IV. Hearing, Filing and Follow-up

A. *The Hearing.* Now that the skids are greased and the pleadings prepared, you are ready for the hearing. . . . [Y]ou should appear wherever you have arranged to meet the judge with your client, Sam Successful. Sam should be prepared to testify to the matters set out in your pleadings. If the judge grants your TRO, he will (a) fill in the amount of the bond; (b) set a date, within ten days, for hearing the application for [preliminary] injunction; and (c) sign the order.

B. *Don't Forget the Filing Fee.* Check state or federal costs schedules to determine the amount of the filing fee. . . .

[Here, the article describes how the attorney should obtain copies of the pleadings and certified copies of the TRO (to convince doubters), use special marshall's forms and form of summons in federal court, and obtain service of the TRO. The lawyer, it suggests, should go to the site of the activity both to help the sheriff or marshal serve defendant and to assist in obtaining compliance. In the rare instance of defiance, the lawyer may draw up an affidavit to support contempt.]

V. Congratulations!

By noon Saturday all is peaceful. Landeater has withdrawn from Sam's land. Sam lost a few trees, but serious damage has been averted. If you have obtained the TRO, had it served, and stopped the cutting smoothly and without a hitch, you have done an outstanding job of legal planning and organization. Sam should be pleased and impressed with a job well done.

Problem B

THE CASE OF THE IMPOUNDED BULLDOG. The City of New London has a provision called Ordinance No. 81-235, which allows impoundment of a dog or other animal that has bitten a human being and, after a hearing with prior notice to the owners if they can be identified through reasonable effort, the eventual destruction of the animal. Wade and Sandra Collins have come to you because their bulldog, Spike, is impounded under the authority of 81-235. The hearing will take place tomorrow, but they have not been able to learn when Spike would be destroyed if the hearing goes against him. With their help, you determine that 81-235 does not have any explicit provision governing who must prove what at the hearing and does not provide for judicial review of the decision at the hearing. The Collinses want you to stop the hearing or, in the alternative, prevent the city from destroying Spike. What papers will you need, what specifics will they contain, and what are your chances?

II. Damages: The Traditional Legal Remedy

[A] Compensatory Damages: Recoverable Elements

MEMPHIS COMMUNITY SCHOOL DISTRICT v. STACHURA, 477 U.S. 299 (1986). Parents' complaints, apparently based largely on inaccurate rumors, resulted in the suspension of tenured teacher Edward Stachura from the Memphis, Michigan, School District after he instructed students on human reproduction in a seventh-grade life sciences class. Stachura was reinstated, but he sued under 28

U.S.C. § 1983 on the allegation that his suspension deprived him of due process and violated the First Amendment to the Constitution. He had received his salary throughout the suspension period but claimed other elements of damage. The Supreme Court did not decide whether Stachura's constitutional claims were valid, because the liability issue was not presented to it; it considered only the correctness of certain instructions given by the trial judge on damages.

During its instructions to the jury, the District Court had made the following remarks regarding (1) compensatory damages: "You should consider in this regard any lost earnings; loss of earning capacity; out-of-pocket expenses; and any mental anguish or emotional distress that you find the plaintiff to have suffered as a result of conduct by the defendants depriving him of his civil rights." In addition, the court instructed the jury that (2) punitive damages could be awarded. Finally, at Stachura's request and over the defendants' objection, the court charged that (3) damages also could be awarded based upon the value or importance of the abstract constitutional rights that were allegedly violated, as follows:

> The precise value you place upon any constitutional right which you find was denied the plaintiff is within your discretion. You may wish to consider the importance of the right in our system of government, the role which this right has played in the history of our republic, [and] the significance of the right in the context of the activities which the plaintiff was engaged in at the time of the violation of the right.

The jury found the defendants liable and awarded a total of $275,000 in compensatory damages and $46,000 in punitive damages. The district court entered judgment against all but one defendant for a slightly reduced amount. The Court of Appeals affirmed. The Supreme Court reversed, holding that it was error to allow the jury to find damages for the alleged constitutional deprivation in the abstract, as opposed to damages suffered by the plaintiff:

> We have repeatedly noted that 42 U.S.C. § 1983 creates a "species of tort liability" in favor of persons who are deprived of "rights, privileges, or immunities secured" to them by the Constitution. *Carey v. Piphus*, 435 U.S. 247, 253 (1978).... Accordingly, when § 1983 plaintiffs seek damages for violations of constitutional rights, the level of damages is ordinarily according to principles derived from the common law of torts....
>
> Punitive damages aside, damages in tort cases are designed to provide "*compensation* for the injury caused to plaintiff by defendant's breach of duty." ... To that end, compensatory damages may include not only out-of-pocket loss and other monetary harms, but also such injuries as "impairment of reputation ..., personal humiliation, and mental anguish and suffering" ... Deterrence is also an important purpose of this system, but it operates through the mechanism of damages that are *compensatory*—damages grounded in determinations of plaintiffs' actual losses. [REVERSED AND REMANDED.]

Notes and Questions

(1) *Nominal Damages: Bayer v. Neiman Marcus Group Inc.*, 861 F.3d 853 (9th Cir. 2017). Although the defendant committed a violation of the Americans with Disabilities Act, the plaintiff suffered no actual compensable damage. (Specifically, the defendant required him to execute an arbitration agreement that was violative of his rights under the Act but never actually affected those rights.) The court of appeals here holds that the plaintiff may recover equitable relief in the form of "nominal damages." This remedy consists of a minimal amount, perhaps $1.00. The purpose of nominal damages, said the court, are first, to clarify who wins and therefore establish the law, and second, to serve as a basis for the recovery of attorney's fees.

(2) *Pain and Suffering as a Compensable Element of Damages.* Perhaps the same kind of "measurement of damages" problem as in *Stachura* arises when the jury is required to determine monetary compensation for plaintiff's pain and suffering. Should the jury go about this task by putting a value on an hour's or day's suffering, and multiplying it by the number of hours or days that plaintiff has endured? Some jurisdictions restrict the plaintiff's attorney from arguing this measure, although many allow it. *Cf. Tate v. Colabello*, 58 N.Y.2d 84, 459 N.Y.S.2d 422, 445 N.E.2d 1101 (1983) (court did not need to determine whether "*per diem*" argument would be approved in New York; it was not improper, however, for plaintiff's counsel to "suggest" a sum based on life expectancy of 64 years and on series of rhetorical questions as to the value of pain over a period of time). If not by a *per diem* method, how should pain and suffering damages be fixed? By a "market value" approach (*i.e.*, the amount of money that a person would accept in exchange for undergoing the same pain)?

(3) *Damage "Caps": Fein v. Permanente Medical Group*, 38 Cal. 3d 137, 211 Cal. Rptr. 368, 695 P.2d 665 (1985). The *Fein* case has been dealt with in several earlier parts of this book, most notably in § 1.07[A] of Chapter 1. The jury found the defendant liable for medical malpractice in failing to diagnose a heart condition of the plaintiff, and earlier excerpts have dealt with jury selection and instructions. There also were important damages issues.

In *Fein*, the court upheld and applied a "cap" on non-economic damages in medical malpractice cases. The California Act in question allowed full recovery for "hard" elements of damages, such as lost earnings or medical expenses, but limited "non-economic damages" by a $250,000 damage "cap." The California Supreme Court, by a four-to-three majority, held that the cap was constitutional. Other jurisdictions have decided the constitutional question differently; for example, some states have interpreted state constitutions as invalidating similar damage caps.

[B] Proof of Economic Damages with Reasonable Certainty

Washington v. Kellwood Company

714 Fed. Appx. 35 (2d Cir. 2017) (unpublished opinion)

Plaintiffs Daryl K. Washington and Sunday Players, Inc. (collectively, "SP") sued defendant Kellwood Company ("Kellwood") for breach of a . . . license agreement . . . , pursuant to which Kellwood became the exclusive manufacturer, licensee, and promoter of SP's athletic compression wear products. SP here appeals from the entry of a $1.00 judgment notwithstanding a jury award of $4.35 million. . . . [The JMOL resulted from the apparent failure of SP to offer sufficient evidence supporting its damages, in spite of the proof of Kellwood's liability. The trial court instead decided that SP's proof of damages was insufficient. The court of appeals here affirms.]

1. Lost Future Profits

Under New York law, a plaintiff deprived of his entire stake in a business by a contractual breach may sue either for lost future profits or the lost value of his business on the date of breach. *See Schonfeld v. Hilliard,* 218 F.3d 164, 172, 175–76 (2d Cir. 2000). To prove lost profits, a plaintiff must demonstrate "both the existence and amount of such damages with reasonable certainty." *Id.* at 172. Although the damages "need not be proven with mathematical precision, they must be capable of measurement based upon known reliable factors without undue speculation." "[E]vidence of lost profits from a new business venture receives greater scrutiny because there is no track record upon which to base an estimate." A new venture whose profits are "purely hypothetical" and that would require "untested" sales to "hypothetical" consumers does not support a damages award.

As the district court correctly observed, SP failed to proffer evidence from which lost profits could be established with reasonable certainty. The sole profits calculations presented to the jury were those of its expert, who testified that, had Kellwood reasonably marketed SP's products, SP's 2005–2007 revenues would have been 50% of those of the compression wear market leader, Under Armour, in 2002–2004. Under Armour was not a reasonable comparator. At the time in question, Under Armour was an established business with annual sales between $49.5 million and $195 million. Indeed, by the end of 2002, it controlled approximately 80% of the market. By contrast, during the two-year comparison period, SP was a small start-up, producing a product similar to brand-name companies, but with no record of notable sales. Throughout its existence, SP sold less than $200,000 in merchandise to only a few small retailers and high school and college athletic teams. The expert's testimony that SP's revenues were reasonably certain to increase from a few hundred thousand dollars to approximately $80,000,000 in two years was so unfounded that it failed to establish any legal basis for awarding lost-profits damages. . . . .

2. Lost Business Value Damages

Where lost future profits cannot be obtained, the "most accurate and immediate measure of damages" of a nascent business is its "market value . . . at the time of breach." *Id.* at 176. Such estimates are "inherently less speculative" than an estimation of future profits, as they may be measured by proof of "what a buyer is willing to pay for the chance" that the business will produce substantial income. In proving such a claim, a plaintiff must nonetheless establish the value lost by the business with "reasonable certainty." *Id.*

As the district court correctly observed, SP's expert's $532,000 lost-business-value calculation fails with the $3.783 million lost-profits calculation, as both were premised on the same "yardstick" comparison to Under Armour's revenues. Nor could such damages be proved, as in *Schonfeld,* by reference to a "price at which the [business] would change hands between a willing buyer and a willing seller." Although Washington himself testified that Kellwood had offered to purchase SP, no evidence was proffered to suggest the price at which the business might have changed hands at that time. . . . [AFFIRMED.]

HAWTHORNE INDUSTRIES, INC. v. BALFOUR MACLAINE INTERNATIONAL LTD., 676 F.2d 1385 (11th Cir. 1982). Balfour contracted to supply Hawthorne with jute carpet backing, which was required to conform to the standards and tolerances of the Jute Carpet Backing Council. The jute failed to conform, and in order to avoid "wrinkles, sagging and other undesirable effects" in its carpets, Hawthorne had to slow its machinery, make hand adjustments, and add extra latex adhesive. Its suit for breach of warranty was made more difficult, however, by the fact that "jute carpet backing is an imperfect commodity in which some deviation in quality and dimension is normally expected."

As evidence of its consequential damages, therefore, Hawthorne offered testimony of three plant supervisors to the effect that the machinery was slowed from 20 feet per minute to only 3 feet per minute to process Balfour's jute; that the plant experienced approximately 30% down time; and that from two to four extra ounces of adhesive were applied per yard. Using these estimates, together with normal weekly production reports, Hawthorne's chief financial officer testified to a cost estimate for the lost efficiency and extra materials, supporting the prayer for $50,000 in Hawthorne's complaint. Balfour, pointing out that Hawthorne had kept no written records of the slowed production rate or additional materials, attacked this evidence as "guesswork and speculation."

The district judge found that Hawthorne suffered "a loss of machine efficiency in processing the Balfour jute," that down time caused "additional cost," and that extra adhesives also required "increased cost." But because Hawthorne's "method of proving consequential damages failed to account adequately for the wide deviation in the rate of production with various types of jute," the District Court concluded that Hawthorne had "failed to prove its damages with a sufficient degree of certainty."

The District Court therefore awarded Hawthorne no damages, but awarded Balfour the contract price. The Court of Appeals remanded, reasoning as follows:

> The District Court's findings plainly indicate that some consequential damages were caused by Balfour's breach. . . . [Under] the Uniform Commercial Code . . . , the rule preventing recovery of "speculative" damages referred "more especially to the uncertainty as to the cause, rather than uncertainty as to the measure or extent of damages." . . . There is no speculation in this case as to the causation of damages. With respect to certainty as to measure or extent of damages, Comment 4 to UCC § 2-715 . . . states the applicable rule as follows:
>
> The burden of proving the extent of loss incurred by way of consequential damage is on the buyer, but the [UCC] section on liberal administration of remedies rejects any doctrine of certainty which requires almost mathematical precision in the proof of loss. Loss may be determined in any manner which is reasonable under the circumstances.
>
> . . . [The applicable] law requires "reasonable certainty" . . .
>
> Balfour is entirely correct that the "question of damages cannot be left to speculation and guesswork." . . . [H]owever, . . . compensation for undisputed injury should not be denied merely because the amount of damages cannot be precisely and exactly determined.
>
> The district court may very well have believed that the proof of damages was insufficient because the estimates of company witnesses were mere conjecture. . . . Unfortunately, we cannot tell from the record as it stands whether this was, in fact, the basis of the district court's opinion. On remand, if the district court feels that proof of extent of damages is lacking, it should enter a finding to that effect. However, if the court determines upon reexamination of the record and its findings that an award of consequential damages can be ascertained with reasonable certainty, the court shall enter such an award. . . .

Notes and Questions

(1) *What Does Substantial Certainty Mean, and What Is Enough? Hawthorne Industries, Inc. v. Balfour Maclaine International Ltd.*, 676 F.2d 1185 (11th Cir. 1982). Balfour contracted to provide jute for carpet manufacturing, but the material it supplied did not meet contract standards. As a result, Hawthorne employees testified, the assembly line slowed from 20 to 3 feet per second, the plant suffered 30% down time, and two to four extra ounces of adhesive were required per yard. They also supplied dollar estimates of the cost increase caused by each of these difficulties. The trial judge denied any damages based on this proof. The court of appeals remanded, stating that the district court must enter a damage award in this evidence unless it concluded that the estimates themselves (as opposed to the method) were too speculative.

What, then, is meant by the words, "reasonably certain," as in *Washington v. Kellwood, supra,* or "substantial certainty," as *Hawthorne* put it? No proof of this kind can approach "certainty." Is this word useful or meaningful at all? Perhaps it would make more sense if the courts were to require a "reasonable estimate," and perhaps that is what they really mean. But the fact remains that lost profits damages for a new venture, as in *Washington v. Kellwood,* are extraordinarily difficult to prove to the satisfaction of the courts, however wronged the plaintiffs may be. *See also Freund v. Washington Square Press, Inc.,* 34 N.Y.2d 379, 357 N.Y.S.2d 857, 314 N.E.2d 419 (1974) (no damages allowed for copyright holder when publisher breached contract because no sufficient proof of market for the book or future sales).

(2) *Proof of "Reasonableness" of Tort Damages: Jackson v. Lewis,* 554 S.W.2d 21 (Tex. Civ. App.-Amarillo 1977, no writ). This case demonstrates, in a tragic way, the technical requirements of proof of damages. In a wrongful death case for personal injuries, the plaintiff sought to recover for medical expenses. The proof for the medical expenses was offered by stipulation, as follows:

> [Counsel for Lewis]: Your Honor, we have agreed that these charges . . . are reasonable, customary, usual, and necessary charges in the vicinities in which they were rendered. [To opposing counsel:] Is that correct?
>
> [Counsel for Jackson]: Yes, sir, that is correct. We want this all to go to the jury, I doubt if any medical charge these days is reasonable, but we are not going to argue about that. But we would like all this to go to the jury, we just don't raise any objection on that.
>
> [Counsel for Lewis]: Okay, your Honor, in other words, so we wouldn't have to call the doctors to testify.
>
> [The Court]: Let the record so show.
>
> [Counsel for Lewis]: We will offer then those bills into evidence.
>
> [The Court]: They will be accepted.

The jury, however, rendered a verdict finding "zero" damages for medical expenses. The trial judge noted that Lewis was required to prove (1) that the medical expenses actually were incurred, (2) that they were reasonable in amount in the place and at the time they were rendered, and (3) that they were reasonably medically necessary for the treatment of injuries resulting from the accident. The trial judge rendered judgment for Lewis in the amount shown by the medical bills. The appellate court reversed and rendered judgment that Lewis take nothing, according to the jury's verdict. Although the stipulation clearly established the reasonableness of the amount of the charges and the bills showed that Lewis had incurred them, there was no proof in the record that they were reasonably necessary to treat injuries resulting from the accident!

Problem C

PROOF OF DAMAGES IN HOWARD v. BACHMAN. The jury instructions contained in Problem C, in Chapter 10, above, are fairly typical for the measurement of damages to a chattel resulting from the defendant's negligence. The instruction reads as follows:

> Find from the preponderance of the evidence the reasonable cost in Manero County, West York, of repairs, if any, necessary to restore Bruce Bachman's vehicle to the condition in which it was, immediately before the occurrence in question.

If you represented the claimant, Bachman, what witness(es) would you call, and what question(s) would you ask of them, to lay a predicate for the recovery of damages to Bachman's vehicle under this instruction?

[C] Punitive or "Exemplary" Damages

SMITH v. WADE, 461 U.S. 30 (1983). Smith, a prison guard, placed two other inmates in Wade's cell with him, who beat and sexually assaulted him. Wade had voluntarily sought administrative segregation because of prior assaults, and a vacant cell was available. Wade sued Smith under 42 U.S.C. § 1983, alleging that Smith violated the Eighth Amendment prohibition on cruel and unusual punishment because he knew or should have known that assault was likely. The trial court instructed the jury that Smith could be liable only if he acted with "gross negligence," defined as "a callous indifference or thoughtless disregard for the consequences of one's act or failure to act." Smith could not be liable even for compensatory damages on mere simple negligence. The trial judge also instructed the jury on punitive damages:

> If you find the issues in favor of the plaintiff, and if the conduct of one or more of the defendants is shown to be a reckless or callous disregard of, or indifference to, the rights or safety of others, then you may assess punitive or exemplary damages in addition to any award of actual damages.
>
> ... The amount of punitive or exemplary damages assessed against any defendant may be such sum as you believe will serve to punish that defendant and to deter him and others from like conduct.

The jury found Smith liable and awarded $25,000 in compensatory and $5,000 in punitive damages. The Supreme Court affirmed a judgment on this verdict.

Smith argued that the punitive damage award should be reversed because the instruction should have limited punitive damages to situations involving "ill will, spite, or intent to injure" in a § 1983 case. The Supreme Court rejected this argument:

> [Smith] concedes, of course, that deterrence of future egregious conduct is a primary purpose of both § 1983 ... and of punitive damages.... But deterrence, he contends, cannot be achieved unless the standard of conduct is stated with sufficient clarity to enable potential defendants to conform to the law and to avoid the proposed sanction....

> ... [W]e are not persuaded that a recklessness standard is too vague to be fair or useful....
>
> ... The need for exceptional clarity in the standard for punitive damages arises only if one assumes that there are substantial numbers of officers who will not be deterred by compensatory damages; only such officers will seek to guide their conduct by the punitive damages standard. The presence of such officers is a powerful argument against raising the threshold for punitive damages....

Justice Rehnquist, joined by the Chief Justice and Justice Powell, dissented. He argued that mature legal systems would require intent or wrongful animus before imposing punishment: "A relation between some mental element and punishment for a harmful act is almost as instinctive as the child's familiar exculpatory 'But I didn't mean to.'" Furthermore, the award of punitive damages on less than proof of intent would provide a powerful incentive to additional § 1983 litigation, which already flooded the courts; and "the uncertainty resulting from largely random awards of punitive damages will have serious effects upon the performance by state and local officers of their official duties."

Note on the Economic Purpose of Compensatory and Punitive Damages

How the Market System Works to Allocate Resources. To an economist, the costs of various resources that a firm uses to provide a product or service are an inducement to efficiency. The market system forces the firm to produce in the most efficient manner possible, and it also induces the firm to provide those products or services that the consumers of a society most want.

The Function of Compensatory Damages in Addressing Market Imperfections. But this theory breaks down if the firm can avoid costs by "externalizing" them. Thus, if cheaper means of production result in environmental pollution or an unacceptably large proportion of accidents and injuries, the market system functions counterproductively to induce the firm to choose this undesirable method of production. The economist would see the law's imposition of damage liability as a counterpart to these externalities. To the economist, the desirable level of damage liability would be reached when it precisely balanced the consumer's desire for cheaply produced products against the desire to avoid the harmful consequences such as pollution or injuries that result from cheap production. But this theory also breaks down, because desirable levels of damage liability might not result. Transaction costs (such as attorney's or experts' fees) and proof difficulties are such that not all injured persons will recover all their losses. This is where the theory of punitive damages comes in, according to an economist. The function of these damages, in the eyes of an economist, is not so much that of "punishing" an individual based upon "wrongful intent" as that of adjusting the level of damage liability to take account of undervaluation of external costs by compensatory damages.

The Need to Limit Punitive Damages. But this theory suggests that punitive damages can be harmful as well as helpful, if they are excessively imposed. Therefore, there is a need to limit their availability and their amount. The economist would see a "gross negligence" threshold as a means of limiting the availability of punitive damages. If this standard did not perfectly calibrate the desired reduction in injuries or pollution with the desired level of production of goods and services, the economist would advise shifting to a different standard—*e.g.*, a requirement of intentional injury, if punitive damages were too high. In addition, the law has evolved various means of limiting the amount of punitive damages (such as requiring a relationship between the amount of actual damages awarded and the amount of punitive damages in some states).

Comparing Smith v. Wade to the Economic Theory. The opinions in *Smith v. Wade* seem to fit these economic theories. The majority speaks in terms of the lack of desirable levels of deterrence of some callous officers if an intent standard is imposed, while the dissent speaks in terms of the discouragement of official government duties if a lower standard is used. *See also* Cooter, *Economic Analysis of Punitive Damages*, 56 So. Cal. L. Rev. 79 (1982).

Notes and Questions

(1) *Limiting Punitive Damages by Relationships between Amounts of Punitive Damages and Amounts of Actual Damages: Doubleday & Co. v. Rogers*, 674 S.W.2d 751 (Tex. 1984). The jury found that Doubleday had libeled Rogers; awarded "zero" in actual damages, finding that he had suffered no harm; and awarded more than $1 million in punitive damages. An intermediate appellate court rendered judgment for Rogers for the amount of punitive damages. The state supreme court reversed on the basis of a rule requiring a relationship between the amount of punitive damages and the amount of actual damages; since there was no actual damage, there could be no recovery of punitive damages. This rule has been rejected in many jurisdictions; is it sound?

(2) *Limiting Punitive Damages as a Part of the "Tort Reform Movement": The Montana Statute.* Montana enacted a statute that limits the recovery of certain kinds of punitive damages to $25,000 or two percent of the defendant's net worth, whichever is larger. Mont. Code Ann. § 27-1-22(6)(b) (1985). As alternative approaches to the call for tort reform, would it make sense to enact specific ratio limitations (say, two-to-one) for punitive as compared to actual damages? Consider the following cases.

EXXON SHIPPING CO. v. BAKER, 554 U.S. 471 (2008). In this case, the Supreme Court applied admiralty or maritime law, which resembles the common law, and which required the Court to set punitive damage limits in the way that a state supreme court might. The Court had already set constitutional standards (in the case that appears below); here, the Court was free to set stricter standards. The case arose from the negligent running aground of the supertanker Exxon Valdez, which spilled millions of gallons of crude oil into Prince William Sound, Alaska, while under the command of a seriously intoxicated captain. The plaintiffs were persons dependent on the waters and shores of the Sound for their livelihood.

In the damages phase of the trial, the jury found compensatory damages exceeding $19 million. And then, in a later phase, the jury assessed punitive damages of $5 billion against Exxon and $5000 against the captain. The Court held that the punitive damage award against Exxon was excessive:

> The real problem, it seems, is the stark unpredictability of punitive awards. . . . A recent comprehensive study of punitive damages awarded by juries in state civil trials found a median ratio of punitive to compensatory awards of just 0.62:1, but a mean ratio of 2.90:1 and a standard deviation of 13.81. . . . Even to those of us unsophisticated in statistics, the thrust of these figures is clear: the spread is great, and the outlier cases subject defendants to punitive damages that dwarf the corresponding compensatories.

The Court pointed out that some states imposed a dollar limit or "cap" on punitive damages, but that method was less acceptable, because it was unresponsive to wide differences in the ratio of punitives to compensatories. Other states limited punitive damages by a maximum ratio to compensatory damages, which ranged from 1:1 to 5:1. This was a better way of addressing the problem of unpredictability. The Court settled upon a maximum ratio of 1 to 1:

> . . . [A] median ratio of punitive to compensatory damages of about 0.65:1 probably marks the line near which cases like this one largely should be grouped. Accordingly, given the need to protect against the possibility . . . of awards that are unpredictable and unnecessary, either for deterrence or for measured retribution, we consider that a 1:1 ratio, which is above the median award, is a fair upper limit in such maritime cases.

But what about a state without limits upon punitive damages? The Court had held that the Due Process Clause of the Constitution provides standards. Consider the next case.

BMW of North America, Inc. v. Gore

517 U.S. 559 (1995)

Justice Stevens delivered the opinion of the Court.

[An automobile purchaser, Dr. Ira Gore, brought an action against the automobile manufacturer, distributor, and dealer based on the distributor's failure to disclose that automobile had been repainted after being damaged prior to delivery. The Alabama Circuit Court entered judgment on a jury verdict awarding compensatory damages of $4,000 and punitive damages of $4 million. The Alabama Supreme Court affirmed the punitive damage award after reducing it to $2 million. The United States Supreme Court here holds the punitive award unconstitutional under the Due Process Clause.] . . .

Elementary notions of fairness enshrined in our constitutional jurisprudence dictate that a person receive fair notice not only of the conduct that will subject him to punishment, but also of the severity of the penalty that a State may impose. Three guideposts, each of which indicates that BMW did not receive adequate notice of the magnitude of the sanction that Alabama might impose . . . , lead us to the conclusion that the $2 million award against BMW is grossly excessive: [1] the degree of reprehensibility of the [conduct]; [2] the disparity between the harm or potential harm suffered by Dr. Gore and his punitive damages award; and [3] the difference between this remedy and the civil penalties authorized or imposed in comparable cases. . . .

Degree of Reprehensibility. . . . In this case, none of the aggravating factors associated with particularly reprehensible conduct is present. The harm BMW inflicted on Dr. Gore was purely economic in nature. The presale refinishing of the car had no effect on its performance or safety features, or even its appearance for at least nine months after his purchase. BMW's conduct evinced no indifference to or reckless disregard for the health and safety of others. To be sure, infliction of economic injury, especially when done intentionally through affirmative acts of misconduct, or when the target is financially vulnerable, can warrant a substantial penalty. But this observation does not convert all acts that cause economic harm into torts that are sufficiently reprehensible to justify a significant sanction in addition to compensatory damages. . . .

Ratio. . . . The $2 million in punitive damages awarded to Dr. Gore by the Alabama Supreme Court is 500 times the amount of his actual harm as determined by the jury. Moreover, there is no suggestion that Dr. Gore or any other BMW purchaser was threatened with any additional potential harm by BMW's nondisclosure policy. The disparity in this case is thus dramatically greater than those considered in [the Court's earlier punitive damage cases]. . . .

Sanctions for Comparable Misconduct. . . . The maximum civil penalty authorized by the Alabama Legislature for a violation of its Deceptive Trade Practices Act is $2,000; other States authorize more severe sanctions, with the maxima ranging from $5,000 to $10,000. None of these statutes would provide an out-of-state distributor with fair notice that the first violation . . . of its provisions might subject an offender to a multimillion dollar penalty. . . .

. . . [W]e are not prepared to draw a bright line marking the limits of a constitutionally acceptable punitive damages award. . . . [H]owever, we are fully convinced that the grossly excessive award imposed in this case transcends the constitutional limit. . . . [REVERSED AND REMANDED.]

[The concurring opinion of Justice Breyer, joined by Justices Souter and O'Connor, is omitted. The dissenting opinion of Justice Scalia, joined by Justice Thomas, and the dissenting opinion of Justice Ginsburg, joined by Chief Justice Rehnquist, are omitted. Justice Scalia wrote, "Since the Constitution does not make [the amount of punitive damages] any of our business, the Court's activities in this area are an unjustified incursion into the province of state governments." Justice Ginsburg, similarly, said, "I would . . . leave the state court's judgment undisturbed, and resist unnecessary intrusion into an area dominantly of state concern."]

Notes and Questions

(1) *Survey Confirmation of the Conditions for "Punitive Damages 'Run Wild'":* Wall St. Journal, Nov. 13, 1991, § B, at 3, col. 1. The California research firm Metricus polled people eligible for jury duty nationwide. Among the findings: (1) 70% were more likely to favor an individual over a corporation even before knowing anything else about the dispute; (2) the respondents were "much more likely" to believe an accusation that a defense lawyer was not telling the truth than the same accusation about a plaintiff's lawyer; and (3) most significantly, "60% of [potential] jurors deemed a $1 million judgment just a 'slap on the wrist' for a corporation."

(2) *Should the Jury Be Told the Defendant's Total Net Worth Whenever Punitive Damages Are Sought?: Lunsford v. Morris,* 746 S.W.2d 471 (Tex. 1988). In this case, a state supreme court held that evidence of the defendant's total net worth was relevant evidence in a case in which punitive damages were at issue. Some states confine consideration of punitive damages to a separate phase after liability and compensatory damages, as in *Exxon, above.* In a case involving a relatively small loss and doubtful liability, what effect would this rule of evidence, admitting total net worth, have in a suit against Microsoft, Exxon, or IBM?

(3) *Settlement Impact: The Effect of Discretionary Punitive Damages.* Most cases are not tried; they are settled. Imagine that you are defending the hypothetical suit, above, for a relatively small loss based on dubious liability, but in which the net worth of your client (Microsoft, Exxon, or IBM) will be presented to the jury in support of the plaintiff's prayer for many millions of dollars in punitive damages. How will the combination of these legal rules affect settlement negotiations?

III. Equitable Remedies

[A] Injunctions

Origins and Nature of Equity. Reconsider § I[B] of Chapter 5, above, which introduced the concept of equity jurisprudence. Equity developed remedies for wrongs that were not adequately addressed by the courts of law, under the stewardship of the Chancellor.

"Irreparable Injury" for Which There Is "No Adequate Remedy at Law." You should remember that jurisdictional disputes between law and equity resulted in the requirement that an equity suitor demonstrate that, in the absence of equitable relief, she would suffer "irreparable injury" for which there was "no adequate remedy at law." For example, if the harm anticipated by the plaintiff could be completely redressed by common law damages, an injunction would not issue.

This requirement is a feature of the case that follows, *MidCon Corp. v. Freeport-McMoran, Inc.*

The Relationship Among Temporary Restraining Orders (TROs), Preliminary Injunctions, and Permanent Injunctions. To preserve the status quo, Rule 65(b) empowers the court to grant a temporary restraining order without notice to the opposing party, which can have a duration of no more than fourteen (14) days. Next, a preliminary injunction under Rule 65(a) is issued with notice and after a hearing for the purpose of preventing irreparable injury during the pendency of suit, before final judgment. A permanent injunction is the final adjudication of the issue.

Flexibility and Conditions; "Balancing the Equities." In granting or denying equitable relief, the court "balances" the equities. For example, in the case that follows, which involves a preliminary injunction, the court invokes a traditional four-part test for the relief, which involves balancing of various possibilities of harm. It also invokes a more novel test. For another example of flexibility in the use of this remedy, and related remedies, see Brill, *The Citizen's Relief Against Inactive Federal Officials: Case Studies in Mandamus, Actions "in the Nature of Mandamus," and Mandatory Injunctions*, 16 Akron L. Rev. 339 (1983).

[1] Preliminary Injunctions: The Requirements

MidCon Corp. v. Freeport-McMoran, Inc.

625 F. Supp. 1475 (N.D. Ill. 1986)

Duff, District Judge.

This matter comes before the court on the plaintiff's motion for a preliminary injunction. Plaintiff MidCon Corporation ("MidCon") is the owner of a pipeline system which supplies natural gas to the St. Louis and Chicago areas, among others. Defendants Freeport-McMoran, Inc. [and other defendants] own or are affiliated with persons owning substantial natural gas properties in the United States.

On December 16, 1985, defendants announced a tender offer to acquire all outstanding shares of common stock of MidCon. MidCon asks this court to enjoin the acquisition alleging that it would violate §§ 1 and 2 of the Sherman Act, 15 U.S.C. §§ 1–2 and § 7 of the Clayton Act, 15 U.S.C. § 18. Section 7 of the Clayton Act provides in relevant part:

> No person engaged in commerce or in any activity affecting commerce shall acquire [t]he whole or any part of the stock or other share capital [o]f another person engaged also in commerce or in any activity affecting commerce, *where, in any line of commerce or in any activity affecting commerce in* any section of the country, the effect of such acquisition may be substantially to lessen competition, or to tend to create a monopoly. (Emphasis added.)

... After hearing two days of live testimony and considering the affidavits and depositions submitted, the court denied plaintiff's motion for a preliminary injunction. The court ruled orally.... As stated then, to the extent that anything in this opinion is contrary to the oral ruling, the written opinion is controlling.

FACTS

Plaintiff bases its antitrust claim on the possibility that the defendants, once they gain control of the pipelines owned by MidCon's subsidiaries, will force those subsidiaries to purchase gas from the defendants at inflated prices, resulting in higher gas prices for MidCon's utility customers and, ultimately, for consumers. Nearly all of plaintiff's evidence was presented in an attempt to support this argument.

One MidCon subsidiary, Natural Gas Pipeline Company of America ("Natural"), supplies natural gas to the Chicago area....

Plaintiff's theory that defendants would force high priced gas into MidCon's pipelines rests on what it called MidCon's "captive market." According to James J. McElligott, Natural's Assistant Vice President for rates, Natural has a captive market in the Chicago area because its competitors have the capacity to supply only 200 to 300 billion cubic feet ("bcf") of the 700 to 900 bcf of gas consumed in the Chicago area. This leaves a demand for 500 to 600 bcf that can be filled only by Natural....

[Plaintiff offered testimony about Natural's policy of purchasing at the lowest available price. But it did not show that defendants would abandon this practice when purchasing, nor did it show that defendants, as sellers, had ever entered into contracts at prices exceeding prevailing market prices.]

In addition to the evidence about the particular policies of these parties, plaintiff's witnesses testified that generally, it is important for a pipeline to be independent from producers. Dan H. Grubb, President of Natural, testified that a pipeline company makes money by investing in pipelines and therefore has an incentive to keep prices low. A producer, on the other hand, makes money on the spread between the cost of finding the gas and the ultimate sales price and, thus, Grubb concluded, defendants would be motivated to keep prices high. Other than this vague speculation, plaintiff failed to provide any real evidence that defendants would, in fact, pursue such a high pricing policy which would be contrary to their own economic interests.

While urging the importance of independence between pipeline and producer, Natural acknowledged that it owns two gas-producing subsidiaries. Grubb testified that in 1985, Natural produced 51 bcf of natural gas. Defendants' combined production for 1984 was approximately 60 bcf. Grubb testified that despite the fact that both MidCon and the defendants are substantial gas producers, the relationship between MidCon and its gas-producing affiliates differs from the relationship MidCon would have with the defendants. Grubb did not adequately explain how or why MidCon's relationship with Natural would be different and seemed to rely on the "great personalities" of the defendants in predicting that they would force Natural to take its gas.

DISCUSSION

In determining whether to issue a preliminary injunction, the court must consider four factors: (1) whether plaintiff has an adequate remedy at law or will suffer irreparable harm if the injunction is denied; (2) whether this harm will be greater than the harm defendant will suffer if the injunction is granted; (3) whether plaintiff has shown a reasonable likelihood of success on the merits; and (4) whether the public interest will be affected by the issuance of an injunction....

In *American Hospital Supply Corporation v. Hospital Products Limited*, 780 F.2d 589, 593 (7th Cir. 1986), Judge Posner reduced these factors to an algebraic formula and directed a district judge to

> ... grant the preliminary injunction if but only if
>
> $$P \times Hp > (1 - P) \times Hd,$$
>
> or, in other words, only if the harm to the plaintiff if the injunction is denied, multiplied by the probability that the denial would be an error (that the plaintiff, in other words, will win at trial), exceeds the harm to the defendant if the injunction is granted, multiplied by the probability that granting the injunction would be an error.

There is the potential here for irreparable injury on both sides of Judge Posner's equation. If this proposed merger violates § 7 of the Clayton Act, and it is not enjoined, plaintiff would suffer an irreparable injury. After the takeover, it would be virtually impossible to "unscramble the eggs" and return the two companies to the status quo.

On the other hand, if the proposed merger does not violate the Clayton Act and the defendants are enjoined, it might be difficult to make the defendants whole with a money judgment. It is difficult for the court to say that these defendants would be injured, however, since the court cannot predict what the loss would be if the takeover were erroneously enjoined. There are incalculable contingencies.... Nonetheless, courts have held that blocking an otherwise lawful tender offer is an irreparable injury.

In *Edgar v. MITE Corp.*, 457 U.S. 624 (1982), the Supreme Court discussed the injuries which flow from an injunction against a takeover as follows:

> The effects of allowing the [injunction of] a nationwide tender offer are substantial. Shareholders are deprived of the opportunity to sell their shares at a premium. The reallocation of economic resources to their highest valued use, a process which can improve efficiency and competition, is hindered. The incentive the tender offer mechanism provides incumbent management to perform well so that stock prices remain high is reduced....

As in *American Hospital Supply Corporation*, the magnitude of injury to the plaintiff if the injunction were erroneously denied is nearly equal to the injury to the defendants if the injunction were erroneously granted. Thus, under Judge

Posner's formula, plaintiff must show "a better than 50 percent chance of winning the case." . . . [I]n this case plaintiff's chances of success can only be characterized as a long shot.

While the traditional threshold for establishing likelihood of success on the merits is low, plaintiff has failed to present any evidence or even any argument to suggest that it could ultimately prevail against these defendants. Under §7 of the Clayton Act as quoted above plaintiff must show that this proposed merger may substantially lessen competition or tend to create a monopoly in any line of commerce and in any section of the country. . . .

. . . Plaintiff's basic argument is that after the merger, defendants would force high-priced gas into MidCon's pipelines. The court cannot determine how this argument . . . establishes that the merger will lessen competition, perhaps because plaintiff's evidence does not support [its] argument. . . .

While the defendants would acquire a substantial percentage of the market at the utility end of the pipeline, it is no different from that percentage of the market now controlled by the plaintiff. The merger will, therefore, not affect the market at the utility end of the pipeline. The vertical merger would appear to have the potential to affect the market at the producer end of the pipeline. Yet, plaintiff provided no evidence on the market of natural gas producers, on defendants' percentage of that market, or on the likelihood that defendants would foreclose any other producers from the natural gas market. . . .

It is clear from the foregoing that plaintiff has a negligible chance of succeeding on the merits. When this is multiplied against the equality of potential injury to each party, Judge Posner's formula looks like this: $P \times Hp > (1 - P) \times Hd$ and plaintiff's request for a preliminary injunction should be denied.

At first blush, Judge Posner's formula seems to ignore the public interest. The public interest, however, may be factored with the injury on either side of the equation, depending on where the public interest lies. *See American Hospital* at 601-602.

[T]he public may be affected by the fact that such a large percentage of the market is supplied by a single pipeline. The court cannot say, however, that the public would be affected by a change in the ownership of that pipeline. [T]hus, an examination of the public interest in the issuance or denial of an injunction in this case does not add anything to either side of the equation.

For these reasons, plaintiff's motion for a preliminary injunction has been denied.

Notes and Questions

(1) *The Traditional "Four Factor Test" and Judge Posner's "Algebraic Formula"—Are They Equivalent?: Lawson Products, Inc. v. Avnet*, 782 F.2d 1429 (7th Cir. 1986). The traditional "four factor" test of equity contains a public interest element

(at least in some cases), and this factor, according to the District Court in *MidCon*, must be added to both sides of Judge Posner's equation where applicable. With this addition, is the algebraic test the same as the traditional test? In *Lawson Products*, a different panel of the Seventh Circuit said that Judge Posner's mathematics "provide important insights which may be helpful in the exercise of a district judge's discretion"—but his test should not be read to undermine the rule that preliminary injunctive relief continues to be governed by the four traditional equitable factors of irreparable injury, the balance of the equities, the likelihood of success, and the public interest. In particular, said the *Lawson Products* court, Judge Posner's *American Hospital* formula "[does] not limit in any way the ability of the district courts to flexibly weigh the competing considerations and mold appropriate relief in preliminary injunction cases." Is this advice helpful—or is it merely reflective of this panel's suspicion of algebra?

(2) *"Irreparable Injury": Los Angeles Memorial Coliseum Comm'n v. National Football League*, 634 F.2d 1197 (9th Cir. 1980). The Oakland Raiders football team proposed to move to Los Angeles, and the Los Angeles Memorial Coliseum Commission sought a preliminary injunction against the National Football League to prevent its potential invocation of a rule requiring a three-fourths vote of all franchises for such a transfer. The Commission claimed that the rule violated the antitrust laws, but the Court of Appeals vacated a preliminary injunction granted by the District Court without reaching the merits of the antitrust claim—because it concluded that the Commission had not shown the requisite "irreparable injury" for which there would be "no adequate remedy at law." It quoted the following from *Sampson v. Murray*, 415 U.S. 61, 90 (1974):

> [T]he temporary loss of income, ultimately to be recovered, does not usually constitute irreparable injury.... "The key word in this consideration is irreparable." Mere injuries, however substantial, ... are not enough. The possibility that adequate compensation or other corrective relief will be available at a later date, in the ordinary course of litigation, weighs heavily against a claim of irreparable injury.

On this basis, the court held that the loss of the Commission's "only opportunity to obtain a professional football tenant" did not constitute "irreparable injury" for which there was no adequate remedy at law. Does this reasoning make sense? For reasoning that may be more realistic (and certainly is more emotionally satisfying), see *City of New York v. New York Yankees*, 117 Misc. 2d 332, 458 N.Y.S.2d 486 (1983), in which the court held that the City would suffer irreparable injury if the Yankees' home opening series were played in Denver, in violation of the baseball team's stadium lease. As the court put it, "The Yankee pin stripes belong to New York like Central Park, like the Statue of Liberty.... Dare one whisper the dreaded words: 'The Denver Yankees'?"

[2] Permanent Injunctions: Shaping the Relief to Balance the Equities

GALELLA v. ONASSIS, 487 F.2d 986 (2d Cir. 1973). Jacqueline Onassis, the widow of President John F. Kennedy, obtained a temporary injunction against Galella, a "paparazzo" photographer, who had "insinuated himself into the very fabric of" the lives of her and her children, often startling or endangering them or interfering with their privacy. Galella contemptuously violated the order. The trial judge consolidated the hearing on preliminary and permanent injunctions. At this hearing, Galella "demonstrated a galling lack of respect for the truth.... Not only did he admit blatantly lying in his testimony, but he admitted attempting to have other witnesses lie for him." After a six-week trial, the District Court granted a permanent injunction ordering Galella not to (1) keep Mrs. Onassis or her children under surveillance; (2) approach within 100 yards of the home of Mrs. Onassis or her children, within 100 yards of either child's school, within 75 yards of either child, or within 50 yards of Mrs. Onassis; (3) use photographs of these persons for advertising; or (4) attempt to communicate with them except through her attorney. The Court of Appeals concluded,

> Injunctive relief is appropriate....
>
> The injunction, however, is broader than is required to protect [Mrs. Onassis]. Relief must be tailored to protect Mrs. Onassis from the "paparazzo" attack which distinguishes Galella's behavior from that of other photographers; it should not unnecessarily infringe on reasonable efforts to "cover" [Mrs. Onassis]. Therefore, we modify the court's order to prohibit only (1) any approach within twenty-five (25) feet of defendant or any touching of the person of... Jacqueline Onassis; (2) any blocking of her movement in public places and thoroughfares; (3) any act foreseeably or reasonably calculated to place the life and safety of [Mrs. Onassis] in jeopardy; and (4) any conduct which would reasonably be foreseen to harass, alarm or frighten [Mrs. Onassis].
>
> Any further restriction on Galella's taking and selling pictures of [Mrs. Onassis] for news coverage is, however, improper and unwarranted by the evidence.... [The Court of Appeals similarly limited the injunction with reference to the children.]

Judge Timbers dissented from the restriction of the injunction. He pointed out that Galella had a "heavy" burden of showing abuse of discretion by the district judge, who had heard the evidence. The repeated violations of earlier orders showed that abstract prohibitions on "harassment" and the like were unworkable; the restraint needed to be clear, simple and effective; Galella's attitude was a proper consideration in tailoring the relief; and the injunction needed to leave no room for quibbling or evasion.

Notes and Questions

(1) *"Balancing the Equities."* Which of the judges "balanced the equities" properly? Should the Court of Appeals have deferred to the findings and holding of the trial judge, or was this question one of law that an appellate court could decide as well as the trial judge? *See also* Urquhart, *The Most Extraordinary Remedy: The Injunction*, 45 Tex. B.J. 358 (1982).

(2) *Enforceability of the Decree by Contempt.* One of the main issues in drafting an injunction is whether it will be enforceable by criminal contempt. If Galella violates this injunction, contempt will be Mrs. Onassis's main remedy. For criminal contempt to lie, the injunction must be specific in its prohibitions. *See* § VI[E] below. Given these principles, what do the prohibitions on "blocking movements," "placing in jeopardy," and "harassment, alarm or fright" add to Mrs. Onassis's relief, in reality?

Problem D

THE CASE OF THE IMPOUNDED BULLDOG (CONTINUED). Reconsider Problem B (in which the Collinses' bulldog has been impounded and is subject to being destroyed after a hearing). Would the Collinses be entitled to a preliminary injunction, given the test for such an injunction? What should the injunction say?

[B] Specific Performance, Equitable Restitution, Constructive Trusts, and Other Equitable Relief: Notes and Questions

(1) *Specific Performance: Centex Homes Corp. v. Boag*, 128 N.J. Super. 385, 320 A.2d 194 (1974). Specific performance is an equitable remedy available when the performance required by a contract is so unique that damages will not provide an adequate remedy, so that equity is justified in intervening to order the performance. In the *Centex Homes* case, Boag signed a contract to purchase a condominium unit in a luxury high-rise building from Centex. The contract provided for Centex's retention of the deposit as liquidated damages upon breach. Boag refused to close the purchase or to make any further payments, thereby breaching the contract. Centex sued—but in order to avoid being limited to liquidated damages, it did not sue for contract damages; instead, it sued for specific performance. The court noted that a purchaser, as distinguished from a seller, of real property, ordinarily could invoke the remedy of specific performance, since parcels of land usually fulfill the "uniqueness" requirement. This rationale, however, did not extend to a seller such as Centex, which would receive money on performance of the contract—the money being "non-unique." The court recognized that remedies available to the parties would not be symmetrical, but held that "mutuality" of remedy was not required. *See generally* Schwartz, *The Case of Specific Performance*, 89 Yale L.J. 271 (1979).

(2) *Restitution: Prevention of "Unjust Enrichment."* Restitution is a complex subject; but put simply, it means "restoration" of something to the plaintiff.

Restitutionary remedies exist both at law and in equity. For example, replevin (for recovering a chattel) and general assumpsit (*e.g.*, for the restoration of money paid by mistake) were common law writs that sometimes involved restitutionary remedies. The goal of restitution, however, may not in some cases be limited to that of restoring something to the plaintiff; often, it is to cause the defendant to disgorge "unjust enrichment." *See also* Kovacic, *A Proposal to Simplify Quantum Meruit Litigation*, 35 Am. U. L. Rev. 547 (1986).

(3) *Equitable Restitution Versus Compensatory Damages: Burger King Corp. v. Mason*, 710 F.2d 1480 (11th Cir. 1983). This case shows, in a striking way, the difference between equitable restitution, which is founded on disgorgement of unjust enrichment, and damages. The District Court found that Mason had breached his contract with Burger King in the operation of a restaurant franchise but rejected Burger King's arguments based upon trademark infringement and unfair competition. Then, in an erroneous effort to compensate for the breach of contract, the District Court awarded Burger King the profits earned by Mason in the operation of the restaurant as "compensatory damages," finding that these profits coincidentally happened to equal Burger King's actual damages. The Court of Appeals reversed:

> As the parties recognize, a trademark infringer can be required to turn over the profits he earns during the period of the infringement subject to the discretion of the district judge and in light of the equities of the case. . . . However, the district judge did not find that Mason infringed upon a trademark. . . .
>
> . . . Disgorgement of profits earned is not the remedy for breach of contract. . . . [A] contract plaintiff may recover damages in an amount which will place him in the position that he would have obtained but for the breach. . . . In some cases, if the offending conduct causes the non-breaching party to lose profits, the defendant can be required to compensate the plaintiff for the [plaintiff's] *lost profits*. . . .
>
> There is no support on the record that the profits owned by Mason equaled [Burger King's] damages from the breach. That would be correct only if [Burger King] proved that it would have taken over the operation of the franchises after termination and [Burger King] reasonably could have earned the profits that were generated by Mason. . . .

(4) *Constructive Trust: An Equitable Restitutionary Remedy.* Judge Cardozo said: "A constructive trust is the formula through which the conscience of equity finds expression. When property has been acquired in such circumstances that the holder of the legal title may not in good conscience retain the beneficial interest, equity converts him into a trustee." *Beatty v. Guggenheim Exploration Co.*, 225 N.Y. 380, 386, 122 N.E. 378, 380 (1919). While there are other equitable restitutionary devices, the flexible constructive trust is one of the most frequently used. It allows the plaintiff to obtain the increase in value of property; it may also enable him to "follow the property into its product" (*i.e.*, to obtain property, or its increased value, into

which his lost property has been transmuted). The remedy is simple: the holder of unjust enrichment is deemed to be a trustee for the proper claimant. A constructive trust may be used, for example, to prevent unjust enrichment of a fiduciary who otherwise would be immune from a damage remedy because of rules such as the statute of frauds. In the case of *Snepp v. United States*, below, the constructive trust was used in a novel context, but in a way consistent with its history, because proof of damages would be difficult and would itself be unduly costly. *See also* Devin & David, *The Constructive Trust—A Valuable Salvage Tool*, 15 Forum 790 (1980).

(5) *Constructive Trust: Snepp v. United States*, 444 U.S. 507 (1979). Snepp's employment with the CIA involved a fiduciary relationship, as the Court put it, to an "extremely high degree." This fiduciary relationship was emphasized in a written contract signed by Snepp. The agreement specifically imposed the obligation not to publish any information relating to the agency without submitting the information for clearance. In breach of this agreement, Snepp published a book about certain CIA activities in South Vietnam. For purposes of the litigation, the government conceded that Snepp's book divulged no classified intelligence. However, it pointed out that a former intelligence agent's publication of unreviewed material is detrimental to vital national interests even if not classified, because it may expose classified information and confidential sources indirectly, may discourage agents from serving in dangerous posts dependent upon confidentiality, and may destroy the confidence of cooperative nations' intelligence sources. The District Court, based upon these findings, imposed a constructive trust on Snepp's profits from the sale of his book. The Court of Appeals agreed that Snepp was liable for the breach, but held that the remedy should be confined to compensatory and punitive damages. The Supreme Court reversed the Court of Appeals and reinstated the constructive trust:

> The government could not pursue the only remedy that the Court of Appeals left it without losing the benefit of the bargain it seeks to enforce. Proof of the tortious conduct necessary to sustain an award of punitive damages might force the government to disclose some of the very confidences that Snepp promised to protect. . . .
>
> A constructive trust, on the other hand, protects both the Government and the former agent from unwarranted risks. . . . If the agent publishes unreviewed material in violation of his fiduciary and contractual obligation, the trust remedy simply requires him to disgorge the benefits of his faithlessness. . . .

(6) *Resulting Trusts (As Compared to Constructive Trusts): Harris v. Sentry Title Co.*, 727 F.2d 1368 (5th Cir. 1984). A "resulting" trust often is prayed for as an alternative to a constructive trust, although the two are different in concept. The resulting trust is a "true" trust, but it is implied rather than created by express contract. For example, in *Harris v. Sentry Title*, the plaintiff gave the defendant money with which to purchase real estate, on the understanding that the defendant would hold the property as a "nominee" for the plaintiff (the wealthy plaintiff was concerned

that, otherwise, his involvement would increase the purchase price). The defendant, however, simply kept the real estate as his own, asserting the statute of frauds as a defense to any legal obligation to convey it to the plaintiff! The trial court imposed a constructive trust, but the Court of Appeals, over a vigorous dissent, reversed—because the duration of the parties' relationship and its fiduciary nature allegedly were not sufficiently strong to comply with constructive trust law. On remand to the District Court, may the plaintiff prevail on the theory of resulting trust? [Do the parties have an implied trust relationship?] You should also consider whether the decision rejecting the constructive trust remedy seems correct.

(7) *Other Restitutionary Equitable Remedies: Equitable Liens, Accountings, Subrogation, Rescission, and Reformation.* An "equitable lien" can be imposed by a court when wrongfully taken property is used to purchase a more substantial asset; the plaintiff has a lien against the asset to secure payment. (This remedy actually is a special case of the constructive trust.) An equitable "accounting" is available in situations of complex accounts (*cf. Dairy Queen v. Wood*, § II[A][1] of Chapter 10, above); and an "accounting for profits" is a slightly different remedy, available for example when the defendant wrongfully has infringed the plaintiff's trademark (*see Burger King Corp. v. Mason*, above). "Subrogation" is analogous to constructive trust, but operates by allowing one person to "step into the shoes of another." The most common example is the casualty insurer who pays an injured person's loss; the remedy of subrogation allows the insurer, in some circumstances, to step into the shoes of its insured and sue a negligent third person for the amount of the loss. "Rescission" is a remedy by which a party to an illegal or otherwise improper transaction may have the court set it aside, and "reformation" is a restructuring of the agreement when the parties have inaccurately expressed it owing to mistake or fraud of a kind that equity will redress. All of these remedies might be loosely described as types of, "restitution."

(8) *The Modern Evolution of Equitable Remedies: Marvin v. Marvin* ["*Marvin II*"], 5 Fam. L. Rep. 3077 (Cal. Super. Ct. April 18, 1979). This famous case dramatically illustrates the continuing evolution of equitable remedies. In *Marvin I* [*Marvin v. Marvin*, 557 P.2d 106 (1976)], the California Supreme Court held that Michelle Triola, also known as Michelle Marvin, could recover from movie star Lee Marvin, with whom she had resided while unmarried, on an implied contract or on various legal or equitable theories. On remand, the trial court held that there was no express or implied contract, and it further found no basis for constructive trust, resulting trust, or any other traditional legal or equitable remedy. The trial court noted, however, that Michelle had resorted to unemployment benefits while Lee had substantial resources. The California Supreme Court's opinion had "[urged] the trial court to employ whatever equitable remedy may be proper." Therefore, the trial court ordered what might be called "equitable rehabilitative alimony." It said: "In view of these circumstances, the court in equity awards plaintiff $104,000 [*i.e.*, $1,000 per week, the highest scale plaintiff ever earned as a singer, paid over a two-year period] for rehabilitation purposes . . . so that she may return from her status

as companion of a motion picture star to a separate, independent, but perhaps more prosaic existence."

The District Court of Appeals reversed this "equitable rehabilitative alimony" award in *Marvin v. Marvin* ["*Marvin III*"], 122 Cal. App. 3d 871, 876, Cal. Rptr. 555 (1981). The majority held that the trial court's findings of no contract, no unjust enrichment, and no wrongful act on Lee's part, gave no substantive basis for any award whatsoever. However, the *Marvin* case remains as an example of the continuing growth of equity.

(9) *Equity's Evolution Continues: Bayer v. Neiman Marcus Group Inc.*, 861 F.3d 853 (9th Cir. 2017). In this case, which is discussed in an earlier section of this chapter, the court awarded nominal damages in the absence of adequate proof of actual damages. The court characterized these particular nominal damages as an "equitable" award, because it allowed the plaintiff to establish a precedent for the point sued upon and provided a basis for the recovery of attorney's fees.

(10) *"Institutional Reform" Remedies in Civil Rights Cases: Williams v. New Orleans*, 729 F.2d 1554 (5th Cir. 1984) (en banc). Black officers sued the city in a class action, claiming longstanding racial discrimination in employment in violation of Title VII of the Civil Rights Act of 1964. The parties agreed on a proposed settlement agreement that governed "virtually every phase of an officer's employment by the New Orleans Police Department." Among other subjects, the decree required recruitment by black officers in black neighborhoods; assignments of "buddies" to guide black applicants through the (shortened) application process; new examination procedures designed to ensure that blacks passed in the same proportion in which they entered the police academy; special training sessions; elimination of general intelligence tests; an "academy review panel" composed half of black officers to review any dismissals; creation of forty-four new supervisory positions, all to be filled by black officers; filling of all supervisory vacancies by fifty percent black officers; extensive reporting obligations; and a $300,000 back-pay fund to be distributed to black officers. The District Court adopted all of the decree except the fifty percent black promotion provision, concluding that it would impact adversely upon members of other minority groups. The en banc Court of Appeals, in a fragmented opinion, affirmed on the ground that the trial judge had the discretion of a court of equity, and he could either enter or reject the decree.

School desegregation cases provide another example of the broad, equitable discretion of the trial judge in "institutional reform" litigation. *Brown v. Board of Education*, 347 U.S. 483 (1954), required equitable remedies of desegregation to be carried out with "all deliberate speed." Later, in response to intractable segregation, the courts created such remedies as faculty ratios, minority-to-majority transfer policies, redrawing of zone lines, pairing of different schools, and "satellite" zoning. This last remedy required busing of children to schools in cross-town zones not contiguous to ones in which they resided, and it was approved in *Swann v. Charlotte-Mecklenburg Board of Education*, 402 U.S. 1 (1971).

IV. Declaratory Judgments

Read 28 U.S.C. §§ 2201–2202 and Fed. R. Civ. P. 57 (declaratory judgments).

Why are Declaratory Judgments Needed?: Beacon Theatres, Inc. v. Westover, 359 U.S. 500 (1958) (reproduced in § II[A][1] of Chapter 10). It sometimes happens that a party needs a declaration of her rights, even though the controversy has not proceeded to a point where traditional coercive relief would be available. For example, Fox West Coast Theatres had exclusive distribution contracts for certain motion pictures. Beacon claimed that the contracts were invalid. It was important to Fox to know whether they were valid and enforceable. The mechanism for finding out was the declaratory judgment.

A Common Use of the Declaratory Judgment: Insurance Duty-to-Defend Cases. Typically, liability insurance contracts impose on the insurer a duty to furnish a defense to the insured in suits covered by the policy. But what if the insured is subjected to a suit that the insurer believes is not covered? The insurer can simply decline to defend—but then might be subjected to liability if it is wrong. The typical solution to these difficulties is for the insurer to furnish a defense to the insured (which customarily is accompanied by a "reservation of rights" agreement, in which the insured and insurer agree that the furnishing of the defense is not a waiver of the insurer's rights), but also bringing a suit for declaratory judgment of nonliability. For an interesting discussion of a different but related issue, see Morris, *Conflicts of Interest in Defending Under Liability Insurance Policies: A Proposed Solution*, 1981 Utah L. Rev. 457 (1981).

V. Attorney's Fees, Interest, and Costs

Perdue v. Kenny A. ex rel. Winn

559 U.S. 542 (2010)

[Title 42 U.S.C. § 1988 authorizes courts to award a "reasonable" attorney's fee for prevailing parties in civil rights actions. Half of respondents' $14 million fee request was based on their calculation of the "lodestar," i.e., the number of hours the attorneys and their employees worked multiplied by the hourly rates prevailing in the community. The other half represented a fee enhancement for superior work and results, supported by affidavits claiming that the lodestar would be insufficient to induce lawyers of comparable skill and experience to litigate this case.]

[Awarding fees of about $10.5 million, the District Court found that the proposed hourly rates were "fair and reasonable," but that some of the entries on counsel's billing records were vague and that the hours claimed for many categories were excessive. The court therefore cut the lodestar to approximately $6 million, but enhanced that award by 75%, or an additional $4.5 million. The Eleventh Circuit affirmed in reliance on its precedent. The Supreme Court reversed in this opinion, holding that the enhancement was unauthorized.] . . .

The general rule in our legal system is that each party must pay its own attorney's fees and expenses, but Congress enacted 42 U.S.C. § 1988 in order to ensure that federal rights are adequately enforced. Section 1988 provides that a prevailing party in certain civil rights actions may recover "a reasonable attorney's fee as part of the costs." . . . Unfortunately, the statute does not explain what Congress meant by a "reasonable" fee, and therefore the task of identifying an appropriate methodology for determining a "reasonable" fee was left for the courts.

One possible method was set out in *Johnson v. Georgia Highway Express, Inc.*, 488 F.2d 714, 717–719 (C.A.5 1974), which listed 12 factors that a court should consider in determining a reasonable fee. This method, however, "gave very little actual guidance to district courts. Setting attorney's fees by reference to a series of sometimes subjective factors placed unlimited discretion in trial judges and produced disparate results."

An alternative, the lodestar approach, was pioneered by the Third Circuit . . . and "achieved dominance in the federal courts" . . . . *Gisbrecht v. Barnhart,* 535 U.S. 789, 801 (2002). "Since that time, '[t]he "lodestar" figure has, as its name suggests, become the guiding light of our fee-shifting jurisprudence.'"

Although the lodestar method is not perfect, it has several important virtues. First, in accordance with our understanding of the aim of fee-shifting statutes, the lodestar looks to "the prevailing market rates in the relevant community." Developed after the practice of hourly billing had become widespread, the lodestar method produces an award that roughly approximates the fee that the prevailing attorney would have received if he or she had been representing a paying client who was billed by the hour in a comparable case. Second, the lodestar method is readily administrable, and unlike the *Johnson* approach, the lodestar calculation is "objective," . . . and thus cabins the discretion of trial judges, permits meaningful judicial review, and produces reasonably predictable results. . . .

. . . [W]e have noted that "the lodestar figure includes most, if not all, of the relevant factors constituting a 'reasonable' attorney's fee" and have held that an enhancement may not be awarded based on a factor that is subsumed in the lodestar calculation. We have thus held that the novelty and complexity of a case generally may not be used as a ground for an enhancement because these factors "presumably [are] fully reflected in the number of billable hours recorded by counsel." . . . We have also held that the quality of an attorney's performance generally should not be used to adjust the lodestar "[b]ecause considerations concerning the quality of a prevailing party's counsel's representation normally are reflected in the reasonable hourly rate." . . .

We reject the suggestion that it is appropriate to grant performance enhancements on the ground that departures from hourly billing are becoming more common. . . .

We are told that, under an increasingly popular arrangement, attorneys are paid at a reduced hourly rate but receive a bonus if certain specified results are obtained, and this practice is analogized to the award of an enhancement such as the one in this case. The analogy, however, is flawed. An attorney who agrees, at the outset of the representation, to a reduced hourly rate in exchange for the opportunity to earn a performance bonus is in a position far different from an attorney in a § 1988 case who is compensated at the full prevailing rate and then seeks a performance enhancement in addition to the lodestar amount after the litigation has concluded. Reliance on these comparisons for the purposes of administering enhancements, therefore, is not appropriate.

[The Court observes that it is not holding that enhancement is never appropriate, but only that it should be "rare." It gives examples of appropriate enhancements such as unusual delay in receiving the fee or unusually high expenses with significant risk advanced by lawyers.] . . . [REVERSED AND REMANDED.]

Notes and Questions

(1) *Should Defendants Recover Attorney's Fees if They Prevail in Civil Rights Actions? Eastway Constr. Corp. v. City of New York*, 762 F.2d 243 (2d Cir. 1985). This case appears above in § V[B][1] of Chapter 5, as a case dealing with sanctions under Rule 11. The court of appeals also recognized that the Civil Rights Attorney's Fees Act provides for awards to prevailing defendants. The court limited such awards to actions that were "frivolous, unreasonable, or without foundation," but it did not require "subjective bad faith." Under this standard, the court held that the trial judge must award fees to the defendant city in a suit in which there was no basis for the claim.

(2) *Who Is a "Prevailing Party," Entitled to Attorney's Fees? Lefemine v. Wideman*, 568 U.S. 1 (2012). Does either party get an award of attorney's fees if the action is settled? (Yes, unless the attorney's fee is also settled.) Or, what about an injunction? (Yes, says the *Lefemine* case.) There is a "prevailing party, entitled to attorney's fees, if there is a "material alteration" in the parties' legal relationship as a result of the litigation, even if there is no damage award. *But see Farrar v. Hobby*, 506 U.6 103 (1992) (nominal damages of $1.00 merited "no fee at all").

(3) *Disproportionate Fees and "Billing Judgment": Must the Fee Be Reduced by Unproductive Hours or Lesser Results?—City of Riverside v. Rivera*, 477 U.S. 561 (1986). Plaintiffs, described as "eight Chicano individuals" at a party that was broken up by the City, obtained a judgment for $13,300 on their federal claims. They then claimed fees for 1,942 hours at $125 per hour, plus 845 hours at $25 for law clerks, or $245,456.25, for prevailing. [Today, a comparable fee request might

be several multiples of these dollar figures.—Eds.] The district court found the hours and rate reasonable and awarded $245,456.25, or more than eighteen (18) times the recovery.

The Supreme Court split three ways. All cited authority to the effect that an attorney must exercise "billing judgment" in submitting a fee request and must eliminate unproductive hours. But Justice Brennan wrote for the Court that a fee exceeding the recovery could be reasonable and upheld the award. Justice Powell concurred on the ground that the district judge's fee award was a fact finding that should not be disturbed unless clearly erroneous. Justice Rehnquist, joined by two other Justices, did not dispute that a reasonable fee could exceed the actual damages, but he argued that a factor of "proportion" should be part of an attorney's "billing judgment" and should restrain the fee.

Note on Availability and Impact of Pre-Judgment Interest

General Rule Against Pre-Judgment Interest. The common law did not authorize recovery of prejudgment interest in most tort cases. Exceptions existed in contract cases and in tort cases in which the damages were liquidated and the harm occurred on a particular date before trial.

Judicial Imposition of Pre-Judgment Interest: Cavnar v. Quality Control Parking, Inc., 696 S.W.2d 549 (Tex. 1985). In *Cavnar*, a parking lot attendant struck the deceased while backing a van, then backed a second time and ran over her again. The deceased's three adult children sued. In addition to awarding damages, the state supreme court held for the first time that "as a matter of law, a prevailing plaintiff may recover prejudgment interest compounded daily (based on a 365-day year) on damages that have accrued by the time of the judgment." The court borrowed from a general statute setting rates of interest not otherwise provided, to set the rate of interest. The court further held that in wrongful death and non-death personal injury actions, interest begins to accrue six months after the occurrence. In survival actions, interest begins to accrue as of the date of death (or, if the deceased does not die within six months of the injury, interest begins as of the date of the occurrence). Pre-judgment interest was not to be permitted on future damages or on punitive damages. (Notice that this holding meant that there must be special verdicts separating survival damages from wrongful death damages and past damages from future damages; a single, lump-sum award would make calculation of pre-judgment interest impossible.)

Pre-Judgment Interest as "Judicial Legislation." The holding in *Cavnar* looks like a statute, with its "daily" compounding, 365-day year, six-month periods, and precise separation of different categories of damages. In fact, it has widely been criticized as "judicial legislation." While courts have generally exercised power to adjust or extend common law claims and remedies, should a matter of this complexity, with so little basis in statute or precedent, have been left to the legislature? Subsequent legislation has modified and superseded *Cavnar.*

Notes and Questions

(1) *Discounting Future Damages to Present Value; Other Adjustments.* If a plaintiff cannot work and has lost income of $50,000 per year, and has a life expectancy of 40 years, is the value of her lost earnings equal to (40 x $50,000), or $2 million? Not in present dollars, because the total must be discounted by a present-value factor (*e.g.*, current market interest rates), since the $50,000 payments in the 39th and 40th years are worth much less today than $50,000 paid today. Litigants frequently offer testimony of labor economists on these issues. The plaintiff will counter the discount by offering evidence that a worker earning $50,000 has a reasonable anticipation of increases in real dollars owing to raises or promotions. These adjustments can be significant in amount (the $2 million, for example, may be reduced to a small fraction of that amount by discounting to present value at a high rate of interest).

(2) *"Costs" to the Prevailing Party.* Most jurisdictions allow a prevailing party to recover "costs" unless the court provides otherwise. But costs of court do not compensate for all expenses, because they do not include the most significant items, such as attorney's fees or amounts paid expert witnesses; instead, they usually include filing fees, deposition reporting costs, witness fees and expenses, payments for record preparation, and the like. Consider the following:

> Bell Helicopter Textron is seeking almost $50,000 in out-of-pocket trial costs . . . from two women who sued the company over their husbands' deaths. . . .
>
> A federal jury ruled in favor of the widows in January 1985 and awarded them $3.65 million after finding that the Bell rotor system was "unreasonably dangerous."
>
> But the Fourth U.S. Circuit Court of Appeals in Richmond recently overturned the case after ruling defense contractors are not liable for defects in aircraft built for the military. . . .
>
> Federal law allows the winners of civil suits to seek certain trial expenses . . . , such as the costs of depositions, witness fees and some travel expenses. The district clerk of each court has wide discretion about which fees to allow. . . .
>
> Many of [Bell's] witnesses flew first-class from Fort Worth to Baltimore and stayed in expensive hotels, racking up airline and hotel bills of $17,145, according to court documents. . . .
>
> "I have talked to numerous judges and lawyers and they're all appalled," [plaintiff's attorney John] Green said. "They're appalled that Bell, who probably has already written off these expenses, and who had over $800 million in sales last year, would come back against two widows of servicemen." . . .

Houston Chronicle, Aug. 29, 1986, § 1, at 33, col. 1 (Scripps-Howard News Service).(*) Should observers be "appalled," or is this an instance of "hard cases make bad law"?

VI. Enforcement of Judgments

[A] Execution and Judicial Sale

GRIGGS v. MILLER, 374 S.W.2d 119 (Mo. 1963), *followed in* **SISK v. McILROY AND ASSOCIATES**, 934 S.W.2d 567 (Mo. App. 1996). Plaintiff Griggs had purchased a 322-acre farm previously owned by W.A. Brookshire at a sheriff's sale following execution. But Brookshire declined to relinquish the premises, so Griggs brought this ejectment action against him. Later, Brookshire was incarcerated in the Missouri penitentiary, and Miller, who was appointed trustee of his estate, was substituted as defendant in the ejectment action. The issue in the ejectment action concerned the validity of the sheriff's sale.

Brookshire had had several judgments against him which he did not pay. In fact, this same parcel of land had been sold at sheriff's sale on a previous occasion; that sale had been set aside on grounds similar to those at issue in this case. On this occasion, Ray Crouch had an outstanding final judgment against Brookshire amounting to just over $2,000 including interest and costs; Dorothy Contestible had an outstanding judgment for $17,000 for wrongful death; there also were judgments for $600 and $13.00. Counsel in these cases sought and obtained general writs of execution, commanding the sheriff to investigate, advertise, seize, and sell property of the judgment debtor sufficient to pay the respective judgments. The sheriff advertised the sale of the 322-acre farm to pay the Crouch judgment (approximately $2,000), but did not advertise it in connection with the Contestible judgment (the one for $17,000). Brookshire appeared at the execution sale and protested to bidders that the farm was clear of liens and was worth $50,000; that he had advised the sheriff in writing to sell only the northeast 40 acres; and that "whoever bought the farm would buy a law suit." The sheriff sold the entire 322 acres to the highest bidder, Griggs, for $20,600.

The Missouri Supreme Court, while recognizing that "[f]orced sales of property usually do not bring full value," set forth several restrictions on execution sales. First, (1) the sheriff is the agent of both the judgment creditor and the property owner, and it is his duty to protect their interests and to see that the property is not sacrificed. Second, (2) a sufficiently large "disparity" between market value and sales price would require setting aside. Third, (3) the sheriff may not levy execution

(*) Copyright 1986 by Scripps-Howard News Service. Reprinted with permission.

upon all the debtor's property, but only so much as is sufficient to satisfy the judgment debt. Fourth, (4) if real property is capable of division, it must be subdivided, and only that portion sold that is necessary to pay the debt. Finally, (5) if the judgment debtor elects in writing three days before sale, the sheriff must follow the order of sale designated by the debtor.

Here, only the $2,000 judgment could be considered since it was the only one that had been advertised, even though the sheriff had levied on the fund for all four judgments. The sheriff's violations of these applicable principles restricting execution sales required the setting aside of the sale, said the court. However, it required Brookshire to "do equity" in order to obtain relief, holding that he would be entitled to a reversal of the lower court's judgment against him if, but only if, he deposited $20,600 plus six percent interest in the registry of the court within thirty days.

Notes and Questions

(1) *Changing the Facts: What if All Judgments Had Been Advertised?* If the sheriff had advertised the sale to pay all of the judgments against Brookshire (particularly the Contestible judgment, for $17,000), should the result have been different? If so, is the holding in *Griggs v. Miller* based on a "technicality"?

(2) *Other Typical Restrictions on Execution Sales.* The restrictions on execution sales set forth in *Griggs v. Miller* are representative of the laws of many states, and there are other restrictions to be found in some states. *Cf. Matter of Silverman*, 6 B.R. 991 (D.N.J. 1980) (under New Jersey law, execution on real property is void unless preceded by good-faith effort to locate and levy upon debtor's personalty first).

(3) *Liability for Wrongful Execution; Sheriff's Insistence on Bond.* A common-law claim exists for wrongful execution. Given this prospect, not to mention federal civil rights liability under statutes such as 42 U.S.C. § 1983, would you be prompt and energetic in enforcing judgments if you were a Missouri sheriff? [Note: In many jurisdictions, it is customary for the sheriff to withhold execution and sale until the judgment creditor furnishes a satisfactory indemnity bond.]

(4) *Are the Restrictions on Execution Sales Set Forth in Griggs v. Miller Appropriate?* There was nothing preventing Brookshire from selling property in whatever order he chose, for the purpose of satisfying each judgment (which, after all, was a court order providing that the plaintiff recover from him). The purchaser, Griggs, sustains a significant net loss, including his attorney's fees (and other purchasers sometimes lose even larger amounts if the setting aside of a sale is not accompanied by an equitable requirement, as here, for repayment of the bid price). The law's protection of Brookshire comes at the expense, also, of judgment creditors (including those holding wrongful death judgments, such as Ms. Contestible). Who else loses? [Note: The Missouri court recognizes that "[f]orced sales of property usually do not bring full value"; isn't that so, because the purchaser knows she is buying a lawsuit? Consequently, the price is discounted even more than for other distress sales, and the judgment debtor whose property is sold has a greater

deficiency than she otherwise might—or receives less than she otherwise would because excess amounts are payable to the judgment debtor.] Do these considerations justify a more absolute sale mechanism, in the interest of both judgment creditors and judgment debtors? The New York legislature has so concluded. Consider the following.

Guardian Loan Co. v. Early

47 N.Y.2d 515, 419 N.Y.S.2d 56, 392 N.E.2d 1240 (1979), *followed in Northern Blvd Corona, LLC v. Northern Blvd Property, LLC,* 569 N.Y.S.3d 866 (N.Y. App. 2018)

Cooke, Chief Judge.

We determine here whether the provisions of CPLR 5240 may be utilized to set aside a lawfully consummated Sheriff's sale once the real property has been struck off and a deed delivered to a stranger to the underlying judgment. We hold that while the statute vests the court with broad discretion to prevent abuse in the use of the enforcement procedures of CPLR article 52, it furnishes no grounds for relief once those procedures have been carried out in accordance with law.

Plaintiff, not a party to this appeal, obtained a judgment against respondents Early for $1,268.93 which was docketed in the office of the Suffolk County Clerk on July 14, 1976. After respondents had failed to satisfy the judgment, plaintiff delivered a real property execution, with notice to respondents, to the Suffolk County Sheriff for the sale of respondents' residence. The sale was duly advertised in accordance with CPLR 5236 (subd. [c]) but was adjourned twice at the request of respondents (*see* CPLR 5236, subd. [d]). Finally, the property was struck off to appellant Berlin, a stranger to the underlying judgment, for the sum of $3,020. Two days later, the Sheriff, after deduction of his proper fees, distributed the proceeds of the sale to judgment creditors who had failed executions and delivered a deed to the property to appellant.

This proceeding to set aside the sale was brought on by order to show cause. In support of their request for relief, respondents averred that they had approximately $1,100 in cash—a sum which would have been inadequate to redeem the property prior to the sale—but were unable to reach the place of sale on time because of a flat tire. It was asserted upon information and belief that the property had a market value of between $55,000 and $60,000 (later revised to $48,000) and was subject to a mortgage balance of approximately $9,000. In opposition, appellant disputed the value of the property .... Supreme Court [the trial court] set aside the sale, relying on CPLR 5240. A divided Appellate Division affirmed. We must now reverse.

The enactment of CPLR article 52 effected sweeping changes of both substance and procedure in the law relating to the satisfaction of money judgments. Nowhere were these changes more apparent than those with respect to the procedures involving the sale of real property. Perhaps the most striking change accomplished by the CPLR was the abolition of the debtor's right of redemption upon sales to enforce money judgments (CPLR 5236). The Civil Practice Act had previously contained a number of rather complex provisions under which the judgment debtor or his creditors could redeem property after it had been sold upon execution (Civ. Prac. Act. §§ 758–763). It was thought that substantially higher prices could be realized upon execution sales were the right to redeem eliminated. While this rationale may not have been borne out in actual experience, the purchaser at a Sheriff's sale now takes immediate title to the property and is placed in the same position as he would have been if the deed had been executed by the judgment debtor himself (*see Hetzel v. Barber*, 69 N.Y. 1, 10).

Any judicial sale, especially one involving the judgment debtor's residence, is a tragic event. Debtors are often divested of their only real asset to satisfy a previous obligation, however small. In many instances, the family home is sold for substantially less than the debtor's equity in it. It is evident, however, that the Legislature was not unaware of this problem. For example, it has recently raised the homestead exemption, which provides that upon a judicial sale of the debtor's principal place of residence, the first $10,000 of the proceeds representing the debtor's equity may not be used in satisfaction of the judgment (CPLR 5205, subd. [a]).

CPLR 5240 is perhaps the most practical method to protect judgment debtors from the often harsh results of lawful enforcement procedures. The statute provides: "The court may at any time, make an order denying, limiting, conditioning, regulating, extending or modifying the use of any enforcement procedure. . . ." CPLR 5240 grants the courts broad discretionary power to control and regulate the enforcement of a money judgment under article 52 to prevent "unreasonable annoyance, expense, embarrassment, disadvantage, or other prejudice to any person or the courts." . . .

. . . [I]n many instances the statute has been applied in an extremely beneficial manner in accordance with its stated purpose. By way of illustration, courts have restrained impending sales of residences on the ground that creditors could easily resort to less intrusive means to satisfy judgments.

But while CPLR 5240 grants the courts broad discretionary power to alter the use of the procedures set forth in article 52, it has no application after a Sheriff's sale has been carried out and the deed delivered to the purchaser, at which time the use of the enforcement procedure will have been completed. . . . After the sale has been consummated, the interests of persons other than the judgment debtor and creditor are implicated. . . .

This is not to say that a judgment debtor is without remedy once a judicial sale has taken place. CPLR 2003 grants the power to set aside such a Sheriff's sale within one year "for a failure to comply with the requirements of the civil practice law and rules as to the notice, time or manner of such sale, if a substantial right of a party was prejudiced by the defect." . . . And, of course, the court may exercise its inherent equitable power over a sale made pursuant to its judgment or decree to ensure that it is not made the instrument of injustice. . . .

In this case, the sale was conducted in strict conformity with statutory procedure (*see* CPLR 5236), rendering CPLR 2003 inapposite. . . . While the sale price was less than respondents' equity in the property, the simple fact is that in most instances the fair market value of the property will exceed the winning bid at an execution sale. For this reason, it is well settled that mere inadequacy of price—the only pertinent showing here—does not furnish sufficient grounds for vacating a sale. . . .

Although respondents' plight is certain to evoke sympathy, here the record is devoid of any showing warranting intervention by a court of equity. . . . Respondents' rights were protected to the fullest extent that the law provides. [Reversed; sale upheld.] . . .

Notes and Questions

(1) *Exempt Property.* At the time of the opinion above, New York's homestead exemption reserved to the judgment debtor the first $10,000 realized from the judicial sale of her principal residence. New York's homestead exemption subsequently was increased to $50,000. CPLR 5206(a). Other states have larger homestead exemptions. For example, Texas exempts "urban" homesteads "of not more than 10 acres of land" and "rural" homesteads for single adults "of not more than 100 acres" and for families of "not more than 200 acres." *See* Tex. Prop. C. § 41.002. Because Texas law also exempts substantial amounts of personal property, including current wages for personal services (*see* Tex. Prop. C. § 42.001), much of what most people own or earn is not subject to the satisfaction of judgments obtained by third parties. Is this result appropriate?

(2) *CPLR 5240: The Court's Discretionary Authority to Protect the Judgment Debtor from Unreasonably Disadvantageous Consequences of Otherwise Lawful Enforcement of Judgments.* Equity courts traditionally have had authority to protect the judgment debtor from unreasonable effects of judgment enforcement (and in fact sometimes enjoined execution of judgments at law before the merger of law and equity). In New York, CPLR 5240 contains a broad express grant of discretion to the trial courts. If you represented the judgment debtors in *Guardian Loan Co. v. Early*, how might you have used this provision? [Note: Would execution on chattels, or income execution, have been preferable for them?]

> Read Fed. R. Civ. P. 69 (execution and other enforcement mechanisms).

Note on the Approach of the Federal Rules in Borrowing State Enforcement Procedures and Provisional Remedies

Rules 64 and 69: Federal Courts Borrow State Enforcement Mechanisms and Provisional Remedies. Rules 64 and 69, respectively, adopt the mechanisms available in the state in which the District Court sits for non-injunctive provisional remedies (such as seizure) and for enforcement of judgment. Thus, in New York, that state's attachment procedure would be available under the same terms as in state courts, and the judicial sale rules illustrated by *Guardian Loan Co. v. Early* would apply, as updated.

Should Federal Courts Have Federal Enforcement Provisions? The borrowing of state law is defensible on the theory that it leads to uniformity in the law that practitioners in a given state must use, and it produces results in conformity with the *Erie* doctrine in diversity cases. But it is open to criticism. Imagine two plaintiffs, one in Texas and one in New York (or California), who had obtained judgments for serious injuries received during the deprivation of their civil rights. The first plaintiff may find enforcement of her judgment impractical because of Texas' exemption of most property and earnings; and the other will find enforcement more readily obtainable. Does the vindication of federal policy call for a uniform federal procedure here?

[B] Judgment Liens

Note on Judgment Liens

Judgment Liens on Realty. In most states, a judgment can be the basis of a lien upon the judgment debtor's real property. The manner in which the lien is perfected varies significantly from state to state. In New York, for example, the judgment lien attaches automatically to any real property within a given county in which the judgment debtor has or acquires an interest, once the judgment is docketed with the clerk of the county. CPLR 5203(a). Texas follows a roughly similar procedure: Tex. Prop. Code Ann. §§ 52.001 *et seq.*

Judgment Liens on Personalty. In some states, judgment liens can be perfected upon personalty, too, usually by delivery of a writ of execution or other appropriate writ to the appropriate officer.

Foreclosure of Judgment Lien; Priorities; Bankruptcy Proceedings. A judgment lien creates a claim against the property as security for the judgment debt. It may create a right of foreclosure against the property—and thus, the judgment debtor may be able to cause its sale not only while it is owned by the judgment debtor, but also while it is owned by most subsequent purchasers or other transferees. Also, a perfected judgment lien may give the judgment creditor the right to have his debt satisfied from the property in question in higher priority than other creditors (for example, the principle of "first in time, first in right" ordinarily will mean that the earliest judgment creditor prevails over later judgment creditors).

TEXACO INC. v. PENNZOIL COMPANY, 784 F.2d 1133 (2d Cir. 1986).[(b)] Reconsider this case (which appears in § II[B] of Chapter 12, above, in connection with

(b) As is indicated in Chapter 12, the Supreme Court reversed on other grounds, but the Second Circuit's analysis of the judgment liens remains useful. *See supra* § II[B] of Chapter 12.

supersedeas bonds). Pennzoil obtained a judgment for $11.12 billion from Texaco in a Texas state court. In order to stay enforcement of the judgment pending appeal, under Texas law, Texaco was required to post a supersedeas bond "in at least the amount of the judgment, interest, and costs," or more than $12 billion. The Second Circuit affirmed a preliminary injunction allowing Texaco to supersede the judgment by filing a bond for only $1 billion. Part of the court's analysis included a finding that Texaco otherwise would suffer irreparable injury, not only from active enforcement of the judgment, but also from the lien on Texaco's real property that would result from the filing of an abstract of the judgment in county deed records:

> It is beyond dispute that absent injunctive relief, enforcement of Texas' lien and supersedeas bond provisions would rapidly produce a catastrophe of major proportions, causing substantial harm to Texaco itself and to thousands of others throughout the United States. . . . Pennzoil concedes that Texaco . . . could not possibly post a bond or security in the sum of the approximately $12 billion that is mandated by [Texas law]. The simultaneous attachment of a lien pursuant to Tex. Prop. Code Ann. §§ 52.001 *et seq.* on Texaco's real property in Texas, valued at $5 billion, would seal the company's fate. Unable to finance its operations or obtain credit lines needed for its continued existence [because of the lien], Texaco, the fifth largest business organization in the United States, would be forced into bankruptcy or liquidation. . . .

Notes and Questions

(1) *Judgment Liens in Bankruptcy Proceedings.* Many of the cases dealing with judgment liens are bankruptcy cases. A properly perfected and enforceable lien is an important advantage in a bankruptcy proceeding because liquidation proceedings generally mean that the debtor's assets will not satisfy all creditors, and "general" or unsecured creditors usually are satisfied only after other creditors with liens against property ("secured" creditors). In fact, the bankruptcy trustee (who is appointed by the court to collect and preserve the estate of the bankrupt) is given, by the Bankruptcy Code, the status of a hypothetical judgment lien creditor whose lien is perfected as of the commencement of the bankruptcy case. Thus, the judgment lien concept is fundamental to the structure of the Bankruptcy Code.

(2) *Judgment Liens as Preventing Purchase and Sale of Realty; Title Insurance or Opinions.* Title insurers, or attorneys rendering title opinions, routinely check judgment records; outstanding judgment liens will appear as exceptions to the title insurance policy or to the opinion of marketable title, and purchasers ordinarily will not complete the transaction until these defects are cured, ordinarily by satisfaction of the judgment and filing of a release.

Problem E

RELEASING THE JUDGMENT LIEN. You are sitting in your office when the telephone rings. "Good afternoon, Mr./Ms. Attorney," says a voice. "I'm Lynn Jones, a closer at East America Title Company. You remember that judgment your client took against Dan Debtor seven years ago? Well, Mr. Debtor is here, ready to close the sale of a parcel of real property, and I have a release of judgment for you and your client to sign, and Mr. Debtor has drafted a personal check to bring to you." You begin to have a warm feeling, based upon the conclusion that justice does exist after all. The closer continues: "Mr. Debtor is on his way over to clear this matter up right now, because we really must close the transaction this afternoon, and it's already four o'clock." What do you say in return?

[C] Post-Judgment Garnishment

United States v. Bankas

717 F.3d 637 (7th Cir. 2018) (unpublished opinion)

... [Ernest] Bankas earned three Master's degrees from different American universities, a law degree from Southern Methodist University, and a doctorate in philosophy and public international law from Durham University in the United Kingdom. But over a two-year period, Bankas also submitted false promissory notes to several lenders. ... Bankas pleaded guilty to one count of fraudulently obtaining student loans. District Judge Barbara Crabb sentenced him to 24 months' imprisonment and ordered him under the Mandatory Victims Restitution Act to pay $340,810 to the U.S. Department of Education.

Once Bankas was released from prison, the government sought to obtain the unpaid restitution through garnishments. ... [T]he district court ordered that the royalties from Bankas's book [about international suits against foreign sovereigns] be garnished and applied to his restitution debt.

Four years later the government discovered that Bankas was working as a health-care aid and initiated proceedings to garnish his wages. The district court issued a writ of garnishment, and garnishments began in early 2017. Bankas objected to the garnishment and filed a form request for a hearing on grounds of financial hardship, specifying that certain expenses—child-support payments and the costs of caring for five children—qualified as exemptions from enforcement. ... District Judge William Conley held a telephonic status conference to assess Bankas's request for a hearing and concluded that one was not warranted. The judge explained that all of Bankas's five children were over eighteen, so their expenses were not exempt. ... He also reminded Bankas that there is no exemption to garnishment solely for financial hardship. ... [Bankas appealed and argued that the absence of a hearing had denied him due process.] ...

Bankas did not base his objection on any of the statute's listed grounds; he was not entitled to a garnishment hearing; the denial of such a hearing, then, did not deprive him of due process. ...

Finally, Bankas challenges the calculation of the garnishment amount in light of fluctuations in his pay, which significantly increased just before the garnishment began in 2017. But the record reflects that Bankas's biweekly disposable income for the relevant time period has been at least $630—a figure greater than the $580 threshold above which the government may garnish 25% of a debtor's income. There is no evidence of any improper calculations. [AFFIRMED.]

Notes and Questions

(1) *How Post-Judgment Garnishment Works.* The judgment creditor, as garnishor, serves the application on a third person, such as a bank or employer, who has funds payable to the judgment debtor. This third person is called the garnishee. In many states, garnishment proceedings technically are a separate suit, ancillary to the main action, in which the garnishee is the named defendant. The proceeding is *in rem*, but the judgment debtor must be provided with notice. The garnishee may have obligations to the judgment debtor to exercise due care to preserve his property (*e.g.*, by filing an answer) and may be entitled to attorney's fees. The result, in the banking situation, is that the judgment debtor's account effectively is frozen, up to the amount of the garnishment plus the bank's attorney's fees, frequently causing unpaid checks and other losses to the judgment debtor; accordingly, the garnishor may be liable for wrongful garnishment, just as for other wrongful use of provisional remedies or enforcement procedures.

Notice that in *Bankas*, the garnishment was limited to 25% of funds exceeding a threshold amount. This limit is imposed on garnishment of "earnings" by the Consumer Credit Act.

(2) *Putting the Judgment Debtor on "a Budget"; The Employer's Position.* In a sense, wage garnishment "puts the judgment debtor on a budget"; if the 25 percent limit insufficiently protects the debtor, notice that a court of equity can further reduce the percentage. The reaction of employer-garnishors, quite understandably, is that the process is a costly nuisance, creating potential liability for failure to withhold the right amounts, undesired and undeserved relationships with courts and lawyers, and complicated paperwork, all for an employee who didn't pay her debts. Most jurisdictions prohibit the employer from taking any adverse action toward the employee, motivated by the garnishment. Would you expect such a prohibition to be 100 percent effective? [Note that the question is one of motive for the termination or other action, and employees who neglect their debts to such a point as to suffer wage garnishment may have neglected other duties, too.]

[D] Turnover Orders, Receiverships, and Other Equitable Supplementary Proceedings

[1] Turnover Orders

Note on the Need for Turnover Relief

Non-Exempt Property that Cannot Readily Be Levied Upon: In re Dunlap, 27 B.R. 728 (Bkrptcy. N.C. 1983). It often happens that a judgment debtor has valuable property or rights that are not exempt from process but are not subject to execution (or cannot easily be executed upon). For example, in the *Dunlap* bankruptcy, the court held that a judgment debtor who had sold his interest in an insurance agency for monthly payments based on 30% of certain other sums, but who had certain contractual obligations himself in exchange (including the obligation not to compete with the sold business), had only a "contingent" right to payment. In accordance with the general rule, the court held that this contingent interest was not subject to execution. But if a judgment creditor had no systematic way of reaching such assets, the debtor could avoid satisfying the judgment simply by secreting and spending the funds as they were received. The law governing what property is subject to execution varies from state to state and is not completely consistent. *Compare, e.g., First Northwestern Trust Co. v. Internal Revenue Serv.*, 622 F.2d 387 (8th Cir. 1980) (income from discretionary trust is not "property" subject to execution); *George v. Kitchens by Rice Bros., Inc.*, 665 F.2d 7 (1st Cir. 1981) (power to revoke a trust is not "property" and cannot be reached by process), *with Springsteen v. Meadows, Inc.*, 534 F. Supp. 504 (D. Mass. 1982) (Massachusetts liquor license was subject to execution as a transferrable asset even though it could be revoked by issuing authority); *New Jersey Bank, N.A. v. Community Association/Farms, Inc.*, 666 F.2d 813 (3d Cir. 1981) (reserve account retained by bank as security for performance was subject to levy even though subject to possible offset for noncompliance with contract obligations).

The Need for Turnover Relief. In situations such as these, the judgment debtor has valuable rights that are not exempt from process but are difficult to reach by ordinary means. The debtor may be able to continue to enjoy the fruits of these rights without satisfying her judgment creditors unless there is a means of requiring her to cooperate with the court in securing them for payment.

The Nature of Turnover Relief: A Statutory Example. The New York statute is an example of broad turnover authority. Also, Tex. Civ. Prac. & Rem. Code § 31.002 (Vernon 1986) provides that if a judgment debtor owns "property, including present or future rights to property, that (1) cannot readily be attached or levied upon by ordinary legal process; and (2) is not exempt from attachment, execution, or seizure for the satisfaction of liabilities," the judgment creditor "is entitled to aid from a court of appropriate jurisdiction through injunction or other means to reach property to obtain satisfaction on the judgment. . . ." The debtor may be required, for example, to assemble and turn over records of various kinds, to pay property into the registry of the court as it is received, or to separate nonexempt property from property claimed to be exempt. In addition, the court may order other persons to perform acts facilitating the collection process, since the statute is not limited to relief directly ordered against the debtor.

CORSAIR SPECIAL SITUATIONS FUND, L.P. v. PESIRI, 887 F.3d 589 (2d Cir. 2018) (***per curiam***). Corsair obtained a judgment from the United States District

Court for the District of Maryland jointly and severally against the defendants in the amount of $5,443,171.33. While attempting to enforce [that] judgment, Corsair learned that one of the defendants had "signed a contract with a Connecticut-based third party, National Resources, entitling [it] to a payment from National Resources of more than $3,000,000." On learning that, Corsair "enrolled its judgment in the United States District Court for the District of Connecticut," which thereupon issued a writ of execution. Corsair engaged State Marshal Mark A. Pesiri to serve a writ of execution on National Resources for a portion of the debt.

> Although Pesiri successfully served the writ, National Resources ignored it, relinquishing the $2,308,504 to Corsair only after Corsair instituted and won a subsequent turnover action for the monies. Despite the intervening legal action taken by Corsair in pursuit of the fruits of its judgment, the district court held that under Connecticut General Statute § 52-261(a), Pesiri was entitled to a full fifteen percent commission on the $2,308,504. It therefore awarded him fees representing that fifteen percent: $346,275.60.
>
> On appeal, Corsair argued that Pesiri was not entitled to the fee because it collected the debt itself through the enforcement proceedings [i.e., by turnover order]. We certified [the question] to the Connecticut Supreme Court. . . . [That court held that the State Marshal was entitled to his fee of 15% under the circumstances and that the fact that it was the plaintiff itself who recovered the property through turnover order, and that the Marshal did very little, did not matter.]

The Connecticut Supreme Court, in reaching that conclusion, relied on its observation that "Pesiri's proper service and demand were essential predicates to recovery of [the] debt [via turnover], a fact made evident by Corsair's own statements in its application for, and memorandum in support of, the turnover order." The court affirmed the award to Pesiri of fees in the amount of $346,275.60.

Notes and Questions

(1) *New York's Income Execution and Installment Payment Order: Schwartz v. Goldberg*, 58 Misc. 2d 308, 295 N.Y.S.2d 245 (Sup. Ct. 1968). In addition to turnover relief, New York provides for execution on income; it also provides for an installment payment order "where it is shown that the judgment debtor is receiving or will receive money from any source, or is attempting to impede the judgment creditor. . . ." CPLR 5231, 5226; *see* O. Chase, *2 Weinstein, Korn & Miller CPLR Manual* §§ 27.13–27.16 (1997). The income execution does not require a particularized court order and is effective as to only ten percent of income, with certain exemptions; the installment payment order, on the other hand, is an order, similar to a turnover order, not subject to the same limitations. In *Schwartz v. Goldberg*, for example, there were six judgment creditors waiting in line for payment by income executions; a seventh creditor obtained an installment payment order and, by virtue of its nature as a court order, was entitled to receive payment before the other six!

(2) *Enforcement of Decrees in Matrimonial (i.e., Divorce) Cases: In re Brecheisen*, 665 S.W.2d 197 (Tex. App. 1984). The *Brecheisen* case is interesting as an example of enforcement of a marital dissolution decree, which several of the authors of this book consider among the most formidable challenges in the enforcement area. Wealthy, determined former spouses who are ill disposed toward each other sometimes fight with primitive energy even after the decree. In this case, the court ordered a noncompliant ex-husband to turn over cash he received on a continuing basis to the registry of the court until a judgment for past amounts was satisfied, and it provided for the ex-wife to withdraw funds. For a discussion of sophisticated uses of such devices as liens, turnover, and the like in the post-divorce context, see George, *After the Divorce—Securing and Obtaining the Property: Post-Judgment Relief in Texas*, 17 TEXAS TECH. L. REV. 1349 (1986).

Problem F

USE OF TURNOVER PROVISIONS TO REACH TRUST PROPERTY IN FIRST NORTHWESTERN TRUST CO. v. IRS AND GEORGE v. KITCHENS BY RICE BROS., INC. You have directed interrogatories to a judgment debtor to locate and identify his property. The answers indicate that he created a trust for the benefit of his 21-year-old son; the trust is revocable at will. Further, he is the beneficiary of a trust that pays income to him in the discretion of the trustee. If you were practicing in a state with a general turnover statute similar to the ones discussed in this subsection, what steps might you take with respect to these trust properties? What orders might you request that the court issue to the judgment debtor and to third parties, and would you expect the court to issue them? [Note: In *First Northwestern Trust Co. v. IRS*, 622 F.2d 387 (8th Cir. 1980), and *George v. Kitchens by Rice Bros., Inc.*, 665 F.2d 7 (1st Cir. 1981), the courts held, respectively, that these rights could not be reached through execution.]

[2] Receivership

> Read Fed. R. Civ. P. 66 (receivers).

Ypsilanti Fire Marshal v. Kircher

730 N.W.2d 481 (Mich. App. 2007)

JANSEN, J.

[In protracted nuisance-abatement litigation concerning repeated serious fire code violations by Kircher's buildings, the trial court granted city's motions for appointment of a receiver and for summary disposition to foreclose on liens for funds expended to repair one of the buildings. The trial court stated, "[Kircher] has not complied with the [c]ourt's [orders]. . . . Furthermore, I'm going to specifically find that the building is in dangerous condition and is a nuisance." The appellate court here upholds the receivership but narrows the scope of the receiver's powers.] . . .

[T]he trial court had the jurisdiction to appoint a receiver for the . . . [b]uilding pursuant to MCL 600.2926. That statute provides that "[c]ircuit court judges in the exercise of their equitable powers, may appoint receivers in all cases pending where appointment is allowed by law." A court-appointed receiver is a ministerial officer of the court. . . . It is well settled that a receiver's possession of assets and property is tantamount to possession by the court itself. *Chronowski v. Park Sproat Corp.*, 11 N.W.2d 286 (1943). . . .

Kircher . . . contends that the trial court's receivership order constituted an abuse of discretion because the creation of a receivership is an extraordinary equitable remedy, and there existed "adequate legal remedies" in this matter. It is true that receivership is a remedy of last resort, and should not be used where another, less drastic remedy exists. . . . *White v. Fulton*, 244 N.W. 498 (1932). However, Kircher does not sufficiently brief this issue by explaining precisely what "adequate legal remedies" were available in this matter. . . . [W]e consider this issue abandoned on appeal. . . .

Kircher [also] contends that the trial court's receivership order constituted an abuse of discretion because it failed to provide for proper judicial supervision and oversight of the receiver's activities and expenditures. We agree. . . .

. . . [T]he trial court's . . . receivership order . . . granted the receiver nearly unfettered authority to make repairs and renovations to the Thompson Building, and nearly unchecked power to charge Kircher for any such work. . . .

By giving the receiver the authority to make the Thompson building "economically viable," the order allows the receiver to make repairs beyond removing the hazards of which plaintiffs originally complained. [Ypsilanti's] reliance on the fire code does not support its argument that the broad scope of the order is appropriate. The quoted portion of the fire code only addresses hazards that endanger human life. It does not address the "economic viability" of the building. Accordingly, we reverse that portion of the . . . order providing "that the Receiver needs to make the building economically viable and functional."

The trial court's order must . . . comply with the provisions of MCL 600.2926 which provides: "In all cases in which a receiver is appointed the court shall provide for bond and shall define the receiver's power and duties where they are not otherwise spelled out by law." [AFFIRMED IN PART AND REVERSED IN PART.]

Notes and Questions

(1) *Receivership as a "Drastic" Remedy for Collecting Money Judgments: Olsan v. Comora*, 140 Cal. Rptr. 835 (Cal. App. 1977). Olsan obtained a judgment for over $380,000 against Cormora, a dentist, but after using both execution and garnishment remedies, she collected less than ten percent of it. The court ordered a receiver to collect and disburse Comora's future earnings. The appellate court recognized

that receivership was a drastic remedy but upheld the receivership, because Comora had stated that he had no assets subject to execution, and if he had any, he would place them beyond collection efforts.

Why do the courts in both *Ypsilanti*, above, and *Olsan*, here, refer to the appointment of a receiver as a "drastic" remedy? [The receiver takes charge of the affairs of an ongoing business. Her decisions displace those of the usual management of the business.]

(2) *Receiverships to Enforce Non-Money Judgments: The South Boston School Desegregation Receivership.* In business litigation, a receivership may be ordered when management seriously has breached its obligations to shareholders or in situations of consumer fraud, if the equities so require. Non-business usage of the receiver may be illustrated by Judge Arthur Garrity's ordering of a receiver for the South Boston schools in desegregation litigation. *Morgan v. Kerrigan*, 401 F. Supp. 216 (D. Mass. 1975).

Problem G

MOTION TO APPOINT RECEIVERSHIP TO ENFORCE DECREE SIMILAR TO THAT IN WILLIAMS v. NEW ORLEANS, 729 F.2d 1554 (5th Cir. 1984) *(en banc)*. Imagine that you are a federal district judge who previously has entered a decree similar to that in *Williams*. The decree is designed to remedy longstanding and serious racial discrimination in employment of black police officers; it contains draconian requirements about recruiting, testing, training, probation, termination, and promotion of black and non-black officers, and governs "virtually every phase of an officer's employment by the . . . Police Department." It also requires extensive and frequent reports by the defendants concerning their compliance. Some of the terms (such as racial quotas) are highly specific; others are general and require cooperative effort.

Representatives of the plaintiff class are now, a year later, claiming massive and deliberate violations of the decree and falsification of the reports. They urge you to appoint a receiver to implement the decree. The defendants argue that while the goals of the decree have not been fully achieved, they have not engaged in any intentional violations, and they vehemently argue that appointment of a receiver would be unlawful, inappropriate and harmful. What considerations militate in favor of appointment of a receiver, and what considerations against?

[3] Discovery in Aid of Enforcement of Judgment

Use of Discovery Devices to Locate Assets and Enforce Judgment. Rule 69 provides for the use of discovery devices in aid of enforcement. It is permissible, for example, to take the deposition of the judgment debtor (or of other persons) to ask about property, interests, or other rights he has or may have; likewise, the judgment creditor may use interrogatories or requests for production. State rules typically contain similar provisions. This type of discovery first was developed by courts of equity in the creditor's bill (as was the turnover order).

MATTER OF SILVERMAN, 6 B.R. 991 (D.N.J. 1980). In this case, the propriety of execution on the judgment debtor's realty depended upon whether the creditor had made a good faith effort first to locate personalty (which in New Jersey must be levied upon first). The creditor, through its attorney, had undertaken an "examination in aid of execution" (equivalent to a deposition) and used "standard form interrogatories prepared by [the creditor's] law firm." This discovery "contain[ed] numerous particular questions about the debtor's ownership of such personalty as motor vehicles, other vehicles or trailers, aircraft, firearms, coin or stamp collections, tools or equipment, sporting goods or equipment, paintings or other art objects, interests in business, bank accounts, securities, patents or copyrights, and insurance policies."

However, "[n]otably missing . . . [were] inquiries into the debtor's cash on hand and ownership of furniture, appliances, and other household goods," and there was "no generalized question as to the personal property owned by the debtor." The court concluded that this discovery was sufficiently "thorough and conscientious" to constitute a good faith effort, so that the levy on the debtor's realty was not unlawful even though he owned leviable personalty. But was the discovery skillfully conducted?

[E] Contempt and Arrest

BELITZ v. BELITZ, 842 N.W.2d 613 (Neb. App. 2017). This case illustrates the character of contempt as a quasi-criminal proceeding, the due process protections attached to it, and the requirement of unusual specificity in orders with which a party must comply. Typically, an order that provides for visitation of a certain number of days will not support criminal contempt against a parent who does not return a child unless the order states, explicitly, that the parent "shall return the child" on a given date. Furthermore, the order will not support contempt if it does not specify a date and time for the return. In this case, the order allegedly violated was not specific enough to support contempt, although it probably could have been understood by a person intending to comply:

> Although Katherine [the child] was not returned to Omaha [at the end of the period of the mother's possession], our de novo review of the record leads us to conclude that the district court did not abuse its discretion in failing to find Kathleen [the mother] in contempt. There was no court order which specifically required Kathleen to return Katherine on a date certain, although there was testimony to an agreed-upon date. . . . Under the particular facts of this case, we affirm the district court's determination that Kathleen's actions did not amount to a clearly willful violation of prior court orders.

Notes and Questions

(1) *The Requirement of Willful Disobedience: Vaughn v. City of Flint,* 752 F.2d 1160 (6th Cir. 1985). Criminal contempt, whether enforced by fine or incarceration, is

a quasi-criminal proceeding, and it requires proof of willful disobedience. Willfulness, in this context, means a deliberate or intended violation, as distinguished from one that is accidental, inadvertent, or negligent. This element, as well as all other elements, must be proved beyond a reasonable doubt to support criminal contempt. Note, however, that contempt validly lies in some instances of willful disobedience even if the underlying injunction is invalid; *see Walker v. City of Birmingham*, 388 U.S. 307 (1967). The issue is a difficult one; *cf. In re Providence Journal Co.*, 820 F.2d 1342 (1st Cir. 1986) (newspaper may challenge press injunction by violating it, without contempt—but only if injunction is not merely invalid, but "transparently" invalid).

(2) *Civil versus Criminal Contempt and Direct versus Indirect Contempt: Charles Manufacturing Co. v. United Furniture Workers*, 367 So. 2d 1033 (Ala. 1978). This case explains that "civil" contempt punishes a party who violates an order on a continuing basis until the party purges herself of contempt by complying. "Criminal" contempt is punishment for a past violation. "Direct" contempt is that which takes place in the presence of the court. "Direct" contempt is conduct that takes place in the presence of the judge, so that lesser proof is necessary. "Indirect" contempt involves conduct outside the presence of the court. In *Charles Manufacturing*, the contempt was criminal and indirect, and therefore it required stringent due process protections.

Problem H

HYPOTHETICAL CRIMINAL CONTEMPT PROCEEDINGS BASED UPON GALELLA v. ONASSIS, SUPRA. In this case, which appears in § III[A][2] of this Chapter, above, the court enjoined a "paparazzo" photographer from approaching closer than 25 feet to the widow of former President Kennedy and from doing certain acts such as harassing, annoying, or frightening her. One judge, who supported the broader injunction issued by the trial court, pointed out that abstract prohibitions had proved unworkable. Imagine that Mrs. Onassis goes swimming in the ocean, whereupon Galella, using a speedboat, circles about her (but never comes closer than 25 feet), and that this conduct in fact harasses, annoys and frightens her. (In fact, Galella had engaged in very similar conduct before issuance of the injunction.) If you represented Mrs. Onassis, and you wished to invoke the court's authority to hold Galella in contempt, what would be the most significant difficulty you would encounter in obtaining an adjudication of contempt?

[F] Interstate Enforcement of Judgments

Note: Action on the Judgment, Registration, and UEFJA

Action on the Judgment. From Chapters 1 and 2, you should recall that a judgment by a court of State X cannot directly be enforced by officers of State Y in State Y. The judgment creditor obtains enforcement by bringing an "action on the judgment" in a court of State Y, which will issue its own judgment based upon the State X judgment.

The Federal Procedure for "Registration" of Judgments. For a judgment taken in a federal court, an action on the judgment is unnecessary. In 1948, Congress streamlined the procedure by providing that a federal judgment may be "registered" in any other District, and it then has the same force as if it had been rendered in that District. 28 U.S.C. § 1963.

The Uniform Enforcement of Foreign Judgments Act. The Commissioners on Uniform State Laws have drafted a Uniform Enforcement of Foreign Judgments Act, which allows sister state judgments to be treated in the same manner as federal judgments. The UEFJA now has been adopted in many of the states, eliminating the need for actions upon judgments in most instances. The same process has produced the Uniform Foreign Country Money Judgment Recognition Act (UFCMJRA), which also has been widely adopted.

L&W AIR CONDITIONING CO., INC. v. VARSITY INN OF ROCHESTER, INC., 82 Misc. 2d 937, 371 N.Y.S.2d 997 (Sup. Ct. Monroe Co. 1975). New York's adoption of the UEFJA allows the judgment creditor simply to file the judgment with the clerk along with an affidavit containing information such as the name and last known address of the judgment debtor and the assertion that the judgment remains unsatisfied. Interestingly, however, New York did not adopt the UEFJA for default judgments, which still required an action on the judgment. In the *L&W Air Conditioning* case, the plaintiff had taken a judgment in Georgia after the defendant had answered but did not appear for trial. When the plaintiff filed the judgment in New York, the defendant moved to stay, on the ground that the judgment was by default; but the court held that the judgment was entitled to enforcement, because New York's exception excluded "only those default judgments where there is no appearance at all in the action." *See also* O. Chase, *2 Weinstein, Korn & Miller CPLR Manual* § 27.28 (1997). Does it make sense to exclude default judgments from the UEFJA? [Note that a defaulting defendant with meritorious grounds could move to stay enforcement even in the absence of such an exception.]

VII. How to Answer the Chapter Summary Problem: Some Suggestions

The Embezzlement From Acme Company: Remedies

1.Devices to secure property before suit, or to prevent Bailey's disappearance or transfer of property either before, during or after suit. One possibility is a TRO and temporary injunction against alienating property. If any of the property can be traced, a writ of sequestration (or its equivalent in the targeted state) can be used; otherwise, one can use a writ of attachment (or its equivalent). If any funds are in a depository institution or otherwise owed to Bailey, a prejudgment writ of garnishment is a possibility. The requirements must be met, including a reason to conclude that the property will disappear or be impaired.

2. Damage and damage-related remedies. The claimant can sue for damages for conversion. This remedy will require proof of the amount of the loss with reasonable certainty. Other possibilities include restitution of the amount taken or the use of an equitable lien or constructive trust (see below).

3. Equitable remedies (might there be some such remedies that would afford greater recovery than damages?). See *2* above. Restitution would provide a greater recovery if the claimant can show the amount taken but cannot prove the amount lost. An equitable lien or constructive trust might provide greater recovery by obtaining the current value of Bailey's investments (because these devices follow the property into its changes).

4. Means of collecting or enforcing a judgment against Bailey at the post-judgment stage, if suit is successful. Conceivably, any of the devices in the last part of the chapter could be used: execution, garnishment, turnover, judgment liens, etc.

Chapter 15

Alternate Methods of Dispute Resolution

I. The Case for and Against, and the Types of, ADRs

[A] The Mechanisms of Alternate Dispute Resolution: An Introduction

Throughout American history, private, community, and religious institutions have furnished forums as alternatives to the courts. *See generally* Stamato & Jaffee, *Dispute Resolution, New Jersey Style*, National Institute of Justice Reports, March 1986, at 6. During the last century, adjudication dominated, but the recent expansion of alternatives has emphasized that it is only one model of litigation.

Arbitration is a contractual proceeding by which the parties submit their dispute to a third-party decisionmaker, often one with special expertise in the subject matter of the dispute. Contractual arbitration usually is binding.

Mediation also involves a third party, who acts as a facilitator rather than as a judge or arbiter, in an effort to assist the parties in reaching a voluntary resolution.

Traditional Negotiation, Compromise, and Settlement. Of course, the prevalent method of dispute resolution (at least in terms of frequency of use) is negotiation and compromise. In fact, it might be said that we have a settlement system, in which adjudicatory processes force the issue and resolve only the unusual case.

Private Judging. Some states, such as California, have "rent-a-judge" statutes, which enable the parties to hire a judge for their particular dispute, who then presides over a traditional trial. The parties gain flexibility in the timing of trial.

Neutral Expert Fact Finding. The parties may hire, or the court may appoint, an expert to conduct an investigation of the matter in dispute. The expert's report may be a tool for use in settlement, or (in some instances) may be admissible in evidence.

Mini-Trial. It may be worthwhile for the parties to a large business dispute to present summary versions of their cases to a neutral person as an adjunct of their settlement efforts. The recent invention of the "mini-trial" fulfills this function.

Screening Panels. Some states require presentation of the claim to a panel or administrative agency before litigation in court. The most common models are worker's compensation boards and medical malpractice screening panels. The usual pattern is that the result is advisory, but some jurisdictions attach conditions such as requirements that the plaintiff advance costs or admit the result into evidence.

Settlement Conference. The court may require the parties to appear for a pretrial conference relating specifically to settlement.

Court-Annexed ADR. The court may require the parties to submit to a given ADR mechanism for an advisory ruling (*e.g.*, nonbinding arbitration).

Industry-Wide Claims Settlement. Asbestos producers have entered into what is known as the "Wellington Agreement," which provides for a number of alternatives to adjudication and is designed to provide flexible, yet consistent and low-cost, means of addressing claims.

The "Multiple-Door Courthouse." Some commentators have advocated the emergence of public or private facilities to which disputants may apply for the furnishing of whichever method of resolution seems most appropriate to their individual circumstances.

A Chart of Some Common ADRs: Green, A Comprehensive Approach to the Theory and Practice of Dispute Resolution, 34 J. Legal Ed. 245, 257–58 (1984).(*)

Figure 15A below contains a chart prepared by Professor Eric Green, setting out the characteristics of some commonly used mechanisms for dispute resolution. *See also* Goldberg, Green & Sander, *ADR Problems and Prospects: Looking to the Future,* 69 Judicature 291 (1985); Ray, *Emerging Options in Dispute Resolution,* ABA Journal, June 1989, at 66.

Problem A: Chapter 15 Summary Problem

WHICH ALTERNATE DISPUTE RESOLUTION DEVICE (IF ANY)—ARBITRATION, MEDIATION, MINI-TRIAL, SUMMARY JURY TRIAL, ETC.? The following are potential disputes. State whether you think a particular alternate dispute resolution device is appropriate—including arbitration, mediation, mini-trial, summary jury trial, etc.—or whether traditional litigation would be most appropriate:

(a) *The Fact-Dispute Price-Fixing Case.* Acme Sales Co., a widget buyer, sues three widget manufacturers under the antitrust laws, accusing them of fixing prices, which is a *per se* antitrust violation. The dispute depends mainly upon whether the fact finder believes the plaintiff's evidence of price fixing (which consists of memoranda of meetings, price similarity, and a few insider witnesses who say the defendants met and verbally agreed on the prices they would charge) or the defendants' (which consists of vehement direct denials by defendants' officers).

(b) *The Interwoven Fact-Law Tying Arrangement Dispute.* Acme Sales Co. sues United States Widget Co. for $50 million, claiming that the defendant refuses to sell widgets to Acme unless Acme also buys a thingummy with each widget (Acme doesn't need any thingummys). Acme claims that this practice constitutes a prohibited "tying arrangement," in violation of the antitrust laws. The facts can be interpreted in various ways to support arguments that the defendant's conduct is, or is

(*) Copyright 1984 by the Journal of Legal Education. Reprinted with permission.

Figure 15A

Green, *A Comprehensive Approach to the Theory and Practice of Dispute Resolution*, 34 J. LEGAL ED. 245, 257–58 (1984)

Appendix

"Primary" Dispute Resolution Processes

ADJUDICATION	ARBITRATION	MEDIATION/ CONCILIATION	TRADITIONAL NEGOTIATION
Nonvoluntary	Voluntary unless contractual or court centered	Voluntary	Voluntary
Binding, subject to appeal	Binding (usually), no appeal	Nonbinding	Nonbinding (except through use of adjudication to enforce agreement)
Imposed third-party neutral decision maker, with no specialized expertise in dispute subject	Party-selected third-party decision maker, usually with specialized subject expertise	Party-selected outside facilitator, often with specialized subject expertise	No third-party facilitator
Highly procedural; formalized and highly structured by predetermined, rigid rules	Procedurally less formal; procedural rules and substantive law may be set by parties	Usually informal, unstructured	Usually informal, unstructured
Opportunity for each party to present proofs supporting decision in its favor	Opportunity for each party to present proofs supporting decision in its favor	Presentation of proofs less important than attitudes of each party; may include principled argument	Presentation of proofs usually indirect or non-existent; may include principled argument
Win/Lose result	Compromise result possible (probable?)	Mutually acceptable agreement sought	Mutually acceptable agreement sought
Expectation of reasoned statement	Reason for result not usually required	Agreement usually embodied in contract of release	Agreement usually embodied in contract or release
Process emphasizes attaining substantive consistency and predictability of results	Consistency and predictability balanced against concern for disputants' relationship	Emphasis on disputants' relationship, not on adherence to or development of consistent rules	Emphasis on disputants' relationship, not on adherence to or development of consistent rules
Public process: lack of privacy of submissions	Private process unless judicial enforcement sought	Private process	Highly private process

Figure 15A (Continued)

Appendix (Page 2)

"Hybrid" Dispute Resolution Processes

PRIVATE JUDGING	NEUTRAL EXPERT FACT FINDING	MINITRIAL	SETTLEMENT CONFERENCE
Voluntary	Voluntary or nonvoluntary under FRE 706	Voluntary	Voluntary or mandatory
Binding but subject to appeal and possibly review by trial court	Nonbinding but results may be admissible	Nonbinding (except through use of adjudication to enforce agreement)	Binding or nonbinding
Party-selected third-party decision maker; may have to be former judge or lawyer	Third-party neutral with specialized subject matter expertise may be selected by the parties	Third-party neutral advisor with specialized subject expertise	Judge, other judge, or third-party neutral selected by parties
Statutory procedure (*see, e.g.*, Cal. Code Civ. Proc. § 638 et seq.) but highly flexible as to timing, place and procedures	Informal	Less formal than adjudication and arbitration but procedural rules and scope of issues may be set by the parties and implemented by neutral advisor	Informal, off-the-record
Opportunity for each party to present proofs supporting decision in its favor	Investigatory	Opportunity and responsibility to present proofs supporting result in its favor	Presentation of proofs may or may not be allowed
Win/lose result (judgment of court)	Report or testimony	Mutually acceptable agreement sought	Mutually acceptable agreement sought; binding conference is similar to arbitration
Findings of fact and conclusions of law possible but not required	May influence result or settlement	Agreement usually embodied in contract or release	Agreement usually embodied in contract or release
Adherence to norms, laws and precedent	Emphasis on reliable fact determination	Emphasis on sound, cost-effective and fair resolution satisfactory to both parties	Emphasis on resolving the dispute
Private process unless judicial enforcement sought	May be highly private or discussed in court	Highly private process	Private process but may be discovered

not, a tying arrangement. The law also is complex and can be applied to the facts in various ways.

(c) *The Antitrust Dispute Overlapped by a Personality Clash.* Acme Sales Co., one of North America's larger widget buyers, often buys from Consolidated Widget, one of the larger sellers. Acme has a longstanding complaint about the sales policy of Consolidated, in that it does not discount for large volumes even though it probably has cost savings. Acme has threatened suit under the antitrust laws (although the claim is weak). The two vice presidents who have responsibility for the purchases and sales have talked about the problem, know it must be resolved and yet have difficulty working with each other personally.

(d) *The Recurrent Commercial Dispute.* Acme Sales Co. buys large quantities of widgets on a long-term contract from Hy-Jinks Widget Corporation. It repeatedly has found that the widgets are defective. It could attempt to terminate the entire contract, but that would be risky; it could sue on each delivery that is nonconforming, but that would be expensive and disruptive of the relationship; it could simply accept the goods, but that would hurt its sales. It has attempted negotiation, but has found that Hy-Jinks' personnel, though friendly, revert to bad habits rapidly and continue to send defective shipments occasionally.

[B] The Case for ADRs; The Disadvantages of Traditional Adjudication

Note on the "BATNA"

(1) *Understanding Your BATNA (Best Alternative to a Negotiated Agreement).* In most instances, civil litigation is the unpleasant alternative to a negotiated agreement. In a classic book on negotiation, this concept was described as the BATNA:

> The reason you negotiate is to produce something better than the results you can obtain without negotiating. What is your BATNA—your Best Alternative To a Negotiated Agreement? That is the standard against which any proposed agreement should be measured. That is the only standard which can protect you both from accepting terms that are too unfavorable and from rejecting terms it would be in your interest to accept.

Roger Fisher & William Ury, *Getting to Yes.*

(2) *Why Your BATNA Is the Best Way to Evaluate a Negotiated Proposal.* Fisher and Ury go on to explain the advantages of BATNA analysis:

> Your BATNA not only is a better measure but also has the advantage of being flexible enough to permit the exploration of imaginative solutions. Instead of ruling out any solution which does not meet your bottom line, you can compare a proposal with your BATNA to see whether it better satisfies your interests.

> If you have not thought carefully about what you will do if you fail to reach an agreement, you are negotiating with your eyes closed. You may, for instance, be too optimistic and assume that you have many other choices: other houses for sale, other buyers for your secondhand car, other plumbers, . . . and so on. Even when your alternative is fixed, you may be taking too rosy a view of the consequences of not reaching agreement. You may not be appreciating the full agony of a lawsuit, a contested divorce, a strike, an arms race, or a War.

Note on Arguments in Favor of ADRs

(1) *The Cost of Traditional Adjudication as an Argument for ADRs.* Whether they agree upon a mini-trial and settle their dispute, or whether they contract for binding arbitration, the parties to major business litigation are likely to be motivated in part by cost savings. A study using 8 years of data showed that litigation may consume as much as 33% of Fortune 500 company profits. John B. Henry, *Fortune 500: The Total Cost of Litigation Estimated at One-Third Profits,* Corporate Counsel Business Journal (Friday, February 1, 2008).

A separate report and survey presented at Duke Law School concluded that multi-national companies "spend a disproportionate amount on litigation in the United States relative to their expenditures in foreign jurisdictions. . . . [R]elative U.S. costs were between four and nine times higher than non-U.S. costs (as a percent of revenue)." Lawyers for Civil Justice, the Civil Justice Reform Group and the U.S. Chamber Institute for Legal Reform, *Litigation Cost Survey of Major Companies,* 2010 Conference on Civil Litigation. Diving deeper into the data, the National Center for State Courts concluded that automobile tort cases cost between $17,598 (25th percentile) and $109,428 (75th percentile), and costs of other types of cases such as property, contract, employment or malpractice disputes, are much higher. Paula Hannaford-Agor & Nicole L. Waters, *Estimating the Cost of Civil Litigation,* CourtStatistics.org (Jan. 2013).

(2) *Partial Settlements and Alternate Processes, Including Arbitration.* In some situations, the choice becomes more complicated that just settle or not. The desired outcome in a multi-party case might be a comprehensive settlement, but the BATNA to that comprehensive settlement might be to obtain a partial settlement with some parties but not all, or to collect on an insurance claim that covers only some of the loss. Civil litigation, and more specifically, losing the litigation, might actually be the WATNA—the Worst Alternative to a Negotiated Agreement. Consider the following:

> One of our country's greatest lawyers, Abraham Lincoln, said: "Discourage litigation. Persuade your neighbors to compromise whenever you can. Point out to them how the nominal winner is often a real loser—in fees, expenses, and waste of time. As a peace-maker the lawyer has a superior opportunity of being a good man." . . . My own experience persuades me

> that in terms of cost, time, and human wear and tear, arbitration is vastly better than conventional litigation for many kinds of cases.

Warren Burger, Speech to Members of the Minnesota Bar Ass'n and American Arbitration Ass'n, *reprinted in Chief Justice Burger: Reflections on ADR, Alternatives to the High Cost of Litigation*, October 10, 1985, at 5 (Center for Public Resources Publication).

(3) *Access to Justice: Claims Too Small for Efficient Adjudication.* A corollary of the expense of traditional adjudication is that many litigants cannot afford it. In particular, a claim under $1,000 is unlikely to support a reasonable fee for a lawyer; in fact, even a claim as large as $20,000 to $50,000 may not. The general view is that litigation costs are disproportionate to the value of small cases but not necessarily to the value of large cases. Emery G. Lee III & Thomas E. Willging, *Defining the Problem of Cost in Federal Civil Litigation*, 60 Duke L.J. 765, 769–770 (2010).

To some extent, technology may provide a solution, and online software systems are helping parties use informal approaches to settle disputes:

> Technology-mediated dispute resolution systems can reduce dispute resolution costs. Existing online systems such as Cybersettle and SmartsettleOne are particularly well-suited for resolving single-issue disputes effectively and efficiently. . . .

David Allen Larsen, *"Brother, Can You Spare a Dime?" Technology Can Reduce Dispute Resolution Costs When Times Are Tough and Improve Outcomes,* 11 Nev. L.J. 523, 559 (2011). But one may question this solution on the ground that small claimants should not be forced into settlement by a high-cost system of adjudication.

Another alternative, therefore, may be improvements to small claims courts. *See* Victoria J. Haneman, *Bridging the Justice Gap With a (Purposeful) Restructuring of Small Claims Courts,* 39 W. New Eng. L. Rev. 457 (2017) (advocating higher small claims limits, advisory services to the self-represented, and assistance with collection of judgments).

(4) *Delay, Uncertainty, and Lost Creative Product.* Imagine a patent dispute delayed for many years in its resolution. The cost attributable to the uncertainty of the outcome may exceed the transaction costs of the litigation itself. All parties may be reluctant to develop needed, valuable products whose commercial viability depends on the outcome of the dispute. Chief Justice Burger also said, "Consider the costs of lost productivity in the IBM antitrust litigation, with six years of discovery leading to a trial that went on for nearly seven years. . . ."

(5) *Enlarging the Size of the Pie: "Polycentric" or "Integrative" Solutions.* It often happens that disputing parties can devise a solution that improves on the result both can expect from litigation. Two parties might bicker over who gets the orange. A distributive solution gives it to one and not the other or cuts the orange in two. But if the two disputants had understood each other, they might have learned that one wanted the orange peel for cooking, and the other wanted the juice. Also, imagine

two museums to which the decedent has bequeathed ten paintings; if they litigate to judgment, one might win all ten (including five it may not really want), but if they divide by compromise, the Museum of Western Art can take the five Remingtons while the French Impressionism Museum takes the five Monets. This approach has been described as "polycentric," or many-centered, or alternatively as "integrative," because it considers everyone's shared, different, and perhaps overlapping rather than competing, interests.

(6) *Party Control: "People's" Solutions, Rather than "Legal" Solutions.* Advocates of ADR sometimes argue that it provides qualitatively better solutions by avoiding the strict mechanisms of the law and substituting solutions chosen by the parties themselves, or by a neutral person less subject to those mechanisms than the traditional judge would be. To some extent, this argument may be a restatement of the "enlarged pie" argument. It also may be the result of suspicion that attorneys will impede actual communication. Finally, it may reflect anomalies in the law that would give unjust results.

(7) *Avoidance of the Harm to Long-Term Relationships that Results from the Highly Adversary Process of Adjudicatory Litigation.* A homeowner allows his dog to bark throughout the night, and a neighbor can think of no better solution than to sue for an injunction. A customer sues the major supplier with whom she has had a ten-year relationship on the theory that a shipment of goods is nonconforming. Obviously, there is something counterproductive about the adjudicatory method of resolving both of these disputes. It maximizes the adversary nature of the dispute and has high potential for injecting unnecessary rancor into the underlying relationship. A less formal method, such as arbitration, might be preferable, and mediation would be better still.

(8) *Privacy.* "A privately selected trier can conduct all proceedings in private with only the parties present, and confidentiality can be preserved where there is a valid basis for it—as in the protection of trade secrets." Burger, *supra*, at 16. Opponents of ADR sometimes criticize its "secrecy," alleging that decisionmaking should be done in the open. Is this argument valid?

(9) *Emotions and "Being Heard."* The importance of emotions in negotiation cannot be overlooked. For some, negotiation is a less painful alternative than the stress of litigation. Scholars writing about therapeutic jurisprudence have noted that the legal system, and the settlement process, are often about validation and being heard, and not necessarily achieving perfect solutions. Nathalie Des Rosiers, *Rights Are Not Enough: Therapeutic Jurisprudence Lessons for Law Reformers*, TOURO LAW REVIEW (2015). Parties often consider that they have been heard when a mediator or the other side has listened.

(10) *Validation and Future Impact.* Lawyers are familiar with claimants who say, "I would like to put them [the defendant] out of business" or "I want to see that they can never do this to anyone else." But lawyers may not perceive the strength of this motivation. "[N]otwithstanding any needs or desires for monetary compensation,

plaintiffs' objectives of obtaining admissions of fault, prevention of recurrences, retribution for defendant conduct, answers, apologies and acknowledgments of harm remained invisible to virtually all lawyers throughout . . . the processing of their cases." Tamara Relis, *It's Not about the Money! A Theory on Misconceptions of Plaintiffs' Litigation Aims*, 68 U. Pitt. L. Rev. 701, 704 (2007). In fact, defendants sometimes can complete a settlement with changes, apologies, and meetings of executives with plaintiffs.

[C] The Case for Caution in Encouraging ADRs

Fiss, *Against Settlement*

93 Yale L.J. 1073 (1984).(*)

In my view, . . . the case for settlement rest[s] on questionable premises. I do not believe that settlement as a generic practice is preferable to judgment or should be institutionalized on a wholesale and indiscriminate basis. It should be treated instead as a highly problematic technique for streamlining dockets. Settlement is for me the civil analogue of plea bargaining: Consent is often coerced; the bargain may be struck by someone without authority; the absence of a trial and judgment renders subsequent judicial involvement troublesome; and although dockets are trimmed, justice may not be done. . . .

[ADR advocates see] adjudication in essentially private terms: The purpose of lawsuits and the civil courts is to resolve disputes, and the amount of litigation we encounter is evidence of the needlessly combative and quarrelsome character of Americans. . . . I, on the other hand, see adjudication in more public terms: Civic litigation is an institutional arrangement for using state power to bring a recalcitrant reality closer to our chosen ideals. . . .

To conceive of the civil lawsuit in public terms as America does might be unique. I am willing to assume that no other country . . . has a case like *Brown v. Board of Education* in which the judicial power is used to eradicate the caste structure. . . . But this should be a source of pride rather than shame. . . .

Notes and Questions

(1) *Litigation for Public Purposes.* Litigation is sometimes a tool to help people be heard when they feel otherwise wronged. Lawsuits alleging civil rights or environmental violations can lead to settlement discussions that would not otherwise occur, but the settlements themselves can also be perceived as controversial, inefficient, or unfair. In fact, the Administrator of the U.S. Environmental Protection Agency has sought to limit the agency's authority to settle cases, purportedly

(*) Copyright 1984. Reprinted with permission.

because of concerns with transparency and public participation. *See* Directive Promoting Transparency and Public Participation in Consent Decrees and Settlement Agreements (October 16, 2017). And the Trump Administration's family separation policies in 2018 had roots in a consent decree that established standards for the detention of non-criminal immigrant children and eliminated some of the administration's alternatives. Rebecca M. López, *Codifying the Flores Settlement Agreement: Seeking to Protect Immigrant Children in U.S. Custody*, 95 MARQ. L. REV. 1635 (2012).

For additional reading regarding the impact of alternative dispute resolution, see Perschbacher & Bassett, *The End of Law*, 84 B.U. L. REV. 1 (2006) (building on Professor Fiss's arguments); *see also* Goldberg, Green & Sander, *Litigation, Arbitration or Mediation: A Dialogue*, ABA JOURNAL, June 1989, at 70 (answering criticisms of ADR in the form of a "dialogue" between a litigator and an ADR specialist).

(2) *But . . . the Case Against Fiss.* Some of Fiss's arguments amount to name-calling (settlement is "the civil analogue of plea bargaining," which is not even an "analogue" but also is settlement) or are so vague or counterproductive that they seem invalid. Fiss says that "justice may not be done," for example; but this assumes that justice always comes from (highly uncertain) litigation, in which five of ten hypothetical juries may rule one way and five the other. And does it seem likely that the Supreme Court will cease to have significant cases on its docket? *Brown v. Board of Education* is an incomplete example, since none of the plaintiffs got any relief, and it seems odd to suggest that such cases will not get to the Supreme Court. A settlement can be more efficient than, and superior to, the outcome of a fully-adjudicated case.

Fiss's effort to conscript litigants who might settle as foot soldiers in a war to create public benefits in the form of precedent visits enormous costs on relatively few citizens, and it contradicts economists' models of public goods in which "free riders" are not a positive feature. Furthermore, the arguments lack perspective. Very little litigation is about public rights or law reform, and discouraging settlement would force wasteful costs on random individuals.

(3) *The Limits of ADR: Consent, Coercion, Ethics, and the Public Purpose.* If expenses of litigation are to be borne by the parties, it does not seem inappropriate for the costs of the system to influence the choice; nor does it seem improper for the judge to counteract the posturing that goes with negotiation or the attitude that some people are suspicious of ADR. But doesn't a mediator—including a judge who encourages settlement—have ethical obligations to avoid overreaching? And isn't it necessary to ensure that important cases affecting the public interest (*e.g.*, *Brown v. Board of Education*) are not shunted off to court-annexed arbitration? But if we institutionalize the encouragement of ADR, can't we still avoid the overreaching judge and the shunting off of future *Brown*-type cases?

(4) *Formal Procedures as Protecting against Prejudice, Unfairness, and Inequality.* One interesting hypothesis is that "formal" adjudication minimizes unfairness,

inequality, and prejudice. *Cf.* Delgado, Dunn, Brown, Lee & Hubbert, *Fairness and Formality: Minimizing the Risk of Prejudice in Alternate Dispute Resolution*, 1985 Wis. L. Rev. 1359. But are juries likely to reflect less prejudice than mediators at dispute resolution centers? Are arbitrators more likely than courtroom judges to be subtly influenced by better presentations made by more expensive counsel? It may be that, whatever the setting, prejudice can be reduced by formal and repeatable procedures. But if there are too many formal procedures, won't the cost and skill required to participate then reintroduce precisely the inequality that formality was designed to remove?

Problem B

THE CASE OF THE TILTED HOUSE—ADJUDICATION OR ARBITRATION? You represent Don and Kathleen Fuller, who purchased a house built by Super Constructors, Inc. The house has a slab that is not level. The discrepancy is significant enough so that it can be perceived by a person sitting in a chair or lying in bed; in fact, the Fullers have found it necessary to prop up some of their furniture with boards, including the bed. There is little controversy about the existence of this defect. In fact, before consulting you, the Fullers availed themselves of the mediation services offered by the Greater Metropolitan Association of Home Builders in the same city, and that body wrote a short report concluding with the words, "Slab is not level. Warrantable." Promptly after undertaking to represent the Fullers, you filed a diversity suit in federal court asserting a claim under the state Consumer Protection Act, which provides liberal recovery of damages, attorney's fees, and (in some instances) punitive damages for breaches of express or implied warranty.

You offer to settle for the current market value of the house and rescission of the contract. The lawyer for Super Constructors refuses this offer and points out that (1) "warrantable" finding is not admissible before a jury (which is true), (2) he has expert witnesses that will deny that there is any defect, and (3) a large proportion of potential jurors will come from home building, sales, or lending industries.

He proposes that, instead of proceeding with the suit, both parties submit to binding arbitration according to a program sponsored by the Greater Metropolitan Association of Home Builders, which can and will consider the "warrantable" finding already made. This program involves a three-person panel; one arbiter is chosen by each of the parties, and these two arbiters then jointly choose the third. Neither formal rules of evidence nor formal rules of law are required to be followed, but the award is enforceable in court unless it is without any rational basis. What factors favor your agreement to submit to arbitration? What disadvantages do you see?

[D] The Reality: Our System Vastly Favors Settlement over Judicial Resolution

Problem C

CAN YOU GUESS WHICH TOTAL IS CLOSEST TO THE NUMBER OF CIVIL JURY TRIALS IN CALIFORNIA SUPERIOR COURTS IN 1990–91? California has fifty-eight (58) superior courts, each with at least one judge (Los Angeles has hundreds). The total in 1991 was 789 judges. Which of the following is closest to the number of California superior court civil jury trials in a typical twelve-month period during 1990–91? The answer is in the margin.[(*)]

a. 1,000 c. 25,000

b. 10,000 d. 50,000

e. 100,000

Samuel R. Gross & Kent D. Syverud, *Don't Try: Civil Verdicts in a System Geared to Settlement*

44 UCLA L. Rev. 1, 2–6 (1996)[(*)]

If it is true, as we often hear, that we are one of the most litigious societies on earth, it is because of our propensity to sue, not our affinity for trials. Of the hundreds of thousands of civil lawsuits that are filed each year in America, the great majority are settled; of those that are not settled, most are ultimately dismissed by the plaintiffs or by the courts; only a few percent are tried to a jury or a judge. This is no accident. We prefer settlements and have designed a system of civil justice that embodies and expresses that preference.... Our culture portrays trial—especially trial by jury—as the quintessential dramatic instrument of justice. Our judicial system operates on a different premise: Trial is a disease, not generally fatal, but serious enough to be avoided at any reasonable cost....

Trials, of course, are important beyond their numbers. For the public, trials have the advantage of visibility. They are open and dramatic, while settlements are usually boring and private—in fact, invisible. Their openness also makes trials attractive subjects for study by scholars, with the added benefit that cases that are fought to the end are likely to present more of the issues that we like to study and need to teach. But for practitioners, trials are important primarily because they influence the terms of settlement for the mass of cases that are not tried; trials cast a major part of the legal shadow within which private bargaining takes place....

(*) The answer is (a) (i.e., 1,000). The actual number is 3,644. If you are surprised by how low the number is, so are most people—but then, that's the point! *See* the authority excerpted in the next item for the backup data.

(*) Copyright 1996. Reprinted with permission of Kent D. Syverud.

... Briefly, we find that most civil jury trials in California (over 70%) concern personal injury claims of one sort or another; that almost all plaintiffs, in trials of every sort, are individuals; that the overwhelming majority of these plaintiffs (especially in personal injury cases) pay their attorneys on a contingent basis; and that almost all defendants, except some large businesses and most government entities, have insurance that covers the cost of defending the lawsuit and all or some of the potential damages. Thus, the typical civil jury trial is a personal injury claim by an individual against a large company, in which neither party is playing with its own money. ...

... [The outcomes of these trials reveal] three notable patterns:

First, most of the total sum of money awarded in these trials is concentrated in a small number of very large cases.

Second, the pattern of outcomes in personal injury trials is very different from that in commercial trials. Plaintiffs lose most personal injury trials—that is, they do less well at trial than they would have by settling—while defendants are more likely to lose in commercial trials. ...

Third, jury verdicts are rarely compromises. Compromise, of course, is the essence of settlement, but compromise judgments are also possible at trial. In fact, they hardly ever happen. When a civil dispute ends in trial there is almost always a clear loser, and usually a clear winner as well. ...

Notes and Questions

(1) *Why So Few Jury Trials?* Which of the following statements do you think is true, and which are related to the reasons for the small number of jury trials? (a) Our society provides too few judges to try many more cases. (b) Judges are lazy. (c) Even if you desire a certain, early date for trial, you can't get one. (d) Judges' time is disproportionately consumed by other matters, including pretrial issues and non-civil trials. (e) Clients are risk-averse. (f) Attorneys are risk-averse. (g) Attorneys are lazy. (h) The expense of litigation makes settlement rational. (i) Settlement is rational in most cases even apart from the expense of litigation. (j) Jury trial, despite our societal adoration of the concept, is less than attractive in reality if you are a participant. (k) Extrinsic factors, such as the attention drained by unresolved grievances or the desire not to discuss sensitive matters with strangers, favor settlement. (l) There are other important factors.

(2) *Why Does One Side or the Other Decline to Settle and Insist on the (Unusual) Resolution of a Trial in a Given Case?* Which of the following do you think are true and related to the reasons why a given case might succumb to (the unusual) resolution of being tried? (a) One side has a bullheaded lawyer. (b) One side has a bullheaded client. (c) The lawyer or the client on one side remains ignorant of the factors that would lead to an accurate assessment of the value of the case. (d) Our society sends everyone the message that it is ethically superior to try the case than to settle. (e) The parties are paying the expenses with someone else's money. (f) There

are structural factors preventing settlement (*e.g.*, only a clean win for plaintiff [or defendant] will result in the payment of enough money to stave off bankruptcy). (g) There are institutional reasons in the form of indecisive or unresponsive management in one client. (h) The judge or lawyers have mismanaged the case. (i) One party or another likes risk. (j) There are other important factors.

(3) *To What Conclusions About Our System Do Your Analyses of the Questions above Lead?* Consider whether your analyses of the above questions might lead to the conclusion that (a) radical or (b) selective reform in our system is warranted or to the conclusion that (c) the system works properly.

(4) *To What Conclusions about Your Role as a Litigation or Trial Lawyer Do Your Analyses of the Questions above Lead?* One possible conclusion is that the typical student in your class who becomes a trial lawyer is actually not going to try very many cases. Consider what other conclusions can be drawn.

II. Negotiation

[A] Methods and Tactics

W. Dorsaneo, D. Crump, E. Carlson & E. Thornburg, *How Does Litigation Get Settled?*

[adapted from] *Texas Civil Procedure: Pretrial Litigation* § 11.06 (4th ed. 1999)(*)

Just how do lawsuits get settled? We all are aware that most disputes are settled rather than tried. How does this happen?

It can happen at almost any stage of the proceedings, in almost any kind of case and in almost any way. The case can be settled before suit is filed, or it may be settled after the Supreme Court has denied certiorari. Small claims cases are settled, and so are death penalty criminal cases. Settlement may be precipitated by a telephone call from defendant to plaintiff, to set up a discovery schedule, culminating in the offhand question: "What will it take to settle this case?" Or it may be precipitated by the stern commands of an irascible federal judge to "sit down and settle this case," together with an implied (or explicit) threat to hold the failure to do so against any party appearing recalcitrant. . . .

The description that follows attempts to catalog and explain certain negotiation techniques. [S]ome of the listed techniques are ethically dubious. However, even an ethical negotiator needs to know *all* of the "tricks of the trade," so that he [or she] can [d]eal with improper ones when they are used by others. Also, this catalog includes several techniques that can only be used in very limited situations. Finally, no claim is made of completeness . . . , because the varieties of successful negotiating behaviors are infinite.

---

[1] The Two Basic Strategies: Refusal to Bargain versus "The" Negotiating Technique (Which Is to Conceal One's Settlement Point and Attempt to Induce the Other Party to Make the First Realistic Offer)

1. REFUSAL TO BARGAIN: THE "FIRM, FAIR OFFER." Conceptually, the simplest negotiating technique is to determine a satisfactory point of resolution, communicate it to one's adversary, and refuse to bargain about it. There are situations in which this technique is the only reasonable approach. For example, the Charles Manson murder case was not plea-bargained, and it could not have been unless the defendant had been willing to accept liability for the maximum sentence. Historically, the "firm, fair offer" is associated with a General Electric Company labor negotiator named Boulware, who customarily figured an acceptable settlement point and communicated it, along with his refusal to bargain, to the union. [T]he technique was so successful at undermining the union's authority that the refusal to bargain has since become the archetypical unfair labor practice. It is sometimes known as "Boulwareism."

The refusal to bargain is effective only if it is convincing enough so that rational negotiators will capitulate to it. Even then, [o]ne may have to litigate often. And if one deals each time with a different adversary who has no reason to know or be convinced of one's track record, the firm, fair offer will not be an effective technique, because many will interpret it as an invitation to bargain further. An institutional litigator with a large volume of claims may successfully use the technique.... The result will be that the litigant will have to try many cases that might more rationally be settled, but it may believe that its "tough" reputation among plaintiff's attorneys has offsetting value.

Frequently, a prosecutor's office may be in a position to use a modified "firm, fair offer" approach. Interestingly, when given descriptions of such a system, law students generally appear to consider it ethically superior for a prosecutor's office, on the theory that variations in sentences owing to negotiating ability should be minimized.

2. CONCEALMENT OF ONE'S OWN SETTLEMENT POINT. This is the opposite result from the firm, fair offer, and in a world of strangers negotiating for maximum advantage, it is generally the more successful approach. The technique works because an opponent who does not know the negotiator's true settlement point may have undervalued his own position, or overvalued the resistance of the negotiator, so that the opponent may make greater concessions than are really necessary to settle the dispute to the satisfaction of the negotiator. Conversely, a negotiator who discloses his true settlement point has indicated to his opponent the maximum concession the opponent need make. An opponent may not believe a statement of one's "true" settlement point and may require one to decide between further concessions and litigation.

3. INDUCING THE OPPONENT TO START THE BARGAINING. There is an advantage to having the opponent state his position first. By doing so, a negotiator

not only can avoid giving away his own settlement point, but he can also begin to assemble data from which he can infer his opponent's settlement point.

An inexperienced opponent may be induced to make the first offer by being asked the question, "What will it take to settle this case?" One with more experience is likely to respond differently. He will make a first offer that is unrealistically high, concealing his realization that it is unrealistically high, and thus he will avoid disclosing any information about his settlement point.... This tactic—that of making an unreasonable offer as the first statement of position and communicating a belief that it is reasonable—is so common that it might be deemed *the* fundamental negotiating technique. The belief in reasonableness (which is frequently deceptive) may be stated explicitly, or it may be implied in non-verbal conduct, but it is an essential part of the technique.

CONCEALMENT AND INDUCEMENT TO START BARGAINING AS "THE" NEGOTIATION TECHNIQUE? Notice that this approach—the exaggerated, unrealistic first offer coupled with efforts to get the opponent to start the real bargaining—is *the* most frequent negotiating technique. If you think about it, the only alternative is for the negotiator to state his or her bottom line immediately and insist on it—and to refuse to bargain from that position.

Many people dislike negotiating because of the prevalence and undeniable success of this simple but seemingly dishonest technique. Several ethical theories have been advanced to justify the technique, including the argument that negotiation is a separate endeavor with rules different from that of other human activity [or] the argument that there may be an element of "self-fulfilling prophecy" in the mere statement of one's true position because it sets, instead, the perimeter of the opponent's maximum concession.

[2] Techniques for Carrying Out the Strategy or for Closing the Gap and Getting to Agreement

4. THE APPEARANCE OF IRRATIONALITY. Negotiation is a rational process. It depends upon the willingness of both parties to concede something to get something in return. If one of the parties is irrational, no negotiation can take place.... [A] person negotiating with another perceived as "crazy" may understand that he will have to make greater concessions than he would against a rational opponent, or will have resort to a test of force.

Anger, cantankerousness, indifference to consequences and even ignorance in some cases enhance a negotiator's bargaining strength.... It follows that the *appearance* of anger, cantankerousness, indifference to consequences or ignorance may likewise create a bargaining advantage. Successful negotiators are often good actors.

5. BLAMING THE CLIENT OR SOME OTHER PERSON OVER WHOM ONE HAS NO CONTROL. This technique is really a different form of irrationality. It puts the opponent in the position of seeming to argue with a rational person, [b]ut with the final result to be determined by another person impervious to rational

arguments. "It's entirely up to him, and he refuses your offer," is a typical way of invoking this technique.... The "Mutt and Jeff Routine" (in which one of a team of negotiators [u]ses the feigned irrationality of another on the same team to induce concessions) is another example.

It should go without saying that blaming it on the client may be a statement of the true facts. But the point is that it may also be a pure negotiating technique. The client may have already given settlement authority to the lawyer or [w]ould accept the advice of the lawyer, but the lawyer pretends that the client is independent.

6. USING A MEDIATOR. Sometimes, a person confronted with an ostensibly irrational opponent may call in a neutral third person to help dispose of the claim. Not infrequently in lawsuit litigation, the trial judge can be induced to occupy this role (assuming he does not naturally undertake it). A mediator is a useful countervailing tool against most of the preceding techniques, undercutting the effort to avoid stating a realistic position as well as blaming the client.

7. APPEALS TO THE MERITS. Inexperienced negotiators tend to place more stock in statements about the merits of the dispute than do experienced negotiators. However, there is an advantage to having one's opponent know the facts advantageous to one's position. Accordingly, even experienced negotiators often take great pains to ensure that the opposing side is aware of all evidence and law that could possibly be helpful. The difference between the inexperienced and experienced negotiator is the former's belief that the latter will accept such information as dispositive.

Experienced negotiators do, however, do a fair amount of posturing over the merits of the suit. This posturing often takes the form of expressing unshakable conviction in the prediction that one will prevail. This approach is an effort to shore up the appearance of reasonableness that is essential to the unrealistically high offer technique. The experienced negotiator will also take a position more extreme than that of the inexperienced negotiator on the merits, and he will advance it with ironclad certainty. These approaches are part of the strategies of concealment of position.

8. THROWING ONESELF ON THE OPPONENT'S MERCY. A negotiator may say, "We can't possibly dispute your claim. You've got us over a barrel. Please don't take advantage of your superior position and punish us." ... [T]he technique is reserved to peculiar situations, specifically those in which one has little or no bargaining strength and the opponent does not seem cold blooded enough to take absolute advantage....

What must be borne in mind is that throwing one's self on the mercy of one's opponent is a bargaining technique.... For example, it is not unheard of for a person using this gambit, and who is successful in inducing a "merciful" offer, to respond by saying, "Oh! That doesn't seem fair. What I had in mind was the following," and then state an unreasonably high counteroffer, having thus induced his opponent to make the first step in the bargaining.

9. INDUCING THE OPPONENT TO BARGAIN AGAINST HERSELF. Sometimes, an inexperienced opponent, having made the first offer, can be induced to make the first concession, too. The methodology is familiar: "Your offer is not even in the ballpark. Come up with something more realistic and then we'll talk."

[A] pattern of concessions by one party not matched by the other tends to carry over into later stages of the process.

10. FORCING TWO OPPONENTS TO BARGAIN AGAINST EACH OTHER. This technique is often used by experienced negotiators in sales situations, sometimes with a "phantom" second bidder. In lawsuits, it requires the presence of multiple parties. The "Mary Carter" agreement, named after a case in which the Mary Carter Paint Company was one of the litigants, enables a plaintiff to settle with one of multiple defendants on the condition that the settling defendant will be repaid out of any recovery from others. [E]ach of the defendants is exposed to the implied threat that such an agreement will be made with the others. Plaintiff may make the threat explicit, saying, "If you don't settle the case, [I]'ll make an agreement with the other defendant and that will give me a war chest to go after you."

11. "GANGING UP." The Mary Carter agreement or, the multiple-party situation in general, carries another implied threat. A settling defendant may be retained in the lawsuit and may assist the plaintiff in pinning blame on the other defendant. A third party impleaded by a defendant may threaten, "If you don't release me, I'm going to cooperate with the plaintiff in pinning blame on you."

12. FLATTERY, CLUBBINESS, AND OTHER ATTITUDES. Experienced negotiators sometimes resort to flattery ("You're too good a lawyer to be handling this kind of case"). Or the negotiator may depict himself and the opposing lawyer as having more in common than the opponent and his client ("You have my sympathies in having to deal with a person as crazy as that. [I] know what you must be going through"). Behind these statements lies the psychological truth that it is easier for a person to make concessions if it can be done in an atmosphere of dignity. . . .

13. TIMING. Time is usually on one side or the other in a negotiation. The person who can afford to wait, who can give the appearance of being able to afford to wait, or who forces himself to wait, has an advantage. . . . A litigant who has just been ordered to prepare a pretrial order that will require the assimilation and labeling of 100,000 documents may be more willing to settle at a reasonable figure than one who has done the work and is prepared for trial.

. . . Bargaining terminated with all parties angry may be resumed at a later session with time having erased the rancor from the process. Experienced negotiators . . . know that repeated statement of the same position, made in several separate sessions with intervening periods of waiting, is an effective negotiating technique.

14. ACTIVITY. Vigorous and aggressive activity moving the litigation toward a point of conclusion can have advantageous effects. Many cases settle on the courthouse steps. [T]he initiation of sequential steps before trial, including discovery, a motion for summary judgment and like steps, communicating to the opponent a

determination to resolve the case and forcing the opponent, repeatedly, to confront and evaluate the situation, is an effective means of precipitating settlement.

At the same time, however, activity must be undertaken with the realization that it often costs money. A litigant who undertakes vigorous and purposeful activity, only to find that he has expended large amounts of money in discovery and in unsuccessful pretrial motions, may find his opponent's settlement position unaffected....

15. COLLATERAL CONSEQUENCES TO THE OPPONENT. There are many litigants whose initial reaction is to "fight it all the way to the Supreme Court" until educated as to the cost of doing so. Some negotiators, taking this fact one step further, tend to increase expense to the opponent by causing collateral consequences to ensue. The drafting of interrogatories that are expensive to answer, the taking of lengthy depositions that tie up the time of the opposing lawyer or make a client himself realize how much of his time is being wasted, or the use of discovery to embarrass, threaten trade secrets and the like are all examples.... Many of these tactics are ethically dubious, but the lawyer needs to know them to defend against them.

16. DEADLINES AND "LOCKING IN." Some negotiators place deadlines upon the acceptance of a given offer in order to avoid the opponent's "riding" the case to get the benefit of future developments. Thus one may say, "If you wait until discovery is finished and I'm ready for trial, my settlement offer is going to go up by $10,000." The effectiveness of this technique is dependent upon its credibility. It is a variant of the "firm, fair offer," and, like that technique, it depends upon the opponent's belief that one is indeed "locked in" to the deadline....

17. FOCAL POINT SOLUTIONS. As differences narrow in the negotiation process, the likelihood of a "splitting of the difference" or adoption of some "standard" solution close to the bargaining position of the parties increases. Round numbers are more likely resolutions.... The experienced negotiator... attempts to make and elicit offers aiming for the elusive "point in the middle" that is advantageous to him. [I]f the parties' latest positions are $5,000 and $12,000, respectively, the... negotiator... will try to keep his position a respectable increment over $10,000, so that this figure, rather than, say, $7,500, will be the natural focal point.

18. DRAFTING THE AGREEMENT. In a straight monetary claim situation, the drafting of the agreement may not be highly important. But in litigation involving a multiplicity of issues, such as a divorce or employment discrimination case, it can be a significant advantage to be the drafter. There are frequently minor points that are incompletely negotiated. The drafter, naturally, drafts these so as to resolve them in her favor. There is always the likelihood that the opponent will not notice the difference... or that some objections may seem too small... to make.

19. CONTROL OF THE AGENDA. In a litigation matter with many issues to resolve, the person who sets the order of discussion may have an advantage. For some reason, concessions seem to come more easily at the beginning of a negotiation process (or at its end, when agreement is approached). Thus the experienced

negotiator attempts to cause those matters most important to him to be considered early. She may even insist that the resolution of a particularly important point is a "precondition" to further negotiation. Conversely, he may suggest with reference to an important, but sticky, point, "Let's put that issue to the side and come back to it later," believing that his opponent will, in the meantime, acquire . . . a stake in preserving agreement. . . .

20. THE "BARGAINING CHIP" OR THE FALSE DEMAND. One may ask for something one does not really want or expect so that one may appear to give it up in exchange for something else. If this happens, one has "given" a concession without really making one. Sometimes, for example, a party to a divorce case who really wants a reasonable property settlement and visitation schedule will demand custody as well. This technique (like the unrealistically high offer) is dependent upon the concealment of one's true position; *i.e.*, it is dependent upon the opponent's belief that the bargaining chip represents a real desire conceded. And it can be ethically dubious.

21. "REVERSE PSYCHOLOGY." Against a perverse opponent, one expected to take a contrary position simply because it is contrary, one can occasionally get what one wants by appearing to be asking for the opposite. "The last thing we want is custody. My client wants to be free of the responsibility." Obviously, this technique [which sometimes is called the "Bre'r Rabbit"; can you see why?] is useful in its purest form only in very limited situations.

22. PHYSICAL FACTORS. Negotiating on familiar ground, among familiar people and under familiar conditions gives one a psychological edge. . . .

23. DIRECT INVOLVEMENT OF THE PRINCIPAL. Occasionally, a negotiator may see some advantage in having his opponent and his principal communicate directly. The opponent may have undervalued the determination or persuasiveness of the principal (or vice versa). In some situations, *e.g.* criminal defense or personal injury plaintiff's litigation, exposure of the opponent to the human qualities of the principal may have a moderating influence. Sometimes direct communication facilitates balanced concessions that would be difficult to obtain through an intermediary. In a divorce case, [t]he "four parties meeting" (with both attorneys and both clients present) may be a way of cutting through the posturing [a]nd animosity.

24. MAKING THE OPPONENT FEEL HE HAS NEGOTIATED CAPABLY. An experienced negotiator generally refrains from "crowing" about an attractive result. Knowing that he may have to meet his opponent again, he instead congratulates the opponent (which is the collegial approach, anyway).

25. THE TEST OF STRENGTH, TOTAL OR PARTIAL. It is worth reemphasizing that not every dispute can be settled by negotiation. Some require a total—or partial—test of strength. The willingness to "go to the mat" is part of the arsenal of the skillful negotiator. However, the hallmark of the good negotiator is the settlement, without the delay or expense or trauma of litigation, of that vast majority of disputes that can be settled. . . .

Notes and Questions

(1) *Negotiation Ethics.* Most of the preceding discussion has been done without consideration of the ethical aspects of each technique. Accordingly, it seems appropriate to ask, which of the preceding techniques seem most vulnerable to ethical criticisms? Actually, the preceding discussion omits some of the most dubious tactics. One team of writers posits the following technique: "After agreement has been reached, have your client reject it and raise his demands." Meltsner & Schrag, *Negotiating Techniques for Legal Services Lawyers*, 7 CLEARINGHOUSE REVIEW 262 (1973). The authors acknowledge that "This is the most ethically dubious of the tactics listed, but there will be occasions where a lawyer will have to defend against it or even employ it." [For further discussion of ethical issues, see subsection [D], below.]

(2) *How Important Are Negotiation Skills to Practicing Lawyers?* Decotiis and Steele observed a sample of skilled general practitioners and recorded how the practitioners spent their professional time. Decotiis & Steele, *The Skills of the Lawyering Process*, 41 TEX. B.J. 483 (1977). They conclude that negotiation is "the most highly developed skill" employed by the lawyers observed.

(3) *What (if Any) Importance Do Negotiating Lawyers Attach to the Underlying Merits (Are the Merits Irrelevant)?: Alexander, Do the Merits Matter? A Study of Settlements in Securities Class Actions*, 43 STAN. L. REV. 497 (1991). Professor Alexander studied this question in the context of securities class actions. Her stunning conclusion: These actions settle for relatively consistent percentages of the projected damages, apparently uninfluenced by the relative merits of the plaintiffs' liability cases! In "big" cases, both sides are risk-averse. The "bet the company" (or "bet the plaintiffs' attorney's fee") approach becomes "unthinkable." In this atmosphere, the lawyers all know that the case will not be tried, and so settlement negotiations tend to be "based on non-merits factors." Question: Has our system reached a point where the merits of litigation are irrelevant?

Problem D

NEGOTIATING TACTICS. Identify the technique that is used in each of the following negotiation statements and explain why the technique may "work," when it would be useful, how it might be defended against and whether it is ethical.

(a) "When we have a case that we don't think there's a good chance of liability on, we always take the position of offering out-of-pocket medical expenses, only."

(b) "This lawsuit's going to cost a lot just to try. Why don't you get with your man and tell me your best shot, and I'll see if I can get my people to take it."

(c) "My client is being totally unreasonable about this case. I'd almost be willing to recommend your last offer, but what it amounts to is that you're really dealing with him. I do think I can get him to take it if you up the offer another $5000, though."

(d) "Well, you keep telling me that we can't win on the merits of the case. Frankly, you're probably correct. But let's talk about what's right. The suit's incidental to the fact that your folks know they owe my man something. Why don't you approach it on that basis? I'm sure my man will take anything that is fair."

(e) "If you guys don't come up with at least a hundred thousand, I'm going to be forced to make a deal with the other defendants and have them testify at the trial."

(f) "My client really doesn't want the corporation to buy her stock back, even though that's what she's suing for, because then she'd miss out on what looks like a really good deal. The last thing she really wants is to be cashed out."

[B] Encouragement by the Court

KOTHE v. SMITH, 771 F.2d 667 (2d Cir. 1985). Read (or re-read) this case, which appears in §III[B] of Chapter 8, above. Judge Sweet recommended that this medical malpractice suit be settled for between $20,000 and $30,000 and warned the parties that if they settled for a comparable amount after trial had begun, he would impose sanctions on the dilatory party. Although the plaintiff's attorney had informed the judge that the plaintiff would settle for $20,000, he had requested confidentiality and had communicated a demand of $50,000 to the defendant. After one day of trial, the case was settled for $20,000, and Judge Sweet imposed sanctions in the form of a requirement that the defendant pay $1,000 each to the plaintiff and the plaintiff's expert witness, plus $480 to the clerk of the court (presumably representing jury fees and other costs to the Government).

The Court of Appeals reversed, reasoning that Rule 16(c)(7) was "designed to encourage pretrial settlement discussions" but not to "impose settlement negotiations on unwilling litigants." Further, settlement was a "two-way street," yet the defendant had never received an offer below $20,000; furthermore, the defendant's attorney should not be condemned "for changing his evaluation of the case after listening to [the plaintiff's] testimony." The Court of Appeals closed with a commendation of Judge Sweet, however, for his efforts.

Notes and Questions

(1) *Permissible Sanctions for Failure to Participate in "Good Faith."* Rule 16 permits sanctions in various situations for failing to participate in good faith in pretrial conference activities. Would sanctions be permissible if the defendant's attorney contemptuously refused even to consider settlement negotiations but then settled after

trial had begun for $20,000? [If not, is there any meaning to the provisions of Rule 16 empowering the judge to encourage settlement?]

(2) *Proper "Persuasion" Versus "Coercion."* Might it be difficult to tell the difference between "encouragement" of settlement and "coercion" by the judge?

(3) *A Case to Contrast with Kothe: Newton v. A.C. & S., Inc.*, 918 F.2d 1121 (3d Cir. 1990). "In an innovative effort to manage its trial docket, the District Court instituted the practice of 'stacking' asbestos cases. Under this practice, the District Court assigned the asbestos injury cases to a designated time slot. As a scheduled case is disposed of, either by trial or settlement, the District Court moves the next case into the allotted slot. To give the parties of the next case in line sufficient notice of their trial date, the District Court judge sets a deadline for settlement negotiations of two weeks prior to the trial date. If the litigants settle after the deadline, the district court imposes a fine regardless of fault and without a prior hearing." This procedure certainly is innovative. But is it lawful? Yes, said the Court of Appeals: "[I]mposing sanctions for unjustified failure to comply with the Court's schedule for settlement is entirely consistent with the spirit of Rule 16." That Rule is designed "to maximize the efficiency of the court system by insisting that attorneys [c]ooperate with the court and abandon practices which unreasonably interfere with [e]xpeditious management." The Court of Appeals nevertheless reversed because the amount of the fine ($1,000) was not tied to any cost factors.

[C] Legal Rules Encouraging Settlement: Pre-Judgment Interest, Attorney's Fee Changes, and Rule 68

Notes and Questions

(1) *The Influence of Pre-Judgment Interest on the Settlement Process.* If a state adopts a rule of substantive law awarding pre-judgment interest to the prevailing plaintiff, what impact would this rule have on the encouragement of settlement? (Would it actually induce settlements more frequently or earlier in litigation—or would it simply shift the balance in favor of plaintiffs to some degree?) Reconsider the materials on pre-judgment interest in §V of Chapter 14, above.

(2) *The Influence of Attorney's Fees.* Would a rule awarding attorney's fees to a prevailing plaintiff encourage settlement (or would it shift the balance of advantages in favor of plaintiffs, so that litigation would settle for greater amounts)? Might such a rule be more effective if it resulted in an award of attorney's fees to the prevailing party, whether plaintiff or defendant, whichever party prevailed? Reconsider the materials on attorney's fees in §V of Chapter 14, above. In *City of Riverside v. Rivera*, reproduced in that section, the Court held that recoverable attorney's fees are not required to be proportional to the amount of the recovery; it upheld an award of attorney's fees of roughly $250,000 where the recovery was roughly $33,000. What effect would you expect that this holding would have upon settlements?

(3) *Rule 68: Direct Encouragement of Settlement by Encouragement of Offers of Judgment.* The *City of Riverside* case, however, is only part of the story. Rule 68 provides for a pretrial offer of judgment and cuts off recovery of costs after the offer if the plaintiff recovers less than the offer. Consider the case that follows; together with the *City of Riverside* case, doesn't it seem likely to exert strong influence on settlements? Is it fair to plaintiffs? Are the two cases, taken together, fair to defendants? *See* Note, *The Impact of Proposed Rule 68 on Civil Rights Litigation*, 34 Colum. L. Rev. 719 (1984).

Read Fed. R. Civ. P. 68 (offer of judgment).

Marek v. Chesny

473 U.S. 1 (1985)

Chief Justice Burger delivered the opinion of the Court.

We granted certiorari to decide whether attorney's fees incurred by a plaintiff subsequent to an offer of settlement under Federal Rule of Civil Procedure 68 must be paid by the defendant under 42 U.S.C. § 1988, when the plaintiff recovers a judgment less than the offer.

I

Petitioners, three police officers, in answering a call on a domestic disturbance, shot and killed respondent's adult son. Respondent [f]iled suit against the officers in the United States District Court under 42 U.S.C. § 1983 and state tort law.

Prior to trial, petitioners made a timely offer of settlement "for a sum, including costs now accrued and attorney's fees, of ONE HUNDRED THOUSAND ($100,000) DOLLARS." Respondent did not accept the offer. The case went to trial and respondent was awarded $5,000 on the state law "wrongful death" claim, $52,000 for the § 1983 violation, and $3,000 in punitive damages.

Respondent filed a request for $171,692.47 in costs, including attorney's fees. This amount included costs incurred after the settlement offer. Petitioners opposed the claim for post-offer costs, relying on Federal Rule of Civil Procedure 68, which shifts to the plaintiff all "costs" incurred subsequent to an offer of judgment not exceeded by the ultimate recovery at trial. Petitioners argued that attorney's fees are part of the "costs" covered by Rule 68. The District Court agreed with petitioners and declined to award respondent "costs, including attorney's fees, incurred after the offer of judgment." ... The parties subsequently agreed that $32,000 fairly represented the allowable costs, including attorney's fees, accrued prior to petitioner's offer of settlement. Respondent appealed the denial of post-offer costs.

The Court of Appeals reversed.... The court rejected what it termed the "rather mechanical linking up of Rule 68 and section 1988." ... Plaintiffs' attorneys, the court reasoned, would be forced to "think very hard" before rejecting even an inadequate offer, and would be deterred from bringing good faith actions because of the prospect of losing the right to attorney's fees if a settlement offer more favorable than the ultimate recovery were rejected. . . . [We reverse.]

II

Rule 68 provides that if a timely pretrial offer of settlement is not accepted and "the judgment finally obtained by the offeree is not more favorable than the offer, the offeree must pay *the costs incurred after the making of the offer.*" Fed. Rule Civ. Proc. 68 (emphasis added). [The 2007 "restyling" amendments changed this language slightly.—Eds.] The plain purpose of Rule 68 is to encourage settlement and avoid litigation. . . .

A

The first question we address is whether petitioners' offer was valid under Rule 68. Respondent contends that the offer was invalid because it lumped petitioners' proposal for damages with their proposal for costs. Respondent argues that Rule 68 requires that an offer must separately recite the amount that the defendant is offering in settlement of the substantive claim and the amount he is offering to cover accrued costs. . . .

The critical feature of this portion of the Rule is that the offer be one that *allows judgment to be taken against the defendant for both the damages caused by the challenged conduct and the costs then accrued.* . . . Accordingly, it is immaterial whether the offer recites that costs are included, whether it specifies the amount the defendant is allowing for costs, or for that matter, whether it refers to costs at all. As long as the offer does not implicitly or explicitly provide that the judgment *not* include costs, a timely offer will be valid.

This construction of the Rule best furthers the objective of the Rule, which is to encourage settlements. . . .

B

The second question we address is whether the term "costs" in Rule 68 includes attorney's fees awardable under 42 U.S.C. § 1988. By the time the Federal Rules of Civil Procedure were adopted in 1938, federal statutes had authorized and defined awards of costs to prevailing parties for more than 85 years. . . . Unlike in England, such "costs" generally had not included attorney's fees; under the "American Rule," each party had been required to bear its own attorney's fees. The "American Rule" as applied in federal courts, however, had become subject to certain exceptions by the late 1930's. [B]ut most of the exceptions were found in federal statutes that directed courts to award attorney's fees as part of costs in particular cases. . . .

The authors of Federal Rule of Civil Procedure 68 were fully aware of these exceptions to the American Rule. . . . In this setting, given the importance of "costs" to the Rule, it is very unlikely that this omission was mere oversight; on the contrary, the most reasonable inference is that the term "costs" in Rule 68 was intended to refer to all costs properly awardable under the relevant substantive statute or other authority.... Thus, absent Congressional expressions to the contrary, where the underlying statute defines "costs" to include attorney's fees, we are satisfied such fees are to be included as costs for purposes of Rule 68.... Here, respondents sued under 42 U.S.C. § 1983. Pursuant to the Civil Rights Attorney's Fees Awards Act of 1976, 42 U.S.C. § 1988, a prevailing party in a § 1983 action may be awarded attorney's fees "as part of the costs." Since Congress expressly included attorney's fees as "costs" available to a plaintiff in a § 1983 suit, such fees are subject to the cost-shifting provision of Rule 68....

To be sure, application of Rule 68 will require plaintiffs to "think very hard" about whether continued litigation is worthwhile; that is precisely what Rule 68 contemplates. This effect of Rule 68, however, is in no sense inconsistent with the congressional policies underlying § 1983 and § 1988.... This case presents a good example: the $139,692 in post-offer legal services resulted in a recovery $8,000 less than petitioner's settlement offer. Given Congress' focus on the success achieved, we are not persuaded that shifting the post-offer costs to respondent in these circumstances would in any sense thwart its intent under § 1988.... [Reversed.]

[The concurring opinions of Justices Powell and Rehnquist are omitted.]

Justice Brennan, with whom Justice Marshall and Justice Blackmun join, dissenting....

Congress has enacted well over 100 attorney's fees statutes, many of which would appear to be affected by today's decision.... Congress has employed a variety of slightly different wordings in these statutes. It sometimes has referred to the awarding of "attorney's fees as *part of* the costs," to "costs *including* attorney's fees," and to "attorney's fees and *other* litigation costs." ... But Congress frequently has referred in other statutes to the awarding of "costs *and* a reasonable attorney's fee," of "costs *together* with a reasonable attorney's fee," or simply of "attorney's fees" without reference to costs. Under the Court's "plain language" analysis, Rule 68 obviously will *not* include [a]ttorney's fees as a settlement incentive [u]nder these statutes because they do not refer to fees "as" costs....

Although the Court's opinion fails to discuss any of the problems reviewed above, it does devote some space to arguing that its interpretation of Rule 68 "is in no sense inconsistent with the Congressional policies underlying § 1983 and § 1988." ...

The Court is wrong. Congress has instructed that attorney's fee entitlement under § 1988 be governed by a *reasonableness* standard. Until today the Court always has recognized that this standard precludes reliance on any mechanical "bright-line" rules automatically denying a portion of fees, acknowledging that such "mathematical approach[es]" provide "little aid in determining what is a reasonable fee in light of all the relevant factors." ...

... Interpreting Rule 68 in its current version to include attorney's fees will lead to a number of skewed settlement incentives that squarely conflict with Congress' intent. To discuss but one example, Rule 68 [g]ives the plaintiff only 10 days to accept or reject. The Court's decision inevitably will encourage defendants who know they have violated the law to make "lowball" offers immediately after suit is filed and before [d]iscovery. . . . Indeed, because Rule 68 offers may be made recurrently without limitation, defendants will be well advised to make ever-slightly larger offers throughout the discovery process and before plaintiffs have conducted all reasonably necessary discovery. . . .

Notes and Questions

(1) *"Costs" in a Suit on a Contract That Provides for Attorney's Fees.* As explained in *Marek v. Chesny,* above, the term "costs" was intended to refer to "all costs properly awardable under the relevant substantive statute or other authority," and thus, when the underlying statute defines "costs" as including attorney fees, such fees are included as costs for Rule 68 purposes. In addition, in *Utility Automation 2000, Inc. v. Choctawhatchee Electric Cooperative, Inc.*, 298 F.3d 1238 (11th Cir. 2002), the Eleventh Circuit held that a contract provision authorizing an award of fees to the prevailing party in any action to enforce the contract may be sufficient to award fees as "costs" under Rule 68. The Eleventh Circuit noted that the underlying contract provided that "the prevailing party shall be entitled to recover such legal expenses, including, without limitation, reasonable attorney's fees, court costs and all related expenses." The circuit court held that this contract provision defined fees as costs, and therefore permitted an award of fees as "costs" under Rule 68.

(2) *What about Rule 68 in a Class Action?* In a case involving a Rule 68 offer of judgment in a class action, the Third Circuit refused to hold that such an offer, made to the named plaintiff before the filing of a class certification motion, mooted the lawsuit. In *Weiss v. Regal Collections,* 385 F.3d 337 (3d Cir. 2004), involving the Fair Debt Collection Practices Act, the court concluded that permitting a defendant to moot the action by picking off the named plaintiff would frustrate the purposes of the class action device.

[D] Ethics and Overreaching

STATE NATIONAL BANK OF EL PASO v. FARAH MANUFACTURING CO., 678 S.W.2d 661 (Tex. App.-El Paso 1984, no writ). This decision took an unusual view of negotiation. The Bank, whose loan to Farah was in default, wanted to remove Farah's president and negotiated with Farah to do so. Farah's lawyer told Farah's representatives that the Bank would shut Farah down if it did not remove the president. Donohoe, an attorney for one of the lenders, wrote a letter to the company's board stating that William Farah's return was "unacceptable to the Banks" and that "the Banks will not grant any waiver of default based thereon." Farah did remove the president, but under its new management, the company produced a product line that was not what the market demanded, priced it inappropriately, and merchandised it poorly, producing mounting losses. William Farah fought to regain his management position. Ultimately, he was successful. After his return, the company was restored to profitability.

Farah then sued the Bank on grounds that the lawyer's representation about shutting down the bank amounted to fraud, because the Bank's administration had not actually decided on that course of action. A jury found the Bank guilty of fraud. A state court of appeals affirmed, leaving a holding that meant that what amounted to "puffing" in negotiations could be fraud. The Bank, it held, "cannot overcome the legal and factual sufficiency of the evidence that the lenders [made representations] which they knew to be false and which, as intended, were relied upon and acted upon by [William] Farah and other board members." The case eventually settled, preventing review of the decision by the state supreme court, leaving the decision to stand.

The decision was widely regarded with astonishment. It meant that normal negotiating behavior was tortious. Bank counsel began giving advice to clients that they should "not negotiate" with troubled borrowers. Either declare default and foreclose or don't, they said; but don't make statements about what you otherwise may do. And that advice, of course, was harmful to borrowers and lenders alike. The *Farah* decision has not been followed, and the state supreme court has treated it as something of an outlier. *See, e.g. Wal-Mart Stores, Inc. v. Sturges,* 52 S.W.3d 711 (Tex. 2001). Consider the following case, which looks at the subject differently.

United States v. Weimert

819 F.3d 351 (7th Cir. 2016)

[In the midst of the 2008–09 financial crisis, a struggling Wisconsin bank called AnchorBank, through its vice president David Weimert, sold its share in a commercial real estate development. The sale exceeded the bank's target price by about one third. Weimert was later charged with and convicted for criminal wire fraud. The court of appeals here sets the conviction aside.] . . .

Federal wire fraud is an expansive tool, but as best we can tell, no previous case at the appellate level has treated as criminal a person's lack of candor about the negotiating positions of parties to a business deal. In commercial negotiations, it is not unusual for parties to conceal from others their true goals, values, priorities, or reserve prices in a proposed transaction. When we look closely at the evidence, the only ways in which Weimert misled anyone concerned such negotiating positions. . . . All the actual terms of the deal, however, were fully disclosed and subject to negotiation. There is no evidence that Weimert misled anyone about any material facts or about promises of future actions. While one can understand the bank's later decision to fire Weimert when the deception about negotiating positions came to light, his actions did not add up to federal wire fraud. Weimert is entitled to judgment of acquittal.

Buyers and sellers negotiate prices and other terms. To state the obvious, they will often try to mislead the other party about the prices and terms they are willing to accept. Such deceptions are not criminal. . . . [S]uppose a seller is willing to accept $28,000 for a new car listed for sale at $32,000. A buyer is actually willing to pay $32,000, but he first offers $28,000. When that offer is rejected and the seller demands $32,000, the buyer responds: "I won't pay more than $29,000." The seller replies: "I'll take $31,000 but not a penny less." After another round of offers and demands, each one falsely labeled "my final offer," the parties ultimately agree on a price of $30,000. Each side has gained from deliberately false misrepresentations about its negotiating position. Each has affected the other side's decisions. If the transaction involves interstate wires, has each committed wire fraud, each defrauding the other of $2,000? Of course not. But why not?

The government's answer at oral argument was the absence of "intent to defraud." That answer begs the question. How do we recognize "intent to defraud" if a party has gained a better deal by misleading the other party about its negotiating position? . . . The better answer is that negotiating parties, and certainly the sophisticated businessmen in this case, do not expect complete candor about negotiating positions, as distinct from facts and promises of future behavior. Deception about negotiating positions—about reserve prices and other terms and their relative importance—should not be considered material for purposes of mail and wire fraud statutes.

In the Restatement (Second) of Torts treatment of fraud, for example, statements about a party's opinions, preferences, priorities, and bottom lines are generally not considered statements of fact material to the transaction. See Restatement (Second) of Torts § 538A cmts. b, g (distinguishing between representations of facts—where the maker has definite knowledge—and opinions—including a "maker's judgment as to quality, value, authenticity or similar matters as to which opinions may be expected to differ"). Rules of professional conduct for attorneys require honesty in dealing with others, but they draw a similar line on negotiation positions. See Model R. Prof. Conduct 4.1(a) cmt. 2 ("[C]ertain types of statements ordinarily are not taken as statements of material fact. Estimates of price or value placed on the subject of a transaction and a party's intentions as to an acceptable settlement of a claim are ordinarily in this category. . . .") . . .

Notes and Questions

(1) *Should It be a Tort to Negotiate?* In both *Farah* and *Weimert*, the parties were accused of wrongdoing because they overstated the strength of their positions and thereby concealed their settlement points. Yet it might be said that the essence of negotiation is the statement of settlement demands in such a way as to assemble information about the opponent's ultimate settlement point while avoiding tipping one's own hand. In fact, a member of the company's board in *Farah* used precisely the same technique against a representative of the bank, for the stated reason of "push[ing] him to the very brink . . . and find[ing] out." Won't the parties necessarily have to "bluff," at least by what they imply to their opponents, if they are to engage in normal negotiating behavior? In fact, *Weimert* shows that the notion of

"puffing" is accepted in the Restatement (Second) of Torts, the ABA Model Rules of Professional Conduct, and other business literature.

(2) *What Reasons or Justifications Underlie the Farah Holding?* What is it about the *Farah* case that explains or justifies the result? Consider the following concepts, all of which can influence the ethical boundaries of a negotiation:

(a) *Donohoe's Status as an Attorney and Spokesperson for the Lender Group.* Do more restrictive ethical norms apply to attorneys than to lay persons? If so, does that difference explain the *Farah* result? *Cf.* Perschbacher, *Regulating Lawyers' Negotiations, supra.*

(b) *The Defendants' Status as Banks.* Were the banks held liable, in part, because they were banks? Is it possible that "bluffing" on the part of debtors is proper, while the same conduct, if engaged in by creditors, is a tortious "misrepresentation"?

(c) *"Bargaining Power."* Did the result follow because the court saw Farah as a debtor in trouble and the banks as solvent, so that they had more "bargaining power"? If your answer is yes, would a different result follow if the banks were in financial trouble themselves and dependent upon recovery of the funds they had loaned to Farah?

(d) *"Oppression."* The court's holding included the conclusion that the default warning could have been considered "oppressive." But what distinguishes oppressive as versus non-oppressive bargaining by a bank with a troubled debtor?

In contrast, in the *Weimert* case, none of these arguments—not even the government's claims of an "intent to defraud"—were persuasive. Instead, the appellate court flatly accepted a degree of deception in negotiation. Where the parties are sufficiently sophisticated, where the actual terms of the deal were adequately disclosed, and where the withheld information is not material, the parties are free to reach an agreement.

Problem E

BUT THERE ARE LIMITS, EVEN IF THEY ARE DIFFICULT TO IDENTIFY. Imagine the following two scenarios. (1) During negotiations, an attorney says, "My client was not driving the car when the accident happened." In her own heart of hearts, this lawyer believes that her client *was* driving the car, although discovery has shown that the client denies it and the evidence is ambiguous. Has the attorney committed fraud or misconduct by being an advocate for his client's position? (2) Immediately before settling, one attorney asks the other, "Has the court entered an order on my motion to exclude evidence?" The other attorney knows that the court *has* entered an order and that it is unfavorable to this attorney's side—but answers, falsely, "No," knowing that his adversary is relying on this false statement. Has this attorney committed fraud or misconduct (is the statement "advocacy"—or something else)? If there is a difference, what is the difference, and what difference in result does it make?

III. Settlement Agreements

[A] Settlement as the Norm in Litigation

"I learned nothing about settlements in law schools, and yet that was the nature of my practice. 90% of all civil lawsuits are settled."—United States District Judge Richard A. Enslen of Kalamazoo, Michigan, at the Conference on Litigation Management at Yale Law School, Oct. 4, 1985, *quoted in Alternatives to the High Cost of Litigation*, Oct. 1985, at 18 (Center for Public Resources publication).

This statement is really about two things. First, it makes the point that settlement is the norm. Second, and less obviously, it makes the point that there are lawyering strategies that must be brought to bear on the settlement process. A person unfamiliar with the process might conclude that settled cases involve trivial attorney input, in comparison to those that are tried—but the conclusion would be erroneous. Consider the following.

Problem F

BLAKE v. WILLISTON PHARMACEUTICALS, INC. Andrew Blake's attorney has written a demand letter to your client, Williston Pharmaceuticals, Inc., claiming damages from the ingestion of an over-the-counter medicine by his son, Andrew Jr. After investigating the matter, you have concluded that the claim is possibly subject to defense, but is substantial. You have negotiated with Blake's attorney and have tentatively agreed to pay $40,000 in exchange for a release of all liability.

In preparing the papers, you begin with a form containing a general release of all claims and an agreement to the entry of a dismissal with prejudice. (An example appears in Litigation Document Example 2.1 at the very end of Chapter 2.) You know that this document has been used for the satisfactory resolution of many other claims. In this case, while you would prefer not to pay anything, you have concluded that the ability to buy peace for a little over the "nuisance value" of the suit makes settlement attractive. Are there any other considerations to which you should be alert in settling this case? See the next section.

[B] The Enforcement and Effects of Releases

Spector v. K-Mart Corporation

99 A.D.2d 605, 471 N.Y.S.2d 711 (1984)

MEMORANDUM DECISION. . . .

Plaintiff allegedly sustained ill effects from the use of Selacryn, a prescription drug manufactured by SmithKline Beckman Corporation, and Colchicine, both of which medications he purchased from K-Mart Corporation between July 2 and November 19, 1979. On January 26, 1982, plaintiff executed a general release to SmithKline in which he settled all of his claims for damages for personal injuries arising out of the ingestion of Selacryn "including, but not limited to, all liability for contribution and/or indemnity." He was paid $40,000 as consideration by SmithKline. By service of a complaint dated October 18, 1982, plaintiff commenced the underlying action against K-Mart, stating causes of action in negligence, strict products liability and breach of warranty. Following joinder of issue, K-Mart served a third-party summons and complaint upon SmithKline seeking contribution or indemnification. Special Term denied SmithKline's CPLR 3211 (subd. [a], par. 5) motion to dismiss both the complaint and third-party complaint. For the reasons which follow, we affirm. [In other words, SmithKline was unsuccessful in "buying peace." Its distributor now is subject to suit, and SmithKline probably will owe the distributor, K-Mart, whatever the distributor loses.]

Essentially, SmithKline reasons that since the subject release, by its terms, also released K-Mart, both the principal action and third-party action must fall pursuant to the mandate of section 15-108 (subd. [a]) of the General Obligations Law. We disagree. That section provides that a release given to one of two or more tort-feasors does not extend to the remaining tort-feasors "unless its terms expressly so provide." The statute was designed to eliminate the inequities existent under the common-law rule where a general release given to one wrongdoer discharged all others (*see Williams v. Pitts*, 40 A.D.2d 1057, 1058, 338 N.Y.S.2d 969). Consistent with this purpose, section 15-108 has been construed to require an express designation by name or other specific identification of which parties are intended to be released....

Here, the release stated that SmithKline and "all other persons, firms, or corporations" were released from liability for plaintiff's ingestion of Selacryn. In our view, this broad language fails to satisfy the statutory requirement....

Where, as here, a product claim against a retailer may give rise to an indemnity claim against the manufacturer (*see Guyot v. Al Charyn, Inc.*, 69 A.D.2d 79, 417 N.Y.S.2d 941; 2 Weinberger, New York Products Liability, § 24.03 p. 3; Restatement Torts 2d, § 886[B]), the third-party complaint should not be dismissed.... [Affirmed; the suit against the distributor, K-Mart, may proceed, and so may K-Mart's suit against SmithKline for indemnity of whatever K-Mart may owe.]

Notes and Questions

(1) *The Parties Released: Generality.* The *Spector* case represents the nightmare of every settling lawyer: the fear that the release, though drafted in the most all-encompassing language, is ineffective to extinguish all claims, or fails to exonerate all persons or entities identified with the defendant, so that the suit must be defended all over again, with the very real possibility of double liability. In the situation shown in *Spector*, the defendant understandably may wish to make the release as global as possible, because it is difficult to anticipate specifically every particular defendant whom the plaintiff might next sue.

However, as *Spector* indicates, that strategy is likely to be ineffective in states that require identification of released parties (a common rule). Consider the language incorporated into the release in Litigation Document Example 2.1 at the end of Chapter 2, which exonerates "each [litigant's] successors and assigns, and each other's related corporations, partnerships, or business entities, through or with which each, respectively, does business, and also all of each other's present and past officers, directors, employees, representatives, and agents," as well as the primary disputants. Would this language be sufficient to prevent a litigant such as Spector from suing the corporation's president on the same claim the very next week? [Probably.] Would it protect a separate corporation that is a subsidiary of the defendant? But wouldn't it be *insufficient* to protect an independent distributor who purchases from the defendant and then sells to retailers? [Note: One solution might be to include a provision for indemnification of the defendant by the plaintiff. *See* section [C] below.]

(2) *The Claims Released: Generality.* For similar reasons, a defendant does not wish to pay money for the release of a given claim only to be sued the next week in the same court by the same plaintiff on a different theory. Thus the Chapter 2 release covers all "claims, demands, controversies, contracts, actions or causes of action which either [litigant] has held or may now or in the future own or hold, or which the heirs, executors, assigns, successors, or administrators of either hereafter can, shall, or may have, own or hold, for or by reason of any matter, cause or thing whatsoever occurring or existing prior to the date of this agreement, whether or not now known, including but not limited to all claims [in the present suit] or which could have been asserted therein by amendment, counterclaim or other addition." (Sometimes the efforts at global coverage describe the bases of the released claims by amusing but vivid language, such as anything existing "from the beginning of the world to the present day.")

A "specific" release, as opposed to these "general" releases, releases only a particular claim. For an example, see *Marchello v. Lenox Hill Hospital*, 107 A.D.2d 566, 483 N.Y.S.2d 305 (1st Dept. 1985) (plaintiff gave release for leg burns due to medical malpractice, but later sued for "drop-foot" condition that developed as result of burns; held, release also extinguished claim in second suit). Should the defendant in *Marchello* have insisted upon a general release in the first place?

(3) *The Persons Whose Claims Are Released: Generality.* In the *Spector* situation, counsel for the defendant should also ask himself whether, under the applicable law, the injured child's father or mother might have their own claims (*e.g.*, for loss of the child's society or companionship), which they might assert in the same court the following week. There may be other potential claimants (*e.g.*, a retailer or other person in the distribution chain with whom the plaintiff has already, previously settled).

(4) *The "Mutual General Release": Should the Plaintiff Demand a Global Release, Too?* In many kinds of litigation, particularly business litigation, the plaintiff should think about future liability, too. If the plaintiff receives payment for goods sold and

gives a "unilateral" general release (as opposed to a mutual one), the defendant may bring suit against the plaintiff the following week on a complex antitrust theory that is not within the compulsory counterclaim rule. If this possibility is suspected, the solution may be for the plaintiff to insist that its consideration include not only payment but also a mutual general release. For an example, see *Sawyer v. First City Financial Corporation*, 124 Cal. App. 3d 390, 177 Cal. Rptr. 398 (1981), in which a mutual general release providing that it would "inure to the benefit of the parties and their respective employees" was held effective to protect the officers of a claiming party in a subsequent suit in which they were defendants.

(5) *Enforceability as to Persons under Disability to Settle: The Need for a "Friendly Suit."* Settlements in some situations or with some parties may be legally ineffective. For example, many jurisdictions have rules requiring court approval of settlements with minors. A mere release signed by the minor or her guardian, even after payment, may not prevent the minor and her guardian from suing again on the same claim. The solution, sometimes, is to file a "friendly suit" even if the parties have agreed upon all the terms of settlement. [How should this consideration affect your analysis of the minor's claim in Problem F, above?] Private settlements that waive certain types of claims, such as labor violations, discrimination, or claims by minors, may be prohibited and require friendly suits. Consider the following case.

BODLE v. TXL MORTGAGE CORPORATION, 788 F.3d 159 (5th Cir. 2015). Bodle and others were former employees of TXL Mortgage Corporation, working under a covenant not to compete. After their employment terminated, TXL sued them on the claim that they were violating the covenant not to compete. The parties settled that case with a broad general release that included both parties' claims of all kinds, including claims under the Fair Labor Standards Act (FLSA). Then, Bodle and the others, as plaintiffs, sued TXL under that same FSLA, claiming that TXL had not properly paid them for overtime. The trial court granted summary judgment for TXL because of the release.

The court of appeals reversed this holding. Pursuant to 29 U.S.C. § 216(b), an employer who violates the FLSA by failing to pay overtime compensation "shall be liable to its employees in the amount of their overtime compensation plus an equal amount of liquidated damages." [Note that the mandatory word "shall" appears in this provision. — Eds.]

> In light of the FLSA's recognition of the unequal bargaining power between employers and employees, the Supreme Court has concluded that the FLSA forbids waiver of the right to statutory wages or to liquidated damages. *Brooklyn Sav. Bank v. O'Neil*, 324 U.S. 697, 706–708 (1945). Accordingly, many courts have held that, in the absence of supervision by the Department of Labor or scrutiny from a court, a settlement of an FLSA claim is prohibited. *See, e.g., Lynn's Food Stores, Inc. v. U.S.*, 679 F.2d 1350, 1355 (11th Cir.1982). To deem the plaintiffs as having fairly bargained

> away unmentioned overtime pay based on a settlement that involves a compromise over wages due for commissions and salary would subvert the purpose of the FLSA: namely, in this case, the protection of the right to overtime pay.

[The court also addressed an exception to this prohibition, involving whether there was a bona fide dispute as to whether certain employees were covered by the FLSA, but it held that the exception did not apply in this case.—Eds.]

Notes and Questions

(1) *The Authority of the Parties to Settle, Free of Interference by the Court.* Traditionally, if the parties can agree to terms, they are free to settle the litigation at any time, and the court need not and should not get involved. *United States v. City of Miami*, 614 F.2d 1322, 1330 & n.16 (5th Cir. 1980) ("the traditional view is that the judge merely resolves issues submitted to him by the parties . . . and stands indifferent when the parties, for whatever reason commends itself to them, choose to settle a litigation.").

(2) *But Some Kinds of Claims Cannot Be Settled by Some Kinds of Parties.* The policy expressed in *Brooklyn Savings Bank* and in *Bodle*, in opposition to settlements unsupervised by a court, is unusual and is a consequence of statutory interpretation of the intent of Congress. But the validity of a settlement can also be influenced by other factors that can fall within the scope of judicial review. For example, a settlement agreement may be subject to ordinary contract principles such as fraud or duress. *See, e.g. Baptist v. City of Kankakee*, 481 F.3d 485, 490 (7th Cir. 2007) (a settlement agreement is "presumptively informed and willing, absent circumstances such as fraud or duress.")

But a sophisticated party might have greater difficulty arguing that a settlement agreement should not be honored. In *Runyan v. National Cash Register Corporation*, 787 F.2d 1039 (6th Cir. 1986), NCR and one of its experienced, in-house labor attorneys reached an agreement regarding termination of the employment relationship. Although the Age Discrimination in Employment Act (ADEA), like the FLSA, has been interpreted to limit unsupervised settlements, the court held that Runyan could not claim that the settlement was void because it "was related to age discrimination." Runyan, the court held, was a well-paid and experienced party who gained the full "benefit of a reasonable and understood bargain."

Litigation Document Example 15.1

Note on the Release and Settlement Agreement in George Miller Co. v. Compudata, Inc.

Read (or re-read) the Release and Settlement Agreement in *George Miller Co. v. Compudata, Inc.*, which appears in Litigation Document Example 2.1 at the end of Chapter 2, *supra*.

[C] Other Common Clauses in Settlement Agreements

"Circular" Indemnity Agreements: A Solution to the Problem of Spector v. K-Mart, supra? It is not uncommon for a settlement agreement to provide that the payee (plaintiff) indemnifies the payor (defendant) for any further claims or expenses that the payor may incur as a result of the incident made the basis of the suit. After all, the defendant is the one paying money to the plaintiff; therefore, it is sometimes not inappropriate for the defendant to insist that the plaintiff ensure that this payment is all that the defendant will be required to pay on account of the plaintiff's claims. The following clause is an example:

> As further part of the consideration for the payment of the above sum of money by KEYWEST SAVINGS ASSOCIATION, we, for ourselves, our heirs, executors, administrators, legal representatives, successors, and assigns, do *hereby agree to indemnify and hold harmless KEYWEST SAVINGS ASSOCIATION from any and all claims*, demands, damages, losses, expenses, actions and causes of action of whatsoever nature or character which have been or which may hereafter be asserted by any person, firm, corporation or any other legal entity whatsoever resulting from either or both of (1) a claim through or under either or both of us arising out of, relating to, in connection with or resulting from the above described, including, but expressly not limited to, any claim for contribution in the above described or any subsequent suit, or (2) a breach of either or both of us of any part of this agreement.

W. Dorsaneo & D. Crump, *Texas Civil Procedure: Pretrial Litigation* § 11.05 (2d ed. 1983) (emphasis added). Notice that this clause covers "expenses" as well as claims; does it cover the defendant's attorney's fees for the defense of a subsequent suit for contribution or indemnity? (It might or might not, depending upon how it is construed.) Would it protect SmithKline in the situation in *Spector v. K-Mart*? (Presumably, after Spector sued K-Mart and K-Mart made its third-party claim against SmithKline, SmithKline would itself file a third-party claim against Spector, completing the circle! And it then would move for summary judgment or judgment on the pleadings.)

Warranties. It is common for the defendant to insist that the plaintiff warrant that she is competent and under no disability to sign the release and has not assigned the claim. This clause may provide some slight protection against the situation in which the plaintiff is prohibited from settling (although a plaintiff disenabled from settling is probably disenabled from giving a warranty of ability to settle).

Attorney's Fees. It is not uncommon for a settlement agreement to provide that a party breaching the agreement is liable for the other party's attorney's fees. The plaintiff should ensure that the provision is mutual.

Prevention of Fraud Claims. One of the ways in which releases can be invalidated is by a showing that they are affected by fraud. The party seeking invalidation is usually the plaintiff, who may claim that suppression of discovery material or statements made during settlement negotiations resulted in misrepresentations that fraudulently induced her to enter into the agreement. To discourage such a claim, the defendant may insist upon a clause to the effect that neither party has relied upon any statement or information provided by the other but instead has made independent investigation of the claim (see Litigation Document Example 2.1 at the end of Chapter 2, above).

"Keep Them Honest" Clause. On the other hand, the plaintiff may be acutely aware that the settlement value of the claim depends upon information known only to the defendant, and may therefore insist upon a warranty by defendant that she has made full disclosure and knows that the plaintiff has relied on the information provided. This approach is sometimes called a "keep them honest" clause. A common usage of it is in divorce settlement agreements, for the protection of the spouse who is less knowledgeable about the extent of the parties' property and is dependent upon the other's inventory.

Disposition of Suit and Tying Up Loose Ends. At the same time that the release and agreement is signed, the parties should execute documents disposing of the suit (a joint agreed motion and either an order of dismissal with prejudice or a take-nothing judgment). It may be necessary to execute other documents to tie up loose ends (*e.g.*, a release of *lis pendens* in a suit affecting land). The defendant may insist that the check be made out jointly to the plaintiff and her attorney (who, if her fee is contingent, may also be a holder of part of the claim). The defendant commonly sends all of the papers, including the executed check, to the plaintiff's attorney with the (often written) understanding that the check will not be negotiated until the plaintiff and her attorney have executed them and the order disposing of the case has been entered.

[D] Adjudicative Effects of Settlement, Structured Settlements, and Trial Agreements between Opponents

Note on Adjudicative Effects of Settlement

(1) *The Basic Notion: Release of One Claim May Extinguish Other Claims against Other Defendants.* The plaintiff should be alert to the possibility that, in releasing her claim against one defendant, she may automatically affect claims against others. For example, the common law followed the "unity of release" rule: A release of one joint tortfeasor automatically was a release of all. This inflexible rule discouraged settlement, and it has been replaced in many jurisdictions.

(2) *Partial Release of Claims against Joint Tortfeasors.* Today, it is common for a jurisdiction to have a rule that partially reduces claims against joint tortfeasors upon the release of any one of them. There are many different patterns, and the rules can be complex. One approach is to reduce the recovery by the percentage of damage found by the jury to have been attributable to the released tortfeasor's negligence, and another is to credit the amount of the settlement to the satisfaction of the judgment. *E.g.*, Tex. Rev. Civ. Stat. Ann. art. 2212a (comparative negligence).

Note on Structured Settlements (Periodic Payments)

Structured Settlements; How to Analyze the Case of Franck v. Polaris E-Z Go Div. of Textron, Inc., Below. The case that follows contains two issues: first, the adjudicative effect of a settlement with one tortfeasor, and second, how to treat the settlement if it provides for periodic future payments rather than for a lump sum (a "structured" settlement). California's settlement provision, in general, is simple. It reduces judgments against other tortfeasors by the amount of the settlement. But how is a structured settlement treated? The defendant argues that all future payments should be added together and subtracted from the award. This approach would make for a large reduction. The plaintiff argues that only the present cash value should be subtracted, since after all, that is the "real" value of the settlement. This approach would result in a much smaller reduction of the judgment.

FRANCK v. POLARIS E-Z GO DIV. OF TEXTRON, INC., 204 Cal. Rptr. 321 (1984). Defendant Polaris was found liable for injuries sustained by Jan Franck while riding on a snowmobile manufactured by Polaris. Damages were assessed at $300,000. But before trial, Franck had settled with other defendants (the driver and owner of the snowmobile) for a total of $215,000. These defendants had agreed to pay $25,000 cash and a total of $190,000 in future periodic payments, structured over eighteen years. These defendants' insurance had a coverage limit of $100,000. After paying $25,000, the insurance company used the balance of $75,000 to purchase an annuity contract that would finance the future payments of $190,000. In addition, the seller of the snowmobile paid $2,500.

The relevant statute provided that a settlement "shall reduce the claims against the others in the amount . . . of the consideration paid for it . . . ." Polaris therefore contended that the $300,000 award should be reduced by the total amount to be paid in settlement ($217,500: $2,500 cash from seller; $25,000 cash from defendants; $190,000 in future payments—a big reduction). The trial court decided in favor of Polaris. The court of appeals here reverses and holds that the present value of future payments is the reduction (a much lesser amount):

> Plaintiff has obtained a judgment of $300,000; therefore she presently is entitled to recover that amount. It is simple economics that money received by plaintiff [after eighteen years] is not worth as much as . . . if she received it today . . . . Only by discounting the future payments to their present cash value and reducing the award by that amount will plaintiff receive the recovery to which she presently is entitled.

Notes and Questions

(1) *Valuation and Settlements: The Present Cash Value of a Structured Settlement May Be Much, Much Less than the Sum of Payments.* Franck's settlement provided for the defendants to pay $190,000 in eighteen annual future payments. A plaintiff's attorney should be careful to evaluate the present cash value of such a settlement.

Valuation consists primarily of an algebraic formula that depends on a chosen rate of interest. Since the algebra involves an exponential function, the discount can be very large, particularly if payments are spread over many years and the interest rate selected is high. For example, at ten percent interest, the value of payments is approximately cut in half after seven years.

(2) *Is the Annuity Provider Going to Remain Solvent?* Another problem is the need to ensure that the annuity provider will be solvent when the last payments are due, years from now. Plaintiff's counsel should consult rating services and refuse agreement to any but high-rated providers.

Note on Opposing-Party Agreements That Disadvantage Other Parties

(1) *Opposing Parties Sometimes Settle by Ganging Up on Other Parties.* In multiparty cases, it is not uncommon for opposing parties to work together against other parties. Some cooperation of this kind is prohibited, some must be disclosed to juries, and some results without overt agreement because of the natural strategies of the parties. Consider, for example, a defendant who brings in a third party. Imagine that the plaintiff and the third party both think the third-party claim is not meritorious. The natural strategy is for the third party to say to the jury, "The plaintiff is hurt, but it's only the defendant that's liable, not us," and for the plaintiff to echo this argument by saying, "I'm badly hurt, but only by the defendant and not the third party." The two allies may carry out this strategy without any agreement, or they may coordinate their jury strikes, witnesses, and arguments.

(2) *The Archetypal Unfair Strategy: "Mary Carter" Agreements.* One kind of agreement that many jurisdictions have prohibited is the Mary Carter agreement, which gets its name from a case in which the Mary Carter Paint Company was a party. The plaintiff sues multiple defendants, then settles with one defendant, but keeps that defendant in the case. The settlement agreement gives the settling defendant a credit for the plaintiff's recovery, so that this defendant has an incentive to help the plaintiff obtain as big a verdict as possible against remaining defendants. At first, the courts required disclosing Mary Carter agreements to juries, but this solution did not work. Courts therefore began declaring Mary Carter agreements against public policy and illegal. *See, e.g., General Motors Corporation v. Simmons,* 558 S.W.2d 855 (Tex. 1977).

(3) *"No Deal" Deals: Secret Cooperation.* A form of cooperation has emerged that is even more threatening to the adversary system: the "no deal" deal. Plaintiff and defendant act in a coordinated way to gang up on a particular defendant or to cut out another plaintiff, without any express agreement. The opposing attorneys know each other, understand the strategy, and trust that the coordinated strategy will work, without words. The parties respond to inquiries by saying that they have "no agreement." The defendant may exercise its jury strikes to benefit the plaintiff and coordinate in other ways. The courts have not really learned to deal with this strategy.

(4) *Other Strategies, Including High-Low Agreements, and Disclosure Requirements.* The varieties of agreements are infinite. Some are lawful but are subject to disclosure requirements. "High-low agreements" are an example. The parties agree that no matter what the verdict is, the judgment will not exceed a specified high number or be less than a specified low number. Sometimes, this strategy is used with one plaintiff and one defendant, because new lawyers want trial experience without risk to their clients. But the high-low agreement can be used to provide a mutual incentive to disadvantage another defendant. Consider the following case.

IN RE EIGHTH JUDICIAL DISTRICT ASBESTOS LITIGATION, 872 N.E.2d 232 (N.Y. 2007). Donald Reynolds and his wife sued multiple defendants, alleging that Mr. Reynolds had contracted mesothelioma from asbestos products while working at an oil refinery. At trial, only two defendants remained: Garlock, a manufacturer of gaskets, and Niagara, a distributor of insulation.

Unbeknownst to Garlock, plaintiffs and Niagara entered into a high-low agreement whereby it was agreed that Niagara's total liability would fall into a predetermined range. If the jury's damage award against Niagara was $155,000 or less, Niagara would pay plaintiffs a minimum of $155,000, even if Niagara was without fault; if the award against Niagara was more than $185,000, Niagara's liability was capped at $185,000; if the award fell within $155,000–$185,000, Niagara would pay the designated amount. Thus, Niagara had only $30,000 at stake, but its participation would likely affect plaintiffs' claims against Garlock, because both parties would be trying to place fault on Garlock. The jury apportioned liability against Garlock and Niagara at 60% and 40%, respectively, and awarded plaintiffs $3,750,000.

The trial court entered judgment for plaintiffs. The appellate division affirmed. The Court of Appeals (New York's highest court) here reverses. The court holds that the failure to disclose the high-low agreement prevented a fair determination of Garlock's liabilities, warranting a new trial:

> [B]etween a plaintiff and a [single] defendant, . . . the high-low agreement affords the parties a means of tempering the . . . risks associated with . . . trial. In a multi-defendant litigation, however, a high-low agreement . . . has the potential of prejudicing the rights of the nonagreeing defendant. . . .
>
> [This] agreement furnished plaintiffs with an incentive to maximize Garlock's liability while minimizing Niagara's. . . . While it is not uncommon for a plaintiff to have a financial incentive to maximize the liability of one particular defendant, . . . Garlock was entitled to disclosure . . . of the high-low agreement . . . . Garlock could have adjusted its trial strategy accordingly and evaluated the risks of going to trial with the knowledge . . . [that it was] the target defendant.

> Nondisclosure also deprived Garlock of the opportunity to seek appropriate . . . rulings from the trial court and [to] argue . . . the high-low agreement to the jury. . . . Garlock may have conducted its jury selection in a different manner, argued that it should not have . . . to share peremptory challenges with Niagara, or brought . . . motions concerning the admissibility of the agreement . . . . Instead, Garlock was compelled to proceed blindly to trial without any meaningful opportunity to defend itself from . . . the secret agreement . . . .

IV. Arbitration and Other Substitutes for Court Adjudication

[A] The Nature of Arbitration

Note on Arbitration

(1) *Arbitration Differs Both from Litigation and from Mediation.* Arbitration is a binding procedure, like litigation, but usually it is carried out in a private setting according to a private agreement. The process is to be distinguished from negotiation and settlement, which is a voluntary process. It also is to be sharply distinguished from mediation, which is discussed below, and which is merely a type of assisted settlement in which the mediator cannot impose a solution. In contrast, an arbitrator (or arbitrators, if there are more than one) have power to decide the dispute between the parties.

(2) *The Agreement to Arbitrate.* Parties may agree to arbitration at the time of making an initial transaction, before any dispute arises, or they can agree to submit a particular dispute to arbitration. An agreement to arbitrate may be tucked into a full contract, even a consumer contract. The possibilities for different kinds of processes under the arbitration agreement are infinite. The procedures may be thoroughly described in the agreement or left more general, and they may be formal or informal.

(3) *The Arbitrator or Arbitrators: A Lesser Standard of Neutrality.* The arbitrator or arbitrators may be required to be "neutral" or not. This feature is sharply different from litigation before a judge. Even a neutral arbitrator does not need to be free of connections with a party to the extent required of a judge.

(4) *Compelling Arbitration, the Arbitral Award, and Confirmation in Court.* If a party to an arbitration agreement instead sues in court, the other party may move to stay or dismiss to compel arbitration. The arbitrator issues a decision, called an "award." This is a private decision, although most parties accept it. If necessary, the prevailing party may sue to "confirm" the award, and the losing party may move to vacate it. If the award is lawful, the court confirms it by an enforceable judgment.

Problem G

THE CASE OF THE TILTED HOUSE, RECONSIDERED. Reconsider Problem B, above, in which Super Constructors, Inc. has proposed to your clients, Don and Kathleen Fuller, an agreement to arbitrate their claim for the tilted slab in the new house they bought from Super. Assume that you have accepted the proposal and have presented your case to the arbitrators, who have been named as indicated in Problem B. The arbiters have considered the case entirely on the basis of written submissions, without hearing live witnesses.

The arbitrators' award requires Super to pay the current market value of the house to the Fullers; however, it expressly states that Super need not pay the Fullers' attorney's fees and is not liable for any penalty or exemplary damages. Under the applicable state law, it appears that a prevailing party is entitled to attorney's fees and to a $2,000 penalty provided for by state consumer protection litigation. Worst of all, you have since discovered that two of the three arbitrators are members of the Greater Metropolitan Association of Home Builders, of which the president of Super is a past president. Was it wise for you to have entered into the agreement to arbitrate? [Don't be too quick to conclude that it was not.—Eds.] If you are dissatisfied with the award, do you have grounds that will suffice for setting it aside and recovering other relief in court? [Probably not.—Eds.] Consider the following materials.

SPRINZEN v. NOMBERG, 389 N.E.2d 456 (N.Y. 1979). As an employee of Local 1115, a union of health-care workers, Nomberg had a contract that contained a covenant not to compete, saying that he would not work as a labor organizer for a period of five years after terminating his employment. The contract also contained what the court called "a sweeping arbitration clause," prescribing that "[a]ll complaints, disputes whatsoever of whatever kind or nature . . . shall be submitted for arbitration" pursuant to a described process. But Nomberg left Local 1115 and began employment with another union that also organized health-care workers, in violation of the restrictive covenant.

Local 1115 demanded arbitration to compel compliance with the restrictive covenant and to enjoin Nomberg from employment at the other union. The parties proceeded to arbitration, where Nomberg, "after unsuccessfully contesting the partiality of the arbitrator named in the . . . agreement, walked out of the hearing." The arbitrator ruled that Local 1115 was entitled to the relief sought and issued an award enjoining Nomberg.

The union brought suit to confirm the award. Nomberg moved to vacate it on grounds that the arbitrator was partial and the award was unjust. The trial court confirmed the award, but the appellate division reversed. The Court of Appeals, New York's highest court, here reverses the reversal and orders the award confirmed:

> [A]n agreement to submit to arbitration . . . is now favorably recognized as an efficacious procedure whereby parties can select their own nonjudicial forum for the "private and practical" resolution of their disputes "with maximum dispatch and at minimum expense." . . .

> An arbitrator's paramount responsibility is to reach an equitable result, and the courts will not assume the role of overseers to mold the award to conform to their sense of justice. Thus, an arbitrator's award will not be vacated for errors of law and fact committed by the arbitrator . . . and "[e]ven where the arbitrator states an intention to apply a law, and then misapplies it, the award will not be set aside." . . .
>
> Despite this policy of according an arbitrator seemingly unfettered discretion . . . , it is the established law in this State that an award which is violative of public policy will not be permitted to stand. [But there are only a few such issues. The court gives examples: punitive damages and claims of usury cannot be arbitrated.] [Ed. Note: these principles may be preempted by the Federal Arbitration Act.] . . .
>
> Applying these principles to this case, we now hold that disputes involving restrictive covenants of employment can be . . . submitted to arbitration, and an arbitrator's award which specifically enforces such covenants, even to the extent of enjoining an individual from engaging in like employment for a reasonable period of years in the future, will not be vacated on public policy grounds. . . .

"In passing," the court rejected Nomberg's objection to the arbitrator. This arbitrator had been named in the contract and was a frequent labor arbitrator, and the circumstance that Local 1115 paid for his services "is not sufficient to constitute bias."

Notes and Questions

(1) *What about a "Completely Irrational" Award?: Lentine v. Fundaro,* 278 N.E.2d 633 (N.Y. 1972). In this case, the New York high court said that an arbitrator exceeds his authority if he makes a "completely irrational" award. For example, another case involved a contract that contained an express damage limit, and the arbitrator simply ignored the limit without finding it to be unenforceable. *See Granite Worsted Mills, Inc. v. Aaronson Cowen, Ltd.*, 255 N.E.2d 168 (N.Y. 1969) (award vacated).

(2) *Legal Limits on Covenants Not to Compete: Should They Be Arbitrable? Sprinzen v. Nomberg* is a dispute about a covenant not to compete. This kind of contract is subject to a variety of legal restrictions, including that it be strictly limited in time length, subject, and geographic scope. If it violates these requirements, many courts will not enforce it. Noncompetes limit entrants in the market, exclude people from the work they know, and often are not needed to protect trade secrets. Should this kind of covenant be subject to arbitration in which an award can fail to conform to the law, or does public policy demand otherwise?

(3) *Arbitration Agreements That are Not Negotiated or Noticed.* An arbitration agreement of the kind at issue in *Sprinzen v. Nomberg* is unlikely to be a subject of great interest at the time of employment, but it can have a significant effect later.

Agreements in consumer contracts are even less likely to attract attention. Should there be a requirement of conspicuousness?

[B] The Federal Arbitration Act (FAA): Controlling over Most Laws

Note on the Basics of the FAA

(1) *The Federal Arbitration Act—Vacating the Award for Corruption, Partiality, Misconduct, or Manifest Disregard of Law: Greenberg v. Bear, Stearns & Co.*, 220 F.3d 22 (2d Cir. 2000). The Federal Arbitration Act requires analogous but different (and perhaps slightly less broad) deference to the arbitrator. An award can be vacated upon a showing of corruption, partiality, or misconduct. This standard cannot be met merely by proof of some relationship to the parties or issues; the evidence must contain some reason for inferring partiality (or corruption or misconduct). The circumstances of *Sprinzen v. Nomberg*, for example, might not have produced any difference on this issue if the FAA had been applicable.

The FAA also allows the award to be vacated if it is based upon "manifest disregard" of the law, as well as if its enforcement would violate public policy. Nevertheless, as the *Greenberg* case shows in upholding an award, the federal standard also is deferential to arbitration. The award is not subject to being vacated as readily as a court of appeals can reverse a district court, because the Act requires not merely an error of law, but "manifest" or obvious disregard of the law.

(2) *Breadth of the Federal Act: Any "Transaction Involving [Interstate] Commerce" That Includes a Written Agreement to Arbitrate.* The FAA enforces written agreements to arbitrate whenever they involve a transaction in interstate commerce. But its coverage is virtually all-encompassing. The scope of the Act is broad, and it displaces state laws that restrict arbitration and that conflict with it.

To understand just how pervasive the FAA is, consider *Allied-Bruce Terminix Companies, Inc. v. Dobson*, 513 U.S. 265 (1995). The case concerned a local termite control contract for a single home: seemingly about as local a commercial transaction as one could imagine. It contained an arbitration clause. The state courts refused to apply the FAA, because they concluded that the transaction did not fit the interstate commerce requirement. The Supreme Court reversed, requiring arbitration under the FAA. "In addition to the multistate nature of Terminix and Allied-Bruce, the termite-treating and house-repairing material used by Allied-Bruce . . . came from outside" the state. After this decision, is there any transaction that the Federal Act does not cover?

Note on Procedure, Evidence, Precedent, and Enforcement

(1) *Procedure.* Arbitration is not rigidly governed by procedural rules such as the federal or state rules of civil procedure. The parties can choose the procedures

they want, although there may be a statutory framework (particularly for enforcement). For example, an arbitrator may not be bound to provide an opinion or statement of reasons; however, since confirmation or vacatur of the award may in some instances depend upon the basis of the award, it may be advisable for the arbitrator to provide an opinion or statement of reasons. Procedures are governed generally by the arbitration agreement and by the organizational meeting of parties and arbitrators.

(2) *Evidence.* The arbitrator may not be bound by the rules of evidence applicable to litigation in court, but may be able to accept reasonable substitutes for that kind of evidence. Ironically, it sometimes happens that arbitrators refuse to receive evidence that would be admissible in court under the rules of evidence. Evidence issues are guided by the arbitration agreement.

(3) *Decisional Law.* The arbitrator may not be bound rigidly by most decisional law. This principle does not mean, however, that the application of precedent is irrelevant to arbitration. The arbitrator normally will be persuaded by judicial or statutory precedent (and indeed her award is subject to vacatur if it is an "irrational" error of law or, under the FAA, if it is a "manifest disregard" of the law). In addition, certain arbitration reports exist, which give the results of arbitrations by reproducing opinions similar to judicial opinions; and the arbitrator very well may regard these precedents as persuasive. Thus, briefing the case may closely resemble briefing the law for judicial adjudication in some cases.

(4) *Scheduling, Discovery, Etc.* Other matters such as scheduling, discovery, pleadings, and order of presentation at hearings may be governed by the agreement upon which arbitration is based, by agreement of the parties during the arbitration process, or by decision of the arbitrators, tailored to the case.

(5) *The Stages in a Typical Arbitration.* The American Arbitration Association has described the arbitration process in seven general stages: (1) case initiation; (2) arbitration selection; (3) preliminary hearing; (4) information exchange; (5) the hearing stage; (6) post hearing submissions; and (7) the award stage. The precise content of each stage, of course, can vary based upon the relevant public statutes and private agreements. *See, e.g.* American Arbitration Association, AAA Arbitration Roadmap (2011) (https://www.adr.org/sites/default/files/document_repository/AAA_Guide_Arbitration_Process_Roadmap_2011_02_16%20(1).pdf).

(6) *Party-Chosen or "Neutral" Arbitrators: They Need Not Be Perfectly Neutral.* Selection of the arbitrator is a critical part of the process. The parties can choose to have one arbitrator or more. A common arrangement is to have three arbitrators, with one chosen by each side and a third chosen by the two party-chosen arbitrators. Arbitrators can choose to use arbitrators who are not neutral. It is assumed that a party-chosen arbitrator will have an orientation that favors that party. But then, the usual practice is for party-chosen arbitrators to disclose conflicts, and the opponent can object to an arbitrator. In the following case, the court considered what to do when a party-chosen arbitrator did not disclose everything.

[C] "Party-Chosen" or "Neutral" Arbitrators: How Neutral?

Certain Underwriting Members of Lloyd's of London v. Florida Department of Financial Services

892 F.3d 501 (2d Cir. 2018)

BACKGROUND

ICA [Insurance Company of the Americas, an insolvent insurer for which the Florida Department of Financial Services is the receiver,] insures workers compensation claims in the construction industry. The Underwriters in turn provide ICA with second and third layer reinsurance under a series of treaties, each of which contains an arbitration clause requiring that disputes be adjudicated by an arbitration panel consisting of three members: one party-appointed arbitrator for each party, and the neutral umpire. The only contractual qualification is that the arbitrators "be active or retired disinterested executive officers of insurance or reinsurance companies or Lloyd's London Underwriters." Each party bears the expense of its own arbitrator and is permitted to engage in ex parte discussion with its party-appointed arbitrators during discovery.

ICA requested coverage from the Underwriters under the treaties [which were the agreed basis for decision] for claims arising out of multiple construction site injuries exceeding in total $12.5 million. The Underwriters declined the claim, citing language in the treaties that (according to the Underwriters) restricts coverage to a single "loss occurrence" involving more than one insured.... ICA demanded arbitration pursuant to the treaty. ICA appointed Alex Campos as its arbitrator, and the two party-appointed arbitrators selected Ben Hernandez as neutral umpire.

At the ... organizational meeting, each arbitrator was called upon to disclose pre-existing or concurrent relationships with a party.... Campos disclaimed any appreciable link to ICA:

> I don't know anyone here except for Mr. [Gary Hirst, Chairman of ICA]. I had some potential business dealings with him about ten years ago that never really materialized.... [A]nd other than that contact I don't have any other related contacts with Mr. Hirst....

[But a]s the district court found, Campos's pre-existing and concurrent relationships with ICA's representatives were considerably more extensive than Campos disclosed. The court emphasized undisclosed dealings between ICA and a human resources firm named Vensure Employee Services ("Vensure") of which Campos was President and CEO. Specifically, the court found that: ICA and Vensure operate out of the same suite in a business park in Mesa, Arizona; John Iorillo, a former director of ICA, was CFO of a firm that provided consulting services to Vensure; and Ricardo Rios, a Director of ICA, was hired as the CFO of Vensure.... Rios testified as a witness at the arbitration, and Iorillo's name was mentioned repeatedly.

The panel favored ICA's interpretation of the treaty language, and the Award granted ICA net damages of over $1.5 million. The Underwriters moved to vacate the Award on several grounds, including "evident partiality" on the part of Alex Campos, manifest disregard of the law, and prejudicial procedural misconduct. ICA cross-moved to confirm.

The district court granted the motion to vacate the award and denied the cross-motion to confirm. . . . Campos's "undisclosed relationships" with ICA representatives were found to be "significant enough to demonstrate evident partiality." . . . The court did not take issue with the substance of the Award, did not connect Campos's conduct to the panel's decision, and made no finding that Campos had a personal or financial interest in the outcome of the arbitration. . . .

I. ["NEUTRAL" ARBITRATORS, WHICH THIS CASE DOES NOT INVOLVE]

Our review of an arbitration award is "severely limited" in view of the strong deference courts afford to the arbitral process. . . . A "stringent standard for vacating awards is a necessary corollary to the federal policy favoring arbitration."

"Under the FAA [Federal Arbitration Act], the validity of an award is subject to attack only on those grounds listed in [Section] 10, and the policy of the FAA requires that the award be enforced unless one of those grounds is affirmatively shown to exist." We may vacate under Section 10 "where there was evident partiality . . . in the arbitrator." . . . The party challenging the award must prove the existence of evident partiality by clear and convincing evidence. . . .

The Supreme Court established in *Commonwealth Coatings* that "an arbitrator's failure to disclose a material relationship with one of the parties can constitute 'evident partiality' requiring vacatur of the award." *Commonwealth Coatings Corp. v. Continental Cas. Co.,* 393 U.S. 145 (1968)). . . . A neutral arbitrator's relationship with a party is material if it goes "so far as to include the rendering of services on the very projects involved in th[e] lawsuit," or contemporaneous investments that create a vested financial stake in that party. A reasonable person could also conclude that the arbitrator is unduly partial to the side of a close family relation.

But even as to neutral arbitrators, "we have not been quick to set aside the results of an arbitration because of an arbitrator's alleged failure to disclose information." . . . For example, past contacts do not amount to material bias. . . . In broader strokes, the FAA does not proscribe all personal or business relationships between arbitrators and the parties. *See Lucent Techs.,* 379 F.3d at 30 (co-ownership of an airplane by arbitrator and party's representative did not indicate evident partiality) . . . .

We . . . "requir[e] a showing of something more than the mere 'appearance of bias' to vacate an arbitration award," and will not vacate arbitration awards for evident partiality when the party opposing the award "identifies no direct connection between [the arbitrator] and the outcome of the arbitration."

Judicial tolerance of relationships between arbitrators and party representatives reflects competing goals in partiality decisions. Complete candor and transparency help root out bias and fraud. But reinsurers and ceding insurers affirmatively seek arbitral panels with expertise. "[T]he best informed and most capable potential arbitrators" are repeat players with deep industry connections." . . .

II. [PARTY-APPOINTED ARBITRATORS (AS HERE)]

Of equal importance, arbitration is a creature of contract, and courts must hold parties to their bargain. ICA and the Underwriters have chosen a tripartite panel with party-appointed arbitrators who are "relieved of all judicial formalities and may abstain from following the strict rules of law." "[P]arties are free to choose for themselves to what lengths they will go in quest of impartiality," including the various degrees of partiality that inhere in the party-appointment feature. . . .

That said, a party-appointed arbitrator is still subject to some baseline limits to partiality. . . . [A]n undisclosed relationship is material if it violates the arbitration agreement. . . . In this case, the qualification in the contract is "disinterested," which would be breached if the party-appointed arbitrator had a personal or financial stake in the outcome of the arbitration.

An undisclosed fact is also material, and therefore warrants vacatur, if the party opposing the award can show that the party-appointed arbitrator's partiality had a prejudicial effect on the award. . . . In the absence of a clear showing that an undisclosed relationship (or the non-disclosure itself) influenced the arbitral proceedings or infected an otherwise-valid award, that award should not be set aside even if a reasonable person (or court) could speculate or infer bias. . . .

We vacate and remand for the district court to determine whether the Underwriters have shown by clear and convincing evidence that the failure to disclose by party-appointed arbitrator Campos either violates the qualification of disinterestedness or had a prejudicial impact on the award. . . . The district court did not consider the Underwriters' challenges as to manifest disregard of the law and prejudicial procedural misconduct; nor do we.

Notes and Questions

(1) *Why Did the Court Not Consider ICA's Arguments That the Award Was in "Manifest Disregard of the Law" or Involved "Prejudicial Procedural Misconduct"?* These arguments were ineffective because the arbitrators did not have to conform to the law. Parties in arbitration can make this choice. The court says, "ICA and the Underwriters have chosen . . . arbitrators who are 'relieved of all judicial formalities and may abstain from following the strict rules of law.'" Why would parties make this choice? First, law-bound litigation is expensive, delay-prone, and very inefficient. Second, they want custom in the industry to control rather than law. Third, they expect that arbitrators acting freely from law can make better mutual decisions by making awards that the law would not contemplate. Finally, they have enough disputes so that apparent injustices tend to even out.

(2) *How Does One Prove That an Arbiter is Not "Neutral" or "Disinterested?": J.P. Stevens & Co. v. Rytex Corp.*, 312 N.E.2d 466 (1974). In this case, the court vacated the award because the arbiter had been appointed "as a neutral," whereas in fact

his firm had done undisclosed business worth millions of dollars with the prevailing party. A failure to disclose business relationships was also an issue in *Certain Underwriters, above.* However, as the Supreme Court noted in *Commonwealth Coatings Corp. v. Continental Cas. Co.,* 393 U.S. 145 (1968), at least for party-chosen arbitrators, it is "the materiality of the undisclosed conflict [that] drives a finding of evident partiality, not the failure to disclose or investigate per se." There is no per se rule requiring vacatur of an award whenever an undisclosed relationship is discovered; rather, it requires an evaluation of the materiality of the bias, and "materiality" means a provable, direct effect on the outcome, not just an inference of bias.

Thus, while the dispute between ICA and the Underwriters was remanded, the award was not set aside; instead, the lower court needed to re-evaluate not only whether Campos failed to disclose relationships with ICA, but also whether the Underwriters could make "a clear showing that an undisclosed relationship (or the non-disclosure itself) influenced the arbitral proceedings." An "inference" of bias is not enough; there must be a direct showing of effect on the award. This kind of showing will be difficult to make.

[D] The Federal Act's Preemption of Other Laws

SOUTHLAND CORPORATION v. KEATING, 465 U.S. 1 (1984). Keating was a franchisee of the Southland Corporation, which was the owner and franchisor of Seven-Eleven convenience stores. Southland's franchise agreements, including the one with Keating, contained a provision requiring arbitration of any dispute. Keating and other franchisees brought a class action in a California state court, alleging various claims, including violation of the California Franchise Investment Law. Southland, the defendant, responded by petitioning the court to compel arbitration, relying on the Federal Arbitration Act ("FAA"), which provides: "A written provision . . . to settle by arbitration a controversy . . . shall be valid, irrevocable, and enforceable, save upon such grounds as exist at law or in equity for the revocation of any contract."

The California courts compelled arbitration of all the claims except the one arising under the California Franchise Investment Law, which provided for judicial consideration and also said that any agreement waiving compliance with the provisions of the Law "is void." But the United States Supreme Court reversed and ordered arbitration of the Franchise Investment Act claim, too, as follows:

> In enacting § 2 of the federal [Arbitration] Act, Congress declared a national policy favoring arbitration and withdrew the power of the states to require a judicial resolution of claims which the contracting parties agreed to resolve by arbitration. . . . Congress thus mandated the enforcement of arbitration agreements. . . .

EPIC SYSTEMS CORPORATION V. LEWIS, 138 S. Ct. 1612 (2018). In this case, the Court considered whether employees were still permitted to bring their claims in class or collective actions pursuant to the National Labor Relations Act (NLRA), even if they had otherwise agreed to resolve disputes through one-on-one arbitration. The NLRA protects employees' right to collective action for "mutual aid and protection," which would seem to protect class actions, but the Court held that the FAA overrode this provision. The opinion by Justice Neal Gorsuch was emphatic:

> [A]s a matter of law the answer is clear. In the Federal Arbitration Act, Congress has instructed federal courts to enforce arbitration agreements according to their terms—including terms providing for individualized proceedings. . . . Not only did Congress require courts to respect and enforce agreements to arbitrate; it also specifically directed them to respect and enforce the parties' chosen arbitration procedures. See § 3 (providing for a stay of litigation pending arbitration "in accordance with the terms of the agreement"); § 4 (providing for "an order directing that . . . arbitration proceed in the manner provided for in such agreement").

The Supreme Court declined to find that the NLRA overrode the FAA, because the NLRA lacked any such "clearly expressed congressional intention," and because the Supreme Court has repeatedly "rejected efforts to conjure conflicts between the Arbitration Act and other federal statutes." In dissent, four Justices emphasized the practical consequences of the decision and the purposes of the statutory schemes. Employees who complained that their employers had underpaid them and violated labor laws, for example, possessed small claims that would not be pursued individually or through arbitration, and thus, depended on class actions. The majority opinion, however, left that policy problem to Congress.

Notes and Questions

(1) *Is There an Arbitration Agreement? Prima Paint Corp. v. Flood & Conklin Mfg. Corp.,* 388 U.S. 395 (1967). In general, the question whether a dispute should be compelled to be submitted to arbitration is a question for the courts; the Arbitration Act provides that an agreement to arbitrate may be attacked "upon such grounds as exist at law or in equity for the revocation of any contract." Thus, if it is unclear whether there really is an agreement to arbitrate, or if the arbitration clause itself allegedly was obtained by fraud, the question is one for the courts. *See AT & T Technologies, Inc. v. Communications Workers,* 475 U.S. 643 (1986) (where arbitration clause was ambiguous as to whether right to lay off workers was arbitrable, court should decide arbitrability).

But the courts have been careful to avoid reading this authority too broadly, so as to defeat the scope of the Arbitration Act. For example, in the *Prima Paint* case, one party alleged that the other had committed fraud in the inducement of the contract, although not of the arbitration clause in particular, and sought to have the claim of fraud adjudicated in federal court. The Court held that consideration of a claim of fraud in the inducement of the whole contract "is for the arbitrators and not for the courts." [But since all the terms of a contract are in some sense interrelated, does this holding make sense?]

(2) *Arbitration Clause and Adhesion Contracts.* Employment or franchise contracts, like the ones at issue in *Southland* and in *EPIC Systems*, can be one-sided. In *Nagrampa v. MailCoups, Inc.*, 413 F.3d 1024 (9th Cir. 2005), the Ninth Circuit held that an arbitrator must not decide whether an agreement containing an arbitration clause is a contract of adhesion, but the court may determine whether an arbitration clause buried within the agreement is procedurally unconscionable and therefore invalid.

[E] Other Streamlined Quasi-Adjudicatory Procedures: "Rent-a-Judge" Statutes and "Court-Annexed Arbitration"

(1) *Private Judging (or "Rent-a-Judge" Statutes).* Some states permit the parties to agree to the appointment of an attorney or judge (usually retired) as the presiding judge in their case. The proceedings closely resemble the trial and (if allowed by governing law) the appeal of any other judicially determined dispute, except with respect to the identity of the judge. By this means, the parties may gain the advantages of speedy disposition, certainty of trial date, and a judge of their choice. The pioneering legislation in this field is that of California. *See* Cal. Code Civ. Pro. § 638; *see also* Note, *The California Rent-A-Judge Experiment: Constitutional and Policy Considerations of Pay-as-You-Go Courts*, 94 Harv. L. Rev. 1592 (1981).

(2) *"Court Annexed Arbitration."* Governing law may authorize or require the court to refer the parties to an arbiter as a preliminary step prior to presentation of the dispute in court. This procedure generally differs sharply from ordinary arbitration in that it is not binding, but is advisory only. It therefore is somewhat related to mediation or to advisory simulations and is treated together with those procedures in § V, below.

V. Mediation and Other Advisory Processes

[A] Mediation: A Method of Assisted Negotiation

Richard S. Weil, *Mediation in a Litigation Culture: The Surprising Growth of Mediation in New York*

17 Dispute Resolution Magazine 8 (2011)*

[This article resulted from a survey conducted by the author. The survey report, *Mediation: Through the Eyes of New York Litigators*, is available at www.nycbar.org/pdf/report/uploads/20072046-MediationThroughtheEyesofNYLitigators.pdf.]

. . . While mediation still may not be as popular in New York as it is in some other places, [this] survey of 485 litigators shows its increasing acceptance. Among lawyers who were interviewed in depth, 90 percent expressed a positive view of mediation, and 97 percent reported that they always or sometimes discuss mediation with their clients. . . .

Two themes that help explain the lawyers' growing acceptance of mediation emerge from the survey data: conventional litigation has become an inefficient way to resolve most disputes, and mediation offers an effective alternative that allows disputants to address personal and emotional barriers to settlement. . . .

. . . [E]discovery has made litigation more burdensome for everyone. Extensive discovery and motions are often unnecessary, as some lawyers observed, because very few cases proceed to trial. In New York City, about two percent of federal civil lawsuits and three percent of state civil suits are tried. For cases that make it to court, the results are difficult to predict, even for experienced litigators. Going to court, one lawyer said, is a "crapshoot." This combination of circumstances (cost, delay, and uncertainty) means that most cases eventually settle but often (according to many respondents) not until after the parties have spent lots of money and devoted substantial amounts of valuable time to litigation-related tasks.

[The article noted that several features of mediation combine to make it an especially effective method for promoting settlement. For example, the parties are encouraged to compare the settlement to the litigation alternative; parties communicate with each other, uninhibited by the rules of evidence; and mediators can provide unbiased evaluations that lead to more realistic views.] . . .

Mediation Allows Litigators to Be Problem Solvers

Some lawyers and clients consider litigation the modern version of trial by combat. While the "warrior" mentality still exists, an important element in many New York litigators' adoption of mediation is that it allows them to be problem solvers. A lawyer's job, said one lawyer in a survey interview, "is to ultimately resolve the dispute, and to use the tools available to you. Mediation is one of those tools." . . .

Concerns Expressed About Mediation . . .

Asked whether court-mandated mediation is worthwhile, an unnerving 40 percent of the 77 respondents who had participated in a court-mandated mediation answered "no." Many felt that courts too often order parties to mediation too soon in the litigation process, before they have sufficient information and before the litigants are emotionally ready to consider settlement on realistic terms. Many also said that the mediators on court panels are not always skilled or committed. This point takes on added significance in light of the fact that in our survey, as in many other studies, the factor most often cited as determinative of the value of a mediation is the quality of the mediator. To remedy these concerns, some respondents suggested that judges might encourage rather than compel parties to mediate and might solicit counsel's views about the most propitious timing of the session. . . .

Kusnetz, *Divorce Mediation*

24 HOUS. LAW. 33 (1986)(*)

The national movement toward alternative methods of dispute resolution now features divorce mediation as one of its components. In an era that has seen major changes in family law, such as no-fault divorce and joint custody, it makes little sense to believe that adversary divorce is the only way to satisfy the legal process. [F]urther impetus comes from new research on the devastating effects of divorce on children. Mediation is one way to reduce the hazards of divorce while helping families to learn constructive problem-solving skills. . . .

Definition

[Although this article addresses the context of divorce and family law, it is useful also for understanding mediation in personal injury, business, or commercial cases.—Eds.]

Mediation is a voluntary process in which parties to a dispute, with the help of a neutral third party, explore ways to negotiate their differences and reach a satisfactory resolution. This resolution is incorporated into a memorandum of agreement which . . . becomes the basis of a court order.

Mediation is not arbitration. In arbitration, a neutral third-party is empowered to decide the issues. In mediation, a neutral third party facilitates negotiations between the parties, but is not empowered to make decisions. All decision-making power stays with the parties.

Mediation is neither traditional legal negotiation nor representation. In the traditional adversarial process, lawyers negotiate for their clients. [I]n mediation, the parties negotiate for themselves, most often face-to-face, with the mediator present. The mediator does not represent either party. . . .

Where Does Mediation Fit?

Divorce mediation is not meant to supplant the adversarial system. For many couples, the traditional adversary system is clearly necessary and desirable; for example, when one party needs physical protection from the other; when there is dependency on drugs or alcohol; or when couples are simply committed to fighting each other. . . .

The Mediation Process

The goal of divorce mediation is an agreement by both parties covering all those issues the parties want to deal with: property, custody, child support, visitation and contractual alimony. . . .

The mediator will usually see the couple together. If this does not work for a particular couple or a particular session, the mediator may separate them and shuttle back and forth. The mediator may try to see each party alone at least once in order to get a clear idea of one's goals and needs, and to gauge where each person is in the emotional process of divorce.

[Note: In the experience of the authors, it is customary for the parties' attorneys to participate, not just the parties, although this description does not follow that pattern.]

In a private mediation setting the process may proceed as follows:

1. The couple meets with the mediator at an orientation session, usually one hour. The process is explained, including rules for the couple's conduct during mediation, full disclosure of assets, confidentiality, the use of outside experts, and the costs anticipated. . . .

2. The parties explain their situation and the problems they need to resolve.

3. If the parties and the mediator agree that mediation is appropriate for them, all sign an agreement to mediate. This agreement is an acceptance of the mediator's rules . . . .

4. A schedule of meetings is outlined and the parties are asked to fill out budget forms, to prepare lists of assets and liabilities, and to produce documents that show the present value of each item. For some this task is sobering as they learn the realistic parameters within which they will negotiate.

5. When information gathering is complete, the parties start to define the issues and formulate agreements. Often the mediator will address an easy issue first to bolster the parties' confidence in their ability to negotiate. The mediator builds on that success for the more difficult issues.

6. Experts are brought in as necessary and may include an accountant, an appraiser, or a child psychiatrist. Children are sometimes brought into the process if a particular issue warrants it. . . .

7. When an agreement is reached, a memorandum of agreement is prepared by the mediator. . . . [T]he document is then signed and given to the attorney who will prepare the court order. . . .

Notes and Questions

(1) *Inequality of Information, Determination, or Negotiating Ability.* In any mediation, one party may have access to much more information than the other. Another frequent problem is the situation in which one party is more used to techniques of negotiation than the other—or is more determined. What should be done if the parties, for example, produce an agreement that is skewed toward one or the other so severely that no person familiar with the court would expect it to be produced in that system? "If an imbalance cannot be rectified to the point where each party can negotiate in his or her interest, serious thought should be given to terminating

the mediation." Kusnetz, *supra*, at 34. A court that orders mediation can avoid this problem by allowing adequate discovery beforehand.

(2) *Are Efforts by the Mediator to Redress Imbalances Appropriate?* The tempting answer to these problems of inequality is for the mediator to redress the imbalance by advocating the rights of one party or the other, invoking "what is customary in this situation," or like behaviors. To some extent, this behavior is unavoidable, but it should be carefully confined.

(3) *Dual Representation.* For an attorney-mediator who also represents one or both parties, professional responsibility rules regarding conflict of interest can be a serious concern. The prevailing opinion appears to be that, in acting solely as a mediator, the attorney represents neither party. But what if, instead of separate attorneys representing both parties, the same mediator-attorney files the divorce complaint, advises either or both parties on their legal rights, comments on the meaning of the settlement agreement or the judgment, appears in court to obtain an uncontested divorce, or advocates one solution or another to the advantage of one spouse or another? The rules do, generally, allow dual representation if each party consents to it after full disclosure of the conflict of interest, but if this route is chosen, the mediator should be very careful about the thoroughness of the disclosure.

(4) *Confidentiality.* Mediation probably works best when both parties feel free to express themselves. Accordingly, there is a need for confidentiality, and mediators seek to provide it by agreement between the parties. Also, statements during settlement negotiations usually are excluded from evidence.

(5) *Representation of Both Parties by Separate Lawyers.* For all of the reasons given above, there is widespread agreement that mediation works best if both parties are represented by counsel of their own choosing, separate and apart from the mediator.

(6) *The Success of Mediation: Expressed Satisfaction of Participants.* Studies show higher rates of satisfaction in mediated settlement agreements than in settlement agreements reached through litigation without mediation. *See generally* Bahr, *Mediation is the Answer*, 3 Family Advocate 32 (1981). In addition, Bahr found that the average couple using mediation paid about $550 less for their divorce than the average non-mediated couple, and effects on children presumably were ameliorated by significantly higher perceptions of fairness as to custody and visitation issues. A study of dispute resolution centers using the multi-door courthouse approach showed that 92 percent of disputants would use the program again, and in the LEAA funded project with the highest rate (Houston), 97 percent reported that they were fully or partially satisfied with the service. Roehl & Cook, *The Multi-Door Dispute Resolution Program: Phase I Assessment, Final Report* (Institute of Social Analysis ed. 1985).

[B] The Mini-Trial (and Neutral Experts)

Eric Green, *The Mini-Trial Approach to Complex Litigation*

in Center for Public Resources, Dispute Management: Corporate Strategies for the Avoidance and Resolution of Legal Disputes I-A.1 (1980)(*)

The dispute resolution model described here has come to be known as a "Mini-Trial," thanks to a creative headline writer for the *New York Times*. It has also been described at various times as an Information Exchange, a Mock Trial, an Advisory Proceeding, and non-binding arbitration. Without getting bogged down in semantics, this model is a dispute-resolution hybrid that merges certain characteristics of adjudicative, arbitral, mediational and negotiational processes into a unique creation....

Properly applied to the right case, at the right time, by parties who genuinely want to resolve their dispute, the mini-trial can produce spectacular results. Experience to date indicates that best results are obtained in mini-trials of cases involving complex questions, of mixed law and fact (for example, patent, products liability, antitrust, unfair competition)—just the kinds of cases in which litigation is often intractable and costly....

Key Ingredients

The key elements of a mini-trial are:

- A voluntary, confidential and non-binding procedure, consisting of
- informal, summary presentations by the lawyers and experts for each party to the dispute of its best case, followed by rebuttal and questions concerning those presentations,
- before top management representatives (with settling authority) of each party,
- presided over a jointly selected "neutral advisor" or moderator who, if necessary, after the mini-trial will advise the parties as to the strengths and weaknesses of their respective cases.

[C] Court-Annexed Arbitration and Summary Jury Trials

In some courts, a non-binding process of "arbitration" has been required. For example, the United States District Court for the Eastern District of New York created a Local Arbitration Rule that allowed for trial *de novo* in court. The rule created a process for "compulsory" arbitration of some civil cases seeking only money damages not in excess of $150,000 and included a procedure for the clerk to initiate the arbitration process and for the conduct of a hearing. Additional excerpts of that rule are included below.

Local Civil Rule 83.7 for the Eastern District of New York (2016) (Arbitration Rule)

. . . (f) Arbitration Hearing.

(1) The arbitration hearing shall take place in the United States Courthouse in a courtroom assigned by the arbitration clerk on the date and at the time set forth in the order of the Court. . . . The arbitration clerk must be notified immediately of any continuance.

(2) Counsel for the parties shall report settlement of the case to the arbitration clerk and all members of the arbitration panel assigned to the case.

(3) The arbitration hearing may proceed in the absence of any party who, after notice, fails to be present. In the event, however, that a party fails to participate in the arbitration process in a meaningful manner, the Court may impose appropriate sanctions, including, but not limited to, the striking of any demand for a trial de novo filed by that party.

(4) Rule 45 of the Federal Rules of Civil Procedure shall apply to subpoenas for attendance of witnesses and the production of documentary evidence at an arbitration hearing under this Rule. Testimony at an arbitration hearing shall be under oath or affirmation.

(5) The Federal Rules of Evidence shall be used as guides to the admissibility of evidence. . . .

(6) A party may have a recording and transcript made of the arbitration hearing, but that party shall make all necessary arrangements and bear all expenses thereof.

(g) Arbitration Award and Judgment.

(1) The arbitration award shall be filed with the Court promptly after the hearing is concluded and shall be entered as the judgment of the Court after the 30 day period for requesting a trial de novo pursuant to Section (h) has expired, unless a party has demanded a trial de novo. The judgment so entered shall be subject to the same provisions of law and shall have the same force and effect as a judgment of the Court . . . , except that it shall not be appealable. . . .

(h) Trial De Novo.

(1) Within 30 days after the arbitration award is entered on the docket, any party may demand in writing a trial de novo in the District Court. . . .

(3) At the trial de novo, the Court shall not admit evidence that there had been an arbitration proceeding, the nature or amount of the award, or any other matter concerning the conduct of the arbitration proceeding.

(4) Upon making a demand for trial de novo the moving party shall, unless permitted to proceed in forma pauperis, deposit with the Clerk of the Court an amount equal to the arbitration fees of the arbitrators as provided in Section (b). [These fees range from $250 to $300.] The sum so deposited shall be returned to the party

demanding a trial de novo in the event that party obtains a final judgment, exclusive of interest and costs, more favorable than the arbitration award. If the party demanding a trial de novo does not obtain a more favorable result after trial or if the Court determines that the party's conduct in seeking a trial de novo was in bad faith, the sum so deposited shall be paid by the Clerk to the Treasury of the United States. . . .

Notes and Questions

(1) *Is Non-Binding Court-Annexed Arbitration Really "Mediation" or "Arbitration"?* After the arbitration award, there is a 30-day period under these rules during which either party may wipe the slate clean and proceed to trial. What will be happening during those 30 days, and what effect will the award have on the parties?

(2) *Criticisms.* For parties who proceed to trial, this local rule arguably imposes an additional layer of bureaucracy. By requiring participation in the arbitration process, it will impose additional costs that could deter a litigant who would otherwise go to trial and win, and it makes the party who rejects the arbitration result responsible to pay an additional fee for the arbitrators if the trial is not more favorable. It also forces on the parties an advisory decisionmaker different from the jury that would decide at trial. Some critics would see disadvantages in the "privatizing" of disputes that ought to be aired in public. Finally, this local rule might induce undesirable kinds of behavior from litigants. Plaintiffs wishing to avoid arbitration may claim artificially inflated damages, and defendants may remove or not remove depending upon their view of this process.

(3) *Advantages.* According to Judge Weinstein, "The court-annexed arbitration program [a]ppears to have worked well. . . . Similar programs in other federal district courts—particularly the Eastern District of Pennsylvania—have reduced the number of cases going to trial by as much as 50%."

Note on Summary Jury Trials

The development of summary jury trials is widely credited to Judge Thomas D. Lambros of the Northern District of Ohio. This procedure is roughly analogous to the substitution of a jury for court-annexed arbitration, with severely limited presentation time. It results in a recommendation for settlement, or for that matter, the parties presumably can agree to be bound by it. The Supreme Court of the State of Michigan, for example, created a pilot project to encourage summary jury trials. An article in the Michigan Bar Journal explained the process as follows:

Summary Jury Trials: How They Work and How They Can Work for You

97 Mich. B.J. 16 (Feb. 2018)
(discussing issued Administrative Order 2015-1 (March 25, 2015))

So how exactly are summary trials different from full-scale jury trials?

First, they are shorter. Full trials can last the better part of a week or more; summary jury trials are typically limited to a single day, with time limits on each component of trial. This necessarily limits the number and length of witnesses and exhibits.

Second, the juries are smaller. Each party is given two peremptory challenges apiece to whittle ten potential jurors down to the six that will be empaneled.

Third, the rules of evidence and procedure are relaxed. There is no need to authenticate documents, and parties are encouraged to stipulate to as much evidence as possible and agree to other tweaks to the rules.

Fourth, although the jury verdicts are binding, both parties must agree to participate in the summary jury trial process.

Fifth, appellate rights are reduced. The only allowable post-trial motion is for a new trial, and this may only be granted for irregularity, jury misconduct, an error of law, or fraud. . . .

. . . But the summary jury trial process has its critics. . . . Richard Posner has noted that the "jury's principal function is to determine the credibility of witnesses, yet there are no witnesses in the summary jury trial."

[Is this procedure superior to court-annexed arbitration—and, perhaps more importantly, is it superior to judicial adjudication? *See also* Lambros, *The Summary Jury Trial and Other Alternative Methods of Dispute Resolution: A Report to the Judicial Conference of the United States Committee on the Operation of the Jury System*, 103 F.R.D. 461 (1985).]

Notes and Questions

(1) *The Court's Authority to Summon Citizens for Summary Jury Trials: The Civil Justice Reform Act and United States v. Exum*, 748 F. Supp. 512 (N.D. Ohio 1990). In this case, the district judge rejected his Chief Judge's (Judge Lambros') approach, holding that the federal law governing jury service did not authorize summonses for service in summary jury trials. He reasoned that the court had no more power to force citizens to serve as settlement advisors than it did to "summon [them] to serve as hand servants." But that was not the extent of his disagreement with Judge Lambros: He also took the extraordinary step of suspending all jury trials on the theory that use of part of the jury pool for summary jury trials would "impermissibly alter" the jury selection process! This approach virtually would have eliminated summary jury trials if upheld. The Civil Justice Reform Act of 1990, however, explicitly encouraged the use of summary jury trials—and after the adoption of this Act, the district judge rescinded his orders.

(2) *What Kinds of Cases Benefit From Summary Jury Trials?: Ray, Emerging Options in Dispute Resolution*, ABA Journal, June 1989, at 66, 68. Mr. Ray reports that Judge Lambros refers a case to summary jury trial by considering the following factors: (1) there is low chance of a liability finding, but damages are potentially high; (2) emotions run high over the issue; and (3) the amount of damages is subject to great uncertainty. Asbestos injury claims seem to fit these criteria.

VI. How to Answer the Chapter Summary Problem: Some Suggestions

Which Alternate Dispute Resolution Device, if Any? (As always, follow your Professor's instructions about how to answer.)

State whether you think a particular alternate dispute resolution device is appropriate—including arbitration, mediation, mini-trial, summary jury trial, etc.—or whether traditional litigation would be most appropriate. The following analyses are merely possible solutions, and actual choices might vary significantly from them.

(a) *The Fact-Dispute Price-Fixing Case.* One alternative is traditional mediation, perhaps with an expert antitrust lawyer as mediator. Yet another alternative is arbitration with three arbitrators designated as neutrals and required to be knowledgeable antitrust expert lawyers, except that these parties probably will not want to give up control to binding arbitration.

(b) *The Interwoven Fact-Law Tying Arrangement Dispute.* The old-time Mini-Trial fits this kind of case. The dispute is complex, big, and ambiguous in both facts and law. But mini-trials are less common today than they once were. An alternative, again, is traditional mediation, perhaps with an expert antitrust lawyer as mediator. Yet another alternative is arbitration with three arbitrators designated as neutrals and required to be knowledgeable antitrust expert lawyers, except that again, parties like these usually do not want to give up control to a binding decision. Traditional adjudication is not an attractive option (it looks like roulette to these parties, is very expensive, and will disrupt all parties for years).

(c) *The Antitrust Dispute Overlapped by a Personality Clash.* Mediation is one way through a personality clash. But traditional adjudication might be a better option than in the situations above. A test case will give a more authoritative answer. Even if these parties mediate and obtain an answer by agreement, it will be doubtful as a guide to the future, whereas a court judgment will provide a more definitive precedent. Litigation of the problem sounds simpler than in the other two situations. It sounds like a matter for summary judgment.

(d) *The Recurrent Commercial Dispute.* This is a situation for arbitration according to a recurring simple plan. Mediation sounds unworkable, and traditional litigation would be expensive and repeatedly require delay and adversary battles over small disputes.

Appendix

The Personal Dimension of Litigation — Or, "Can a Litigator Be Competent, Adversarial, Professional, Successful, and Altruistic … and Also Live a Full Life?"

I. Why We Have Included This (Unusual) Appendix

[A] A Disclaimer

This Appendix is Subject to Disagreement, Contains Controversial Opinions, and Requires Individualized Adaptation to Your Personal Circumstances. It is inherently difficult to describe the job satisfactions and dissatisfactions of litigators. To say what clients are "like," or to identify what to watch out for in your dealings with judges, obstreperous opponents, or (for that matter) alcohol, obviously will result in some ill-fitting advice. Nevertheless, the effort may be worthwhile. Today, for example, the State of California has decided to require — not to suggest, but to *require* — every single practicing lawyer to undertake regular instruction in substance abuse avoidance, stress reduction, and office management. In fact, litigators' complaints in many respects are surprisingly uniform. The life of a litigator can be very hard if one does it the wrong way, and our modest goal in this Appendix is to help you confront the consequences of the choices you must make.

[B] The Depth of Lawyer Dissatisfaction — and, the Good News

(1) *Lawyer Dissatisfaction Is Surprisingly Prevalent: An ABA Survey Showed That Only About Half Were Satisfied with Their Career.* An ABA survey revealed that

about half (55%) of the 800 lawyers surveyed were satisfied with their career; the least satisfied were in large firms, while two-thirds (68%) of lawyers in the public sector reported career satisfaction. Stephanie Francis Ward, *Pulse of the Legal Profession*, ABA JOURNAL, Oct. 2007, at 30. Of the lawyers surveyed, less than half (44%) "would recommend a legal career to young people." *Id.* In 2008, the American Bar Association said flatly, "Lawyers are not happy." ABA JOURNAL, Sept. 2008, at 39. Other surveys, too, have shown surprisingly large percentages of lawyer discontent. *See, e.g.*, Grimes, *Are There Too Many Lawyers (And Are They Happy?)*, HOUSTON LAWYER, Sept.-Oct. 1990, at 6 (43% of lawyers wouldn't enter the legal profession if they had to make the choice again); Robert A. Stein, *Help Is Available*, ABA JOURNAL, June 2005, at 64 (one in four "lawyers suffers from stress," lawyers rank highest in depression among 105 occupations, and have disproportionately high suicide rates).

(2) *The Good News.* The same surveys also showed, however, that most lawyers were basically content with the profession they had chosen. Eighty percent of respondents in the ABA survey stated they were proud to be lawyers and eighty-one percent believe the practice of law is intellectually stimulating. Stephanie Francis Ward, *Pulse of the Legal Profession*, ABA JOURNAL, Oct. 2007, at 30. Again, these lawyers clearly share many of the same problems. What distinguishes the malcontents?

(3) *A Variety of Causes That, Unfortunately, Are Built into the System.* Lawyers complain bitterly about opposing counsel, whom they see as "dumb," or "pushy," or "sneaky." (See below.) They also are disappointed in judges, possibly because the societal image of judges is inflated. Clients are unappreciative, uncooperative, and enthralled with unrealistic expectations; partners or employers are exploitative; and the adversary system produces constant stress, injustice and oppression. There is no time for the lawyer's own concerns — not for hobbies, not even for errands. *Cf.* ABA JOURNAL, Sept. 1986, at 44; ABA JOURNAL, Oct. 1991, at 42-43.

[C] Life, Litigation and Law School: How Much Correlation Between Your Preparation and the Real World?

(1) *Decotiis & Steele, The Skills of the Lawyering Process*, 40 TEX. B.J. 483 (1977). These two researchers observed five general practitioners of high reputation to find how they spent their time on a day-to-day basis. The results were surprising. The lawyers did very little reading, "except proofreading." They also did very little expository writing, except for short letters, although they did exercise a different kind of skill that the researchers called "document preparation" (which differed from writing because it normally involved the "cannibalizing" of clauses from existing documents, although it sometimes required a high degree of experience, knowledge and judgment). As for legal research (the only skill other than appellate opinion analysis that universally is taught to all law students), these practitioners eschewed it as a low-level endeavor. They hired others, such as law clerks, to do their research. The most highly developed skill, according to Decotiis and Steele:

negotiation. The lawyers also were adept at interviewing and at explaining the legal system and legal choices to others (such as clients).

(2) *The Implications: Practice Requires a Greater Adjustment than You Might Expect, and Career Choices Are More Difficult* — *Cf. Biehl, Things They Didn't Teach You in Law School*, ABA JOURNAL, Jan. 1989, at 52. Thus, law school may provide an idealized view of the profession — one in which the more prosaic and the more seamy side is underexplored. New lawyers also sometimes are surprised about the depth and persistence of their skill deficiencies (especially in litigation). Finally, because law school course content does not correspond to the daily tasks of lawyering, new lawyers lack a basis for career choices (or for daily choices that a career presents, such as whether to accept a given contingent fee case). The point, however, is not that there is something "wrong" with the material selected for teaching in law school. The ability to analyze an appellate decision, for example, is essential, because one must appreciate legal analysis before knowing how to go about "fact gathering." Rather, the point is that there are aspects of the legal profession that law school does not aspire to teach.

[D] Coping with a Changing Litigation Marketplace

(1) *Are There Really "Too Many" Litigators?* The legal market is projected to grow at about the same rate as all occupations until at least 2014, primarily due to population and business growth. U.S. Dep't of Labor, Bureau of Labor Statistics, *Occupational Outlook Handbook* (2006). Much of the growth will be in services for the middle class, as a result of "wider availability and affordability of legal clinics." *Id.* Businesses, however, are reducing their legal costs by using accounting firms and even paralegals to accomplish some of the tasks historically left to lawyers. *Id.* Increased reliance on ADR, such as mediation and arbitration, is also decreasing the amount of traditional litigation word. *Id.* As a result of the increases prevalence of large law firms, the number of solo practitioners is expected to slowly decline and solo practitioners will be more successful in smaller communities. *Id.* As the number of law school graduates continues to rise, there has been rigorous competition for available jobs, suppressing wages and forcing some to accept jobs for which they may be overqualified and even filling legal positions through temporary staffing agencies. *Id.*

(2) *The Solutions: Flexibility about Professional Prospects and Careful Study of New Market Conditions in Litigation.* The legal market is cyclical and when discretionary demand decreases during recessionary periods, demand will increase in other areas as disputes arise in areas "such as bankruptcies, foreclosure, and divorces requiring legal action" *Id.* The practice areas that have seen declines in recent years include personal injury and medical malpractice claims, which have been affected by tort reform movements. Amir Efrati, *Hard Case: Job Market Wanes for U.S. Lawyers*, WALL ST. J., September 24, 2007, at A1. Other practice areas are either currently

booming or expected to be hot in the future. These include complex litigation, asbestos, antitrust, immigration, family law, nursing home litigation, and employment law. Robert W. Denney, *What's Hot and What's Not in the Legal Profession*, No. 1 ABA LAW PRACTICE 10 (Jan./Feb. 2007). Environmental law has been declining in importance, but with growing global warming concerns, this practice may also be on an uptrend in the near future. *Id.* Other trends to keep in mind are technological development, globalization, and upcoming retirement of baby boomers. *See id.* In addition to varying demand among practice groups, demand for lawyers varies depending on geographic location, so the ability to relocate can be beneficial to one's job search. *See* U.S. Dep't of Labor, Bureau of Labor Statistics, *Occupational Outlook Handbook* (2006). In summary, you will need to be flexible and maximize opportunities by studying market conditions carefully. But if you do so, and if you have the makeup of a litigator, you can develop sound prospects of finding job satisfaction in the field.

II. Litigation in Human Terms: The "Down Side"

This Section Gives You the Bad News First, Then the Good News. The materials that follow may appear unrelentingly gloomy. For three reasons, they are not. First, if you anticipate these problems, you will have a better chance of avoiding them. Second, we plan to offer solutions when they are available (and often, even for the most serious problems, they are). Third, remember the disclaimer, above: There are two sides to this picture, and we plan to give you the "up" side, also, after we finish with the "down" side.

Problem A

A CAUTIONARY TALE ABOUT A FAST-LANE DIVORCE, adapted from Houston Chronicle, Sept. 20, 1994, at 4A (New York Times report).

> "When [wife] surrendered her two sons to her former husband's custody 11 days ago, it was the climactic act in a cautionary tale of two-career couples in the 1990's.
>
> "To [wife], 43, a counsel to [the United States Senator who chairs the Senate Judiciary Committee], and [to] the feminist legal groups rallying around her, the decision by a Washington judge to award custody to the father is chilling evidence of a judicial backlash against professional women.
>
> "... [But] her former husband, ... 48, the assistant executive director of the American Federation of Television and Radio Artists, [sees the matter differently]. ...
>
> "The battle lines were drawn after a July decision by Judge Harriet Taylor of the District of Columbia Superior Court.

> "In a sharply worded opinion, ... [Judge] Taylor painted [the wife] as a driven workaholic who seldom arrived home before dinner and [the husband] as a doting father who put his children first.
>
> "In her opinion [Judge] Taylor quotes friends and relatives of [the husband's], as well as a baby-sitter who said [the wife] often ate dinner alone and very late at night, 'while sitting on the kitchen floor, with her plate on the floor, talking on the telephone or writing while she was eating.' Friends of [the husband] described [the wife] as working even during her children's birthday parties, of 'barking orders,' and of being 'very tightly wound.'
>
> "... Taylor said [the wife] was 'more devoted and absorbed by her work and her career than anything else in her life, including her health, her children, and her family.' "

(1) *First Question: Why Did This Sad Divorce Decision Occur?* Consider the following hypotheses as reasons for this result. (a) Has the wife's training made her take on counterproductive behaviors? [Before you reject this hypothesis, wait to read Problem B, below, which considers whether law school "teaches" obsessive-compulsive personality characteristics.] (b) Is the wife the victim of gender bias? (c) Did the wife's decision to combine a legal career with a family create the problem? (d) Was the wife's decision to take on a particularly all-consuming position inconsistent with being a good custodial mother (or for that matter, for a man, a good custodial father)? (e) Could the wife have handled the balance by changing some of her behaviors or circumstances? (f) Are all of the above possibly true (or partially true)? (g) Are there other possibilities that you can think of?

(2) *Second Question: Can a Lawyer Avoid This Sort of Outcome?* Consider the following possibilities as a means of avoiding a similarly unfortunate result in your own life and career. (a) Good time management (as you will see below, some people consider this the single biggest factor within a lawyer's control). (b) Stress management. (c) Business management. (d) Effective dealings with adversaries, with the adversary system, and with the people on your side. (e) Finding a position that fits your life and personality. (f) Avoiding dysfunctional dependencies (on drugs or on work). (g) Recognizing what the problems are. (h) Other possibilities that you may recognize.

[A] Institutional Causes of Lawyer Dissatisfaction (and Solutions)

[1] Time: How Lawyers Measure, Manage, and Use It

(1) *Time, and Keeping "Time Records": The Negative Psychological Effects* — Hecht, *Lawyer's Life Governed by the Tick of the Clock*, NAT'L L.J., April 21, 1986, at 17, col. 1. The evidence strongly indicates that lawyers who keep time records are more effective than lawyers who do not. (Time records are the only accepted billing method

for major areas of practice.) Even contingent-fee lawyers need to record time regularly because "reasonable" attorney's fees so frequently are part of the remedy, and government or corporate employers often require time keeping by their in-house lawyers as a means of efficient resource allocation. But a new lawyer who never has experienced the negative personal effects of dividing her professional life into tenths of an hour is in for a shock. For example, one lawyer who left the practice says she felt "worn away in six-minute increments." Jefferson, above, ABA JOURNAL, Dec. 1991, at 60. Interruptions become intolerable because they sidetrack the lawyer's record keeping; the learning curve with unfamiliar law becomes a source of frustration (and so does the series of short telephone calls that the lawyer did not immediately memorialize); and at the end of the day, the lawyer faces major gaps that are impossible to reconstruct. The temptation toward "padding" is enormous. But perhaps the worst effect surfaces when the lawyer's spouse or friend calls to discuss this evening's social engagement, or just to talk. At that point, the lawyer's values turn upside down. Glancing continuously at her watch, the lawyer struggles with the question: "How am I going to bill this time?" while attempting in frustration to end the conversation!

(2) *Time as "Stock in Trade": Not Enough Time for Avocations, People, or Even Personal Errands — see id.; see also* Blodgett, *Time and Money: A Look at Today's Lawyer,* ABA JOURNAL, Sept. 1986, at 47. Time keeping leads to yet another problem. The focus is not how valuable is the time the lawyer has spent, or even whether it was effective; and it certainly is not whether the lawyer has enough time left for personal pursuits. In recent years, it appears that lawyer billable hours have increased. *See* Jefferson, above, ABA JOURNAL, Dec. 1991, at 60 ("As overhead went up through the Eighties, firms kept upping the number of hours people were required to bill .... That's how we ended up with this 2500-hour-a-year rat race"). Many lawyers who once were avid pleasure-readers virtually stop reading non-law books, and many have little time for hobbies, avocations, or personal (non-business) friends. Not only is it difficult to find time to take an art class (for example); the lawyer cannot even find time for car repairs, exercise, or necessary personal errands. And this problem may be getting worse instead of better. *See Look at the Time,* ABA JOURNAL, December 1989, at 88 (reporting that many firms now insist on posting all lawyers' time daily, rather than weekly); Jefferson, above, at 64 (to bill 1,900 or 2,000 hours a year, "[Y]ou're probably going to be in the office at least 10 hours a day." [What about to bill 2,500?]).

(3) *Deadlines and the Court Management Revolution: See Chapter 8, Above.* Statutes of limitation and time limits for post-trial motions have long existed, and pretrial cutoffs have existed for some time. These deadlines have always meant that a lawyer with (say) 200 active matters needs to be alert to the calendar, and many lawyers have suffered the experience of time-barring a client's rights by inadvertence. But today, the consequences of inadvertent noncompliance have increased exponentially with the court management revolution, which includes such innovations as differential case management, staging and fast-tracking. The ultimate

result: The lawyer must spend much more time managing calendar systems. And worst of all, the lawyer inevitably feels a twinge in his stomach while locking the office door to leave for the night. He fears that a glitch in his time management system will cause one of his clients' rights to be "adjudicated" by deadline when the clock strikes midnight.

(4) *The Solution: Short-Term Time Management, Long-Term Time Management, and Vigorous Self-Discipline* — Hanson, *Laughing All the Way Home: A "Tickler" System That Works*, 29 TEX. B.J. 568 (1966). Numerous systems are on the market for time keeping. Initial negotiation with the client of how time billing should be submitted is essential. When the client's demands for billing detail become excessive, the lawyer should consider declining the representation or altering the fee arrangement to reflect increased *de facto* costs. As for deadline management, the lawyer should set up a "double entry tickler system" and a device called a "perpetual calendar" because some deadlines may span as much as ten years (*e.g.*, execution on an existing judgment). [These are paper-and-pencil systems for low-tech lawyers. Recall that increased technology may not be the trend.] Finally, the lawyer must use rigorous self-discipline about time. *See also* Brill, *How Planning Your Priorities Will Improve Your Pleasure and Profitability*, 44 TEX. B.J. 1360 (1981). Careful attention to selection and refusal of representation, attention to the quality of results from different kinds of efforts, reservation of time for non-billable matters, and (perhaps most importantly) insistence upon time for exercise, family, friends and avocations, are all important.

(5) *But Time also Involves Cancellations, Washouts, Unexpected Events, and Chaos: The Paradox of Time Management.* Yet efficient time management is not enough. You must have patience, too. A deposition that you had scheduled for this morning washes out because the "Rambo" litigator on the other side instructed his client not to appear, and the two conflicting meetings that you had scheduled for two o'clock this afternoon both cancelled. You must adjust quickly if you are to avoid wasting your "stock in trade." Here is the paradox: You must be rigorous in insisting on time management, but at the same time you must be flexible. You must be able to tolerate the frustration of your time plans. Again, self-discipline is a key attribute.

[2] The Dark Side of the Adversary System

(1) *The Loss of Civility.* The American Bar Association reports that 69% of lawyers agree that "lawyers have become less civil to each other over time." ABA J., October 2007, at 31.

(2) *Does the System Ever Work?* The ABA also reports that 80% of lawyers agree that "the cost of litigation has become prohibitive in recent years." *Id.*

(3) *Failure and Loss — It Occurs Frequently: Can You Deal With It?* A trial is a zero-sum game. Logically, one side has to lose what the other side wins. And it is difficult to overstate how bad it feels to some lawyers to lose a jury trial. Almost always, the losing lawyer perceives the loss as an injustice; the defeat is public; it

may be published in trial reports in many jurisdictions; the fact that it actually is the loss of the client, who trusted the lawyer, makes matters worse; all too often, the lawyer identifies something he "could have done" to avoid disaster; and sometimes, the opposing (winning) lawyer has seemed to be obstreperous, condescending, and (occasionally) sleazy. The good lawyer's personal commitment works against him, here: It elevates the defeat to a personal rejection. In fact, some lawyers, after losing a jury trial, actually experience the stages of grief that are associated with much more serious losses: denial ("the judge will give me a new trial"); anger ("the other side's witnesses didn't tell the truth and the judge didn't let me show that"); self-abnegation ("I could have hired a metallurgy expert — but then, maybe that wouldn't have made any difference either"); and finally, acceptance ("well, I'll take it as a learning experience").

(4) *The Vince Lombardi Approach: "Winning [Is] the Only Thing."* "Winning isn't everything; it's the only thing," said legendary Green Bay Packer Coach Vince Lombardi. (From Lombardi's standpoint, that astounding statement probably made sense: Instilling into young professional football players an instinctive rejection of anything associated with failure probably motivated them to win, but it did so at a high cost, because of the inevitability of some losses.)

(5) *How Effective Will You Be After Law School in Dealing with Losses or Failures?* Imagine that your professor asks, "Now, this lawyer lost the case. What could he have done to win it?" This is a useful question to expose the impact of substantive law or litigation choices. But you should not misunderstand the professor's question as an indication that all trial losses are the fault of lawyers. You should not, for example, infer that favorable verdicts result from sheer lawyer cleverness uninfluenced by the case facts. Furthermore, you should not assume that the trial result was completely predictable, because litigation often is unavoidably chaotic. (Thus, chances are good that any given "solution" was foreclosed by events not contained in the casebook — which, after all, reflects only a tiny fraction of the lawyering by the parties.) Above all, you should avoid assuming that the lawyer "lost" the case through misfeasance. Quite possibly, two skillful lawyers battled vigorously to a close victory for one of them, and there are many choices that "could" have made a difference — just as Lombardi's Packers could have lost to any other professional team on a given Sunday.

(6) *Dealing with Frequent Losses: Do a Good Job Anyway.* In fact, in some areas of practice, lawyers lose trials much more often than they win them. "We lose 90 percent of the time, so if you're a person who hates to lose, you're going to have a lot of dissatisfaction," says one public defender who nevertheless is happy with her job. Jefferson, above, at 64. The point is that frequent failures and losses are inherent in litigation, and law school may not prepare you for them. Living a satisfying life as a litigator requires learning to deal with them on your own. Lawyers, like other people, can and should get satisfaction from doing the job well: We guarantee effort, but not results.

(7) *The Opposite Problem — Oppression of Innocent People: Benson, Why I Quit Practicing Law*, NEWSWEEK, Nov. 4, 1991, at 10. In this remarkable essay, former Colorado lawyer Sam Benson describes the instant when he realized he was going to quit. He was weary of what he saw as trickery and deception; he did not like pushy lawyers and clients; but his most significant source of discontent was the oppression that was inevitable in the adversary system. "Most of all," he writes, "I was tired of the misery my job caused other people." The problem is that most professional codes require lawyers to represent their clients "zealously" within the bounds of the law. Many if not most litigators interpret this command as requiring them to stretch both facts and law just short of ethical limits, and unfortunately, says Benson, "they may be right." The result is the litigator as a "hired gun" who thinks only about winning cases without actually breaking enforceable rules, not about avoiding oppression of innocent people or solving problems cooperatively. Benson adds: "A nice guy does not usually make a good attorney in the adversarial system." [Do you think Benson's description is too starkly pessimistic? (We do, at least in some respects — Eds.) Even if so, isn't it clear that a person who makes his living as a litigator in the real world regularly will be subject to a perceived "duty to oppress"?]

(8) *Truthtelling, Falsification, and "Zealous" Advocacy — Do the Difficulty of Line-Drawing and the Infrequency of Detection Lead to Cynical Toleration?* In one (real) case, an interrogatory asked, "Identify all photographs of the relevant event." The responding lawyer (who later became president of a major bar association) had a professionally-produced videotape of the entire event — but he answered, with technical correctness, "I know of none." Under applicable discovery rules, it is difficult to argue that this response was anything other than proper. In another case, the interrogatory asked, "Identify all depictions of the product's packaging," and the responding lawyer attempted to justify a similar "no" answer by the argument that the photographs in his possession were not technically "depictions." [One of the authors of this book, as co-counsel, insisted on a "yes" answer, which actually is the answer that the other co-counsel would have arrived at anyway.] The trouble is that the difference between these two definitional problems turns on matters of degree, about which argument is possible in both cases. And often, even looser standards of "reasonableness" or the like govern the propriety of an argument.

(9) *The Mushiness of Standards — and the Result: Burke, "Truth in Lawyering": An Essay on Lying and Deceit in the Practice of Law*, 38 ARK. L. REV. 1 (1984). These circumstances breed cynicism as lawyers see adversaries define terms aggressively and succeed at it. Their own experience calls for similar kinds of self-serving interpretation — with only a blurred line, representing vague matters of degree, demarcating what is forbidden. The result? "For years we have 'winked, blinked, and nodded' at blatant if not outrageous lying and deception in pleading, negotiating, investigating, testifying and bargaining. [W]e have come to accept, in fact, to expect, a certain amount of lying and deception ...," according to Professor Burke, above. But perhaps the worst news is that Professor Burke sees lawyers' codes of ethics, as

well as the rules of evidence and procedure, as "largely responsible" for this ethical confusion! [Are these conclusions justified? Probably, many lawyers would disagree with some of what Professor Burke says, but his essay is valuable even if only to demonstrate the moral conflict. And, consider: "[I]t is easy to tell a lie, but harder to tell only one … . [A]fter the first lies, [o]thers come more easily." S. Bok, *Lying: Moral Choice in Public and Private Life* 25 (1978); *see also* Tuohy & Warden, *The Fall from Grace of a Greylord Judge*, ABA JOURNAL, Feb. 1989, at 60.]

(10) *Injustice: Its Incidence and Its Effects.* Injustice, or at least perceived injustice, is a frequent condition of litigation. The object, after all, is resolving disputes, and that is a messy business. To avoid becoming consumed by stress, the litigator must prevent himself from feeling responsible for every injustice that happens to occur. But the trouble is, he also must prevent this attitude from subtly developing into toleration of (or willing participation in) those injustices. And that is not as easy as it sounds.

(11) *The Spectre of Malpractice — and the Situations in Which You are "Damned If You Do and Damned If You Don't."* A young litigator perceives the testimony of an opposing party as willful perjury and believes that his duty is to expose it. After several months of vigorous effort, he is sanctioned under Rule 11 for an amount in the hundreds of thousands of dollars because the court found the allegation unreasonable. [This example is taken from a real case, or at least is taken from the "real" version given by the young lawyer.] Situations like this one, in which you are "damned if you do and damned if you don't," occur sometimes in litigation. (Consider, for another example, Alice Delagroi's medical malpractice claim, which is the focus of the Chapter 5 summary problem, above. *See also Costly Errors*, ABA JOURNAL, June 1989, at 28.)

(12) *Solutions ("Am I Insured for This?") — Cross, The Spectre of the Malpractice Suit: Increasingly Visible*, LEGAL ADVOCATE, Mar. 1979, at 3, col. 1. How can the lawyer avoid disaster in these problem situations? Experience is helpful, as is hard work; the humility of a lawyer who recognizes that she is not omniscient may be even more important, because it helps her to recognize the impending disaster. But even competent, ethical lawyers make mistakes, especially in today's climate, with occasionally disastrous losses to their clients, and with the spectre of malpractice liability more real today than ever. As for malpractice insurance, it is only a partial solution. It is sufficiently expensive so that lawyers in less lucrative practices may determine that they cannot afford it. Increasingly, too, malpractice insurers are insisting on "claims made" policies, covering only claims that are asserted against the insured during the policy period. *See Bar Plan v. Campbell*, at the end of Section 5.05 in Chapter 5, above. If the act of malpractice or the loss occurred in an earlier year and the lawyer no longer is insured, there is no coverage under such a policy. And since the annual application requires disclosure of prior conduct that might give rise to claims, the insurer may be in a position to refuse the coverage. *See also* Mary Kathleen Hartley, *Top Trends in Malpractice*, GP SOLO, April/May 2003, at 22.

[3] People Problems, Part I: The People on Your Side

(1) *Clients Who Are Difficult or Uncooperative: Hecht,* NAT'L L.J., Mar. 9, 1987, at 11, col. 2. "The case may be good. The issues may be interesting and important. The pot of gold at the end of the rainbow may be attractive. But what can you do when the client doesn't help you represent him?" Hecht identifies "four categories" of uncooperative clients: (1) the "Never-in Nellie," who is never in and who "never returns your phone calls" (send the client a "please call me" letter after three attempts), (2) "the great Houdini," who is reachable on the telephone but "never appears for depositions, contract signings, court dates and the like," (3) "Mal Content," who "disagrees with everything you do and, if that isn't enough, despises you," (solution: "don't even try" to please this client), and (4) "Double-Dealing Debbie," who generates second opinions herself (or obtains them from dubious sources) and asks questions like "Why didn't you raise the defense of collateral estoppel?" The result may be that "your Rolaids bill" may exceed the fee you earn. Hecht suggests: first, transferring these clients to a colleague; second, telling the client that the case is "flawed (even if it isn't)" to make the client feel a degree of responsibility; and third, making the client "an adversary." This last solution is accomplished by a lengthy series of letters warning the client that "unless X is provided, the case may be dismissed." Hecht's conclusion: "At least estate attorneys do not have these problems since their clients [n]ever utter a complaint, since they are dead. Lucky guys." [What do you think of this advice — is it ethical? And if so, is it unduly cynical?]

(2) *"Cases and Clients That Should Be Turned Down," in J. Foonberg, How to Start and Build a Law Practice, 51-54 (1976).* Foonberg's ostensibly cynical (but more often sensible) advice is that the beginning lawyer should refuse employment in certain situations, including: (1) "When you are the second or third lawyer on the case" (earlier lawyers may have had honest differences with the client but often they indicate "a. a nonmeritorious case[;] b. an uncooperative client[; or] c. a nonpaying client"); (2) " 'hurt feeling' cases" such as cases of libel, brawls, or assault and battery (which have arguably wrongful conduct, but "nominal damages at best"); (3) "landlord-tenant cases (unless you are paid in full in advance)," in which representing either party is equally undesirable ("each side wants to use the lawyer for revenge if he can use the lawyer for free"). In addition, Foonberg recommends against acceptance of bankruptcy cases unless the lawyer is prepaid in full ("It was embarrassing when my client amended his bankruptcy schedules to include the unpaid balance of the fee due me"), clients who "use your telephones, secretary and offices to do their business" (this client, he says, somehow always ends up being "trouble"), and the like. For cases totally without merit, Foonberg's solution is, "Tell your client the truth."

(3) *"Firing the Client": The Solution of Withdrawal.* Some commentators recommend liberal use of the withdrawal option for serious problem clients, unless withdrawal is impractical or unethical (*e.g.*, it would prejudice the client's case). *See* Foonberg, above, at 102; *cf.* Hecht, above, at 14. Often, conflict or nonpayment

makes the client avoid the lawyer; in that situation, a "due process trail" of letters may be necessary to avoid prejudicing the client and to protect the lawyer.

(4) *"The Client's Curve of Gratitude."* Foonberg reproduces this "curve," which is similar to the Bell curve familiar to statisticians. The curve begins with the day the complaint is served on the client, who recognizes that he is in trouble: "I didn't know [those pulleys I sold and didn't check] were defective and would be used in a jet airplane which crashed." The curve reaches its topmost point on the day when the lawyer's hard work produces a favorable settlement on the courthouse steps: "No other lawyer could have done what he did. I owe him my business, my career, everything." Mysteriously, the curve turns downward, until, ten weeks later, the client considers the lawyer "crazy if he thinks I'm going to pay" and, eventually, decides to complain to the bar association and sue the lawyer "for malpractice." Foonberg's message is simple: the lawyer should insist on payment in advance (or bill monthly and take steps to collect). For reasons that involve the client's welfare as well as his own, Foonberg implies that the sensible lawyer never lets the client get "too far ahead" of him.

(5) *Fee Disputes.* A large percentage of complaints or grievances presented by clients to disciplinary boards originate in fee disputes. A partial solution lies in the nearly universal advice that the attorney insist upon a written fee agreement in every case (which is more difficult that it might appear). Another partial solution is the practice of regular billing and collection, which tends to ensure that disputes are confronted early.

(6) *Clients in Divorce, Personal Injury and Criminal Cases: A Special Problem — Buchmeyer, How to Avoid Grievance Complaints*, 47 TEX. B.J. 162 (1983). Consider the following client dilemma. The only sensible course is for your client to accept insurance policy limits of $20,000, even though he is horribly disfigured, because his case is weak on liability and there is no defendant who even approaches solvency. Naturally, the client objects to the proposed settlement. But assuming that trial absolutely cannot produce more money and that a zero verdict is a real possibility, your duty is to persist in your advice. Here is the point: If you must overcome strong client resistance, watch out, even though there clearly is no other alternative. In this area of practice (personal injury) — and in divorce and criminal law — clients make disciplinary complaints at a much higher rate than in other areas, even where monetary losses are larger. In these areas, lawyers deal almost invariably with unsophisticated clients who are unfamiliar with the litigation system and have unrealistic expectations. (Incidentally, Buchmeyer convincingly refutes the hypothesis that there is a lesser standard among these practitioners.) The solutions: consider declining representation; don't promise the moon; help your client to confront the weaknesses in the case; don't coerce settlement; seek another lawyer's assistance in explaining the problems to the client when necessary; and treat the client with respect. *See also* Mary Kathleen Hartley, *Top Trends in Malpractice*, GP SOLO, April/May 2003, at 22.

(7) *Pick Your Mentor Carefully for Courage, Time Availability, and Willingness to Give Support: The Problems of Co-Counsel, Employers and Supervisors.* In addition to trouble with opposing counsel, lawyers often have trouble with counsel who ostensibly are on the same side. To take a situation that (we hope) is infrequent: If a superior is untrustworthy or mendacious, it can be surprisingly difficult for a beginning lawyer to avoid entanglement in ethical violations or sanctionable conduct. The beginner's inexperience and subordinate position makes the subordinate eager to please. Sometimes, the problem is even worse: The superior who lacks integrity also lacks courage, and may take steps to insure that his subordinate is the one in the compromised position. The solution: Pick your mentors with care. Look for the time availability that will let you obtain guidance (although this quality is not as abundant as one might hope in experienced attorneys). Look to see whether she takes the responsibility herself rather than placing it on subordinates. And, finally, look for integrity.

Problem B

MILGRAM'S EXPERIMENTS WITH AUTHORITY AND OBEDIENCE. The social psychology of authority and obedience has produced some disturbing results. For example, Stanley Milgram's authority experiment is a classic. Milgram set up a phony "experimenter" in an official-looking white lab coat, who actually was a stooge, and who instructed subjects to administer electrical "shocks" to a strapped-down "learner" whenever the learner made errors. The scale for the "shocks" began at "15 Volts — 'Slight' Shock" and went through 150 Volts ("'Strong' Shock"), all the way to 450 Volts.

But in reality, there were no shocks, and the learner was a stooge, who both erred intentionally and grunted or gasped in pain at the lower settings. At 120 volts, the stooge playing the part of the learner protested that the shocks were painful; at 150, the stooge (through a voice recorder) shouted "Get me out of here! ... I refuse!" But if the subject faltered, the experimenter responded firmly that "the experiment requires that you go on." At "180 volts," the learner shouted that he "couldn't stand" the pain; at 300, responses stopped, and the experimenter told the subject to treat a non-response as a wrong answer. Most subjects who "prematurely" terminated this charade were highly agitated, and so were those who continued, protesting all the way, to 450 volts. The white-jacketed "experimenter" used a simple technique, simply telling the subject that "the experiment requires you to continue," or words to that effect.

But astonishingly, more than 60 percent of the subjects continued to the end of the scale, hearing increasingly agonized cries from the stooge. Milgram's conclusion was that "ordinary people" were sufficiently obedient to purported authority that they could be readily engaged in a "terribly destructive process."

(1) *First Question: What Significance Does This Have for Lawyers?* A new lawyer will encounter many authority figures, ranging from clients to judges to employers to partners. Does Milgram's experiment demonstrate that these authoritative

people might succeed to a surprising degree in inducing the new lawyer to behave dysfunctionally?

(2) *Second Question: What Factors or Behaviors Increase or Decrease the Likelihood That an Authority Can Induce Bad Behavior in You?* Milgram's experiments also showed some of the factors that affected obedience to commands to shock. Obedience increased (a) when the authority (the white-coated "experimenter") had high status, (b) when there was no disobeying role model, (c) when the experimenter was physically close, (d) when the victim was distant, and (e) when the subject was depersonalized (*e.g.*, when the subject wore a mask). Other experiments have shown that conformity increases (f) when the subject has no clear commitment against the suggestion, (g) when the subject belongs to a culture that values conformity, (h) when a sizable group is the authority, and (i) when the correctness or wrongness of the suggested behavior is ambiguous. What do these factors suggest about how you can avoid being led into destructive behavior by the people on your side?

[4] People Problems, Part II: The Other Participants

(1) *Disappointments with Judges and Courts: Report of the Texas Judicial Qualification Commission*, 58 TEX. B.J. 1095 (1991). The public impression of judges is that they are selfless and scholarly. Courtroom etiquette reinforces the natural tendency to hold judges in esteem. Perhaps for that reason, judges often are sources of attorney disappointment. First, in today's disposition-oriented climate, docket pressures often motivate judges to become abusive, to cut off arguments, to refuse relief, and to treat disputants like feuding children even when they have honest differences requiring adjudication. (Thus, the above report notes one judge who "used profanity and became personally abusive toward a defendant when the judge lost his temper in the course of a judicial proceeding." *See also Kothe v. Smith*, above.) Second, sometimes the judge acts energetically and with good motives, but with an unfortunate disassociation from rules and consequences: "In an effort to avoid further conflict between the parties, a judge heard evidence from each party outside the presence of the other party, thereby failing to allow cross-examination." Another judge "personally conducted a field investigation concerning a case pending in his court, which included surveillance of the defendant's home and interviewing the defendant's neighbors." *Id.* (If that last report troubles you, consider the *Business Guides* case, § V[B][1] in Chapter 5, above, in which the Supreme Court apparently condoned extensive telephone detective work by the trial court.) Third, judges sometimes abuse their positions: "A judge telephoned a member of a law firm, which had other cases pending in the judge's court, to inquire into the progress of a civil matter, on behalf of a friend who had an interest in that civil matter." *Id.* Fourth, judges sometimes have garden-variety prejudices. These kinds of disappointing conduct occur in every state and are especially troublesome when the judge cannot be removed. Often, the inexperienced lawyer is helpless to counteract judicial misbehavior. *See also, e.g.*, Gilbert, *Difficult Judges: How to Survive Them*, CALIFORNIA LITIGATION, Winter 1991, at

3 (even if the judge acts in a blatantly sexist manner toward you or your client in front of the jury, "a quick lesson on the evils of sexism may hurt rather than help your client"); Smolin, *Thirteen Deadly Sins: How Lawyers Irritate Judges*, CALIFORNIA LITIGATION, Winter 1991 at 11 (the "greatest" deadly sin, according to this article: "boring the judge"(!)).

(2) *Opposing Counsel Who Are Uncooperative, Unresponsive or Incompetent.* Unless the trial judge has the time, the experience, and the fortitude to impose sanctions, dealing with such an adversary can be maddeningly frustrating. Often, the judge chooses forbearance, rather than visitation of the sins from the opposing lawyer's ignorance on his client — although the judge perhaps should be aware that this forbearance visits them instead on the competent lawyer's client. The only solution, then, is patience.

(3) *The Difficult Problem of the "Rambo" Litigator.* Imagine the following scenario. Your client has cancelled a potentially profitable meeting to be present for his deposition, and you have taken several hours to prepare him. The Rambo litigator on the other side, of course, set it up by notice without calling you beforehand. Together with your client, you wait ... and you wait. After almost an hour, you call Rambo's office, only to hear an unconcerned receptionist explain that Rambo is vacationing in Steamboat Springs! Surprise: You have just experienced one of Rambo's favorite tactics, which is to notice depositions and not show up. (You can file a motion for sanctions, but don't place inordinate faith in it: Rambo knows how to stop just short of conduct that will truly invoke sanctions. He will have an excuse, which perhaps will involve a telephone call in which he left a message with "someone" in your office cancelling the deposition.)

(4) *The Varieties of Rambo Tactics: Lynn, Handling the Obstructionist Litigator, in University of Houston, Advanced Civil Discovery (D. Crump ed. 1990).* Rambo's client declines to answer deposition questions about documents, because he "doesn't know what the word 'document' means." When you define it as any paper he uses in his business, he again will demur, feigning ignorance of what the word "business" means to a lawyer. This conduct is not accidental but results from Rambo's tutelage. When it comes to pushing, Rambo knows how to draft an interrogatory that will require you to assemble information from every one of your client's 10,000 installations. He knows how to set depositions on five days' notice, to force your hand in attending them, and to threaten his own motion for sanctions if you insist on terminating at 3:00 p.m. for a previous engagement. He is abusive to your client, repeatedly calling him (or you) a "liar" during the deposition.

(5) *What Can You Do, In the Real World, About the Rambo Lawyer?: Cardwell, Dealing With Rambo Lawyers, in University of Houston, Advanced Civil Discovery (D. Crump ed. 1991).* First, slow down. Painstaking care and patience pay off. There may be no way to avoid the additional dollars that Rambo will cost your client, in that all other alternatives may cost even more. Second, avoid trying to out-Rambo Rambo. Most of us are not as good at it as he is, and your inept imitations will

give Rambo his best arguments for avoiding sanctions (or for imposing sanctions on you; remember, motions for sanctions are another favorite arrow in Rambo's quiver). Third, proceed methodically but relentlessly. Fourth, advise your client of the reasons you have chosen this course and of the need for perseverance. Fifth, do not file a motion for sanctions at the first slight opportunity. You invite the judge (who, after all, does not assume that Rambo is Rambo) to treat your complaints as the initiation of a childish squabble, diminishing the credibility of later, more serious motions. Ted Allen, *Your First Deposition*, 224 N.Y.L.J. 24, Sept. 15, 2000, col. 1 (calling the judge to whine about opposing counsel being mean at a deposition will irritate the judge). Finally, document the offending behavior carefully, and seek sanctions only when the conduct is egregious, persistent, and indisputably provable to the neutral observer. Lawrence D. Rosenberg, *Aristotle's Methods for Outstanding Oral Arguments*, 33 No. 4 LITIGATION 33 (2007) (failing to answer or providing evasive answers may irritate the judge and influence his opinion). Set the motion far enough in the future so that you can invite compliance by Rambo in the meantime. If you must present the motion, handle it with professional restraint. Remember, as far as this motion is concerned, you're the prosecutor, the "heavy," and you must avoid overstatement. *See Abraham v. Super Buy Tires, Inc.*, No. 05CV1296-B(NLS), 2007 U.S. Dist. LEXIS 2229, at *13-14 (S.D. Cal. 2007) (court denied sanctions even where attorney's conduct violated the rules of professionalism through "gratuitous, rude, unsubstantiated, and impertinent remarks"); *Ofoedu v. St. Francis Hosp.*, 234 F.R.D. 26, 34-35 (D. Conn. 2006) (court declined to award sanctions despite abusive conduct of opposing counsel and failure of production during discovery, although the court noted that such sanctions could be properly awarded).

(6) *Avoid Confusing "Negotiating Behavior" with Malfeasance or Rambo Tactics.* Consider these scenarios: Your opponent identifies internal investigative documents but declines to produce them on a marginal claim of work product. Or: In an antitrust case, your opponent seeks documents relevant to "every meeting" participated in by your client's bidding agent over a ten-year period. Or: Your opponent communicates the insurance adjuster's settlement offer of $5,000 for your client's paraplegic injuries. Pause before you react to this conduct; in each instance, it may be the opening of a normal course of negotiation. If the work product claim is "marginal," that still means it is subject to reasonable argument, and your adversary may be able to make reciprocal concessions with you during discovery. The $5,000 offer represents the opening of a channel of communication, and you are perfectly at liberty to respond with your demand of $10 million. The distinction between negotiation and Rambo tactics is important, but it often eludes beginning lawyers. *See also, e.g., In re Snyder*, 472 U.S. 634 (1985) (even if opponent is rude or lacks professional courtesy, a single incident may not invoke sanctions).

[5] Business Management in the Law Practice

(1) *Litigation Management (and the Impact of Money Concerns).* Imagine that your client has suffered an adverse jury verdict in a case with clear error. But the

difficulty of showing harm reduces the likelihood of reversal to less than 25%. The posting of a supersedeas bond (at a premium of 10% of the judgment), plus the costs of preparing the record, printing briefs, and attorney's fees for the appeal, exceed the mathematical expectancy of the gain that might result from reversal. In another case, the judge indicates that he will grant your client's request for a temporary restraining order, but he sets a bond that your client cannot afford. Many lawyers suffer severe frustration with these kinds of money-driven dispositions. But don't let it get to you: Like these examples, much of the decisionmaking in litigation is economically determined, and the only solutions are anticipation of these bottlenecks — and acceptance. (After all, if litigation were cost-free it would inundate us all.)

(2) *The Cost of Accomplishing Even Small Steps Seems Inordinately Large.* Filing and serving a complaint may seem easy, but the number of steps required in some instances to serve even a non-evasive out-of-state defendant can be formidable. And one of the authors had the experience of having a complaint rejected for filing three times for noncompliance with local rules, each time producing wasted (and expensive, non-billable) effort. The costs of taking depositions in another city for two days readily can exceed $5,000, and experts in a serious personal injury case may well exceed $50,000 (which the lawyer, as a practical matter, must advance). The solution is not to take these steps for granted and to deal with clients and opponents accordingly.

(3) *Money in the Law Practice.* One partner practices law diligently, billing thousands of hours over the year. Another partner has frequent 3-hour lunches and bills a fraction of the first partner's production — but this partner is the "rainmaker," the one who has the clients. How should these two partners divide the pie? This question, and others like it, are what bitter partnership dissolutions are made of. The truth may well be that both partners work hard, both have something valuable to offer, and each needs the other. [In declining economic times, the calculus becomes even more difficult, because there is no attractive way to allocate the losses attributable to a shrinking pie.] The best solution is to recognize the problem, to avoid egocentricism when recognizing the other partner's worth, and to negotiate without attributing motives.

(4) *Management Systems (and Lawyers' Aversion to Them): See Special Bar Journal Section [on Professional Management]: An Introduction*, 53 Tex. B.J. 204 et seq. (1990). The values of efficient timekeeping, standardized office procedures, personnel management, and other organizational devices are clear. They become obscured, however, by deadlines and daily production needs. Furthermore, legal education contains little that concerns office management — and, indeed, the every-case-is-unique approach of the Socratic dialogue tends to depreciate the value of management, which is concerned with efficient handling of repetitive problems. The solution to this problem is to have the self-discipline to investigate and implement office systems — by setting aside the time to do so.

[B] The Personal Costs of the Litigator's Life — and Solutions

[1] Stress

(1) *What Stress Is and What It Does: Finney, The Stressful Workplace, Management Digest,* NEWSWEEK, Nov. 4, 1991, at A-6. Stress is caused partly by external stimuli, such as conflicting demands, unreasonable expectations, unclear directions, and frequent frustrations or "hassles." Lawyers are more susceptible to stress than most other professions, likely due to "the unique interplay of the legal profession and lawyer personality." Jennifer Pirtle, *Stressing Yourself Sick*, ABA JOURNAL, Sept. 2006, at 34. The adversarial nature of the legal profession is likely to cause stressful situations, and lawyers are generally "thinkers" instead of "feelers," and therefore, do not tend to recognize or understand stress-related emotions when they occur. *Id.* When faced with a stressful situation, the brain releases adrenaline, which increases one's heart rate, and cortisol, which provides an energy boost. *Id.* After the stress subsides, the body relaxes and normalizes hormone levels; but since lawyers experience frequent stressors, their hormone levels often remain elevated, resulting in symptoms of chronic stress. Such symptoms include an accelerated aging process, a weakened immune system, sleep disorders, gastrointestinal disorders, hypertension, and heart disease. *Id.* Stress also affects one's mood, with short term effects "such as low self-esteem, irritability, guilt, pessimism, procrastination and general grouchiness"; whereas chronic stress can lead to "depression and anxiety." *Id.*

Additional causes of stress, ironically, are self-imposed: They include poor self-image, anger, impatience and intolerance. Finally, there are life change stressors, which the Holmes-Rahe "Social Readjustment Rating Scale" measures (in this scale, the death of a spouse is the highest stressor, at 100 points, with divorce, promotion, intercity moves, and other life events occupying lower ratings; the cumulative total over a period of time is what indicates disadvantageous stress). Dysfunctional stress interferes with relationships as well as job performance.

(2) *What Conditions are Correlated With Dysfunctional Stress?: A Multiple-Choice Test.* Which of the following is most likely to produce conditions of dysfunctional stress?

(a) Learning that a friend who lives in a distant city has died.

(b) Hearing from a lawyer who recently opposed you in a case that he has referred a client to you.

(c) Receiving an adverse jury verdict in a case in which you expended a large effort and which represents a major loss to the client.

(d) After running behind and missing meetings all day because you are trying to prepare for a hearing early tomorrow morning, having the temporary secretary tell you that the computer lost the only copy of the brief you must file tomorrow.

(e) Learning that you did not make partner this year.

[Note: The above source suggests that the correct answer is (d). Repetitive, cumulative assaults by life's smaller hassles, according to consistent research, often creates more dysfunctional stress than a single (even very serious) event. *See* MANAGEMENT DIGEST, above.]

(3) *"But Wait — Those 'Stress-Producing Conditions' Are Exactly What Litigation Itself Inevitably Produces!"* Exactly. That's the point. Litigators are particularly prone to stress because they are constantly in ambiguous, conflicted, acrimonious, irritating, unjust and often humiliating situations. It is for this reason that California now requires every practicing lawyer to take regular instruction in stress reduction (see above) — and it also is why this section is in this book.

(4) *But Some Stress is "Good," Some People Thrive on It, and Even Dysfunctional Stress Has Its Uses.* Exciting, interesting experiences often are stressful. Most people would find a stress-free existence to be intolerably boring. (See below.) And even dysfunctional stress has its uses; without the stress of confronting a jury trial together with you, your client might never evaluate the settlement offer that is his best alternative. [Incidentally, the Rambo litigator is unethical and unpleasant, but he's no fool; he knows about stress, and he uses it.]

(5) *A Multiple-Choice Test About Stressor Effects.* Lawyer Brown and Lawyer Green both are handling large dockets of difficult cases. Brown seems to thrive on it, while Green is becoming depressed and frustrated. Why?

(a) Brown went to a better law school.

(b) Brown is older.

(c) Brown functions happily under stress while Green does not.

(d) Brown is more motivated by prestige and money.

(e) Brown took a trial practice course in law school.

[Undoubtedly, you have guessed that the answer is (c). Some individuals enjoy a work environment that others would find dysfunctionally stressful. If Brown were deprived of the excitement he gets at work, he might seek his stress by skydiving or gaming in Las Vegas.]

(6) *Dealing With Stress: Some Solutions.* Effective time management can help reduce stress by making the individual "feel more in control" and helping him realize when to decline a task that would leave him overextended. *See* Jennifer Pirtle, *Stressing Yourself Sick*, ABA JOURNAL, Sept. 2006, at 34. Learning to recognize stressors and stress signals allows an individual to learn to avoid or better respond to stressful situations. *Id.* Other stress management techniques include keeping a positive outlook, taking short breaks to relax during the day, diet, and exercise. *Id.* Social relationships can also relieve stress by boosting the body's oxytocin levels. *Id.*

Problem C

THE EXECUTIVE MONKEY EXPERIMENT. The famous "executive monkey" experiment paired two monkeys, both of which were subject to a series of electric shocks, but one of which, the executive monkey, controlled the timing of each shock.

The difference in manifestations of stress between the two monkeys was dramatic. This was so even though there was no difference in the number or intensity of the shocks. Photographs clearly show the executive monkey, which differed only in having the ability to determine when the shocks occurred, as relatively relaxed. The other monkey, which was unable to control the shocks, remained rigidly anxious.

Question: Given that a litigator often is subject to unpleasant stimuli delivered unpredictably by judges, juries, adversaries, clients, and employers and cannot very well control his or her schedule, what does the executive monkey experiment suggest about the resultant stress on a litigator?

[2] Secondary Effects: Substance Abuse and Dysfunctional Personal Relationships

(1) *Substance Abuse: Alcohol and Beyond.* Whereas studies indicate that "10 percent of the general population" suffers from alcohol or substance abuse, it is estimated that the percentage of lawyers is nearly double that of the general population. Michael J. Flaherty & Richard J. Jacobson, *Smart Practices: Confronting Alcoholism in the Legal Profession*, Law Practice Mgmt., Oct. 2001, at 39. Of 105 occupations surveyed, lawyers ranked at the top of the list for depression and have disproportionately high suicide rates. Robert A. Stein, *Help Is Available*, ABA Journal, June 2005, at 64. A lawyer assistance program now exists in every state to help lawyers fight not only their addiction problems but also to cope with stress and depression. *Id.*

(2) *Effects of Stress, Time Management and the Adversary System on the Lawyer's Personal Relationships: Divorce, Children and Friends.* Litigators often have days that they feel have been consumed entirely in fighting with other people. (After all, one of the main things a lawyer has to offer to a client is the ability to induce a third person or entity to do something that that person otherwise would not do.) It is difficult for human beings to "turn off" this kind of behavior immediately upon leaving the job, and therefore, lawyers tend to extend their argumentation to spouses, children, and friends. Thus, "battles in the courtroom" become "battles in the bedroom." Likewise, the difficulties that lawyers have in reserving time for personal obligations lead to neglect of spouses, children and friends. Among the results: a high divorce rate for the legal profession. The solution? Again, it is self-discipline, good time management, stress control, professional counseling when one can benefit from it — and an awareness of the problem in the first place. *See generally* Steven Keeva, *Why Lawyers Lose in Love*, ABA Journal, May 2005, at 76.

Problem D

DSM-IV AND THE OBSESSIVE-COMPULSIVE PERSONALITY DISORDER: CAN LAW SCHOOL INDUCE SOME DYSFUNCTIONAL CHARACTERISTICS? The American Psychiatric Association's Diagnostic and Statistical Manual of Mental Disorders is knowns as "DSM" for short. The fourth edition, DSM-IV, is the current Bible for diagnosticians of clinical psychological disorders. Under the heading, "Obsessive-Compulsive Disorder," DSM sets forth the following diagnostic criteria:

> **301.4 Obsessive-Compulsive Personality Disorder**
>
> A pervasive pattern of preoccupation with orderliness, perfectionism, and mental and interpersonal control, at the expense of flexibility, openness, and efficiency, beginning by early adulthood and present in a variety of contexts, as indicated by four (or more) of the following:
>
> (1) is preoccupied with details, rules, lists, order, organization, or schedules to the extent that the major point of the activity is lost
>
> (2) shows perfectionism that interferes with task completion (e.g., is unable to complete a project because his or her own overly strict standards are not met)
>
> (3) is excessively devoted to work and productivity to the exclusion of leisure activities and friendships (not accounted for by obvious economic necessity)
>
> (4) is overconscientious, scrupulous, and inflexible about matters of morality, ethics, or values (not accounted for by cultural or religious identification)
>
> (5) is unable to discard worn-out or worthless objects even when they have no sentimental value
>
> (6) is reluctant to delegate tasks or to work with others unless they submit to exactly his or her way of doing things
>
> (7) adopts a miserly spending style toward both self and others; money is viewed as something to be hoarded for future catastrophes
>
> (8) shows rigidity and stubbornness

Other sources suggest that, in moderation, some measure of these characteristics may be functional (perhaps in a lawyer, for example). Excessive manifestation of these behaviors, however, has a number of unpleasant results, not the least of which is that it drives to distraction anyone close to such a person.

(1) *Can Law School "Teach" You These Characteristics in a Dysfunctional Way?* No one is suggesting that everyone who emerges from law school is clinically obsessive-compulsive (or even a significant percentage) or that your professors are setting out to "teach" you how to be dysfunctional. But doesn't DSM's list display a striking coincidence with some of what law school seems to inculcate, such as "preoccup[ation] with details, rules, lists, order," etc. that often departs from the "major point" (the just outcome), or "excessive devot[ion] to work and productivity"?

(2) *How Can You Maintain "Good" Compulsiveness (Meticulous Professionalism) but Keep It in Balance?* No one is saying that a law school education is a bad thing, either. In context, concentration on rules and devotion to work are good things.

Maybe the meticulous professional simply is bound to appear a little obsessive at times. But how can you ensure that your compulsivity won't get out of balance?

[3] Lack of Significance in One's Work

(1) *There are Boring Jobs In Litigation, and Boring Parts of Any Job.* Civil procedure courses often treat discovery as though beginning lawyers spent the bulk of their time drafting interrogatories or motions to produce. On the contrary, they spend a great deal more time *responding* to interrogatories or motions to produce (or sifting through the results) — which is a much less exciting task. Indeed, like any endeavor, litigation is composed in large percentage of tasks that are neither interesting nor inherently valuable in isolation.

(2) *The Deeper Problem of Lack of Significance.* Benson's explanation, cited above, of his reasons for quitting the practice of law indicates a deeper kind of dissatisfaction than intermittent boredom. Benson, *Why I Quit Practicing Law*, NEWSWEEK, Nov. 4, 1991, at 10. Many lawyers are not only bored and stressed, but convinced that their efforts do not matter. Sometimes, this perception results from the enormous costs of discovery in proportion to the perceived gains. Because many cases take years to resolve, our system creates the impression that litigation is ineffective to resolve real disputes.

(3) *The Solutions: Information, Flexibility, Persistence.* The solution to this problem is to learn as much as possible about the job, including what lawyers who do it really do on a daily basis, *before* accepting the position. A second solution is to avoid prejudice about what you really would like to do. Sometimes, a law student who seems to have the soul of a poet thrives in a large competitive law firm, where he finds that the interests he serves ultimately benefit society, and that his own abilities are well used. Sometimes such a lawyer even finds caring mentors in that "impersonal" law firm. On the other hand, it is surprising how often a law student who seems drawn to prestige and financial rewards is happier in the district attorney's office — or in a solo practice, or in a setting that more explicitly claims to serve the public interest. Likewise, another attorney may be astounded to find that, for him, a corporate legal department offers a better combination of lifestyle and professional interest. *Cf.* Machlovitz, *Lawyers Move In-House*, ABA JOURNAL, May 1989, at 66 (reporting, counterintuitively, that the buildup of corporate legal departments may mean not only that that is where jobs are, but also a better quality of life for many lawyers). Thus, a full exploration of the alternatives, without prejudice, pays enormous dividends later in life. Third, it is inadvisable to forsake a chosen path at the first sign of boredom or conflict, because those conditions are unavoidable in any legal career. Finally, persistent conviction that one's work lacks significance should lead, as it did in Benson's case, to a decision to forsake litigation. After all, there are many other worthwhile things to do.

III. Updating the Personal Dimension: Justice O'Connor's View

(1) *Justice O'Connor's View, Expressed in 1999: Reports Say That "More than Half" of Lawyers Call Themselves Dissatisfied*, HOUSTON CHRONICLE, May 24, 1999, at 8A. In a speech at American University's Washington College of Law on May 23, 1999, Justice Sandra Day O'Connor reportedly cited surveys concluding that "more than half" the country's lawyers say that they are dissatisfied at work. The Justice mentioned such irritants as money, public perceptions of lawyers, and frustration at lack of social worth in lawyers' work. Her reported solution: civility, and devoting more time to pro bono work. Justice O'Connor particularly emphasized providing more legal services to the poor as a means of reducing frustration. *See also* Sandra Day O'Connor, *Professionalism*, 78 ORE. L. REV. 385, 386, 390-91 (1999) (speech at University of Oregon Law School, citing a RAND study concluding that "only half would choose to become lawyers if they had to do it over," and repeating the call for pro bono services as part of a solution).

(2) *Skepticism About Justice O'Connor's Proposed Solution.* Some authors of this book, having been involved extensively in pro bono work, are skeptical of Justice O'Connor's proposed solution. These authors advocate pro bono work for its own sake, but the source of the skepticism is doubt that doing more pro bono will decrease dissatisfaction. Representing the poor, unfortunately, is itself frustrating, difficult, stressful, and disappointing. Therefore, while endorsing the idea of performing pro bono, these authors caution that the work should not be viewed as a ready means of decreasing frustration or stress, because it may have the opposite effect.

IV. The "Up" Side: Positive Reasons for Practicing Law

[A] "Good" Stress: Challenge and Adventure

(1) *Practicing Law Can Involve "Good" Stress — Or, Work That Is Interesting and Exciting.* In explaining the significance of his work, a personal injury lawyer asks: "Where else could I depose a safety expert from [a major automobile manufacturer], and make him answer my questions about defects in the way his company designs cars?" Short of election to Congress (and perhaps not even then), he is right. There are few other positions offering such an opportunity to make a difference, to deal with issues of significance, and, indeed, to have such interesting experiences. Even in cases that themselves seem to be devoid of social significance, issues about an obscure security interest provision in the UCC can be fantastically interesting, when coupled with the stimulus provided by the adversary system.

(2) *Interest and Excitement as the Number One Reason Given by Lawyers for Entering the Profession*, ABA JOURNAL, Sept. 1986, at 44. People go to law school because

they think it will be interesting. "Roughly three in five lawyers (58.4%) said they studied law because the subject interested them, and more than half (58.1%) did so in the expectation that their work as lawyers would be interesting." This reason — interest and excitement — was mentioned by more lawyers in this survey than income potential (46.3%), prestige (43.1%), or the desire to improve society (23.4%). In fact, the "interesting subject matter" motivation prevailed over wanting to "see justice done" (21.6%) by more than 2 to 1. Therefore, you should seek work that interests you, whether it is bankruptcy, environmental litigation (where lawyers go to court infrequently), personal injury defense in a small-to-medium sized firm (where trial work is much more frequent) or something else.

[B] Service

(1) *A High Proportion of Civic Activities: Blodgett, Time and Money: A Look at Today's Lawyer,* ABA Journal, Sept. 1, 1986, at 47. Today's lawyer "would like to spend more time with his family yet willingly assumes a host of duties and civic activities." These activities included not only *pro bono* litigation, but serving upon local boards of directors of hospitals and other nonprofit organizations. It appears that these kinds of organizations value lawyers because of their organizational ability, practical approach to getting things done and dedication to service. Consider, also, the following:

> Lawyers make things work. They may do it in a variety of ways. They may do it by sabbaticals and periodic service in government. They may do it by commissions and boards and special roles. They may do it solely in their community or in their church, or in fund-raising or legislative activities, reforms or programs within the system. They certainly serve the public interest day in and day out by guaranteeing due process and protecting the rights and liberties of our citizens.

Civiletti, *Projecting Law Practice in the 1990's,* Nat'l L.J., Aug. 10, 1987, at 22.

(2) *Public Service Through Service to Clients.* Furthermore, *pro bono* efforts are not the only way in which lawyers are of service. The plaintiff's attorney who deposed the safety expert, referred to above, provided a service to his client, and in the traditional manner, thereby indirectly served the larger public by advocating safer products — as did his counterpart on the defense side, who advocated products that were functional and affordable. As Civiletti says, lawyers "make things work" as well as preserving values such as due process — and they do it by doing their jobs.

(3) *Service to a Legal System That "Works" Overall and That Is a Part of Democratic Government, Even Though It Miscarries in Some Cases.* Every society must have a system of dispute resolution that has public confidence. It is an essential part of the "glue" that allows the society to function. Our own legal system reflects such deeply held values as the individual's right to be heard before an impartial decision-maker

subject to a neutral body of norms applicable to all. The lawyer, as advocate, plays an indispensable role in that system. Thus, the work of the litigator contributes to the function of our democracy and to a system that "works," at least in the overall sense — even when the particular case is only of routine importance and even though the system has imperfections.

[C] Financial Rewards (or, How Real Is "L.A. Law"?)

(1) *Personal Wealth.* According to the Occupational Outlook Handbook of the Department of Labor, Bureau of Labor Statistics, the median salary of all lawyers was $94,930 in 2004, with the middle fifty percent earning between $64,620 and $143,620. The median salary for new attorneys nine months after graduation was $55,000, including great disparity between the median salary in private practice ($80,000) and the median salary in government positions ($44,700). *Id.* In 2007, large firms increased starting salaries for new associates to $160,000, but those positions are generally filled with the top graduates of the top law schools. Amir Efrati, *Hard Case: Job Market Wanes for U.S. Lawyers*, WALL ST. J., Sept. 24, 2007, A1. A national oversupply of lawyers, in conjunction with weakened demand, is keeping wages suppressed for all but the top paying jobs, leaving many new graduates struggling to repay law school debt that can often exceed $100,000. *Id.*

(2) *Independence and Self-Development.* But these financial factors understate a distinct advantage: The lawyer has greater independence than many other workers. He can choose to establish his own practice, but this is generally "easiest in small towns and expanding suburban areas" where there is likely to be less competition from large, established firms, which dominate the legal market in big cities. Bureau of Labor Statistics, *Occupational Outlook Handbook: Lawyers* (2006). A law degree is also an attractive asset, although not a necessity, for positions in "nontraditional areas" such as "administrative, managerial, and business positions in banks, insurance firms, real estate companies, government agencies, and other organizations." *Id.* The dues that lawyers pay as they struggle with time pressures, adversaries and stress give them a freedom that is unusual.

[D] The Profession — And the Fellowship of Other Lawyers

(1) *A Profession with a History: Trevathan, No More Lawyer-Bashing*, HOUS. LAWYER, Nov. 1991, at 11. "Our 'ancestors' include Cicero, Patrick Henry, Justice Louis D. Brandeis, and Oliver Wendell Holmes" — to which we could add Sir Thomas More and Abraham Lincoln.

(2) *The Fellowship of Other Lawyers.* As one California lawyer put it: "If I scored big in the lottery, I'd still keep practicing law." Blodgett, above, ABA JOURNAL at 48. Lawyers make wonderful company to work with or to know socially. Even the less professional and altruistic members of the profession tend, at least, to be interesting.

[E] It's Up to You

The Point of This Appendix. The point is that the choices you make in how you select your career, the organization in which you undertake it, the way you manage it, and the ways you balance it with your personal life, all will make a difference in whether you can find the elusive path to combining competence, adversary practice, ethics, altruism and success with a full life as a lawyer. And you can enhance the quality of your choices by careful examination and self-discipline. You will have to live with the consequences, but you can make them turn out positively. It's up to you.

Table of Cases

B

Index

[References are to sections.]

F

G

I

J

P

Personal Jurisdiction

Pleadings